The Bible of the world; ed. by Robert O.
Ballou in collaboration with Friedrich
Spiegelberg and with the assistance and
advice of Horace L. Friess.   New York,
Viking Press, 1939.
xxi, 1415 p. illus. 24cm.
"The scriptural essence of eight great
living source religions."--Introd.
Bibliographical references in "Notes":
p. [1343]-1379; "Condensed bibliography":
p. 1380-1384.
1. Sacred books (Selections, extracts,
etc.) I. Bal-   lou, Robert Oleson,
1892-   ed.   II. Spiegelberg,
Friedrich, 1897-   ed.   III. Friess,
Horace Leland, 1900-   ed.

The
BIBLE
of the World

The BIBLE OF THE WORLD

Edited by ROBERT O. BALLOU
in collaboration with FRIEDRICH SPIEGELBERG,
PH.D., S.T.M. (Columbia University) and
with the assistance and advice of HORACE
L. FRIESS, PH.D. (Columbia University)

New York - THE VIKING PRESS - Mcmxxxix

The jacket, binding, title page, and halftitles for

this volume were hand-lettered by Arnold Bank

FIRST PUBLISHED IN OCTOBER 1939

NINTH PRINTING FEBRUARY 1967

PRINTED IN U.S.A. BY VAIL-BALLOU PRESS, INC.

DISTRIBUTED IN CANADA BY THE MACMILLAN COMPANY OF CANADA, LTD.

TABLE OF CONTENTS

Mohammedan Scriptures

"As one can ascend to the top of a house by means of a ladder or a bamboo or a staircase or a rope, so divers are the ways and means to approach God, and every religion in the world shows one of these ways.

"Different creeds are but different paths to reach the Almighty. Various and different are the ways that lead to the temple of Mother Kali at Kalighat. Similarly, various are the ways that lead to the house of the Lord. Every religion is nothing but one of such paths that lead to God.

"It is one and the same Avatara that, having plunged into the ocean of life, rises up in one place and is known as Krishna, and diving down again rises in another place and is known as Christ.

"Bow down and worship where others kneel, for where so many have been paying the tribute of adoration the kind Lord must manifest himself, for he is all mercy."

—From the Sayings of Sri Ramakrishna.

"There is one body, and one spirit . . . one Lord, one faith, one baptism, one God and Father of all, who is above all, and through all, and in you all."

—Paul's Epistle to the Ephesians, 4.4-6.

'We hold that there is but one religion for humanity; the many faiths and creeds are all streams or streamlets of this great river. This may perhaps seem a hard saying to some, but let us briefly consider its meaning. The Sun of Truth is one. His rays stream forth into the minds and hearts of men; surely if we believe anything at all, we hold this faith in the Fatherhood of God. Must we not then believe that our common Father is no respecter of persons and that at all times, in all lands, he has loved and loves and will love his children?"

—G. R. S. MEAD in *Fragments of a Faith Forgotten*.

ACKNOWLEDGMENTS

The editors and publishers of *The Bible of the World* acknowledge their indebtedness and extend their thanks to the following:

Mrs. C. A. F. Rhys Davids, for her checking of parts of the Buddhist scriptures; Professor Arthur Jeffrey of Columbia University, for invaluable advice concerning selections from *The Koran;* Professor Louis H. Gray of Columbia University, for critical examination of the Zoroastrian scriptural selections; the Reverend Edward M. Chapman of New London, Connecticut, and the Reverend Raymond C. Knox, Chaplain of Columbia University, for advice as to the arrangement of the books of the Old Testament; Lillian E. Ballou, a devoted reader of the Psalms for more than seventy-five years, whose favourite Psalms became the basis of the selection for *The Bible of the World;* Miss Ruth Smith, for her work of editing, checking, typing, and proofreading, which is beyond measuring by any acknowledgment; and the following publishers or authors, for texts reprinted from their books: Alice A. Bailey, of New York; Bernard Quaritch, of London; Dr. Eric F. F. Bishop, of Palestine; the Bombay Theosophical Publication Fund, of Bombay, India; the Buddhist Lodge, of London; Chapman and Hall, of London; the University Press, Cambridge; the Clarendon Press, of Oxford; H. C. Dass, of Calcutta, India; E. P. Dutton and Company, of New York; the Eastern Buddhist Society, of Kyoto, Japan; Kenneth Sylvan Guthrie, of Yonkers, N. Y.; Harvard University Press, of Cambridge, Massachusetts; Henry Frowde, of London; Humphrey Milford, of London; Kegan Paul, Trench, Trubner and Company, of London; George Routledge and Sons, Ltd., of London; E. J. Lazarus and Company, of Benares, India; Lucis Publishing Company, of New York; Luzac and Company, of London; *The Moslem World,* Hartford Seminary Foundation, Hartford, Connecticut; John Murray, of London; the Oxford University Press, of London and New York; the Pali Text Society, of London; Probsthain and Company, of London; Charles Scribner's Sons, of New York; Society for the Resuscitation of Indian Literature, of Calcutta, India; the Theosophical Press, of Wheaton, Illinois; the Theosophical Publishing House, of London; the Vedanta Society, of New York; Charles A. Wong; Kelly and Walsh, Ltd., of Shanghai.

Introduction

THE BIBLE OF THE WORLD is the result of a diligent attempt on the part of a lay editor, with the advice of two scholars, to put into one volume the scriptural essence of eight great living source religions for the use of the modern English reader. It would be difficult to separate and state the many reasons for entering upon so challenging, so attractive, and at the same time so difficult a project, but some of the impelling stimulants are apparent.

Most obvious of these are the facts that the material involved is superb from a purely literary point of view, and that by far the greatest part of it included here is little known to the average reader. Nowhere in literature is there more profound or beautiful poetry than that contained in the earliest scriptures of Hinduism, the Vedic hymns, composed no one knows when, but certainly more than a millennium before the birth of Christ; in the Chinese odes and the Tao-Te-King; or in the best of the Psalms of the Judeo-Christian Bible. There are no better stories anywhere than those of the Upanishads, the Bhagavad-Gita, the Puranas, the Hitopadesa, and the Parables of Sri Ramakrishna in Hinduism; the Pali Tripitaka, the Jataka birth stories and Buddhaghosha's Parables of Buddhism; the Zendavesta and Pahlavi texts of Zoroastrianism; the book of Chuang Tze of Taoism; and the Jewish Old Testament. There is nowhere a more profound or timeless philosophy than is embodied in the more thoughtful and philosophic scriptures of all of these religions.[1]

---

[1] For those who would like to approach *The Bible of the World* purely as a collection of literary masterpieces, a good beginning could be made by reading the following: Poetry: "Prayer of a Gambler," p. 19; "To Aranyani," p. 23; "A Charm against Fear," p. 28; "Plea to an Ancestor," p. 385; "Sorrow," p. 396; "Beauty," p. 396; *The Tao-Te-King*, pp. 471 ff.; *The Psalms*, pp. 879 ff.; *The Song of Solomon*, pp. 933 ff.; "The Hymn of the Soul," pp. 1281 ff. Prose: the story of Arjuna, conscientious objector to war, pp. 85 ff.; Sumati's account of hell, which, in form and content, is much like Dante's *Inferno*, p. 132; *The Works of Sri Ramakrishna*, especially the first few pages, beginning 161, and the stories on pp. 168, 175, and 176; "The Conception and Birth

Yet in the great bulk of scriptural literature the poetry, the stories, the religious exaltation, and the philosophy must be sought out within a maze of passages which are dull and meaningless to the average modern reader. He fails to find the central themes which he can accept seriously, for want of an adequate volume in which the essential scriptures of the great religions are presented without the accumulations that hinder his reading and distract his interest.

It seems to me that the choice open to an intelligent man to-day is evidenced not in the question: "Must I have any religion at all, and if so, which one?" but rather in this: "What have these profoundly felt religions, which have influenced all mankind, that will help me in my own search for revelation of eternal truth?"

At no time has understanding among the nations of the world been more obviously vital to civilization than now. Year by year, the social and political necessity of sympathetic communication between East and West increases, as the significance of spatial distance lessens. But political, social, and economic knowledge arrived at without consideration of the inmost religious and philosophical beliefs of the peoples concerned is knowledge of circumstances without a basic focus for understanding.

"It is well said, in every sense, that a man's religion is the chief fact with regard to him," wrote Carlyle in *Heroes and Hero-Worship.* "A man's or a nation of men's. By religion I do not mean here the church creed which he professes, the articles of faith which he will sign and, in words or otherwise, assert; not this wholly, in many cases not this at all. We see men of all kinds of professed creeds attain to almost all degrees of worth or worthlessness under each or any of them. This is not what I call religion, this profession and assertion; which is often

of the Buddha," pp. 181 ff.; "The Great Retirement," pp. 192 ff.; "The Plaint of Yasodhara," p. 201; "Rebirth and Karma," pp. 287 ff.; *The Dhammapada,* pp. 295 ff.; the Buddhist creation story, pp. 263 ff.; "The Elephant and the Blind Men," p. 277; "The Story of Maddhakundali," p. 304; "The Story of Kisagotami," p. 306; "The Story of the Hen and the Little Sow," p. 309; "The Story of Chuang Tze's dream," p. 512; "Prince Hui's Excellent Cook," p. 513; "The Choice of Chuang Tze," p. 538; "The Grand Augur and the Pigs," p. 542; "The Man Who Fished for Fun," p. 545; "The Wise Tender of Horses," p. 550; the story of Joseph and his brothers, pp. 677 ff.; the story of Balaam, pp. 737 ff.; the story of Samson, pp. 774 ff.; the story of Absalom, pp. 802 ff.; "The Story of Jezebel," p. 825; *The Book of Esther,* pp. 843 ff.; *The Book of Ruth,* pp. 852 ff.; *Judith,* pp. 1032 ff.; *The History of Susanna,* pp. 1046 ff.; "The Sermon on the Mount," pp. 1123 ff.; "The Woman Taken in Adultery," p. 1093; the Apocryphal story of the birth of the Virgin Mary, pp. 1247 ff.; the Apocryphal story of the trial of Jesus, pp. 1258 ff.; "The Dance of Praise," p. 1278; and "A Mouse Draws the Leading Rein of a Camel," p. 1332. If you are interested in Christian Science, read *Sankaracharya's Atma Bodha,* p. 141. And if you like dogs, read "Of the Dog," pp. 601 ff., and "The Independence of the Dog," p. 637.

only a profession and assertion from the outworks of the man, from the mere argumentative region of him, if even so deep as that. But the thing a man does practically believe (and this is often enough without asserting it even to himself, much less to others); the thing a man does practically lay to heart, and know for certain, concerning his vital relations to this mysterious universe and his duty and destiny there, that is in all cases the primary thing for him, and creatively determines all the rest. That is his religion; or, it may be, his mere scepticism and no-religion: the manner in which he feels himself to be spiritually related to the Unseen World or No-World; and I say, if you tell me what that is, you tell me to a very great extent what the man is, what the kind of things he will do is. Of a man or of a nation we inquire, therefore, first of all, what religion they had."

It is partly to tell what the worshippers of Brahma and Allah and Jehovah, and the followers of Christ, Buddha, Confucius, Zoroaster, and Lao Tze, were, and are, that *The Bible of the World* has been compiled. But there is a reason for its existence which seems to me to be more important.

In times of world stress such as this second quarter of the twentieth century men's minds and hearts instinctively rise in revolt against the materialistic temper to which they justifiably charge much of social disaster, and seek knowledge of the roots of life, the sources of their beings. Seeking at first release from their uncertainty, insecurity, and pain, they find in their search a need for something more than mere escape. They must go on to a positive identification with the power which is within and behind and surrounding everything.

These are the true radicals of every age—not those who would merely escape or overthrow the existing order, but those who would find the basic truth, the laws of which any order must obey or perish, those who must, in the words of the Oberlin Theological Seminary's statement of purpose, "search for the truth regardless of where the search may lead."

Everywhere throughout the world there is evidence of this groping return to a search for universal truth as it is manifested in the religious impulse. Even the passionate desire of great numbers of persons to save democracy, which at first glance is a social and political phenomenon, is actually closely connected with this return, for the ideal of democracy is itself a natural flowering of the social idealism inherent in every great religion.

But the religious need of a man to-day is for something greater than the dogma of a single sectarian church. Many deeply religious persons, whether churchmen or not, have constructed for themselves eclectic religions which, even though those who hold to them may not be aware of it, are probably composed of parts of the traditional beliefs of many other people, and probably include the strong faith in an intangible universal divine realm which is basic to most religions, but which does not necessarily have within it any of the bigoted quality of narrow sectarianism. It is the hope and belief of the editors of *The Bible of the World* that such persons will find within this book expression of many of their most dearly held (though perhaps inarticulate) beliefs, and a deeper realization of man's heritage of faith.

The religions of the East have always taken into account this universality of the religious impulse, and the unity of the basic search for eternal truth, regardless of the differences of form which mark the search. Krishna, speaking in the Bhagavad-Gita (the Lord's Song), says: "Wherever there is a decay of righteousness, and there is exaltation of unrighteousness, then I, myself, come forth; for the protection of the good, for the destruction of evil-doers, for the sake of firmly established righteousness, I am born from age to age. He who thus knows my divine birth and action in its essence cometh to me. Freed from passion, fear, and anger, filled with me, taking refuge in me, purified in the fire of wisdom, many have entered my being. However men approach me, even so do I welcome them, for the path men take from every side is mine."

A philosophy for to-day needs knowledge of mankind's many paths to God. It needs, to be sure, the compassionate humanity of Christ, his conception of the Father-God, and the passion for justice in the Jewish prophets, but it needs, too, the all-embracing vision of life and respect for other religions found in Hinduism and Buddhism, the wise and timeless social precepts of Confucianism, especially in reference to government, the mysticism and sense of co-operation with nature in Taoism, the reverence for work and the adoration of earth and its fruits which mark Zoroastrianism. Each of these religions has the strength and the weakness inherent in its particular emphasis, which often gives importance to one phase of spiritual need to the neglect of other equally vital phases. We need the strength inherent in each of these emphases to counteract the weaknesses in our own biases.

Tolerance of religions other than our own has probably increased during the past century, partly as a result of the painstaking work of scholars who have replaced many of our misconceptions by facts. But to become merely tolerant is to take but a single halting step away from the impoverishing force of intolerance. Only when the mind is freed from all sense of religious "tolerance," of condescension, out of a sense of duty to a creed which we actually feel is on a lower plane than that occupied by our traditional religion, can the constructive state of appreciation be entered, in which true and useful meaning may be found.

In this state the point of view toward disagreements between the four Gospels of the New Testament, between the Old and the New Testaments, between the Hebrew-Christian scriptures, and those of Hinduism, Buddhism, Confucianism, and other religions, becomes a constructive one. Such disagreements between honest and intelligent expressions of deep spiritual insight as are found in the scriptures are among the greatest stimulants to intellectual and spiritual growth—through which humanity may eventually find salvation. Examined from this point of view such disagreements confirm, rather than deny, basic truth.

Man is incapable of grasping pure truth in its entirety. The very search for it, if it is uncompromising, and conducted in humility, constitutes the most intimate contact with eternal verity which he will ever know. Exposed to this search in the mind and heart of another, he is exalted and feels the cleansing breath of truth itself, even though the other's point of view may differ radically in details from his own. And he will find, too, strangely insistent notes of that cosmic music of the soul the elusiveness of which has always tortured his desire.

There is, in the Upanishads, in the words of Gotama Buddha, in the Book of the Second Isaiah, and the Tao-Te-King a sense of purity and eternal might and beauty familiar to any one who knows the Sermon on the Mount. It is impossible to read these, or the Bhagavad-Gita, or the words of Chuang Tze and Sri Ramakrishna, with an unprejudiced mind without hearing a timeless voice speaking through each of them, the voice of an intangible spirit, the essence of universal divinity. It speaks not to one group of persons alone—not to Hindus or Taoists or Mohammedans or Jews or Christians only—but to all mankind. For those who have truly listened to it with understanding, there is no sectarianism, no division of any kind—yet for too many understanding has been confused by narrow interpretations of Hindu dogma and ritual, by the misinterpretation of Buddhist doctrine which represents it as pessimism and nihilism, by the racial exclusiveness of the Jew, the fanatic intolerance of the Moslem, and the sectarianism which has ever divided the Christian Church.

One must push through the limitations of organized dogmas and seek the sources themselves if one would find the heart of the world's religions. Only when he has done that will he have prepared himself to be at home with Christ, and at home when he has reached the heart of Buddha or Brahma, or has set the feet of his spirit upon Tao. I was reminded forcefully of this universality and timelessness of religious feeling when, in selecting the material for *The Bible of the World,* we came upon and I read for the first time the song from the ancient Chinese book of poetry in which the following lines occur:

> Alas for me, who am a little child,
> On whom has devolved the unsettled state!
> Solitary am I and full of distress,
> O my great Father.

Immediately I thought of the American Negro spiritual:

> Sometimes I feel like a motherless child,
> A long way from home.

It would be difficult to imagine two men more widely removed from each other by time, place, and circumstance than a Chinese sovereign or minister who lived several thousand years ago, educated and steeped in the ancient ceremonial traditions of China, living in ease in the midst of many servants, and the illiterate, simple, American Negro slave who knew only ceaseless toil and hardship, who constantly obeyed, but never issued orders, completely without that surface polish which we wrongly call culture. Yet from the hearts of the exalted yellow man and the submerged black man came the same piteous cry of longing for a divine parent.

At a famous meeting of the Free Religious Association of America held in Boston during the latter half of the nineteenth century, a somewhat overzealous minister quoted certain passages from the Gospels, adding that these could not be matched in the sacred books of any of the other religions. At this point Ralph Waldo Emerson, who was in the audience, rose and said quietly: "The gentleman's remark only proves how narrowly he has read."

These, then, have been the stimulants to the compilation of *The Bible of the World*. The difficulties involved were obviously great. When it is realized that the scriptures of India alone consist of more than a thousand volumes, not all of which are available in English translations, some idea of the task may be understood.

However, all the scriptures are repetitive. Just as the Jewish Old Testament tells the same stories and repeats the same concepts many times, and as each of the four Gospels tells fundamentally the same story of the life of Christ, so the same narratives and the same philosophies are repeated over and over in the texts of the Hindu, Buddhist, Zoroastrian, and Mohammedan sacred books. The first task in the editing of *The Bible of the World* has been to eliminate most of these repetitions.

In choosing what has been included the editors have been guided by a desire to put into one volume for the modern Western reader those concepts which are essential to his understanding of the eight most important and influential of the world's living religions, and that poetry and prose of great and enduring beauty which has ever made, and will always make, sacred books one of the world's most fertile literary sources.

It has been the aim of the book to give the reader the essential scriptures of each of these eight religions. The editors believe that, through reading *The Bible of the World,* it will be possible (for one who is not devoting his life to scholarship) to achieve a deeper and more intimate understanding of the scriptures than he is likely to gain through an attempt to read the hundreds of books which would be necessary if he were to seek the same material in complete form.

The Old and New Testaments of the Hebrew-Christian scriptures, for instance, have been reduced from about 750,000 to about 225,000 words, yet if a reader were to make his first acquaintance with our Bible in this form, he would be able to acquire from these 225,000 words probably as intimate a knowledge of this great library of books as that of the man in whose childhood and youth the King James Bible was the most familiar book.

Those of us who were brought up on the Bible have long since discarded such slight memories as we may have had of special outworn rituals and religious laws which no longer have meaning, of the Chronicles of the Jews, of much of the less important warfare of the Old Testament, of the detailed architectural descriptions of temples and altars. These, and similar passages from other scriptures, have been omitted from *The Bible of the World*. On the other hand, those basic principles of social and ethical conduct, and that timeless music of religious exaltation which rings for ever in the words of the Vedic poets, the Psalmists, Isaiah, Jesus, Buddha, Confucius, Lao Tze, Chuang Tze, and Sri Ramakrishna, have been given new emphasis through omission of what is less vital.

In the preparation of *The Bible of the World* more than a thousand books have been examined. Where more than one translation of a desired text is in existence different translations have been compared and one chosen which combines sound scholarship with readable English rendering. In each field specialists have been consulted.

For the Hebrew-Christian scriptures the King James translation has been used. Although more accurate translations than this have been made, and although the synagogues use a slightly different translation of the Old Testament and the Catholic Church a different translation of both Testaments, the King James—even with its specific errors—remains the English Bible to such a predominant majority of English-speaking persons that the use of any other seemed less desirable. Though the author of the Twenty-Third Psalm (according to the translation of Dr. J. M. P. Smith) wrote: "Even though I walk in the darkest valley" and "I shall dwell in the house of the Lord down to old age," the King James rendering: "Yea, though I walk through the valley of the shadow of death" and "I shall dwell in the house of the Lord for ever," are imperishable parts of the Judeo-Christian tradition, with their intimations of immortality which the psalmist probably never intended.

A word of justification may be necessary for excluding canonical scriptures of such less well-known religions as Jainism (save for a few brief passages which occur as an addition to the Buddhist section), Sikhism, Shintoism, Bahai, Swedenborgianism, Mormonism, Christian Science, and others. In consideration of the limited space available, a decision had to be made to include only the scriptures of those religions whose basic sacred books were compiled during the great scriptural era between 2000 B.C. and A.D. 1000. These are the scriptures which have most greatly influenced the world's thought. In them will be found the sources of most of the faiths which may to-day bear different names.

But why, one may ask, exclude these and include apocryphal Judeo-Christian scriptures? The Old Testament books now excluded from the King James Bible were at one time a part of the canon of the entire

Christian Church. A number of those books which were finally dropped from the Protestant English canon only in 1648 by the Westminster Assembly of the Church of England are still included as canonical in the Vulgate version used by the Roman Catholic Church. Some of them, not now included in the King James Bible, are nevertheless acknowledged in the Book of Common Prayer of the American Protestant Episcopal Church, as books to be read "for example of life and instruction of manners."

The position in regard to the much less known New Testament Apocrypha is somewhat different. The Old Testament apocryphal books —the Second Book of Esdras, Tobit, Ecclesiasticus, Susanna and the Elders, and the others—are simply additions to the basic traditions and theology of the Old Testament. The discarded books which deal with the lives and teachings of Christ and his disciples, on the other hand, present many concepts and legends which must be considered heretical in the light of Christian Church dogma, and in this fact we find the reason for their exclusion from our traditional Bible and our lack of familiarity with them.

Yet some of the dearest traditions of the Christian Church come from these heretical books rather than from those of the canonical scriptures. Christ's descent into Hell (p. 1268), mentioned in the Catholic and Episcopal (and formerly in other Protestant) versions of the Apostles' Creed, is documented not by a book in the King James Bible but by a long apocryphal story. The story of the mother of the Virgin Mary (p. 1247), so important to Catholic theology, is only in the Apocrypha.

Further interest in the New Testament Apocrypha is added by the fact that many of these books formed an important part of the scriptures of Manichæism and Gnosticism, which, while not living religions to-day in the sense of having organizations and churches, are very much alive in their profound influence on modern religious thought.

As to the canonical books of the Old Testament, the editors, after consideration, decided to abandon the order in which they appear in the King James translation, so as to present the prophets in that order which is now believed to be approximately chronological. Between the time of Amos, Hosea, and Micah, and the time of Daniel, a great deal had happened to Jewish social and religious thought. A gradual transition had taken place in the conception of God, until the vengeful and still somewhat tribal Jehovah of the earlier prophets had assumed many of the aspects of the universal Father-God of the New Testament. The arrangement of the books of the prophets in *The Bible of the World*, based upon contemporary judgments of the approximate order in which the books were written, presents a record of this transition somewhat as it occurred. This has involved a division of the book of Isaiah, the first and last parts of which are now considered as two distinct books written by two prophets separated in time by perhaps two hundred years, whose writings are markedly different in style and feeling.

The arrangement of material taken from the four canonical Gospels which contain most of our conceptions of the life and teachings of Jesus was made entirely from the point of view of a layman, with full consideration for objections which may be made, in the light of exegesis, to mixing the material of the synoptic Gospels (Matthew, Mark, and Luke) with that of John, which is considerably later, which has fewer evidences of historicity, and which reflects a somewhat different theology. The possibility was also considered that the arrangement here presented might create the false impression of attempting to present the life of Jesus in exact chronological sequence.

Actually the intent of *The Bible of the World* arrangement is not to attempt a synthesis or reconciliation of the four Gospels, nor to select those passages which have any special claim to historicity, nor to intimate that there is any scholarly basis for belief that this arrangement presents the acts and sayings of Jesus in their actual chronological order.

Here, as elsewhere, our object has been to present, in restricted space, and in as convenient an arrangement as possible, scriptural material as the great mass of scripture readers have been influenced by it. The story of Christ, which has so deeply influenced human thought and the course of civilization, falls naturally into two parts—the story of the things he did and the things which were done to him, and the record of the things he said.

But neither all of the Gospel record of his life nor that of his sayings, nor that of the attitude of his contemporary world toward him, is contained in any one of the Gospels, nor even in all the synoptics. The Sermon on the Mount, for instance, occurs as a whole only in Matthew; the story of the woman taken in adultery, and the theological conception of the Word as God, occur only in John. And throughout the four Gospels there are many differences in the record of details.

The story which the average lay Christian knows of the life of Jesus is a synthetic story made up of bits of all four of these books. He makes no special distinction between the three earlier synoptic Gospels and the later Gospel of John. To each of the four sacred books he attaches equal authority and the same theological significance. Indeed he is often scarcely conscious of the detailed differences that exist between them. If John has been his favourite Gospel, he believes that Jesus carried his cross to Calvary; if he has learned more thoroughly the tradition of Matthew, Mark, or Luke, he believes that another carried it, and if his memory is especially good, that the cross-bearer's name was Simon.

The differences in these details seem to me of no importance to one seeking the basic meaning of Christ, save that they evidence our lack of absolute historical knowledge of the ordinary everyday life of Jesus. It is spiritually healthful for us to accept that lack. Since we have no absolute knowledge, belief in the historical accuracy of the Gospels and a desire to hold to a complete factual consistency are detrimental to the perception of the truths and healing goodness of Christ. Only by wiping out of our minds that desire, by accepting the fact that it can never be realized, can the significance of Christ be found. It is for this reason that variant versions of the same stories will be found together in *The Bible of the World* rendering of Gospel material, so that the reader may easily compare them and discover the differences himself.

Any criticism of this handling of the Gospels should be directed at the lay editor and not at the scholars who have worked in the compilation of this volume.

For greater convenience in reading, identification of sources and explanatory and critical material usually found in footnotes have not been printed with the text pages, but put in an appendix, in which attention is called also to many of the fascinating parallels which exist between all of the world's scriptures.

ROBERT O. BALLOU

July 1939

HINDU
Scriptures

HINDU SCRIPTURES

The Hymns of the Rig-Veda

Creation

Then was not non-existent nor existent: there was no realm of air,
no sky beyond it.
What covered in, and where? and what gave shelter? Was water there,
unfathomed depth of water?

Death was not then, nor was there aught immortal: no sign was there,
the day's and night's divider.
That One Thing, breathless, breathed by its own nature: apart from it
was nothing whatsoever.

Darkness there was: at first concealed in darkness this All was undis-
criminated chaos.
All that existed then was void and formless: by the great power of
warmth was born that unit.

Thereafter rose desire in the beginning, desire, the primal seed and
germ of spirit.
Sages who searched with their heart's thought discovered the existent's
kinship in the non-existent.

Transversely was their severing line extended: what was above it then,
and what below it?
There were begetters, there were mighty forces, free action here and
energy up yonder.

Who verily knows and who can here declare it, whence it was born and
whence comes this creation?
The gods are later than this world's production. Who knows then whence
it first came into being?

He, the first origin of this creation, whether he formed it all or did not
form it,
Whose eye controls this world in highest heaven, he verily knows it, or
perhaps he knows not.

To Dawn

This light is come, amid all lights the fairest; born is the brilliant, far-
extending brightness.
Night, sent away for Savitar's uprising, hath yielded up a birthplace
for the morning.

The fair, the bright is come with her white offspring; to her the dark one
hath resigned her dwelling.
Akin, immortal, following each other, changing their colours both the
heavens move onward.

Common, unending is the sisters' pathway; taught by the gods, alternately they travel.
Fair-formed, of different hues and yet one-minded, Night and Dawn
clash not, neither do they tarry.

Bright leader of glad sounds, our eyes behold her; splendid in hue she
hath unclosed the portals.
She, stirring up the world, hath shown us riches: Dawn hath awakened
every living creature.

Rich Dawn, she sets afoot the coiled-up sleeper, one for enjoyment, one
for wealth or worship,
Those who saw little for extended vision. All living creatures hath the
dawn awakened.

One to high sway, one to exalted glory, one to pursue his gain, and
one his labour:
All to regard their different vocations, all moving creatures hath the
dawn awakened.

We see her there, the child of heaven, apparent, the young maid, flushing
in her shining raiment.

Thou sovran lady of all earthly treasure, flush on us here, auspicious
    Dawn, this morning.

She, first of endless morns to come hereafter, follows the path of morns
    that have departed.
Dawn, at her rising, urges forth the living: him who is dead she wakes
    not from his slumber.

Gone are the men who in the days before us looked on the rising of
    the earlier morning.
We, we the living, now behold her brightness, and they come nigh who
    shall hereafter see her.

Arise! the breath, the life, again hath reached us: darkness hath passed
    away, and light approacheth.
She for the sun hath left a path to travel: we have arrived where men
    prolong existence.

Singing the praises of refulgent mornings with his hymn's web the
    priest, the poet, rises.
Shine then to-day, rich maid, on him who lauds thee, shine down on us
    the gift of life and offspring.

To Indra

I will declare the manly deeds of Indra, the first that he achieved, the
    thunder-wielder.
He slew the dragon, then disclosed the waters, and cleft the channels of
    the mountain torrents.

He slew the dragon lying on the mountain: his heavenly bolt of thunder
    Tvashtar fashioned.
Like lowing kine in rapid flow descending the waters glided downward
    to the ocean.

Impetuous as a bull, he chose the Soma, and in three sacred beakers
    drank the juices.
The Bounteous One grasped the thunder for his weapon, and smote to
    death this firstborn of the dragons.

When, Indra, thou hadst slain the dragons' firstborn, and overcome the
     charms of the enchanters,
Then, giving life to sun and dawn and heaven, thou foundest not one
     foe to stand against thee.

Indra with his own great and deadly thunder smote into pieces Vritra,
     worst of Vritras.
As trunks of trees, what time the axe hath felled them, low on the earth
     so lies the prostrate dragon.

He, like a mad weak warrior, challenged Indra, the great impetuous
     many-slaying hero.
He, brooking not the clashing of the weapons, crushed—Indra's foe—
     the shattered forts in falling.

Footless and handless still he challenged Indra, who smote him with his
     bolt between the shoulders.
Emasculate yet claiming manly vigour, thus Vritra lay with scattered
     limbs dissevered.

There as he lies like a bank-bursting river, the waters taking courage
     flow above him.
The dragon lies beneath the feet of torrents which Vritra with his
     greatness had encompassed.

Then humbled was the strength of Vritra's mother: Indra hath cast his
     deadly bolt against her.
The mother was above, the son was under, and like a cow beside her
     calf lay Danu.

Rolled in the midst of never-ceasing currents flowing without a rest for
     ever onward,
The waters bear off Vritra's nameless body: the foe of Indra sank to
     during darkness.

Guarded by Ahi stood the thralls of Dasas, the waters stayed like kine
     held by the robber.
But he, when he had smitten Vritra, opened the cave wherein the floods
     had been imprisoned.

A horse's tail wast thou when he, O Indra, smote on thy bolt; thou,
     god without an equal,

Thou hast won back the kine, hast won the Soma; thou hast let loose
to flow the seven rivers.

Nothing availed him lightning, nothing thunder, hailstorm or mist
which he had spread around him:
When Indra and the dragon strove in battle, Maghavan gained the
victory for ever.

Whom sawest thou to avenge the dragon, Indra, that fear possessed thy
heart when thou hadst slain him;
That, like a hawk affrighted through the regions, thou crossedst nine-
and-ninety flowing rivers?

Indra is king of all that moves and moves not of creatures tame and
horned, the thunder-wielder.
Over all living men he rules as sovran, containing all as spokes within
the felly.

To Varuna

This laud of the self-radiant wise Aditya shall be supreme o'er all that
is in greatness.
I beg renown of Varuna the mighty, the god exceeding kind to him who
worships.

Having extolled thee, Varuna, with thoughtful care may we have high
fortune in thy service,
Singing thy praises like the fires at coming, day after day, of mornings
rich in cattle.

May we be in thy keeping, O thou leader, wide-ruling Varuna, lord of
many heroes.
O sons of Aditi, for ever faithful, pardon us, gods, admit us to your
friendship.

He made them flow, the Aditya, the sustainer: the rivers run by Varuna's
commandment.
These feel no weariness, nor cease from flowing: swift have they flown
like birds in air around us.

Loose me from sin as from a bond that binds me: may we swell, Varuna, thy spring of order.

Let not my thread, while I weave song, be severed, nor my work's sum, before the time, be shattered.

Far from me, Varuna, remove all danger: accept me graciously, thou holy sovran.

Cast off, like cords that hold a calf, my troubles: I am not even mine eyelid's lord without thee.

Strike us not, Varuna, with those dread weapons which, Asura, at thy bidding wound the sinner.

Let us not pass away from light to exile. Scatter, that we may live, the men who hate us.

O mighty Varuna, now and hereafter, even as of old, will we speak forth our worship.

For in thyself, invincible god, thy statutes ne'er to be moved are fixed as on a mountain.

Move far from me what sins I have committed: let me not suffer, king, for guilt of others.

Full many a morn remains to dawn upon us: in these, O Varuna, while we live direct us.

O King, whoever, be he friend or kinsman, hath threatened me affrighted in my slumber—

If any wolf or robber fain would harm us, therefore, O Varuna, give thou us protection.

May I not live, O Varuna, to witness my wealthy, liberal, dear friend's destitution.

King, may I never lack well-ordered riches. Loud may we speak, with heroes, in assembly.

To Varuna

Sing forth a hymn sublime and solemn, grateful to glorious Varuna, imperial ruler,

Who hath struck out, like one who slays the victim, earth as a skin to
   spread in front of Surya.

In the tree-tops the air he hath extended, put milk in kine and vigorous
   speed in horses,
Set intellect in hearts, fire in the waters, Surya in heaven and Soma on
   the mountain.

Varuna lets the big cask, opening downward, flow through the heaven
   and earth and air's mid-region.
Therewith the universe's sovran waters earth as the shower of rain
   bedews the barley.

When Varuna is fain for milk he moistens the sky, the land, and earth
   to her foundation.
Then straight the mountains clothe them in the rain-cloud: the heroes,
   putting forth their vigour, loose them.

I will declare this mighty deed of magic, of glorious Varuna the lord
   immortal,
Who standing in the firmament hath meted the earth out with the sun
   as with a measure.

None, verily, hath ever let or hindered this the most wise god's mighty
   deed of magic,
Whereby with all their flood, the lucid rivers fill not one sea wherein
   they pour their waters.

If we have sinned against the man who loves us, have ever wronged
   a brother, friend, or comrade,
The neighbour ever with us, or a stranger, O Varuna, remove from us
   the trespass.

If we, as gamesters cheat at play, have cheated, done wrong unwittingly
   or sinned of purpose,
Cast all these sins away like loosened fetters, and, Varuna, let us be
   thine own beloved.

To Agni

Dear, ageless sacrificial drink is offered in light-discovering, heaven-
pervading Agni.
The gods spread forth through his celestial nature, that he might bear
the world up and sustain it.

The world was swallowed and concealed in darkness; Agni was born,
and light became apparent.
The deities, the broad earth, and the heavens, and plants, and waters
gloried in his friendship.

Inspired by gods who claim our adoration, I now will laud eternal lofty
Agni,
Him who hath spread abroad the earth with lustre, this heaven, and both
the worlds, and air's mid-region.

Earliest priest whom all the gods accepted, and chose him, and anointed
him with butter,
He swiftly made all things that fly, stand, travel, all that hath motion,
Agni Jatavedas.

Because thou, Agni Jatavedas, stoodest at the world's head with thy refulgent splendour,
We sent thee forth with hymns and songs and praises: thou filledst
heaven and earth, God meet for worship.

Head of the world is Agni in the night-time; then, as the sun, at morn
springs up and rises.
Then to his task goes the prompt priest foreknowing the wondrous
power of gods who must be honoured.

Lovely is he who, kindled in his greatness, hath shone forth, seated in
the heavens, refulgent.
With resonant hymns all gods who guard our bodies have offered up
oblation in this Agni.

First the gods brought the hymnal into being; then they engendered
Agni, then oblation.

He was their sacrifice that guards our bodies; him the heavens know, the earth, the waters know him.

He, Agni, whom the gods have generated, in whom they offered up all worlds and creatures,
He with his bright glow heated earth and heaven, urging himself right onward in his grandeur.

Then by the laud the gods engendered Agni in heaven, who fills both worlds through strength and vigour.
They made him to appear in threefold essence; he ripens plants of every form and nature.

What time the gods, whose due is worship, set him as sun-god, son of Aditi, in heaven,
When the pair, ever wandering, sprang to being, all creatures that existed looked upon them.

For all the world of life the gods made the universal Agni to be the days' bright banner—
Him who hath spread abroad the radiant mornings, and, coming with his light, unveils the darkness.

The wise and holy deities engendered the universal Agni whom age ne'er touches,
The ancient star that wanders on for ever, lofty and strong, lord of the living being.

We call upon the sage with holy verses, the universal Agni, the ever-beaming,
Who hath surpassed both heaven and earth in greatness: he is a god below, a god above us.

I have heard mention of two several pathways, ways of the fathers and of gods and mortals.
On these two paths each moving creature travels, each thing between the father and the mother.

These two united paths bear him who journeys born from the head and pondered with the spirit.
He stands directed to all things existing, hasting, unresting in his fiery splendour.

Which of us twain knows where they speak together, upper and lower
    of the two rite-leaders?
Our friends have helped to gather our assembly. They came to sacrifice;
    who will announce it?

How many are the fires and suns in number? What is the number of
    the dawns and waters?
Not jestingly I speak to you, O fathers. Sages, I ask you this for in-
    formation.

As great as is the fair-winged morning's presence to him who dwells
    beside us, Matarisvan!
Is what the Brahmana does when he approaches to sacrifice and sits
    below the Hotar.

To Agni, in Praise of Night and Day

One-half of day is dark, and bright the other: both atmospheres move
    on by sage devices.
Agni Vaisvanara, when born as sovran, hath with his lustre overcome
    the darkness.

I know not either warp or woof, I know not the web they weave when
    moving to the contest.
Whose son shall here speak words that must be spoken without assist-
    ance from the Father near him?

For both the warp and woof he understandeth, and in due time shall
    speak what should be spoken,
Who knoweth as the immortal world's protector, descending, seeing
    with no aid from other.

He is the priest, the first of all: behold him. Mid mortal men he is the
    light immortal.
Here was he born, firm-seated in his station, immortal, ever waxing in
    his body.

A firm light hath been set for men to look on: among all things that fly
    the mind is swiftest.

All gods of one accord, with one intention, move unobstructed to a
single purpose.

Mine ears unclose to hear, mine eye to see him; the light that harbours
in my spirit broadens.
Far roams my mind, whose thoughts are in the distance. What shall I
speak, what shall I now imagine?

All the gods bowed them down in fear before thee, Agni, when thou
wast dwelling in the darkness.
O Universal One, be gracious to assist us, may the Immortal favour us
and help us.

To the Waters

Forth from the middle of the flood the waters—their chief the sea—
flow cleansing, never sleeping.
Indra, the bull, the thunderer, dug their channels: here let those waters,
goddesses, protect me.

Waters which come from heaven, or those that wander dug from the
earth, or flowing free by nature,
Bright, purifying, speeding to the ocean, here let those waters, goddesses, protect me.

Those amid whom goes Varuna the sovran, he who discriminates men's
truth and falsehood—
Distilling meath, the bright, the purifying, here let those waters, goddesses, protect me.

They from whom Varuna the king, and Soma, and all the deities drink
strength and vigour,
They into whom the universal Agni entered, here let those waters, goddesses, protect me.

To Varuna

Wise, verily, are creatures through his greatness who stayed even spacious
heaven and earth asunder;

Who urged the high and mighty sky to motion, the star of old, and
    spread the earth before him.

With mine own heart I commune on the question how Varuna and I may
    be united.
What gift of mine will he accept unangered? When may I calmly look
    and find him gracious?

Fain to know this my sin I question others: I seek the wise, O Varuna,
    and ask them.
This one same answer even the sages gave me, Surely this Varuna is
    angry with thee.

What, Varuna, hath been my chief transgression, that thou wouldst slay
    the friend who sings thy praises?
Tell me, unconquerable lord, and quickly sinless will I approach thee
    with mine homage.

Free us from sins committed by our fathers, from those wherein we have
    ourselves offended.
O king, loose, like a thief who feeds the cattle, as from the cord a calf,
    set free Vasishtha.

Not our own will betrayed us, but seduction, thoughtlessness, Varuna!
    wine, dice, or anger.
The old is near to lead astray the younger: even sleep removeth not all
    evil doing.

Slavelike may I do service to the Bounteous, serve, free from sin, the
    god inclined to anger.
This gentle lord gives wisdom to the simple: the wiser god leads on
    the wise to riches.

O lord, O Varuna, may this laudation come close to thee and lie within
    thy spirit.
May it be well with us in rest and labour. Preserve us evermore, ye gods,
    with blessings.

To Frogs

They who lay quiet for a year, the Brahmanas who fulfil their vows,
The frogs have lifted up their voice, the voice the rain god hath
    inspired.

What time on these, as on a dry skin lying in the pool's bed, the floods
    of heaven descend,
The music of the frogs comes forth in concert like the cows' lowing
    with their calves beside them.

When at the coming of the rains the water has poured upon them as they
    yearned and thirsted,
One seeks another as he talks and greets him with cries of pleasure as a
    son his father.

Each of these twain receives the other kindly, while they are revelling in
    the flow of waters,
When the frog moistened by the rain springs forward, and green and
    spotty both combine their voices.

When one of these repeats the other's language, as he who learns the
    lesson of the teacher,
Your every limb seems to be growing larger as ye converse with elo-
    quence on the waters.

One is Cow-bellow and Goat-bleat the other, one frog is green and one
    of them is spotty.
They bear one common name, and yet they vary, and, talking, modulate
    the voice diversely.

As Brahmanas, sitting round the brimful vessel, talk at the Soma-rite of
    nightly worship,
So, frogs, ye gather round the pool to honour this day of all the year,
    the first of rain-time.

These Brahmanas with the Soma juice, performing their year-long rite,
    have lifted up their voices;
And these performers, sweating with their kettles, come forth and show
    themselves, and none are hidden.

They keep the twelvemonth's God-appointed order, and never do the
    men neglect the season.
Soon as the rain-time in the year returneth, these who were heated
    kettles gain their freedom.

Cow-bellow and Goat-bleat have granted riches, and green and spotty
    have vouchsafed us treasure.
The frogs who give us cows in hundreds lengthen our lives in this most
    fertilizing season.

To Indra

I from my father have received deep knowledge of the holy law:
I was born like unto the sun.

After the lore of ancient time I make, like Kanva, beauteous songs,
And Indra's self gains strength thereby.

Whatever Rishis have not praised thee, Indra, or have lauded thee,
By me exalted wax thou strong.

Indra, these spotted cows yield thee their butter and the milky draught,
Aiders, thereby, of sacrifice;

Which, teeming, have received thee as a life-germ, Indra, with their
    mouth,
Like Surya who sustaineth all.

Accept this eulogy of mine, Indra, and guard me carefully:
Strengthen my thought and prosper it.

For thee, O mighty, thunder-armed, we singers through devotion have
Fashioned the hymn that we may live.

Come with thy lovely bay steeds, come to us from regions far away:
O Indra, drink this Soma juice.

Dialogue between Yama and Yami

Fain would I win my friend to kindly friendship. So may the sage, come
   through the air's wide ocean,
Remembering the earth and days to follow, obtain a son, the issue of his
   father.

Thy friend loves not the friendship which considers her who is near
   in kindred as a stranger.
Sons of the mighty Asura, the heroes, supporters of the heavens, see far
   around them.

Yea, this the immortals seek of thee with longing, progeny of the sole
   existing mortal.
Then let thy soul and mine be knit together, and as a loving husband
   take thy consort.

Shall we do now what we ne'er did aforetime? we who spake righteously
   now talk impurely?
Gandharva in the floods, the dame of waters—such is our bond, such our
   most lofty kinship.

Even in the womb god Tvashtar, vivifier, shaping all forms, creator,
   made us consorts.
None violates his holy ordinances: that we are his the heavens and earth
   acknowledge.

Who knows that earliest day whereof thou speakest? Who hath beheld
   it? Who can here declare it?
Great is the law of Varuna and Mitra. What, wanton! wilt thou say to
   men to tempt them?

I, Yami, am possessed by love of Yama, that I may rest on the same
   couch beside him.
I as a wife would yield me to my husband. Like car-wheels let us speed
   to meet each other.

They stand not still, they never close their eyelids, those sentinels of
   gods who wander round us.

Not me—go quickly, wanton, with another, and hasten like a chariot
    wheel to meet him.

May Surya's eye with days and nights endow him, and ever may his light
    spread out before him.
In heaven and earth the kindred pair commingle. On Yami be the un-
    brotherly act of Yama.

Sure there will come succeeding times when brothers and sisters will do
    acts unmeet for kinsfolk.
Not me, O fair one,—seek another husband, and make thine arm a pillow
    for thy consort.

Is he a brother when no lord is left her? Is she a sister when destruction
    cometh?
Forced by my love these many words I utter. Come near, and hold me
    in thy close embraces.

I will not fold mine arms about thy body; they call it sin when one comes
    near his sister.
Not me,—prepare thy pleasures with another: thy brother seeks not this
    from thee, O fair one.

Alas! thou art indeed a weakling, Yama; we find in thee no trace of
    heart or spirit.
As round the tree the woodbine clings, another will cling about thee
    girt as with a girdle.

Embrace another, Yami; let another, even as the woodbine rings the
    tree, enfold thee.
Win thou his heart and let him win thy fancy, and he shall form with
    thee a blest alliance.

Funeral Hymn

For some is Soma purified, some sit by sacrificial oil:
To those for whom the meath flows forth, even to those let him depart.

Invincible through fervour, those whom fervour hath advanced to
    heaven,
Who showed great fervour in their lives,—even to those let him depart.

The heroes who contend in war and boldly cast their lives away,
Or who give guerdon thousandfold,—even to those let him depart.

Yea, the first followers of law, law's pure and holy strengtheners,
The fathers, Yama! fervour-moved,—even to those let him depart.

Skilled in a thousand ways and means, the sages who protect the sun,
The Rishis, Yama! fervour-moved,—even to those let him depart.

Prayer of a Gambler

Sprung from tall trees on windy heights, these rollers transport me as
    they turn upon the table.
Dearer to me the die that never slumbers than the deep draught of
    Mujavan's own Soma.

She never vexed me nor was angry with me, but to my friends and me
    was ever gracious.
For the die's sake, whose single point is final, mine own devoted wife
    I alienated.

My wife holds me aloof, her mother hates me: the wretched man finds
    none to give him comfort.
As of a costly horse grown old and feeble, I find not any profit of the
    gamester.

Others caress the wife of him whose riches the die hath coveted, that
    rapid courser:
Of him speak father, mother, brothers saying, We know him not: bind
    him and take him with you.

When I resolve to play with these no longer, my friends depart from me
    and leave me lonely.
When the brown dice, thrown on the board, have rattled, like a fond
    girl I seek the place of meeting.

The gamester seeks the gambling-house, and wonders, his body all afire,
    Shall I be lucky?
Still do the dice extend his eager longing, staking his gains against his
    adversary.

Downward they roll, and then spring quickly upward, and, handless,
    force the man with hands to serve them.
Cast on the board, like lumps of magic charcoal, though cold themselves
    they burn the heart to ashes.

Play not with dice: no, cultivate thy corn-land. Enjoy the gain, and
    deem that wealth sufficient.
There are thy cattle, there thy wife, O gambler. So this good Savitar
    himself hath told me.

Make me your friend: show us some little mercy. Assail us not with your
    terrific fierceness.
Appeased be your malignity and anger, and let the brown dice snare
    some other captive.

To Purusha

A thousand heads hath Purusha, a thousand eyes, a thousand feet.
On every side pervading earth he fills a space ten fingers wide.

This Purusha is all that yet hath been and all that is to be;
The lord of immortality which waxes greater still by food.

So mighty is his greatness; yea, greater than this is Purusha.
All creatures are one-fourth of him, three-fourths eternal life in heaven.

With three-fourths Purusha went up: one-fourth of him again was here.
Thence he strode out to every side over what eats not and what eats.

From him Viraj was born; again Purusha from Viraj was born.
As soon as he was born he spread eastward and westward o'er the earth.

When gods prepared the sacrifice with Purusha as their offering,
Its oil was spring, the holy gift was autumn; summer was the wood.

From that great general sacrifice the dripping fat was gathered up.
He formed the creatures of the air, and animals both wild and tame.

From that great general sacrifice Rig-Veda and Sama-Veda were born:
Therefrom were spells and charms produced; the Yajur-Veda had its
    birth from it.

From it were horses born, from it all cattle with two rows of teeth:
From it were generated kine, from it the goats and sheep were born.

When they divided Purusha how many portions did they make?
What do they call his mouth, his arms? What do they call his thighs
and feet?

The Brahman was his mouth, of both his arms was the Rajanya made.
His thighs became the Vaisya, from his feet the Sudra was produced.

The moon was gendered from his mind, and from his eye the sun had
birth;
Indra and Agni from his mouth were born, and Vayu from his breath.

Forth from his navel came mid-air; the sky was fashioned from his head;
Earth from his feet, and from his ear the regions. Thus they formed the
worlds.

Seven fencing-sticks had he, thrice seven layers of fuel were prepared,
When the gods, offering sacrifice, bound, as their victim, Purusha.

Gods, sacrificing, sacrificed the victim: these were the earliest holy
ordinances.
The mighty ones attained the height of heaven, there where the Sadhyas,
gods of old, are dwelling.

To Liberality

The gods have not ordained hunger to be our death: even to the well-fed
man comes death in varied shape.
The riches of the liberal never waste away, while he who will not give
finds none to comfort him.

The man with food in store who, when the needy comes in miserable
case begging for bread to eat,
Hardens his heart against him—even when of old he did him service—
finds not one to comfort him.

Bounteous is he who gives unto the beggar who comes to him in want of
food and feeble.
Success attends him in the shout of battle. He makes a friend of him in
future troubles.

No friend is he who to his friend and comrade who comes imploring
    food will offer nothing.
Let him depart—no home is that to rest in—, and rather seek a stranger
    to support him.

Let the rich satisfy the poor implorer, and bend his eye upon a longer
    pathway.
Riches come now to one, now to another, and like the wheels of cars
    are ever rolling.

The hands are both alike: their labour differs. The yield of sister milch-
    kine is unequal.
Twins even differ in their strength and vigour: two, even kinsmen,
    differ in their bounty.

To Night

With all her eyes the goddess Night looks forth approaching many a
    spot:
She hath put all her glories on.

Immortal, she hath filled the waste, the goddess hath filled height and
    depth:
She conquers darkness with her light.

The goddess as she comes hath set the Dawn her sister in her place:
And then the darkness vanishes.

So favour us this night, O thou whose pathways we have visited
As birds their nest upon the tree.

The villagers have sought their homes, and all that walks and all that
    flies,
Even the falcons fain for prey.

Keep off the she-wolf and the wolf, O Night, and keep the thief away:
Easy be thou for us to pass.

Clearly hath she come nigh to me who decks the dark with richest hues:
O Morning, cancel it like debts.

These have I brought to thee like kine. O Night, thou child of heaven, accept
    This laud as for a conqueror.

To Aranyani, the Woods Goddess

Goddess of wild and forest who seemest to vanish from the sight,
How is it that thou seekest not the village? Art thou not afraid?

What time the grasshopper replies and swells the shrill cicala's voice,
Seeming to sound with tinkling bells, the lady of the wood exults.

And, yonder, cattle seem to graze, what seems a dwelling-place appears:
Or else at eve the lady of the forest seems to free the wains.

Here one is calling to his cow, another there hath felled a tree:
At eve the dweller in the wood fancies that somebody hath screamed.

The goddess never slays, unless some murderous enemy approach.
Man eats of savoury fruit and then takes, even as he wills, his rest.

Now have I praised the forest queen, sweet-scented, redolent of balm,
The mother of all sylvan things, who tills not but hath stores of food.

The Atharva-Veda

Blessing for a Child

This child, old age! shall grow to meet thee only: none of the hundred
    other deaths shall harm him.
From trouble caused by friends let Mitra guard him, as a kind mother
    guards the son she nurses.

Mitra or Varuna the foe-destroyer, accordant, grant him death in course
    of nature!
Thus Agni, Hotar-priest, skilled in high statutes, declareth all the deities'
    generations.

Thou art the lord of all terrestrial cattle, of cattle born and to be born
    hereafter.
Let not breath drawn or breath emitted fail him. Let not his friends, let
    not his foemen slay him.

Let heaven thy father and let earth thy mother, accordant, give thee
    death in course of nature,
That thou mayst live on Aditi's bosom, guarded, a hundred winters,
    through thy respirations.

Lead him to life, O Agni, and to splendour, this dear child, Varuna!
    and thou, King Mitra!
Give him protection, Aditi! as a mother; all gods, that his be life of
    long duration!

A Love Charm

Let the impeller goad thee on. Rest not in peace upon thy bed.
Terrible is the shaft of love: therewith I pierce thee to the heart.

That arrow winged with longing thought, its stem desire, its neck
    resolve,
Let Kama, having truly aimed, shoot forth and pierce thee in the heart.

The shaft of Kama, pointed well, that withers and consumes the spleen,
With hasty feathers, all aglow, therewith I pierce thee to the heart.

Pierced through with fiercely-burning heat, steal to me with thy parch-
    ing lips,
Gentle and humble, all mine own, devoted, with sweet words of love.

Away from mother and from sire I drive thee hither with a whip,
That thou mayst be at my command and yield to every wish of mine.

Mitra and Varuna, expel all thought and purpose from her heart.
Deprive her of her own free-will and make her subject unto me.

To a Magical Plant, That It Heal a Broken Bone

Thou art the healer, making whole, the healer of the broken bone:
Make thou this whole, Arundhati!

Whatever bone of thine within thy body hath been wrenched or cracked,
May Dhatar set it properly, and join together limb by limb.

With marrow be thy marrow joined, thy limb united with the limb.
Let what hath fallen of thy flesh, and the bone also, grow again.

Let marrow close with marrow, let skin grow united with the skin.
Let blood and bone grow strong in thee, flesh grow together with the
    flesh.

Join thou together hair with hair, join thou together skin with skin.
Let blood and bone grow strong in thee. Unite the broken part, O plant.

Arise, advance, speed forth: the car hath goodly fellies, naves, and
    wheels.
Stand up erect upon thy feet.

If he be torn and shattered, having fallen into a pit, or a cast stone have
    struck him,
Let the skilled leech join limb with limb, as 'twere the portions of a car.

A Charm to Destroy Hostile Priests

Whatever plot from yonder, O ye gods, that godless man would frame,
Let not the gods come to his call, nor Agni bear his offering up. Come
    ye, come hither to my call.

Run, ye exertions, farther on. By Indra's order smite and slay.
As a wolf worrieth a sheep, so let not him escape from you while life
    remains. Stop fast his breath.

The Brahmana whom those yonder have appointed priest, for injury,
He, Indra! is beneath thy feet. I cast him to the god of death.

Exertions which that man hath made, exertions which he yet will make—
Turn them, O Indra, back again, O Vritra-slayer, back again on him that
      they may kill that man.

Here, Indra, Vritra-slayer, in thy strength pierce thou their vital parts.
Here, even here, attack them, O Indra. Thine own dear friend am I.
Indra, we closely cling to thee. May we be in thy favouring grace.

To Heaven and Earth

All hail to heaven!

All hail to earth!

All hail to air!

All hail to air!

All hail to heaven!

All hail to earth!

Mine eye is sun and my breath is wind, air is my soul and earth my body.
I verily who never have been conquered give up my life to heaven and
      earth for keeping.

Exalt my life, my strength, my deed and action; increase my understand-
      ing and my vigour.
Be ye my powerful keepers, watch and guard me, ye mistresses of life
      and life's creators! Dwell ye within me, and forbear to harm me.

A Charm against Witchcraft

An eagle found thee: with his snout a wild boar dug thee from the earth.
Harm thou, O plant, the mischievous, and drive the sorcerer away.

As 'twere a strip cut round from skin of a white-footed antelope,
Bind, like a golden chain, O God, his witchcraft on the sorcerer.

Take thou his sorcery by the hand, and to the sorcerer lead it back.
Lay it before him, face to face, that it may kill the sorcerer.

Back on the wizard fall his craft, upon the curser light his curse!
Let witchcraft, like a well-naved car, roll back upon the sorcerer.

Whoso, for other's harm hath dealt—woman or man—in magic arts,
To him we lead the sorcery back, even as a courser with a rope.

Thou who hast piercing weapons, pierce him who hath wrought it;
    conquer him.
We do not sharpen thee to slay the man who hath not practised it.

Go as a son goes to his sire: bite as a trampled viper bites.
As one who flies from bonds, go back, O witchcraft, to the sorcerer.

Let it go contrary like flame, like water following its course.
Let witchcraft, like a well-naved car, roll back upon the sorcerer.

A Charm to Grow Hair

Born from the bosom of wide earth the goddess, godlike plant, art thou:
So we, Nitatni! dig thee up to strengthen and fix fast the hair.

Make the old firm, make new hair spring, lengthen what has already
    grown.

Thy hair where it is falling off, and with the roots is torn away,
I wet and sprinkle with the plant, the remedy for all disease.

To Bless a Child's First Teeth

Two tigers have grown up who long to eat the mother and the sire:
Soothe, Brahmanaspati, and thou, O Jatavedas, both these teeth.

Let rice and barley be your food, eat also beans and sesamum.
This is the share allotted you, to be your portion, ye two teeth. Harm
    not your mother and your sire.

Both fellow teeth have been invoked, gentle and bringing happiness.
Elsewhither let the fierceness of your nature turn away, O teeth! Harm
    not your mother or your sire.

A Water Charm

That little spring of water which is running downward from the hill
I turn to healing balm for thee that thou mayst be good medicine.

Hither and onward! Well! Come on! Among thy hundred remedies
Most excellent of all art thou, curing disease and morbid flow.

Mighty is this wound-healing balm: from out the earth was it produced.
This is the cure for morbid flow, this driveth malady away.

Bless us the waters! be the plants auspicious!
May Indra's thunderbolt drive off the demons. Far from us fall the
　　　shafts they shoot against us!

A Charm against Fear

As heaven and earth are not afraid, and never suffer loss or harm,
Even so, my spirit, fear not thou.

As day and night are not afraid, nor ever suffer loss or harm,
Even so, my spirit, fear not thou.
As sun and moon are not afraid, nor ever suffer loss or harm,
Even so, my spirit, fear not thou.

As Brahmanhood and princely power fear not, nor suffer loss or harm,
Even so, my spirit, fear not thou.
As truth and falsehood have no fear, nor ever suffer loss or harm,
Even so, my spirit, fear not thou.

As what hath been and what shall be fear not, nor suffer loss or harm,
Even so, my spirit, fear not thou.

A Charm against Sterility

From thee we banish and expel the cause of thy sterility.
This in another place we lay apart from thee and far removed.

As arrow to the quiver, so let a male embryo enter thee.
Then from thy side be born a babe, a ten-month child, thy hero son.

Bring forth a male, bring forth a son. Another male shall follow him.
The mother shalt thou be of sons born and hereafter to be born.

With that auspicious genial flow wherewith bulls propagate their kind,
Do thou obtain thyself a son: be thou a fruitful mother-cow.

I give thee power to bear a child: within thee pass the germ of life!
Obtain a son, O woman, who shall be a blessing unto thee. Be thou a
    blessing unto him.

May those celestial herbs whose sire was heaven, the earth their mother,
    and their root the ocean,
May those celestial healing plants assist thee to obtain a son.

A Blessing on Barley

Spring high, O barley, and become much through thine own magnifi-
    cence:
Burst all the vessels; let the bolt from heaven forbear to strike thee down.

As we invite and call to thee, barley, a god who heareth us,
Raise thyself up like heaven on high and be exhaustless as the sea.

Exhaustless let thine out-turns be, exhaustless be thy gathered heaps,
Exhaustless be thy givers, and exhaustless those who eat of thee.

One Common Spirit

Prajapati engenders earthly creatures: may the benevolent ordainer form
    them,
Having one common womb, and mind, and spirit. He who is lord of
    plenty give me plenty!

To Time

Prolific, thousand-eyed, and undecaying, a horse with seven reins, Time
bears us onward.
Sages inspired with holy knowledge mount him: his chariot wheels are
all the worlds of creatures.

This Time hath seven rolling wheels and seven naves: immortality is
the chariot's axle.
This Time brings hitherward all worlds about us: as primal deity is he
entreated.

On Time is laid an overflowing beaker: this we behold in many a place
appearing.
He carries from us all these worlds of creatures. They call him Kala in
the loftiest heaven.

He only made the worlds of life, he only gathered the worlds of living
things together.
Their son did he become who was their father: no other higher power
than he existeth.

Kala created yonder heaven, and Kala made these realms of earth.
By Kala, stirred to motion, both what is and what shall be expand.

Kala created land: the sun in Kala hath his light and heat.
In Kala rest all things that be: in Kala doth the eye discern.

In Kala mind, in Kala breath, in Kala name are fixt and joined.
These living creatures, one and all, rejoice when Kala hath approached.

Kala embraces holy fire, the highest, Brahma, in himself.
Yea, Kala, who was father of Prajapati, is lord of all.

He made, he stirred this universe to motion, and on him it rests.
He, Kala, having now become Brahma, holds Parameshthin up.

Kala created living things and, first of all, Prajapati.
From Kala, self-made Kasyapa, from Kala holy fire was born.

The Satapatha-Brahmana

The Creation of Prajapati and the Gods

Verily, in the beginning this universe was water, nothing but a sea of water. The waters desired, "How can we be reproduced?" They toiled and performed fervid devotions; when they were becoming heated, a golden egg was produced. The year, indeed, was not then in existence: this golden egg floated about for as long as the space of a year.

In a year's time a man, this Prajapati, was produced therefrom; and hence a woman, a cow, or a mare brings forth within the space of a year; for Prajapati was born in a year. He broke open this golden egg. There was then, indeed, no resting-place: only this golden egg, bearing him, floated about for as long as the space of a year.

At the end of a year he tried to speak. He said "bhuh": this word became this earth;—"bhuvah": this became this air;—"svah": this became yonder sky. Therefore a child tries to speak at the end of a year, for at the end of a year Prajapati tried to speak.

When he was first speaking Prajapati spoke words of one syllable and of two syllables; whence a child, when first speaking, speaks words of one syllable and of two syllables.

These three words consist of five syllables: he made them to be the five seasons, and thus there are these five seasons. At the end of the first year, Prajapati rose to stand on these worlds thus produced; whence a child tries to stand up at the end of a year, for at the end of a year Prajapati stood up.

He was born with a life of a thousand years: even as one might see in the distance the opposite shore, so did he behold the opposite shore, the end of his own life.

Desirous of offspring, he went on singing praises and toiling. He laid the power of reproduction into his own self. By the breath of his mouth he created the gods: the gods were created on entering the sky; and this is the godhead of the gods (deva) that they were created on entering the sky (div). Having created them, there was, as it were, daylight for him; and this also is the godhead of the gods that, after creating them, there was, as it were, daylight (diva) for him.

And by the downward breathing (flatulence) he created the Asuras: they were created on entering this earth. Having created them there was, as it were, darkness for him.

He knew, "Verily, I have created evil for myself since, after creating, there has come to be, as it were, darkness for me." Even then he smote them with evil, and owing to this it was that they were overcome; whence people say, "Not true is that regarding the fight between the gods and Asuras which is related partly in the tale and partly in the legend; for it was even then that Prajapati smote them with evil, and it was owing to this that they were overcome."

Therefore it is with reference to this that the Rishi has said, "Not for a single day hast thou fought, nor hast thou any enemy, O Maghavan: illusion is what they say concerning thy battles; no foe hast thou fought either to-day or aforetime."

Now what daylight, as it were, there was for him, on creating the gods, of that he made the day; and what darkness, as it were, there was for him on creating the Asuras, of that he made the night: they are these two, day and night.

Now, these are the deities who were created out of Prajapati,—Agni, Indra, Soma, and Parameshth in Prajapatya.

They were born with a life of a thousand years: even as one would see in the distance the opposite shore, so did they behold the opposite shore of their own life.

Manu's Escape from the Flood

In the morning they brought to Manu water for washing, just as now also they are wont to bring water for washing the hands. When he was washing himself, a fish came into his hands.

It spoke to him the word, "Rear me, I will save thee!" "Wherefrom wilt thou save me?" "A flood will carry away all these creatures: from that I will save thee!" "How am I to rear thee?"

It said, "As long as we are small, there is great destruction for us: fish devours fish. Thou wilt first keep me in a jar. When I outgrow that, thou wilt dig a pit and keep me in it. When I outgrow that, thou wilt take me down to the sea, for then I shall be beyond destruction."

It soon became a large fish. Thereupon it said, "In such and such a year that flood will come. Thou shalt then attend to me (to my advice) by preparing a ship; and when the flood has risen thou shalt enter into the ship, and I will save thee from it."

After he had reared it in this way, he took it down to the sea. And in the same year which the fish had indicated to him, he attended to the advice of the fish by preparing a ship; and when the flood had risen, he entered into the ship. The fish then swam up to him, and to its horn he tied the rope of the ship, and by that means he passed swiftly up to yonder northern mountain.

It then said, "I have saved thee. Fasten the ship to a tree; but let not the water cut thee off, whilst thou art on the mountain. As the water subsides, thou mayest gradually descend!" Accordingly he gradually descended, and hence that slope of the northern mountain is called "Manu's descent." The flood then swept away all these creatures, and Manu alone remained here.

Being desirous of offspring, he engaged in worshipping and austerities. During this time he also performed a paka-sacrifice: he offered up in the waters clarified butter, sour milk, whey, and curds. Thence a woman was produced in a year: becoming quite solid, she rose; clarified butter gathered in her footprint. Mitra and Varuna met her.

They said to her, "Who art thou?" "Manu's daughter," she replied. "Say thou art ours," they said. "No," she said, "I am the daughter of him who begat me." They desired to have a share in her. She either agreed or did not agree, but passed by them. She came to Manu.

Manu said to her, "Who art thou?" "Thy daughter," she replied. "How, illustrious one, art thou my daughter?" he asked. She replied, "Those offerings of clarified butter, sour milk, whey, and curds, which thou madest in the waters, with them thou hast begotten me. I am the blessing (benediction): make use of me at the sacrifice! If thou wilt make use of me at the sacrifice, thou wilt become rich in offspring and cattle. Whatever blessing thou shalt invoke through me, all that shall be granted to thee!" He accordingly made use of her as the benediction in the middle of the sacrifice; for what is intermediate between the fore-offerings and the after-offerings, is the middle of the sacrifice.

With her he went on worshipping and performing austerities, wishing for offspring. Through her he generated this race, which is this race of Manu; and whatever blessing he invoked through her, all that was granted to him.

The Fire-Altar, the Universe

Verily, this brick-built fire-altar is this terrestrial world:—the waters of the encircling ocean are its circle of enclosing-stones; the men its Yajushmati bricks, the cattle its Sudadohas; the plants and trees its earth-fillings between the layers of bricks, its oblations and fire-logs; Agni, the terrestrial fire, its space-filling brick;—thus this comes to make up the whole Agni, and the whole Agni comes to be the space-filler; and, verily, whosoever knows this, thus comes to be that whole Agni who is the space-filler.

But, indeed, that fire-altar also is the air:—the junction of heaven and earth, the horizon, is its circle of enclosing-stones, for it is beyond the air that heaven and earth meet, and that junction is the circle of enclosing-stones; the birds are its Yajushmati bricks, the rain its Suda-dohas, the rays of light its earth-fillings, oblations and fire-logs; Vayu, the wind, is its space-filler; thus this comes to make up the whole Agni, and the whole Agni comes to be the space-filler; and, verily, whosoever knows this, thus comes to be that whole Agni who is the space-filler.

But, indeed, that fire-altar also is the sky:—the heavenly waters are its enclosing-stones, for even as a case here is closed up so are these worlds enclosed within the waters; and the waters beyond these worlds are the enclosing-stones;—the gods are the Yajushmati bricks; what food there is in that world is its Sudadohas; the lunar mansions are the earth-fillings, the oblations and the fire-logs; and Aditya, the sun, is the space-filler;—thus this comes to make up the whole Agni; and the whole Agni comes to be the space-filler; and, verily, whosoever knows this, thus comes to be that whole Agni who is the space-filler.

But, indeed, that fire-altar also is the sun:—the regions are its enclosing-stones, and there are three hundred and sixty of these, because three hundred and sixty regions encircle the sun on all sides;—the rays are its Yajushmati bricks, for there are three hundred and sixty of these, and three hundred and sixty rays of the sun; and in that he establishes the Yajushmatis within the enclosing-stones thereby he establishes the rays in the regions. And what is between the regions and the rays is its Sudadohas; and what food there is in the regions and rays, that is the earth-fillings, the oblations and the fire-logs; and that which is called both "regions" and "rays" is the space-filling brick:—thus this comes to make up the whole Agni; and the whole Agni comes to be the space-filler; and, verily, whosoever knows this, thus comes to be that whole Agni who is the space-filler.

But, indeed, that fire-altar also is the year:—the nights are its enclosing-stones, and there are three hundred and sixty of these, because there are three hundred and sixty nights in the year; and the days are its Yajushmati bricks, for there are three hundred and sixty of these, and three hundred and sixty days in the year; and those thirty-six bricks which are over are the thirteenth month, the body of the year and the altar, the half-months and months,—there being twenty-four half-months, and twelve months. And what there is between day and night, that is the Sudadohas; and what food there is in the days and nights is the earth-fillings, the oblations, and the fire-logs; and what is called "days and nights" that constitutes the space-filling brick:—thus this comes to make up the whole Agni, and the whole Agni comes to be the space-filler; and, verily, whosoever knows this, thus comes to be that whole Agni who is the space-filler.

But, indeed, that fire-altar also is the body:—the bones are its enclosing-stones, and there are three hundred and sixty of these, because there are three hundred and sixty bones in man; the marrow parts are the Yajushmati bricks, for there are three hundred and sixty of these, and three hundred and sixty parts of marrow in man; and those thirty-six bricks which are over, are the thirteenth month, the trunk, the vital air of the altar,—in his body there are thirty parts, in his feet two, in his vital airs two, and in his head two,—as to there being two of these, it is because the head consists of two skull-bones. And that whereby these joints are held together is the Sudadohas; and those three whereby this body is covered—to wit, hair, skin, and flesh—are the earth-fillings; what he drinks is the oblations, and what he eats the fire-logs; and what is called the "body," that is the space-filling brick:—thus this comes to make up the whole Agni, and the whole Agni comes to be the space-filler; and, verily, whosoever knows this, thus comes to be that whole Agni who is the space-filler.

But, indeed, that which built Agni (the fire-altar) is all beings, all the gods; for all the gods, all beings are the waters, and that built fire-altar is the same as those waters;—the navigable streams round the sun are its enclosing-stones, and there are three hundred and sixty of these, because three hundred and sixty navigable streams encircle the sun on all sides; and the navigable streams, indeed, are also the Yajushmati bricks, and there are three hundred and sixty of these, because three hundred and sixty navigable streams flow towards the sun. And what is between each two navigable rivers is the Sudadohas; and those thirty-six bricks which remain over are the same as that thirteenth month, and the body of this altar, the waters, is the same as this gold man.

His feet are that gold plate and lotus-leaf—that is, the waters and the sun's orb are his feet; his arms are the two spoons, and they are Indra and Agni; the two naturally perforated bricks are this earth and the air; and the three all-light bricks are these deities—Agni, Vayu, and Aditya, for these deities, indeed, are all the light; and the twelve seasonal bricks are the year, the body of the altar, and the gold man; and the five celestials and five Pankakudas are the sacrifice, the gods; and the Vikarni, the third Svayamatrinna and the variegated stone; and the fire which is deposited on the altar is the thirty-fifth; and the formula of the space-filling brick is the thirty-sixth;—that gold man, indeed, the body of the altar, is the end of everything here: he is in the midst of all the waters, endowed with all objects of desire—for all objects of desire are the waters; whilst possessed of all objects of desire he is without desire, for no desire of anything troubles him.

Regarding this there is this verse—"By knowledge they ascend that state where desires have vanished: sacrificial gifts go not thither, nor the fervid practisers of rites without knowledge";—for, indeed, he who does not know this does not attain to that world either by sacrificial gifts or by devout practices, but only to those who know does that world belong.

The welkin is the earth-fillings between the layers of brick; the moon the oblations; the lunar mansions the fire-logs,—because the moon resides in the lunar mansions, therefore the oblation resides in the fire-wood: that, indeed, is the food of the oblation, and its support; whence the oblation does not fail, for that is its food and its support. And what are called "the gods" they are the space-filling brick; for by naming the gods everything here is named.

It is regarding this that it is said by the Ric, "The All-gods have gone after this thy Yajur"—for all beings, all the gods, indeed, become the Yajur here. Thus this whole Agni comes to be the space-filler; and, verily, whosoever knows this, thus comes to be that whole Agni who is the space-filler.

The Sacrificial Horse, the Universe

Verily, the dawn is the head of the sacrificial horse, the sun its eye, the wind its breath, Agni, the fire belonging to all men, its open mouth. The year is the body of the sacrificial horse, the sky its back, the air its belly, the earth the under part of its belly, the quarters its flanks, the intermediate quarters its ribs, the seasons its limbs, the months and half-months its joints, the days and nights its feet, the stars its bones, the welkin its flesh, the sand its intestinal food, the rivers its bowels, the mountains its liver and lungs, the herbs and trees its hair, the rising sun the forepart, and the setting sun the hindpart of its body, the lightning its yawning, the thundering its whinnying, the raining its voiding urine, and speech its voice. The day, indeed, was produced as the cup before the horse, and its birthplace is in the eastern sea. The night was produced as the cup behind it, and its birthplace is in the western sea: these two cups, indeed, came to be on both sides of the horse. As a steed it carried the gods; as a racer, the Gandharvas; as a courser, the Asuras; as a horse, men. The sea, indeed, is its kindred, the sea its birthplace.

The Upanishads

The Universal Self[1]

I

In the beginning this was Self alone, in the shape of a person. He looking round saw nothing but his Self. He first said, "This is I"; therefore he became I by name. Therefore even now, if a man is asked, he first says, "This is I," and then pronounces the other name which he may have. And because before (purva) all this, he, the Self, burnt down (ush) all evils, therefore he was a person (pur-usha). Verily he who knows this, burns down every one who tries to be before him.

He feared, and therefore any one who is lonely fears. He thought, "As there is nothing but myself, why should I fear?" Thence his fear passed away. For what should he have feared? Verily fear arises from a second only.

But he felt no delight. Therefore a man who is lonely feels no delight. He wished for a second. He was so large as man and wife together. He then made this his Self to fall in two, and thence arose husband and wife. Therefore Yajnavalkya said: "We two are thus, each of us, like half a shell." Therefore the void which was there is filled by the wife. He embraced her, and men were born.

---

[1] The word "Self" here must not be interpreted to mean the individual personal self, as we use the word in English. Nor is "soul," as it is sometimes translated, an adequate rendering. What is meant here is the universal soul, or universal self which is in each of us, that "Self" which existed before all else, which is the source of all life and being. Perhaps the conception in Western thought most nearly akin to it is "God within us." Instead of being the egotistic conception which on casual inspection it may seem to be, it is, on the contrary, the most extreme humility before that essence of divinity which pervades the human soul and mind.

She thought, "How can he embrace me, after having produced me from himself? I shall hide myself."

She then became a cow, the other became a bull and embraced her, and hence cows were born. The one became a mare, the other a stallion; the one a male ass, the other a female ass. He embraced her, and hence one-hoofed animals were born. The one became a she-goat, the other a he-goat; the one became a ewe, the other a ram. He embraced her, and hence goats and sheep were born. And thus he created everything that exists in pairs, down to the ants.

He knew, "I indeed am this creation, for I created all this." Hence he became the creation, and he who knows this lives in this his creation.

Next he thus produced fire by rubbing. From the mouth, as from the fire-hole, and from the hands he created fire. Therefore both the mouth and the hands are inside without hair, for the fire-hole is inside without hair.

And when they say, "Sacrifice to this or sacrifice to that god," each god is but his manifestation, for he is all gods.

Now, whatever there is moist, that he created from seed; this is Soma. So far verily is this universe either food or eater. Soma indeed is food, Agni eater. This is the highest creation of Brahman, when he created the gods from his better part, and when he, who was then mortal, created the immortals. Therefore it was the highest creation. And he who knows this lives in this his highest creation.

Now all this was then undeveloped. It became developed by form and name, so that one could say, "He, called so and so, is such a one." Therefore at present also all this is developed by name and form, so that one can say, "He, called so and so, is such a one."

He (Brahman or the Self) entered thither, to the very tips of the fingernails, as a razor might be fitted in a razor-case, or as fire in a fire-place.

He cannot be seen, for, in part only, when breathing, he is breath by name; when speaking, speech by name; when seeing, eye by name; when hearing, ear by name; when thinking, mind by name. All these are but the names of his acts. And he who worships (regards) him as the one or the other, does not know him, for he is apart from this when qualified by the one or the other. Let men worship him as Self, for in the Self all these are one. This Self is the footstep of everything, for through it one knows everything. And as one can find again by footsteps what was lost, thus he who knows this finds glory and praise.

This, which is nearer to us than anything, this Self, is dearer than a son, dearer than wealth, dearer than all else.

And if one were to say to one who declares another than the Self dear, that he will lose what is dear to him, very likely it would be so. Let him worship the Self alone as dear. He who worships the Self alone as dear, the object of his love will never perish.

Here they say: "If men think that by knowledge of Brahman they will become everything, what then did that Brahman know, whence all this sprang?"

Verily in the beginning this was Brahman, that Brahman knew its Self only, saying, "I am Brahman." From it all this sprang. Thus, whatever Deva was awakened so as to know Brahman, he indeed became that Brahman; and the same with Rishis and men. The Rishi Vamadeva saw and understood it, singing, "I was Manu (moon), I was the sun." Therefore now also he who thus knows that he is Brahman, becomes all this, and even the Devas cannot prevent it, for he himself is their Self.

Now if a man worships another deity, thinking the deity is one and he another, he does not know. He is like a beast for the Devas. For verily, as many beasts nourish a man, thus does every man nourish the Devas. If only one beast is taken away, it is not pleasant; how much more when many are taken! Therefore it is not pleasant to the Devas that men should know this.

Verily in the beginning this was Brahman, one only. That being one, was not strong enough. It created still further the most excellent Kshatra (power), viz. those Kshatras (powers) among the Devas—Indra, Varuna, Soma, Rudra, Parjanya, Yama, Mrityu, Isana. Therefore there is nothing beyond the Kshatra, and therefore at the Rajasuya sacrifice the Brahmana sits down below the Kshatriya. He confers that glory on the Kshatra alone. But Brahman is nevertheless the birthplace of the Kshatra. Therefore though a king is exalted, he sits down at the end of the sacrifice below the Brahmana, as his birthplace. He who injures him, injures his own birthplace. He becomes worse, because he has injured one better than himself.

He was not strong enough. He created the Vis (people), the classes of Devas which in their different orders are called Vasus, Rudras, Adityas, Visve Devas, Maruts.

He was not strong enough. He created the Sudra colour, caste, as Pushan (as nourisher). This earth verily is Pushan, the nourisher; for the earth nourishes all this whatsoever.

He was not strong enough. He created still further the most excellent law (dharma). Law is the power of powers; therefore there is nothing higher than the law. Thenceforth even a weak man rules a stronger with the help of the law, as with the help of a king. Thus the law is what is called the true. And if a man declares what is true, they say he declares the law; and if he declares the law, they say he declares what is true. Thus both are the same.

In the beginning this was Self alone, one only. He desired, "Let there be a wife for me that I may have offspring, and let there be wealth for me that I may offer sacrifices." Verily this is the whole desire, and, even if wishing for more, he would not find it. Therefore now also a lonely person desires, "Let there be a wife for me that I may have offspring, and let there be wealth for me that I may offer sacrifices." And so long as he does not obtain either of these things, he thinks he is incomplete. Now his completeness is made up as follows: mind is his Self (husband); speech the wife; breath the child; the eye all worldly wealth, for he finds it with the eye; the ear his divine wealth, for he hears it with the ear. The body (atman) is his work, for with the body he works. This is the fivefold sacrifice, for fivefold is the animal, fivefold man, fivefold all this whatsoever. He who knows this, obtains all this.

II

Now when Yajnavalkya was going to enter upon another state, he said: "Maitreyi, verily I am going away from this my house into the forest. Forsooth, let me make a settlement between thee and that Katyayani, my other wife."

Maitreyi said: "My lord, if this whole earth, full of wealth, belonged to me, tell me, should I be immortal by it?"

"No," replied Yajnavalkya; "like the life of rich people will be thy life. But there is no hope of immortality by wealth."

And Maitreyi said: "What should I do with that by which I do not become immortal? What my lord knoweth of immortality, tell that to me."

Yajnavalkya replied: "Thou who art truly dear to me, thou speakest dear words. Come, sit down, I will explain it to thee, and mark well what I say."

And he said: "Verily, a husband is not dear, that you may love the husband; but that you may love the Self[1] through the husband, therefore a husband is dear.

"Verily, a wife is not dear, that you may love the wife; but that you may love the Self through the wife, therefore a wife is dear.

"Verily, sons are not dear, that you may love the sons; but that you may love the Self through the sons, therefore sons are dear.

"Verily, wealth is not dear, that you may love wealth; but that you may love the Self through the wealth, therefore wealth is dear.

"Verily, the Brahman-class is not dear, that you may love the Brahman-class; but that you may love the Self through the Brahman-class, therefore the Brahman-class is dear.

"Verily, the Kshatriya-class is not dear, that you may love the Kshatriya-class; but that you may love the Self through the Kshatriya-class, therefore the Kshatriya-class is dear.

"Verily, the worlds are not dear, that you may love the worlds; but that you may love the Self through the worlds, therefore the worlds are dear.

"Verily, the Devas are not dear, that you may love the Devas; but that you may love the Self through the Devas, therefore the Devas are dear.

"Verily, creatures are not dear, that you may love the creatures; but that you may love the Self through the creatures, therefore are creatures dear.

"Verily, everything is not dear, that you may love everything; but that you may love the Self through everything, therefore everything is dear.

"Verily, the Self is to be seen, to be heard, to be perceived, to be marked, O Maitreyi! When we see, hear, perceive, and know the Self, then all this is known.

"Whosoever looks for the Brahman-class elsewhere than in the Self, was abandoned by the Brahman-class. Whosoever looks for the Kshatriya-class elsewhere than in the Self, was abandoned by the Kshatriya-class. Whosoever looks for the worlds elsewhere than in the Self, was abandoned by the worlds. Whosoever looks for the Devas elsewhere than in the Self, was abandoned by the Devas. Whosoever looks for creatures elsewhere than in the Self, was abandoned by the creatures.

---

[1] For meaning of the word "Self" as used here, see footnote on page 38.

Whosoever looks for anything elsewhere than in the self, was abandoned by everything. This Brahman-class, this Kshatriya-class, these worlds, these Devas, these creatures, this everything, all is that Self.

"As all waters find their centre in the sea, all touches in the skin, all tastes in the tongue, all smells in the nose, all colours in the eye, all sounds in the ear, all percepts in the mind, all knowledge in the heart, all actions in the hands, all movements in the feet, and all the Vedas in speech;

"As a lump of salt, when thrown into water, becomes dissolved into water, and could not be taken out again, but wherever we taste (the water) it is salt—thus verily, O Maitreyi, does this great Being, endless, unlimited, consisting of nothing but knowledge, rise from out these elements, and vanish again in them. When he has departed, there is no more knowledge (name), I say, O Maitreyi." Thus spoke Yajnavalkya.

Then Maitreyi said: "Here thou has bewildered me, Sir, when thou sayest that having departed, there is no more knowledge."

But Yajnavalkya replied: "O Maitreyi, I say nothing that is bewildering. This is enough, O beloved, for wisdom.

"For when there is as it were duality, then one sees the other, one smells the other, one hears the other, one salutes the other, one perceives the other, one knows the other; but when the Self only is all this, how should he smell another, how should he see another, how should he hear another, how should he salute another, how should he perceive another, how should he know another? How should he know him by whom he knows all this? How, O beloved, should he know himself, the knower?"

The House of Death

I

(*Vajasravasa, desirous of heavenly rewards, surrenders at a sacrifice all that he possesses. He has a son named Nachiketas. When the promised presents are being given to the priests, faith enters into the heart of Nachiketas, who is still a boy.*)

Nachiketas (*thinking*): Unblessed, surely, are the worlds to which a man goes by giving as his promised present at a sacrifice cows which have drunk water, eaten hay, given their milk, and are barren.

(*Knowing that his father has promised to give up all that he possesses, and therefore his son also, he speaks to his father.*)

Nachiketas (*speaking*): Dear father, to whom wilt thou give me?

(*His father does not answer.*)

Nachiketas (*again*): Dear father, to whom wilt thou give me?

(*Still his father does not answer.*)

Nachiketas (*for the third time*): Dear father, to whom wilt thou give me?

Vajasravasa (*angrily*): I shall give thee unto Death!

Nachiketas (*as if to himself*): I go as the first, at the head of many who have still to die; I go in the midst of many who are now dying. What will be the work of Yama, the ruler of the departed, which to-day he has to do unto me? Look back how it was with those who came before, look forward how it will be with those who come hereafter. A mortal ripens like corn, like corn he springs up again.

(*Nachiketas enters into the abode of Yama [Death], and there is no one to receive him. Thereupon one of the attendants of Yama speaks.*)

Attendant: Fire enters into the houses, when a Brahmana enters as a guest. That fire is quenched by this peace-offering—bring water, O Vaivasvata! A Brahmana that dwells in the house of a foolish man without receiving food to eat destroys his hopes and expectations, his possessions, his righteousness, his sacred and his good deeds, and all his sons and cattle.

(*Yama, returning to his house after an absence of three nights, during which time Nachiketas has received no hospitality from him, speaks in apology.*)

Death: O Brahmana, as thou, a venerable guest, hast dwelt in my house three nights without eating, therefore choose now three boons. Hail to thee! and welfare to me!

Nachiketas: O Death, as the first of the three boons I choose that Gautama, my father, be pacified, kind, and free from anger towards me; and that he may know me and greet me, when I shall have been dismissed by thee.

Death: Through my favour thy father will know thee, and be again towards thee as he was before. He shall sleep peacefully through the night, and free from anger, after having seen thee freed from the mouth of death.

Nachiketas: In the heaven-world there is no fear; thou art not there,

O Death, and no one is afraid on account of old age. Leaving behind both hunger and thirst, and out of the reach of sorrow, all rejoice in the world of heaven. Thou knowest, O Death, the fire-sacrifice which leads us to heaven; tell it to me, for I am full of faith. Those who live in the heaven-world reach immortality—this I ask as my second boon.

Death: I tell it thee, learn it from me, and when thou understandest that fire-sacrifice which leads to heaven, know, O Nachiketas, that it is the attainment of the endless worlds, and their firm support, hidden in darkness.

(*Death then tells him of that fire-sacrifice, the beginning of all the worlds, and what bricks are required for the altar, and how many, and how they are to be placed. And Nachiketas repeats all as it has been told to him.*)

Death: I give thee now another boon; that fire-sacrifice shall be named after thee, take also this many-coloured chain. He who has three times performed this Nachiketa rite, and has been united with the three (father, mother, and teacher), and has performed the three duties (study, sacrifice, almsgiving), overcomes birth and death. When he has learnt and understood this fire, which knows (or makes us know) all that is born of Brahman, which is venerable and divine, then he obtains everlasting peace. He who knows the three Nachiketa fires, and knowing the three piles up the Nachiketa sacrifice, he, having first thrown off the chains of death, rejoices in the world of heaven, beyond the reach of grief. This, O Nachiketas, is thy fire which leads to heaven, and which thou hast chosen as thy second boon. That fire all men will proclaim. Choose now, O Nachiketas, thy third boon.

Nachiketas: There is that doubt, when a man is dead—some saying, he is; others, he is not. This I should like to know, taught by thee; this is the third of my boons.

Death: On this point even the gods have doubted formerly; it is not easy to understand. That subject is subtle. Choose another boon, O Nachiketas, do not press me, and let me off that boon.

Nachiketas: On this point even the gods have doubted indeed, and thou, Death, hast declared it to be not easy to understand, and another teacher like thee is not to be found—surely no other boon is like unto this.

Death: Choose sons and grandsons who shall live a hundred years, herds of cattle, elephants, gold, and horses. Choose the wide abode of earth, and live thyself as many harvests as thou desirest. If thou canst think of any boon equal to that, choose wealth, and long life. Be king, Nachiketas, on the wide earth. I make thee the enjoyer of all desires. Whatever desires are difficult to attain among mortals, ask for them according to thy wish; these fair maidens with their chariots and musical instruments—such are indeed not to be obtained by men—be waited on by them whom I give to thee, but do not ask me about dying.

Nachiketas: These things last till to-morrow, O Death, for they wear out this vigour of all the senses. Even the whole of life is short. Keep thou thy horses, keep dance and song for thyself. No man can be made happy by wealth. Shall we possess wealth, when we see thee? Shall we live, as long as thou rulest? Only that boon which I have chosen is to be chosen by me. What mortal, slowly decaying here below, and knowing, after having approached them, the freedom from decay enjoyed by the immortals, would delight in a long life, after he has pondered on the pleasures which arise from beauty and love? No, that on which there is this doubt, O Death, tell us what there is in that great hereafter. Nachiketas does not choose another boon but that which enters into the hidden world.

II

Death: The good is one thing, the pleasant another; these two, having different objects, chain a man. It is well with him who clings to the good; he who chooses the pleasant, misses his end. The good and pleasant approach man: the wise goes round about them and distinguishes them. Yea, the wise prefers the good to the pleasant, but the fool chooses the pleasant through greed and avarice.

Thou, O Nachiketas, after pondering all pleasures that are or seem delightful, hast dismissed them all. Thou hast not gone into the road that leadeth to wealth, in which many men perish.

Wide apart and leading to different points are these two, ignorance, and what is known as wisdom. I believe Nachiketas to be one who desires knowledge, for even many pleasures did not tear thee away. Fools dwelling in darkness, wise in their own conceit, and puffed up with vain knowledge, go round and round, staggering to and fro, like blind men led by the blind. The hereafter never rises before the eyes of the careless child, deluded by the delusion of wealth. "This is the world," he thinks, "there is no other"—thus he falls again and again under my sway.

He (the Self) of whom many are not even able to hear, whom many, even when they hear of him, do not comprehend; wonderful is a man, when found, who is able to teach him (the Self); wonderful is he who comprehends him, when taught by an able teacher. That (Self), when taught by an inferior man, is not easy to be known, even though often thought upon; unless it be taught by another, there is no way to it, for it is inconceivably smaller than what is small. That doctrine is not to be obtained by argument, but when it is declared by another, then, O dearest, it is easy to understand. Thou hast obtained it now; thou art truly a man of true resolve. May we have always an inquirer like thee!

Nachiketas: I know that what is called a treasure is transient, for that eternal is not obtained by things which are not eternal. Hence the Nachiketa fire-sacrifice has been laid by me first; then, by means of transient things, I have obtained what is not transient, the teaching of Yama.

Death: Though thou hadst seen the fulfilment of all desires, the foundation of the world, the endless rewards of good deeds, the shore where there is no fear, that which is magnified by praise, the wide abode, the rest, yet being wise thou hast with firm resolve dismissed it all. The wise who, by means of meditation on his Self, recognizes the Ancient, who is difficult to be seen, who has entered into the dark, who is hidden in the cave, who dwells in the abyss, as God, he indeed leaves joy and sorrow far behind.

A mortal who has heard this and embraced it, who has separated from it all qualities, and has thus reached the subtle Being, rejoices, because he has obtained what is a cause for rejoicing. The house of Brahman is open, I believe, O Nachiketas.

Nachiketas: That which thou seest as neither this nor that, as neither effect nor cause, as neither past nor future, tell me that.

Death: That word or place which all the Vedas record, which all penances proclaim, which men desire when they live as religious students, that word I tell thee briefly, it is Om. That imperishable syllable means

Brahman, that syllable means the highest Brahman; he who knows that syllable, whatever he desires, is his. This is the best support, this is the highest support; he who knows that support is magnified in the world of Brahma.

The knowing Self is not born, it dies not; it sprang from nothing, nothing sprang from it. The Ancient is unborn, eternal, everlasting; he is not killed, though the body is killed. If the killer thinks that he kills, if the killed think that he is killed, they do not understand; for this one does not kill, nor is that one killed.

The Self, smaller than small, greater than great, is hidden in the heart of that creature. A man who is free from desires and free from grief sees the majesty of the Self by the grace of the Creator.

Though sitting still, he walks far; though lying down, he goes everywhere. Who, save myself, is able to know that God who rejoices and rejoices not?

The wise who knows the Self as bodiless within the bodies, as unchanging among changing things, as great and omnipresent, does never grieve. That Self cannot be gained by the Veda, nor by understanding, nor by much learning. He whom the Self chooses, by him the Self can be gained. The Self chooses him (his body) as his own.

But he who has not first turned away from his sickness, who is not tranquil, and subdued, or whose mind is not at rest, he can never obtain the Self (even) by knowledge.

Who then knows where he is, he to whom the Brahmanas and Kshatriyas are (as it were) but food, and death itself a condiment?

III

(Death continues)

There are the two, drinking their reward in the world of their own works, entered into the cave of the heart, dwelling on the highest summit. Those who know Brahman call them shade and light; likewise, those householders who perform the Trinachiketa sacrifice. May we be able to master that Nachiketa rite which is a bridge for sacrificers; also that which is the highest, imperishable Brahman for those who wish to cross over to the fearless shore.

Know the Self to be sitting in the chariot, the body to be the chariot, the intellect (buddhi) the charioteer, and the mind the reins. The senses they call the horses, the objects of the senses their roads. When he (the highest Self) is in union with the body, the senses, and the mind, then wise people call him the Enjoyer.

He who has no understanding and whose mind (the reins) is never firmly held, his senses (horses) are unmanageable, like vicious horses of a charioteer. But he who has understanding and whose mind is always firmly held, his senses are under control, like good horses of a charioteer.

He who has no understanding, who is unmindful and always impure, never reaches that place, but enters into the round of births. But he who has understanding, who is mindful and always pure, reaches indeed that place, whence he is not born again. But he who has understanding for his charioteer, and who holds the reins of the mind, he reaches the end of his journey, and that is the highest place of Vishnu.

Beyond the senses there are the objects, beyond the objects there is the mind, beyond the mind there is the intellect, the Great Self is beyond the intellect. Beyond the Great there is the Undeveloped, beyond the Undeveloped there is the Person (purusha). Beyond the Person there is nothing—this is the goal, the highest road. That Self is hidden in all beings and does not shine forth, but it is seen by subtle seers through their sharp and subtle intellect.

A wise man should keep down speech and mind; he should keep them within the Self which is knowledge; he should keep knowledge within the Self which is the Great; and he should keep that (the Great) within the Self which is the Quiet.

Rise, awake! having obtained your boons, understand them! The sharp edge of a razor is difficult to pass over; thus the wise say the path to the Self is hard.

He who has perceived that which is without sound, without touch, without form, without decay, without taste, eternal, without smell, without beginning, without end, beyond the Great, and unchangeable, is freed from the jaws of death.

(*A wise man who has repeated or heard the ancient story of Nachiketas told by Death is magnified in the world of Brahman. And he who repeats this greatest mystery in an assembly of Brahmanas, or full of devotion at the time of the Sraddha sacrifice, obtains thereby infinite rewards.*)

IV

(Death still speaks)

The Self-existent pierced the openings of the senses so that they turn forward: therefore man looks forward, not backward into himself. Some wise man, however, with his eyes closed and wishing for immortality, saw the Self behind.

Children follow after outward pleasures, and fall into the snare of widespread death. Wise men only, knowing the nature of what is immortal, do not look for anything stable here among things unstable. That by which we know form, taste, smell, sounds, and loving touches, by that also we know what exists besides. This is that which thou hast asked for. The wise, when he knows that that by which he perceives all objects in sleep or in waking is the great omnipresent Self, grieves no more. He who knows this living soul which eats honey (perceives objects) as being the Self, always near, the lord of the past and the future, henceforward fears no more. He who knows him who was born first from the brooding heat, for he was born before the water, who, entering into the heart, abides therein, and was perceived from the elements. He who knows Aditi also, who is one with all deities, who arises with Prana (breath), who, entering into the heart, abides therein, and was born from the elements.

There is Agni (fire), the all-seeing, hidden in the two fire-sticks, well-guarded like a child in the womb by the mother, day after day to be adored by men when they awake and bring oblations. And that whence the sun rises and whither it goes to set, there all the Devas are contained, and no one goes beyond.

What is here visible in the world, the same is there invisible in Brahman; and what is there, the same is here. He who sees any difference here, between Brahman and the world, goes from death to death. Even by the mind this Brahman is to be obtained, and then there is no difference whatsoever. He goes from death to death who sees any difference here.

The person (purusha), of the size of a thumb, stands in the middle of the Self, as lord of the past and the future, and henceforward fears no more. That person, of the size of a thumb, is like a light without smoke, lord of the past and the future, he is the same to-day and to-morrow.

As rain-water that has fallen on a mountain-ridge runs down the rocks on all sides, thus does he, who sees a difference between qualities, run after them on all sides. As pure water poured into pure water remains the same, thus, O Gautama, is the Self of a thinker who knows.

V

(*Death continues to speak*)

There is a town with eleven gates belonging to the Unborn (Brahman), whose thoughts are never crooked. He who approaches it, grieves no more, and liberated from all bonds of ignorance, becomes free.

He (Brahman) is the swan (sun), dwelling in the bright heaven; he is the Vasu (air), dwelling in the sky; he is the sacrificer (fire), dwelling on the hearth; he is the guest (Soma), dwelling in the sacrificial jar; he dwells in men, in gods, in the sacrifice, in heaven; he is born in the water, on earth, in the sacrifice, on the mountains; he is the true and the great. He (Brahman) it is who sends up the breath (prana), and who throws back the breath (apana). All the Devas (senses) worship him, the dwarf, who sits in the centre.

When that incorporated (Brahman) who dwells in the body is torn away and freed from the body, what remains then? No mortal lives by the breath that goes up and by the breath that goes down. We live by another, in whom these two repose.

Well then, O Gautama, I shall tell thee this mystery, the old Brahman, and what happens to the Self, after reaching death. Some enter the womb in order to have a body, as organic beings, others go into inorganic matter, according to their work and according to their knowledge.

He, the highest Person, who is awake in us while we are asleep, shaping one lovely sight after another, that indeed is the Bright, that is Brahman, that alone is called the Immortal. All worlds are contained in it, and no one goes beyond.

As the one fire, after it has entered the world, though one, becomes different according to whatever it burns, thus the one Self within all things becomes different, according to whatever it enters, and exists also without. As the one air, after it has entered the world, though one, becomes different according to whatever it enters, thus the one Self within all things becomes different, according to whatever it enters, and exists also without. As the sun, the eye of the whole world, is not contaminated by the external impurities seen by the eyes, thus the one Self within all things is never contaminated by the misery of the world, being himself without.

There is one ruler, the Self within all things, who makes the one form manifold. The wise who perceive him within their Self, to them belongs eternal happiness, not to others. There is one eternal thinker, thinking non-eternal thoughts, who, though one, fulfils the desires of many. The wise who perceive him within their Self, to them belongs eternal peace, not to others.

They perceive that highest indescribable pleasure, saying, This is that. How then can I understand it? Has it its own light, or does it reflect light?

The sun does not shine there, nor the moon and the stars, nor these lightnings, and much less this fire. When he shines, everything shines after him; by his light all this is lighted.

VI

(Death concludes his discourse)

There is that ancient tree, whose roots grow upward and whose branches grow downward—that indeed is called the Bright, that is called Brahman, that alone is called the Immortal. All worlds are contained in it, and no one goes beyond.

Whatever there is, the whole world, when gone forth from the Brahman, trembles in its breath. That Brahman is a great terror, like a drawn sword. Those who know it become immortal. From terror of Brahman fire burns, from terror the sun burns, from terror Indra and Vayu, and Death, as the fifth, run away.

If a man could not understand it before the falling asunder of his body, then he has to take body again in the worlds of creation.

As in a mirror, so Brahman may be seen clearly here in this body; as in a dream, in the world of the fathers; as in the water, he is seen about in the world of the Gandharvas; as in light and shade, in the world of Brahma.

Having understood that the senses are distinct from the Atman, and that their rising and setting, their waking and sleeping, belong to them in their distinct existence and not to the Atman, a wise man grieves no more.

Beyond the senses is the mind, beyond the mind is the highest created Being, higher than that Being is the Great Self, higher than the Great, the highest Undeveloped. Beyond the Undeveloped is the Person, the all-pervading and entirely imperceptible. Every creature that knows him is liberated, and obtains immortality. His form is not to be seen, no one beholds him with the eye. He is imagined by the heart, by wisdom, by the mind. Those who know this, are immortal.

When the five instruments of knowledge stand still together with the mind, and when the intellect does not move, that is called the highest state. This, the firm holding back of the senses, is what is called Yoga. He must be free from thoughtlessness then, for Yoga comes and goes.

He, the Self, cannot be reached by speech, by mind, or by the eye. How can it be apprehended except by him who says: "He is"? By the words "He is," is he to be apprehended, and by admitting the reality of both the invisible Brahman and the visible world, as coming from Brahman. When he has been apprehended by the words "He is," then his reality reveals itself.

When all desires that dwell in his heart cease, then the mortal becomes immortal, and obtains Brahman. When all the ties of the heart are severed here on earth, then the mortal becomes immortal—here ends the teaching.

There are a hundred and one arteries of the heart, one of them penetrates the crown of the head. Moving upwards by it, a man at his death reaches the Immortal; the other arteries serve for departing in different directions.

The Person not larger than a thumb, the inner Self, is always settled in the heart of men. Let a man draw that Self forth from his body with steadiness, as one draws the pith from a reed. Let him know that Self as the Bright, as the Immortal; yes, as the Bright, as the Immortal.

(*Having received this knowledge taught by Death and the whole rule of Yoga [meditation], Nachiketas became free from passion and death, and obtained Brahman. Thus it will be with another also who knows thus*

what relates to the Self. May he protect us both! May he enjoy us both!
May we acquire strength together! May our knowledge become bright!
May we never quarrel! Om! Peace! peace! peace! Hari, Om!)

How Many Gods?

Then Vidagdha Sakalya asked him: "How many gods are there, O
Yajnavalkya?" He replied with this formula: "As many as are mentioned
in the formula of the hymn of praise addressed to the Visvedevas, viz.
three and three hundred, three and three thousand."

"Yes," he said, and asked again: "How many gods are there really,
O Yajnavalkya?"

"Thirty-three," he said.

"Yes," he said, and asked again: "How many gods are there really,
O Yajnavalkya?"

"Six," he said.

"Yes," he said, and asked again: "How many gods are there really,
O Yajnavalkya?"

"Three," he said.

"Yes," he said, and asked again: "How many gods are there really,
O Yajnavalkya?"

"Two," he said.

"Yes," he said, and asked again: "How many gods are there really,
O Yajnavalkya?"

"One and a half (adhyardha)," he said.

"Yes," he said, and asked again: "How many gods are there really,
O Yajnavalkya?"

"One," he said.

"Yes," he said, and asked: "Who are these three and three hundred,
three and three thousand?"

Yajnavalkya replied: "They are only the various powers."

The Light of Man

Yajnavalkya came to Janaka Vaideha, and he did not mean to speak
with him. But when formerly Janaka Vaideha and Yajnavalkya had a

disputation on the Agnihotra, Yajnavalkya had granted him a boon, and he chose that he might be free to ask him any question he liked. Yajnavalkya granted it, and thus the king was the first to ask him a question.

"Yajnavalkya," he said, "what is the light of man?"

Yajnavalkya replied: "The sun, O king; for, having the sun alone for his light, man sits, moves about, does his work, and returns."

Janaka Vaideha said: "So indeed it is, O Yajnavalkya. When the sun has set, O Yajnavalkya, what is then the light of man?"

Yajnavalkya replied: "The moon indeed is his light; for, having the moon alone for his light, man sits, moves about, does his work, and returns."

Janaka Vaideha said: "So indeed it is, O Yajnavalkya. When the sun has set, O Yajnavalkya, and the moon has set, what is the light of man?"

Yajnavalkya replied: "Fire indeed is his light; for, having fire alone for his light, man sits, moves about, does his work, and returns."

Janaka Vaideha said: "When the sun has set, O Yajnavalkya, and the moon has set, and the fire is gone out, what is then the light of man?"

Yajnavalkya replied: "Sound indeed is his light; for, having sound alone for his light, man sits, moves about, does his work, and returns. Therefore, O king, when one cannot see even one's own hand, yet when a sound is raised, one goes towards it."

Janaka Vaideha said: "So indeed it is, O Yajnavalkya. When the sun has set, O Yajnavalkya, and the moon has set, and the fire is gone out, and the sound hushed, what is then the light of man?"

Yajnavalkya said: "The Self indeed is his light; for, having the Self alone as his light, man sits, moves about, does his work, and returns."

Janaka Vaideha said: "Who is that Self?"

Yajnavalkya replied: "He who is within the heart, surrounded by the pranas (senses), the person of light, consisting of knowledge. He, remaining the same, wanders along the two worlds, as if thinking, as if moving. During sleep (in dream) he transcends this world and all the forms of death (all that falls under the sway of death, all that is perishable).

"On being born, that person, assuming his body, becomes united with all evils; when he departs and dies, he leaves all evils behind.

"And there are two states for that person, the one here in this world, the other in the other world, and as a third an intermediate state, the state of sleep. When in that intermediate state, he sees both those states together, the one here in this world, and the other in the other world. Now whatever his admission to the other world may be, having gained that admission, he sees both the evils and the blessings.

"And when he falls asleep, then after having taken away with him the material from the whole world, destroying and building it up again, he sleeps (dreams) by his own light. In that state the person is self-illuminated.

"There are no real chariots in that state, no horses, no roads, but he himself creates chariots, horses, and roads. There are no blessings there, no happiness, no joys, but he himself creates blessings, happiness, and joys. There are no tanks there, no lakes, no rivers, but he himself creates tanks, lakes, and rivers. He indeed is the maker.

"On this there are these verses:

" 'After having subdued by sleep all that belongs to the body, he, not asleep himself, looks down upon the sleeping (senses). Having assumed light, he goes again to his place, the golden person, the lonely bird.

" 'Guarding with the breath (prana, life) the lower nest, the immortal moves away from the nest; that immortal one goes wherever he likes, the golden person, the lonely bird.

" 'Going up and down in his dream, the god makes manifold shapes for himself, either rejoicing together with women, or laughing with his friends, or seeing terrible sights.

" 'People may see his playground, but himself no one ever sees.'

"Therefore they say, 'Let no one wake a man suddenly, for it is not easy to remedy, if he does not get back rightly to his body.'

"Here some people object and say, 'No, this sleep is the same as the place of waking, for what he sees while awake, that only he sees when asleep.' No, here in sleep the person is self-illuminated."

Janaka Vaideha said: "I give you, Sir, a thousand. Speak on for the sake of my emancipation."

Yajnavalkya said: "That person having enjoyed himself in sleep, having moved about and seen both good and evil, hastens back again as he came, to the place from which he started, to be awake. And whatever he may have seen there, he is not followed (affected) by it, for that person is not attached to anything.

"That person having enjoyed himself in that state of waking, having moved about and seen both good and evil, hastens back again as he came, to the place from which he started, to the state of sleeping.

"There are in his body the veins called Hita, which are as small as a hair divided a thousandfold, full of white, blue, yellow, green, and red. Now when, as it were, they kill him, when, as it were, they overcome him, when, as it were, an elephant chases him, when, as it were, he falls into a well, he fancies, through ignorance, that danger which he commonly sees in waking. But when he fancies that he is, as it were, a god, or that he is, as it were, a king, or 'I am this altogether,' that is his highest world.

"This indeed is his true form, free from desires, free from evil, free from fear. Now as a man, when embraced by a beloved wife, knows nothing that is without, nothing that is within, thus this person, when embraced by the intelligent (prajna) Self, knows nothing that is without, nothing that is within. This indeed is his true form, in which his wishes are fulfilled, in which the Self only is his wish, in which no wish is left—free from any sorrow.

"Then a father is not a father, a mother not a mother, the worlds not worlds, the gods not gods, the Vedas not Vedas. Then a thief is not a thief, a murderer not a murderer, a Chandala not a Chandala, a Paulkasa not a Paulkasa, a Sramana not a Sramana, a Tapasa not a Tapasa. He is not followed by good, not followed by evil, for he has then overcome all the sorrows of the heart.

"And when there (in the Sushupti) he does not see, yet he is seeing, though he does not see. For sight is inseparable from the seer, because it cannot perish. But there is then no second, nothing else different from him that he could see. And when there (in the Sushupti) he does not smell, yet he is smelling, though he does not smell. For smelling is inseparable from the smeller, because it cannot perish. But there is then no second, nothing else different from him that he could smell. And when there (in the Sushupti) he does not taste, yet he is tasting, though he does not taste. For tasting is inseparable from the taster, because it cannot perish. But there is then no second, nothing else different from him that he could taste.

"And when there (in the Sushupti) he does not think, yet he is thinking, though he does not think. For thinking is inseparable from the thinker, because it cannot perish. But there is then no second, nothing

else different from him that he could think. And when it is said that
there (in the Sushupti) he does not know, yet he is knowing, though he
does not know. For knowing is inseparable from the knower, because it
cannot perish. But there is then no second, nothing else different from
him that he could know.

"When in waking and dreaming there is, as it were, another, then can
one see the other, then can one smell the other, then can one speak to
the other, then can one hear the other, then can one think the other,
then can one touch the other, then can one know the other. An ocean is
that one seer, without any duality; this is the Brahma-world, O king.
This is his highest goal, this is his highest success, this is his highest
world, this is his highest bliss. All other creatures live on a small portion
of that bliss.

" 'If a man clearly beholds this Self as Brahman, and as the lord of
all that is and will be, then he is no more afraid.

" 'He behind whom the year revolves with the days, him the gods
worship as the light of lights, as immortal time.

" 'He in whom the five beings and the ether rest, him alone I believe
to be the Self—I, who know, believe him to be Brahman; I, who am
immortal, believe him to be immortal.

" 'They who know the life of life, the eye of the eye, the ear of the
ear, the mind of the mind, they have comprehended the ancient, primeval Brahman.

" 'By the mind alone it is to be perceived, there is in it no diversity.
He who perceives therein any diversity goes from death to death.

" 'This eternal being that can never be proved, is to be perceived in
one way only; it is spotless, beyond the ether, the unborn Self, great and
eternal.

" 'Let a wise Brahmana, after he has discovered him, practise wisdom.
Let him not seek after many words, for that is mere weariness of the
tongue.'

"And he is that great unborn Self, who consists of knowledge, is surrounded by the pranas, the ether within the heart. In it there reposes
the ruler of all, the lord of all, the king of all. He does not become
greater by good works, nor smaller by evil works. He is the lord of all,
the king of all things, the protector of all things. He is a bank and a
boundary, so that these worlds may not be confounded. Brahmanas seek
to know him by the study of the Veda, by sacrifice, by gifts, by penance,

by fasting, and he who knows him becomes a Muni. Wishing for that world (for Brahman) only, mendicants leave their homes.

"Knowing this, the people of old did not wish for offspring. What shall we do with offspring, they said, we who have this Self and this world (of Brahman)? And they, having risen above the desire for sons, wealth, and new worlds, wander about as mendicants. For desire for sons is desire for wealth, and desire for wealth is desire for worlds. Both these are indeed desires only. He, the Self, is to be described by No, no! He is incomprehensible, for he cannot be comprehended; he is imperishable, for he cannot perish; he is unattached, for he does not attach himself; unfettered, he does not suffer, he does not fail. Him who knows, these two do not overcome, whether he says that for some reason he has done evil, or for some reason he has done good—he overcomes both, and neither what he has done, nor what he has omitted to do, burns (affects) him.

"This has been told by a verse: 'This eternal greatness of the Brahmana does not grow larger by work, nor does it grow smaller. Let man try to find its trace, for having found it, he is not sullied by any evil deed.'

"He therefore that knows it, after having become quiet, subdued, satisfied, patient, and collected, sees self in Self, sees all as Self. Evil does not overcome him, he overcomes all evil. Evil does not burn him, he burns all evil. Free from evil, free from spots, free from doubt, he becomes a true Brahmana; this is the Brahma-world, O king"—thus spoke Yajnavalkya.

Janaka Vaideha said: "Sir, I give you the Videhas, and also myself, to be together your slaves."

This indeed is the great, the unborn Self, the strong, the giver of wealth. He who knows this obtains wealth.

This great, unborn Self, undecaying, undying, immortal, fearless, is indeed Brahman. Fearless is Brahman, and he who knows this becomes verily the fearless Brahman.

My Self within the Heart

All this is Brahman. Let a man meditate on that visible world as beginning, ending, and breathing in it, the Brahman.

Now man is a creature of will. According to what his will is in this world, so will he be when he has departed this life. Let him therefore have this will and belief:

The intelligent, whose body is spirit, whose form is light, whose thoughts are true, whose nature is like ether, omnipresent and invisible, from whom all works, all desires, all sweet odours and tastes proceed; he who embraces all this, who never speaks, and is never surprised, he is my self within the heart, smaller than a corn of rice, smaller than a corn of barley, smaller than a mustard seed, smaller than a canary seed or the kernel of a canary seed. He also is my self within the heart, greater than the earth, greater than the sky, greater than heaven, greater than all these worlds.

He from whom all works, all desires, all sweet odours and tastes proceed, who embraces all this, who never speaks and who is never surprised, he, my self within the heart, is that Brahman. When I shall have departed hence, I shall obtain him (that Self). He who has this faith has no doubt; thus said Sandilya, yea, thus he said.

When the Sun Rises

Aditya (the sun) is Brahman, this is the doctrine, and this is the fuller account of it:

In the beginning this was non-existent. It became existent, it grew. It turned into an egg. The egg lay for the time of a year. The egg broke open. The two halves were one of silver, the other of gold.

The silver one became this earth, the golden one the sky, the thick membrane of the white the mountains, the thin membrane of the yolk the mist with the clouds, the small veins the rivers, the fluid the sea.

And what was born from it that was Aditya, the sun. When he was born shouts of hurrah arose, and all beings arose, and all things which they desired. Therefore whenever the sun rises and sets, shouts of hurrah arise, and all beings arise, and all things which they desire.

If any one knowing this meditates on the sun as Brahman, pleasant shouts will approach him and will continue, yea, they will continue.

Quarrel of the Senses

He who knows the oldest and the best becomes himself the oldest and the best. Breath indeed is the oldest and the best. He who knows the richest, becomes himself the richest. Speech indeed is the richest. He who knows the firm rest, becomes himself firm in this world and in the next. The eye indeed is the firm rest. He who knows success, his wishes succeed, both his divine and human wishes. The ear indeed is success. He who knows the home, becomes a home of his people. The mind indeed is the home.

The five senses quarrelled together, who was the best, saying, I am better, I am better.

They went to their father Prajapati and said: "Sir, who is the best of us?" He replied: "He by whose departure the body seems worse than worst, he is the best of you."

The tongue (speech) departed, and having been absent for a year, it came round and said: "How have you been able to live without me?" They replied: "Like mute people, not speaking, but breathing with the breath, seeing with the eye, hearing with the ear, thinking with the mind. Thus we lived." Then speech went back.

The eye (sight) departed, and having been absent for a year, it came round and said: "How have you been able to live without me?" They replied: "Like blind people, not seeing, but breathing with the breath, speaking with the tongue, hearing with the ear, thinking with the mind. Thus we lived." Then the eye went back.

The ear (hearing) departed, and having been absent for a year, it came round and said: "How have you been able to live without me?" They replied: "Like deaf people, not hearing, but breathing with the breath, speaking with the tongue, thinking with the mind. Thus we lived." Then the ear went back.

The mind departed, and having been absent for a year, it came round and said: "How have you been able to live without me?" They replied: "Like children whose mind is not yet formed, but breathing with the breath, speaking with the tongue, seeing with the eye, hearing with the ear. Thus we lived." Then the mind went back.

The breath, when on the point of departing, tore up the other senses, as a horse, going to start, might tear up the pegs to which he is tethered. They came to him and said: "Sir, be thou our lord; thou art the best among us. Do not depart from us!"

Then the tongue said to him: "If I am the richest, thou art the richest." The eye said to him: "If I am the firm rest, thou art the firm rest." The ear said to him: "If I am success, thou art success." The mind said to him: "If I am the home, thou art the home."

And people do not call them, the tongues, the eyes, the ears, the minds, but the breaths (prana, the senses). For breath are all these.

The Education of Svetaketu

Hari, Om. There lived once Svetaketu Aruneya, the grandson of Aruna. To him his father, Uddalaka, the son of Aruna, said: "Svetaketu, go to school; for there is none belonging to our race, darling, who, not having studied the Veda, is, as it were, a Brahmana by birth only."

Having begun his apprenticeship with a teacher when he was twelve years of age, Svetaketu returned to his father when he was twenty-four, having then studied all the Vedas—conceited, considering himself well-read, and stern.

His father said to him: "Svetaketu, as you are so conceited, considering yourself so well-read, and so stern, my dear, have you ever asked for that instruction by which we hear what cannot be heard, by which we perceive what cannot be perceived, by which we know what cannot be known?"

"What is that instruction, Sir?" he asked.

The father replied: "My dear, as by one clod of clay all that is made of clay is known, the difference being only a name, arising from speech, but the truth being that all is clay; and as, my dear, by one nugget of gold all that is made of gold is known, the difference being only a name, arising from speech, but the truth being that all is gold; and as, my dear, by one pair of nail-scissors all that is made of iron is known, the difference being only a name, arising from speech, but the truth being that all is iron—thus, my dear, is that instruction."

The son said: "Surely those venerable men, my teachers, did not know that. For if they had known it, why should they not have told it me? Do you, Sir, therefore tell me that." "Be it so," said the father.

"In the beginning, my dear, there was that only which is, one only, without a second. Others say, in the beginning there was that only which is not, one only, without a second; and from that which is not, that which is was born.

"But how could it be thus, my dear?" the father continued. "How could that which is, be born of that which is not? No, my dear, only that which is, was in the beginning, one only, without a second.

"It thought, May I be many, may I grow forth. It sent forth fire. That fire thought, may I be many, may I grow forth. It sent forth water. And therefore whenever anybody anywhere is hot and perspires, water is produced on him from fire alone.

"Water thought, may I be many, may I grow forth. It sent forth earth (food). Therefore whenever it rains anywhere, most food is then produced. From water alone is eatable food produced.

"Of all living things there are indeed three origins only, that which springs from an egg, that which springs from a living being, and that which springs from a germ.

"That Being (i.e. that which had produced fire, water, and earth) thought, Let me now enter those three beings (fire, water, earth) with this living Self, and let me then develop names and forms.

"Then that Being having said, Let me make each of these three tripartite, so that fire, water, and earth should each have itself for its principal ingredient, besides an admixture of the other two, entered into those three beings with this living Self only, and revealed names and forms. He made each of these tripartite; and how these three beings become each of them tripartite, that learn from me now, my friend!

"The red colour of burning fire (agni) is the colour of fire, the white colour of fire is the colour of water, the black colour of fire the colour of earth. Thus vanishes what we call fire, as a mere variety, being a name, arising from speech. What is true is the three colours (or forms). The red colour of the sun (aditya) is the colour of fire, the white of water, the black of earth. Thus vanishes what we call the sun, as a mere variety, being a name, arising from speech. What is true is the three colours. The red colour of the moon is the colour of fire, the white of water, the black of earth. Thus vanishes what we call the moon, as a mere variety, being a name, arising from speech. What is true is the three colours. The red colour of the lightning is the colour of fire, the white of water, the black of earth. Thus vanishes what we call the lightning, as a mere variety, being a name, arising from speech. What is true is the three colours.

"Great householders and great theologians of olden times who knew this have declared the same, saying, 'No one can henceforth mention to us anything which we have not heard, perceived, or known.' Out of these (three colours or forms) they knew all. Whatever they thought looked red, they knew was the colour of fire. Whatever they thought looked white, they knew was the colour of water. Whatever they thought looked black, they knew was the colour of earth. Whatever they thought was altogether unknown, they knew was some combination of those three beings (devata).

"Now learn from me, my friend, how those three beings, when they reach man, become each of them tripartite.

"The earth (food) when eaten becomes threefold; its grossest portion becomes fæces, its middle portion flesh, its subtilest portion mind. Water when drunk becomes threefold; its grossest portion becomes water, its middle portion blood, its subtilest portion breath. Fire (i.e. in oil, butter, etc.) when eaten becomes threefold; its grossest portion becomes bone, its middle portion marrow, its subtilest portion speech.

"For truly, my child, mind comes of earth, breath of water, speech of fire."

"Please, Sir, inform me still more," said the son.

"Be it so, my child," the father replied.

"That which is the subtile portion of curds, when churned, rises upwards, and becomes butter. In the same manner, my child, the subtile portion of earth (food), when eaten, rises upwards, and becomes mind. That which is the subtile portion of water, when drunk, rises upwards, and becomes breath. That which is the subtile portion of fire, when consumed, rises upwards, and becomes speech. For mind, my child, comes of earth, breath of water, speech of fire."

"Please, Sir, inform me still more," said the son.

"Be it so, my child," the father replied.

"Man (purusha), my son, consists of sixteen parts. Abstain from food for fifteen days, but drink as much water as you like, for breath comes from water, and will not be cut off, if you drink water."

Svetaketu abstained from food for fifteen days. Then he came to his father and said: "What shall I say?" The father said: "Repeat the Ric, Yajur and Sama verses." He replied: "They do not occur to me, Sir."

The father said to him: "As of a great lighted fire one coal only of the size of a firefly may be left, which would not burn much more than this (i.e. very little), thus, my dear son, one part only of the sixteen parts of you is left, and therefore with that one part you do not remember the Vedas. Go and eat! Then wilt thou understand me."

Then Svetaketu ate, and afterwards approached his father. And whatever his father asked him, he knew it all by heart. Then his father said to him:

"As of a great lighted fire one coal of the size of a firefly, if left, may be made to blaze up again by putting grass upon it, and will thus burn more than this, thus, my dear son, there was one part of the sixteen parts left to you, and that, lighted up with food, burnt up, and by it you remember now the Vedas." After that, he understood what his father meant when he said: "Mind, my son, comes from food, breath from water, speech from fire." He understood what he said, yea, he understood it.

"Please, Sir, inform me still more," said the son.

"Be it so, my child," the father replied.

"As the bees, my son, make honey by collecting the juices of distant trees, and reduce the juice into one form. And as these juices have no discrimination, so that they might say, I am the juice of this tree or that, in the same manner, my son, all these creatures, when they have become merged in the True (either in deep sleep or in death), know not that they are merged in the True. Whatever these creatures are here, whether a lion, or a wolf, or a boar, or a worm, or a midge, or a gnat, or a mosquito, that they become again and again. Now that which is that subtile essence, in it all that exists has its self. It is the True. It is the Self, and thou, O Svetaketu, art it."

"Please, Sir, inform me still more," said the son.

"Be it so, my child," the father replied.

"These rivers, my son, run, the eastern like the Ganga, toward the east, the western like the Sindhu, toward the west. They go from sea to sea (i.e. the clouds lift up the water from the sea to the sky, and send it back as rain to the sea). They become indeed sea. And as those rivers, when they are in the sea, do not know, I am this or that river, in the same manner, my son, all these creatures, when they have come back from the True, know not that they have come back from the True. Whatever these creatures are here, whether a lion, or a wolf, or a boar, or a worm, or a midge, or a gnat, or a mosquito, that they become again and again.

"That which is that subtile essence, in it all that exists has its self. It is the True. It is the Self, and thou, O Svetaketu, art it."

"Please, Sir, inform me still more," said the son.

"Be it so, my child," the father replied.

"If someone were to strike at the root of this large tree here, it would bleed, but live. If he were to strike at its stem, it would bleed, but live. If he were to strike at its top, it would bleed, but live. Pervaded by the living Self that tree stands firm, drinking in its nourishment and re-joicing; but if the life (the living Self) leaves one of its branches, that branch withers; if it leaves a second, that branch withers; if it leaves a third, that branch withers. If it leaves the whole tree, the whole tree withers.

"In exactly the same manner, my son, know this. This body indeed withers and dies when the living Self has left it; the living Self dies not.

"That which is that subtile essence, in it all that exists has its self. It is the True. It is the Self, and thou, O Svetaketu, art it."

"Please, Sir, inform me still more," said the son.

"Be it so, my child," the father replied.

"Fetch me thence a fruit of the nyagrodha tree."

"Here is one, Sir."

"Break it."

"It is broken, Sir."

"What do you see there?"

"These seeds, almost infinitesimal."

"Break one of them."

"It is broken, Sir."

"What do you see there?"

"Not anything, Sir."

The father said: "My son, that subtile essence which you do not perceive there, of that very essence this great nyagrodha tree exists.

"Believe it, my son. That which is the subtile essence, in it all that exists has its self. It is the True. It is the Self, and thou, O Svetaketu, art it."

"Please, Sir, inform me still more," said the son.

"Be it so, my child," the father replied.

"Place this salt in water, and then wait on me in the morning."

The son did as he was commanded.

The father said to him: "Bring me the salt which you placed in the water last night."

The son having looked for it, found it not, for, of course, it was melted.

The father said: "Taste it from the surface of the water. How is it?"

The son replied: "It is salt."

"Taste it from the middle. How is it?"

The son replied: "It is salt."

"Taste it from the bottom. How is it?"

The son replied: "It is salt."

The father said: "Throw it away and then wait on me."

He did so; but salt exists for ever.

Then the father said: "Here also, in this body, forsooth, you do not perceive the True, my son; but there indeed it is.

"That which is the subtile essence, in it all that exists has its self. It is the True. It is the Self, and thou, O Svetaketu, art it."

"Please, Sir, inform me still more," said the son.

"Be it so, my child," the father replied.

"My child, they bring a man hither whom they have taken by the hand, and they say: 'He has taken something, he has committed a theft.' When he denies, they say, 'Heat the hatchet for him.' If he committed the theft, then he makes himself to be what he is not. Then the false-minded, having covered his true Self by a falsehood, grasps the heated hatchet—he is burnt, and he is killed.

"But if he did not commit the theft, then he makes himself to be what he is. Then the true-minded, having covered his true Self by truth, grasps the heated hatchet—he is not burnt, and he is delivered.

"As that truthful man is not burnt, thus has all that exists its self in that. It is the True. It is the Self, and thou, O Svetaketu, art it." He understood what he said, yea, he understood it.

The Power of God

Those who know the High Brahman, the vast, hidden in the bodies of all creatures, and alone enveloping everything, as the Lord, they become immortal.

I know that great person (purusha) of sunlike lustre beyond the darkness. A man who knows him truly, passes over death; there is no other path to go. This whole universe is filled by this person (purusha), to whom there is nothing superior, from whom there is nothing different, than whom there is nothing smaller or larger, who stands alone, fixed like a tree in the sky.

That which is beyond this world is without form and without suffering. They who know it, become immortal, but others suffer pain indeed. That Bhagavat exists in the faces, the heads, the necks of all, he dwells in the cave (of the heart) of all beings, he is all-pervading, therefore he is the omnipresent Siva. That person (purusha) is the great lord; he is the mover of existence, he possesses that purest power of reaching everything; he is light, he is undecaying.

The person (purusha), not larger than a thumb, dwelling within, always dwelling in the heart of man, is perceived by the heart, the thought, the mind; they who know it become immortal.

The person (purusha) with a thousand heads, a thousand eyes, a thousand feet, having compassed the earth on every side, extends beyond it by ten fingers' breadth. That person alone (purusha) is all this, what has been and what will be; he is also the lord of immortality; he is whatever grows by food. Its hands and feet are everywhere, its eyes and head are everywhere, its ears are everywhere, it stands encompassing all in the world. Separate from all the senses, yet reflecting the qualities of all the senses, it is the lord and ruler of all, it is the great refuge of all.

The embodied spirit within the town with nine gates, the bird, flutters outwards, the ruler of the whole world, of all that rests and of all that moves. Grasping without hands, hasting without feet, he sees without eyes, he hears without ears. He knows what can be known, but no one knows him; they call him the first, the great person (purusha).

The Self, smaller than small, greater than great, is hidden in the heart of the creature. A man who has left all grief behind sees the majesty, the Lord, the passionless, by the grace of the creator, the Lord. I know this undecaying, ancient one, the self of all things, being infinite and omnipresent. They declare that in him all birth is stopped, for the Brahma-students proclaim him to be eternal.

That living soul is to be known as part of the hundredth part of the point of a hair, divided a hundred times, and yet it is to be infinite. It is not woman, it is not man, nor is it neuter; whatever body it takes, with that it is joined only. By means of thoughts, touching, seeing, and passions, the incarnate Self assumes successively in various places various forms, in accordance with his deeds, just as the body grows when food and drink are poured into it.

Some wise men, deluded, speak of nature, and others of time (as the cause of everything); but it is the greatness of God by which this Brahma-wheel is made to turn. It is at the command of him who always covers this world, the knower, the time of time, who assumes qualities and all knowledge, it is at his command that this work, creation, unfolds itself, which is called earth, water, fire, air, and ether; he who, after he has done that work and rested again, and after he has brought together one essence (the self) with the other (matter), with one, two, three, or eight, with time also and with the subtile qualities of the mind, who, after starting the works endowed with the three qualities, can order all things, yet when, in the absence of all these, he has caused the destruction of the work, goes on, being in truth different from all that he has produced; he is the beginning, producing the causes which unite the soul with the body, and, being above the three kinds of time, past, present, future, he is seen as without parts, after we have first worshipped that adorable god, who has many forms, and who is the true source of all things, as dwelling in our own mind.

He is beyond all the forms of the world and of time, he is the other, from whom this world moves round, when one has known him who brings good and removes evil, the lord of bliss, as dwelling within the self, the immortal, the support of all. Let us know that highest great lord of lords, the highest deity of deities, the master of masters, the highest above, as god, the lord of the world, the adorable.

There is no effect and no cause known of him, no one is seen like unto him or better; his high power is revealed as manifold, as inherent, acting as force and knowledge. There is no master of his in the world, no ruler of his, not even a sign of him. He is the cause, the lord of the lords of the organs, and there is of him neither parent nor lord.

That only god who spontaneously covered himself, like a spider, with threads drawn from the first cause, grant us entrance into Brahman.

He is the one God, hidden in all beings, all-pervading, the self within all beings, watching over all works, dwelling in all beings, the witness, the perceiver, the only one, free from qualities. He is the one ruler of many who seem to act, but really do not act; he makes the one seed manifold. The wise who perceive him within their self, to them belongs eternal happiness, not to others. He is the eternal among eternals, the thinker among thinkers, who, though one, fulfils the desires of many. He who has known that cause which is to be apprehended by Samkhya (philosophy) and Yoga (religious discipline), he is freed from all fetters.

The sun does not shine there, nor the moon and the stars, nor these lightnings, and much less this fire. When he shines, everything shines after him; by his light all this is lightened.

He is the one bird in the midst of the world; he is also like the fire of the sun that has set in the ocean. A man who knows him truly, passes over death; there is no other path to go.

He makes all, he knows all, the self-caused, the knower, the time of time, who assumes qualities and knows everything, the master of nature and of man, the lord of the three qualities, the cause of the bondage, the existence, and the liberation of the world.

He who has become that, he is the immortal, remaining the lord, the knower, the ever-present guardian of this world, who rules this world for ever, for no one else is able to rule it.

Seeking for freedom I go for refuge to that God who is the light of his own thoughts, he who first creates Brahman and delivers the Vedas to him; who is without parts, without actions, tranquil, without fault, without taint, the highest bridge to immortality—like a fire that has consumed its fuel.

Only when men shall roll up the sky like a hide, will there be an end of misery, unless God has first been known.

Through the power of his penance and through the grace of God has the wise Svetasvatara truly proclaimed Brahman, the highest and holiest, to the best of ascetics, as approved by the company of Rishis.

This highest mystery in the Vedanta, delivered in a former age, should not be given to one whose passions have not been subdued, nor to one who is not a son, or who is not a pupil. If these truths have been told to a high-minded man, who feels the highest devotion for God, and for his Guru as for God, then they will shine forth—then they will shine forth indeed.

Father and Son

I

Now, when one has been away, on coming back he should kiss his son's head and say:

> "From every limb of mine you come!
> Right from my heart you are born forth!
> You are myself, indeed, my son!
> So live a hundred autumns long!

"So-and-so!"—He takes his name.

> "Become a stone! Become an axe!
> Become unconquerable gold!
> A brilliance, son, indeed you are!
> So live a hundred autumns long!

"So-and-so!"—He takes his name.

Then he embraces him, saying: "Wherewith Prajapati embraced his creatures for their security, therewith I embrace you, So-and-so!"—He takes his name.

Then he mutters in his right ear:—

"Confer on him, O generous one, onrushing . . ."

and in the left ear:—

"O Indra, grant most excellent possessions!"

and says: "Be not cut off! Be not perturbed. Live a hundred autumns of life. Son, I kiss your head with your name, So-and-so!"—Thrice he should kiss his head.

"I make a lowing over you with the lowing of cows."—Thrice he should make a lowing over his head.

II

Now next, the father-and-son ceremony, or the transmission, as they call it.

A father, when about to decease, summons his son. Having strewn the house with new grass, having built up the fire, having set down near it a vessel of water together with a dish, the father, wrapped around with a fresh garment, remains lying. The son, having come, lies down on top, touching organs with organs. Or he may, even, transmit to him seated face to face. Then he delivers over to him thus:—

Father: "My speech in you I would place!"
Son: "Your speech in me I take."
Father: "My breath in you I would place!"
Son: "Your breath in me I take."
Father: "My eye in you I would place!"
Son: "Your eye in me I take."
Father: "My ear in you I would place!"
Son: "Your ear in me I take."
Father: "My tastes in you I would place!"
Son: "Your tastes in me I take."
Father: "My deeds in you I would place!"
Son: "Your deeds in me I take."
Father: "My pleasure and pain in you I would place!"
Son: "Your pleasure and pain in me I take."
Father: "My bliss, delight, and procreation in you I would place!"
Son: "Your bliss, delight, and procreation in me I take."

Father: "My goings in you I would place!"
Son: "Your goings in me I take."
Father: "My mind in you I would place!"
Son: "Your mind in me I take."
Father: "My intelligence in you I would place!"
Son: "Your intelligence in me I take."

If, however, he should be unable to speak much, let the father say summarily: "My vital breaths in you I would place!" and the son reply: "Your vital breaths in me I take."

Then, turning to the right, he goes forth toward the east.

The father calls out after him: "May glory, sacred lustre, and fame delight in you!"

Then the other looks over his left shoulder. Having hid his face with his hand, or having covered it with the edge of his garment, he says: "Heavenly worlds and desires do you obtain!"

If he should become well, the father should dwell under the lordship of his son, or he should wander around as a religious mendicant. If, however, he should decease, so let them furnish him as he ought to be furnished—as he ought to be furnished.

III

When a father who knows this departs this world, then he enters into his son together with his own spirits, with speech, mind, and breath. If there is anything done amiss by the father, of all that the son delivers him, and therefore he is called Putra, son. By help of his son the father stands firm in this world. Then these divine immortal spirits, speech, mind, and breath, enter into him.

From the earth and from fire, divine speech enters into him. And verily that is divine speech whereby whatever he says comes to be. From heaven and the sun, divine mind enters into him. And verily that is divine mind whereby he becomes joyful, and grieves no more. From water and the moon, divine breath (spirit) enters into him. And verily that is divine breath which, whether moving or not moving, does not tire, and therefore does not perish. He who knows this becomes the Self of all beings. As that deity (Hiranyagarbha) is, so does he become. And as all beings honour that deity with sacrifice, etc., so do all beings honour him who knows this. Whatever grief these creatures suffer, that is all one and therefore disappears. Only what is good approaches him; verily, evil does not approach the Devas.

The Blessed Triad

The threefold descendants of Prajapati, gods, men, and Asuras, dwelt as Brahmacharins (students) with their father Prajapati. Having finished their studentship the gods said: "Tell us something, Sir." He told them the syllable da. Then he said: "Did you understand?" They said: "We did understand. You told us, 'Damyata,' Be subdued." "Yes," he said, "you have understood."

Then the men said to him: "Tell us something, Sir." He told them the same syllable da. Then he said: "Did you understand?" They said: "We did understand. You told us, 'Datta,' Give." "Yes," he said, "you have understood."

Then the Asuras said to him: "Tell us something, Sir." He told them the same syllable da. Then he said: "Did you understand?" They said: "We did understand. You told us, 'Dayadham,' Be merciful." "Yes," he said, "you have understood."

The divine voice of thunder repeats the same, Da da da, that is, Be subdued, give, be merciful. Therefore let that triad be taught, subduing, giving, and mercy.

The Way of Truth

Truly, it is life that shines forth in all things!
Understanding this, one becomes a knower. There is no superior speaker.
Having delight in the soul, having pleasure in the soul, doing the rites,
Such a one is the best of Brahma-knowers.

This soul is obtainable by truth, by austerity,
By proper knowledge, by the student's life of chastity constantly prac-
    tised.
Within the body, consisting of light, pure is he
Whom the ascetics, with imperfections done away, behold.

Truth alone conquers, not falsehood.
By truth is laid out the path leading to the gods
By which the sages whose desire is satisfied ascend
To where is the highest repository of truth.

Vast, heavenly, of unthinkable form,
And more minute than the minute, it shines forth.
It is farther than the far, yet here near at hand,
Set down in the secret place of the heart, even here among those who
        behold it.

Not by sight is it grasped, not even by speech,
Not by any other sense-organs, austerity, or work.
By the peace of knowledge, one's nature purified—
In that way, however, by meditating, one does behold him who is with-
        out parts.

That subtile soul is to be known by thought
Wherein the senses fivefoldly have entered.
The whole of men's thinking is interwoven with the senses.
When that is purified, the soul shines forth.

Whatever world a man of purified nature makes clear in mind,
And whatever desires he desires for himself—
That world he wins, those desires too.
Therefore he who is desirous of welfare should praise the knower of
        the soul.

The Glory of God

Behold the universe in the glory of God: and all that lives and moves
on earth. Leaving the transient, find joy in the eternal: set not your
heart on another's possession.

Working thus, a man may wish for a life of a hundred years. Only
actions done in God bind not the soul of man.

There are demon-haunted worlds, regions of utter darkness. Whoever
in life neglects the Spirit goes to that darkness after death.

The Spirit, without moving, is swifter than the mind; the senses cannot reach him: he is ever beyond them. Standing still, he overtakes
those who run. To the ocean of his being the spirit of life leads the
streams of action.

He moves, and he moves not. He is far, and he is near. He is within
all, and he is outside all.

Who sees all beings in his own Self, and his own Self in all beings,
loses all fear.

When a sage sees this great unity and his Self has become all beings,
what delusion and what sorrow can ever be near him?

The Spirit filled all with his radiance. He is incorporeal and invulnerable, pure and untouched by evil. He is the supreme seer and thinker,
immanent and transcendent. He placed all things in the path of eternity.

Into deep darkness fall those who follow action. Into deeper darkness fall those who follow knowledge.

One is the outcome of knowledge, and another is the outcome of
action. Thus have we heard from the ancient sages who explained this
truth to us.

He who knows both knowledge and action, with action overcomes
death and with knowledge reaches immortality.

Into deep darkness fall those who follow the immanent. Into deeper
darkness fall those who follow the transcendent.

One is the outcome of the transcendent, and another is the outcome
of the immanent. Thus have we heard from the ancient sages who explained this truth to us.

He who knows both the transcendent and the immanent, with the
immanent overcomes death and with the transcendent reaches immortality.

The face of truth remains hidden behind a circle of gold. Unveil it,
O god of light, that I who love the true may see!

O life-giving sun, offspring of the lord of creation, solitary seer of
heaven! Spread thy light and withdraw thy blinding splendour that I
may behold thy radiant form: that Spirit far away within thee is my own
inmost Spirit.

May life go to immortal life, and the body go to ashes. OM. O my
soul, remember past strivings, remember! O my soul, remember past
strivings, remember!

By the path of good lead us to final bliss, O fire divine, thou god who knowest all ways. Deliver us from wandering evil. Prayers and adoration we offer unto thee.

The Ordinances of Manu

Creation

The great seers having approached Manu seated intent, having reverenced him, duly spoke this speech. Lord! deign to tell us truly in order the rules of all the castes, and of all the castes that arise between (them). For thou, Lord, alone knowest the true sense of the objects of this universal, self-existent system, unattainable by (simple) reason, not to be reasoned out.

He whose glory is unmeasured, being duly questioned by those magnanimous ones, having saluted all the great seers, answered them: Hear!

This (All) was darkness, imperceptible, without definite qualities, undiscoverable, unknowable, as if wholly in sleep. Then the self-existent Lord became manifest, making this undiscrete (All) discernible with his power, unobstructed by the chief elements and the like, removing the darkness. He who can be apprehended by the suprasensual, (who is) subtile, undiscrete, eternal, who consists of all elements, incomprehensible, he verily became manifest of himself.

Wishing to produce different beings from his own body, he having desired, first created water alone; in that he cast seed. That became a golden egg, like in splendour to the thousand-rayed (sun); in that was born spontaneously Brahma, the grandparent of all the worlds.

That Lord having dwelt in that egg for a year, spontaneously, by his own meditation, split that egg in two. And with those two shares he formed the heaven and the earth, in the middle the sky and the eight regions, and the perpetual place of waters.

From himself he created mind, which is and is not; and from mind egoism, the ruler, the lord. And likewise the great self, and all (things) with the three qualities, and, severally, the five organs of sense, the apprehenders of sensible objects.

He, in the beginning, from the words of the Vedas, appointed the names and functions of all beings severally, and their several conditions.

He created time and the divisions of time, the lunar zodiac, also the planets; rivers, oceans, rocks, plains, and uneven ground; austerity, speech, and sexual enjoyment, desire also as well as anger: and desiring to create these beings, he created this creation. And he made distinct dharma and non-dharma in order to a distinction of deeds. And he endowed these beings with the pairs—pleasure and pain, and the like.

Now in what action that Lord first employed any creature, that creature being reproduced again and again, spontaneously followed just that course of action. Baneful or harmless; gentle or savage; right or wrong; true or false; whatever he, at the creation, assigned to any that quality spontaneously entered it.

Having divided his own body into two, he became a male by half, by half a female: on her that Lord begot Viraj. But, O best of twice-born men! know that I am he, the creator of all this world, whom that male Viraj, having practised austerity, spontaneously produced.

Now I, desirous of creating beings, having performed very severe austerity, first created the ten lords of beings, great seers. They, very glorious, produced seven other Manus, together with gods and the abodes of gods, and great seers unlimited in glory. Yakshas, Rakshasas, Picacas, Gandharvas, Apsarasas, Asuras, Nagas, serpents, eagles, and the different hosts of manes. Lightnings, thunderbolts, and clouds, Indra's bent and unbent bows, meteors, comets, and various luminaries. Kinnaras, apes, fishes, and all kinds of birds; cattle, deer, and men, beasts of prey, and animals with two rows of teeth. Worms, grubs, and winged insects, lice, flies, and bugs, with all biting gnats, and innumerable things of different kinds. Thus was this All (consisting of things), stationary and movable according to their acts, created by those great beings at my command, through the force of austerity.

Cattle and also deer, and wild beasts with two rows of teeth, demons and devils, and men, are born from a caul. Produced from eggs are birds, snakes, crocodiles, and fish, and tortoises; and likewise all other kinds of reptiles which are produced on land or are aquatic. From moisture are produced gnats and flies, lice, fleas, and bugs; and from heat is produced whatever else is of this kind.

Plants with one stem and many stems are of many kinds; so also grasses: but convolvulus and creepers spring from seed or a slip. These creatures, enveloped by a manifold darkness caused by past deeds, have an internal conscience, and are endowed with pleasure and pain.

Having thus created all this and me, he of unthinkable powers was again absorbed into himself, alternating a time of creation by a time of repose.

When a Brahmana is born, he is born above the world, the chief of all creatures, to guard the treasury of dharma. Thus, whatever exists in the universe is all the property of the Brahmana; for the Brahmana is entitled to it all by his superiority and eminence of birth.

For the ascertainment of his duties and those of the other castes in order, the prudent Manu Svayam composed this treatise.

Laws

I

A Brahmana having lived the first quarter of his life with a Guru, should live, having taken a wife, the second quarter of his life in his own house. A Brahmana should live, except in distress, following the calling which is his, without doing any injury to beings, or with little injury.

A twice-born man who keeps sacred fires, if he desires long life, should not eat new grain or flesh if he has not sacrificed with the new grain or cattle. For his fires, not honoured with new grain or an offering of cattle, being eager for new rice-food and flesh, desire to devour his breath.

According to his ability, a householder must give to beggars, and a portion is to be made for beings as well as he can without inconvenience to his family.

Although wild with passion, he must not approach his wife on the appearance of her courses; nor must he even sleep with her on a common bed. For a man who approaches a woman when menstruating, the learning, glory, strength, sight, and also longevity, are destroyed.

One should not eat with his wife, nor look at her eating, sneezing, yawning, or sitting at her ease. A good Brahmana desirous of glory may not see her adorning her eyes (with collyrium), smeared with oil, naked, or bringing forth a child.

One should never recite the Vedas indistinctly or in presence of a Sudra; nor having recited the Veda at the end of the night, though fatigued, may one sleep again. When wind is audible at night, when dust is collected by day, those are two occasions during the rainy season not fit for recitation; so declare those who understand recitations. When there is a storm, an earthquake, or an eclipse of the heavenly bodies, even in season, one should know recitals to be unseasonable. One may not recite the Veda when lying down, when with the feet raised, or having put a cloth over the loins, nor having eaten meat or rice and food at events involving pollution; nor if there be a fog, or sound of arrows, nor at the morning and evening twilights, nor at the conjunction of sun and moon, nor on the fourteenth lunar day, nor on the day of the full moon, nor on the eighth lunar day. One may not recite the Veda near a burning-ground, near a village, or even in a cow-pen, when one has put on a cloth worn in copulation, and when one has received a present at a sraddha. One should not recite when mounted on a horse, and on a tree or on an elephant; nor on a ship, nor on an ass, nor on a camel, nor standing on a salt waste, nor riding in a vehicle; nor in a dispute, nor in a fight, nor with an army, nor in battle, nor having just eaten, nor during indigestion, nor having vomited, nor in a state of pollution; nor without having warned a guest, nor when a wind blows strongly, nor when blood flows from a limb, nor when wounded by a weapon.

One should speak truth, and speak what is pleasant; one should not speak unpleasant truth: one should not speak pleasant falsehood. This is fixed law.

II

Garlic, onions also, leeks and mushrooms, are not to be eaten by the twice-born, as well as things arising from impurity. Milk from a cow which has not passed the ten days of impurity after calving, camel's milk, milk of an animal with a solid hoof also, ewe's milk, milk of a cow in heat, or milk of a cow that has no calf; also that of all forest animals except the buffalo; women's milk also, and all sour liquids must be avoided.

One should avoid all carnivorous birds, so also those that abide in towns, and beasts with solid hoofs not permitted by this law, tittibhas also. The sparrow, plava, flamingo, the cuckoo, the tame town-cock, the sarasa, and rajjuvala, the parrot and sarika; birds that peck, and web-footed birds, the paddy-bird, birds that tear with their claws, fish-eating divers; butcher's meat and dried meat also; also the crane, the small crane, and the raven, khanjaritaka, fish-eaters, tame swine, and fish of all kinds.

The wise have pronounced eatable, among five-toed animals, the hedgehog (or boar) and porcupine, the iguana, rhinoceros, tortoise, and hare also, and, except camels, animals which have one row of teeth.

Having considered the source of flesh, and the slaughter and confinement of animals, one should cease from eating all flesh. There is no fault in eating flesh, nor in drinking intoxicating liquor, nor in copulation, for that is the occupation of beings, but cessation from them produces great fruit.

The learned become pure by tranquillity; those doing what is not to be done, by gifts; those with concealed sin, by muttering sacred texts; the most learned in the Vedas, by austerity. By earth and water what is to be purified is made pure; a river becomes pure by its velocity; a woman defiled by her mind becomes pure by her courses; a Brahmana, by renunciation of the world. The limbs become pure by water; the mind becomes pure by truth; the self of beings by knowledge and austerity; the intellect becomes pure by knowledge.

No act is to be done according to her own will by a young girl, a young woman, or even by an old woman, though in their own houses. In her childhood a girl should be under the will of her father; in her youth, of her husband; her husband being dead, of her sons; a woman should never enjoy her own will. She must never wish separation of her self from her father, husband, or sons, for by separation from them a woman would make both families contemptible. She must always be cheerful and clever in household business, with the furniture well cleaned, and with not a free hand in expenditure.

The good wife of a husband, be he living or dead, if she desire the world where her husband is, must never do anything disagreeable to him. But she may at will when he is dead emaciate her body by living on pure flowers, fruits, and roots. She may not, however, when her husband is dead, mention even the name of another man. She must be till death subdued, intent, chaste, following that best law which is the rule of wives of a single husband. But the woman who, from desire of offspring, is unfaithful to her dead husband, meets with blame here, and is deprived of her husband's place in the next world.

She who, restrained in mind, speech, and body, is not unfaithful to her husband, attains the abode of her husband, and is called virtuous by the good. A twice-born man must burn a wife of such behaviour and of the same caste, if dying before him, by means of the sacred fire and sacrificial vessels, according to rule.

Having used the fires for the last rites to his wife dying before him, he may marry again, and again establish the sacred fires also.

III

Now a king, desirous to inspect suits, should, subdued, enter the assembly with Brahmanas and ministers who know mantras. There, seated or standing, having stretched forth his right hand, with humble vesture and ornaments, he should inspect the affairs of the parties. Day by day he should judge separately cases under the eighteen titles by reasons drawn from local usage and the treatises.

Of these titles, the first is non-payment of debt; next pledges; sale without ownership; partnership and non-delivery of what has been given; also non-payment of wages; breach of contract; revocation of sale and purchase; disputes between master and servant; also the law of disputes about boundaries; assault and slander; theft; violence; also adultery; the law between man and woman; partition; dicing; and games with animals. These eighteen topics occur in the settlements of suits here.

One should not enter the court or what is correct must be spoken; a man who speaks not, or speaks perversely, is sinful.

The king should cause a Brahmana to swear by truth; a Kshatriya by his steed and his weapons; a Vaisya by his cows, his seed, and his gold; but a Sudra by all wicked deeds. Or he may cause him to hold fire, or cause him to dive into the water, or even let him touch the heads of his wife and son one after the other. He whom the lighted fire does not burn, he whom the water does not cause to rise to the surface, and he who within a short time meets with no misfortune,—these must be recognized as pure in respect to their oath.

A business transaction is not legal when it has been performed by a drunken person, a crazy person, a person in distress, a slave, a child, an old man, or one not duly authorized.

What is given by force, used by force, and also what is written by force—in short all things done by force, Manu said, are as if not done.

A decision in regard to the boundary-lines of a field, spring, pond, garden, or house, shall be established by an appeal to the neighbours. If the neighbours lie concerning the boundary over which men are disputing, each one of them shall be fined the medium fine by the king. If it is impossible to settle the boundary-line, a king who knows the right should himself, and alone, in order to do them a kindness, point out the ground: so stands the law.

A thief must, with loosened hair and a firm bearing, approach the king and proclaim his theft, saying: "Thus have I done; punish me"; while he bears to the king upon his shoulder a club, or a staff of acacia wood, a spear sharp at both ends, or an iron rod. By being punished or by being released the thief is freed from the crime of theft; but if the king does not punish him, he himself receives the crime of the thief.

He who takes from a spring either the rope or the bucket, and he who breaks open a water-tank, should receive a fine of one masa, and replace it in this place.

Death is the penalty if one steals more than ten measures of grain; where the amount is less he must pay a fine eleven times the value of the grain, and in either case be made to return the property to that owner. But cutting off the hand is enjoined for stealing less than one hundred but more than fifty palas; where the amount is less, however, one should ordain a fine eleven times as great as the worth of the things stolen.

Wherever right is oppressed, there may the twice-born take arms; also where, brought on by some unlucky time, calamity has come upon the twice-born castes. And in self-defence, in a struggle for gifts, and when peril threatens a woman or a Brahmana, he who thus kills a man in a just cause does no wrong. Thus let him, without hesitating, kill any one attacking him with a weapon in his hand, even if it be a Guru, a child, an old man, or a Brahmana who is very learned. No sin comes at any time upon the slayer for causing, whether openly or in secret, the death of one who attacks him with a weapon in his hand, for thus anger meets anger.

He who addressed the wife of another at a watering-place, in a forest or wood, or at the union of rivers, would incur the sin of adultery. Attendance upon her, sporting with her, touching her ornaments or clothes, sitting upon a bed with her, all this is called adultery. If any man touches a woman upon an improper part of her body, or being thus touched by her submits to it with patience, this is all called adultery, if done by mutual consent. One who is not a Brahmana deserves capital punishment for committing adultery. The wives of all the four castes must always be most carefully guarded.

The king should not cause a girl who tries to seduce a man of high caste to pay any fine at all; but he ought to compel a girl to live confined at home if she make love to a man of low caste.

A Brahmana should support both a Kshatriya and Vaisya whose means of livelihood have been diminished, making them attend each to his respective duties, but without causing them any cruelty. But if a Brahmana through avarice, and because he possesses the power, compel twice-born men who have received the initiation into the caste order to do the work of a slave when they do not wish it, he shall be fined six hundred panas by the king. But a Sudra, whether bought or not bought, the Brahmana may compel to practise servitude; for that Sudra was created by the Self-existent merely for the service of the Brahmana.

Wife, son, and slave, these three are said to be without property: whatever property they acquire is his to whom they belong.

IV

One should give a girl in marriage according to rule to that suitor who is of high family, handsome, and of like caste, even though she has not reached the age of puberty. Better that the girl, even if she has arrived at the age of puberty, should remain at home till her death than that one should ever give her to a suitor lacking in good qualities.

At thirty years of age a man may marry a beloved girl of twelve years, or, if he is thrice eight years, he may marry a girl of eight years; if his religious duties would otherwise be unfulfilled he may marry at once.

Let there be mutual fidelity ending in death alone; this, in few words, should be recognized as the highest law of duty for man and wife.

The Bhagavad-Gita
(THE LORD'S SONG)

Revolt against War

Having seen arrayed the army of the Pandavas, the Prince Duryodhana approached his teacher, and spake these words:

"Behold this mighty host of the sons of Pandu, O teacher, arrayed by the son of Drupada, thy wise disciple. Insufficient seems this army of ours, though marshalled by Bhishma, while that army of theirs seems sufficient, though marshalled by Bhima; therefore in the rank and file let all, standing firmly in their respective divisions, guard Bhishma, even all ye generals."

To enhearten him, the Ancient of the Kurus, the grandsire, the glorious, blew his conch, sounding on high a lion's roar. Then conches and kettledrums, tabours and drums and cowhorns, suddenly blared forth, and the sound was tumultuous.

Then, stationed in their great war-chariot, yoked to white horses, Madhava and the son of Pandu blew their divine conches. Drupada and the Draupadeyas, and Saubhadra, the mighty-armed, on all sides their several conches blew. That tumultuous uproar rent the hearts of the sons of Dhritarashtra, filling the earth and sky with sound.

Then, beholding the sons of Dhritarashtra standing arrayed, and the flight of missiles about to begin, he whose crest is an ape, the son of Pandu, took up his bow, and spake this word to Hrishikesa:

"In the midst, between the two armies, stay my chariot, O Achyuta, that I may behold these standing, longing for battle, with whom I must strive in this outbreaking war. And gaze on those here gathered together, ready to fight, desirous of pleasing in battle the evil-minded son of Dhritarashtra."

Thus addressed by Arjuna, Hrishikesa, having stayed that best of chariots in the midst, between the two armies, over against Bhishma, Drona and all the rulers of the world, said:

"O Partha, behold these Kurus gathered together."

Then saw Partha standing there, uncles and grandfathers, teachers, mother's brothers, cousins, sons and grandsons, comrades, fathers-in-law and benefactors also in both armies; seeing all these kinsmen thus standing arrayed, Arjuna, deeply moved to pity, this uttered in sadness:

"Seeing these my kinsmen, O Krishna, arrayed, eager to fight, my limbs fail and my mouth is parched, my body quivers, and my hair stands on end, Gandiva slips from my hand, and my skin burns all over, I am not able to stand, my mind is whirling, and I see adverse omens, O Kesava. Nor do I foresee any advantage from slaying kinsmen in battle.

"For I desire not victory, O Krishna, nor kingdom, nor pleasures; what is kingdom to us, O Govinda, what enjoyment, or even life? Those for whose sake we desire kingdom, enjoyments and pleasures, they stand here in battle, abandoning life and riches—teachers, fathers, sons, as well as grandfathers, mother's brothers, fathers-in-law, grandsons, brothers-in-law, and other relatives. These I do not wish to kill, though myself slain, O Madhusudana, even for the sake of the kingship of the three worlds; how then for earth?

"Slaying these sons of Dhritarashtra, what pleasure can be ours, O Janardana? Killing these desperadoes, sin will but take hold of us. Therefore we should not kill the sons of Dhritarashtra, our relatives; for how, killing our kinsmen, may we be happy, O Madhava? Although these, with intelligence overpowered by greed, see no guilt in the destruction of a family, no crime in hostility to friends, why should not we learn to turn away from such a sin, O Janardana, who see the evils in the destruction of a family? In the destruction of a family the immemorial family traditions perish; in the perishing of tradition, lawlessness overcomes the whole family; owing to predominance of lawlessness, O Krishna, the women of the family become corrupt; women corrupted, O Varshneya, there ariseth caste-confusion; this confusion draggeth to hell the slayers of the family, and the family; for their ancestors fall, deprived of rice-balls and libations. By these caste-confusing misdeeds of the slayers of the family, the everlasting caste customs and family customs are abolished. The abode of the men whose family customs are extinguished, O Janardana, is everlastingly in hell. Thus have we heard. Alas! in committing a great sin are we engaged, we who are endeavouring to kill our kindred from greed of the pleasures of kingship. If the sons of Dhritarashtra, weapon in hand, should slay me, unresisting, unarmed, in the battle, that would for me be the better."

Having thus spoken on the battlefield, Arjuna sank down on the seat of the chariot, casting away his bow and arrow, his mind overborne by grief.

The Blessed Lord said: "Whence hath this dejection befallen thee in this perilous strait, ignoble, heaven-closing, infamous, O Arjuna? Yield not to impotence, O Partha! it doth not befit thee. Shake off this paltry faintheartedness! Stand up, Parantapa!"

Arjuna said: "How, O Madhusudana, shall I attack Bhishma and Drona with arrows in battle, they who are worthy of reverence, O slayer of foes? Better in this world to eat even the beggar's crust than to slay these most noble Gurus. Slaying these Gurus, our well-wishers, I should taste of blood-besprinkled feasts. Nor know I which for us be the better, that we conquer them or they conquer us—these, whom having slain we should not care to live, even these arrayed against us, the sons of Dhritarashtra. My heart is weighed down with the vice of faintness; my mind is confused as to duty. I ask thee which may be the better—that tell me decisively. I am thy disciple, suppliant to thee; teach me. For I see not that it would drive away this anguish that withers up my senses, if I should attain unrivalled monarchy on earth, or even the sovereignty of the shining ones."

The Blessed Lord said: "Thou grievest for those that should not be grieved for, yet speakest words of wisdom. The wise grieve neither for the living nor for the dead. Nor at any time verily was I not, nor thou, nor these princes of men, nor verily shall we ever cease to be, here-after. As the dweller in the body experienceth in the body childhood, youth, old age, so passeth he on to another body; the steadfast one grieveth not thereat. The contacts of matter, O son of Kunti, giving cold and heat, pleasure and pain, they come and go, impermanent; endure them bravely, O Bharata.

"The man whom these torment not, O chief of men, balanced in pain and pleasure, steadfast, he is fitted for immortality. The unreal hath no being; the real never ceaseth to be; the truth about both hath been perceived by the seers of the essence of things. Know THAT to be indestructible by whom all this is pervaded. Nor can any work the destruction of that imperishable One. These bodies of the embodied One, who is eternal, indestructible and immeasurable, are known as finite. Therefore fight, O Bharata. He who regardeth this as a slayer, and he who thinketh he is slain, both of them are ignorant. He slayeth not, nor is he slain. He is not born, nor doth he die; nor having been, ceaseth he any more to be; unborn, perpetual, eternal and ancient, he is not slain when the body is slaughtered. Who knoweth him indestructible, perpetual, unborn, undiminishing, how can that man slay, O Partha, or cause to be slain?

"As a man, casting off worn-out garments, taketh new ones, so the dweller in the body, casting off worn-out bodies, entereth into others that are new. Weapons cleave him not, nor fire burneth him, nor waters wet him, nor wind drieth him away. Uncleavable he, incombustible he, and indeed neither to be wetted nor dried away; perpetual, all-pervasive, stable, immovable, ancient. Unmanifest, unthinkable, immutable, he is called; therefore knowing him as such, thou shouldst not grieve. Or if thou thinkest of him as being constantly born and constantly dying, even then, O mighty-armed, thou shouldst not grieve. For certain is death for the born, and certain is birth for the dead; therefore over the inevitable thou shouldst not grieve.

"Beings are unmanifest in their origin, manifest in their midmost state, O Bharata, unmanifest likewise are they in dissolution. What room then for lamentation? As marvellous one regardeth him; as marvellous another speaketh thereof; as marvellous another heareth thereof; yet having heard, none indeed understandeth. This dweller in the body of every one is ever invulnerable, O Bharata; therefore thou shouldst not grieve for any creature."

The Rule of Action

Arjuna said: "With these perplexing words thou only confusest my understanding; therefore tell me with certainty the one way by which I may reach bliss."

The Blessed Lord said: "In this world there is a twofold path, as I before said, O sinless one: that of yoga by knowledge, of the Sankhyas; and that of yoga by action, of the Yogis.

"Man winneth not freedom from action by abstaining from activity, nor by mere renunciation doth he rise to perfection. Nor can any one, even for an instant, remain really actionless; for helplessly is every one driven to action by the qualities born of nature. Who sitteth, controlling the organs of action, but dwelling in his mind on the objects of the senses, that bewildered man is called a hypocrite. But who, controlling the senses by the mind, O Arjuna, with the organs of action without attachment, performeth yoga by action, he is worthy. Perform thou right action, for action is superior to inaction, and, inactive, even the maintenance of thy body would not be possible.

"The world is bound by action, unless performed for the sake of sacrifice; for that sake, free from attachment, O son of Kunti, perform thou action. Having in ancient times emanated mankind together with sacrifice, the lord of emanation said: 'By this shall ye propagate; be this to you the giver of desires; with this nourish ye the shining ones, and may the shining ones nourish you; thus nourishing one another, ye shall reap the supremest good. For nourished by sacrifice, the shining ones shall bestow on you the enjoyments you desire.' A thief verily is he who enjoyeth what is given by them without returning them aught. The righteous, who eat the remains of the sacrifice, are freed from all sins; but the impious, who dress food for their own sakes, they verily eat sin. From food creatures become; from rain is the production of food; rain proceedeth from sacrifice; sacrifice ariseth out of action. Know thou that from Brahma action groweth, and Brahma from the Imperishable cometh. Therefore the ETERNAL, the all-permeating, is ever present in sacrifice.

"He who on earth doth not follow the wheel thus revolving, sinful of life and rejoicing in the senses, he, O son of Pritha, liveth in vain. But the man who rejoiceth in the SELF with the SELF is satisfied, and is content in the SELF, for him verily there is nothing to do; for him there is no interest in things done in this world, nor any in things not done, nor doth any object of his depend on any being. Therefore, without attachment, constantly perform action which is duty, for, by performing action without attachment, man verily reacheth the Supreme.

"Whatsoever a great man doeth, that other men also do; the standard he setteth up, by that the people go. Let no wise man unsettle the mind of ignorant people attached to action; but acting in harmony with me let him render all action attractive.

"All actions are wrought by the qualities of nature only. The self, deluded by egoism, thinketh: 'I am the doer.' But he, O mighty-armed, who knoweth the essence of the divisions of the qualities and functions, holding that 'the qualities move amid the qualities,' is not attached. Those deluded by the qualities of nature are attached to the functions of the qualities. The man of perfect knowledge should not unsettle the foolish whose knowledge is imperfect. Surrendering all actions to me, with thy thoughts resting on the supreme SELF, from hope and egoism freed, and of mental fever cured, engage in battle.

"Who abide ever in this teaching of mine, full of faith and free from cavilling, they too are released from actions. Who carp at my teaching and act not thereon, senseless, deluded in all knowledge, know thou these mindless ones as fated to be destroyed.

"Even the man of knowledge behaves in conformity with his own nature; beings follow nature; what shall restraint avail? Affection and aversion for the objects of sense abide in the senses; let none come under the dominion of these two; they are obstructors of the path. Better one's own duty though destitute of merit, than the duty of another, well-discharged. Better death in the discharge of one's own duty; the duty of another is full of danger."

Arjuna said: "But dragged on by what does a man commit sin, reluctantly indeed, O Varshneya, as it were by force constrained?"

The Blessed Lord said: "It is desire, it is wrath, begotten by the quality of motion; all-consuming, all-polluting, know thou this as our foe here on earth. As a flame is enveloped by smoke, as a mirror by dust, as an embryo is wrapped by the amnion, so this is enveloped by it. Enveloped is wisdom by this constant enemy of the wise in the form of desire, which is insatiable as a flame.

"The senses, the mind and the reason are said to be its seat; by these enveloping wisdom it bewilders the dweller in the body. Therefore, O best of the Bharatas, mastering first the senses, do thou slay this thing of sin, destructive of wisdom and knowledge. It is said that the senses are great; greater than the senses is the mind: greater than the mind is the reason; but what is greater than the reason, is HE.

"Thus understanding him as greater than the reason, restraining the self by the SELF, slay thou, O mighty-armed, the enemy in the form of desire, difficult to overcome."

The Rule of Wisdom

The Blessed Lord said: "Many births have been left behind by me and by thee, O Arjuna. I know them all, but thou knowest not thine, O Parantapa. Though unborn, the imperishable SELF, and also the lord of all beings, brooding over nature, which is mine own, yet I am born through my own power.

"Whenever there is decay of righteousness, O Bharata, and there is exaltation of unrighteousness, then I myself come forth; for the protection of the good, for the destruction of evil-doers, for the sake of firmly establishing righteousness, I am born from age to age.

"He who thus knoweth my divine birth and action, in its essence, having abandoned the body, cometh not to birth again, but cometh unto me, O Arjuna. Freed from passion, fear and anger, filled with me, taking refuge in me, purified in the fire of wisdom, many have entered into my being. However men approach me, even so do I welcome them, for the path men take from every side is mine, O Partha.

"They who long after success in action on earth worship the shining ones; for in brief space verily, in this world of men, success is born of action.

"The four castes were emanated by me, by the different distribution of qualities and actions; know me to be the author of them, though the actionless and inexhaustible. Nor do actions affect me, nor is the fruit of action desired by me. He who thus knoweth me is not bound by actions.

"Having thus known, our forefathers, ever seeking liberation, performed action; therefore do thou also perform action, as did our forefathers in the olden time.

" 'What is action, what inaction?' Even the wise are herein perplexed. Therefore I will declare to thee the action by knowing which thou shalt be loosed from evil. It is needful to discriminate action, to discriminate unlawful action, and to discriminate inaction; mysterious is the path of action. He who seeth inaction in action, and action in inaction, he is wise among men, he is harmonious, even while performing all action.

"Whose works are all free from the moulding of desire, whose actions are burned up by the fire of wisdom, him the wise have called a sage. Having abandoned attachment to the fruit of action, always content, nowhere seeking refuge, he is not doing anything, although doing actions. Hoping for naught, his mind and self controlled, having abandoned all greed, performing action by the body alone, he doth not commit sin. Content with whatsoever he obtaineth without effort, free from the pairs of opposites, without envy, balanced in success and failure, though acting he is not bound. Of one with attachment dead, harmonious, with his thoughts established in wisdom, his works sacrifices, all action melts away.

"Even if thou art the most sinful of all sinners, yet shalt thou cross over all sin by the raft of wisdom. As the burning fire reduces fuel to ashes, O Arjuna, so doth the fire of wisdom reduce all actions to ashes. Verily, there is no purifier in this world like wisdom; he that is perfected in yoga finds it in the SELF in due season.

"The man who is full of faith obtaineth wisdom, and he also who hath mastery over his senses; and, having obtained wisdom, he goeth swiftly to the supreme peace. But the ignorant, faithless, doubting self goeth to destruction; nor this world, nor that beyond, nor happiness, is there for the doubting self.

"He who hath renounced actions by yoga, who hath cloven asunder doubt by wisdom, who is ruled by the SELF, actions do not bind him, O Dhananjaya.

"Therefore, with the sword of the wisdom of the SELF cleaving asunder this ignorance-born doubt, dwelling in thy heart, be established in yoga. Stand up, O Bharata."

The Nature of God

The Blessed Lord said: "With the mind clinging to me, O Partha, performing yoga, refuged in me, how thou shalt without doubt know me to the uttermost, that hear thou. I will declare to thee this knowledge and wisdom in its completeness, which, having known, there is nothing more here needeth to be known. Among thousands of men scarce one striveth for perfection; of the successful strivers scarce one knoweth me in essence.

"Earth, water, fire, air, ether, mind, and reason also and egoism—these are the eightfold division of my nature.

"This the inferior. Know my other nature, the higher, the life-element, O mighty-armed, by which the universe is upheld.

"Know this to be the womb of all beings. I am the source of the forthgoing of the whole universe and likewise the place of its dissolving. There is naught whatsoever higher than I, O Dhananjaya. All this is threaded on me, as rows of pearls on a string.

"I am the sapidity in waters, O son of Kunti, I the radiance in moon and sun; the word of power in all the Vedas, sound in ether, and virility in men; the pure fragrance of earths and the brilliance in fire am I; the life in all beings am I, and the austerity in ascetics. Know me, O Partha! as the eternal seed of all beings. I am the reason of the reason-endowed, the splendour of splendid things am I. And I the strength of the strong, devoid of desire and passion. In beings I am desire not contrary to duty, O Lord of the Bharatas. The natures that are harmonious, active, slothful, these know as from me; not I in them, but they in me.

"All this world, deluded by these natures made by the three qualities, knoweth not me, above these, imperishable. This divine illusion of mine, caused by the qualities, is hard to pierce; they who come to me, they cross over this illusion."

The Imperishable

The Blessed Lord said: "The indestructible, the supreme is the ETERNAL; his essential nature is called SELF-knowledge; the emanation that causes the birth of beings is named action; knowledge of the elements concerns my perishable nature, and knowledge of the shining ones concerns the life-giving energy; the knowledge of sacrifice tells of me, as wearing the body, O best of living beings.

"And he who, casting off the body, goeth forth thinking upon me only at the time of the end, he entereth into my being: there is no doubt of that. Whosoever at the end abandoneth the body, thinking upon any being, to that being only he goeth, O Kaunteya, ever to that conformed in nature. Therefore at all times think upon me only, and fight. With mind and reason set on me, without doubt thou shalt come to me. With the mind not wandering after aught else, harmonized by continual

practice, constantly meditating, O Partha, one goeth to the Spirit
supreme, divine.

"He who thinketh upon the Ancient, the Omniscient, the All-Ruler,
minuter than the minute, the supporter of all, of form unimaginable,
refulgent as the sun beyond the darkness, in the time of forthgoing,
with unshaken mind, fixed in devotion, by the power of yoga drawing
together his life-breath in the centre of the two eyebrows, he goeth to
this Spirit, supreme, divine.

"That which is declared indestructible by the Veda-knowers, that
which the controlled and passion-free enter, that desiring which Brahma-
charya is performed, that path I will declare to thee with brevity.

"All the gates closed, the mind confined in the heart, the life-breath
fixed in his own head, concentrated by yoga. 'Aum!' the one-syllabled
ETERNAL, reciting, thinking upon me, he who goeth forth, abandoning the body, he goeth on the highest path. He who constantly thinketh
upon me, not thinking ever of another, of him I am easily reached,
O Partha, of this ever-harmonized Yogi.

"Having come to me, these Mahatmas come not again to birth, the
place of pain, non-eternal; they have gone to the highest bliss. The
worlds, beginning with the world of Brahma, they come and go, O
Arjuna; but he who cometh unto me, O Kaunteya, he knoweth birth
no more.

"The people who know the day of Brahma, a thousand ages in duration, and the night, a thousand ages in ending, they know day and night.

"From the unmanifested all the manifested stream forth at the coming
of day; at the coming of night they dissolve, even in that called the
unmanifested. This multitude of beings, going forth repeatedly, is dissolved at the coming of night: by ordination, O Partha, it streams forth
at the coming of day. Therefore verily there existeth, higher than that
unmanifested, another unmanifested, eternal, which, in the destroying
of all beings, is not destroyed. That unmanifested, 'the Indestructible,'
it is called; it is named the highest path. They who reach it return not.
That is my supreme abode.

"He, the highest Spirit, O Partha, may be reached by unswerving
devotion to him alone, in whom all beings abide, by whom all this is
pervaded."

The Lord of All

The Blessed Lord said: "By me all this world is pervaded in my unmanifested aspect; all beings have root in me, I am not rooted in them. As the mighty air everywhere moving is rooted in the ether, so all beings rest rooted in me—thus know thou.

"Hidden in nature, which is mine own, I emanate again and again all this multitude of beings, helpless, by the force of nature. Under me as supervisor nature sends forth the moving and unmoving; because of this, O Kaunteya, the universe revolves.

"The foolish disregard me, when clad in human semblance, ignorant of my supreme nature, the great Lord of beings; empty of hope, empty of deeds, empty of wisdom, senseless, partaking of the deceitful, brutal and demoniacal nature.

"Others also, sacrificing with the sacrifice of wisdom, worship me as the One and the Manifold everywhere present.

"I the oblation; I the sacrifice; I the ancestral offering; I the fire-giving herb; the mantram I; I also the butter; I the fire; the burnt offering I; I the Father of this universe, the Mother, the Supporter, the Grandsire, the Holy One to be known, the Word of Power, and also the Ric, Sama, and Yajur, the Path, Husband, Lord, Witness, Abode, Shelter, Lover, Origin, Dissolution, Foundation, Treasure-house, Seed imperishable. I give heat; I hold back and send forth the rain; immortality and also death, being and non-being am I, Arjuna.

"To those men who worship me alone, thinking of no other, to those ever harmonious, I bring full security. They who worship the shining ones go to the shining ones; to the ancestors go the ancestor-worshippers; to the elementals go those who sacrifice to elementals; but my worshippers come unto me. He who offereth to me with devotion a leaf, a flower, a fruit, water, that I accept from the striving self, offered as it is with devotion.

"The same am I to all beings; there is none hateful to me nor dear. They verily who worship me with devotion, they are in me, and I also in them. Even if the most sinful worship me, with undivided heart, he too must be accounted righteous, for he hath rightly resolved; speedily he becometh dutiful and goeth to eternal peace, O Kaunteya, know thou for certain that my devotee perisheth never. They who take refuge with me, O Partha, though of the womb of sin, women, Vaisyas, even Sudras, they also tread the highest path.

"On me fix thy mind; be devoted to me; sacrifice to me; prostrate thyself before me; harmonized thus in the SELF, thou shalt come unto me, having me as thy supreme goal."

The Form of God

Arjuna said: "This word of the supreme secret concerning the SELF, thou hast spoken out of compassion; by this my delusion is taken away. The production and destruction of beings have been heard by me in detail from thee, O Lotus-eyed, and also thy imperishable greatness. O supreme Lord, even as thou describest thyself, O best of beings, I desire to see thy form omnipotent. If thou thinkest that by me it can be seen, O Lord, Lord of Yoga, then show me thine imperishable SELF."

The Blessed Lord said: "Behold, O Partha, a form of me, a hundred-fold, a thousandfold, various in kind, divine, various in colours and shapes. Behold the Adityas, the Vasus, the Rudras, the two Asvins and also the Maruts; behold many marvels never seen ere this, O Bharata. Here, to-day, behold the whole universe, movable and immovable, standing in one in my body, O Gudakesa, with aught else thou desirest to see. But verily thou art not able to behold me with these thine eyes; the divine eye I give unto thee. Behold my sovereign Yoga."

Having thus spoken, the great Lord of Yoga, Hari, showed to Partha his supreme form as Lord. With many mouths and eyes, with many visions of marvel, with many divine ornaments, with many upraised divine weapons; wearing divine necklaces and vestures, anointed with divine unguents, the God all-marvellous, boundless, with face turned everywhere.

If the splendour of a thousand suns were to blaze out together in the sky, that might resemble the glory of that Mahatma.

There Pandava beheld the whole universe, divided into manifold parts, standing in one in the body of the Deity of Deities. Then he, Dhananjaya, overwhelmed with astonishment, his hair upstanding, bowed down his head to the shining one, and with joined palms spake.

The Blessed Lord said:

"Arjuna, by my favour thou hast seen
This loftiest form by yoga's self revealed!
Radiant, all-penetrating, endless, first,
That none except thyself hath ever seen.
Nor sacrifice, nor Vedas, alms, nor works,
Nor sharp austerity, nor study deep,
Can win the vision of this form for man,
Foremost of Kurus, thou alone hast seen.
Be not bewildered, be thou not afraid,
Because thou hast beheld this awful form;
Cast fear away, and let thy heart rejoice;
Behold again mine own familiar shape."

Arjuna said: "Beholding again thy gentle human form, O Janardana, I am now collected, and am restored to my own nature."

The Blessed Lord said: "This form of mine beholden by thee is very hard to see. Verily the shining ones ever long to behold this form. Nor can I be seen as thou hast seen me by the Vedas, nor by austerities, nor by alms, nor by offerings: but by devotion to me alone I may thus be perceived, Arjuna, and known and seen in essence, and entered, O Parantapa. He who doeth actions for me, whose supreme good I am, my devotee, freed from attachment, without hatred of any being, he cometh unto me, O Pandava."

The Rule of Devotion

Arjuna said: "Those devotees who ever harmonized worship thee, and those also who worship the Indestructible, the Unmanifested, whether of these is the more learned in yoga?"

The Blessed Lord said: "They who with mind fixed on me, ever harmonized worship me, with faith supreme endowed, these in my opinion are best in yoga.

"They who worship the Indestructible, the Ineffable, the Unmanifested, Omnipresent, and Unthinkable, the Unchanging, Immutable, Eternal, restraining and subduing the senses, regarding everything equally, in the welfare of all rejoicing, these also come unto me.

"The difficulty of those whose minds are set on the Unmanifested is greater; for the path of the Unmanifested is hard for the embodied to reach.

"Those verily who, renouncing all actions in me and intent on me, worship meditating on me, with wholehearted yoga, these I speedily lift up from the ocean of death and existence, O Partha, their minds being fixed on me.

"Place thy mind in me, into me let thy reason enter; then without doubt thou shalt abide in me hereafter. And if thou art not able firmly to fix thy mind on me, then by the yoga of practice seek to reach me, O Dhananjaya.

"If also thou art not equal to constant practice, be intent on my service; performing actions for my sake, thou shalt attain perfection. If even to do this thou hast not strength, then, taking refuge in union with me, renounce all fruit of action with the self controlled.

"Better indeed is wisdom than constant practice; than wisdom, meditation is better; than meditation, renunciation of the fruit of action; on renunciation follows peace.

"He who beareth no ill-will to any being, friendly and compassionate, without attachment and egoism, balanced in pleasure and pain, and forgiving, ever content, harmonious with the self controlled, resolute, with mind and reason dedicated to me, he, my devotee, is dear to me.

"He from whom the world doth not shrink away, who doth not shrink away from the world, freed from the anxieties of joy, anger, and fear, he is dear to me.

"He who wants nothing, is pure, expert, passionless, untroubled, renouncing every undertaking, he, my devotee, is dear to me. He who neither loveth nor hateth, nor grieveth, nor desireth, renouncing good and evil, full of devotion, he is dear to me.

"Alike to foe and friend, and also in fame and ignominy, alike in cold and heat, pleasures and pain, destitute of attachment, taking equally praise and reproach, silent, wholly content with what cometh, homeless, firm in mind, full of devotion, that man is dear to me.

"They verily who partake of this life-giving wisdom as taught herein, endued with faith, I their supreme object, devotees, they are surpassingly dear to me."

The Good Man and the Evil

"Fearlessness, cleanness of life, steadfastness in the Yoga of wisdom, alms-giving, self-restraint and sacrifice and study of the scriptures, austerity and straightforwardness, harmlessness, truth, absence of wrath, renunciation, peacefulness, absence of crookedness, compassion to living beings, uncovetousness, mildness, modesty, absence of fickleness, vigour, forgiveness, fortitude, purity, absence of envy and pride—these are his who is born with the divine properties, O Bharata.

"Hypocrisy, arrogance and conceit, wrath and also harshness and un-wisdom are his who is born, O Partha, with demoniacal properties.

"The divine properties are deemed to be for liberation, the demonia-cal for bondage. Grieve not, thou art born with divine properties, O Pandava.

"Twofold is the animal creation in this world, the divine and the demoniacal: the divine hath been described at length: hear from me, O Partha, the demoniacal. Demoniacal men know neither right energy nor right abstinence; nor purity, nor even propriety, nor truth is in them. 'The universe is without truth, without basis,' they say, 'without a god; brought about by mutual union, and caused by lust and nothing else.'

"Holding this view, these ruined selves of small understanding, of fierce deeds, come forth as enemies for the destruction of the world. Surrendering themselves to insatiable desires, possessed with vanity, conceit and arrogance, holding evil ideas through delusion, they engage in action with impure resolves. Giving themselves over to unmeasured thought whose end is death, regarding the gratification of desires as the highest, feeling sure that this is all, held in bondage by a hundred ties of expectation, given over to lust and anger, they strive to obtain by unlawful means hoards of wealth for sensual enjoyments.

" 'This to-day by me hath been won, that purpose I shall gain; this wealth is mine already, and also this shall be mine in future. I have slain this enemy, and others also I shall slay. I am the lord, I am the enjoyer, I am perfect, powerful, happy; I am wealthy, well-born; what other is there that is like unto me? I will sacrifice, I will give alms, I will rejoice.' Thus deluded by unwisdom, bewildered by numerous thoughts, enmeshed in the web of delusion, addicted to the gratification of desire, they fall downwards into a foul hell.

"Self-glorifying, stubborn, filled with the pride and intoxication of wealth, they perform lip-sacrifices for ostentation, contrary to scriptural ordinance. Given over to egoism, power, insolence, lust and wrath, these malicious ones hate me in the bodies of others and in their own.

"These haters, evil, pitiless, vilest among men in the world, I ever throw down into demoniacal wombs. Cast into demoniacal wombs, deluded birth after birth, attaining not to me, O Kaunteya, they sink into the lowest depths. Triple is the gate of this hell, destructive of the self— lust, wrath, and greed; therefore let man renounce these three.

"A man liberated from these three gates of darkness, O son of Kunti, accomplisheth his own welfare, and thus reacheth the highest goal.

"He who, having cast aside the ordinances of the scriptures, followeth the promptings of desire, attaineth not to perfection, nor happiness, nor the highest goal.

"Therefore let the scriptures be thy authority, in determining what ought to be done, or what ought not to be done. Knowing what hath been declared by the ordinances of the scriptures, thou oughtest to work in this world."

The Way of Deliverance

"Man reacheth perfection by each being intent on his own duty. Listen thou how perfection is won by him who is intent on his own duty. He from whom is the emanation of beings, by whom all this is pervaded, by worshipping him in his own duty a man winneth perfection. Better is one's own duty though destitute of merits than the well-executed duty of another. He who doeth the duty laid down by his own nature incurreth not sin. Congenital duty, O son of Kunti, though defective, ought not to be abandoned. All undertakings indeed are clouded by defects as fire by smoke.

"He whose reason is everywhere unattached, the self subdued, dead to desires, he goeth by renunciation to the supreme perfection of freedom from obligation. How he who hath attained perfection obtaineth the ETERNAL, that highest state of wisdom, learn thou from me only succinctly, O Kaunteya.

"United to the reason, purified, controlling the self by firmness, having abandoned sound and the other objects of the senses, having laid aside passion and malice, dwelling in solitude, abstemious, speech, body and mind subdued, constantly fixed in meditation and yoga, taking refuge in dispassion, having cast aside egoism, violence, arrogance, desire, wrath, covetousness, selfless and peaceful—he is fit to become the ETERNAL.

"Becoming the ETERNAL, serene in the SELF, he neither grieveth nor desireth; the same to all beings, he obtaineth supreme devotion unto me. By devotion he knoweth me in essence, who and what I am; having thus known me in essence he forthwith entereth into the Supreme. Though ever performing all actions, taking refuge in me, by my grace he obtaineth the eternal indestructible abode.

"Renouncing mentally all works in me, intent on me, resorting to the yoga of discrimination, have thy thought ever on me. Thinking on me, thou shalt overcome all obstacles by my grace: but if from egoism thou wilt not listen, thou shalt be destroyed utterly. Entrenched in egoism, thou thinkest, 'I will not fight'; to no purpose thy determination, nature will constrain thee.

"O son of Kunti, bound by thine own duty born of thine own nature, that which from delusion thou desirest not to do, even that helplessly thou shalt perform. The Lord dwelleth in the hearts of all beings, O Arjuna, by his illusive power, causing all beings to revolve, as though mounted on a potter's wheel.

"Flee unto him for shelter with all thy being, O Bharata; by his grace thou shalt obtain supreme peace, the everlasting dwelling-place. Thus hath wisdom, more secret than secrecy itself, been declared unto thee by me; having reflected on it fully, then act thou as thou listest."

The Vishnu Purana

The Sacred Ganges

O great Muni, from clouds proceed the rains; from them the water which is the nutriment and delight of all the celestials and the rest. The celestials who receive oblations, being pleased by burnt offerings, cause the rain to fall for the support of created beings. This holy seat of Vishnu is the stay of the three worlds as it is the source of the rain.

From this region proceeds the river Ganges, that removes all sins, embrowned with the unguents of the nymphs of heaven. She issues from the nail of the great toe of Vishnu's left foot.

Saints, who are purified by bathing in the waters of this river, and whose minds are devoted to Kesava, obtain final liberation. The sacred river, when heard of, desired, seen, touched, bathed in, or hymned, day by day purifies all beings. And those who living even at a distance of a hundred yoyanas exclaim "Ganga and Ganga" are relieved of the sins committed during the three previous existences. The place from which this river has issued for the purification of the three worlds is the third division of the celestial region—the seat of Vishnu.

The General Duties of Man

Aurva said: Vishnu being worshipped, a man obtains the consummation of all earthly desires and attains to the regions of the celestials and of Brahma and even final liberation. O king of kings, whatever a man desires, either small, or great, he gets by the worship of Achyuta. O king of earth, you have asked me how Vishnu can be worshipped. Hear, I shall relate all that to you. He is the true worshipper of Vishnu who

observes duly the duties of the four castes and rules of four Asramas.
There is no other means of satisfying Vishnu. He who offers sacrifices,
sacrifices to him; he who recites prayers, prays to him; he who injures
living beings, injures him; for Hari is identical with all living beings.
Therefore, he who observes duly the duties of his caste is said to
worship the glorious Janardana. O lord of earth, the Brahmana, the
Kshatriya, the Vaisya, the Sudra, by attending to the duties prescribed
by his caste, best worships Vishnu. He who does not vilify another either
in his presence, or in his absence, who does not speak untruth, does not
injure others, pleases Kesava the best. Kesava is best pleased with him,
O king, who does not covet another's wife, wealth, and who does not
bear ill feeling towards any. O lord of men, Kesava is pleased with him
who neither beats nor slays any animate or inanimate thing. O lord of
men, Govinda is pleased with that man who is ever intent upon serving
the gods, the Brahmanas and his spiritual preceptor. Hari is always satisfied with him who is ever anxious for the welfare of all creatures, his
children and his own soul. Vishnu is always pleased with that pure-
minded man whose mind is not sullied with anger and other passions.
He best worships Vishnu, O king, who observes the duties laid down by
scripture for every caste and condition of life; there is no other mode.

Sagara said: O foremost of twice-born ones, I wish to hear of the
duties of caste and condition. Relate them to me.

Aurva said: Hear attentively from me in order the duties of the
Brahmana, the Kshatriya, the Vaisya and the Sudra. The duties of the
Brahmanas consist in making gifts, worshipping the celestials with sacrifices, studying the Vedas, performing oblations and libations with water
and preserving the sacred fire. For maintenance, he may offer sacrifices
for others, teach others and may accept liberal presents in a becoming
manner. He must advance the well-being of all and do injury to none—
for the greatest wealth of a Brahmana consists in cherishing kind feelings
towards all. He must consider with an equal eye the jewel and stone
belonging to another. He should at proper seasons beget offspring on his
wife, O king of earth.

The duties of the Kshatriya consist in making gifts to the Brahmanas
at pleasure, in worshipping Vishnu with various sacrifices and receiving
instructions from the preceptor. His principal sources of maintenance are
arms and protection of the earth. But his greatest duty consists in guarding the earth. By protecting the earth a king attains his objects, for he

gets a share of the merit of all sacrifices. If a king, by maintaining the order of caste, represses the wicked, supports the pious, he proceeds to whatever region he desires.

O lord of men, the great patriarch Brahma has assigned to the Vaisyas, for their maintenance, the feeding of the cattle, commerce, and agriculture. Study, sacrifice, and gift are also within the duties of the Vaisyas: besides these, they may also observe the other fixed and occasional rites.

The Sudra must maintain himself by attending upon the three castes, or by the profits of trade, or the earnings of mechanical labour. He may also make gifts, offer the sacrifices in which food is presented, and he may also make obsequial offerings.

Besides these, the four castes have got other duties, namely—the acquisition of wealth for the support of servants, cohabitation with their wives for the sake of children, kindness towards all creatures, patience, humility, truth, purity, contentment, decorum of manners, gentleness of speech, friendliness, freedom from envy or avarice and the habit of vilifying. These also constitute the duties of every condition of life.

In cases of emergency a Brahmana may follow the occupations of a Kshatriya or Vaisya; the Kshatriya may adopt those of Vaisya and the Vaisya those of Kshatriya: but the last two should never adopt the functions of the Sudra if they can avoid them. And if that be not possible they must at any rate avoid the functions of the mined caste.

The Duties of Householders

Aurva said: As soon as a son is born his father should perform the ceremonies consequent upon the birth of a child and all other initiatory ceremonies as well as a Sraddha, which is the source of prosperity.

Upon the tenth day after birth the father should give a name to the child, the first term of which shall be the name of a god and the second of a man as Sarman or Varman. The former is the proper designation of a Brahmana, and the second of a Kshatriya. And Vaisyas and Sudras should have the designation of Gupta and Dasa. A name should not be devoid of any meaning, should not be indecent, absurd, inauspicious, or dreadful. It should contain an even number of syllables; it should not be too long nor too short, nor too full of long vowels, but contain a due proportion of short vowels and be easily articulated.

After going through these initiatory ceremonies and being purified the youth should acquire knowledge from his preceptor. And having acquired knowledge from the preceptor and given him presents, O king, he should, desirous of entering the order of householders, marry.

He must marry a maiden who is of a third of his age, one who has not too much of hair, but is not without any, one who is not very black or yellow-complexioned and who is not from birth a cripple or deformed. He must not marry a girl who is vicious or unhealthy, born of a low family, or suffering from any disease; one who may have been badly trained, one who talks improperly, one who has inherited some disease from father or mother; one who has a beard and has got a masculine appearance; one who speaks thick or thin or croaks like a craven, who has got eyes without eyelashes, or insufficiently covered with them; one who has got legs covered with hairs, thick ankles; one who has dimples in her cheeks when laughing. The learned should not marry a girl who has not got a tender countenance, who has got white nails, and who has got red eyes. The wise and prudent should not marry one whose hands and legs are heavy, who is a dwarf, or who is very tall or one whose eyebrows meet, or whose teeth are far apart and resemble tusks. O king, a householder should marry a girl who is at least five degrees distant in descent from his mother and seven degrees from his father.

Having bathed and offered duly libations to the celestials, Rishis and manes and adorned his hand with precious jewels, having recited introductory prayers, offered oblations with fire, food to guests, to Brahmanas, to his elders and to his family, the householder should take his meal, wearing unsullied cloth, excellent garlands, and sprinkled with perfumes. He must not eat, O lord of men, with a single garment on, nor with wet hands and feet.

He must not eat with his face directed to any intermediate point of the horizon, but facing the east or the north; and with a smiling countenance, happy and attentive, let him take good and wholesome food boiled with clean water, procured from no mean person, nor by improper means, nor improperly cooked. Having given a part to his hungry companions he should take food without reproach from a clean, handsome vessel which must not be placed upon a low stool or bed.

He must not take his food in an unbecoming place or out of season or in an unsuitable mood, giving the first morsel to fire. His food, O king, must be consecrated with suitable texts, must be good and must not be stale except in the case of fruit or meat. Nor should it be made of dry vegetable substances other than jujubes or preparation of molasses. And a man should never eat that of which the juices have been extracted. Nor should a man so eat as nothing will be left of his meal except in the case of flour, cakes, honey, water, curds and butter.

He should with a devoted mind first taste that which has good flavour; in the middle he should take salt and sour things and in the end he should take those which are pungent and bitter. The person who begins his food with fluid things, takes solid food in the middle, and finishes with fluid things, will ever be strong and healthy. In this wise he should take such food as is not prohibited, should be silent at the time of eating, and should take five handfuls for the nutriment of the vital principle.

After he has taken his food, he should, facing the east or the north, rinse his mouth, and having washed his hands up to the wrist, he should again sip water.

Then with a satisfied and calm mind he should take his seat, meditate upon his tutelary deity and pray: "May fire excited by air cause this food to digest in the space afforded by the ethereal atmosphere, convert this into the earthly elements of this body, and give me satisfaction. May this food, when assimilated, contribute to the vigour of the earth, water, fire, and air of my body and afford unmixed satisfaction. May Agasti, Agni and submarine fire bring about the digestion of the food I have taken and may I enjoy happiness consequent thereupon, and may my body be freed from all ills. May Vishnu, who is the chief principle of all senses, of all bodies and souls, be propitiated with my faith and cause such assimilation of the food I have eaten as may invigorate my health. Verily Vishnu is the eater, the food and the nourishment; may the food I have taken through this faith be digested."

Having recited this prayer he should rub his stomach with his hand, and renouncing idleness should engage in such action as can easily be performed. He should spend the day in the reading of sacred writings and in such amusements as are authorized by the righteous, and when the Sandhya sets in he must engage in devotion. O king, he must perform the morning rites before the stars have disappeared and perform the evening rites before the sun has quite set. The morning and evening rites should never be neglected except at seasons of impurity, anxiety, sickness or alarm. He who but for illness lies in bed at the hours of sunrise and sunset is guilty of iniquity. Therefore a man should rise before the sun in the morning and sleep not until after it has set. Those who sinfully neglect the performance of both the morning and evening rites, go to the hell of darkness after death. And having prepared food in the evening, the wife of the householder, with a view to obtain the fruit of the Visvedeva rite, should give food, without offering any prayers, to outcasts or unclean persons.

The householder, as his means allow, should again show hospitality to any guest who may come, receiving him with the salutation of evening, and offering him water to wash his feet, a seat, a supper and a bed. The sin consequent upon not receiving hospitably a guest who comes after sunset is eight times greater than that of turning away one who comes during the day. A person should therefore particularly show respect to him who seeks refuge after sunset, for the respect, given to his satisfaction, will afford pleasure to all the celestials. The householder should, therefore, as his means permit him, give a guest food, potherbs, water, a bed, a mat, or if he cannot give anything more, ground only on which to lie.

Having taken his evening meal and washed his feet, a householder should take rest. His bed must be complete and made of wood, it must have ample space, must not be cracked nor uneven, nor dirty nor infested by insects, and must have a bedding. The householder must sleep with his head either to the east or to the south; any other position is unhealthy.

In proper time, under the influence of an auspicious planet and in an auspicious moment, he should go to his wife if she is not unbathed, sick, unwell, unwilling, angry, pregnant, hungry or over-fed. He should also be free from all these imperfections and should be neatly dressed and adorned and excited by tenderness and affection. Having bathed, wearing garlands, using perfumes, delighted and animated by desire, he should go to his wife—not being hungry and excited with anxiety. There are certain days on which the use of unguents, flesh and women is prohibited, as the eighth and fourteenth lunar days, new-moon and full-moon and the entrance of the sun into a new sign. On these occasions the wise should control their appetites and engage in the worship of the celestials as laid down in scripture, in meditation and prayer. And he who acts otherwise will be doomed to a hell where he will be constrained to live upon ordure. A man should not excite his desires by medicines nor satisfy them with unnatural objects or in public or holy places. A man should not go to a woman under a huge tree, in the courtyard, in a place of pilgrimage, in pasturage, where four streets meet, in a cremation ground, in a garden or in the waters. On all these occasions mentioned before, in the morning or in the evening, or being unclean, the wise should not cohabit with women. If a man goes to a woman during the Parva he loses wealth, if during the day he is visited with sin, if he cohabits with a woman on ground he loses his fame. A man should not think voluptuously of another's wife, nor should he speak to her for that purpose; for such a wight will be born in his next life as a creeping insect. The cohabitation with another's wife is a source of fear to him both in this life and in the next—for in this he loses his longevity and in the next he is doomed to hell. Considering all these things a man should approach his own wife in proper season or even at other times.

The householder should venerate gods, king, Brahmanas, saints, aged persons and holy preceptors. He should also observe duly the two Sandhyas and offer oblations to fire. He should use untorn garments, delicate herbs and flowers, wear emeralds and other precious stones, keep his hair neat and clean, perfume his body with delicious unguents and should always go out handsomely dressed and decorated with garlands and white flowers. He should not misappropriate another's property nor should treat him unkindly. He should always speak amiably and the truth, and should not speak out publicly another's faults.

A man should not bathe in a river when it is ebb-tide, should not enter a house when it is on fire nor climb to the top of a tree; nor (when in the company of others) clean his teeth, nor blow his nose nor gape without covering his mouth, nor clear his throat, nor cough, nor laugh loudly, nor emit wind with noise, nor bite his nails, nor cut grass, nor scratch ground, nor put his beard into his mouth, nor crumble a clod of clay, nor look upon the planets when he is unclean.

He should not see another's wife when she is naked nor see the sun at the time of its rising or setting. He should not express disgust at a dead body, for the odour of it is the produce of the moon. He should avoid, during the night, the place where four roads meet, the village tree, the forest adjacent to a cremation ground and a loose woman.

The wise should not pass across the shadow of a venerable person, of an image of a deity, of a flag, of a heavenly luminary.

He who, having controlled himself, puts a stop to the sources of all these imperfections, meets with no obstacle in the acquisition of piety, wealth and desire. Final emancipation is in his grasp who is sinless towards them who commit mischief by him, who speaks amicably to them who use harsh words and whose soul melts with benevolence. The earth is upheld by the truthfulness of those who have controlled their passions, and who, always following pious observances, are not sullied by desire, covetousness and anger. A prudent man should always cultivate that in act, thought and speech, which conduces to the well-being of all living creatures both in this world and the next.

The Burden of Life

Parasara said: O Maitreya, having investigated three kinds of worldly pain and having acquired true wisdom and detachment from worldly objects, the wise man obtains final liberation. The first of the three pains, or Adhyatmika, is of two kinds—physical and mental. Bodily pain, as you shall hear, is of many sorts. Affections of the head, catarrh, fever, cholic, fistula, spleen, hæmorrhoids, intumescence, sickness, ophthalmia, dysentery, leprosy, and many other diseases constitute physical affliction. Mental pains are love, anger, fear, hate, covetousness, stupefaction, despair, sorrow, malice, disdain, jealousy, envy and many other passions that are created in the mind. These and diverse other afflictions, mental or physical, are comprised under the class of worldly sufferings which is called Adhyatmika. The pain Adhibhautika, O excellent Brahmana, is every kind of evil that is inflicted upon men by beasts, birds, men, goblins, snakes, fiends or reptiles, and the pain that is called Adhidauvika or superhuman is the work of cold, heat, wind, rain, lightning and other phenomena. Affliction, O Maitreya, is multiplied in thousands of shapes in the progress of conception, birth, decay, disease, death and hell. The tender animal exists in the embryo surrounded by abundant filth, floating in water and distorted in its back, neck and bones; enduring severe pain even in the course of its development, and disordered by the acid, bitter, pungent and saline articles of its mother's food; incapable of extending or contracting its limbs, reposing amidst slime of ordure and urine; every way incommoded with consciousness and calling to memory many hundred previous births. Thus exists the embryo in profound affliction bound to the world by its former works.

When the child is about to be born, its face is besmeared by excrement, urine, blood, mucus, and semen; its attachment to the uterus is ruptured by the Prajapati wind; it is turned head downwards and violently expelled from the womb by the powerful and painful winds of parturition; and the infant, losing for a time all sensation when brought in contact with the external air, is immediately deprived of its intellectual knowledge. Then born, the child is tortured in every limb, as if pierced with thorns or cut to pieces with a saw, and falls from its fetid lodgment as from a sore, like a crawling thing upon the earth. Unable to feel itself, unable to turn itself, it is dependent on the will of others for being bathed and nourished. Laid upon a dirty bed, it is bitten by insects and mosquitoes and has not power to drive them away. Many are the pangs attending birth and many are those which succeed to birth; and many are the afflictions that are inflicted by elemental and superhuman powers in the state of childhood covered by the gloom of ignorance; and internally bewildered, man knows not whence he is, who he is, whither he goeth nor what is his nature; by what bonds he is bound; what is cause and what is not cause; what is to be done and what is to be left undone; what is to be said and what is to be kept silent; what is righteousness and what is iniquity; in what it consists or how; what is right, what is wrong; what is virtue, what is vice. Thus man, like a brute beast addicted only to animal gratification, suffers the pain that ignorance brings about. Ignorance, darkness, inactivity influence those devoid of knowledge so that pious works are neglected; but hell is the consequence of neglect of religious acts, according to the great sages, and the ignorant therefore suffer affliction both in this world and in the next.

When old age comes in, the body is infirm, the limbs are relaxed; the face is emaciate and shrivelled; its skin is wrinkled and scantily covers the veins and sinews; the eyes discern not afar off, and the pupil gazes on vacuity, the nostrils are stuffed with hair; the trunk trembles as it moves; the bones appear beneath the surface; the back is bowed and the joints are bent; the digestive fire is extinct and there is little appetite and little vigour; walking, rising, sitting, sleeping, are all painful efforts; the ear is dull; the eye is dim; the mouth is disgusting with dribbling saliva; the senses no longer are obedient to the will; and as death approaches, the things that are perceived even are immediately forgotten. The utterance of a single sentence is fatiguing, and wakefulness is perpetuated by difficult breathing, coughing and painful exhaustion. The old man is lifted up by somebody else; he is an object of contempt to his servants, his children and his wife. Incapable of cleanliness, of amusement, or food, or desire, he is laughed at by his dependants, and disregarded by his kin; and dwelling on the exploits of his youth, as on the actions of a past life, he sighs deeply and is sorely distressed. Such are some of the pains to which old age is doomed. I will now describe to you the agonies of death.

The neck droops, the feet and hands are relaxed; the man is repeatedly exhausted, subdued and visited with interrupted knowledge; the principle of selfishness afflicts him, and he thinks, What will become of my wealth, my lands, my children, my wife, my servants, my house? The joints of his limbs are tortured with severe pains as if cut by a saw or as if they were pierced by the sharp arrows of the destroyer; he rolls his eyes and tosses about his hands and feet; his lips and palate are parched and dry, and his throat, obstructed by foul humours and deranged vital airs, emits a rattling sound; he is afflicted with burning heat, thirst and hunger; and he at last passes away tortured by the servants of the judge of the dead, to undergo a renewal of his sufferings in another body.

Death sooner or later is inevitable. As long as he lives he is immersed in manifold afflictions, like the seed of the cotton amidst the down that is to be spun into thread. In acquiring, losing, and preserving wealth there are many griefs; and so there are in the misfortunes of our friends. Whatever is produced that is most acceptable to man; that, Maitreya, becomes a seed whence springs the tree of sorrow. Wife, children, servants, houses, lands, riches, contribute much more to the misery than to the happiness of mankind. Where could man, scorched by fires of the sun of this world, look for felicity, were it not for the shade afforded by the tree of emancipation? Attainment of the divine being is considered by the wise as the remedy of the threefold class of ills that beset the different stages of life, conception, birth and decay, as characterized by that only happiness which effaces all other kinds of felicity however abundant, and as being absolute and final.

It should therefore be the assiduous endeavour of wise men to attain unto God. He dwelleth eternally in all beings and all things dwell in him; and thence the lord Vasudeva is the creator and preserver of the world. He, though identical with all beings, is beyond and separate from material nature, from its products, from properties and from imperfections; he is beyond all investing substance; he is universal soul; all the interstices of the universe are filled up by him; he is one with all good qualities; and all created beings are endowed with but a small portion of his individuality. Assuming various shapes, he bestows benefits on the whole world, which was his work. Glory, might, dominion, wisdom, energy, power and other attributes are collected in him. Supreme of the supreme, in whom no imperfections abide, lord over finite and infinite, god in individuals and universals, visible and invisible, omnipotent, omnipresent, omniscient, almighty. The wisdom, perfect, pure, supreme, undefiled and one only by which he is conceived, contemplated and known, that is wisdom; all else is ignorance.

Benediction

Salutation unto the first of gods, Purusottama, who is without end and beginning, without growth and decay and death, who is substance that knows no change. Salutation unto that undecaying Purusha, Vishnu, who assumed sensible qualities, who though pure became as if impure, assuming various shapes, who is gifted with divine wisdom and who is the lord of the preservation of all creatures. Salutation unto him who is the instrument of meditative wisdom and active virtue; who confers enjoyments upon human beings; who is identical with threefold qualities; who is without any change and is the cause of the evolution of the world, and who is without any birth or decay. Salutation unto him who is called heaven, air, fire, water, earth and ether, who confers all objects that satisfy sense, who benefits mankind, and who is perceptible, subtle, and imperceptible. May that unborn eternal Hari, who is seen in manifold forms, whose essence consists of both nature and spirit, confer upon humanity that blessed condition which is without birth or decay.

The Garuda Purana

The Duties of the Four Castes

(Brahma speaks)

Celebrating sacrifices for themselves and others, making gifts and accepting them, study and teaching constitute the sixfold duties of the Brahmanas. Making gifts, studying and celebrating sacrifices are the duties of the Kshatriyas and the Vaisyas. To govern is also the duty of a Kshatriya, whereas cultivation constitutes that of a Vaisya. To serve the twice-born is the duty of the Sudras. Handicraft and menial service are also their duties. Begging, attending the preceptor, Vedic study, abandonment of worldly affections and possessions and the preservation of the sacred fire constitute the duties of a Brahmacharin.

All the four Ashramas (orders) have twofold conditions. They are called Brahmacharin (religious student), Upakurvana (householder), Vaishthika and Brahmatatpara. He who having duly studied the Vedas enters into the order of the householder is called Upakurvanaka. He who continues the life of the religious student till his death is called Vaishthika. O foremost of the twice-born, the preservation of sacred fire, the entertainment of the guests, the celebration of sacrifices, making gifts, and the adoration of the deities constitute the duties of a householder. A Udasina (one disassociated from the world) and a Sadhaka (one devoted exclusively to religious practices) become householders in two ways. A Sadhaka, while he is busy with maintaining his relations, becomes a householder. He who, having neglected the payment of threefold debts and renounced wife and earthly possessions, etc., roves about alone, is a nominal Udasina.

The duty of a dweller of the forest (hermit) consists in duly sleeping

on earth, living on roots and fruits, and studying the Vedas. He is the
best of ascetics living in the forest who practises austerities in the forest,
worships the gods, offers oblations to fire and studies the Vedas. Being
emaciated greatly by practising hardest austerities, he who is engaged
solely in the meditation of the deity is known as a Sannyasin stationed in
the Vanaprastha order. The Bhikkhu or the mendicant, who daily practises Yoga, is self-controlled and follows the light of Jnana (knowledge), is called Parameshthika. The great ascetic, who delights in self
and is ever gratified and besmeared with sandal, is called Bhikkhu. Begging alms, Vedic studies, vow of silence, asceticism, meditation, perfect
knowledge and disassociation from the world constitute the duties of a
Bhikkhu. Parameshthikas are divided into three classes—viz., Jnana
Sannyasins, Veda Sannyasins, and Karma Sannyasins. Yoga is also threefold—Bhoutika, Kshatra; and the third is Antashrami. Abstract meditation of the deity is also threefold—Prathama, Duskara, Antima. Religious rites beget emancipation and pursuance of worldly objects creates
desire. Vedic rites are twofold—Pravritti and Nivritti. Nivritti or extinction of desire is preceded by Jnana or knowledge, and Pravritti is
worked out by the worship of sacred fire.

Forgiveness, self-restraint, compassion, charity, want of avarice, simplicity, want of jealousy, visiting sacred shrines, truthfulness, contentment, faith in the existence of God, the subjugation of senses, the adoration of the deities, the worship of the Brahmanas, abstinence from doing
injury, speaking sweet words, not to slander, and amiability,—these are
the duties of the various orders of the four castes. The region of Brahma
is reserved for those Brahmanas who perform sacrificial rites. That of
Indra is intended for those Kshatriyas who never fly away from the
battlefield. That of the Gandharva is reserved for the Sudras who steadfastly serve the three higher castes.

The Worship of Ancestors

Said the God Brahma: The city of Gaya is a sacred sanctuary in the
country of Kikata and likewise is the forest of Rajagriha (modern
Rajgir) in that part of the continent of India. Sacred is the place called
the Vishaya Charana, and the rivers which drain the aforesaid tracts are

the holiest of the holies. A man, by simply making a pilgrimage to Gaya, stands absolved from all debts due by him to his forefathers.

Similarly, by witnessing the images of the gods Rudra, Kaleshvara and Kedara at Gaya, a man is supposed to pay off the debts he owes to his fathers. By seeing the image of the celestial grandfather at Gaya, a man is absolved from all sins, whereas by repairing to the presence of the divine image of the great-grandfather at Gaya, a man is sure to enter the sinless region after death.

The holy pool known as the Nabhi-tirtham lies to the north of the river Kanaka, and occupies a middle place between that river and the holy well of Brahma-Sada, an ablution wherein leads the bather to the region of Brahma after death. The man who offers oblations or obsequious cakes to his departed manes on the rim of that sacred well, and casts them in its holy waters, is freed from all moral indebtedness to his forefathers. Similarly a Sraddha ceremony, performed by a man at the shrine of the immortal Vata tree, leads the souls of his departed forefathers to the region of Brahma. The man who bathes in the holy pool, known as the Hansa-tirtham, is absolved from all sins. A Sraddha ceremony performed by a man at any of the following sacred spots or shrines, such as the Koti-tirtham, the Gayaloka, the Vaitarini, and the Gomaka, leads the souls of his ancestors, removed even to the twenty-first degree in the ascending line, to the region of Brahma.

By passing through the hill crevice or the natural tunnel known as the Brahma-Yoni, with his mind absorbed in the contemplation of his forefathers, a man is exempted for good from the trouble of passing through the uterine canal of any woman in the shape of a child. Libations of water, offered by a man to his departed manes at the shrine of Kaka-jangha, give them infinite and perpetual satisfaction. The man who performs a Sraddha ceremony at the well of Matanga in the holy forest of Dharmaranya, ascends to heaven after death. A similar ceremony performed at the well of virtue or at the shrine of the stake of virtue (Dharma Yupa) absolves a man from all obligations to the souls of his forefathers. The gods should be invoked to bear testimony to the fact as follows: "Witness, O ye gods, and the guardian angels of the different regions or abodes, that I have come to the well of Matanga in this holy forest and have brought about the liberation of my departed manes."

The man who contemplates that a visit to Gaya is not a matter of everyday probability, and that it does not fall to the lot of every one to offer obsequious cakes at Gaya to one's departed manes more than once in life, shall do well to touch the holy waters of the river Mahanadi and to offer libations of the same to his departed manes, whereby they would be enabled to ascend to the regions of eternity, accompanied by the souls of all the departed cognates of the offerer. The man who recites at the shrine of the goddess Gayatri the Vedic hymns and verses composing the rite of his daily Sandhya is sure to acquire the merit of such continuous recitation for the period of twelve consecutive years.

Once on a time, a ghost met a certain merchant in the way and addressed him as follows:

"Cast some obsequious cakes in my name at the sanctuary of Gayashirsha, since both the offerer and the receiver of such cakes are liberated from the confines of the nether regions and are admitted into the abodes of the gods." The merchant did as he was requested to do by the departed spirit, and subsequently offered obsequious cakes to his own forefathers jointly with his younger brothers, who were immediately released from the mansion of death. The merchant in his turn was blessed with the birth of a male child named Vishala. His wife Vishala bore him that son. Vishala, who was childless up to that time, asked the Brahmanas how he could beget children, and the Brahmanas replied that a pilgrimage to Gaya would remove all impediments in the way of having offspring of his own. Vishala went to Gaya and offered obsequious cakes to his departed fathers at the sanctuary of Gayashirsha. Whereupon a son was born to him. One day Vishala saw three shadowy images, white, red, and black, reflected in the sky just before his eyes. He questioned them as to their identity and whereabouts, whereupon the white one replied, "I am thy father, O Vishala, and am at present residing in the region of Indra through the merit of my good deeds in life. O son, the red spectre thou findest is my father, who killed a Brahmana in his human existence and was a man of the blackest iniquity on earth. The black one is my grandfather, who had taken by forcible hands the life of many holy sages in their hermitage. They are now doomed to the torments of that particular quarter of the sea of hell whose dire monotony is not broken by the rising of a single wave and which hides within its lethean and unfathomable depth an eternity of impious misery and wailing. Release them, O thou the offerer of our obsequious cakes, from the dismal confines of that infernal world and send them happy and emancipated to the region of the immortal gods."

Now Vishala did what he was requested to do by his father, and ascended heaven after a prosperous sovereignty on earth.

Having performed a ceremonial ablution with the Varunastra Mantra, the pilgrim should offer obsequious cakes to his departed manes at the sanctuary of the hill of spirits (Pretasila) and invoke them as follows:

"On the blades of Kusa grass extended in my front, and with this libation of water containing sesamum, I invoke the presence of the souls of those who have been born in my family and subsequently died without any means of succour from the shades of the infernal region.

"I offer these obsequious cakes for the liberation of those spirits who have once been born in flesh in the family of my father or mother. I offer this obsequious cake to those spirits who have once taken their birth in the family of my maternal grandfather and who are divested of all means of liberation from their infernal confines.

"I offer these obsequious cakes for the release of those of my relations who have died in their mother's womb, or have found an untimely grave even without cutting a single tooth. I have offered this obsequious cake for the succour of those my friends, whether born in my family or otherwise, and even whose names and spiritual clanship have escaped from my memory.

"I offer this cake to the souls of those who have committed suicide or met a violent death either by water, poison, blow, or strangulation. I offer this obsequious cake to the spirits of those who have been burnt to death, or devoured by lions and tigers, or killed by horned cattle, or expired under the bites of fanged or sharp-toothed beasts. I offer this obsequious cake to the spirits of those whose earthly remains have been cremated in unconsecrated fire, or have not been consigned to the flames of any fire at all, as well as to the souls of those who have been killed by thieves or lightning.

"I offer this obsequious cake for the liberation of those spirits who have been kept confined within the dark walls of the hells known as the Raurava and the Kalasutra. I offer this obsequious cake for the liberation of those spirits who are at present doomed to the tortures of those divisions of hell which are known as the Kumbhipaka (hell of whirling eddies) and Asipatra Vanam (forest of sword blades). I offer this obsequious cake for the liberation of spirits who are tortured in other quarters of hell.

"I offer this obsequious cake for the emancipation of those spirits who have been reincarnated as serpents, birds, or other lower animals, or have been consigned to the voiceless agonies of vegetable life.

"I offer this obsequious cake for the liberation of those spirits who, under the ordination of the god of death, have been consigned to suffer eternal tortures in hell.

"I offer this obsequious cake for the elevation of those spirits in the astral plane who, for their countless misdeeds in successive rebirths, and through the workings of the propulsions of ignoble passions turned into dynamics of fate, are perpetually getting down in the graduated scale of life, and to whom a working upward to the plane of human existence has become a thing of rarest impossibility.

"May the souls of those who were friends to me in this life, or have been my friends in any other existence, or of those who are not related to me in that capacity and are utterly friendless for the present, be propitiated and liberated by this obsequious cake which I have offered at the present sanctuary in Gaya. May the souls of any of my forefathers who might be staying at present in the shape of astral beings derive perpetual satisfaction from the obsequious cake which I have offered.

"I have offered obsequious cakes for the satisfaction of all those spirits who have once taken their birth in the family of my father or mother, or who were related to my preceptors, or father-in-law or any other relations in life, or who have died without having any issue of their own, and accordingly stand, at present, divested of their specific shares of funeral cakes and libations of water, or who have been born deaf, dumb, blind, crippled or idiotic in life, whether they are any way related to me or not, or who have died in the womb without ever seeing the light of god (whether do I know them or not), and may they derive eternal felicity from this cake which I have offered to them.

"May the gods and Brahma and Isana, in particular, bear testimony to the fact that I have come to Gaya, and effected the liberation of my fathers from the confines of the nether world. Witness, O thou mace-bearing god, that I have arrived at Gaya, done all the needful rites for the emancipation of my departed manes, and stand fully absolved from the threefold debt of human existence."

Of Associates

Double-tongued are the snakes and the malicious; their cruel mouths are the source of many an evil to man. Avoid the company of an erudite miscreant: is not the serpent that bears a gem on its hood doubly dangerous for the stone? Who is he that dreadeth not the malicious who work mischief without any provocation and who are but the serpents in human form? Words of spite drop down from the mouths of the malicious; the fangs of serpents secrete deadly venom.

Sit in the assembly of the honest; combine with those that are good and virtuous; nay, seek out a noble enemy where enmity cannot be helped and have nothing to do with the wicked and the unrighteous. Even in bondage thou shalt live with the virtuous, the erudite and the truthful; but not for a kingdom shalt thou stay with the wicked and the malicious.

The vile are ever prone to detect the faults of others, though they be as small as mustard seeds, and persistently shut their eyes against their own, though they be as large as Vilva fruits. I come to the conclusion, after much deliberation, that pleasure exists not where desire or affection has room to be. True happiness lies in the extinction of all emotions. Apprehension is where affection is. Where there is affection there is misery. Pain has its root in love or affection. Renounce affection and you shall be happy. This human body is a theatre of pleasure and pain, and they come into being with the self of a man. Dependence or bondage is misery. Liberty or emancipation is the only happiness vouchsafed to man.

Nobody is any one's friend. Nobody is any one's enemy. Friendship and enmity are bound to each other by a distinct chain of cause and effect (self-interest). A source of solace in grief, a succour in distress, and a repository of happiness and confidence:—O who has created the two letters "Mitram" (friend), which are more precious than a mine of gems! By the single utterance of the two letters "Hari" a fettered self makes a step towards emancipation. A man does not repose so much confidence in his sons, wives and brothers as he implicitly places in his own natural friend. Gamble not and make no pecuniary transactions with a man, nor see his wife in his absence; these three being the essentials of a permanent amity.

Never stay in a lonely place with your own daughters, sisters or step-mothers. The fiend of lust takes advantage of solitude and pleads evil counsel to the heart to which the learned have been known to yield. How absurd is the love god in his frolics! A man naturally shuns a woman who loves him and is easily available to him, and covets one whose touch is the forfeit of life. Easier it is to determine the velocity of a horse or of a storm, or even the depth of an unfathomable ocean; but how puerile is the attempt at sounding a heart that loves not. It is the absence of a nook of vantage, or the want of leisure or of a person mak-ing love-overtures to her, that mainly accounts for the chastity of a woman. It is only rarely when a couple is fondly attached to each other that the wife is true at heart. A son should not think, out of a sense of decorum, what is done by his mother in a passion of love.

A courtesan is a dependant even in respect of her sleep, the sole aim of her life being to regale the hearts of her visitors as long as they can decently bear their wine. She is a sort of perpetual smiling machine, being obliged to hammer out a horse-laugh, even with the weight of a life-long grief, misery and futility lying heavy on her heart. Her person is sold to others for money, while she often meets a violent death. Fire, water, a king, a woman, a fool, or a serpent used or provoked by another, should be regarded as fatal. What wonder is it that a man well-versed in letters will pass as an erudite one? What is surprising in the fact that a king who is learned in the science of politics will rule justly as a virtuous prince? What is there to wonder, if a young and beautiful woman, proud and conscious of her charms, leads a gay and fast life? What is there to surprise, if an indigent person commits a crime? Let not your neighbour know of your weakness, but rather observe his weak points unseen, like a turtle, from your own housetop. Amorous fancies spontaneously occur even in the mind of a girl who has been incarcerated from her infancy in a moated castle in the nether worlds. Who can pretend to conquer a woman?

How can I believe a rich man to be an anchorite, and a drunken woman chaste? Trust not the untrustworthy nor confide any secret in your friend, lest he might betray you in a fit of anger. A vast, deep and child-like faith in all, a universal clemency, and a close and watchful veiling of his own god-like inherent virtues, are the traits which mark a noble soul.

What wise man will believe in a woman, in a serpent, in a king, in the services done by his own enemy, in the infallible nature of his own knowledge and memory and in the enjoyment of the worldly pleasures, even for once in life? Trust not those who are unworthy of credence. Do not repose unbounded faith even in the trustworthy, lest they might bring about your ruin and overthrow by betraying it.

He who rests confident after having made a reconciliation with his enemy, is sure to a fall one day like a man who peacefully reposes on a tree-top. Be not too mild nor too fierce, but subdue a mild enemy with a mild means and a fierce one with fierce measures. Be not too straight nor too crooked. Crooked trees are left standing while the straight ones are felled by a forester. Trees that are laden with fruits are bent under their burden, a heavy rain-cloud seems to touch the ground with the weight of its charge; but a fool and a dry wood break under pressure but know no bending. Pleasure and pain come and go without asking. Men, like cats, are ever ready to pounce upon happiness. Many a happiness walks before and after a virtuous man, the contrary being the case with the iniquitous. A counsel heard by six ears (discussed among three men) is soon divulged; heard by four it is kept secret for a while. He who keeps his own counsel baffles the scrutiny of the god Brahma.

Karma

A man is the creator of his own fate, and even in his fœtal life he is affected by the dynamics of the works of his prior existence. Whether confined in a mountain fastness or lulling on the bosom of a sea, whether secure in his mother's lap or held high above her head, a man cannot fly from the effects of his own prior deeds. Ravana had his fortress on the summits of the mount Trikruta, moated by the deep sea; and innumerable hosts of valiant Rakshasas were ever ready to lay their lives for him. The wise sage Ushana himself tutored him well in ethics, politics and social economy. Time has killed even that mighty Ravana. Whatever is to befall a man on any particular age or time will surely overtake him then and on that date. Scale the heavens, or plunge into the nether regions, or enfilade the quarters of the skies, a thing which you have once given away can never be yours. Knowledge acquired by a man in his prior birth, wealth given away in charity in his prior existence, and works done by him in a previous incarnation, go ahead of his soul in its sojourn. A person's Karma is the principal factor in determining his happiness or unhappiness in life, inasmuch as Janaki, though joined in wedlock under the auspices of blissful asterisms by the holy Vasishta himself, had nothing but misery for her portion in life. (A good physiognomy does not necessarily ensure a happy life on earth.) Rama was round-thighed, Lakshmana was fleet-coursing as the wind, and Sita had a crown of fine, thick-set hair, yet they were all unhappy. A son cannot relieve the misery of his father's spirit by performing proper obsequies, nor can a fond father, with all his anxious care for his good, and due performance of his paternal duties, lead him in the path of happiness.

This human body entombs a self which is nothing if not emphatically a worker. It is the works of this self in a prior existence which determine the nature of its organism in the next, as well as the character of the diseases, whether physical or mental, which it is to fall a prey to. Shafts discharged even by strong-armed archers fall to the ground, and wise men even with their knowledge and forethought are sometimes vanquished. Hence all projects should be carefully judged and deliberated in the light of the Shastras.

A man reaps that at that age, whether infancy, youth or old age, at which he had sowed it in his previous birth. The Karma of a man draws him away from a foreign country and makes him feel its consequence even in spite of his will. A man gets in life what he is fated to get, and even a god cannot make it otherwise. Thus neither do I wonder nor mourn my lot, O Sounaka. What is lotted cannot be blotted. A frightened mouse runs to its hole; a scared serpent, to a well; a terrified elephant, to its stake—but where can a man fly from his Karma?

Knowledge imparted is knowledge gained. Fresh water springs up from beneath the well that has been bored out. Riches earned honestly and fairly are true riches; opulence acquired by honest means is true opulence:—do not lose sight of the fact, when you try to acquire anything in life. The amount of hardship which a man undergoes in order to earn his bread is infinitely greater than what is necessary for acquiring religious merit, which can grant him an immunity from such troubles in his births to come.

Sometimes I have got a thing without seeking it. Sometimes my fervent prayer for a thing has rested unanswered. A thing goes there where it is wanted:—what is there to mourn for in this?

Our life comes from the unseen and goes to the unseen, its middle part being only patent and manifest:—what is there to mourn for in this, O Shounaka?

A man dies not before the appointed time, even if he is riddled with shafts. A wound from the tip of a Kusa sprout proves fatal at the right moment. A man receives that which he is fated to receive, goes only there where fate leads him to, and finds only that much pleasure or pain which he is destined to meet in this life:—what is there to mourn for in this life?

Flowers bloom and fruits ripen in their appointed time and of their own accord without waiting for anybody's bidding; and the effects of one's Karma, O Shounaka, bide their time and become patent only on the right occasion. Birth, education, conduct, character, virtue or connexion avails not a man in this life. The effects of one's Karma and penance, done in a prior existence, fructify, like a tree at the appointed time, in the next.

Learn this to be a general synopsis, O Shounaka, of the rules of pleasure and pain. Misery follows happiness and happiness follows misery like the spokes of a wheel. What is gone is gone for good. What is future is still remote. He who acts only in the living present knows no affliction.

The shadow of a cloud, the love of the malicious, an intimacy with another man's wife, youth and opulence, are the five equally transitory things in the world. Life is transitory. Transient are the youth and opulence of a man. Wives, children, friends, and relations are but passing shadows in the phantasmagoria of life. Only virtue and good deeds endure. Even a centenarian has but a short space of life, the one-half of which is covered by the night, the other half being rendered fruitless by disease, grief, imbecility and toil. Night covers the one-half of the hundred years allotted to man and is spent in sleep. Infancy and boyhood cover the half of the other moiety, a part of its remaining half being clouded by grief, misery and service. The rest is but changeful and transient like a wave of the ocean. Ah, what is the end of life? What does glory, fame, or honour signify? Death with his attendants Day and Night is perpetually travelling the world in the guise of Old

Age, and is devouring all created beings, as a serpent gulps down a gust of wind.

A Duty to Children

The parents of a child are but his enemies when they fail to educate him properly in his boyhood. An illiterate boy, like a heron amidst swans, cannot shine in the assembly of the learned. Learning imparts a heightened charm to a homely face. Knowledge is the best treasure that a man can secretly hoard up in life. Learning is the revered of the revered. Knowledge makes a man honest, virtuous and endearing to the society. It is learning alone that enables a man to better the condition of his friends and relations. Knowledge is the holiest of the holies, the god of the gods, and commands the respect of crowned heads; shorn of it a man is but an animal. The fixtures and furniture of one's house may be stolen by thieves; but knowledge, the highest treasure, is above all stealing.

The Markandeya Purana

Sumati Instructs His Father

I

A certain high-minded Brahmana, born in the race of Bhrigu, said to his gentle son Sumati, resembling one void of sense at the time of his investiture with the sacred thread:

Study the Vedas, O Sumati, in due order being intent upon serving your preceptor and depending upon alms. Then entering the life of a householder do you celebrate excellent sacrifices and beget desirable offspring and then enter into woods. When you shall live in the forest, O child, and, leaving the company of your wife, lead the life of a mendicant, you will attain to that Brahman, approaching whom no one grieves. Being thus urged on by his father out of parental affection with nectarine words, he, smiling, said:

O father, all that you advise me to study has been exhaustively read by me together with various other branches of learning and diverse mechanical arts. Ten thousand births more come to my recollection. I was conversant with happiness and misery and was engaged in destruction, progress and prosperity. I had union with enemies, friends, and wives, as well as separation from them. I saw many a mother as well as many a father. I experienced thousands of miseries and happiness. I had a great many friends and different kinds of fathers. I lived in a female womb sullied by urine and excreta and I suffered from severe diseases and ailments in thousands. I suffered numberless miseries in the womb, in infancy and youth, and in old age; all these I now recollect.

I was born as a Brahmana, a Kshatriya, a Vaisya and a Sudra, and again as a beast, a worm, a deer and a bird. I was born in the houses of the royal entertainers and war-like kings, as I have been born in your house. I became servants and slaves of many men and I came by mastery, lordship, and poverty.

I slew many and in turn was slain and struck down by them. My wealth was given away by many to others and I also gave away much. I was always pleased by fathers, mothers, friends, brothers and wives; and when I became poor I bathed my countenance with tears.

Thus revolving on the perilous wheel of the world, I have attained to this knowledge, O father, which is instrumental to the attainment of liberation. Acquiring this knowledge all the actions sanctioned by Ric, Yajur and Sama appear to me as shorn of any virtue and inadequate. Therefore of what use are the Vedas to me who have acquired understanding, have been satiated with the wisdom of the preceptor, am devoid of exertion and am fond of the soul? I shall attain that most excellent Brahma state which is shorn of the six kinds of action, misery, happiness, delight, sentiment, and attributes.

Therefore I shall go, O father, renouncing the collection of evils, as is well-known, originating from sentiment, joy, fear, anxiety, anger, spite, decrepitude, and casting off the three Vedas which are like the Kimpaka fruit and lead to demerit.

Hearing his words, the great father with delighted heart said to his own son, being filled with joy and wonder: What is it that you say, O my son? Whence has this your knowledge come? By what has your previous dullness been changed into wisdom? Is it that on the wane of the curse of an ascetic or a deity, your knowledge that was once lost to you has come back? I wish to hear all this; great is my curiosity. Tell me, O my child, all that you did formerly.

The son said: Hear, O father, a true account of what I have experienced again and again. This wheel of a world is undecaying, still it has no existence. Commanded by you, O father, I shall communicate to you all from the time coming out, which no one else can speak.

In this body, the bile, growing angry, being fanned by a strong wind and flaming, although nearly no fuel, pierces the very vitals. Then the wind named Udana moves over it and obstructs the passage of the meat and drink taken. Only those persons that have given away food and drink to others, enjoy comfort at that precious moment. He who has given away food with a meat purified by reverence obtains satisfaction even without food.

He who has never uttered a falsehood, he who has not made a distinction of love, he who believes in God and who is reverential, meets with happy death. Those who are intent upon adoring the deities and Brahmanas, who are free from spite, who are pure in spirit, are liberal and bashful, meet with easy death. He who does not forsake virtue through lust, anger or spite, he who keeps his promise and is gentle, meets with easy death. But he who does not give water to one who is thirsty, food to one who is hungry, is assailed by them when death presents itself. Those who give fuel conquer cold, those who give sandal conquer heat; but those who afflict people come by a dreadful pain destroying the very life.

Those worst of men, who cause ignorance and stupefaction, attain great fear and are crushed by fierce pangs. Those that give false evidence, or speak false, or satisfy the orders of a wicked man, or disregard the Vedas, die in ignorance. The dreadful and vicious-souled followers of Yama, breathing hellish smell around, with nooses and maces in hands, approach them. And when they come within the range of their vision they all tremble and continually bewail for their brothers, mothers and sons. Then their speech becomes indistinct, O father, and is composed of one letter; their eyes roll and their faces are dried up with fear and sighs. Then with breath running high, sight dimmed and assailed by pain, he renounces his body. Then going before the body, for undergoing affliction consequent upon his acts, he assumes another body not sprung from a father or a mother but which has the same age, condition and habitation as assigned to the other body.

Then the emissaries of Yama quickly bind him with dreadful nooses and drag him to the south, trembling with the stroke of the rod. Then he is dragged by the emissaries of Yama, sending out dreadful, inauspicious yells through grounds rough with Kusa, thorns, ant-hills, pins and stones, glowing with flames at places, covered with pits, blazing with the heat of the sun and burning with its rays. Dragged by the dreadful emissaries and eaten by hundreds of jackals, the sinful person goes to Yama's house through a fearful passage.

But those who have distributed umbrellas and shoes, those who have given away cloth, as well as those who have given away food, go easily by that way.

Going through such sufferings, losing all control over self and assailed by sin, a man is taken, on the twelfth day, to the city of Dharma. When his body is burnt he experiences a great burning sensation; and when his body is beaten or cut he feels a great pain.

His body being thus destroyed, a creature, although walking into another body, suffers eternal misery on account of his own adverse actions. Going there he feeds on the sesame and water or the ball of boiled rice offered by his descendants.

A person receives comforts from his relations' rubbing their bodies with oil, from their kneading their limbs and from their taking their food. He enjoys rest by his relations' lying down on the ground. A dead man is pleased with his relations by their performance of charitable works.

Taken to his own home on the twelfth day he sees it and feeds on the Pinda and water that are offered on the earth. After the twelfth day, being drawn, a man beholds the dreadful and terrible-looking iron city of Yama. As soon as he enters there he beholds Yama in the midst of the Destroyers, Death and others having blood-red eyes, and resembling a mass of crushed collyrium, with face with dreadful teeth, and a dreadful frowning countenance;—the lord, encircled by hundreds of distempers having disfigured and dreadful visages, carrying his rod, mighty-armed, with the noose in his hand and highly fearful to look at. A creature attains to a state, good or bad, assigned by him. One giving false evidence or uttering falsehood goes to Raurava.

Hear now, I will give what is the true description of Raurava. It measures two thousand yoyanas. There is a pit which is knee-deep and difficult of being crossed. Levelled with heaps of flaming charcoal it is heated by a piece of land burning dreadfully with coal. Into it the followers of Yama throw the perpetrator of impious deeds. And burnt by the dreadful fire he runs about. His feet get torn and injured at every step and within a day and night he can but once take away his feet.

When he thus goes over a thousand yoyanas he is let alone. Then to have his sins washed off he is taken to another such hell. After having gone through all the hells the sinner takes upon a beastly life. Then going through the lives of worms, insects, and flies, beasts of prey, gnats, elephants, trees, horses, cows, and through diverse other sinful and miserable lives, he, coming to the race of men, is born as a hunchback, or an ugly person or a dwarf or a Chandala Pukkasa.

Then carrying the remnant of his virtue and vice he goes up gradually to the higher castes, Sudras, Vaisyas, Kshatriyas, Brahmanas, and the state of the king of gods; sometimes perpetrating iniquities he falls into the hell beneath.

Hear, I shall now describe how virtuous people proceed. These persons follow the pious course laid down by Yama. With Gandharvas singing, Apsaras dancing, wearing many a beautiful and shining garland, they proceed in excellent cars embellished with chains, bangles and other beautiful ornaments. Coming down therefore they are born in the families of other high-souled kings and protect people engaged in noble works. After having enjoyed all the best things of life they go upward; but if they go down they fare as before.

I have thus described to you all about the sufferings of creatures. Hear now, O Brahmana saint, how embryos are created.

II

As soon as the male seed is mixed with female blood, one, released from heaven or hell, enters into it. O father, the two kinds of seed being influenced by him, he attains stability. He then grows into protoplasm, next into a bubble and then into a lump of flesh. The germ that grows up in the lumps of flesh is called Ankura, and then are gradually produced the five limbs. Then the minor limbs, fingers, eyes, nose, face, and ears are developed from principal limbs, and from them the nails, etc. Then hairs grow on the skin and then those on the head.

Thus does the embryo grow up along with the uterus. As a coco-nut fruit grows along with its case so does this increase along with its case, with its face bent downwards. It grows, keeping its hands downwards to its thighs and sides; the thumbs are placed on the thighs and the other fingers before them. The eyes are behind the thighs and the nose is within the thighs. The hips are between the two heels; the arms and legs remain outside.

Thus a creature, lying in the womb of a female, grows up gradually; the embryos of other creatures lie in the womb according to their forms. It gets hardened by fire and lives by what is eaten and drunk; the embryo exists in the womb depending upon virtue and vice. The entrail called Apyayani fixed to its navel is attached to the entrail of the female and it grows there. Having its body nourished while in the womb by the food and drink a creature gradually grows up. It then gets the recollection of its many births and then pushed hither and thither it comes to entertain a distaste for such a state.

Having been released from the womb—"I shall never do it again—I shall so strive that I shall not have to enter into the womb any more"— thus does it think remembering a hundred miseries of births originating from destiny which he had experienced before.

Then in the course of time, the creature, with its face bent downwards, turns itself and is then born in the ninth or the tenth month. And coming out it is assailed by the Prajapatya wind, and tormented by the grief that is in its heart it bewails. Coming out of the womb, it falls into an unbearable trance; it regains its consciousness when it feels the surrounding air.

Then the enchanting illusion of Vishnu takes possession of it; having its soul possessed by it, it sustains a bewilderment of sense. With the loss of sense the creature comes of infancy, boyhood, youth and old age.

A man repeatedly goes through a cycle of births and deaths. In this way, he rolls like a clock on the wheel of the world. Sometimes a man attains heaven, sometimes he goes to hell and sometimes a dead man reaps both heaven and hell. And sometimes born again in this earth he

reaps the fruits of his own acts. And sometimes enjoying the fruits of
his own acts within a short time he breathes his last. Sometimes, O best
of Brahmanas, living in heaven or hell for a short time on account of
his limited merit or demerit he is born in this earth.

O father, the dwellers of heaven are seen by them to enjoy happiness
—and then those, brought down to perdition, think that there is a great
misery in hell. Even in heaven there is incomparable misery, for from
the time of ascension every one conceives in his mind, "I shall fall."
Beholding the people of hell, they attain to mighty misery thinking day
and night, "I shall be brought to this condition."

Mighty is the pain of living in the womb, of being born from a
female, of the infancy of one when born, and that of decrepitude as
well. There is also great misery in youth influenced by lust, malice and
anger; old age is also full of miseries and the culmination of this is
death. Mighty is the pain of those who are carried away by force by the
emissaries of Yama and thrown into hell; then again is birth in the
womb and death and hell.

In this wise bound by the fetters of nature the creatures revolve on
the wheel of the world like a clock and suffer miseries. O father, there
is not the least happiness in this world abounding in a hundred miseries.
Why then shall I, exerting for emancipation, follow the three Vedas?

III

The father said: Glory be to you, O my child; in the shape of imparting instructions, you have given a highly useful discourse on the wilderness of the world. In this you have described Raurava and all the other
hells. Do you describe them now at length, O you of great intelligence.

The son said: I have first described to you the hell called Raurava;
then hear of the hell, O father, known as Maharaurava. It extends, on
all sides, over twelve thousand yoyanas. There the ground is coppery
and underneath is the flaming fire. Heated by that fire, all the ground,
having the resplendence of the rising moon, appears dreadful to look
at or feel. There the sinner, bound hand and foot, is left by the envoy of
Yama and he rolls in it. Being eaten by crows, herons, owls, scorpions,
gnats and vultures he is pulled by them on the way. Being bewildered
and greatly agitated he continually cries out, "O father, O mother,
O brother, O child" and does not obtain any respite.

It is after ayuta and ayuta of years that the wicked sinners find release from those sufferings. There is another hell called Tama, bitterly cold by nature; it is as spacious as Maharaurava and enshrouded by darkness. Stricken with cold, people run about in that dreadful darkness and remain clasping each other. Stricken with cold and trembling, their teeth break up and they suffer from hunger, thirst and other afflictions. A dreadful wind, blowing over the cold tract, cuts asunder their bones; and they, assailed by hunger, feed on the fat and blood coming out therefrom. And they, collected together, while licking it, are whirled away. In this way, O best of Brahmanas, do the people suffer greatly, so long as their sins are not washed away.

There is another principal hell called Nikrintana; in it, O father, potters' wheels are continually rolling. Getting upon them, people are cut off from the soles of their feet to their heads by the dreadful threads held by the fingers of Yama's envoy. These do not, however, perish, O foremost of the twice-born, and the portions of their bodies, sundered into hundreds, are again combined. Thus the sinners are sundered for a thousand years, so long as their sin is not completely washed off.

Hear, I shall now describe the hell, Apratishtha; living in it, people suffer afflictions hard to bear. There are wheels at places—and the clocks at others—the instruments of afflictions to persons of impious deeds. Some men, fast fixed on the wheels, are whirled on and they cannot come out even for a thousand years. Firmly fixed on the machinery of the clock even as a clock is fixed in water, people are whirled on, continually vomiting blood. Vomiting forth blood through their mouths and having eyes overflowing with tears, these creatures suffer intolerable afflictions.

Hear again, I shall describe another hell, the forest of sword blades, which is all fire, covering the earth for a thousand yoyanas. Scorched by the terrible and fierce rays of the sun, creatures dwelling in hell always drop there. In it there is a beautiful forest covered with cool foliage. The leaves and fruits thereof, O foremost of the twice-born, consist of sword blades. There bark a million of powerful dogs, with large mouths, huge teeth and dreadful like tigers to look at. Beholding before them the forest covered with dews and shades, creatures afflicted with thirst rush towards it. Having their feet burnt by the fire raging underneath, they, greatly afflicted, cry out, "O father, O mother!"

As soon as they reach there, the wind blows, shaking the sword leaves, and the swords fall on them. They then drop down on earth—here a collection of fire and there all ablaze with flames spreading all over the surface. The dreadful dogs then quickly tear into pieces their bodies and numberless limbs as they cry in agony. I have described to you, O father, the forest of sword blades.

Hear now from me of the far more dreadful Taptakumbha. It has all around it heated pans, encircled by flames of fire, filled with iron dust and boiling oil resembling flames. In these vessels are thrown by the envoys of Yama perpetrators of wicked deeds with their faces bent towards the ground; they are fried there with their bodies bursting and rendered foul with fatty excretions. With their heads, eyes and bones coming out, they are forcibly taken up by ferocious vultures and are again thrown into them. Then accompanied by hissing sounds and converted into liquid, their heads, bodies, tendons, flesh, skin and bones are mixed up with oil. Then the perpetrators of iniquities are pounded in these volumes of eddying oil with a ladle by the emissaries of Yama. Thus I have described to you at length, O father, the hell Taptakumbha.

IV

The son said: In the seventh birth preceding this, I was born in the Vaisya race. Formerly I obstructed the approach of kine to a reservoir. From that adverse action, I was thrown into a dreadful hell, terrific with flames and abounding in iron-beaked birds; covered with mire of the streams of blood coming out from bodies crushed by instruments of torture and filled with the cries of sinners dropping down sundered. Thrown there and oppressed by powerful heat and thirst and burning, I remained a hundred years and more.

It so happened that one day came to me a fresh cool breeze delighting my heart, flowing from an earthen vessel filled with meals mixed with curds. By its touch the numberless afflictions of the people were brought to a close and I too attained that excellent joy which is enjoyed by the inhabitants of the celestial region. Thinking, "What is this?" with eyes expanded and shaking with joy we saw near us a most excellent man, the jewel of the race. A dreadful emissary of Yama, resplendent like lightning, with a rod in his hand, waited before him showing him the way and saying, "Come this way." Beholding the hell abounding in a hundred miseries, he, filled with compassion, said to the follower of Yama:

"I shall go, O emissary of the deity Yama, wherever you will take me; I shall ask you something and you should speak to me the truth. These crows, having beaks like adamant, are plucking out the eyes of men; but they are regaining their eyes again and again. Tell me what an iniquity they had perpetrated? These crows are also taking out their tongues growing anew again and again. Why are these unfortunate men being severed by saws? And why, thrown in oil, are they being boiled in earthen vessels filled with meal mixed with curd? Tell me why are these afflicted having the joints of their bodies loosened and being dragged by iron-beaked birds? And why are they uttering shrieks of pain? Having their bodies cut all over with the iron, and afflicted, these men are suffering day and night; what iniquity had they perpetrated? Describe to me at length by what adverse actions these sinful men are undergoing miseries which I see?"

The emissary of Yama said: "The adamant-beaked birds pluck out the eyes of those wretched men who look at others' wives with evil eyes as well as those of covetous people who desire others' property with impious thoughts; and their eyes grow again and again. They will suffer from their eyes as many thousand years as these men had winks when they perpetrated the crime. For so many years the dreadful adamant-beaked birds will pluck out the tongues growing anew again and again of those persons who, for destroying completely the spiritual sight of the enemies, instructed people in bad scriptures, gave dishonest counsels, explained the scriptures falsely, uttered untruths, reviled the Vedas, the deities, the twice-born ones and the preceptors.

"Behold, O king, those wretched men severed by saws, who brought about dissension amongst friends, separation of a father from his son, that amongst relatives, that between a priest and a sacrificer, that of a mother from her son, that of companions from each other, or that between a husband and a wife.

"Those who afflict others, those who obstruct the enjoyment of others, those who deprive people of palmyra fans, air-passages, sandal, Ucira (a fragrant grass), and those wretched people who bring sufferings destroying even life, on innocent persons, reap their sins by being placed on sand vessels full of meals mixed with curds.

"Those persons who, being invited by others, feed on the Sraddha performed by another, either for the ancestral manes or deities, are dragged by these birds in two opposite directions.

"Those who pierce the vitals of the pious with their own hands, have their own in return pierced, without any obstruction, by these birds.

"He who by his perverted mind and word commits an iniquity, has his tongue severed in twain by sharpened razors.

"Those that through haughtiness of heart disregard their fathers, or mothers, or preceptors, are plunged, with their faces bent downwards, into pits filled with pus, urine and excretion.

"Those wicked people that take their food before the deities, guests, servants, newcomers, ancestral manes, the fires and birds are fed, are born as Suchimukhas (birds) huge as hills and take delight in eating pus and dung. Those who, while observing a vow, feed with partiality the Brahmanas and persons born of any other order, feed on dung like these. Those who take their food without treating the poor and beggars and those who drive the same interest, feed, like these, on phlegm. O lord of men, those who, while unclean from eating, touch kine, Brahmanas or fire, have their hands burnt in this flaming pit. Those who, while unclean from eating, willingly see the sun, moon or stars, have their eyes cast into fire by the envoys of Yama and are purified there.

"Those men that have with their feet touched kine, fire, their mothers, inspired sages, their elder brothers, fathers, sisters, good wives, preceptors or elderly men, have their limbs bound by chains of heated fire; and being placed in heaps of burning coal, burn up to their knees.

"He that, having given away his daughter to one, again gives her to a second man, being sundered in pieces, is thrown into a river of alkali.

"Those that, possessed by anger, forsake helpless sons, servants, wives or friends on the occasion of a famine or any calamity, being thus sundered by Yama's retainers, feed on their own flesh in hunger and again gorge it out.

"He who forsakes, out of cupidity, dependants living upon service, is assailed with engines by the servants of Yama.

"Those persons who sell their religious merit acquired all through their lives are pressed with stones like those perpetrators of iniquities.

"Those who misappropriate deposit money, bound all over, are constrained to feed day and night on worms, scorpions, crows and owls.

"Those sinful persons who visit women by day or who live with others' wives are subject to afflictions and have their tongues and palates dried up with hunger and thirst. See, they have been fixed on Shalmali trees with long iron pins and their bodies have been severed and are bathed in streams of blood. And see, O foremost of men, those who ravished others' wives, killed by Yama's servants, being thrown in crucibles.

"The man who, putting his preceptor to shame or striking him dumb, receives lessons or learns any mechanical art from him, suffers misery by carrying stones on his head and is greatly assailed in the way of men; he suffers day and night from hunger and fatigue and his head aches for carrying the load.

"Those that discharge urine, phlegm, stool, etc., in water, are doomed to this hell filled with the bad smell of phlegm, excreta and urine.

"Those who never treated before each other with hospitality are now possessed by hunger, eating each other's flesh.

"Those that vilified the Vedas and those that, lighting sacrificial fire, disregarded it, are repeatedly being thrown down from mountain peaks.

"Those who passed their days as the husbands of widows, being emaciated, are reduced to those worms that are being eaten up by ants.

"Those who accept gifts from an outcast, who officiate as his priests and those who serve him, become worms living inside the rocks.

"Those who take sweets in the presence of their servants, friends, and guests, have got to swallow burning coal down their throats.

"O king, those who feed on the flesh of another's back, have their own daily eaten by dreadful wolves.

"The cursed men who turn ungrateful to persons who do them good, roam about, being stricken with hunger, or being blind, deaf and dumb. This highly vicious-minded, ungrateful wretch, injuring his friends, is thrown into a heated vessel and pounded there. He is then tortured by the engines in the sand vessels containing milk with curd and is then severed with saws in the forest of sword blades. He will be then hewn by the thread of time; thus undergoing various afflictions, I do not know how he will be freed therefrom.

"Those wicked Brahmanas, leaping over one another, ate the food of a sacrificial offering. They now drink the foam coming out from all their limbs.

"That stealer of gold, that killer of a Brahmana, that consumer of strong drinks, and that ravisher of his preceptor's wife, are being burnt for many thousand years by a fire flaming above and below: these are again born as men marked with leprosy, consumption and other diseases. When dead they go to hell and are again born in the same manner. O king, they will suffer from diseases till the end of the Kalpa.

"One who kills a cow goes to hell for three successive births—this is also the fate of the perpetrators of minor crimes."

V

The son said: Then flowers were showered upon the king; and placing him upon his car Hari took him to his own region. Myself and others there being freed from sufferings came by other births appointed by our own actions. I have thus described to you, O foremost of the twice-born, all the hells; and I have described to you all as seen before by me, all the births taken in pursuance of their respective sins; I have given you a truthful account based on my previous experience.

The Development of Creatures

From the mouth of Brahma, meditating on truth and entering upon the functions of creation, were produced a thousand pairs. They, thus born, were all moved by the quality of Satwa, and were joined to the right understanding. Another thousand pairs he created from his breast. They all were moved by the quality of Rajas, and were full of strength and invincible. Another thousand pairs he created again from his thigh. They were moved by the two qualities of Rajas and Tamas, and were full of energy and enterprise. From his two feet he created another thousand pairs. They were all moved by the quality of Tamas, and were without beauty, and of little understanding. Then these beings, thus produced in pairs, were moved by delight, and being desirous of one another, commenced to come together. Since then, in this Kalpa, creatures are born in pairs.

In those days the females did not keep time every month, therefore, though the pairs came together, they never procreated. Only once, at the close of their life, they would give birth to pairs. Since then, in this Kalpa, creatures are born in pairs.

This then is the mental creation of the lord of creatures, as it took place in the beginning; subsequent to that were produced those creatures by whom this world is filled. The creatures could then use and enjoy the rivers, the oceans, the lakes and the mountains at their pleasure, and in that cycle both heat and cold were moderate, therefore the creatures could move about everywhere. O thou of high aspirations! having found natural gratification in the objects, they had no obstacles in their way, and no envy, and no anger.

They were entirely without any habitation, they used to live in mountains or in the oceans, they moved about without any desire, and their minds were constantly full of delight.

Picacas, serpents, Raksasas, as well as envious beings, beasts, birds, alligators, fishes, reptiles all, whether born of mothers or from eggs, were produced by unrighteousness.

In those days there were neither roots nor fruits nor flowers of herbs and trees, nor were there the seasons nor the years. All times were pleasant, and there was neither excessive heat nor excessive cold; in due time their wishes would attain wonderful fulfilment. Then again whether in the forenoon, or at noon, whenever they felt any want, it would be satisfied without any effort, even as they asked. And similarly, whenever they wished, they could put forth their intellectual efforts. Then again, owing to the subtle powers of the waters in those days, the attainment of their various wishes full of delight would be secured, such as would fulfil all their desires. Those creatures had no need of sacraments for the purification of their bodies, and their youth was permanent.

Without any determination they would beget creatures in pairs, who were like them in the process of their birth, in their form and beauty, and they would also die like them. They were without any conflicts of desires, and without envy or ill-will, and in this way they would live with one another; the term of their life was the same, and they were all without any distinction of superior or inferior among them. They would live for four thousand years, measured by human measurement, and were without any misery, and did not come by any harmful accident.

Now and then they would come into being a second time, always owing to the good fortune of this earth, just as in course of time human beings are reborn.

Similarly they, whose objects were attained always, would gradually die; and on all of them being destroyed, men would drop down from the sky. Generally they would appear with the heavenly tree that satisfied all wishes, called the household Kalpa-tree, and from it they would gain the satisfaction of all their desires. In those days, at the commencement of the Treta-Yuga, they lived holding on to these heavenly trees.

Afterwards, in course of time, of a sudden, attachment grew upon them. This caused the repetition of the monthly courses, which led to repeated child-bearing. Then owing to the birth of attachment in them, those trees, called the household trees, next began to throw out other branches, and also produce garments and ornaments and fruits;—in those fruits of those trees was produced honey in quantities measured by putahas (a sort of cup) and which was full of sweet smell and flavour and of beautiful colour, which was highly strengthening and which was not produced by bees. At the commencement of the Treta-Yuga, they lived on this honey.

Then, in course of time, they were overtaken by greed. And on their heart being overcome by the sense of ownership of these trees, they took possession of them, and on account of the wrong thus committed by them, those trees were destroyed. Then came conflicts between cold and heat, etc., and to overcome those conflicts they, for the first time, built houses. In deserts, passes, mountains, and caves, they took shelter, also in fortresses built in trees, mountains, and on water. Similarly, they made artificial fortresses.

Having thus made towns, etc., for their own residence, they made houses for the habitation of the pairs. Those creatures, remembering the house-like trees that they inhabited of old, made all their present habitations after the same model. Just as the tree sends forth its branches, the new house also similarly sent out its branches, one standing below the other, and they similarly made coverings for the house like the barks of trees.

Having thus adopted means to overcome the conflicts between heat and cold, they began to meditate upon the means of protecting their cattle and crops, because of the entire destruction of the Kalpa-trees with all the honey they produced.

The creatures became downcast and distracted through being pressed by hunger and thirst. Then at the commencement of the Treta-Yuga in those days, they attained to miraculous powers in agriculture. The cattle and the crops were obtained by them, and for them the rains came down at their will; and on earth those rain-waters began to flow downwards. With the obstruction of this down-flowing rain-water, rivers and canals were made. The rain-water that had previously found the level of the earth, afterwards coming in contact with the earth, became faultless.

Then fourteen kinds of trees and herbs that had not been cultivated by the plough, that had not been sown, and that put forth flowers and fruits at all seasons, were created. At the commencement of the Treta-Yuga, season-flowers and herbs also came into existence, and on those herbs did the creatures live in the Treta-Yuga.

All of a sudden the creatures, being moved by attachment and greed in those days, began to appropriate to themselves rivers and fields, and mountains, and trees and herbs, according to each person's might. On account of that wrong the vegetables were destroyed. At that time those herbs were, all of a sudden, eaten up by the earth. At the destruction of those herbs and vegetables those bewildered beings, driven by hunger, sought the protection of Brahma, of most superior will. By virtue of his spiritual insight he too, having then known of the eating up of the herbs by the earth, the lord, the possessor of all the powers and riches, milched the earth, having made a calf of the northern pole. By him was this cow thus milched of seed-grains; those seeds, being of two kinds, those that grew near human habitations (cultured) and those that grew in the jungles (wild), were created on the surface of the earth.

When, though thus fully brought forth, the herbs did not again germinate, then he, the Brahma, created means for their growth and subsistence. The self-created lord Brahma created the skill of hand born of work. Since then the herbs began to grow, and became difficult of decomposition. In this way, after the establishment of the means of subsistence for them, the lord himself established honour and precedence among them according to their respective rights and qualifications.

Brahma's Petition to the Sun

When the sky and the earth were heated by the rays of the sun, the lotus-sprung grandfather, with a desire to create progeny, began to think: "As soon as I will create it, everything will be destroyed by the heat of the divine sun, the cause of the creation, preservation and destruction. All the creatures will be deprived of their lives, the water will be dried up by his heat, and without water it will be impossible to carry on the creation of the universe."

Thinking thus, the divine Brahma, the grandfather of the world, with his mind fixed on him, began to chant the glories of the divine sun.

Brahma said: "Salutation unto him who is identical with this whole universe, who is identical with all who have the universe for their form, who is the great light which is meditated on by the Yogins; who is identical with Ric, who is the root of Yajur, who is the origin of Sama, who is of inconceivable energy, who, for his grossness, is identical with three, whose great form is the half matra, and who is beyond all qualities; who is the cause of all, who is worthy of being eulogized greatly and being known, who is the great light Avanhi in the beginning, who is gross being identical with the gross—I bow unto that greatest of the great, the sun, the first of all.

"Urged on by this prime energy, I create water, earth, air, fire, gods, and various other endless objects beginning with Om; and in due order preserve and destroy them. I can never do so of my own accord. Thou art fire. By thy prowess I dry up the water and create the world and perform the first cooking process of the world. Thou art, O lord, manifest over the universe and identical with Akasa (space). Thou art protecting this universe in fivefold ways. By undertaking sacrifices, persons conversant with great soul worship thee; thou art Vivaswan— thou art Vishnu—thou art the lord of all, and the greatest of the great. Desirous of emancipation and controlling their mind and soul, even the ascetics meditate on thee.

"Salutation unto thee who art in the form of sacrifice, art the great Brahman and being, meditated upon by the Yogins. O lord, I am engaged in creation—this bundle of effulgence has stood in my way— do thou withdraw it."

Having been thus eulogized in a most excellent manner by Brahma, the creator of the universe, the divine sun withdrew his own great effulgence and held a little. Then the lotus-sprung great Brahma, O great Muni, created, as in the previous Kalpa, the similar gods, Asuras, men, beasts and others, trees, creepers and hells.

Sankaracharya's Atma Bodha
(KNOWLEDGE OF SPIRIT)

The spirit is smothered, as it were, by ignorance, but so soon as ignorance is destroyed, spirit shines forth, like the sun when released from clouds. After the soul, afflicted by ignorance, has been purified by knowledge, knowledge disappears, as the seed or berry of the Kataka after it has purified water.

Like an image in a dream the world is troubled by love, hatred, and other poisons. So long as the dream lasts, the image appears to be real; but on awaking it vanishes.

The world appears real, as an oyster-shell appears to be silver; but only so long as the Brahman remains unknown, he who is above all, and indivisible. That Being, true, intelligent, comprehends within itself every variety of being, penetrating and permeating all as a thread which strings together beads.

In consequence of possessing diverse attributes, the supreme existence appears manifold, but when the attributes are annihilated, unity is restored. In consequence of those diverse attributes, a variety of names and conditions are supposed proper to the spirit, just as a variety of tastes and colours are attributed to water.

The body, formed by the union of five elements produced by the effect of action, is considered to be the seat of perceptions of pleasure and pain. The subtile body, which is not formed by the five (gross) elements, but by the union of the five breaths (of life) with manas, intelligence, and the ten organs, is the instrument of sensuous perception.

All that belongs to the body (must be considered) as the product of ignorance. It is visible; it is perishable as bubbles of air (on the surface of water) ; but that which has not these signs must be recognized as pure spirit which says of itself, "I am Brahman. Because I am distinct from body, I experience neither birth, old age, decrepitude, nor extinction, and detached from organs of sense, I have no longer any connexion with their objects, such as sound."

This conception, "I am Brahman itself," incessantly entertained, disperses the hallucinations born of ignorance, as medicine disperses sickness.

Seated in a desert place, exempt from passion, master of his senses, let man represent to himself this spirit, one and infinite, without allowing his thoughts to stray elsewhere.

Considering the visible universe as annihilated in spirit, let a man, pure through intelligence, constantly contemplate the One Spirit, as he might contemplate luminous ether.

The Yogin, possessing perfect discernment, contemplates all things as subsisting in himself, and thus, by the eye of knowledge, discovers that all is the One Spirit. He knows that all this movable world is spirit or that beyond spirit there is nothing; as all varieties of vase are clay, so all things he sees are spirit.

The Hathayoga Pradipika of Swatmaram Swami

Exercises of a Yogin

To those who wander in the darkness of the conflicting sects unable to obtain Raja Yoga, the most merciful Swatmarama Yogi offers the light of Hatha knowledge.

The Yogi desirous of obtaining higher powers should keep the Hathayoga very secret. For it is effectual only when it is kept secret, and becomes vain when injudiciously revealed.

The practicer of Hathayoga should live alone in a small hermitage or monastery situated in a place free from rocks, water and fire; of the extent of a bow's length and in a fertile country ruled over by a virtuous king where he will not be disturbed.

The hermitage should have a very small door, and should be without any windows; it should be level and without any holes; it should be neither too high nor too long. It should be very clean, being daily smeared over with cow dung, and should be free from all insects. Outside it should have a small corridor with a raised seat and a well, and the whole should be surrounded by a wall. These are the characteristics of a Yoga hermitage as laid down by those who have attained higher powers, who have practised Hathayoga.

Living in such a place, the Yogin should free his mind from all cares and practise the Yoga as taught by his spiritual leader.

The Yogi succeeds by cheerfulness, perseverance, courage, true knowledge, firm belief in the words of the Guru, and by abandoning company.

To do no harm to any object, to speak the truth, to refrain from taking what belongs to another, to preserve continence, to practise forbearance and fortitude, to be merciful to all, to walk straightforwardly, to be moderate in diet, and to purify oneself, constitute control.

Postures are treated of in the first place as they form the first stage of Hathayoga. So one should practise postures that make him firm, free from diseases, and light of limb.

I proceed to give out some of the postures that are accepted by sages.

Having firmly inserted both insteps between the thighs and the calves of the legs, he should sit straight on a level place. This is Svastika position.

Place the right sole under the left posterior and the left sole under the right posterior. This position resembles the face of a cow.

Place one foot on the other thigh and the other foot under the other thigh.

Place the right foot at the foot of the left thigh and the left foot outside the right knee. Take hold of the right foot by the left hand and the left foot by the right hand and turn your head towards the left completely.

This posture increases appetite by fanning the gastric fire and destroys terrible diseases in the body: when practised it rouses the serpent power and makes the moon steady.

Plant your hands firmly on the ground and support your body upon your elbows pressing against the side of your loins. Raise your feet in the air stiff and straight on a level with the head.

Lying upon one's back on the ground at full length like a corpse is another position. This removes the fatigue caused by the other postures, and induces calmness of mind.

Place the right heel at the root of the left thigh and the left heel at the root of the right, cross the hands behind the back and take hold of the toes, the right toe with the right hand and the left toe with the left. Place the chin firmly on the breast and look fixedly at the tip of the nose. This is called the Lotus-seat, and destroys all diseases.

Moderate diet is defined to mean taking pleasant and sweet food, leaving one-fourth of the stomach free, and offering up the act to Siva.

The following things are considered as unsalutary to the Yogis: things that are sharp, sour, pungent and hot, myrobalans, betel-nut and leaves, the ordinary conjee oil, sesamum, mustard, liquors, fish, flesh of animals like the goat, curds, buttermilk, gram, fruit of the jujube, oil-cakes, asafœtida and garlic.

Diet of the following nature should be avoided as being unhealthy: food that having been once cooked has grown cold and is heated again; that has an excess of salt and sourness; that is indigestible, and that has the leaves of the woody quassia mixed with it.

Goraksha says he should avoid in the beginning bad company, basking near the fire during winter, sexual relations and long journeys, bathing early in the morning, fasting, and hard physical work.

Any person if he actively practises Yoga, achieves higher powers, be he young, old or even very old, sickly or weak.

One who practises will obtain higher powers, but not one who is idle. Yoga powers are not obtained by a mere theoretical reading of the scriptures.

Higher powers are not obtained by wearing the dress of a Yogi, or by talking about them, but untiring practice is the secret of success. There is no doubt about this.

All the processes with regard to the breath should be gone through with a mind concentrated on the subject. The wise man should not allow his mind to wander away during that time.

After making the mind supportless (by removing it from every object of conception) he should not think of anything. He certainly then remains like a pot filled inside and outside with world-space.

One should saturate the body from the head to the foot with the stream of nectar. He then becomes endowed with an excellent body, great strength and valour.

Place your spirit in the midst of the world-space and the world-space in the midst of your spirit; and on reducing everything to the form of world-space one must not think of anything else.

The Yogi in highest meditation is void within and without like a pot in the world-space. He is also, like a pot in the ocean, full within and without.

He should think of nothing in the outside nature; so also he should give up personal thoughts. He should abandon all thoughts subjective and objective.

The external universe is created by our thoughts, as also the imaginary world. Having abandoned the idea of permanency in these creations of thought, and concentrating your mind upon that which is not subject to any change, obtain everlasting and certain peace.

The mind, when concentrated on one's spirit, becomes one with it, like camphor with the flame, and like salt with the water of the ocean.

Everything that is seen and experienced is called the known, and the faculty of knowing is called the mind. When the known and the knowledge are lost there is no duality.

When the mind becomes one with the object concentrated upon, this process is called Raja Yoga. The Yogi, being the master of creation and destruction, becomes the equal of the highest lord.

There are many who are merely Hatha Yogis without the knowledge of Raja Yoga. I think them to be simply practicers who do not get the fruit of their pains.

All the Hathayoga practices are only for the attainment of Raja Yoga. The man perfect in Raja Yoga deceives death.

A Yogi in highest meditation feels neither smell, taste, touch, sound, shape, nor colour; he does not know himself and others.

A Yogi in Samadhi does not feel heat or cold, pain or pleasure, honour or disgrace.

A Yogi in Samadhi is invulnerable to all weapons; all the world cannot overpower him; and he is beyond the powers of incantations and magical diagrams.

The Yoga Sutras of Patanjali

I

AUM. The following instruction concerneth the science of union. This union (or Yoga) is achieved through the subjugation of the psychic nature, and the restraint of the chitta (or mind). When this has been accomplished, the Yogi knows himself as he is in reality.

The mind states are five, and are subject to pleasure or pain; they are painful or not painful. These modifications (activities) are correct knowledge, incorrect knowledge, fancy, passivity (sleep) and memory. The basis of correct knowledge is correct perception, correct deduction, and correct witness (or accurate evidence).

The control of these modifications of the internal organ, the mind, is to be brought about through tireless endeavour and through non-attachment.

When the object to be gained is sufficiently valued, and the efforts towards its attainment are persistently followed without intermission, then the steadiness of the mind (restraint of the vrittis) is secured.

Non-attachment is freedom from longing for all objects of desire, either earthly or traditional, either here or hereafter. The consummation of this non-attachment results in an exact knowledge of the spiritual man when liberated from the qualities or gunas.

The consciousness of an object is attained by concentration upon its fourfold nature: the form, through examination; the quality (or guna), through discriminative participation; the purpose, through inspiration (or bliss); and the soul, through identification.

A further stage of Samadhi is achieved when, through one pointed thought, the outer activity is quieted. In this stage, the chitta is responsive only to subjective impressions.

Other Yogins achieve Samadhi and arrive at a discrimination of pure spirit through belief, followed by energy, memory, meditation and right perception.

The attainment of this state (spiritual consciousness) is rapid for those whose will is intensely alive.

By intense devotion to Isvara, knowledge of Isvara is gained. This Isvara is the soul, untouched by limitation, free from karma, and desire.

The word of Isvara is AUM (or OM). This is the Pranava. Through the sounding of the word and through reflection upon its meaning, the way is found. From this comes the realization of the Self (the soul) and the removal of all obstacles.

The obstacles to soul cognition are bodily disability, mental inertia, wrong questioning, carelessness, laziness, lack of dispassion, erroneous perception, inability to achieve concentration, failure to hold the meditative attitude when achieved. Pain, despair, misplaced bodily activity and wrong direction (or control) of the life currents are the results of the obstacles in the lower psychic nature. To overcome the obstacles and their accompaniments, the intense application of the will to some one truth (or principle) is required.

The peace of the chitta (or mind stuff) can be brought about through the practice of sympathy, tenderness, steadiness of purpose, and dispassion in regard to pleasure or pain, or towards all forms of good or evil. The peace of the chitta is also brought about by the regulation of the prana or life breath.

By meditation upon light and upon radiance, knowledge of the spirit can be reached and thus peace can be achieved.

Peace (steadiness of the chitta) can be reached through meditation on the knowledge which dreams give.

Peace can also be reached through concentration upon that which is dearest to the heart.

To him whose vrittis (modifications of the substance of the mind) are entirely controlled, there eventuates a state of identity with and similarity to that which is realized. The knower, knowledge and the field of knowledge become one, just as the crystal takes to itself the colours of that which is reflected in it.

When this super-contemplative state is reached, the Yogi acquires pure spiritual realization through the balanced quiet of the chitta (or mind stuff). His perception is now unfailingly exact (or his mind reveals only the truth).

II

The Yoga of action, leading to union with the soul, is fiery aspiration, spiritual reading and devotion to Isvara. The aim of these three is to bring about soul vision and to eliminate obstructions.

These are the difficulty-producing hindrances: avidya (ignorance), the sense of personality, desire, hate and the sense of attachment. These five hindrances, when subtly known, can be overcome by an opposing mental attitude. Karma itself has its root in these five hindrances and must come to fruition in this life or in some later life.

To the illuminated man all existence (in the three worlds) is considered pain owing to the activities of the gunas. These activities are threefold, producing consequences, anxieties and subliminal impressions. Pain which is yet to come may be warded off. The illusion that the perceiver and that which is perceived are one and the same is the cause (of the pain-producing effects) which must be warded off.

All that is exists for the sake of the soul.

In the case of the man who has achieved Yoga (or union) the objective universe has ceased to be. Yet it existeth still for those who are not yet free.

The association of the soul with the mind and thus with that which the mind perceives produces an understanding of the nature of that which is perceived and likewise of the perceiver. The cause of this association is ignorance or avidya. This has to be overcome. When ignorance is brought to an end through non-association with the things perceived, this is the great liberation.

The eight means of Yoga are, the commandments or Yama, the rules or Niyama, posture or Asana, right control of life-force or Pranayama, abstraction or Pratyahara, attention or Dharana, meditation or Dhyana, contemplation or Samadhi. Harmlessness, truth to all beings, abstention from theft, from incontinence and from avarice, constitute Yama or the five commandments. Yama (or the five commandments) constitutes the universal duty and is irrespective of race, place, time or emergency.

When thoughts which are contrary to Yoga are present there should be the cultivation of their opposite. Thoughts contrary to Yoga are harmfulness, falsehood, theft, incontinence, and avarice, whether committed personally, caused to be committed or approved of, whether arising from avarice, anger or delusion (ignorance); whether slight in the doing, middling or great. These result always in excessive pain and ignorance. For this reason, the contrary thoughts must be cultivated.

In the presence of him who has perfected harmlessness, all enmity ceases. When truth to all beings is perfected, the effectiveness of his words and acts is immediately to be seen. When abstention from theft is perfected, the Yogi can have whatever he desires. By abstention from incontinence, energy is acquired. When abstention from avarice is perfected, there comes an understanding of the law of rebirth.

The posture assumed must be steady and easy. Steadiness and ease of posture is to be achieved through persistent slight effort and through the concentration of the mind upon the infinite. When this is attained, the pairs of opposites no longer limit. When right posture (asana) has been attained there follow right control of prana and proper inspiration and expiration of the breath.

Right control of prana (or the life currents) is external, internal or motionless; it is subject to place, time and number and is also protracted or brief.

There is a fourth stage which transcends those dealing with the internal and external phases. Through this, that which obscures the light is gradually removed. And the mind is prepared for concentrated meditation.

III

Concentration is the fixing of the chitta (mind stuff) upon a particular object. This is dharana. Sustained concentration (dharana) is meditation (dhyana). When the chitta becomes absorbed in that which is the reality (or idea embodied in the form), and is unaware of separateness or the personal self, this is contemplation or Samadhi. When concentration, meditation and contemplation form one sequential act, then is sanyama achieved. As a result of sanyama comes the shining forth of the light.

The sequence of mental states is as follows: the mind reacts to that which is seen; then follows the moment of mind control. Then ensues a moment wherein the chitta (mind stuff) responds to both these factors. Finally these pass away, and the perceiving consciousness has full sway. Through the cultivation of this habit of mind there will eventuate a steadiness of spiritual perception. The establishing of this habit, and the restraining of the mind from its thought-form-making tendency, result eventually in the constant power to contemplate.

Through concentrated meditation upon the triple nature of every form comes the revelation of that which has been and of that which will be. The sound (or word), that which it denotes (the object) and the embodied spiritual essence (or idea) are usually confused in the mind of the perceiver. By concentrated meditation on these three aspects comes an (intuitive) comprehension of the sound uttered by all forms of life.

Through concentrated meditation, the thought images in the minds of other people become apparent. As, however, the object of those thoughts is not apparent to the perceiver, he sees only the thought and not the object. His meditation excludes the tangible.

By concentrated meditation upon the distinction between form and body, those properties of the body which make it visible to the human eye are negated (or withdrawn) and the Yogi can render himself invisible.

Karma (or effects) are of two kinds: immediate karma or future karma. By perfectly concentrated meditation on these, the Yogi knows the term of his experience in the three worlds. This knowledge comes also from signs.

Union with others is to be gained through one-pointed meditation upon the three states of feeling—compassion, tenderness and dispassion.

Understanding of the mind-consciousness comes from one-pointed meditation upon the heart centre.

By liberation from the causes of bondage through their weakening and by an understanding of the mode of transference (withdrawal or entrance), the mind stuff (or chitta) can enter another body.

One-pointed meditation upon the five forms which every element takes produces mastery over every element. These five forms are the gross nature, the elemental form, the quality, the pervasiveness and the basic purpose. Through this mastery, minuteness and the other siddhis (or powers) are attained, likewise bodily perfection and freedom from all hindrances. Symmetry of form, beauty of colour, strength and the compactness of the diamond, constitute bodily perfection.

Mastery over the senses is brought about through concentrated meditation upon their nature, peculiar attributes, egoism, pervasiveness and useful purpose. As a result of this perfection, there come rapidity of action like that of mind, perception independent of the organs, and mastery over root substance.

There should be entire rejection of all allurements from all forms of being, even the celestial, for the recurrence of evil contacts remains possible.

When the objective forms and the soul have reached a condition of equal purity, then is at-one-ment achieved and liberation results.

The Sarva-Darsana-Samgraha
(THE PHILOSOPHICAL SYSTEMS)

Prologue

I worship Siva, the abode of eternal knowledge, the storehouse of supreme felicity; by whom the earth and the rest were produced, in him only has this all a maker.

Daily I follow my Guru Sarvajna-Vishnu, who knows all the Agamas, the son of Sarngapani, who has gone to the further shore of the seas of all the systems, and has contented the hearts of all mankind by the proper meaning of the term soul.

The synopsis of all the systems is made by the venerable Madhava, mighty in power, the Kaustubha-jewel of the milk-ocean of the fortunate Sayana.

Having thoroughly searched the Sastras of former teachers, very hard to be crossed, the fortunate Sayana-Madhava the lord has expounded them for the delight of the good. Let the virtuous listen with a mind from which all envy has been far banished; who finds not delight in a garland strung of various flowers?

The Lokayata System

We have said in our preliminary invocation "salutation to Siva, the abode of eternal knowledge, the storehouse of supreme felicity," but how can we attribute to the divine being the giving of supreme felicity, when such a notion has been utterly abolished by Charvaka, the crest-gem of the atheistical school, the follower of the doctrine of Brihaspati? The efforts of Charvaka are indeed hard to be eradicated, for the majority of living beings hold by the current refrain—

> While life is yours, live joyously;
> None can escape Death's searching eye:
> When once this frame of ours they burn,
> How shall it e'er again return?

The mass of men, in accordance with the Sastras of policy and enjoyment, considering wealth and desire the only ends of man, and denying the existence of any object belonging to a future world, are found to follow only the doctrine of Charvaka. Hence another name for that school is Lokayata,—a name well accordant with the thing signified.

In this school the four elements, earth, etc., are the original principles; from these alone, when transformed into the body, intelligence is produced, just as the inebriating power is developed from the mixing of certain ingredients; and when these are destroyed, intelligence at once perishes also.

The only end of man is enjoyment produced by sensual pleasures. Nor may you say that such cannot be called the end of man as they are always mixed with some kind of pain, because it is our wisdom to enjoy the pure pleasure as far as we can, and to avoid the pain which inevitably accompanies it; just as the man who desires fish takes the fish with their scales and bones, and having taken as many as he wants, desists; or just as the man who desires rice, takes the rice, straw and all, and having taken as much as he wants, desists. It is not therefore for us, through a fear of pain, to reject the pleasure which our nature instinctively recognizes as congenial. Men do not refrain from sowing rice because forsooth there are wild animals to devour it; nor do they refuse to set the cooking-pots on the fire because forsooth there are beggars to pester us for a share of the contents. If any one were so timid as to forsake a visible pleasure, he would indeed be foolish like a beast.

There is no heaven, no final liberation, nor any soul in another world,
Nor do the actions of the four castes, orders, etc., produce any real effect.
The Agnihotra, the three Vedas, the ascetic's three staves, and smearing
        one's self with ashes,
Were made by nature as the livelihood of those destitute of knowledge
        and manliness.
If a beast slain in the Jyotishtoma rite will itself go to heaven,
Why then does not the sacrificer forthwith offer his own father?

The Jaina System

The Gymnosophists (Jainas), maintaining continued existence to a certain extent, overthrow the doctrine of the momentariness of everything. (They say): If no continuing soul is accepted, then even the arrangement of the means for attaining worldly fruit in this life will be useless. But surely this can never be imagined as possible—that one should act and another reap the consequences! Therefore as this conviction, "I who previously did the deed am the person who now reap its consequences," establishes undoubtedly the existence of a continuing soul, which remains constant through the previous and the subsequent period, the discriminating Jaina Arhats reject as untenable the doctrine of momentary existence, i.e., an existence which lasts only an instant, and has no previous or subsequent part.

Asrava is described as the movement of the soul called yoga, through its participation in the movement of its various bodies, audarika, etc. As a door opening into the water is called asrava, because it causes the stream to descend through it, so this yoga is called asrava, because by it as by a pipe actions and their consequences flow in upon the soul. Or, as a wet garment collects the dust brought to it from every side by the wind, so the soul, wet with previous sins, collects, by its manifold points of contact with the body, the actions which are brought to it by yoga.

Asrava is twofold, as good or evil. Thus abstaining from doing injury is a good yoga of the body; speaking what is true, measured, and profitable is a good yoga of the speech.

The Saiva-Darsana

Certain of the Mahesvara sect hold the opinion that "the Supreme Being is a cause in dependence on our actions, etc."; and they maintain that there are three categories distinguished as the Lord, the soul, and the world (or literally "the master," "the cattle," and "the fetter"). As has been said by those well versed in the Tantra doctrines—

> "The Guru of the world, having first condensed in one sutra the great tantra, possessed of three categories and four feet, has again declared the same at full length."

The meaning of this is as follows: its three categories are the three before mentioned; its four feet are learning, ceremonial action, meditation, and morality, hence it is called the great tantra, possessed of three categories and four feet. Now the "souls" are not independent, and the "fetters" are unintelligent, hence the Lord, as being different from these, is first declared; next follows the account of the souls as they agree with him in possessing intelligence; lastly follow the "fetters" or matter, such is the order of the arrangement. Since the ceremony of initiation is the means to the highest human end, and this cannot be accomplished without knowledge which establishes the undoubted greatness of the hymns, the lords of the hymns, etc., and is a means for the ascertainment of the real nature of the "cattle," the "fetter," and the "master," we place as first the "foot" of knowledge (jnana), which makes known all this unto us. Next follows the "foot" of ceremonial action (kriya), which declares the various rules of initiation with the divers component parts thereof. Without meditation the end cannot be attained, hence the "foot" of meditation (yoga) follows next, which declares the various kinds of yoga with their several parts. And as meditation is worthless without practice, i.e., the fulfilling what is enjoined and the abstaining from what is forbidden, lastly follows the fourth "foot" of practical duty (charya), which includes all this.

Now Siva is held to be the lord (or master). Although participation in the divine nature of Siva belongs to liberated souls and to such beings as Vidyesvara, etc., yet these are not independent, since they depend on the Supreme Being; and the nature of an effect is recognized to belong to the worlds, etc., which resemble him, from the very fact of the orderly arrangement of their parts. And from their thus being effects we infer that they must have been caused by an intelligent being. By the strength of this inference is the universal acknowledgment of a Supreme Being confirmed.

From the Hitopadesa

The Sweet Way of Learning

Amongst all things, knowledge, they say, is truly the best thing; from its not being liable ever to be stolen, from its not being purchasable, and from its being imperishable.

What benefit accrues by a son being born, who is neither learned nor virtuous? Or what is the use of a sightless eye? It is merely trouble.

Of a son unborn, dead, or a fool,—better the two first than the last. The two first cause unhappiness once; but the last, perpetually.

Food, sleep, fear, propagation;—each is the common property of men with brutes. Virtue is really their additional distinction; devoid of virtue, they are equal with brutes.

Glass, from the nearness of gold, acquires an emerald lustre: so by the proximity of the excellent a fool attains to cleverness.

The mind is lowered, O son, through association with inferiors. With equals it attains equality; and with superiors, superiority.

No labour bestowed upon a worthless thing can be productive of fruit; even by a hundred efforts a crane cannot be made to talk like a parrot.

Thousands of occasions of sorrow, and hundreds of occasions of fear, day by day assail the fool, not the sage.

As one's life is dear to himself, so also are those of all beings. The good show compassion towards all living beings because of their resemblance to themselves.

He who looks on another's wife as a mother, on another's goods as a clod of earth, and on all creatures as himself, is a wise man.

Confidence should never be put in rivers, in armed men, in creatures with claws or horns, in women, and in kings' households.

From covetousness anger proceeds; from covetousness lust is born; from covetousness come delusion and perdition. Covetousness is the cause of sin.

Want of control over the senses is called the road to ruin; victory over them, the path to fortune. Go then by which you please.

Six faults ought to be avoided by a man seeking prosperity in this world: sleep, sloth, fear, anger, laziness, prolixity.

In this life there is none more happy than he who has a friend to converse with, a friend to live with, and a friend to chat with.

As long as danger is at a distance, it should be dreaded: but when a man perceives danger to be present, he should act in a becoming manner.

Fitting hospitality must be shown even towards an enemy arrived at the house. The tree does not withdraw from the wood-cutter the shade at its side.

Straw, room, water, and fourthly, pleasant speech: these things are never withheld in the house of the good.

If either a boy, or an old man, or a youth, come to a house, respect must be paid to him. The visitor is every one's superior.

The good show pity even to worthless beings. The moon withholds not its light from the hovel of the outcast.

Who would commit an enormous crime for the sake of this evil belly, which can be satisfied by vegetables growing wild in the wood?

"Is this one of our tribe or a stranger?" is the calculation of the narrow-minded; but to those of a noble disposition the earth itself is but one family.

In misfortunes a man may know a friend; in battle, a hero; in a loan, an honest man; in diminished fortunes, a wife; and in afflictions, kinsmen.

What cannot be done, cannot be done: what may be done, may be done. A cart goes not on the water, neither does a ship sail on dry land.

The evil man is like a pot of clay, easily breaking, but reunited with difficulty; whilst a good man is like a jar of gold, hard to break and quickly to be joined again.

Neither a bath in very cool waters, nor a necklace of pearls, nor sandal-ointment applied to every limb, so refreshes one oppressed with heat as good men's conversation, polished with good argument, and resembling a magic charm of attraction, generally avails to delight the mind of the righteous.

In the mind of the wicked there is one thing; in their discourse another; their conduct is another. In the heart, in the speech, and in the conduct of the magnanimous there is one and the same thing.

With one foot a wise man moves, with one stands still. Until he has examined another place, he should not leave his former abode.

One should not fix one's abode there where five things are not found: a moneyed man, a student of scripture, a king, a river, and, fifthly, a physician.

When without any apparent cause a young wife, pulling her old husband by the hair and hugging him unmercifully, kisses him, there will be a reason for it.

As the mind of those pinched with cold delights not in the moon, nor the mind of those oppressed with heat in the sun, so the heart of woman delights not in a husband stricken with old age.

If there is no place, if there is no opportunity, if there is no man to be their suitor, thus, O Narada, do women become chaste.

The high-spirited man may indeed die, but he will not stoop to meanness. Fire, though it may be quenched, will not become cool.

Whoever has a contented mind has all riches. To him whose foot is enclosed in a shoe is not the earth as it were carpeted with leather?

One should leave a single person for the sake of a family; for the sake of a village he should abandon a family; a village he should renounce for the sake of a country, and for the sake of his soul, the earth.

Men of scholarly mind hanker not after what is unattainable, nor are they inclined to grieve for what is lost, nor are they perplexed even in calamities.

One should attend to pleasure when it arrives, and likewise to pain when it arrives. Pains and pleasures have their revolutions like a wheel.

The shadow of a cloud, the affection of the deceitful, new corn, women, youth, and riches are to be enjoyed but a short time.

One should not strive overmuch for a subsistence, for it is provided by the creator. As soon as a living being has dropped from the womb, both teats of the mother stream.

Well-water, the shade of a banyan tree, a brunette, and a brick house will be warm in cold weather and cool in warm weather.

On the touchstone of misfortune a man discovers the strength of understanding and of spirit in kinsmen, wife, servants, and himself.

Kesava vouchsafed not a reply to the king of Chedi when he cursed him; for the lion echoes the sound of the thundercloud, not the yells of the jackal.

The tempest uproots not the soft grasses that bow low on all sides; on the lofty trees it strikes hard. It is against the mighty that the mighty puts forth his prowess.

An embankment is broken by waters; and so is secret counsel that is not kept. Friendship is broken by tale-bearing; and a coward may be broken down by words.

Every one who is affluent will always be unmanageable in the long run. It is a maxim of the seers that prosperity perverts the mind.

Ingenious men can make even falsehoods look like truths, as skilled painters can make hollows and eminences appear on an even surface.

Fire is never satisfied with fuel, nor the ocean with rivers, nor death with all creatures, nor bright-eyed women with men.

Through fear, humility is assumed in the hope of life; but if I must perish, why need I cringe to the lion?

To pull out by the roots poisoned food, a loose tooth, and a wicked minister, gives ease.

There is no man in the world who is not enamoured of fortune, who looks not with desire on the young and charming wife of his neighbour.

He who is beloved, is still beloved, though he acts falsely. To whom is not the body dear, although it be corrupted by all kinds of faults?

At any other time, patience is the ornament of a man, as modesty is of a woman; but valour at an insult befits a man, as boldness in embraces a woman.

A store of grain, O king, is better than every other store; for a gem cast into the mouth cannot sustain life.

The natural disposition of any one, whatever it may be, cannot be suppressed by him. If a dog were made king, would he not gnaw his shoe?

What is not to be, will not be; if it is to be, it cannot be otherwise; why do you not drink this antidote that destroys the poison of care?

Of all gifts the greatest, as they say here, is neither the gift of land, nor the gift of gold, nor the gift of cattle, nor the gift of food, but the gift of security.

As one plank of timber and another may meet in the mighty ocean, and, having met, may again separate, even such is the meeting of living beings.

They whose eating is but for the sustaining of life, whose cohabitation is but for the sake of offspring, and whose speech is only to declare truth, make their way even through hard paths.

Happiness hath he who renounces this cycle of being, which is utterly unsubstantial and overwhelmed by the pains of birth, death, old age and disease.

The Lion, the Mouse, and the Cat

"A master ought never to be made free from cares by his servants. By making his lord free from cares, a servant would be like Dadhikarna.

"In the North, upon a mountain called Arbudasikhara, there was a lion, named Maha-vikrama (Great of valour). As he lay asleep in the mountain-cave, a certain mouse was wont to nibble the tip of his mane. The lion, noticing that the tip of his mane was gnawed, became angry; but not being able to catch the mouse, who slipped into his hole, he said to himself: 'What is to be done here?—Well, it is commonly said:

" 'If one has an insignificant foe who is not to be overcome by valour, a combatant who is a match for him must be employed to catch him.'

"Meditating thus, he went to a village, and having won the heart of a cat named Dadhi-karna with flesh and other kinds of food, he brought him thence with some trouble and kept him in his cave. After that, the mouse through fear of him never ventured out; the lion therefore slept comfortably with his mane unnipped. As often as he heard the noise of the mouse, he would then notably regale the cat with a present of animal food. But one day, as the famishing mouse was sneaking out, he was caught, killed, and devoured by the cat. After that the lion never heard the noise of the mouse; and then, as there was no use for his help, he became neglectful in feeding the cat. Therefore I say, 'A master ought never to be made free from cares,' and so forth."

The Lion and the Rabbit

"He who hath sense, hath strength; but whence hath a fool strength? See, a lion, intoxicated with pride, was defeated by a rabbit.

"Upon a mountain called Mandara there was a lion, by name Durdanta (Hard-to-tame). He was ever making a slaughter of the beasts. At length all the beasts meeting in assembly thus petitioned the lion: 'Your Majesty, wherefore are all the beasts being slaughtered? We will ourselves, as a free gift, daily furnish a single beast for your meal.' 'If that is agreeable to you,' said the lion, 'then be it so.' Thenceforward he used daily to feed upon the single beast supplied. Now on a certain day the turn fell on an old rabbit. So he thought to himself:

" 'Through fear, humility is assumed in the hope of life; but if I must perish, why need I cringe to the lion?

Then I will approach him very leisurely.'

"Now the lion, being tormented with hunger, cried to him in a rage: 'Why have you delayed in coming?' The rabbit replied: 'I am not in fault. On the road I was forcibly detained by another lion; I have taken an oath before him to return, and I am come here to inform my lord.' The lion angrily exclaimed: 'Go quickly and show me where that wretch is!' Then the rabbit took him, and came near a deep well. Saying, 'Let my lord come here and see,' he showed him his own image reflected in the water of the well. Thereupon, being inflated with pride, he flung himself upon it, and perished. Therefore I say, 'He who hath sense,' and so forth."

The Works of Sri Ramakrishna

The Sayings of Sri Ramakrishna

You see many stars at night in the sky but find them not when the sun rises; can you say that there are no stars in the heaven of day? So, O man! because you behold not God in the days of your ignorance, say not that there is no god.

As one and the same material, water, is called by different names by different peoples, one calling it water, another eau, a third aqua, and another pani, so the one Sat-chit-ananda, the everlasting-intelligent-bliss, is invoked by some as God, by some as Allah, by some as Jehovah, by some as Hari, and by others as Brahman.

As one can ascend to the top of a house by means of a ladder or a bamboo or a staircase or a rope, so divers are the ways and means to approach God, and every religion in the world shows one of these ways.

Different creeds are but different paths to reach the Almighty. Various and different are the ways that lead to the temple of Mother Kali at Kalighat (Calcutta). Similarly, various are the ways that lead to the house of the Lord. Every religion is nothing but one of such paths that lead to God.

As the young wife in a family shows her love and respect to her father-in-law, mother-in-law, and every other member of the family, and at the same time loves her husband more than these; similarly, being firm in thy devotion to the deity of thy own choice (Ishta-Devata), do not despise other deities, but honour them all.

Bow down and worship where others kneel, for where so many have been paying the tribute of adoration the kind Lord must manifest himself, for he is all mercy.

Two persons were hotly disputing as to the colour of a chameleon. One said, "The chameleon on that palm tree is of a beautiful red colour." The other, contradicting him, said, "You are mistaken, the chameleon is not red but blue." Not being able to settle the matter by arguments, both went to the person who always lived under that tree and had watched the chameleon in all its phases of colour. One of them said, "Sir, is not the chameleon on that tree of a red colour?" The person replied, "Yes, sir." The other disputant said, "What do you say? How is it? It is not red, it is blue." That person again humbly replied, "Yes, sir." The person knew that the chameleon is an animal that constantly changes colour; thus it was that he said "yes" to both of these conflicting statements.

The Sat-chit-ananda likewise has many forms. The devotee who has seen God in one aspect only, knows him in that aspect alone. But he who has seen him in manifold aspects is alone in a position to say, "All these forms are of one god and God is multiform." He is formless and with form, and many are his forms which no one knows.

He who tries to give an idea of God by mere book learning is like the man who tries to give an idea of Kasi (Benares) by means of a map or picture.

The Vedas, Tantras, and the Puranas and all the sacred scriptures of the world have become as if defiled (as food thrown out of the mouth becomes polluted), because they have been constantly repeated by and have come out of human mouths. But the Brahman or the Absolute has never been defiled, for no one as yet has been able to express it by human speech.

So long as one is not blessed with the divine vision, so long as the base metal is not turned into gold by touching the philosopher's stone, there will be the delusion of "I am the doer," and so long must there necessarily remain the idea of the distinction between "I have done this good work" and "I have done that bad work." This idea of duality or distinction is the Maya which is responsible for the continuance of the world current. By taking refuge in Vidyamaya (the Maya having preponderance of satva), which follows the adoption of the right path, one can reach him. He alone crosses the ocean of Maya who comes face to face with God, who realizes him. He is truly free, living even in this body, who knows that God is the doer and he is the non-doer.

The magnetic needle always points towards the north, and hence it is that the sailing vessel does not lose her course. So long as the heart of man is directed towards God, he cannot be lost in the ocean of wordliness.

Men weep rivers of tears because a son is not born to them, others wear away their hearts with sorrow because they cannot get riches. But how many are there who weep and sorrow because they have not seen God? He finds who seeks him; he who with intense longing weeps for God has found God.

Verily, verily, I say unto thee, he who longs for him, finds him. Go and verify this in thine own life; try for three consecutive days with genuine earnestness and thou art sure to succeed.

God cannot be seen so long as there is the slightest taint of desire; therefore have thy small desires satisfied, and renounce the big desires by right reasoning and discrimination.

It is the nature of the lamp to give light. With its help some may cook food, some may forge a deed, and the third may read the word of God. So with the help of the Lord's name some try to attain salvation, others try to serve their evil purposes and so on. His holy name, however, remains unaffected.

The truly wise man is he who has seen the Lord. He becomes like a child. The child, no doubt, seems to have an Ahamkara, an egoism, of its own; but that egoism is a mere appearance, it is not selfish egotism. The self of a child is nothing like the self of a grown-up man.

O heart! Call out truly to thy Almighty Mother, and thou shalt see how she will come quickly running to thee. When one calls out to God with all one's heart and soul, he can no longer remain unmoved.

Knowledge and love of God are ultimately one and the same. There is no difference between pure knowledge and pure love.

The master said, "Everything that exists is God." The pupil understood it literally, but not in the right spirit. While he was passing through the street he met an elephant. The driver shouted aloud from his high place, "Move away! Move away!" The pupil argued in his mind, "Why should I move away? I am God, so is the elephant God; what fear has God of himself?" Thinking thus, he did not move. At last the elephant took him up in his trunk and dashed him aside. He was hurt severely, and going back to his master, he related the whole adventure. The master said: "All right. You are God, the elephant is God also, but God in the shape of the elephant-driver was warning you from above. Why did you not pay heed to his warnings?"

The Avatara or Saviour is the messenger of God. He is like the viceroy of a mighty monarch. As when there is some disturbance in a far-off province, the king sends his viceroy to quell it, so whenever there is a decline of religion in any part of the world, God sends his Avatara there. It is one and the same Avatara that, having plunged into the ocean of life, rises up in one place and is known as Krishna, and diving down again rises in another place and is known as Christ.

The Avataras (like Rama, Krishna, Buddha, Christ) stand in relation to the Absolute Brahman as the waves of the ocean are to the ocean.

On the tree of absolute existence-knowledge-bliss (Sat-chit-ananda) there hang innumerable Ramas, Krishnas, Buddhas, Christs, etc., out of which one or two come down to this world now and then and produce mighty changes and revolutions.

There is a fabled species of birds called "Homa," which live so high up in the heavens, and so dearly love those regions, that they never condescend to come down to the earth. Even their eggs, which when laid in the sky begin to fall down to the earth attracted by gravity, are said to get hatched in the middle of their downward course and give birth to the young ones. The fledgelings at once find out that they are falling down and immediately change their course and begin to fly upwards towards their home, drawn thither by instinct. Men such as Suka Deva, Narada, Jesus, Sankaracharya, and others, are like those birds, who even in their boyhood give up all attachments to the things of this world and betake themselves to the highest regions of true knowledge and divine light.

As an aquatic bird, such as a pelican, dives into water, but the water does not wet its plumage, so the emancipated soul lives in the world, but the world does not affect him.

Ornaments cannot be made of pure gold. Some alloy must be mixed with it. A man totally devoid of Maya will not survive more than twenty-one days. So long as the man has a body, he must have some Maya, however small it may be, to carry on the functions of the body.

Hast thou got, O preacher, the badge of authority? As the humblest servant of the king authorized by him is heard with respect and awe, and can quell the riot by showing his badge; so must thou, O preacher, obtain first the order and inspiration from God. So long as thou hast not this badge of divine inspiration thou mayest preach all thy life, but only in vain.

What is true preaching like? Instead of preaching to others, if one worships God all that time, that is enough preaching. He who strives to make himself free is the real preacher. Hundreds come from all sides, no one knows whence, to him who is free, and are taught by him. When a rosebud blooms, the bees come from all sides uninvited and unasked.

Throw an unbaked cake of flour into hot butter, it will make a sort of boiling noise. But the more it is fried, the less becomes the noise; and when it is fully fried, the bubbling ceases altogether. So long as a man has little knowledge, he goes about lecturing and preaching, but when the perfection of knowledge is obtained, man ceases to make vain displays.

As many have merely heard of snow but not seen it, so many are the religious preachers who have read only in books about the attributes of God, but have not realized them in their lives. And as many have seen but not tasted it, so many are the religious teachers who have got only a glimpse of divine glory, but have not understood its real essence. He only who has tasted the snow can say what it is like. Similarly, he alone can describe the attributes of God who has associated with him in his different aspects, now as a servant of God, then as a friend of God, then as a lover of God, or as being absorbed in him.

The seeds of Vajrabantul do not fall to the bottom of the tree. They are carried by the wind far off and take root there. So the spirit of a prophet manifests itself at a distance and he is appreciated there.

The sunlight is one and the same wherever it falls, but only bright surfaces like water, mirrors and polished metals can reflect it fully. So is the divine light. It falls equally and impartially on all hearts, but only the pure and clean hearts of the good and holy can fully reflect it.

Every man should follow his own religion. A Christian should follow Christianity, a Mohammedan should follow Mohammedanism, and so on. For the Hindus the ancient path, the path of the Aryan Rishis, is the best.

People partition off their lands by means of boundaries, but no one can partition off the all-embracing sky overhead. The indivisible sky surrounds all and includes all. So common man in ignorance says, "My religion is the only one, my religion is the best." But when his heart is illumined by true knowledge, he knows that above all these wars of sects and sectarians presides the one indivisible, eternal, all-knowing bliss.

As a mother, in nursing her sick children, gives rice and curry to one, and sago arrowroot to another and bread and butter to a third, so the Lord has laid out different paths for different men suitable to their natures.

Dispute not. As you rest firmly on your own faith and opinion, allow others also the equal liberty to stand by their own faiths and opinions. By mere disputation you will never succeed in convincing another of his error. When the grace of God descends on him, each one will understand his own mistakes.

So long as the bee is outside the petals of the lily, and has not tasted the sweetness of its honey, it hovers round the flower emitting its buzzing sound; but when it is inside the flower, it noiselessly drinks its nectar. So long as a man quarrels and disputes about doctrines and dogmas, he has not tasted the nectar of true faith; when he has tasted it, he becomes quiet and full of peace.

People of this age care for the essence of everything. They will accept the essential of religion and not its non-essentials (that is, the rituals, ceremonials, dogmas and creeds).

Although in a grain of paddy the germ is considered the only necessary thing (for germination and growth), while the husk or chaff is considered to be of no importance; still if the husked grain be put into the ground, it will not sprout up and grow into a plant and produce rice. To get a crop one must needs sow the grain with the husk on. But if one wants to get at the kernel itself, he must remove the husk of the grain. So rites and ceremonies are necessary for the growth and perpetuation of a religion. They are the receptacles that contain the kernel of truth, and consequently every man must perform them before he reaches the central truth.

Honour spirit and form, both sentiment within and symbol without.

Common men talk bagfuls of religion but act not a grain of it, while the wise man speaks little, but his whole life is a religion acted out.

What you wish others to do, do yourself.

The tender bamboo can be easily bent, but the full grown bamboo breaks when attempt is made to bend it. It is easy to bend young hearts towards God, but the heart of the old escapes the hold when so drawn.

The new-born calf looks very lively, blithe, and merry. It jumps and runs all day long, and only stops to suck the sweet milk from its dam. But no sooner is the rope placed round its neck than it begins to pine away gradually, and, far from being merry, wears a dejected and sorry appearance, and gets almost reduced to a skeleton. So long as a boy has no concern with the affairs of the world, he is as merry as the day is long. But when he once feels the weight of responsibilities of a man of family, by binding himself in time to the world by the indissoluble tie of wedlock, then he no longer appears jolly, but wears the look of dejection, care, and anxiety, and is seen to lose the glow of health from his cheeks, while wrinkles gradually make their appearance on the forehead. Blessed is he that remains a boy throughout his life, free as the morning air, fresh as a newly-blown flower, and pure as a dew-drop.

Worldly men repeat the name of Hari and perform various pious and charitable deeds with the hope of worldly rewards, but when misfortune, sorrow, poverty, death approach them, they forget them all. They are like the parrot that repeats by rote the divine name "Radha Krishna, Radha Krishna" the livelong day, but cries "Kaw, Kaw," when caught by a cat, forgetting the divine name.

Flies sit at times on the sweet-meats kept exposed for sale in the shop of a confectioner; but no sooner does a sweeper pass by with a basketful of filth than the flies leave the sweet-meats and sit upon the filth-basket. But the honey-bee never sits on filthy objects, and always drinks honey from the flowers. The worldly men are like flies. At times they get a momentary taste of divine sweetness, but their natural tendency for filth soon brings them back to the dunghill of the world. The good man, on the other hand, is always absorbed in the beatific contemplation of divine beauty.

It is true that God is even in the tiger, but we must not go and face the animal. So it is true that God dwells even in the most wicked, but it is not meet that we should associate with the wicked.

A young plant should be always protected by a fence from the mischief of goats and cows and little urchins. But when once it becomes a big tree, a flock of goats or a herd of cows may find shelter under its spreading boughs, and fill their stomachs with its leaves. So when you have but little faith within you, you should protect it from the evil influences of bad company and worldliness. But when once you grow strong in faith, no worldliness or evil inclination will dare approach your holy presence; and many who are wicked will become godly through your holy contact.

If you have a mind to live unattached from the world, you should first practise devotion in solitude for some time,—say a year, or six months, or a month, or at least twelve days. During the period of retirement you should meditate constantly upon God and pray to him for divine love. You should revolve in your mind the thought that there is nothing in the world that you may call your own; those whom you think your own will pass away in no time. God is really your own, he is your all-in-all. How to obtain him should be your only concern.

Those who live in the world and try to find salvation are like soldiers that fight protected by the breastwork of a fort, while the ascetics who renounce the world in search of God are like soldiers fighting in the open field. To fight from within the fort is more convenient and safer than to fight in the open field.

The spiritual gain of a person depends upon his sentiments and ideas, proceeds from his heart and not from his visible actions. Two friends, while strolling about, happened to pass by a place where Bhagavat (the word of God) was being preached. One of them said: "Brother, let us go there for a while and hear the good words spoken." The other replied, "No friend, what is the use of hearing the Bhagavatam? Let us spend the time in yonder public-house in amusement and pleasure." The first one did not consent to this. He went to the place where the Bhagavatam was being read and began to hear it. The other went to the public-house, but did not find the pleasure that he had anticipated there and was thinking all the while, "Alas, me! Why have I come here? How happy is my friend hearing all the while the sacred life and deeds of Hari (Lord)." Thus he meditated on Hari even though in a public-house. The other man who was hearing the Bhagavatam also did not find pleasure in it. Sitting there, he began to blame himself, saying, "Alas! Why did I not accompany my friend to the public-house? What a great pleasure he must be enjoying at this time there!" The result was that he who was sitting where the Bhagavatam was preached meditated on the pleasure of the public-house and acquired the fruit of the sin of going to the public-house because of his bad thoughts; while the man who had gone to the public-house acquired the merit of hearing the Bhagavatam because of his good heart.

It is the mind that makes one wise or ignorant, bound or emancipated. One is holy because of his mind, one is wicked because of his mind, one is a sinner because of his mind, and it is the mind that makes one vir-

tuous. So he whose mind is always fixed on God requires no other practices, devotion, or spiritual exercises.

The faith-healers of India order their patients to repeat with full conviction the words, "There is no illness in me, there is no illness at all."
The patient repeats it, and thus mentally denying the illness goes off. So
if you think yourself mortally weak, sinful and without goodness, you
will really find yourself to be so in time. Know and believe that you are
of immense power and the power will come to you at last.

A wife once spoke to her husband, saying, "My dear, I am very anxious
about my brother. For the last few days he has been thinking of renouncing the world and of becoming a Sannyasin, and has begun preparations
for it. He has been trying gradually to curb his desires and reduce his
wants." The husband replied, "You need not be anxious about your
brother. He will never become a Sannyasin. No one has ever renounced
the world by making long preparations." The wife asked, "How then
does one become a Sannyasin?" The husband answered, "Do you wish
to see how one renounces the world? Let me show you." Saying this, instantly he tore his flowing dress into pieces, tied one piece round his
loins, told his wife that she and all women were henceforth his mother,
and left the house never to return.

There is nothing to be proud of in money. If you say that you are rich,
there are richer and richer men than you, in comparison with whom you
are a mere beggar. After dusk, when the glow-worms make their appearance, they think, "We are giving light to the world." But when the
stars rise, their pride is gone. Then the stars begin to think, "We are
shedding light on the universe." After some time the moon ascends the
sky, and the stars are humiliated and look melancholy. So again the moon
begins to be proud and think that by her light the world is lighted, and
smiles and bathes in beauty and cheerfulness. But lo! the dawn proclaims
the advent of the rising sun on the eastern horizon. Where is the moon
now? If they who think themselves rich ponder over these natural facts,
they will never, never boast of their riches again.

If I hold up this cloth before me, you will not see me any more,
though I shall be as near you. So also God is nearer to you than anything
else, yet because of the screen of egoism you cannot see him.

Sankaracharya had a disciple who served him for a long time, but he
did not give any instructions to him. Once when Sankara was seated
alone, he heard the footsteps of someone coming behind. He called out,

"Who is there?" The disciple answered, "It is I." The Acharya said, "If the word 'I' is so dear to thee, then either expand it indefinitely, that is, know the universe as thyself, or renounce it altogether."

If you find that you cannot make this "I" go, then let it remain as the "servant I." There is not much to fear of mischief in the "I" which knows itself as "I am the servant of God; I am his devotee." Sweets beget dyspepsia, but the crystallized sugar candy is not among the sweets, for it has not that injurious property.

The "servant I," the "I" of a devotee, or the "I" of a child is like the line drawn with a stick on a sheet of water. It does not last long.

If you feel proud, feel so in the thought that you are the servant of God, the son of God. Great men have the nature of children. They are always children before God, so they have no egoism. All their strength is of God, belonging to and coming from him, nothing of themselves.

There are two egos—one ripe and the other unripe. "Nothing is mine; whatever I see, feel or hear, nay, even this body, is not mine. I am always eternal, free, and all-knowing"—the ego that has this idea is the ripe one, while the unripe ego is that which thinks, "This is my house, my child, my wife, my body, etc."

When shall I be free? When the "I" has vanished. "I and mine" is ignorance; "Thou and thine" is true knowledge. The true devotee always says, "O Lord, thou art the doer, thou doest everything. I am only a machine. I do whatever thou makest me to do. And all this is thy glory. This home and this family are thine, not mine; I have only the right to serve as thou ordainest."

As a wet-nurse in a rich family brings up the child of her master, loving the baby as if it were her own, but knows well that she has no claim upon it; so think ye also that you are but trustees and guardians of your children whose real father is the Lord God in heaven.

When the knowledge of Self is gained, all fetters fall off of themselves. Then there is no distinction between a Brahmana and a Sudra, a high caste or a low caste. In that state the sacred-thread-sign of caste falls away of itself. But so long as a man has the consciousness of distinction and difference, he should not forcibly throw it off.

The spiritual-minded belong to a caste of their own irrespective of all social conventions.

When a man is on the plains he sees the lowly grass and the mighty pine tree and says, "How big is the tree and how small is the grass!" But when he ascends the mountain and looks from its high peak on the plain below, the mighty pine tree and the lowly grass blend into one indistinguishable mass of green verdure. So in the sight of the worldly there are differences of rank and position—one is a king, another is a cobbler, one a father, another a son, and so on—but when the divine sight is opened, all appear as equal and one, and there remains no distinction of good and bad, high and low.

When I look upon chaste women of respectable families, I see in them the divine Mother arrayed in the garb of a chaste lady; and again, when I look upon the public women of the city, sitting in their verandas, arrayed in the garb of immorality and shamelessness, I see in them also the divine Mother sporting in a different way.

Man is like a pillow-case. The colour of the one may be red, that of another blue, that of a third black, but all contain the same cotton. So it is with man,—one is beautiful, another is black, a third holy, a fourth wicked, but the divine One dwells within them all.

God tells the thief to go and steal, and at the same time warns the householder against the thief.

If you fill an earthen vessel with water and set it apart upon a shelf, the water in it will dry up in a few days; but if you place the same vessel immersed in water, it will remain filled as long as it is kept there. Even so is the case of your love for the Lord God. Fill and enrich your bosom with the love of God for a time and then employ yourself in other affairs, forgetting him all the while, and then you are sure to find within a short time that your heart has become poor and vacant and devoid of that precious love. But if you keep your heart immersed always in the ocean of divine love, your heart is sure to remain ever full to overflowing with the water of the divine love.

There are three kinds of love,—unselfish, mutual, and selfish. The unselfish love is of the highest kind. The lover only minds the welfare of the beloved and does not care for his own sufferings. In mutual love the lover not only wants the happiness of his beloved but has an eye towards his own happiness also. It is middling. The selfish love is the lowest. It only looks towards its own happiness, no matter whether the beloved suffers weal or woe.

A man after fourteen years' penance in a solitary forest obtained at last the power of walking on water. Overjoyed at this, he went to his Guru and said, "Master, master, I have acquired the power of walking on water." The master rebukingly replied, "Fie, O child! is this the result of thy fourteen years' labours? Verily thou hast obtained only that which is worth a penny; for what thou hast accomplished after fourteen years' arduous labour ordinary men do by paying a penny to the boatman."

Fans should be discarded when the wind blows. Prayers and penances should be discarded when the grace of God descends.

So long as one does not become simple like a child, one does not get divine illumination. Forget all the worldly knowledge that thou hast acquired and become as ignorant as a child, and then wilt thou get the divine wisdom.

Lunatics, drunkards and children sometimes give out the truth unconsciously, as if inspired by heaven.

To kill another swords and shields are needed, whilst to kill one's own self even a pin will do; so to teach others one must study many scriptures and sciences, whilst to acquire self-illumination firm faith in a single motto will suffice.

The Parables of Sri Ramakrishna

The Saints and the Saviours

A place was enclosed by means of a high wall. The men outside did not know what sort of place it was. Once four persons determined to find out what was inside by scaling the wall with a ladder. As soon as the first man ascended to the top of the wall, he laughed out, "Ha, ha, ha!" and jumped in. The second also, as soon as he ascended, similarly laughed aloud and jumped in, and so did the third. When the fourth and last man got up to the top of the wall, he found stretched beneath him a large and beautiful garden containing pleasant groves and delicious fruits. Though strongly tempted to jump down and enjoy the scene, he resisted the temptation, and coming down the ladder, preached the glad tidings about the beautiful garden to all outsiders. The Brahman is like the walled garden. He who sees it forgets his own existence and with ecstatic joy rushes headlong unto it to attain to Moksha or absolute freedom. Such are the holy men and liberated saints of the world. But the saviours of humanity are those who see God and, being at the same time anxious to share their happiness of divine vision with others, refuse the final liberation (Moksha), and willingly undergo the troubles of rebirth in the world in order to teach and lead struggling humanity to its ultimate goal.

The Fortunate Wood-Cutter

A wood-cutter led a very miserable life with the small means he could procure by daily selling the load of wood brought from a neighbouring forest. Once a Sannyasin, who was wending his way through the forest, saw him at work and advised him to proceed onward into the interior recesses of the forest, intimating to him that he would be a gainer thereby. The wood-cutter obeyed the injunction and proceeded onward until he came to a sandalwood tree, and being much pleased, he took away with him as many sandal logs as he could carry and sold them in the market and derived much profit. Then he began to think within himself why the good Sannyasin did not tell him anything about the wood of the sandal trees, but simply advised him to proceed onward into the interior of the forest. So the next day he went on beyond the place of the sandalwood, and at last came upon a copper mine, and he took with him as much copper as he could carry, and, selling it in the market, got much money by it. Next day, without stopping at the copper mine, he proceeded further still, as the Sadhu had advised him to do, and came upon a silver mine, and took with him as much of it as he could carry and sold it all and got even more money; and so daily proceeding further and further, he got at gold mines and diamond mines and at last became exceedingly rich. Such is also the case with the man who aspires after true knowledge. If he does not stop in his progress after attaining a few extraordinary and supernatural powers, he at last becomes really rich in the eternal knowledge of truth.

The Power of Faith

A disciple, having firm faith in the infinite power of his Guru, walked over a river even by pronouncing his name. The Guru, seeing this, thought within himself, "Well, is there such a power even in my name? Then I must be very great and powerful, no doubt!" The next day he also tried to walk over the river pronouncing "I, I, I," but no sooner had he stepped into the waters than he sank and was drowned. Faith can achieve miracles, while vanity or egoism is the death of man.

Of Worldly Demands

It is said that when a Tantrika tries to invoke the deity through the medium of the spirit of the dead, he sits over a fresh human corpse and keeps near him food and wine. During the invocation, if at any time the corpse is vivified (though temporarily) and opens its mouth, the intrepid invoker must pour the wine and the food into its gaping mouth at the time to appease the elemental that has, for the time being, taken possession of the dead body. If he does not do so, the invocation is interrupted by this elemental and the higher spirit does not descend. So, dwelling in the bosom of the carcass of the world, if thou wantest to attain beatitude, thou must first provide thyself beforehand with everything necessary to pacify the clamour of all worldly demands on thee, otherwise thy devotions will be broken and interrupted by worldly cares and anxieties.

The Ocean of Bliss

The alligator loves to swim on the surface of the water, but as soon as he rises up he is made a mark of by the hunters. Necessarily he is obliged to remain under water and cannot rise to the surface. Still, whenever he finds an opportunity, he rises up with a deep whizzing noise and swims happily on the wide watery expanse. O man, entangled in the meshes of the world! Thou too art anxious to swim on the surface of the ocean of bliss, but art prevented from doing so by the importunate demands of thy family. But be of good cheer, and whenever thou findest any leisure call intensely upon thy God, pray to him earnestly, and tell him all thy sorrows. In his proper time he will surely emancipate thee and enable thee to swim merrily on the surface of the ocean of bliss.

The Protection of God

A Jnani (knower of God) and a Premika (lover of God) were once passing through a forest. On the way they saw a tiger at a distance. The Jnani said, "There is no reason why we should flee; the Almighty God will certainly protect us." At this the Premika said, "No, brother, come, let us run away. Why should we trouble the Lord for what can be accomplished by our own exertions?"

The Aspects of God

Be not like Ghanta Karna in thy bigotry. There was a man who worshipped Shiva but hated all other deities. One day Shiva appeared to him and said, "I shall never be pleased with thee so long as thou hatest the other gods." But the man was inexorable. After a few days Shiva again appeared to him and said, "I shall never be pleased with thee so long as thou hatest." The man kept silent. After a few days Shiva again appeared to him. This time he appeared as Hari-har, namely, one side of his body was that of Shiva, and the other side that of Vishnu. The man was half pleased and half displeased. He laid his offerings on the side representing Shiva, and did not offer anything to the side representing Vishnu. Then Shiva said, "Thy bigotry is unconquerable. I, by assuming this dual aspect, tried to convince thee that all gods and goddesses are but various aspects of the one Absolute Brahman."

The Converted Snake

A snake dwelt in a certain place. No one dared to pass by that way; for whoever did so was instantaneously bitten to death. Once a Mahatman (high-souled one) passed by that road, and the serpent ran after the sage in order to bite him. But when the snake approached the holy man he lost all his ferocity and was overpowered by the gentleness of the Yogin. Seeing the snake, the sage said: "Well, friend, thinkest thou to bite me?" The snake was abashed and made no reply. At this the sage said: "Hearken, friend; do not injure anybody in the future." The snake bowed and nodded assent. The sage went his own way, and the snake entered his hole, and thenceforward began to live a life of innocence and purity without even attempting to harm any one. In a few days all the neighbourhood began to think that the snake had lost all his venom and was no more dangerous, and so every one began to tease him. Some pelted him; others dragged him mercilessly by the tail, and in this way there was no end to his troubles. Fortunately the sage again passed by that way and, seeing the bruised and battered condition of the good snake, was very much moved, and inquired the cause of his distress. At this the snake replied: "Holy Sir, this is because I do not injure any one after your advice. But alas! they are so merciless!" The sage smilingly said: "My dear friend, I simply advised you not to bite any one, but I did not tell you not to frighten others. Although you should not bite any creature, still you should keep every one at a considerable distance by hissing at him."

Similarly, if thou livest in the world, make thyself feared and respected. Do not injure any one, but be not at the same time injured by others.

The Fisherwoman's Sleeplessness

A fisherwoman on her way home from a distant market was overtaken by a storm at nightfall, so she was compelled to take refuge in a florist's house near at hand. The hospitable florist received her very kindly and allowed her to spend the night in a room next to his garden. But the fragrant atmosphere of the place was too good for the fisherwoman. She could not sleep for a long time. At last when she discovered that the sweet aroma of the flowers in the garden kept her awake, she sprinkled water on her empty basket of fish, placed it close to her nose, and immediately fell into a sound sleep. Such indeed is the power and influence of bad habits over all those who are addicted to them. They cannot enjoy the uplifting influence of the spiritual atmosphere.

The Diamond and the Dust

A husband and wife renounced the world and jointly undertook a pilgrimage to various religious shrines. Once, as they were walking on a road, the husband, being a little ahead of the wife, saw a piece of diamond on the road. Immediately he scratched the ground to hide the diamond, thinking that, if his wife saw it, she might perchance be moved by avarice and thus lose the merit of her renunciation. While he was thus busy, the wife came up and asked him what he was doing. In an apologetic tone he gave her an evasive reply. She noticed the diamond, however, and reading his thoughts, asked him, "Why have you left the world, if you still feel the difference between the diamond and the dust?"

The Hurt of the Divine Mother

The god Kartikeya, the leader of the heavenly army, once happened to scratch a cat with his nail. On going home he saw there was the mark of a scratch on the cheek of his mother. Seeing this, he asked of her, "Mother, dear, how have you got that ugly scratch on your cheek?" The goddess Durga replied: "Child, this is thy own handiwork—the mark scratched by thy own nail." Kartikeya asked in wonder, "Mother, how is it? I never remember to have scratched thee!" The mother replied, "Darling, hast thou forgotten having scratched a cat this morning?" Kartikeya said, "Yes, I did scratch a cat; but how did your cheek get marked?" The mother replied, "Dear child, nothing exists in this world but myself. I am all creation. Whomsoever thou hurtest, thou hurtest me." Kartikeya was greatly surprised at this, and determined never to marry; for whom would he marry? Every woman was mother to him. I am like Kartikeya. I consider every woman as my divine mother.

The Seven Jars of Gold

Greed brings woe, while contentment is all happiness. A barber was once passing under a haunted tree when he heard a voice say, "Wilt thou accept of seven jars of gold?" The barber looked round, but could see no one. The mysterious voice again repeated the words, and the cupidity of the barber being greatly roused by the spontaneous offer of such wealth, he spoke aloud, "When the merciful God is so good as to take pity even on a poor barber like me, is there anything to be said as to my accepting the kind offer so generously made?" At once the reply came, "Go home, I have already carried the jars thither." The barber ran in hot haste to his house and was transported to see the promised jars there. He opened them one after another and saw them all filled, save one which was half filled. Now arose in the heart of the barber the desire of filling this last jar. So he sold all his gold and silver ornaments and converted them into coins and threw them into the jar. But the jar still remained empty. He now began to starve himself and his family by living upon insufficient, coarse, and cheap food, throwing all his savings into the jar, but the jar remained as empty as ever. The barber then requested the king to increase his pay as it was not sufficient to maintain him and his family. As he was a favourite of the king, the latter granted his request. The barber now began to save all his pay and emoluments and throw them all into the jar, but the greedy jar showed no sign of being filled. He now began to live by begging, and became as wretched and miserable as possible. One day the king, seeing his sad plight, inquired of him by saying, "Hallo! when thy pay was half of what thou gettest now, thou wast far happier and more cheerful, contented, and healthy; but with double that pay I see thee morose, careworn, and dejected. Now what is the matter with thee? Hast thou accepted the seven jars of gold?" The barber was taken aback by this home-thrust, and with clasped hands asked the king as to who had informed his majesty about the matter. The king answered, "Whosoever accepts the riches of a Yaksha is sure to be reduced to such an abject and wretched plight. I have known thee through this invariable sign. Do away with the money at once. Thou canst not spend a farthing of it. That money is for hoarding and not for spending." The barber was brought to his senses by this advice and went to the haunted tree and said, "O Yaksha, take back thy gold," and he returned home to find the seven jars vanished, taking with them his lifelong savings. Nevertheless he began to live happily thereafter.

BUDDHIST
Scriptures

BUDDHIST SCRIPTURES

The Life of the Buddha

The Conception and Birth of the Buddha

Now while the future Buddha was still dwelling in the city of the Tusita gods, the "Buddha-Uproar," as it is called, took place. For there are three uproars which take place in the world,—the Cyclic-Uproar, the Buddha-Uproar, and the Universal-Monarch-Uproar. They occur as follows:

When it is known that after the lapse of a hundred thousand years the cycle is to be renewed, the gods called Loka-byuhas, inhabitants of a heaven of sensual pleasure, wander about through the world, with hair let down and flying in the wind, weeping and wiping away their tears with their hands, and with their clothes red and in great disorder. And thus they make announcement:

"Sirs, after the lapse of a hundred thousand years, the cycle is to be renewed; this world will be destroyed; also the mighty ocean will dry up; and this broad earth, and Sineru, the monarch of the mountains, will be burnt up and destroyed,—up to the Brahma heavens will the destruction of the world extend. Therefore, sirs, cultivate friendliness; cultivate compassion, joy, and indifference; wait on your mothers; wait on your fathers; and honour your elders among your kinsfolk."

This is called the Cyclic-Uproar.

Again, when it is known that after a lapse of a thousand years an omniscient Buddha is to arise in the world, the guardian angels of the world wander about, proclaiming:

"Sirs, after the lapse of a thousand years a Buddha will arise in the world."

This is called the Buddha-Uproar.

181

And lastly, when they realize that after the lapse of a hundred years a universal monarch is to arise, the terrestrial deities wander about, proclaiming:

"Sirs, after the lapse of a hundred years a universal monarch is to arise in the world."

This is called the Universal-Monarch-Uproar. And these three are mighty uproars.

When of these three uproars they hear the sound of the Buddha-Uproar, the gods of all ten thousand worlds come together into one place, and having ascertained what particular being is to be the Buddha, they approach him, and beseech him to become one. But it is not till after omens have appeared that they beseech him.

At that time, therefore, having all come together in one world, with the Chatum-Maharajas, and with the Sakka, the Suyama, the Santusita, the Paranimmita-Vasavatti, and the Maha-Brahma of each several world, they approached the future Buddha in the Tusita heaven, and besought him, saying,

"Sir, it was not to acquire the glory of a Sakka, or of a Mara, or of a Brahma, or of a universal monarch, that you fulfilled the ten perfections; but it was to gain omniscience in order to save the world, that you fulfilled them. Sir, the time and fit season for your Buddhaship has now arrived."

But the great being, before assenting to their wish, made what is called the five great observations. He observed, namely, the time, the continent, the country, the family, and the mother and her span of life.

Having thus made the five great observations, he kindly made the gods the required promise, saying,

"Sirs, you are right. The time has come for my Buddhaship."

Then, surrounded by the gods of the Tusita heaven, and dismissing all the other gods, he entered the Nandana Grove of the Tusita capital, —for in each of the heavens there is a Nandana Grove. And here the gods said, "Attain in your next existence your high destiny," and kept reminding him that he had already paved the way to it by his accumulated merit. Now it was while he was thus dwelling, surrounded by these deities, and continually reminded of his accumulated merit, that he died, and was conceived in the womb of queen Maha-Maya. And in order that this matter may be fully understood, I will give the whole account in due order.

It is related that at that time the midsummer festival had been proclaimed in the city of Kapilavatthu, and the multitude were enjoying the feast. And queen Maha-Maya, abstaining from strong drink, and brilliant with garlands and perfumes, took part in the festivities for the six days previous to the day of full moon. And when it came to be the day of full moon, she rose early, bathed in perfumed water, and dispensed four hundred thousand pieces of money in great largess. And decked in full gala attire, she ate of the choicest food; after which she took the eight vows, and entered her elegantly furnished chamber of state. And lying down on the royal couch, she fell asleep and dreamed the following dream:

The four guardian angels came and lifted her up, together with her couch, and took her away to the Himalaya Mountains. There, in the Manosila table-land, which is sixty leagues in extent, they laid her under a prodigious sal-tree, seven leagues in height, and took up their positions respectfully at one side. Then came the wives of these guardian angels, and conducted her to Anotatta Lake, and bathed her, to remove every human stain. And after clothing her with divine garments, they anointed her with perfumes and decked her with divine flowers. Not far off was Silver Hill, and in it a golden mansion. There they spread a divine couch with its head towards the east, and laid her down upon it. Now the future Buddha had become a superb white elephant, and was wandering about at no great distance, on Gold Hill. Descending thence, he ascended Silver Hill, and approaching from the north, he plucked a white lotus with his silvery trunk, and trumpeting loudly, went into the golden mansion. And three times he walked round his mother's couch, with his right side towards it, and striking her on her right side, he seemed to enter her womb. Thus the conception took place in the midsummer festival.

On the next day the queen awoke, and told the dream to the king. And the king caused sixty-four eminent Brahmanas to be summoned, and spread costly seats for them on ground festively prepared with green leaves, dalbergia flowers, and so forth. The Brahmanas being seated, he filled gold and silver dishes with the best of milk-porridge compounded with ghee, honey, and treacle; and covering these dishes with others, made likewise of gold and silver, he gave the Brahmanas to eat. And not only with food, but with other gifts, such as new garments, tawny cows, and so forth, he satisfied them completely. And when their every desire had been satisfied, he told them the dream and asked them what would come of it.

"Be not anxious, great king!" said the Brahmanas; "a child has planted itself in the womb of your queen, and it is a male child and not a female. You will have a son. And he, if he continue to live the household life, will become a universal monarch; but if he leave the household life and retire from the world, he will become a Buddha, and roll back the clouds of sin and folly of this world."

Now the instant the future Buddha was conceived in the womb of his mother, all the ten thousand worlds suddenly quaked, quivered, and shook. And the thirty-two prognostics appeared, as follows: an immeasurable light spread through ten thousand worlds; the blind recovered their sight, as if from desire to see this his glory; the deaf received their hearing; the dumb talked; the hunchbacked became straight of body; the lame recovered the power to walk; all those in bonds were freed from their bonds and chains; the fires went out in all the hells; the hunger and thirst of the departed ancestors was stilled; wild animals lost their timidity; diseases ceased among men; all mortals became mild-spoken; horses neighed and elephants trumpeted in a manner sweet to the ear; all musical instruments gave forth their notes without being played upon; bracelets and other ornaments jingled; in all quarters of the heavens the weather became fair; a mild, cool breeze began to blow, very refreshing to men; rain fell out of season; water burst forth from the earth and flowed in streams; the birds ceased flying through the air; the rivers checked their flowing; in the mighty ocean the water became sweet; the ground became everywhere covered with lotuses of the five different colours; all flowers bloomed, both those on land and those that grow in the water; trunk-lotuses bloomed on the trunks of trees, branch-lotuses on the branches, and vine-lotuses on the vines; on the ground, stalk-lotuses, as they are called, burst through the overlying rocks and came up by sevens; in the sky were produced others, called hanging-lotuses; a shower of flowers fell all about; celestial music was heard to play in the sky; and the whole ten thousand worlds became one mass of garlands of the utmost possible magnificence, with waving chowries, and saturated with the incense-like fragrance of flowers, and resembled a bouquet of flowers sent whirling through the air, or a closely woven wreath, or a superbly decorated altar of flowers.

From the time the future Buddha was thus conceived, four angels with swords in their hands kept guard, to ward off all harm from both the future Buddha and the future Buddha's mother. No lustful thought sprang up in the mind of the future Buddha's mother; having reached the pinnacle of good fortune and of glory, she felt comfortable and well, and experienced no exhaustion of body. And within her womb she could distinguish the future Buddha, like a white thread passed through a transparent jewel. And whereas a womb that has been occupied by a future Buddha is like the shrine of a temple, and can never be occupied or used again, therefore it was that the mother of the future Buddha died when he was seven days old, and was reborn in the Tusita heaven.

Now other women sometimes fall short of and sometimes run over the term of ten lunar months, and then bring forth either sitting or lying down; but not so the mother of a future Buddha. She carries the future Buddha in her womb for just ten months, and then brings forth while standing up. This is a characteristic of the mother of a future Buddha. So also queen Maha-Maya carried the future Buddha in her womb, as it were oil in a vessel, for ten months; and being then far gone with child, she grew desirous of going home to her relatives, and said to king Suddhodana,

"Sire, I should like to visit my kinsfolk in their city Devadaha."

"So be it," said the king; and from Kapilavatthu to the city of Devadaha he had the road made even, and garnished it with plantain-trees set in pots, and with banners, and streamers; and, seating the queen in a golden palanquin borne by a thousand of his courtiers, he sent her away in great pomp.

Now between the two cities, and belonging to the inhabitants of both, there was a pleasure-grove of sal-trees, called Lumbini Grove. And at this particular time this grove was one mass of flowers from the ground to the topmost branches, while amongst the branches and flowers hummed swarms of bees of the five different colours, and flocks of various kinds of birds flew about warbling sweetly. Throughout the whole of Lumbini Grove the scene resembled the Chittalata Grove in Indra's paradise, or the magnificently decorated banqueting pavilion of some potent king.

When the queen beheld it she became desirous of disporting herself therein, and the courtiers therefore took her into it. And going to the foot of the monarch sal-tree of the grove, she wished to take hold of one of its branches. And the sal-tree branch, like the tip of a well-stemmed reed, bent itself down within reach of the queen's hand. Then she reached out her hand, and seized hold of the branch, and immediately her pains came upon her. Thereupon the people hung a curtain about her, and retired. So her delivery took place while she was standing up, and keeping fast hold of the sal-tree branch.

At that very moment came four pure-minded Maha-Brahma angels bearing a golden net; and, receiving the future Buddha on this golden net, they placed him before his mother and said,

"Rejoice, O queen! A mighty son has been born to you."

Now other mortals on issuing from the maternal womb are smeared with disagreeable, impure matter; but not so the future Buddha. He issued from his mother's womb like a preacher descending from his preaching-seat, or a man coming down a stair, stretching out both hands and both feet, unsmeared by any impurity from his mother's womb, and flashing pure and spotless, like a jewel thrown upon a vesture of Benares cloth. Notwithstanding this, for the sake of honouring the future Buddha and his mother, there came two streams of water from the sky, and refreshed the future Buddha and his mother.

Then the Brahma angels, after receiving him on their golden net, delivered him to the four guardian angels, who received him from their hands on a rug which was made of the skins of black antelopes, and was soft to the touch, being such as is used on state occasions; and the guardian angels delivered him to men who received him on a coil of fine cloth; and the men let him out of their hands on the ground, where he stood and faced the east. There, before him, lay many thousands of worlds, like a great open court; and in them, gods and men, making offerings to him of perfumes, garlands, and so on, were saying,

"Great Being! There is none your equal, much less your superior."

When he had in this manner surveyed the four cardinal points, and the four intermediate ones, and the zenith, and the nadir, in short, all the ten directions in order, and had nowhere discovered his equal, he exclaimed, "This is the best direction," and strode forward seven paces, followed by Maha-Brahma holding over him the white umbrella, Suyama bearing the fan, and other divinities having the other symbols of royalty in their hands. Then, at the seventh stride, he halted, and with a noble voice he shouted the shout of victory, beginning,

"The chief am I in all the world."

Now at the very time that our future Buddha was born in Lumbini Grove there also came into existence the mother of Rahula, and Channa the courtier, Kaludayi the courtier, Kanthaka the king of horses, the great Bo-tree, and the four urns full of treasure. Of these last, one was a quarter of a league in extent, another a half-league, the third three-quarters of a league, and the fourth a league. These seven are called the connate ones.

Then the inhabitants of both cities took the future Buddha, and carried him to Kapilavatthu.

The Holy Child

On this same day the happy and delighted hosts of the heaven of the thirty-three held a celebration, waving their cloaks and giving other signs of joy, because to king Suddhodana in Kapilavatthu had been born a son who should sit at the foot of the Bo-tree, and become a Buddha.

Now it came to pass at that time that an ascetic named Kaladevala, who was an intimate friend of king Suddhodana, and practised in the eight stages of meditation, went, after his daily meal, to the heaven of the thirty-three to take his noon-day rest. And as he was sitting there resting, he noticed these gods, and said,

"Why do you frolic so joyously? Let me too know the reason."

"Sir," replied the gods, "it is because a son has been born to king Suddhodana, who shall sit at the foot of the Bo-tree, and become a Buddha, and cause the wheel of the doctrine to roll; in him we shall be permitted to behold the infinite and masterful ease of a Buddha, and shall hear the doctrine."

On hearing this, the ascetic descended from the world of the gods in haste, and entered the dwelling of the king; and having seated himself on the seat assigned to him, he said,

"Great king, I hear that a son has been born to you. I would see him."

Then the king had the prince magnificently dressed, and brought in, and carried up to do reverence to the ascetic. But the feet of the future Buddha turned and planted themselves in the matted locks of the ascetic. For in that birth there was no one worthy of the future Buddha's reverence; and if these ignorant people had succeeded in causing the future Buddha to bow, the head of the ascetic would have split in seven pieces.

"It is not meet that I compass my own death," thought the ascetic, and rose from his seat, and with joined hands did reverence to the future Buddha. And when the king had seen this wonder, he also did reverence to his son.

Then said the king, "What shall my son see to make him retire from the world?"

"The four signs."

"What four?"

"A decrepit old man, a diseased man, a dead man, and a monk."

"From this time forth," said the king, "let no such persons be allowed to come near my son. It will never do for my son to become a Buddha. What I would wish to see is my son exercising sovereign rule and authority over the four great continents and the two thousand attendant isles, and walking through the heavens surrounded by a retinue thirty-six leagues in circumference." And when he had so spoken he placed guards for a distance of a quarter of a league in each of the four directions, in order that none of these four kinds of men might come within sight of his son.

He Sees the Four Signs

Now on a certain day the future Buddha wished to go to the park, and told his charioteer to make ready the chariot. Accordingly the man brought out a sumptuous and elegant chariot, and adorning it richly, he harnessed to it four state-horses of the Sindhava breed, as white as the petals of the white lotus, and announced to the future Buddha that everything was ready. And the future Buddha mounted the chariot, which was like to a palace of the gods, and proceeded towards the park.

"The time for the enlightenment of prince Siddhattha draweth nigh," thought the gods; "we must show him a sign": and they changed one of their number into a decrepit old man, broken-toothed, grey-haired, crooked and bent of body, leaning on a staff, and trembling, and showed him to the future Buddha, but so that only he and the charioteer saw him.

Then said the future Buddha to the charioteer, in the manner related in the Mahapadana,

"Friend, pray, who is this man? Even his hair is not like that of other men." And when he heard the answer, he said, "Shame on birth, since to every one that is born old age must come." And agitated in heart, he thereupon returned and ascended his palace.

"Why has my son returned so quickly?" asked the king.

"Sire, he has seen an old man," was the reply; "and because he has seen an old man, he is about to retire from the world."

"Do you want to kill me, that you say such things? Quickly get ready some plays to be performed before my son. If we can but get him to enjoying pleasure, he will cease to think of retiring from the world." Then the king extended the guard to half a league in each direction.

Again, on a certain day, as the future Buddha was going to the park, he saw a diseased man whom the gods had fashioned; and having again made inquiry, he returned, agitated in heart, and ascended his palace.

And the king made the same inquiry and gave the same orders as before; and again extending the guard, placed them for three-quarters of a league around.

And again on a certain day, as the future Buddha was going to the park, he saw a dead man whom the gods had fashioned; and having again made inquiry, he returned, agitated in heart, and ascended his palace.

And the king made the same inquiry and gave the same orders as before; and again extending the guard, placed them for a league around.

And again on a certain day, as the future Buddha was going to the park, he saw a monk, carefully and decently clad, whom the gods had fashioned; and he asked his charioteer, "Pray, who is this man?"

Now although there was no Buddha in the world, and the charioteer had no knowledge of either monks or their good qualities, yet by the power of the gods he was inspired to say, "Sire, this is one who has retired from the world"; and he thereupon proceeded to sound the praises of retirement from the world. The thought of retiring from the world was a pleasing one to the future Buddha, and this day he went on until he came to the park. The repeaters of the Digha, however, say that he went to the park after having seen all the four signs on one and the same day.

The World about Him

Hearing the news, "The prince is going out," from the attendants of the female apartments, the women hastened to the roofs of the different mansions, having obtained the leave of their lords. Hindered by the strings of their girdles which had slipped down, with their eyes bewildered as just awakened from sleep, and with their ornaments hastily put on in the stir of the news, and filled with curiosity, they crowded round, frightening the flocks of birds which lived in the houses with the noise of their girdles and the jingling of their anklets which resounded on the staircases and roofs of the mansions, and mutually reproaching one another for their hurry. Some of these women, even in their haste as they rushed longing to see, were delayed in their going by the weight of their hips and full bosoms.

There they were restlessly swaying about in the windows, crowded together in the mutual press, with their earrings polished by the continual collision and their ornaments all jingling. The lotus-like faces of the women gleamed while they looked out from the windows, with their earrings coming into mutual proximity, as if they were real lotuses fastened upon the houses. Gazing down upon the prince in the road, the women appeared as if longing to fall to the earth; gazing up to him with upturned faces, the men seemed as if longing to rise to heaven.

Then from that city-garden, with their eyes restless in excitement, the women went out to meet the prince as a newly-arrived bridegroom; and when they came up to him, their eyes wide open in wonder, they performed their due homage with hands folded like a lotus-calyx. Then they stood surrounding him, their minds overpowered by passion, as if they were drinking him in with their eyes motionless and blossoming wide with love. Some of the women verily thought that he was Kama incarnate,—decorated as he was with his brilliant signs as with connate ornaments. Others thought from his gentleness and majesty that it was the moon with its ambrosial beams as it were visibly come down to the earth. Others, smitten by his beauty, yawned as if to swallow him, and fixing their eyes on each other, softly sighed. Thus the women only looked upon him, simply gazing with their eyes,—they spoke not, nor did they smile, controlled by his power.

But having seen them thus listless, bewildered in their love, the wise son of the family priest, Udayin, thus addressed them: "Ye are all skilled in all the graceful arts, proficients in understanding the language of amorous sentiments, possessed of beauty and gracefulness, thorough masters in your own styles. With these graces of yours ye may embellish even the northern Kurus, yea, even the dances of Kuvera, much more this little earth. This being so, boldly put forth your efforts that the prosperity of the king's family may not be turned away from him. Ordinary women captivate similar lovers; but they are truly women who subdue the natures of high and low."

Having heard these words of Udayin these women as stung to the heart rose even above themselves for the conquest of the prince. With their brows, their glances, their coquetries, their smiles, their delicate movements, they made all sorts of significant gestures like women utterly terrified. But they soon regained their confidence through the command of the king and the gentle temperament of the prince, and through the power of intoxication and of love. Then surrounded by troops of women the prince wandered in the wood like an elephant in the forests of Himavat accompanied by a herd of females.

There some of them, urged by passion, pressed him with their full firm bosoms in gentle collisions. Another violently embraced him after making a pretended stumble,—leaning on him with her shoulders drooping down, and with her gentle creeper-like arms dependent. Another with her mouth smelling of spirituous liquor, her lower lip red like copper, whispered in his ear, "Let my secret be heard." Another, with her blue garments continually slipping down in pretended intoxication, stood conspicuous with her tongue visible like the night with its lightning flashing. Others, with their golden zones tinkling, wandered about here and there, showing to him their hips veiled with thin cloth. Another sang a sweet song easily understood and with the proper gesticulations, rousing him, self-subdued though he was, by her glances, as saying, "O how thou art deluded!" Another, having armed herself with her bright face, with its brow-bow drawn to its full, imitated his action, as playing the hero. Another, with beautiful full bosoms, and having her earrings waving in the wind, laughed loudly at him, as if saying, "Catch me, sir, if you can!"

Thus these young women, their souls carried away by love, assailed the prince with all kinds of stratagems. But although thus attacked, he, having his senses guarded by self-control, neither rejoiced nor smiled, thinking anxiously, "One must die."

Then the prince uttered a discourse full of resolve and abolishing the objects of desire; and the lord of day, whose orb is the worthy centre of human eyes, departed to the western mountain. And the women, having worn their garlands and ornaments in vain, with their graceful arts and endearments all fruitless, concealing their love deep in their hearts, returned to the city with broken hopes. Having thus seen the beauty of the troop of women who had gone out to the city-garden, now withdrawn in the evening,—the prince, pondering the transitoriness which envelops all things, entered his dwelling.

Then the king, when he heard how his mind turned away from all objects of sense, could not lie down all that night, like an elephant with an arrow in its heart; but wearied in all sorts of consultation, he and his ministers could find no other means besides these despised pleasures to restrain his son's purpose.

The Great Retirement

At this juncture, Suddhodana the king, having heard that the mother of Rahula had brought forth a son, sent a messenger, saying, "Announce the glad news to my son."

On hearing the message, the future Buddha said, "An impediment (rahula) has been born; a fetter has been born."

"What did my son say?" questioned the king; and when he had heard the answer, he said, "My grandson's name shall be prince Rahula from this very day."

But the future Buddha in his splendid chariot entered the city with a pomp and magnificence of glory that enraptured all minds. At the same moment Kisa Gotami, a virgin of the warrior caste, ascended to the roof of her palace, and beheld the beauty and majesty of the future Buddha, as he circumambulated the city; and in her pleasure and satisfaction at the sight, she burst forth into this song of joy:

"Full happy now that mother is,
Full happy now that father is,
Full happy now that woman is,
Who owns this lord so glorious!"

On hearing this, the future Buddha thought, "In beholding a handsome figure the heart of a mother attains Nirvana, the heart of a father attains Nirvana, the heart of a wife attains Nirvana. This is what she says. But wherein does Nirvana consist?" And to him, whose mind was already averse to passion, the answer came: "When the fire of lust is extinct, that is Nirvana; when the fires of hatred and infatuation are extinct, that is Nirvana; when pride, false belief, and all other passions and torments are extinct, that is Nirvana. She has taught me a good lesson. Certainly, Nirvana is what I am looking for. It behoves me this very day to quit the household life, and to retire from the world in quest of Nirvana. I will send this lady a teacher's fee." And loosening from his neck a pearl necklace worth a hundred thousand pieces of money, he sent it to Kisa Gotami. And great was her satisfaction at this, for she thought, "Prince Siddhattha has fallen in love with me, and has sent me a present."

And the future Buddha entered his palace in great splendour, and lay on his couch of state. And straightway richly dressed women, skilled in all manner of dance and song, and beautiful as celestial nymphs, gathered about him with all kinds of musical instruments, and with dance, song, and music they endeavoured to please him. But the future Buddha's aversion to passion did not allow him to take pleasure in the spectacle, and he fell into a brief slumber. And the women, exclaiming, "He for whose sake we should perform has fallen asleep. Of what use is it to weary ourselves any longer?" threw their various instruments on the ground, and lay down. And the lamps fed with sweet-smelling oil continued to burn. And the future Buddha awoke, and seating himself cross-legged on his couch, perceived these women lying asleep, with their musical instruments scattered about them on the floor,—some with their bodies wet with trickling phlegm and spittle; some grinding their teeth, and muttering and talking in their sleep; some with their mouths open; and some with their dress fallen apart so as plainly to disclose their loathsome nakedness. This great alteration in their appearance still further increased his aversion for sensual pleasures. To him that magnificent apartment, as splendid as the palace of Sakka, began to seem like a cemetery filled with dead bodies impaled and left to rot; and the three modes of existence appeared like houses all ablaze. And breathing forth the solemn utterance, "How oppressive and stifling is it all!" his mind turned ardently to retiring from the world. "It behoves me to go forth on the great retirement this very day," said he; and he arose from his couch, and coming near the door, called out,—

"Who's there?"

"Master, it is I, Channa," replied the courtier who had been sleeping with his head on the threshold.

"I wish to go forth on the great retirement to-day. Saddle a horse for me."

"Yes, sire." And taking saddle and bridle with him, the courtier started for the stable. There, by the light of lamps fed with sweet-smelling oils, he perceived the mighty steed Kanthaka in his pleasant quarters, under a canopy of cloth beautified with a pattern of jasmine flowers. "This is the one for me to saddle to-day," thought he; and he saddled Kanthaka.

"He is drawing the girth very tight," thought Kanthaka, whilst he was being saddled; "it is not at all as on other days, when I am saddled for rides in the park and the like. It must be that to-day my master wishes to issue forth on the great retirement." And in his delight he neighed a loud neigh. And that neigh would have spread through the whole town, had not the gods stopped the sound, and suffered no one to hear it.

Now the future Buddha, after he had sent Channa on his errand, thought to himself, "I will take just one look at my son"; and, rising from the couch on which he was sitting, he went to the suite of apartments occupied by the mother of Rahula, and opened the door of her chamber. Within the chamber was burning a lamp fed with sweet-smelling oil, and the mother of Rahula lay sleeping on a couch strewn deep with jasmine and other flowers, her hand resting on the head of her son. When the future Buddha reached the threshold, he paused, and gazed at the two from where he stood.

"If I were to raise my wife's hand from off the child's head, and take him up, she would awake, and thus prevent my departure. I will first become a Buddha, and then come back and see my son." So saying, he descended from the palace.

When the future Buddha had thus descended from the palace, he came near to his horse, and said,

"My dear Kanthaka, save me now this one night; and then, when thanks to you I have become a Buddha, I will save the world of gods and men." And thereupon he vaulted upon Kanthaka's back.

Now Kanthaka was eighteen cubits long from his neck to his tail, and of corresponding height; he was strong and swift, and white all over like a polished conch-shell. If he neighed or stamped, the sound was so loud as to spread through the whole city; therefore the gods exerted their power, and muffled the sound of his neighing, so that no one heard it; and at every step he took they placed the palms of their hands under his feet.

The future Buddha rode on the mighty back of the mighty steed, made Channa hold on by the tail, and so arrived at midnight at the great gate of the city.

Now the king, in order that the future Buddha should not at any time go out of the city without his knowledge, had caused each of the two leaves of the gate to be made so heavy as to need a thousand men to move it. But the future Buddha had a vigour and a strength that was equal, when reckoned in elephant-power, to the strength of ten thousand million elephants, and, reckoned in man-power, to the strength of a hundred thousand million men.

"If," thought he, "the gate does not open, I will straightway grip tight hold of Kanthaka with my thighs, and, seated as I am on Kanthaka's back, and with Channa holding on by the tail, I will leap up and carry them both with me over the wall, although its height be eighteen cubits."

"If," thought Channa, "the gate is not opened, I will place my master on my shoulder, and tucking Kanthaka under my arm by passing my right hand round him and under his belly, I will leap up and carry them both with me over the wall."

"If," thought Kanthaka, "the gate is not opened, with my master seated as he is on my back, and with Channa holding on by my tail, I will leap up and carry them both with me over the wall."

Now if the gate had not opened, verily one or another of these three persons would have accomplished that whereof he thought; but the divinity that inhabited the gate opened it for them.

At this moment came Mara, with the intention of persuading the future Buddha to turn back; and standing in the air, he said,

"Sir, go not forth! For on the seventh day from now the wheel of empire will appear to you, and you shall rule over the four great continents and their two thousand attendant isles. Sir, turn back!"

"Who are you?"

"I am Vasavatti."

"Mara, I knew that the wheel of empire was on the point of appearing to me; but I do not wish for sovereignty. I am about to cause the ten thousand worlds to thunder with my becoming a Buddha."

"I shall catch you," thought Mara, "the very first time you have a lustful, malicious, or unkind thought." And, like an ever-present shadow, he followed after, ever on the watch for some slip.

Advancing in this glory, the future Buddha in one night passed through three kingdoms, and at the end of thirty leagues he came to the river named Anoma.

And the future Buddha, stopping on the river-bank, said to Channa,

"What is the name of this river?"

"Sire, its name is Anoma (Illustrious)."

"And my retirement from the world shall also be called Anoma," replied the future Buddha. Saying this, he gave the signal to his horse with his heel; and the horse sprang over the river, which had a breadth of eight usabhas, and landed on the opposite bank. And the future Buddha, dismounting and standing on the sandy beach that stretched away like a sheet of silver, said to Channa,

"My good Channa, take these ornaments and Kanthaka and go home. I am about to retire from the world."

"Sire, I also will retire from the world."

Three times the future Buddha refused him, saying, "It is not for you to retire from the world. Go now!" and made him take the ornaments and Kanthaka.

And Channa did obeisance to the future Buddha; and keeping his right side towards him, he departed.

Buddha Is Instructed and Instructs

Then having left the weeping tear-faced Channa,—indifferent to all things in his longing for the forest, he by whom all objects are accomplished, overpowering the place by his beauty, entered a hermitage as if it were fully blessed. And the Brahmanas who had gone outside for the sake of fuel, having come with their hands full of fuel, flowers, and kusa grass,—pre-eminent as they were in penances, and proficients in wisdom, went to see him, and went not to their cells. Delighted, the peacocks uttered their cries, as if they had seen a dark-blue cloud rising up; and leaving the young grass and coming forward, the deer with restless eyes and the ascetics who grazed like deer stood still.

Then he, being duly honoured and invited to enter by those dwellers in the hermitage, paid his homage to the saints, with a voice like a cloud in the rainy season. He, the wise one, longing for liberation, traversed that hermitage filled with the holy company desirous of heaven,—gazing at their strange practices. He, the gentle one, having seen the different kinds of practices carried out by the ascetics in that sacred grove,—desiring to know the truth, thus addressed one of the ascetics who was following him:

"Since this to-day is my first sight of a hermitage I do not understand this rule of practice; therefore will your honour kindly explain to me what resolve possesses each one of you."

Then the Brahmana well-versed in practice told in order to that bull of the Sakyas, a very bull in prowess, all the various kinds of practice and the fruit thereof.

"Uncultivated food, growing out of the water, leaves, water, and roots and fruits,—this is the fare of the saints according to the sacred texts; but the different alternatives of practice vary. Some live like the birds on gleaned corn, others graze on grass like the deer, others live on air with the snakes, as if turned into ant-hills. Others win their nourishment with great effort from stones, others eat corn ground with their own teeth; some, having boiled for others, dress for themselves what may chance to be left. Others, with their tufts of matted hair continually wet with water, twice offer oblations to Agni with hymns; others plunging like fishes into the water dwell there with their bodies scratched by tortoises. By such penances endured for a time,—by the higher they attain heaven, by the lower the world of men; by the path of pain they eventually dwell in happiness,—pain, they say, is the root of merit."

The king's son, having heard this speech of the ascetic, even though he saw no lofty truth in it, was not content, but gently uttered these thoughts to himself:

"The practice is full of pain and of many kinds, and the fruit of the practice is mainly heaven at its best, and all the worlds are subject to change; verily the labour of the hermitages is spent for but little gain. Those who, abandoning wealth, kindred, and worldly objects, undertake vows for the sake of heaven,—they, when parted, only wish to go to a still greater wood of their own again. There is ever to living creatures fear from death, and they with all their efforts seek to be born again; where there is action, there must inevitably be death,—he is always drowned therein, just because he is afraid."

He spent several nights there, himself like the moon, examining their practices; and he departed from that practice-field, feeling that he had comprehended the whole nature of practice. The dwellers of the hermitage followed him with their minds fixed on the greatness of soul visible in his person, as if they were great seers beholding Religion herself, withdrawn from a land invaded by the base. Then he looked on all those ascetics with their matted hair, bark garments, and rag-strips waving, and he stood considering their practices under an auspicious and noble tree by the way-side.

Then the hermits having approached stood surrounding the best of men; and an old man from among them thus addressed him respectfully in a gentle voice:

"At thy coming the hermitage seems to have become full, it becomes as it were empty when thou art gone,—therefore, my son, thou wilt not surely desert it, as the loved life the body of one who wishes to live. Hast thou seen in this sacred grove one who neglects all ceremonies or who follows confused ceremonies or an outcast or one impure, that thou dost not desire to dwell here? Speak it out, and let the abode be welcomed."

He, the chief of the wise, when thus addressed in the midst of the ascetics by their chief—having resolved in his mind to put an end to all existence—thus uttered his inward thought:

"The upright-souled saints, the upholders of religion, become the very ideal of our own kindred through their delight in showing hospitality; by all these kind feelings of thine towards me affection is produced in me and the path which regards the Self as supreme is revealed. I seem to be all at once bathed by these gentle heart-touching words of thine, and the joy now throbs in me once more which I felt when I first grasped the idea of dharma. There is sorrow to me when I reflect that I shall have to depart, leaving you who are thus engaged, you who are such a refuge and who have shown such excessive kindness to me,—just as there was when I had to leave my kindred behind. But this devotion of yours is for the sake of heaven,—while my desire is that there may be no fresh birth; therefore I wish not to dwell in this wood; the nature of cessation is different from that of activity. It is not therefore any dislike on my part or the wrong conduct of another which makes me go away from this wood; for ye are all like great sages, standing fast in the religious duties which are in accordance with former ages."

Then having heard the prince's discourse, gracious and of deep meaning, gentle, strong, and full of dignity, the ascetics paid him especial honour. But a certain Brahmana who was lying there in the ashes, tall and wearing his hair in a tuft, and clothed in the bark of trees, with reddish eyes and a thin long nose, and carrying a pot with water in his hand, thus lifted his voice:

"With the nose of a well-fed horse, large long eyes, a red lower lip, white sharp teeth, and a thin red tongue,—this face of thine will drink up the entire ocean of what is to be known. That unfathomed depth which characterizes thee, that majesty and all those signs of thine,—they shall win a teacher's chair in the earth which was never won by sages even in a former age."

The prince replied, "Very well," and having saluted the company of sages he departed; the hermits also having duly performed to him all the rites of courtesy entered again into the ascetic-grove.

Sad Homecoming

Meanwhile the attendant of the horse, in deep distress, when his unselfish master thus went into the forest, made every effort in the road to dissolve his load of sorrow, and yet in spite of it all not a tear dropped from him. But the road which by his lord's command he had traversed in one night with that horse,—that same road he now travelled in eight days, pondering his lord's absence.

And the horse Kanthaka, though he still went on bravely, flagged and had lost all spirit in his heart; and decked though he was with ornaments, he had lost all his beauty when bereft of his master. And turning round towards that ascetic-grove, he neighed repeatedly with a mournful sound; and though pressed with hunger, he welcomed not nor tasted any grass or water on the road, as before.

Slowly they two at last came back to the city called after Kapila, which seemed empty when deserted by that hero who was bent on the salvation of the world,—like the sky bereft of the sun. Bright as it was with lotus-covered waters, adorned also with trees full of flowers, that garden of his, which was now like a forest, was no longer gay with citizens, who had lost all their gladness.

Then those two,—who were as it were silently forbidden by the sad inhabitants who were wandering in that direction, their brightness gone and their eyes dim with tears,—slowly entered the city which seemed all bathed in gloom.

And entering the royal stable, looking about with his eyes full of tears, Kanthaka uttered a loud sound, as if he were uttering his woe to the people. Then the birds that fed in the middle of the house, and the carefully cherished horses that were tied near by, re-echoed the sound of that horse, thinking that it might be the return of the prince.

And the people, deceived by an excessive joy, who were in the neighbourhood of the king's inner apartments, thought in their hearts, "Since the horse Kanthaka neighs, it must be that the prince is coming."

But when they saw Channa standing helpless, his eyes filled with tears, and the horse, the noble women wept with pale faces, like cows abandoned by the bull in the midst of the forest.

Gautami's Lament

Then the king's principal queen Gautami, like a fond cow that has lost her calf, fell bursting into tears on the ground with outstretched arms, like a golden plantain-tree with trembling leaves.

With her eyes filled with the tears of despondency, wretched like an osprey who has lost her young,—Gautami abandoning all self-control wailed aloud,—she fainted, and with a weeping face exclaimed:

"Beautiful, soft, black, and all in great waves, growing each from its own special root,—those hairs of his are tossed on the ground, worthy to be encircled by a royal diadem. With his long arms and lion-gait, his bull-like eye, and his beauty bright like gold, his broad chest, and his voice deep as a drum or a cloud,—should such a hero as this dwell in a hermitage?

"Those two feet of his, tender, with their beautiful web spread between the toes, with their ankles concealed, and soft like a blue lotus,—how can they, bearing a wheel marked in the middle, walk on the hard ground of the skirts of the forest? That body, which deserves to sit or lie on the roof of a palace,—honoured with costly garments, aloes, and sandal-wood,—how will that manly body live in the woods, exposed to the attacks of the cold, the heat, and the rain?

"He who was proud of his family, goodness, strength, energy, sacred learning, beauty, and youth,—who was ever ready to give, not to ask,—how will he go about begging alms from others?

"He who, lying on a spotless golden bed, was awakened during the night by the concert of musical instruments,—how alas! will he, my ascetic, sleep to-day on the bare ground with only one rag of cloth interposed?"

The Plaint of Yasodhara

Then thus spoke Yasodhara, shedding tears with deep sorrow, her bosom heaving with her sighs, her eyes discoloured with anger, and her voice choking with emotion through the influence of despondency:

"Leaving me helplessly asleep in the night, whither, O Channa, is he, the desire of my heart, gone? and when thou and Kanthaka are alone come back, while three went away together, my mind trembles.

"Why dost thou weep to-day, O cruel one, having done a dishonourable, pitiless, and unfriendly deed to me? Cease thy tears and be content in thy heart,—tears and that deed of thine ill agree. Through thee, his dear obedient faithful loyal companion, always doing what was right, the son of my lord is gone never to return,—rejoice,—all hail! thy pains have gained their end. Better for a man a wise enemy rather than a foolish friend unskilled in emergencies; by thee, the unwise self-styled friend, a great calamity has been brought upon this family.

"These women are sorely to be pitied who have put away their ornaments, having their eyes red and dimmed with continuous tears, who are as it were desolate widows, though their lord still stands as unshaken as the earth or Mount Himavat.

"And these lines of palaces seem to weep aloud, flinging up their dovecots for arms, with the long unbroken moan of their doves,—separated verily, with him, from all who could restrain them.

"Even that horse Kanthaka without doubt desired my utter ruin; for he bore away from hence my treasure when all were sound asleep in the night,—like one who steals jewels. When he was able to bear even the onsets of arrows, and still more the strokes of whips,—how then for fear of the fall of a whip could he go carrying with him my prosperity and my heart together? The base creature now neighs loudly, filling the king's palace with the sound; but when he carried away my beloved, then this vilest of horses was dumb. If he had neighed and so woke up the people, or had even made a noise with his hoofs on the ground, or had made the loudest sound he could with his jaws, my grief would not have been so great."

Then Yasodhara fell upon the ground, like the ruddy goose parted from her mate, and in utter bewilderment she slowly lamented, with her voice repeatedly stopped by sobs:

"If he wishes to practise a religious life after abandoning me his lawful wife widowed,—where is his religion, who wishes to follow practices without his lawful wife to share them with him? He surely has never heard of the monarchs of olden times, his own ancestors, Mahasudarsa and the rest,—how they went with their wives into the forest,—that he thus wishes to follow a religious life without me. He does not see that husband and wife are both consecrated in sacrifices, and both purified by the performance of the rites of the Veda, and both destined to enjoy the same results afterwards,—he therefore grudges me a share in his merit.

"Surely it must be that this fond lover of religion, knowing that my mind was secretly quarrelling even with my beloved, lightly and without fear has deserted me thus angry, in the hope to obtain heavenly nymphs in Indra's world!

"But what kind of a thought is this of mine? those women even there have the attributes which belong to bodies,—for whose sake he thus practises austerities in the forest, deserting his royal magnificence and my fond devotion.

"I have no such longing for the joy of heaven, nor is that hard for even common people to win if they are resolute; but my one desire is how he my beloved may never leave me either in this world or the next.

"Even if I am unworthy to look on my husband's face with its long eyes and bright smile, still is this poor Rahula never to roll about in his father's lap? Alas! the mind of that wise hero is terribly stern,—gentle as his beauty seems, it is pitilessly cruel,—who can desert of his own accord such an infant son with his inarticulate talk, one who would charm even an enemy.

"My heart too is certainly most stern, yea, made of rock or fashioned even of iron, which does not break when its lord is gone to the forest, deserted by his royal glory like an orphan,—he so well worthy of happiness."

The Firm Resolve

Then on the pure bank of the Nairangana the saint whose every effort was pure fixed his dwelling, bent as he was on a lonely habitation.

Five mendicants, desiring liberation, came up to him when they beheld him there, just as the objects of the senses come up to a percipient who has gained wealth and health by his previous merit.

Being honoured by these disciples who were dwelling in that family, as they bowed reverently with their bodies bent low in humility, as the mind is honoured by the restless senses, and thinking, "This may be the means of abolishing birth and death," he at once commenced a series of difficult austerities by fasting.

For six years, vainly trying to attain merit, he practised self-mortification, performing many rules of abstinence, hard for a man to carry out. At the hours for eating, he, longing to cross the world whose farther shore is so difficult to reach, interrupted his fast with single jujube fruits, sesame seeds, and rice. Having only skin and bone remaining, with his fat, flesh and blood entirely wasted, yet, though diminished, he still shone with undiminished grandeur like the ocean.

Then the seer, having his body evidently emaciated to no purpose in a cruel self-mortification,—dreading continued existence, thus reflected in his longing to become a Buddha: "This is not the way to passionlessness, nor to perfect knowledge, nor to liberation; that was certainly the true way which I found at the root of the Jambu tree. But that cannot be attained by one who has lost his strength,"—so resuming his care for his body, he next pondered thus, how best to increase his bodily vigour:

"Wearied with hunger, thirst, and fatigue, with his mind no longer self-possessed through fatigue, how should one who is not absolutely calm reach the end which is to be attained by his mind? True calm is properly obtained by the constant satisfaction of the senses; the mind's self-possession is only obtained by the senses' being perfectly satisfied. True meditation is produced in him whose mind is self-possessed and at rest,—to him whose thoughts are engaged in meditation the exercise of perfect contemplation begins at once. By contemplation are obtained those conditions through which is eventually gained that supreme calm, undecaying, immortal state, which is so hard to be reached."

Having thus resolved, "This means is based upon eating food," the wise seer of unbounded wisdom, having made up his mind to accept the continuance of life, and having bathed, thin as he was, slowly came up the bank of the Nairangana, supported as by a hand by the trees on the shore, which bent down the ends of their branches in adoration.

Now at that time Nandabala, the daughter of the leader of the herds-men, impelled by the gods, with a sudden joy risen in her heart, had just come near, her arm gay with a white shell, and wearing a dark blue woollen cloth, like the river Yamuna, with its dark blue water and its wreath of foam. She, having her joy increased by her faith, with her lotus-like eyes opened wide, bowed down before him and persuaded him to take some milk. By partaking that food, having made her obtain the full reward of her birth, he himself became capable of gaining the highest knowledge, all his six senses being now satisfied.

The seer, having his body now fully robust, together with his glorious fame, one beauty and one majesty being equally spread in both, shone like the ocean and the moon.

Thinking that he had returned to the world, the five mendicants left him, as the five elements leave the wise soul when it is liberated. Accompanied only by his own resolve, having fixed his mind on the attainment of perfect knowledge, he went to the root of an Asvattha tree, where the surface of the ground was covered with young grass. Then he sat down on his hams in a posture, immovably firm and with his limbs gathered into a mass like a sleeping serpent's hood, exclaiming, "I will not rise from this position on the earth until I have obtained my utmost aim."

Then the dwellers in heaven burst into unequalled joy; the herds of beasts and the birds uttered no cry; the trees moved by the wind made no sound, when the holy one took his seat firm in his resolve.

Assault by Mara

When the great sage, sprung from a line of royal sages, sat down there with his soul fully resolved to obtain the highest knowledge, the whole world rejoiced; but Mara, the enemy of the good law, was afraid. He whom they call in the world Kamadeva, the owner of the various weapons, the flower-arrowed, the lord of the course of desire,—it is he whom they also style Mara the enemy of liberation. His three sons, Confusion, Gaiety, and Pride, and his three daughters, Lust, Delight, and Thirst, asked of him the reason of his despondency, and he thus made answer unto them:

"This sage, wearing the armour of resolution, and having drawn the arrow of wisdom with the barb of truth, sits yonder intending to conquer my realms,—hence is this despondency of my mind. If he succeeds in overcoming me and proclaims to the world the path of final bliss, all this my realm will to-day become empty, as did that of the disembodied lord when he violated the rules of his station. While, therefore, he stands within my reach and while his spiritual eyesight is not yet attained, I will assail him to break his vow as the swollen might of a river assails a dam."

Then having seized his flower-made bow and his five infatuating arrows, he drew near to the root of the Asvattha tree with his children, he the great disturber of the minds of living beings. Having fixed his left hand on the end of the barb and playing with the arrow, Mara thus addressed the calm seer as he sat on his seat, preparing to cross to the further side of the ocean of existence:

"Up, up, O thou Kshatriya, afraid of death! follow thine own duty and abandon this law of liberation! and having conquered the lower worlds by thy arrows, proceed to gain the higher worlds of Indra. That is a glorious path to travel, which has been followed by former leaders of men; this mendicant life is ill-suited for one born in the noble family

of a royal sage to follow. But if thou wilt not rise, strong in thy purpose,—then be firm if thou wilt and quit not thy resolve,—this arrow is
uplifted by me,—it is the very one which was shot against Suryaka, the
enemy of the fish. So too, I think, when somewhat probed by this
weapon, even the son of Ida, the grandson of the moon, became mad;
and Samtanu also lost his self-control,—how much more then one of
feebler powers now that the age has grown degenerate? Therefore
quickly rise up and come to thyself,—for this arrow is ready, darting out
its tongue, which I do not launch even against the kakravaka birds, tenderly attached as they are and well deserving the name of lovers."

But when, even though thus addressed, the Sakya saint unheeding did
not change his posture, then Mara discharged his arrow at him, setting
in front of him his daughters and his sons.

But even when that arrow was shot he gave no heed and swerved not
from his firmness; and Mara, beholding him thus, sank down, and slowly
thus spoke, full of thought: "He is not worthy of my flower-shaft, nor
my arrow 'gladdener,' nor the sending of my daughter Rati to tempt
him; he deserves the alarms and rebukes and blows from all the gathered
hosts of the demons."

Then Mara called to mind his own army, wishing to work the overthrow of the Sakya saint; and his followers swarmed round, wearing
different forms and carrying arrows, trees, darts, clubs, and swords in
their hands; having the faces of boars, fishes, horses, asses, and camels,
of tigers, bears, lions, and elephants,—one-eyed, many-faced, three-
headed,—with protuberant bellies and speckled bellies; blended with
goats, with knees swollen like pots, armed with tusks and with claws,
carrying headless trunks in their hands, and assuming many forms, with
half-mutilated faces, and with monstrous mouths; copper-red, covered
with red spots, bearing clubs in their hands, with yellow or smoke-
coloured hair, with wreaths dangling down, with long pendulous ears
like elephants, clothed in leather or wearing no clothes at all; having
half their faces white or half their bodies green,—red and smoke-col-
oured, yellow and black,—with arms reaching out longer than a serpent, and with girdles jingling with rattling bells; with dishevelled hair,
or with topknots, or half-bald, with rope-garments or with head-dress all
in confusion,—with triumphant faces or frowning faces,—wasting the
strength or fascinating the mind.

Some as they went leaped about wildly, others danced upon one another, some sported about in the sky, others went along on the tops of the trees. One danced, shaking a trident, another made a crash, dragging a club, another bounded for joy like a bull, another blazed out flames from every hair. Such were the troops of demons who encircled the root of the Bodhi tree on every side, eager to seize it and to destroy it, awaiting the command of their lord.

But the great sage having beheld that army of Mara thus engaged in an attack on the knower of the law, remained untroubled and suffered no perturbation, like a lion seated in the midst of oxen.

Then Mara commanded his excited army of demons to terrify him; and forthwith that host resolved to break down his determination with their various powers. Some with many tongues hanging out and shaking, with sharp-pointed savage teeth and eyes like the disk of the sun, with wide-yawning mouths and upright ears like spikes,—they stood round trying to frighten him. Before these monsters standing there, so dreadful in form and disposition, the great sage remained unalarmed and untroubled, sporting with them as if they had been only rude children.

Then some being of invisible shape, but of pre-eminent glory, standing in the heavens,—beholding Mara thus malevolent against the seer,— addressed him in a loud voice, unruffled by enmity:

"Take not on thyself, O Mara, this vain fatigue,—throw aside thy malevolence and retire to peace; this sage cannot be shaken by thee any more than the mighty mountain Meru by the wind. Even fire might lose its hot nature, water its fluidity, earth its steadiness, but never will he abandon his resolution, who has acquired his merit by a long course of actions through unnumbered æons. Such is that purpose of his, that heroic effort, that glorious strength, that compassion for all beings,— until he attains the highest wisdom, he will never rise from his seat, just as the sun does not rise, without dispelling the darkness.

"Pitying the world lying distressed amidst diseases and passions, he, the great physician, ought not to be hindered, who undergoes all his labours for the sake of the remedy knowledge. He who toilsomely pursues the one good path, when all the world is carried away in devious tracks,—he the guide should not be disturbed, like a right informant when the caravan has lost its way. He who is made a lamp of knowledge when all beings are lost in the great darkness,—it is not for a right-minded soul to try to quench him,—like a lamp kindled in the gloom of night. He who, when he beholds the world drowned in the great flood of existence and unable to reach the further shore, strives to bring them safely across,—would any right-minded soul offer him wrong? The tree of knowledge, whose roots go deep in firmness, and whose fibres are patience,—whose flowers are moral actions and whose branches are memory and thought,—and which gives out the law as its fruit,—surely when it is growing it should not be cut down.

"To-day is the appointed period of all those actions which have been performed by him for the sake of knowledge,—he is now seated on this seat just as all the previous saints have sat. This is the navel of the earth's surface, endued with all the highest glory; there is no other spot of the earth than this,—the home of contemplation, the realm of well-being. Give not way, then, to grief, but put on calm; let not thy greatness, O Mara, be mixed with pride; it is not well to be confident,—fortune is unstable,—why dost thou accept a position on a tottering base?"

Having listened to these words, and having seen the unshaken firmness of the great saint, Mara departed dispirited and broken in purpose with those very arrows by which, O world, thou art smitten in thy heart.

Attainment of Knowledge

Thus he, the holy one, sitting there on his seat of grass at the root of the tree, pondering, by his own efforts attained at last perfect knowledge. Then bursting the shell of ignorance, having gained all the various kinds of perfect intuition, he attained all the partial knowledge of alternatives which is included in perfect knowledge. He became the perfectly wise, the Bhagavat, the Arhat, the king of the law, the Tathagata, he who has attained the knowledge of all forms, the lord of all science.

Having beheld all this, the spirits standing in heaven spoke one to another, "Strew flowers on this all-wise monarch of saints." While other immortals exclaimed, who knew the course of action of the greatest among the former saints, "Do not now strew flowers,—no reason for it has been shown."

Then the Buddha, mounted on a throne, up in the air to the height of seven palm-trees, addressed all those Nirmita Bodhisattvas, illumining their minds,

"Ho! ho! listen ye to the words of me who have now attained perfect knowledge; everything is achieved by meritorious works, therefore as long as existence lasts acquire merit. Since I ever acted as liberal, pure-hearted, patient, skilful, devoted to meditation and wisdom,—by these meritorious works I became a Bodhisattva. After accomplishing in due order the entire round of the preliminaries of perfect wisdom,—I have now attained that highest wisdom and I am become the all-wise Arhat and Jaina. My aspiration is thus fulfilled; this birth of mine has borne its fruit; the blessed and immortal knowledge which was attained by former Buddhas is now mine. As they through the good law achieved the wel-fare of all beings, so also have I; all my sins are abolished, I am the destroyer of all pains. Possessing a soul now of perfect purity, I urge all living beings to seek the abolition of worldly existence through the lamps of the law." Having worshipped him as he thus addressed them, those sons of the Jainas disappeared.

The gods then with exultation paid him worship and adoration with divine flowers; and all the world, when the great saint had become all-wise, was full of brightness.

Then the holy one descended and stood on his throne under the tree; there he passed seven days filled with the thought, "I have here attained perfect wisdom."

When the Bodhisattva had thus attained perfect knowledge, all beings became full of great happiness; and all the different universes were illu-mined by a great light. The happy earth shook in six different ways like an overjoyed woman, and the Bodhisattvas, each dwelling in his own special abode, assembled and praised him.

The Aliment of Joy

Daily praised by all the various heavenly beings, the perfectly wise one thus passed that period of seven days which is designated "the aliment of joy." He then passed the second week, while he was bathed with jarfuls of water by the heavenly beings, the Bodhisattvas and the rest. Then hav-ing bathed in the four oceans and being seated on his throne, he passed the third week restraining his eyes from seeing. In the fourth week, assuming many forms, he stood triumphant on his throne, having deliv-ered a being who was ready to be converted.

Then Mara, utterly despondent in soul, thus addressed the Tathagata, "O holy one, be pleased to enter Nirvana, thy desires are accomplished."

"I will first establish in perfect wisdom worlds as numerous as the sand, and then I will enter Nirvana," thus did the Buddha reply, and with a shriek Mara went to his home.

The Great Ministry Begins

Then seated under a palm-tree the holy one pondered: "The profound wisdom so hard to be understood is now known by me. These sin-defiled worlds understand not this most excellent law, and the unenlightened shamelessly censure both me and my wisdom. Shall I proclaim the law? It is only produced by knowledge; having attained it thus in my lonely pondering, do I feel strong enough to deliver the world?" Having remembered all that he had heard before, he again pondered; and resolving, "I will explain it for the sake of delivering the world," Buddha, the chief of saints, absorbed in contemplation, shone forth, arousing the world, having emitted in the darkness of the night a light from the tuft of hair between his eyebrows.

Then Buddha set out to go joyfully to Benares, manifesting as he went the manifold supernatural course of life of Magadha. Having made a mendicant whom he met happy in the path of those who are illustrious through the law, the glorious one went on, illumining the country which lies to the north of Gaya. Having stayed in the dwelling of the prince of the Nagas, named Sudarsana, on the occurrence of night, he ate a morning meal consisting of the five kinds of ambrosia, and departed, gladdening him with his blessing. Near Vanara he went under the shadow of a tree and there he established a poor Brahmana named Nandin in sacred knowledge.

In Vanara in a householder's dwelling he was lodged for the night; in the morning he partook of some milk and departed, having given his blessing. In the village called Vumdadvira he lodged in the abode of a Yaksha named Vumda, and in the morning after taking some milk and giving his blessing he departed.

Having delivered various beings in every place, the compassionate saint journeyed on to Gandhapura and was worshipped there by the Yaksha Gandha.

When he arrived at the city Sarathi, the citizens volunteered to be charioteers in his service; thence he came to the Ganges, and he bade the ferryman cross. "Good man, convey me across the Ganges, may the seven blessings be thine." "I carry no one across unless he pays the fee." "I have nothing, what shall I give?" So saying he went through the sky like the king of birds; and from that time Bimbisara abolished the ferry-fee for all ascetics.

The next day at the end of the second watch, having gone his begging round collecting alms, he, the unequalled one, like Hari, proceeded to the Deer Park.

The five disciples united in a worthy society, when they beheld him, said to one another, "This is Gotama who has come hither, the ascetic who has abandoned his self-control. He wanders about now, greedy, of impure soul, unstable, and with his senses under no firm control, devoted to inquiries regarding the frying-pan. We will not ask after his health, nor rise to meet him, nor address him, nor offer him a welcome, nor a seat, nor bid him enter into our dwelling."

Having understood their agreement, with a smiling countenance, spreading light all around, Buddha advanced gradually nearer, holding his staff and his begging-pot. Forgetful of their agreement, the five friends, under his constraining majesty, rose up like birds in their cages when scorched by fire. Having taken his begging-bowl and staff, they gave him an arghya, and water for washing his feet and rinsing his mouth; and bowing reverentially they said to him, "Honoured Sir, health to thee."

"Health in every respect is ours,—that wisdom has been attained which is so hard to be won," so saying, the holy one thus spoke to the five worthy associates: "But address me not as 'Worthy Sir,'—know that I am a Jaina,—I have come to give the first wheel of the law to you. Receive initiation from me,—ye shall obtain the place of Nirvana."

Then the five, pure in heart, begged leave to undertake his vow of a religious life; and the Buddha, touching their heads, received them into the mendicant order. Then at the mendicants' respectful request the chief of saints bathed in the tank, and after eating ambrosia he reflected on the field of the law.

The Foundation of the Kingdom of Righteousness

(The first sermon ascribed to Gotama Buddha)

And the Blessed One thus addressed the five monks: "There are two extremes, monks, which he who has given up the world, ought to avoid.

"What are these two extremes? A life given to pleasures, devoted to pleasures and lusts; this is degrading, sensual, vulgar, ignoble, and profitless.

"And a life given to mortifications; this is painful, ignoble, and profitless.

"By avoiding these two extremes, monks, the Tathagata has gained the knowledge of the middle path which leads to insight, which leads to wisdom, which conduces to calm, to knowledge, to Sambodhi (supreme enlightenment), to Nirvana.

"Which, monks, is this middle path the knowledge of which the Tathagata has gained, which leads to insight, which leads to wisdom, which conduces to calm, to knowledge, to Sambodhi, to Nirvana?

"It is the noble eightfold path, namely: right views, right intent, right speech, right conduct, right means of livelihood, right endeavour, right mindfulness, right meditation.

"This, monks, is the middle path the knowledge of which the Tathagata has gained, which leads to insight, which leads to wisdom, which conduces to calm, to knowledge, to perfect enlightenment, to Nirvana.

"This, monks, is the noble truth of suffering: birth is suffering; decay is suffering; death is suffering; presence of objects we hate, is suffering; separation from objects we love, is suffering; not to obtain what we desire, is suffering.

"In brief, the five aggregates which spring from grasping, they are painful.

"This, monks, is the noble truth concerning the origin of suffering: verily it originates in that craving which causes the renewal of becomings, is accompanied by sensual delight, and seeks satisfaction now here, now there; that is to say, craving for pleasures, craving for becoming, craving for not becoming.

"This, monks, is the noble truth concerning the cessation of suffering.

Verily, it is passionlessness, cessation without remainder of this very craving; the laying aside of, the giving up, the being free from, the harbouring no longer of, this craving.

"This, monks, is the noble truth concerning the path which leads to the cessation of suffering. Verily, it is this noble eightfold path, that is to say, right views, right intent, right speech, right conduct, right means of livelihood, right endeavour, right mindfulness and right meditation.

"As long, monks, as I did not possess with perfect purity this true knowledge and insight into these four noble truths, with its three modifications and its twelve constituent parts, so long, monks, I knew that I had not yet obtained the highest absolute enlightenment in the world of men and gods, in Mara's and in Brahma's world, among all beings, samanas, and brahmanas, gods and men.

"But when I possessed, monks, with perfect purity this true knowledge and insight into these four noble truths, with its three modifications and its twelve constituent parts, then I knew, monks, that I had obtained the highest, universal enlightenment in the world of men and gods, in Mara's and in Brahma's world, among all beings, samanas, and brahmanas, gods and men.

"And this knowledge and insight arose in my mind: 'The emancipation of my mind cannot be shaken; this is my last birth; now shall I not be born again.' "

Thus the Blessed One spoke. The five monks were delighted, and they rejoiced at the words of the Blessed One. And when this exposition was propounded, the venerable Kondanna obtained the pure and spotless dhamma-eye (that is to say, the following knowledge): "Whatsoever is an arising thing, all that is a ceasing thing."

And as the Blessed One had set going the wheel of the dhamma, the earth-inhabiting devas shouted: "Truly the Blessed One has set going at Benares, in the deer park Isipatana, the wheel of the dhamma, which may be opposed neither by a samana, nor by a brahmana, neither by a deva, nor by Mara, nor by Brahma, nor by any being in the world."

Hearing the shout of the earth-inhabiting devas, the four firmament-devas shouted. . . . Hearing their shout the Tavatimsa devas, . . . the Yama devas, . . . the Tusita devas, . . . the Nimmanarati devas, . . . the Paranimmitavasavatti devas, . . . the Brahma-world devas shouted: "Truly the Blessed One has set going at Benares, in the deer park Isipatana, the wheel of the dhamma, which may be opposed neither by a samana nor by a brahmana, neither by a deva, nor by Mara, nor by Brahma, nor by any being in the world."

Thus in that moment, in that instant, in that second, the shout reached the Brahma world; and this whole system of ten thousand worlds quaked, was shaken, and trembled; and an infinite, mighty light was seen through the world, which surpassed the light that can be produced by the divine power of the devas.

Return

Making millions of ascetics, disciples, Arhats, sages, mendicants, and fasters,—and delivering from their ills the blind, the humpbacked, the lame, the insane, the maimed as well as the destitute,—and having established many persons of the fourth caste in the true activity and inaction and in the three yanas, with the four samgrahas and the eight amgas,— going on from place to place, delivering, and confirming the Bhikkhus, in the twelfth year he went to his own city.

Day by day confirming the Bhikkhus, and providing food for the congregation, in an auspicious moment he made a journey to Lumbini with the Bhikkhus and the citizens, Brahma and Rudra being at their head, with great triumph and noise of musical instruments. There he saw the holy fig-tree and he stood by it remembering his birth, with a smile; and rays of light streamed from his mouth and went forth illumining the earth; and he uttered a discourse to the goddess of the wood, giving her the serenity of faith.

Having come to the Lumbini fig-tree he spoke to Paurvika the daughter of Rahula, and Gopika the daughter of Maitra, and his own Saudhani Kausika; and he uttered an affectionate discourse honouring his mother by the tank Vasatya; then speaking with Ekasamgi the daughter of Mahakautuka and Sautasomi in the wood Nigrodha, he received into the community some members of his own family, headed by Sundarananda, and one hundred and seven citizens.

Having declared the glory of the law of Buddha, he built a round stupa and gave a royal coronation to Saunu, sending him into the wood pre-eminent with the holiest saints and Kaityas, and bidding him worship the sacred relics; and commanded Rahula, Gautami, and the other women led by Gopika, with staves in their hands, as shaven ascetics, to practise the vow of fasting called ahoratra, and after that the laksha-kaitya ceremony and then the rite called sringabheri, and that called vasumdharika.

After displaying miracles in the city of Kapila, and having paid honour to his father, and having made Rahula and his companions Arhats, and also the Bhikkhunis with Gautami and Gopika at their head, and various women of all the four castes; and having established Saunu on his imperial throne, and the people in the Jaina doctrine, and having abolished poverty and darkness, and then remembering his mother, he set forth, after worshipping Svayambhu, towards the northern region with Brahma, Vishnu, and Siva as mendicants in his train.

The Buddha's Daily Habits

Habits are of two kinds, the profitable, and the unprofitable. Of these, the unprofitable habits of the Blessed One had been extirpated by his attainment of saintship at the time he sat cross-legged under the Bo-tree. Profitable habits, however, remained to the Blessed One.

These were fivefold: his habits before eating; his habits after eating; his habits of the first part of the afternoon; his habits of the middle part of the afternoon; his habits of the last part of the afternoon.

His habits before eating were as follows:

The Blessed One would rise early in the morning, and when, out of kindness to his body-servant and for the sake of bodily comfort, he had rinsed his mouth and otherwise cared for his person, he would sit retired until it was time to go begging. And when it came time, he would put on his tunic, girdle, and robes, and taking his bowl, he would enter the village or the town for alms. Sometimes he went alone, sometimes sur-rounded by a congregation of priests; sometimes without anything especial happening, sometimes with the accompaniment of many prodigies.

While, namely, the Lord of the World is entering for alms, gentle winds clear the ground before him; the clouds let fall drops of water to lay the dust in his pathway, and then become a canopy over him; other winds bring flowers and scatter them in his path; elevations of ground depress themselves, and depressions elevate themselves; wherever he places his foot, the ground is even and pleasant to walk upon, or lotus-flowers receive his tread. No sooner has he set his right foot within the city-gate than the rays of six different colours which issue from his body race hither and thither over palaces and pagodas, and deck them, as it were, with the yellow sheen of gold, or with the colours of a painting. The elephants, the horses, the birds, and other animals give forth melodious sounds; likewise the tom-toms, lutes, and other musical instruments, and the ornaments worn by the people.

By these tokens the people would know, "The Blessed One has now entered for alms"; and in their best tunics and best robes, with perfumes, flowers, and other offerings, would issue forth from their houses into the street. Then, having zealously paid homage to the Blessed One with the perfumes, flowers, and other offerings, and done him obeisance, some would implore him, "Reverend Sir, give us ten priests to feed"; some, "Give us twenty"; and some, "Give us a hundred priests." And they would take the bowl of the Blessed One, and prepare a seat for him, and zealously show their reverence for him by placing food in the bowl.

When he had finished his meal, the Blessed One, with due consideration for the different dispositions of their minds, would so teach them the doctrine that some would become established in the refuges, some in the five precepts, some would become converted, some would attain to the fruit of either once returning, or of never returning, while some would become established in the highest fruit, that of saintship, and would retire from the world. Having shown this kindness to the multitude, he would rise from his seat, and return to the monastery.

On his arrival there, he would take his seat in a pavilion, on the excellent Buddha-mat which had been spread for him, where he would wait for the priests to finish their meal. When the priests had finished their meal, the body-servant would announce the fact to the Blessed One. Then the Blessed One would enter the perfumed chamber.

These, then, were his habits before eating.

Then the Blessed One, having thus finished his duties before eating, would first sit in the perfumed chamber, on a seat that had been spread for him by his body-servant, and would wash his feet. Then, taking up his stand on the landing of the jewelled staircase which led to the perfumed chamber, he would exhort the congregation of the priests, saying,

"O priests, diligently work out your salvation; for not often occur the appearance of a Buddha in the world and existence among men and the propitious moment and retirement from the world and the opportunity to hear the true doctrine."

At this point some would ask the Blessed One for exercises in meditation, and the Blessed One would assign them exercises suited to their several characters. Then all would do obeisance to the Blessed One, and go to the places where they were in the habit of spending the night or the day—some to the forest, some to the foot of trees, some to the hills, and so on, some to the heaven of the four great kings, . . . and some to Vasavatti's heaven.

Then the Blessed One, entering the perfumed chamber, would, if he wished, lie down for a while, mindful and conscious, and on his right side after the manner of a lion. And secondly, his body being now refreshed, he would rise, and gaze over the world. And thirdly, the people of the village or town near which he might be dwelling, who had given him breakfast, would assemble after breakfast at the monastery, again in their best tunics and their best robes, and with perfumes, flowers, and other offerings.

Thereupon the Blessed One, when his audience had assembled, would approach in such miraculous manner as was fitting; and taking his seat in the lecture-hall, on the excellent Buddha-mat which had been spread for him, he would teach the doctrine, as suited the time and occasion. And when he perceived it was time, he would dismiss the audience, and the people would do obeisance to the Blessed One, and depart.

These were his habits after eating.

When he had thus finished his duties after eating, he would rise from the excellent Buddha-seat, and if he desired to bathe, he would enter the bathhouse, and cool his limbs with water made ready by his body-servant. Then the body-servant would fetch the Buddha-seat, and spread it in the perfumed chamber. And the Blessed One, putting on a tunic of double red cloth, and binding on his girdle, and throwing his upper robe over his right shoulder, would go thither and sit down, and for a while remain solitary, and plunged in meditation. After that would come the priests from here and from there to wait on the Blessed One. And some would propound questions, some would ask for exercises in meditation, and some for a sermon; and in granting their desires the Blessed One would complete the first part of the afternoon.

And now, when the Blessed One had finished his duties of the first part of the afternoon, and when the priests had done him obeisance and were departing, the deities throughout the entire system of ten thousand worlds would seize the opportunity to draw near to the Blessed One and ask him any questions that might occur to them, even such as were but four syllables long. And the Blessed One in answering their questions would complete the middle part of the afternoon.

These were his habits of the middle part of the afternoon.

The last part of the afternoon he would divide into three parts, and as his body would be tired from so much sitting since the morning, he would spend one part in pacing up and down to free himself from the discomfort. In the second part he would enter the perfumed chamber, and would lie down mindful and conscious, and on his right side after the manner of a lion. In the third part he would rise, and taking his seat, he would gaze over the world with the eye of a Buddha, in order to discover any individual who, under some former Buddha, with alms-giving, or keeping the precepts, or other meritorious deeds, might have made the earnest wish.

These were his habits of the last part of the afternoon.

The Gift of Ambapali

Now the courtesan Ambapali heard that the Exalted One had arrived at Vesali, and was staying there at her mango grove. And ordering a number of state vehicles to be made ready, she mounted one of them, and went forth with her train from Vesali towards her garden. She went in the carriage as far as the ground was passable for carriages; there she alighted; and she proceeded on foot to the place where the Exalted One was, and took her seat respectfully on one side. And when she was thus seated the Exalted One instructed, aroused, incited, and gladdened her with religious discourse.

Then she—instructed, aroused, incited, and gladdened with his words—addressed the Exalted One, and said:

"May the Exalted One do me the honour of taking his meal, together with the brethren, at my house to-morrow?"

And the Exalted One gave, by silence, his consent. Then when Ambapali the courtesan saw that the Exalted One had consented, she rose from her seat and bowed down before him, and keeping him on her right hand as she passed him, she departed thence.

And at the end of the night Ambapali the courtesan made ready in her mansion sweet rice and cakes, and announced the time to the Exalted One, saying: "The hour, lord, has come, and the meal is ready!"

And the Exalted One, who had dressed himself early in the morning, took his bowl, and his robe, and went with the brethren to the place where Ambapali's mansion was: and when he had come there he seated himself on the seat prepared for him. And Ambapali the courtesan set the sweet rice and cakes before the Order, with the Buddha at their head, and waited upon them till they refused any more.

And when the Blessed One had quite finished his meal, and had cleansed the bowl and his hands, the courtesan had a low stool brought, and sat down at his side, and addressed the Exalted One, and said: "Lord, I present this pleasance to the order of mendicants, of which the Buddha is the chief." And the Exalted One accepted the gift; and after instructing, and rousing, and inciting, and gladdening her with religious discourse, he rose from his seat and departed thence.

Hold Fast to the Truth

Now when the Exalted One had remained so long as he wished at Ambapali's grove, he addressed Ananda, and said: "Come, Ananda, let us go on to Beluva."

"So be it, lord," said Ananda, in assent, to the Exalted One.

Then the Exalted One proceeded, with a great company of the brethren, to Beluva, and there the Exalted One stayed in the village itself.

Now the Exalted One there addressed the brethren, and said: "O mendicants, do you take up your abode round about Vesali, each according to the place where his friends, acquaintances, and intimates may live, for the retreat in the rainy season. I shall enter upon the rainy season here at Beluva."

"So be it, lord!" said those brethren, in assent, to the Exalted One. And they entered upon the rainy season round about Vesali, each according to the place where his friends, acquaintances, and intimates lived: whilst the Exalted One stayed even there at Beluva.

Now when the Exalted One had thus entered upon the rainy season, there fell upon him a dire sickness, and sharp pains came upon him, even unto death. But the Exalted One, mindful and self-possessed, bore them without complaint.

Then this thought occurred to the Exalted One: "It would not be right for me to pass away without addressing the disciples, without taking leave of the Order. Let me now, by a strong effort of the will, bend this sickness down again, and keep my hold on life till the allotted time be come."

And the Exalted One, by a strong effort of the will, bent that sickness down again, and kept his hold on life till the time he fixed upon should come. And the sickness abated upon him.

Now very soon after the Blessed One began to recover. And when he had quite got rid of the sickness, he came out from his lodging, and sat down in the shadow thereof on a seat spread out there. And the venerable Ananda went to the place where the Exalted One was, and saluted him, and took a seat respectfully on one side, and addressed the Exalted One, and said: "I have beheld, lord, how the Exalted One was in health, and I have beheld how the Exalted One had to suffer. And though at the sight of the sickness of the Exalted One my body became weak as a creeper, and the horizon became dim to me, and my faculties were no longer clear, yet notwithstanding I took some little comfort from the thought that the Exalted One would not pass away until at least he had left instructions as touching the Order."

"What, then, Ananda? Does the Order expect that of me? I have preached the truth without making any distinction between exoteric and esoteric doctrine; for in respect of the truths, Ananda, the Tathagata has no such thing as the closed fist of a teacher, who keeps some things back. Surely, Ananda, should there be any one who harbours the thought, 'It is I who will lead the brotherhood,' or, 'The Order is dependent upon me,' it is he who should lay down instructions in any matter concerning the Order. Now the Tathagata, Ananda, thinks not that it is he who should lead the brotherhood, or that the Order is dependent upon him. Why then should he leave instructions in any matter concerning the Order? I too, O Ananda, am now grown old, and full of years, my journey is drawing to its close, I have reached my sum of days, I am turning eighty years of age; and just as a worn-out cart, Ananda, can be kept going only with the help of thongs, so, methinks, the body of the Tathagata can only be kept going by bandaging it up. It is only, Ananda, when the

Tathagata, by ceasing to attend to any outward thing, becomes plunged by the cessation of any separate sensation in that concentration of heart which is concerned with no material object—it is only then that the body of the Tathagata is at ease.

"Therefore, O Ananda, live as having the Self as lamp. Live as having the Self as refuge, and no other. Live as having Dhamma as lamp. Live as having Dhamma as refuge, and no other. And how, Ananda, is one to live having the Self as lamp, having the Self as refuge, as having no other refuge? How is one to live having Dhamma as lamp, having Dhamma as refuge, as having no other refuge?

"Herein, Ananda, a brother continues living, as to the body, so to look upon the body that he remains strenuous, self-possessed, and mindful, having overcome both the hankering and the dejection common in the world. And in the same way as to feelings . . . moods . . . ideas, he continues so to look upon each that he remains strenuous, self-possessed, and mindful, having overcome both the hankering and the dejection common in the world.

"And whosoever, Ananda, either now or after I am dead, shall live as having the Self as lamp, the Self as refuge, as having no other refuge, shall live as having Dhamma as lamp, Dhamma as refuge, as having no other refuge, the Peak of the Undying, Ananda, will those brethren become!—but they must be anxious to learn."

Announcement of Death

Now the Exalted One robed himself early in the morning, and taking his bowl in the robe, went into Vesali for alms. When, after he had returned from the round for alms, he had finished eating the rice, he addressed the venerable Ananda, and said: "Take up the mat, Ananda; I will go and spend the day at the Chapala Shrine."

"So be it, lord!" said the venerable Ananda, in assent, to the Exalted One. And taking up the mat he followed step for step behind the Exalted One.

So the Exalted One proceeded to the Chapala Shrine, and when he had come there he sat down on the mat spread out for him, and the venerable Ananda took his seat respectfully beside him. Then the Exalted One addressed the venerable Ananda, and said: "How delightful a spot, Ananda, is Vesali, and how charming the Udena Shrine, and the Gota-maka Shrine, and the Shrine of the Seven Mangoes, and the Shrine of Many Sons, and the Sarandada Shrine, and the Chapala Shrine!

"Ananda, whosoever has developed, practised, dwelt on, expanded, and ascended to the very heights of the four paths to Iddhi, and so mastered them as to be able to use them as a vehicle, and as a basis, he, should he desire it, could remain in the same birth for an æon, or for that portion of the æon which had yet to run. Now the Tathagata has thoroughly practised and developed them, and he could, therefore, should he desire it, live on yet for an æon, or for that portion of the æon which has yet to run."

But even though a suggestion so evident and a hint so clear were thus given by the Exalted One, the venerable Ananda was incapable of comprehending them; and he besought not the Exalted One, saying: "Vouchsafe, lord, to remain during the æon! Live on through the æon, O Happy One! for the good and the happiness of the great multitudes, out of pity for the world, for the good and the gain and the weal of gods and men!" So far was his heart possessed by the Evil One.

A second and a third time did the Exalted One say the same thing, and a second and a third time was Ananda's heart thus hardened.

Then the Exalted One addressed the venerable Ananda, and said: "You may leave me, Ananda, awhile, and do whatsoever now seemeth to thee fit."

"So be it, lord!" said the venerable Ananda, in assent, to the Exalted One, and passing him on the right sat down at the foot of a certain tree not far off thence.

Now not long after the venerable Ananda had been gone, Mara, the Evil One, approached the Exalted One and stood beside him. And so standing there, he addressed the Exalted One in these words:

"Pass away now, lord; let the Exalted One now die. Now is the time for the Exalted One to pass away—even according to the word which the Exalted One spoke when he said: 'I shall not die, O Evil One! until the brethren and sisters of the Order, and until the lay-disciples of either sex shall have become true hearers, wise and well trained, ready and learned, carrying the doctrines well in their memory, masters of the lesser corollaries that follow from the larger doctrine, correct in life, walking according to the precepts—until they, having thus themselves learned the doctrine, shall be able to tell others of it, preach it, make it known, establish it, open it, minutely explain it and make it clear—until they, when others start vain doctrine easy to be refuted by the truth, shall be able in refuting it, to spread the wonder-working truth abroad!'

"And now, lord, the brethren and sisters of the Order and the lay-disciples of either sex have become all this, are able to do all this. Pass away now therefore, lord; let the Exalted One now die! The time has come for the Exalted One to pass away."

And when he had thus spoken, the Exalted One addressed Mara, the Evil One, and said: "O Evil One! make thyself happy, the death of the Tathagata shall take place before long. At the end of three months from this time the Tathagata will pass away."

Thus the Exalted One while at the Shrine of Chapala deliberately and consciously let go interest in life's conditions. And on his so rejecting it there arose a mighty earthquake, awful and terrible, and the thunders of heaven burst forth. And when the Exalted One beheld this, he broke out at that time into this hymn of exultation:

> "His sum of life the sage renounced,
>   What may be reckoned and what not,
>   With inward joy and calm, he broke,
>   Like coat of mail, the self-compound!"

And when he had thus spoken the venerable Ananda addressed the Exalted One, and said: "Vouchsafe, lord, to remain during the æon: live on through the kalpa, O Exalted One! for the good and the happiness of the great multitudes, out of pity for the world, for the good and the gain and the weal of gods and men!"

"Enough now, Ananda, beseech not the Tathagata!" was the reply. "The time for making such request is past."

And again, the second time, and the third time, the venerable Ananda besought the Exalted One in the same words.

"Hast thou faith, Ananda, in the wisdom of the Tathagata?"

"Even so, lord!"

"Now why, then, Ananda, dost thou trouble the Tathagata even until the third time?"

"From his own mouth have I heard from the Exalted One, from his own mouth have I received this saying: 'Whosoever has developed, practised, dwelt on, expanded, and ascended to the very heights of the four paths to Iddhi, and so mastered them as to be able to use them as a vehicle, and as a basis, he, should he desire it, could remain in the same birth for an æon, or for that portion of the æon which had yet to run.' Now the Tathagata has thoroughly practised and developed them, and he could, therefore, should he desire it, live on yet for an æon, or for that portion of the æon which has yet to run.''

"Hast thou faith, Ananda?"

"Even so, lord!"

"Then, O Ananda, thine is the fault, thine is the offence—in that when a suggestion so evident and a hint so clear were thus given thee by the Tathagata, thou wast yet incapable of comprehending them, and thou besoughtest not the Tathagata, saying: 'Vouchsafe, lord, to remain during the æon for the good and the happiness of the great multitudes, out of pity for the world, for the good and the gain and the weal of gods and men.' If thou shouldst then have so besought the Tathagata, the Tathagata might have rejected the appeal even to the second time, but the third time he would have granted it. Thine, therefore, O Ananda, is the fault, thine is the offence!

"On one occasion, Ananda, I was dwelling at Rajagaha, on the hill called the Vulture's Peak—on one occasion at that same Rajagaha in the Banyan Grove—on one occasion at that same Rajagaha at the Robbers' Cliff—on one occasion at that same Rajagaha in the Sattapanni Cave on the slope of Mount Vebhara—on one occasion at that same Rajagaha at the Black Rock on the slope of Mount Isigili—on one occasion at that same Rajagaha in the Sitavana Grove in the mountain cave Sappasondika—on one occasion at that same Rajagaha in the Tapoda Grove—on one occasion at that same Rajagaha in the Bambu Grove in the Squirrels' Feeding Ground—on one occasion at that same Rajagaha in Jivaka's Mango Grove—on one occasion at that same Rajagaha in the Deer Forest at Maddakucchi.

"Now there too, Ananda, I spoke to thee. . . . But even when a suggestion so evident and a hint so clear were thus given thee by the Tathagata, thou wast yet incapable of comprehending them, and thou besoughtest not the Tathagata, saying: 'Vouchsafe, lord, to remain during the æon. Live on, O Exalted One! through the æon for the good and the happiness of the great multitudes, out of pity for the world, for the good and the gain and the weal of gods and men.' If thou shouldst then have so besought the Tathagata, the Tathagata might have rejected the appeal even to the second time, but the third time he would have granted it. Thine, therefore, O Ananda, is the fault, thine is the offence!

"But now, Ananda, have I not formerly declared to you that it is in the very nature of all things, near and dear unto us, that we must divide ourselves from them, leave them, sever ourselves from them? How, then, Ananda, can this be possible—whereas anything whatever born, brought into being, and organized, contains within itself the inherent necessity of dissolution—how then can this be possible that such a being should not be dissolved? No such condition can exist! And that which, Ananda, has been relinquished, cast away, renounced, rejected, and abandoned by the Tathagata—the remaining sum of life surrendered by him—verily with regard to that the word has gone forth from the Tathagata, saying: 'The passing away of the Tathagata shall take place before long. At the end of three months from this time the Tathagata will die!' That the Tathagata for the sake of living should repent him again of that saying—this can no wise be!

"Come, Ananda, let us go to the Kutagara Hall, to the Mahavana."

"Even so, lord!" said the venerable Ananda, in assent, to the Exalted One.

Then the Exalted One proceeded, and Ananda with him, to the Mahavana, to the Kutagara Hall: and when he had arrived there he addressed the venerable Ananda, and said:

"Go now, Ananda, and assemble in the Service Hall such of the brethren as reside in the neighbourhood of Vesali."

"Even so, lord!" said the venerable Ananda, in assent, to the Exalted One. And when he had assembled in the Service Hall such of the brethren as resided in the neighbourhood of Vesali, he went to the Exalted One and saluted him and stood beside him. And standing beside him, he addressed the Exalted One, and said:

"Lord! the assembly of the brethren has met together. Let the Exalted One do even as seemeth to him fit."

Then the Exalted One proceeded to the Service Hall, and sat down there on the mat spread out for him. And when he was seated the Exalted One addressed the brethren, and said:

"Which then, O brethren, are the things which, when I had perceived, I made known to you, which when you have mastered it behoves you to practise, meditate upon, and spread abroad, in order that pure religion may last long and be perpetuated, in order that it may continue to be for the good and the happiness of the great multitudes, out of pity for the world, to the good and the gain and the weal of gods and men?

"They are these:

> The four earnest meditations,
> The fourfold great struggle,
> The four roads to iddhi,
> The five moral powers,
> The five organs of spiritual sense,
> The seven kinds of wisdom, and
> The Aryan eightfold path.

These, O brethren, are the truths which, when I had perceived, I made known to you, which when you have mastered it behoves you to practise, meditate upon, and spread abroad, in order that pure religion may last long and be perpetuated, in order that it may continue to be for the good and the happiness of the great multitudes, out of pity for the world, to the good and the gain and the weal of gods and men!"

And the Exalted One exhorted the brethren, and said:

"Behold now, O brethren, I exhort you, saying: 'All component things must grow old. Work out your salvation with diligence. The final extinction of the Tathagata will take place before long. At the end of three months from this time the Tathagata will die!'

> "My age is now full ripe, my life draws to its close:
> Leaving you I shall go, relying on the Self, virtuous,
> Be earnest then, O brethren, holy, full of thought!
> Be steadfast in resolve! Keep watch o'er your own hearts!
> Who wearies not, but earnest keeps in Right and Rule,
> Shall cross this sea of life, shall make an end of grief."

The Food of Chunda the Smith

Now Chunda, the worker in metals, heard that the Exalted One had come to Pava, and was staying there in his Mango Grove.

And Chunda, the worker in metals, went to the place where the

Exalted One was, and saluting him took his seat respectfully on one side. And when he was thus seated, the Exalted One instructed, aroused, incited, and gladdened him with religious discourse.

Then he, instructed, aroused, incited, and gladdened by the religious discourse, addressed the Exalted One, and said: "May the Exalted One do me the honour of taking his meal together with the brethren, at my house to-morrow?"

And the Exalted One signified, by silence, his consent.

Now at the end of the night, Chunda, the worker in metals, made ready in his dwelling-place sweet rice and cakes, and a quantity of truffles. And he announced the hour to the Exalted One, saying: "The hour, lord, has come, and the meal is ready."

And the Exalted One robed himself early in the morning, and taking his bowl, went with the brethren to the dwelling-place of Chunda, the worker in metals. When he had come thither he seated himself on the seat prepared for him. And when he was seated he addressed Chunda, the worker in metals, and said: "As to the truffles you have made ready, serve me with them, Chunda: and as to the other food, the sweet rice and cakes, serve the brethren with it."

"Even so, lord!" said Chunda, the worker in metals, in assent, to the Blessed One. And the truffles he had made ready he served to the Exalted One; whilst the other food, the sweet rice and cakes, he served to the members of the Order.

Now the Exalted One addressed Chunda, the worker in metals, and said: "Whatever truffles, Chunda, are left over to thee, those bury in a hole. I see no one, Chunda, on earth nor in Mara's heaven, nor in Brahma's heaven, no one among Samanas and Brahmanas, among gods, and men, by whom, when he has eaten it, that food can be properly assimilated, save by a Tathagata."

"Even so, lord!" said Chunda, the worker in metals, in assent, to the Exalted One. And whatever truffles remained over those he buried in a hole. And he went to the place where the Exalted One was; and when he had come there, took his seat respectfully on one side. And when he was seated, the Exalted One instructed and aroused and incited and gladdened Chunda, the worker in metals, with religious discourse. And the Exalted One then rose from his seat and departed thence.

Now when the Exalted One had eaten the rice prepared by Chunda, the worker in metals, there fell upon him a dire sickness, the disease of dysentery, and sharp pain came upon him, even unto death. But the Exalted One, mindful and self-possessed, bore it without complaint.

And the Exalted One addressed the venerable Ananda, and said: "Come, Ananda, let us go on to Kusinara."

And the Exalted One addressed the venerable Ananda, and said: "Now it may happen, Ananda, that someone should stir up remorse in Chunda the smith, by saying: 'This is evil to thee, Chunda, and loss to thee in that when the Tathagata had eaten his last meal from thy provision, then he died.' Any such remorse, Ananda, in Chunda the smith should be checked by saying: 'This is good to thee, Chunda, and gain to thee, in that when the Tathagata had eaten his last meal from thy provision, then he died. From the very mouth of the Exalted One, Chunda, have I heard, from his own mouth have I received this saying: "These two offerings of food are of equal fruit, and of equal profit, and of much greater fruit and much greater profit than any other—and which are the two? The offering of food which, when a Tathagata has eaten, he attains to supreme and perfect insight; and the offering of food which, when a Tathagata has eaten, he passes away by that utter passing away in which nothing whatever remains behind—these two offerings of food are of equal fruit and of equal profit, and of much greater fruit and much greater profit than any others. There has been laid up by Chunda the smith a karma redounding to length of life, redounding to good birth, redounding to good fortune, redounding to good fame, redounding to the inheritance of heaven, and of sovereign power." ' In this way, Ananda, should be checked any remorse in Chunda the smith."

Preparation for Death

Now the Exalted One addressed the venerable Ananda, and said: "Come, Ananda, let us go on to the Sala Grove of the Mallas, the Upavattana of Kusinara, on the further side of the river Hiranyavati."

"Even so, lord!" said the venerable Ananda, in assent, to the Exalted One.

And the Exalted One proceeded with a great company of the brethren to the Sala Grove of the Mallas, the Upavattana of Kusinara, on the further side of the river Hiranyavati: and when he had come there he addressed the venerable Ananda, and said:

"Spread over for me, I pray you, Ananda, the couch with its head to the north, between the twin Sala trees. I am weary, Ananda, and would lie down."

"Even so, lord!" said the venerable Ananda, in assent, to the Exalted One. And he spread a covering over the couch with its head to the north, between the twin Sala trees. And the Exalted One laid himself down on his right side, with one leg resting on the other; and he was mindful and self-possessed.

Now at that time the twin Sala trees were all one mass of bloom with flowers out of season; and all over the body of the Tathagata these dropped and sprinkled and scattered themselves, out of reverence for the successor of the Buddhas of old. And heavenly mandarava flowers, too, and heavenly sandalwood powder came falling from the sky, and all over the body of the Tathagata they descended and sprinkled and scattered themselves, out of reverence for the successor of the Buddhas of old. And heavenly music was sounded in the sky, out of reverence for the successor of the Buddhas of old. And heavenly songs came wafted from the skies, out of reverence for the successor of the Buddhas of old!

Then the Exalted One addressed the venerable Ananda and said:

"Now it is not thus, Ananda, that the Tathagata is rightly honoured, reverenced, venerated, held sacred or revered. But the brother or the sister, the devout man or the devout woman, who continually fulfils all the greater and the lesser duties, who is correct in life, walking according to the precepts—it is he who rightly honours, reverences, venerates, holds sacred, and reveres the Tathagata with the worthiest homage. Therefore, O Ananda, be ye constant in the fulfilment of the greater and of the lesser duties, and be ye correct in life, walking according to the precepts; and thus, Ananda, should it be taught."

Now at that time the venerable Upavana was standing in front of the Exalted One, fanning him. And the Exalted One was not pleased with Upavana, and he said to him: "Stand aside, O brother, stand not in front of me!"

And the venerable Ananda said to the Exalted One: "This venerable Upavana has long been in close personal attendance and service on the Exalted One. What may be the cause and what the reason that the Exalted One is not pleased with Upavana, and speaks thus with him?"

"In great numbers, Ananda, are the gods of the ten world-systems assembled together to behold the Tathagata. For twelve leagues, Ananda, around the Sala Grove of the Mallas, the Upavattana of Kusinara, there is no spot in size even as the pricking of the point of the tip of a hair which is not pervaded by powerful spirits. And the spirits, Ananda, are murmuring, and say: 'From afar have we come to behold the Tathagata. Few and far between are the Tathagatas, the Arahant Buddhas who appear in the world: and now to-day, in the last watch of the night, the death of a Tathagata will take place; and this eminent brother stands in front of the Tathagata, concealing him, and in his last hour we are prevented from beholding the Tathagata'; thus, Ananda, do the spirits murmur."

The Establishment of Pilgrimage Places

Ananda said: "In times past, lord, the brethren, when they had spent the rainy season in different districts, used to come to see the Tathagata, and we used to receive those very reverend brethren to audience, and to wait upon the Exalted One. But, lord, after the end of the Exalted One, we shall not be able to receive those very reverend brethren to audience, and to wait upon the Exalted One."

"There are these four places, Ananda, which the believing clansman should visit with feelings of reverence. Which are the four?

"The place, Ananda, at which the believing man can say: 'Here the Tathagata was born!' is a spot to be visited with feelings of reverence.

"The place, Ananda, at which the believing man can say: 'Here the Tathagata attained to the supreme and perfect insight!' is a spot to be visited with feelings of reverence.

"The place, Ananda, at which the believing man can say: 'Here was the kingdom of righteousness set on foot by the Tathagata!' is a spot to be visited with feelings of reverence.

"The place, Ananda, at which the believing man can say: 'Here the Tathagata passed finally away in that utter passing away which leaves nothing whatever to remain behind!' is a spot to be visited with feelings of reverence. These are the four places, Ananda, which the believing clansman should visit with feelings of reverence.

"And they, Ananda, who shall die while they, with believing heart, are journeying on such pilgrimage, shall be reborn after death, when the body shall dissolve, in the happy realms of heaven."

"How are we to conduct ourselves, lord, with regard to womankind?"
"As not seeing them, Ananda."
"But if we should see them, what are we to do?"
"No talking, Ananda."
"But if they should speak to us, lord, what are we to do?"
"Keep wide awake, Ananda."

"What are we to do, lord, with the remains of the Tathagata?"
"Hinder not yourselves, Ananda, by honouring the remains of the Tathagata. Be zealous, I beseech you, Ananda, in your own behalf! Devote yourselves to your own good! Be earnest, be zealous, be intent on your own good! There are wise men, Ananda, among the nobles, among the Brahmanas, among the heads of houses, who are firm believers in the Tathagata; and they will do due honour to the remains of the Tathagata."

"But what should be done, lord, with the remains of the Tathagata?"
"As men treat the remains of a king of kings, so, Ananda, should they treat the remains of the Tathagata."

"And how, lord, do they treat the remains of a king of kings?"
"They wrap the body of a king of kings, Ananda, in a new cloth. When that is done they wrap it in carded cotton wool. When that is done they wrap it in a new cloth, and so on till they have wrapped the body in five hundred successive layers of both kinds. Then they place the body in an oil vessel of iron, and cover that close up with another oil vessel of iron. They then build a funeral pyre of all kinds of perfume, and burn the body of the king of kings. And then at the four cross roads they erect a cairn to the king of kings. This, Ananda, is the way in which they treat the remains of a king of kings.

"And as they treat the remains of a king of kings, so, Ananda, should they treat the remains of the Tathagata. At the four cross roads a cairn should be erected to the Tathagata. And whosoever shall there place garlands or perfumes or paint, or make salutation there, or become in its presence calm in heart—that shall long be to them for a profit and a joy."

Ananda Weeps

Now the venerable Ananda went into the Vihara, and stood leaning against the lintel of the door, and weeping at the thought: "Alas! I remain still but a learner, one who has yet to work out his own perfection. And the Master is about to pass away from me—he who is so kind!"

Now the Exalted One called the brethren, and said: "Where then, brethren, is Ananda?"

"The venerable Ananda, lord, has gone into the Vihara, and stands leaning against the lintel of the door, weeping."

And the Exalted One called a certain brother, and said: "Go now, brother, and call Ananda in my name, and say: 'Brother Ananda, the Master calls for thee.'"

"Even so, lord!" said that brother, in assent, to the Exalted One. And he went up to the place where Ananda was: and when he had come there, he said to the venerable Ananda: "Brother Ananda, the Master calls for thee."

"Very well, brother," said the venerable Ananda, in assent, to that brother. And he went up to the place where the Exalted One was, and when he had come there, he bowed down before the Exalted One, and took his seat respectfully on one side.

Then the Exalted One said to the venerable Ananda, as he sat there by his side: "Enough, Ananda! Do not let yourself be troubled; do not weep! Have I not already, on former occasions, told you that it is in the very nature of all things most near and dear unto us that we must divide ourselves from them, leave them, sever ourselves from them? How, then, Ananda, can this be possible—whereas anything whatever born, brought into being, and organized, contains within itself the inherent necessity of dissolution—how, then, can this be possible, that such a being should not be dissolved? No such condition can exist! For a long time, Ananda, have you been very near to me by acts of love, kind and good, that never varies, and is beyond all measure. For a long time, Ananda, have you been very near to me by words of love, kind and good, that never varies, and is beyond all measure. For a long time, Ananda, have you been very near to me by thoughts of love, kind and good, that never varies, and is beyond all measure. You have done well, Ananda! Be earnest in effort, and you too shall soon be free from the intoxications—of sensuality, and individuality, and delusion, and ignorance!"

Admission of Women

Now the Blessed Buddha was staying among the Sakyas in Kapilavatthu, in the Nigrodharama. And Maha-Prajapati the Gotami went to the place where the Blessed One was, and on arriving there, bowed down before the Blessed One, and remained standing on one side. And so standing she spake thus to the Blessed One:

"It would be well, lord, if women should be allowed to renounce their homes and enter the homeless state under the doctrine and discipline proclaimed by the Tathagata."

"Enough, Gotami. Let it not please thee that women should be allowed to do so."

(And a second and a third time did Maha-Prajapati the Gotami make the same request in the same words, and receive the same reply.)

Then Maha-Prajapati the Gotami, sad and sorrowful for that the Blessed One would not permit women to enter the homeless state, bowed down before the Blessed One, and keeping him on her right hand as she passed him, departed thence weeping and in tears.

Now when the Blessed One had remained at Kapilavatthu as long as he thought fit, he set out on his journey towards Vesali; and travelling straight on he in due course arrived thereat. And there at Vesali the Blessed One stayed, in the Mahavana in the Kutagara Hall.

And Maha-Prajapati the Gotami cut off her hair, and put on orange-coloured robes, and set out, with a number of women of the Sakya clan, towards Vesali; and in due course she arrived at Vesali, at the Mahavana, at the Kutagara Hall. And Maha-Prajapati the Gotami, with swollen feet and covered with dust, sad and sorrowful, weeping and in tears, took her stand outside under the entrance porch.

And the venerable Ananda saw her so standing there, and on seeing her so he said to Maha-Prajapati: "Why standest thou there, outside the porch, with swollen feet and covered with dust, sad and sorrowful, weeping and in tears?"

"Inasmuch, Ananda, as the lord, the Blessed One, does not permit women to renounce their homes and enter the homeless state under the doctrine and discipline proclaimed by the Tathagata."

Then did the venerable Ananda go up to the place where the Blessed One was, and bow down before the Blessed One, and take his seat on one side. And, so sitting, the venerable Ananda said to the Blessed One:

"Behold, lord, Maha-Prajapati the Gotami is standing outside under the entrance porch, with swollen feet and covered with dust, sad and sorrowful, weeping and in tears, inasmuch as the Blessed One does not permit women to renounce their homes and enter the homeless state under the doctrine and discipline proclaimed by the Blessed One.

"It were well, lord, if women were to have permission granted to them to do as she desires."

"Enough, Ananda. Let it not please thee that women should be allowed to do so."

(And a second and a third time did Ananda make the same request, in the same words, and receive the same reply) . . .

Then the venerable Ananda thought: "The Blessed One does not give his permission, let me now ask the Blessed One on another ground." And the venerable Ananda said to the Blessed One:

"Are women, lord, capable when they have gone forth from the household life and entered the homeless state, under the doctrine and discipline proclaimed by the Blessed One—are they capable of realizing the fruit of conversion, or of the second path, or of the third path, or of Arahantship?"

"They are capable, Ananda."

"If then, lord, they are capable thereof, since Maha-Prajapati the Gotami has proved herself of great service to the Blessed One, when as aunt and nurse she nourished him and gave him milk, and on the death of his mother suckled the Blessed One at her own breast, it were well, lord, that women should have permission to go forth from the household life and enter the homeless state under the doctrine and discipline proclaimed by the Tathagata."

"If then, Ananda, Maha-Prajapati the Gotami take upon herself the eight chief rules, let that be reckoned to her as her ordination. They are these:

"A nun, even if of a hundred years standing, shall make salutation to, shall rise up in the presence of, shall bow down before, and shall per-

form all proper duties towards a monk, if only just initiated. This is a
rule to be revered and reverenced, honoured and observed, and her life
long never to be transgressed.

"A nun is not to spend the rainy season in a district in which there is
no monk. This is a rule . . . never to be transgressed.

"Every half month a nun is to await from the order of Bhikkhus two
things, the asking as to the date of the uposatha ceremony, and the time
when the monk will come to give the exhortation. This is a rule . . .
never to be transgressed.

"After keeping the rainy season the nun is to hold Pavarana, to
inquire whether any fault can be laid to her charge, before both orders
—as well that of the monks as that of nuns—with respect to three
matters, namely, what has been seen, and what has been heard, and
what has been suspected. This is a rule . . . never to be transgressed.

"A nun who has been guilty of a serious offence is to undergo suitable discipline towards both orders, monks and nuns. This is a rule . . .
never to be transgressed.

"When a nun, as novice, has been trained for two years in the six
rules, she is to ask leave for the upasampada ordination from both
orders, as well that of monks as that of nuns. This is a rule . . . never
to be transgressed.

"A nun is on no pretext to revile or abuse a monk. This is a rule . . .
never to be transgressed.

"From henceforth official admonition by nuns of monks is forbidden,
whereas the official admonition of nuns by monks is not forbidden. This
is a rule . . . never to be transgressed.

"If, Ananda, Maha-Prajapati the Gotami take upon herself these
eight chief rules, let that be reckoned to her as her ordination."

Then the venerable Ananda, when he had learnt from the Blessed One
these eight chief rules, went to Maha-Prajapati the Gotami and told her
all that the Blessed One had said, to which she replied:

"Just, Ananda, as a man or a woman, when young and of tender
years, accustomed to adorn himself, would, when he had bathed his
head, receive with both hands a garland of lotus flowers or jasmine
flowers or atimuttaka flowers, and place it on the top of his head; even
so do I, Ananda, take upon me these eight chief rules never to be transgressed my life long."

Then the venerable Ananda returned to the Blessed One, and bowed down before him, and took his seat on one side. And, so sitting, the venerable Ananda said to the Blessed One: "Maha-Prajapati the Gotami, lord, has taken upon herself the eight chief rules, the aunt of the Blessed One has received the upasampada ordination."

"If, Ananda, women had not received permission to go out from the household life and enter the homeless state, under the doctrine and discipline proclaimed by the Tathagata, then would the pure religion, Ananda, have lasted long, the good law would have stood fast for a thousand years. But since, Ananda, women now have received that permission, the pure religion, Ananda, will not now last so long, the good law will now stand fast for only five hundred years. Just, Ananda, as houses in which there are many women and but few men, are easily violated by robbers, by burglars; just so, Ananda, under whatever doctrine and discipline women are allowed to go out from the household life into the homeless state, that religion will not last long.

"And just, Ananda, as when disease, called mildew, falls upon a field of rice in fine condition, that field of rice does not continue long; just so, Ananda, under whatsoever doctrine and discipline women are allowed to go forth from the household life into the homeless state, that religion will not last long. And just, Ananda, as when disease, called blight, falls upon a field of sugar-cane in good condition, that field of sugar-cane does not continue long; just so, Ananda, under whatsoever doctrine and discipline women are allowed to go forth from the household life into the homeless state, that religion does not last long. And just, Ananda, as a man would in anticipation build an embankment to a great reservoir, beyond which the water should not overpass; just even so, Ananda, have I in anticipation laid down these eight chief rules for the nuns, their life long not to be overpassed."

Now Maha-Prajapati the Gotami went up to the place where the Blessed One was, and bowed down before him, and stood respectfully on one side.

And, so standing, Maha-Prajapati the Gotami spoke thus to the Blessed One: "What course, lord, should I pursue towards these women of the Sakya clan?" Then the Blessed One taught Maha-Prajapati the Gotami and incited her and aroused her, and gladdened her with religious discourse; and she, so taught, incited, aroused, gladdened, bowed down before the Blessed One, and keeping him on her right hand as she passed him, she departed thence.

The Last Conversion

Now at that time a wanderer named Subhadda, who was not a believer, was dwelling at Kusinara. And the wanderer Subhadda heard the news: "This very day, they say, in the third watch of the night, will take place the final passing away of the Samana Gotama."

Then the wanderer Subhadda went to the Sala Grove of the Mallas, to the Upavattana of Kusinara, to the place where the venerable Ananda was.

And when he had come there he said to the venerable Ananda: "Thus have I heard from fellow wanderers, old and well stricken in years, teachers and disciples, when they said: 'Sometimes and full seldom do Tathagatas appear in the world, the able Awakened Ones.' Yet this day, in the last watch of the night, the final passing away of the Samana Gotama will take place. Now a certain feeling of uncertainty has sprung up in my mind; and this faith have I in the Samana Gotama, that he, methinks, is able so to present the truth that I may get rid of this feeling of uncertainty. O that I, even I, Ananda, might be allowed to see the Samana Gotama!"

And when he had thus spoken the venerable Ananda said to the wanderer Subhadda: "Enough! friend Subhadda. Trouble not the Tathagata. The Exalted One is weary."

And again the wanderer Subhadda made the same request in the same words, and received the same reply; and the third time the wanderer Subhadda made the same request in the same words, and received the same reply.

Now the Exalted One overheard this conversation of the venerable Ananda with the wanderer Subhadda. And the Exalted One called the venerable Ananda, and said: "It is enough, Ananda! Do not keep out Subhadda. Subhadda, Ananda, may be allowed to see the Tathagata. Whatever Subhadda may ask of me, he will ask from a desire for knowledge, and not to annoy me. And whatever I may say in answer to his questions, that he will quickly understand."

Then the venerable Ananda said to Subhadda, the wanderer: "Enter in, friend Subhadda; for the Exalted One gives you leave."

Then Subhadda, the wanderer, went in to the place where the Exalted One was, and saluted him courteously, and after exchanging with him the compliments of esteem and of civility, he took his seat on one side. And when he was thus seated, Subhadda, the wanderer, said to the Exalted One: "The leaders in religious life who are heads of companies of disciples and students, teachers of students, well known, renowned, founders of schools of doctrine, esteemed as good men by the multitude —to wit, Purana Kassapa, Makkhali of the cattle-pen, Ajita of the garment of hair, Kakkayana of the Pakudha tree, Sanjaya the son of the Belatthi slave-girl, and Niggantha of the Natha clan—have they all, according to their own assertion, thoroughly understood things? or have they not? or are there some of them who have understood, and some who have not?"

And the Exalted One spake: "In whatsoever doctrine and discipline, Subhadda, the Aryan eightfold path is not found, neither in it is there found a man of true saintliness of the first, or of the second, or of the third, or of the fourth degree. And in whatsoever doctrine and discipline, Subhadda, the Aryan eightfold path is found, in it is found the man of true saintliness of the first, and the second, and the third, and the fourth degree. Now in this doctrine and discipline, Subhadda, is found the Aryan eightfold path, and in it too, are found, Subhadda, the men of true saintliness of all the four degrees. Void are the systems of other teachers—void of true saints. And in this one, Subhadda, may the brethren live the life that's right, so that the world be not bereft of Arahants."

And when he had thus spoken, Subhadda, the wanderer, said to the Exalted One: "Most excellent, lord, are the words of thy mouth, most excellent! Just as if a man were to set up that which is thrown down, or were to reveal that which is hidden away, or were to point out the right road to him who has gone astray, or were to bring a lamp into the darkness, so that those who have eyes can see external forms;—just even so, lord, has the truth been made known to me, in many a figure, by the Exalted One. And I, even I, betake myself, lord, to the Exalted One as my refuge, to the truth, and to the Order. I would fain be accepted as a probationer under the Exalted One, as a full member in his Order."

"Whosoever, Subhadda, has formerly been a follower of another doctrine, and thereafter desires to be received into the higher or the lower grade in this doctrine and discipline, he remains on probation for the space of four months; and at the end of the four months, the brethren, exalted in spirit, receive him into the lower or into the higher grade of the Order. Nevertheless in this case I acknowledge the difference in persons."

"I too, then, will remain on probation for the space of four months; and at the end of the four months let the brethren, exalted in spirit, receive me into the lower or into the higher grade of the Order!"

But the Exalted One called the venerable Ananda, and said: "As it is, Ananda, receive Subhadda into the Order!"

"Even so, lord!" said the venerable Ananda, in assent, to the Exalted One.

So the venerable Subhadda became yet another among the Arahants; and he was the last disciple whom the Exalted One himself converted.

Death of the Buddha

Now the Exalted One addressed the venerable Ananda, and said: "It may be, Ananda, that in some of you the thought may arise, 'The word of the master is ended, we have no teacher more!' But it is not thus, Ananda, that you should regard it. It is Dhamma, and the rules of the Order, which I have set forth and laid down for you all; let them, after I am gone, be the teacher to you.

"Ananda! when I am gone address not one another in the way in which the brethren have heretofore addressed each other—with the epithet, that is, of 'Avuso' (Friend). A younger brother may be addressed by an elder with his name, or his family name, or the title 'Friend.' But an elder should be addressed by a younger brother as 'Sir' or as 'Venerable Sir.'

"When I am gone, Ananda, let the Order, if it should so wish, abolish all the lesser and minor precepts."

Then the Exalted One addressed the brethren, and said: "It may be, brethren, that there may be doubt or misgiving in the mind of some brother as to the Buddha, or the doctrine, or the path, or the method.

Inquire, brethren, freely. Do not have to reproach yourselves afterwards with the thought: 'Our teacher was face to face with us, and we could not bring ourselves to inquire of the Exalted One when we were face to face with him.' "

And when he had thus spoken the brethren were silent.

And again the second and the third time the Exalted One addressed the brethren.

And even the third time the brethren were silent.

Then the Exalted One addressed the brethren, and said: "It may be, brethren, that you put no questions out of reverence for the teacher. Let comrade communicate to comrade."

And when he had thus spoken the brethren were silent.

And the venerable Ananda said to the Exalted One: "How wonderful a thing is it, lord, and how marvellous! Verily, I believe that in this whole assembly of the brethren there is not one brother who has any doubt or misgiving as to the Buddha, or the doctrine, or the path, or the method!"

"It is out of the fullness of faith that thou hast spoken, Ananda! But, Ananda, the Tathagata knows for certain that in this whole assembly of the brethren there is not one brother who has any doubt or misgiving as to the Buddha, or the doctrine, or the path, or the method! For even the most backward, Ananda, of all these five hundred brethren has become converted, is no longer liable to be born in a state of suffering, and is assured of hereafter attaining to the enlightenment of Arahantship."

Then the Exalted One addressed the brethren, and said: "Behold now, brethren, I exhort you, saying: *'Decay is inherent in all component things! Work out your salvation with diligence!'* "

This was the last word of the Tathagata!

Then the Exalted One entered into the first stage of rapture. And rising out of the first stage he passed into the second. And rising out of the second he passed into the third. And rising out of the third stage he passed into the fourth. And rising out of the fourth stage of rapture, he entered into the state of mind to which the infinity of space is alone present. And passing out of the mere consciousness of the infinity of space he entered into the state of mind to which the infinity of thought is alone present. And passing out of the mere consciousness of the infinity of thought he entered into a state of mind to which nothing at

all was specially present. And passing out of the consciousness of no
special object he fell into a state between consciousness and unconsciousness. And passing out of the state between consciousness and
unconsciousness he fell into a state in which the consciousness both
of sensations and of ideas had wholly passed away.

Then the venerable Ananda said to the venerable Anuruddha: "O my
lord, O Anuruddha, the Exalted One is dead!"

"Nay! brother Ananda, the Exalted One is not dead. He has entered
into that state in which both sensations and ideas have ceased to be!"

Then the Exalted One, passing out of the state in which both sensations and ideas have ceased to be, entered into the state between consciousness and unconsciousness. And passing out of the state between
consciousness and unconsciousness he entered into the state of mind to
which nothing at all is specially present. And passing out of the consciousness of no special object he entered into the state of mind to which
the infinity of thought is alone present. And passing out of the mere
consciousness of the infinity of thought he entered into the state of
mind to which the infinity of space is alone present. And passing out
of the mere consciousness of the infinity of space he entered into the
fourth stage of rapture. And passing out of the fourth stage he entered
into the third. And passing out of the third stage he entered into the
second. And passing out of the second he entered into the first. And
passing out of the first stage of rapture he entered into the second. And
passing out of the second stage he entered into the third. And passing
out of the third stage he entered into the fourth stage of rapture. And
passing out of the last stage of rapture he immediately expired.

The Doctrine of the Buddha

The Thirty-Two Marks

Thus have I heard:

The Exalted One was once staying near Savatthi, in Anathapindika's park, the Jeta-Vana. And there the Exalted One addressed the monks, saying Bhikkhus! Yea, lord! they responded. And he said: There are thirty-two special marks of the superman, brethren, and for the superman possessing them two careers lie open, and none other. If he live the life of the house, he becomes monarch, turner of the wheel, a righteous lord of the right, ruler of the four quarters, conqueror, guardian of the people's good, owner of the seven treasures. But if such a boy go forth from the life of the house into the homeless state, he becomes arahant, a Buddha supreme, rolling back the veil from the world.

And what, brethren, are the thirty-two marks of the superman, wherewith endowed two careers lie open to him and none other: that of a monarch, turner of the wheel . . . that of Buddha supreme?

(1) He hath feet with level tread. That this is so counts to him as one of the marks of the superman.

(2) Moreover, beneath, on the soles of his feet, wheels appear thousand-spoked, with tire and hub, in every way complete and well divided. That this is so counts to him as one of the marks of the superman.

(3) He has projecting heels. That this is so, etc.

(4) He is long in the fingers and toes. . . .

(5) Soft and tender in hands and feet. . . .

(6) With hands and feet like a net. . . .

(7) His ankles are like rounded shells. . . .

(8) His legs are like an antelope's. . . .

(9) Standing and without bending he can touch and rub his knees with either hand. . . .

(10) His male organs are concealed in a sheath. . . .

(11) His complexion is like bronze, the colour of gold. . . .

(12) His skin is so delicately smooth that no dust cleaves to his body. . . .

(13) The down on it grows in single hairs one to each pore. . . .

(14) The down on his body turns upward, every hair of it, blue black in colour like eye-paint, in little curling rings, curling to the right. . . .

(15) He has a frame divinely straight. . . .

(16) He has the seven convex surfaces. . . .

(17) The front half of his body is like a lion's. . . .

(18) There is no furrow between his shoulders. . . .

(19) His proportions have the symmetry of the banyan-tree: the length of his body is equal to the compass of his arms, and the compass of his arms is equal to his height. . . .

(20) His bust is equally rounded. . . .

(21) His taste is supremely acute. . . .

(22) His jaws are as a lion's. . . .

(23) He has forty teeth. . . .

(24) Regular teeth. . . .

(25) Continuous teeth. . . .

(26) The eyeteeth are very lustrous. . . .

(27) His tongue is long. . . .

(28) He has a divine voice like the karavika bird's. . . .

(29) His eyes are intensely blue. . . .

(30) He has eyelashes like a cow's. . . .

(31) Between the eyebrows appears a hairy mole white and like soft cotton down. . . .

(32) His head is like a royal turban. . . .

The Nine Incapabilities

(Words ascribed to Gotama Buddha)

The brother who is arahant, in whom the intoxicants are destroyed, who has lived the life, who has done his task, who has laid low his burden, who has attained salvation, who has utterly destroyed the fetter of rebirth, who is emancipated by the true gnosis, he is incapable of perpetrating nine things:

1. He is incapable of deliberately depriving a living creature of life.
2. He is incapable of taking what is not given so that it constitutes theft.
3. He is incapable of sexual impurity.
4. He is incapable of deliberately telling lies.
5. He is incapable of laying up treasure for indulgence in worldly pleasure as he used to do in the life of the house.
6. He is incapable of taking a wrong course through partiality.
7. He is incapable of taking a wrong course through hate.
8. He is incapable of taking a wrong course through stupidity.
9. He is incapable of taking a wrong course through fear.

These nine things the arahant in whom the mental intoxicants are destroyed, who has lived the life, whose task is done, whose burden is laid low, who has attained salvation, who has utterly destroyed the fetter of becoming, who is emancipated by the true gnosis, is incapable of perpetrating.

Setting-Up of Mindfulness

Thus have I heard.

The Exalted One was once staying among the Kurus. Kammassadhamma is a city of the Kuru country. There the Exalted One addressed the brethren, saying, "Bhikkhus!" "Reverend sir!" responded the brethren. And the Exalted One said:

"The one and only path, bhikkhus, leading to the purification of beings, to passing far beyond grief and lamentation, to the dying-out of ill and misery, to the attainment of right method, to the realization of Nirvana, is that of the fourfold setting up of mindfulness.

"Which are the four? Herein, O bhikkhus, let a brother, as to the body, continue so to look upon the body that he remains ardent, self-possessed, and mindful, so as to overcome both the hankering and the dejection common in the world.

"And how, bhikkhus, does a brother so continue to consider the body?

"Herein, O bhikkhus, let a brother, going into the forest, or to the roots of a tree, or to an empty chamber, sit down cross-legged, holding the body erect, and set his mindfulness alert.

"Mindful let him inhale, mindful let him exhale. Whether he inhale a long breath, let him be conscious thereof; or whether he exhale a long breath, let him be conscious thereof. Whether he inhale a short breath or exhale a short breath, let him be conscious thereof. Let him practise with the thought 'Conscious of my whole body will I inhale'; let him practise with the thought 'Conscious of my whole body will I exhale.' Let him practise with the thought 'I will inhale tranquillizing my bodily organism'; let him practise with the thought 'I will exhale tranquillizing my bodily organism.'

"Even as a skilful turner, or turner's apprentice, drawing his string out at length, or drawing it out short, is conscious that he is doing one or the other, so let a brother practise inhaling and exhaling.

"So does he, as to the body, continue to consider the body, either internally or externally, or both internally and externally. He keeps on considering how the body is something that comes to be, or again he keeps on considering how the body is something that passes away; or again he keeps on considering the coming to be with the passing away; or again, conscious that 'There is the body,' mindfulness hereof becomes thereby established, far enough for the purposes of knowledge and of self-collectedness. And he abides independent, grasping after nothing in the world whatever. Thus, bhikkhus, does a brother continue to regard the body.

"And moreover, bhikkhus, a brother, when he is walking, is aware of it thus: 'I walk'; or when he is standing, or sitting, or lying down, he is aware of it. However he is disposing the body, he is aware thereof.

"And moreover, bhikkhus, a brother—whether he departs or returns, whether he looks at or looks away from, whether he has drawn in or stretched out his limbs, whether he has donned under-robe, over-robe, or bowl, whether he is eating, drinking, chewing, reposing, or whether he is obeying the calls of nature—is aware of what he is about. In going, standing, sitting, sleeping, watching, talking, or keeping silence, he knows what he is doing.

"And moreover, bhikkhus, a brother reflects upon this very body, from the soles of his feet below upward to the crown of his head, as something enclosed in skin and full of divers impurities: 'Here is in this body hair and down, nails, teeth, skin, flesh, sinews, bones, marrow, kidney, heart, liver, membranes, spleen, lungs, stomach, bowels, intestines; excrement, bile, phlegm, pus, blood, sweat, fat, tears, serum, saliva, mucus, synovic fluid, urine.'

"Just as if there were a double-mouthed sample-bag, bhikkhus, full of various sorts of grain, such as rice, paddy, beans, vetches, sesamum or rice husked for boiling; and a keen-eyed man were to reflect as he poured them out: 'That's rice, that's paddy, those are beans,' and so forth. Even so, bhikkhus, does a brother reflect upon the body, from the soles of the feet below upward to the crown of the head, as something enclosed in skin and full of divers impurities.

"And moreover, bhikkhus, a brother reflects upon this very body, however it be placed or disposed, with respect to its fundamentals: 'There are in this body the four primary elements of earth, water, heat, and air.' Just as a cattle-butcher, or his apprentice, when he has slain an ox, displays the carcass piece-meal at the crossways as he sits, even so, bhikkhus, does a brother reflect upon this very body . . . with respect to its fundamental constituents. . . .

"And moreover, bhikkhus, a brother, just as if he had seen a body abandoned in the charnel-field, dead for one, two, or three days, swollen, turning black and blue, and decomposed, applies that perception to this very body of his own, reflecting: 'This body, too, is even so constituted, is of even such a nature, has not got beyond that.'

"And how, bhikkhus, does a brother, as to the feelings, continue to consider the feelings?

"Herein, O bhikkhus, is a brother when affected by a feeling of pleasure, aware of it, reflecting: 'I feel a pleasurable feeling.' So, too, is he aware when affected by a painful feeling, or by a neutral feeling, or by a pleasant or painful or neutral feeling concerning material things, or by a pleasant or painful or neutral feeling concerning spiritual things.

"So does he, as to the feelings, continue to consider feeling, both internally and externally, or internally and externally together. He keeps on considering how the feelings are something that comes to be, or again he keeps on considering how the feelings are something that passes away, or he keeps on considering their coming to be with their passing away.

"Or again, with the consciousness: 'There is feeling,' mindfulness thereof becomes thereby established far enough for the purposes of knowledge and of self-collectedness. And he abides independent, grasping after nothing in the world whatever. Thus, bhikkhus, does a brother, with respect to the feelings, continue to consider feeling.

"And how, bhikkhus, does a brother, as to thought, continue to consider thought?

"Herein, O bhikkhus, a brother, if his thought be lustful, is aware that it is so, or if his thought be free from lust, is aware that it is so; or if his thought be full of hate, or free from hate, or dull, or intelligent, or attentive, or distrait, or exalted, or not exalted, or mediocre, or ideal, or composed, or discomposed, or liberated, or bound, he is aware in each case that his thought is so, reflecting: 'My thought is lustful,' and so on.

"So does he, as to thought, continue to consider thought, internally or externally, or internally and externally together. He keeps on considering how thought is something that comes to be, or again he keeps on considering how a thought is something that passes away, or again he ever considers its coming to be and passing away together. Or again, with the consciousness: 'There is a thought,' mindfulness thereof becomes thereby established, far enough for the purposes of knowledge and of self-possession. And he abides independent, grasping after nothing in the world whatever. Thus, bhikkhus, does a brother, with respect to thought, continue to consider thought.

"And how, bhikkhus, does a brother, as to ideas, continue to consider ideas?

"Herein, O bhikkhus, a brother, as to ideas, continues to consider ideas from the point of view of the five hindrances.

"And how, bhikkhus, does a brother, as to ideas, continue to consider ideas relating to the five hindrances?

"Herein, O bhikkhus, a brother, when within him is sensuous desire, is aware of it, reflecting: 'I have within me sensuous desire.' Or again, when within him is no sensuous desire, he is aware of this. And he knows of the uprising of such desire unfelt before, knows too of his putting aside that uprisen sensuous desire, knows too of the non-arising in future of that banished sensuous desire.

"And moreover, bhikkhus, a brother, as to ideas, continues to consider ideas from the point of view of the six internal and external spheres of sense. And how does he do this?

"Herein, O bhikkhus, a brother is aware of the organ of sight, is aware of the objects of sight, and any fetter which arises on account of them both—of that, too, is he aware; and how there comes an uprising of a fetter not arisen before—of that, too, is he aware; and how there comes a putting-aside of a fetter that has arisen—of that, too, is he aware; and how in the future there shall arise no fetter that has been put aside—of that, too, is he aware.

"And so, too, with respect to the organ of hearing and sounds, to the organ of smell and odours, to the organ of taste and tastes, to the organ of touch and tangibles, to the sensorium and images, he is aware of the sense and of the object, of any fetter which arises on account of both, of how there comes an uprising of a fetter not arisen before, of how there comes a putting-aside of a fetter that has arisen, and of how in the future there shall arise no fetter that has been put aside.

"So does he, as to ideas, continue to consider ideas, from the point of view of the six internal and external spheres of sense.

"And moreover, bhikkhus, a brother, as to ideas, continues to consider ideas from the point of view of the four Aryan truths. And how does he do this?

"Herein, O bhikkhus, a brother at the thought: 'This is ill!' is aware of it as it really is;—at the thought: 'This is the coming to be of ill!' is aware of it as it really is;—at the thought: 'This is the cessation of ill!' is aware of it as it really is;—at the thought: 'This is the way leading to the cessation of ill!' is aware of it as it really is.

"And what, bhikkhus, is the Aryan truth concerning the way that leads to the cessation of ill?

"This is that Aryan eightfold path, to wit, right view, right aspiration, right speech, right doing, right livelihood, right effort, right mindfulness, right rapture.

"And what, bhikkhus, is right view?

"Knowledge, bhikkhus, about ill, knowledge about the coming to be of ill, knowledge about the cessation of ill, knowledge about the way that leads to the cessation of ill. This is what is called right view.

"And what, bhikkhus, is right aspiration?

"The aspiration towards renunciation, the aspiration towards benevolence, the aspiration towards kindness. This is what is called right aspiration.

"And what, bhikkhus, is right speech?

"Abstaining from lying, slander, abuse and idle talk. This is what is called right speech.

"And what, bhikkhus, is right doing?

"Abstaining from taking life, from taking what is not given, from carnal indulgence. This is what is called right doing.

"And what, bhikkhus, is right livelihood?

"Herein, O bhikkhus, the Aryan disciple, having put away wrong livelihood, supports himself by right livelihood.

"And what, bhikkhus, is right effort?

"Herein, O bhikkhus, a brother makes effort in bringing forth will that evil and bad states that have not arisen within him may not arise; to that end he stirs up energy, he grips and forces his mind. That he may put away evil and bad states that have arisen within him he puts forth will, he makes effort, he stirs up energy, he grips and forces his mind. That good states which have not arisen may arise he puts forth will, he makes effort, he stirs up energy, he grips and forces his mind. That good states which have arisen may persist, may not grow blurred, may multiply, grow abundant, develop and come to perfection, he puts forth will, he makes effort, he stirs up energy, he grips and forces his mind. This is what is called right effort.

"And what, bhikkhus, is right mindfulness?

"Herein, O bhikkhus, a brother, as to the body, continues so to look upon the body, that he remains ardent, self-possessed and mindful, having overcome both the hankering and the dejection common in the world. And in the same way as to feelings, thoughts and ideas, he so looks upon each, that he remains ardent, self-possessed and mindful, having overcome the hankering and the dejection that is common in the world. This is what is called right mindfulness.

"And what, bhikkhus, is right rapture?

"Herein, O bhikkhus, a brother, aloof from sensuous appetites, aloof from evil ideas, enters into and abides in the first Jhana, wherein there is cogitation and deliberation, which is born of solitude and is full of joy and ease. Suppressing cogitation and deliberation, he enters into and abides in the second Jhana, which is self-evoked, born of concentration, full of joy and ease, in that, set free from cogitation and deliberation, the mind grows calm and sure, dwelling on high. And further, disenchanted with joy, he abides calmly contemplative while, mindful and self-possessed, he feels in his body that ease whereof Aryans declare: 'He that is calmly contemplative and aware, he dwelleth at ease.' So does he enter into and abide in the third Jhana. And further, by putting aside ease and by putting aside malaise, by the passing away of the happiness and of the melancholy he used to feel, he enters into and abides in the fourth Jhana, rapture of utter purity of mindfulness and equanimity, wherein neither ease is felt nor any ill. This is what is called right rapture.

"This, bhikkhus, is the Aryan truth concerning the way leading to the cessation of ill.

"Bhikkhus! whoso shall thus practise these four applications of mindfulness for seven years, in him one of two kinds of fruition may be looked for: either in this present life the Knowledge, or, if there be yet residuum for rebirth, the state of him who returns no more. Or, not to speak of seven years, bhikkhus, whoso shall thus practise these four for six years, for five only, for four only, for three only, for two only, for one year only, in him one of two kinds of fruition may be looked for: either in this present life the Knowledge, or, if there be yet residuum for rebirth, the state of him who returns no more. Or not to speak of one year, bhikkhus, whoso shall thus practise these four for six months, or for five months, for four only, or three, or two, or one month only, or half a month only, in him one of two kinds of fruition may be looked for: either in this present life the Knowledge, or, if there be yet residuum for rebirth, the state of him who returns no more. Or not to speak of half a month, bhikkhus, whoso shall thus practise these four for seven days, in him one of two kinds of fruition may be looked for: either in this present life the Knowledge, or, if there be yet residuum for rebirth, the state of him who returns no more. It was on account of this that that was said which was said (at the beginning): 'The one and only path, bhikkhus, leading to the purification of beings, to passing far beyond

grief and lamentation, to the dying out of ill and misery, to the attainment of right method, to the realization of Nirvana, is that of the four
settings-up of mindfulness.' "

Thus spake the Exalted One. Pleased were the brethren, delighting in
that which was spoken by the Exalted One.

The Perfect Net

Thus have I heard. The Blessed One was once going along the high
road between Rajagaha and Nalanda with about five hundred brethren.
And Suppiya the mendicant too was going along the high road between
Rajagaha and Nalanda with his disciple the youth Brahmadatta. Now
just then Suppiya the mendicant was speaking in many ways in dispraise of the Buddha, in dispraise of the doctrine, in dispraise of the
Order. But young Brahmadatta, his pupil, gave utterance, in many ways,
to praise of the Buddha, to praise of the doctrine, to praise of the Order.
Thus they two, teacher and pupil, holding opinions in direct contradiction one to the other, were following step by step, after the Blessed One
and the company of the brethren.

Now the Blessed One put up at the royal rest-house in the Ambalat-
thika pleasance to pass the night, and with him the company of the
brethren. And so also did Suppiya the mendicant, and with him his
young disciple Brahmadatta. And there, at the rest-house, these two
carried on the same discussion as before.

And in the early dawn a number of the brethren assembled, as they
rose up, in the pavilion; and this was the trend of the talk that sprang
up among them, as they were seated there. "How wonderful a thing
is it, brethren, and how strange that the Blessed One, he who knows
and sees, the Arahant, the Buddha supreme, should so clearly have perceived how various are the inclinations of men! For see how while Suppiya the mendicant speaks in many ways in dispraise of the Buddha, the
doctrine, and the Order, his own disciple, young Brahmadatta, speaks,
in as many ways, in praise of them. So do these two, teacher and pupil,
follow step by step after the Blessed One and the company of the brethren, giving utterance to views in direct contradiction one to the other."

Now the Blessed One, on realizing what was the drift of their talk,
went to the pavilion, and took his seat on the mat spread out for him.

And when he had sat down he said: "What is the talk on which you are engaged sitting here, and what is the subject of the conversation between you?" And they told him all. And he said:

"Brethren, if outsiders should speak against me, or against the doctrine, or against the Order, you should not on that account either bear malice, or suffer heart-burning, or feel illwill. If you, on that account, should be angry and hurt, that would stand in the way of your own self-conquest. If, when others speak against us, you feel angry at that, and displeased, would you then be able to judge how far that speech of theirs is well said or ill?"

"That would not be so, Sir."

"But when outsiders speak in dispraise of me, or of the doctrine, or of the Order, you should unravel what is false and point it out as wrong, saying: 'For this or that reason this is not the fact, that is not so, such a thing is not found among us, is not in us.'

"But also, brethren, if outsiders should speak in praise of me, in praise of the doctrine, in praise of the Order, you should not, on that account, be filled with pleasure or gladness, or be lifted up in heart. Were you to be so that also would stand in the way of your self-conquest. When outsiders speak in praise of me, or of the doctrine, or of the Order, you should acknowledge what is right to be the fact, saying: 'For this or that reason this is the fact, that is so, such a thing is found among us, is in us.'

"It is in respect only of trifling things, of matters of little value, of mere morality, that an unconverted man, when praising the Tathagata, would speak. And what are such trifling, minor details of mere morality that he would praise?

" 'Putting away the killing of living things, Gotama the recluse holds aloof from the destruction of life. He has laid the cudgel and the sword aside, and ashamed of roughness, and full of mercy, he dwells compassionate and kind to all creatures that have life.' It is thus that the unconverted man, when speaking in praise of the Tathagata, might speak.

"Or he might say: 'Putting away the taking of what has not been given, Gotama the recluse lives aloof from grasping what is not his own. He takes only what is given, and expecting that gifts will come, he passes his life in honesty and purity of heart.'

"Or he might say: 'Putting away unchastity, Gotama the recluse is chaste. He holds himself aloof, far off, from the vulgar practice, from the sexual act.'

"Or he might say: 'Putting away lying words, Gotama the recluse holds himself aloof from falsehood. He speaks truth, from the truth he never swerves; faithful and trustworthy, he breaks not his word to the world.'

"Or he might say: 'Putting away slander, Gotama the recluse holds himself aloof from calumny. What he hears here he repeats not elsewhere to raise a quarrel against the people here; what he hears elsewhere he repeats not here to raise a quarrel against the people there. Thus does he live as a binder together of those who are divided, an encourager of those who are friends, a peacemaker, a lover of peace, impassioned for peace, a speaker of words that make for peace.'

"Or he might say: 'Putting away rudeness of speech, Gotama the recluse holds himself aloof from harsh language. Whatsoever word is blameless, pleasant to the ear, lovely, reaching to the heart, urbane, pleasing to the people, beloved of the people—such are words he speaks.'

"Or he might say: 'Putting away frivolous talk, Gotama the recluse holds himself aloof from vain conversation. In season he speaks, in accordance with the facts, words full of meaning, on religion, on the discipline of the Order. He speaks, and at the right time, words worthy to be laid up in one's heart, fitly illustrated, clearly divided, to the point.'[1]

"There are, brethren, other things, profound, difficult to realize, hard to understand, tranquillizing, sweet, not to be grasped by mere logic, subtle, comprehensible only by the wise. These things the Tathagata, having himself realized them and seen them face to face, hath set forth;

---

[1] Here we have omitted nineteen pages in which are listed further minor moralities for which the unconverted might praise the Buddha, such as taking but one meal a day; refraining from seeing "shows at fairs, with nautch dances, singing, and music"; abstaining from ornamentation, scents, and unguents; from the use of large and lofty beds; from accepting silver or gold, raw meat, uncooked grain, women or girls; from cheating, from bribery, from games such as "blowing through toy pipes made of leaves, ploughing with toy ploughs, turning somersaults, guessing at letters traced in the air," etc.; from telling ghost stories, or engaging in futile and wrangling argument and speculations about the creation of land and sea; from earning a living by wrong means, such as divining, prophesying, interpreting dreams, sacrificing to Agni, laying demons and ghosts, snake charming, poison craft, selling charms, weather prophecies, using charms to procure abortions, using charms to make people unlucky, vowing gifts to a god in exchange for benefits, causing virility or impotence, administering purges and emetics, etc.

and it is of them that they, who would rightly praise the Tathagata in accordance with the truth, should speak.

"And what are they?

"There are recluses and Brahmanas, brethren, who reconstruct the ultimate beginnings of things, whose speculations are concerned with the ultimate past, and who on eighteen grounds put forward various assertions regarding it. And about what, with reference to what, do those venerable ones do so?

"There are, brethren, some recluses and Brahmanas who are Eternalists, and who proclaim that both the soul and the world are eternal. And about what, with reference to what, do those venerable ones do so?

"In the first place, brethren, some recluse or Brahmana by means of ardour, of exertion, of application, of earnestness, of careful thought, reaches up to such rapture of heart that, rapt in heart, he calls to mind his various dwelling-places in times gone by—in one birth, or in two, or three, or four, or five, or ten, or twenty, or thirty, or forty, or fifty, or a hundred, or a thousand, or in several hundreds or thousands or lacs of births. And he says to himself: 'Eternal is the soul; and the world, giving birth to nothing new, is steadfast as a mountain peak, as a pillar firmly fixed; and though these living creatures transmigrate and pass away, fall from one state of existence and spring up in another, yet they are for ever and ever. And why must that be so? Because I, by means of ardour, of exertion, of application, of earnestness, of careful thought, can reach up to such rapture of heart that, rapt in heart, I can call to mind, and in full detail both of condition and of custom, my various dwelling-places in times gone by.'

"This, brethren, is the first state of things on account of which, starting from which, some recluses and Brahmanas are Eternalists, and maintain that both the soul and the world are eternal.

"And in the next place, brethren, on what ground is it, starting from what, that those venerable ones are Eternalists, and maintain that the soul and the world are eternal?

"In this case, brethren, some recluse or Brahmana is addicted to logic and reasoning. He gives utterance to the following conclusion of his own, beaten out by his argumentations and based on his sophistry: 'Eternal is the soul; and the world, giving birth to nothing new, is steadfast as a mountain peak, as a pillar firmly fixed; and these living creatures, though they transmigrate and pass away, fall from one state of existence and spring up in another, yet they are for ever and ever.'

"This, brethren, is another state of things on the ground of which, starting from which, some recluses and Brahmanas are Eternalists, and maintain that the soul and the world are eternal.

"Now of these, brethren, the Tathagata knows that these speculations thus arrived at, thus insisted on, will have such and such a result, such and such an effect on the future condition of those who trust in them. That does he know, and he knows also other things far beyond, far better than those speculations; and having that knowledge he is not puffed up, and thus untarnished he has, in his own heart, realized the way of escape from them, has understood, as they really are, the rising up and passing away of sensations, their sweet taste, their danger, how they cannot be relied on; and not grasping after any of those things men are eager for, he, the Tathagata, is quite set free.

"These, brethren, are those other things, profound, difficult to realize, hard to understand, tranquillizing, sweet, not to be grasped by mere logic, subtle, comprehensible only by the wise, which the Tathagata, having himself realized and seen face to face, hath set forth; and it is concerning these that they who would rightly praise the Tathagata in accordance with the truth, should speak.[1]

"For whosoever, brethren, whether recluses or Brahmanas, are thus reconstructors of the past or arrangers of the future, or who are both, whose speculations are concerned with both, who put forward various propositions with regard to the past and to the future, they, all of them, are entrapped in the net of these sixty-two modes; this way and that they plunge about, but they are in it; this way and that they may flounder, but they are included in it, caught in it.

---

[1] Between this and the final paragraphs of the Sutta (here given) are long expositions by the Buddha of those recluses and Brahmanas who are Eternalists with regard to some things and in regard to others, Non-Eternalists, maintaining that the soul and the world are partly eternal and partly not; of those who are Extensionists, and who set forth the infinity or finiteness of the world; of those "who wriggle like eels" when a question is put to them, and resort to equivocation; of those recluses and Brahmanas who are Fortuitous-Originists, and who maintain that the soul and the world arise with a cause; of those "who reconstruct the ultimate beginnings of things, whose speculations are concerned with the ultimate past, and who put forward various assertions of the past"; of those recluses and Brahmanas who arrange the future, and who put forward various assertions regarding the future; of those who hold the doctrine of an unconscious existence after death and who maintain that the soul after death is unconscious; and of recluses and Brahmanas who hold the doctrine of happiness in this life, "who maintain the complete salvation, in this visible world, of a living being."

"Just, brethren, as when a skilful fisherman or fisherlad should drag a tiny pool of water with a fine-meshed net he might fairly think: 'Whatever fish of size may be in this pond, every one will be in this net; flounder about as they may, they will be included in it, and caught'— just so is it with these speculators about the past and the future, in this net, flounder as they may, they are included and caught.

"The outward form, brethren, of him who has won the truth, stands before you, but that which binds it to rebirth is cut in twain. So long as his body shall last, so long do gods and men behold him. On the dissolution of the body, beyond the end of his life, neither gods nor men shall see him.

"Just, brethren, as when the stalk of a bunch of mangoes has been cut, all the mangoes that were hanging on that stalk go with it; just so, brethren, though the outward form of him who has won the truth stands before you, that which binds it to rebirth has been cut in twain. So long as his body shall last, so long do gods and men behold him. On the dissolution of the body, beyond the end of his life, neither gods nor men shall see him."

When he had thus spoken, the venerable Ananda said to the Blessed One: "Strange, Lord, is this, and wonderful! And what name has this exposition of the truth?"

"Ananda, you may remember this exposition as the Net of Advantage, and as the Net of Truth, and as the Supreme Net, and as the Net of Theories; remember it even as the glorious victory in the day of battle!"

Thus spake the Blessed One, and glad at heart the brethren exalted his word. And on the delivery of this discourse the thousandfold world-system shook.

Questions Which Tend Not to Edification

Thus have I heard.

On a certain occasion the Blessed One was dwelling at Savatthi in Jetavana monastery in Anathapindika's Park. Now it happened to the venerable Malunkyaputta, being in seclusion and plunged in meditation, that a consideration presented itself to his mind, as follows:

"These theories which the Blessed One has left unelucidated, has set aside and rejected,—that the world is eternal, that the world is not eternal, that the world is finite, that the world is infinite, that the soul and the body are identical, that the soul is one thing and the body another, that the saint exists after death, that the saint does not exist after death, that the saint both exists and does not exist after death, that the saint neither exists nor does not exist after death,—these the Blessed One does not elucidate to me. And the fact that the Blessed One does not elucidate them to me does not please me nor suit me. Therefore I will draw near to the Blessed One and inquire of him concerning this matter. If the Blessed One will elucidate them to me, in that case will I lead the religious life under the Blessed One. If the Blessed One will not elucidate them to me, in that case will I abandon religious training and return to the lower life of a layman."

Then the venerable Malunkyaputta arose at eventide from his seclusion, and drew near to where the Blessed One was; and having drawn near and greeted the Blessed One, he sat down respectfully at one side. And seated respectfully at one side, the venerable Malunkyaputta spoke to the Blessed One as follows:

"Reverend Sir, it happened to me, as I was just now in seclusion and plunged in meditation, that a consideration presented itself to my mind, as follows: 'These theories which the Blessed One has left unelucidated, has set aside and rejected,—that the world is eternal, that the world is not eternal, . . . that the saint neither exists nor does not exist after death,—these the Blessed One does not elucidate to me. And the fact that the Blessed One does not elucidate them to me does not please me nor suit me. I will draw near to the Blessed One and inquire of him concerning this matter. If the Blessed One will elucidate them to me, in that case will I lead the religious life under the Blessed One. If the Blessed One will not elucidate them to me, in that case will I abandon religious training and return to the lower life of a layman.'

"If the Blessed One knows that the world is eternal, let the Blessed One elucidate to me that the world is eternal; if the Blessed One knows that the world is not eternal, let the Blessed One elucidate to me that the world is not eternal. If the Blessed One does not know either that the world is eternal or that the world is not eternal, the only upright thing for one who does not know, or who has not that insight, is to say, 'I do not know; I have not that insight.'"

"Pray, Malunkyaputta, did I ever say to you, 'Come, Malunkyaputta, lead the religious life under me, and I will elucidate to you either that the world is eternal, or that the world is not eternal, . . . or that the saint neither exists nor does not exist after death'?"

"Nay, verily, Reverend Sir."

"Or did you ever say to me, 'Reverend Sir, I will lead the religious life under the Blessed One, on condition that the Blessed One elucidate to me either that the world is eternal, or that the world is not eternal, . . . or that the saint neither exists nor does not exist after death'?"

"Nay, verily, Reverend Sir."

"That being the case, vain man, whom are you so angrily denouncing?

"Malunkyaputta, any one who should say, 'I will not lead the religious life under the Blessed One until the Blessed One shall elucidate to me either that the world is eternal, or that the world is not eternal, . . . or that the saint neither exists nor does not exist after death;'—that person would die, Malunkyaputta, before the Tathagata had ever elucidated this to him.

"It is as if, Malunkyaputta, a man had been wounded by an arrow thickly smeared with poison, and his friends and companions, his relatives and kinsfolk, were to procure for him a physician or surgeon; and the sick man were to say, 'I will not have this arrow taken out until I have learnt whether the man who wounded me belonged to the warrior caste, or to the Brahmana caste, or to the agricultural caste, or to the menial caste.'

"Or again he were to say, 'I will not have this arrow taken out until I have learnt whether the arrow which wounded me was an ordinary arrow, or a claw-headed arrow, or a vekanda, or an iron arrow, or a calf-tooth arrow, or a karavirapatta.' That man would die, Malunkyaputta, without ever having learnt this.

"In exactly the same way, Malunkyaputta, any one who should say, 'I will not lead the religious life under the Blessed One until the Blessed One shall elucidate to me either that the world is eternal, or that the world is not eternal, . . . or that the saint neither exists nor does not exist after death;'—that person would die, Malunkyaputta, before the Tathagata had ever elucidated this to him.

"The religious life, Malunkyaputta, does not depend on the dogma that the world is eternal; nor does the religious life, Malunkyaputta, depend on the dogma that the world is not eternal. Whether the dogma obtain, Malunkyaputta, that the world is eternal, or that the world is not eternal, there still remain birth, old age, death, sorrow, lamentation, misery, grief, and despair, for the extinction of which in the present life I am prescribing.

"Accordingly, Malunkyaputta, bear always in mind what it is that I have not elucidated, and what it is that I have elucidated. And what, Malunkyaputta, have I not elucidated? I have not elucidated, Malunkya-putta, that the world is eternal; I have not elucidated that the world is not eternal. . . . I have not elucidated that the saint neither exists nor does not exist after death. And why, Malunkyaputta, have I not eluci-dated this? Because, Malunkyaputta, this profits not, nor has to do with the fundamentals of religion, nor tends to aversion, absence of passion, cessation, quiescence, the supernatural faculties, supreme wisdom, and Nirvana; therefore have I not elucidated it.

"And what, Malunkyaputta, have I elucidated? Misery, Malunkya-putta, have I elucidated; the origin of misery have I elucidated; the cessa-tion of misery have I elucidated; and the path leading to the cessation of misery have I elucidated. And why, Malunkyaputta, have I elucidated this? Because, Malunkyaputta, this does profit, has to do with the funda-mentals of religion, and tends to aversion, absence of passion, cessation, quiescence, knowledge, supreme wisdom, and Nirvana; therefore have I elucidated it. Accordingly, Malunkyaputta, bear always in mind what it is that I have not elucidated, and what it is that I have elucidated."

Thus spake the Blessed One; and, delighted, the venerable Malunkya-putta applauded the speech of the Blessed One.

Discussion of Dependent Origination

Thus have I heard.

On a certain occasion the Blessed One was dwelling among the Kurus where was the Kuru-town named Kammasadhamma.

Then drew near the venerable Ananda to where the Blessed One was; and having drawn near and greeted the Blessed One, he sat down respect-fully at one side. And seated respectfully at one side, the venerable Ananda spoke to the Blessed One as follows:

"O wonderful is it, Reverend Sir! O marvellous is it, Reverend Sir!

How profound, Reverend Sir, is dependent origination, and of how profound an appearance! To me, nevertheless, it is as clear as clear can be."

"O Ananda, say not so! O Ananda, say not so! Profound, Ananda, is dependent origination, and profound of appearance. It is through not understanding this doctrine, Ananda, through not penetrating it, that thus mankind is like to an entangled warp, or to an ensnarled web, or to munja-grass and pabbaja-grass, and fails to extricate itself from punishment, suffering, perdition, rebirth.

"Ananda, if it be asked, 'Do old age and death depend on anything?' the reply should be, 'They do.' And if it be asked, 'On what do old age and death depend?' the reply should be, 'Old age and death depend on birth.'

"Ananda, if it be asked, 'Does birth depend on anything?' the reply should be, 'It does.' And if it be asked, 'On what does birth depend?' the reply should be, 'Birth depends on existence.'

"Ananda, if it be asked, 'Does existence depend on anything?' the reply should be, 'It does.' And if it be asked, 'On what does existence depend?' the reply should be, 'Existence depends on attachment.'

"Ananda, if it be asked, 'Does attachment depend on anything?' the reply should be, 'It does.' And if it be asked, 'On what does attachment depend?' the reply should be, 'Attachment depends on desire.'

"Ananda, if it be asked, 'Does desire depend on anything?' the reply should be, 'It does.' And if it be asked, 'On what does desire depend?' the reply should be, 'Desire depends on sensation.'

"Ananda, if it be asked, 'Does sensation depend on anything?' the reply should be, 'It does.' And if it be asked, 'On what does sensation depend?' the reply should be, 'Sensation depends on contact.'

"Ananda, if it be asked, 'Does contact depend on anything?' the reply should be, 'It does.' And if it be asked, 'On what does contact depend?' the reply should be, 'Contact depends on the mental and physical phenomena.'

"Ananda, if it be asked, 'Do the mental and physical phenomena depend on anything?' the reply should be, 'They do.' And if it be asked, 'On what do the mental and physical phenomena depend?' the reply should be, 'The mental and physical phenomena depend on consciousness.'

"Ananda, if it be asked, 'Does consciousness depend on anything?' the reply should be, 'It does.' And if it be asked, 'On what does consciousness depend?' the reply should be, 'Consciousness depends on the mental and physical phenomena.'

"Thus, Ananda, on the mental and physical phenomena depends consciousness;

"On consciousness depend the mental and physical phenomena;

"On the mental and physical phenomena depends contact;

"On contact depends sensation;

"On sensation depends desire;

"On desire depends attachment;

"On attachment depends existence;

"On existence depends birth;

"On birth depend old age and death, sorrow, lamentation, misery, grief, and despair. Thus does this entire aggregation of misery arise."

On Theology

Then the young Brahmana Vasettha and the young Brahmana Bharadvaga went on to the place where the Exalted One was.

And when they had come there, they exchanged with the Exalted One the greetings and compliments of politeness and courtesy, and sat down beside him.

And while they were thus seated the young Brahmana Vasettha said to the Exalted One:

"As we, Gotama, were taking exercise and walking up and down, there sprang up a conversation between us on which was the true path, and which the false. I said thus:

" 'This is the straight path, this the direct way which makes for salvation, and leads him, who acts according to it, into a state of union with Brahma. I mean that which has been announced by the Brahmana Pokkharasadi.'

"Bharadvaga said thus:

" 'This is the straight path, this the direct way which makes for salvation, and leads him, who acts according to it, into a state of union with Brahma. I mean that which has been announced by the Brahmana Tarukkha.'

"Regarding this matter, Gotama, there is a strife, a dispute, a difference of opinion between us."

"Wherein, then, O Vasettha, is there a strife, a dispute, a difference of opinion between you?"

"Concerning the true path and the false, Gotama. Various Brahmanas, Gotama, teach various paths. The Addhariya Brahmanas, the Tittiriya Brahmanas, the Khandoka Brahmanas (the Khandava Brahmanas), the Bavhariga Brahmanas. Are all those saving paths? Are they all paths which will lead him, who acts according to them, into a state of union with Brahma?

"Just, Gotama, as near a village or a town there are many and various paths, yet they all meet together in the village—just in that way are all the various paths taught by various Brahmanas. Are all these saving paths? Are they all paths which will lead him, who acts according to them, into a state of union with Brahma?"

"Do you say that they all lead aright, Vasettha?"

"I say so, Gotama."

"Do you really say that they all lead aright, Vasettha?"

"So I say, Gotama."

"But yet, Vasettha, is there a single one of the Brahmanas versed in the three Vedas who has ever seen Brahma face to face?"

"No, indeed, Gotama."

"Or is there then, Vasettha, a single one of the teachers of the Brahmanas versed in the three Vedas who has seen Brahma face to face?"

"No, indeed, Gotama!"

"Or is there then, Vasettha, a single one of the pupils of the teachers of the Brahmanas versed in the three Vedas who has seen Brahma face to face?"

"No, indeed, Gotama!"

"Or is there then, Vasettha, a single one of the Brahmanas up to the seventh generation who has seen Brahma face to face?"

"No, indeed, Gotama!"

"Well, then, Vasettha, those ancient Rishis of the Brahmanas versed in the three Vedas, the authors of the verses, the utterers of the verses, whose ancient form of words so chanted, uttered, or composed, the Brahmanas of to-day chant over again or repeat; intoning or reciting exactly as has been intoned or recited; did even they speak thus, saying: 'We know it, we have seen it, where Brahma is, whence Brahma is, whither Brahma is'?"

"Not so, Gotama!"

"Then you say, Vasettha, that none of the Brahmanas, or of their teachers, or of their pupils, even up to the seventh generation, has ever seen Brahma face to face. And that even the Rishis of old, the authors and utterers of the verses, of the ancient form of words which the Brahmanas of to-day so carefully intone and recite precisely as they have been handed down—even they did not pretend to know or to have seen where or whence or whither Brahma is. So that the Brahmanas versed in the three Vedas have forsooth said thus: 'What we know not, what we have not seen, to a state of union with that we can show the way, and can say: "This is the straight path, this is the direct way which makes for salvation, and leads him, who acts according to it, into a state of union with Brahma!" '

"Now what think you, Vasettha? Does it not follow, this being so, that the talk of the Brahmanas, versed though they be in the three Vedas, turns out to be foolish talk?"

"In sooth, Gotama, that being so, it follows that the talk of the Brahmanas versed in the three Vedas is foolish talk!"

The Passing Away and Becoming of the World

Thus have I heard:

The Exalted One was once staying near Savatthi, in the East Park, at the mansion of the mother of Migara. Then the Exalted One said to Vasettha:

There comes a time, Vasettha, when, sooner or later, after the lapse of a long, long period, this world passes away. And when this happens, beings have mostly been reborn in the World of Radiance; and there they dwell, made of mind, feeding on rapture, self-luminous, traversing the air, continuing in glory; and thus they remain for a long, long period of time. There comes also a time, Vasettha, when sooner or later this world begins to re-evolve. When this happens, beings who have deceased from the World of Radiance usually come to life as humans. And they become made of mind, feeding on rapture, self-luminous, traversing the air, continuing in glory, and remain thus for a long, long period of time.

Now at that time, all had become one world of water, dark, and of darkness that maketh blind. No moon nor sun appeared, no stars were seen nor constellations, neither was night manifest nor day, neither months nor half-months, neither years nor seasons, neither female nor male. Beings were reckoned just as beings only. And to those beings, Vasettha, sooner or later after a long time, earth with its savour was spread out in the waters. Even as a scum forms on the surface of boiled milky rice that is cooling, so did the earth appear. It became endowed with colour, with odour, and with taste. Even as well-made ghee or pure butter, so was its colour; even as the flawless honey of the bee, so sweet was it.

Then, Vasettha, some being of greedy disposition, said: Lo now! what will this be? and tasted the savoury earth with his finger. He thus, tasting, became suffused with the savour, and craving entered into him. And other beings, following his example, tasted the savoury earth with their fingers. They thus, tasting, became suffused with the savour, a craving entered into them. Then those beings began to feast on the savoury earth, breaking off lumps of it with their hands. And from the doing thereof the self-luminance of those beings faded away. As their self-luminance faded away, the moon and the sun became manifest. Thereupon star-shapes and constellations became manifest. Thereupon night and day became manifest, months too and half-months, the seasons and the years. Thus far then, Vasettha, did the world evolve again.

Now those beings, Vasettha, feasting on the savoury earth, feeding on it, nourished by it, continued thus for a long long while. And in measure as they thus fed, did their bodies become solid, and did variety in their comeliness become manifest. Some beings were well favoured, some were ill favoured. And herein they that were well favoured despised them that were ill favoured, thinking: We are more comely than they; they are worse favoured than we. And while they through pride in their beauty thus became vain and conceited, the savoury earth disappeared. At the disappearance of the savoury earth, they gathered themselves together and bewailed it: Alas for the savour! alas for the savour! Even so now when men having gotten a good savour say: Ah, the savour of it! ah, the savour of it! they do but follow an ancient primordial saying, not recognizing the significance thereof.

Then, Vasettha, when the savoury earth had vanished for those beings, outgrowths appeared in the soil. The manner of the rising up thereof was as the springing up of the mushroom, it had colour, odour and taste; even as well-formed ghee or fine butter so was the colour thereof, and even as flawless honeycomb so was the sweetness thereof. Then those beings began to feast on these outgrowths of the soil. And they, feasting on them, finding food and nourishment in them, continued for a long long while. And in measure as they thus fed and were thus nourished, so did their bodies grow ever more solid, and the difference in their comeliness more manifest, some becoming well favoured, some ill favoured. Then they that were well favoured despised them that were ill favoured, thinking: We are more comely than they; they are worse favoured than we. And while they, through pride in their beauty, thus became vain and conceited, these outgrowths of the soil disappeared. Thereupon creeping plants appeared, and the manner of the growth thereof was as that of the bamboo, and they had colour, odour and taste. Even as well-made ghee or fine butter so was the colour thereof; even as flawless honeycomb so was the sweetness thereof.

Then, Vasettha, those beings began to feast on the creepers. And they, feasting on them, feeding on them, nourished by them, continued so for a long long while. And in measure as they thus fed and were nourished did their bodies wax more solid, and the divergence in their comeliness increase, so that, as before, the better favoured despised the worse favoured. And while those, through pride in their beauty, became vain and conceited, the creepers disappeared. At the disappearance thereof they gathered themselves together and bewailed, saying: Verily it was ours, the creeper! Now it has vanished away! Alas and O me! we have lost! Even so now when men, being asked what is the matter, say: Alas and O me! what we had that have we lost! they do but follow an ancient primordial saying, not recognizing the significance thereof.

Then, Vasettha, when the creepers had vanished for those beings, rice appeared ripening in open spaces,

> No powder had it and no husk.
> Pure, fragrant and clean grained.

Where of an evening they gathered and carried away for supper, there next morning the rice stood ripe and grown again. Where in the morning they gathered and carried away for breakfast, there in the evening it stood ripe and grown again. No break was to be seen where the husks had been broken off.

Then those beings feasting on this rice in the clearings, feeding on

it, nourished by it, so continued for a long long while. And in measure
as they, thus feeding, went on existing, so did the bodies of those beings
become even more solid, and the divergence in their comeliness more
pronounced. In the female appeared the distinctive features of the
female, in the male those of the male. Then truly did woman contemplate man too closely, and man, woman. In their contemplating
over-much the one the other, passion arose and burning entered their
body. They in consequence thereof followed their lusts. And beings
seeing them so doing threw, some, sand, some, ashes, some, cowdung,
crying: Perish, foul one! perish, foul one! How can a being treat a
being so? Even so now when men, in certain districts, when a bride is
led away, throw either sand, or ashes, or cowdung, they do but follow
an ancient enduring primordial form, not recognizing the significance
thereof.

That which was reckoned immoral at that time, Vasettha, is now
reckoned to be moral. Those beings who at that time followed their
lusts, were not allowed to enter village or town either for a whole
month or even for two months. And inasmuch as those beings at that
time quickly incurred blame for immorality, they set to work to make
huts, to conceal just that immorality.

Then Vasettha, this occurred to some being of a lazy disposition:
Lo now! why do I wear myself out fetching rice for supper in the
evening, and in the morning for breakfast? What if I were to fetch
enough rice for supper and breakfast together? So he gathered at one
journey enough rice for the two meals together.

Then some being came to him and said: Come, good being, let us go
rice-gathering. That's not wanted, good being, I have fetched rice for
the evening and morning meal. Then the former followed his example
and fetched rice for two days at once, saying: So much, they say, will
about do. Then some other being came to this one and said: Come,
good being, let us go rice-gathering. And he: Never mind, good being,
I have fetched rice enough for two days. And so, in like manner, they
stored up rice enough for four, and then for eight days.

Now from the time, Vasettha, that those beings began to feed on
hoarded rice, powder enveloped the clean grain, and husk enveloped
the grain, and the reaped or cut stems did not grow again; a break
became manifest where the reaper had cut; the rice-stubble stood in
clumps.

Then those beings, Vasettha, gathered themselves and bewailed this, saying: Evil customs, sirs, have appeared among men. For in the past, we were made of mind, we fed on rapture, self-luminous, we traversed the air in abiding loveliness; long long the period we so remained. For us sooner or later, after a long long while the savoury earth had arisen over the waters. Colour it had, and odour and taste. We set to work to make the earth into lumps, and feast on it. As we did so our self-luminance vanished away. When it was gone, moon and sun became manifest, star-shapes and constellations, night and day, the months and half-months, the seasons and the years. We, enjoying the savoury earth, feeding on it, nourished by it, continued so for a long long while. But since evil and immoral customs became rife among us, the savoury earth disappeared. When it had ceased outgrowths of the soil became manifest, clothed with colour, odour and taste. Them we began to enjoy; and fed and nourished thereby, we continued so for a long long while. But when evil and immoral customs arose among us, these outgrowths disappeared. When they had vanished, creepers appeared clothed with colour, odour and taste. Them we turned to enjoy; and fed and nourished thereby we continued so for a long long while. But since evil and immoral customs became prevalent among us, the creepers also disappeared. When they had ceased rice appeared, ripening in open spaces, without powder, without husk, pure, fragrant and clean grained. Where we plucked and took away for the evening meal every evening, there next morning it had grown ripe again. Where we plucked and took away for the morning meal, there in the evening it had grown ripe again. There was no break visible. Enjoying this rice, feeding on it, nourished by it, we have so continued a long long while. But from evil and immoral customs becoming manifest among us, powder has enveloped the clean grain, husk too has enveloped the clean grain, and where we have reaped is no re-growth; a break has come, and the rice-stubble stands in clumps. Come now, let us divide off the rice fields and set boundaries thereto! And so they divided off the rice and set up boundaries round it.

Now some being, Vasettha, of greedy disposition, watching over his own plot, stole another plot and made use of it. They took him and holding him fast, said: Truly, good being, thou hast wrought evil in that, while watching thine own plot, thou hast stolen another plot and made use of it. See, good being, that thou do not such a thing again!

Aye, sirs, he replied. And a second time he did so. And yet a third. And again they took him and admonished him. Some smote him with the hand, some with clods, some with sticks. With such a beginning, Vasettha, did stealing appear, and censure and lying and punishment became known.

Now those beings, Vasettha, gathered themselves together, and bewailed these things, saying: From our evil deeds, sirs, becoming manifest, inasmuch as stealing, censure, lying, punishment have become known, what if we were to select a certain being, who should be wrathful when indignation is right, who should censure that which should rightly be censured and should banish him who deserves to be banished? But we will give him in return a proportion of the rice.

Then, Vasettha, those beings went to the being among them who was the handsomest, the best favoured, the most attractive, the most capable, and said to him: Come now, good being, be indignant at that whereat one should rightly be indignant, censure that which should rightly be censured, banish him who deserves to be banished. And we will contribute to thee a proportion of our rice.

And he consented, and did so, and they gave him a proportion of their rice.

Chosen by the whole people, Vasettha, is what is meant by Maha Sammata; so Maha Sammata (the Great Elect) was the first standing phrase to arise for such an one. Lord of the fields is what is meant by Khattiya; so Khattiya (Noble) was the next expression to arise. He charms the others by Dhamma—by what ought to charm—is what is meant by Raja; so this was the third standing phrase to arise.

Thus then, Vasettha, was the origin of this social circle of the nobles, according to the ancient primordial phrases (by which they were known). Their origin was from among those very beings, and no others; like unto themselves, not unlike; and it took place according to Dhamma (according to what ought to be, justly), not unfittingly.

For, Vasettha:

> Dhamma's the best among this folk,
> Both in this world and in the next.

Now it occurred, Vasettha, to some of those beings, as follows: Evil deeds, sirs, have become manifest among us, inasmuch as stealing, censure, lying, punishment can be noticed, and banishment. Let us now put away from us evil and immoral customs. And they put away from them such customs. They put away evil, immoral customs, Vasettha, is what is meant by Brahmanas, and thus was it that Brahmanas became the earliest standing phrase for those who did so.

The Fall and Rise of Social Behaviour

(*Words ascribed to Gotama Buddha*)

When poverty was become rife, a certain man took that which others had not given him, what people call by theft. Him they caught, and brought before the king, saying: This man, O king, has taken that which was not given him, and that is theft.

Thereupon the king spake thus to the man: Is it true, sirrah, that thou hast taken what no man gave thee, hast committed what men call theft?

It is true, O king.

But why?

O king, I have nothing to keep me alive.

Then the king bestowed wealth on that man, saying: With this wealth, sirrah, do thou both keep thyself alive, maintain thy parents, maintain children and wife, carry on thy business, and keep up such alms for holy men as shall be of value in the realms above, heavenly gifts, the result whereof shall be happiness here and rebirth in the heavenly worlds.

Even so, O king, replied the man.

Now another man, brethren, took by theft what was not given him. Him they caught and brought before the king, the anointed Kshatriya, and told him, saying: This man, O king, hath taken by theft what was not given him.

And the king spoke and did even as he had spoken and done to the former man.

Now men heard, brethren, that to them who had taken by theft what was not given them, the king was giving wealth. And hearing they thought: Let us then take by theft what has not been given us.

Now a certain man did so. And him they caught and charged before the king, the anointed Kshatriya, who, as before, asked him why he had stolen.

Because, O king, I cannot maintain myself.

Then the king thought: If I bestow wealth on any one soever who has taken by theft what was not given him, there will be hereby an increase of this stealing. Let me now put a final stop to this, inflict condign punishment on him, have his head cut off!

So he bade his men saying: Now, look ye! bind this man's arms behind him with a strong rope and a tight knot, shave his head bald, lead him around with a harsh sounding drum, from road to road, from crossways to crossways, take him out by the southern gate, and to the south of the town, put a final stop to this, inflict on him the uttermost penalty, cut off his head.

Even so, O king, answered the men, and carried out his commands.

Now men heard, brethren, that they who took by theft what was not given them, were thus put to death. And hearing, they thought: Let us also now have sharp swords made ready for ourselves, and them from whom we take what is not given us—what they call theft—let us put a final stop to them, inflict on them the uttermost penalty, and cut their heads off.

And they gat themselves sharp swords, and came forth to sack village and town and city, and to work highway robbery. And them whom they robbed they made an end of, cutting off their heads.

Thus, brethren, from goods not being bestowed on the destitute poverty grew rife; from poverty growing rife stealing increased, from the spread of stealing violence grew apace, from the growth of violence the destruction of life became common, from the frequency of murder both the span of life in those beings and their comeliness also wasted away, so that, of humans whose span of life was eighty thousand years, the sons lived but forty thousand years.

Now among humans of the latter span of life, brethren, a certain man took by theft what was not given him and, even as those others, was accused before the king and questioned if it was true that he had stolen.

Nay, O king, he replied, thus deliberately telling a lie.

Thus, from goods not being bestowed on the destitute, poverty grew rife . . . stealing . . . violence . . . murder . . . until lying grew common. And from lying growing common both the span of life in those beings and the comeliness of them wasted away, so that of humans whose span of life was forty thousand years, the sons lived but twenty thousand years.

Now among humans of the latter life-span, a certain man took by theft what was not given him. Him a certain man reported to the king, the anointed Kshatriya, saying: Such and such a man, O king, has taken by theft what was not given him—thus speaking evil of him.

And so, brethren, from goods not being bestowed on the destitute, poverty grew rife . . . stealing . . . violence . . . murder . . . lying . . . evil speaking grew abundant. And from evil speaking growing abundant, both the life-span of those beings and also the comeliness of them wasted away, so that, of humans whose life-span was twenty thousand years, the sons lived but ten thousand years.

Now among humans of the latter span of life, brethren, some were comely and some were ugly. And so those who were ugly, coveting them that were comely, committed adultery with their neighbours' wives.

Thus from goods not being bestowed on the destitute, poverty . . . stealing . . . violence . . . murder . . . lying . . . evil speaking . . . immorality grew rife. And from the increase of immorality, both the life-span of those beings and also the comeliness of them wasted away, so that, of humans whose life-span was ten thousand years, the sons lived but five thousand years.

Now among humans of the latter span of life, brethren, two things increased, abusive speech and idle talk. And from these two things increasing, both the life-span of those beings and the comeliness of them wasted away, so that, of humans whose life-span was five thousand years, some sons lived but two and a half, some but two, thousand years.

Among humans of a life-span of two thousand years and a half, covetousness and ill-will waxed great. And thereby . . . the sons lived but a thousand years.

Among humans of the latter span of life, brethren, false opinions grew. And thereby the life-span of those beings and the comeliness of them wasted, so that, of humans whose span of life was a thousand years, the sons lived but five hundred years.

Among humans of the latter span of life, brethren, three things grew apace: incest, wanton greed, and perverted lust. Thereby the life-span of those beings and their comeliness wasted, so that, of humans whose span of life was five hundred years, some sons lived but two and a half centuries, some only two centuries.

Among humans of a life-span, brethren, of two and a half centuries, these things grew apace—lack of filial piety to mother and father, lack of religious piety to holy men, lack of regard for the head of the clan.

Thus, brethren, from goods not being bestowed on the destitute, poverty grew great . . . stealing . . . violence . . . murder . . . lying . . . evil speaking . . . adultery . . . abusive and idle talk . . . covetousness and ill-will . . . false opinions . . . incest, wanton greed and perverted lust . . . till finally lack of filial and religious piety and lack of regard for the head of the clan grew great. From these things growing, the life-span of those beings and the comeliness of them wasted, so that, of humans whose span of life was two and a half centuries, the sons lived but one century.

There will come a time, brethren, when the descendants of those humans will have a life-span of ten years. Among humans of this life-span, maidens of five years will be of a marriageable age. Among such humans these kinds of tastes (savours) will disappear: ghee, butter, oil of tila, sugar, salt. Among such humans kudrusa grain will be the highest kind of food. Even as to-day, rice and curry is the highest kind of food, so will kudrusa grain be then. Among such humans the ten moral courses of conduct will altogether disappear, the ten immoral courses of action will flourish excessively; there will be no word for moral among such humans—far less any moral agent. Among such humans, brethren, they who lack filial and religious piety, and show no respect for the head of the clan—'tis they to whom homage and praise will be given, just as to-day homage and praise are given to the filial-minded, to the pious and to them who respect the heads of their clans.

Among such humans, brethren, there will be no such thoughts of reverence as are a bar to inter-marriage with mother, or mother's sister, or mother's sister-in-law, or teacher's wife, or father's sister-in-law. The world will fall into promiscuity, like goats and sheep, fowls and swine, dogs and jackals.

Among such humans, brethren, keen mutual enmity will become the rule, keen ill-will, keen animosity, passionate thoughts even of killing, in a mother towards her child, in a child towards its mother, in a father towards his child and a child towards its father, in brother to brother, in brother to sister, in sister to brother. Just as a sportsman feels towards the game that he sees, so will they feel.

Among such humans, brethren, there will arise a sword-period of seven days, during which they will look on each other as wild beasts; sharp swords will appear ready to their hands, and they, thinking, This is a wild beast, this is a wild beast, will with their swords deprive each other of life.

Then to some of those beings it will occur: Let us not slay just any one; nor let just any one slay us! Let us now, therefore, betake ourselves to dens of grass, or dens in the jungle, or holes in trees, or river fastnesses, or mountain clefts, and subsist on roots and fruits of the jungle. And they will do so for those seven days. And at the end of those seven days, coming forth from those dens and fastnesses and mountain clefts, they will embrace each other, and be of one accord comforting one another, and saying: Hail, O mortal, that thou livest still! O happy sight to find thee still alive!

Then this, brethren, will occur to those beings: Now, only because we had gotten into evil ways, have we had this heavy loss of kith and kin. Let us therefore now do good. What can we do that is good? Let us now abstain from taking life. That is a good thing that we may take up and do. And they will abstain from slaughter, and will continue in this good way. Because of their getting into this good way, they will increase again both as to their span of life and as to their comeliness. And to them thus increasing in life and comeliness, to them who lived but one decade, there will be children who will live for twenty years.

Then this, brethren, will occur to those beings: Now we, because we have gotten into good ways, increase in length of life and comeliness. Let us now do still more good. Let us now abstain from taking what is not given, let us abstain from adultery, let us now abstain from lying, let us now abstain from evil speaking, let us now abstain from abuse and from idle talk, let us now abstain from covetousness, from ill-will, from false opinions, let us now abstain from the three things— incest, wanton greed and perverted desires; let us now be filial towards our mothers, and our fathers, let us be pious towards holy men, let us respect the heads of clans, yea, let us continue to practise each of these good things.

So they will practise these virtues. And because of the good they do they will increase in length of life, and in comeliness, so that the sons of them who lived but twenty years will come to live forty years. And the sons of these sons will come to live eighty years; their sons to one hundred and sixty years; their sons to three hundred and twenty years; their sons to six hundred and forty years; their sons to two thousand years; their sons to four thousand years; their sons to eight thousand years; their sons to twenty thousand years; their sons to forty thousand years; and the sons of those that lived forty thousand years will come to live eighty thousand years.

Among humans living eighty thousand years, brethren, maidens are marriageable at five hundred years of age. Among such humans there will be only three kinds of disease—appetite, non-assimilation and old age. Among such humans, this India will be mighty and prosperous, the villages, towns and royal cities will be so close that a cock could fly from each one to the next.

The Buddha and the Elephant

Thus have I heard: On a certain occasion the Exalted One was staying at Kosambi in Ghosita Park. Now on that occasion the Exalted One was worried by monks and nuns, lay-followers, both men and women, by rajas and royal ministers, by sectarians and their followers, and lived in discomfort, not at ease. Then the Exalted One thought: Here am I living worried by monks and nuns . . . by sectarians and their followers. I live in discomfort, not at ease. Suppose I were to live remote from the crowd alone.

So the Exalted One, robing himself in the forenoon and taking bowl and robe, entered Kosambi to quest for alms-food; and having done his rounds for alms-food in Kosambi, after returning and eating his meal, he himself set his bed and lodging in order, and taking bowl and robe, without informing his attendant or giving notice to the order of monks, alone and unattended, started on his rounds for Parileyya village, and later on, while on his rounds, reached that place. There the Exalted One took up his dwelling in Guarded Forest Glade, at the foot of a lovely sal tree.

Now a certain bull-elephant was living worried by elephants and she-elephants, by calf-elephants and sucklings, and had to feed on grass already cropped by them. They ate the bundles of branches as he broke them off. He had to drink muddied water, and when he crossed over by the ford the she-elephants went pushing against his body. So he lived in discomfort, not at ease. So this bull-elephant thought: Here am I living worried by elephants and she-elephants, by calf-elephants and sucklings. I have to feed on grass already cropped. They eat the bundles of branches as I break them off. I have to drink muddied water, and when I cross over by the ford the she-elephants go pushing against my body. Thus I live in discomfort, not at ease. Suppose now I were to live remote from the crowd alone.

Accordingly that bull-elephant left the herd and started for Parileyya village and Guarded Forest Glade and the foot of the lovely sal tree where was the Exalted One. On reaching that place he kept the spot where the Exalted One was staying free from grass, and with his trunk brought water for the use of the Exalted One.

Thus the Exalted One lived in seclusion and solitude, and there arose in him this thought: Formerly I dwelt worried by monks and nuns . . . I lived in discomfort, not at ease. But now here am I dwelling unworried by monks and nuns . . . by sectarians and their followers. Unworried, I dwell in comfort and at ease. Likewise that bull-elephant thought: Formerly I dwelt worried by elephants . . . Now I dwell unworried, in comfort and at ease.

And the Exalted One, observing his own seclusion and knowing with his mind the thought of that bull-elephant, at that time gave utterance to this verse of uplift:

> Herein agreeth mind with mind, of sage
> And elephant whose tusks are like a plough pole,
> Since both alike love forest solitude.

The Mighty Ocean of Dhamma

Then the Exalted One admonished the monks, saying:
"Just as, monks, the mighty ocean flows down, slides and tends downward gradually, and there is no abrupt precipice, so also in this dhamma-discipline the training is gradual, the action is gradual, the procedure is gradual; there is no abrupt penetration of knowledge. Since this is so

. . . this is the first strange and wonderful thing, seeing which monks take delight in this dhamma-discipline.

"Just as, monks, the mighty ocean is of a stable nature, since it overpasses not its boundary, even so, monks, my disciples transgress not, even at cost of life, the training enjoined on them by me. Since this is so . . . this is the second strange and wonderful thing. . . .

"Just as, monks, the mighty ocean consorts not with a dead body; for when a dead body is found in the mighty ocean it quickly wafts it ashore, throws it up on the shore; even so, monks, whatsoever person is immoral, of a wicked nature, impure, of suspicious behaviour, of covert deeds, one who is no recluse though claiming to be such, one who is no liver of the Brahma-life though claiming to be such, one rotten within, full of lusts, a rubbish-heap of filth,—with such the Order consorts not, but gathering together quickly throws him out. Though, monks, he be seated in the midst of the Order, yet is he far away from the Order; far away is the Order from him. Since this is so . . . this is the third strange and wonderful thing. . . .

"Just as, monks, whatsoever great rivers there are—namely, Ganga, Yamuna, Aciravati, Sarabhu, Mahi—these, on reaching the mighty ocean, abandon their former names and lineage, and henceforth go by the name of just 'mighty ocean,' even so, monks, the four castes— namely, the nobles, the Brahmanas, the merchants and the serfs—on going forth from home to the homeless in the dhamma-discipline proclaimed by the Wayfarer, abandon their former names and lineage and go by the name of just 'recluses who are Sakya sons.' Since this is so, this is the fourth strange and wonderful thing. . . .

"Just as, monks, whatsoever streams flow into the mighty ocean and whatsoever floods fall from the sky, there is no shrinkage nor overflow seen thereby in the mighty ocean,—even so, monks, though many monks pass finally away in that condition of Nirvana which has no remainder, yet is there no shrinkage nor overflow in that condition of Nirvana seen thereby. Since this is so . . . this is the fifth strange and wonderful thing. . . .

"Just as, monks, the mighty ocean is of one flavour, the flavour of salt, even so, monks, this dhamma is of one flavour, the flavour of release. Since this is so . . . this is the sixth strange and wonderful thing. . . .

"Just as, monks, the mighty ocean has many gems, divers gems . . .

even so in this dhamma are many gems, divers gems; therein are the four arisings of mindfulness, the four best efforts, the four bases of psychic power, the five faculties, the five powers, the seven limbs of wisdom, the Aryan eightfold way. Since this is so . . . this is the seventh strange and wonderful thing. . . .

"Just as, monks, the mighty ocean is the abode of great creatures, therein are these creatures,—the leviathan, the fish-eater . . . Gandharvas; even so, monks, this dhamma-discipline is the abode of great creatures; therein are these creatures: the stream-winner, he who fares on by realizing the fruits of stream-winning; the once-returner, he who fares on by realizing the fruits of once-returning; the no-returner, he who fares on by realizing the fruits of no-return; the arahant, he who fares on by arahantship. Since this is so . . . this, monks, is the eighth strange and wonderful thing about this dhamma-discipline, beholding which again and again monks take delight in this dhamma-discipline.

"These, then, monks, are the eight strange and wonderful things in this dhamma-discipline, beholding which again and again monks take delight in this dhamma-discipline."

The Elephant and the Blind Men

Thus have I heard: On a certain occasion the Exalted One was staying near Savatthi . . . in Anathapindika's Park.

Now on that occasion a great number of recluses and Brahmanas, who were wanderers holding various views, entered Savatthi to quest for alms-food. They held various views, were tolerant of various things, favoured various things, inclined to rely on various views. Some recluses and Brahmanas spoke in favour of this, and held this view;—that the world is eternal, that this is the truth, that any other view is infatuation. Other recluses and Brahmanas . . . that the world is not eternal; that this is truth, any other view infatuation. Some . . . that the world is limited . . . others that it is unlimited. . . . Some held that the living principle is body . . . others that the living principle is one thing, body another. Some held that the self is beyond death, others that the self is not beyond death . . . that it both is and is not beyond death . . . that it neither is nor is not beyond death . . . that this is truth, that any other view is infatuation. So they, by nature quarrelsome, wrangling and disputatious, lived wounding one another with the weapons of the tongue, maintaining: "Dhamma is such and such, dhamma is not such and such; it is, it is not."

Now a great number of monks, robing themselves in the forenoon and taking bowl and robe, entered Savatthi to quest for alms, and, after their rounds and eating their meal, went to the Exalted One . . . and said: "Sir, there are living here in Savatthi a great number of recluses and Brahmanas who are wanderers holding various views to the following effect": (and they detailed the various views). Then said the Exalted One:

"Monks, the wanderers holding other views are blind, unseeing. They know not the profitable, they know not the unprofitable. They know not dhamma, they know not what is not dhamma. In their ignorance of these things they are by nature quarrelsome, wrangling and disputatious in maintaining their several views thus and thus. Formerly, monks, there was a certain raja of this same Savatthi. Then, monks, that raja called to a certain man, saying, 'Come thou, good fellow, go and gather together in one place all the men in Savatthi who were born blind.'

" 'Very good, sire,' replied that man, and in obedience to the raja gathered together all the men born blind in Savatthi, and having done so went to the raja and said, 'Sire, all the men born blind in Savatthi are assembled.'

" 'Then, my good man, show the blind men an elephant.'

" 'Very good, sire,' said the man, and did as he was told, and said to them, 'O blind, such as this is an elephant'; and to one man he presented the head of the elephant, to another its ear, to another a tusk, to another the trunk, the foot, back, tail and tuft of the tail, saying to each one that that was the elephant.

"Now, monks, that man, having thus presented the elephant to the blind men, came to the raja and said, 'Sire, the elephant has been presented to the blind men. Do what is your will.'

"Thereupon, monks, that raja went up to the blind men and said to each, 'Well, blind man, have you seen the elephant?'

" 'Yes, sire.'

" 'Then tell me, blind men, what sort of thing is an elephant.'

"Thereupon those who had been presented with the head answered, 'Sire, an elephant is like a pot.' And those who had observed an ear only replied, 'An elephant is like a winnowing-basket.' Those who had been presented with a tusk said it was a ploughshare. Those who knew only the trunk said it was a plough; they said the body was a granary; the foot, a pillar; the back, a mortar; the tail, a pestle; the tuft of the tail, just a besom.

"Then they began to quarrel, shouting, 'Yes, it is!' 'No, it is not!' 'An elephant is not that!' 'Yes, it's like that!' and so on, till they came to fisti-cuffs over the matter.

"Then, monks, that raja was delighted with the scene.

"Just so are these wanderers holding other views, blind, unseeing, knowing not the profitable, knowing not the unprofitable. They know not dhamma. They know not what is not dhamma. In their ignorance of these things they are by nature quarrelsome, wrangling and disputatious, each maintaining it is thus and thus."

Thereupon the Exalted One at that time, seeing the meaning of it, gave utterance to this verse of uplift:

> O how they cling and wrangle, some who claim
> Of Brahmana and recluse the honoured name!
> For, quarrelling, each to his view they cling.
> Such folk see only one side of a thing.

Death of the Insects

Thus have I heard: On a certain occasion the Exalted One was staying near Savatthi . . . in Anathapindika's Park.

On that occasion the Exalted One was seated in the open air, on a night of inky darkness, and oil-lamps were burning.

And at that time swarms of winged insects kept falling into those oil-lamps and thereby met their end, came to destruction and utter ruin. And the Exalted One saw those swarms of winged insects so doing, and at that time, seeing the meaning of it, gave utterance to this verse of uplift:

> They hasten up and past, but miss the real;
> A bondage ever new they cause to grow.
> Just as the flutterers fall into the lamp,
> So some are bent on what they see and hear.

The Sorrow of Visakha

Thus have I heard: On a certain occasion the Exalted One was staying near Savatthi in East Park, at the storied house of Migara's mother.

Now at that time the dear and lovely grand-daughter of Visakha, Migara's mother, had died. So Visakha, Migara's mother, with clothes and hair still wet from washing, came at an unseasonable hour to see the Exalted One, and on coming to him, saluted him and sat down at one side. As she sat thus the Exalted One said this to Visakha, Migara's mother:

"Why, Visakha! How is it that you come here with clothes and hair still wet at an unseasonable hour?"

"O, sir, my dear and lovely grand-daughter is dead! That is why I come here, with hair and clothes still wet at an unseasonable hour."

"Visakha, would you like to have as many sons and grandsons as there are men in Savatthi?"

"Yes, sir, I would indeed!"

"But how many men do you suppose die daily in Savatthi?"

"Ten, sir, or maybe nine, or eight. Maybe seven, six, five or four, three, two; maybe one a day dies in Savatthi, sir. Savatthi is never free from men dying, sir."

"What think you, Visakha? In such case would you ever be without wet hair and clothes?"

"Surely not, sir! Enough for me, sir, of so many sons and grandsons!"

"Visakha, whoso have a hundred things beloved, they have a hundred sorrows. Whoso have ninety, eighty . . . thirty, twenty things beloved . . . whoso have ten . . . whoso have but one thing beloved, have but one sorrow. Whoso have no one thing beloved, they have no sorrow. Sorrowless are they and passionless. Serene are they, I declare."

> All griefs or lamentations whatsoe'er
> And divers forms of sorrow in the world,—
> Because of what is dear do these become.
> Thing dear not being, these do not become.
> Happy are they therefore and free from grief
> To whom is naught at all dear in the world.

Wherefore aspiring for the griefless, sorrowless,
Make thou in all the world naught dear to thee.

A Sermon to the Monks

This was said by the Exalted One, said by the Arahant, so I have
heard:

Monks, I am your surety for not returning to birth. Do ye give up lust,
ill-will, delusion, wrath, spite, pride. I am your surety for not returning.

Monks, the man who does not understand and comprehend the all,
who has not detached his mind therefrom, who has not abandoned the
all, can make no growth in extinguishing ill. But, monks, he who does
understand and comprehend the all, who has detached his mind therefrom, who has abandoned the all, he makes growth in extinguishing ill.

Who, knowing the all in all its parts,
For all its phases hath no lust,
By comprehension of the all
He truly hath escaped all-ill.

Monks, for the monk who is a learner not yet come to mastery of
mind, but who dwells aspiring for peace from the bond, making it a
matter concerning what is outside the self, I see no other single factor so
helpful as friendship with the lovely. Monks, one who is a friend of the
lovely abandons the unprofitable and makes the profitable to become.

The monk who has a lovely friend, who pays
Deference and reverence to him, who does
What friends advise,—if mindful and composed
Such in due course shall win all fetters' end.

Here, monks, I discern a certain person with mind at peace to be such
because I compass his thoughts with my mind; and, if at this moment this
person were to make an end, he would be put just so into the heaven-
world according to his deserts. What is the reason for that? His mind at
peace. Indeed it is because of a mind at peace, monks, that in this way
certain beings, when body breaks up, after death arise again in the happy
bourn, in the heaven-world.

Here seeing a certain one with mind at peace,
The Teacher 'mid the monks set forth this saying:
"If at this time this person were to die,
In the happy bourn he would arise again.
Indeed the mind of him has come to peace.
Thro' peace of mind men reach the happy bourn.
As one lays down what he has taken up,
So such an one, when body breaks up, strong
In wisdom rises up in the heaven-world."

Monks, if beings knew, as I know, the ripening of sharing gifts, they would not enjoy their use without sharing them, nor would the taint of stinginess obsess the heart and stay there. Even if it were their last bit, their last morsel of food, they would not enjoy its use without sharing it, if there were any one to receive it. But inasmuch, monks, as beings do not know, as I know, the ripening of sharing gifts, therefore they enjoy their use without sharing them, and the taint of stinginess obsesses their heart and stays there.

If only beings knew—as said the mighty sage—
The ripening of sharing gifts, how great the fruit thereof,
Putting away the taint of stinginess, with heart
Made pure within, they would bestow in season due
When great the fruit of charity on Aryans.
And giving food as gift to those deserving much
From man-state falling hence givers to heaven go.
And they, to heaven gone, rejoice and there enjoy
In the fullness of their hearts' desire the ripening
Of sharing gifts, the fruit of their unselfishness.

Monks, whatsoever grounds there be for good works undertaken with a view to rebirth, all of them are not worth one sixteenth part of that goodwill which is the heart's release; goodwill alone, which is the heart's release, shines and burns and flashes forth in surpassing them. Just as, monks, the radiance of all the starry bodies is not worth one sixteenth part of the moon's radiance, but the moon's radiance shines and burns and flashes forth in surpassing them, even so, monks, goodwill . . . flashes forth in surpassing good works undertaken with a view to rebirth.

Just as, monks, in the last month of the rains, in autumn time, when the sky is opened up and cleared of clouds, the sun, leaping up into the firmament, drives away all darkness from the heavens and shines and burns and flashes forth,—even so, monks, whatsoever grounds there be for good works . . . goodwill . . . flashes forth in surpassing them.

Just as, monks, in the night at time of daybreak the star of healing shines and burns and flashes forth, even so, whatsoever grounds there be for good works undertaken with a view to rebirth, all of them are not worth one sixteenth part of that goodwill which is the heart's release. Goodwill, which is the heart's release, alone shines and burns and flashes forth in surpassing them.

Monks, two dhamma-teachings of the wayfarer arahant, a rightly awakened one, take place one after the other. What two? "Look at evil as evil" is the first dhamma-teaching. "Seeing evil as evil, be disgusted therewith, be cleansed of it, be freed of it" is the second dhamma-teaching. These two dhamma-teachings of the wayfarer take place one after the other.

> Of the wayfarer, the awakened one,
> Who hath compassion on all things that be,
> Behold the way of speech and teachings twain:
> "Evil behold for what it is, and then
> Conceive disgust for it: with heart made clean
> Of evil, ye shall make an end of ill."

Monks, ignorance leads the way to the attainment of unprofitable things; shamelessness and disregard of blame follow after. But, monks, knowledge leads the way to the attainment of profitable things, shrinking and fear of blame follow after.

> Whatso be these ill-bourns in this world and the next,
> All rooted are in ignorance, of lust compounded.
> And since the wicked man is void of shame, and hath
> No reverence, therefore he worketh wickedness,
> And through that wickedness he to the downfall goes.
> Wherefore forsaking longing, lust and ignorance
> And causing knowledge to arise in him, a monk
> Should give up, leave behind, the ill-bourns one and all.

Monks, there are these two conditions of Nirvana. What two? The condition of Nirvana with the basis still remaining and that without basis. Of what sort, monks, is the condition of Nirvana which has the basis still remaining? Herein, monks, a monk is arahant, one who has destroyed the cankers, who has lived the life, done what was to be done, laid down the burden, won the goal, worn out the fetter of becoming, one released by perfect knowledge. In him the five sense-faculties still remain, through which, as they have not yet departed, he experiences sensations pleasant and unpleasant, undergoes pleasure and pain. In him the end of lust, malice and delusion, monks, is called "the condition of Nirvana with the basis still remaining."

And of what sort, monks, is the condition of Nirvana that is without basis?

Herein a monk is arahant . . . released by perfect knowledge, but in him in this very life all things that are sensed have no delight for him, they have become cool. This is called "the condition of Nirvana without basis." So, monks, these are the two conditions of Nirvana.

> These two Nirvana-states are shown by him
> Who seeth, who is such and unattached.
> One state is that in this same life possessed
> With base remaining, tho' becoming's stream
> Be cut off. While the state without a base
> Belongeth to the future, wherein all
> Becomings utterly do come to cease.

Monks, do ye delight in solitary communing; delighted by solitary communing, given to mental calm in the inner self, not neglecting musing, possessed of insight, do ye foster resort to empty places? One of two fruits is to be looked for in those who do these things, namely, gnosis in this very life or, if there be still a basis, not-return to this world.

> They who with heart at peace discriminate,
> Thoughtful and musing, rightly dhamma see,
> Their passions they do closely scrutinize.
> For being fain for seriousness and seeing
> Peril in wantonness, they are not the sort
> To fail, but to Nirvana they are close.

Monks, there are these three persons found existing in the world.

What three? The one who is like a drought, the one who rains locally and the one who pours down everywhere.

And how, monks, is a person like a drought?

Herein, monks, a certain person is not a giver to all alike, no giver of food and drink, clothing and vehicle, flowers, scents and unguents, bed, lodging and light to recluses and Brahmanas, to wretched and needy beggars. In this way, monks, a person is like a drought.

And how, monks, is a person like a local rainfall?

In this case a person is a giver to some, but to others he gives not; be they recluses and Brahmanas or wretched, needy beggars, he is no giver of food and drink . . . lodging and lights. In this way a person is like a local rainfall.

And how, monks, does a person rain down everywhere?

In this case a certain person gives to all, be they recluses and Brahmanas or wretched, needy beggars; he is a giver of food and drink . . . lodging and lights. In this way a person rains down everywhere.

So these are the three sorts of persons found existing in the world.

Monks, even if a monk should seize the hem of my garment and walk behind me step for step, yet if he be covetous in his desires, fierce in his longing, malevolent of heart, of mind corrupt, careless and unrestrained, not quieted but scatter-brained and uncontrolled in sense, that monk is far from me and I am far from him. What is the cause of that? Monks, that monk sees not dhamma. Not seeing dhamma he sees not me. Monks, even though a monk should dwell a hundred yoyanas away, yet if he be not covetous in his desires, not fierce in his longing, not malevolent of heart, not of mind corrupt, but with mindfulness set up and composed, calmed, one-pointed in mind and restrained in sense,—then indeed that one is nigh unto me and I am nigh unto him. What is the cause of that? Monks, that monk sees dhamma. Seeing dhamma he sees me.

> Tho' following in his steps, if he be passionate,
> Vexatious—lo! how far away the follower
> Of lust from him that lusteth not. How far
> The not-waned from the waned! How far the greedy
> From him that hath no greed is separate!
>
> But dhamma comprehending thoroughly,
> The prudent man, by insight into dhamma,
> Lustless, like pool unstirred by wind, is calmed.

That lustless to the lustless, lo! how near.
That waned one to the waned! That one not greedy,—
How near to him that hath put greed away.

Monks, there are these two gifts, the carnal and the spiritual. Of these two gifts the spiritual gift is pre-eminent. Monks, there are these two sharings together, the sharing of the carnal and the sharing of the spiritual. Of these two sharings together the sharing of the spiritual is pre-eminent. Monks, there are these two acts of kindness, the carnal and the spiritual. Of these two acts of kindness the spiritual is pre-eminent.

That which men call "the best gift, unsurpassed,"
That sharing which the Exalted One has praised,—
With heart of faith in that best merit-field,
If he but understand and know it well,
Who would not offer it in season due?

They who both hear it and who speak thereof,
With heart of faith in the Wayfarer's teaching,
In them their highest profit is made pure
Who set themselves to the Wayfarer's teaching.

Monks, I am a Brahmana, one to ask a favour of, ever clean-handed, wearing my last body, incomparable physician and surgeon. Ye are my own true sons, born of my mouth, born of dhamma, created by dhamma, my spiritual heirs, not carnal heirs.

Monks, do ye live perfect in virtue, do ye live perfect in the performance of the obligations, restrained with the restraint of the obligations, perfect in the practice of right behaviour; seeing danger in the slightest faults, undertake and train yourselves in the training of the precepts. For him who so lives . . . so restrained . . . who undertakes the training of the precepts, what else remains to be done?

Whether he walk or stand or rest or lie
Or stretch his limbs or draw them in again,
Let him do all these things composedly;
Above, across, and back again returning—
Whatever be one's bourn in all the world—
Let him be one who views the rise-and-fall
Of all compounded things attentively.

So dwelling ardent, living a life of peace
And not elated, but to calmness given,
For mind's composure doing what is right,
Ever and always training,—"ever intent"—
That is the name men give to such a monk.

Rebirth and Karma

Thus have I heard.

The venerable Kumara Kassapa was once walking on tour in Kosala together with a great company of bhikkhus, to the number of about five hundred, and coming to the Kosalese city named Setavya, he there abode. And there the venerable Kumara Kassapa dwelt to the north of Setavya, in the Simsapa-tree Grove. Now at that time the chieftain Payasi was residing at Setavya, a spot teeming with life, with much grass-land and wood-land, with water and corn, on a royal domain granted him by King Pasenadi of Kosala, as a royal gift, with power over it as if he were the king.

Now at that time there came over Payasi an evil view of things to this effect: "Neither is there any other world, nor are there beings reborn otherwise than from parents, nor is there fruit or result of deeds well done or ill done."

Now at that time Payasi, the chieftain, had gone apart to the upper terrace of his house for siesta. And seeing the people thus go by he said to his doorkeeper: "Why are the people of Setavya going forth like this towards the Simsapa-tree Grove?" Then the doorkeeper told him the news. And he said: "Then, good doorkeeper, go to the Brahmanas and householders of Setavya and say to them: 'Payasi, sirs, bids you wait; he will come himself to see the wanderer Master Kassapa.' That boy Kassapa will be winning over at the outset those foolish and inexpert Brahmanas and householders of Setavya to think: 'There is both another world and there are beings who are born not of parents, and there is fruit and result of deeds well done and ill done.' But, my good doorkeeper, these three things do not exist."

"Even so, sir," said the doorkeeper, and carried out his master's bidding.

So Payasi, the chieftain, surrounded by the Brahmanas and house-holders of Setavya, came to the Simsapa-tree Grove, and finding the venerable Kassapa, exchanged with him the greetings and compliments of politeness and courtesy, and took his seat on one side.

And when he was seated Payasi spoke thus to the venerable Master Kassapa:

"I, Master Kassapa, am of this opinion, of these views: Neither is there another world, nor are there beings reborn not of parents, nor is there fruit or result of deeds well done or ill done."

"I, prince, have neither seen or heard of any one holding such a view, such an opinion. Wherefore, prince, I will cross-question you herein, and do you reply in what way you may approve. What think you, yon moon and sun, are they in this world or in another world, are they divine or human?"

"This moon and sun, Master Kassapa, are in another world, not in this, they are gods, not human."

"Then, prince, let this be taken as evidence that there is both another world, and rebirth as inheritor of the highest heavens, and fruit and result of deeds done well or ill."

"Even though Master Kassapa says thus, it still appears to me that not one of these things exists."

"Have you, prince, any proof to establish that they do not exist?"

"Here it is, Master Kassapa. I have had friends, companions, rela-tives, men of the same blood as myself, who have taken life, committed thefts, or fornication, have uttered lying, slanderous, abusive, gossiping speech, have been covetous, of malign thoughts, of evil opinions. They anon have fallen ill of mortal suffering and disease. When I have under-stood that they would not recover from that illness, I have gone to them and said: 'According to the views and opinion held, sirs, by certain wanderers and Brahmanas, they who break the precepts of morality, when the body breaks up after death, are reborn into the waste, the woeful way, the fallen place, the pit. Now you, sirs, have broken those precepts. If what those reverend wanderers and Brahmanas say is true, this, sirs, will be your fate. If these things should befall you, sirs, come to me and tell me!' They have consented to do this, saying, 'Very good,' but they have neither come themselves, nor dispatched a messenger."

"Well then, prince, I will yet ask you this, and do you answer even as you think fit. What think you? Take the case of men who have taken a felon red-handed and bring him up saying: 'My lord, this felon was caught in the act; inflict what penalty you wish.' He replies: 'Well then, sirs, bind this man securely, his arms behind him, with a strong cord; shave his head; lead him around, to the sound of a sharp drum, from street to street, from cross-road to cross-road, and out at the southern gate; there, south of the town in the place of execution, cut off his head.' They, assenting with 'Very good,' proceed to carry out these orders, and, in the place of execution, make him sit down. Now would the felon gain permission of this sort from his executioners: 'Let my masters, the executioners, wait till I have visited my friends and advisers, my kinsmen by blood, in this or that village or town, and come back'? Or would the executioners cut off the head of this vain talker?"

"They would not grant the permission, Master Kassapa; they would cut off his head."

"But this felon, prince, is human and cannot get leave from human executioners. How much less then would your friends and relatives, after death, in the pit, gain permission from the keepers of the pit, saying: 'Let my masters, the pit-keepers, wait till we have gone and told the chieftain Payasi, that there is both another world and rebirth other than of parents, and fruit and result of deeds well-done and ill'! Be this exposition a proof to you, prince, that these things exist."

"Even though Master Kassapa says thus, it still appears to me that not one of these things exists."

"Have you, prince, any further proof to establish that they do not exist?"

"Here it is, Master Kassapa. I have had friends and companions, kinsmen, men of the same blood as myself, who have abstained from taking life, from committing thefts, or fornication, from lying, slandering, rude, or frivolous speech, who have not coveted, or had malign thoughts or evil opinions. They anon have fallen ill of mortal suffering and disease. When I have understood that they would not recover from that illness, I have gone to them and said: 'According, sirs, to the views and opinions held by some wanderers and Brahmanas, they who keep the precepts of morality, when the body breaks up, are after death reborn into the bright and happy world. Now you, sirs, have kept those precepts. If what those reverend Samanas and Brahmanas say is true, this, sirs, will be your fate. If these things should befall you, sirs, when you have been there reborn, come to me and let me know.' They have consented to do this, but they have not come and let me know, nor have they dispatched a messenger."

"Well then, prince, I will make you a simile, for by a simile some intelligent persons will recognize the meaning of what is said. Just as if a man were plunged head-under in a pit of mire. And you were to order men saying: 'Well now, masters, pull the man out of that pit.' They, saying 'Very good,' were to comply and pull him out. You were then to say to them: 'Well now, masters, brush the mire smearing him from off his body with split bamboo.' And they were to obey you. And you were to say to them: 'Well now, masters, shampoo this man's body a treble massage with yellow shampoo powder.' And they were to do so. And you were to say to them: 'Now, masters, rub him with oil, and bathe him three times using fine chunam.' And they were to do so. And you were to say to them: 'Well, masters, now dress his hair.' And they were to do so. And you were to say to them: 'Now, masters, deck him with a costly garland and costly unguent and costly garments.' And they were to do so. And you were to say to them: 'Well, masters, take him up on to the palace and amuse him with the pleasures of the five senses.' And they were to do so. Now what think you, O chieftain? Would this man, well bathed, well anointed, shaved and combed, dressed, wreathed and adorned, clad in clean raiment, taken to the upper palace, and indulging in, surrounded by, treated to, the five pleasures of sense, be desirous of being plunged once more into that pit of mire?"

"No indeed, Master Kassapa."

"And why?"

"Foul, Master Kassapa, is a pit of mire, foul and counted as such, stinking, disgusting, repulsive, and counted as such."

"Even so, prince, are human beings in the eyes of the gods, foul and counted as such, stinking, disgusting, repulsive, and counted as such. The smell of man offends the gods a hundred leagues away. What then? Shall your friends and companions, your kinsmen and connexions who, having kept the precepts, are reborn into the bright and happy place, come and bring you word that there is another world, that there is rebirth other than by parentage, that there is fruit and result of deeds well-done and ill-done? Let this exposition, chieftain, be evidence to you that these things exist."

"Even though Master Kassapa says so, it still appears to me that not one of these things exists."

"Well then, prince, I will reply by asking you something, and do you answer as you think fit. That which, humanly speaking, is a century, this to the three-and-thirty gods is one night and day. Of such a night thirty nights are the month—of such a month twelve months are the year—of such a year the celestial thousand years are the life-span of the three-and-thirty gods. Those of whom you now speak will have attained rebirth into the communion of these gods. If it should occur to them thus: 'Let us for two or three days indulge ourselves, surrounded by and steeped in the five pleasures of sense, and thereafter let us go and tell the chieftain Payasi that there is another world, rebirth other than of parents, and fruit and result of deeds well-done and ill-done'—would they then have come to you, and told you so?"

"Certainly not, Master Kassapa; for we should have been dead long before. But who lets Master Kassapa know all these things: that there are three-and-thirty gods, or that the three-and-thirty gods live so many years? We do not believe him when he says these things."

"That, prince, is just as if there were a man born blind who could not see objects as dark or bright, as blue, yellow, red or brown; who could not see things as smooth or rough, nor the stars, nor moon, nor sun. And he were to say: 'There are none of these things, nor any one capable of seeing them. I don't know them, I don't see them; therefore they don't exist.' Would one so speaking, speak rightly, prince?"

"Not so, Master Kassapa. The visual objects of which you speak do exist, and so does the faculty of seeing them. To say: 'I don't know them, I don't see them; therefore they don't exist': that would not be speaking rightly."

"But even so, methinks, do you, prince, talk like the blind man in my parable when you say: 'But who lets Master Kassapa know that there are three-and-thirty gods, or that the three-and-thirty gods live so many years? We do not believe him when he says these things.' For, prince, the other world is not, as you imagine, to be regarded with this fleshly eye. Those wanderers and Brahmanas who haunt the lonely and remote recesses of the forest, where noise, where sound there hardly is, they there abiding strenuous, ardent, aloof, purify the eye divine; they by that purified eye divine, passing the vision of men, see both this world and that other world, and beings reborn not of parents. In this way, prince, is the other world to be seen, and not, even as you imagine, by this fleshly eye. Let this be a proof to you that there is another world, that there are beings reborn not of parents, that there is fruit and result of deeds well-done and ill-done."

"Even though Master Kassapa says so, yet it still appears to me that not one of these things exists."

"Have you any further evidence, prince?"

"Here it is, Master Kassapa. I see wanderers and Brahmanas moral and of virtuous dispositions, fond of life, averse from dying, fond of happiness, shrinking from sorrow. Then I think, Master Kassapa: 'If these good wanderers and Brahmanas were to know this—"When once we are dead we shall be better off"—then these good men would take poison, or stab themselves, or put an end to themselves by hanging, or throw themselves from precipices. And it is because they do not know that, once dead, they will be better off, that they are fond of life, averse from dying, fond of happiness, disinclined for sorrow.' "

"Well then, prince, I will make you a simile, for by way of a simile some wise men discern the meaning of what is spoken. Once upon a time, prince, there was a Brahmana who had two wives. By one he had a son, ten or twelve years of age; the other was pregnant and near her time. Then the Brahmana died. Now the boy said to his mother's co-wife: 'Whatever treasure there is, lady, or grain, or silver, or gold, all that is mine. There is nothing here for you whatever; make over to me, lady, the heritage of my father!' Then the Brahmana-wife made answer to him: 'Wait, my lad, till my child is born. If 'twill be a boy, one portion shall be his; if a girl, she shall wait on you.'

"But the boy reiterated his claim again and yet again. Then the Brahmana-wife, taking a sword, entered an inner room and ripped up her belly, saying: 'If I can only find out whether 'tis a boy or a girl.' Thus did she destroy both her own life and her unborn infant, and her wealth also, through the foolish and thoughtless way in which, seeking a heritage, she met with ruin and disaster. Even so you, prince, foolish and thoughtless that you are, will meet with ruin and disaster by seeking without wisdom for another world. Moral and virtuous wanderers and Brahmanas do not force maturity on that which is unripe; they, being wise, wait for that maturity. The virtuous have need of their life. In proportion to the length of time such men abide here, is the abundant merit that they produce and accomplish for the welfare of many, for the happiness of many, out of compassion for the world, for the advantage, the welfare, the happiness of gods and men. Let this then be a

proof to you, prince, that there is another world, that there is rebirth
other than of parentage, that there is fruit and result of deeds well and
ill-done.''

"Even though Master Kassapa says so, it still appears to me that not
one of these things exists.''

"Have you further evidence, prince?''

"Here it is, Master Kassapa. Take the case of men who having taken
a felon red-handed bring him up, saying: 'This felon, my lord, was
caught in the act. Inflict on him what penalty you wish.' And I should
say: 'Well then, my masters, throw this man alive into a jar; close the
mouth of it and cover it over with wet leather, put over that a thick
cement of moist clay, put it on to a furnace and kindle a fire.' They
saying 'Very good' would obey me and . . . kindle a fire. When we
knew that the man was dead, we should take down the jar, unbind and
open the mouth, and quickly observe it, with the idea: 'Perhaps we
may see the soul of him coming out!' We don't see the soul of him
coming out!''

"Well then, prince, I will in reply ask you something, and do you
answer as you may please. Do you not admit, prince, that, when you
are taking siesta, you see dreams of enjoyment in garden, grove, country, or lake side?''

"I do admit it, Master Kassapa.''

"Are you at that time watched over by attendant women—hunchbacks
and dwarfs, and maidens and girls?''

"That is so, Master Kassapa.''

"Do they see your soul entering or leaving you?''

"Not so, Master Kassapa.''

"So they who are living do not see the soul of you who are living
entering or leaving you when you dream. How then will you see the
soul of a dead person entering or leaving him? Let this be a proof to
you, prince, that those things do exist.''

"Even though Master Kassapa says this, I still cannot bring myself to
renounce this evil set of opinions. King Pasenadi the Kosalan knows
me, and so do foreign kings, as holding to the creed and the opinion
that there is neither another world nor rebirth other than of parents, nor
fruit or result of deeds well and ill-done. If I, Master Kassapa, renounce these opinions, people will say of me: 'How silly is Prince
Payasi, how unintelligent, how badly he grasps anything!' In wrath

thereat will I keep to it. In guile will I keep to it. In self-respect will I keep to it!"

"Well then, prince, I will give you a simile, for it is by way of a simile that some intelligent men discern the meaning of what is said. Once upon a time, prince, a certain country-side migrated. And one man said to his crony: 'Let's go, friend, to that country-side; perhaps we may come upon some treasure.' 'Good, friend,' assented the other. And they came to where, in that country-side, there was a certain village street. There they saw a heap of hemp thrown away. Then one said to the other: 'Here's a heap of hemp: do you make some into a bundle, I'll do the same and we'll carry it away.' The other consented, and they did so.

"Bearing this burden they went on to another village street. There they saw a heap of hempen thread thrown away, and one said to the other: 'This heap of hempen thread thrown away is just the thing we want hemp for. Well then, friend, you throw away your load of hemp, I'll throw away mine, and we'll take away each a load of hempen thread.' 'I've brought this load of hemp a long way, friend, and it's well tied up—that's enough for me; you choose for yourself.' So the former changed his load for one of hempen thread.

"Then they came to another village street. There they saw a heap of hempen cloths. And the one said to the other: 'This heap of hempen cloths is just the thing we want hemp for, or hempen thread for. Well then, friend, do you throw away your load of hemp, I'll throw away my load of hempen thread, and we'll each take a load of hempen cloth.' 'I've brought this load of hemp a long way, friend, and it's well tied up —that's enough for me; you choose for yourself.' So the former changed his load for one of hempen cloth.

"Then they came to another village street. There they saw a heap of flax. And to another where they saw linen thread; and to another where they saw linen cloth. And at each place the one crony made a change for the better, the other retained his hemp. Further they saw cotton-down, cotton thread and calico; and the same thing happened. Further they saw iron, copper, tin, lead, silver, gold. So that in the end the one crony had a load of gold, the other of hemp.

"So they came to their own village. There the crony who brought a load of hemp pleased neither his parents, nor his own family, nor his friends, and won neither pleasure nor happiness. But the other with his load of gold both gave and won pleasure.

"Even like the simile of the load of hemp, methinks, prince, is what you say. Renounce, prince, this evil set of opinions, renounce them, I say! Let them not be long a source of bale and sorrow to you."

"With Master Kassapa's first simile I was pleased, I was charmed; moreover, I wanted to hear his ready wit in questions, for I regarded Master Kassapa as one who was to be opposed. It is wonderful, Master Kassapa, it is marvellous! just as if one were to set up what has been upset, or were to reveal that which has been hidden away, or were to point out the road to the bewildered, or were to bring a lamp into the darkness, so that they that have eyes may see—even so has the truth been declared in many a figure by Master Kassapa. And I, even I, betake myself for refuge to Gotama the Exalted One, to the doctrine and to the brotherhood."

The Dhammapada

The Twin-Verses

All that we are is the result of what we have thought: it is founded on our thoughts, it is made up of our thoughts. If a man speaks or acts with an evil thought, pain follows him, as the wheel follows the foot of the ox that draws the carriage.

All that we are is the result of what we have thought: it is founded on our thoughts, it is made up of our thoughts. If a man speaks or acts with a pure thought, happiness follows him, like a shadow that never leaves him.

"He abused me, he beat me, he defeated me, he robbed me"—in those who harbour such thoughts hatred will never cease.

"He abused me, he beat me, he defeated me, he robbed me"—in those who do not harbour such thoughts hatred will cease.

For hatred does not cease by hatred at any time: hatred ceases by love —this is an old rule.

The world does not know that we must all come to an end here; but those who know it, their quarrels cease at once.

He who lives looking for pleasures only, his senses uncontrolled, immoderate in his food, idle, and weak, Mara will certainly overthrow him, as the wind throws down a weak tree.

He who lives without looking for pleasures, his senses well controlled, moderate in his food, faithful and strong, him Mara will certainly not overthrow, any more than the wind throws down a rocky mountain.

They who imagine truth in untruth, and see untruth in truth, never arrive at truth, but follow vain desires.

They who know truth in truth, and untruth in untruth, arrive at truth, and follow true desires.

As rain breaks through an ill-thatched house, passion will break through an unreflecting mind.

As rain does not break through a well-thatched house, passion will not break through a well-reflecting mind.

On Earnestness

Earnestness is the path of Nirvana, thoughtlessness the path of death. Those who are in earnest do not die, those who are thoughtless are as if dead already.

Having understood this clearly, those who are advanced in earnestness delight in earnestness, and rejoice in the knowledge of the elect.

These wise people, meditative, steady, always possessed of strong powers, attain to Nirvana, the highest happiness.

If an earnest person has roused himself, if he is not forgetful, if his deeds are pure, if he acts with consideration, if he restrains himself, and lives according to law—then his glory will increase.

By rousing himself, by earnestness, by restraint and control, the wise man may make for himself an island which no flood can overwhelm.

Earnest among the thoughtless, awake among the sleepers, the wise man advances like a racer, leaving behind the hack.

Thought

As a fletcher makes straight his arrow, a wise man makes straight his trembling and unsteady thought, which is difficult to guard, difficult to hold back.

As a fish taken from his watery home and thrown on the dry ground, our thought trembles all over in order to escape the dominion of Mara, the tempter.

It is good to tame the mind, which is often difficult to hold in and flighty, rushing wherever it listeth; a tamed mind brings happiness.

Let the wise man guard his thoughts, for they are difficult to perceive, very artful, and they rush wherever they list: thoughts well guarded bring happiness.

Before long, alas! this body will lie on the earth, despised, without understanding, like a useless log.

Whatever a hater may do to a hater, or an enemy to an enemy, a wrongly-directed mind will do him greater mischief.

Not a mother, not a father, will do so much, nor any other relatives; a well-directed mind will do us greater service.

Flowers

Who shall overcome this earth, and the world of Yama, the lord of the departed, and the world of the gods? Who shall find out the plainly shown path of virtue, as a clever man finds the right flower?

The disciple will overcome the earth, and the world of Yama, and the world of the gods. The disciple will find out the plainly shown path of virtue, as a clever man finds the right flower.

He who knows that this body is like froth, and has learnt that it is as unsubstantial as a mirage, will break the flower-pointed arrow of Mara, and never see the king of death.

Death carries off a man who is gathering flowers, and whose mind is distracted, as a flood carries off a sleeping village.

Death subdues a man who is gathering flowers, and whose mind is distracted, before he is satiated in his pleasures.

As the bee collects nectar and departs without injuring the flower, or its colour or scent, so let a sage dwell in his village.

As on a heap of rubbish cast upon the highway the lily will grow full of sweet perfume and delight, thus among those who are mere rubbish the disciple of the truly enlightened Buddha shines forth by his knowledge above the blinded worldling.

The Fool

Long is the night to him who is awake; long is a mile to him who is tired; long is life to the foolish who do not know the true law.

If a traveller does not meet with one who is his better, or his equal, let him firmly keep to his solitary journey; there is no companionship with a fool.

"These sons belong to me, and this wealth belongs to me"; with such thoughts a fool is tormented. He himself does not belong to himself; how much less sons and wealth?

The fool who knows his foolishness, is wise at least so far. But a fool who thinks himself wise, he is called a fool indeed.

If a fool be associated with a wise man even all his life, he will perceive the truth as little as a spoon perceives the taste of soup.

If an intelligent man be associated for one minute only with a wise man, he will soon perceive the truth, as the tongue perceives the taste of soup.

Fools of poor understanding have themselves for their greatest enemies, for they do evil deeds which bear bitter fruits.

That deed is not well done of which a man must repent, and the reward of which he receives crying and with a tearful face.

No, that deed is well done of which a man does not repent, and the reward of which he receives gladly and cheerfully.

As long as the evil deed done does not bear fruit, the fool thinks it is like honey; but when it ripens, then the fool suffers grief.

"One is the road that leads to wealth, another the road that leads to Nirvana"—if the Bhikkhu, the disciple of Buddha, has learnt this, he will not yearn for honour, he will strive after separation from the world.

The Thousands

Even though a speech be a thousand words, but made up of senseless words, one word of sense is better, which if a man hears, he becomes quiet.

Even though a poem be a thousand words, but made up of senseless words, one word of a poem is better, which if a man hears, he becomes quiet.

One's own self conquered is better than all other people; not even a god, a Gandharva, not Mara (with Brahman) could change into defeat the victory of a man who has vanquished himself, and always lives under restraint.

If a man for a hundred years sacrifice month by month with a thousand, and if he but for one moment pay homage to a man whose soul is grounded in true knowledge, better is that homage than a sacrifice for a hundred years.

And he who lives a hundred years, idle and weak, a life of one day is better if a man has attained firm strength.

And he who lives a hundred years, not seeing the highest law, a life of one day is better if a man sees the highest law.

Punishment

All men tremble at punishment, all men fear death; remember that you are like unto them, and do not kill, nor cause slaughter.

All men tremble at punishment, all men love life; remember that thou art like unto them, and do not kill, nor cause slaughter.

He who, seeking his own happiness, punishes or kills beings who also long for happiness, will not find happiness after death.

He who, seeking his own happiness, does not punish or kill beings who also long for happiness, will find happiness after death.

Do not speak harshly to any one; those who are spoken to will answer thee in the same way. Angry speech is painful: blows for blows will touch thee.

Old Age

How is there laughter, how is there joy, as this world is always burning? Do you not seek a light, ye who are surrounded by darkness?

Look at this dressed-up lump, covered with wounds, joined together, sickly, full of many schemes, but which has no strength, no hold!

This body is wasted, full of sickness, and frail; this heap of corruption breaks to pieces, life indeed ends in death.

After one has looked at those grey bones, thrown away like gourds in the autumn, what pleasure is there left in life?

After a stronghold has been made of the bones, it is covered with flesh and blood, and there dwell in it old age and death, pride and deceit.

The brilliant chariots of kings are destroyed, the body also approaches destruction, but the virtue of good people never approaches destruction —thus do the good say to the good.

A man who has learnt little, grows old like an ox; his flesh grows, but his knowledge does not grow.

Looking for the maker of this tabernacle, I have run through a course of many births, not finding him; and painful is birth again and again. But now, maker of the tabernacle, thou hast been seen; thou shalt not make up this tabernacle again. All thy rafters are broken, thy ridge-pole is sundered; the mind, approaching the Eternal, has attained to the extinction of all desires.

Anger

Let a man leave anger, let him forsake pride, let him overcome all bondage! No sufferings befall the man who is not attached to name and form, and who calls nothing his own.

He who holds back rising anger like a rolling chariot, him I call a real driver; other people are but holding the reins.

Let a man overcome anger by love, let him overcome evil by good; let him overcome the greedy by liberality, the liar by truth!

Speak the truth, do not yield to anger; give, if thou art asked for little; by these three steps thou wilt go near the gods.

The Way

The best of ways is the eightfold; the best of truths the four words; the best of virtues passionlessness; the best of men he who has eyes to see.

This is the way, there is no other that leads to the purifying of intelligence. Go on this path! This is the confusion of Mara, the tempter.

If you go on this way, you will make an end of pain! The way preached by me, when I had understood the removal of the thorns in the flesh.

You yourself must make an effort. The Tathagatas are only preachers. The thoughtful who enter the way are freed from the bondage of Mara.

He who does not rouse himself when it is time to rise, who, though young and strong, is full of sloth, whose will and thought are weak, that lazy and idle man never finds the way to knowledge.

So long as the desire of man towards women, even the smallest, is not destroyed, so long is his mind in bondage, as the calf that drinks milk is to its mother.

A wise and well-behaved man who knows the meaning of this should quickly clear the way that leads to Nirvana.

Proverbs

If by leaving a small pleasure one sees a great pleasure, let a wise man leave the small pleasure, and look to the great.

He who, by causing pain to others, wishes to obtain pleasure for himself, he, entangled in the bonds of hatred, will never be free from hatred.

What ought to be done is neglected, what ought not to be done is done; the desires of unruly, thoughtless people are always increasing.

But they whose whole watchfulness is always directed to their body, who do not follow what ought not to be done, and who steadfastly do what ought to be done, the desires of such watchful and wise people will come to an end.

The Downward Course

He who says what is not goes to hell; he also who, having done a thing, says I have not done it. After death both are equal: they are men with evil deeds in the next world.

Many men whose shoulders are covered with the yellow gown are ill-conditioned and unrestrained; such evil-doers by their evil deeds go to hell.

Better it would be to swallow a heated iron ball, like flaring fire, than that a bad unrestrained fellow should live on the charity of the land.

Four things does a reckless man gain who covets his neighbour's wife—demerit, an uncomfortable bed, thirdly, punishment, and lastly, hell.

There is demerit, and the evil way to hell: there is the short pleasure of the frightened in the arms of the frightened, and the king imposes heavy punishment; therefore let no man think of his neighbour's wife.

As a grass-blade, if badly grasped, cuts the arm, badly-practised asceticism leads to hell.

If anything is to be done, let a man do it, let him attack it vigorously! A careless pilgrim only scatters the dust of his passions more widely.

They who are ashamed of what they ought not to be ashamed of, and are not ashamed of what they ought to be ashamed of, such men, embracing false doctrines, enter the evil path.

They who fear when they ought not to fear, and fear not when they ought to fear, such men, embracing false doctrines, enter the evil path.

They who see sin where there is no sin, and see no sin where there is sin, such men, embracing false doctrines, enter the evil path.

They who see sin where there is sin, and no sin where there is no sin, such men, embracing the true doctrine, enter the good path.

The Brahmana

A man does not become a Brahmana by his plaited hair, by his family, or by birth; in whom there is truth and righteousness, he is blessed, he is a Brahmana.

What is the use of plaited hair, O fool! what of the raiment of goatskins? Within thee there is ravening, but the outside thou makest clean.

The man who wears dirty raiments, who is emaciated and covered with veins, who meditates alone in the forest, him I call indeed a Brahmana.

I do not call a man a Brahmana because of his origin or of his mother. He is indeed arrogant, and he is wealthy; but the poor, who is free from all attachments, him I call indeed a Brahmana.

Him I call indeed a Brahmana who, though he has committed no offence, endures reproach, stripes, and bonds: who has endurance for his force, and strength for his army.

Him I call indeed a Brahmana who is free from anger, dutiful, virtuous, without appetites, who is subdued, and has received his last body.

Him I call indeed a Brahmana who does not cling to sensual pleasures, like water on a lotus leaf, like a mustard seed on the point of a needle.

Him I call indeed a Brahmana who without hurting any creatures, whether feeble or strong, does not kill nor cause slaughter.

Him I call indeed a Brahmana who is tolerant with the intolerant, mild with the violent, and free from greed among the greedy.

Him I call indeed a Brahmana from whom anger and hatred, pride and hypocrisy have dropped like a mustard seed from the point of a needle.

Him I call indeed a Brahmana who utters true speech, instructive and free from harshness, so that he offend no one.

Him I call indeed a Brahmana who takes nothing in the world that is not given him, be it long or short, small or large, good or bad.

Him I call indeed a Brahmana who fosters no desires for this world or for the next, has no inclinations, and is unshackled.

Him I call indeed a Brahmana who has no interests, and when he has understood the truth, does not say How, how? and who has reached the depth of the Immortal.

Him I call indeed a Brahmana who in this world has risen above both ties, good and evil, who is free from grief, from sin, and from impurity.

Buddhaghosha's Parables

The Story of Maddhakundali

Gotama, while he was in the Savatthi country, preached the law as follows, giving as an illustration of it an account of the Thuthe's son, Maddhakundali.

In the Savatthi country there lived a Thuthe named Adinnapubbaka; he was called by this name because he would never give away anything to any one. This Thuthe had an only son, whom he loved very dearly, but he was so niggardly that, rather than pay a goldsmith for his work, he made him a pair of earrings with his own hands, and on that account his son received the name of Maddhakundali.

One day Maddhakundali became very seriously ill, when his father, fearing the expense of medicine and attendance, shut the boy up in the house, in order that no one should know anything about it; the mother, seeing the child so ill, begged him to send for a doctor, but the Thuthe cried out, "Woman! would you squander all my wealth?" Then he went himself to a doctor, and, explaining the symptoms of the disease, asked him what remedy should be employed: the doctor, seeing what a hard man he was, told him that the root and bark of the Hu-Hu-Nya-Nya tree would be beneficial. The Thuthe went home and treated the invalid as he had been directed, but the disease increased in severity, and became beyond all remedy; then, when it was too late, he sent for the doctor. The doctor, the moment he saw the lad, knew at once that there was no hope, so he said, "I am very busy just now, and have no time to attend to this case; you had better send for someone else." The Thuthe then, fearing that all his relatives and friends might get a sight of his wealth, had the boy carried into one of the outer rooms of the house.

At daybreak on the following morning when Gotama arose with the perfected spirit of charity and love, his first thought was as to whom he should deliver from a state of punishment; on looking around him he beheld the Thuthe's son Maddhakundali, who he at once knew was about to become a Sotapan; then he considered, "Has this dead lad perfect faith and love in me?" and finding that he had, and seeing that he was about to enjoy the happiness of the Nats in the Tavatinsa region, he took with him the whole of his attendant priesthood and went into the Savatthi country. As soon as he reached the door of the house of the Thuthe Adinnapubbaka, he dispatched his sacred appearance to the Thuthe's son, who directly he saw him, with his heart full of faith and love, raised his hands and paid him homage. Gotama then left, and the boy dying with his heart full of faith and love passed as it were from sleeping to waking, and found himself in a palace thirty yoyanas in extent in the midst of the Tavatinsa Nat country.

After burning the body of his son, Adinnapubbaka used to go every day to the tomb weeping bitterly for his loss. When Maddhakundali from his palace in the Nat country saw his father weeping over his tomb, he formed the resolution of going to him, to reason with him, and bringing him to a better frame of mind, rescue him from his errors. Accordingly, assuming the appearance he had borne among men, he descended to earth, and throwing himself down near the tomb where his father was, began to weep with violence; on this, the Thuthe said, "Young man, why are you weeping?" "I am weeping," he replied, "because I want the sun and the moon to make a pair of wheels for my cart." "Young man," said the Thuthe, "you must be mad: who can make cart-wheels out of the sun and moon!" The son of the Nat rejoined, "You are weeping for a mortal whose transient life has passed away, but I weep for the sun and moon which I continually have before me." The Thuthe on hearing this began to recall to his mind the law of the righteous, and took comfort; then he said, "Are you a Katu Maharaga Nat, or are you the Sakka King?" The Nat's son replied, "I was Maddhakundali, the Thuthe's son. Because at the point of death my heart was filled with faith and love towards Gotama, I have become a Nat's son and live in the Tavatinsa country in a palace thirty yoyanas in extent." When the Thuthe heard this, his heart was filled with joy, and he determined to go that very day and contemplate Gotama. The Nat's son, after bidding the Thuthe go and make an offering in token of homage to Gotama and keep steadily the five commandments, returned to the Nat country.

The Thuthe after contemplating with reverence Gotama asked him this question, "Can a man without performing any good works at all, by a pure and loving heart alone, obtain the happiness of the Nats?" Gotama replied, "Why do you ask me this? Your son Maddhakundali told you that because he died with his heart full of love and faith towards me, he was now enjoying the happiness of the Nats." "When was it," said the Thuthe, "that he told me this?" "This very day at the tomb," replied Gotama.

Once again Gotama related the story of Maddhakundali, and seeing that the mind of the Thuthe Adinnapubbaka (the boy's father) was still full of error, he commanded that Maddhakundali with his palace should descend to earth. Maddhakundali appeared in his palace, and descending from it made his obeisance to Gotama. Gotama said to him, "Young Nat, by means of what offerings and other good works did you obtain the happiness of the Nats?" The Nat's son replied, "Without performing one good work, but from dying in faith and love to my lord and master I obtained the happiness of the Nats." Then Gotama said, "It is the heart of love and faith accompanying good actions which spreads as it were a beneficent shade from the world of men to the world of Nats." This divine utterance was like the stamp of a king's seal upon a royal edict.

When Gotama had finished his discourse, 84,000 of the congregation were converted. Maddhakundali obtained the reward due to Sotapatti, and Adinnapubbaka becoming a Sotapan, and sedulous in the performance of his duties as such, spent large sums of money in the performance of good works.

The Story of Kisagotami

Gotama, while he was staying in the Jetavana monastery in the Savatthi country, preached the following discourse on the subject of Kisagotami:

In the Savatthi country there was a Thuthe who was worth four

hundred millions. One day all the wealth in his house turned into charcoal. The Thuthe, seeing this, was so wretched that he refused food and
took to his bed. A friend of his, paying him a visit, seeing the miserable
expression of his face, asked him why he was so wretched, and he told
him that he was miserable because all his wealth had been changed into
charcoal. His friend, who was also a Thuthe, seeing that this had happened to him because he was not worthy of his wealth, said to him, "My
friend Thuthe, have no anxiety about this; I know a plan; will you do
as I direct?" The Thuthe said, "I will." "Then," said his friend,
"spread some mats in the bazaar, and pile up upon them all your wealth
that has turned into charcoal, and pretend to be trafficking in it. People
seeing the heap will say to you, 'O you Thuthe, every one else sells
clothes, tobacco, oil, honey, and treacle; why do you sell charcoal?' Then
you reply to them, 'I am selling my goods.' If any one say to you, 'Why
do you sell so much gold and silver?' say to them, 'Bring it to me'; then
take what they bring in their hand, and in your hand it will become gold
and silver. If the person be a woman, marry her to your son; and making
over to her the four hundred millions of your property make use of
whatever she shall give you. If it be a man, marry your daughter to him,
and making over the property to him, make use of what he shall give
you."

The Thuthe, following his friend's instructions, spread some mats in
the bazaar, and piling upon them a large heap of his property which
was turned into charcoal, pretended to be selling it. Some people, seeing it, said, "Why does he sell charcoal?" Just at this time a young girl
named Kisagotami, who was worthy to be the owner of the property,
and who having lost both her parents was in a wretched condition, happened to come to the bazaar on some business. When she saw the heap,
she said, "My lord Thuthe, all the people sell clothes, tobacco, oil,
honey, and treacle; how is it that you pile up gold and silver for sale?"
The Thuthe said, "Madam, give me that gold and silver." Kisagotami,
taking up a handful of it, brought it to him; what the young girl had
in her hand no sooner touched the Thuthe's hand than it became gold
and silver. The Thuthe married the girl to his son, and having delivered
over to her the whole of the four hundred millions of his property,
made use daily of the gold and silver which she gave him.

Some time after this, Kisagotami became in the family way, and when
the ten months were completed, gave birth to a son. When the boy was

able to walk by himself, he died. The young girl, in her love for it, carried the dead child clasped to her bosom, and went about from house to house asking if any one would give her some medicine for it. When the neighbours saw this, they said, "Is the young girl mad that she carries about on her breast the dead body of her son!" But a wise man thinking to himself, "Alas! this Kisagotami does not understand the law of death, I must comfort her," said to her, "My good girl, I cannot myself give medicine for it, but I know of a doctor who can attend to it." The young girl said, "If so, tell me who it is." The wise man continued, "Gotama can give medicine, you must go to him."

Kisagotami went to Gotama, and doing homage to him, said, "Lord and master, do you know any medicine that will be good for my boy?" Gotama replied, "I know of some." She asked, "What medicine do you require?" He said, "I want a handful of mustard seed." The girl promised to procure it for him, but Gotama continued, "I require some mustard seed taken from a house where no son, husband, parent, or slave has died." The girl said, "Very good," and went to ask for some at the different houses, carrying the dead body of her son astride on her hip. The people said, "Here is some mustard seed, take it." Then she asked, "In my friend's house has there died a son, a husband, a parent, or a slave?" They replied, "Lady, what is this that you say! The living are few, but the dead are many." Then she went to other houses, but one said, "I have lost a son"; another, "I have lost my parents"; another, "I have lost my slave." At last, not being able to find a single house where no one had died, from which to procure the mustard seed, she began to think, "This is a heavy task that I am engaged in. I am not the only one whose son is dead. In the whole of the Savatthi country, everywhere children are dying, parents are dying." Thinking thus, she acquired the law of fear, and putting away her affection for her child, she summoned up resolution, and left the dead body in a forest; then she went to Gotama and paid him homage. He said to her, "Have you procured the handful of mustard seed?" "I have not," she replied; "the people of the village told me, 'The living are few, but the dead are many.'" Gotama said to her, "You thought that you alone had lost a son; the law of death is that among all living creatures there is no permanence." When Gotama had finished preaching the law, Kisagotami was established in the reward of Sotapatti; and all the assembly who heard the law were also established in the reward of Sotapatti.

Some time afterwards, when Kisagotami was one day engaged in the performance of her religious duties, she observed the lights in the houses now shining, now extinguished, and began to reflect, "My state is like these lamps." Gotama, who was then in the Gandhakuti building, sent his sacred appearance to her, which said to her, just as if he himself were preaching, "All living beings resemble the flame of these lamps, one moment lighted, the next extinguished; those only who have arrived at Nirvana are at rest." Kisagotami, on hearing this, reached the stage of a Rahanda possessed of intuitive knowledge.

The Story of the Hen and the Little Sow

At another time, Gotama, when he was in the Jetavana monastery, preached a discourse about a little sow.

Gotama, one day, as he was entering the Rajagaha city to collect food, seeing a little sow at the gate of the city, smiled. My lord Ananda asked him why he smiled. "Ananda," he replied, "I am smiling at this little sow." Ananda asked him what there was about the sow to make him smile, and he said:

"Ananda, this little sow, in the time of the Buddha Kakusandha was a hen; hearing a Rahan in a forest-monastery repeating the Vipassana Kammaṭṭhana, and knowing that it was the law, she listened to it; from the influence of this good deed, when she died, she became the princess Upari. The princess, going one day to a certain place, saw there a heap of maggots; repeating the Puluvakasana, she obtained the first state of Dhyana. After her death she was born again in the Brahma country. Now this princess, from an inhabitant of the Brahma country, has, by transition to another existence, been changed into a little sow; it was this that made me smile. When, upon her death, she leaves the condition of a sow, she will become the wife of the prime minister."

When the Rahans heard Gotama say this, they acquired the law of Samvega.

After the little sow died, and had become the wife of the prime minister residing in the village of Mahapunna, the Rahans, on their way to collect food, seeing her standing at the door of her house, said, "My masters, the little sow has become the prime minister's wife." The prime minister's wife no sooner heard this than she trembled, and becoming impressed with the law of Samvega, and acquiring the Gatisara knowledge, which enables the possessor to see his past existences, she saw that in the time of the Buddha Kakusandha she was a hen; dying from the condition of a hen, she became in the time of Gotama the princess Upari; dying from the condition of the princess Upari, she existed again in the Brahma country; dying out of the Brahma country, she became a little sow; dying out of the condition of the little sow, she became the wife of the prime minister.

The moment that she saw all this, she asked her husband's permission, and became a Rahan under the priest Pankapathaka, and directly after listening to the Satipatthana law in the Tissamahavihara monastery, she was established in the reward of Sotapatti. After becoming a Sotapan, and while she was living in the village of Gandha, to which she had gone and where her relatives resided, she listened to the law of Asivisut in the Kamlakamahavihara monastery, and immediately afterwards became a Rahanda.

The Path of Purity
(BUDDHAGHOSHA'S VISUDDHIMAGGA)

The Restraint of Covetousness

In this religion a brother lives, being restrained by the restraint of the Patimokkha, is possessed of good behaviour and lawful resort, sees danger in the smallest faults, trains himself in the observance of the precepts"—this is virtue "as restraint according to the Patimokkha." Virtue "as restraint of the controlling faculties" is that virtue which has been declared thus: "When he sees an object with his eye, he is not entranced by the general appearance or the details of it. He sets himself to restrain that which might give occasion for immoral states, covetousness, and grief to flow in over him while he dwells unrestrained as to the faculty of sight." He seizes only what appears (as the abominable thirty-two parts) in the body, like Mahatissa the Elder who lived at Mount Chetiya. It is said that a certain daughter-in-law, having broken with her husband and having well beautified and dressed herself like a celestial nymph, left Anuradhapura betimes, and, while going to the home of her relatives, saw on the way the Elder, who was coming to Anuradhapura from Mount Chetiya for the sake of alms, and with corrupt thoughts laughed aloud. The Elder, wondering what it was, looked up, and acquiring the perception of the foul in her teeth, attained sanctity. Hence it has been said:

> "Those bones, her teeth, he saw, and called to mind
> His first perception. Even where he stood
> The Elder thus attained to sanctity."

And the husband, following the same road, saw the Elder and inquired: "Perhaps your Reverence has met a certain lady?" The Elder replied:

> "I know not whether man or woman passed.
> A certain lump of bones went by this way."

The Trickery of Roundabout Talk

"What is the basis of trickery that is called roundabout talk?"

On seeing cowherds tending calves, a member of the Order asks: "Are these calves sucking the mother's milk or drinking diluted buttermilk?"

"They are calves sucking the mother's milk, sir," the cowherds reply.

Then he says: "They are not milk-sucking calves. If they were milk-sucking calves, the brethren also would receive milk." And in this way he makes the lads inform their parents so that they have to offer milk.

"Roundabout talk" is talk bordering on the object wanted. Here the story of the brother, frequenter of a family, should be considered.

It is said that a certain brother, a frequenter of a family, enters the house and sits down wishing for food. The lady of the house seeing him and not wishing to give food, says: "There is no rice," and goes to a neighbour's house as though to bring rice.

Then the brother enters the interior of the house, and looking about, sees sugar-cane in a door-corner, molasses in a bowl, flat pieces of salt fish in a basket, rice in a pot, butter in a jar, and comes out and sits down. The lady comes back saying she has not obtained any rice.

And the brother says: "Madam, I already saw a sign that to-day my alms-begging would not be successful."

"What may it be, sir?"

"I saw a snake like the sugar-cane lying there in the door-corner. Looking about with the intention of striking it, I saw a stone like the molasses kept there in the bowl. And the snake, struck by the stone, spread a hood like the flat pieces of salt-fish kept there in the basket. The teeth of the snake wanting to bite the stone were like the rice kept there in the pot. And the saliva mixed with poison issuing from its mouth in its state of anger was like the butter kept there in the jar."

Then the housewife, unable to impose upon the bald-pate, presents him with the sugar-cane, cooks the rice, and gives everything, butter, molasses, fish and all.

Thus a talk bordering on what one desires is "roundabout talk."

The Elder Chittagutta

"By mindfulness is restraint of the controlling faculties to be attained. Better it were to grasp a heated iron wire, molten and incandescent, than that the faculty of sight should grasp details and signs in visible objects, and so achieve covetousness and other evil states of consciousness which come in at the eye door. A brother who restrains the controlling faculties should be like the Elder Chittagutta who lived in the great Kurandaka cave."

It is said that there was a beautiful painting of the Renunciation of Seven Buddhas in the great Kurandaka cave. And many of the brethren, wandering round the dwellings, saw the painting, and said: "Sir, beautiful is the painting." The Elder said, "Lads, I have lived in the cave for over sixty years and I did not even know whether the painting existed or not. Now I know to-day through you who possess eyes." Thus it is said that for so long the Elder living there never lifted his eyes and looked up. And at the cave-entrance there was a great ironwood tree. But the

Elder had never looked up at it. It is said that he knew that it was in blossom when each spring he saw the filaments that fell to the ground.

Shrichakrasambhara Tantra

Yoga-Practices in Buddhism

Having been duly initiated into the outer and inner Mandalas, which constitute the very self of Chakra Sambhara, by a competent teacher, and having been further developed by the Mandalas' own grace or blessing, one speedily sets forth to obtain the special teachings, and to learn their practical results. Assuming that he has attained to the stage of firm concentration of the mind and that he wishes to proceed further in the perfect or final stage (meditation on the formless) he should proceed thus: Either in the morning or any other time let him take an easy position, cross-legged. Having thought of oneself as the two-handed (Heruka), imagine the Guru (teacher) on one's head. Put forth intense faith in him, and pray, "I beseech thee, cause pure enlightenment to grow in my mind." Then imagine on the letter "A" a lunar disk, red and white, about the size of the half of a pea, inside one's heart. Upon the lunar disk imagine a light-point about the size of a mustard seed which is the concentrated form of one's mind. Fix the mind on that and regulate the breath gently. When one is well practised, the mind is held and does not run astray but remains fixed. Then one attains the blissful and clear enlightenment. When one attains stability or firmness in that, then transfer the imagination to another of the sense organs.

Imagine within the two pupils of the eyes, that there are two very fine bright white points, one in each eye. Close the eyes and imagine in your mind that the points are there. When the mind gets accustomed to that, then look on various objects. Whilst all the while keeping the points before the mind, let it stray upon other objects. On being well practised the point is constantly and vividly present to the mind's eye. No matter on whatever object the eye may fall, enlightenment is produced. Having attained stability in that, draw in the point within the heart, and imagine that the latter gains greater brilliancy and clearness, and keep the mind tranquil; this will produce enlightenment of the most excellent kind, or the state of tranquillity.

After this, transfer the imagination to the ears. Imagine two blue points or dots upon two lunar disks the size of a half-pea inside each ear and meditate upon them, in a place free from noise. When you have succeeded in fixing the mind upon them, listen to sounds, at the same time keeping the mind fixed upon the two points and not letting it stray away from them. On being practised in that, one attains vividness of the mind-picture and enlightenment follows on hearing sound. When one has gained stability in this, withdraw the points inside the heart and imagine that the points have gained blazing brilliancy and vividness. From this the excellent enlightenment or tranquillity is produced.

Then transfer the imagination to the nose. Imagine a yellow point on a lunar disk in the cavity of each nostril in a place free from any odour, and concentrate your mind on that. When the mind is fixed, smell various odours, keeping the mind fixed on the yellow points, not letting the mind stray away. When one gets used to that, on perception of odours there is produced enlightenment. When firmness is gained in this, draw the points into the heart. By this, brilliancy and vividness of the point is produced, and practice in this produces enlightenment.

Next transfer the imagination to the tongue. Imagine a red point on a lunar disk at the root of the tongue, and meditate on it without tasting any flavour. Concentrate your mind on it, do not let it stray. Then, when the mind is fixed on the point, taste various flavours, keeping your mind concentrated on the point. Then draw it inside the heart. When the point attains brilliancy and vividness, enlightenment is produced through the sense of taste.

Then transfer your imagination to the body. Either at the root of the secret parts, or on your forehead, imagine a green point on a lunar disk, and fix your mind on it without touching anything. When your mind has attained some degree of fixity on that spot, try concentration, touching various things and keeping the mind from straying. When vividness of the point is obtained, practise until it is quite firm, then draw the point in the place of touch into the point within the heart, and meditate upon that until great brilliance and vividness is obtained, which will produce tranquillity or excellent enlightenment.

Then after that, transfer the imagination to the mind, which moves everywhere. Imagine a very small pink point on the top of that already imagined as being within the heart. Try the meditation in a very quiet place at first. When you have succeeded in concentrating your mind, try the meditation in company where you are sure that some evil passions will be excited, such as lust or the like. Then imagine that the chief passion—infatuation—which accompanies all other evil passions, is concentrated in it. Think that it is absorbed into a blue point. Fix the mind on that. On getting accustomed in that practice, passions will not arise; or should they do so, they are controlled by the mind. When one has attained firmness in that, sink the blue point into the pink point, and that into the white and red point below it. Then the last sinks into the moon-disk; which in its turn is dissolved or disappears in the sky like a cloud. Then there remains only emptiness, in which the mind is to be kept at a level. This will produce the profound tranquil state of enlightenment called resting-in-peace. Then rising from the state of tranquillity, again imagine the lunar disks and the points to be present or springing forth simultaneously; and that one's own self, too, is at once transformed into the Heruka. Regard external objects as being only visible and apparently true, but having no independent and absolute reality in themselves. Meditating thus till each stage has shown its sign of perfection or proficiency, one at last attains proficiency or perfection in the whole, as a result of which one obtains profound tranquillity, which is realization of the Sunyata, which is bliss and clarity.

Continuation in these practices produces the knowledge of the path, from which is produced Buddhahood. This is the stage of conferring grace and blessing on oneself.

The Sleeping and Waking of a Yogi

He whose mind is firm in Bodhisattva resolve, who has obtained the highest initiation, who understands the Mantras and is foremost among Yogis, will of a surety obtain the highest boons, both temporal and spiritual, if he follows the course prescribed, namely, the imaginative and meditative; if he practises to make his mind tranquil; if he offers rice cakes and other food offerings; and if in short he assiduously applies himself to all the four branches of a Yogi's duty.

The devotee when about to go to sleep should firstly imagine his body to be that of Buddha Vajra-Sattva and then at length merge into the tranquil state of the void. Arising from that state he should think that the double drums are resounding from the midst of the heavens proclaiming the Mantras of the twenty-four heroes. Arising from his sleep in this state of divine body he should regard all things around him as constituting the Mandala of himself as Vajra-Sattva.

The Lotus of the True Law

The Wheel of the Law

Thus have I heard. Once upon a time the Lord was staying at Rajagaha, on the Gridhrakuta mountain, with a numerous assemblage of monks, twelve hundred monks, all of them Arhats, stainless, free from depravity, self-controlled, thoroughly emancipated in thought and knowledge, of noble breed, like unto great elephants, having done their task, done their duty, acquitted their charge, reached the goal; in whom the ties which bound them to existence were wholly destroyed, whose minds were thoroughly emancipated by perfect knowledge, who had reached the utmost perfection in subduing all their thoughts; who were possessed of the transcendent faculties; eminent disciples, such as the venerable Subhuti, the venerable Rahula; with them yet other great disciples, as the venerable Ananda, still under training, and two thousand other monks, some of whom were still under training, the others masters; with six thousand nuns having at their head Maha-Prajapati, and the nun Yasodhara, the mother of Rahula, along with her train;

further with eighty thousand Bodhisattvas, all unable to slide back, endowed with the spells of supreme, perfect enlightenment, firmly standing in wisdom.

Now at that time it was that the Lord, surrounded, attended, honoured, revered, venerated, worshipped by the four classes of hearers, after expounding the Dharmaparyaya called "the Great Exposition," a text of great development, serving to instruct Bodhisattvas and proper to all Buddhas, sat cross-legged on the seat of the law and entered upon the meditation termed "the station of the exposition of infinity"; his body was motionless and his mind had reached perfect tranquillity. And as soon as the Lord had entered upon his meditation, there fell a great rain of divine flowers, covering the Lord and the four classes of hearers, while the whole Buddha-field shook in six ways: it moved, removed, trembled, trembled from one end to the other, tossed, tossed along.

And at that moment there issued a ray from within the circle of hair between the eyebrows of the Lord. It extended over eighteen hundred thousand Buddha-fields in the eastern quarter, so that all those Buddha-fields appeared wholly illuminated by its radiance, down to the great hell Avichi and up to the limit of existence. And the beings in any of the six states of existence became visible, all without exception. Likewise the Lords Buddhas staying, living, and existing in those Buddha-fields became all visible, and the law preached by them could be entirely heard by all beings. And the monks, nuns, lay devotees male and female, Yogins and students of Yoga, those who had obtained the fruition of the paths of sanctification and those who had not, they, too, became visible. And the Bodhisattvas Mahasattvas in those Buddha-fields who plied the Bodhisattva-course with ability, due to their earnest belief in numerous and various lessons and the fundamental ideas, they, too, became all visible. Likewise the Lords Buddhas in those Buddha-fields who had reached final Nirvana became visible, all of them. And the Stupas made of jewels and containing the relics of the extinct Buddhas became all visible in those Buddha-fields.

Whereupon Manjusri, the prince royal, addressed Maitreya, the Bodhisattva Mahasattva, and the whole assembly of Bodhisattvas in these words: It is the intention of the Tathagata, young men of good family, to begin a grand discourse for the teaching of the law, to pour the great rain of the law, to make resound the great drum of the law, to raise the great banner of the law, to kindle the great torch of the law, to blow the great conch trumpet of the law, and to strike the great timbal of the law. Again, it is the intention of the Tathagata, young men of good family, to make a grand exposition of the law this very day. Thus it appears to me, young men of good family, as I have witnessed a similar sign of the former Tathagatas, the Arhats, the perfectly enlightened. Those former Tathagatas, they, too, emitted a lustrous ray, and I am convinced that the Tathagata is about to deliver a grand discourse for the teaching of the law and make his grand speech on the law everywhere heard, he having shown such a fore-token. And because the Tathagata wishes that this turning of the wheel of the law, which meets opposition in all the world, be heard everywhere, therefore does he display so great a miracle and this fore-token consisting in the lustre occasioned by the emission of a ray.

The Lord then rose with recollection and consciousness from his meditation, and forthwith addressed the venerable Sariputra:[1]

It is not by reasoning, Sariputra, that the law is to be found: it is beyond the pale of reasoning, and must be learnt from the Tathagata. For, Sariputra, it is for a sole object, a sole aim, verily a lofty object, a lofty aim, that the Buddha, the Tathagata, appears in the world. To show all creatures the sight of Tathagata-knowledge does the Buddha, the Tathagata, appear in the world; to open the eyes of creatures for the sight of Tathagata-knowledge does the Buddha, the Tathagata, appear in the world.

Why should not the mighty one, after having waited for the right time, speak, now that he perceives the right moment is come? This is the fit opportunity, met somehow, of commencing the exposition of what really is.

Now the word of my commandment, as contained in nine divisions, has been published according to the varying degree of strength of creatures. Such is the device I have shown in order to introduce creatures to the knowledge of the giver of boons. And to those in the world who have always been pure, wise, good-minded, compassionate sons of Buddha and done their duty under many kotis of Buddhas will I make known amplified Sutras. For they are endowed with such gifts of mental disposition and such advantages of a blameless outward form that I can

---

[1] Here is omitted a long passage in which the Buddha refuses to expound the law, for, he says, it will not be understood. Thereupon many of the congregation, offended, leave, after which he considers his congregation pure, and speaks. This sutra is aggressively *Mahayanist,* and those who withdraw from hearing it are *Hinayana* monks.

announce to them: in future ye shall become Buddhas benevolent and compassionate.

There is, indeed, but one vehicle; there is no second, nor a third anywhere in the world, apart from the case of the Purushottamas using an expedient to show that there is a diversity of vehicles. The Chief of the world appears in the world to reveal the Buddha-knowledge. He has but one aim, indeed, no second; the Buddhas do not bring over creatures by an inferior vehicle.

There is no envy whatever in me; no jealousy, no desire, nor passion. Therefore I am the Buddha, because the world follows my teaching.

If, O son of Sari, I spoke to the creatures, "Vivify in your minds the wish for enlightenment," they would in their ignorance all go astray and never catch the meaning of my good words. And considering them to be such, and that they have not accomplished their course of duty in previous existences, I see how they are attached and devoted to sensual pleasures, infatuated by desire and blind with delusion.

From lust they run into distress; they are tormented in the six states of existence and people the cemetery again and again; they are overwhelmed with misfortune, as they possess little virtue. They are continually entangled in the thickets of sectarian theories, such as, "It is and it is not; it is thus and it is not thus." In trying to get a decided opinion on what is found in the sixty-two heretical theories they come to embrace falsehood and continue in it. They are hard to correct, proud, hypocritical, crooked, malignant, ignorant, dull; hence they do not hear the good Buddha-call, not once in kotis of births.

To those, son of Sari, I show a device and say: Put an end to your trouble. When I perceive creatures vexed with mishap I make them see Nirvana.

And all in the world who are hearing or have heard the law from the mouth of the Tathagatas, given alms, followed the moral precepts, and patiently accomplished the whole of their religious duties; who have acquitted themselves in point of zeal and meditation, with wisdom reflected on those laws, and performed several meritorious actions, have all of them reached enlightenment.

Others also, who paid worship to the relics of the departed Jainas, erected many thousands of Stupas made of gems, gold, silver, or crystal, or built Stupas of emerald, cat's eye, pearls, egregious lapis lazuli, or sapphire; they have all of them reached enlightenment.

The little boys even, who in playing erected here and there heaps of sand with the intention of dedicating them as Stupas to the Jainas, they have all of them reached enlightenment.

Or by worshipping were it but with a single flower, by drawing on a wall the images of the Sugatas, by doing worship were it even with distracted thoughts, one shall in course of time see kotis of Buddhas.

I reveal the law in its multifariousness with regard to the inclinations and dispositions of creatures. I use different means to rouse each according to his own character. Such is the might of my knowledge.

I likewise see the poor wretches, deficient in wisdom and conduct, lapsed into the mundane whirl, retained in dismal places, plunged in affliction incessantly renewed. Fettered as they are by desire like the yak by its tail, continually blinded by sensual pleasure, they do not seek the Buddha, the mighty one; they do not seek the law that leads to the end of pain. Staying in the six states of existence, they are benumbed in their senses, stick unmoved to the low views, and suffer pain on pain. For those I feel a great compassion.

Many years have I preached and pointed to the stage of Nirvana, the end of wretchedness and mundane existence. Thus I used to speak at all times.

And when I saw, Sariputra, the children of the highest of men by many thousands of kotis, numberless, striving after the supreme, the highest enlightenment; and when such as had heard the law of the Jainas, owing to the many-sidedness of their skilfulness, had approached me and stood before my face, all of them with joined hands, and respectful; then I conceived the idea that the time had come for me to announce the excellent law and to reveal supreme enlightenment, for which task I had been born in the world.

This event to-day will be hard to be understood by the ignorant who imagine they see here a sign, as they are proud and dull. But the Bodhisattvas, they will listen to me.

At certain times, at certain places, somehow do the leaders appear in the world, and after their appearance will they whose view is boundless at one time or another preach a similar law. Just as the blossom of the glomerous fig-tree is rare, albeit sometimes, at some places, and somehow it is met with, as something pleasant to see for everybody, as a wonder to the world including the gods; so wonderful and far more wonderful is the law I proclaim. Any one who, on hearing a good exposition of it, shall cheerfully accept it and recite but one word of it, will have done honour to all Buddhas.

Let this mystery be for thee, Sariputra, for all disciples of mine, and for the eminent Bodhisattvas, who are to keep this mystery.

For the creatures, when at the period of the five depravities, are vile and bad; they are blinded by sensual desires, the fools, and never turn their minds to enlightenment. Some beings, having heard this one and sole vehicle manifested by the Jaina, will in days to come swerve from it, reject the Sutra, and go down to hell. But those beings who shall be modest and pure, striving after the supreme and the highest enlightenment, to them shall I unhesitatingly set forth the endless forms of this one and sole vehicle.

Ye are my children, I am your father, who has removed you from pain, from the triple world, from fear and danger, when you had been burning for many kotis of æons. And I am teaching blessed rest (Nirvana) in so far as, though you have not yet reached final rest, you are delivered from the trouble of the mundane whirl, provided you seek the vehicle of the Buddhas.

When the creatures in this world delight in low and contemptible pleasures, then the Chief of the world, who always speaks the truth, indicates pain as the first great truth. And to those who are ignorant and too simple-minded to discover the root of that pain I lay open the way: "Awaking of full consciousness, strong desire is the origin of pain."

Always try, unattached, to suppress desire. This is my third truth, that of suppression. It is an infallible means of deliverance; for by practising this method one shall become emancipated. And from what are they emancipated, Sariputra? They are emancipated from chimeras. Yet they are not wholly freed; the Chief declares that they have not yet reached final and complete rest in this world.

Why is it that I do not pronounce one to be delivered before one's having reached the highest, supreme enlightenment? Because such is my will; I am the ruler of the law, who is born in this world to lead to beatitude.

This, Sariputra, is the closing word of my law which now at the last time I pronounce for the weal of the world including the gods. Preach it in all quarters. And if some one speaks to you these words, "I joyfully accept," and with signs of utmost reverence receives this Sutra, thou mayst consider that man to be unable to slide back.

But do not speak of this matter to haughty persons, nor to conceited ones, nor to Yogins who are not self-restrained; for the fools, always revelling in sensual pleasures, might in their blindness scorn the law manifested.

Now hear the dire results when one scorns my skilfulness and the Buddha-rules for ever fixed in the world; when one, with sullen brow, scorns the vehicle. Hear the destiny of those who have scorned such a Sutra as this, whether during my lifetime or after my Nirvana, or who have wronged the monks.

After having disappeared from amongst men, they shall dwell in the lowest hell during a whole kalpa, and thereafter they shall fall lower and lower, the fools, passing through repeated births for many intermediate kalpas. And when they have vanished from amongst the inhabitants of hell, they shall further descend to the condition of brutes, be even as dogs and jackals, and become a sport to others.

And whenever they assume a human shape, they are born crippled, maimed, crooked, one-eyed, blind, dull, and low, they having no faith in my Sutra.

And since I am fully aware of it, I command thee, Sariputra, that thou shalt not expound a Sutra like this before foolish people.

But those who are sensible, instructed, thoughtful, clever, and learned, who strive after the highest supreme enlightenment, to them expound its real meaning. Those who, full of energy and ever kind-hearted, have a long time been developing the feeling of kindness, have given up body and life, in their presence thou mayst preach this Sutra. Those who show mutual love and respect, keep no intercourse with ignorant people, and are content to live in mountain caverns, to them expound this hallowed Sutra. Those who are not irascible, ever sincere, full of compassion for all living beings, and respectful towards the Sugata, before those thou mayst propound this Sutra.

As the venerable Subhuti, the venerable Maha-Katyayana, the venerable Maha-Kasyapa, and the venerable Maha-Maudgalyayana heard this law unheard of before, and as from the mouth of the Lord they heard the future destiny of Sariputra to superior perfect enlightenment, they were struck with wonder, amazement, and rapture. They instantly rose from their seats and went up to the place where the Lord was sitting; after throwing their cloak over one shoulder, fixing the right knee on the ground and lifting up their joined hands before the Lord, looking up to him, their bodies bent, bent down and inclined, they addressed the Lord in this strain:

Lord, we are old, aged, advanced in years; honoured as seniors in this assemblage of monks. Worn out by old age we fancy that we have attained Nirvana; we make no efforts, O Lord, for supreme perfect enlightenment; our force and exertion are inadequate to it. Though the Lord preaches the law and has long continued sitting, and though we have attended to that preaching of the law, yet, O Lord, as we have so long been sitting and so long attended the Lord's service, our greater and minor members, as well as the joints and articulations, begin to ache. Hence, O Lord, we are unable, in spite of the Lord's preaching, to realize the fact that all is vanity, purposeless, and unfixed; we have conceived no longing after the Buddha-laws, the divisions of the Buddha-fields, the sports of the Bodhisattvas or Tathagatas. For by having fled out of the triple world, O Lord, we imagined having attained Nirvana, and we are decrepit from old age. Hence, O Lord, though we have exhorted other Bodhisattvas and instructed them in supreme perfect enlightenment, we have in doing so never conceived a single thought of longing. And just now, O Lord, we are hearing from the Lord that disciples also may be predestined to supreme perfect enlightenment. We are astonished and amazed, and deem it a great gain, O Lord, that to-day, on a sudden, we have heard from the Lord a voice such as we never heard before. We have acquired a magnificent jewel, O Lord, an incomparable jewel. We had not sought, nor searched, nor expected, nor required so magnificent a jewel. It has become clear to us, O Lord; it has become clear to us, O Sugata.

It is a case, O Lord, as if a certain man went away from his father and betook himself to some other place. He lives there in foreign parts for many years, twenty or thirty or forty or fifty. In course of time the one, the father, becomes a great man; the other, the son, is poor; in seeking a livelihood for the sake of food and clothing he roams in all directions and goes to some place, whereas his father removes to another country. The latter has much wealth, gold, corn, treasures, and granaries; possesses much wrought gold and silver, many gems, pearls, lapis lazuli, conch shells, and stones, corals, gold and silver; many slaves male and female, servants for menial work and journeymen; is rich in elephants, horses, carriages, cows, and sheep. He keeps a large retinue; has his money invested in great territories, and does great things in business, money-lending, agriculture, and commerce.

In course of time, Lord, that poor man, in quest of food and clothing, roaming through villages, towns, boroughs, provinces, kingdoms, and royal capitals, reaches the place where his father, the owner of much wealth and gold, treasures and granaries, is residing. Now the poor man's father, Lord, the owner of much wealth and gold, treasures and granaries, who was residing in that town, had always and ever been thinking of the son he had lost fifty years ago, but he gave no utterance to his thoughts before others, and was only pining in himself and thinking: I am old, aged, advanced in years, and possess abundance of bullion, gold, money and corn, treasures and granaries, but have no son. It is to be feared lest death shall overtake me and all this perish unused. Repeatedly he was thinking of that son: O how happy should I be, were my son to enjoy this mass of wealth!

Meanwhile, Lord, the poor man in search of food and clothing was gradually approaching the house of the rich man, the owner of abundant bullion, gold, money and corn, treasures and granaries. And the father of the poor man happened to sit at the door of his house, surrounded and waited upon by a great crowd of Brahmanas, Kshatriyas, Vaisyas, and Sudras; he was sitting on a magnificent throne with a footstool decorated with gold and silver, while dealing with hundred thousands of kotis of gold-pieces, and fanned with a chowrie, on a spot under an extended awning inlaid with pearls and flowers and adorned with hanging garlands of jewels; sitting, in short, in great pomp. The poor man, Lord, saw his own father in such pomp sitting at the door of the house, surrounded with a great crowd of people and doing a householder's business. The poor man, frightened, terrified, alarmed, seized with a feeling of goose-flesh all over the body, and agitated in mind, reflects thus: Unexpectedly have I here fallen in with a king or grandee. People like me have nothing to do here; let me go; in the street of the poor I am likely to find food and clothing without much difficulty. Let me no longer tarry at this place, lest I be taken to do forced labour or incur some other injury.

Thereupon, Lord, the poor man quickly departs, runs off, does not tarry from fear of a series of supposed dangers. But the rich man, sitting on the throne at the door of his mansion, has recognized his son at first sight, in consequence whereof he is content, in high spirits, charmed, delighted, filled with joy and cheerfulness. He thinks: Wonderful! he who is to enjoy this plenty of bullion, gold, money and corn, treasures and granaries, has been found! He of whom I have been thinking again and again is here now that I am old, aged, advanced in years.

At the same time, moment, and instant, Lord, he dispatches couriers, to whom he says: Go, sirs, and quickly fetch me that man. The fellows thereon all run forth in full speed and overtake the poor man, who, frightened, terrified, alarmed, seized with a feeling of goose-flesh all over his body, agitated in mind, utters a lamentable cry of distress, screams, and exclaims: I have given you no offence. But the fellows drag the poor man, however lamenting, violently with them. He, frightened, terrified, alarmed, seized with a feeling of goose-flesh all over his body, and agitated in mind, thinks by himself: I fear lest I shall be punished with capital punishment; I am lost. He faints away, and falls on the earth. His father, dismayed and near despondency, says to those fellows: Do not carry the man in that manner. With these words he sprinkles him with cold water without addressing him any further. For that householder knows the poor man's humble disposition and his own elevated position; yet he feels that the man is his son.

The householder, Lord, skilfully conceals from every one that it is his son. He calls one of his servants and says to him: Go, sirrah, and tell that poor man: Go, sirrah, whither thou likest; thou art free. The servant obeys, approaches the poor man and tells him: Go, sirrah, whither thou likest; thou art free. The poor man is astonished and amazed at hearing these words; he leaves that spot and wanders to the street of the poor in search of food and clothing. In order to attract him the householder practises an able device. He employs for it two men ill-favoured and of little splendour. Go, says he, go to the man you saw in this place; hire him in your own name for a double daily fee, and order him to do work here in my house. And if he asks: What work shall I have to do? tell him: Help us in clearing the heap of dirt. The two fellows go and seek the poor man and engage him for such work as mentioned. Thereupon the two fellows conjointly with the poor man clear the heap of dirt in the house for the daily pay they receive from the rich man, while they take up their abode in a hovel of straw in the neighbourhood of the rich man's dwelling. And that rich man beholds through a window his own son clearing the heap of dirt, at which sight he is anew struck with wonder and astonishment.

Then the householder descends from his mansion, lays off his wreath and ornaments, parts with his soft, clean, and gorgeous attire, puts on dirty raiment, takes a basket in his right hand, smears his body with dust, and goes to his son, whom he greets from afar, and thus addresses: Please, take the baskets and without delay remove the dust. By this device he manages to speak to his son, to have a talk with him and say: Do, sirrah, remain here in my service; do not go again to another place; I will give thee extra pay, and whatever thou wantest thou mayst confidently ask me, be it the price of a pot, a smaller pot, a boiler or wood, or be it the price of salt, food, or clothing. I have got an old cloak, man; if thou shouldst want it, ask me for it, I will give it. Any utensil of such sort, when thou wantest to have it, I will give thee. Be at ease, fellow; look upon me as if I were thy father, for I am older and thou art younger, and thou hast rendered me much service by clearing this heap of dirt, and as long as thou hast been in my service thou hast never shown nor art showing wickedness, crookedness, arrogance, or hypocrisy; I have discovered in thee no vice at all of such as are commonly seen in other men-servants. From henceforward thou art to me like my own son.

From that time, Lord, the householder addresses the poor man by the name of son, and the latter feels in presence of the householder as a son to his father. In this manner, Lord, the householder, affected with longing for his son, employs him for the clearing of the heap of dirt during twenty years, at the end of which the poor man feels quite at ease in the mansion to go in and out, though he continues taking his abode in the hovel of straw.

After a while, Lord, the householder falls sick, and feels that the time of his death is near at hand. He says to the poor man: Come hither, man, I possess abundant bullion, gold, money and corn, treasures and granaries. I am very sick, and wish to have one upon whom to bestow my wealth; by whom it is to be received, and with whom it is to be deposited. Accept it. For in the same manner as I am the owner of it, so art thou, but thou shalt not suffer anything of it to be wasted.

And so, Lord, the poor man accepts the abundant bullion, gold, money and corn, treasures and granaries of the rich man, but for himself he is quite indifferent to it, and requires nothing from it, not even so much as the price of a prastha of flour; he continues living in the same hovel of straw and considers himself as poor as before.

After a while, Lord, the householder perceives that his son is able to save, mature and mentally developed; that in the consciousness of his nobility he feels abashed, ashamed, disgusted, when thinking of his former poverty. The time of his death approaching, he sends for the poor man, presents him to a gathering of his relations, and before the king or king's peer and in the presence of citizens and country-people makes the following speech: Hear, gentlemen! this is my own son, by me begotten. It is now fifty years that he disappeared from such and such a town. He is called so and so, and myself am called so and so. In searching after him I have from that town come hither. He is my son, I am his father. To him I leave all my revenues, and all my personal or private wealth shall he acknowledge his own.

The poor man, Lord, hearing this speech, was astonished and amazed; he thought by himself: Unexpectedly have I obtained this bullion, gold, money and corn, treasures and granaries.

Even so, O Lord, do we represent the sons of the Tathagata, and the Tathagata says to us: Ye are my sons, as the householder did.

Thereupon the Lord addressed the venerable Maha-Kasyapa and the other senior great disciples, and said: Very well, very well, Kasyapa; you have done very well to proclaim the real qualities of the Tathagata. They are the real qualities of the Tathagata, Kasyapa, but he has many more, innumerable, incalculable, the end of which it would be difficult to reach, even were one to continue enumerating them for immeasurable æons.

It is a case, Kasyapa, similar to that of a great cloud big with rain, coming up in this wide universe over all grasses, shrubs, herbs, trees of various species and kind, families of plants of different names growing on earth, on hills, or in mountain caves, a cloud covering the wide universe to pour down its rain everywhere and at the same time. Then, Kasyapa, the grasses, shrubs, herbs, and wild trees in this universe, such as have young and tender stalks, twigs, leaves, and foliage, and such as have middle-sized stalks, twigs, leaves, and foliage, and such as have the same fully developed, all those grasses, shrubs, herbs, and wild trees, smaller and greater other trees, will each, according to its faculty and power, suck the humid element from the water emitted by that great cloud, and by that water which, all of one essence, has been abundantly poured down by the cloud, they will each, according to its germ, acquire a regular development, growth, shooting up, and bigness; and so they will produce blossoms and fruits, and will receive, each severally, their names. Rooted in one and the same soil, all those families of plants and germs are drenched and vivified by water of one essence throughout.

I am the Tathagata, O ye gods and men! the Arhat, the perfectly enlightened one; having reached the shore myself, I carry others to the shore; being free, I make free; being comforted, I comfort; being perfectly at rest, I lead others to rest. By my perfect wisdom I know both this world and the next, such as they really are. I am all-knowing, all-seeing. Come to me, ye gods and men! hear the law. I am he who indicates the path; who shows the path, as knowing the path, being acquainted with the path.

I shall refresh all beings whose bodies are withered, who are clogged to the triple world. I shall bring to felicity those that are pining away with toils, give them pleasures and final rest.

Hearken to me, ye hosts of gods and men; approach to behold me: I am the Tathagata, the Lord, who has no superior, who appears in this world to save. To thousands of kotis of living beings I preach a pure and most bright law that has but one scope, to wit, deliverance and rest.

I preach with ever the same voice, constantly taking enlightenment as my text. For this is equal for all; no partiality is in it, neither hatred nor affection. I am inexorable, bear no love nor hatred towards any one, and proclaim the law to all creatures without distinction, to the one as well as the other.

I re-create the whole world like a cloud shedding its water without distinction; I have the same feelings for respectable people as for the low; for moral persons as for the immoral; for the depraved as for those who observe the rules of good conduct; for those who hold sectarian views and unsound tenets as for those whose views are sound and correct. I preach the law to the inferior in mental culture as well as to persons of superior understanding and extraordinary faculties; inaccessible to weariness, I spread in season the rain of the law.

The Lord having thus spoken, the venerable Maha-Kasyapa said: Lord, if the beings are of different disposition, will there be for those who have left the triple world one Nirvana, or two, or three? The Lord replied: Nirvana, Kasyapa, is a consequence of understanding that all laws (things) are equal. Hence there is but one Nirvana, not two, not three.

As the rays of the sun and moon descend alike on all men, good and bad, without deficiency in one case or surplus in the other; so the wisdom of the Tathagata shines like the sun and moon, leading all beings without partiality.

As the potter, making clay vessels, produces from the same clay pots for sugar, milk, ghee, or water; some for impurities, others for curdled milk, the clay used by the artificer for the vessels being of but one sort; as a vessel is made to receive all its distinguishing qualities according to the quality of the substance laid into it, so the Tathagatas, on account of the diversity of taste, mention a diversity of vehicles, though the Buddha-vehicle be the only indisputable one.

He who ignores the rotation of mundane existence has no perception of blessed rest; but he who understands that all laws are void and without reality and without individual character penetrates the enlightenment of the perfectly enlightened lords in its very essence.

The strength of charity or kindness is my abode; the apparel of forbearance is my robe; and voidness or complete abstraction is my seat; let the preacher take his stand on this and preach. My body has existed entire in thousands of kotis of regions; during a number of kotis of æons beyond comprehension I teach the law to creatures.

To that courageous man who shall proclaim this Sutra after my complete extinction I will also send many creations. And should there be some to attack him with clods, sticks, injurious words, threats, taunts, then the creations shall defend him. And when he shall stay alone, engaged in study, in a lonely place, in the forest or the hills, then will I show him my luminous body and enable him to remember the lesson he forgot.

He who keeps this Sutra, the veritable law, will fathom the mystery of the highest man; will soon comprehend what truth it was that was arrived at on the terrace of enlightenment. The quickness of his apprehension will be unlimited; like the wind he will nowhere meet impediments; he knows the purport and interpretation of the law, he who keeps this exalted Sutra.

Of the Regarder-of-the-Cries-of-the-World

(Words ascribed to Gotama Buddha)

If there be any who hold fast to the name of that Bodhisattva, Regarder-of-the-Cries-of-the-World, though they fall into a great fire, the fire will not be able to burn them, by virtue of the august supernatural power of that Bodhisattva. If any, carried away by a flood, call upon his name, they will immediately reach the shallows. If there be hundreds, thousands, myriads, kotis of beings, who in search of gold, silver, lapis lazuli, moon-stones, agate, coral, amber, pearls, and other treasures, go out on the ocean, and if a black gale blows their ships adrift upon the land of the Rakshasa-demons, and if amongst them there be even a single person who calls the name of the Bodhisattva Regarder-of-the-Cries-of-the-World, all those people will be delivered from the woes of the Rakshasas. It is for this cause that he is named Regarder-of-the-Cries-of-the-World.

Or if any one cries who is in deadly peril by the sword, the sword will be snapped asunder. If wicked demons attack, the one who cries will become invisible to them. Whether guilty or innocent, if he cry, though loaded with manacles, fetters, cangues or chains, all will be broken and he will be set free. A train of jewel-merchants, passing along a road infested with robbers, have but to cry with one voice and they will be protected. Those possessed by carnal passions, anger, or infatuation have but to remember and revere this Bodhisattva and they will be set free. If a woman desires a son, worships and pays homage, she will bear a son, virtuous and wise; or if a daughter, then of good demeanour and looks.

The merit attained by worship of other Bodhisattvas, in number as sands of sixty-two kotis of Ganges, just equals the merit of him who but for one moment worships the Regarder-of-the-Cries-of-the-World.

The Diamond Sutra

The Transcendent Wisdom

Thus have I heard concerning our Lord Buddha:

Upon a memorable occasion, the Lord Buddha sojourned in the kingdom of Sravasti, lodging in the grove of Jeta, a park within the imperial domain, which Jeta, the heir-apparent, bestowed upon Sutana, a benevolent minister of state, renowned for his charities and benefactions.

With the Lord Buddha, there were assembled together twelve hundred and fifty mendicant disciples, all of whom had attained to eminent degrees of spiritual wisdom.

Upon that occasion, the venerable Subhuti occupied a place in the midst of the assembly. Rising from his seat, with cloak arranged in such manner that his right shoulder was disclosed, Subhuti knelt upon his right knee, then pressing together the palms of his hands, he respectfully raised them towards Lord Buddha, saying: "Thou art of transcendent wisdom, honoured of the worlds! With wonderful solicitude, thou dost preserve in the faith, and instruct in the law, this illustrious assembly of enlightened disciples. Honoured of the worlds! if a good disciple, whether man or woman, seeks to obtain supreme spiritual wisdom, what immutable law shall sustain the mind of that disciple, and bring into subjection every inordinate desire?"

The Lord Buddha replied to Subhuti, saying: "Truly a most excellent theme! As you affirmed, I preserve in the faith, and instruct in the law, this illustrious assembly of enlightened disciples. Attend diligently unto me, and I shall enunciate a law whereby the mind of a good disciple, whether man or woman, seeking to obtain supreme spiritual wisdom, shall be adequately sustained, and enabled to bring into subjection every inordinate desire." Subhuti was gratified, and signified glad consent.

Thereupon, the Lord Buddha, with majesty of person, and perfect articulation, proceeded to deliver the text of this scripture, saying:

"By this wisdom shall enlightened disciples be enabled to bring into subjection every inordinate desire! Every species of life, whether hatched in the egg, formed in the womb, evolved from spawn, produced by metamorphosis, with or without form or intelligence, possessing or devoid of natural instinct—from these changeful conditions of being, I command you to seek deliverance, in the transcendental concept of Nirvana. Thus, you shall be delivered from an immeasurable, innumerable, and illimitable world of sentient life; but, in reality, there is no world of sentient life from which to seek deliverance. And why? Because, in the minds of enlightened disciples, there have ceased to exist such arbitrary concepts of phenomena as an entity, a being, a living being, or a personality.

"Moreover, Subhuti, an enlightened disciple ought to act spontaneously in the exercise of charity, uninfluenced by sensuous phenomena such as sound, odour, taste, touch, or law. Subhuti, it is imperative that an enlightened disciple, in the exercise of charity, should act independently of phenomena. And why? Because, acting without regard to illusive forms of phenomena, he will realize in the exercise of charity a merit inestimable and immeasurable.

"Subhuti, what think you? Is it possible to estimate the distance comprising the illimitable universe of space?" Subhuti replied, saying: "Honoured of the worlds! It is impossible to estimate the distance comprising the illimitable universe of space." The Lord Buddha thereupon discoursed, saying: "It is equally impossible to estimate the merit of an enlightened disciple, who discharges the exercise of charity, unperturbed by the seductive influences of phenomena. Subhuti, the mind of an enlightened disciple ought thus to be indoctrinated."

The Lord Buddha interrogated Subhuti, saying: "What think you? Is it possible that by means of his physical body, the Lord Buddha may be clearly perceived?" Subhuti replied, saying: "No! Honoured of the worlds! It is impossible that by means of his physical body, the Lord Buddha may be clearly perceived. And why? Because what the Lord Buddha referred to as a physical body is in reality not merely a physical body." Thereupon the Lord Buddha addressed Subhuti, saying: "Every form or quality of phenomena is transient and illusive. When the mind realizes that the phenomena of life are not real phenomena, the Lord Buddha may then be clearly perceived."

Subhuti inquired of the Lord Buddha, saying: "Honoured of the worlds! In future ages, when this scripture is proclaimed, amongst those beings destined to hear, shall any conceive within their minds a sincere, unmingled faith?"

The Lord Buddha replied to Subhuti, saying: "Have no such apprehensive thought! Even at the remote period of five centuries subsequent to the Nirvana of the Lord Buddha, there will be many disciples observing the monastic vows, and assiduously devoted to good works. These, hearing this scripture proclaimed, will believe in its immutability, and similarly conceive within their minds a pure, unmingled faith. Besides, it is important to realize that faith thus conceived is not exclusively in virtue of the insular thought of any particular Buddha, but because of its affiliation with the concrete thoughts of myriad Buddhas, throughout infinite ages. Therefore, amongst the beings destined to hear this scripture proclaimed, many, by momentary reflection, will intuitively conceive a pure and holy faith."

The Lord Buddha addressed Subhuti, saying: "What think you? Has the Lord Buddha really attained to supreme spiritual wisdom? Or has he a system of doctrine which can be specifically formulated?"

Subhuti replied, saying: "As I understand the meaning of the Lord Buddha's discourse, he has no system of doctrine which can be specifically formulated; nor can the Lord Buddha express, in explicit terms, a form of knowledge which can be described as supreme spiritual wisdom. And why? Because what the Lord Buddha adumbrated in terms of the law is transcendental and inexpressible. Being a purely spiritual concept, it is neither consonant with law, nor synonymous with anything apart from the law. Thus is exemplified the manner by which wise disciples and holy Buddhas, regarding intuition as the law of their minds, severally attained to different planes of spiritual wisdom."

The Lord Buddha addressed Subhuti, saying: "What think you? If a benevolent person bestowed as alms an abundance of the seven treasures sufficient to fill the universe, would there accrue to that person a considerable merit?"

Subhuti replied, saying: "A very considerable merit, honoured of the worlds! And why? Because what is referred to does not partake of the nature of ordinary merit, and in this sense the Lord Buddha made mention of a 'considerable' merit."

The Lord Buddha rejoined, saying: "If a disciple adhered with implicit faith to a stanza of this scripture, and diligently explained it to others, the intrinsic merit of that disciple would be relatively greater. And why? Because, Subhuti, the holy Buddhas, and the law by which they attained to supreme spiritual wisdom, severally owe their inception to the truth of this sacred scripture. Subhuti, what is ordinarily termed the Buddhic law is not really a law attributive to Buddha."

The Lord Buddha inquired of Subhuti, saying: "What think you? May a Srotapatti (that is, one who has entered the stream which bears on to Nirvana) thus moralize within himself, 'I have obtained the fruits commensurate with the merit of a Srotapatti'?" Subhuti replied, saying: "No! honoured of the worlds! And why? Because Srotapatti is simply a descriptive term signifying 'having entered the stream.' A disciple who avoids the seductive phenomena of form, sound, odour, taste, touch, and law, is named a Srotapatti."

The Lord Buddha yet again inquired of Subhuti, saying: "What think you? May an Arhat (having attained to absolute quiescence of mind) thus meditate within himself, 'I have obtained the condition of an Arhat'?" Subhuti replied, saying: "No! honoured of the worlds! And why? Because there is not in reality a condition synonymous with the term Arhat. Honoured of the worlds! if an Arhat thus meditates within himself, 'I have obtained the condition of an Arhat,' there would be obvious recurrence of such arbitrary concepts as an entity, a being, a living being, and a personality."

Upon that occasion, Subhuti inquired of the Lord Buddha, saying: "Honoured of the worlds! by what name shall this scripture be known, that we may regard it with reverence?" The Lord Buddha replied, saying: "Subhuti, this scripture shall be known as The Diamond Sutra, 'The Transcendent Wisdom,' by means of which we reach 'The Other Shore.' By this name you shall reverently regard it! And why? Subhuti, what the Lord Buddha declared as 'transcendent wisdom' by means of which we reach 'the other shore' is not essentially 'transcendent wisdom'—in its essence it transcends all wisdom."

The Lord Buddha addressed Subhuti, saying: "What think you? You disciples, do not affirm that the Lord Buddha reflects thus within himself, 'I bring salvation to every living being.' Subhuti, entertain no such delusive thought! And why? Because in reality there are no living beings to whom the Lord Buddha can bring salvation. If there were living beings to whom the Lord Buddha could bring salvation, the Lord Buddha would necessarily assume the reality of such arbitrary concepts as an entity, a being, a living being, and a personality. Subhuti, what the Lord Buddha adverted to as an entity is not in reality an entity; it is only understood to be an entity, and believed in as such, by the common, uneducated people. Subhuti, what are ordinarily referred to as the 'common, uneducated people,' these the Lord Buddha declared to be not merely 'common, uneducated people.' "

The Lord Buddha addressed Subhuti, saying: "Can the Lord Buddha be perceived by means of his thirty-two bodily distinctions?" Subhuti replied, saying: "Even so, the Lord Buddha can be perceived by means of his thirty-two bodily distinctions."

The Lord Buddha, continuing, said unto Subhuti: "If by means of his thirty-two bodily distinctions it were possible to perceive the Lord Buddha, then the Lord Buddha would merely resemble one of the great wheel-turning kings."

Subhuti thereupon addressed the Lord Buddha, saying: "Honoured of the worlds! According as I am able to interpret the Lord Buddha's instruction, it is improbable that the Lord Buddha may be perceived by means of his thirty-two bodily distinctions."

Thereafter, the "Honoured of the Worlds" delivered this sublime Gatha:

"I am not to be perceived by means of any visible form,
 Nor sought after by means of any audible sound;
 Whosoever walks in the way of iniquity,
 Cannot perceive the blessedness of the Lord Buddha."

The Lord Buddha said unto Subhuti: "If you think thus within yourself 'The Lord Buddha did not, by means of his perfect bodily distinctions, obtain supreme spiritual wisdom,' Subhuti, have no such deceptive thought! Or if you think thus within yourself, 'In obtaining supreme spiritual wisdom, the Lord Buddha declared the abrogation of every law,' Subhuti, have no such delusive thought! And why? Because, those disciples who obtain supreme spiritual wisdom, neither affirm the abrogation of any law, nor the destruction of any distinctive quality of phenomena."

The Lord Buddha thereupon declared unto Subhuti, "Belief in the unity or eternity of matter is incomprehensible; and only common, worldly-minded people, for purely materialistic reasons, covet this hypothesis."

The Lord Buddha addressed Subhuti, saying: "If a disciple, having immeasurable spheres filled with the seven treasures, bestowed these in the exercise of charity; and if a disciple, whether man or woman, having aspired to supreme spiritual wisdom, selected from this scripture a stanza comprising four lines, then rigorously observed it, studied it, and diligently explained it to others; the cumulative merit of such a disciple would be relatively greater than that of the other.

"In what attitude of mind should it be diligently explained to others? Not assuming the permanency or the reality of earthly phenomena, but in the conscious blessedness of a mind at perfect rest. And why? Because, the phenomena of life may be likened unto a dream, a phantasm, a bubble, a shadow, the glistening dew, or lightning flash, and thus they ought to be contemplated."

When the Lord Buddha concluded his enunciation of this scripture, the venerable Subhuti, the monks, nuns, lay-brethren and sisters, all mortals, and the whole realm of spiritual beings, rejoiced exceedingly, and consecrated to its practice, they received it and departed.

Asvaghosha's Discourse on the Awakening of Faith

The Conversion of Asvaghosha

Asvaghosha, who felt extremely ashamed of his former self-assumption, was thinking of attempting his own life. Punyayacas, his teacher, however, attaining arhatship, entered into a samadhi and divined what was going on in the mind of Asvaghosha. He ordered him to go and bring some books out of the library. Asvaghosha said to the Acarya: "The room is perfectly dark; how can I get in there?" To this Punyayacas answered: "Just go in, and I shall let you have light." Then the Acarya through his supernatural power stretched far into the room his right hand whose five fingers each radiating with light illuminated everything inside of the walls. Asvaghosha thought it a mental hallucination, and knowing the fact that a hallucination as a rule disappears when one is conscious of it, he was surprised to see the light glowing more and more. He tried his magical arts to extinguish it till he felt utterly exhausted, for the mysterious light suffered no change whatever. Finally coming to realize that it was the work of no other person than his teacher, his spirit was filled with remorse, and he thenceforth applied himself diligently to religious discipline and never relapsed.

The Purchase of Asvaghosha

After that a king of the smaller Tukhara country in North India invaded the middle country, Magadha. When the besieging had continued for some time, the king of Central India sent a message to the invader, saying: "If there be anything you want, I will supply it; do not disturb the peace of my people by thus long staying here." To which this reply was given: "If you really ask a surrender, send me 300,000,000 gold pieces; I will release you." The besieged king said: "Even this entire kingdom cannot produce 100,000,000 gold pieces; how can I supply you with 300,000,000?" The answer was: "There are in your country two great treasures: (1) the Buddha-bowl, (2) a Bhikkhu of wonderful talent (i.e., Asvaghosha). Give them to me, they are worth 300,000,000 gold pieces." The besieged king said: "Those two treasures are what I most revere, I cannot give them up." Thereupon the Bhikkhu said to the king in explanation of the Dharma:

"All sentient beings are everywhere the same, while Buddhism, deep and comprehensive, aims at universal salvation, and the highest virtue of a great man consists in delivering all beings. As our temporal administration is very liable to meet obstructions, even your rule does not extend itself outside of this one kingdom. If you, on the other hand, propose a wide propagation of Buddhism, you would naturally be a Dharmaraja over the four oceans. The duty of a Bhikkhu is to save all the people and not to give preference to one or the other. Merits lie in our heart; truth makes no distinction. Pray, be far-sighted, and do not think only of the present."

The king, who was from the first a great admirer of him, respectfully followed his advice and delivered him to the king of Tukhara, who returned with him to his own kingdom.

Asvaghosha's Doctrine of Suchness

After the Nirvana of the Buddha there were men who possessed in themselves the intellectual power to understand the many-sided meanings of the Sutras, even if they read only a few of them. There were others who by their own intellectual powers could understand the meanings of the Sutras only after an extensive reading of many of them. Still others lacking in intellectual powers of their own could understand the meanings of the Sutras only through the assistance of elaborate commentaries. But there are some who, lacking in intellectual powers of their own, shun the perusal of elaborate commentaries and take delight in studying and cultivating inquiries which present the many-sidedness and universality of the doctrine in a concise form.

For the sake of the people of the last class I write this discourse, in which the most excellent, the deepest, and the most inexhaustible doctrine of the Tathagata will be treated in comprehensive brevity.

In the one soul we may distinguish two aspects. The one is the soul as suchness, the other is the soul as birth-and-death. Each in itself constitutes all things, and both are so closely interrelated that one cannot be separated from the other.

What is meant by the soul as suchness, is the oneness of the totality of things, the great all-including whole, the quintessence of the doctrine. For the essential nature of the soul is uncreate and eternal.

Therefore all things in their fundamental nature are not nameable or explicable. They cannot be adequately expressed in any form of language. They are without the range of apperception. They are universals. They have no signs of distinction. They possess absolute sameness. They are universals. They are subject neither to transformation, nor to destruction. They are nothing but the one soul, for which suchness is another designation. Therefore they cannot be fully explained by words or exhausted by reasoning.

In the essence of suchness, there is neither anything which has to be excluded, nor anything which has to be added.

The soul as birth-and-death comes forth (as the law of causation) from the Tathagata's womb. But the immortal (i.e., suchness) and the mortal (i.e., birth-and-death) coincide with each other. Though they are not identical, they are not a duality. Thus when the absolute soul assumes a relative aspect by its self-affirmation it is called the all-conserving mind.

The same mind has a twofold significance as the organizer and the producer of all things.

Again it embraces two principles: (1) enlightenment; (2) non-enlightenment.

Enlightenment is the highest quality of the mind. As it is free from all limiting attributes of subjectivity, it is like unto space, penetrating everywhere, as the unity of all. That is to say, it is the universal Dharmakaya of all Tathagatas.

The multitude of people are said to be lacking in enlightenment, because ignorance prevails there from all eternity, because there is a constant succession of confused subjective states from which they have never been emancipated.

But when they transcend their subjectivity, they can then recognize that all states of mentation, viz., their appearance, presence, change, and disappearance (in the field of consciousness) have no genuine reality. They are neither in a temporal nor in a spatial relation with the one soul, for they are not self-existent.

When you understand this, you also understand that enlightenment in appearance cannot be manufactured, for it is no other thing than enlightenment in its suchness, which is uncreate and must be discovered.

To illustrate: a man who is lost goes astray because he is bent on pursuing a certain direction; and his confusion has no valid foundation other than that he is bent on a certain direction.

It is even the same with all beings. They become unenlightened, foster their subjectivity and go astray, because they are bent on enlightenment.

While the essence of the mind is eternally clean and pure, the influence of ignorance makes possible the existence of a defiled mind. But in spite of the defiled mind, the mind itself is eternal, clear, pure, and not subject to transformation.

When the oneness of the totality of things is not recognized, then ignorance as well as particularization arises, and all phases of the defiled mind are thus developed. But the significance of this doctrine is so extremely deep and unfathomable that it can be fully comprehended by Buddhas and by no others.

When the mind is disturbed, it fails to be a true and adequate knowledge; it fails to be a pure, clean essence; it fails to be eternal, blissful, self-regulating, and pure; it fails to be tranquil. On the contrary, it will become transient, changeable, unfree, and therefore the source of falsity and defilement, while its modifications outnumber the sands of the Ganges. But when there is no disturbance in the essence of the mind, we speak of suchness as being the true, adequate knowledge, and as possessing pure and clean merits that outnumber the sands of the Ganges.

When the mind is disturbed it will strive to become conscious of the existence of an external world and will thus betray the imperfection of its inner condition. But as all infinite merits in fact constitute the one mind which, perfect in itself, has no need of seeking after any external things other than itself, so suchness never fails to actualize all those Buddha-dharmas, that, outnumbering the sands of the Ganges, can be said to be neither identical nor non-identical with the essence of the mind, and that therefore are utterly out of the range of our comprehension. On that account suchness is designated the Tathagata's womb or the Tathagata's Dharmakaya.

The body has infinite forms. The form has infinite attributes. The attribute has infinite excellencies. And the accompanying rewards of Bodhisattvas, that is, the region where they are predestined to be born by their previous karma, also has infinite merits and ornamentations. Manifesting itself everywhere, the body of Bliss is infinite, boundless, limitless, unintermittent in its action, directly coming forth from the mind.

The Tibetan Doctrine

The "Elegant Sayings" of the Lamas

A hen, when at rest, produceth much fruit;
A peacock, when it remaineth still, hath a handsome tail;
A gentle horse hath a swift pace;
The quiescence of a holy man is the sign of his being a sage.

Not to be cheered by praise,
Not to be grieved by blame,
But to know thoroughly one's own virtues or powers
Are the characteristics of an excellent man.

In the same place where the great Lord Buddha is present
Who would acknowledge any other man?
When the sun hath arisen, though there be many bright stars in the sky,
Not one of them is visible.

A foolish man proclaimeth his qualifications;
A wise man keepeth them secret within himself;
A straw floateth on the surface of water,
But a precious gem placed upon it sinketh.

It is only narrow-minded men that make such distinctions
As "This is our friend, this our enemy";
A liberal-minded man showeth affection for all,
For it is uncertain who may yet be of aid to one.

An excellent man, like precious metal,
Is in every way invariable;

A villain, like the beams of a balance,
Is always varying, upwards and downwards.

The greatest wealth consisteth in being charitable,
And the greatest happiness in having tranquillity of mind.
Experience is the most beautiful adornment;
And the best comrade is one that hath no desires.

Men of little ability, too,
By depending upon the great, may prosper;
A drop of water is a little thing,
But when will it dry away if united to a lake?

Hurtful expressions should never be used,
Not even against an enemy;
For inevitably they will return to one,
Like an echo from a rock.

When about to perform any great work,
Endeavour to have a trustworthy associate;
If one would burn down a forest,
The aid of a wind is, of course, needed.

To him who knoweth the true nature of things,
What need is there of a teacher?
To him who hath recovered from illness,
What need is there of a physician?
To him who hath crossed the river,
What need is there of a boat?

An astronomer maketh calculations and divinations concerning the mo-
        tions of the moon and the stars,
But he doth not divine that in his own household his own womenfolk,
        being at variance, are misbehaving.

In eating, sleeping, fearing, and copulating, men and beasts are alike;
Man excelleth the beast by engaging in religious practices.
So why should a man, if he be without religion, not be equal to the beast?

Although many stars shine, and that ornament of the earth, the moon,
        also shineth,
Yet when the sun setteth, it becometh night.

The science which teacheth arts and handicrafts
Is merely science for the gaining of a living;
But the science which teacheth deliverance from worldly existence,
Is not that the true science?

That which one desireth not for oneself,
Do not do unto others.

The foolish are like ripples on water,
For whatsoever they do is quickly effaced;
But the righteous are like carvings upon stone,
For their smallest act is durable.

The supreme path of altruism is a short-cut,
Leading to the realm of the conquerors,—
A track more speedy than that of a racing horse;
The selfish, however, know naught of it.

Charity produceth the harvest in the next birth.
Chastity is the parent of human happiness.
Patience is an adornment becoming to all.
Industry is the conductor of every personal accomplishment.
Meditation is the clarifier of a beclouded mind.
Intellect is the weapon which overcometh every enemy.

Gloat not, even though death and misfortune overwhelm thine enemies;
Boast not, even though thou equal Indra in greatness.

Some there are who turn inside out their whole interior
By means of over-talkativeness.

Be humble and meek if thou would be exalted;
Praise every one's good qualities if thou would have friends.

Relinquish an evil custom even though it be of thy fathers and ancestors;
Adopt a good custom even though it be established among thine enemies:
Poison is not to be taken even though offered by one's mother;
But gold is acceptable even from one who is inimical.

Be not too quick to express the desire of thy heart.
Be not short-tempered when engaged in a great work.
Be not jealous of a devotee who is truly religious and pious.
Consult not him who is habituated and hardened to evil-doing.

Rogues there are even in religious orders;
Poisonous plants grow even on hills of medicinal herbs.

Some there are who marvel not at others removing mountains,
But who consider it a heavy task when obliged to carry a bit of fleece.

He who is ever ready to take the credit for any action when it hath proved
　　　successful
And is equally ready to throw the blame on others when it goeth wrong
　　　in the least,
And who is ever looking for faults in those who are learned and
　　　righteous,
Possesseth the nature of a crow.

Preaching religious truths to an unbeliever is like feeding a venomous
　　　serpent with milk.

Although a cloth be washed a hundred times,
How can it be rendered clean and pure
If it be washed in water which is dirty?

He who knoweth the precepts by heart, but faileth to practise them,
Is like unto one who lighteth a lamp and then shutteth his eyes.

Who can say with certainty that one will live to see the morrow?

How can it be just to kill helpless and inoffensive creatures?

The Voice of the Silence

　　The mind is the great slayer of the real. Let the disciple slay the slayer.
　　Compassion speaketh and saith: "Can there be bliss when all that lives
must suffer? Shalt thou be saved and hear the whole world cry?"
　　Let not the fierce sun dry one tear of pain before thyself has wiped it
from the sufferer's eye.
　　The pupil must regain the child state he has lost ere the first sound can
fall upon his ear.
　　Kill in thyself all memory of past experiences. Look not behind or
thou art lost.
　　Both action and inaction may find room in thee; thy body agitated, thy
mind tranquil, thy soul as limpid as a mountain lake.

To live to benefit mankind is the first step. To practise the six glorious virtues is the second.

If sun thou canst not be, then be the humble planet.

The path is one for all, the means to reach the goal must vary with the pilgrims.

Thou shalt not let thy senses make a playground of thy mind.

Hast thou attuned thy being to humanity's great pain, O candidate for light?

For know, that the ETERNAL knows no change.

Jaina Sutras

Who Knows One Thing

He who knows one thing, knows all things; and he who knows all things, knows one thing. He who is careless in all respects, is in danger; he who is not careless in all respects, is free from danger.

He who conquers one passion, conquers many; and he who conquers many, conquers one. "Knowing the misery of the world," rejecting the connection with the world, "the heroes go on the great journey," they rise gradually; "they do not desire life."

He who avoids one passion, avoids them all severally; and he who avoids them severally, avoids one. Faithful according to the commandment of the Tirthakaras, wise, and understanding the world according to the commandment—such a man is without danger from anywhere. There are degrees in injurious acts, but there are no degrees in control.

He who knows wrath, knows pride; he who knows pride, knows deceit; he who knows deceit, knows greed; he who knows greed, knows love; he who knows love, knows hate; he who knows hate, knows delusion; he who knows delusion, knows conception; he who knows conception, knows birth; he who knows birth, knows death; he who knows death, knows hell; he who knows hell, knows animal existence; he who knows animal existence, knows pain.

Therefore, a wise man should avoid wrath, pride, deceit, greed, love, hate, delusion, conception, birth, death, hell, animal existence, and pain.

The Way of a Jaina Monk

The wise ones who attain in due order to one of the unerring states in which suicide is prescribed, those who are rich in control and endowed with knowledge, knowing the incomparable religious death, should continue their contemplation.

Knowing the twofold obstacles, bodily and mental, the wise ones, having thoroughly learned the law, perceiving in due order that the time for their death has come, get rid of karman. Subduing the passions and living on little food, they should endure hardships. If a mendicant falls sick, let him again take food. He should not long for life, nor wish for death; he should yearn after neither, life or death.

He who is indifferent and wishes for the destruction of karman, should continue his contemplation. Becoming unattached internally and externally, he should strive after absolute purity. Whatever means one knows for calming one's own life, that a wise man should learn in order to gain time for continuing practice.

In a village or in a forest, examining the ground and recognizing it as free from living beings, the sage should spread the straw. Without food he should lie down and bear the pains which attack him. He should not for too long time give way to worldly feelings which overcome him. When crawling animals or such as live on high or below, feed on his flesh and blood, he should neither kill them nor rub the wound. Though these animals destroy the body, he should not stir from his position.

We shall now describe a more exalted method for a well-controlled and instructed monk.

He should give up all motions except his own in the thrice threefold way. He should not lie on sprouts of grass, but inspecting the bare ground he should lie on it. Without any comfort and food, he should there bear pain. When the sage becomes weak in his limbs, he should strive after calmness. For he is blameless, who is well fixed and immovable in his intention to die. He should move to and fro on his ground, contract and stretch his limbs for the benefit of the whole body; or he should remain quiet as if he were lifeless. He should walk about, when tired of lying, or stand with passive limbs; when tired of standing, he should sit down. Intent on such an uncommon death, he should regulate the motions of his organs.

Having attained a place swarming with insects, he should search for a clean spot. He should not remain there whence sin would rise. He should raise himself above sinfulness, and bear all pains.

And this is a still more difficult method, when one lives according to it: not to stir from one's place, while checking all motions of the body.

This is the highest law, exalted above the preceding method: having examined a spot of bare ground he should remain there; stay O Brahmana! Having attained a place free from living beings, he should there fix himself. He should thoroughly mortify his flesh, thinking: There are no obstacles in my body. Knowing as long as he lives the dangers and troubles, the wise and restrained ascetic should bear them as being instrumental to the dissolution of the body. He should not be attached to the transitory pleasures, nor to the greater ones; he should not nourish desire and greed, looking only for eternal praise. He should be enlightened with eternal objects, and not trust in the delusive power of the gods; a Brahmana should know of this and cast off all inferiority. Not devoted to any of the external objects he reaches the end of his life; thinking that patience is the highest good, he should choose one of the described three good methods of entering Nirvana. Thus I say.

The Five Vows

The first great vow, sir, runs thus:

I renounce all killing of living beings, whether subtile or gross, whether movable or immovable. Nor shall I myself kill living beings, nor cause others to do it, nor consent to it. As long as I live, I confess and blame, repent and exempt myself of these sins, in the thrice threefold way, in mind, speech, and body.

There are five clauses.

A Nirgrantha is careful in his walk, not careless. The Kevalin assigns as the reason, that a Nirgrantha, careless in his walk, might with his feet hurt or displace or injure or kill living beings. Hence a Nirgrantha is careful in his walk, not careless in his walk.

A Nirgrantha searches into his mind (i.e. thoughts and intentions). If his mind is sinful, blamable, intent on works, acting on impulses, produces cutting and splitting, or division and dissension, quarrels, faults, and pains, injures living beings, or kills creatures, he should not employ such a mind in action; but if, on the contrary, it is not sinful, then he may put it in action.

A Nirgrantha searches into his speech; if his speech is sinful, blamable, intent on works, acting on impulses, produces cutting and splitting, quarrels, faults, and pains, injures living beings, or kills creatures, he should not utter that speech. But if, on the contrary, it is not sinful, then he may utter it.

A Nirgrantha is careful in laying down his utensils of begging, he is not careless in it. The Kevalin says: A Nirgrantha who is careless in laying down his utensils of begging, might hurt or displace or injure or kill all sorts of living beings. Hence a Nirgrantha is careful in laying down his utensils of begging, he is not careless in it.

A Nirgrantha eats and drinks after inspecting his food and drink; he does not eat and drink without inspecting his food and drink. The Kevalin says: If a Nirgrantha would eat and drink without inspecting his food and drink, he might hurt and displace or injure or kill all sorts of living beings. Hence a Nirgrantha eats and drinks after inspecting his food and drink, not without doing so.

In this way the great vow is correctly practised, followed, executed, explained, established, effected according to the precept.

The second great vow runs thus:

I renounce all vices of lying speech arising from anger or greed or fear or mirth. I shall neither myself speak lies, nor cause others to speak lies, nor consent to the speaking of lies by others. I confess and blame, repent and exempt myself of these sins in the thrice threefold way, in mind, speech, and body.

There are five clauses.

A Nirgrantha speaks after deliberation, not without deliberation. The Kevalin says: Without deliberation a Nirgrantha might utter a falsehood in his speech. A Nirgrantha speaks after deliberation, not without deliberation.

A Nirgrantha comprehends and renounces anger, greed, fear, and mirth. The Kevalin says: A Nirgrantha who is moved by anger, greed, fear, and mirth, might utter a falsehood in his speech.

In this way the great vow is correctly practised, followed, executed, explained, established, effected according to the precept.

The third great vow runs thus:

I renounce all taking of anything not given, either in a village or a town or a wood, either of little or much, of small or great, of living or lifeless things. I shall neither take myself what is not given, nor cause others to take it, nor consent to their taking it. As long as I live, I confess and blame, repent and exempt myself of these sins in the thrice threefold way, in mind, speech, and body.

There are five clauses.

A Nirgrantha begs after deliberation, for a limited ground, not without deliberation. The Kevalin says: If a Nirgrantha begs without deliberation for a limited ground, he might take what is not given.

A Nirgrantha consumes his food and drink with permission of his superior, not without his permission. The Kevalin says: If a Nirgrantha consumes his food and drink without the superior's permission, he might eat what is not given.

A Nirgrantha who has taken possession of some ground, should always take possession of a limited part of it and for a fixed time. The Kevalin says: If a Nirgrantha who has taken possession of some ground, should take possession of an unlimited part of it and for an unfixed time, he might take what is not given.

A Nirgrantha who has taken possession of some ground, should constantly have his grant renewed. The Kevalin says: If a Nirgrantha has not constantly his grant renewed, he might take possession of what is not given.

A Nirgrantha begs for a limited ground for his co-religionists after deliberation, not without deliberation. The Kevalin says: If a Nirgrantha should beg without deliberation, he might take possession of what is not given.

In this way the great vow is correctly practised, followed, executed, explained, established, effected according to the precept.

The fourth great vow runs thus:

I renounce all sexual pleasures, either with gods or men or animals. I shall not give way to sensuality, nor cause others to do it, nor consent to it. As long as I live, I confess and blame, repent and exempt myself of these sins, in the thrice threefold way, in mind, speech, and body.

There are five clauses.

A Nirgrantha does not continually discuss topics relating to women. The Kevalin says: If a Nirgrantha discusses such topics, he might fall from the law declared by the Kevalin, because of the destruction or disturbance of his peace.

A Nirgrantha does not regard and contemplate the lovely forms of women; a Nirgrantha does not recall to his mind the pleasures and amusements he formerly had with women; a Nirgrantha does not eat and drink too much, nor does he drink liquors or eat highly-seasoned dishes; a Nirgrantha does not occupy a bed or couch affected by women, animals, or eunuchs. The Kevalin says: If a Nirgrantha did so, he might fall from the law declared by the Kevalin, because of the destruction or disturbance of his peace.

In this way the great vow is correctly practised, followed, executed, explained, established, effected according to the precept.

The fifth great vow runs thus:

I renounce all attachments, whether little or much, small or great, living or lifeless; neither shall I myself form such attachments, nor cause others to do so, nor consent to their doing so. As long as I live, I confess and blame, repent and exempt myself of these sins, in the thrice threefold way, in mind, speech, and body.

There are five clauses.

If a creature with ears hears agreeable and disagreeable sounds, it should not be attached to, nor delighted with, nor desiring of, nor infatuated by, nor covetous of, nor disturbed by the agreeable or disagreeable sounds. The Kevalin says: If a Nirgrantha is thus affected by the pleasant or unpleasant sounds, he might fall from the law declared by the Kevalin, because of the destruction or disturbance of his peace.

If it is impossible not to hear sounds which reach the ear, the mendicant should avoid love or hate originated by them.

A creature with ears hears agreeable and disagreeable sounds.

If a creature with eyes sees agreeable and disagreeable forms or colours, if a creature with an organ of smell smells agreeable or disagreeable smells, if a creature with a tongue tastes agreeable or disagreeable tastes, if a creature with an organ of feeling feels agreeable or disagreeable touches, it should not be attached to, nor delighted with, nor desiring of, nor infatuated by, nor covetous of, nor disturbed by the agreeable or disagreeable impressions. The Kevalin says: If a Nirgrantha is thus affected by the pleasant or unpleasant impressions, he might fall from the law declared by the Kevalin, because of the destruction or disturbance of his peace.

If it is impossible not to have all those impressions which reach the organs of the senses, the mendicant should avoid love or hate originated by them.

In this way the great vow is correctly practised, followed, executed, explained, established, effected according to the precept.

He who is well provided with these great vows and their twenty-five clauses is really Houseless, if he, according to the sacred lore, the precepts, and the way, correctly practises, follows, executes, explains, establishes, and, according to the precept, effects them.

A Manual of Zen Buddhism

The Lankavatara Sutra

Those who, afraid of sufferings arising from the discrimination of birth and death, seek for Nirvana, do not know that birth and death and Nirvana are not to be separated the one from the other; and, seeing that all things subject to discrimination have no reality, imagine that Nirvana consists in the further annihilation of the senses and their fields. They are not aware, Mahamati, of the fact that Nirvana is the superior wisdom where a revulsion takes place by self-realization. Therefore, Mahamati, those who are stupid talk of the trinity of vehicles and not of the state of mind-only where there are no shadows. Therefore, Mahamati, those who do not understand the teachings of the Tathagatas of the past, present, and future, concerning the external world, which is of mind itself, cling to the notion that there is a world outside what is seen of the mind and, Mahamati, go on rolling themselves along the wheel of birth and death.

Further, Mahamati, according to the teaching of the Tathagatas of the past, present, and future, all things are unborn. Why? Because they have no reality, being manifestations of mind itself, and Mahamati, as they are not born of being and non-being, they are unborn. Mahamati, all things are like the horns of the hare, horse, donkey, or camel, but the ignorant and simple-minded who are given up to their false and erroneous imaginations, discriminate things where they are not; therefore, all things are unborn.

Mahamati, since the ignorant and the simple-minded, not knowing that the world is what is seen of mind itself, cling to the multitudinousness of external objects, cling to the notions of being and non-being, oneness and otherness, bothness and not-bothness, existence and non-existence, eternity and non-eternity, as having the character of self-substance, which idea rises from discrimination based on habit-energy, they are addicted to false imaginings. Mahamati, it is like a mirage in which the springs are seen as if they were real. They are imagined so by the animals who, thirsty from the heat of the season, would run after them. Not knowing that the springs are their own mental illusions, the animals do not realize that there are no such springs.

In the same way, Mahamati, the ignorant and simple-minded with their minds impressed by various erroneous speculations and discriminations since beginningless time; with their minds burning with the fire of greed, anger, and folly; delighted in a world of multitudinous forms; with their thoughts saturated with the ideas of birth, destruction, and subsistence; not understanding well what is meant by existent and non-existent, by inner and outer; the ignorant and simple-minded fall into the way of grasping at oneness and otherness, being and non-being as realities.

Mahamati, it is like the city of the Gandharvas which the unwitted take for a real city, though it is not so in fact. This city appears in essence owing to their attachment to the memory of a city preserved in seed from beginningless time. This city is thus neither existent nor non-existent.

In the same way, Mahamati, clinging to the memory of erroneous speculations and doctrines since beginningless time, they hold fast to ideas such as oneness and otherness, being and non-being, and their thoughts are not at all clear about what is seen of mind-only.

Mahamati, it is like a man, who, dreaming in his sleep of a country variously filled with women, men, elephants, horses, cars, pedestrians, villages, towns, hamlets, cows, buffalos, mansions, woods, mountains, rivers, and lakes, enters into its inner apartments and is awakened. While awakened thus, he recollects the city and its inner apartments. What do you think, Mahamati? Is this person to be regarded as wise, who is recollecting the various unrealities he has seen in his dream?

Said Mahamati: Indeed, he is not, Blessed One.

The Blessed One continued: In the same way the ignorant and simple-minded who are bitten by erroneous views and inclined towards the philosophers, do not recognize that things seen of the mind itself are like a dream, and are held fast by the notions of oneness and otherness, of being and non-being. Mahamati, it is like the painter's canvas on which there is neither depression nor elevation as imagined by the ignorant. In the same way, Mahamati, there may be in the future some people brought up in the habit-energy, mentality, and imagination based on the philosophers' erroneous views; clinging to the ideas of oneness and otherness, or bothness and not-bothness, they may bring themselves and others to ruin; they may declare those people nihilists who hold the doctrine of no-birth apart from the category of being and non-being. They argue against cause and effect, they are followers of the wicked views whereby they uproot meritorious causes of unstained purity. They are to be kept away by those whose desires are for things excellent. They are those whose thoughts are entangled in the error of self, other, and both, entangled in the error of imagining being and non-being, assertion and refutation; and hell will be their final refuge.

Mahamati, it is like the dim-eyed ones who, seeing a hair-net, would exclaim to one another, saying: "It is wonderful! it is wonderful! Look, O honourable sirs!" And the said hair-net has never been brought into existence. It is in fact neither an entity nor a non-entity, because it is seen and not seen. In the same manner, Mahamati, those whose minds are addicted to discrimination of the erroneous views as cherished by the philosophers, and who are also given up to the realistic ideas of being and non-being, oneness and otherness, bothness and not-bothness, will contradict the good Dharma, ending in the destruction of themselves and others.

Mahamati, it is like a firebrand-wheel which is no real wheel but which is imagined to be of such character by the ignorant, but not by the wise. In the same manner, Mahamati, those whose minds have fallen into the erroneous views of the philosophers will falsely imagine in the rise of all beings the reality of oneness and otherness, bothness and not-bothness.

Mahamati, it is like those water-bubbles in a rainfall which have the appearance of crystal gems, and the ignorant taking them for real crystal gems run after them. Mahamati, they are no more than water-bubbles, they are not gems, nor are they not-gems, because of their being so comprehended by one party and being not so comprehended by another. In the same manner, Mahamati, those whose minds are impressed by the habit-energy of the philosophical views and discriminations will regard things born as non-existent and those destroyed by causation as existent.

On Believing in Mind

The perfect Way knows no difficulties
Except that it refuses to make preferences;
Only when freed from hate and love,
It reveals itself fully and without disguise;
A tenth of an inch's difference,
And heaven and earth are set apart;
If you wish to see it before your own eyes,
Have no fixed thoughts either for or against it.

To set up what you like against what you dislike—
This is the disease of the mind:
When the deep meaning of the Way is not understood
Peace of mind is disturbed to no purpose.

The Way is perfect like unto vast space,
With nothing wanting, nothing superfluous:
It is indeed due to making choice
That its suchness is lost sight of.

Pursue not the outer entanglements,
Dwell not in the inner void;

Be serene in the oneness of things,
And dualism vanishes by itself.

When you strive to gain quiescence by stopping motion,
The quiescence thus gained is ever in motion;
As long as you tarry in the dualism,
How can you realize oneness?

And when oneness is not thoroughly understood,
In two ways loss is sustained:
The denying of reality is the asserting of it,
And the asserting of emptiness is the denying of it.

Wordiness and intellection—
The more with them the further astray we go;
Away therefore with wordiness and intellection,
And there is no place where we cannot pass freely.

When we return to the root, we gain the meaning;
When we pursue external objects, we lose the reason.
The moment we are enlightened within,
We go beyond the voidness of a world confronting us.

Transformations going on in an empty world which confronts us
Appear real all because of ignorance:
Try not to seek after the true,
Only cease to cherish opinions.

Abide not with dualism,
Carefully avoid pursuing it;
As soon as you have right and wrong,
Confusion ensues, and Mind is lost.

The two exist because of the One,
But hold not even to this One;
When a mind is not disturbed,
The ten thousand things offer no offence.

No offence offered, and no ten thousand things;
No disturbance going, and no mind set up to work:
The subject is quieted when the object ceases,
The object ceases when the subject is quieted.

The object is an object for the subject,
The subject is a subject for the object:
Know that the relativity of the two
Rests ultimately on one emptiness.

In one emptiness the two are not distinguished,
And each contains in itself all the ten thousand things;
When no discrimination is made between this and that,
How can a one-sided and prejudiced view arise?

The great Way is calm and large-hearted,
For it nothing is easy, nothing is hard;
Small views are irresolute,
The more in haste the tardier they go.

Clinging is never kept within bounds,
It is sure to go the wrong way;
Quit it, and things follow their own courses,
While the essence neither departs nor abides.

Obey the nature of things, and you are in concord with the Way,
Calm and easy and free from annoyance;
But when your thoughts are tied, you turn away from the truth,
They grow heavier and duller and are not at all sound.

When they are not sound, the spirit is troubled;
What is the use of being partial and one-sided then?
If you want to walk the course of the One Vehicle,
Be not prejudiced against the six sense-objects.

The ignorant cherish the idea of rest and unrest,
The enlightened have no likes and dislikes:
All forms of dualism
Are contrived by the ignorant themselves.
They are like unto visions and flowers in the air:
Why should we trouble ourselves to take hold of them?
Gain and loss, right and wrong—
Away with them once for all!

If an eye never falls asleep,
All dreams will by themselves cease:

If the mind retains its absoluteness,
The ten thousand things are of one suchness.

The ultimate end of things where they cannot go any further,
Is not bound by rules and measures:
In the mind harmonious with the Way we have the principle of identity,
In which we find all strivings quieted;
Doubts and irresolutions are completely done away with,
And the right faith is straightened;
There is nothing left behind,
There is nothing retained,
All is void, lucid, and self-illuminating,
There is no exertion, no waste of energy—
This is where thinking never attains,
This is where the imagination fails to measure.

In the higher realm of true suchness
There is neither "self" nor "other":
When direct identification is sought,
We can only say, "Not two."

What is is the same as what is not,
What is not is the same as what is:
Where this state of things fails to obtain,
Indeed, no tarrying there.

One in all,
All in One—
If only this is realized,
No more worry about your not being perfect!

Where Mind and each believing mind are not divided,
And undivided are each believing mind and Mind,
This is where words fail;
For it is not for the past, present, and future.

On the Absolute

The great Master died on the third day of the eighth month of the second year of Hsien-t'ien. On the eighth day of the seventh month this year, he had a farewell gathering of his followers, as he felt that he was to leave them for ever in the following month, and told them to have all the doubts they might have about his teaching once for all settled on this occasion. As he found them weeping in tears he said: "You are all weeping, but for whom are you so sorry? If you are sorry for my not knowing where I am to depart, you are mistaken; for I know where I am going. Indeed, if I did not, I would not part with you. The reason why you are in tears is probably that you do not yourselves know whither I am going. If you did, you would not be weeping so. The essence of the Dharma knows no birth-and-death, no coming-and-going. You all sit down, and let me give you a gatha with the title, "On the Absolute":

There is nothing true anywhere,
The true is nowhere to be seen;
If you say you see the true,
This seeing is not the true one.

Where the true is left to itself,
There is nothing false in it, which is mind itself.
When mind in itself is not liberated from the false,
There is nothing true, nowhere is the true to be found.

A conscious being alone understands what is meant by "moving";
To those not endowed with consciousness, the moving is unintelligible;
If you exercise yourself in the practice of keeping your mind unmoved,
          (in a quietistic meditation),
The immovable you gain is that of one who has no consciousness.

If you are desirous for the truly immovable,
The immovable is in the moving itself,
And this immovable is the truly immovable one;
There is no seed of Buddhahood where there is no consciousness.

Mark well how varied are aspects of the immovable one,
And know that the first reality is immovable;

Only when this insight is attained,
The true working of suchness is understood.

I advise you, O students of the truth,
To exert yourselves in the proper direction;
Do not in the teaching of the Mahayana
Commit the fault of clinging to the relative knowledge of birth and
    death.
Where there is an all-sided concordance of views
You may talk together regarding the Buddha's teaching;
Where there is really no such concordance,
Keep your hands folded and your joy within yourself.

There is really nothing to argue about in this teaching,
Any arguing is sure to go against the intent of it:
Doctrines given up to confusion and argumentation,
Lead by themselves to birth and death.

Yoka Daishi's "Song of Enlightenment"

Knowest thou that leisurely philosopher who has gone beyond learning
    and is not exerting himself in anything?
He neither endeavours to avoid idle thoughts nor seeks after the truth;
For he knows that ignorance in reality is the Buddha-nature,
And that this empty visionary body is no less than the Dharma-body.

When one knows what the Dharma-body is, there is not an object to be
    known as such,
The source of all things, as far as its self-nature goes, is the Buddha in
    his absolute aspect;
The five aggregates are like a cloud floating hither and thither with no
    fixed purpose,
The three poisons are like foams appearing and disappearing as it so
    happens to them.

When reality is attained, it is seen to be without an ego-substance and
    devoid of all forms of objectivity,
And thereby all the karma which leads us to the lowest hell is instantly
    wiped out;

Those, however, who cheat beings with their false knowledge,
Will surely see their tongues pulled out for innumerable ages to come.

Let the four elements go off your hold,
And in the midst of the eternally serene allow yourself to quaff or to
          peck, as you like;
Where all things of relativity are transient and ultimately empty,
There is seen the great perfect enlightenment of the Tathagata realized.

True monkhood consists in having a firm conviction;
If, however, you fail to have it, ask me according to your ideas, and you
          will be enlightened.
To have a direct understanding in regard to the root of all things, this
          is what the Buddha affirms;
If you go on gathering leaves and branches, there is no help for you.

Sons of the Sakya are known to be poor;
But their poverty is of the body, their spiritual life knows no poverty;
The poverty-stricken body is wrapped in rags,
But their spirit holds within itself a rare invaluable gem.

The superior one has it settled once for all and for ever,
The middling one learns much and holds much in doubt;
The point is to cast aside your soiled clothes you so dearly keep with you;
What is the use of showing off your work before others?

Let others speak ill of me, let others spite me;
Those who try to burn the sky with a torch end in tiring themselves out;
I listen to them and taste their evil-speaking as nectar;
All melts away and I find myself suddenly within the unthinkable itself.

Seeing others talk ill of me, I acquire the chance of gaining merit,
For they are really my good friends;
When I cherish, being vituperated, neither enmity nor favouritism,
There grows within me the power of love and humility which is born
          of the unborn.

I crossed seas and rivers, climbed mountains, and forded freshets,
In order to interview the masters, to inquire after truth, to delve into
          the secrets of Zen;
And ever since I was enabled to recognize the path of Sokei,
I know that birth-and-death is not the thing I have to be concerned with.

For walking is Zen, sitting is Zen,
Whether talking or remaining silent, whether moving or standing quiet,
    the essence itself is ever at ease;
Even when greeted with swords and spears it never loses its quiet way,
So with poisonous drugs, they fail to perturb its serenity.

Our Master, (Sakyamuni), anciently served Dipankara the Buddha,
And again for many kalpas disciplined himself as an ascetic called
    Kshanti.
I have also gone through many a birth and many a death;
Births and deaths—how endlessly they recur!

But ever since my realization of no-birth, which quite abruptly came
    on me,
Vicissitudes of fate, good and bad, have lost their power over me.
Far away in the mountains I live in an humble hut;
High are the mountains, thick the arboreous shades, and under an old
    pine-tree
I sit quietly and contentedly in my monkish home;
Perfect tranquillity and rustic simplicity rules here.

Only let us take hold of the root and not worry about the branches;
It is like a crystal basin reflecting the moon,
And I know now what this mani-gem is,
Whereby not only oneself is benefited but others, inexhaustibly,
The moon is serenely reflected on the stream, the breeze passes softly
    through the pines,
Perfect silence reigning unruffled—what is it for?

The morality-jewel inherent in the Buddha-nature stamps itself on the
    mind-ground of the enlightened one;
Whose robe is cut out of mists, clouds, and dews,
Whose bowl anciently pacified the fiery dragons, and whose staff once
    separated the fighting tigers,
And listen to the golden rings of his staff giving out mellifluous tunes.
These are not, however, mere symbolic expressions, devoid of historical
    contents;
Wherever the holy staff of Tathagatahood moves, the traces are distinctly
    marked.

He neither seeks the true nor severs himself from the defiled,
He clearly perceives that dualities are empty and have no reality,
That to have no reality means not to be one-sided, neither empty nor
     not-empty,
For this is the genuine form of Tathagatahood.

The mind like a mirror is brightly illuminating and knows no obstruc-
     tions,
It penetrates the vast universe to its minutest crevices;
All its contents, multitudinous in form, are reflected in the mind,
Which, shining like a perfect gem, has no surface, nor the inside.

Hini the herb grows on the Himalaya where no other grasses are found,
And the cows feeding on it give the purest of milk, and this I always
     enjoy.
One nature, perfect and pervading, circulates in all natures;
One reality, all comprehensive, contains within itself all realities;
The one moon reflects itself wherever there is a sheet of water,
And all the moons in the waters are embraced within the one moon;
The Dharma-body of all the Buddhas enters into my own being,
And my own being is found in union with theirs.

Alas! this age of degeneration is full of evils;
Beings are most poorly endowed and difficult to control;
Being further removed from the ancient Sage, they deeply cherish false
     views;
The Evil One is gathering up his forces while the Dharma is weakened,
     and hatred is growing rampant;
Even when they learn of the "abrupt" school of the Buddhist teaching,
What a pity that they fail to embrace it and thereby to crush evils like a
     piece of brick!

The mind is the author of all works and the body the sufferer of all ills;
Do not blame others plaintively for what properly belongs to you;
If you desire not to incur upon yourself the karma for a hell,
Cease from blaspheming the Tathagata-wheel of the good Dharma.

There are no inferior trees in the grove of sandal-woods,
Among its thickly-growing primeval forest lions alone find their abode;

Where no disturbances reach, where peace only reigns, there is the place
   for lions to roam;
All the other beasts are kept away, and birds do not fly in the vicinity.

It is only their own cubs that follow their steps in the woods,
When the young ones are only three years old, they roar.
How can jackals pursue the king of the Dharma?
With all their magical arts the elves gape to no purpose.

"No" is not necessarily "No," nor is "Yes" "Yes";
But when you miss even a tenth of an inch, the difference widens up to
   one thousand miles;
When it is "Yes," a young Naga girl in an instant attains Buddhahood,
When it is "No," the most learned Zensho while alive falls into hell.

Since early years I have been eagerly after scholarly attainment,
I have studied the sutras and sastras and commentaries,
I have been given up to the analysis of names and forms, and never
   known what fatigue meant;
But diving into the ocean to count up its sands is surely an exhausting
   task and a vain one;
The Buddha has never spared such, his scolding are just to the point,
For what is the use of reckoning the treasures that are not mine?
All my past achievements have been efforts vainly and wrongly applied—
   I realize it fully now,
I have been a vagrant monk for many years to no end whatever.

When the notion of the original family is not properly understood,
You never attain to the understanding of the Buddha's perfect "abrupt"
   system;
The two Vehicles exert themselves enough, but lack in the aspirations
   of the Bodhisattva;
The philosophers are intelligent enough but wanting in Prajna;
As to the rest of us, they are either ignorant or puerile;
They take an empty fist as containing something real, and the pointing
   finger for the object pointed;
When the finger is adhered to as the moon itself, all their efforts are
   lost;
They are indeed idle dreamers lost in a world of senses and objects.

A royal table is set before the hungry, but they refuse to eat;

If the sick turn away from a good physician, how are they cured?

Practise Zen while in a world of desires, and the genuine power of intuition is manifested;

When the lotus blooms in the midst of a fire, it is never destroyed.

Yuse the Bhikkhu was the offender of one of the gravest crimes, but when he had an enlightened insight into no-birth,

He instantly attained to Buddhahood and is still living in another world.

However rapidly revolves the iron-wheel over my head,

The perfect brightness of Dhyana and Prajna in me is never effaced;

The sun may turn cold and the moon hot;

With all the power of the evil ones the doctrine true remains for ever indestructible.

The elephant-carriage steadily climbs up the steepest hill,

Before whose wheels how can the beetle stand?

The great elephant does not walk on the hare's lane,

Supreme enlightenment goes beyond the narrow range of intellection;

Cease from measuring heaven with a tiny piece of reed;

If you have no insight yet, I will have the matter settled for you.

Dai-o Kokushi "On Zen"

There is a reality even prior to heaven and earth;

Indeed, it has no form, much less a name;

Eyes fail to see it;

It has no voice for ears to detect;

To call it Mind or Buddha violates its nature,

For it then becomes like a visionary flower in the air;

It is not Mind, nor Buddha;

Absolutely quiet, and yet illuminating in a mysterious way,

It allows itself to be perceived only by the clear-eyed.

It is Dharma truly beyond form and sound;

It is Tao having nothing to do with words.

Wishing to entice the blind,

The Buddha has playfully let words escape his golden mouth;

Heaven and earth are ever since filled with entangling briars.

O my good worthy friends gathered here,
If you desire to listen to the thunderous voice of the Dharma,
Exhaust your words, empty your thoughts,
For then you may come to recognize this one essence.
Says Hui the Brother, "The Buddha's Dharma
Is not to be given up to mere humanly sentiments."

Hakuin's Song of Meditation

Sentient beings are primarily all the Buddhas:
It is like ice and water,
Apart from water no ice can exist,
Outside sentient beings, where do we find the Buddhas?
Not knowing how near the truth is,
People seek it far away,—what a pity!
They are like him who, in the midst of water,
Cries in thirst so imploringly;
They are like the son of a rich man
Who wandered away among the poor.
The reason why we transmigrate through the six worlds,
Is because we are lost in the darkness of ignorance;
Going astray further and further in the darkness,
When are we able to get away from birth-and-death?

As regards the meditation practised in the Mahayana,
We have no words to praise it fully:
The virtues of perfection such as charity, morality,
And the invocation of the Buddha's name, confession, and ascetic dis-
        cipline,
And many other good deeds of merit,—
All these issue from the practice of meditation;
Even those who have practised it just for one sitting,
Will see all their evil karma wiped clean;
Nowhere will they find the evil paths,
But the pure land will be near at hand.
With a reverential heart, let them to this truth
Listen even for once,

And let them praise it, and gladly embrace it,
And they will surely be blessed most infinitely.

For such as, reflecting within themselves,
Testify to the truth of Self-nature,
To the truth that Self-nature is no-nature,
They have really gone beyond the ken of sophistry.
For them opens the gate of the oneness of cause and effect,
And straight runs the path of non-duality and non-trinity.
Abiding with the not-particular which is in particulars,
Whether going or returning, they remain for ever unmoved;
Taking hold of the not-thought which lies in thoughts,
In every act of theirs they hear the voice of the truth.
How boundless the sky of Samadhi unfettered!
How transparent the perfect moon-light of the fourfold wisdom!
At that moment what do they lack?
As the truth eternally calm reveals itself to them,
This very earth is the lotus land of purity,
And this body is the body of the Buddha.

The Ten Oxherding Pictures

1. *Undisciplined*

With his horns fiercely projected in the air the beast snorts,
Madly running over the mountain paths, farther and farther he goes
    astray!
A dark cloud is spread across the entrance of the valley,
And who knows how much of the fine fresh herb is trampled under his
    wild hoofs!

2. *Discipline Begun*

I am in possession of a straw rope, and I pass it through his nose,
For once he makes a frantic attempt to run away, but he is severely
      whipped and whipped;
The beast resists the training with all the power there is in a nature wild
      and ungoverned,
But the rustic oxherd never relaxes his pulling tether and ever-ready
      whip.

3. *In Harness*

Gradually getting into harness the beast is now content to be led by the
nose,
Crossing the stream, walking along the mountain path, he follows
every step of the leader;
The leader holds the rope tightly in his hand never letting it go,
All day long he is on the alert almost unconscious of what fatigue is.

4. *Faced Round*

After long days of training the result begins to tell and the beast is faced
round,

A nature so wild and ungoverned is finally broken, he has become
gentler;

But the tender has not yet given him his full confidence,

He still keeps his straw rope with which the ox is now tied to a tree.

5. *Tamed*

Under the green willow tree and by the ancient mountain stream,
The ox is set at liberty to pursue his own pleasures;
At the eventide when a grey mist descends on the pasture,
The boy wends his homeward way with the animal quietly following.

6. *Unimpeded*

On the verdant field the beast contentedly lies idling his time away,
No whip is needed now, nor any kind of restraint;
The boy too sits leisurely under the pine tree,
Playing a tune of peace, overflowing his joy.

7. *Laissez Faire*

The spring stream in the evening sun flows languidly along the willow-
    lined bank,
In the hazy atmosphere the meadow grass is seen growing thick;
When hungry he grazes, when thirsty he quaffs, as time sweetly slides,
While the boy on the rock dozes for hours not noticing anything that
    goes about him.

8. *All Forgotten*

The beast all in white now is surrounded by the white clouds,
The man is perfectly at his ease and care-free, so is his companion;
The white clouds penetrated by the moon-light cast their white shadows
    below,
The white clouds and the bright moon-light—each following its course
    of movement.

9. *The Solitary Moon*

Nowhere is the beast, and the oxherd is master of his time,
He is a solitary cloud wafting lightly along the mountain peaks;
Clapping his hands he sings joyfully in the moon-light,
But remember a last wall is still left barring his homeward walk.

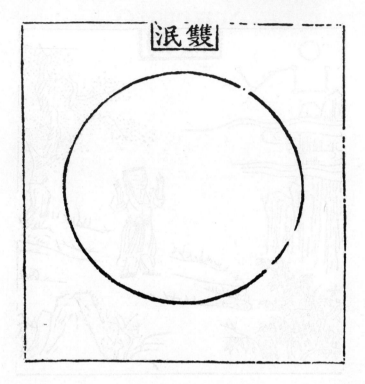

10. *Both Vanished*

Both the man and the animal have disappeared, no traces are left,
The bright moon-light is empty and shadowless with all the ten-thousand
    objects in it;
If any one should ask the meaning of this,
Behold the lilies of the field and their fresh sweet-scented verdure.

CONFUCIANIST
Scriptures

CONFUCIANIST SCRIPTURES
The Li Ki

The Nature of the Universe and Man

Man is the product of the attributes of heaven and earth, by the interaction of the dual forces of nature, the union of the animal and intelligent souls, and the finest subtle matter of the five elements.

Heaven exercises the control of the strong and light force, and hangs out the sun and stars. Earth exercises the control of the dark and weaker force, and gives vent to it in the hills and streams. The five elements are distributed through the four seasons, and it is by their harmonious action that the moon is produced, which therefore keeps waxing for fifteen days and waning for fifteen.

The five elements in their movements alternately displace and exhaust one another. Each one of them, in the revolving course of the twelve months of the four seasons, comes to be in its turn the fundamental one for the time.

The five notes of harmony, with their six upper musical accords, and the twelve pitch tubes, come each, in their revolutions among themselves, to be the first note of the scale.

The five flavours, with the six condiments, and the twelve articles of diet, come each one, in their revolutions in the course of a year, to give its character to the food.

The five colours, with the six elegant figures, which they form on the two robes, come each one, in their revolutions among themselves, to give the character of the dress that is worn.

Therefore man is the heart and mind of heaven and earth, and the visible embodiment of the five elements. He lives in the enjoyment of all flavours, the discriminating of all notes of harmony, and the enrobing of all colours.

Thus it was that when the sages would make rules for men, they felt it necessary to find the origin of all things in heaven and earth; to make the two forces of nature the commencement of all; to use the four seasons as the handle of their arrangements; to adopt the sun and stars as the recorders of time, the moon as the measurer of work to be done, the spirits breathing in nature as associates, the five elements as giving substance to things, rules of propriety and righteousness as their instruments, the feelings of men as the field to be cultivated, and the four intelligent creatures as domestic animals to be reared.

The origin of all things being found in heaven and earth, they could be taken in hand, one after the other.

The Feelings of Men

What are the feelings of men? They are joy, anger, sadness, fear, love, disliking, and liking. These seven feelings belong to men without their learning them. What are "the things which men consider right"? Kindness on the part of the father, and filial duty on that of the son; gentleness on the part of the elder brother, and obedience on that of the younger; righteousness on the part of the husband, and submission on that of the wife; kindness on the part of elders, and deference on that of juniors; with benevolence on the part of the ruler, and loyalty on that of the minister;—these ten are the things which men consider to be right.

Truthfulness in speech and the cultivation of harmony constitute what are called "the things advantageous to men." Quarrels, plundering, and murders are "the things disastrous to men."

Hence when a ruler would regulate the seven feelings of men, cultivate the ten virtues that are right, promote truthfulness of speech, and the maintenance of harmony, show his value for kindly consideration and complaisant courtesy, and put away quarrelling and plundering: if he neglect the rules of propriety, how shall he succeed?

The things which men greatly desire are comprehended in meat and drink and sexual pleasure; those which they greatly dislike are comprehended in death, exile, poverty, and suffering. Thus liking and disliking are the great elements in men's minds. But men keep them hidden in their minds, where they cannot be fathomed or measured. The good and the bad of them being in their minds, and no outward manifestation of them being visible, if it be wished to determine these qualities in one uniform way, how can it be done without the rules of propriety?

The Functions of the Ruler

Heaven produces the seasons. Earth produces all the sources of wealth. Man is begotten by his father, and instructed by his teacher. The ruler correctly uses these four agencies, and therefore he stands in the place where there is no error.

Hence the ruler is he to whose brightness men look; he does not seek to brighten men. It is he whom men support; he does not seek to support men. It is he whom men serve; he does not seek to serve men. If the ruler were to seek to brighten men he would fall into errors. If he were to seek to nourish men, he would be unequal to the task. If he were to seek to serve men, he would be giving up his position. Therefore the people imitate the ruler and we have their self-government; they nourish the ruler, and they find their security in doing so; they serve the ruler, and find their distinction in doing so. Thus it is by the universal application of the rules of propriety that the lot and duty of different classes are fixed; thus it is that men acting contrary to those rules would all have to account death a boon, and life an evil.

Therefore the ruler, making use of the wisdom of others, will put away the cunning to which that wisdom might lead him; using their courage, he will put away passion; and using their benevolence, he will put away covetousness.

Therefore when it is said that the ruler, being a sage, can look on all under the sky as one family, and on all in the middle states as one man, this does not mean that he will do so on premeditation and purpose. He must know men's feelings, lay open to them what they consider right, show clearly to them what is advantageous, and comprehend what are their calamities. Being so furnished, he is then able to effect the thing.

The Meaning of Sacrifice

Of all the methods for the good ordering of men, there is none more urgent than the use of ceremonies. Ceremonies are of five kinds, and there is none of them more important than sacrifices.

Sacrifice is not a thing coming to a man from without; it issues from within him, and has its birth in his heart. When the heart is deeply moved, expression is given to it by ceremonies; and hence, only men of ability and virtue can give complete exhibition to the idea of sacrifice.

The sacrifices of such men have their own blessing;—not indeed what the world calls blessing. Blessing here means perfection;—it is the name given to the complete and natural discharge of all duties. When nothing is left incomplete or improperly discharged;—this is what we call perfection, implying the doing everything that should be done in one's internal self, and externally the performance of everything according to the proper method. There is a fundamental agreement between a loyal subject in his service of his ruler and a filial son in his service of his parents. In the supernal sphere there is a compliance with what is due to the repose and expansion of the energies of nature; in the external sphere, a compliance with what is due to rulers and elders; in the internal sphere, the filial service of parents;—all this constitutes what is called perfection.

It is only the able and virtuous man who can attain to this perfection; and can sacrifice when he has attained to it. Hence in the sacrifices of such a man he brings into exercise all sincerity and good faith, with all right-heartedness and reverence; he offers the proper things; accompanies them with proper rites; employs the soothing of music; does everything suitably to the season. Thus intelligently does he offer his sacrifices, without seeking for anything to be gained by them:—such is the heart and mind of a filial son.

The Shih King

The Song of How-tsieh

The first birth of our people
Was from Keang Yuen.
How did she give birth to our people?
She had presented a pure offering and sacrificed,
That her childlessness might be taken away.
She then trod on a toe-print made by God, and was moved,
In the large place where she rested.
She became pregnant; she dwelt retired;
She gave birth to, and nourished a son,
Who was How-tsieh.

When she had fulfilled her months,
Her first-born son came forth like a lamb,
There was no bursting, nor rending,
No injury, no hurt;—
Showing how wonderful he would be.
Did not God give her the comfort?
Had he not accepted her pure offering and sacrifice,
So that thus easily she brought forth her son?

He was placed in a narrow lane,
But the sheep and oxen protected him with loving care.
He was placed in a wide forest,
Where he was met with by the woodcutters.
He was placed on the cold ice,
And a bird screened and supported him with its wings.

When the bird went away,
How-tsieh began to wail;
His cry was long and loud,
So that his voice filled the whole way.

When he was able to crawl,
He looked majestic and intelligent.
When he was able to feed himself,
He fell to planting large beans.
The beans grew luxuriantly;
His rows of paddy shot up beautifully;
His hemp and wheat grew strong and close;
His gourds yielded abundantly.

We load the stands with the offerings,
The stands both of wood and of earthenware.
As soon as the fragrance ascends,
God, well pleased, smells the sweet savour.
Fragrant is it, and in its due season!
How-tsieh founded the sacrifice,
And no one, we presume, has given occasion for blame or regret
    In regard to it, down to the present day.

The Wisdom of Yu

Profoundly wise were the lords of Shang,
And long had there appeared the omens of their dignity.

When the waters of the deluge spread vast abroad,
Yu arranged and divided the regions of the land,
And assigned to the exterior great states their boundaries,
With their borders extending all over the kingdom.
Even then the chief of Sung was beginning to be great,
And God raised up the son of his daughter, and founded the line of
    Shang.

The dark king exercised an effective sway.
Charged with a small state, he commanded success;

Charged with a large state, he commanded success.
He followed his rules of conduct without error;
Wherever he inspected the people, they responded to his instructions.
Then came Hsiang-thu all ardent,
And all within the four seas, beyond the middle regions, acknowledged
     his restraints.

Spring Song

Ah! ah! ministers and officers,
Reverently attend to your public duties.
The king has given you perfect rules;—
Consult about them, and consider them.

Ah! ah! ye assistants,
It is now the end of spring;
And what have ye to seek for?
Only how to manage the new fields and those of the third year.
How beautiful are the wheat and the barley!
The bright and glorious God
Will in them give us a good year.
Order all our men
To be provided with their spuds and hoes:—
Anon we shall see the sickles at work.

Plea to an Ancestor

Alas for me, who am a little child,
On whom has devolved the unsettled state!
Solitary am I and full of distress.
Oh! my great father,
All thy life long, thou wast filial.

Thou didst think of my great grandfather,
Seeing him, as it were, ascending and descending in the court;
I, the little child,
Day and night will be as reverent.

Oh! ye great kings,
As your successor, I will strive not to forget you.

Lamentation

Great heaven, unjust,
Is sending down these exhausting disorders.
Great heaven, unkind,
Is sending down these great miseries.
Let superior men come into office,
And that would bring rest to the people's hearts.
Let superior men execute their justice,
And the animosities and angers would disappear.

O unpitying great heaven,
There is no end to the disorder!
With every month it continues to grow,
So that the people have no repose.
I am as if intoxicated with the grief of my heart.
Who holds the ordering of the kingdom?
He attends not himself to the government,
And the result is toil and pain to the people.

Heavenly Disaster

At the conjunction of the sun and moon in the tenth month,
On the first day of the moon, which was hsin-mao,
The sun was eclipsed,
A thing of very evil omen.
Before, the moon became small,
And now the sun became small.
Henceforth the lower people
Will be in a very deplorable case.

The sun and moon announce evil,
Not keeping to their proper paths.
Throughout the kingdom there is no proper government,

Because the good are not employed.
For the moon to be eclipsed
Is but an ordinary matter.
Now that the sun has been eclipsed,—
How bad it is!

Grandly flashes the lightning of the thunder.
There is a want of rest, a want of good.
The streams all bubble up and overflow.
The crags on the hill-tops fall down.
High banks become valleys;
Deep valleys become hills.
Alas for the men of this time!
How does the king not stop these things?

Distant far is my village,
And my dissatisfaction is great.
In other quarters there is ease,
And I dwell here, alone and sorrowful.
Everybody is going into retirement,
And I alone dare not seek rest.
The ordinances of heaven are inexplicable,
But I will not dare to follow my friends, and leave my post.

Accusation of Heaven

Great and wide heaven,
How is it you have contracted your kindness,
Sending down death and famine,
Destroying all through the kingdom?
Compassionate heaven, arrayed in terrors,
How is it you exercise no forethought, no care?
Let alone the criminals:—
They have suffered for their guilt.
But those who have no crime
Are indiscriminately involved in ruin.
How is it, O great heaven,
That the king will not hearken to the justest words?

He is like a man going astray,
Who knows not where he will proceed to.
All ye officers,
Let each of you attend to his duties.
How do ye not stand in awe of one another?
Ye do not stand in awe of heaven.

Warning to Governors

God has reversed his usual course of procedure,
And the lower people are full of distress.
The words which you utter are not right;
The plans which you form are not far-reaching.
As there are not sages, you think you have no guidance;—
You have no real sincerity.
Thus your plans do not reach far,
And I therefore strongly admonish you.

Heaven is now sending down calamities;—
Do not be so complacent.
Heaven is now producing such movements;—
Do not be so indifferent.
If your words were harmonious,
The people would become united.
If your words were gentle and kind,
The people would be settled.

Though my duties are different from yours,
I am your fellow-servant.
I come to advise with you,
And you hear me with contemptuous indifference.
My words are about the present urgent affairs;—
Do not think them matter for laughter.
The ancients had a saying:—"Consult the gatherers of
          grass and firewood."

Heaven is now exercising oppression;—
Do not in such a way make a mock of things.
An old man, I speak with entire sincerity;

But you, my juniors, are full of pride.
It is not that my words are those of age,
But you make a joke of what is sad.
But the troubles will multiply like flames,
Till they are beyond help or remedy.

Heaven is now displaying its anger;—
Do not be either boastful or flattering,
Utterly departing from all propriety of demeanour,
Till good men are reduced to personators of the dead.
The people now sigh and groan,
And we dare not examine into the causes of their trouble.
The ruin and disorder are exhausting all their means of living,
And we show no kindness to our multitudes.

Heaven enlightens the people,
As the bamboo flute responds to the earthen whistle;
As two half-maces form a whole one;
As you take a thing, and bring it away in your hand,
Bringing it away, without any more ado.
The enlightenment of the people is very easy.
They have now many perversities;—
Do not you set up your perversity before them.

Good men are a fence;
The multitudes of the people are a wall;
Great states are screens;
Great families are buttresses;
The cherishing of virtue secures repose;
The circle of the king's relatives is a fortified wall.
We must not let the fortified wall get destroyed;
We must not let the king be solitary and consumed with terrors.

Revere the anger of heaven,
And presume not to make sport or be idle.
Revere the changing moods of heaven,
And presume not to drive about at your pleasure.
Great heaven is intelligent,
And is with you in all your goings.
Great heaven is clear-seeing,
And is with you in your wanderings and indulgences.

How Vast Is God!

How vast is God,
The ruler of men below!
How arrayed in terrors is God,
With many things irregular in his ordinations.
Heaven gave birth to the multitudes of the people,
But the nature it confers is not to be depended on.
All are good at first,
But few prove themselves to be so at the last.

King Wan said, "Alas!
Alas! you sovereign of Shang,
People have a saying,
'When a tree falls utterly,
While its branches and leaves are yet uninjured,
It must first have been uprooted.'
The beacon of Yiu is not far distant;—
It is in the age of the last sovereign of Hsia."

Drought

Bright was the milky way,
Shining and revolving in the sky.
The king said, "Oh!
What crime is chargeable on us now,
That heaven thus sends down death and disorder?
Famine comes again and again.
There is no spirit I have not sacrificed to;
There is no victim I have grudged;
Our jade symbols, oblong and round, are exhausted;—
How is it that I am not heard?

"The drought is excessive;
Its fervours become more and more tormenting.
I have not ceased offering pure sacrifices;

From the border altars I have gone to the ancestral temple.
To the powers above and below I have presented my offerings
        and then buried them;—
There is no spirit whom I have not honoured.
Hau-ki is not equal to the occasion;
God does not come to us.
This wasting and ruin of our country,—
Would that it fell only on me!

"The drought is excessive;—
Parched are the hills, and the streams are dried.
The demon of drought exercises his oppression,
As if scattering flames and fire.
My heart is terrified with the heat;
My sorrowing heart is as if on fire.
The many dukes and their ministers of the past
Do not hear me.
O God, from thy great heaven,
Grant me the liberty to withdraw into retirement.

"I look up to the great heaven,
But its stars sparkle bright.
My great officers and excellent men,
Ye have reverently drawn near to heaven with all your powers.
Death is approaching,
But do not cast away what you have done.
You are seeking not for me only,
But to give rest to all our departments.
I look up to the great heaven;—
When shall I be favoured with repose?"

Widow's Plaint

It floats about, that boat of cypress wood,
There in the middle of the Ho.
With his two tufts of hair falling over his forehead,
He was my mate;
And I swear that till death I will have no other.

O mother, O heaven,
Why will you not understand me?

It floats about, that boat of cypress wood,
There by the side of the Ho.
With his two tufts of hair falling over his forehead,
He was my only one;
And I swear that till death I will not do the evil thing.
O mother, O heaven,
Why will you not understand me?

Brothers Are Best

The flowers of the cherry tree—
Are they not gorgeously displayed?
Of all the men in the world
There are none equal to brothers.

Brothers may quarrel inside the walls,
But they will oppose insult from without,
When friends, however good they may be,
Will not afford help.

When death and disorder are past,
And there are tranquillity and rest,
Although they have brothers,
Some reckon them not equal to friends.

Loving union with wife and children
Is like the music of lutes;
But it is the accord of brothers
Which makes the harmony and happiness lasting.

For the ordering of your family,
For your joy in your wife and children,
Examine this and study it;—
Will you not find that it is truly so?

Blessing

Heaven protects and establishes thee,
With the greatest security;
Makes thee entirely virtuous,
That thou mayest enjoy every happiness;
Grants thee much increase,
So that thou hast all in abundance.

Heaven protects and establishes thee,
So that in everything thou dost prosper,
Like the high hills, and the mountain masses,
Like the topmost ridges, and the greatest bulks;
That, as the stream ever coming on,
Such is thine increase.

With happy auspices and purifications, thou bringest the offerings,
And dost filially present them,
In spring, summer, autumn, and winter,
To the dukes and former kings,
Who say, "We give to thee
Myriads of years of duration unlimited."

The spirits come
And confer on thee many blessings.
The people are simple and honest,
Daily enjoying their meat and drink.
All the black-haired race, in all their surnames,
Universally practise your virtue.

Like the moon advancing to the full,
Like the sun ascending the heavens,
Like the age of the southern hills,
Never waning, never falling,
Like the luxuriance of the fir and the cypress;—
May such be thy succeeding line!

In Praise of Ancestors

Small is the cooing dove,
But it flies aloft up to heaven.
My heart is wounded with sorrow,
And I think of our forefathers.
When the dawn is breaking, and I cannot sleep,
The thoughts in my breast are of our parents.

Men who are grave and wise,
Though they drink, are mild and masters of themselves;
But those who are benighted and ignorant
Are devoted to drink, and more so daily.
Be careful, each of you, of your deportment;—
What heaven confers, when once lost, is not regained.

We must be mild, and humble,
As if we were perched on trees.
We must be anxious and careful,
As if we were on the brink of a valley.
We must be apprehensive and cautious,
As if we were treading upon thin ice.

On Letting Alone

Do not push forward a wagon;—
You will only raise the dust about yourself.
Do not think of all your anxieties;—
You will only make yourself ill.

The Nature of People and Things

Well fashioned is the bow adorned with horn,
And swift is its recoil.

Brothers and relatives by affinity
Should not be treated distantly.

When you keep yours at a distance,
The people all do the same with theirs.
What you teach
The people all imitate.

An old horse, notwithstanding, thinks himself a colt,
And has no regard to the future.
It is like craving a superabundance of food,
And an excess of drink.

Do not teach a monkey to climb trees;—
You act like adding mud to one in the mud.
If the sovereign have good ways,
The small people will accord with them.

The snow may have fallen abundantly,
But when it feels the sun's heat, it dissolves.
You are not willing to discountenance those parties,
And so they become more troublesome and arrogant.

The Necessity of Propriety

Look at a rat,—it has its skin;
But a man shall be without dignity of demeanour.
If a man have no dignity of demeanour,
What should he do but die?

Look at a rat,—it has its teeth;
But a man shall be without any right deportment.
If a man have not right deportment,
What should he wait for but death?

Look at a rat,—it has its limbs;
But a man shall be without any rules of propriety.
If a man observe no rules of propriety,
Why does he not quickly die?

Sorrow

There was the millet with its drooping heads;
There was the sacrificial millet coming into blade.
Slowly I moved about,
In my heart all-agitated.
Those who knew me
Said I was sad at heart.
Those who did not know me
Said I was seeking for something.
O distant and azure heaven!
By what man was this brought about?

Admonition

Do not try to cultivate fields too large;—
The weeds will only grow luxuriantly.
Do not think of winning people far away;—
Your toiling heart will be grieved.

How young and tender
Is the child with his two tufts of hair!
When you see him after not a long time,
Lo! he is wearing the cap!

Beauty

Round and round the firewood is bound;
And the Three Stars appear in the sky.
This evening is what evening,
That I see this good man?
O me! O me!
That I should get a good man like this!

Round and round the grass is bound;
And the Three Stars are seen from the corner.
This evening is what evening,
That we have this unexpected meeting?
Happy pair! Happy pair!
That we should have this unexpected meeting!

Round and round the thorns are bound;
And the Three Stars are seen from the door.
This evening is what evening,
That I see this beauty?
O me! O me!
That I should see a beauty like this!

The King's Affairs

Suh-suh go the feathers of the wild geese,
As they settle on the bushy oaks.
The king's affairs must not be slackly discharged,
And so we cannot plant our sacrificial millet and millet;—
What will our parents have to rely on?
O thou distant and azure heaven!
When shall we be in our places again?

Suh-suh go the wings of the wild geese,
As they settle on the bushy jujube trees.
The king's affairs must not be slackly discharged,
And so we cannot plant our millet and sacrificial millet;—
How shall our parents be supplied with food?
O thou distant and azure heaven!
When shall our service have an end?

Suh-suh go the rows of the wild geese,
As they rest on the bushy mulberry trees.
The king's business must not be slackly discharged,
And so we cannot plant our rice and maize;—
How shall our parents get food?
O thou distant and azure heaven!
When shall we get back to our ordinary lot?

Pattern

In hewing the wood for an axe-handle, how do you proceed?
Without another axe it cannot be done.
In taking a wife, how do you proceed?
Without a go-between it cannot be done.

In hewing an axe-handle, in hewing an axe-handle,
The pattern is not far off.
I see the lady,
And forthwith the vessels are arranged in rows.

Analects of Confucius

Book I

The Master said, "Is it not pleasant to learn with a constant persever-ance and application? Is it not delightful to have friends coming from distant quarters? Is he not a man of complete virtue who feels no dis-composure though men may take no note of him?

"Fine words and an insinuating appearance are seldom associated with true virtue."

The philosopher Tsang said, "I daily examine myself on three points:—whether, in transacting business for others, I may have been not faithful;—whether, in intercourse with friends, I may have been not sincere;—whether I may have not mastered and practised the instructions of my teacher."

The Master said, "To rule a country of a thousand chariots, there must be reverent attention to business, and sincerity; economy in expenditure, and love for men; and the employment of the people at the proper seasons."

Tsze-hsia said, "If a man withdraws his mind from the love of beauty, and applies it as sincerely to the love of the virtuous; if, in serving his parents, he can exert his utmost strength; if, in serving his prince, he can devote his life; if, in his intercourse with his friends, his words are sincere:—although men say that he has not learned, I will certainly say that he has."

The philosopher Yu said, "When agreements are made according to what is right, what is spoken can be made good. When respect is shown according to what is proper, one keeps far from shame and disgrace. When the parties upon whom a man leans are proper persons to be intimate with, he can make them his guides and masters."

The Master said, "He who aims to be a man of complete virtue in his food does not seek to gratify his appetite, nor in his dwelling-place does he seek the appliances of ease; he is earnest in what he is doing, and careful in his speech; he frequents the company of men of principle that he may be rectified:—such a person may be said indeed to love to learn.

"I will not be afflicted at men's not knowing me; I will be afflicted that I do not know men."

Book II

The Master said, "He who exercises government by means of his virtue may be compared to the north polar star which keeps its place and all the stars turn towards it.

"If the people be led by laws, and uniformity sought to be given them by punishments, they will try to avoid the punishment, but have no sense of shame. If they be led by virtue, and uniformity sought to be given them by the rules of propriety, they will have the sense of shame, and moreover will become good.

"At fifteen, I had my mind bent on learning. At thirty, I stood firm. At forty, I had no doubts. At fifty, I knew the decrees of heaven. At sixty, my ear was an obedient organ for the reception of truth. At seventy, I could follow what my heart desired, without transgressing what was right.

"I have talked with Hui for a whole day, and he has not made any objection to anything I said;—as if he were stupid. He has retired, and I have examined his conduct when away from me, and found him able to illustrate my teachings. Hui!—He is not stupid.

"See what a man does. Mark his motives. Examine in what things he rests. How can a man conceal his character?

"If a man keeps cherishing his old knowledge, so as continually to be acquiring new, he may be a teacher of others."

Tsze-kung asked what constituted the superior man. The Master said, "He acts before he speaks, and afterwards speaks according to his actions. The superior man is universally minded and no partisan. The inferior man is a partisan and not universal."

The Master said, "Yu, shall I teach you what knowledge is? When you know a thing, to hold that you know it; and when you do not know a thing, to allow that you do not know it;—this is knowledge."

The duke Ai asked, saying, "What should be done in order to secure the submission of the people?" Confucius replied, "Advance the upright and set aside the crooked, then the people will submit. Advance the crooked and set aside the upright, then the people will not submit."

The Master said, "For a man to sacrifice to a spirit which does not belong to him is flattery.

"To see what is right and not to do it is lack of courage."

Book III

The Master said, "If a man be without the virtues proper to humanity, what has he to do with the rites of propriety? If a man be without the virtues proper to humanity, what has he to do with music?"

Tsze-kung wished to do away with the offering of a sheep connected with the inauguration of the first day of each month. The Master said, "Tsze, you love the sheep; I love the ceremony."

The duke Ai asked Tsai Wo about the altars of the spirits of the land. Tsai Wo replied, "The Hsia sovereign planted the pine tree about them; the men of the Yin planted the cypress; and the men of the Chau planted the chestnut tree, meaning thereby to cause the people to be in awe."

When the Master heard it, he said, "Things that are done, it is needless to speak about; things that have had their course, it is needless to remonstrate about; things that are past, it is needless to blame."

The Master said, "High station filled without indulgent generosity; ceremonies performed without reverence; mourning conducted without sorrow;—wherewith should I contemplate such ways?"

Book IV

The Master said, "It is virtuous manners which constitute the excellence of a neighbourhood. If a man in selecting a residence do not fix on one where such prevail, how can he be wise?

"Those who are without virtue cannot abide long either in a condition of poverty and hardship, or in a condition of enjoyment. The virtuous rest in virtue; the wise desire virtue. It is only the truly virtuous man who can love, or who can hate, others.

"A scholar whose mind is set on truth, and who is ashamed of bad clothes and bad food, is not fit to be discoursed with.

"The superior man, in the world, does not set his mind either for anything, or against anything; what is right he will follow. The superior man thinks of virtue; the small man thinks of comfort. The superior man thinks of the sanctions of law; the small man thinks of favours which he may receive.

"He who acts with a constant view to his own advantage will be much murmured against.

"A man should say, I am not concerned that I have no place, I am concerned how I may fit myself for one. I am not concerned that I am not known, I seek to be worthy to be known.

"The reason why the ancients did not readily give utterance to their words, was that they feared lest their actions should not come up to them.

"Virtue is not left to stand alone. He who practises it will have neighbours."

Tsze-yu said, "In serving a prince, frequent remonstrances lead to disgrace. Between friends, frequent reproofs make the friendship distant."

Book V

Someone said, "Yung is truly virtuous, but he is not ready with his tongue." The Master said, "What is the good of being ready with the tongue? They who encounter men with smartness of speech for the most part procure themselves hatred. I know not whether he be truly virtuous, but why should he show readiness of the tongue?"

The Master was wishing Ch'i-tiao K'ai to enter on official employment. He replied, "I am not yet able to rest in the assurance of THIS." The Master was pleased.

The Master said of Tsze-ch'an that he had four of the characteristics of a superior man:—in his conduct of himself, he was humble; in serving his superiors, he was respectful; in nourishing the people, he was kind; in ordering the people, he was just.

Chi Wan thought thrice, and then acted. When the Master was informed of it, he said, "Twice may do."

The Master said, "When good order prevailed in this country, Ning Wu acted the part of a wise man. When his country was in disorder, he acted the part of a stupid man. Others may equal his wisdom, but they cannot equal his stupidity."

Yen Yuan and Chi Lu being by his side, the Master said to them, "Come, let each of you tell his wishes."

Tsze-lu said, "I should like, having chariots and horses, and light fur dresses, to share them with my friends, and though they should spoil them, I would not be displeased."

Yen Yuan said, "I should like not to boast of my excellence, nor to make a display of my meritorious deeds."

Tsze-lu then said, "I should like, sir, to hear your wishes." The Master said, "They are, in regard to the aged, to give them rest; in regard to friends, to show them sincerity; in regard to the young, to treat them tenderly."

The Master said, "In a hamlet of ten families, there may be found one honourable and sincere as I am, but not so fond of learning."

Book VI

The Master said, "Mang Chih-fan does not boast of his merit. Being in the rear on an occasion of flight, when they were about to enter the gate, he whipped up his horse, saying, 'It is not that I dare to be last. My horse would not advance.'

"They who know the truth are not equal to those who love it, and they who love it are not equal to those who delight in it."

Fan Ch'ih asked what constituted wisdom. The Master said, "To give one's self earnestly to the duties due to men, and, while respecting spiritual beings, to keep aloof from them, may be called wisdom." He asked about perfect virtue. The Master said, "The man of virtue makes the difficulty to be overcome his first business, and success only a subsequent consideration;—this may be called perfect virtue."

Tsai Wo asked, saying, "A benevolent man, though it be told him—'There is a man in the well,' will go in after him, I suppose." Confucius said, "Why should he do so? A superior man may be made to go to the well, but he cannot be made to go down into it. He may be imposed upon, but he cannot be befooled."

Tsze-kung said, "Suppose the case of a man extensively conferring benefits on the people, and able to assist all, what would you say of him? Might he be called perfectly virtuous?" The Master said, "Why speak only of virtue in connexion with him? Must he not have the qualities of a sage? Even Yao and Shun were still solicitous about this. Now the man of perfect virtue, wishing to be established himself, seeks also to establish others; wishing to be enlarged himself, he seeks also to enlarge others. To be able to judge of others by what is nigh in ourselves;—this may be called the art of virtue."

Book VII

The Master said, "From the man bringing his bundle of dried flesh for my teaching upwards, I have never refused instruction to any one.

I do not open up the truth to one who is not eager to get knowledge, nor help out any one who is not anxious to explain himself. When I have presented one corner of a subject to any one, and he cannot from it learn the other three, I do not repeat my lesson."

When the Master was eating by the side of a mourner, he never ate to the full. He did not sing on the same day in which he had been weeping.

Tsze-lu said, "If you had the conduct of the armies of a great state, whom would you have to act with you?" The Master said, "I would not have him to act with me, who will unarmed attack a tiger, or cross a river without a boat, dying without any regret. My associate must be the man who proceeds to action full of solicitude, who is fond of adjusting his plans, and then carries them into execution."

The Master said, "If the search for riches is sure to be successful, though I should become a groom with whip in hand to get them, I will do so. As the search may not be successful, I will follow after that which I love."

When the Master was in company with a person who was singing, if he sang well, he would make him repeat the song, while he accompanied it with his own voice.

The Master said, "In letters I am perhaps equal to other men, but the character of the superior man, carrying out in his conduct what he professes, is what I have not yet attained to."

Book VIII

The Master said, "Respectfulness, without the rules of propriety, becomes laborious bustle; carefulness, without the rules of propriety, becomes timidity; boldness, without the rules of propriety, becomes insubordination; straightforwardness, without the rules of propriety, becomes rudeness. When those who are in high stations perform well all their duties to their relations, the people are aroused to virtue. When old friends are not neglected by them, the people are preserved from inferiority.

"Though a man have abilities as admirable as those of the duke of Chau, yet if he be proud and niggardly, those other things are really not worth being looked at."

Book IX

The Master said, "The linen cap is that prescribed by the rules of ceremony, but now a silk one is worn. It is economical, and I follow the common practice. The rules of ceremony prescribe the bowing below the hall, but now the practice is to bow only after ascending it. That is arrogant. I continue to bow below the hall, though I oppose the common practice."

There were four things from which the Master was entirely free. He had no foregone conclusions, no arbitrary pre-determinations, no obstinacy, and no egoism.

The Master said, "Am I indeed possessed of knowledge? I am not knowing. But if a mean person, who appears quite empty-like, ask anything of me, I set it forth from one end to the other, and exhaust it."

Yen Yuan, in admiration of the Master's doctrines, sighed and said, "I looked up to them, and they seemed to become more high; I tried to penetrate them, and they seemed to become more firm; I looked at them before me, and suddenly they seemed to be behind. The Master, by orderly method, skilfully leads men on. He enlarged my mind with learning, and taught me the restraints of propriety. When I wish to give over the study of his doctrines, I cannot do so, and having exerted all my ability, there seems something to stand right up before me; but though I wish to follow and lay hold of it, I really find no way to do so."

Tsze-kung said, "There is a beautiful gem here. Should I lay it up in a case and keep it? or should I seek for a good price and sell it?" The Master said, "Sell it! Sell it! But I would wait for one to offer the price."

The Master standing by a stream, said, "It passes on just like this, not ceasing day or night!"

The Master said, "I have not seen one who loves virtue as he loves beauty.

"A youth is to be regarded with respect. How do we know that his future will not be equal to our present? If he reach the age of forty or fifty, and has not made himself heard of, then indeed he will not be worth being regarded with respect.

"Hold faithfulness and sincerity as first principles. Have no friends not equal to yourself. When you have faults, do not fear to abandon them.

"Dressed himself in a tattered robe quilted with hemp, yet standing by the side of men dressed in furs, and not ashamed;—ah, it is Yu who is equal to this! 'He dislikes none, he covets nothing;—what can he do but what is good?' "

Book X

Confucius, in his village, looked simple and sincere, and as if he were not able to speak.

When he was in the prince's ancestorial temple, or in the court, he spoke minutely on every point, but cautiously.

When he was waiting at court, in speaking with the great officers of the lower grade, he spake freely, but in a straightforward manner; in speaking with those of the higher grade, he did so blandly, but precisely.

When the ruler was present, his manner displayed respectful uneasiness; it was grave, but self-possessed.

When the prince called him to employ him in the reception of a visitor, his countenance appeared to change, and his legs to move forward with difficulty.

He inclined himself to the other officers among whom he stood, moving his left or right arm, as their position required, but keeping the skirts of his robe before and behind evenly adjusted.

He hastened forward, with his arms like the wings of a bird.

When the guest had retired, he would report to the prince, "The visitor is not turning round any more."

When he entered the palace gate, he seemed to bend his body, as if it were not sufficient to admit him.

When he was standing, he did not occupy the middle of the gateway; when he passed in or out, he did not tread upon the threshold.

When he was passing the vacant place of the prince, his countenance appeared to change, and his legs to bend under him, and his words came as if he hardly had breath to utter them.

He ascended the reception hall, holding up his robe with both his hands, and his body bent; holding in his breath also, as if he dared not breathe.

When he came out from the audience, as soon as he had descended one step, he began to relax his countenance, and had a satisfied look. When he had got to the bottom of the steps, he advanced rapidly to his place, with his arms like wings, and on occupying it, his manner still showed respectful uneasiness.

When he was carrying the sceptre of his ruler, he seemed to bend his body, as if he were not able to bear its weight. He did not hold it higher than the position of the hands in making a bow, nor lower than their position in giving anything to another. His countenance seemed to change, and look apprehensive, and he dragged his feet along as if they were held by something to the ground.

In presenting the presents with which he was charged, he wore a placid appearance.

At his private audience, he looked highly pleased.

The stable being burned down, when he was at court, on his return he said, "Has any man been hurt?" He did not ask about the horses.

When any of his friends died, if he had no relations who could be depended on for the necessary offices, he would say, "I will bury him."

When he saw any one in a mourning dress, though it might be an acquaintance, he would change countenance; when he saw any one wearing the cap of full dress, or a blind person, though he might be in his undress, he would salute them in a ceremonious manner.

Book XI

The Master said, "The men of former times, in the matters of ceremonies and music, were rustics, it is said, while the men of these latter times, in ceremonies and music, are accomplished gentlemen. If I have occasion to use those things, I follow the men of former times."

Chi Lu asked about serving the spirits of the dead. The Master said, "While you are not able to serve men, how can you serve their spirits?" Chi Lu added, "I venture to ask about death." He was answered, "While you do not know life, how can you know about death?"

Tsze-kung asked which of the two, Shih or Shang, was the superior. The Master said, "Shih goes beyond the due mean, and Shang does not come up to it." "Then," said Tsze-kung, "the superiority is with Shih, I suppose." The Master said, "To go beyond is as wrong as to fall short."

Tsze-lu asked whether he should immediately carry into practice what he heard. The Master said, "There are your father and elder brothers to be consulted;—why should you act on that principle of immediately carrying into practice what you hear?" Yen Yu asked the same, whether he should immediately carry into practice what he heard, and the Master answered, "Immediately carry into practice what you hear." Kung-hsi Hwa said, "Yu asked whether he should carry immediately into practice what he heard, and you said, 'There are your father and elder brothers to be consulted.' Ch'iu asked whether he should immediately carry into practice what he heard, and you said, 'Carry it immediately into practice.' I, Ch'ih, am perplexed, and venture to ask you for an explanation." The Master said, "Ch'iu is retiring and slow; therefore, I urged him forward. Yu has more than his own share of energy; therefore, I kept him back."

Tsze-lu, Tsang Hsi, Yen Yu, and Kung-hsi Hwa were sitting by the Master. He said to them, "Though I am a day or so older than you, do not think of that. From day to day you are saying, 'We are not known.' If some ruler were to know you, what would you like to do?"

Tsze-lu hastily and lightly replied, "Suppose the case of a state of ten thousand chariots; let it be straitened between other large states; let it be suffering from invading armies; and to this let there be added a famine in corn and in all vegetables:—if I were entrusted with the government of it, in three years' time I could make the people to be bold, and to recognize the rules of righteous conduct." The Master smiled at him.

Turning to Yen Yu, he said, "Ch'iu, what are your wishes?" Ch'iu replied, "Suppose a state of sixty or seventy li square, or one of fifty or sixty, and let me have the government of it;—in three years' time, I could make plenty to abound among the people. As to teaching them the principles of propriety, and music, I must wait for the rise of a superior man to do that."

"What are your wishes, Ch'ih," said the Master next to Kung-hsi Hwa. Ch'ih replied, "I do not say that my ability extends to these things, but I should wish to learn them. At the services of the ancestral temple, and at the audiences of the princes with the sovereign, I should like, dressed in the dark square-made robe and the black linen cap, to act as a small assistant."

Last of all, the Master asked Tsang Hsi, "Tien, what are your wishes?" Tien, pausing as he was playing on his lute, while it was yet twanging, laid the instrument aside, and rose. "My wishes," he said, "are different from the cherished purposes of these three gentlemen." "What harm is there in that?" said the Master; "do you also, as well as they, speak out your wishes." Tien then said, "In this, the last month of spring, with the dress of the season all complete, along with five or six young men who have assumed the cap, and six or seven boys, I would wash in the I, enjoy the breeze among the rain altars, and return home singing." The Master heaved a sigh and said, "I give my approval to Tien."

Book XII

Yen Yuan asked about perfect virtue. The Master said, "To subdue one's self and return to propriety, is perfect virtue. If a man can for one day subdue himself and return to propriety, all under heaven will ascribe perfect virtue to him. Is the practice of perfect virtue from a man himself, or is it from others?"

Chung-kung asked about perfect virtue. The Master said, "It is, when you go abroad, to behave to every one as if you were receiving a great guest; to employ the people as if you were assisting at a great sacrifice; not to do to others as you would not wish done to yourself; to have no murmuring against you in the country, and none in the family." Chung-kung said, "Though I am deficient in intelligence and vigour, I will make it my business to practise this lesson."

Sze-ma Niu asked about the superior man. The Master said, "The superior man has neither anxiety nor fear." "Being without anxiety or fear!" said Niu;—"does this constitute what we call the superior man?" The Master said, "When internal examination discovers nothing wrong, what is there to be anxious about, what is there to fear?"

Tsze-chang asked what constituted intelligence. The Master said, "He with whom neither slander that gradually soaks into the mind, nor statements that startle like a wound in the flesh, are successful, may be called intelligent indeed. Yea, he with whom neither soaking slander, nor startling statements, are successful, may be called far-seeing."

Tsze-kung asked about government. The Master said, "The requisites of government are that there be sufficiency of food, sufficiency of military equipment, and the confidence of the people in their ruler."

Tsze-kung said, "If it cannot be helped, and one of these must be dispensed with, which of the three should be foregone first?" "The military equipment," said the Master.

Tsze-kung again asked, "If it cannot be helped, and one of the remaining two must be dispensed with, which of them should be foregone?" The Master answered, "Part with the food. From of old, death has been the lot of all men; but if the people have no faith in their rulers, there is no standing for the state."

The Master said, "In hearing litigations, I am like any other body. What is necessary, however, is to cause the people to have no litigations."

Chi K'ang asked Confucius about government, saying, "What do you say to killing the unprincipled for the good of the principled?" Confucius replied, "Sir, in carrying on your government, why should you use killing at all? Let your evinced desires be for what is good, and the people will be good. The relation between superiors and inferiors is like that between the wind and the grass. The grass must bend, when the wind blows across it."

Tsze-chang asked, "What must the officer be, who may be said to be distinguished?" The Master said, "What is it you call being distinguished?" Tsze-chang replied, "It is to be heard of through the state, to be heard of throughout his clan." The Master said, "That is notoriety, not distinction. Now the man of distinction is solid and straightforward, and loves righteousness. He examines people's words, and looks at their countenances. He is anxious to humble himself to others. Such a man will be distinguished in the country; he will be distinguished in his clan."

Fan Ch'ih asked about benevolence. The Master said, "It is to love all men." He asked about knowledge. The Master said, "It is to know all men."

Tsze-kung asked about friendship. The Master said, "Faithfully admonish your friend, and skilfully lead him on. If you find him impracticable, stop. Do not disgrace yourself."

Book XIII

Tsze-lu said, "The ruler of Wei has been waiting for you, in order with you to administer the government. What will you consider the first thing to be done?"

The Master replied, "What is necessary is to rectify names."

"So, indeed!" said Tsze-lu. "You are wide of the mark! Why must there be such rectification?"

The Master said, "How uncultivated you are, Yu! A superior man, in regard to what he does not know, shows a cautious reserve.

"If names be not correct, language is not in accordance with the truth of things. If language be not in accordance with the truth of things, affairs cannot be carried on to success.

"When affairs cannot be carried on to success, proprieties and music will not flourish. When proprieties and music do not flourish, punishments will not be properly awarded. When punishments are not properly awarded, the people do not know how to move hand or foot.

"Therefore a superior man considers it necessary that the names he uses may be spoken appropriately, and also that what he speaks may be carried out appropriately. What the superior man requires is just that in his words there may be nothing incorrect."

Fan Ch'ih requested to be taught husbandry. The Master said, "I am not so good for that as an old husbandman." He requested also to be taught gardening, and was answered, "I am not so good for that as an old gardener." Fan Ch'ih having gone out, the Master said, "A small man, indeed, is Fan Hsu!"

When the Master went to Wei, Zan Yu acted as driver of his carriage. The Master observed, "How numerous are the people!" Yu said, "Since they are thus numerous, what more shall be done for them?" "Enrich them," was the reply. "And when they have been enriched, what more shall be done?" The Master said, "Teach them."

The duke of Sheh informed Confucius, saying, "Among us here there are those who may be styled upright in their conduct. If their father have stolen a sheep, they will bear witness to the fact." Confucius said, "Among us, in our part of the country, those who are upright are different from this. The father conceals the misconduct of the son, and the son conceals the misconduct of the father. Uprightness is to be found in this."

Tsze-kung asked, saying, "What do you say of a man who is loved by all the people of his neighbourhood?" The Master replied, "We may not for that accord our approval of him." "And what do you say of him who is hated by all the people of his neighbourhood?" The Master said, "We may not for that conclude that he is bad. It is better than either of these cases that the good in the neighbourhood love him, and the bad hate him."

The Master said, "The superior man is easy to serve and difficult to please. If you try to please him in any way which is not accordant with right, he will not be pleased. But in his employment of men, he uses them according to their capacity. The inferior man is difficult to serve, and easy to please. If you try to please him, though it be in a way which is not accordant with right, he may be pleased. But in his employment of men, he wishes them to be equal to everything.

"The superior man has a dignified ease without pride. The inferior man has pride without a dignified ease."

Book XIV

Someone said, "What do you say concerning the principle that injury should be recompensed with kindness?" The Master said, "With what then will you recompense kindness? Recompense injury with justice, and recompense kindness with kindness."

The Master said, "Alas! there is no one that knows me." Tsze-kung said, "What do you mean by thus saying—that no one knows you?" The Master replied, "I do not murmur against heaven. I do not grumble against men. My studies lie low, and my penetration rises high. But there is heaven;—that knows me!"

Yuan Zang was squatting on his heels, and so waited the approach of the Master, who said to him, "In youth, not humble as befits a junior; in manhood, doing nothing worthy of being handed down; and living on to old age:—this is to be a pest." With this he hit him on the shank with his staff.

Book XV

The Master said, "The determined scholar and the man of virtue will not seek to live at the expense of injuring their virtue. They will even sacrifice their lives to preserve their virtue complete."

Tsze-kung asked about the practice of virtue. The Master said, "The mechanic, who wishes to do his work well, must first sharpen his tools. When you are living in any state, take service with the most worthy among its great officers, and make friends of the most virtuous among its scholars."

The Master said, "If a man take no thought about what is distant, he will find sorrow near at hand.

"He who requires much from himself and little from others, will keep himself from being the object of resentment.

"When a man is not in the habit of saying—'What shall I think of this? What shall I think of this?' I can indeed do nothing with him!

"When a number of people are together for a whole day without their conversation turning on righteousness, and when they are fond of carrying out the suggestions of a small shrewdness;—theirs is indeed a hard case.

"The superior man in everything considers righteousness to be essential. He performs it according to the rules of propriety. He brings it forth in humility. He completes it with sincerity. This is indeed a superior man.

"The superior man is distressed by his want of ability. He is not distressed by men's not knowing him.

"The superior man is dignified, but does not wrangle. He is sociable, but not a partisan."

Tsze-kung asked, saying, "Is there one word which may serve as a rule of practice for all one's life?" The Master said, "Is not RECIPROCITY such a word? What you do not want done to yourself, do not do to others."

The Master said, "Specious words confound virtue. Want of forbearance in small matters confounds great plans.

"When the multitude hate a man, it is necessary to examine into the case. When the multitude like a man, it is necessary to examine into the case.

"The object of the superior man is truth. Food is not his object. There is ploughing;—even in that there is sometimes want. So with learning;—emolument may be found in it. The superior man is anxious lest he should not get truth; he is not anxious lest poverty should come upon him.

"In teaching there should be no distinction of classes."

Book XVI

Confucius said, "There are three friendships which are advantageous, and three which are injurious. Friendship with the upright; friendship with the sincere; and friendship with the man of much observation:—these are advantageous. Friendship with the man of specious airs; friendship with the insinuatingly soft; and friendship with the glib-tongued:—these are injurious.

"There are three things men find enjoyment in which are advantageous, and three things they find enjoyment in which are injurious. To find enjoyment in the discriminating study of ceremonies and music; to find enjoyment in speaking of the goodness of others; to find enjoyment in having many worthy friends:—these are advantageous. To find enjoyment in extravagant pleasures; to find enjoyment in idleness and sauntering; to find enjoyment in the pleasures of feasting:—these are injurious.

"There are three errors to which they who stand in the presence of a man of virtue and station are liable. They may speak when it does not come to them to speak;—this is called rashness. They may not speak when it comes to them to speak;—this is called concealment. They may speak without looking at the countenance of their superior;—this is called blindness.

"There are three things which the superior man guards against. In youth, when the physical powers are not yet settled, he guards against lust. When he is strong, and the physical powers are full of vigour, he guards against quarrelsomeness. When he is old, and the animal powers are decayed, he guards against covetousness.

"There are three things of which the superior man stands in awe. He stands in awe of the ordinances of heaven. He stands in awe of great men. He stands in awe of the words of sages. The inferior man does not know the ordinances of heaven, and consequently does not stand in awe of them. He is disrespectful to great men. He makes sport of the words of sages.

"The superior man has nine things which are subjects with him of thoughtful consideration. In regard to the use of his eyes, he is anxious to see clearly. In regard to the use of his ears, he is anxious to hear distinctly. In regard to his countenance, he is anxious that it should be benign. In regard to his demeanour, he is anxious that it should be respectful. In regard to his speech, he is anxious that it should be sincere. In regard to his doing of business, he is anxious that it should be reverently careful. In regard to what he doubts about, he is anxious to question others. When he is angry, he thinks of the difficulties his anger may involve him in. When he sees gain to be got, he thinks of righteousness!"

Ch'an K'ang asked Po-yu, saying, "Have you heard any lessons from your father different from what we have all heard?"

Po-yu replied, "No. He was standing alone once, when I passed below the hall with hasty steps, and said to me, 'Have you learned the Odes?' On my replying 'Not yet,' he added, 'If you do not learn the Odes, you will not be fit to converse with.' I retired and studied the Odes.

"Another day, he was in the same way standing alone, when I passed by below the hall with hasty steps, and said to me, 'Have you learned the rules of propriety?' On my replying 'Not yet,' he added, 'If you do not learn the rules of propriety, your character cannot be established.' I then retired, and learned the rules of propriety.

"I have heard only these two things from him."

Ch'an K'ang retired, and, quite delighted, said, "I asked one thing, and I have got three things. I have heard about the Odes. I have heard about the rules of propriety. I have also heard that the superior man maintains a distant reserve towards his son."

Book XVII

Yang Ho wished to see Confucius, but Confucius would not go to see him. On this, he sent a present of a pig to Confucius, who, having chosen a time when Ho was not at home, went to pay his respects for the gift. He met him, however, on the way.

Ho said to Confucius, "Come, let me speak with you." He then asked, "Can he be called benevolent who keeps his jewel in his bosom, and leaves his country to confusion?" Confucius replied, "No." "Can he be called wise, who is anxious to be engaged in public employment, and yet is constantly losing the opportunity of being so?" Confucius again said, "No." "The days and months are passing away; the years do not wait for us." Confucius said, "Right; I will go into office."

Tsze-chang asked Confucius about perfect virtue. Confucius said, "To be able to practise five things everywhere under heaven constitutes perfect virtue." He begged to ask what they were, and was told, "Gravity, generosity of soul, sincerity, earnestness, and kindness. If you are grave you will not be treated with disrespect. If you are generous, you will win all. If you are sincere, people will repose trust in you. If you are earnest, you will accomplish much. If you are kind, this will enable you to employ the services of others."

The Master said, "Yu, have you heard the six words to which are attached six becloudings?" Yu replied, "I have not." "Sit down and I will tell them to you.

"There is the love of being benevolent without the love of learning; —the beclouding here leads to a foolish simplicity. There is the love of knowing without the love of learning;—the beclouding here leads to dissipation of mind. There is the love of being sincere without the love of learning;—the beclouding here leads to an injurious disregard of consequences. There is the love of straightforwardness without the love of learning;—the beclouding here leads to rudeness. There is the love of boldness without the love of learning;—the beclouding here leads to insubordination. There is the love of firmness without the love of learning;—the beclouding here leads to extravagant conduct."

The Master said, "Your good, careful people of the villages are the thieves of virtue.

"Fine words and an insinuating appearance are seldom associated with virtue."

The Master said, "I would prefer not speaking." Tsze-kung said, "If you, Master, do not speak, what shall we, your disciples, have to record?" The Master said, "Does heaven speak? The four seasons pursue their courses, and all things are continually being produced, but does heaven say anything?"

The Master said, "Hard is it to deal with him, who will stuff himself with food the whole day, without applying his mind to anything good! Are there not gamesters and chessplayers? To be one of these would still be better than doing nothing at all."

Tsze-lu said, "Does the superior man esteem valour?" The Master said, "The superior man holds righteousness to be of highest importance. A man in a superior situation, having valour without righteous-ness, will be guilty of insubordination; one of the lower people, having valour without righteousness, will commit robbery."

Tsze-kung said, "Has the superior man his hatreds also?" The Master said, "He has his hatreds. He hates those who proclaim the evil of others. He hates the man who, being in a low station, slanders his superiors. He hates those who have valour merely, and are unobservant of propriety. He hates those who are forward and determined, and, at the same time, of contracted understanding."

The Master then inquired, "Ts'ze, have you also your hatreds?" Tsze-kung replied, "I hate those who pry out matters, and ascribe the knowledge to their wisdom. I hate those who are only not modest, and think that they are valorous. I hate those who make known secrets, and think that they are straightforward."

The Master said, "Of all people, girls and servants are the most diffi-cult to behave to. If you are familiar with them, they lose their humility. If you maintain a reserve towards them, they are discontented."

Book XVIII

The madman of Ch'u, Chieh-yu, passed by Confucius, singing and saying, "O Fang! O Fang! How is your virtue degenerated! As to the past, reproof is useless; but the future may still be provided against. Give up your vain pursuit. Give up your vain pursuit. Peril awaits those who now engage in affairs of government." Confucius alighted and wished to converse with him, but Chieh-yu hastened away, so that he could not talk with him.

The duke of Chau addressed his son, the duke of Lu, saying, "The virtuous prince does not neglect his relations. He does not cause the great ministers to repine at his not employing them. Without some great cause, he does not dismiss from their offices the members of old families. He does not seek in one man talents for every employment."

Book XIX

Tsze-chang said, "The scholar, trained for public duty, seeing threat-ening danger, is prepared to sacrifice his life. When the opportunity of gain is presented to him, he thinks of righteousness. In sacrificing, his thoughts are reverential. In mourning, his thoughts are about the grief which he should feel. Such a man commands our approbation indeed."

The disciples of Tsze-hsia asked Tsze-chang about the principles that should characterize mutual intercourse. Tsze-chang asked, "What does Tsze-hsia say on the subject?" They replied, "Tsze-hsia says:—'Associate with those who can advantage you. Put away from you those who cannot do so.'" Tsze-chang observed, "This is different from what I have learned. The superior man honours the talented and virtuous, and bears with all. He praises the good, and pities the incompetent. Am I possessed of great talents and virtue?—who is there among men whom I will not bear with? Am I devoid of talents and virtue?—men will put me away from them. What have we to do with the putting away of others?"

Tsze-hsia said, "Even in inferior studies and employments there is something worth being looked at; but if it be attempted to carry them out to what is remote, there is a danger of their proving inapplicable. Therefore, the superior man does not practise them."

Book XX

Yao said, "Oh! you, Shun, the heaven-determined order of succession now rests in your person. Sincerely hold fast the due Mean. If there shall be distress and want within the four seas, the heavenly revenue will come to a perpetual end."

Shun also used the same language in giving charge to Yu.

T'ang said, "I, the child Li, presume to use a dark-coloured victim, and presume to announce to thee, O most great and sovereign God, that the sinner I dare not pardon, and thy ministers, O God, I do not keep in obscurity. The examination of them is by thy mind, O God. If, in my person, I commit offences, they are not to be attributed to you, the people of the myriad regions. If you in the myriad regions commit offences, these offences must rest on my person."

Tsze-chang asked Confucius, saying, "In what way should a person in authority act in order that he may conduct government properly?" The Master replied, "Let him honour the five excellent, and banish away the four bad, things;—then may he conduct government properly."

Tsze-chang said, "What are meant by the five excellent things?" The Master said, "When the person in authority is beneficent without great expenditure; when he lays tasks on the people without their repining; when he pursues what he desires without being covetous; when he maintains a dignified ease without being proud; when he is majestic without being fierce."

Tsze-chang said, "What is meant by being beneficent without great expenditure?" The Master replied, "When the person in authority makes more beneficial to the people the things from which they naturally derive benefit;—is not this being beneficent without great expenditure? When he chooses the labours which are proper, and makes them labour on them, who will repine? When his desires are set on benevolent government, and he secures it, who will accuse him of covetousness? Whether he has to do with many people or few, or with things great or small, he does not dare to indicate any disrespect;—is not this to maintain a dignified ease without any pride? He adjusts his clothes and cap, and throws a dignity into his looks, so that, thus dignified, he is looked at with awe;—is not this to be majestic without being fierce?"

Tsze-chang then asked, "What are meant by the four bad things?" The Master said, "To put the people to death without having instructed them;—this is called cruelty. To require from them, suddenly, the full tale of work, without having given them warning;—this is called oppression. To issue orders as if without urgency, at first, and, when the time comes, to insist on them with severity;—this is called injury. And, generally, in the giving pay or rewards to men, to do it in a stingy way; —this is called acting the part of a mere official."

The Master said, "Without recognizing the ordinances of heaven, it is impossible to be a superior man. Without an acquaintance with the rules of propriety, it is impossible for the character to be established. Without knowing the force of words, it is impossible to know men."

The Great Learning

What the Great Learning teaches, is—to illustrate illustrious virtue; to renovate the people; and to rest in the highest excellence.

The point where to rest being known, the object of pursuit is then determined; and, that being determined, a calm unperturbedness may be attained to. To that calmness there will succeed a tranquil repose. In that repose there may be careful deliberation, and that deliberation will be followed by the attainment of the desired end.

Things have their root and their branches. Affairs have their end and their beginning. To know what is first and what is last will lead near to what is taught in the Great Learning.

The ancients who wished to illustrate illustrious virtue throughout the kingdom first ordered well their own states. Wishing to order well their states, they first regulated their families. Wishing to regulate their families, they first cultivated their persons. Wishing to cultivate their persons, they first rectified their hearts. Wishing to rectify their hearts, they first sought to be sincere in their thoughts. Wishing to be sincere in their thoughts, they first extended to the utmost their knowledge. Such extension of knowledge lay in the investigation of things.

Things being investigated, knowledge became complete. Their knowledge being complete, their thoughts were sincere. Their thoughts being sincere, their hearts were then rectified. Their hearts being rectified, their persons were cultivated. Their persons being cultivated, their families were regulated. Their families being regulated, their states were rightly governed. Their states being rightly governed, the whole kingdom was made tranquil and happy.

From the Son of Heaven down to the mass of the people, all must consider the cultivation of the person the root of everything besides.

It cannot be, when the root is neglected, that what should spring from it will be well ordered. It never has been the case that what was of great importance has been slightly cared for, and, at the same time, that what was of slight importance has been greatly cared for.

The Doctrine of the Steadfast Mean
(CHUNG YUNG)

My master, the philosopher Ch'ang, says:—"Being without inclination to either side is called CHUNG; admitting of no change is called YUNG. By CHUNG is denoted the correct course to be pursued by all under heaven; by YUNG is denoted the fixed principle regulating all under heaven. This work contains the law of the mind, which was handed down from one to another, in the Confucian school, till Tsze-sze, fearing lest in the course of time errors should arise about it, committed it to writing, and delivered it to Mencius. The book first speaks of one principle; it next spreads this out, and embraces all things; finally, it returns and gathers them all up under the one principle. Unroll it, and it fills the universe; roll it up, and it retires and lies hid in mysteriousness. The relish of it is inexhaustible. The whole of it is solid learning. When the skilful reader has explored it with delight till he has apprehended it, he may carry it into practice all his life, and will find that it cannot be exhausted."

What heaven has conferred is called THE NATURE; an accordance with this nature is called THE PATH OF DUTY; the regulation of this path is called INSTRUCTION. The path may not be left for an instant. If it could be left, it would not be the path. On this account, the superior man does not wait till he sees things, to be cautious, nor till he hears things, to be apprehensive.

There is nothing more visible than what is secret, and nothing more manifest than what is minute. Therefore the superior man is watchful over himself, when he is alone.

While there are no stirrings of pleasure, anger, sorrow, or joy, the mind may be said to be in the state of EQUILIBRIUM. When those feelings have been stirred, and they act in their due degree, there ensues what may be called the state of HARMONY. This EQUILIBRIUM is the great root from which grow all the human actings in the world, and this HARMONY is the universal path which they all should pursue. Let the states of equilibrium and harmony exist in perfection, and a happy order will prevail throughout heaven and earth, and all things will be nourished and flourish.

The Master said, "Perfect is the virtue which is according to the Mean! Rare have they long been among the people, who could practise it!

"I know how it is that the path of the Mean is not walked in:—The knowing go beyond it, and the stupid do not come up to it. I know how it is that the path of the Mean is not understood:—The men of talents and virtue go beyond it, and the worthless do not come up to it.

"Men all say, 'We are wise'; but being driven forward and taken in a net, a trap, or a pitfall, they know not how to escape. Men all say, 'We are wise'; but happening to choose the course of the Mean, they are not able to keep it for a round month.

"The kingdom, its states, and its families, may be perfectly ruled; dignities and emoluments may be declined; naked weapons may be trampled under the feet;—but the course of the Mean cannot be attained to."

Tsze-lu asked about energy. The Master said, "Do you mean the energy of the South, the energy of the North, or the energy which you should cultivate yourself?

"To show forbearance and gentleness in teaching others; and not to revenge unreasonable conduct:—this is the energy of southern regions, and the good man makes it his study.

"To lie under arms and meet death without regret:—this is the energy of northern regions, and the forceful make it their study.

"Therefore, the superior man cultivates a friendly harmony, without being weak. How firm is he in his energy! He stands erect in the middle, without inclining to either side. How firm is he in his energy! When good principles prevail in the government of his country, he does not change from what he was in retirement.—How firm is he in his energy! When bad principles prevail in the country, he maintains his course to death without changing.—How firm is he in his energy!"

The way which the superior man pursues, reaches wide and far, and yet is secret. Common men and women, however ignorant, may inter-meddle with the knowledge of it; yet in its utmost reaches, there is that which even the sage does not know. Common men and women, how-ever much below the ordinary standard of character, can carry it into practice; yet in its utmost reaches there is that which even the sage is not able to carry into practice. Great as heaven and earth are, men still find some things in them with which to be dissatisfied. Thus it is that, were the superior man to speak of his way in all its greatness, nothing in the world would be found able to embrace it, and were he to speak of it in its minuteness, nothing in the world would be found able to split it.

The Master said, "The path is not far from man. When men try to pursue a course which is far from the common indications of con-sciousness, this course cannot be considered THE PATH. When one cultivates to the utmost the principles of his nature, and exercises them on the principle of reciprocity, he is not far from the path. What you do not like when done to yourself, do not do to others.

"In the way of the superior man there are four things, to not one of which have I as yet attained.—To serve my father, as I would require my son to serve me: to this I have not attained; to serve my prince, as I would require my minister to serve me: to this I have not attained; to serve my elder brother, as I would require my younger brother to serve me: to this I have not attained; to set the example in behaving to a friend, as I would require him to behave to me: to this I have not attained. Earnest in practising the ordinary virtues, and careful in speak-ing about them, if in his practice he has anything defective, the superior man dares not but exert himself; and if, in his words, he has any excess, he dares not allow himself such licence. Thus his words have respect to his actions, and his actions have respect to his words; is it not just an entire sincerity which marks the superior man?"

The superior man does what is proper to the station in which he is; he does not desire to go beyond this.

In a position of wealth and honour, he does what is proper to a posi-tion of wealth and honour. In a poor and low position, he does what is proper to a poor and low position. Situated among barbarous tribes, he does what is proper to a situation among barbarous tribes. In a position of sorrow and difficulty, he does what is proper to a position of sorrow and difficulty. The superior man can find himself in no situation in which he is not himself.

In a high situation, he does not treat with contempt his inferiors. In a low situation, he does not court the favour of his superiors. He rectifies himself, and seeks for nothing from others, so that he has no dissatisfactions. He does not murmur against heaven, nor grumble against men.

Thus it is that the superior man is quiet and calm, waiting for the appointments of heaven, while the inferior man walks in dangerous paths, looking for lucky occurrences.

It is said in the Book of Poetry, "Happy union with wife and children is like the music of lutes and harps. When there is concord among brethren, the harmony is delightful and enduring. Thus may you regulate your family, and enjoy the pleasure of your wife and children."

The duke Ai asked about government.

The Master said, "The government of Wan and Wu is displayed in the records,—the tablets of wood and bamboo. Let there be the men and the government will flourish; but without the men, their government decays and ceases. With the right men the growth of government is rapid, just as vegetation is rapid in the earth; and moreover their government might be called an easily-growing rush. Therefore the administration of government lies in getting proper men. Such men are to be got by means of the ruler's own character. That character is to be cultivated by his treading in the ways of duty. And the treading those ways of duty is to be cultivated by the cherishing of benevolence.

"Benevolence is the characteristic element of humanity, and the great exercise of it is in loving relatives. Righteousness is the accordance of actions with what is right, and the great exercise of it is in honouring the worthy. The decreasing measures of the love due to relatives, and the steps in the honour due to the worthy, are produced by the principle of propriety.

"The duties of universal obligation are five, and the virtues wherewith they are practised are three. The duties are those between sovereign and minister, between father and son, between husband and wife, between elder brother and younger, and those belonging to the intercourse of friends. Those five are the duties of universal obligation. Knowledge, magnanimity, and energy, these three, are the virtues universally binding. And the means by which they carry the duties into practice is singleness. Some are born with the knowledge of those duties; some know them by study; and some acquire the knowledge after a painful feeling of their ignorance. But the knowledge being possessed, it comes to the same thing. Some practise them with a natural ease; some from a desire for their advantages; and some by strenuous effort. But the achievement being made, it comes to the same thing."

The Master said, "To be fond of learning is to be near to knowledge. To practise with vigour is to be near to magnanimity. To possess the feeling of shame is to be near to energy. He who knows these three things, knows how to cultivate his own character. Knowing how to cultivate his own character, he knows how to govern other men. Knowing how to govern other men, he knows how to govern the kingdom with all its states and families.

"All who have the government of the kingdom with its states and families have nine standard rules to follow;—viz., the cultivation of their own characters; the honouring of men of virtue and talents; affection towards their relatives; respect towards the great ministers; kind and considerate treatment of the whole body of officers; dealing with the mass of the people as children; encouraging the resort of all classes of artisans; indulgent treatment of men from a distance; and the kindly cherishing of the princes of the states.

"In all things success depends on previous preparation, and without such previous preparation there is sure to be failure. If what is to be spoken be previously determined, there will be no stumbling. If affairs be previously determined, there will be no difficulty with them. If one's actions have been previously determined, there will be no sorrow in connexion with them. If principles of conduct have been previously determined, the practice of them will be inexhaustible.

"Sincerity is the way of heaven. The attainment of sincerity is the way of men. He who possesses sincerity is he who, without an effort, hits what is right, and apprehends without the exercise of thought;—he is the sage who naturally and easily embodies the right way. He who attains to sincerity is he who chooses what is good, and firmly holds it fast. To this attainment there are requisite the extensive study of what is good, accurate inquiry about it, careful reflection on it, the clear discrimination of it, and the earnest practice of it.

"The superior man, while there is anything he has not studied, or while in what he has studied there is anything he cannot understand, will not intermit his labour. While there is anything he has not inquired about, or anything in what he has inquired about which he does not know, he will not intermit his labour. While there is anything which he has not reflected on, or anything in what he has reflected on which he does not apprehend, he will not intermit his labour. While there is anything which he has not discriminated, or his discrimination is not clear, he will not intermit his labour. If there be anything which he has not practised, or his practice fails in earnestness, he will not intermit his labour. If another man succeed by one effort, he will use a hundred efforts. If another man succeed by ten efforts, he will use a thousand. Let a man proceed in this way, and, though dull, he will surely become intelligent; though weak, he will surely become strong."

Sincerity is that whereby self-completion is effected, and its way is that by which man must direct himself. Sincerity is the end and beginning of things; without sincerity there would be nothing. On this account, the superior man regards the attainment of sincerity as the most excellent thing. The possessor of sincerity does not merely accomplish the self-completion of himself. With this quality he completes other men and things also. The completing himself shows his perfect virtue. The completing other men and things shows his knowledge. Both these are virtues belonging to the nature, and this is the way by which a union is effected of the external and internal. Therefore, whenever he—the entirely sincere man—employs them,—that is, these virtues,—their action will be right.

The heaven now before us is only this bright shining spot; but when viewed in its inexhaustible extent, the sun, moon, stars, and constellations of the zodiac are suspended in it, and all things are overspread by it. The earth before us is but a handful of soil; but when regarded in its breadth and thickness, it sustains mountains like the Hwa and the Yo, without feeling their weight, and contains the rivers and seas, without their leaking away. The mountain now before us appears only a stone; but when contemplated in all the vastness of its size, we see how the grass and trees are produced on it, and birds and beasts dwell on it, and precious things which men treasure up are found on it. The water now before us appears but a ladleful; yet extending our view to its unfathomable depths, the largest tortoises, iguanas, iguanodons, dragons, fishes, and turtles are produced in them, articles of value and sources of wealth abound in them.

The Master said, "Let a man who is ignorant be fond of using his own judgment; let a man without rank be fond of assuming a directing power to himself; let a man who is living in the present age go back to the ways of antiquity;—on the persons of all who act thus calamities will be sure to come."

All things are nourished together without their injuring one another. The courses of the seasons, and of the sun and moon, are pursued without any collision among them. The smaller energies are like river currents; the greater energies are seen in mighty transformations. It is this which makes heaven and earth so great.

It is only he possessed of all sagely qualities that can exist under heaven, who shows himself quick in apprehension, clear in discernment, of far-reaching intelligence, and all-embracing knowledge, fitted to exercise rule; magnanimous, generous, benign, and mild, fitted to exercise forbearance; impulsive, energetic, firm, and enduring, fitted to maintain a firm hold; self-adjusted, grave, never swerving from the Mean, and correct, fitted to command reverence; accomplished, distinctive, concentrative, and searching, fitted to exercise discrimination.

All-embracing is he and vast, deep and active as a fountain, sending forth in their due season his virtues.

All-embracing and vast, he is like heaven. Deep and active as a fountain, he is like the abyss. He is seen, and the people all reverence him; he speaks, and the people all believe him; he acts, and the people all are pleased with him.

Therefore his fame overspreads the Middle Kingdom, and extends to all barbarous tribes. Wherever ships and carriages reach; wherever the strength of man penetrates; wherever the heavens overshadow and the earth sustains; wherever the sun and moon shine; wherever frosts and dews fall:—all who have blood and breath unfeignedly honour and love him. Hence it is said,—"He is the equal of heaven."

It is only the individual possessed of the most entire sincerity that can exist under heaven, who can adjust the great invariable relations of mankind, establish the great fundamental virtues of humanity, and know the transforming and nurturing operations of heaven and earth; —shall this individual have any being or anything beyond himself on which he depends?

Call him man in his ideal, how earnest is he! Call him an abyss, how deep is he! Call him heaven, how vast is he!

Who can know him, but he who is indeed quick in apprehension, clear in discernment, of far-reaching intelligence and all-embracing knowledge, possessing all heavenly virtue?

The Works of Mencius

Book I

The Perfect Government

Mencius went to see king Hwuy of Leang. The king said, "Venerable sir, since you have not counted it far to come here, a distance of a thousand le, may I presume that you are likewise provided with counsels to profit my kingdom?" Mencius replied, "Why must your Majesty use that word profit? What I am 'likewise' provided with, are counsels to benevolence and righteousness, and these are my only topics.

"If your Majesty say, 'What is to be done to profit my kingdom?' the great officers will say, 'What is to be done to profit our families?' and the inferior officers and the common people will say, 'What is to be done to profit our persons?' Superiors and inferiors will try to snatch this profit the one from the other, and the kingdom will be endangered. In the kingdom of ten thousand chariots, the murderer of his sovereign shall be the chief of a family of a thousand chariots. In a kingdom of a thousand chariots, the murderer of his prince shall be the chief of a family of a hundred chariots. To have a thousand in ten thousand, and a hundred in a thousand, cannot be said not to be a large allotment, but if righteousness be put last, and profit be put first, they will not be satisfied without snatching all.

"There never has been a man trained to benevolence who neglected his parents. There never has been a man trained to righteousness who made his sovereign an after consideration.

"Let your Majesty also say, 'Benevolence and righteousness, and these shall be the only themes.' Why must you use that word—'profit'?"

Mencius, another day, saw king Hwuy of Leang. The king went and stood with him by a pond, and, looking round at the large geese and deer, said, "Do wise and good princes also find pleasure in these things?"

Mencius replied, "Being wise and good, they have pleasure in these things. If they are not wise and good, though they have these things, they do not find pleasure."

King Hwuy of Leang said, "Small as my virtue is, in the government of my kingdom I do indeed exert my mind to the utmost. If the year be bad on the inside of the river, I remove as many of the people as I can to the east of the river, and convey grain to the country in the inside. When the year is bad on the east of the river, I act on the same plan. On examining the government of the neighbouring kingdoms, I do not find that there is any prince who employs his mind as I do. And yet the people of the neighbouring kingdoms do not decrease, nor do my people increase. How is this?"

Mencius replied, "Your Majesty is fond of war;—let me take an illustration from war.—The soldiers move forward to the sound of the drums; and after their weapons have been crossed, on one side they throw away their coats of mail, trail their arms behind them, and run. Some run a hundred paces and stop; some run fifty paces and stop. What would you think if those who run fifty paces were to laugh at those who run a hundred paces?" The king said, "They may not do so. They only did not run a hundred paces; but they also ran away." "Since your Majesty knows this," replied Mencius, "you need not hope that your people will become more numerous than those of the neighbouring kingdoms.

"If the seasons of husbandry be not interfered with, the grain will be more than can be eaten. If close nets are not allowed to enter the pools and ponds, the fishes and turtles will be more than can be consumed. If the axes and bills enter the hills and forests only at the proper time, the wood will be more than can be used. When the grain and fish and turtles are more than can be eaten, and there is more wood than can be used, this enables the people to nourish their living and bury their dead, without any feeling against any. This condition, in which the people nourish their living and bury their dead without any feeling against any, is the first step of royal government.

"Let mulberry trees be planted about the homesteads with their five *mow*, and persons of fifty years may be clothed with silk. In keeping fowls, pigs, dogs, and swine, let not their times of breeding be neglected, and persons of seventy years may eat flesh. Let there not be taken away the time that is proper for the cultivation of the farm with its hundred *mow*, and the family of several mouths that is supported by it shall not suffer from hunger. Let careful attention be paid to education in schools, inculcating in it especially the filial and fraternal duties, and grey-haired men will not be seen upon the roads, carrying burdens on their backs or on their heads. It never has been that the ruler of a state where such results were seen,—persons of seventy wearing silk and eating flesh, and the black-haired people suffering neither from hunger nor cold,—did not attain to the imperial dignity.

"Your dogs and swine eat the food of men, and you do not know to make any restrictive arrangements. There are people dying from famine on the roads, and you do not know to issue the stores of your granaries for them. When people die, you say, 'It is not owing to me; it is owing to the year.' In what does this differ from stabbing a man and killing him, and then saying, 'It was not I; it was the weapon'? Let your Majesty cease to lay the blame on the year, and instantly from all the empire the people will come to you."

King Hwuy of Leang said, "I wish quietly to receive your instructions."

Mencius replied, "Is there any difference between killing a man with a stick and with a sword?" The king said, "There is no difference." "Is there any difference between doing it with a sword and with the style of government?" "There is no difference," was the reply.

Mencius then said, "In your kitchen there is fat meat; in your stables there are fat horses. But your people have the look of hunger, and on the wilds there are those who have died of famine. This is leading on beasts to devour men. Beasts devour one another, and men hate them for doing so. When a prince, being the parent of his people, administers his government so as to be chargeable with leading on beasts to devour men, where is that parental relation to the people?"

Mencius went to see the king Seang of Leang. On coming out from the interview, he said to some persons, "When I looked at him from a distance, he did not appear like a sovereign; when I drew near to him, I saw nothing venerable about him. Abruptly he asked me, 'How can the empire be settled?' I replied, 'It will be settled by being united under one sway.'

" 'Who can so unite it?'

"I replied, 'He who has no pleasure in killing men can so unite it.'

" 'Who can give it to him?'

"I replied, 'All the people of the empire will unanimously give it to him. Does your Majesty understand the way of the growing grain? During the seventh and eighth months, when drought prevails, the plants become dry. Then the clouds collect densely in the heavens, they send down torrents of rain, and the grain erects itself, as if by a shoot. When it does so, who can keep it back? Now among the shepherds of men throughout the empire, there is not one who does not find pleasure in killing men. If there were one who did not find pleasure in killing men, all the people in the empire would look towards him with out-stretched necks. Such being indeed the case, the people would flock to him, as water flows downwards with a rush, which no one can repress.' "

The king said, "What virtue must there be in order to the attain-ment of imperial sway?" Mencius answered, "The love and protection of the people; with this there is no power which can prevent a ruler from attaining it."

The king asked again, "Is such an one as I competent to love and protect the people?" Mencius said, "Yes." "From what do you know that I am competent to that?" "I heard the following incident from Hoo Heih:—'The king,' said he, 'was sitting aloft in the hall, when a man appeared, leading an ox past the lower part of it. The king saw him, and asked, Where is the ox going? The man replied, We are going to consecrate a bell with its blood. The king said, Let it go. I cannot bear its frightened appearance as if it were an innocent person going

to the place of death. The man answered, Shall we then omit the consecration of the bell? The king said, How can that be omitted? Change
it for a sheep.' I do not know whether this incident really occurred."

The king replied, "It did," and then Mencius said, "The heart seen in
this is sufficient to carry you to the imperial sway. The people all supposed that your Majesty grudged the animal, but your servant knows
surely, that it was your Majesty's not being able to bear the sight, which
made you do as you did."

The king said, "You are right. And yet there really was an appearance
of what the people condemned. But though Ts'e be a small and narrow
state, how should I grudge one ox? Indeed it was because I could not
bear its frightened appearance, as if it were an innocent person going to
the place of death, that therefore I changed it for a sheep."

Mencius pursued, "Let not your Majesty deem it strange that the
people should think you were grudging the animal. When you changed
a large one for a small, how should they know the true reason. If you
felt pained by its being led without guilt to the place of death, what was
there to choose between an ox and a sheep?" The king laughed and said,
"What really was my mind in the matter? I did not grudge the expense
of it, and changed it for a sheep!—There was reason in the people's saying that I grudged it."

"There is no harm in their saying so," said Mencius. "Your conduct
was an artifice of benevolence. You saw the ox, and had not seen the
sheep. So is the superior man affected towards animals, that, having seen
them alive, he cannot bear to see them die; having heard their dying
cries, he cannot bear to eat their flesh. Therefore he keeps away from his
cook-room."

The king was pleased, and said, "It is said in the Book of Poetry, 'The
minds of others, I am able by reflection to measure';—this is verified,
my Master, in your discovery of my motive. I indeed did the thing, but
when I turned my thoughts inward, and examined into it, I could not
discover my own mind. When you, Master, spoke those words, the movements of compassion began to work in my mind. How is it that this
heart has in it what is equal to the imperial sway?"

Mencius replied, "Suppose a man were to make this statement to your
Majesty: 'My strength is sufficient to lift three thousand catties, but it is
not sufficient to lift one feather;—my eye-sight is sharp enough to examine the point of an autumn hair, but I do not see a wagon-load of fag-

gots';—would your Majesty allow what he said?" "No" was the answer, on which Mencius proceeded, "Now here is kindness sufficient to reach to animals, and no benefits are extended from it to the people. How is this? Is an exception to be made here? The truth is, the feather's not being lifted is because the strength is not used; the wagon-load of fire-wood's not being seen is because the vision is not used; and the people's not being loved and protected is because the kindness is not employed. Therefore your Majesty's not exercising the imperial sway is because you do not do it, not because you are not able to do it."

The king asked, "How may the difference between the not doing a thing, and the not being able to do it, be represented?" Mencius replied, "In such a thing as taking the T'ae mountain under your arm, and leap-ing over the north sea with it, if you say to people—'I am not able to do it,' that is a real case of not being able. In such a matter as breaking off a branch from a tree at the order of a superior, if you say to people—'I am not able to do it,' that is a case of not doing it, it is not a case of not being able to do it. Therefore your Majesty's not exercising the imperial sway is not such a case as that of taking the T'ae mountain under your arm, and leaping over the north sea with it. Your Majesty's not exercis-ing the imperial sway is a case like that of breaking off a branch from a tree.

"Treat with the reverence due to age the elders in your own family, so that the elders in the families of others shall be similarly treated; treat with the kindness due to youth the young in your own family, so that the young in the families of others shall be similarly treated:—do this, and the empire may be made to go round in your palm. It is said in the Book of Poetry, 'His example affected his wife. It reached to his brothers, and his family of the state was governed by it.' The language shows how king Wan simply took this kindly heart, and exercised it towards those parties. Therefore the carrying out his kindly heart by a prince will suffice for the love and protection of all within the four seas, and if he do not carry it out, he will not be able to protect his wife and children. The way in which the ancients came greatly to surpass other men was no other than this:—simply that they knew well how to carry out, so as to affect others, what they themselves did. Now your kindness is sufficient to reach to animals, and no benefits are extended from it to reach the people.—How is this? Is an exception to be made here?

"You collect your equipments of war, endanger your soldiers and officers, and excite the resentment of the other princes;—do these things cause you pleasure in your mind?"

The king replied, "No. How should I derive pleasure from these things? My object in them is to seek for what I greatly desire."

Mencius said, "May I hear from you what it is that you greatly desire?" The king laughed and did not speak. Mencius resumed, "Are you led to desire it, because you have not enough of rich and sweet food for your mouth? Or because you have not enough of light and warm clothing for your body? Or because you have not enough of beautifully coloured objects to delight your eyes? Or because you have not voices and tones enough to please your ears? Or because you have not enough of attendants and favourites to stand before you and receive your orders? Your Majesty's various officers are sufficient to supply you with those things. How can your Majesty be led to entertain such a desire on account of them?" "No," said the king; "my desire is not on account of them." Mencius added, "Then, what your Majesty greatly desires may be known. You wish to enlarge your territories, to have Ts'in and Ts'oo wait at your court, to rule the Middle Kingdom, and to attract to you the barbarous tribes that surround it. But to do what you do to seek for what you desire, is like climbing a tree to seek for fish."

The king said, "Is it so bad as that?" "It is even worse," was the reply. "If you climb a tree to seek for fish, although you do not get the fish, you will not suffer any subsequent calamity. But if you do what you do to seek for what you desire, doing it moreover with all your heart, you will assuredly afterwards meet with calamities." The king asked, "May I hear from you the proof of that?" Mencius said, "If the people of Tsow should fight with the people of Ts'oo, which of them does your Majesty think would conquer?" "The people of Ts'oo would conquer." "Yes;— and so it is certain that a small country cannot contend with a great, that few cannot contend with many, that the weak cannot contend with the strong. The territory within the four seas embraces nine divisions, each of a thousand le square. All Ts'e together is but one of them. If with one part you try to subdue the other eight, what is the difference between that and Tsow's contending with Ts'oo? For, with the desire which you have, you must likewise turn back to the radical course for its attainment.

"Now, if your Majesty will institute a government whose action shall all be benevolent, this will cause all the officers in the empire to wish to stand in your Majesty's court, and the farmers all to wish to plough in your Majesty's fields, and the merchants, both travelling and stationary, all to wish to store their goods in your Majesty's market-places, and travelling strangers all to wish to make their tours on your Majesty's roads, and all throughout the empire who feel aggrieved by their rulers to wish to come and complain to your Majesty. And when they are so bent, who will be able to keep them back?''

The king said, "I am stupid, and not able to advance to this. I wish you, my Master, to assist my intentions. Teach me clearly; although I am deficient in intelligence and vigour, I will essay and try to carry your instructions into effect."

Mencius replied, "They are only men of education, who, without a certain livelihood, are able to maintain a fixed heart. As to the people, if they have not a certain livelihood, it follows that they will not have a fixed heart. And if they have not a fixed heart, there is nothing which they will not do, in the way of self-abandonment, of moral deflexion, of depravity, and of wild licence. When they thus have been involved in crime, to follow them up and punish them;—this is to entrap the people. How can such a thing as entrapping the people be done under the rule of a benevolent man?

"Therefore an intelligent ruler will regulate the livelihood of the people, so as to make sure that, above, they shall have sufficient wherewith to serve their parents, and, below, sufficient wherewith to support their wives and children; that in good years they shall always be abundantly satisfied, and that in bad years they shall escape the danger of perishing. After this he may urge them, and they will proceed to what is good, for in this case the people will follow after that with ease.

"Now, the livelihood of the people is so regulated that, above, they have not sufficient wherewith to serve their parents, and, below, they have not sufficient wherewith to support their wives and children. Notwithstanding good years, their lives are continually embittered, and, in bad years, they do not escape perishing. In such circumstances they only try to save themselves from death, and are afraid they will not succeed. What leisure have they to cultivate propriety and righteousness?

"If your Majesty wishes to effect this regulation of the livelihood of the people, why not turn to that which is the essential step to it?

"Let mulberry-trees be planted about the homesteads with their five *mow*, and persons of fifty years may be clothed with silk. In keeping fowls, pigs, and swine, let not their times of breeding be neglected, and persons of seventy years may eat flesh. Let there not be taken away the time that is proper for the cultivation of the farm with its hundred *mow,* and the family of eight mouths that is supported by it shall not suffer from hunger. Let careful attention be paid to education in schools,—the inculcation in it especially of the filial and fraternal duties, and grey-haired men will not be seen upon the roads, carrying burdens on their backs or on their heads. It never has been that the ruler of a state where such results were seen,—the old wearing silk and eating flesh, and the black-haired people suffering neither from hunger nor cold,—did not attain to the imperial dignity."

The king, Seuen, of Ts'e asked, "Was it so, that the park of king Wan contained seventy square le?" Mencius replied, "It is so in the records."

"Was it so large as that?" exclaimed the king. "The people," said Mencius, "still looked on it as small." The king added, "My park contains only forty square le, and the people still look on it as large. How is this?" "The park of king Wan," was the reply, "contained seventy square le, but the grass-cutters and fuel-gatherers had the privilege of entrance into it; so also had the catchers of pheasants and hares. He shared it with the people, and was it not with reason that they looked on it as small?

"When I first arrived at the borders of your state, I inquired about the great prohibitory regulations, before I would venture to enter it; and I heard that inside the border-gates there was a park of forty square le, and that he who killed a deer in it was held guilty of the same crime as if he had killed a man. Thus those forty square le are a pitfall in the middle of the kingdom. Is it not with reason that the people look upon them as large?"

Book II

The Path to Peace

Kung-sun Ch'ow asked Mencius, saying, "Master, if you were to be appointed a high noble and the prime minister of Ts'e, so as to be able to carry your principles into practice, though you should thereupon raise the prince to the headship of all the other princes, or even to the imperial dignity, it would not be to be wondered at.—In such a position would your mind be perturbed or not?" Mencius replied, "No. At forty, I attained to an unperturbed mind."

Ch'ow said, "Since it is so with you, my Master, you are far beyond Mang Pun." "The mere attainment," said Mencius, "is not difficult. The scholar Kaou had attained to an unperturbed mind at an earlier period of life than I did."

Ch'ow asked, "Is there any way to an unperturbed mind?" The answer was, "Yes.

"Pih-kung Yew had this way of nourishing his valour:—He did not flinch from any strokes at his body. He did not turn his eyes aside from any thrusts at them. He considered that the slightest push from any one was the same as if he were beaten before the crowds in the market-place, and that what he would not receive from a common man in his loose large garments of hair, neither should he receive from a prince of ten thousand chariots. He viewed stabbing a prince of ten thousand chariots just as stabbing a fellow dressed in cloth of hair. He feared not any of all the princes. A bad word addressed to him he always returned.

"Mang She-shay had this way of nourishing his valour: He said, 'I look upon not conquering and conquering in the same way. To measure the enemy and then advance; to calculate the chances of victory and then engage:—this is to stand in awe of the opposing force. How can I make certain of conquering? I can only rise superior to all fear.'

"Formerly, the philosopher Tsang said to Tsze-seang, 'Do you love valour?' I heard an account of great valour from the Master. It speaks thus:—'If, on self-examination, I find that I am not upright, shall I not be in fear even of a poor man in his loose garments of hair-cloth? If, on self-examination, I find that I am upright, I will go forward against thousands and tens of thousands.' "

"I venture to ask," said Ch'ow again, "wherein you, Master, surpass Kaou." Mencius told him, "I understand words. I am skilful in nourishing my vast, flowing passion-nature."

Ch'ow pursued, "I venture to ask what you mean by your vast, flowing passion-nature!" The reply was, "It is difficult to describe it.

"This is the passion-nature:—It is exceedingly great, and exceedingly strong. Being nourished by rectitude, and sustaining no injury, it fills up all between heaven and earth.

"This is the passion-nature:—It is the mate and assistant of righteousness and reason. Without it, man is in a state of starvation.

"It is produced by the accumulation of righteous deeds; it is not to be obtained by incidental acts of righteousness. If the mind does not feel complacency in the conduct, the nature becomes starved. I therefore said, 'Kaou has never understood righteousness, because he makes it something external.'

"There must be the constant practice of this righteousness, but without the object of thereby nourishing the passion-nature. Let not the mind forget its work, but let there be no assisting the growth of that nature. Let us not be like the man of Sung. There was a man of Sung, who was grieved that his growing corn was not longer, and so he pulled it up. Having done this, he returned home, looking very stupid, and said to his people, 'I am tired to-day. I have been helping the corn to grow long.' His son ran to look at it, and found the corn all withered. There are few in the world who do not deal with their passion-nature as if they were assisting the corn to grow long. Some indeed consider it of no benefit to them, and let it alone:—they do not weed their corn. They who assist it to grow long, pull out their corn. What they do is not only of no benefit to the nature, but it also injures it."

Mencius said, "He who, using force, makes a pretence to benevolence, is the leader of the princes. A leader of the princes requires a large kingdom. He who, using virtue, practises benevolence—is the sovereign of the empire. To become the sovereign of the empire, a prince need not wait for a large kingdom. T'ang did it with only seventy le, and king Wan with only a hundred.

"When one by force subdues men, they do not submit to him in heart. They submit because their strength is not adequate to resist. When one subdues men by virtue, in their hearts' core they are pleased, and sincerely submit, as was the case with the seventy disciples in their submission to Confucius. What is said in the Book of Poetry,

> 'From the west, from the east,
> From the south, from the north,
> There was not one who thought of refusing submission,'

is an illustration of this."

Mencius said, "All men have a mind which cannot bear to see the sufferings of others.

"The ancient kings had this commiserating mind, and they, as a matter of course, had likewise a commiserating government. When with a commiserating mind was practised a commiserating government, the government of the empire was as easy a matter as the making anything go round in the palm.

"When I say that all men have a mind which cannot bear to see the sufferings of others, my meaning may be illustrated thus:—even nowadays, if men suddenly see a child about to fall into a well, they will without exception experience a feeling of alarm and distress. They will feel so, not as a ground on which they may seek the praise of their neighbours and friends, nor from a dislike to the reputation of having been unmoved by such a thing.

"From this case we may perceive that the feeling of commiseration is essential to man, that the feeling of shame and dislike is essential to man, that the feeling of modesty and complaisance is essential to man, and that the feeling of approving and disapproving is essential to man.

"The feeling of commiseration is the principle of benevolence. The feeling of shame and dislike is the principle of righteousness. The feeling of modesty and complaisance is the principle of propriety. The feeling of approving and disapproving is the principle of knowledge."

"From the want of benevolence and the want of wisdom will ensue the entire absence of propriety and righteousness;—he who is in such a case must be the servant of other men. To be the servant of men and yet ashamed of such servitude is like a bow-maker's being ashamed to make bows, or an arrow-maker's being ashamed to make arrows.

"If he be ashamed of his case, his best course is to practise benevolence.

"The man who would be benevolent is like the archer. The archer adjusts himself and then shoots. If he misses, he does not murmur against those who surpass himself. He simply turns round and seeks the cause of his failure in himself."

Mencius said, "When any one told Tsze-loo that he had a fault, he rejoiced.

"The great Shun had a still greater delight in what was good. He regarded virtue as the common property of himself and others, giving up his own way to follow that of others, and delighting to learn from others to practise what was good.

"To take example from others to practise virtue, is to help them in the same practice. Therefore, there is no attribute of the superior man greater than his helping men to practise virtue."

As Mencius was about to go to court to see the king, the king sent a person to him with this message,—"I was wishing to come and see you. But I have got a cold, and may not expose myself to the wind. In the morning I will hold my court. I do not know whether you will give me the opportunity of seeing you then." Mencius replied, "Unfortunately, I am unwell, and not able to go to the court."

Next day, he went out to pay a visit of condolence to someone of the Tung-kwoh family, when Kung-sun Ch'ow said to him, "Yesterday, you declined going to the court on the ground of being unwell, and to-day you are going to pay a visit of condolence. May this not be regarded as improper?" "Yesterday," said Mencius, "I was unwell; to-day, I am better:—why should I not pay this visit?"

In the meantime, the king sent a messenger to inquire about his sickness, and also a physician. Mang Chung replied to them, "Yesterday, when the king's order came, he was feeling a little unwell, and could not go to the court. To-day he was a little better, and hastened to go to court. I do not know whether he can have reached it by this time or not." Having said this, he sent several men to look for Mencius on the way, and say to him, "I beg that, before you return home, you will go to the court."

On this, Mencius felt himself compelled to go to king Ch'ow's, and there stop the night. King said to him, "In the family, there is the relation of father and son; abroad, there is the relation of prince and minister. These are the two great relations among men. Between father and son the ruling principle is kindness. Between prince and minister the ruling principle is respect. I have seen the respect of the king to you, sir, but I have not seen in what way you show respect to him." Mencius replied, "Oh! what words are these? Among the people of Ts'e there is no one who speaks to the king about benevolence and righteousness. Are they thus silent because they do not think that benevolence and righteousness are admirable? No, but in their hearts they say, 'This man is not fit to be spoken with about benevolence and righteousness.' Thus they manifest a disrespect than which there can be none greater. I do not dare to set forth before the king any but the ways of Yaou and Shun. There is therefore no man of Ts'e who respects the king so much as I do."

King said, "Not so. That was not what I meant. In the Book of Rites it is said, 'When a father calls, the answer must be without a moment's hesitation. When the prince's order calls, the carriage must not be waited for.' You were certainly going to the court, but when you heard the king's order, then you did not carry your purpose out. This does seem as if it were not in accordance with that rule of propriety."

Mencius answered him, "How can you give that meaning to my conduct? The philosopher Tsang said, 'The wealth of Tsin and Ts'oo cannot be equalled. Let their rulers have their wealth:—I have my benevolence. Let them have their nobility:—I have my righteousness. Wherein should I be dissatisfied as inferior to them?' Now shall we say that these sentiments are not right? Seeing that the philosopher Tsang spoke them, there is in them, I apprehend, a real principle. In the empire there are three things universally acknowledged to be honourable. Nobility is one of them; age is one of them; virtue is one of them. In courts, nobility holds the first place of the three; in villages, age holds the first place; and for helping one's generation and presiding over the people, the other two are not equal to virtue. How can the possession of only one of these be presumed on to despise one who possesses the other two?"

Book III

Of Co-operation in Agriculture

The duke Wan of T'ang asked Mencius about the proper way of governing a kingdom.

Mencius said, "The business of the people may not be remissly attended to. It is said in the Book of Poetry,

> 'In the daylight go and gather the grass,
> And at night twist your ropes;
> Then get up quickly on the roofs;—
> Soon must we begin sowing again the grain.'

"Lung said, 'For regulating the lands, there is no better system than that of mutual aid, and none which is not better than that of taxing. By the tax system, the regular amount was fixed by taking the average of several years. In good years, when the grain lies about in abundance, much might be taken without its being oppressive, and the actual exaction would be small. But in bad years, the produce being not sufficient to repay the manuring of the fields, this system still requires the taking of the full amount. When the parent of the people causes the people to wear looks of distress, and, after the whole year's toil, yet not to be able to nourish their parents, so that they proceed to borrowing to increase their means, till the old people and children are found lying in the ditches and water-channels:—where, in such a case, is his parental relation to the people?'

"It is said in the Book of Poetry,

> 'May the rain come down on our public field,
> And then upon our private fields!'

It is only in the system of mutual aid that there is a public field, and from this passage we perceive that even in the Chow dynasty this system has been recognized."

The Distribution of Labour

There came from Ts'oo to T'ang one Heu Hing, who gave out that he acted according to the words of Shin-nung. Coming right to his gate, he addressed the duke Wan, saying, "A man of a distant region, I have heard that you, Prince, are practising a benevolent government, and I wish to receive a site for a house, and to become one of your people." The duke Wan gave him a dwelling-place. His disciples, amounting to several tens, all wore clothes of haircloth, and made sandals of hemp and wove mats for a living.

At the same time, Ch'in Seang, a disciple of Ch'in Leang, and his younger brother, Sin, with their plough-handles and shares on their backs, came from Sung to T'ang, saying, "We have heard that you, Prince, are putting into practice the government of the ancient sages, showing that you are likewise a sage. We wish to become the subjects of a sage."

When Ch'in Seang saw Heu Hing, he was greatly pleased with him, and, abandoning entirely whatever he had learned, became his disciple. Having an interview with Mencius, he related to him with approbation the words of Heu Hing to the following effect:—"The prince of T'ang is indeed a worthy prince. He has not yet heard, however, the real doctrines of antiquity. Now, wise and able princes should cultivate the ground equally and along with their people, and eat the fruit of their labour. They should prepare their own meals, morning and evening, while at the same time they carry on their government. But now, the prince of T'ang has his granaries, treasuries, and arsenals, which is an oppressing of the people to nourish himself.—How can he be deemed a real worthy prince?"

Mencius said, "I suppose that Heu Hing sows grain and eats the produce. Is it not so?" "It is so," was the answer. "I suppose also he weaves cloth, and wears his own manufacture. Is it not so?" "No. Heu wears clothes of haircloth." "Does he wear a cap?" "He wears a cap." "What kind of cap?" "A plain cap." "Is it woven by himself?" "No. He gets it in exchange for grain." "Why does Heu not weave it himself?" "That would injure his husbandry." "Does Heu cook his food in boilers and earthen-ware pans, and does he plough with an iron share?" "Yes." "Does he make those articles himself?" "No. He gets them in exchange for grain."

Mencius then said, "The getting those various articles in exchange for grain is not oppressive to the potter and the founder, and the potter and the founder in their turn, in exchanging their various articles for grain, are not oppressive to the husbandman. How should such a thing be supposed? And moreover, why does not Heu act the potter and founder, supplying himself with the articles which he uses solely from his own establishment? Why does he go confusedly dealing and exchanging with the handicraftsmen? Why does he not spare himself so much trouble?" Ch'in Seang replied, "The business of the handicraftsman can by no means be carried on along with the business of husbandry."

Mencius resumed, "Then, is it the government of the empire which alone can be carried on along with the practice of husbandry? Great men have their proper business, and little men have their proper business. Moreover, in the case of any single individual, whatever articles he can require are ready to his hand, being produced by the various handicraftsmen:—if he must first make them for his own use, this way of doing would keep the whole empire running about upon the roads. Hence, there is the saying, 'Some labour with their minds, and some labour with their strength. Those who labour with their minds govern others; those who labour with their strength are governed by others. Those who are governed by others support them; those who govern others are supported by them.' This is a principle universally recognized.

Ch'in Seang said, "If Heu's doctrines were followed, then there would not be two prices in the market, nor any deceit in the kingdom. If a boy of five cubits were sent to the market, no one would impose on him; linen and silk of the same length would be of the same price. So it would be with bundles of hemp and silk, being of the same weight; with the different hanks of grain, being the same in quantity; and with shoes which were of the same size."

Mencius replied, "It is the nature of things to be of unequal quality. Some are twice, some five times, some ten times, some a hundred times, some a thousand times, some ten thousand times as valuable as others. If you reduce them all to the same standard, that must throw the empire into confusion. If large shoes and small shoes were of the same price, who would make them? For people to follow the doctrines of Heu, would be for them to lead one another on to practise deceit. How can they avail for the government of a state?"

The Story of Yaou and Shun

The disciple Kung-too said to Mencius, "Master, the people beyond our school all speak of you as being fond of disputing. I venture to ask whether it be so." Mencius replied, "Indeed, I am not fond of disputing, but I am compelled to do it.

"A long time has elapsed since this world of men received its being, and there has been along its history now a period of good order, and now a period of confusion.

"In the time of Yaou, the waters, flowing out of their channels, inundated the Middle Kingdom. Snakes and dragons occupied it, and the people had no place where they could settle themselves. In the low grounds they made nests for themselves, and in the high grounds they made caves. It is said in the Book of History, 'The waters in their wild course warned me.' Those 'waters in their wild course' were the waters of the great inundation.

"Shun employed Yu to reduce the waters to order. Yu dug open their obstructed channels, and conducted them to the sea. He drove away the snakes and dragons, and forced them into the grassy marshes. On this, the waters pursued their course through the country, even the waters of the Keang, the Hwae, the Ho, and the Han, and the dangers and obstructions which they had occasioned were removed. The birds and beasts which had injured the people also disappeared, and after this men found the plains available for them, and occupied them.

"After the death of Yaou and Shun, the principles that mark sages fell into decay. Oppressive sovereigns arose one after another, who pulled down houses to make ponds and lakes, so that the people knew not where they could rest in quiet, and threw fields out of cultivation to form gardens and parks, so that the people could not get clothes and food. Afterwards, corrupt speakings and oppressive deeds became more rife; gardens and parks, ponds and lakes, thickets and marshes, became more numerous, and birds and beasts swarmed. By the time of Chow the empire was again in a state of great confusion.

"Chow-kung assisted king Woo, and destroyed Chow. He smote Yen, and after three years put its sovereign to death. He drove Fei-leen to a corner by the sea, and slew him. The states which he extinguished amounted to fifty. He drove far away also the tigers, leopards, rhinoceroses, and elephants;—and the empire was greatly delighted. It is said in the Book of History, 'Great and splendid were the plans of king Wan! Greatly were they carried out by the energy of king Woo! They are for the assistance and instruction of us who are of an after day. They are all in principle correct, and deficient in nothing.'

"Again the world fell into decay, and principles faded away. Perverse speakings and oppressive deeds waxed rife again. There were instances of ministers who murdered their sovereigns, and of sons who murdered their fathers.

"Confucius was afraid, and made the 'Spring and Autumn.' What the 'Spring and Autumn' contains are matters proper to the emperor. On this account Confucius said, 'Yes! It is the Spring and Autumn which will make men know me, and it is the Spring and Autumn which will make men condemn me.'"

Book IV

The Root of the State

Mencius said, "The power of vision of Le Low, and skill of hand of Kung-shoo, without the compass and square, could not form squares and circles. The acute ear of the music-master K'wang, without the pitch-tubes, could not determine correctly the five notes. The principles of Yaou and Shun, without a benevolent government, could not secure the tranquil order of the empire.

"There are now princes who have benevolent hearts and a reputation for benevolence, while yet the people do not receive any benefits from them, nor will they leave any example to future ages;—all because they do not put into practice the ways of the ancient kings.

"Hence we have the saying:—'Virtue alone is not sufficient for the exercise of government; laws alone cannot carry themselves into practice.'

"When the prince has no principles by which he examines his administration, and his ministers have no laws by which they keep themselves in the discharge of their duties, then in the court obedience is not paid to principle, and in the office obedience is not paid to rule. Superiors violate the laws of righteousness, and inferiors violate the penal laws. It is only by a fortunate chance that a kingdom in such a case is preserved."

"Confucius said, 'There are but two courses which can be pursued, that of virtue and its opposite.'

"A sovereign who carries the oppression of his people to the highest pitch will himself be slain, and his kingdom will perish. If one stop short of the highest pitch, his life will notwithstanding be in danger, and his kingdom will be weakened. He will be styled 'The dark,' or 'The cruel,' and though he may have filial sons and affectionate grandsons, they will not be able in a hundred generations to change the designation."

"It is said in the Book of Poetry,
" 'Be always studious to be in harmony with the ordinances of God,
And you will obtain much happiness.' "

Mencius said, "People have this common saying,—'The empire, the state, the family.' The root of the empire is in the state. The root of the state is in the family. The root of the family is in the person of its head.

"There was a boy singing,

" 'When the water of the Ts'ang-lang is clear,
It does to wash the strings of my cap;
When the water of the Ts'ang-lang is muddy,
It does to wash my feet.'

"Confucius said, 'Hear what he sings, my children. When clear, then he will wash his cap-strings, and when muddy, he will wash his feet with it. This different application is brought by the water on itself.'

"A man must first despise himself, and then others will despise him. A family must first destroy itself, and then others will destroy it. A kingdom must first smite itself, and then others will smite it."

Mencius said, "With those who do violence to themselves, it is impossible to speak. With those who throw themselves away, it is impossible to do anything. To disown in his conversation propriety and righteousness, is what we mean by doing violence to one's self. To say—'I am not able to dwell in benevolence or pursue the path of righteousness,' is what we mean by throwing one's self away.

"Benevolence is the tranquil habitation of man, and righteousness is his straight path.

"Alas for them, who leave the tranquil dwelling empty, and do not reside in it, and who abandon the right path and do not pursue it!"

Mencius said, "When those occupying inferior situations do not obtain the confidence of the sovereign, they cannot succeed in governing the people. There is a way to obtain the confidence of the sovereign:— if one is not trusted by his friends, he will not obtain the confidence of his sovereign. There is a way of being trusted by one's friends:—if one do not serve his parents so as to make them pleased, he will not be trusted by his friends. There is a way to make one's parents pleased:— if one, on turning his thoughts inwards, finds a want of sincerity, he will not give pleasure to his parents. There is a way to the attainment of sincerity in one's self:—if a man do not understand what is good, he will not attain sincerity in himself.

"Therefore, sincerity is the way of heaven. To think how to be sincere is the way of man.

"Never has there been one possessed of complete sincerity, who did not move others. Never has there been one who had not sincerity who was able to move others."

Mencius said, "Of all the parts of a man's body there is none more excellent than the pupil of the eye. The pupil cannot be used to hide a man's wickedness. If within the breast all be correct, the pupil is bright. If within the breast all be not correct, the pupil is dull.

"Listen to a man's words and look at the pupil of his eye. How can a man conceal his character?"

Kung-sun Ch'ow said, "Why is it that the superior man does not himself teach his son?"

Mencius replied, "The circumstances of the case forbid its being done. The teacher must inculcate what is correct. When he inculcates what is correct and his lessons are not practised, he follows them up with being angry. When he follows them up with being angry, then, contrary to what should be, he is offended with his son. At the same time, the pupil says, 'My master inculcates on me what is correct, and he himself does not proceed in a correct path.' The result of this is, that father and son are offended with each other. When father and son come to be offended with each other, the case is evil.

"The ancients exchanged sons, and one taught the son of another.

"Between father and son, there should be no reproving admonitions to what is good. Such reproofs lead to alienation, and than alienation there is nothing more inauspicious."

Mencius said, "When scholars are put to death without any crime, the great officers may leave the country. When the people are slaughtered without any crime, the scholars may remove.

"If the sovereign be benevolent, all will be benevolent. If the sovereign be righteous, all will be righteous.

"Acts of propriety which are not really proper, and acts of righteousness which are not really righteous, the great man does not do.

"Those who keep the Mean, train up those who do not, and those who have abilities, train up those who have not, and hence men rejoice in having fathers and elder brothers who are possessed of virtue and talent. If they who keep the Mean spurn those who do not, and they who have abilities spurn those who have not, then the space between them—those so gifted and the ungifted—will not admit an inch.

"Men must be decided on what they will NOT do, and then they are able to act with vigour in what they ought to do.

"The great man does not think beforehand of his words that they may be sincere, nor of his actions that they may be resolute;—he simply speaks and does what is right.

"The great man is he who does not lose his child's-heart.

"That whereby man differs from the lower animals is but small. The mass of people cast it away, while superior men preserve it.

"When it appears proper to take a thing, and afterwards not proper, to take it is contrary to moderation. When it appears proper to give a thing and afterwards not proper, to give it is contrary to kindness. When it appears proper to sacrifice one's life, and afterwards not proper, to sacrifice it is contrary to bravery.

"He who loves others is constantly loved by them. He who respects others is constantly respected by them.

"Here is a man who treats me in a perverse and unreasonable manner. The superior man in such a case will turn round upon himself—'I must have been wanting in benevolence; I must have been wanting in propriety:—how should this have happened to me?'

"He examines himself, and is specially benevolent. He turns round upon himself, and is specially observant of propriety. The perversity and unreasonableness of the other, however, are still the same. The superior man will again turn round on himself—'I must have been failing to do my utmost.'

"He turns round upon himself, and proceeds to do his utmost, but still the perversity and unreasonableness of the other are repeated. On this the superior man says, 'This is a man utterly lost indeed! Since he conducts himself so, what is there to choose between him and a brute? Why should I go to contend with a brute?' "

Book V

Of Friendships and Gifts

Wan Chang asked Mencius saying, "I venture to ask the principles of friendship." Mencius replied, "Friendship should be maintained without any presumption on the ground of one's superior age, or station, or the circumstances of his relatives. Friendship with a man is friendship with his virtue, and does not admit of assumptions of superiority.

"Respect shown by inferiors to superiors is called giving to the noble the observance due to rank. Respect shown by superiors to inferiors is called giving honour to talents and virtue. The rightness in each case is the same."

Wan Chang asked Mencius, saying, "I venture to ask what feeling of the mind is expressed in the presents of friendship." Mencius replied, "The feeling of respect."

"How is it," pursued Chang, "that the declining a present is accounted disrespectful?" The answer was, "When one of honourable rank presents a gift, to say in the mind, 'Was the way in which he got this righteous or not? I must know this before I can receive it';—this is deemed disrespectful, and therefore presents are not declined."

Chang said, "The princes of the present day take from their people just as a robber despoils his victim. Yet if they put a good face of propriety on their gifts, then the superior man receives them. I venture to ask how you explain this." Mencius answered, "Do you think that, if there should arise a truly imperial sovereign, he would collect the princes of the present day, and put them all to death? Or would he admonish them, and then, on their not changing their ways, put them to death? Indeed, to call every one who takes what does not properly belong to him a robber, is pushing a point of resemblance to the utmost, and insisting on the most refined idea of righteousness. When Confucius was in office in Loo, the people struggled together for the game taken in hunting, and he also did the same. If that struggling for the captured game was proper, how much more may the gifts of the princes be received!"

Mencius said to Wan Chang, "The scholar whose virtue is most distinguished in a village shall make friends of all the virtuous scholars in the village. The scholar whose virtue is most distinguished throughout a state shall make friends of all the virtuous scholars of that state. The scholar whose virtue is most distinguished throughout the empire shall make friends of all the virtuous scholars of the empire.

"When a scholar feels that his friendship with all the virtuous scholars of the empire is not sufficient to satisfy him, he proceeds to ascend to consider the men of antiquity. He repeats their poems, and reads their books, and as he does not know what they were as men, to ascertain this he considers their history. This is to ascend and make friends of the men of antiquity."

Book VI

Man's Nature Is Good

The philosopher Kaou said, "Man's nature is like the willow, and righteousness is like a cup or a bowl. The fashioning benevolence and righteousness out of man's nature is like the making cups and bowls from the willow."

Mencius replied, "Can you, leaving untouched the nature of the willow, make with it cups and bowls? You must do violence and injury to the willow, before you can make cups and bowls with it. If you must do violence and injury to the willow in order to make cups and bowls with it, on your principles you must in the same way do violence and injury to humanity in order to fashion from it benevolence and righteousness! Your words, alas! would certainly lead all men on to reckon benevolence and righteousness to be calamities."

The philosopher Kaou said, "Man's nature is like water whirling round in a corner. Open a passage for it to the east, and it will flow to the east; open a passage for it to the west, and it will flow to the west. Man's nature is indifferent to good and evil, just as the water is indifferent to the east and west."

Mencius replied, "Water indeed will flow indifferently to the east or west, but will it flow indifferently up or down? The tendency of man's nature to good is like the tendency of water to flow downwards. There are none but have this tendency to good, just as all water flows downwards.

"Now by striking water and causing it to leap up, you may make it go over your forehead, and, by damming and leading it, you may force it up a hill;—but are such movements according to the nature of water? It is the force applied which causes them. When men are made to do what is not good, their nature is dealt with in this way."

The disciple Kung-too said, "The philosopher Kaou says 'Man's nature is neither good nor bad.' Some say, 'Man's nature may be made to practise good, and it may be made to practise evil, and accordingly, under Wan and Woo, the people loved what was good, while under Yew and Le, they loved what was cruel.' Some say, 'The nature of some is good, and the nature of others is bad. Hence it was that under such a sovereign as Yaou there yet appeared Seang; that with such a father as Koo-sow there yet appeared Shun; and that with Chow for their sovereign, and the son of their elder brother besides, there were found K'e, the viscount of Wei, and the prince Pe-kan.' And now you say, 'The nature is good.' Then are all those wrong?"

Mencius said, "From the feelings proper to it, it is constituted for the practise of what is good. This is what I mean in saying that the nature is good. If men do what is not good, the blame cannot be imputed to their natural powers. The feeling of commiseration belongs to all men; so does that of shame and dislike; and that of reverence and respect; and that of approving and disapproving. The feeling of commiseration implies the principle of benevolence; that of shame and dislike, the principle of righteousness; that of reverence and respect, the principle of propriety; and that of approving and disapproving, the principle of knowledge. Benevolence, righteousness, propriety, and knowledge are not infused into us from without. We are certainly furnished with them. And a different view is simply from want of reflection. Hence it is said, 'Seek and you will find them. Neglect and you will lose them.' Men differ from one another in regard to them;—some as much again as others, some five times as much, and some to an incalculable amount:—it is because they cannot carry out fully their natural powers."

Mencius said, "In good years the children of the people are most of them good, while in bad years the most of them abandon themselves to evil. It is not owing to their natural powers conferred by heaven that they are thus different. The abandonment is owing to the circumstances through which they allow their minds to be ensnared and drowned in evil.

"There now is barley.—Let it be sown and covered up; the ground being the same, and the time of sowing likewise the same, it grows rapidly up, and when the full time is come, it is all found to be ripe. Although there may be inequalities of produce, that is owing to the difference of the soil, as rich or poor, to the unequal nourishment afforded by the rains and dews, and to the different ways in which man has performed his business in reference to it.

"Thus all things which are the same in kind are like to one another; —why should we doubt in regard to man, as if he were a solitary exception to this? The sage and we are the same in kind."

Mencius said, "The trees of the New mountain were once beautiful. Being situated, however, in the borders of a large state, they were hewn down with axes and bills;—and could they retain their beauty? Still through the activity of the vegetative life day and night, and the nourishing influence of the rain and dew, they were not without buds and sprouts springing forth, but then came the cattle and goats and browsed upon them. To these things is owing the bare and stript appearance of the mountain, which when people see, they think it was never finely wooded. But is this the nature of the mountain?

"And so also of what properly belongs to man;—shall it be said that the mind of any man was without benevolence and righteousness? The way in which a man loses his proper goodness of mind is like the way in which the trees are denuded by axes and bills. Hewn down day after day, can it—the mind—retain its beauty? But there is a development of its life day and night, and in the calm air of the morning, just between night and day, the mind feels in a degree those desires and aversions which are proper to humanity, but the feeling is not strong, and it is fettered and destroyed by what takes place during the day. This fettering taking place again and again, the restorative influence of the night is not sufficient to preserve the proper goodness of the mind; and when this proves insufficient for that purpose, the nature becomes not much different from that of the irrational animals, which when people see, they think that it never had those powers which I assert. But does this condition represent the feelings proper to humanity?"

Mencius said, "It is not to be wondered at that the king is not wise! Suppose the case of the most easily growing thing in the world;—if you let it have one day's genial heat, and then expose it for ten days to cold, it will not be able to grow. It is but seldom that I have an audience of the king, and when I retire, there come all those who act upon him like the cold. Though I succeed in bringing out some buds of goodness, of what avail is it!

"Now chess-playing is but a small art, but without his whole mind being given, and his will bent to it, a man cannot succeed at it. Chess Ts'ew is the best chess-player in all the kingdom. Suppose that he is teaching two men to play.—The one gives to the subject his whole mind and bends to it all his will, doing nothing but listening to Chess Ts'ew. The other, although he seems to be listening to him, has his whole mind running on a swan which he thinks is approaching, and wishes to bend his bow, adjust the string to the arrow, and shoot it. Although he is learning along with the other, he does not come up to him. Why?—because his intelligence is not equal? Not so."

Mencius said, "I like fish and I also like bear's paws. If I cannot have the two together, I will let the fish go, and take the bear's paws. So, I like life, and I also like righteousness. If I cannot keep the two together, I will let life go and choose righteousness.

"I like life indeed, but there is that which I like more than life, and therefore I will not seek to possess it by any improper ways. I dislike death indeed, but there is that which I dislike more than death, and therefore there are occasions when I will not avoid danger.

"If among the things which man likes there were nothing which he liked more than life, why should he not use every means by which he could preserve it? If among the things which man dislikes there were nothing which he disliked more than death, why should he not do everything by which he could avoid danger?

"There are cases when men by a certain course might preserve life, and they do not employ it; when by certain things they might avoid danger, and they will not do them.

"Therefore, men have that which they like more than life, and that which they dislike more than death. They are not men of distinguished talents and virtue only who have this mental nature. All men have it; what belongs to such men is simply that they do not lose it.

"Here are a small basket of rice and a platter of soup, and the case is one in which the getting them will preserve life, and the want of them will be death;—if they are offered with an insulting voice, even a tramper will not receive them, or if you first tread upon them, even a beggar will not stoop to take them.

"And yet a man will accept of ten thousand chung, without any consideration of propriety or righteousness. What can the ten thousand chung add to him? When he takes them, is it not that he may obtain beautiful mansions, that he may secure the services of wives and concubines, or that the poor and needy of his acquaintance may be helped by him?

"In the former case the offered bounty was not received, though it would have saved from death, and now the emolument is taken for the sake of beautiful mansions. The bounty that would have preserved from death was not received, and the emolument is taken to get the service of wives and concubines. The bounty that would have saved from death was not received, and the emolument is taken that one's poor and needy acquaintance may be helped by him. Was it then not possible likewise to decline this? This is a case of what is called—'Losing the proper nature of one's mind.' "

The disciple Kung-too said, "All are equally men, but some are great men, and some are little men;—how is this?" Mencius replied, "Those who follow that part of themselves which is great are great men; those who follow that part which is little are little men."

Kung-too pursued, "All are equally men, but some follow that part of themselves which is great, and some follow that part which is little;—how is this?" Mencius answered, "The senses of hearing and seeing do not think, and are obscured by external things. When one thing comes into contact with another, as a matter of course it leads it away. To the mind belongs the office of thinking. By thinking, it gets the right view of things; by neglecting to think, it fails to do this. These—the senses and the mind—are what heaven has given to us. Let a man first stand fast in the supremacy of the nobler part of his constitution, and the inferior part will not be able to take it from him. It is simply this which makes the great man."

Mencius said, "Benevolence subdues its opposite just as water subdues fire. Those, however, who nowadays practise benevolence do it as if with one cup of water they could save a whole wagon-load of fuel which was on fire, and when the flames were not extinguished, were to say that water cannot subdue fire. This conduct, moreover, greatly encourages those who are not benevolent. The final issue will simply be this—the loss of that small amount of benevolence."

Convention and Emergency

A man of Jin asked the disciple Uh-loo, saying, "Is an observance of the rules of propriety in regard to eating, or the eating, the more important?" The answer was, "The observance of the rules of propriety is the more important."

"Is the gratifying the appetite of sex, or the doing so only according to the rules of propriety, the more important?" The answer again was, "The observance of the rules of propriety in the matter is the more important."

The man pursued, "If the result of eating only according to the rules of propriety will be death by starvation, while by disregarding those rules we may get food, must they still be observed in such a case? If according to the rule that he shall go in person to meet his wife a man cannot get married, while by disregarding that rule he may get married, must he still observe the rule in such a case?"

Uh-loo was unable to reply to these questions, and the next day he went to Tsow, and told them to Mencius. Mencius said, "What difficulty is there in answering these inquiries?

"If you do not adjust them at their lower extremities, but only put their tops on a level, a piece of wood an inch square may be made to be higher than the pointed peak of a high building.

"Gold is heavier than feathers;—but does that saying have reference, on the one hand, to a single clasp of gold, and, on the other, to a wagon-load of feathers?

"If you take a case where the eating is of the utmost importance and the observing the rules of propriety is of little importance, and compare the things together, why stop with saying merely that the eating is more important? So, taking the case where the gratifying the appetite of sex is of the utmost importance and the observing the rules of propriety is of little importance, why stop with merely saying that the gratifying the appetite is the more important?

"Go and answer him thus, 'If, by twisting your elder brother's arm, and snatching from him what he is eating, you can get food for yourself, while, if you do not do so, you will not get anything to eat, will you so twist his arm? If by getting over your neighbour's wall, and dragging away his virgin daughter, you can get a wife, while if you do not do so, you will not be able to get a wife, will you so drag her away?' "

Man His Own Teacher

Keaou said, "I shall be having an interview with the prince of Tsow, and can ask him to let me have a house to lodge in. I wish to remain here, and receive instruction at your gate."

Mencius replied, "The way of truth is like a great road. It is not difficult to know it. The evil is only that men will not seek it. Do you go home and search for it, and you will have abundance of teachers."

The Awakening of Right Motives

Sung K'ang being about to go to Ts'oo, Mencius met him in Shih-k'ew. "Master, where are you going?" asked Mencius.

K'ang replied, "I have heard that Ts'in and Ts'oo are fighting together, and I am going to see the king of Ts'oo and persuade him to cease hostilities. If he shall not be pleased with my advice, I shall go to see the king of Ts'in, and persuade him in the same way. Of the two kings I shall surely find that I can succeed with one of them."

Mencius said, "I will not venture to ask about the particulars, but I should like to hear the scope of your plan. What course will you take to try to persuade them?" K'ang answered, "I will tell them how unprofitable their course is to them." "Master," said Mencius, "your aim is great, but your argument is not good.

"If you, starting from the point of profit, offer your persuasive counsels to the kings of Ts'in and Ts'oo, and if those kings are pleased with the consideration of profit so as to stop the movements of their armies, then all belonging to those armies will rejoice in the cessation of war, and find their pleasure in the pursuit of profit. Ministers will serve their sovereign for the profit of which they cherish the thought; sons will serve their fathers, and younger brothers will serve their elder brothers, from the same consideration:—and the issue will be, that, abandoning benevolence and righteousness, sovereign and minister, father and son, younger brother and elder, will carry on all their intercourse with this thought of profit cherished in their breasts. But never has there been such a state of society, without ruin being the result of it.

"If you, starting from the ground of benevolence and righteousness, offer your counsels to the kings of Ts'in and Ts'oo, and if those kings are pleased with the consideration of benevolence and righteousness so as to stop the operations of their armies, then all belonging to those armies will rejoice in the stopping from war, and find their pleasure in benevolence and righteousness. Ministers will serve their sovereign, cherishing the principles of benevolence and righteousness; sons will serve their fathers, and younger brothers will serve their elder brothers, in the same way:—and so, sovereign and minister, father and son, elder brother and younger, abandoning the thought of profit, will cherish the principles of benevolence and righteousness, and carry on all their intercourse upon them. But never has there been such a state of society, without the state where it prevailed rising to imperial sway. Why must you use that word 'profit'?"

Mencius said, "Those who nowadays serve their sovereigns say, 'We can for our sovereign enlarge the limits of the cultivated ground, and fill his treasuries and arsenals.' Such persons are nowadays called 'Good ministers,' but anciently they were called 'Robbers of the people.' Or they will say, 'We can for our sovereign form alliances with other states, so that our battles must be successful.' Such persons are nowadays called 'Good ministers,' but anciently they were called 'Robbers of the people.'"

The prince of Loo wanting to commit the administration of his government to the disciple Yo-ching, Mencius said, "When I heard of it, I was so glad that I could not sleep."

Kung-sun Ch'ow asked, "Is Yo-ching a man of vigour?" and was answered, "No." "Is he wise in council?" "No." "Is he possessed of much information?" "No."

"What then made you so glad that you could not sleep?"

"He is a man who loves what is good."

"Is the love of what is good sufficient?"

"The love of what is good is more than a sufficient qualification for the government of the empire;—how much more is it so for the state of Loo!"

Book VII

All Things Are Complete in Us

Mencius said, "He who has exhausted all his mental constitution knows his nature. Knowing his nature, he knows heaven. To preserve one's mental constitution, and nourish one's nature, is the way to serve heaven.

"There is an appointment for everything. A man should receive submissively what may be correctly ascribed thereto. Therefore, he who has the true idea of what is heaven's appointment will not stand beneath a precipitous wall. Death sustained in the discharge of one's duties may correctly be ascribed to the appointment of heaven. Death under handcuffs and fetters cannot correctly be so ascribed.

"All things are already complete in us.

"If one acts with a vigorous effort at the law of reciprocity, when he seeks for the realization of perfect virtue, nothing can be closer than his approximation to it.

"To act without understanding, and to do so habitually without examination, pursuing the proper path all the life without knowing its nature;—this is the way of multitudes.

"Kindly words do not enter so deeply into men as a reputation for kindness. Good government does not lay hold of the people so much as good instructions. Good government is feared by the people, while good instructions are loved by them. Good government gets the people's wealth, while good instructions get their hearts."

Mencius said, "When Shun was living amid the deep retired mountains, dwelling with the trees and rocks, and wandering among the deer and swine, the difference between him and the rude inhabitants of those remote hills appeared very small. But when he heard a single good word, or saw a single good action, he was like a stream or a river bursting its banks, and flowing out in an irresistible flood."

Mencius said, "Let a man not do what his own sense of righteousness tells him not to do, and let him not desire what his sense of righteousness tells him not to desire;—to act thus is all he has to do.

"Men who are possessed of intelligent virtue and prudence in affairs will generally be found to have been in sickness and troubles. They are the friendless minister and concubine's son, who keep their hearts under a sense of peril, and use deep precautions against calamity. On this account they become distinguished for their intelligence.

"There are persons who serve the prince;—they serve the prince, that is, for the sake of his countenance and favour. There are ministers who seek the tranquillity of the state, and find their pleasure in securing that tranquillity. There are those who are the people of heaven. They, judging that, if they were in office, they could carry out their principles throughout the empire, proceed so to carry them out. There are those who are great men. They rectify themselves and others are rectified.

"Wide territory and a numerous people are desired by the superior man, but what he delights in is not here.

"To stand in the centre of the empire, and tranquillize the people within the four seas;—the superior man delights in this, but the highest enjoyment of his nature is not here.

"What belongs by his nature to the superior man cannot be increased by the largeness of his sphere of action, nor diminished by his dwelling in poverty and retirement;—for this reason, that it is determinately apportioned to him by heaven.

"What belong by his nature to the superior man are benevolence, righteousness, propriety, and knowledge. These are rooted in his heart; their growth and manifestation are a mild harmony appearing in the countenance, a rich fullness in the back, and the character imparted to the four limbs. Those limbs understand to arrange themselves, without being told."

Mencius said, "The principle of the philosopher Yang was—'Each one for himself.' Though he might have benefited the whole empire by plucking out a single hair, he would not have done it. The philosopher Mih loves all equally. If by rubbing smooth his whole body from the crown to the heel, he could have benefited the empire, he would have done it. Tsze-moh holds a medium between these. By holding that medium, he is nearer the right. But by holding it without leaving room for the exigency of circumstances, it becomes like their holding their one point. The reason why I hate that holding to one point is the injury it does to the way of right principle. It takes up one point and disregards a hundred others.

"The hungry think any food sweet, and the thirsty think the same of any drink, and thus they do not get the right taste of what they eat and drink. The hunger and thirst, in fact, injure their palate. And is it only the mouth and belly which are injured by hunger and thirst? Men's minds are also injured by them. If a man can prevent the evils of hunger and thirst from being any evils to his mind, he need not have any sorrow about not being up with other men.

"To feed a scholar and not love him, is to treat him as a pig. To love him and not respect him, is to keep him as a domestic animal. Honouring and respecting are what exist before any offering of gifts. If there be honouring and respecting without the reality of them, a superior man may not be retained by such empty demonstrations."

Kung-sun Ch'ow said, "Lofty are your principles and admirable, but to learn them may well be likened to ascending the heavens, something which cannot be reached. Why not adapt your teachings so as to cause learners to consider them attainable, and so daily exert themselves?"

Mencius said, "A great artificer does not, for the sake of a stupid workman, alter or do away with the marking line. E did not, for the sake of a stupid archer, change his rule for drawing the bow.

"The superior man draws the bow, but does not discharge the arrow. The whole thing seems to leap before the learner. Such is his standing exactly in the middle of the right path. Those who are able, follow him."

Mencius said, "There are men who say—'I am skilful at marshalling troops, I am skilful at conducting a battle!'—They are great criminals. If the sovereign of a state love benevolence, he will have no enemy in the empire.

"A carpenter or a carriage-maker may give a man the circle and square, but cannot make him skilful in the use of them.

"Anciently, the establishment of the frontier-gates was to guard against violence. Nowadays, it is to exercise violence.

"If men of virtue and ability be not confided in, a state will become empty and void. Without the rules of propriety and distinctions of right, the high and the low will be thrown into confusion. Without the great principles of government and their various business, there will not be wealth sufficient for the expenditure.

"Anciently, men of virtue and talents by means of their own enlightenment made others enlightened. Nowadays, it is tried, while they are themselves in darkness, and by means of that darkness, to make others enlightened.

"There are the foot-paths along the hills;—if suddenly they be used, they become roads; and if as suddenly they are not used, the wild grass fills them up. Now, the wild grass fills up your mind.

"Words which are simple, while their meaning is far-reaching, are good words. Principles which, as held, are compendious, while their application is extensive, are good principles. The words of the superior man do not go below the girdle, but great principles are contained in them. The principle which the superior man holds is that of personal cultivation, but the empire is thereby tranquillized. The disease of men is this:—that they neglect their own fields, and go to weed the fields of others, and that what they require from others is great, while what they lay upon themselves is light.

"Those who give counsel to the great should despise them, and not look at their pomp and display. Halls several times eight cubits high, with beams projecting several cubits;—these, if my wishes were to be realized, I would not have. Food spread before me over ten cubits square, and attendant girls to the amount of hundreds;—these, though my wishes were realized, I would not have. Pleasure and wine, and the dash of hunting, with thousands of chariots following after me;—these, though my wishes were realized, I would not have. What they esteem are what I would have nothing to do with; what I esteem are the rules of the ancients. Why should I stand in awe of them?"

Mencius said, "From Yaou and Shun down to T'ang were 500 years and more. As to Yu and Kaou-yaou, they saw those earliest sages, and so knew their doctrines, while T'ang heard their doctrines as transmitted, and so knew them.

"From T'ang to king Wan were 500 years and more. As to E Yin, and Lae Choo, they saw T'ang and knew his doctrines, while king Wan heard them as transmitted, and so knew them.

"From king Wan to Confucius were 500 years and more. As to T'ae-kung Wang and San E-sang, they saw Wan, and so knew his doctrines, while Confucius heard them as transmitted, and so knew them.

"From Confucius downwards until now, there are only 100 years and somewhat more. The distance in time from the sage is so far from being remote, and so very near at hand was the sage's residence. In these circumstances, is there no one to transmit his doctrines? Yea, is there no one to do so?"

The Book of Filial Piety
(THE HSIAO KING)

The Meaning of Filial Duty

Once upon a time Confucius was sitting in his study, having his disciple Tseng Ts'an to attend upon him. He asked Tseng Ts'an: "Do you know by what virtue and power the good emperors of old made the world peaceful, the people to live in harmony with one another, and the inferior contented under the control of their superiors?" To this Tseng Ts'an, rising from his seat, replied: "I do not know this, for I am not clever." Then said Confucius: "The duty of children to their parents is the fountain whence all other virtues spring, and also the starting-point from which we ought to begin our education. Now take your seat, and I will explain this. Our body and hair and skin are all derived from our parents, and therefore we have no right to injure any of them in the least. This is the first duty of a child.

"To live an upright life and to spread the great doctrines of humanity must win good reputation after death, and reflect great honour upon our parents. This is the last duty of a son.

"Hence the first duty of a son is to pay a careful attention to every want of his parents. The next is to serve his government loyally; and the last to establish a good name for himself.

"So it is written in the Ta Ya: 'You must think of your ancestors and continue to cultivate the virtue which you inherit from them.' "

The Filial Duty of Common People

To do the necessary in every season (such as growing crops in spring and reaping harvest in autumn), to do the utmost to make lands as fertile as possible, and to be frugal in their expense, in order to keep their parents in comfort, is the filial duty of the common people.

From the emperor downwards to the common people, every one has the same duty imposed upon him, and there is no instance in which we can find that a man cannot fulfil this duty.

The Three Powers

On hearing what Confucius said about filial duty, Tseng Tze remarked: "How great is the use of filial duty!" Here Confucius continued: "Filial duty is the constant doctrine of heaven, the natural righteousness of earth, and the practical duty of man. Every member of the community ought to observe it with the greatest care. We do what is dictated by heaven and what is good for the general public in order to organize the community. On this account our education is widespread, though it is not compulsory, and our government is sound, though it is not rigorous. The effect of education upon the minds of the people was well known to the good emperors of old. They made every person love his parents by loving their own parents first. They induced every person to cultivate his virtue by expounding the advantages of virtue to him. They behaved themselves respectfully and humbly, so that the people might not quarrel with one another. They trained the people with ceremonial observances, and educated them with music so that they might live in harmony. They told the people what things they liked or disliked to see done, so that they might understand what they were forbidden to do."

In the Shih King it is thus written: "The dignified statesman is always the subject of the attention of the people."

Filial Duty in Government

The good emperors of old ruled the Empire by means of filial duty, and dared not neglect the ministers of their vassal states. How much less the dukes, marquises, earls, viscounts, and barons! They thereby gained the goodwill of all their vassal states, which sent their deputies to represent them in any sacrifice offered to the ancestors of their Supreme Master. This is what we mean by saying that the good emperors of old governed the world by filial duty.

As to the vassal states, their rulers dared not treat widowers and widows with insolence; how then could they dare act so towards the literary class and the people? Hence they gained the goodwill of their subjects, and the latter would join them in offering sacrifices to their ancestors.

Now we may say a word about a family. If the head of a family do not act haughtily towards his servant, he cannot act so to his wife and children. Hence he will gain the goodwill of all his people, and they will help him in the fulfilment of his filial duty. In such a family the parents must feel happy when they are living, and their spirits must come to enjoy the sacrifice when they are dead. By the principle of filial duty the whole world can be made happy and all calamities and dangers can be averted. Such was the government of the Empire by the enlightened rulers of old, in accordance with the principle of filial duty.

In the Shih King it is thus written: "If you adorn yourself with the highest virtue, the whole world will follow you."

The Question of Remonstrance

Tseng Tze said: "I have heard all that you said about parental love, filial love, reverence to elders, how to treat parents every day, and how to please them by making oneself known for good conduct; and now I will venture to ask you whether it is filial that a son should obey every command of his father, whether right or wrong?"

"What do you say?—what do you say?" replied Confucius. "Once upon a time there was a certain emperor who would have lost his empire through his wickedness but that he had seven good ministers who often checked his illegal actions by strong protests; there was also a feudal baron who would have lost his feudal estate through wantonness, but for the fact that he had five good men who often made strong remonstrances to him; and there was also a statesman who would have brought frightful calamity upon his family, but for the fact that he had three good servants who often strongly advised him not to do what he ought not.

"If a man has a good friend to resist him in doing bad actions, he will have his reputation preserved; so if a father has a son to resist his wrong commands, he will be saved from committing serious faults.

"When the command is wrong, a son should resist his father, and a minister should resist his august master.

"The maxim is, 'Resist when wrongly commanded.' Hence how can he be called filial who obeys his father when he is commanded to do wrong?"

The Obliging Lao Lai Tze

In the country of Ch'u lived Lao Lai Tze, who, when so old that he had lost nearly all his teeth, made every effort to rejoice and comfort his parents, constantly endeavouring to gladden their hearts. At times he imitated the playfulness of a little child, and arraying himself in gaudy and variegated clothes, amused them by his strutting and gambols. He would likewise purposely fall on the ground, kicking and wailing to the utmost of his power. His mother was delighted, and manifested her joy in her countenance. Thus did Lai forget his age in order to rejoice the hearts of his parents; and affection, harmony, and joy prevailed among the family. If this ardent love for his parents had been insincere and constrained, how could it be referred to as worthy of imitation?

With Deer's Milk He Supplied His Parents

In the time of the Chou dynasty lived Yen, who possessed a very filial disposition. His father and mother were aged, and both were afflicted with sore eyes, to cure which they desired to have some deer's milk. Yen concealed himself in the skin of a deer, and went deep into the forests, among the herds of deer, to obtain some of their milk for his parents. While amongst the trees the hunters saw him, and were about to shoot at him with their arrows, when Yen disclosed to them his true character and related the history of his family, with the reasons for his conduct.

The Miracle of the Bamboo Shoots

Meng Tsung, who lived in the Chin Dynasty, lost his father when young. His mother was very ill, and one winter's day she longed to taste a soup made of bamboo shoots, but Meng could not procure any. At last he went into the bamboo grove, and, clasping the bamboos with his hands, wept bitterly. His filial love moved nature, and the ground slowly opened, sending forth several shoots, which he gathered and carried home. He made a soup of them, which his mother tasted, and immediately recovered from her malady.

Taoist
Scriptures

TAOIST SCRIPTURES

The Tao-Te-King

I

The Tao that can be expressed is not the eternal Tao;
The name that can be defined is not the unchanging name.
Non-existence is called the antecedent of heaven and earth;
Existence is the mother of all things.
From eternal non-existence, therefore, we serenely observe the mysterious beginning of the universe;
From eternal existence we clearly see the apparent distinctions.
These two are the same in source and become different when manifested.
This sameness is called profundity. Infinite profundity is the gate whence comes the beginning of all parts of the universe.

II

When all in the world understand beauty to be beautiful, then ugliness exists.
When all understand goodness to be good, then evil exists.
Thus existence suggests non-existence;
Easy gives rise to difficult;
Short is derived from long by comparison;
Low is distinguished from high by position;
Resonance harmonizes sound;
After follows before.
Therefore, the sage carries on his business without action, and gives his teaching without words.

III

Not exalting the worthy keeps the people from emulation. Not valuing
rare things keeps them from theft. Not showing what is desirable keeps
their hearts from confusion. Therefore the sage rules

By emptying their hearts,
Filling their stomachs,
Weakening their ambitions
And strengthening their bones.

He always keeps them from knowing what is evil and desiring what is
good; thus he gives the crafty ones no chance to act. He governs by
non-action; consequently there is nothing un-governed.

IV

Tao, when put in use for its hollowness, is not likely to be filled.
In its profundity it seems to be the origin of all things.
In its depth it seems ever to remain.
I do not know whose offspring it is;
But it looks like the predecessor of nature.

V

Heaven and earth do not own their benevolence;
To them all things are straw-dogs.
The sage does not own his benevolence;
To him the people are straw-dogs.

The space between heaven and earth is like a blacksmith's bellows.
Hollow as it seems, nothing is lacking.
If it is moved, more will it bring forth.

He who talks more is sooner exhausted.
It is better to keep what is within himself.

VI

"The Valley and the Spirit never die."
They form what is called the Mystic Mother,
From whose gate comes the origin of heaven and earth.
This (the origin) seems ever to endure.
In use it can never be exhausted.

VII

Heaven is lasting and earth enduring.
The reason why they are lasting and enduring is that they do not live
        for themselves;
Therefore they live long.
In the same way the sage keeps himself behind and he is in the front;
He forgets himself and he is preserved.
Is it not because he is not self-interested
That his self-interest is established?

VIII

The highest goodness is like water. Water is beneficent to all things but
does not contend. It stays in places which others despise. Therefore it is
near Tao.

In dwelling, think it a good place to live;
In feeling, make the heart deep;
In friendship, keep on good terms with men;
In words, have confidence;
In ruling, abide by good order;
In business, take things easy;
In motion, make use of the opportunity.
Since there is no contention, there is no blame.

IX

Holding and keeping a thing to the very full—it is better to leave it
    alone;
Handling and sharpening a blade—it cannot be long sustained;
When gold and jade fill the hall, no one can protect them;
Wealth and honour with pride bring with them destruction:
To have accomplished merit and acquired fame, then retire—
This is the Tao of heaven.

X

Can you keep the soul always concentrated from straying?
Can you regulate the breath and become soft and pliant like an infant?
Can you clear and get rid of the unforeseen and be free from fault?
Can you love the people and govern the state by non-action?
Can you open and shut the gates of nature like a female?
Can you become enlightened and penetrate everywhere without knowl-
    edge?

XI

Thirty spokes unite in one nave,
And because of the part where nothing exists we have the use of a
    carriage wheel.
Clay is moulded into vessels,
And because of the space where nothing exists we are able to use them
    as vessels.
Doors and windows are cut out in the walls of a house,
And because they are empty spaces, we are able to use them.
Therefore, on the one hand we have the benefit of existence, and on the
    other, we make use of non-existence.

XII

The five colours will blind a man's sight.
The five sounds will deaden a man's hearing.
The five tastes will spoil a man's palate.
Chasing and hunting will drive a man wild.
Things hard to get will do harm to a man's conduct.
Therefore the sage makes provision for the stomach and not for the eye.
He rejects the latter and chooses the former.

XIII

"Favour and disgrace are like fear; fortune and disaster are like our body."

What does it mean by "Favour and disgrace are like fear"? Favour is in a higher place, and disgrace in a lower place. When you win them you are like being in fear, and when you lose them you are also like being in fear. So favour and disgrace are like fear.

What does it mean by "Fortune and disaster are like our body"? We have fortune and disaster because we have a body. When we have no body, how can fortune or disaster befall us?

Therefore he who regards the world as he does the fortune of his own body can govern the world. He who loves the world as he does his own body can be entrusted with the world.

XIV

That which we look at and cannot see is called plainness.
That which we listen to and cannot hear is called rareness.
That which we grope for and cannot get is called minuteness.

These three cannot be closely examined;
So they blend into One.
Revealed, it is not dazzling;
Hidden, it is not dark.
Infinite, it cannot be defined.
It goes back to non-existence.
It is called the form of the formless,
And the image of non-existence.
It is called mystery.
Meet it, you cannot see its face;
Follow it, you cannot see its back.

By adhering to the Tao of the past
You will master the existence of the present
And be able to know the origin of the past.
This is called the clue of Tao.

XV

In old times the perfect man of Tao was subtle, penetrating and so profound that he can hardly be understood. Because he cannot be understood, I shall endeavour to picture him:

He is cautious, like one who crosses a stream in winter;
He is hesitating, like one who fears his neighbours;
He is modest, like one who is a guest;
He is yielding, like ice that is going to melt;
He is simple, like wood that is not yet wrought;
He is vacant, like valleys that are hollow;
He is dim, like water that is turbid.

For who is able to purify the dark till it becomes slowly light?
Who is able to calm the turbid till it slowly clears?
Who is able to quicken the stagnant till it slowly makes progress?
He who follows these principles does not desire fullness.
Because he is not full, therefore when he becomes decayed he can renew.

XVI

Attain to the goal of absolute vacuity;
Keep to the state of perfect peace.
All things come into existence,
And thence we see them return.
Look at the things that have been flourishing;
Each goes back to its origin.
Going back to the origin is called peace;
It means reversion to destiny.
Reversion to destiny is called eternity.
He who knows eternity is called enlightened.
He who does not know eternity is running blindly into miseries.
Knowing eternity he is all-embracing.
Being all-embracing he can attain magnanimity.
Being magnanimous he can attain omnipresence.
Being omnipresent he can attain supremacy.
Being supreme he can attain Tao.
He who attains Tao is everlasting.
Though his body may decay he never perishes.

XVII

The great rulers—the people do not notice their existence;
The lesser ones—they attach to and praise them;
The still lesser ones—they fear them;
The still lesser ones—they despise them.
For where faith is lacking,
It cannot be met by faith.
Now how much importance must be attributed to words!

XVIII

When the great Tao is lost, spring forth benevolence and righteousness.
When wisdom and sagacity arise, there are great hypocrites.

When family relations are no longer harmonious, we have filial children
and devoted parents.
When a nation is in confusion and disorder, patriots are recognized.
Where Tao is, equilibrium is. When Tao is lost, out come all the differences of things.

XIX

Do away with learning, and grief will not be known.
Do away with sageness and eject wisdom, and the people will be more
benefited a hundred times.
Do away with benevolence and eject righteousness, and the people will
return to filial duty and parental love.
Do away with artifice and eject gains, and there will be no robbers and
thieves.
These four, if we consider them as culture, are not sufficient.
Therefore let there be what the people can resort to:
Appear in plainness and hold to simplicity;
Restrain selfishness and curtail desires.

XX

Between yea and nay, how much difference is there?
Between good and evil, how much difference is there?
What are feared by others we must fear;
Vastly are they unlimited!
The people in general are so happy as if enjoying a great feast,
Or, as going up a tower in spring.
I alone am tranquil, and have made no signs,
Like a baby who is yet unable to smile;
Forlorn as if I had no home to go to.
Others all have more than enough,
And I alone seem to be in want.
Possibly mine is the mind of a fool,
Which is so ignorant!
The vulgar are bright,

And I alone seem to be dull.
The vulgar are discriminative, and I alone seem to be blunt.

I am negligent as if being obscure;
Drifting, as if being attached to nothing.
The people in general all have something to do,
And I alone seem to be impractical and awkward.
I alone am different from others.
But I value seeking sustenance from the Mother.

XXI

The great virtue as manifested is but following Tao.
Tao is a thing that is both invisible and intangible.
Intangible and invisible, yet there are forms in it;
Invisible and intangible, yet there is substance in it;
Subtle and obscure, there is essence in it;
This essence being invariably true, there is faith in it.
From of old till now, it has never lost its (nameless) name,
Through which the origin of all things has passed.
How do I know that it is so with the origin of all things?
By this (Tao).

XXII

"Be humble, and you will remain entire."
Be bent, and you will remain straight.
Be vacant, and you will remain full.
Be worn, and you will remain new.
He who has little will receive.
He who has much will be embarrassed.
Therefore the sage keeps to One and becomes the standard for the world.
He does not display himself; therefore he shines.
He does not approve himself; therefore he is noted.

He does not praise himself; therefore he has merit.
He does not glory in himself; therefore he excels.
And because he does not compete; therefore no one in the world can
      compete with him.
The ancient saying "Be humble, and you will remain entire"—
Can this be regarded as mere empty words?
Indeed he shall return home entire.

XXIII

To be sparing of words is natural.

A violent wind cannot last a whole morning; pelting rain cannot last
a whole day. Who have made these things but heaven and earth? Inasmuch as heaven and earth cannot last for ever, how can man? He who
engages himself in Tao is identified with Tao. He who engages himself
in virtue is identified with virtue. He who engages himself in abandonment is identified with abandonment. Identified with Tao he will be
well received by Tao. Identified with virtue he will be well received by
virtue. Identified with abandonment he will be well received by abandonment.

XXIV

A man on tiptoe cannot stand firm;
A man astride cannot walk on;
A man who displays himself cannot shine;
A man who approves himself cannot be noted;
A man who praises himself cannot have merit;
A man who glories in himself cannot excel:
These, when compared with Tao, are called:
      "Excess in food and overdoing in action."
Even in other things, mostly, they are rejected;
Therefore the man of Tao does not stay with them.

XXV

There is a thing inherent and natural,
Which existed before heaven and earth.
Motionless and fathomless,
It stands alone and never changes;
It pervades everywhere and never becomes exhausted.
It may be regarded as the Mother of the Universe.
I do not know its name.
If I am forced to give it a name,
I call it Tao, and I name it as supreme.
Supreme means going on;
Going on means going far;
Going far means returning.
Therefore Tao is supreme; heaven is supreme; earth is supreme; and
      man is also supreme. There are in the universe four things
      supreme, and man is one of them.
Man follows the laws of earth;
Earth follows the laws of heaven;
Heaven follows the laws of Tao;
Tao follows the laws of its intrinsic nature.

XXVI

Heaviness is the basis of lightness;
Calmness is the controlling-power of hastiness.
Therefore the sage, though travelling all day long,
Never separates from his baggage-wagon;
Though surrounded with magnificent sights,
He lives in tranquillity.
How is it, then, that a king of ten thousand chariots
Should conduct himself so lightly in the empire?
To be light is to lose the basis;
To be hasty is to lose the controlling power.

XXVII

A good traveller leaves no track;
A good speaker leaves no error;
A good reckoner needs no counter;
A good closer needs no bars or bolts,
And yet it is impossible to open after him.
A good fastener needs no cords or knots,
And yet it is impossible to untie after him.
Even if men be bad, why should they be rejected?
Therefore the sage is always a good saviour of men,
And no man is rejected;
He is a good saviour of things,
And nothing is rejected:
This is called double enlightenment.
Therefore good men are bad men's instructors,
And bad men are good men's materials.
Those who do not esteem their instructors,
And those who do not love their materials,
Though expedient, are in fact greatly confused.
This is essential subtlety.

XXVIII

He who knows the masculine and yet keeps to the feminine
Will become a channel drawing all the world towards it;
Being a channel of the world, he will not be severed from the eternal
        virtue,
And then he can return again to the state of infancy.
He who knows the white and yet keeps to the black
Will become the standard of the world;
Being the standard of the world, with him eternal virtue will never
        falter,
And then he can return again to the absolute.
He who knows honour and yet keeps to humility

Will become a valley that receives all the world into it;
Being a valley of the world, with him eternal virtue will be complete,
And then he can return again to wholeness.
Wholeness, when divided, will make vessels of utility;
These when employed by the sage will become officials and chiefs.
However, for a great function no discrimination is needed.

XXIX

When a man is to take the world over and shape it,
I see that he must be obliged to do it.
For the world is a divine vessel:
It cannot be shaped;
Nor can it be insisted upon.
He who shapes it damages it;
He who insists upon it loses it.
Therefore the sage does not shape it, so he does not damage it;
He does not insist upon it, so he does not lose it.
For, among all things, some go ahead, while others lag behind;
Some keep their mouths shut, while others give forth puffs;
Some are strong, while others are weak;
Some are on the cart, while others fall off.
Therefore the sage avoids excess, extravagance and indulgence.

XXX

He who assists a ruler of men with Tao does not force the world with
    arms.
He aims only at carrying out relief, and does not venture to force his
    power upon others.
When relief is done, he will not be assuming,
He will not be boastful; he will not be proud;
And he will think that he was obliged to do it.
So it comes that relief is done without resorting to force.
When things come to the summit of their vigour, they begin to grow old.

This is against Tao.
What is against Tao will soon come to an end.

XXXI

So far as arms are concerned, they are implements of ill-omen. They are not implements for the man of Tao. For the actions of arms will be well requited: where armies have been quartered brambles and thorns grow. Great wars are for certain followed by years of scarcity. The man of Tao when dwelling at home makes the left as the place of honour, and when using arms makes the right as the place of honour. He uses them only when he cannot avoid it. In his conquests he takes no delight. If he took delight in them, it would mean that he enjoys the slaughter of men. He who takes delight in the slaughter of men cannot have his will done in the world.

XXXII

Tao was always nameless.
When for the first time applied to function, it was named.
Inasmuch as names are given, one should also know where to stop.
Knowing where to stop one can become imperishable.

XXXIII

He who knows others is wise;
He who knows himself is enlightened.
He who conquers others is strong;
He who conquers himself is mighty.
He who knows contentment is rich.
He who keeps on his course with energy has will.
He who does not deviate from his proper place will long endure.
He who may die but not perish has longevity.

XXXIV

The great Tao pervades everywhere, both on the left and on the right.
By it all things came into being, and it does not reject them.
Merits accomplished, it does not possess them.
It loves and nourishes all things but does not dominate over them.
It is always non-existent; therefore it can be named as small.
All things return home to it, and it does not claim mastery over them;
      therefore it can be named as great.
Because it never assumes greatness, therefore it can accomplish greatness.

XXXV

To him who holds to the Great Form all the world will go.
It will go and see no danger, but tranquillity, equality and community.
Music and dainties will make the passing stranger stop.
But Tao when uttered in words is so pure and void of flavour.
When one looks at it, one cannot see it;
When one listens to it, one cannot hear it.
However, when one uses it, it is inexhaustible.

XXXVI

In order to contract a thing, one should surely expand it first.
In order to weaken, one will surely strengthen first.
In order to overthrow, one will surely exalt first.
"In order to take, one will surely give first."
This is called subtle wisdom.
The soft and weak can overcome the hard and strong.
As the fish should not leave the deep
So should the sharp implements of a nation not be shown to any one.

XXXVII

Tao is ever inactive, and yet there is nothing that it does not do.
If princes and kings could keep to it, all things would of themselves
        become developed.
When they are developed, desire would stir in them;
I would restrain them by the nameless Simplicity,
In order to make them free from desire.
Free from desire, they would be at rest;
And the world would of itself become rectified.
However insignificant Simplicity seems, the whole world cannot make
        it submissive.
If princes and kings could keep to it,
All things in the world would of themselves pay homage.
Heaven and earth would unite to send down sweet dew.
The people with no one to command them would of themselves become
        harmonious.
When merits were accomplished and affairs completed,
The people would speak of themselves as following nature.

XXXVIII

The superior virtue is not conscious of itself as virtue;
Therefore it has virtue.
The inferior virtue never lets off virtue;
Therefore it has no virtue.
The superior virtue seems inactive, and yet there is nothing that it does
        not do.
The inferior virtue acts, and yet in the end leaves things undone.
The superior benevolence acts without a motive.
The superior righteousness acts with a motive.
The superior ritual acts, but at first no one responds to it;
Gradually people raise their arms and follow it.
Therefore when Tao is lost, virtue follows.

When virtue is lost, benevolence follows,

When benevolence is lost, righteousness follows.

When righteousness is lost, ritual follows.

Ritual, therefore, is the attenuation of loyalty and faith and the outset
of confusion.

Fore-knowledge is the flower of Tao and the beginning of folly.

Therefore the truly great man keeps to the solid and not to the tenuous;

Keeps to the fruit and not to the flower.

Thus he rejects the latter and takes the former.

XXXIX

From of old the things that have acquired unity are these:

Heaven by unity has become clear;

Earth by unity has become steady;

The Spirit by unity has become spiritual;

The Valley by unity has become full;

All things by unity have come into existence;

Princes and kings by unity have become rulers of the world.

If heaven were not clear, it would be rent;

If earth were not steady, it would be tumbled down;

If the Spirit were not active, it would pass away;

If the Valley were not full, it would be dried up;

If all things were not existing, they would be extinct;

If princes and kings were not rulers, they would be overthrown.

The noble must be styled in the terms of the humble;

The high must take the low as their foundation.

Therefore princes and kings call themselves "the ignorant," "the virtueless" and "the unworthy."

Does this not mean that they take the humble as their root?

What men hate most are "the ignorant," "the virtueless" and "the unworthy."

And yet princes and kings choose them as their titles.

Therefore the highest fame is to have no fame.

Thus kings are increased by being diminished;

They are diminished by being increased.

It is undesirable to be as prominent as a single gem,
Or as monotonously numerous as stones.

XL

Returning is the motion of Tao,
Weakness is the appliance of Tao.
All things in the universe come from existence,
And existence from non-existence.

XLI

When the superior scholar is told of Tao,
He works hard to practise it.
When the middling scholar is told of Tao,
It seems that sometimes he keeps it and sometimes he loses it.
When the inferior scholar is told of Tao,
He laughs aloud at it.
If it were not laughed at, it would not be sufficient to be Tao.
Therefore the proverb says:
"Tao in enlightenment seems obscure;
Tao in progress seems regressive;
Tao in its straightness seems rugged.
The highest virtue seems like a valley;
The purest white seems discoloured;
The most magnificent virtue seems insufficient;
The solidest virtue seems frail;
The simplest nature seems changeable;
The greatest square has no angles;
The largest vessel is never complete;
The loudest sound can scarcely be heard;
The biggest form cannot be visualized.
Tao, while hidden, is nameless."
Yet it is Tao alone that is good at imparting and completing.

XLII

Tao begets One; one begets two; two begets three; three begets all things. All things are backed by the Shade (yin) and faced by the Light (yang), and harmonized by the immaterial Breath (ch'i).

What others teach, I also teach: "The daring and violent do not die a natural death." This (maxim) I shall regard as my instructor.

XLIII

The non-existent can enter into the impenetrable.
By this I know that non-action is useful.
Teaching without words, utility without action—
Few in the world have come to this.

XLIV

Fame or your person, which is nearer to you?
Your person or wealth, which is dearer to you?
Gain or loss, which brings more evil to you?
Over-love of anything will lead to wasteful spending;
Amassed riches will be followed by heavy plundering.
Therefore, he who knows contentment can never be humiliated:
He who knows where to stop can never be perishable;
He will long endure.

XLV

The greatest perfection seems imperfect;
Yet its use will last without decay.
The greatest fullness seems empty;
Yet its use cannot be exhausted.
The greatest straightness seems crooked;

The greatest dexterity seems awkward;
The greatest eloquence seems stammering.
Activity overcomes cold;
Quietness overcomes heat.
Only through purity and quietude can the world be ruled.

XLVI

When Tao reigns in the world
Swift horses are curbed for hauling the dung-carts in the field.
When Tao does not reign in the world,
War horses are bred on the commons outside the cities.
There is no greater crime than seeking what men desire;
There is no greater misery than knowing no content;
There is no greater calamity than indulging in greed.
Therefore the contentment of knowing content will ever be contented.

XLVII

Without going out of the door
One can know the whole world;
Without peeping out of the window
One can see the Tao of heaven.
The further one travels
The less one knows.
Therefore the sage knows everything without travelling;
He names everything without seeing it;
He accomplishes everything without doing it.

XLVIII

He who pursues learning will increase every day;
He who pursues Tao will decrease every day.

He will decrease and continue to decrease,
Till he comes at non-action;
By non-action everything can be done.

XLIX

The sage has no self to call his own;
He makes the self of the people his self.
To the good I act with goodness;
To the bad I also act with goodness:
Thus goodness is attained.
To the faithful I act with faith;
To the faithless I also act with faith:
Thus faith is attained.
The sage lives in the world in concord, and rules over the world in
     simplicity.
Yet what all the people turn their ears and eyes to,
The sage looks after as a mother does her children.

L

Men go out of life and enter into death.

The parts (proportions) of life are three in ten; the parts of death are
also three in ten. Men that from birth move towards the region of death
are also three in ten. Why is it so? Because of their redundant effort in
seeking to live. But only those who do nothing for the purpose of living
are better than those who prize their lives. For I have heard that he who
knows well how to conserve life, when travelling on land does not meet
the rhinoceros or the tiger; when going to a battle he is not attacked by
arms and weapons. The rhinoceros can find nowhere to drive his horn;
the tiger can find nowhere to put his claws; the weapons can find nowhere
to thrust their blades. Why is it so? Because he is beyond the region
of death.

LI

Tao produces them (all things);
Virtue feeds them;
All of them appear in different forms;
Each is perfected by being given power.
Therefore none of the numerous things does not honour Tao and esteem
       virtue.
The honouring of Tao and the esteem of virtue are done, not by com-
       mand, but always of their own accord.
Therefore Tao produces them, makes them grow, nourishes them, shel-
       ters them, brings them up and protects them.
When all things come into being Tao does not reject them.
It produces them without holding possession of them.
It acts without depending upon them, and raises without lording it over
       them.
When merits are accomplished it does not lay claim to them.
Because it does not lay claim to them, therefore it does not lose them.

LII

The beginning of the universe, when manifested, may be regarded as
       its Mother.
When a man has found the Mother, he will know the children accord-
       ingly;
Though he has known the children, he still keeps to the Mother:
Thus, however his body may decay, he will never perish.
If he shuts his mouth and closes his doors,
He can never be exhausted.
If he opens his mouth and increases his affairs,
He can never be saved.
To see the minuteness of things is called clarity of sight;
To keep to what is weak is called power.
Use your light, but dim your brightness;

Thus you will cause no harm to yourself.
This is called following the eternal (Tao).

LIII

Let me have sound knowledge and walk on the great way (Tao);
Only I am in fear of deviating.
The great way is very plain and easy,
But the people prefer by-paths.
While the royal palaces are very well kept,
The fields are left weedy
And the granaries empty.
To wear embroidered clothes,
To carry sharp swords,
To be satiated in drink and food,
To be possessed of redundant riches—
This is called encouragement to robbery.
Is it not deviating from Tao?

LIV

What is planted by the best planter can never be removed;
What is embraced by the best embracer can never be loosened.
Thus his children and grandchildren will be able to continue their ances-
      tral sacrifice for endless generations.
If he applies Tao to himself his virtue will be genuine;
If he applies it to his family his virtue will be abundant;
If he applies it to his village his virtue will be lasting;
If he applies it to his country his virtue will be full;
If he applies it to the world his virtue will be universal.
Therefore by one's person one may observe persons;
By one's family one may observe families;
By one's village one may observe villages;
By one's country one may observe countries;
By one's world one may observe worlds.

How do I know that the world may be so governed by Tao?
By this observation.

LV

He who is endowed with ample virtue may be compared to an infant.
No venomous insects sting him;
Nor fierce beasts seize him;
Nor birds of prey strike him.
His bones are frail, his sinews tender, but his grasp is strong.
He does not know the conjugation of male and female, and yet he has
      sexual development;
It means he is in the best vitality.
He may cry all day long without growing hoarse.
It means that he is in the perfect harmony.
To know this harmony is to approach eternity;
To know eternity is to attain enlightenment.
To increase life is to lead to calamity;
To let the heart exert the breath is to become stark.

LVI

Blunt all that is sharp;
Cut all that is divisible;
Blur all that is brilliant;
Mix with all that is humble as dust;
This is called absolute equality.
Therefore it cannot be made intimate;
Nor can it be alienated.
It cannot be benefited;
Nor can it be harmed.
It cannot be exalted;
Nor can it be debased.
Therefore it is the most valuable thing in the world.

LVII

Albeit one governs the country by rectitude,
And carries on wars by stratagems,
Yet one must rule the empire by meddling with no business.
The empire can always be ruled by meddling with no business.
Otherwise, it can never be done.
How do I know it is so?
By this:
The more restrictions and avoidances are in the empire,
The poorer become the people;
The more sharp implements the people keep,
The more confusions are in the country;
The more arts and crafts men have,
The more are fantastic things produced;
The more laws and regulations are given,
The more robbers and thieves there are.
Therefore the sage says:
Inasmuch as I betake myself to non-action, the people of themselves become developed.
Inasmuch as I love quietude, the people of themselves become righteous.
Inasmuch as I make no fuss, the people of themselves become wealthy.
Inasmuch as I am free from desire, the people of themselves remain simple.

LVIII

When the government is blunt and inactive the people will be happy and prosperous;
When the government is discriminative, the people will be dissatisfied and restless.
It is upon misery that happiness rests;
It is under happiness that misery lies.
Who then can know the supremacy (good government)?
Only when the government does no rectifying.

Otherwise, rectitude will again become stratagem,
And good become evil.
Men have been ignorant of this, since long ago.
Therefore the sage is square but does not cut others;
He is angled but does not chip others;
He is straight but does not stretch others;
He is bright but does not dazzle others.

LIX

In ruling men and in serving heaven, the sage uses only moderation.
By moderation alone he is able to have conformed early to Tao.
This early conformity is called intensive accumulation of virtue.
With this intensive accumulation of virtue, there is nothing that he
     cannot overcome.
Because there is nothing that he cannot overcome, no one will be able to
     know his supremacy.
Because no one knows his supremacy he can take possession of a country.
Because what he does is identified with the Mother in taking possession
     of a country, he can long endure.
This means that he is deep rooted and firmly based, and knows the way
     of longevity and immortality.

LX

Govern a great state as you would cook a small fish (do it gently).
Let Tao reign over the world, and no spirits will show their ghostly
     powers.
Not that the spirits have no more powers,
But their powers will not harm men.
Neither will they harm men,
Nor will the sage harm the people.
Inasmuch as none of them harms anybody,
Therefore virtue belongs to them both.

LXI

A great state is the world's low-stream to which all the river flows down, the world's field and the world's female. The female always conquers the male by quietude, which is employed as a means to lower oneself. Thus a great state lowers itself towards a small state before it takes over the small state. A small state lowers itself towards a great state before it takes over the great state. Therefore some lower themselves to take, while others lower themselves to gather. A great state wishes nothing more than to have and keep many people, and a small state wishes nothing more than to get more things to do. When the two both mean to obtain their wishes, the greater one should lower itself.

LXII

Tao is the source of all things, the treasure of good men, and the sustainer of bad men.

Therefore at the enthronement of an emperor and the appointment of the three ministers, better still than those who present jewels followed by horses, is the one who sitting presents (propounds) this Tao. Why did the ancients prize this Tao? Was it not because it could be attained by seeking and thus sinners could be freed? For this reason it has become the most valuable thing in the world.

Good words will procure one honour; good deeds will get one credit.

LXIII

Act non-action; undertake no undertaking; taste the tasteless.
The sage desires the desireless, and prizes no articles that are difficult to get.
He learns no learning, but reviews what others have passed through.

Thus he lets all things develop in their natural way, and does not venture
        to act.
Regard the small as great; regard the few as many.
Manage the difficult while they are easy;
Manage the great while they are small.
All difficult things in the world start from the easy;
All great things in the world start from the small.
The tree that fills a man's arms arises from a tender shoot;
The nine-storied tower is raised from a heap of earth;
A thousand miles' journey begins from the spot under one's feet.
Therefore the sage never attempts great things, and thus he can achieve
        what is great.
He who makes easy promises will seldom keep his word;
He who regards many things easy will find many difficulties.
Therefore the sage regards things difficult, and consequently never has
        difficulties.

LXIV

What is motionless is easy to hold;
What is not yet foreshadowed is easy to form plans for;
What is fragile is easy to break;
What is minute is easy to disperse.
Deal with a thing before it comes into existence;
Regulate a thing before it gets into confusion.
The common people in their business often fail on the verge of suc-
        ceeding.
Take care with the end as you do with the beginning,
And you will have no failure.

LXV

In olden times the best practicers of Tao did not use it to awaken the
        people to knowledge,
But used it to restore them to simplicity.
People are difficult to govern because they have much knowledge.

Therefore to govern the country by increasing the people's knowledge is
      to be the destroyer of the country;
To govern the country by decreasing their knowledge is to be the blesser
      of the country.
To be acquainted with these two ways is to know the standard;
To keep the standard always in mind is to have sublime virtue.
Sublime virtue is infinitely deep and wide.
It goes reverse to all things;
And so it attains perfect peace.

LXVI

As Tao is to the world so are streams and valleys to rivers and seas.
Rivers and seas can be kings to all valleys because the former can well
      lower themselves to the latter.
Thus they become kings to all valleys.
Therefore the sage, in order to be above the people, must in words keep
      below them;
In order to be ahead of the people, he must in person keep behind them.
Thus when he is above, the people do not feel his burden;
When he is ahead, the people do not feel his hindrance.
Therefore all the world is pleased to hold him in high esteem and never
      get tired of him.
Because he does not compete; therefore no one competes with him.

LXVII

All the world says to me: "Great as Tao is, it resembles no description
      (form)." Because it is great, therefore it resembles no descrip-
      tion. If it resembled any description it would have long since
      become small.

I have three treasures, which I hold and keep safe:
The first is called love;
The second is called moderation;

The third is called not venturing to go ahead of the world.
Being loving, one can be brave;
Being moderate, one can be ample;
Not venturing to go ahead of the world, one can be the chief of all
        officials.
Instead of love, one has only bravery;
Instead of moderation, one has only amplitude;
Instead of keeping behind, one goes ahead:
These lead to nothing but death.
For he who fights with love will win the battle;
He who defends with love will be secure.
Heaven will save him, and protect him with love.

LXVIII

The best soldier is not soldierly;
The best fighter is not ferocious;
The best conqueror does not take part in war;
The best employer of men keeps himself below them.
This is called the virtue of not contending;
This is called the ability of using men;
This is called the supremacy of consorting with heaven.

LXIX

An ancient tactician has said:
"I dare not act as a host but would rather act as a guest;
I dare not advance an inch but would rather retreat a foot."
This implies that he does not marshal the ranks as if there were no ranks;
He does not roll up his sleeves as if he had no arms;
He does not seize as if he had no weapons;
He does not fight as if there were no enemies.
No calamity is greater than underestimating the enemy;

To underestimate the enemy is to be on the point of losing our treasure
    (love).
Therefore when opposing armies meet in the field the ruthful will win.

LXX

Words have an ancestor; deeds have a governor.
My words are very easy to know, and very easy to practise.
Yet all men in the world do not know them, nor do they practise them.
It is because they have knowledge that they do not know me.
When those who know me are few, eventually I am beyond all praise.
Therefore the sage wears clothes of coarse cloth but carries jewels in his
    bosom;
He knows himself but does not display himself;
He loves himself but does not hold himself in high esteem.
Thus he rejects the latter and takes the former.

LXXI

Not knowing that one knows is best;
Thinking that one knows when one does not know is sickness.
Only when one becomes sick of this sickness can one be free from
    sickness.
The sage is never sick; because he is sick of this sickness, therefore he is
    not sick.

LXXII

If the people have no fear of their ruling authority, still greater fear will
    come.
Be sure not to give them too narrow a dwelling;
Nor make their living scanty.
Only when their dwelling place is no longer narrow will their dissatisfac-
    tion come to an end.

LXXIII

He who shows courage in daring will perish;
He who shows courage in not-daring will live.
To know these two is to distinguish the one, benefit, from the other,
        harm.
Who can tell that one of them should be loathed by heaven?
The Tao of heaven does not contend; yet it surely wins the victory.
It does not speak; yet it surely responds.
It does not call; yet all things come of their own accord.
It remains taciturn; yet it surely makes plans.
The net of heaven is vast, and its meshes are wide;
Yet from it nothing escapes.

LXXIV

When the people are not afraid of death, what use is it to frighten them with the punishment of death? If the people were constantly afraid of death and we could arrest and kill those who commit treacheries, who then would dare to commit such? Only the Supreme Executioner kills. To kill in place of the Supreme Executioner is to hack instead of a greater carpenter. Now if one hacks in place of a great carpenter one can scarcely avoid cutting one's own hand.

LXXV

The people starve. Because their officials take heavy taxes from them, therefore they starve. The people are hard to rule. Because their officials meddle with affairs, therefore they are hard to rule. The people pay no heed to death. Because they endeavour to seek life; therefore they pay no heed to death.

LXXVI

Man when living is soft and tender; when dead he is hard and tough. All animals and plants when living are tender and fragile; when dead they become withered and dry. Therefore it is said: the hard and tough are parts of death; the soft and tender are parts of life. This is the reason why the soldiers when they are too tough cannot carry the day; the tree when it is too tough will break. The position of the strong and great is low, and the position of the weak and tender is high.

LXXVII

Is not the Tao of heaven like the drawing of a bow? It brings down the part which is high; it raises the part which is low; it lessens the part which is redundant (convex); it fills up the part which is insufficient (concave). The Tao of heaven is to lessen the redundant and fill up the insufficient. The Tao of man, on the contrary, is to take from the insufficient and give to the redundant. Who can take from the redundant and give to the insufficient? Only he who has Tao can. Therefore the sage does not hoard. The more he helps others, the more he benefits himself; the more he gives to others, the more he gets himself. The Tao of heaven does one good but never does one harm; the Tao of the sage acts but never contends.

LXXVIII

The weakest things in the world can overmatch the strongest things in
   the world.
Nothing in the world can be compared to water for its weak and yielding
   nature; yet in attacking the hard and the strong nothing proves
   better than it. For there is no other alternative to it.
The weak can overcome the strong and the yielding can overcome the
   hard:

This all the world knows but does not practise.

Therefore the sage says:

He who sustains all the reproaches of the country can be the master of
    the land;

He who sustains all the calamities of the country can be the king of the
    world.

These are words of truth,

Though they seem paradoxical.

LXXIX

Return love for great hatred.

Otherwise, when a great hatred is reconciled, some of it will surely
    remain.

How can this end in goodness?

Therefore the sage holds to the left half of an agreement but does not
    exact what the other holder ought to do.

The virtuous resort to agreement;

The virtueless resort to exaction.

"The Tao of heaven shows no partiality;

It abides always with good men."

LXXX

Supposing here is a small state with few people.

Though there are various vessels I will not have them put in use.

I will make the people regard death as a grave matter and not go far
    away.

Though they have boats and carriages they will not travel in them;

Though they have armours and weapons they will not show them.

I will let them restore the use of knotted cords (instead of writing).

They will be satisfied with their food;

Delighted in their dress;

Comfortable in their dwellings;

Happy with their customs.

Though the neighbouring states are within sight

And their cocks' crowing and dogs' barking within hearing;
The people (of the small state) will not go there all their lives.

LXXXI

He who knows does not speak;
He who speaks does not know.
He who is truthful is not showy;
He who is showy is not truthful.
He who is virtuous does not dispute;
He who disputes is not virtuous;
He who is learned is not wise;
He who is wise is not learned.
Therefore the sage does not display his own merits.

The Works of Chuang Tze

The Music of Earth and Heaven

Tze Ch'i of Nan-kuo sat leaning on a table. Looking up to heaven, he sighed and became silent, as though soul and body had parted.

Yen Ch'eng Tze Yu, who was standing by him, exclaimed, "What are you thinking about that your body should become thus like dry wood, your mind like dead ashes? Surely the man now leaning on the table is not he who was here just now."

"My friend," replied Tze Ch'i, "your question is apposite. To-day I have buried myself. . . . Do you understand? . . . Ah! perhaps you only know the music of man, and not that of earth. Or even if you have heard the music of earth, you have not heard the music of heaven."

"Pray explain," said Tze Yu.

"The breath of the universe," continued Tze Ch'i, "is called wind. At times, it is inactive. But when active, every aperture resounds to the blast. Have you never listened to its growing roar?

"Caves and dells of hill and forest, hollows in huge trees of many a span in girth;—these are like nostrils, like mouths, like ears, like beam-sockets, like goblets, like mortars, like ditches, like bogs. And the wind goes rushing through them, sniffing, snoring, singing, soughing, puffing, purling, whistling, whirring, now shrilly treble, now deeply bass, now soft, now loud; until, with a lull, silence reigns supreme. Have you never witnessed among the trees such a disturbance as this?"

"Well, then," inquired Tze Yu, "since the music of earth consists of nothing more than holes, and the music of man of pipes and flutes,—of what consists the music of heaven?"

"The effect of the wind upon these various apertures," replied Tze Ch'i, "is not uniform. But what is it that gives to each the individuality, to all the potentiality, of sound?

"Great knowledge embraces the whole: small knowledge, a part only. Great speech is universal: small speech is particular.

"For whether when the mind is locked in sleep or whether when in waking hours the body is released, we are subject to daily mental pertur-bations,—indecision, want of penetration, concealment, fretting fear, and trembling terror. Now like a javelin the mind flies forth, the arbiter of right and wrong. Now like a solemn covenanter it remains firm, the guardian of rights secured. Then, as under autumn and winter's blight, comes gradual decay, a passing away, like the flow of water, never to return. Finally, the block when all is choked up like an old drain,—the failing mind which shall not see light again.

"Joy and anger, sorrow and happiness, caution and remorse, come upon us by turns, with ever-changing mood. They come like music from hollowness, like mushrooms from damp. Daily and nightly they alter-nate within us, but we cannot tell whence they spring. Can we then hope in a moment to lay our finger upon their very cause?

"But for these emotions I should not be. But for me, they would have no scope. So far we can go; but we do not know what it is that brings them into play. 'Twould seem to be a soul; but the clue to its existence is wanting. That such a power operates, is credible enough, though we cannot see its form. It has functions without form.

"Take the human body with all its manifold divisions. Which part of it does a man love best? Does he not cherish all equally, or has he a preference? Do not all equally serve him? And do these servitors then govern themselves, or are they subdivided into rulers and subjects? Surely there is some soul which sways them all.

"But whether or not we ascertain what are the functions of this soul, it matters but little to the soul itself. For coming into existence with this mortal coil of mine, with the exhaustion of this mortal coil its mandate will also be exhausted. To be harassed by the wear and tear of life, and to pass rapidly through it without possibility of arresting one's course,—is not this pitiful indeed? To labour without ceasing, and then, without living to enjoy the fruit, worn out, to depart, suddenly, one knows not whither,—is not that a just cause for grief?

"What advantage is there in what men call not dying? The body decomposes, and the mind goes with it. This is our real cause for sorrow. Can the world be so dull as not to see this? Or is it I alone who am dull, and others not so?

"Speech is not mere breath. It is differentiated by meaning. Take away that, and you cannot say whether it is speech or not. Can you even distinguish it from the chirping of young birds?

"But how can TAO be so obscured that we speak of it as true and false? And how can speech be so obscured that it admits the idea of contraries? How can TAO go away and yet not remain? How can speech exist and yet be impossible?

"TAO is obscured by our want of grasp. Speech is obscured by the gloss of this world.

"There is nothing which is not objective: there is nothing which is not subjective. But it is impossible to start from the objective. Only from subjective knowledge is it possible to proceed to objective knowledge.

"When subjective and objective are both without their correlates, that is the very axis of TAO. And when that axis passes through the centre at which all infinities converge, positive and negative alike blend into an infinite ONE.

"Therefore it is that, viewed from the standpoint of TAO, a beam and a pillar are identical. So are ugliness and beauty, greatness, wickedness, perverseness, and strangeness. Separation is the same as construction: construction is the same as destruction. Nothing is subject either to construction or to destruction, for these conditions are brought together into ONE.

"Only the truly intelligent understand this principle of the identity of all things. They do not view things as apprehended by themselves, sub-jectively; but transfer themselves into the position of the things viewed. And viewing them thus they are able to comprehend them, nay, to master them;—and he who can master them is near. So it is that to place oneself in subjective relation with externals, without consciousness of their objec-tivity,—this is TAO. But to wear out one's intellect in an obstinate adherence to the individuality of things, not recognizing the fact that all things are ONE,—this is called *Three in the Morning.*"

"What is *Three in the Morning?*" asked Tze Yu.

"A keeper of monkeys," replied Tze Ch'i, "said with regard to their rations of chestnuts that each monkey was to have three in the morning and four at night. But at this the monkeys were very angry, so the keeper said they might have four in the morning and three at night, with which arrangement they were all well pleased. The actual number of the chest-nuts remained the same, but there was an adaptation to the likes and dis-likes of those concerned. Such is the principle of putting oneself into subjective relation with externals.

"Therefore what the true sage aims at is the light which comes out of darkness. He does not view things as apprehended by himself, subjec-tively, but transfers himself into the position of the things viewed. This is called using the light.

"If there was a beginning, then there was a time before that begin-ning. And a time before the time which was before the time of that beginning.

"If there is existence, there must have been non-existence. And if there was a time when nothing existed, then there must have been a time before that—when even nothing did not exist. Suddenly, when nothing came into existence, could one really say whether it belonged to the category of existence or of non-existence? Even the very words I have just now uttered,—I cannot say whether they have really been uttered or not.

"There is nothing under the canopy of heaven greater than the tip of an autumn spikelet. A vast mountain is a small thing. Neither is there any age greater than that of a child cut off in infancy. P'eng Tsu himself died young. The universe and I came into being together; and I, and everything therein, are ONE.

"If then all things are ONE, what room is there for speech? On the other hand, since I can utter these words, how can speech not exist?

"If it does exist, we have ONE and speech = two; and two and one = three. From which point onwards even the best mathematicians will fail to reach:

TAO.

How much more then will ordinary people fail?

"Hence, if from nothing you can proceed to something, and subsequently reach three, it follows that it would be still more easy if you were to start from something. To avoid such progression you must put yourself into subjective relation with the external.

"Before conditions existed, TAO was. Before definitions existed, speech was. Subjectively, we are conscious of certain delimitations which are,—

Right	and Left
Relationship	and Obligation
Division	and Discrimination
Emulation	and Contention

These are called the Eight Predicables. For the true sage, beyond the limits of an external world, they exist, but are not recognized. By the true sage, within the limits of an external world, they are recognized, but are not assigned. And so, with regard to the wisdom of the ancients, as embodied in the canon of Spring and Autumn, the true sage assigns, but does not justify by argument. And thus, classifying, he does not classify; arguing, he does not argue."

"How can that be?" asked Tze Yu.

"The true sage," answered Tze Ch'i, "keeps his knowledge within him, while men in general set forth theirs in argument, in order to convince each other. And therefore it is said that in argument he does not manifest himself.

"Perfect TAO does not declare itself. Nor does perfect argument express itself in words. Nor does perfect charity show itself in act. Nor is perfect honesty absolutely incorruptible. Nor is perfect courage absolutely unyielding.

"For the TAO which shines forth is not TAO. Speech which argues falls short of its aim. Charity which has fixed points loses its scope. Honesty which is absolute is wanting in credit. Courage which is absolute misses its object. These five are, as it were, round, with a strong bias towards squareness. Therefore that knowledge which stops at what it does not know, is the highest knowledge.

"Who knows the argument which can be argued without words?—the TAO which does not declare itself as TAO? He who knows this may be said to be of God. To be able to pour in without making full, and pour out without making empty, in ignorance of the power by which such results are accomplished,—this is accounted Light."

There Is No Absoluteness

Yeh Ch'ueh asked Wang I, saying, "Do you know for certain that all things are subjectively the same?"

"How can I know?" answered Wang I. "Do you know what you do not know?"

"How can I know?" replied Yeh Ch'ueh. "But can then nothing be known?"

"How can I know?" said Wang I. "Nevertheless, I will try to tell you. How can it be known that what I call knowing is not really not knowing, and that what I call not knowing is not really knowing? Now I would ask you this. If a man sleeps in a damp place, he gets lumbago and dies. But how about an eel? And living up in a tree is precarious and trying to the nerves;—but how about monkeys? Of the man, the eel, and the monkey, whose habitat is the right one, absolutely? Human beings feed on flesh, deer on grass, centipedes on snakes, owls and crows on mice. Of these four, whose is the right taste, absolutely? Monkey mates with monkey, the buck with the doe; eels consort with fishes, while men admire Mao Ch'iang and Li Chi, at the sight of whom fishes plunge deep down in the water, birds soar high in the air, and deer hurry away. Yet who shall say which is the correct standard of beauty? In my opinion, the standard of human virtue, and of positive and negative, is so obscured that it is impossible to actually know it as such."

"If you then," asked Yeh Ch'ueh, "do not know what is bad for you, is the perfect man equally without this knowledge?"

"The perfect man," answered Wang I, "is a spiritual being. Were the ocean itself scorched up, he would not feel hot. Were the Milky Way frozen hard, he would not feel cold. Were the mountains to be riven with thunder, and the great deep to be thrown up by storm, he would not tremble. In such case, he would mount upon the clouds of heaven, and driving the sun and the moon before him, would pass beyond the limits of this external world, where death and life have no more victory over man;—how much less what is bad for him?"

Life Is a Great Dream

Chu Ch'iao addressed Chang Wu Tze as follows:—"I heard Confucius say, 'The true sage pays no heed to mundane affairs. He neither seeks gain nor avoids injury. He asks nothing at the hands of man. He adheres, without questioning, to TAO. Without speaking, he can speak; and he can speak and yet say nothing. And so he roams beyond the limits of this dusty world. These,' added Confucius, 'are wild words.' Now to me they are the skilful embodiment of TAO. What, sir, is your opinion?"

"Points upon which the Yellow Emperor doubted," replied Chang Wu Tze, "how should Confucius know? You are going too fast. You see your egg, and expect to hear it crow. You look at your cross-bow, and expect to have broiled duck before you. I will say a few words to you at random, and do you listen at random.

"How does the sage seat himself by the sun and moon, and hold the universe in his grasp? He blends everything into one harmonious whole, rejecting the confusion of this and that. Rank and precedence, which the vulgar prize, the sage stolidly ignores. The revolutions of ten thousand years leave his unity unscathed. The universe itself may pass away, but he will flourish still.

"How do I know that love of life is not a delusion after all? How do I know but that he who dreads to die is not as a child who has lost the way and cannot find his home?

"The lady Li Chi was the daughter of Ai Feng. When the Duke of Chin first got her, she wept until the bosom of her dress was drenched with tears. But when she came to the royal residence, and lived with the Duke, and ate rich food, she repented of having wept. How then do I know but that the dead repent of having previously clung to life?

"Those who dream of the banquet, wake to lamentation and sorrow.

Those who dream of lamentation and sorrow wake to join the hunt. While they dream, they do not know that they dream. Some will even interpret the very dream they are dreaming; and only when they awake do they know it was a dream. By and by comes the Great Awakening, and then we find out that this life is really a great dream. Fools think they are awake now, and flatter themselves they know if they are really princes or peasants. Confucius and you are both dreams; and I who say you are dreams,—I am but a dream myself. This is a paradox. To-morrow a sage may arise to explain it; but that to-morrow will not be until ten thousand generations have gone by.

"Granting that you and I argue. If you beat me, and not I you, are you necessarily right and I wrong? Or if I beat you and not you me, am I necessarily right and you wrong? Or are we both partly right and partly wrong? Or are we both wholly right and wholly wrong? You and I cannot know this, and consequently the world will be in ignorance of the truth.

"Whom shall I employ as arbiter between us? If I employ someone who takes your view, he will side with you. How can such a one arbitrate between us? If I employ someone who takes my view, he will side with me. How can such a one arbitrate between us? And if I employ someone who either differs from, or agrees with, both of us, he will be equally unable to decide between us. Since then you, and I, and man, cannot decide, must we not depend upon Another? Such dependence is as though it were not dependence. We are embraced in the obliterating unity of God. There is perfect adaptation to whatever may eventuate; and so we complete our allotted span.

"But what is it to be embraced in the obliterating unity of God? It is this. With reference to positive and negative, to that which is so and that which is not so,—if the positive is really positive, it must necessarily be different from its negative: there is no room for argument. And if that which is so really is so, it must necessarily be different from that which is not so: there is no room for argument.

"Take no heed of time, nor of right and wrong. But passing into the realm of the Infinite, take your final rest therein."

Once upon a time, I, Chuang Tze, dreamt I was a butterfly, fluttering hither and thither, to all intents and purposes a butterfly. I was conscious only of following my fancies as a butterfly, and was unconscious of my individuality as a man. Suddenly, I awaked, and there I lay, myself again.

Now I do not know whether I was then a man dreaming I was a butterfly, or whether I am now a butterfly dreaming I am a man.

The Worthless Tree

Hui Tze said to Chuang Tze, "Sir, I have a large tree, of a worthless kind. Its trunk is so irregular and knotty that it cannot be measured out for planks; while its branches are so twisted as to admit of no geometrical subdivision whatever. It stands by the roadside, but no carpenter will look at it. And your words, sir, are like that tree;—big and useless, not wanted by anybody."

"Sir," rejoined Chuang Tze, "have you never seen a wild cat, crouching down in wait for its prey? Right and left it springs from bough to bough, high and low alike,—until perchance it gets caught in a trap or dies in a snare. On the other hand, there is the yak with its great huge body. It is big enough in all conscience, but it cannot catch mice.

"Now if you have a big tree and are at a loss what to do with it, why not plant it in the domain of non-existence, whither you might betake yourself to inaction by its side, to blissful repose beneath its shade? There it would be safe from the axe and from all other injury; for being of no use to others, itself would be free from harm."

The Middle Course

My life has a limit, but my knowledge is without limit. To drive the limited in search of the limitless, is fatal; and the knowledge of those who do this is fatally lost.

In striving for others, avoid fame. In striving for self, avoid disgrace. Pursue a middle course. Thus you will keep a sound body, and a sound mind, fulfil your duties, and work out your allotted span.

Prince Hui's Excellent Cook

Prince Hui's cook was cutting up a bullock. Every blow of his hand, every heave of his shoulders, every tread of his foot, every thrust of his knee, every *whshh* of rent flesh, every *chhk* of the chopper, was in perfect harmony,—rhythmical like the dance of the Mulberry Grove, simultaneous like the chords of the Ching Shou.

"Well done!" cried the Prince. "Yours is skill indeed."

"Sire," replied the cook; "I have always devoted myself to TAO. It is better than skill. When I first began to cut up bullocks, I saw before me simply whole bullocks. After three years' practice, I saw no more whole animals. And now I work with my mind and not with my eye. When my senses bid me stop, but my mind urges me on, I fall back upon eternal principles. I follow such openings or cavities as there may be, according to the natural constitution of the animal. I do not attempt to cut through joints: still less through large bones.

"A good cook changes his chopper once a year,—because he cuts. An ordinary cook, once a month,—because he hacks. But I have had this chopper nineteen years, and although I have cut up many thousand bullocks, its edge is as if fresh from the whetstone. For at the joints there are always interstices, and the edge of a chopper being without thickness, it remains only to insert that which is without thickness into such an interstice. By these means the interstices will be enlarged, and the blade will find plenty of room. It is thus that I have kept my chopper for nineteen years as though fresh from the whetstone.

"Nevertheless, when I come upon a hard part where the blade meets with a difficulty, I am all caution. I fix my eye on it. I stay my hand, and gently apply my blade, until with a *hwah* the part yields like earth crumbling to the ground. Then I take out my chopper, and stand up, and look around, and pause, until with an air of triumph I wipe my chopper and put it carefully away."

"Bravo!" cried the Prince. "From the words of this cook I have learnt how to take care of my life."

The Shang Mountain Tree

Tze Ch'i of Nan-poh was travelling on the Shang mountain when he saw a large tree which astonished him very much. A thousand chariot teams could have found shelter under its shade.

"What tree is this?" cried Tze Ch'i. "Surely it must have unusually fine timber." Then looking up, he saw that its branches were too crooked for rafters; while as to the trunk he saw that its irregular grain made it valueless for coffins. He tasted a leaf, but it took the skin off his lips; and its odour was so strong that it would make a man as it were drunk for three days together.

"Ah!" said Tze Ch'i. "This tree is good for nothing, and that is how it has attained this size. A wise man might well follow its example."

The Deformed Councillors

A certain hunchback, named Wu Ch'un, whose heels did not touch the ground, had the ear of Duke Ling of Wei. The Duke took a great fancy to him; and as for well-formed men, he thought their necks were too short.

Another man, with a goitre as big as a large jar, had the ear of Duke Huan of Ch'i. The Duke took a great fancy to him; and as for well-formed men, he thought their necks were too thin.

Thus it is that virtue should prevail and outward form be forgotten. But mankind forgets not that which is to be forgotten, forgetting that which is not to be forgotten. This is forgetfulness indeed! And thus with the truly wise, wisdom is a curse, sincerity like glue, virtue only a means to acquire, and skill nothing more than a commercial capacity. For the truly wise make no plans, and therefore require no wisdom. They do not separate, and therefore require no glue. They want nothing, and therefore need no virtue. They sell nothing, and therefore are not in want of a commercial capacity. These four qualifications are bestowed upon them by God and serve as heavenly food to them. And those who thus feed upon the divine have little need for the human. They wear the forms of men, without human passions. Because they wear the forms of men, they associate with men. Because they have not human passions, positives and negatives find in them no place. Infinitesimal indeed is that which makes them man: infinitely great is that which makes them divine!

The Nature of God

He who knows what God is, and who knows what man is, has attained. Knowing what God is, he knows that he himself proceeded therefrom.

Knowing what man is, he rests in the knowledge of the known, waiting for the knowledge of the unknown. Working out one's allotted span, and not perishing in mid career,—this is the fullness of knowledge.

God is a principle which exists by virtue of its own intrinsicality, and operates spontaneously, without self-manifestation.

Herein, however, there is a flaw. Knowledge is dependent upon fulfilment. And as this fulfilment is uncertain, how can it be known that my divine is not really human, my human really divine?

The Four Friends

Four men were conversing together, when the following resolution was suggested: "Whosoever can make inaction the head, life the backbone, and death the tail, of his existence,—that man shall be admitted to friendship with us." The four looked at each other and smiled; and tacitly accepting the conditions, became friends forthwith.

By and by, one of them, named Tze Yu, fell ill, and another, Tze Ssu, went to see him. "Verily God is great!" said the sick man. "See how he has doubled me up. My back is so hunched that my viscera are at the top of my body. My cheeks are level with my navel. My shoulders are higher than my neck. My hair grows up towards the sky. The whole economy of my organism is deranged. Nevertheless, my mental equilibrium is not disturbed." So saying, he dragged himself painfully to a well, where he could see himself, and continued, "Alas, that God should have doubled me up like this!"

"Are you afraid?" asked Tze Ssu.

"I am not," replied Tze Yu. "What have I to fear? Ere long I shall be decomposed. My left shoulder will become a cock, and I shall herald the approach of morn. My right shoulder will become a cross-bow, and I shall be able to get broiled duck. My buttocks will become wheels; and with my soul for a horse, I shall be able to ride in my own chariot. I obtained life because it was my time: I am now parting with it in accordance with the same law. Content with the natural sequence of these states, joy and sorrow touch me not. I am simply, as the ancients expressed it, hanging in the air, unable to cut myself down, bound with the trammels of material existence. But man has ever given way before God: why, then, should I be afraid?"

By and by, another of the four, named Tze Lai, fell ill, and lay gasping for breath, while his family stood weeping around. The fourth friend, Tze Li, went to see him. "Chut!" cried he to the wife and children; "begone! you balk his decomposition." Then, leaning against the door, he said, "Verily, God is great! I wonder what he will make of you now. I wonder whither you will be sent. Do you think he will make you into a rat's liver or into the shoulders of a snake?"

"A son," answered Tze Lai, "must go whithersoever his parents bid him. Nature is no other than a man's parents. If she bid me die quickly, and I demur, then I am an unfilial son. She can do me no wrong. TAO gives me this form, this toil in manhood, this repose in old age, this rest in death. And surely that which is such a kind arbiter of my life is the best arbiter of my death.

"Suppose that the boiling metal in a smelting-pot were to bubble up and say, 'Make of me an Excalibur'; I think the caster would reject that metal as uncanny. And if a sinner like myself were to say to God, 'Make of me a man, make of me a man'; I think he too would reject me as uncanny. The universe is the smelting-pot, and God is the caster. I shall go whithersoever I am sent, to wake unconscious of the past, as a man wakes from a dreamless sleep."

On Charity

Intentional charity and intentional duty to one's neighbour are surely not included in our moral nature. Yet what sorrow these have involved. Divide your joined toes and you will howl: bite off your extra finger and you will scream. In one case there is too much, in the other too little; but the sorrow is the same. And the charitable of the age go about sorrowing over the ills of the age, while the non-charitable cut through the natural conditions of things in their greed after place and wealth. Surely then intentional charity and duty to one's neighbour are not included in our moral nature. Yet from the time of the Three Dynasties downwards what a fuss has been made about them!

Tsang and Ku were shepherds, both of whom lost their flocks. On inquiry, it appeared that Tsang had been engaged in reading, while Ku had gone to take part in some trials of strength. Their occupations had been different, but the result was in each case loss of the sheep.

Poh I died for fame at the foot of Mount Shouyang. Robber Che died for gain on Mount T'ai. Their deaths were not the same, but the injury to their lives and natures was in each case the same. How then can we applaud the former and blame the latter?

And so, if a man dies for charity and duty to his neighbour the world calls him a noble fellow; but if he dies for gain, the world calls him a low fellow. The dying being the same, one is nevertheless called noble and the other low. But in point of injury to life and nature, the robber Che and Poh I are one. Where then does the distinction of noble and low come in?

Were a man to apply himself to charity and duty towards his neighbour until he were the equal of Tseng or Shih, this would not be what I mean by perfection. Or to flavours, until he were the equal of Yu Erh. Or to sounds, until he were the equal of Shih K'uang. Or to colours, until he were the equal of Li Chu. What I mean by perfection is not what is meant by charity and duty to one's neighbour. It is found in the cultivation of TAO. And those whom I regard as cultivators of TAO are not those who cultivate charity and duty to one's neighbour. They are those who yield to the natural conditions of things. What I call perfection of hearing is not hearing others but oneself. What I call perfection of vision is not seeing others but oneself. For a man who sees not himself but others, takes not possession of himself but of others, thus taking what others should take and not what he himself should take. Instead of being himself, he in fact becomes someone else. And if a man thus becomes someone else instead of himself, this is a fatal error of which both the robber Che and Poh I can be equally guilty.

And so, conscious of my own deficiency in regard to TAO, I do not venture at my best to practise the principles of charity and duty to my neighbour, nor at my worst to fall into the fatal error above-mentioned.

The Degradation of Horses and Men

Horses have hoofs to carry them over frost and snow; hair, to protect them from wind and cold. They eat grass and drink water, and fling up their heels over the champaign. Such is the real nature of horses. Palatial dwellings are of no use to them.

One day Poh Loh appeared, saying, "I understand the management of horses."

So he branded them, and clipped them, and pared their hoofs, and put halters on them, tying them up by the head and shackling them by the feet, and disposing them in stables, with the result that two or three in every ten died. Then he kept them hungry and thirsty, trotting them and galloping them, and grooming, and trimming, with the misery of the tasselled bridle before and the fear of the knotted whip behind, until more than half of them were dead.

The potter says, "I can do what I will with clay. If I want it round, I use compasses; if rectangular, a square."

The carpenter says, "I can do what I will with wood. If I want it curved, I use an arc; if straight, a line."

But on what grounds can we think that the natures of clay and wood desire this application of compasses and square, of arc and line? Nevertheless, every age extols Poh Loh for his skill in managing horses, and potters and carpenters for their skill with clay and wood. Those who *govern* the empire make the same mistake.

Now I regard government of the empire from quite a different point of view.

The people have certain natural instincts;—to weave and clothe themselves, to till and feed themselves. These are common to all humanity, and all are agreed thereon. Such instincts are called "Heaven-sent."

And so in the days when natural instincts prevailed, men moved quietly and gazed steadily. At that time, there were no roads over mountains, nor boats, nor bridges over water. All things were produced, each for its own proper sphere. Birds and beasts multiplied; trees and shrubs grew up. The former might be led by the hand; you could climb up and peep into the raven's nest. For then man dwelt with birds and beasts, and all creation was one. There were no distinctions of good and bad men. Being all equally without knowledge, their virtue could not go astray. Being all equally without evil desires, they were in a state of natural integrity, the perfection of human existence.

But when sages appeared, tripping people over charity and fettering with duty to one's neighbour, doubt found its way into the world. And then with their gushing over music and fussing over ceremony, the empire became divided against itself.

Were the natural integrity of things left unharmed, who could make sacrificial vessels? Were white jade left unbroken, who could make the regalia of courts? Were TAO not abandoned, who could introduce charity and duty to one's neighbour? Were man's natural instincts his guide, what need would there be for music and ceremonies? Were the five colours not confused, who would practise decoration? Were the five notes not confused, who would adopt the six pitch-pipes?

Destruction of the natural integrity of things, in order to produce articles of various kinds,—this is the fault of the artisan. Annihilation of TAO in order to practise charity and duty to one's neighbour,—this is the error of the sage.

Horses live on dry land, eat grass and drink water. When pleased, they rub their necks together. When angry, they turn round and kick up their heels at each other. Thus far only do their natural dispositions carry them. But bridled and bitted, with a plate of metal on their foreheads, they learn to cast vicious looks, to turn the head to bite, to resist, to get the bit out of the mouth or the bridle into it. And thus their natures become depraved,—the fault of Poh Loh.

In the days of Ho Hsu the people did nothing in particular when at rest, and went nowhere in particular when they moved. Having food, they rejoiced; having full bellies, they strolled about. Such were the capacities of the people. But when the sages came to worry them with ceremonies and music in order to rectify the form of government, and dangled charity and duty to one's neighbour before them in order to satisfy their hearts,—then the people began to develop a taste for knowledge and to struggle one with the other in their desire for gain. This was the error of the sages.

On Letting Alone

There has been such a thing as letting mankind alone; there has never been such a thing as governing mankind.

Letting alone springs from fear lest men's natural dispositions be perverted and their virtue laid aside. But if their natural dispositions be not perverted nor their virtue laid aside, what room is there left for government?

Because men are made to rejoice and to sorrow and to displace their centre of gravity, they lose their steadiness, and are unsuccessful in thought and action. And thus it is that the idea of surpassing others first came into the world, followed by the appearance of such men as Robber Che, Tseng, and Shih, the result being that the whole world could not furnish enough rewards for the good nor distribute punishments enough for the evil among mankind. And as this great world is not equal to the demand for rewards and punishments; and as, ever since the time of the Three Dynasties downwards, men have done nothing but struggle over rewards and punishments,—what possible leisure can they have had for adapting themselves to the natural conditions of their existence?

Besides, over-refinement of vision leads to debauchery in colour; over-refinement of hearing leads to debauchery in sound; over-refinement of charity leads to confusion in virtue; over-refinement of duty towards one's neighbour leads to perversion of principle; over-refinement of cere-monial leads to divergence from the true object; over-refinement of music leads to lewdness of thought; over-refinement of wisdom leads to an extension of mechanical art; and over-refinement of shrewdness leads to an extension of vice.

If people adapt themselves to the natural conditions of existence, the above eight may be or may not be; it matters not. But if people do not adapt themselves to the natural conditions of existence, then these eight become hindrances and spoilers, and throw the world into confusion.

In spite of this, the world reverences and cherishes them, thereby greatly increasing the sum of human error. And not as a passing fashion, but with admonitions in words, with humility in prostrations, and with the stimulus of music and song. What then is left for me?

Therefore, for the perfect man who is unavoidably summoned to power over his fellows, there is naught like inaction. By means of inac-tion he will be able to adapt himself to the natural conditions of exist-ence. And so it is that he who respects the state as his own body is fit to support it, and he who loves the state as his own body is fit to govern it. And if I can refrain from injuring my internal economy, and from tax-ing my powers of sight and hearing, sitting like a corpse while my dragon-power is manifested around, in profound silence while my thunder-voice resounds, the powers of heaven responding to every phase of my will, as under the yielding influence of inaction all things are brought to maturity and thrive,—what leisure then have I to set about governing the world?

Ts'ui Chu asked Lao Tze, saying, "If the empire is not to be governed, how are men's hearts to be kept in order?"

"Be careful," replied Lao Tze, "not to interfere with the natural goodness of the heart of man. Man's heart may be forced down or stirred up. In each case the issue is fatal.

"By gentleness, the hardest heart may be softened. But try to cut and polish it,—'twill glow like fire or freeze like ice. In the twinkling of an eye it will pass beyond the limits of the Four Seas. In repose, profoundly still; in motion, far away in the sky. No bolt can bar, no bond can bind,— such is the human heart."

The Yellow Emperor sat on the throne for nineteen years, and his laws obtained all over the empire.

Hearing that Kuang Ch'eng Tze was living on Mount K'ung-t'ung, he went thither to see him, and said, "I am told, sir, that you are in possession of perfect TAO. May I ask in what perfect TAO consists? I desire to avail myself of the good influence of heaven and earth in order to secure harvests and feed my people. I should also like to control the two powers of nature in order to assure the protection of all living things. How can I accomplish this?"

"What you desire to avail yourself of," replied Kuang Ch'eng Tze, "is the primordial integrity of matter. What you wish to control are the disintegrators thereof. Ever since the empire has been governed by you, the clouds have rained without waiting to thicken, the foliage of trees has fallen without waiting to grow yellow, the brightness of the sun and moon has paled, and the voice of the flatterer is heard on every side. How then speak of perfect TAO?"

The Yellow Emperor withdrew. He resigned the throne. He built himself a solitary hut. He lay upon straw. For three months he remained in seclusion, and then went again to see Kuang Ch'eng Tze.

The latter was lying down with his face to the south. The Yellow Emperor approached after the manner of an inferior, upon his knees. Prostrating himself upon the ground he said, "I am told, sir, that you are in possession of perfect TAO. May I ask how my self may be preserved so as to last?"

Kuang Ch'eng Tze jumped up with a start. "A good question indeed!" cried he. "Come, and I will speak to you of perfect TAO.

"The essence of perfect TAO is profoundly mysterious; its extent is lost in obscurity.

"See nothing; hear nothing, let your soul be wrapped in quiet; and your body will begin to take proper form. Let there be absolute repose and absolute purity; do not weary your body nor disturb your vitality,— and you will live for ever. For if the eye sees nothing, and the ear hears nothing, and the mind thinks nothing, the soul will preserve the body, and the body will live for ever.

"Cherish that which is within you, and shut off that which is without; for much knowledge is a curse. Then I will place you upon that abode of great light which is the source of the positive power, and escort you through the gate of profound mystery which is the source of the negative power. These powers are the controllers of heaven and earth, and each contains the other.

"Cherish and preserve your own self, and all the rest will prosper of itself. I preserve the original ONE, while resting in harmony with externals. It is because I have thus cared for my self now for twelve hundred years that my body has not decayed."

The Yellow Emperor prostrated himself and said, "Kuang Ch'eng Tze is surely God. . . ."

Whereupon the latter continued, "Come, I will tell you. That self is eternal; yet all men think it mortal. That self is infinite; yet all men think it finite. Those who possess TAO are princes in this life and rulers in the hereafter. Those who do not possess TAO behold the light of day in this life and become clods of earth in the hereafter.

"Nowadays, all living things spring from the dust and to the dust return. But I will lead you through the portals of eternity into the domain of infinity. My light is the light of sun and moon. My life is the life of heaven and earth. I know not who comes nor who goes. Men may all die, but I endure for ever."

The Infinite Tao

The Master said, "How profound in its repose, how infinite in its purity, is TAO!

"If metal and stone were without TAO, they would not be capable of emitting sound. And just as they possess the property of sound but will not emit sound unless struck, so surely is the same principle applicable to all creation.

"The man of complete virtue remains blankly passive as regards what goes on around him. He is as originally by nature, and his knowledge extends to the supernatural. Thus, his virtue expands his heart, which goes forth to all who come to take refuge therein.

"Without TAO, form cannot be endued with life. Without virtue, life cannot be endued with intelligence. To preserve one's form, live out one's life, establish one's virtue, and realize TAO,—is not this complete virtue?

"Issuing forth spontaneously, moving without premeditation, all things following in his wake,—such is the man of complete virtue!

"He can see where all is dark. He can hear where all is still. In the darkness he alone can see light. In the stillness he alone can detect harmony. He can sink to the lowest depths of materialism. To the highest heights of spirituality he can soar. This because he stands in due relation to all things. Though a mere abstraction, he can minister to their wants, and ever and anon receive them into rest,—the great, the small, the long, the short, for ever without end."

Divine Virtue

At the beginning of the beginning, even nothing did not exist. Then came the period of the Nameless.

When ONE came into existence, there was ONE, but it was formless. When things got that by which they came into existence, it was called their virtue. That which was formless, but divided, though without interstice, was called destiny.

Then came the movement which gave life, and things produced in accordance with the principles of life had what is called form. When form encloses the spiritual part, each with its own characteristics, that is its nature. By cultivating this nature, we are carried back to virtue; and if this is perfected, we become as all things were in the beginning. We become unconditioned, and the unconditioned is great. As birds unconsciously join their beaks in chirping, and beaks to chirp must be joined,—to be thus joined with the universe without being more conscious of it than an idiot, this is divine virtue, this is accordance with the eternal fitness of things.

The Gardener

When Tze Kung went south to the Ch'u State on his way back to the Chin State, he passed through Han-yin. There he saw an old man engaged in making a ditch to connect his vegetable garden with a well. He had a pitcher in his hand, with which he was bringing up water and pouring it into the ditch,—great labour with very little result.

"If you had a machine here," cried Tze Kung, "in a day you could irrigate a hundred times your present area. The labour required is trifling as compared with the work done. Would you not like to have one?"

"What is it?" asked the gardener.

"It is a contrivance made of wood," replied Tze Kung, "heavy behind and light in front. It draws up water as you do with your hands, but in a constantly overflowing stream. It is called a well-sweep."

Thereupon the gardener flushed up and said, "I have heard from my teacher that those who have cunning implements are cunning in their dealings, and that those who are cunning in their dealings have cunning in their hearts, and that those who have cunning in their hearts cannot be pure and incorrupt, and that those who are not pure and incorrupt are restless in spirit, and that those who are restless in spirit are not fit vehicles for TAO. It is not that I do not know of these things. I should be ashamed to use them."

At this Tze Kung was much abashed, and said nothing. Then the gardener asked him who he was, to which Tze Kung replied that he was a disciple of Confucius.

"Are you not one who extends his learning with a view to being a sage; who talks big in order to put himself above the rest of mankind; who plays in a key to which no one can sing so as to spread his reputation abroad? Rather become unconscious of self and shake off the trammels of the flesh,—and you will be near. But if you cannot govern your own self, what leisure have you for governing the empire? Begone! Do not interrupt my work."

Tze Kung changed colour and slunk away, being not at all pleased with this rebuff; and it was not before he had travelled some thirty li that he recovered his usual appearance.

"What did the man we met do," asked a disciple, "that you should change colour and not recover for such a long time?"

"I used to think there was only one man in all the world," replied Tze Kung. "I did not know that there was also this man. I have heard the Master say that the test of a scheme is its practicability, and that success must be certain. The minimum of effort with the maximum of success,—such is the way of the Sage.

"Not so this manner of man. Aiming at TAO, he perfects his virtue. By perfecting his virtue he perfects his body, and by perfecting his body he perfects his spiritual part. And the perfection of the spiritual part is the TAO of the sage. Coming into life he is as one of the people, knowing not whither he is bound. How complete is his purity? Success, profit, skill,—these have no place in his heart. Such a man, if he does not will it, he does not stir; if he does not wish it, he does not act. If all the world praises him, he does not heed. If all the world blames him, he does not repine. The praise and the blame of the world neither advantage him nor otherwise. He may be called a man of perfect virtue. As for me, I am but a mere creature of impulse."

The Tao of God

The TAO of GOD operates ceaselessly; and all things are produced. The TAO of the sovereign operates ceaselessly; and the empire rallies around him. The TAO of the sage operates ceaselessly; and all within the limit of surrounding ocean acknowledge his sway. He who apprehends God, who is in relation with the sage, and who recognizes the radiating virtue of the sovereign,—his actions will be to him unconscious, the actions of repose.

The repose of the sage is not what the world calls repose. His repose is the result of his mental attitude. All creation could not disturb his equilibrium: hence his repose.

When water is still, it is like a mirror, reflecting the beard and the eyebrows. It gives the accuracy of the water-level, and the philosopher makes it his model. And if water thus derives lucidity from stillness, how much more the faculties of the mind? The mind of the sage being in repose becomes the mirror of the universe, the speculum of all creation.

Repose, tranquillity, stillness, inaction,—these were the levels of the universe, the ultimate perfection of TAO. Therefore wise rulers and sages rest therein. Resting therein they reach the unconditioned, from which springs the conditioned; and with the conditioned comes order. Again, from the unconditioned comes repose, and from repose comes movement, and from movement comes attainment. Further, from repose comes inaction, and from inaction comes potentiality of action. And inaction is happiness; and where there is happiness no cares can abide, and life is long.

Repose, tranquillity, stillness, inaction,—these were the source of all things. Due perception of this was the secret of Yao's success as a ruler, and of Shun's success as his minister. Due perception of this constitutes the virtue of sovereigns on the throne, the TAO of the inspired sage and of the uncrowned king below. Keep to this in retirement, and the lettered denizens of sea and dale will recognize your power. Keep to this when coming forward to pacify a troubled world, and your merit shall be great and your name illustrious, and the empire united into one. In your repose you will be wise; in your movements, powerful. By inaction you will gain honour; and by confining yourself to the pure and simple, you will hinder the whole world from struggling with you for show.

To fully apprehend the scheme of the universe, this is called the great secret of being in accord with GOD, whereby the empire is so administered that the result is in accord with man. To be in accord with man is human happiness; to be in accord with God is the happiness of God.

Appeal to arms is the lowest form of virtue. Rewards and punishments are the lowest form of education. Ceremonies and laws are the lowest form of government. Music and fine clothes are the lowest form of happiness. Weeping and mourning are the lowest form of grief. These five should follow the movements of the mind.

The ancients indeed cultivated the study of accidentals, but they did not allow it to precede that of essentials. The prince precedes, the minister follows. The father precedes, the son follows. The elder brother precedes, the younger follows. Seniors precede, juniors follow. Men precede, women follow. Husbands precede, wives follow. Distinctions of rank and precedence are part of the scheme of the universe, and the sage adopts them accordingly. In point of spirituality, heaven is honourable, earth is lowly. Spring and summer precede autumn and winter: such is the order of the seasons. In the constant production of all things, there are phases of existence. There are the extremes of maturity and decay, the perpetual tide of change. And if heaven and earth, divinest of all, admit of rank and precedence, how much more man?

In the ancestral temple, parents rank before all; at court, the most honourable; in the village, the elders; in matters to be accomplished, the most trustworthy. Such is the order which appertains to TAO. He who in considering TAO disregards this order, thereby disregards TAO; and he who in considering TAO disregards TAO,—whence will he secure TAO?

Therefore, those of old who apprehended TAO, first apprehended God. TAO came next, and then charity and duty to one's neighbour, and then the functions of public life, and then forms and names, and then employment according to capacity, and then distinctions of good and bad, and then discrimination between right and wrong, and then rewards and punishments. Thus wise men and fools met with their dues; the exalted and the humble occupied their proper places. And the virtuous and the worthless being each guided by their own natural instincts, it was necessary to distinguish capabilities, and to adopt a corresponding nomenclature, in order to serve the ruler, nourish the ruled, administer things generally, and elevate self. Where knowledge and plans are of no avail, one must fall back upon the natural. This is perfect peace, the acme of good government.

Of old, Shun asked Yao, saying, "How does your Majesty employ your faculties?"

"I am not arrogant towards the defenceless," replied Yao. "I do not neglect the poor. I grieve for those who die. I pity the orphan. I sympathize with the widow. Beyond this, nothing."

"Good indeed!" cried Shun, "but yet not great."

"How so?" inquired Yao.

"Be passive," said Shun, "like the virtue of God. The sun and moon shine; the four seasons revolve; day and night alternate; clouds come and rain falls."

"Alas!" cried Yao, "what a muddle I have been making. You are in accord with God; I am in accord with man."

Of old, heaven and earth were considered great; and the Yellow Emperor and Yao and Shun all thought them perfection. Consequently, what did those do who ruled the empire of old? They did what heaven and earth do; no more.

Lao Tze said, "TAO is not too small for the greatest, nor too great for the smallest. Thus all things are embosomed therein; wide indeed its boundless capacity, unfathomable its depth.

"Form, and virtue, and charity, and duty to one's neighbour, these are the accidentals of the spiritual. Except he be a perfect man, who shall determine their place? The world of the perfect man, is not that vast? And yet it is not able to involve him in trouble. All struggle for power, but he does not join. Though discovering nothing false, he is not tempted astray. In spite of the utmost genuineness, he still confines himself to essentials.

"He thus places himself outside the universe, beyond all creation, where his soul is free from care. Apprehending TAO, he is in accord with virtue. He leaves charity and duty to one's neighbour alone. He treats ceremonies and music as adventitious. And so the mind of the perfect man is at peace.

"Books are what the world values as representing TAO. But books are only words, and the valuable part of words is the thought therein contained. That thought has a certain bias which cannot be conveyed in words, yet the world values words as being the essence of books. But though the world values them, they are not of value; as that sense in which the world values them is not the sense in which they are valuable.

"That which can be seen with the eye is form and colour; that which can be heard with the ear is sound and noise. But alas! the people of this generation think that form, and colour, and sound, and noise, are means by which they can come to understand the essence of TAO. This is not so. And as those who know do not speak, while those who speak do not know, whence should the world derive its knowledge?"

The Circling Sky

The sky turns round; the earth stands still; sun and moon pursue one another. Who causes this? Who directs this? Who has leisure enough to see that such movements continue?

Some think there is a mechanical arrangement which makes these bodies move as they do. Others think that they revolve without being able to stop.

The clouds cause rain; rain causes clouds. Whose kindly bounty is this? Who has leisure enough to see that such result is achieved?

Wind comes from the north. It blows now east, now west; and now it whirls aloft. Who puffs it forth? Who has leisure enough to be flapping it this way or that? I should like to know the cause of all this.

The Music of God

Pei Men Ch'eng said to the Yellow Emperor, "When your Majesty played the Han-ch'ih in the wilds of Tung-t'ing, the first time I heard it I was afraid, the second time I was amazed, and the last time I was confused, speechless, overwhelmed."

"You are not far from the truth," replied the Yellow Emperor. "I played as a man, drawing inspiration from God. The execution was punctilious, the expression sublime.

"Perfect music first shapes itself according to a human standard; then it follows the lines of the divine; then it proceeds in harmony with the five virtues; then it passes into spontaneity. The four seasons are then blended, and all creation is brought into accord. As the seasons come forth in turn, so are all things produced. Now fullness, now decay, now soft and loud in turn, now clear, now muffled, the harmony of Yin and Yang. Like a flash was the sound which roused you as the insect world is roused, followed by a thundering peal, without end and without beginning, now dying, now living, now sinking, now rising, on and on without a moment's break. And so you were afraid.

"When I played again, it was the harmony of the Yin and Yang, lighted by the glory of sun and moon; now broken, now prolonged, now gentle, now severe, in one unbroken, unfathomable volume of sound. Filling valley and gorge, stopping the ears and dominating the senses, adapting itself to the capacities of things,—the sound whirled around on all sides, with shrill note and clear. The spirits of darkness kept to their domain. Sun, moon, and stars, pursued their appointed course. When the melody was exhausted I stopped; if the melody did not stop, I went on. You would have sympathized, but you could not understand. You would have looked, but you could not see. You would have pursued, but you could not overtake. You stood dazed in the middle of the wilderness, leaning against a tree and crooning, your eye conscious of exhausted vision, your strength failing for the pursuit, and so unable to overtake me. Your frame was but an empty shell. You were completely at a loss, and so you were amazed.

"Then I played in sounds which produce no amazement, the melodious law of spontaneity, springing forth like nature's countless buds, in manifold but formless joy, as though poured forth to the dregs, in deep but soundless bass. Beginning nowhere, the melody rested in void; some would say dead, others alive, others real, others ornamental, as it scattered itself on all sides in never-to-be-anticipated chords.

"The wondering world inquires of the sage. He is in relation with its variations and follows the same eternal law.

"When no machinery is set in motion, and yet the instrumentation is complete, this is the music of God. The mind awakes to its enjoyment without waiting to be called. Accordingly, Yu Piao praised it, saying, 'Listening you cannot hear its sound; gazing you cannot see its form. It fills heaven and earth. It embraces the six cardinal points.' Now you desired to listen to it, but you were not able to grasp its existence. And so you were confused.

"My music first induced fear; and as a consequence, respect. I then added amazement, by which you were isolated. And lastly, confusion; for confusion means absence of sense, and absence of sense means TAO, and TAO means absorption therein."

Confucius and Lao Tze

Confucius had lived to the age of fifty-one without hearing TAO, when he went south to P'ei, to see Lao Tze.

Lao Tze said, "So you have come, sir, have you? I hear you are considered a wise man up north. Have you got TAO?"

"Not yet," answered Confucius.

"In what direction," asked Lao Tze, "have you sought for it?"

"I sought it for five years," replied Confucius, "in the science of numbers, but did not succeed."

"And then? . . ." continued Lao Tze.

"Then," said Confucius, "I spent twelve years seeking for it in the doctrine of the Yin and Yang, also without success."

"Just so," rejoined Lao Tze. "Were TAO something which could be presented, there is no man but would present it to his sovereign, or to his parents. Could it be imparted or given, there is no man but would impart it to his brother or give it to his child. But this is impossible, for the following reason. Unless there is a suitable endowment within, TAO will not abide. Unless there is outward correctness, TAO will not operate. The external being unfitted for the impression of the internal, the true sage does not seek to imprint. The internal being unfitted for the reception of the external, the true sage does not seek to receive.

"Reputation is public property; you may not appropriate it in excess. Charity and duty to one's neighbour are as caravanserais established by wise rulers of old; you may stop there one night, but not for long, or you will incur reproach.

"The perfect men of old took their road through charity, stopping a night with duty to their neighbour, on their way to ramble in transcendental space. Feeding on the produce of non-cultivation, and establishing themselves in the domain of no obligations, they enjoyed their transcendental inaction. Their food was ready to hand; and being under no obligations to others, they did not put any one under obligation to themselves. The ancients called this the outward visible sign of an inward and spiritual grace.

"Those who make wealth their all in all, cannot bear loss of money. Those who make distinction their all in all, cannot bear loss of fame. Those who affect power will not place authority in the hands of others. Anxious while holding, distressed if losing, yet never taking warning from the past and seeing the folly of their pursuit,—such men are the accursed of God.

"Resentment, gratitude, taking, giving, censure of self, instruction of others, power of life and death,—these eight are the instruments of right; but only he who can adapt himself to the vicissitudes of fortune, without being carried away, is fit to use them. Such a one is an upright man among the upright. And he whose heart is not so constituted,— the door of divine intelligence is not yet opened for him."

Confucius visited Lao Tze, and spoke of charity and duty to one's neighbour.

Lao Tze said, "The chaff from winnowing will blind a man's eyes so that he cannot tell the points of the compass. Mosquitoes will keep a man awake all night with their biting. And just in the same way this talk of charity and duty to one's neighbour drives me nearly crazy. Sir!

strive to keep the world to its own original simplicity. And as the wind bloweth where it listeth, so let virtue establish itself. Wherefore such undue energy, as though searching for a fugitive with a big drum?

"The snow-goose is white without a daily bath. The raven is black without daily colouring itself. The original simplicity of black and of white is beyond the reach of argument. The vista of fame and reputation is not worthy of enlargement. When the pond dries up and the fishes are left upon dry ground, to moisten them with the breath or to damp them with a little spittle is not to be compared with leaving them in the first instance in their native rivers and lakes."

On returning from this visit to Lao Tze, Confucius did not speak for three days. A disciple asked him, saying, "Master, when you saw Lao Tze, in what direction did you admonish him?"

"I saw a dragon," replied Confucius, "—a dragon which by convergence showed a body, by radiation became colour, and riding upon the clouds of heaven, nourished the two principles of creation. My mouth was agape: I could not shut it. How then do you think I was going to admonish Lao Tze?"

Self-Conceit

Self-conceit and assurance, which lead men to quit society, and be different from their fellows, to indulge in tall talk and abuse of others, —these are nothing more than personal over-estimation, the affectation of recluses and those who have done with the world and have closed their hearts to mundane influences.

Preaching of charity and duty to one's neighbour, of loyalty and truth, of respect, of economy, and of humility,—this is but moral culture, affected by would-be pacificators and teachers of mankind, and by scholars at home or abroad.

Preaching of meritorious services, of fame, of ceremonial between sovereign and minister, of due relationship between upper and lower classes,—this is mere government, affected by courtiers or patriots who strive to extend the boundaries of their own state and to swallow up the territory of others.

Living in marshes or in wildernesses, and passing one's days in fishing,—this is mere inaction, affected by wanderers who have turned their backs upon the world and have nothing better to do.

Exhaling and inhaling, getting rid of the old and assimilating the new, stretching like a bear and craning like a bird,—this is but valetudinarianism, affected by professors of hygiene and those who try to preserve the body to the age of P'eng Tsu.

But in self-esteem without self-conceit, in moral culture without charity and duty to one's neighbour, in government without rank and fame, in retirement without solitude, in health without hygiene,—there we have oblivion absolute coupled with possession of all things; an infinite calm which becomes an object to be attained by all.

Such is the TAO of the universe, such is the virtue of the sage. Wherefore it has been said, "In tranquillity, in stillness, in the unconditioned, in inaction, we find the levels of the universe, the very constitution of TAO."

Wherefore it has been said, "The sage is a negative quantity, and is consequently in a state of passivity. Being passive he is in a state of repose. And where passivity and repose are, there sorrow and anxiety do not enter, and foul influences do not collect. And thus his virtue is complete and his spirituality unimpaired."

Wherefore it has been said, "The birth of the sage is the will of God; his death is but a modification of existence. In repose, he shares the passivity of the Yin; in action, the energy of the Yang. He will have nothing to do with happiness, and so has nothing to do with misfortune. He must be influenced ere he will respond. He must be urged ere he will move. He must be compelled ere he will arise. Ignoring the future and the past, he resigns himself to the laws of God.

"And therefore no calamity comes upon him, nothing injures him, no man is against him, no spirit punishes him. He floats through life to rest in death. He has no anxieties; he makes no plans. His honour does not make him illustrious. His good faith reflects no credit upon himself. His sleep is dreamless, his awaking without pain. His spirituality is pure, and his soul vigorous. Thus unconditioned and in repose, he is a partaker of the virtue of God."

Wherefore it has been said, "Sorrow and happiness are the heresies of virtue; joy and anger lead astray from TAO; love and hate cause the loss of virtue. The heart unconscious of sorrow and happiness,—that is perfect virtue. ONE, without change,—that is perfect repose. Without any obstruction,—that is the perfection of the unconditioned. Holding no relations with the external world,—that is perfection of the negative state. Without blemish of any kind,—that is the perfection of purity."

Autumn Floods

It was the time of autumn floods. Every stream poured into the river, which swelled in its turbid course. The banks receded so far from one another that it was impossible to tell a cow from a horse.

Then the Spirit of the River laughed for joy that all the beauty of the earth was gathered to himself. Down with the stream he journeyed east, until he reached the ocean. There, looking eastwards and seeing no limit to its waves, his countenance changed. And as he gazed over the expanse, he sighed and said to the Spirit of the Ocean, "A vulgar proverb says that he who has heard but part of the truth thinks no one equal to himself. And such a one am I.

"When formerly I heard people detracting from the learning of Confucius or underrating the heroism of Poh I, I did not believe. But now that I have looked upon your inexhaustibility—alas for me, had I not reached your abode, I should have been for ever a laughing-stock to those of comprehensive enlightenment!"

To which the Spirit of the Ocean replied, "You cannot speak of ocean to a well-frog,—the creature of a narrower sphere. You cannot speak of ice to a summer insect,—the creature of a season. You cannot speak of TAO to a pedagogue: his scope is too restricted. But now that you have emerged from your narrow sphere and have seen the great ocean, you know your own insignificance, and I can speak to you of great principles.

"Dimensions are limitless; time is endless. Conditions are not invariable; terms are not final. Thus, the wise man looks into space, and does not regard the small as too little, nor the great as too much; for he knows that there is no limit to dimension. He looks back into the past, and does not grieve over what is far off, nor rejoice over what is near; for he knows that time is without end. He investigates fullness and decay, and does not rejoice if he succeeds, nor lament if he fails; for he knows that conditions are not invariable. He who clearly apprehends the scheme of existence, does not rejoice over life, nor repine at death; for he knows that terms are not final.

"What man knows is not to be compared with what he does not know. The span of his existence is not to be compared with the span of his non-existence.

"I have heard say, the man of TAO has no reputation; perfect virtue acquires nothing; the truly great man ignores self;—this is the height of self-discipline."

"But how then," asked the Spirit of the River, "are the internal and external extremes of value and worthlessness, of greatness and small·ness, to be determined?"

"From the point of view of TAO," replied the Spirit of the Ocean, "there are no such extremes of value or worthlessness. Men individually value themselves and hold others cheap. The world collectively withholds from the individual the right of appraising himself.

"If we say that a thing is great or small because it is relatively great or small, then there is nothing in all creation which is not great, nothing which is not small.

"The life of man passes by like a galloping horse, changing at every turn, at every hour. What should he do, or what should he not do, other than let his decomposition go on?"

"If this is the case," retorted the Spirit of the River, "pray what is the value of TAO?"

"Those who understand TAO," answered the Spirit of the Ocean, "must necessarily apprehend the eternal principles above mentioned and be clear as to their application. Consequently, they do not suffer any injury from without.

"The man of perfect virtue cannot be burnt by fire, nor drowned in water, nor hurt by frost or sun, nor torn by wild bird or beast. Not that he makes light of these; but that he discriminates between safety and danger.

"Happy under prosperous and adverse circumstances alike, cautious as to what he discards and what he accepts;—nothing can harm him.

"Therefore it has been said that the natural abides within, the artificial without. Virtue abides in the natural. Knowledge of the action of the natural and of the artificial has its root in the natural, its development in virtue. And thus, whether in motion or at rest, whether in expansion or in contraction, there is always a reversion to the essential and to the ultimate."

"What do you mean," inquired the Spirit of the River, "by the natural and the artificial?"

"Horses and oxen," answered the Spirit of the Ocean, "have four feet. That is the natural. Put a halter on a horse's head, a string through a bullock's nose,—that is the artificial.

"Therefore it has been said, do not let the artificial obliterate the natural; do not let will obliterate destiny; do not let virtue be sacrificed to fame. Diligently observe these precepts without fail, and thus you will revert to the divine."

Each in Its Own Way

The walrus envies the centipede; the centipede envies the snake; the snake envies the wind; the wind envies the eye; the eye envies the mind.

The walrus said to the centipede, "I hop about on one leg, but not very successfully. How do you manage all these legs you have?"

"I don't manage them," replied the centipede. "Have you never seen saliva? When it is ejected, the big drops are the size of pearls, the small ones like mist. They fall promiscuously on the ground and cannot be counted. And so it is that my mechanism works naturally, without my being conscious of the fact."

The centipede said to the snake, "With all my legs I do not move as fast as you with none. How is that?"

"One's natural mechanism," replied the snake, "is not a thing to be changed. What need have I for legs?"

The snake said to the wind, "I can manage to wriggle along, but I have a form. Now you come blustering down from the north sea to bluster away to the south sea, and you seem to be without form. How is that?"

"'Tis true," replied the wind, "that I bluster as you say; but any one who can point at me or kick at me, excels me. On the other hand, I can break huge trees and destroy large buildings. That is my strong point. Out of all the small things in which I do not excel I make one great one in which I do excel. And to excel in great things is given only to the sages."

The Choice of Chuang Tze

Chuang Tze was fishing in the P'u when the prince of Ch'u sent two high officials to ask him to take charge of the administration of the Ch'u State.

Chuang Tze went on fishing, and without turning his head said, "I have heard that in Ch'u there is a sacred tortoise which has been dead now some three thousand years. And that the prince keeps this tortoise carefully enclosed in a chest on the altar of his ancestral people. Now would this tortoise rather be dead and have its remains venerated, or be alive and wagging its tail in the mud?"

"It would rather be alive," replied the two officials, "and wagging its tail in the mud."

"Begone!" cried Chuang Tze. "I too will wag my tail in the mud."

Perfect Happiness

Is perfect happiness to be found on earth, or not? Are there those who can enjoy life, or not? If so, what do they do, what do they affect, what do they avoid, what do they rest in, accept, reject, like, and dislike?

What the world esteems comprises wealth, rank, old age, and goodness of heart. What it enjoys comprises comfort, rich food, fine clothes, beauty, and music. What it does not esteem comprises poverty, want of position, early death, and evil behaviour. What it does not enjoy comprises lack of comfort for the body, lack of rich food for the palate, lack of fine clothes for the back, lack of beauty for the eye, and lack of music for the ear. If men do not get these, they are greatly miserable. Yet from the point of view of our physical frame, this is folly.

Wealthy people who toil and moil, putting together more money than they can possibly use,—from the point of view of our physical frame, is not this going beyond the mark?

Officials of rank who turn night into day in their endeavours to compass the best ends;—from the point of view of our physical frame, is not this a divergence?

Man is born to sorrow, and what misery is theirs whose old age with dulled faculties only means prolonged sorrow! From the point of view of our physical frame, this is going far astray.

Patriots are in the world's opinion admittedly good. Yet their goodness does not enable them to enjoy life; and so I know not whether theirs is veritable goodness or not. If the former, it does not enable them to enjoy life; if the latter, it at any rate enables them to cause others to enjoy theirs.

It has been said, "If your loyal counsels are not attended to, depart quietly without resistance." Thus, when Tze Hsu resisted, his physical frame perished; yet had he not resisted, he would not have made his name. Is there then really such a thing as this goodness, or not?

As to what the world does and the way in which people are happy now, I know not whether such happiness be real happiness or not. The happiness of ordinary persons seems to me to consist in slavishly following the majority, as if they could not help it. Yet they all say they are happy.

But I cannot say that this is happiness or that it is not happiness. Is there then, after all, such a thing as happiness?

I make true pleasure to consist in inaction, which the world regards as great pain. Thus it has been said, "Perfect happiness is the absence of happiness; perfect renown is the absence of renown."

Now in this sublunary world of ours it is impossible to assign positive and negative absolutely. Nevertheless, in inaction they can be so assigned. Perfect happiness and preservation of life are to be sought for only in inaction.

Let us consider. Heaven does nothing; yet it is clear. Earth does nothing; yet it enjoys repose. From the inaction of these two proceed all the modifications of things. How vast, how infinite is inaction, yet without source! How infinite, how vast, yet without form!

The endless varieties of things around us all spring from inaction. Therefore it has been said, "Heaven and earth do nothing, yet there is nothing which they do not accomplish." But among men, who can attain to inaction?

The Death of Chuang Tze's Wife

When Chuang Tze's wife died, Hui Tze went to condole. He found the widower sitting on the ground, singing, with his legs spread out at a right angle, and beating time on a bowl.

"To live with your wife," exclaimed Hui Tze, "and see your eldest son grow up to be a man, and then not to shed a tear over her corpse,—this would be bad enough. But to drum on a bowl, and sing; surely this is going too far."

"Not at all," replied Chuang Tze. "When she died, I could not help being affected by her death. Soon, however, I remembered that she had already existed in a previous state before birth, without form, or even substance; that while in that unconditioned condition, substance was added to spirit; that this substance then assumed form; and that the next stage was birth. And now, by virtue of a further change, she is dead, passing from one phase to another like the sequence of spring, summer, autumn, and winter. And while she is thus lying asleep in eternity, for me to go about weeping and wailing would be to proclaim myself ignorant of these natural laws. Therefore I refrain."

The Wisdom of the Skull

Chuang Tze one day saw an empty skull, bleached but still preserving its shape. Striking it with his riding whip, he said, "Wert thou once some ambitious citizen whose inordinate yearnings brought him to this pass?—some statesman who plunged his country into ruin and perished in the fray?—some wretch who left behind him a legacy of shame?—some beggar who died in the pangs of hunger and cold? Or didst thou reach this state by the natural course of old age?"

When he had finished speaking, he took the skull, and placing it under his head as a pillow, went to sleep. In the night, he dreamt that the skull appeared to him and said, "You speak well, sir; but all you say has reference to the life of mortals, and to mortal troubles. In death there are none of these. Would you like to hear about death?"

Chuang Tze having replied in the affirmative, the skull began:—"In death, there is no sovereign above, and no subject below. The workings of the four seasons are unknown. Our existences are bounded only by eternity. The happiness of a king among men cannot exceed that which we enjoy."

Chuang Tze, however, was not convinced, and said, "Were I to prevail upon God to allow your body to be born again, and your bones and flesh to be renewed, so that you could return to your parents, to your wife, and to the friends of your youth,—would you be willing?"

At this, the skull opened its eyes wide and knitted its brows and said, "How should I cast aside happiness greater than that of a king, and mingle once again in the toils and troubles of mortality?"

The Great Scheme

Certain germs, falling upon water, become duckweed. When they reach the junction of the land and the water, they become lichen. Spreading up the bank, they become the dog-tooth violet. Reaching rich soil, they become su-tsu, the root of which becomes grubs, while the leaves become butterflies, or hsu. These are changed into insects, born in the chimney corner, which look like skeletons. Their name is ch'u-to. After a thousand days, the ch'u-to becomes a bird, called Kan-yu-ku, the spittle of which becomes the ssu-mi. The ssu-mi becomes a wine fly, and that comes from an i-lu. The huang-k'uang produces the chiu-yu and the mou-jui produces the glow-worm. The yang-ch'i grafted to an old bamboo which has for a long time put forth no shoots, produces the ch'ing-ning, which produces the leopard, which produces the horse, which produces man.

Then man goes back into the great scheme, from which all things come and to which all things return.

The Secret of Life

"A drunken man who falls out of a cart, though he may suffer, does not die. His bones are the same as other people's; but he meets his accident in a different way. His spirit is in a condition of security. He is not conscious of riding in the cart; neither is he conscious of falling out of it. Ideas of life, death, fear, etc., cannot penetrate his breast; and so he does not suffer from contact with objective existences. And if such security is to be got from wine, how much more is it to be got from God. It is in God that the sage seeks his refuge, and so he is free from harm."

The Grand Augur and the Pigs

The Grand Augur, in his ceremonial robes, approached the shambles and thus addressed the pigs:

"How can you object to die? I shall fatten you for three months. I shall discipline myself for ten days and fast for three. I shall strew fine grass, and place you bodily upon a carved sacrificial dish. Does not this satisfy you?"

Then speaking from the pigs' point of view, he continued, "It is better perhaps after all to live on bran and escape the shambles. . . .

"But then," added he, speaking from his own point of view, "to enjoy honour when alive one would readily die on a war-shield or in the headsman's basket."

So he rejected the pigs' point of view and adopted his own point of view. In what sense then was he different from the pigs?

The Fighting Cocks

Chi Hsing Tze was training fighting cocks for the prince. At the end of ten days the latter asked if they were ready. "Not yet," replied Chi; "they are still excited by the sounds and shadows of other cocks."

Ten days more, and the prince asked again. "Not yet," answered Chi; "the sight of an enemy is still enough to excite them to rage."

But after another ten days, when the prince again inquired, Chi said, "They will do. Other cocks may crow, but they will take no notice. To look at them one might say they were of wood. Their virtue is complete. Strange cocks will not dare meet them, but will run."

Confucius at the Cataract

Confucius was looking at the cataract at Lu-liang. It fell from a height of thirty jen, and its foam reached forty li away. No scaly, finny creature could enter therein. Yet Confucius saw an old man go in, and thinking that he was suffering from some trouble and desirous of ending his life, bade a disciple run along the side to try to save him. The old man emerged about a hundred paces off, and with flowing hair went carolling along the bank. Confucius followed him and said, "I had thought, sir, you were a spirit, but now I see you are a man. Kindly tell me, is there any way to deal thus with water?"

"No," replied the old man; "I have no way. There was my original condition to begin with; then habit growing into nature; and lastly acquiescence in destiny. Plunging in with the whirl, I come out with the swirl. I accommodate myself to the water, not the water to me. And so I am able to deal with it after this fashion."

"What do you mean," inquired Confucius, "by your original condition to begin with, habit growing into nature, and acquiescence in destiny?"

"I was born," replied the old man, "upon dry land, and accommodated myself to dry land. That was my original condition. Growing up on the water, I accommodated myself to the water. That was what I meant by nature. And doing as I did without being conscious of any effort so to do, that was what I meant by destiny."

The Way of the Good Carpenter

Ch'ing, the chief carpenter, was carving wood into a stand for hanging musical instruments. When finished, the work appeared to those who saw it as though of supernatural execution. And the prince of Lu asked him, saying, "What mystery is there in your art?"

"No mystery, your Highness," replied Ch'ing; "and yet there is something.

"When I am about to make such a stand, I guard against any diminution of my vital power. I first reduce my mind to absolute quiescence.

Three days in this condition, and I become oblivious of any reward to be gained. Five days, and I become oblivious of any fame to be acquired. Seven days, and I become unconscious of my four limbs and my physical frame. Then, with no thought of the Court present to my mind, my skill becomes concentrated, and all disturbing elements from without are gone. I enter some mountain forest. I search for a suitable tree. It contains the form required, which is afterwards elaborated. I see the stand in my mind's eye, and then set to work. Otherwise, there is nothing. I bring my own natural capacity into relation with that of the wood. What was suspected to be of supernatural execution in my work was due solely to this."

Chuang Tze and the Strange Bird

When Chuang Tze was wandering in the park at Tiao-ling, he saw a strange bird which came from the south. Its wings were seven feet across. Its eyes were an inch in circumference. And it flew close past Chuang Tze's head to alight in a chestnut grove.

"What manner of bird is this?" cried Chuang Tze. "With strong wings it does not fly away. With large eyes it does not see."

So he picked up his skirts and strode towards it with his cross-bow, anxious to get a shot. Just then he saw a cicada enjoying itself in the shade, forgetful of all else. And he saw a mantis spring and seize it, forgetting in the act its own body, which the strange bird immediately pounced upon and made its prey. And this it was which had caused the bird to forget its own nature.

"Alas!" cried Chuang Tze with a sigh, "how creatures injure one another. Loss follows the pursuit of gain."

So he laid aside his bow and went home, driven away by the park-keeper who wanted to know what business he had there.

The Beautiful and Ugly Concubines

The innkeeper had two concubines, one beautiful, the other ugly. The latter he loved; the former, he hated.

Yang Tze asked how this was; whereupon one of the inn servants said, "The beautiful one is so conscious of her beauty that one does not think her beautiful. The ugly one is so conscious of her ugliness that one does not think her ugly."

"Note this, my disciples!" cried Yang Tze. "Be virtuous, but without being consciously so; and wherever you go, you will be beloved."

The Man Who Fished for Fun

When Wen Wang was on a tour of inspection in Tsang, he saw an old man fishing. But his fishing was not real fishing, for he did not fish to catch fish, but to amuse himself.

So Wen Wang wished to employ him in the administration of government, but feared lest his own ministers, uncles, and brothers, might object. On the other hand, if he let the old man go, he could not bear to think of the people being deprived of such an influence.

Accordingly, that very morning he informed his ministers, saying, "I once dreamt that a sage of a black colour and with a large beard, riding upon a parti-coloured horse with red stockings on one side, appeared and instructed me to place the administration in the hands of the old gentleman of Tsang, promising that the people would benefit greatly thereby."

The ministers at once said, "It is a command from your Highness' father."

"I think so," answered Wen Wang. "But let us try by divination."

"It is a command from your Highness' late father," said the ministers, "and may not be disobeyed. What need for divination?"

So the old man of Tsang was received and entrusted with the administration. He altered none of the existing statutes. He issued no unjust regulations. And when, after three years, Wen Wang made another inspection, he found all dangerous organizations broken up, the officials doing their duty as a matter of course, while the use of measures of grain was unknown within the four boundaries of the state. There was thus unanimity in the public voice, singleness of official purpose, and identity of interests to all.

So Wen Wang appointed the old man Grand Tutor; and then, standing with his face to the north, asked him, saying, "Can such government be extended over the empire?"

The old man of Tsang was silent and made no reply. He then abruptly took leave, and by the evening of that same day had disappeared, never to be heard of again.

The Law of Creation

The universe is very beautiful, yet it says nothing. The four seasons abide by a fixed law, yet they are not heard. All creation is based upon absolute principles, yet nothing speaks.

And the true sage, taking his stand upon the beauty of the universe, pierces the principles of created things. Hence the saying that the perfect man does nothing, the true sage performs nothing, beyond gazing at the universe.

For man's intellect, however keen, face to face with the countless evolutions of things, their death and birth, their squareness and roundness,—can never reach the root. There creation is, and there it has ever been.

The six cardinal points, reaching into infinity, are ever included in TAO. An autumn spikelet, in all its minuteness, must carry TAO within itself. There is nothing on earth which does not rise and fall, but it never perishes altogether. The Yin and the Yang, and the four seasons, keep to their proper order. Apparently destroyed, yet really existing; the material gone, the immaterial left;—such is the law of creation, which passeth all understanding. This is called the root, whence a glimpse may be obtained of God.

The Impossibility of Possessing

Shun asked Ch'eng, saying, "Can one get TAO so as to have it for one's own?"

"Your very body," replied Ch'eng, "is not your own. How should TAO be?"

"If my body," said Shun, "is not my own, pray whose is it?"

"It is the delegated image of God," replied Ch'eng. "Your life is not your own. It is the delegated harmony of God. Your individuality is

THE WORKS OF CHUANG TZE

not your own. It is the delegated adaptability of God. Your posterity is not your own. It is the delegated exuviae of God. You move, but know not how. You are at rest, but know not why. You taste, but know not the cause. These are the operation of God's laws. How then should you get TAO so as to have it for your own?''

All Things after Their Kind

Confucius said to Lao Tze, "To-day you are at leisure. Pray tell me about perfect TAO."

"Purge your heart by fasting and discipline," answered Lao Tze. "Wash your soul as white as snow. Discard your knowledge. TAO is abstruse and difficult of discussion. I will try, however, to speak to you of its outline.

"Light is born of darkness. Classification is born of formlessness. The soul is born of TAO. The body is born of the vital essence.

"Thus all things produce after their kind. Creatures with nine channels of communication are born from the womb. Creatures with eight are born from the egg. Of their coming there is no trace. In their departure there is no goal. No entrance gate, no dwelling house, they pass this way and that, as though at the meeting of cross-roads.

"Those who enter herein become strong of limb, subtle of thought, and clear of sight and hearing. They suffer no mental fatigue, nor meet with physical resistance.

"Heaven cannot but be high. Earth cannot but be broad. The sun and moon cannot but revolve. All creation cannot but flourish. To do so is their TAO.

"But it is not from extensive study that this may be known, nor by dialectic skill that this may be made clear. The true sage will have none of these. It is in addition without gain, in diminution without loss, that the true sage finds salvation.

"Unfathomable as the sea, wondrously ending only to begin again, informing all creation without being exhausted, the TAO of the perfect man is spontaneous in its operation. That all creation can be informed by it without exhaustion, is its TAO.

"In the Middle Kingdom there are men who recognize neither positive nor negative. They abide between heaven and earth. They act their part as mortals, and then return to the Cause.

"From that standpoint, life is but a concentration of the vital fluid, whose longest and shortest terms of existence vary by an inappreciable space,—hardly enough for the classification of Yao and Chieh.

"Tree-fruits and plant-fruits exhibit order in their varieties; and the relationships of man, though more difficult to be dealt with, may still be reduced to order. The true sage who meets with these, does not violate them. Neither does he continue to hold fast by them. Adaptation by arrangement is TE. Spontaneous adaptation is TAO, by which sovereigns flourish and princes succeed.

"Man passes through this sublunary life as a white horse passes a crack. Here one moment, gone the next. Neither are there any not equally subject to the ingress and egress of mortality. One modification brings life; then another, and it is death. Living creatures cry out; human beings sorrow. The bow-sheath is slipped off; the clothes-bag is dropped; and in the confusion the soul wings its flight, and the body follows, on the great journey home!

"The reality of the formless, the unreality of that which has form,—this is known to all. Those who are on the road to attainment care not for these things, but the people at large discuss them. Attainment implies non-discussion: discussion implies non-attainment. Manifested, TAO has no objective value; hence silence is better than argument. It cannot be translated into speech; better then say nothing at all. This is called the great attainment."

Where Tao Is

Tung Kuo Tze asked Chuang Tze, saying, "What you call TAO,—where is it?"

"There is nowhere," replied Chuang Tze, "where it is not."

"Tell me one place at any rate where it is," said Tung Kuo Tze.

"It is in the ant," replied Chuang Tze.

"Why go so low down?" asked Tung Kuo Tze.

"It is in a tare," said Chuang Tze.

"Still lower," objected Tung Kuo Tze.

"It is in a potsherd," said Chuang Tze.

"Worse still!" cried Tung Kuo Tze.

"It is in ordure," said Chuang Tze. And Tung Kuo Tze made no reply.

"Sir," continued Chuang Tze, "your question does not touch the essential. When Huo, inspector of markets, asked the managing director about the fatness of pigs, the test was always made in parts least likely to be fat. Do not therefore insist in any particular direction; for there is nothing which escapes. Such is perfect TAO; and such also is ideal speech. *Whole, entire, all,* are three words which sound differently but mean the same. Their purport is ONE.

"Try to reach with me the palace of Nowhere, and there, amidst the identity of all things, carry your discussions into the infinite. Try to practise with me inaction, wherein you may rest motionless, without care, and be happy. For thus my mind becomes an abstraction. It wanders not, and yet is not conscious of being at rest. It goes and comes and is not conscious of stoppages. Backwards and forwards without being conscious of any goal. Up and down the realms of infinity, wherein even the greatest intellect would fail to find an end.

"That which makes things the things they are, is not limited to such things. The limits of things are their own limits in so far as they are things. The limits of the limitless, the limitlessness of the limited,— these are called fullness and emptiness, renovation and decay. TAO causes fullness and emptiness, but it is not either. It causes renovation and decay, but it is not either. It causes beginning and end, but it is not either. It causes accumulation and dispersion, but it is not either."

The Invisibility of Nothing

Light asked Nothing, saying, "Do you, sir, exist, or do you not exist?"

But getting no answer to his question, Light set to work to watch for the appearance of Nothing.

Hidden, vacuous,—all day long he looked but could not see it, listened but could not hear it, grasped at but could not seize it.

"Bravo!" cried Light. "Who can equal this? I can get to be Nothing, but I cannot get as far as the absence of Nothing. Assuming that Nothing has an objective existence, how can it reach this next stage?"

No Past, No Present

Jen Ch'iu asked Confucius, saying, "Can we know about the time before the universe existed?"

"We can," replied Confucius. "Time was of old precisely what it is now."

At this rebuff, Jen Ch'iu withdrew. Next day he again visited Confucius and said, "Yesterday when I asked you that question and you answered me, I was quite clear about it. To-day I am confused. How is this?"

"Your clearness of yesterday," answered Confucius, "was because my answer appealed direct to your natural intelligence. Your confusion of to-day results from the intrusion of something other than the natural intelligence. There is no past, no present, no beginning, no end. To have posterity before one has posterity,—is that possible?"

Jen Ch'iu made no answer, and Confucius continued, "That will do. Do not reply. If life did not give birth to death, and if death did not put an end to life, surely life and death would be no longer correlates, but would each exist independently. What there was before the universe, was TAO. TAO makes things what they are, but is not itself a thing. Nothing can produce TAO; yet everything has TAO within it, and continues to produce it without end. And the endless love of the sage for his fellow-man is based upon the same principle."

The Wise Tender of Horses

When the Yellow Emperor went to see TAO upon the Chu-tz'u Mountain, Fang Ming was his charioteer, Ch'ang Yu sat on his right, Chang Jo and Hsi P'eng were his outriders, and K'un Hun and Hua Chi brought up the rear. On reaching the wilds of Hsiang-ch'eng, these seven sages lost their way and there was no one of whom to ask the road. By and by, they fell in with a boy who was grazing horses, and asked him, saying, "Do you know the Chu-tz'u Mountain?"

"I do," replied the boy.

"And can you tell us," continued the Sages, "where TAO abides?"

"I can," replied the boy.

"This is a strange lad," cried the Yellow Emperor. "Not only does he know where the Chu-tz'u Mountain is, but also where TAO abides! Come tell me, pray, how would you govern the empire?"

"I should govern the empire," said the boy, "just the same as I look after my horses. What else should I do?

"When I was a little boy and used to live within the points of the compass, my eyes got dim of sight. An old man advised me to mount the chariot of the sun and visit the wilds of Hsiang-ch'eng. My sight is now much better, and I continue to dwell without the points of the compass. I should govern the empire in just the same way. What else should I do?"

"Of course," said the Yellow Emperor, "government is not your trade. Still I should be glad to hear what you would do."

The boy declined to answer, but on being again urged, cried out, "What difference is there between governing the empire and looking after horses? See that no harm comes to the horses, that is all!"

Thereupon the Emperor prostrated himself before the boy; and addressing him as Divine Teacher, took his leave.

The Value of Hsi P'eng

Kuan Chung being at the point of death, Duke Huan went to see him.

"You are ill, venerable sir," said the Duke, "really ill. You had better say to whom, in the event of your getting worse, I am to entrust the administration of the state."

"Whom does your Highness wish to choose?" inquired Kuan Chung.

"Will Pao Yu do?" asked the Duke.

"He will not," said Kuan Chung. "He is pure, incorruptible, and good. With those who are not like himself, he will not associate. And if he has once heard of a man's wrong-doing, he never forgets it. If you employ him in the administration of the empire, he will get to loggerheads with his prince and to sixes and sevens with the people. It would not be long before he and your Highness fell out."

"Whom then can we have?" asked the Duke.

"There is no alternative," replied Kuan Chung; "it must be Hsi

P'eng. He is a man who forgets the authority of those above him, and makes those below him forget his. Ashamed that he is not the peer of the Yellow Emperor, he grieves over those who are not the peers of himself.

"To share one's virtue with others is called true wisdom. To share one's wealth with others is reckoned meritorious. To exhibit superior merit is not the way to win men's hearts. To exhibit inferior merit is the way. There are things in the state he does not hear; there are things in the family he does not see. There is no alternative; it must be Hsi P'eng."

The Stickleback Out of Water

Chuang Tze's family being poor, he went to borrow some corn from the prince of Chien-ho.

"Yes," said the prince. "I am just about collecting the revenue of my fief, and will then lend you three hundred ounces of silver. Will that do?"

At this Chuang Tze flushed with anger and said, "Yesterday, as I was coming along, I heard a voice calling me. I looked round, and in the cart-rut I saw a stickleback.

" 'And what do you want, stickleback?' said I.

" 'I am a denizen of the eastern ocean,' replied the stickleback. 'Pray, sir, a pint of water to save my life.'

" 'Yes,' said I. 'I am just going south to visit the princes of Wu and Yueh. I will bring you some from the west river. Will that do?'

"At this the stickleback flushed with anger and said, 'I am out of my element. I have nowhere to go. A pint of water would save me. But to talk to me like this,—you might as well put me in a dried-fish shop at once.' "

Shan Chuan's Choice

Shun offered to resign the empire to Shan Chuan. Shan Chuan said, "I am a unit in the sum of the universe. In winter I wear fur clothes. In summer I wear grass-cloth. In spring I plough and sow, toiling with my body. In autumn I gather in the harvest, and devote myself to rest and enjoyment. At dawn I go to work; at sunset I leave off. Contented with my lot I pass through life with a light heart. Why then should I trouble myself with the empire? Ah, sir, you do not know me."

So he declined, and subsequently hid himself among the mountains, nobody knew where.

Chuang Tze on Death

When Chuang Tze was about to die, his disciples expressed a wish to give him a splendid funeral. But Chuang Tze said, "With heaven and earth for my coffin and shell; with the sun, moon, and stars as my burial regalia; and with all creation to escort me to the grave,—are not my funeral paraphernalia ready to hand?"

"We fear," argued the disciples, "lest the carrion kite should eat the body of our Master"; to which Chuang Tze replied, "Above ground I shall be food for kites; below I shall be food for mole-crickets and ants. Why rob one to feed the other?

"If you adopt, as absolute, a standard of evenness which is so only relatively, your results will not be absolutely even. If you adopt, as absolute, a criterion of right which is so only relatively, your results will not be absolutely right. Those who trust to their senses become slaves to objective existences. Those alone who are guided by their intuitions find the true standard. So far are the senses less reliable than the intuitions. Yet fools trust to their senses to know what is good for mankind, with alas! but external results."

Keng Sang Ch'u

Among the disciples of Lao Tze was one named Keng Sang Ch'u. He alone had attained to the TAO of his Master. He lived up north, on the Wei-lei Mountains. Of his attendants, he dismissed those who were systematically clever or conventionally charitable. The useless remained with him; the incompetent served him. And in three years the district of Wei-lei was greatly benefited.

One of the inhabitants said in conversation, "When Mr. Keng Sang first came among us, we did not know what to make of him. Now, we could not say enough about him in a day, and even a year would leave something unsaid. Surely he must be a true sage. Why not pray to him as to the spirits, and honour him as a tutelary god of the land?"

On hearing of this, Keng Sang Ch'u turned his face to the south in shame, at which his disciples were astonished. But Keng Sang said, "What cause have you for astonishment? The influence of spring quickens the life of plants, and autumn brings them to maturity. In the absence of any agent, how is this so? It is the operation of TAO.

"I have heard that the perfect man may be pent up like a corpse in a tomb, yet the people will become unartificial and without care. But now these poor people of Wei-lei wish to exalt me among their wise and good. Surely then I am but a shallow vessel; and therefore I was shamed for the doctrine of Lao Tze."

Nan Yung

Nan Yung took some provisions, and after a seven days' journey arrived at the abode of Lao Tze.

"Have you come from Keng Sang Ch'u?" said the latter.

"I have," replied Nan Yung.

"But why," said Lao Tze, "bring all these people with you?"

Nan Yung looked back in alarm, and Lao Tze continued, "Do you not understand what I say?"

Nan Yung bent his head abashed, and then looking up, said with a sigh, "I have now forgotten how to answer, in consequence of missing what I came to ask."

"What do you mean?" said Lao Tze.

"If I do not know," replied Nan Yung, "men call me a fool. If I do know, I injure myself. If I am not charitable, I injure others. If I am, I injure myself. If I do not do my duty to my neighbour, I injure others. If I do it, I injure myself. My trouble lies in not seeing how to escape from these three dilemmas. On the strength of my connexion with Keng Sang, I would venture to ask advice."

"When I saw you," said Lao Tze, "I knew in the twinkling of an eye what was the matter with you. And now what you say confirms my view. You are confused, as a child that has lost its parents. You would fathom the sea with a pole. You are astray. You are struggling to get back to your natural self, but cannot find the way. Alas! alas!"

Nan Yung begged to be allowed to remain, and set to work to cultivate the good and eliminate the evil within him. At the expiration of ten days, with sorrow in his heart, he again sought Lao Tze.

"Have you thoroughly cleansed yourself?" said Lao Tze. "But this grieved look . . . There is some evil obstruction yet.

"If the disturbances are external, do not be always combating them, but close the channels to the mind. If the disturbances are internal, do not strive to oppose them, but close all entrance from without. If the disturbances are both internal and external, then you will not even be able to hold fast to TAO, still less practise it."

"If a rustic is sick," said Nan Yung, "and another rustic goes to see him; and if the sick man can say what is the matter with him,—then he is not seriously ill. Yet my search after TAO is like swallowing drugs which only increase the malady. I beg therefore merely to ask the art of preserving life."

"The art of preserving life," replied Lao Tze, "consists in being able to keep all in ONE, to lose nothing, to estimate good and evil without divination, to know when to stop, and how much is enough, to leave others alone and attend to oneself, to be without cares and without knowledge,—to be in fact as a child. A child will cry all day and not become hoarse, because of the perfection of its constitutional harmony. It will keep its fist tightly closed all day and not open it, because of the concentration of its virtue. It will gaze all day without taking off its eyes, because its sight is not attracted by externals. In motion, it knows not whither it is bound; at rest, it is not conscious of doing anything; but unconsciously adapts itself to the exigencies of its environment. This is the art of preserving life."

"Is this then the virtue of the perfect man?" cried Nan Yung.

"Not so," said Lao Tze. "I am, as it were, but breaking the ice.

"The perfect man shares the food of this earth, but the happiness of God. He does not incur trouble either from men or things. He does not join in censuring, in plotting, in toadying. Free from care he comes, and unconscious he goes;—this is the art of preserving life."

"This then is perfection?" inquired Nan Yung.

"Not yet," said Lao Tze. "I specially asked if you could be as a child. A child acts without knowing what it does; moves without knowing whither. Its body is like a dry branch; its heart like dead ashes. Thus, good and evil fortune find no lodgment therein; and there where good and evil fortune are not, how can the troubles of mortality be?

"Those whose hearts are in a state of repose give forth a divine radiance, by the light of which they see themselves as they are. And only by cultivating such repose can man attain to the constant.

"Those who are constant are sought after by men and assisted by God. Those who are sought after by men are the people of God; those who are assisted by God are his chosen children.

"To study this is to study what cannot be learnt. To practise this is to practise what cannot be accomplished. To discuss this is to discuss what can never be proved. Let knowledge stop at the unknowable. That is perfection. And for those who do not follow this, God will destroy them!

"With such defences for the body, ever prepared for the unexpected, deferential to the rights of others,—if then calamities overtake you, these are from God, not from man. Let them not disturb what you have already achieved. Let them not penetrate into the soul's abode. For there resides the will. And if the will knows not what to will, it will not be able to will.

"Whatsoever is not said in all sincerity, is wrongly said. And not to be able to rid oneself of this vice is only to sink deeper towards perdition.

"Those who do evil in the open light of day,—men will punish them. Those who do evil in secret,—God will punish them. Who fears both man and God, he is fit to walk alone. Those who are devoted to the internal, in practice acquire no reputation. Those who are devoted to the external, strive for pre-eminence among their fellows. Practice without reputation throws a halo around the meanest. But he who strives for pre-eminence among his fellows, he is as a huckster whose weariness all perceive though he himself puts on an air of gaiety.

"He who is naturally in sympathy with man, to him all men come. But he who forcedly adapts, has no room even for himself, still less for others. And he who has no room for others, has no ties. It is all over with him.

"TAO informs its own subdivisions, their successes and their failures. What is feared in sub-division is separation. What is feared in separation, is further separation. Thus, to issue forth without return, this is development of the supernatural. To issue forth and attain the goal, this is called death. To be annihilated and yet to exist, this is convergence of the supernatural into ONE. To make things which have form appear to all intents and purposes formless,—this is the sum of all things.

"Birth is not a beginning; death is not an end. There is existence without limitation; there is continuity without a starting-point. Existence without limitation is space. Continuity without a starting-point is time. There is birth, there is death, there is issuing forth, there is entering in. That through which one passes in and out without seeing its form, that is the Portal of God.

"The Portal of God is non-existence. All things sprang from non-existence. Existence could not make existence existence. It must have proceeded from non-existence, and non-existence and nothing are ONE. Herein is the abiding-place of the sage.

"The knowledge of the ancients reached the highest point,—the time before anything existed. This is the highest point. It is exhaustive. There is no adding to it.

"The second best was that of those who started from existence. Life was to them a misfortune. Death was a return home. There was already separation.

"The next in the scale said that at the beginning there was nothing. Then life came, to be quickly followed by death. They made nothing the head, life the trunk, and death the tail of existence, claiming as friends whoever knew that existence and non-existence, and life and death were all ONE.

"These three classes, though different, were of the same clan; as were Chao Ching who inherited fame, and Chia who inherited territory.

"Man's life is as the soot on a kettle. Yet men speak of the subjective point of view. But this subjective point of view will not bear the test. It is a point of knowledge we cannot reach.

"At the winter sacrifice, the tripe may be separated from the great toe; yet these cannot be separated. He who looks at a house, visits the ancestral hall, and even the latrines. Thus every point is the subjective point of view.

"Let us try to formulate this subjective point of view. It originates with life, and, with knowledge as its tutor, drifts into the admission of right and wrong. But one's own standard of right is the standard, and others have to adapt themselves to it. Men will die for this. Such people look upon the useful as appertaining to wisdom, the useless as appertaining to folly; upon success in life as honourable, upon failure as dishonourable. The subjective point of view is that of the present generation, who like the cicada and the young dove see things only from their own standpoint.

"If a man treads upon a stranger's toe in the market-place, he apologizes on the score of hurry. If an elder brother does this, he is quit with an exclamation of sympathy. And if a parent does so, nothing whatever is done.

"Therefore it has been said, 'Perfect politeness is not artificial; perfect duty to one's neighbour is not a matter of calculation; perfect wisdom takes no thought; perfect charity recognizes no ties; perfect trust requires no pledges.'

"Discard the stimuli of purpose. Free the mind from disturbances. Get rid of entanglements to virtue. Pierce the obstructions to TAO.

"Honours, wealth, distinction, power, fame, gain,—these six stimulate purpose.

"Mien, carriage, beauty, arguments, influence, opinions,—these six disturb the mind.

"Hate, ambition, joy, anger, sorrow, pleasure,—these six are entanglements to virtue.

"Rejecting, adopting, receiving, giving, knowledge, ability,—these six are obstructions to TAO.

"If these twenty-four be not allowed to run riot, then the mind will be duly ordered. And being duly ordered, it will be in repose. And being in repose, it will be clear of perception. And being clear of perception, it will be unconditioned. And being unconditioned, it will be in that state of inaction by which there is nothing which cannot be accomplished."

Zoroastrian
Scriptures

ZOROASTRIAN
SCRIPTURES

The Hymns of Zoroaster
(The Gathas)

Exhortation to the Faithful

Now will I speak out: listen and hear,
You who, from far and near, have come to seek my word;
Now I exhort you clearly to impress on your memory the evil teacher
     and his faults; for
No longer shall the evil teacher—Druj that he is!—destroy the second
    life,
In the speech of his tongue misleading to the evil life.

Now will I speak out: At the beginning of life
The holier Mentality said to the opposing Mentality who was more
    hostile,
"Neither our thoughts, doctrines, plans,
Beliefs, utterances, deeds,
Individualities, nor souls agree."

Now will I speak out! Of that which at the beginning of life
The knowing Ahura Mazda said:
"Those who do not practise the Word,
As I consider and declare it,
They shall have woe at the end of life."

Now will I speak out what is the best of life:
Through Justice, O Mazda, have I discovered thee, who hast created him;
That Mazda is the father of the working Good Disposition;
And that Love, who produces good deeds, is his daughter;
And that the all-detecting Ahura is not to be deceived.

Now will I, who am the utterer of this Word which is the best for
      mortal men to hear,
Speak out what the most bounteous Ahura Mazda said to me:
"Those who, for the attainment of this mystic manthric Word grant me
      their obedience,
They shall come up with Health, and Immortality,
With the deeds of the good Mentality."

Now will I speak out about the greatest being of all
Through Justice praising Mazda, who blesses all existent beings!
Let Ahura Mazda hear, through the bounteous Mentality, the fact
That I consulted Good Disposition as to how I should adore Mazda;
Through Mazda's understanding, may he, Good Disposition, teach me
      the best teachings!

Let the preparers for the conversion of the world, both those who were,
      and those who are yet becoming
Wish for the profits of the compensations;
The successful soul of the Ashaist abiding in Immortality
With enduringness; while the Drujists shall endure griefs,
And all this Ahura Mazda creates through the coming of the Kingdom.

Thou shalt seek to win Mazda with such praises of reverence as for
      instance this psalm:
"With my own eyes shall I now behold the heaven
Of the good Mentality of word and deed;
Having, through Justice, known Ahura Mazda,
To whom let us, in heaven, set down adorations for the filling of the
      paradise Garodman."

Him, Mazda, along with Good Disposition, shalt thou seek to satisfy
      for us,
Because it is he who, by his will, makes our fortune or misfortune.
May Ahura Mazda through his realm
Grant, for the group of herdsmen, prospering of our cattle and men
By the proficiency of Good Disposition, through Justice.

How shalt thou, O individual believer, with hymns of Love, magnify
Him who is reputed to be Ahura Mazda for eternity;
Since through Justice and Good Disposition he has promised us

That in his realm we shall obtain Health and Immortality;
But we shall obtain that his heavenly dwelling through vitality and
enduringness.

Whoever, therefore, in the future scorns the Daevas
And the men who scorn Zarathushtra,
And all others—lukewarm neutrals—except whoever is devoted to
Zarathushtra,
Shall be considered, by the bounteous individuality of Zarathushtra, who
is Saviour and Master-of-the-house
As his friend, brother, or father,—O Ahura Mazda!

A Prayer for Guidance

O Ahura Mazda, this I ask of thee: speak to me truly!
How should I pray, when I wish to pray to one like you?
May one like you, O Mazda, who is friendly, teach one like me?
And may you give us supporting aids through the friendly Justice,
And tell us how you may come to us with Good Disposition?

O Ahura Mazda, this I ask of thee: speak to me truly!
Whether at the beginning of the best life
The retributions will be of profit to their recipients?
And whether he, who is bounteous to all through Justice, and who
watches the end
Through his Mentality,—whether he is the life-healing friend of the
people?

O Ahura Mazda, this I ask of thee: speak to me truly!
Who was the first father of Justice by giving birth to him?
Who established the sunlit days and the star glistering sphere and the
Milky Way?
Who, apart from thee, established the law by which the moon waxes
and wanes?
These and other things would I like to know!

O Ahura Mazda, this I ask of thee: speak to me truly!
Who was from beneath sustaining the earth and the clouds
So that they would not fall down? Who made the waters and the plants?

Who yoked the two swift ones, thunder and lightning, to the wind and
    to the clouds?
Who is the creator of Good Disposition?

O Ahura Mazda, this I ask of thee: speak to me truly!
Who produced well-made lights and darkness?
Who produced sleep, well-induced through laborious waking?
Who produced the dawns and the noon through the contrast with the
    night
Whose daily changes act for the enlightened believers as monitors of
    their interests?

O Ahura Mazda, this I ask of thee: speak to me truly!
Is the message I am about to proclaim genuine?
Does Love support Justice through deeds?
Dost thou with Good Disposition destine the realm for these believers?
For whom but these believers didst thou shape the fortune-bringing
    cattle?

O Ahura Mazda, this I ask of thee: speak to me truly!
Who shaped prized Love with Power?

Who, by guidance, rendered sons reverent to their fathers?
It is I who strive to learn to recognize thee
Through the bounteous Mentality, as giver of all good things!

O Ahura Mazda, this I ask of thee: speak to me truly!
I would like to know what sort of a purpose is thine, that I may be
    mindful of it;
What are thy utterances, about which I asked through the aid of Good
    Disposition;
The proper knowledge of life through Justice—
How shall my soul, encouraged by bliss, arrive at that good reward?

O Ahura Mazda, this I ask of thee: speak to me truly!
How may I accomplish the sanctification of those spirits
To whom thou, the well-disposed Master of the coming Kingdom,
Hast pronounced promises about its genuine blessings,
Promising that those spirits shall dwell in the same dwelling with
    Justice and Good Disposition?

O Ahura Mazda, this I ask of thee: speak to me truly!
How will Love actually, in deeds, extend over those persons
To whom thy spirit was announced as a doctrine?
On account of whom I first was elected, and whom I love;
All others I look upon with hostility of mentality!

O Ahura Mazda, this I ask of thee: speak to me truly!
How shall I carry out the object inspired by you,
Namely, my attachment to you, in order that my speech may grow
    mighty, and
That by that word of mine the adherent of Justice
May in the future commune with Health, and Immortality?

The Choice between Right and Wrong

But thus, O souls desirous of hearing, I will utter those things worthy
    to be remembered by the expert-knower,
The praises for Ahura, and hymns worthy of Good Disposition,
And things well remembered with the aid of Justice, and the propitious
    omens beheld through the lights of the stars, or of the altar-
    flames.

Listen with your ears to the best information; behold with your sight,
    and with your mind;
Man by man, each for his own person, distinguishing between both
    confessions,
Before this great crisis. Consider again!

At the beginning both these Mentalities became conscious of each other,
The one being a Mentality better in thought, and word, and deed, than
    the other Mentality who is bad.
Now let the just man discriminate between these two, and choose the
    benevolent one, not the bad one.

But when the twin-Mentalities came together, they produced
The first life, and lifelessness, and settled on the state of the last con-
    dition of existence,
The worst for the Drujists, but for the Ashaists the best mind.

The Drujist chose between these twin-Mentalities, the one who perpetrated the worst deeds,

But he who was inspired by the most bountiful Mentality that is clothed upon by the most adamantine stone-quarried heavens as a garment,

And he who cheerfully satisfied Ahura Mazda with sincere deeds, chose Justice.

The Daevaists did not discriminate accurately between these two, because

Just as they were deliberating, there came upon them a delusion so that they should choose the worst Mind,

So that, all together, they rushed over to Fury, through which they afflict the life of man with disease.

And to this man now sick came Mazda Ahura with the Power realm, with Good Disposition, and with Justice,

And Love endowed the sick body of man with firmness and endurance

So that he may become the first of those surviving the tests of passing through the metallic trials and through the retributions.

And thereupon, when the punishments of those malefactors shall occur,

Then the saved man shall obtain for thee, O Mazda, with the help of Good Disposition, the Power realm,

Which will be the fulfilment of the world's destiny, and this will be obtained by those who shall deliver the Druj into the two hands of Justice.

And may we be those who shall make life progressive or purposeful!

Assemble together, along with Justice, O Ahuras Mazda, and come hither

So that here where our thoughts formerly developed separately, they may now mature together, fuse, and become wisdom.

Then shall the success of the Druj break down,

And all those who shall be attaining a good renown

Shall obtain their reward, meeting at the good dwelling of Good Disposition, Mazda, and Justice.

When, O you mortals, you have familiarized yourselves with these commandments of Mazda about the twin-Mentalities, which mean Prosperity as opposed to adversity, and the length of the suffering of

the Drujists as contrasted with the useful progress of the
Ashaists;

When, I repeat, you have fully realized the significance of this contrast,
I feel quite sure none of you all will hesitate or delay to enter
into the desired abode of praise.

A Prayer for Enlightenment

Minding these your commands, O gods, let us pronounce speeches
Unheeded by those who would, by the commands of Druj, destroy the
substance of Justice,
But most acceptable to them who will trust in Mazda.

But since the preferable path is not always obvious
Therefore, as heaven appointed arbiter and judge over both parties,
Will I go to you, that we may live in accordance with Justice.

In order that I may cause all men to choose aright, I pray thee O Ahura
Mazda, with the tongue of thy mouth to tell
What satisfaction, taught through Justice, thou wilt give to both con-
tending parties, through Mentality and fire;
What is thy command for the enlightened, that we may understand that
command.

And this command is, that as far as Justice and the other Ahuras Mazda
are willing to be invoked
Through Compensation and Love and the best Disposition,
So far shall I seek for myself the Power of Realm by the vigorous increase whereof we may defeat the Druj.

Tell me, O Ahura Mazda, what is not to occur, and what is to occur,
In order that I may distinguish that, whatever success therein you may
have given me through Justice, was the better thing,
In order that I may understand it through Good Disposition, and may
ponder over this so that by understanding it fully I may gather
therefrom a reward.

This is the best reward of life: namely, that realm which the man who
receives it may for his own concurrent advantage increase for
Mazda, through Good Disposition;

May this best reward be granted to him who after having discovered for
      himself the right solution to these following problems that dis-
      tress me, will tell me sincerely
Justice's mystic Word which is the secret of Health and Immortality.

Whether Mazda was the first one to fill the glories of heaven with
      lights of stars,
Whether Mazda through understanding created Justice, and whether
      Justice will maintain the best activity of Good Disposition,
Whether Mazda shall cause these to prosper through the holy Mentality,
      which is ever the same until the present time.

Whereupon, when Zarathushtra with his own eye by looking at nature
      and through his mind by puzzling out its significance, compre-
      hended Mazda and Disposition,
Then Zarathushtra understood that Mazda was both the first and young-
      est of creation and the father of Good Disposition;
The genuine creator of Justice and the ruling lord in the deeds of life;

That, O Mazda Ahura, to thee belongs both Love and the shaper of the
      bovine creation which was part of the understanding of the
      holy Mentality.
That when for the cow thou didst ordain a path of freedom of will,
      following which
She might repudiate the herdsman, and go to abide with the nomad

Then she chose for herself from among the two possible lords, the
      herdsman or nomad, the herdsman who would follow her,
Namely, the Ashaist, who feels that it is his mission to see to it that all
      things that belong to Good Disposition prosper, and who in
      return is prospered by him,
Whereas the nomad shall not get a share of Good Disposition's favour-
      able report at the judgment, even though he should urge for it,
      so long as he will not herd cattle.

That at first thou, O Mazda, with thy mind and understanding,
Thou didst shape substance and spirits, and didst establish body and life,
And deeds and doctrines whereby men who exercised their faculties of
      choice might develop convictions.

Amidst such sublime issues, vulgar men who speak either falsely or
justly, the expert-knower or the ignorant,
Each, according to the fancy of his heart and mind, dares to raise his
impudent voice
Where Love councils successively with the spirits who yet are wavering.

O Mazda, thou with Justice keepest a watch with thy watchful gleam-
ing eyes
Over all these men who ask questions openly or furtively; and
Over all officials who inflict the greatest penance for even a small transgression.

O Ahura Mazda, I ask thee about these conditions, present and future—
Namely, what compensations will be given to satisfy the claims of the
Ashaist,
And what compensations shall be enforced from the Drujist:—How
shall both stand at the time of awarding the compensations?

O Ahura, I ask thee what shall be the punishments of those who encourage the dominion of the Drujist, of those who cannot make
their living
Without violence to cattle and to men devoted to herding them.

O Mazda Ahura, I ask thee whether the well-disposed man who may
strive
To improve the houses, the villages, the clans and the provinces, through
Justice,
Whether he may at all become a being like unto thee; if so, when he shall
arise unto this likeness and what deeds he shall do to become
such.

Tell me, O Lord, which is the more important object of choice—that of
the Ashaist or that of the Drujist?
Do thou who art the expert-knower inform me who would become one,
and do not permit the ignorant man to continue deluding such
as me who would like to learn,
O Ahura Mazda, be thou to us an instructor of Good Disposition!

Therefore O well disposed believer, hearken not to the mystic-words or
teachings of any of the Drujists,

For these would reduce house, village, clan or province, to misfortune or
   death;
Therefore, rather oppose them with the weapon!

But hearken to him who thought out Justice; that is, Zarathushtra who is
   the life healing expert-knower;
Him who is able to vindicate his tongue's speeches at will, at the latter
   day
When, O Ahura Mazda, with thy red fire the good compensations of
   the two contending parties are to be distributed; with thy red
   fire, produced by the two good rubbing sticks.

Destruction, lasting darkness, bad food, and imprecations
Shall at the latter day be kept away from whomsoever identifies himself
   with the Ashaists;
Beware, O Drujists: it is to that sort of existence that your evil spirit
   may lead you!

From the resources of his innate glory, Ahura Mazda shall grant sustained communion
And fullness of Health, and Immortality, and of Justice and of Power
   and Good Disposition
To whomsoever is a friend to Ahura Mazda in mind and deeds.

The man who is well-disposed, understands this as clearly as does Mazda,
   who knows with the divine Disposition.
It is this well-disposed man who holds Justice in union with the good
   Political Power, through his speech and deeds.
It is this well-disposed man who is the most prospering companion to
   thee, O Ahura Mazda.

The Zendavesta

The Fatherhood of God

Yea, I will speak forth; hear ye; now listen, ye who from near, and ye who from afar have come seeking the knowledge. Now ponder ye clearly all that concerns him. Not for a second time shall the false teacher slay our life of the mind, or the body. The wicked is hemmed in with his faith and his tongue!

Yea, I will declare the world's two first spirits, of whom the more bountiful thus spake to the harmful: Neither our thoughts, nor commands, nor our understandings, nor our beliefs, nor our deeds, nor our consciences, nor our souls, are at one.

Thus I will declare this world's first teaching, that which the all-wise Mazda Ahura hath told me. And they among you who will not so fulfil and obey this Mathra, as I now shall conceive and declare it, to these shall the end of life issue in woe.

Thus I will declare forth this world's best being. From the insight of his righteousness Mazda, who hath appointed these things, hath known what he utters to be true; yea, I will declare him the father of the toiling Good Mind within us. So is his daughter through good deeds our Piety. Not to be deceived is the all-viewing Lord.

Yea, thus I will declare that which the most bountiful One told me, that word which is the best to be heeded by mortals. They who therein grant me obedient attention, upon them cometh weal to bless, and the immortal being, and in the deeds of his Good Mind cometh the Lord.

Aye, thus I will declare forth him who is of all the greatest, praising through my righteousness, I who do aright, those who dispose of all as well aright. Let Ahura Mazda hear with his bounteous spirit, in whose homage what I asked was asked with the Good Mind. Aye, let him exhort me through his wisdom which is ever the best.

Yea, I will declare him whose blessings the offerers will seek for, those who are living now, as well as those who have lived aforetime, as will they also who are coming hereafter. Yea, even the souls of the righteous will desire them in the eternal immortality. Those things they will desire which are blessings to the righteous but woes to the wicked. And these hath Ahura Mazda established through his kingdom, he, the creator of all.

Him in our hymns of homage and of praise would I faithfully serve, for now with mine eye, I see him clearly, Lord of the good spirit, of word, and action, I knowing through my righteousness him who is Ahura Mazda. And to him not here alone, but in his home of song, his praise we shall bear.

Yea, him with our better mind we seek to honour, who desiring good, shall come to us to bless in weal and sorrow. May he, Ahura Mazda, make us vigorous through Khshathra's royal power, our flocks and men in thrift to further, from the good support and bearing of his Good Mind, itself born in us by his righteousness.

Him in the Yasnas of our piety we seek to praise with homage, who in his persistent energy was famed to be in truth the Lord Ahura Mazda, for he hath appointed in his kingdom, through his holy Order and his Good Mind, both Weal and Immortality, to grant the eternal mighty pair to this our land and the creation.

Him would we magnify and praise who hath despised the Daeva-gods and alien men, them who before held him in their derision. Far different are these from him who gave him honour. This latter one is through the Saoshyant's bounteous faith, who likewise is the Lord of saving power, a friend, brother, or a father to us, Mazda Lord!

The Mazdayasnian Confession

I drive the Daevas hence; I confess as a Mazda-worshipper of the order of Zarathushtra, estranged from the Daevas, devoted to the lore of the Lord, a praiser of the bountiful Immortals; and to Ahura Mazda, the good and endowed with good possessions, I attribute all things good, to the Holy One, the resplendent, to the glorious, whose are all things whatsoever which are good; whose is the kine, whose is Asha (the righteous order pervading all things pure), whose are the stars, in whose lights the glorious beings and objects are clothed.

And I choose Piety, the bounteous and the good, mine may she be. And therefore I loudly deprecate all robbery and violence against the sacred kine, and all drought to the wasting of the Mazdayasnian villages.

Away from their thoughts do I wish to lead the thought of wandering at will, away the thought of free nomadic pitching of the tent, for I wish to remove all wandering from their kine which abide in steadfastness upon this land; and bowing down in worship to Righteousness I dedicate my offerings with praise so far as that. Never may I stand as a source of wasting, never as a source of withering to the Mazdayasnian villages, not for the love of body or of life.

Away do I abjure the shelter and headship of the Daevas, evil as they are; aye, utterly bereft of good, and void of virtue, deceitful in their wickedness, of all beings those most like the Demon-of-the-Lie, the most loathsome of existing things, and the ones the most of all bereft of good.

Off, off, do I abjure the Daevas and all possessed by them, the sorcerers and all that hold to their devices, and every existing being of the sort; their thoughts do I abjure, their words and actions, and their seed that propagate their sin; away do I abjure their shelter and their headship, and the iniquitous of every kind who act as Rakhshas act!

Thus and so in very deed might Ahura Mazda have indicated to Zarathushtra in every question which Zarathushtra asked, and in all the consultations in which they two conversed together. Thus and so might Zarathushtra have abjured the shelter and the headship of the Daevas in all the questions, and in all the consultations with which they two conversed together, Zarathushtra and the Lord.

And so I myself, in whatsoever circumstances I may be placed, as a worshipper of Mazda, and of Zarathushtra's order, would so abjure the Daevas and their shelter, as he who was the holy Zarathushtra abjured them once of old.

To that religious sanctity to which the waters appertain, do I belong, to that sanctity to which the plants, to that sanctity to which the kine of blessed gift, to that religious sanctity to which Ahura Mazda, who made both kine and holy men, belongs, to that sanctity do I. Of that creed which Zarathushtra held, which Kavi Vistaspa, and those two, Frashaostra and Gamaspa; yea, of that religious faith which every Saoshyant who shall yet come to save us, the holy ones who do the deeds of real significance, of that creed, and of that lore, am I.

A Mazda-worshipper I am, of Zarathushtra's order; so do I confess, as a praiser and confessor, and I therefore praise aloud the well-thought thought, the word well spoken, and the deed well done.

Yet, I praise at once the faith of Mazda, the faith which has no faltering utterance, the faith that wields the felling halbert, the faith of kindred marriage, the holy creed, which is the most imposing, best, and most beautiful of all religions which exist, and of all that shall in future come to knowledge, Ahura's faith, the Zarathushtrian creed. Yea, to Ahura Mazda do I ascribe all good, and such shall be the worship of the Mazdayasnian belief!

The Earth

O Maker of the material world, thou Holy One! Which is the first place where the earth feels most happy? Ahura Mazda answered: It is the place whereon one of the faithful steps forward, O Spitama Zarathushtra! with the log in his hand, the Baresma in his hand, the milk in his hand, the mortar in his hand, lifting up his voice in good accord with religion, and beseeching Mithra, the lord of the rolling country-side, and Rama Hvastra.

O Maker of the material world, thou Holy One! Which is the second place where the earth feels most happy? Ahura Mazda answered: It is the place whereon one of the faithful erects a house with a priest within, with cattle, with a wife, with children, and good herds within; and wherein afterwards the cattle continue to thrive, virtue to thrive, fodder to thrive, the dog to thrive, the wife to thrive, the child to thrive, the fire to thrive, and every blessing of life to thrive.

O Maker of the material world, thou Holy One! Which is the third place where the earth feels most happy? Ahura Mazda answered: It is the place where one of the faithful sows most corn, grass, and fruit, O Spitama Zarathushtra! where he waters ground that is dry, or drains ground that is too wet.

O Maker of the material world, thou Holy One! Which is the fourth place where the earth feels most happy? Ahura Mazda answered: It is the place where there is most increase of flocks and herds.

O Maker of the material world, thou Holy One! Which is the fifth place where the earth feels most happy? Ahura Mazda answered: It is the place where flocks and herds yield most dung.

O Maker of the material world, thou Holy One! Which is the first place where the earth feels sorest grief? Ahura Mazda answered: It is the neck of Arezura, whereon the hosts of fiends rush forth from the burrow of the Drug.

O Maker of the material world, thou Holy One! Which is the second place where the earth feels sorest grief? Ahura Mazda answered: It is the place wherein most corpses of dogs and of men lie buried.

O Maker of the material world, thou Holy One! Which is the third place where the earth feels sorest grief? Ahura Mazda answered: It is the place whereon stand most of those Dakhmas on which the corpses of men are deposited.

O Maker of the material world, thou Holy One! Which is the fourth place where the earth feels sorest grief? Ahura Mazda answered: It is the place wherein are most burrows of the creatures of Angra Mainyu.

O Maker of the material world, thou Holy One! Which is the fifth place where the earth feels sorest grief? Ahura Mazda answered: It is the place whereon the wife and children of one of the faithful, O Spitama Zarathushtra! are driven along the way of captivity, the dry, the dusty way, and lift up a voice of wailing.

O Maker of the material world, thou Holy One! Who is the first that rejoices the earth with greatest joy? Ahura Mazda answered: It is he who digs out of it most corpses of dogs and men.

O Maker of the material world, thou Holy One! Who is the second that rejoices the earth with greatest joy? Ahura Mazda answered: It is he who pulls down most of those Dakhmas on which the corpses of men are deposited. Let no man alone by himself carry a corpse. If a man alone by himself carry a corpse, the Nasu rushes upon him. This Drug Nasu falls upon and stains him, even to the end of the nails, and he is unclean, thenceforth, for ever and ever.

O Maker of the material world, thou Holy One! What shall be the place of that man who has carried a corpse alone? Ahura Mazda answered: It shall be the place on this earth wherein is least water and fewest plants, whereof the ground is the cleanest and the driest and the least passed through by flocks and herds, by the fire of Ahura Mazda, by the consecrated bundles of Baresma, and by the faithful.

O Maker of the material world, thou Holy One! Who is the third that rejoices the earth with greatest joy? Ahura Mazda answered: It is he who fills up most burrows of the creatures of Angra Mainyu.

O Maker of the material world, thou Holy One! Who is the fourth that rejoices the earth with greatest joy? Ahura Mazda answered: It is he who sows most corn, grass, and fruit, O Spitama Zarathushtra! who waters ground that is dry, or drains ground that is too wet. Unhappy is the land that has long lain unsown with the seed of the sower and wants a good husbandman, like a well-shapen maiden who has long gone child-less and wants a good husband. He who would till the earth, O Spitama Zarathushtra! with the left arm and the right, with the right arm and the left, unto him will she bring forth plenty of fruit: even as it were a lover sleeping with his bride on her bed; the bride will bring forth children, the earth will bring forth plenty of fruit. He who would till the earth, O Spitama Zarathushtra! with the left arm and the right, with the right arm and the left, unto him thus says the earth: "O thou man! who dost till me with the left arm and the right, with the right arm and the left, here shall I ever go on bearing, bringing forth all manner of food, bringing corn first to thee." He who does not till the earth, O Spitama Zarathushtra! with the left arm and the right, with the right arm and the left, unto him thus says the earth: "O thou man! who dost not till me with the left arm and the right, with the right arm and the left, ever shalt thou stand at the door of the stranger, among those who beg for bread; the refuse and the crumbs of the bread are brought unto thee, brought by those who have profusion of wealth."

O Maker of the material world, thou Holy One! What is the food that fills the religion of Mazda? Ahura Mazda answered: It is sowing corn again and again, O Spitama Zarathushtra! He who sows corn, sows right-eousness: he makes the religion of Mazda walk, he suckles the religion of Mazda; as well as he could do with a hundred man's feet, with a thou-sand woman's breasts, with ten thousand sacrificial formulas. When barley was created, the Daevas started up; when it grew, then fainted the Daevas' hearts; when the knots came, the Daevas groaned; when the ear came, the Daevas flew away. In that house the Daevas stay, wherein wheat perishes. It is as though red hot iron were turned about in their throats, when there is plenty of corn. Then let people learn by heart this holy saying: "No one who does not eat, has strength to do heavy works of holiness, strength to do works of husbandry, strength to beget children. By eating every material creature lives, by not eating it dies away."

O Maker of the material world, thou Holy One! Who is the fifth that rejoices the earth with greatest joy? Ahura Mazda answered: It is he who kindly and piously gives to one of the faithful who tills the earth, O Spitama Zarathushtra! He who would not kindly and piously give to one of the faithful who tills the earth, O Spitama Zarathushtra! Spenta Armaiti will throw him down into darkness, down into the world of woe, the world of hell, down into the deep abyss.

Funerals and Purification

If a dog or a man die under a hut of wood or a hut of felt, what shall the worshippers of Mazda do?

Ahura Mazda answered: They shall search for a Dakhma, they shall look for a Dakhma all around. If they find it easier to remove the dead, they shall take out the dead, they shall let the house stand, and shall perfume it with Urvasna or Vohu-gaona, or Vohu-kereti, or Hadha-naepata, or any other sweet-smelling plant. If they find it easier to remove the house, they shall take away the house, they shall let the dead lie on the spot, and shall perfume the house with Urvasna, or Vohu-gaona, or Vohu-kereti, or Hadha-naepata, or any other sweet-smelling plant.

O Maker of the material world, thou Holy One! If in the house of a worshipper of Mazda a dog or a man happens to die, and it is raining, or snowing, or blowing, or it is dark, or the day is at its end, when flocks and men lose their way, what shall the worshippers of Mazda do?

Ahura Mazda answered: The place in that house whereof the ground is the cleanest and the driest, and the least passed through by flocks and herds, by the fire of Ahura Mazda, by the consecrated bundles of Baresma, and by the faithful.

O Maker of the material world, thou Holy One! How far from the fire? How far from the water? How far from the consecrated bundles of Baresma? How far from the faithful?

Ahura Mazda answered: Thirty paces from the fire; thirty paces from the water; thirty paces from the consecrated bundles of Baresma; three paces from the faithful;—on that place they shall dig a grave, half a foot deep if the earth be hard, half the height of a man if it be soft; they shall cover the surface of the grave with ashes or cow-dung; they shall cover the surface of it with dust of bricks, of stones, or of dry earth. And they shall let the lifeless body lie there, for two nights, or three nights, or a month long, until the birds begin to fly, the plants to grow, the hidden floods to flow, and the wind to dry up the earth. And when the birds begin to fly, the plants to grow, the hidden floods to flow, and the wind to dry up the earth, then the worshippers of Mazda shall make a breach in the wall of the house, and two men, strong and skilful, having stripped their clothes off, shall take up the body from the clay or the stones, or from the plastered house, and they shall lay it down on a place where they know there are always corpse-eating dogs and corpse-eating birds. Afterwards the corpse-bearers shall sit down, three paces from the dead, and the holy Ratu shall proclaim to the worshippers of Mazda thus: "Worshippers of Mazda, let the urine be brought here wherewith the corpse-bearers there shall wash their hair and their bodies."

O Maker of the material world, thou Holy One! Which is the urine wherewith the corpse-bearers shall wash their hair and their bodies? Is it of sheep or of oxen? Is it of man or of woman?

Ahura Mazda answered: It is of sheep or of oxen; not of man nor of woman, except a man or a woman who has married the next-of-kin; these shall therefore procure the urine wherewith the corpse-bearers shall wash their hair and their bodies.

The Sixteen Perfect Lands

Ahura Mazda spake unto Spitama Zarathushtra, saying:

I have made every land dear to its people, even though it had no charms whatever in it: had I not made every land dear to its people, even though it had no charms whatever in it, then the whole living world would have invaded the Airyana Vaego.

The first of the good lands and countries which I, Ahura Mazda, created, was the Airyana Vaego, by the Vanguhi Daitya.

Thereupon came Angra Mainyu, who is all death, and he counter-created the serpent in the river, and winter, a work of the Daevas.

There are ten winter months there, two summer months; and those are cold for the waters, cold for the earth, cold for the trees. Winter falls there, the worst of all plagues.

The second of the good lands and countries which I, Ahura Mazda, created, was the plain which the Sughdhas inhabit.

Thereupon came Angra Mainyu who is all death, and he counter-created the locust, which brings death unto cattle and plants.

The third of the good lands and countries which I, Ahura Mazda, created, was the strong, holy Mouru.

Thereupon came Angra Mainyu, who is all death, and he counter-created plunder and sin.

The fourth of the good lands and countries which I, Ahura Mazda, created, was the beautiful Bakhdhi with high-lifted banners.

Thereupon came Angra Mainyu, who is all death, and he counter-created the ants and the ant-hills.

The fifth of the good lands and countries which I, Ahura Mazda, created, was Nisaya, that lies between Mouru and Bakhdhi.

Thereupon came Angra Mainyu, who is all death, and he counter-created the sin of unbelief.

The sixth of the good lands and countries which I, Ahura Mazda, created, was the house-deserting Haroyu.

Thereupon came Angra Mainyu, who is all death, and he counter-created tears and wailing.

The seventh of the good lands and countries which I, Ahura Mazda, created, was Vaekereta, of the evil shadows.

Thereupon came Angra Mainyu, who is all death, and he counter-created the Pairika Knathaiti, who clave unto Keresaspa.

The eighth of the good lands and countries which I, Ahura Mazda, created, was Urva of the rich pastures.

Thereupon came Angra Mainyu, who is all death, and he counter-created the sin of pride.

The ninth of the good lands and countries which I, Ahura Mazda, created, was Khnenta which the Vehrkanas inhabit.

Thereupon came Angra Mainyu, who is all death, and he counter-created a sin for which there is no atonement, the unnatural sin.

The tenth of the good lands and countries which I, Ahura Mazda, created, was the beautiful Harahvaiti.

Thereupon came Angra Mainyu, who is all death, and he counter-created a sin for which there is no atonement, the burying of the dead.

The eleventh of the good lands and countries which I, Ahura Mazda, created, was the bright, glorious Haetumant.

Thereupon came Angra Mainyu, who is all death, and he counter-created the evil work of witchcraft.

And this is the sign by which it is known, this is that by which it is seen at once: wheresoever they may go and raise a cry of sorcery, there the worst works of witchcraft go forth. From there they come to kill and strike at heart, and they bring locusts as many as they want.

The twelfth of the good lands and countries which I, Ahura Mazda, created, was Ragha of the three races.

Thereupon came Angra Mainyu, who is all death, and he counter-created the sin of utter unbelief.

The thirteenth of the good lands and countries which I, Ahura Mazda, created, was the strong, holy Kakhra.

Thereupon came Angra Mainyu, who is all death, and he counter-created a sin for which there is no atonement, the cooking of corpses.

The fourteenth of the good lands and countries which I, Ahura Mazda, created, was the four-cornered Varena, for which was born Thraetaona, who smote Azi Dahaka.

Thereupon came Angra Mainyu, who is all death, and he counter-created abnormal issues in women and barbarian oppression.

The fifteenth of the good lands and countries which I, Ahura Mazda, created, was the Seven Rivers.

Thereupon came Angra Mainyu, who is all death, and he counter-created abnormal issues in women and excessive heat.

The sixteenth of the good lands and countries which I, Ahura Mazda, created, was the land by the sources of the Rangha, where people live who have no chiefs.

Thereupon came Angra Mainyu, who is all death, and he counter-created winter, a work of the Daevas.

There are still other lands and countries, beautiful and deep, longing and asking for the good, and bright.

The First Man

Zarathushtra asked Ahura Mazda:

O Ahura Mazda, most beneficent Spirit, Maker of the material world, thou Holy One!

Who was the first mortal, before myself, Zarathushtra, with whom thou, Ahura Mazda, didst converse, whom thou didst teach the religion of Ahura, the religion of Zarathushtra?

Ahura Mazda answered:

The fair Yima, the good shepherd, O holy Zarathushtra! he was the first mortal, before thee, Zarathushtra, with whom I, Ahura Mazda, did converse, whom I taught the religion of Ahura, the religion of Zarathushtra.

Unto him, O Zarathushtra, I, Ahura Mazda, spake, saying: "Well, fair Yima, son of Vivanghat, be thou the preacher and the bearer of my religion!"

And the fair Yima, O Zarathushtra, replied unto me, saying:

"I was not born, I was not taught to be the preacher and the bearer of thy religion."

Then I, Ahura Mazda, said thus unto him, O Zarathushtra:

"Since thou dost not consent to be the preacher and the bearer of my religion, then make thou my world increase, make my world grow: consent thou to nourish, to rule, and to watch over my world."

And the fair Yima replied unto me, O Zarathushtra, saying:

"Yes! I will make thy world increase, I will make thy world grow. Yes! I will nourish, and rule, and watch over thy world. There shall be, while I am king, neither cold wind nor hot wind, neither disease nor death."

Then I, Ahura Mazda, brought two implements unto him: a golden seal and a poniard inlaid with gold. Behold, here Yima bears the royal sway!

Thus, under the sway of Yima, three hundred winters passed away, and the earth was replenished with flocks and herds, with men and dogs and birds and with red blazing fires, and there was room no more for flocks, herds, and men.

Then I warned the fair Yima, saying: "O fair Yima, son of Vivanghat, the earth has become full of flocks and herds, of men and dogs and birds and of red blazing fires, and there is room no more for flocks, herds, and men."

Then Yima stepped forward, in light, southwards, on the way of the sun, and afterwards he pressed the earth with the golden seal, and bored it with the poniard, speaking thus:

"O Spenta Armaiti, kindly open asunder and stretch thyself afar, to bear flocks and herds and men."

And Yima made the earth grow larger by one-third than it was before, and there came flocks and herds and men, at their will and wish, as many as he wished.

Thus, under the sway of Yima, six hundred winters passed away, and the earth was replenished with flocks and herds, with men and dogs and birds and with red blazing fires, and there was room no more for flocks, herds, and men.

And I warned the fair Yima, saying: "O fair Yima, son of Vivanghat, the earth has become full of flocks and herds, of men and dogs and birds and of red blazing fires, and there is room no more for flocks, herds, and men."

Then Yima stepped forward, in light, southwards, on the way of the sun, and afterwards he pressed the earth with the golden seal, and bored it with the poniard, speaking thus:

"O Spenta Armaiti, kindly open asunder and stretch thyself afar, to bear flocks and herds and men."

And Yima made the earth grow larger by two-thirds than it was before, and there came flocks and herds and men, at their will and wish, as many as he wished.

Thus, under the sway of Yima, nine hundred winters passed away, and the earth was replenished with flocks and herds, with men and dogs and birds and with red blazing fires, and there was room no more for flocks, herds, and men.

And I warned the fair Yima, saying: "O fair Yima, son of Vivanghat, the earth has become full of flocks and herds, of men and dogs and birds and of red blazing fires, and there is room no more for flocks, herds, and men."

Then Yima stepped forward, in light, southwards, on the way of the sun, and afterwards he pressed the earth with the golden seal, and bored it with the poniard, speaking thus:

"O Spenta Armaiti, kindly open asunder and stretch thyself afar, to bear flocks and herds and men."

And Yima made the earth grow larger by three-thirds than it was before, and there came flocks and herds and men, at their will and wish, as many as he wished.

The Evil Winters

The Maker, Ahura Mazda, called together a meeting of the celestial Yazatas in the Airyana Vaego of high renown, by the Vanguhi Daitya.

The fair Yima, the good shepherd, called together a meeting of the best of the mortals, in the Airyana Vaego of high renown, by the Vanguhi Daitya.

To that meeting came Ahura Mazda, in the Airyana Vaego of high renown, by the Vanguhi Daitya; he came together with the celestial Yazatas.

To that meeting came the fair Yima, the good shepherd, in the Airyana Vaego of high renown, by the Vanguhi Daitya; he came together with the best of the mortals.

And Ahura Mazda spake unto Yima, saying:

"O fair Yima, son of Vivanghat! Upon the material world the evil winters are about to fall, that shall bring the fierce, deadly frost; upon the material world the evil winters are about to fall, that shall make snow-flakes fall thick, even an aredvi deep on the highest tops of mountains.

"And the beasts that live in the wilderness, and those that live on the tops of the mountains, and those that live in the bosom of the dale shall take shelter in underground abodes.

"Before that winter, the country will bear plenty of grass for cattle, before the waters have flooded it. Now after the melting of the snow, O Yima, a place wherein the footprint of a sheep may be seen will be a wonder in the world.

"Therefore make thee a Vara, long as a riding-ground on every side of the square, and thither bring the seeds of sheep and oxen, of men, of dogs, of birds, and of red blazing fires.

"Therefore make thee a Vara, long as a riding-ground on every side of the square, to be an abode for men; a Vara, long as a riding-ground on every side of the square, for oxen and sheep.

"There thou shalt make waters flow in a bed a hathra long; there thou shalt settle birds, on the green that never fades, with food that never fails. There thou shalt establish dwelling-places, consisting of a house with a balcony, a courtyard, and a gallery.

"Thither thou shalt bring the seeds of men and women, of the greatest, best, and finest on this earth; thither thou shalt bring the seeds of every kind of cattle, of the greatest, best, and finest on this earth.

"Thither thou shalt bring the seeds of every kind of tree, of the highest of size and sweetest of odour on this earth; thither thou shalt bring the seeds of every kind of fruit, the best of savour and sweetest of odour. All those seeds shalt thou bring, two of every kind, to be kept inexhaustible there, so long as those men shall stay in the Vara.

"There shall be no humpbacked, none bulged forward there; no impotent, no lunatic; no one malicious, no liar; no one spiteful, none jealous; no one with decayed tooth, no leprous to be pent up, nor any of the brands wherewith Angra Mainyu stamps the bodies of mortals.

"In the largest part of the place thou shalt make nine streets, six in the middle part, three in the smallest. To the streets of the largest part thou shalt bring a thousand seeds of men and women; to the streets of the middle part, six hundred; to the streets of the smallest part, three hundred. That Vara thou shalt seal up with thy golden seal, and thou shalt make a door, and a window self-shining within."

Then Yima said within himself: "How shall I manage to make that Vara which Ahura Mazda has commanded me to make?"

And Ahura Mazda said unto Yima: "O fair Yima, son of Vivanghat! Crush the earth with a stamp of thy heel, and then knead it with thy hands, as the potter does when kneading the potter's clay."

And Yima did as Ahura Mazda wished; he crushed the earth with a stamp of his heel, he kneaded it with his hands, as the potter does when kneading the potter's clay.

And Yima made a Vara, long as a riding-ground on every side of the square. There he brought the seeds of sheep and oxen, of men, of dogs, of birds, and of red blazing fires. He made a Vara, long as a riding-ground on every side of the square, to be an abode for men; a Vara, long as a riding-ground on every side of the square, for oxen and sheep.

There he made waters flow in a bed a hathra long; there he settled birds, on the green that never fades, with food that never fails. There he established dwelling-places, consisting of a house with a balcony, a courtyard, and a gallery.

There he brought the seeds of men and women, of the greatest, best, and finest on this earth; there he brought the seeds of every kind of cattle, of the greatest, best, and finest on this earth.

There he brought the seeds of every kind of tree, of the highest of size and sweetest of odour on this earth; there he brought the seeds of every kind of fruit, the best of savour and sweetest of odour. All those seeds he brought, two of every kind, to be kept inexhaustible there, so long as those men should stay in the Vara.

And there were no humpbacked, none bulged forward there; no impotent, no lunatic; no one malicious, no liar; no one spiteful, none jealous; no one with decayed tooth, no leprous to be pent up, nor any of the brands wherewith Angra Mainyu stamps the bodies of mortals.

In the largest part of the place he made nine streets, six in the middle part, three in the smallest. To the streets of the largest part he brought a thousand seeds of men and women; to the streets of the middle part, six hundred; to the streets of the smallest part, three hundred. That Vara he sealed up with the golden ring, and he made a door, and a window self-shining within.

O Maker of the material world, thou Holy One! What are the lights that give light in the Vara which Yima made?

Ahura Mazda answered: There are uncreated lights and created lights. The one thing missed there is the sight of the stars, the moon, and the sun, and a year seems only as a day.

Every fortieth year, to every couple two are born, a male and a female. And thus it is for every sort of cattle. And the men in the Vara which Yima made live the happiest life.

O Maker of the material world, thou Holy One! Who is he who brought the religion of Mazda into the Vara which Yima made?

Ahura Mazda answered: It was the bird Karshipta, O holy Zarathushtra!

O Maker of the material world, thou Holy One! Who are the Lord and the Master there?

Ahura Mazda answered: Urvatad-nara, O Zarathushtra! and thyself, Zarathushtra.

Assault on Zarathushtra

From the region of the north, from the regions of the north, forth rushed Angra Mainyu, the deadly, the Daeva of the Daevas. And thus spake the evil-doer Angra Mainyu, the deadly: "Drug, rush down and kill him," O holy Zarathushtra! The Drug came rushing along, the demon Buiti, who is deceiving, unseen death.

Zarathushtra chanted aloud the Ahuna-Vairya: "The will of the Lord is the law of righteousness. The gifts of Vohumano to the deeds done in this world for Mazda. He who relieves the poor makes Ahura king."

He offered the sacrifice to the good waters of the good Daitih! He recited the profession of the worshippers of Mazda!

The Drug dismayed, rushed away, the demon Buiti, who is deceiving, unseen death.

And the Drug said unto Angra Mainyu: "Thou, tormenter, Angra Mainyu! I see no way to kill Spitama Zarathushtra, so great is the glory of the holy Zarathushtra."

Zarathushtra saw all this within his soul: "The wicked, the evil-doing Daevas," thought he, "take council together for my death."

Up started Zarathushtra, forward went Zarathushtra, unabated by Akemmano, by the hardness of his malignant riddles; he went swinging stones in his hand, stones as big as a house, which he obtained from the Maker, Ahura Mazda, he the holy Zarathushtra.

"Whereat on this wide, round earth, whose ends lie afar, whereat dost thou swing those stones, thou who standest by the upper bank of the river Darega, in the mansion of Pourusaspa?"

Thus Zarathushtra answered Angra Mainyu: "O evil-doer, Angra Mainyu! I will smite the creation of the Daeva; I will smite the Nasu, a creature of the Daeva; I will smite the Pairika Knathaiti, till the victorious Saoshyant come up to life out of the lake Kasava, from the region of the dawn, from the regions of the dawn."

Again to him said the maker of the evil world, Angra Mainyu: "Do not destroy my creatures, O holy Zarathushtra! Thou art the son of Pourusaspa; by thy mother I was invoked. Renounce the good religion of the worshippers of Mazda, and thou shalt gain such a boon as Vadhaghna gained, the ruler of the nations."

Spitama Zarathushtra said in answer: "No! never will I renounce the good religion of the worshippers of Mazda, either for body or life, though they should tear away the breath!"

Again to him said the maker of the evil world, Angra Mainyu: "By whose word wilt thou strike, by whose word wilt thou repel, by whose weapon will the good creatures strike and repel my creation, who am Angra Mainyu?"

Spitama Zarathushtra said in answer: "The sacred mortar, the sacred cups, the Haoma, the Word taught by Mazda, these are my weapons, my best weapons! By this Word will I strike, by this Word will I repel, by this weapon will the good creatures strike and repel thee, O evil-doer, Angra Mainyu! The Good Spirit made the creation; he made it in the boundless Time. The Amesha-Spentas made the creation, the good, the wise sovereigns."

Zarathushtra asked Ahura Mazda: "O Maker of the good world, Ahura Mazda! With what manner of sacrifice shall I worship, with what manner of sacrifice shall I make people worship this creation of Ahura Mazda?"

Ahura Mazda answered: "Go, O Spitama Zarathushtra! towards the high-growing trees, and before one of them that is beautiful, high-growing, and mighty, say thou these words: 'Hail to thee! O good, holy tree, made by Mazda! Ashem vohu!'

"The priest shall cut off a twig of Baresma, long as an aesha, thick as a yava. The faithful one, holding it in his left hand, shall keep his eyes upon it without ceasing, whilst he is offering up to Ahura Mazda and to the Amesha-Spentas, the high and beautiful golden Haomas, and Good Thought and the good Rata, made by Mazda, holy and excellent."

Zarathushtra asked Ahura Mazda: "O thou all-knowing Ahura Mazda: Should I urge upon the godly man, should I urge upon the godly woman, should I urge upon the wicked Daeva-worshipper who lives in sin, to give the earth made by Ahura, the water that runs, the corn that grows, and all the rest of their wealth?"

Ahura Mazda answered: "Thou shouldst, O holy Zarathushtra."

"O Maker of the material world, thou Holy One! Where are the rewards given? Where does the rewarding take place? Where is the rewarding fulfilled? Whereto do men come to take the reward that, during their life in the material world, they have won for their souls?"

Ahura Mazda answered: "When the man is dead, when his time is over, then the wicked, evil-doing Daevas cut off his eyesight. On the third night, when the dawn appears and brightens up, when Mithra, the god with beautiful weapons, reaches the all-happy mountains, and the sun is rising:

"Then the fiend, named Vizaresha, O Spitama Zarathushtra, carries off in bonds the souls of the wicked Daeva-worshippers who live in sin. The soul enters the way made by Time, and open both to the wicked and to the righteous. At the head of the Chinvad bridge, the holy bridge made by Mazda, they ask for their spirits and souls the reward for the worldly goods which they gave away here below.

"Then comes the beautiful, well-shapen, strong and well-formed maid, with the dogs at her sides, one who can distinguish, who has many children, happy, and of high understanding.

"She makes the soul of the righteous one go up above the Hara-berezaiti; above the Chinvad bridge she places it in the presence of the heavenly gods themselves.

"Up rises Vohumano from his golden seat; Vohumano exclaims: 'How hast thou come to us, thou holy one, from that decaying world into this undecaying one?'

"Gladly pass the souls of the righteous to the golden seat of Ahura Mazda, to the golden seat of the Amesha-Spentas, to the Garo-nmanem, the abode of Ahura Mazda, the abode of the Amesha-Spentas, the abode of all the other holy beings.

"As to the godly man that has been cleansed, the wicked evil-doing Daevas tremble at the perfume of his soul after death, as doth a sheep on which a wolf is pouncing.

"The souls of the righteous are gathered together there: Nairyo-sangha is with them; a messenger of Ahura Mazda is Nairyo-sangha."

And the evil-doing Daeva, Angra Mainyu, the deadly, said: "What! let the wicked, evil-doing Daevas gather together at the head of Arezura!"

They rush away shouting, the wicked, evil-doing Daevas; they run away shouting, the wicked, evil-doing Daevas; they run away casting the evil eye, the wicked, evil-doing Daevas: "Let us gather together at the head of Arezura!

"For he is just born, the holy Zarathushtra, in the house of Pourusapa. How can we procure his death? He is the weapon that fells the fiends: he is a counter-fiend to the fiends; he is a Drug to the Drug. Vanished are the Daeva-worshippers, the Nasu made by the Daeva, the false-speaking Lie!"

They rush away shouting, the wicked, evil-doing Daevas, into the depths of the dark, raging world of hell.

The One of Whom Questions Are Asked

Zarathushtra asked Ahura Mazda: "O Ahura Mazda, most beneficent Spirit, Maker of the material world, thou Holy One! What of the Holy Word is the strongest? What is the most victorious? What is the most glorious? What is the most effective?

"What is the most fiend-smiting? What is the best-healing? What destroyeth best the malice of Daevas and men? What maketh the material world best come to the fulfilment of its wishes? What freeth the material world best from the anxieties of the heart?"

Ahura Mazda answered: "Our name, O Spitama Zarathushtra! who are the Amesha-Spentas, that is the strongest part of the Holy Word; that is the most victorious; that is the most glorious; that is the most effective; that is the most fiend-smiting; that is the best-healing; that destroyeth best the malice of Daevas and men; that maketh the material world best come to the fulfilment of its wishes; that freeth the material world best from the anxieties of the heart."

Then Zarathushtra said: "Reveal unto me that name of thine, O Ahura Mazda! that is the greatest, the best, the fairest, the most effective, the most fiend-smiting, the best-healing, that destroyeth best the malice of Daevas and men; that I may afflict all Daevas and men; that I may afflict all Yatus and Pairikas; that neither Daevas nor men may be able to afflict me; neither Yatus nor Pairikas."

Ahura Mazda replied unto him: "My name is the One of whom questions are asked, O holy Zarathushtra!

"My second name is the Herd-giver.

"My third name is the Strong One.

"My fourth name is Perfect Holiness.

"My fifth name is All good things created by Mazda, the offspring of the holy principle.

"My sixth name is Understanding;

"My seventh name is the One with understanding.

"My eighth name is Knowledge;

"My ninth name is the One with knowledge.

"My tenth name is Weal;

"My eleventh name is He who produces weal.

"My twelfth name is AHURA (the Lord).

"My thirteenth name is the Most Beneficent.

"My fourteenth name is He in whom there is no harm.

"My fifteenth name is the Unconquerable One.

"My sixteenth name is He who makes the true account.

"My seventeenth name is the All-seeing One.

"My eighteenth name is the Healing One.

"My nineteenth name is the Creator.

"My twentieth name is MAZDA (the All-knowing One).

"Worship me, O Zarathushtra, by day and by night, with offerings of libations well accepted. I will come unto thee for help and joy, I, Ahura Mazda; the good, holy Sraosha will come unto thee for help and joy; the waters, the plants, and the Fravashis of the holy ones will come unto thee for help and joy."

The Best Healing

One may heal with holiness, one may heal with the law, one may heal with the knife, one may heal with herbs, one may heal with the Holy Word: amongst all remedies this one is the healing one that heals with the Holy Word; this one it is that will best drive away sickness from the body of the faithful: for this one is the best-healing of all remedies.

Sickness fled away before it, death fled away; the Daeva fled away, the Daeva's counter-work fled away; the unholy Ashemaogha fled away, the oppressor of men fled away. The brood of the snake fled away; the brood of the wolf fled away; the brood of the two-legged fled away. Pride fled away; scorn fled away; hot fever fled away; slander fled away; discord fled away; the evil eye fled away.

Hymn to the Sun

We sacrifice unto the undying, shining, swift-horsed Sun.

When the light of the sun waxes warmer, when the brightness of the sun waxes warmer, then up stand the heavenly Yazatas, by hundreds and thousands: they gather together its glory, they make its glory pass down, they pour its glory upon the earth made by Ahura, for the increase of the world of holiness, for the increase of the creatures of holiness, for the increase of the undying, shining, swift-horsed Sun.

And when the sun rises up, then the earth, made by Ahura, becomes clean; the running waters become clean, the waters of the wells become clean, the waters of the sea become clean, the standing waters become clean; all the holy creatures, the creatures of the Good Spirit, become clean.

Should not the sun rise up, then the Daevas would destroy all the things that are in the seven Karshvares, nor would the heavenly Yazatas find any way of withstanding or repelling them in the material world.

He who offers up a sacrifice unto the undying, shining, swift-horsed Sun—to withstand darkness, to withstand the Daevas born of darkness, to withstand the robbers and bandits, to withstand the Yatus and Pairikas, to withstand death that creeps in unseen—offers it up to Ahura Mazda, offers it up to the Amesha-Spentas, offers it up to his own soul. He rejoices all the heavenly and worldly Yazatas, who offers up a sacrifice unto the undying, shining, swift-horsed Sun.

I will sacrifice unto Mithra, the lord of wide pastures, who has a thousand ears, ten thousand eyes.

I will sacrifice unto the club of Mithra, the lord of wide pastures, well struck down upon the skulls of the Daevas.

I will sacrifice unto that friendship, the best of all friendships, that reigns between the moon and the sun.

I bless the sacrifice and the invocation, and the strength and vigour of the undying, shining, swift-horsed Sun.

The Glory of God

We sacrifice unto the awful glory, that cannot be forcibly seized, made by Mazda . . . for which the Good Spirit and the Evil One did struggle with one another: for that glory that cannot be forcibly seized they flung each of them their darts most swift.

The Good Spirit flung a dart, and so did Vohumano, and Asha-Vahista and Atar, the son of Ahura Mazda.

The Evil Spirit flung a dart, and so did Akem-Mano, and Aeshma of the wounding spear, and Azi Dahaka and Spityura, he who sawed Yima in twain.

Then forward came Atar, the son of Ahura Mazda, thinking thus in his heart: "I want to seize that glory that cannot be forcibly seized."

But Azi Dahaka, the three-mouthed, he of the evil law, rushed on his back, thinking of extinguishing it:

"Here give it up to me, O Atar, son of Ahura Mazda: if thou seizest that glory that cannot be forcibly seized, I shall rush upon thee, so that thou mayest never more blaze on the earth made by Ahura and protect the world of the good principle."

And Atar took back his hands, as the instinct of life prevailed, so much had Azi affrighted him.

Then Azi, the three-mouthed, he of the evil law, rushed forward, thinking thus in his heart: "I want to seize that glory that cannot be forcibly seized."

But Atar, the son of Ahura Mazda, advanced behind him, speaking in these words:

"There give it up to me, thou three-mouthed Azi Dahaka. If thou seizest that glory that cannot be forcibly seized, then I will enter thy hinder part, I will blaze up in thy jaws, so that thou mayest never more rush upon the earth made by Mazda and destroy the world of the good principle."

Then Azi took back his hands, as the instinct of life prevailed, so much had Atar affrighted him.

That glory swells up and goes to the sea Vouru-Kasha. The swift-horsed Son of the Waters seizes it at once: this is the wish of the Son of the Waters, the swift-horsed: "I want to seize that glory that cannot be forcibly seized, down to the bottom of the sea Vouru-Kasha, in the bottom of the deep rivers."

We sacrifice unto the Son of the Waters, the swift-horsed, the tall and shining lord, the lord of females; the male god, who helps one at his appeal; who made man, who shaped man, a god who lives beneath waters, and whose ear is the quickest to hear when he is worshipped.

"And whosoever of you, O men,"—thus said Ahura Mazda,—"O holy Zarathushtra! shall seize that glory that cannot be forcibly seized, he has the gifts of an Athravan; whosoever shall long for the illumination of knowledge, he has the gifts of an Athravan; whosoever shall long for fullness of knowledge, he has the gifts of an Athravan;

"And riches will cleave unto him, giving him full welfare, holding a shield before him, powerful, rich of cattle and garments; and victory will cleave unto him, day after day; and likewise strength, that smites more than a year. Attended by that victory, he will conquer the havocking hordes; attended by that victory, he will conquer all those who hate him."

The Praise of Holiness

Zarathushtra asked Ahura Mazda: "O Ahura Mazda, most beneficent Spirit, Maker of the material world, thou Holy One!

"What is the only word in which is contained the glorification of all good things, of all the things that are the offspring of the good principle?"

Ahura Mazda answered: "It is the praise of holiness, O Spitama Zarathushtra!

"He who recites the praise of holiness, in the fullness of faith and with a devoted heart, praises me, Ahura Mazda; he praises the waters, he praises the earth, he praises the cattle, he praises the plants, he praises all good things made by Mazda, all the things that are the offspring of the good principle. For the reciting of that word of truth, O Zarathushtra! the pronouncing of that formula, the Ahuna Vairya, increases strength and victory in one's soul, and piety."

The Fravashis of the Faithful

Ahura Mazda spake unto Spitama Zarathushtra, saying: "Do thou proclaim, O pure Zarathushtra! the vigour and strength, the glory, the help and the joy that are in the Fravashis of the faithful, the awful and overpowering Fravashis; do thou tell how they come to help me, how they bring assistance unto me, the awful Fravashis of the faithful.

"Through their brightness and glory, O Zarathushtra! I maintain that sky, there above, shining and seen afar, and encompassing this earth all around.

"It looks like a palace, that stands built of a heavenly substance, firmly established, with ends that lie afar, shining in its body of ruby over the three-thirds of the earth; it is like a garment inlaid with stars, made of a heavenly substance, that Mazda puts on, along with Mithra and Rashnu and Spenta-Armaiti, and on no side can the eye perceive the end of it.

"Through their brightness and glory, O Zarathushtra! I maintain Ardvi Sura Anahita, the wide-expanding and health-giving, who hates the Daevas and obeys the laws of Ahura, who is worthy of sacrifice in the material world, worthy of prayer in the material world; the life-increasing and holy, the flocks-increasing and holy, the fold-increasing and holy, the wealth-increasing and holy, the country-increasing and holy;

"Who makes the seed of all males pure, who makes the womb of all females pure for bringing forth, who makes all females bring forth in safety, who puts milk in the breasts of all females in the right measure and the right quality;

"The large river, known afar, that is as large as the whole of all the waters that run along the earth; that runs powerfully from the height Hukairya down to the sea Vouru-Kasha.

"All the shores of the sea Vouru-Kasha are boiling over, all the middle of it is boiling over, when she runs down there, when she streams down there, she, Ardvi Sura Anahita, who has a thousand cells and a thousand channels; the extent of each of those cells, of each of those channels, is as much as a man can ride in forty days, riding on a good horse.

"From this river of mine alone flow all the waters that spread all over the seven Karshvares; this river of mine alone goes on bringing waters, both in summer and in winter. This river of mine purifies the seed in males, the womb in females, the milk in females' breasts.

"Through their brightness and glory, O Zarathushtra! I maintain the wide earth made by Ahura, the large and broad earth, that bears so much that is fine, that bears all the bodily world, the live and the dead, and the high mountains, rich in pastures and waters;

"Upon which run the many streams and rivers; upon which the many kinds of plants grow up from the ground, to nourish animals and men, to nourish the Aryan nations, to nourish the five kinds of animals, and to help the faithful.

"Through their brightness and glory, O Zarathushtra! I maintain in the womb the child that has been conceived, so that it does not die from the assaults of Vidotu, and I develop in it the bones, the hair, the entrails, the feet, and the sexual organs.

"Had not the awful Fravashis of the faithful given help unto me, those animals and men of mine, of which there are such excellent kinds, would not subsist; strength would belong to the Drug, the dominion would belong to the Drug, the material world would belong to the Drug.

"Between the earth and the sky the immaterial creatures would be harassed by the Drug; between the earth and the sky the immaterial creatures would be smitten by the Drug; and never afterwards would Angra-Mainyu give way to the blows of Spenta-Mainyu.

"Through their brightness and glory the waters run and flow forward from the never-failing springs; through their brightness and glory the plants grow up from the earth, by the never-failing springs; through their brightness and glory the winds blow, driving down the clouds towards the never-failing springs.

"Through their brightness and glory the females conceive offspring; through their brightness and glory they bring forth in safety; it is through their brightness and glory when they become blessed with children.

"Through their brightness and glory a man is born who is a chief in assemblies and meetings, who listens well to the holy words, whom wisdom holds dear, and who returns a victor from discussions with Gaotema, the heretic.

"Through their brightness and glory the sun goes his way; through their brightness and glory the moon goes her way; through their brightness and glory the stars go their way.

"In fearful battles they are the wisest for help, the Fravashis of the faithful.

"The most powerful amongst the Fravashis of the faithful, O Spitama! are those of the men of the primitive law or those of the Saoshyants not yet born, who are to restore the world. Of the others, the Fravashis of the living faithful are more powerful, O Zarathushtra! than those of the dead, O Spitama!

"And the man who in life shall treat the Fravashis of the faithful well, will become a ruler of the country with full power, and a chief most strong; so shall any man of you become, who shall treat Mithra well, the lord of wide pastures, and Arstat, who makes the world grow, who makes the world increase.

"Thus do I proclaim unto thee, O pure Spitama! the vigour and strength, the glory, the help, and the joy that are in the Fravashis of the faithful, the awful and overpowering Fravashis; and how they come to help me, how they bring assistance unto me, the awful Fravashis of the faithful."

We worship the good, strong, beneficent Fravashis of the faithful, who show beautiful paths to the waters, made by Mazda, which had stood before for a long time in the same place without flowing: and now they flow along the path made by Mazda, along the way made by the gods, the watery way appointed to them, at the wish of Ahura Mazda, at the wish of the Amesha-Spentas.

We worship the good, strong, beneficent Fravashis of the faithful, who show a beautiful growth to the fertile plants, which had stood before for a long time in the same place without growing: and now they grow up along the path made by Mazda, along the way made by the gods, in the time appointed to them, at the wish of Ahura Mazda, at the wish of the Amesha-Spentas.

We worship the good, strong, beneficent Fravashis of the faithful, who showed their paths to the stars, the moon, the sun, and the endless lights, that had stood before for a long time in the same place, without moving forwards, through the oppression of the Daevas and the assaults of the Daevas. And now they move around in their far-revolving circle for ever, till they come to the time of the good restoration of the world.

We worship the perception; we worship the intellect; we worship the conscience; we worship those of the Saoshyants; we worship the souls;

those of the tame animals; those of the wild animals; those of the animals that live in the waters; those of the animals that live under the ground; those of the flying ones; those of the running ones; those of the grazing ones.

We worship the spirit, conscience, perception, soul, and Fravashi of men of the primitive law, of the first who listened to the teaching of Ahura, holy men and holy women, who struggled for holiness; we worship the spirit, conscience, perception, soul, and Fravashi of our next-of-kin, holy men and holy women, who struggled for holiness.

We worship the men of the primitive law who will be in these houses, boroughs, towns, and countries; we worship the men of the primitive law who have been in these houses, boroughs, towns, and countries; we worship the men of the primitive law who are in these houses, boroughs, towns, and countries.

We worship the men of the primitive law in all houses, boroughs, towns, and countries, who obtained these houses, who obtained these boroughs, who obtained these towns, who obtained these countries, who obtained holiness, who obtained the Mathra, who obtained the blessedness of the soul, who obtained all the perfections of goodness.

We worship Zarathushtra, the lord and master of all the material world, the man of the primitive law; the wisest of all beings, the best-ruling of all beings, the brightest of all beings, the most glorious of all beings, the most worthy of sacrifice amongst all beings, the most worthy of prayer amongst all beings, the most worthy of propitiation amongst all beings, the most worthy of glorification amongst all beings, whom we call well-desired and worthy of sacrifice and prayer as much as any being can be, in the perfection of his holiness.

We worship this earth; we worship those heavens; we worship those good things that stand between the earth and the heavens and that are worthy of sacrifice and prayer and are to be worshipped by the faithful man.

We worship the souls of the wild beasts and of the tame.

We worship the souls of the holy men and women, born at any time, whose consciences struggle, or will struggle, or have struggled, for the good.

We worship the spirit, conscience, perception, soul, and Fravashi of the holy men and holy women who struggle, will struggle, or have struggled, and teach the law, and who have struggled for holiness.

The Fravashis of the faithful, awful and overpowering, awful and victorious; the Fravashis of the men of the primitive law; the Fravashis of the next-of-kin; may these Fravashis come satisfied into this house; may they walk satisfied through this house!

The Abodes of the Soul

Zarathushtra asked Ahura Mazda: "O Ahura Mazda, most beneficent Spirit, Maker of the material world, thou Holy One! When one of the faithful departs this life, where does his soul abide on that night?"

Ahura Mazda answered: "It takes its seat near the head, singing and proclaiming happiness: 'Happy is he, happy the man, whoever he be, to whom Ahura Mazda gives the full accomplishment of his wishes!' On that night his soul tastes as much of pleasure as the whole of the living world can taste."

"On the second night where does his soul abide?"

Ahura Mazda answered: "It takes its seat near the head, singing and proclaiming happiness: 'Happy is he, happy the man, whoever he be, to whom Ahura Mazda gives the full accomplishment of his wishes!' On that night his soul tastes as much of pleasure as the whole of the living world can taste."

"On the third night where does his soul abide?"

Ahura Mazda answered: "It takes its seat near the head, singing and proclaiming happiness: 'Happy is he, happy the man, whoever he be, to whom Ahura Mazda gives the full accomplishment of his wishes!' On that night his soul tastes as much of pleasure as the whole of the living world can taste."

At the end of the third night, when the dawn appears, it seems to the soul of the faithful one as if it were brought amidst plants and scents: it seems as if a wind were blowing from the region of the south, from the regions of the south, a sweet-scented wind, sweeter-scented than any other wind in the world.

And it seems to the soul of the faithful one as if he were inhaling that wind with the nostrils, and he thinks: "Whence does that wind blow, the sweetest-scented wind I ever inhaled with my nostrils?"

And it seems to him as if his own conscience were advancing to him in that wind, in the shape of a maiden fair, bright, white-armed, strong, tall-formed, high-standing, thick-breasted, beautiful of body, noble, of a glorious seed, of the size of a maid in her fifteenth year, as fair as the fairest things in the world.

And the soul of the faithful one addresses her, asking: "What maid art thou, who art the fairest maid I have ever seen?"

And she, being his own conscience, answers him: "O thou youth of good thoughts, good words, and good deeds, of good religion, I am thy own conscience!

"Everybody did love thee for that greatness, goodness, fairness, sweet-scentedness, victorious strength and freedom from sorrow, in which thou dost appear to me;

"And so thou, O youth of good thoughts, good words, and good deeds, of good religion! didst love me for that greatness, goodness, fair-ness, sweet-scentedness, victorious strength, and freedom from sorrow, in which I appear to thee.

"When thou wouldst see a man making derision and deeds of idolatry, or rejecting the poor and shutting his door, then thou wouldst sit singing the Gathas and worshipping the good waters and Atar, the son of Ahura Mazda, and rejoicing the faithful that would come from near or from afar.

"I was lovely and thou madest me still lovelier; I was fair and thou madest me still fairer; I was desirable and thou madest me still more desirable; I was sitting in a forward place and thou madest me sit in the foremost place, through this good thought, through this good speech, through this good deed of thine; and so henceforth men worship me for my having long sacrificed unto and conversed with Ahura Mazda."

The first step that the soul of the faithful man made, placed him in the good-thought paradise; the second step that the soul of the faithful man made, placed him in the good-word paradise; the third step that the soul of the faithful man made, placed him in the good-deed paradise; the fourth step that the soul of the faithful man made, placed him in the endless lights.

Then one of the faithful, who had departed before him, asked him, saying: "How didst thou depart this life, thou holy man? How didst thou come, thou holy man! from the abodes full of cattle and full of the wishes and enjoyments of love? From the material world into the world of the spirit? From the decaying world into the undecaying one? How long did thy felicity last?"

And Ahura Mazda answered: "Ask him not what thou askest him, who has just gone the dreary way, full of fear and distress, where the body and the soul part from one another.

"Let him eat of the food brought to him, of the oil of Zaremaya: this is the food for the youth of good thoughts, of good words, of good deeds, of good religion, after he has departed this life; this is the food for the holy woman, rich in good thoughts, good words, and good deeds, well-principled and obedient to her husband, after she has departed this life."

Zarathushtra asked Ahura Mazda: "O Ahura Mazda, most beneficent Spirit, Maker of the material world, thou Holy One! When one of the wicked perishes, where does his soul abide on that night?"

Ahura Mazda answered: "It rushes and sits near the skull, singing the Kima Gatha, O holy Zarathushtra! 'To what land shall I turn, O Ahura Mazda? To whom shall I go with praying?'

"On that night his soul tastes as much of suffering as the whole of the living world can taste."

"On the second night, where does his soul abide?"

Ahura Mazda answered: "It rushes and sits near the skull, singing the Kima Gatha, O holy Zarathushtra! 'To what land shall I turn, O Ahura Mazda? To whom shall I go with praying?'

"On that night his soul tastes as much of suffering as the whole of the living world can taste."

"On the third night, where does his soul abide?"

Ahura Mazda answered: "It rushes and sits near the skull, singing the Kima Gatha, O holy Zarathushtra! 'To what land shall I turn, O Ahura Mazda? To whom shall I go with praying?'

"On that night his soul tastes as much of suffering as the whole of the living world can taste."

At the end of the third night, when the dawn appears, it seems to the soul of the wicked one as if it were brought amidst snow and stench, and as if a wind were blowing from the region of the north, from the regions of the north, a foul-scented wind, the foulest-scented of all the winds in the world.

And it seems to the soul of the wicked man as if he were inhaling wind with the nostrils, and he thinks: "Whence does that wind the foulest-scented wind that I ever inhaled with my nostrils?"

The first step that the soul of the wicked man made laid him in the evil-thought hell; the second step that the soul of the wicked man made laid him in the evil-word hell; the third step that the soul of the wicked man made laid him in the evil-deed hell; the fourth step that the soul of the wicked man made laid him in the endless darkness.

Then one of the wicked who departed before him addressed him, saying: "How didst thou perish, O wicked man? How didst thou come, O fiend! from the abodes full of cattle and full of the wishes and enjoyments of love? From the material world into the world of the spirit? From the decaying world into the undecaying one? How long did thy suffering last?"

Angra Mainyu, the lying one, said: "Ask him not what thou askest him, who has just gone the dreary way, full of fear and distress, where the body and the soul part from one another.

"Let him eat of the food brought unto him, of poison and poisonous stench: this is the food, after he has perished, for the youth of evil thoughts, evil words, evil deeds, evil religion, after he has perished; this is the food for the fiendish woman, rich in evil thoughts, evil words, and evil deeds, evil religion, ill-principled, and disobedient to her husband."

Of the Dog

"Which is the good creature among the creatures of the Good Spirit that from midnight till the sun is up goes and kills thousands of the creatures of the Evil Spirit?"

Ahura Mazda answered: "The dog with the prickly back, with the long and thin muzzle, the dog Vanghapara, which evil-speaking people call the Duzaka; this is the good creature among the creatures of the Good Spirit that from midnight till the sun is up goes and kills thousands of the creatures of the Evil Spirit.

"And whosoever, O Zarathushtra! shall kill the dog kills his own soul for nine generations, nor shall he find a way over the Chinvad bridge, unless he has, while alive, atoned for his sin."

"O Maker of the material world, thou Holy One! If a man kill the dog, what is the penalty that he shall pay?"

Ahura Mazda answered: "A thousand stripes with the Aspahe-astra, a thousand stripes with the Sraosho-karana.

"Whosoever shall smite either a shepherd's dog, or a house-dog, or a Vohunazga dog, or a trained dog, his soul when passing to the other world, shall fly howling louder and more sorely grieved than the sheep does in the lofty forest where the wolf ranges.

"No soul will come and meet his departing soul and help it, howling and grieved in the other world; nor will the dogs that keep the Chinvad bridge help his departing soul howling and grieved in the other world."

"O Maker of the material world, thou Holy One! What is the place of the shepherd's dog?"

Ahura Mazda answered: "He comes and goes a Yugyesti round about the fold, watching for the thief and the wolf."

"O Maker of the material world, thou Holy One! What is the place of the house-dog?"

Ahura Mazda answered: "He comes and goes a Hathra round about the house, watching for the thief and the wolf."

"O Maker of the material world, thou Holy One! What is the place of the Vohunazga dog?"

Ahura Mazda answered: "He claims none of those talents, and only seeks for his subsistence."

"O Maker of the material world, thou Holy One! If a man give bad food to a shepherd's dog, of what sin does he make himself guilty?"

Ahura Mazda answered: "He makes himself guilty of the same guilt as though he should serve bad food to a master of a house of the first rank.

"For in this material world, O Spitama Zarathushtra! it is the dog, of all the creatures of the Good Spirit, that most quickly decays into age while not eating near eating people, and watching goods none of which it receives. Bring ye unto him milk and fat with meat; this is the right food for the dog."

"O Maker of the material world, thou Holy One! If there be in the house of a worshipper of Mazda a mad dog, who has no scent, what shall the worshippers of Mazda do?"

Ahura Mazda answered: "They shall attend him to heal him, in the same manner as they would do for one of the faithful."

"O Maker of the material world, thou Holy One! If they try to heal him and fail, what shall the worshippers of Mazda do?"

Ahura Mazda answered: "They shall put a wooden collar around his neck, and they shall tie thereto a muzzle, an asti thick if the wood be hard, two astis thick if it be soft. To that collar they shall tie it; by the two sides of the collar they shall tie it.

"If they shall not do so, the scentless dog may fall into a hole, or a well, or a precipice, or a river, or a canal, and come to grief: if he come to grief so, they shall be therefore Peshotanus.

"The dog, O Spitama Zarathushtra! I, Ahura Mazda, have made self-clothed and self-shod; watchful and wakeful; and sharp-toothed; born to take his food from man and to watch over man's goods. I, Ahura Mazda, have made the dog strong of body against the evil-doer, when sound of mind and watchful over your goods.

"And whosoever shall awake at his voice, O Spitama Zarathushtra! neither shall the thief nor the wolf carry anything from his house, without his being warned; the wolf shall be smitten and torn to pieces; he is driven away, he melts away like snow.

"A dog has the characters of eight sorts of people:

"He has the character of a priest, of a warrior, of a husbandman, of a strolling singer, of a thief, of a disu, of a courtesan, and of a child.

"He eats the refuse, like a priest; he is easily satisfied, like a priest; he is patient, like a priest; he wants only a small piece of bread, like a priest; in these things he is like unto a priest.

"He marches in front, like a warrior; he fights for the beneficent cow, like a warrior; he goes first out of the house, like a warrior; in these things he is like unto a warrior.

"He is watchful and sleeps lightly, like a husbandman; he goes first out of the house, like a husbandman; he returns last into the house, like a husbandman; in these things he is like unto a husbandman.

"He is fond of singing, like a strolling singer; he wounds him who gets too near, like a strolling singer; he is ill-trained, like a strolling singer; he is changeful, like a strolling singer; in these things he is like unto a strolling singer.

"He is fond of darkness, like a thief; he prowls about in darkness, like a thief; he is a shameless eater, like a thief; he is therefore an unfaithful keeper, like a thief; in these things he is like unto a thief.

"He is fond of darkness like a disu; he prowls about in darkness, like a disu; he is a shameless eater, like a disu; he is therefore an unfaithful keeper, like a disu; in these things he is like unto a disu.

"He is fond of singing, like a courtesan; he wounds him who gets too near, like a courtesan; he roams along the roads, like a courtesan; he is ill-trained, like a courtesan; he is changeful, like a courtesan; in these things he is like unto a courtesan.

"He is fond of sleep, like a child; he is tender like snow, like a child; he is full of tongue, like a child; he digs the earth with his paws, like a child; in these things he is like unto a child!

"If those two dogs of mine, the shepherd's dog and the house-dog, pass by any one of my houses, let them never be kept away from it.

"For no house could subsist on the earth made by Ahura, but for those two dogs of mine, the shepherd's dog and the house-dog."

"O Maker of the material world, thou Holy One! When a dog dies, with marrow and seed dried up, whereto does his ghost go?"

Ahura Mazda answered: "It passes to the spring of the waters, O Spitama Zarathushtra! and there out of them two water-dogs are formed: out of every thousand dogs and every thousand she-dogs, a couple is formed, a water-dog and a water she-dog.

"He who kills a water-dog brings about a drought that dries up pastures.

"Until then, O Spitama Zarathushtra! sweetness and fatness would flow out from that land and from those fields, with health and healing, with fullness and increase and growth, and a growing of corn and grass."

"O Maker of the material world, thou Holy One! When are sweetness and fatness to come back again to that land and to those fields, with health and healing, with fullness and increase and growth, and a growing of corn and grass?"

Ahura Mazda answered: "Sweetness and fatness will never come back again to that land and to those fields, with health and healing, with fullness and increase and growth, and a growing of corn and grass, until the murderer of the water-dog has been smitten to death on the spot, and the holy soul of the dog has been offered up a sacrifice, for three days and three nights, with fire blazing, with Baresma tied up, and with Haoma prepared.

"Then sweetness and fatness will come back again to that land and to those fields, with health and healing, with fullness and increase and growth, and a growing of corn and grass."

"O Maker of the material world, thou Holy One! If a bitch be near her time, which is the worshipper of Mazda that shall support her?"

Ahura Mazda answered: "He whose house stands nearest, the care of supporting her is his; so long shall he support her, until the whelps be born.

"If he shall not support her, so that the whelps come to grief, for want of proper support, he shall pay for it the penalty for wilful murder.

"He shall take her to rest upon a litter of nemovanta or of any foliage fit for a litter; so long shall he support her, until the young dogs are capable of self-defence and self-subsistence.

"It lies with the faithful to look in the same way after every pregnant female, either two-footed or four-footed, two-footed woman or four-footed bitch."

The Pahlavi Texts

The Conception and Birth of Zarathushtra

About the marvellousness of the manifestations before the birth of that most auspicious of offsprings from his mother, one marvel is this which is declared, that the creator passed on that glory of Zarathushtra through the material existences of the creatures to Zarathushtra; when the command arose from Ahura Mazda, the coming of that glory from the spiritual existence to the worldly, and to the material substance of Zarathushtra, was manifested as a great wonder to the multitude. Just as revelation mentions it thus: "Thereupon, when Ahura Mazda had produced the material of Zarathushtra, the glory then, in the presence of Ahura Mazda, fled on towards the material of Zarathushtra, on to that germ; from that germ it fled on, on to the light which is endless; from the light which is endless it fled on, on to that of the sun; from that of the sun it fled on, on to the moon; from that moon it fled on, on to those stars; from those stars it fled on, on to the fire which was in the house of Zois; and from that fire it fled on, on to the wife of Frahimrvana-zois, when she brought forth that girl who became the mother of Zarathushtra.

Of that splendour, escaped at the same time into the earth and into the sky, the father-in-law's ignorance is declared, so that it is said by those in the village of the more instructed and invoking Zois, as to the self-combustion which burns the fire, that fuel is not necessary for its use. Then they went on to the governor, and he explained to them concerning that same, thus: "The full glory of embodied existence is the glory of life apart from the body, so that all diligence devoid of this is only movement."

And it is declared that the demons, on account of their defeat by that glory in maintaining adversity for the girl, were bringing on to that district three armaments, winter, the demon of pestilence, and oppressive enemies; and a suspicion was cast by them into the minds of those of the district, that this harm happened to the district owing to the witchcraft of this girl; so that those of the district quarrelled dreadfully with the parents, as to the witchcraft of antagonism in the girl, and about putting her out from that district.

And the father of that girl spoke even these words to those of the district, with much reason, about the unjust assertion of witchcraft relative to the girl, that is: "When this girl was brought forth among those of mine, her whole destiny was afterwards set forth by that manifest radiance of fire, where it brought out radiance from all over her in the dark night. When this girl sits in the interior of the house, wherein there is no fire, and in the chamber of fire they increase its intensity, it is lighter there, where and when this girl sits, than there where they increase the intensity of the fire; one is dazzled by the radiance from her body, and that of a wizard would not have been so glorious."

Even then, owing to the influence of the demons, and the Kavig and Karap of the district, they did not become satisfied; so the father ordered the girl to go to Padiragtaraspo, the father of a family in the country of the Spitamas, in the district of Alak; and the girl obeyed the command of her father. That disturbance which the demons caused, with evil intention, for the expatriation of that girl, the sacred beings assiduously made the reason for the coming of the girl for marriage to Porushaspo, the father of Zarathushtra, through her father sending the girl to the dwelling of Padiragtaraspo, the father of Porushaspo.

One marvel is this which is declared, that when that girl, in going to that family, stood on the loftiest place in the country of the Spitamas, and it was surveyed by her, a great wonder was manifested to the girl, just as revelation mentions: "It is their voice is carried away to her from them; 'do thou proceed to that village which is theirs; it is very depressed in height and very wide in breadth, in which he who is living and the cattle mostly walk together; besides, for thy assistance that village is divinely fashioned and compassionate.'" Thereupon that damsel stopped, and also fully observed that "Their recital seems to be for the conveyance of this statement, that my action should be such as was ordered me by my father also." Then that damsel thoroughly washed her hands, and proceeded from them to that village which was Padiragtaraspo's, and the glory came to Porushaspo, the son of Padiragtaraspo.

One marvel is this which is declared, that the creator Ahura Mazda passed on the guardian spirit of Zarathushtra, to the parents of Zarathushtra, through Hom (a sacred tree) by a marvel produced by cultivation. Again, too, revelation says that, when the separation of the third millennium occurred, at the end of the 3,000 years of spiritual existence without a destroyer (after the creatures were in spiritual existence and before the arrival of the fiend); then the archangels framed Zarathushtra together, and they seated the guardian spirit within, having a mouth, having a tongue, and the proclaimer of the celestial mansions.

Then the three millenniums of Zarathushtra were the number manifest to them through observation by the eye, and it seemed that he became just like an archangel through bodily contact with the archangels. And when the separation of the third millennium occurred, after the framing of Zarathushtra together, and before the conveying of Zarathushtra down to the worldly state, at the end of the 3,000 years of worldly existence with a destroyer, then Ahura Mazda argued with Vohumano and Ashavahisto thus: "Is his mother beheld by you, so that we may produce Zarathushtra?"

And Ashavahisto spoke in reply thus: "Thou art aware even of that, O propitious one! about the Zarathushtra we shall produce, and thou and we have produced, thou knowest, O Ahura Mazda! and to us who are the other archangels do thou announce the place, because its appearance thou knowest, thou propitious spirit Ahura Mazda!"

Then Ahura Mazda argued with Vohumano and Ardavahisto, Sha-traver, Spendarmad, Khurdad, and Amurdad, saying: "The conveying of Zarathushtra down does not seem to be for me, because, having a mouth and having a tongue, he will be a proclaimer to the world of embodied beings. If we convey Zarathushtra down on to the world of embodied beings, having a mouth and having a tongue, as a proclaimer of the celestial mansion, this is evident: they will say, concerning the origin of him who is my righteous man, that we frame him together with the water, with the land, with the plants, and with the animals. Therefore we will carry off there, to the village of Porushaspo, him whom they will call Zarathushtra of good lineage of both natures, both of Neryosang who is of the archangels, and of Yim who is of mankind."

Then the archangels framed together a stem of Hom the height of a man, excellent in colour, and juicy where fresh; also to carry off the guardian spirit of Zarathushtra to that stem of theirs, the archangels made it go forth thither from that endless light, and gave it up there also to the instinctive intellect. Likewise their carrying off was manifest around, and a wall was openly displayed round them, but a restless one; the Hom was constantly provided with a mouth, where it was suitable, and sap constantly oozed from the Hom where it was moist.

One marvel is this which is declared, that the coming of the nature of the body of Zarathushtra, through water and vegetation, to the bodies of his parents, was manifested as a great wonder of the creator to the multi-tude. As revelation mentions it thus: "Thereupon, when Ahura Mazda had produced the material of Zarathushtra, the nature of his body then, in the presence of Ahura Mazda, fled on towards the material of Zarathushtra."

About Khurdad and Murdad bringing the cloud-water down in a com-passionate manner ever anew, drop by drop, and completely warm, for the delight of sheep and men, and—with as much seed as the roving of two rampant bulls would thereby cast upon the plants which have grown, all of every species—they are casting it upon those other plants at that time, even upon the dry ones; and the nature of Zarathushtra comes from that water to those plants.

One marvel is this which is declared, that, in order that the nature of Zarathushtra shall come unto his parents, after the mounting of the archangels Porushaspo drives six white cows, with yellow ears, up to those plants. And here is manifested a great wonder, such as revelation mentions thus: Two of those cows, unimpregnated, had become full of milk, and the nature of Zarathushtra came from the plants to those cows, and was mingled with the cows' milk; it is owing thereto that Porushaspo drove those cows back. And Porushaspo spoke to Dukdaub thus: "O Dukdaub! in two of those cows, which are unimpregnated and have not calved, milk has appeared; do thou milk those cows, which are the splendour and glory of the cows and of any embodied existence whatever." And Dukdaub arose and, taking that pail of hers which had a four-fold capacity, she also milked from them the milk which was in them, and a great part of what they gave up to her she had to throw away; and the nature of Zarathushtra was in that milk.

One marvel is this which is manifested in the struggle of the adversary for concealing and spoiling that milk, just as revelation mentions thus: Thereupon, at that time, the demons formed themselves into an assembly, and the demon of demons growled thus: "You demons become quite unobservant: that food is really supplied fresh, so that the formation is settled which will extend as far as to that man who will be the righteous Zarathushtra; which of you will undertake his destruction, all the while that he exists for mankind, so as to make him more contemptibly impotent?" Keshmak, astute in evil, growled thus: "I will undertake his destruction." Astute in evil, he rushed away with thrice fifty of the demons who are Karaps of Keshmak; and that village was partly uprooted and partly destroyed by him, fellow-workers were ruined, and the number of fellow-eaters of broken victuals, attending the great, was not broken up, among whom was he that had repelled his authority.

It is declared that, afterwards, Porushaspo asked again for that Hom from Dukdaub, and he pounded it, and with that cows' milk, into which the nature of the body of Zarathushtra had come, he here mingled the guardian spirit of Zarathushtra, and the nature of the body came at once into union with it.

One marvel is this which is declared, that Porushaspo and Dukdaub drank up that Hom and milk, when they were mingled together and announced to Ahura Mazda; and here occurred a combination of the glory, guardian spirit, and bodily nature of Zarathushtra into a manchild. And a great wonder was manifested to both of them, through that which revelation mentions thus: Thereupon, both have embraced the first time with desire for a son, and the demons shouted out unto them, in the villainous speech of sinfulness, thus: "Why shouldst thou act like this, vile Porushaspo?" whereupon they started up like people who are ashamed. A second time they have embraced, and the demons shouted out unto them, in villainous speech; whereupon they started up like people who are ashamed. A third time they have embraced thus, with desire for a son; and the demons shouted out unto them, in villainous speech; whereupon they started up like people who are ashamed. And they spoke with one another about it, and continued at this duty, and accomplished it, saying: "We will not so stop without accomplishing something, not even though both Rak and Nodar should arrive here together." Then that manchild who was the righteous Zarathushtra became complete, and here below there came together the nature of the body, the guardian spirit, and the glory of Zarathushtra in the womb of his mother.

One marvel is this which is declared, that, after the combination of Zarathushtra in the womb of his mother, the demons strove anew wonderfully to cause the death of Zarathushtra in his mother's womb, and she who bore him was rendered sickly by them through the sharpest of sharp and afflictive pain, until she wished to ask the wizard physicians for a desirable remedy. And here is manifested a great wonder, just as revelation says: It is then a voice of theirs is carried away there to her from the higher region, from Ahura Mazda and from the archangels, thus: "Thou damsel who goest! do not proceed thither, because anything of theirs is destruction through wizard medical treatment; for healthfulness wash thy hands thoroughly, and those hands shall take firewood, and upon it thou shalt offer meat for the sake of the infant, thou shalt offer up cows' butter to the fire for his sake; thou shalt likewise heat it at the fire for his sake, and shalt quaff it off at the proper time for his sake, and thou wilt become well." Then at once that damsel washed her hands thoroughly, and she did just as she had heard, and became well.

One marvel is this which was manifested to the multitude when three days remained to his coming forth; in the manner of the sun, at the approach of its uprising, when its first advancing twilight is diffused, his body was then announced as revelation says: It was then in those last three nights during which Zarathushtra was in the womb, where he still subsisted three days till afterwards born, that the village of Porushaspo became all luminous. Then spoke the horse-owners and cattle-owners of the Spitamas, in running away, thus: "It is requisite to be forgiven; the village of Porushaspo, on which that fire is in every crevice, is disturbed by confusion." Then, on running together again, they said: "It is not fully forgiven for the village of Porushaspo; fire is on it in every crevice and it is disturbed by confusion; unto him is born, at his house, a brilliant manchild."

One marvel is this which is declared, that on being born he laughed outright; the seven midwives, who sat around him, were quite frightened thereby; and those terrified ones spoke thus: "What was this, on account of grandeur or contempt? when, like the worthy man whose pleasure is due to activity, the man's child so laughs at the birth owing to him." Porushaspo also spoke thus: "Bring out this manchild to the sheepskin clothing which is soft; the affair was owing to thee, owing to the virtue of thee who art Dukdaub, that the advent of glory and coming of radiance to this manchild was openly seen when he laughed outright at his birth."

Hazards of the Infant Zarathushtra

About the trials which occurred to him whose practice was lawful, and the signs of prophecy that are seen therein, it is thus declared, namely; Another day, when the child had been born, Porushaspo called one of those five brothers of the race of Karaps, and spoke thus: "Fully observe the marks and specks of my son Zarathushtra."

The Karap went and sat down before Zarathushtra, and the head of Zarathushtra was thereupon severely twisted by him, in order that he should be killed; but he, being fearless, watched the wizards whose terror was distressing. As it was in those ten nights for hospitality, Ahura Mazda sent Spendarmad, Aredvisur, and Ardai-fravard down to the earth, by way of female care; thereupon no variation occurred to the child, and, further, the hand of that Karap was withered, and that wizard demanded the life of Zarathushtra from Porushaspo for the harm from him, which sprang upon himself from his own action.

At the same time Porushaspo took Zarathushtra, and gave him to the Karap, that he might do with him according to his own will. He seized him and threw him out, at the feet of the oxen who were going on a path to the water; the leader of that drove of oxen stood still beside him, and 150 oxen, which walked behind it, were kept away from him thereby; and Porushaspo took him, and carried him back to the house.

he second day, the Karap threw him out at the feet of the horses; leader of the horses stood still beside Zarathushtra, and 150 ...hich walked behind it, were kept away from him thereby; and Porushaspo took him, and carried him back to the house.

Also the third day, firewood was gathered together by the Karap, and Zarathushtra was deposited on it by him, the fire was stirred up by him, yet with the same result, the child was not burnt by it; and those marks, which existed and were made upon him, were a preservation from it.

And the fourth day, he was thrown by the Karap into the lair of a wolf; the wolf was not in the lair, and when it wished to go back to the den, it stopped when it came in front of some radiance, in the manner of a mother, at the place where its cub was. In the night, Vohumano and Srosh the righteous brought a woolly sheep with udder full of milk into the den, and it gave milk to Zarathushtra, in digestible draughts, until daylight.

In the dawn, the mother of Zarathushtra went to that place, in the expectation that it would be necessary to bring a skeleton out of the den, and the woolly sheep came out and ran away; his mother supposed that it was the wolf, and she spoke thus: "Thou hast devoured to repletion; mayst thou endure for ever without it!" She went farther, and when she saw Zarathushtra quite safe, she then took him up and spoke thus: "I will not give thee to any one during life, not though both the provinces of Ragh and Nodar should arrive here together."

The Vision of the Child

These were his tokens at birth:—One day, one of those five brothers of the Karaps saw Zarathushtra, and he looked a long while upwards, downwards, and on all sides around.

Porushaspo inquired thus: "What was there when thou lookedst upwards, what when thou lookedst downwards, and what when thou lookedst on all sides?"

And he replied thus, namely: "When I looked upwards, it was for this reason, when I saw that our souls that go up to the sky, will go up to the best existence, owing to the words of this soul of mankind. When I looked downwards, I saw that, owing to the action of this one, the demon and fiend, the wizard and witch become buried below the earth, and fall paralyzed back to hell. And when I looked on all sides, I saw that the words of this one will extend through the whole earth; and when they have become as the law of the seven regions, each person is kept clothed with a robe of seven skins, in which the glory of the seven archangels has arisen."

Announcement of Purpose

And on the completion of thirty years beyond his birth, the archangel Vohumano came on in commemoration of Ahura Mazda, when he was bringing his Hom-water from the river Aevatak, just as this which revelation mentions thus: When Zarathushtra came forth to the third effluent, that of the good Daitih, he further proceeded through that; and when he marched onwards from that, a man was seen by him, who marched from the southern quarter. That was Vohumano, and it seemed to him that Vohumano was of earthly form, so that he was more discerning as to a person, and foreseeing; it seemed to him that Vohumano was as much in height as three men's spears; and it seemed to him, as to Vohumano, that a glossy twig was brought by him in his hand, through carrying off which branch the plant was not injured by him; that became the spiritual twig of the religion, and this was indicated by it, that it is necessary to proceed as uninjuriously by the religion. There is some one who says that it became a reminder of the spiritual existence, and this was indicated by it, that it is necessary to proceed as uninjuriously in the world, so that peace may exist with every one.

When he came onward to the fourth effluent, as far as the Aushan-rud of the good Daitih, which was the name of it, and he was in it, Zarathushtra was bringing the Hom-water from the middle of it; and on the ascent Zarathushtra, bringing his right foot out of the Aushan-rud, covered himself with his clothes, and upon that Vohumano, advancing, joined him in front.

And that man inquired of him thus: "Who art thou; from whom of them art thou?" He replied: "I am Zarathushtra of the Spitamas."

The words of Vohumano were: "O Zarathushtra of the Spitamas!

about what is thy foremost distress; about what is thy foremost endeavour; and for what is the tendency of thy desire?" The reply of Zarathushtra was thus: "About righteousness, I consider my foremost distress; about righteousness my foremost endeavour; and for righteousness the tendency of my desire."

The words of Vohumano were: "O Zarathushtra of the Spitamas! that which is righteousness is existing (a real thing is, as it were, that which is righteousness), so that whatever is that which is righteousness is thus what is one's own." And Zarathushtra spoke thus: "That which is righteousness exists, and concerning that I am completely clear and aware, but where and how is that radiance which is that whose arrival is through Vohumano."

And Vohumano spoke to him thus: "O Zarathushtra of the Spitamas! deposit this one garment which thou carriest, so that we may confer with him by whom thou art produced and by whom I am produced, who is the most propitious of spirits, who is the most beneficent of existences, and who is he that I, who am Vohumano, am testifying."

Thereupon, Zarathushtra thought thus: "Good is he who is the creator, who is better than this reminder." Then they proceeded in company, Vohumano and Zarathushtra; Vohumano first and Zarathushtra after.

And Vohumano directed Zarathushtra thus: "Do thou proceed to an assembly of the spirits!" As much as Vohumano walked on in nine steps, Zarathushtra did in ninety steps, and when he had gone ninety steps farther than him, he saw the assembly of the seven archangels. When he came within twenty-four feet of the archangels, he then did not see his own shadow on the ground, on account of the great brilliancy of the archangels; the position of the assembly was in Iran, and in the direction of the districts on the bank of the water of the Daitih. Zarathushtra offered homage, and spoke thus: "Homage to Ahura Mazda, and homage to the archangels!" and he went forward and sat down in the seat of the inquirers.

As to the asking of questions by Zarathushtra, he inquired of Ahura Mazda thus: "In the embodied world which is the first of the perfect ones, which the second, and which the third?" And Ahura Mazda replied thus: "The first perfection is good thoughts, the second good words, and the third good deeds."

Zarathushtra also inquired thus: "Which thing is good, which is better, and which is the best of all habits?" And Ahura Mazda replied thus: "The title of the archangels is good, the sight of them is better, and carrying out their commands is the best of all habits."

Afterwards he demonstrated the duality of the original evolutions, and the divergence in each control, and spoke thus: "Of those spirits, he who was wicked preferred the practice which is iniquitous (Aharman's desire was for the practice which is iniquitous), and the spirit of righteousness, the propitious (Ahura Mazda), prefers righteousness." Specially he demonstrated the divergence in each control of the exhibitors of light, and he spoke thus: "Neither our thoughts, nor desires, nor words, nor deeds, nor religion, nor spiritual faculties agree; he who loves light, his place is with the luminaries; and he who loves darkness is with the dark ones."

Temptation by a Demon

Zarathushtra proceeded to the habitable and friendly world, for the purpose of fully observing that beaten track of the embodied existence; then that fiend came forward when he sat in the vicinity of a garment— that garment which, when Vohumano was conveying him to the conference, was deposited by him—a female, golden-bodied and full-bosomed, and companionship, conversation, and co-operation were requested by her from him; she also whined: "I am Spendarmad."

And Zarathushtra spoke thus: "She who is Spendarmad was fully observed by me in the light of a cloudless day, and that Spendarmad appeared to me fine behind and fine before and fine all round; do thou turn thy back, and I shall know if thou art Spendarmad."

And the fiend spoke to him thus: "O Zarathushtra of the Spitamas! where we are, those who are females are handsome in front, but frightfully hideous behind; so do not make a demand for my back." After she had protested a third time, the fiend turned her back, and she was seen by Zarathushtra behind in the groin; and when matter was exuded, it was full of serpents, toads, lizards, centipedes, and frogs.

And that triumphant saying, the Yatha-ahuvairyo, was uttered aloud by Zarathushtra; then that fiend was annihilated.

The Joyousness of Religion

One marvel is this which is declared that, when Zarathushtra chanted revelation in the abode of Vistasp, it was manifest to the eye that it is danced to with joyfulness, both by the cattle and beasts of burden, and by the spirit of the fires which are in the abode. By which, too, a great wonder is proclaimed, like this which revelation mentions thus: There seemed a righteous joyfulness of all the cattle, beasts of burden, and fires of the place, and there seemed a powerfulness of every kind of well-prepared spirits and of those quitting the abode, "that will make us henceforth powerful through religion," when they fully heard those words which were spoken by the righteous Zarathushtra of the Spitamas.

The Death of Zarathushtra

In the forty-seventh year Zarathushtra passes away, who attains seventy-seven years and forty days in the month Ardavahisto, on the day Khur; and for eight rectified months, till the month Dadvo and day Khur, he should be brought forward as to be reverenced.

The Apostasy of the Iron Age

This, too, is a statement as to them, which revelation mentions thus: That is the age mingled with iron in which they bring forth into life him who is a sturdy praying apostate. This is their sturdiness, that their approval is unobservant of both doctrines; and this is their praying, that whenever it is possible for them they shall cause misery to others; also when an old man publicly advances into a crowd of youths, owing to the evil times in which that man who is learned is born, they are unfriendly to him. They are freely speaking, they are wicked and are fully maliciously talking, so that they shall make the statements of priests and high-priests useless; they also tear asunder the spiritual lordship and priestly authority, and shall bring the ruler and priestly authority into evil behaviour as vicious, but they bring together those who are singular. Anything they say is always mischief, and that district which had a judge they cast into the smiting precinct, into hell; it is misery without any inter-mission they shall inflict therein, till they attain unto damnation through the recitation they persevere in, both he who is the evil progeny dissemi-nated by the apostate and he who is the villainous wolf full of disaster and full of depravity.

Here below they fight, the friend with him who is a friend, they also defraud him of his own work, and they give it to him from whom they obtain prosperity in return; if not, they seek him who is acting as a con-federate, and they make that other one defraud the poor man; they also cheat him when he shall make complaint. I shall not again produce such for thee, no friend here for him who is a friend, no brother for him who is a brother, no son for him who is a father, nor yet a father for him who is a son; admonished, but not convinced, they become the abode of the will of the place, so that they subsist in every single place where it is necessary for them to be, in each that is necessary for them they march on together, and on the way they reflect upon the path of blessedness and the manifold learning they utter owing to knowledge of me.

The Essence of Zarathushtra's Religion

About the five dispositions of priests, and the ten admonitions with which all instruction as to religion is connected:

Of those five dispositions the first is innocence.

The second is discrimination among thoughts, words, and deeds; to fully distinguish the particulars of destruction from indestructiveness, such as noxious creatures from cattle; and of production from unproduc-tiveness, such as the righteous and worthy from the wicked and un-worthy.

The third is authoritativeness, because that priestly master is always wiser and speaking more correctly who is taught wisely and teaches with more correct words.

The fourth is to understand and consider the ceremonial as the cere-monial of Ahura Mazda, and the essentials with all goodness, benefi-cence, and authority; to be steadfast in his religion, and to consider the indications of protection which are established for his religion. To maintain the reverence of the luminaries prayerfully, also the reverence of the emanations from the six archangels, be they fire, be they earth, or be they of bodily form, and of the creatures which are formed by them; also the pure cleansing from dead matter, menstruation, bodily refuse, and other hurtfulness; this is in order that they may be characterized, and thereby constituted, as better-principled, more sensible, and purer, and they may become less faulty. The reverence of mankind is to consider authoritatively about knowledge and property; the reverence of cattle is about fodder, little hardship, and moderate maintenance; the reverence of plants is about sowing and ripening for the food of the worthy. The ceremonial which is glorifying all the sacred beings, praises the luminaries and worldly creations improperly, and is antagonistic to them, because complete glorification is proper through complete recitation of the ritual; and the ceremonial of any one whatever is his own proper duty professionally, so long as it is possible to keep proceeding with very little sinfulness.

The fifth is to struggle prayerfully, day and night, with your own fiend, and all life long not to depart from steadfastness, nor allow your proper duty to go out of your hands.

And the first of those ten admonitions is to proceed with good repute, for the sake of occasioning approving remarks as to the good repute of your own guardian and teacher, high-priest and master.

The second is to become awfully refraining from evil repute, for the sake of evil repute not occurring to relations and guardians.

The third is not to beat your own teacher with a snatched-up stick, and not to bring scandal upon his name, for the sake of annoying him, by uttering that which was not heard from your own teacher.

The fourth is that whatever is taught liberally by your own teacher, you have to deliver back to the worthy, for the sake of not extorting a declaration of renown from the righteous.

The fifth is that the reward of doers of good works and the punishment of criminals have to be established by law, for the sake of progress.

The sixth is to keep the way of the good open to your house, for the sake of making righteousness welcome in your own abode.

The seventh is that, for the sake of not developing the fiend insensibly in your reason, you are not to keep it with the religion of the good, nor to remain in impenitence of sin.

The eighth is that, for the sake of severing the fiend from the reason, you have to force malice away from your thoughts, and to become quickly repentant of sin.

The ninth is to fully understand the forward movement of the religion, also to keep the advancing of the religion further forwards, and to seek your share of duty therein; and on a backward movement, when adversity happens to the religion, to have the religion back again, and to keep your body in the continence of religion.

The tenth is that there is to be a period of obedience towards the ruler and priestly authority, the high-priesthood of the religious.

The Function of the Righteous

For what purpose is a righteous man created for the world, and in what manner is it necessary for him to exist in the world?

The reply is this, that the creator created the creatures for progress, which is his wish; and it is necessary for us to promote whatever is his wish, so that we may obtain whatever is our wish. And, since that persistent creator is powerful, whatever is our wish, and so far as we remain very faithful, such is as it were deserving of his wish, which is for our obtainment of whatever is our wish.

The creatures are for the performance of what is desirable for the creator, and the performance of what is desirable for the creator is necessary for two purposes, which are the practice of worship and contention. As the worship is that of the persistent creator, who is a friend to his own creatures, and the contention is that with the fiend—the contender who is an enemy to the creation of the creator—that great worship is a pledge, most intimate to one's self, of the utmost contention also, and a pledge for the prosperity owing to the friend subjugating by a look which is a contender with the enemy, the great endeavour of the acquirers of reliance upon any mortals whatever.

For when the persistent one accomplished that most perfect and wholly miraculous creation of the lord, and his unwavering look—which was upon the coming on of the wandering evil spirit, the erratic, unobservant spirit—was unmingled with the sight of an eye, he made a spirit of observant temperament, which was the necessary soul, the virtuous lord of the body moving into the world. And the animating life, the preserving guardian spirit, the acquiring intellect, the protect-

ing understanding, the deciding wisdom, the demeanour which is itself
a physician, the impelling strength, the eye for what is seen, the ear for
what is heard, the nose for what is smelt, the mouth for recognizing
flavour, the body for approaching the assembly of the righteous, the
heart for thinking, the tongue for speaking, the hand for working, the
foot for walking, these which make life comfortable, these which are
developments in creating, these which are to join the body, these which
are to be considered perfected, are urged on by him continuously, and
the means of industry of the original body are arranged advisedly. And
by proper regulation, and the recompense of good thoughts, good words,
and good deeds, he announced and adorned conspicuous, patient, and
virtuous conduct; and that procurer of the indispensable did not forget
to keep men in his own true service and proper bounds, the supreme
sovereignty of the creator.

And man became a pure glorifier and pure praiser of that all-good
friend, through the progress which is his wish. Because pure friendship
is owing to sure meditation on every virtue, and from its existence no
harm whatever arose; pure glorifying is owing to glorifying every goodness, and from its existence no vileness whatever arose; and pure praising
is owing to all prosperity, and from its existence no distress whatever
arose.

A more concise reply is this, that a righteous man is the creature by
whom is accepted that occupation which is provided for him, and is
fully watchful in the world as to his not being deceived by the rapacious
fiend. And as a determiner, by wisdom, of the will of the creator—one
who is himself a propitiator and understander, and a promoter of the
understanding of goodness—and of whatever pertains to him, the
creator, he is a giver of heed thereto; and it is necessary for him to be
thus, so that such greatness and goodness may also be his more securely
in the spiritual existence.

Evil to the Good

Why does evil always happen more to the good than to the bad?
The reply is this, that not at every time and every place, and not to
all the good, does evil happen more—for the spiritual welfare of the

good is certainly more—but in the world it is very much more mani
And the reasons for it are many; one which is conclusive is even
that the modes and causes of its occurrence are more; for the occurrence of evil is more particularly appointed by two modes, one by the
demons, the appointers of evil, and one by the vile, the doers of evil;
even to the vileness of creation and the vile they cause vexation. Moreover, incalculable is the evil which happens to the vile from the demons,
and that to the good from the demons and also from the vile, and the
mode of its occurrence is in the same way without a demon.

This, too, is more particularly such as the ancients have said, that the
labour and trouble of the good are much more in the world, and their
reward and recompense are more certain in the spiritual existence; and
the comfort and pleasure of the vile are more in the world, and their
pain and punishment in the spiritual existence are more severe. And
this, too, is the case, that the good, through fear of the pain and punishment of hell, should forsake the comfort and ease in the world, and
should not think, speak, or do anything improper whatever. And through
hope for the comfort and pleasure in heaven they should accept willingly, for the neck, much trouble and fear in the practice of virtue in
thought, word, and deed.

The vile, through provision with temporary enjoyment—even that
enjoyment of improprieties for which eventually there is hell—then
enjoy themselves therein temporarily, and lustfully on account of selfishness; those various actions also, through which there would be a way to
heaven, they do not trouble themselves with.

And in this way, in the world, the comfort and pleasure of the vile
are more, and the anxiety, vexation, despondency, and distress of the
good have become more; the reason is revealed by the stars.

The Chinvad Bridge

How are the Chinvad bridge, the Daitih peak, and the path of the
righteous and wicked; how are they when one is righteous, and how
when one is wicked?

The reply is this, that thus the high-priests have said, that the Daitih
peak is in Airyana-Vaego, in the middle of the world; reaching unto the

vicinity of that peak is that beam-shaped spirit, the Chinvad bridge, which is thrown across from the Alburz enclosure back to the Daitih peak. As it were that bridge is like a beam of many sides, of whose edges there are some which are broad, and there are some which are thin and sharp; its broad sides are so large that its width is twenty-seven reeds, and its sharp sides are so contracted that in thinness it is just like the edge of a razor. And when the souls of the righteous and wicked arrive it turns to that side which is suitable to their necessities, through the great glory of the creator and the command of him who takes the just account.

Moreover, the bridge becomes a broad bridge for the righteous, as much as the height of nine spears—and the length of those which they carry is each separately three reeds—; and it becomes a narrow bridge for the wicked, even unto a resemblance to the edge of a razor. And he who is of the righteous passes over the bridge, and a worldly similitude of the pleasantness of his path upon it is when thou shalt eagerly and unweariedly walk in the golden-coloured spring, and with the gallant body and sweet-scented blossom in the pleasant skin of that maiden spirit, the price of goodness. He who is of the wicked, as he places a footstep on to the bridge, on account of affliction and its sharpness, falls from the middle of the bridge, and rolls over head-foremost. And the unpleasantness of his path to hell is in similitude such as the worldly one in the midst of that stinking and dying existence, there where numbers of the sharp-pointed darts are planted out inverted and point upwards, and they come unwillingly running; they shall not allow them to stay behind, or to make delay. So much greater than the worldly similitude is that pleasantness and unpleasantness unto the souls, as such as is fit for the spirit is greater than that fit for the world.

The Nature of Heaven

How are the nature of heaven and the comfort and pleasure which are in heaven?

The reply is this, that it is lofty, exalted, and supreme, most brilliant, most fragrant, and most pure, most supplied with beautiful existences, most desirable, and most good, and the place and abode of the sacred beings. And in it are all comfort, pleasure, joy, happiness, and welfare, more and better even than the greatest and supremest welfare and pleasure in the world; and there is no want, pain, distress, or discomfort whatever in it; and its pleasantness and the welfare of the angels are from that constantly beneficial place, the full and undiminishable space, the good and boundless world.

And the freedom of the heavenly from danger from evil in heaven is like unto their freedom from disturbance, and the coming of the good angels is like unto the heavenly ones' own good works provided. This prosperity and welfare of the spiritual existence is more than that of the world, as much as that which is unlimited and everlasting is more than that which is limited and demoniacal.

The Nature of Hell

How are the nature of hell, and the pain, discomfort, punishment, and stench of hell?

The reply is this, that it is sunken, deep, and descending, most dark, most stinking, and most terrible, most supplied with wretched existences, and most bad, the place and cave of the demons and fiends. And in it is no comfort, pleasantness, or joy whatever; but in it are all stench, filth, pain, punishment, distress, profound evil, and discomfort; and there is no resemblance of it whatever to worldly stench, filthiness, pain, and evil. And since there is no resemblance of the mixed evil of the world to that which is its sole-indicating good, there is also a deviation of it from the origin and abode of evil.

And so much more grievous is the evil in hell than even the most grievous evil on earth, as the greatness of the spiritual existence is more than that of the world; and more grievous is the terror of the punishment on the soul than that of the vileness of the demons on the body. And the punishment on the soul is from those whose abode it has become, from the demons and darkness—a likeness of that evil to hell —the head of whom is Aharman the deadly.

And the words of the expressive utterance of the high-priests are these, that where there is a fear of every other thing it is more than the thing itself, but hell is a thing worse than the fear of it.

Reception in Heaven

When a soul of the righteous goes on to heaven, in what manner does it go; also, who receives it, who leads it, and who makes it a household attendant of Ahura Mazda? Also, does any one of the righteous in heaven come out to meet it, and shall any thereof make inquiry of it, or how?

The reply is this, that a soul of the righteous steps forth unto heaven through the strength of the spirit of good works, along with the good spirit which is the escort of the soul, into its allotted station and the uppermost which is for its own good works; along with the spiritual good works, without those for the world, and a crown and coronet, a turban-sash and a fourfold fillet-pendant, a decorated robe and suitable equipments, spiritually flying unto heaven, or to the supreme heaven, there where its place is. And Vohumano, the archangel, makes it a household attendant to Ahura Mazda the creator, and by order of Ahura Mazda announces its position and reward; and it becomes glad to beg for the position of household attendant of Ahura Mazda, through what it sees and knows.

Ahura Mazda the creator of good producers is a spirit even among spirits, and spirits even have looked for a sight of him; which spirits are manifestly above worldly existences. But when, through the majesty of the creator, spirits put on worldly appearances, or are attending to the world and spirit, and put away appearance, then he whose patron spirit is in the world is able to see the attending spirits, in such similitude as when they see bodies in which is a soul, or when they see a fire in which is Varahran, or see water in which is its own spirit. Moreover, in that household attendance, that Ahura Mazda has seen the soul is certain, for Ahura Mazda sees all things; and many even of the fiend's souls, who are put away from those of Ahura Mazda in spiritual understanding, are delighted by the appearance of those of Ahura Mazda.

And the righteous in heaven, who have been his intimate friends, of the same religion and like goodness, speak to him of the display of affection, the courteous inquiry, and the suitable eminence from coming to heaven, and his everlasting well-being in heaven.

The Sin of Profiteering

As to them who shall buy corn and keep it in store until it shall become dear, and shall then sell it at a high price, what is the nature of the decision?

The reply is this, that when there is nothing therein on account of which I should so deem it otherwise than due to the eating of the requisite amount of food for one's self, that which is his controlling impulse, and not the teachings of the worthy and good, is the internal instruction which a time of scarcity has taught by means of the occurrences during that time; but clamorous worldly profit is want of diligence, for they would buy to make people distressed, and in order that they may sell again dearer. Moreover, the store one keeps, and keeps as closed even unto the good as unto the bad—and though it be necessary for a man of the good and worthy, and they beg for some of the food, they shall not sell at the price it is worth at that time, on account of its becoming dearer—one keeps in store unauthorizedly and grievously sinfully, and every calamity of those good people they shall suffer who would not sell it at the price they beg.

The First Man

Whence was the first creation of mankind, and how was the formation of the original race of men? What issued from Gayomard, and what did it really become; and from what have Mashya and Mashyoi arisen?

The reply is this, that Ahura Mazda, the all-ruling, produced from the endless light the shape of a fire-priest whose name was that of Ahura Mazda, and its brilliance that of fire; its incombustibility was like that inside the light, and its expansion like the western land. And in the shape of the fire-priest was created by him the material existence that is called man, and for three thousand years, when it did not progress and did not eat, it did not speak; likewise, it did not utter, but it thought of, the righteousness of the perfect and true religion, the desire for the pure glorification of the creator.

Afterwards, the contentious promise-breaker injured the life of it, and produced a burdensome mortality; and the mortality is clear from the appellation, Gayomard, of the nature produced. The seed which was the essence of the life of the leader of life, who was Gayomard, flowed forth on his passing away, came on to the earth of the beneficent angel, and was preserved in the earth until, through the protection of the angels, a brother and sister of mankind, connected together, had grown from it, had attained to movement and walking upon the earth, and had advanced even to intercourse and also procreation.

The ground where the life of Gayomard departed is gold, and from the other land, where the dissolution of his various members occurred, as many kinds of decorative metals flowed forth, it is said.

The Propagation of Man

Where and from what did the origin of race, which they say was next-of-kin marriage, arise; and from what place did it arise?

The reply is this, that the first consummation of next-of-kin marriage was owing to that which Mashya and Mashyoi did, who were brother and sister together, and their consummation of intercourse produced a son as a consummation of the first next-of-kin marriage. So that they effected the first intercourse of man with woman, and the entire progress of the races of every kind of lineage of men arose from that, and all the men of the world are of that race.

It is truly said, that it was the joy of the lord and creator after the creation of the creatures, and, owing to that, its consummation, which was his complete accomplishment of the existence of the creatures, was owing to him. And its occurrence, too, is an evidence that the creator, who is so with unflinching will, is as much the cause of the begetting and entire progress of his own perfect creatures, in whom begetting is by destiny, as Hoshang by whom two-thirds of the demons were smitten, Takhmorup who overturned Aharman through the power of the angels, Yim by whom order was arranged and death was driven away, Fredun who fettered Az-i Dahak and stripped his blaspheming from the world, and the many princes and high-priests of grave spirit who were, and are, and will be.

The Rainbow

What is this appearance which is girded on the sky?

The reply is this, that it is a mingling of the brilliance of the sun with mist and cloud that is seen, of which it is at all times and seasons, more-over, a characteristic appearance, whereby it has become their sign above from spiritual to earthly beings. That which is earthly is the water above to which its brilliance is acceptable; and the many brilliant colours which are formed from that much mingling of brilliance and water, and are depicted, are the one portion for appearing.

The Two Regions

It is in scripture thus declared, that light was above and darkness below, and between those two was open space. Ahura Mazda was in the light, and Aharman in the darkness; Ahura Mazda was aware of the existence of Aharman and of his coming for strife; Aharman was not aware of the existence of light and of Ahura Mazda. It happened to Aharman, in the gloom and darkness, that he was walking humbly on the borders, and meditating other things he came up to the top, and a ray of light was seen by him; and because of its antagonistic nature to him he strove that he might reach it, so that it might also be within his absolute power. And as he came forth to the boundary, accompanied by certain others, Ahura Mazda came forth to the struggle for keeping Aharman away from his territory; and he did it through pure words, confounding witchcraft, and cast him back to the gloom.

The Order of Creation

The first of Ahura Mazda's creatures of the world was the sky, and his good thought, by good procedure, produced the light of the world, along with which was the good religion of the Mazdayasnians; this was because the renovation which happens to the creatures was known to him. Afterwards arose Ardavahist, and then Shatvairo, and then Spendarmad, and then Horvadad, and then Amerodad.

From the dark world of Aharman were Akoman and Andar, and then Sovar, and then Nakahed, and then Tairev and Zairik.

Of Ahura Mazda's creatures of the world, the first was the sky; the second, water; the third, earth; the fourth, plants; the fifth, animals; the sixth, mankind.

Ahura Mazda produced illumination between the sky and the earth, the constellation stars and those also not of the constellations, then the moon, and afterwards the sun, as I shall relate.

First he produced the celestial sphere, and the constellation stars are assigned to it by him; especially these twelve whose names are Varak (the Lamb), Tora (the Bull), Do-patkar (the two-figures of Gemini), Kalakang (the Crab), Ser (the Lion), Khusak (Virgo), Tarazuk (the Balance), Gazdum (the Scorpion), Nimasp (the Centaur or Sagittarius), Vahik (Capricornus), Dul (the Waterpot), and Mahik (the Fish); which, from their original creation, were divided into the twenty-eight sub-divisions of the astronomers, of which the names are Padevar, Pesh-Parviz, Parviz, Paha, Avesar, Besn, Rakhvad, Taraha, Avra, Nahn, Miyan, Avdem, Mashaha, Spur, Husru, Srob, Nur, Gel, Garafsa, Varant, Gau, Goi, Muru, Bunda, Kahtsar, Vaht, Miyan, Kaht. And all his original creations, residing in the world, are committed to them; so that when the destroyer arrives they overcome the adversary and their own persecution, and the creatures are saved from those adversities.

The Flood

On the conflict of the creations of the world with the antagonism of the evil spirit it is said in revelation, that the evil spirit, even as he rushed in and looked upon the pure bravery of the angels and his own violence, wished to rush back. The spirit of the sky is himself like one of the warriors who has put on armour; he arrayed the sky against the evil spirit, and led on in the contest, until Ahura Mazda had completed a rampart around, stronger than the sky and in front of the sky. And his guardian spirits of warriors and the righteous, on war horses and spear in hand, were around the sky; such-like as the hair on the head is the similitude of those who held the watch of the rampart. And no passage was found by the evil spirit, who rushed back; and he beheld the annihilation of the demons and his own impotence, as Ahura Mazda did his own final triumph, producing the renovation of the universe for ever and everlasting.

The second conflict was waged with the water, because, as the star Tistar was in Cancer, the water which is in the subdivision they call Avrak was pouring, on the same day when the destroyer rushed in, and came again into notice for mischief in the direction of the west. For every single month is the owner of one constellation; the month Tir is the fourth month of the year, and Cancer the fourth constellation from Aries, so it is the owner of Cancer, into which Tistar sprang, and displayed the characteristics of a producer of rain; and he brought on the water aloft by the strength of the wind. Co-operators with Tistar were Vohumano and the angel Hom, with the assistance of the angel Burg and the righteous guardian spirits in orderly arrangement.

Tistar was converted into three forms, the form of a man and the form of a horse and the form of a bull; thirty days and nights he was distinguished in brilliance, and in each form he produced rain ten days and nights; as the astrologers say that every constellation has three forms. Every single drop of that rain became as big as a bowl, and the water stood the height of a man over the whole of this earth; and the noxious creatures on the earth being all killed by the rain, went into the holes of the earth.

And afterwards the wind spirit, so that it might not be contaminated, stirred up the wind and atmosphere as the life stirs in the body; and the water was all swept away by it, and was brought out to the borders of the earth, and the wide-formed ocean arose therefrom. The noxious creatures remained dead within the earth, and their venom and stench were mingled with the earth, and in order to carry that poison away from the earth Tistar went down into the ocean in the form of a white horse with long hoofs.

And Apaosh, the demon, came meeting him in the likeness of a black horse with clumsy hoofs; a mile away from him fled Tistar, through the fright which drove him away. And Tistar begged for success from Ahura Mazda, and Ahura Mazda gave him strength and power, as it is said, that unto Tistar was brought at once the strength of ten vigorous horses, ten vigorous camels, ten vigorous bulls, ten mountains, and ten rivers. A mile away from him fled Apaosh, the demon, through fright at his strength; on account of this they speak of an arrow-shot with Tistar's strength in the sense of a mile.

Afterwards, with a cloud for a jar—thus they call the measure which was a means of the work—he seized upon the water and made it rain most prodigiously, in drops like bulls' heads and men's heads, pouring in handfuls and pouring in armfuls, both great and small. On the production of that rain the demons Aspengargak and Apaosh contended with it, and the fire Vazist turned its club over; and owing to the blow of the club Aspengargak made a very grievous noise, as even now, in a conflict with the producer of rain, a groaning and raging are manifest. And ten nights and days rain was produced by him in that manner, and the poison and venom of the noxious creatures which were in the earth were all mixed up in the water, and the water became quite salt, because there remained in the earth some of those germs which noxious creatures ever collect.

Afterwards, the wind, in the same manner as before, restrained the water, at the end of three days, on various sides of the earth; and the three great seas and twenty-three small seas arose therefrom, and two fountains of the sea thereby became manifest, one the Kekast lake, and one the Sovbar, whose sources are connected with the fountain of the sea. And at its north side two rivers flowed out, and went one to the east and one to the west; they are the Arag river and the Veh river; as it is said thus: "Through those finger-breadth tricklings do thou pour and draw forth two such waters, O Ahura Mazda!" Both those rivers wind about through all the extremities of the earth, and intermingle again with the water of the wide-formed ocean. As those two rivers flowed out, and from the same place of origin as theirs, eighteen navigable rivers flowed out, and after the other waters have flowed out from those navigable streams they all flow back to the Arag river and Veh river, whose fertilization of the world arises therefrom.

The Resurrection

On the nature of the resurrection and future existence it says in revelation that, whereas Mashya and Mashyoi, who grew up from the earth, first fed upon water, then plants, then milk, and then meat, men also, when their time of death has come, first desist from eating meat, then milk, then from bread, till when they shall die they always feed upon water. So, likewise, in the millennium of Hushedar-mah, the strength of appetite will thus diminish, when men will remain three days and nights in superabundance through one taste of consecrated food. Then they will desist from meat food, and eat vegetables and milk; afterwards, they abstain from milk food and abstain from vegetable food, and are feeding on water; and for ten years before Soshyans comes they remain without food, and do not die.

After Soshyans comes they prepare the raising of the dead, as it says, that Zarathushtra asked of Ahura Mazda thus: "Whence does a body form again, which the wind has carried and the water conveyed? and how does the resurrection occur?" Ahura Mazda answered thus: "When through me the sky arose from the substance of the ruby, without columns, on the spiritual support of far-compassed light; when through me the earth arose, which bore the material life, and there is no maintainer of the worldly creation but it; when by me the sun and moon and stars were conducted in the firmament of luminous bodies; when by me corn was created so that, scattered about in the earth, it grew again and returned with increase; when by me colour of various kinds was created in plants; when by me fire was created in plants and other things without combustion; when by me a son was created and fashioned in the womb of a mother, and the structure severally of the skin, nails, blood, feet, eyes, ears, and other things was produced; when by me legs were created for the water, so that it flows away, and the cloud was created which carries the water of the world and rains there where it has a purpose; when by me the air was created which conveys in one's eyesight, through the strength of the wind, the lowermost upwards according to its will, and one is not able to grasp it with the hand outstretched; each one of them, when created by me, was herein more difficult than causing the resurrection, for it is an assistance to me in the resurrection that they exist, but when they were formed it was not forming the future out of the past.

"Observe that when that which was not was then produced, why is it not possible to produce again that which was? for at that time one will demand the bone from the spirit of earth, the blood from the water, the hair from the plants, and the life from fire, since they were delivered to them in the original creation."

First, the bones of Gayomard are roused up, then those of Mashya and Mashyoi, then those of the rest of mankind; in the fifty-seven years of Soshyans they prepare all the dead, and all men stand up; whoever is righteous and whoever is wicked, every human creature, they rouse up from the spot where its life departs.

Afterwards, when all material living beings assume again their bodies and forms, then they assign them a single class.

Of the light accompanying the sun, one-half will be for Gayomard, and one-half will give enlightenment among the rest of men, so that the soul and body will know that this is my father, and this is my mother, and this is my brother, and this is my wife, and these are some other of my nearest relations.

Then is the assembly of the Sadvastaran, where all mankind will stand at this time; in that assembly every one sees his own good deeds and his own evil deeds; and then, in that assembly, a wicked man becomes as conspicuous as a white sheep among those which are black.

In that assembly whatever righteous man was friend of a wicked one in the world, and the wicked man complains of him who is righteous, thus: "Why did he not make me acquainted, when in the world, with the good deeds which he practised himself?" if he who is righteous did not inform him, then it is necessary for him to suffer shame accordingly in that assembly.

Afterwards, they set the righteous man apart from the wicked; and then the righteous is for heaven, and they cast the wicked back to hell. Three days and nights they inflict punishment bodily in hell, and then he beholds bodily those three days' happiness in heaven. As it says that, on the day when the righteous man is parted from the wicked, the tears of every one, thereupon, run down unto his legs.

When, after, they set apart a father from his consort, a brother from his brother, and a friend from his friend, they suffer, every one for his own deeds, and weep, the righteous for the wicked, and the wicked about himself; for there may be a father who is righteous and a son wicked, and there may be one brother who is righteous and one wicked. Those for whose peculiar deeds it is appointed, such as Dahak and Frasiyav of Tur, and others of this sort, as those deserving death, undergo a punishment no other men undergo; they call it "the punishment of the three nights."

Among his producers of the renovation of the universe, those righteous men of whom it is written that they are living, fifteen men and fifteen damsels, will come to the assistance of Soshyans. As Gokihar falls in the celestial sphere from a moonbeam on to the earth, the distress of the earth becomes such-like as that of a sheep when a wolf falls upon it. Afterwards, the fire and halo melt the metal of Shatvairo, in the hills and mountains, and it remains on this earth like a river. Then all men will pass into that melted metal and will become pure; when one is righteous, then it seems to him just as though he walks continually in warm milk; but when wicked, then it seems to him in such manner as though, in the world, he walks continually in melted metal.

Afterwards, with the greatest affection, all men come together, father and son and brother and friend ask one another thus: "Where hast thou been these many years, and what was the judgment upon thy soul? hast thou been righteous or wicked?" The first soul the body sees, it inquires of it with those words. All men become of one voice and administer loud praise to Ahura Mazda and the archangels.

Ahura Mazda completes his work at that time, and the creatures become so that it is not necessary to make any effort about them; and among those by whom the dead are prepared, it is not necessary that any effort be made.

Soshyans, with his assistants, performs a Yazisn ceremony in preparing the dead, and they slaughter the ox Hadhayos in that Yazisn; from the fat of that ox and the white Hom they prepare Hush, and give it to all men, and all men become immortal for ever and everlasting.

This, too, it says, that whoever has been the size of a man, they restore him then with an age of forty years; they who have been little when not dead, they restore then with an age of fifteen years; and they give every one his wife, and show him his children with the wife; so they act as now in the world, but there is no begetting of children.

Afterwards, Soshyans and his assistants, by order of the creator Ahura Mazda, give every man the reward and recompense suitable to his deeds; this is even the righteous existence where it is said that they convey him to paradise, and the heaven of Ahura Mazda takes up the body as itself requires; with that assistance he continually advances for ever and everlasting.

This, too, it says, that whoever has performed no worship, and has ordered no Geti-kharid, and has bestowed no clothes as a righteous gift, is naked there; and he performs the worship of Ahura Mazda, and the heavenly angels provide him the use of his clothing.

Afterwards, Ahura Mazda seizes on the evil spirit, Vohumano on Akoman, Ashavahist on Andar, Shatvairo on Savar, Spendarmad on Taromat who is Naunghas, Horvadad and Amerodad on Tairev and Zairik, true-speaking on what is evil-speaking, Srosh on Aeshm. Then two fiends remain at large, Aharman and Az; Ahura Mazda comes to the world, himself the Zota and Srosh the Raspi, and holds the Kusti in his hand; defeated by the Kusti formula the resources of the evil spirit and Az act most impotently, and by the passage through which he rushed into the sky he runs back to gloom and darkness. Gokihar burns the serpent in the melted metal, and the stench and pollution which were in hell are burned in that metal, and hell becomes quite pure. Ahura Mazda sets the vault into which the evil spirit fled in that metal; he brings the land of hell back for the enlargement of the world; the renovation arises in the universe by his will, and the world is immortal for ever and everlasting.

This, too, it says, that this earth becomes an iceless, slopeless plain; even the mountain whose summit is the support of the Chinvad bridge, they keep down, and it will not exist.

The Reproduction of Species

On the nature of generation it says in revelation that a woman when she comes out from menstruation, during ten days and nights, when they go near unto her, soon becomes pregnant. When she is cleansed from her menstruation, and when the time for pregnancy has come, always when the seed of the man is the more powerful a son arises from it; when that of the woman is the more powerful, a daughter; when both seeds are equal, twins and triplets. If the male seed comes the sooner, it adds to the female, and she becomes robust; if the female seed comes the sooner, it becomes blood, and the leanness of the female arises therefrom.

The female seed is cold and moist, and its flow is from the loins, and the colour is white, red, and yellow; and the male seed is hot and dry, its flow is from the brain of the head, and the colour is white and mud-coloured. All the seed of the females which issues beforehand, takes a place within the womb, and the seed of the males will remain above it, and will fill the space of the womb; whatever refrains therefrom becomes blood again, enters into the veins of the females, and at the time any one is born it becomes milk and nourishes him, as all milk arises from the seed of the males, and the blood is that of the females.

These four things, they say, are male, and these female: the sky, metal, wind, and fire are male, and are never otherwise; the water, earth, plants, and fish are female, and are never otherwise; the remaining creation consists of male and female.

As regards the fish it says that, at the time of excitement, they go forwards and come back in the water, two and two, the length of a mile, which is one-fourth of a league, in the running water; in that coming and going they then rub their bodies together, and a kind of sweat drops out betwixt them, and both become pregnant.

The Ancestry of the World

On the nature of men it says in revelation, that Gayomard, in passing away, gave forth seed; that seed was thoroughly purified by the motion of the light of the sun, and Neryosang kept charge of two portions, and Spendarmad received one portion. And in forty years, with the shape of a one-stemmed Rivas-plant, and the fifteen years of its fifteen leaves, Matro and Matroyao grew up from the earth in such a manner that their arms rested behind on their shoulders, and one joined to the other they were connected together and both alike. And the waists of both of them were brought close and so connected together that it was not clear which was the male and which the female, and which was the one whose living soul of Ahura Mazda was not away. As it is said thus: "Which is created before, the soul or the body?" And Ahura Mazda said that the soul is created before, and the body after, for him who was created; it is given into the body that it may produce activity, and the body is created only for activity; hence the conclusion is this, that the soul is created before and the body after.

And both of them changed from the shape of a plant into the shape of a man, and the breath went spiritually into them, which is the soul; and now, moreover, in that similitude a tree had grown up whose fruit was the ten varieties of man.

Ahura Mazda spoke to Mashya and Mashyoi thus: "You are man, you are the ancestry of the world, and you are created perfect in devotion by me; perform devotedly the duty of the law, think good thoughts, speak good words, do good deeds, and worship no demons!"

Both of them first thought this, that one of them should please the other, as he is a man for him; and the first deed done by them was this, when they went out they washed themselves thoroughly; and the first words spoken by them were these, that Ahura Mazda created the water and earth, plants and animals, the stars, moon, and sun, and all prosperity whose origin and effect are from the manifestation of righteousness.

And, afterwards, antagonism rushed into their minds, and their minds were thoroughly corrupted, and they exclaimed that the evil spirit created the water and earth, plants and animals, and the other things as aforesaid. That false speech was spoken through the will of the demons, and the evil spirit possessed himself of this first enjoyment from them; through that false speech they both became wicked, and their souls are in hell until the future existence.

And they had gone thirty days without food, covered with clothing of herbage; and after the thirty days they went forth into the wilderness, came to a white-haired goat, and milked the milk from the udder with their mouths. When they had devoured the milk Mashya said to Mashyoi thus: "My delight was owing to it when I had not devoured the milk, and my delight is more delightful now when it is devoured by my vile body."

That second false speech enhanced the power of the demons, and the taste of the food was taken away by them, so that out of a hundred parts one part remained.

Afterwards, in another thirty days and nights, they came to a sheep, fat and white-jawed, and they slaughtered it; and fire was extracted by them out of the wood of the lote-plum and box-tree, through the guidance of the heavenly angels, since both woods were most productive of fire for them; and the fire was stimulated by their mouths; and the first fuel kindled by them was dry grass, kendar, lotos, date palm leaves, and myrtle; and they made a roast of the sheep.

And they dropped three handfuls of the meat into the fire, and said: "This is the share of the fire." One piece of the rest they tossed to the sky, and said: "This is the share of the angels." A bird, the vulture, advanced and carried some of it away from before them, as a dog ate the first meat.

And first a clothing of skins covered them; afterwards, it is said, woven garments were prepared from a cloth woven in the wilderness.

And they dug out a pit in the earth, and iron was obtained by them and beaten out with a stone, and without a forge they beat out a cutting edge from it; and they cut wood with it, and prepared a wooden shelter from the sun.

Owing to the gracelessness which they practised, the demons became more oppressive, and they themselves carried on unnatural malice between themselves; they advanced one against the other, and smote and tore their hair and cheeks.

Then the demons shouted out of the darkness thus: "You are man; worship the demon! so that your demon of malice may repose."

Mashya went forth and milked a cow's milk, and poured it out towards the northern quarter; through that the demons became more powerful, and owing to them they both became so dry-backed that in fifty winters they had no desire for intercourse, and though they had had intercourse they would have had no children.

And on the completion of fifty years the source of desire arose, first in Mashya and then in Mashyoi, for Mashya said to Mashyoi thus: "When I see thy shame my desires arise." Then Mashyoi spoke thus: "Brother Mashya! when I see thy great desire I am also agitated." Afterwards, it became their mutual wish that the satisfaction of their desires should be accomplished, as they reflected thus: "Our duty even for those fifty years was this."

From them was born in nine months a pair, male and female; and owing to tenderness for offspring the mother devoured one, and the father one. And afterwards Ahura Mazda took tenderness for offspring away from them, so that one may nourish a child, and the child may remain.

The Independence of the Dog

Of the dog they say that out of the star station, that is, away from the direction of the constellation Haptok-ring, was given to him further by a stage than to men, on account of his protection of sheep, and as associating with sheep and men; for this the dog is purposely adapted, as three more kinds of advantage are given to him than to man: he has his own boots, his own clothing, and may wander about without self-exertion.

JUDEO = CHRISTIAN
Scriptures

THE OLD TESTAMENT

The First Book of Moses, Called
GENESIS

The Creation

In the beginning God created the heaven and the earth. And the earth was without form, and void; and darkness was upon the face of the deep: and the Spirit of God moved upon the face of the waters.

And God said, Let there be light: and there was light. And God saw the light, that it was good: and God divided the light from the darkness. And God called the light Day, and the darkness he called Night: and the evening and the morning were the first day.

And God said, Let there be a firmament in the midst of the waters: and let it divide the waters from the waters. And God made the firmament, and divided the waters which were under the firmament from the waters which were above the firmament: and it was so. And God called the firmament Heaven: and the evening and the morning were the second day.

And God said, Let the waters under the heaven be gathered together unto one place, and let the dry land appear: and it was so. And God called the dry land Earth; and the gathering together of the waters called he Seas: and God saw that it was good.

And God said, Let the earth bring forth grass, the herb yielding seed, and the fruit-tree yielding fruit after his kind, whose seed is in itself, upon the earth: and it was so. And the earth brought forth grass, and herb yielding seed after his kind, and the tree yielding fruit, whose seed was in itself, after his kind: and God saw that it was good.

And the evening and the morning were the third day.

And God said, Let there be lights in the firmament of the heaven, to divide the day from the night; and let them be for signs, and for seasons, and for days, and years. And let them be for lights in the firmament of the heaven to give light upon the earth: and it was so. And God made two great lights; the greater light to rule the day, and the lesser light to rule the night: he made the stars also. And God set them in the firmament of the heaven to give light upon the earth, and to rule over the day, and over the night, and to divide the light from the darkness: and God saw that it was good.

And the evening and the morning were the fourth day.

And God said, Let the waters bring forth abundantly the moving creature that hath life, and fowl that may fly above the earth in the open firmament of heaven. And God created great whales, and every living creature that moveth, which the waters brought forth abundantly after their kind, and every winged fowl after his kind: and God saw that it was good. And God blessed them, saying, Be fruitful and multiply, and fill the waters in the seas, and let fowl multiply in the earth.

And the evening and the morning were the fifth day.

And God said, Let the earth bring forth the living creature after his kind, cattle, and creeping thing, and beast of the earth after his kind: and it was so. And God made the beast of the earth after his kind, and cattle after their kind, and everything that creepeth upon the earth after his kind: and God saw that it was good.

And God said, Let us make man in our image, after our likeness: and let them have dominion over the fish of the sea, and over the fowl of the air, and over the cattle, and over all the earth, and over every creeping thing that creepeth upon the earth. So God created man in his own image, in the image of God created he him; male and female created he them. And God blessed them, and God said unto them, Be fruitful, and multiply, and replenish the earth, and subdue it: and have dominion over the fish of the sea, and over the fowl of the air, and over every living thing that moveth upon the earth.

And God said, Behold, I have given you every herb bearing seed, which is upon the face of all the earth, and every tree, in the which is the fruit of a tree yielding seed; to you it shall be for meat. And to every beast of the earth, and to every fowl of the air, and to every thing that creepeth upon the earth, wherein there is life, I have given every green herb for meat: and it was so.

And God saw every thing that he had made: and behold, it was very good. And the evening and the morning were the sixth day.

The Garden of Eden

Thus the heavens and the earth were finished, and all the host of them. And on the seventh day God ended his work which he had made; and he rested on the seventh day from all his work which he had made. And God blessed the seventh day, and sanctified it: because that in it he had rested from all his work which God created and made.

These are the generations of the heavens and of the earth when they were created, in the day that the Lord God made the earth and the heavens, and every plant of the field before it was in the earth, and every herb of the field before it grew: for the Lord God had not caused it to rain upon the earth, and there was not a man to till the ground. But there went up a mist from the earth, and watered the whole face of the ground. And the Lord God formed man of the dust of the ground, and breathed into his nostrils the breath of life; and man became a living soul.

And the Lord God planted a garden eastward in Eden; and there he put the man whom he had formed. And out of the ground made the Lord God to grow every tree that is pleasant to the sight, and good for food; the tree of life also in the midst of the garden, and the tree of knowledge of good and evil.

And a river went out of Eden to water the garden: and from thence it was parted, and became into four heads. The name of the first is Pison: that is it which compasseth the whole land of Havilah, where there is gold; and the gold of that land is good: there is bdellium and the onyx-stone. And the name of the second river is Bihon: the same is it that compasseth the whole land of Ethiopia. And the name of the third river is Hiddekel: that is it which goeth toward the east of Assyria. And the fourth river is Euphrates.

And the Lord God took the man, and put him into the garden of Eden, to dress it, and to keep it.

And the Lord God commanded the man, saying, Of every tree of the garden thou mayest freely eat: but of the tree of the knowledge of good and evil, thou shalt not eat of it: for in the day that thou eatest thereof thou shalt surely die.

And the Lord God said, It is not good that the man should be alone: I will make him an help meet for him.

And out of the ground the Lord God formed every beast of the field, and every fowl of the air, and brought them unto Adam to see what he would call them; and whatsoever Adam called every living creature, that was the name thereof. And Adam gave names to all cattle, and to the fowl of the air, and to every beast of the field: but for Adam there was not found an help meet for him.

And the Lord God caused a deep sleep to fall upon Adam, and he slept; and he took one of his ribs, and closed up the flesh instead thereof: and the rib, which the Lord God had taken from man, made he a woman, and brought her unto the man.

And Adam said, This is now bone of my bones, and flesh of my flesh: she shall be called Woman, because she was taken out of man. Therefore shall a man leave his father and his mother, and shall cleave unto his wife: and they shall be one flesh. And they were both naked, the man and his wife, and were not ashamed.

The Fall of Man

Now the serpent was more subtile than any beast of the field which the Lord God had made: and he said unto the woman, Yea, hath God said, Ye shall not eat of every tree of the garden?

And the woman said unto the serpent, We may eat of the fruit of the trees of the garden: but of the fruit of the tree which is in the midst of the garden, God hath said, Ye shall not eat of it, neither shall ye touch it, lest ye die.

And the serpent said unto the woman, Ye shall not surely die: for God doth know, that in the day ye eat thereof, then your eyes shall be opened; and ye shall be as gods, knowing good and evil.

And when the woman saw that the tree was good for food, and that it was pleasant to the eyes, and a tree to be desired to make one wise; she took of the fruit thereof, and did eat; and gave also unto her husband with her, and he did eat. And the eyes of them both were opened, and they knew that they were naked: and they sewed fig-leaves together, and made themselves aprons.

And they heard the voice of the Lord God walking in the garden in the cool of the day: and Adam and his wife hid themselves from the presence of the Lord God amongst the trees of the garden.

And the Lord God called unto Adam, and said unto him, Where art thou?

And he said, I heard thy voice in the garden: and I was afraid, because I was naked; and I hid myself.

And he said, Who told thee that thou wast naked? Hast thou eaten of the tree whereof I commanded thee, that thou shouldest not eat?

And the man said, The woman whom thou gavest to be with me, she gave me of the tree, and I did eat.

And the Lord God said unto the woman, What is this that thou hast done? And the woman said, The serpent beguiled me, and I did eat.

And the Lord God said unto the serpent, Because thou hast done this, thou art cursed above all cattle, and above every beast of the field: upon thy belly shalt thou go, and dust shalt thou eat all the days of thy life: and I will put enmity between thee and the woman, and between thy seed and her seed: it shall bruise thy head, and thou shalt bruise his heel.

Unto the woman he said, I will greatly multiply thy sorrow and thy conception; in sorrow thou shalt bring forth children: and thy desire shall be to thy husband, and he shall rule over thee.

And unto Adam he said, Because thou hast hearkened unto the voice of thy wife, and hast eaten of the tree of which I commanded thee, saying, Thou shalt not eat of it: cursed is the ground for thy sake; in sorrow shalt thou eat of it all the days of thy life; thorns also and thistles shall it bring forth to thee; and thou shalt eat the herb of the field: in the sweat of thy face shalt thou eat bread, till thou return unto the ground; for out of it wast thou taken: for dust thou art, and unto dust shalt thou return.

And Adam called his wife's name Eve, because she was the mother of all living.

Unto Adam also and to his wife did the Lord God make coats of skins, and clothed them.

And the Lord God said, Behold, the man is become as one of us, to know good and evil: and now, lest he put forth his hand, and take also of the tree of life, and eat, and live for ever: therefore the Lord God sent him forth from the garden of Eden, to till the ground from whence he was taken.

So he drove out the man: and he placed at the east of the garden of Eden Cherubims, and a flaming sword which turned every way, to keep the way of the tree of life.

The Murder of Abel

And Adam knew Eve his wife; and she conceived, and bare Cain, and said, I have gotten a man from the Lord. And she again bare his brother Abel: and Abel was a keeper of sheep, but Cain was a tiller of the ground.

And in process of time it came to pass, that Cain brought of the fruit of the ground an offering unto the Lord. And Abel, he also brought of the firstlings of his flock, and of the fat thereof. And the Lord had respect unto Abel, and to his offering: but unto Cain, and to his offering, he had not respect: and Cain was very wroth, and his countenance fell.

And the Lord said unto Cain, Why art thou wroth? And why is thy countenance fallen? If thou doest well, shalt thou not be accepted? and if thou doest not well, sin lieth at the door: and unto thee shall be his desire, and thou shalt rule over him.

And Cain talked with Abel his brother: and it came to pass when they were in the field, that Cain rose up against Abel his brother, and slew him.

And the Lord said unto Cain, Where is Abel thy brother? And he said, I know not: Am I my brother's keeper?

And he said, What hast thou done? the voice of thy brother's blood crieth unto me from the ground. And now art thou cursed from the earth, which hath opened her mouth to receive thy brother's blood from thy hand. When thou tillest the ground, it shall not henceforth yield unto thee her strength: A fugitive and a vagabond shalt thou be in the earth.

And Cain said unto the Lord, My punishment is greater than I can bear. Behold, thou hast driven me out this day from the face of the earth; and from thy face shall I be hid; and I shall be a fugitive and a vagabond in the earth; and it shall come to pass, that every one that findeth me shall slay me.

And the Lord said unto him, Therefore, whosoever slayeth Cain, vengeance shall be taken on him seven-fold. And the Lord set a mark upon Cain, lest any finding him should kill him.

And Cain went out from the presence of the Lord, and dwelt in the land of Nod, on the east of Eden.

The Making of the Ark

And it came to pass, when men began to multiply on the face of the earth, and daughters were born unto them, that the sons of God saw the daughters of men that they were fair; and they took them wives of all which they chose.

And the Lord said, My Spirit shall not always strive with man, for that he also is flesh: yet his days shall be an hundred and twenty years.

There were giants in the earth in those days, and also after that, when the sons of God came in unto the daughters of men, and they bare children to them: the same became mighty men, which were of old, men of renown.

And God saw that the wickedness of man was great in the earth, and that every imagination of the thoughts of his heart was only evil continually. And it repented the Lord that he had made man on the earth, and it grieved him at his heart.

And the Lord said, I will destroy man whom I have created from the face of the earth; both man and beast, and the creeping thing, and the fowls of the air; for it repenteth me that I have made them.

But Noah found grace in the eyes of the Lord.

These are the generations of Noah: Noah was a just man, and perfect in his generations, and Noah walked with God. And Noah begat three sons, Shem, Ham, and Japheth.

And God said unto Noah, The end of all flesh is come before me; for the earth is filled with violence through them: and behold, I will destroy them with the earth. Make thee an ark of gopher-wood: rooms shalt thou make in the ark, and shalt pitch it within and without with pitch.

A window shalt thou make to the ark, and in a cubit shalt thou finish it above; and the door of the ark shalt thou set in the side thereof: with lower, second, and third stories shalt thou make it.

And behold, I, even I, do bring a flood of waters upon the earth, to destroy all flesh, wherein is the breath of life, from under heaven: and everything that is in the earth shall die.

But with thee will I establish my covenant: and thou shalt come into the ark, thou, and thy sons, and thy wife, and thy sons' wives with thee. And of every living thing of all flesh, two of every sort shalt thou bring into the ark, to keep them alive with thee: they shall be male and female. Of fowls after their kind, and of cattle after their kind, of every creeping thing of the earth after his kind; two of every sort shall come unto thee, to keep them alive.

And take thou unto thee of all food that is eaten, and thou shalt gather it to thee; and it shall be for food for thee, and for them.

Thus did Noah; according to all that God commanded him, so did he.

The Flood

And the Lord said unto Noah, Come thou and all thy house into the ark: for thee have I seen righteous before me in this generation.

And Noah did according unto all that the Lord commanded him. And Noah was six hundred years old when the flood of waters was upon the earth.

And Noah went in, and his sons, and his wife, and his sons' wives with him, into the ark, because of the waters of the flood. Of clean beasts, and of beasts that are not clean, and of fowls, and of everything that creepeth upon the earth, there went in two and two unto Noah into the ark, the male and the female, as God had commanded Noah.

And it came to pass, after seven days, that the waters of the flood were upon the earth. And the rain was upon the earth forty days and forty nights. And the waters prevailed, and were increased greatly upon the earth: and the ark went upon the face of the waters.

And the waters prevailed exceedingly upon the earth: and all the high hills that were under the whole heaven were covered. Fifteen cubits upward did the waters prevail: and the mountains were covered. And all flesh died that moved upon the earth, both of fowl, and of cattle, and of beast, and of every creeping thing that creepeth upon the earth, and every man: all in whose nostrils was the breath of life, of all that was in the dry land, died. Noah only remained alive, and they that were with him in the ark.

And the waters prevailed upon the earth an hundred and fifty days.

And God remembered Noah, and every living thing, and all the cattle that was with him in the ark: and God made a wind to pass over the earth, and the waters assuaged. The fountains also of the deep, and the windows of heaven were stopped, and the rain from heaven was restrained. And the waters returned from off the earth continually: and after the end of the hundred and fifty days the waters were abated.

And the ark rested in the seventh month, on the seventeenth day of the month, upon the mountains of Ararat. And the waters decreased continually, until the tenth month: in the tenth month, on the first day of the month, were the tops of the mountains seen.

And he (Noah) sent forth a raven, which went forth to and fro, until the waters were dried up from off the earth. Also he sent forth a dove from him, to see if the waters were abated from off the face of the ground. But the dove found no rest for the sole of her foot, and she returned unto him into the ark; for the waters were on the face of the whole earth. Then he put forth his hand, and took her, and pulled her in unto him into the ark.

And he stayed yet other seven days; and again he sent forth the dove out of the ark. And the dove came in to him in the evening, and lo, in her mouth was an olive-leaf pluckt off. So Noah knew that the waters were abated from off the earth.

And he stayed yet other seven days, and sent forth the dove; which returned not again unto him any more.

And it came to pass in the six hundredth and first year, in the first month, the first day of the month, the waters were dried up from off the earth: and Noah removed the covering of the ark, and looked, and behold, the face of the ground was dry. And in the second month, on the seven and twentieth day of the month, was the earth dried.

And God spake unto Noah, saying, Go forth of the ark, thou, and thy wife, and thy sons, and thy sons' wives with thee. Bring forth with thee every living thing that is with thee, of all flesh, both of fowl, and of cattle, and of every creeping thing that creepeth upon the earth; that they may breed abundantly in the earth, and be fruitful, and multiply upon the earth.

And Noah went forth, and his sons, and his wife, and his sons' wives with him: every beast, every creeping thing, and every fowl, and whatsoever creepeth upon the earth, after their kinds, went forth out of the ark.

And Noah builded an altar unto the Lord, and took of every clean beast, and of every clean fowl, and offered burnt-offerings on the altar.

And the Lord smelled a sweet savour; and the Lord said in his heart, I will not again curse the ground any more for man's sake; for the imagination of man's heart is evil from his youth: neither will I again smite any more every thing living, as I have done. While the earth remaineth, seed-time and harvest, and cold and heat, and summer and winter, and day and night, shall not cease.

God's Covenant with Noah

And God blessed Noah and his sons, and said unto them, Be fruitful, and multiply, and replenish the earth. And the fear of you, and the dread of you, shall be upon every beast of the earth, and upon every fowl of the air, upon all that moveth upon the earth, and upon all the fishes of the sea; into your hand are they delivered. Every moving thing that liveth shall be meat for you; even as the green herb have I given you all things. But flesh with the life thereof, which is the blood thereof, shall ye not eat.

And surely your blood of your lives will I require: at the hand of every beast will I require it, and at the hand of man; at the hand of every man's brother will I require the life of man. Whoso sheddeth man's blood, by man shall his blood be shed: for in the image of God made he man.

And God spake unto Noah, and to his sons with him, saying: And I, behold, I establish my covenant with you, and with your seed after you; and with every living creature that is with you, of the fowl, of the cattle, and of every beast of the earth with you, from all that go out of the ark, to every beast of the earth. And I will establish my covenant with you; neither shall all flesh be cut off any more by the waters of a flood; neither shall there any more be a flood to destroy the earth.

And God said: This is the token of the covenant which I make between me and you, and every living creature that is with you, for perpetual generations. I do set my bow in the cloud, and it shall be for a token of a covenant between me and the earth. And it shall come to pass, when I bring a cloud over the earth, that the bow shall be seen in the cloud: and I will remember my covenant, which is between me and you, and every living creature of all flesh; and the waters shall no more become a flood to destroy all flesh.

And the sons of Noah that went forth of the ark, were Shem, and Ham, and Japheth: and Ham is the father of Canaan. These are the three sons of Noah: and of them was the whole earth overspread.

And Noah began to be a husbandman, and he planted a vineyard.

And he drank of the wine, and was drunken; and he was uncovered within his tent. And Ham, the father of Canaan, saw the nakedness of his father, and told his two brethren without.

And Shem and Japheth took a garment, and laid it upon both their shoulders, and went backward, and covered the nakedness of their father: and their faces were backward, and they saw not their father's nakedness.

And Noah awoke from his wine, and knew what his younger son had done unto him. And he said, Cursed be Canaan: a servant of servants shall he be unto his brethren.

And he said, Blessed be the Lord God of Shem; and Canaan shall be his servant. God shall enlarge Japheth, and he shall dwell in the tents of Shem; and Canaan shall be his servant.

And Noah lived after the flood three hundred and fifty years. And all the days of Noah were nine hundred and fifty years: and he died.

The Tower of Babel

And the whole earth was of one language, and of one speech. And it came to pass, as they journeyed from the east, that they found a plain in the land of Shinar; and they dwelt there.

And they said one to another, Go to, let us make brick, and burn them thoroughly. And they had brick for stone, and slime had they for mortar.

And they said, Go to, let us build us a city, and a tower, whose top may reach unto heaven; and let us make us a name, lest we be scattered abroad upon the face of the whole earth.

And the Lord came down to see the city and the tower, which the children of men builded.

And the Lord said, Behold, the people is one, and they have all one language; and this they begin to do: and now nothing will be restrained from them, which they have imagined to do. Go to, let us go down, and there confound their language, that they may not understand one another's speech.

So the Lord scattered them abroad from thence upon the face of all the earth: and they left off to build the city. Therefore is the name of it called Babel, because the Lord did there confound the language of all the earth: and from thence did the Lord scatter them abroad upon the face of all the earth.

God's Promise to Abraham

Now the Lord had said unto Abram, Get thee out of thy country, and from thy kindred, and from thy father's house, unto a land that I will shew thee: and I will make of thee a great nation, and I will bless thee, and make thy name great; and thou shalt be a blessing: and I will bless them that bless thee, and curse him that curseth thee: and in thee shall all families of the earth be blessed.

So Abram departed, as the Lord had spoken unto him, and Lot went with him: and Abram was seventy and five years old when he departed out of Haran. And Abram took Sarai his wife, and Lot his brother's son, and all their substance that they had gathered, and the souls that they had gotten in Haran; and they went forth to go into the land of Canaan; and into the land of Canaan they came.

And Abram passed through the land unto the place of Sichem, unto the plain of Moreh. And the Canaanite was then in the land.

And the Lord appeared unto Abram, and said, Unto thy seed will I give this land: and there builded he an altar unto the Lord, who appeared unto him.

And he removed from thence unto a mountain on the east of Beth-el, and pitched his tent, having Beth-el on the west, and Hai on the east:

and there he builded an altar unto the Lord, and called upon the name of the Lord.

And Abram journeyed, going on still toward the south.

And there was a famine in the land: and Abram went down into Egypt to sojourn there; for the famine was grievous in the land.

Sarai and Hagar

Now Sarai, Abram's wife, bare him no children: and she had an handmaid, an Egyptian, whose name was Hagar.

And Sarai said unto Abram, Behold now, the Lord hath restrained me from bearing: I pray thee go in unto my maid; it may be that I may obtain children by her. And Abram hearkened to the voice of Sarai.

And Sarai, Abram's wife, took Hagar her maid the Egyptian, after Abram had dwelt ten years in the land of Canaan, and gave her to her husband Abram to be his wife.

And he went in unto Hagar, and she conceived: and when she saw that she had conceived, her mistress was despised in her eyes.

And Sarai said unto Abram, My wrong be upon thee: I have given my maid into thy bosom; and when she saw that she had conceived, I was despised in her eyes: the Lord judge between me and thee.

But Abram said unto Sarai, Behold, thy maid is in thy hand; do to her as it pleaseth thee. And when Sarai dealt hardly with her, she fled from her face.

And the Angel of the Lord found her by a fountain of water in the wilderness, by the fountain in the way to Shur. And he said, Hagar, Sarai's maid, whence camest thou? And whither wilt thou go? And she said, I flee from the face of my mistress Sarai.

And the angel of the Lord said unto her, Return to thy mistress, and submit thyself under her hands. I will multiply thy seed exceedingly, that it shall not be numbered for multitude. Behold, thou art with child, and shalt bear a son, and shalt call his name Ishmael; because the Lord hath heard thy affliction. And he will be a wild man; his hand will be against every man, and every man's hand against him; and he shall dwell in the presence of all his brethren.

And Hagar bare Abram a son; and Abram called his name Ishmael. And Abram was fourscore and six years old.

The Law of Circumcision

And when Abram was ninety years old and nine, the Lord appeared to Abram, and said unto him, I am the Almighty God; walk before me, and be thou perfect. And I will make my covenant between me and thee, and will multiply thee exceedingly.

And Abram fell on his face: and God talked with him, saying, As for me, behold, my covenant is with thee, and thou shalt be a father of many nations. Neither shall thy name any more be called Abram; but thy name shall be Abraham: for a father of many nations have I made thee. And I will make thee exceedingly fruitful, and I will make nations of thee; and kings shall come out of thee.

And I will establish my covenant between me and thee, and thy seed after thee, in their generations, for an everlasting covenant; to be a God unto thee, and to thy seed after thee. And I will give unto thee, and to thy seed after thee, the land wherein thou art a stranger, all the land of Canaan, for an everlasting possession; and I will be their God.

This is my covenant, which ye shall keep, between me and you, and thy seed after thee; Every man-child among you shall be circumcised. And ye shall circumcise the flesh of your foreskin; and it shall be a token of the covenant betwixt me and you. And he that is eight days old shall be circumcised among you, every man-child in your generations, he that is born in the house, or bought with money of any stranger, which is not of thy seed. He that is born in thy house, and he that is bought with thy money, must needs be circumcised: and my covenant shall be in your flesh for an everlasting covenant. And the uncircumcised man-child, whose flesh of his foreskin is not circumcised, that soul shall be cut off from his people; he hath broken my covenant.

And God said unto Abraham, As for Sarai thy wife, thou shalt not call her name Sarai, but Sarah shall her name be. And I will bless her, and give thee a son also of her: yea, I will bless her, and she shall be a mother of nations; kings of people shall be of her.

Then Abraham fell upon his face, and laughed, and said in his heart, Shall a child be born unto him that is an hundred years old? and shall Sarah, that is ninety years old, bear?

And Abraham said unto God, O that Ishmael might live before thee!

And God said, Sarah thy wife shall bear thee a son indeed; and thou shalt call his name Isaac: and I will establish my covenant with him for an everlasting covenant, and with his seed after him. And as for Ishmael, I have heard thee: Behold, I have blessed him, and will make him fruitful, and will multiply him exceedingly: twelve princes shall he beget, and I will make him a great nation.

But my covenant will I establish with Isaac, which Sarah shall bear unto thee at this set time in the next year. And he left off talking with him, and God went up from Abraham.

And Abraham took Ishmael his son, and all that were born in his house, and all that were bought with his money, every male among the men of Abraham's house; and circumcised the flesh of their foreskin, in the self-same day, as God had said unto him. And Abraham was ninety years old and nine, when he was circumcised in the flesh of his foreskin.

Abraham Entertains the Lord

And the Lord appeared unto him in the plains of Mamre: and he sat in the tent-door in the heat of the day; and he lifted up his eyes and looked, and lo, three men stood by him: and when he saw them, he ran to meet them from the tent door, and bowed himself toward the ground, and said, My Lord, if now I have found favour in thy sight, pass not away, I pray thee, from thy servant: let a little water, I pray you, be fetched, and wash your feet, and rest yourselves under the tree: and I will fetch a morsel of bread, and comfort ye your hearts; after that ye shall pass on: for therefore are ye come to your servant. And they said, So do, as thou hast said.

And Abraham hastened into the tent unto Sarah, and said, Make ready quickly three measures of fine meal, knead it, and make cakes upon the hearth. And Abraham ran unto the herd, and fetched a calf tender and good, and gave it unto a young man; and he hasted to dress it. And he took butter, and milk, and the calf which he had dressed, and set it before them; and he stood by them under the tree, and they did eat.

And they said unto him, Where is Sarah thy wife? And he said, Behold, in the tent.

And he said, I will certainly return unto thee according to the time of life; and lo, Sarah thy wife shall have a son. And Sarah heard it in the tent-door, which was behind him.

Now Abraham and Sarah were old and well stricken in age; and it ceased to be with Sarah after the manner of women. Therefore Sarah laughed within herself, saying, After I am waxed old shall I have pleasure, my lord being old also?

And the Lord said unto Abraham, Wherefore did Sarah laugh, saying, Shall I of a surety bear a child, which am old? Is anything too hard for the Lord? At the time appointed I will return unto thee, according to the time of life, and Sarah shall have a son.

Then Sarah denied, saying, I laughed not; for she was afraid. And he said, Nay; but thou didst laugh.

Abraham Intercedes for Sodom

And the Lord said, Because the cry of Sodom and Gomorrah is great, and because their sin is very grievous, I will go down now, and see whether they have done altogether according to the cry of it, which is come unto me; and if not, I will know.

And Abraham drew near, and said, Wilt thou also destroy the righteous with the wicked? Peradventure there be fifty righteous within the city: wilt thou also destroy and not spare the place for the fifty righteous that are therein? That be far from thee to do after this manner, to slay the righteous with the wicked; and that the righteous should be as the wicked, that be far from thee: Shall not the Judge of all the earth do right?

And the Lord said, If I find in Sodom fifty righteous within the city, then I will spare all the place for their sakes.

And Abraham answered and said, Behold now, I have taken upon me to speak unto the Lord, which am but dust and ashes: peradventure there shall lack five of the fifty righteous: wilt thou destroy all the city for lack of five?

And he said, If I find there forty and five, I will not destroy it.

And he spake unto him yet again, and said, Peradventure there shall be forty found there.

And he said, I will not do it for forty's sake.

And he said unto him, Oh, let not the Lord be angry, and I will speak: Peradventure there shall thirty be found there.

And he said, I will not do it if I find thirty there.

And he said, Behold now, I have taken upon me to speak unto the Lord: Peradventure there shall be twenty found there.

And he said, I will not destroy it for twenty's sake.

And he said, Oh, let not the Lord be angry, and I will speak yet but this once: Peradventure ten shall be found there.

And he said, I will not destroy it for ten's sake.

And the Lord went his way, as soon as he had left communing with Abraham: and Abraham returned unto his place.

The Destruction of Sodom and Gomorrah

And there came two angels to Sodom at even; and Lot sat in the gate of Sodom; and Lot, seeing them, rose up to meet them; and he bowed himself with his face toward the ground; and he said, Behold now, my lords, turn in, I pray you, into your servant's house, and tarry all night, and wash your feet, and ye shall rise up early, and go on your ways. And they said, Nay; but we will abide in the street all night.

And he pressed upon them greatly; and they turned in unto him, and entered into his house; and he made them a feast, and did bake unleavened bread, and they did eat.

But before they lay down, the men of the city, even the men of Sodom, compassed the house round, both old and young, all the people from every quarter: and they called unto Lot, and said unto him, Where are the men which came in to thee this night? bring them out unto us, that we may know them.

And Lot went out at the door unto them, and shut the door after him, and said, I pray you, brethren, do not so wickedly. Behold now, I have two daughters which have not known man; let me, I pray you, bring them out unto you, and do ye to them as is good in your eyes: only unto these men do nothing; for therefore came they under the shadow of my roof.

And they said, Stand back. And they said again, This one fellow came in to sojourn, and he will needs be a judge: now will we deal worse with thee than with them. And they pressed sore upon the man, even Lot, and came near to break the door.

But the men put forth their hand, and pulled Lot into the house to them, and shut to the door. And they smote the men that were at the door of the house with blindness, both small and great: so that they wearied themselves to find the door.

And the men said unto Lot, Hast thou here any besides? son-in-law, and thy sons, and thy daughters, and whatsoever thou hast in the city, bring them out of this place: for we will destroy this place, because the cry of them is waxen great before the face of the Lord; and the Lord hath sent us to destroy it.

And Lot went out, and spake unto his sons-in-law, which married his daughters, and said, Up, get you out of this place; for the Lord will destroy this city: but he seemed as one that mocked unto his sons-in-law.

And when the morning arose, then the angels hastened Lot, saying, Arise, take thy wife, and thy two daughters which are here, lest thou be consumed in the iniquity of the city. And while he lingered, the men laid hold upon his hand, and upon the hand of his wife, and upon the hand of his two daughters; the Lord being merciful unto him; and they brought him forth, and set him without the city.

And it came to pass, when they had brought them forth abroad, that he said, Escape for thy life; look not behind thee, neither stay thou in all the plain: escape to the mountain, lest thou be consumed.

And Lot said unto them, Oh, not so, my Lord! Behold now, thy servant hath found grace in thy sight, and thou hast magnified thy mercy, which thou hast showed unto me in saving my life: and I cannot escape to the mountain, lest some evil take me, and I die: Behold now, this city is near to flee unto, and it is a little one: Oh, let me escape thither! (is it not a little one?) and my soul shall live.

And he said unto him, See, I have accepted thee concerning this thing also, that I will not overthrow this city, for the which thou hast spoken. Haste thee, escape thither; for I cannot do anything till thou be come thither. Therefore the name of the city was called Zoar.

The sun was risen upon the earth when Lot entered into Zoar. Then the Lord rained upon Sodom and upon Gomorrah brimstone and fire from the Lord out of heaven; and he overthrew those cities, and all the plain, and all the inhabitants of the cities, and that which grew upon the ground.

But his wife looked back from behind him, and she became a pillar of salt.

And Lot went up out of Zoar, and dwelt in the mountain, and his two daughters with him; for he feared to dwell in Zoar: and he dwelt in a cave, he and his two daughters.

And the first-born said unto the younger, Our father is old, and there is not a man in the earth to come in unto us after the manner of all the earth: come, let us make our father drink wine, and we will lie with him, that we may preserve seed of our father.

And they made their father drink wine that night: and the first-born went in, and lay with her father; and he perceived not when she lay down, nor when she arose.

And it came to pass on the morrow, that the first-born said unto the younger, Behold, I lay yesternight with my father: let us make him drink wine this night also; and go thou in, and lie with him, that we may preserve seed of our father.

And they made their father drink wine that night also: and the younger arose, and lay with him; and he perceived not when she lay down, nor when she arose.

Thus were both the daughters of Lot with child by their father. And the first-born bare a son, and called his name Moab: the same is the father of the Moabites unto this day. And the younger, she also bare a son, and called his name Ben-ammi: the same is the father of the children of Ammon unto this day.

The Birth of Isaac

And Abraham journeyed from thence toward the south country, and dwelled between Kadesh and Shur, and sojourned in Gerar.

And the Lord visited Sarah as he had said, and the Lord did unto Sarah as he had spoken. For Sarah conceived, and bare Abraham a son in his old age, at the set time of which God had spoken to him. And Abraham called the name of his son that was born unto him, whom Sarah bare to him, Isaac. And Abraham circumcised his son Isaac, being eight days old, as God had commanded him. And Abraham was an hundred years old, when his son Isaac was born unto him.

And Sarah said, God hath made me to laugh, so that all that hear will laugh with me. Who would have said unto Abraham, that Sarah should have given children suck? for I have borne him a son in his old age.

And Sarah saw the son of Hagar the Egyptian, which she had borne unto Abraham, mocking. Wherefore she said unto Abraham, Cast out this bond-woman and her son: for the son of this bond-woman shall not be heir with my son, even with Isaac. And the thing was very grievous in Abraham's sight because of his son.

And God said unto Abraham, Let it not be grievous in thy sight, because of the lad, and because of thy bond-woman; in all that Sarah hath said unto thee, hearken unto her voice; for in Isaac shall thy seed be called. And also of the son of the bond-woman will I make a nation, because he is thy seed.

And Abraham rose up early in the morning, and took bread, and a bottle of water, and gave it unto Hagar, putting it on her shoulder, and the child, and sent her away: and she departed, and wandered in the wilderness of Beer-sheba.

And the water was spent in the bottle, and she cast the child under one of the shrubs, and sat her down over against him, a good way off, as it were a bow-shot: for she said, Let me not see the death of the child. And she sat over against him, and lifted up her voice, and wept.

And God heard the voice of the lad; and the angel of God called to Hagar out of heaven, and said unto her, What aileth thee, Hagar? Fear not; for God hath heard the voice of the lad where he is. Arise, lift up the lad, and hold him in thine hand; for I will make him a great nation.

And God opened her eyes, and she saw a well of water; and she went, and filled the bottle with water, and gave the lad drink. And God was with the lad; and he grew, and dwelt in the wilderness, and became an archer. And he dwelt in the wilderness of Paran: and his mother took him a wife out of the land of Egypt.

Abraham Offers Isaac

And it came to pass after these things, that God did tempt Abraham, and said unto him, Abraham: and he said, Behold, here I am.

And he said, Take now thy son, thine only son Isaac, whom thou lovest, and get thee into the land of Moriah; and offer him there for a burnt-offering upon one of the mountains which I will tell thee of.

And Abraham rose up early in the morning, and saddled his ass, and took two of his young men with him, and Isaac his son, and clave the wood for the burnt-offering, and rose up, and went unto the place of which God had told him. Then on the third day Abraham lifted up his eyes, and saw the place afar off.

And Abraham said unto his young men, Abide ye here with the ass; and I and the lad will go yonder and worship, and come again to you.

And Abraham took the wood of the burnt-offering, and laid it upon Isaac his son; and he took the fire in his hand, and a knife; and they went both of them together.

And Isaac spake unto Abraham his father, and said, My father: and he said, Here am I, my son. And he said, Behold the fire and the wood: but where is the lamb for a burnt-offering?

And Abraham said, My son, God will provide himself a lamb for a burnt-offering: so they went both of them together.

And they came to the place which God had told him of; and Abraham built an altar there, and laid the wood in order, and bound Isaac his son, and laid him on the altar upon the wood. And Abraham stretched forth his hand, and took the knife to slay his son.

And the angel of the Lord called unto him out of heaven, and said, Abraham, Abraham: and he said, Here am I.

And he said, Lay not thine hand upon the lad, neither do thou anything unto him: for now I know that thou fearest God, seeing thou hast not withheld thy son, thine only son from me.

And Abraham lifted up his eyes, and looked, and behold behind him a ram caught in a thicket by his horns: and Abraham went and took the ram, and offered him up for a burnt-offering in the stead of his son.

And Abraham called the name of that place Jehovah-jireh: as it is said to this day, In the mount of the Lord it shall be seen.

Rebekah at the Well

And Abraham was old, and well stricken in age: and the Lord had blessed Abraham in all things. And Abraham said unto his eldest servant of his house, that ruled over all that he had, Put, I pray thee, thy hand under my thigh: and I will make thee swear by the Lord, the God of heaven, and the God of the earth, that thou shalt not take a wife unto my son of the daughters of the Canaanites, among whom I dwell: but thou shalt go unto my country, and to my kindred, and take a wife unto my son Isaac.

And the servant put his hand under the thigh of Abraham his master, and sware to him concerning that matter.

And the servant took ten camels, of the camels of his master, and departed; for all the goods of his master were in his hand: and he arose, and went to Mesopotamia, unto the city of Nahor.

And he made his camels to kneel down without the city by a well of water at the time of the evening, even the time that women go out to draw water: and he said, O Lord God of my master Abraham, I pray thee, send me good speed this day, and shew kindness unto my master Abraham. Behold, I stand here by the well of water; and the daughters of the men of the city come out to draw water: and let it come to pass, that the damsel to whom I shall say, Let down thy pitcher, I pray thee, that I may drink; and she shall say, Drink, and I will give thy camels drink also: let the same be she that thou hast appointed for thy servant Isaac; and thereby shall I know that thou hast shewed kindness unto my master.

And it came to pass, before he had done speaking, that, behold, Rebekah came out, who was born to Bethuel, son of Milcah, the wife of Nahor, Abraham's brother, with her pitcher upon her shoulder. And the damsel was very fair to look upon, a virgin, neither had any man known her: and she went down to the well, and filled her pitcher, and came up.

And the servant ran to meet her, and said, Let me, I pray thee, drink a little water of thy pitcher.

And she said, Drink, my lord: and she hasted, and let down her pitcher upon her hand, and gave him drink.

And when she had done giving him drink, she said, I will draw water for thy camels also, until they have done drinking.

And she hasted, and emptied her pitcher into the trough, and ran again unto the well to draw water, and drew for all his camels. And the man wondering at her held his peace, to wit whether the Lord had made his journey prosperous or not.

And it came to pass, as the camels had done drinking, that the man took a golden ear-ring of half a shekel weight, and two bracelets for her hands of ten shekels weight of gold; and said, Whose daughter art thou? tell me, I pray thee: is there room in thy father's house for us to lodge in?

And she said unto him, I am the daughter of Bethuel the son of Milcah, which she bare unto Nahor. We have both straw and provender enough, and room to lodge in.

And the man bowed down his head, and worshipped the Lord. And the damsel ran, and told them of her mother's house these things.

And the man came into the house: and he ungirded his camels, and gave straw and provender for the camels, and water to wash his feet, and the men's feet that were with him. And there was set meat before him to eat: but he said, I will not eat, until I have told mine errand. And he said, Speak on.

And he said, I am Abraham's servant. The Lord hath blessed my master greatly; and he is become great: and he hath given him flocks, and herds, and silver, and gold, and men-servants, and maid-servants, and camels, and asses. And Sarah my master's wife bare a son to my master when she was old: and unto him hath he given all that he hath.

And my master made me swear, saying, Thou shalt not take a wife to my son of the daughters of the Canaanites, in whose land I dwell: but thou shalt go unto my father's house, and to my kindred, and take a wife unto my son.

And now if ye will deal kindly and truly with my master, tell me: and if not, tell me; that I may turn to the right hand, or to the left.

Then Laban and Bethuel answered and said, The thing proceedeth from the Lord: we cannot speak unto thee bad or good. Behold, Rebekah is before thee, take her, and go, and let her be thy master's son's wife, as the Lord hath spoken.

And it came to pass, that, when Abraham's servant heard their words, he worshipped the Lord, bowing himself to the earth.

And the servant brought forth jewels of silver, and jewels of gold, and raiment, and gave them to Rebekah: he gave also to her brother and to her mother precious things. And they did eat and drink, he and the men that were with him, and tarried all night; and they rose up in the morning, and he said, Send me away unto my master.

And her brother and her mother said, Let the damsel abide with us a few days, at the least ten; after that she shall go.

And he said unto them, Hinder me not, seeing the Lord hath prospered my way; send me away, that I may go to my master.

And they said, We will call the damsel, and inquire at her mouth. And they called Rebekah, and said unto her, Wilt thou go with this man? And she said, I will go.

And they blessed Rebekah, and said unto her, Thou art our sister, be thou the mother of thousands of millions, and let thy seed possess the gate of those which hate them.

And Rebekah arose, and her damsels, and they rode upon the camels, and followed the man: and the servant took Rebekah, and went his way.

And Isaac came from the way of the well Lahai-roi; for he dwelt in the south country, and went out to meditate in the field at the eventide: and he lifted up his eyes, and saw, and, behold, the camels were coming.

And Rebekah lifted up her eyes, and when she saw Isaac, she lighted off the camel.

For she had said unto the servant, What man is this that walketh in the field to meet us? And the servant had said, It is my master: therefore she took a vail and covered herself.

And Isaac brought her into his mother Sarah's tent, and took Rebekah, and she became his wife; and he loved her: and Isaac was comforted after his mother's death.

Esau Sells His Birthright

Then again Abraham took a wife, and her name was Keturah. And she bare him Zimran, and Jokshan, and Medan, and Midian, and Ishbak, and Shuah.

And Abraham gave all that he had unto Isaac.

And these are the days of the years of Abraham's life which he lived, an hundred threescore and fifteen years.

Then Abraham gave up the ghost, and died in a good old age, an old man, and full of years; and was gathered to his people. And his sons Isaac and Ishmael buried him in the cave of Machpelah, in the field of Ephron the son of Zohar the Hittite, which is before Mamre; the field which Abraham purchased of the sons of Heth: there was Abraham buried, and Sarah his wife.

And it came to pass after the death of Abraham, that God blessed his son Isaac; and Isaac dwelt by the well Lahai-roi.

And these are the generations of Isaac, Abraham's son: Abraham begat Isaac: and Isaac was forty years old when he took Rebekah to wife, the daughter of Bethuel the Syrian of Padan-aram, the sister to Laban the Syrian.

And Isaac entreated the Lord for his wife, because she was barren: and the Lord was entreated of him, and Rebekah his wife conceived. And the children struggled together within her; and she said, If it be so, why am I thus? And she went to inquire of the Lord.

And the Lord said unto her, Two nations are in thy womb, and two manner of people shall be separated from thy bowels: and the one people shall be stronger than the other people; and the elder shall serve the younger.

And when her days to be delivered were fulfilled, behold, there were twins in her womb. And the first came out red, all over like an hairy garment: and they called his name Esau. And after that came his brother out, and his hand took hold on Esau's heel; and his name was called Jacob: and Isaac was three-score years old when she bare them.

And the boys grew: and Esau was a cunning hunter, a man of the field; and Jacob was a plain man, dwelling in tents. And Isaac loved Esau, because he did eat of his venison: but Rebekah loved Jacob.

And Jacob sod pottage: and Esau came from the field, and he was faint: and Esau said to Jacob, Feed me, I pray thee, with that same red pottage; for I am faint: therefore was his name called Edom.

And Jacob said, Sell me this day thy birthright.

And Esau said, Behold, I am at the point to die: and what profit shall this birthright do to me?

And Jacob said, Swear to me this day; and he sware unto him: and he sold his birthright unto Jacob. Then Jacob gave Esau bread and pottage of lentiles; and he did eat and drink, and rose up, and went his way: thus Esau despised his birthright.

Isaac Blesses Jacob

And it came to pass, that when Isaac was old, and his eyes were dim, so that he could not see, he called Esau his eldest son, and said unto him, My son: and he said unto him, Behold, here am I.

And he said, Behold now, I am old, I know not the day of my death: now therefore take, I pray thee, thy weapons, thy quiver and thy bow, and go out to the field, and take me some venison; and make me savoury meat, such as I love, and bring it to me, that I may eat; that my soul may bless thee before I die.

And Rebekah heard when Isaac spake to Esau his son. And Esau went to the field to hunt for venison, and to bring it.

And Rebekah spake unto Jacob her son, saying, Behold, I heard thy father speak unto Esau thy brother, saying, Bring me venison, and make me savoury meat, that I may eat, and bless thee before the Lord before my death. Now therefore, my son, obey my voice according to that which I command thee. Go now to the flock, and fetch me from thence two good kids of the goats; and I will make them savoury meat for thy father, such as he loveth: and thou shalt bring it to thy father, that he may eat, and that he may bless thee before his death.

And Jacob said to Rebekah his mother, Behold, Esau my brother is a hairy man, and I am a smooth man: my father peradventure will feel me, and I shall seem to him as a deceiver; and I shall bring a curse upon me, and not a blessing.

And his mother said unto him, Upon me be thy curse, my son: only obey my voice, and go fetch me them.

And he went, and fetched, and brought them to his mother: and his mother made savoury meat, such as his father loved. And Rebekah took goodly raiment of her eldest son Esau, which were with her in the house, and put them upon Jacob her younger son. And she put the skins of the kids of the goats upon his hands, and upon the smooth of his neck: and she gave the savoury meat and the bread, which she had prepared, into the hand of her son Jacob.

And he came unto his father, and said, My father: and he said, Here am I; who art thou, my son?

And Jacob said unto his father, I am Esau thy first-born; I have done according as thou badest me: arise, I pray thee, sit and eat of my venison, that thy soul may bless me.

And Isaac said unto his son, How is it that thou hast found it so quickly, my son?

And he said, Because the Lord thy God brought it to me.

And Isaac said unto Jacob, Come near, I pray thee, that I may feel thee, my son, whether thou be my very son Esau or not.

And Jacob went near unto Isaac his father; and he felt him, and said, The voice is Jacob's voice, but the hands are the hands of Esau. And he discerned him not, because his hands were hairy, as his brother Esau's hands: so he blessed him.

And he said, Art thou my very son Esau?

And he said, I am.

And he said, Bring it near to me, and I will eat of my son's venison, that my soul may bless thee. And he brought it near to him, and he did eat: and he brought him wine, and he drank.

And his father Isaac said unto him, Come near now, and kiss me, my son.

And he came near, and kissed him: and he smelled the smell of his raiment, and blessed him, and said, See, the smell of my son is as the smell of a field which the Lord hath blessed: therefore God give thee of the dew of heaven, and the fatness of the earth, and plenty of corn and wine: let people serve thee, and nations bow down to thee: be lord over thy brethren, and let thy mother's sons bow down to thee: cursed be every one that curseth thee, and blessed be he that blesseth thee.

And it came to pass, as soon as Isaac had made an end of blessing Jacob, and Jacob was yet scarce gone out from the presence of Isaac his father, that Esau his brother came in from his hunting. And he also had made savoury meat, and brought it unto his father, and said unto his father, Let my father arise, and eat of his son's venison, that thy soul may bless me.

And Isaac his father said unto him, Who art thou? And he said, I am thy son, thy first-born Esau.

And Isaac trembled very exceedingly, and said, Who? Where is he that hath taken venison, and brought it me, and I have eaten of all before thou camest, and have blessed him? Yea, and he shall be blessed.

And when Esau heard the words of his father, he cried with a great and exceeding bitter cry, and said unto his father, Bless me, even me also, O my father!

And he said, Thy brother came with subtilty, and hath taken away thy blessing.

And he said, Is not he rightly named Jacob? for he hath supplanted me these two times: he took away my birthright; and, behold, now he hath taken away my blessing. And he said, Hast thou not reserved a blessing for me?

And Isaac answered and said unto Esau, Behold, I have made him thy lord, and all his brethren have I given to him for servants; and with corn and wine have I sustained him: and what shall I do now unto thee, my son?

And Esau said unto his father, Hast thou but one blessing, my father? bless me, even me also, O my father! And Esau lifted up his voice, and wept.

And Isaac his father answered, and said unto him, Behold, thy dwelling shall be the fatness of the earth, and of the dew of heaven from above; and by thy sword shalt thou live, and shalt serve thy brother; and it shall come to pass when thou shalt have the dominion, that thou shalt break his yoke from off thy neck.

And Esau hated Jacob because of the blessing wherewith his father blessed him: and Esau said in his heart, The days of mourning for my father are at hand; then will I slay my brother Jacob.

And these words of Esau her elder son were told to Rebekah: and she sent and called Jacob her younger son, and said unto him, Behold, thy brother Esau, as touching thee, doth comfort himself, purposing to kill thee. Now therefore, my son, obey my voice; and arise, flee thou to Laban my brother to Haran; and tarry with him a few days, until thy brother's fury turn away; until thy brother's anger turn away from thee, and he forget that which thou hast done to him: then I will send, and fetch thee from thence: why should I be deprived also of you both in one day?

The Vision of Jacob's Ladder

And Jacob went out from Beer-sheba, and went toward Haran. And he lighted upon a certain place, and tarried there all night, because the sun was set; and he took of the stones of that place, and put them for his pillows, and lay down in that place to sleep.

And he dreamed, and behold a ladder set up on the earth, and the top of it reached to heaven: and behold the angels of God ascending and descending on it.

And, behold, the Lord stood above it, and said, I am the Lord God of Abraham thy father, and the God of Isaac: the land whereon thou liest, to thee will I give it, and to thy seed; and thy seed shall be as the dust of the earth, and thou shalt spread abroad to the west, and to the east, and to the north, and to the south: and in thee and in thy seed shall all the families of the earth be blessed. And, behold, I am with thee, and will keep thee in all places whither thou goest, and will bring thee again into this land; for I will not leave thee, until I have done that which I have spoken to thee of.

And Jacob awaked out of his sleep, and he said, Surely the Lord is in this place; and I knew it not. And he was afraid, and said, How dreadful is this place! this is none other but the house of God, and this is the gate of heaven.

And Jacob rose up early in the morning, and took the stone that he had put for his pillows, and set it up for a pillar, and poured oil upon the top of it. And he called the name of that place Beth-el: but the name of that city was called Luz at the first.

Jacob Earns Two Wives

Then Jacob went on his journey, and came into the land of the people of the east. And he looked, and behold a well in the field, and, lo, there were three flocks of sheep lying by it; for out of that well they watered the flocks: and a great stone was upon the well's mouth. And thither were all the flocks gathered: and they rolled the stone from the well's mouth, and watered the sheep, and put the stone again upon the well's mouth in his place.

And Jacob said unto them, My brethren, whence be ye? And they said, Of Haran are we.

And he said unto them, Know ye Laban the son of Nahor? And they said, We know him.

And he said unto them, Is he well? And they said, He is well: and, behold, Rachel his daughter cometh with the sheep.

And while he yet spake with them, Rachel came with her father's sheep: for she kept them. And it came to pass, when Jacob saw Rachel the daughter of Laban his mother's brother, and the sheep of Laban his mother's brother, that Jacob went near, and rolled the stone from the well's mouth, and watered the flock of Laban his mother's brother. And Jacob kissed Rachel, and lifted up his voice, and wept.

And Jacob told Rachel that he was her father's brother, and that he was Rebekah's son; and she ran and told her father. And it came to pass, when Laban heard the tidings of Jacob his sister's son, that he ran to meet him, and embraced him, and kissed him, and brought him to his house. And he told Laban all these things.

And Laban said to him, Surely thou art my bone and my flesh. And he abode with him the space of a month.

And Laban said unto Jacob, Because thou art my brother, shouldest thou therefore serve me for nought? tell me, what shall thy wages be?

And Laban had two daughters: the name of the elder was Leah, and the name of the younger was Rachel. Leah was tender-eyed; but Rachel was beautiful and well-favoured.

And Jacob loved Rachel; and said, I will serve thee seven years for Rachel thy younger daughter.

And Laban said, It is better that I give her to thee, than that I should give her to another man: abide with me.

And Jacob served seven years for Rachel; and they seemed unto him but a few days, for the love he had to her.

And Jacob said unto Laban, Give me my wife, for my days are fulfilled, that I may go in unto her.

And Laban gathered together all the men of the place, and made a feast. And it came to pass in the evening, that he took Leah his daughter, and brought her to him; and he went in unto her.

And it came to pass, that in the morning, behold, it was Leah: and he said to Laban, What is this thou hast done unto me? did not I serve with thee for Rachel? wherefore then hast thou beguiled me?

And Laban said, It must not be so done in our country, to give the younger before the first-born. Fulfil her week, and we will give thee this also for the service which thou shalt serve with me yet seven other years.

And Jacob did so, and fulfilled her week: and he gave him Rachel his daughter to wife also.

And he went in also unto Rachel, and he loved also Rachel more than Leah, and served with him yet seven other years.

And when the Lord saw that Leah was hated, he opened her womb: but Rachel was barren.

The Birth of Joseph

And when Rachel saw that she bare Jacob no children, Rachel envied her sister; and said unto Jacob, Give me children, or else I die.

And Jacob's anger was kindled against Rachel: and he said, Am I in God's stead, who hath withheld from thee the fruit of the womb?

And she said, Behold my maid Bilhah, go in unto her; and she shall bear upon my knees, that I may also have children by her. And she gave him Bilhah her handmaid to wife: and Jacob went in unto her. And Bilhah conceived, and bare Jacob a son.

And Rachel said, God hath judged me, and hath also heard my voice, and hath given me a son: therefore called she his name Dan.

And Bilhah, Rachel's maid, conceived again, and bare Jacob a second son.

And Rachel said, With great wrestlings have I wrestled with my sister, and I have prevailed: and she called his name Naphtali.

When Leah saw that she had left bearing, she took Zilpah, her maid, and gave her Jacob to wife. And Zilpah, Leah's maid, bare Jacob a son.

And Leah said, A troop cometh: and she called his name Gad.

And God remembered Rachel, and God hearkened to her, and opened her womb. And she conceived, and bare a son; and said, God hath taken away my reproach: and she called his name Joseph; and said, The Lord shall add to me another son.

And it came to pass, when Rachel had borne Joseph, that Jacob said unto Laban, Send me away, that I may go unto mine own place, and to my country. Give me my wives and my children, for whom I have served thee, and let me go: for thou knowest my service which I have done thee.

And Laban said unto him, I pray thee, if I have found favour in thine eyes, tarry: for I have learned by experience that the Lord hath blessed me for thy sake.

And he said, Appoint me thy wages, and I will give it.

And he said unto him, Thou knowest how I have served thee, and how thy cattle was with me. For it was little which thou hadst before I came, and it is now increased unto a multitude; and the Lord hath blessed thee since my coming: and now, when shall I provide for mine own house also?

And he said, What shall I give thee? And Jacob said, Thou shalt not give me any thing: if thou wilt do this thing for me, I will again feed and keep thy flock. I will pass through all thy flock to-day, removing from thence all the speckled and spotted cattle, and all the brown cattle among the sheep, and the spotted and speckled among the goats: and of such shall be my hire. So shall my righteousness answer for me in time to come, when it shall come for my hire before thy face: every one that is not speckled and spotted among the goats, and brown among the sheep, that shall be counted stolen with me.

And Laban said, Behold, I would it might be according to thy word. And he removed that day the he-goats that were ring-streaked and spotted, and all the she-goats that were speckled and spotted, and every one that had some white in it, and all the brown among the sheep, and gave them into the hand of his sons. And he set three days' journey betwixt himself and Jacob: and Jacob fed the rest of Laban's flocks.

And Jacob took him rods of green poplar, and of the hazel and chestnut-tree; and pilled white streaks in them, and made the white appear which was in the rods. And he set the rods which he had pilled before the flocks in the gutters in the watering-troughs when the flocks came to drink, that they should conceive when they came to drink. And the flocks conceived before the rods, and brought forth cattle ring-streaked, speckled, and spotted.

And Jacob did separate the lambs, and set the faces of the flocks toward the ring-streaked, and all the brown in the flock of Laban; and he put his own flocks by themselves, and put them not unto Laban's cattle.

And it came to pass, whensoever the stronger cattle did conceive, that Jacob laid the rods before the eyes of the cattle in the gutters, that they might conceive among the rods. But when the cattle were feeble, he put them not in: so the feebler were Laban's, and the stronger Jacob's.

And the man increased exceedingly, and had much cattle, and maid-servants, and men-servants, and camels, and asses.

Jacob and Laban Are Estranged

And he heard the words of Laban's sons, saying, Jacob hath taken away all that was our father's; and of that which was our father's hath he gotten all this glory. And Jacob beheld the countenance of Laban, and, behold, it was not toward him as before.

And the Lord said unto Jacob, Return unto the land of thy fathers, and to thy kindred; and I will be with thee.

And Jacob sent and called Rachel and Leah to the field unto his flock, and said unto them, I see your father's countenance, that it is not toward me as before; but the God of my father hath been with me. And ye know that with all my power I have served your father. And your father hath deceived me, and changed my wages ten times; but God suffered him not to hurt me. If he said thus, The speckled shall be thy wages; then all the cattle bare speckled: and if he said thus, The ring-streaked shall be thy hire; then bare all the cattle ring-streaked. Thus God hath taken away the cattle of your father, and given them to me.

And it came to pass at the time that the cattle conceived, that I lifted up mine eyes, and saw in a dream, and, behold, the rams which leaped upon the cattle were ring-streaked, speckled, and grizzled. And the angel of God spake unto me in a dream, saying, Jacob: and I said, Here am I. And he said, Lift up now thine eyes, and see, all the rams which leap upon the cattle are ring-streaked, speckled, and grizzled: for I have seen all that Laban doeth unto thee. I am the God of Beth-el, where thou anointedst the pillar, and where thou vowedst a vow unto me: now arise, get thee out from this land, and return unto the land of thy kindred.

And Rachel and Leah answered, and said unto him, Is there yet any portion or inheritance for us in our father's house? Are we not counted of him strangers? for he hath sold us, and hath quite devoured also our money. For all the riches which God hath taken from our father, that is ours, and our children's: now then, whatsoever God hath said unto thee, do.

Jacob and Esau Make Peace

Then Jacob rose up, and set his sons and his wives upon camels; and he carried away all his cattle, and all his goods which he had gotten, the cattle of his getting, which he had gotten in Padan-aram: for to go to Isaac his father in the land of Canaan.

And Jacob sent messengers before him to Esau his brother unto the land of Seir, the country of Edom. And he commanded them, saying, Thus shall ye speak unto my lord Esau; thy servant Jacob saith thus, I have sojourned with Laban, and stayed there until now: and I have oxen, and asses, flocks, and men-servants, and women-servants: and I have sent to tell my lord, that I may find grace in thy sight.

And the messengers returned to Jacob, saying, We came to thy brother Esau, and also he cometh to meet thee, and four hundred men with him.

Then Jacob was greatly afraid, and distressed: and he divided the people that was with him, and the flocks, and herds, and the camels, into two bands; and said, If Esau come to the one company, and smite it, then the other company which is left shall escape.

And he lodged there that same night; and took of that which came to his hand a present for Esau his brother; two hundred she-goats and twenty he-goats, two hundred ewes and twenty rams, thirty milch camels with their colts, forty kine and ten bulls, twenty she-asses and ten foals.

And he commanded the foremost (servant), saying, When Esau my brother meeteth thee, and asketh thee, saying, Whose art thou? and whither goest thou? and whose are these before thee? Then thou shalt say, They be thy servant Jacob's; it is a present sent unto my lord Esau: and, behold, also he is behind us.

So went the present over before him; and himself lodged that night in the company. And he rose up that night, and took his two wives, and his two women-servants, and his eleven sons, and passed over the ford Jabbok. And he took them, and sent them over the brook, and sent over that he had.

And Jacob was left alone; and there wrestled a man with him, until the breaking of the day. And when he saw that he prevailed not against him, he touched the hollow of his thigh: and the hollow of Jacob's thigh was out of joint, as he wrestled with him.

And he said, Let me go, for the day breaketh: and he said, I will not let thee go, except thou bless me.

And he said unto him, What is thy name? And he said, Jacob.

And he said, Thy name shall be called no more Jacob, but Israel: for as a prince hast thou power with God, and with men, and hast prevailed.

And Jacob asked him, and said, Tell me, I pray thee, thy name: and he said, Wherefore is it that thou dost ask after my name? And he blessed him there.

And Jacob called the name of the place Peniel: for I have seen God face to face, and my life is preserved. And as he passed over Penuel, the sun rose upon him, and he halted upon his thigh. Therefore the children of Israel eat not of the sinew which shrank, which is upon the hollow of the thigh, unto this day; because he touched the hollow of Jacob's thigh in the sinew that shrank.

And Jacob lifted up his eyes, and looked, and, behold, Esau came, and with him four hundred men. And he divided the children unto Leah, and unto Rachel, and unto the two handmaids. And he put the handmaids and their children foremost, and Leah and her children after, and Rachel and Joseph hindermost. And he passed over before them, and bowed himself to the ground seven times, until he came near to his brother.

And Esau ran to meet him, and embraced him, and fell on his neck, and kissed him: and they wept.

And he lifted up his eyes, and saw the women and the children; and said, Who are those with thee? And he said, The children which God hath graciously given thy servant.

Then the handmaidens came near, they and their children, and they bowed themselves. And Leah also with her children came near, and bowed themselves; and after came Joseph near and Rachel, and they bowed themselves.

And he said, What meanest thou by all this drove which I met? And he said, These are to find grace in the sight of my lord.

And Esau said, I have enough, my brother; keep that thou hast unto thyself.

And Jacob said, Nay, I pray thee, if now I have found grace in thy sight, then receive my present at my hand: for therefore I have seen thy face, as though I had seen the face of God, and thou wast pleased with me. Take, I pray thee, my blessing that is brought to thee; because God hath dealt graciously with me, and because I have enough: and he urged him, and he took it.

The Family of Jacob

And God said unto Jacob, Arise, go up to Beth-el, and dwell there: and make there an altar unto God, that appeared unto thee when thou fleddest from the face of Esau thy brother.

Then Jacob said unto his household, and to all that were with him, Put away the strange gods that are among you, and be clean and change your garments: and let us arise, and go up to Beth-el; and I will make there an altar unto God, who answered me in the day of my distress, and was with me in the way which I went.

And they gave unto Jacob all the strange gods which were in their hand, and all their ear-rings which were in their ears; and Jacob hid them under the oak which was by Shechem.

And they journeyed: and the terror of God was upon the cities that were round about them, and they did not pursue after the sons of Jacob. So Jacob came to Luz, which is in the land of Canaan, that is Beth-el, he and all the people that were with him.

And God appeared unto Jacob again when he came out of Padan-aram; and blessed him. And God said unto him, Thy name is Jacob: thy name shall not be called any more Jacob, but Israel shall be thy name; and he called his name Israel. And God said unto him, I am God Almighty: be fruitful and multiply; a nation and a company of nations shall be of thee, and kings shall come out of thy loins.

And they journeyed from Beth-el; and there was but a little way to come to Ephrath; and Rachel travailed, and she had hard labour. And it came to pass, when she was in hard labour, that the midwife said unto her, Fear not; thou shalt have this son also. And it came to pass, as her soul was in departing (for she died), that she called his name Benoni: but his father called him Benjamin.

And Rachel died, and was buried in the way to Ephrath, which is

Beth-lehem. And Jacob set a pillar upon her grave: that is the pillar of Rachel's grave unto this day.

And Israel journeyed, and spread his tent beyond the tower of Edar.

And it came to pass, when Israel dwelt in that land, that Reuben went and lay with Bilhah his father's concubine: and Israel heard it.

Now the sons of Jacob were twelve: the sons of Leah: Reuben, Jacob's first-born, and Simeon, and Levi, and Judah, and Issachar, and Zebulun; the sons of Rachel: Joseph, and Benjamin; and the sons of Bilhah, Rachel's handmaid: Dan, and Naphtali; and the sons of Zilpah, Leah's handmaid: Gad, and Asher. These are the sons of Jacob, which were born to him in Padan-aram.

Joseph Is Sold by His Brothers

And Jacob dwelt in the land wherein his father was a stranger, in the land of Canaan. Joseph being seventeen years old, was feeding the flock with his brethren; and the lad was with the sons of Bilhah, and with the sons of Zilpah, his father's wives: and Joseph brought unto his father their evil report.

Now Israel loved Joseph more than all his children, because he was the son of his old age: and he made him a coat of many colours. And when his brethren saw that their father loved him more than all his brethren, they hated him, and could not speak peaceably unto him.

And Joseph dreamed a dream. And he said unto them, Hear, I pray you, this dream which I have dreamed: for, behold, we were binding sheaves in the field, and, lo, my sheaf arose, and also stood upright; and, behold, your sheaves stood round about, and made obeisance to my sheaf.

And his brethren said to him, Shalt thou indeed reign over us? Or shalt thou indeed have dominion over us? And they hated him yet the more for his dreams, and for his words.

And he dreamed yet another dream, and told it his brethren, and said, Behold, I have dreamed a dream more: and, behold, the sun and the moon and the eleven stars made obeisance to me. And he told it to his father, and to his brethren: and his father rebuked him, and said unto him, What is this dream that thou hast dreamed? Shall I and thy mother and thy brethren indeed come to bow down ourselves to thee to the earth? And his brethren envied him; but his father observed the saying.

And his brethren went to feed their father's flock in Shechem.

And Israel said unto Joseph, Do not thy brethren feed the flock in Shechem? Come, and I will send thee unto them. And he said to him, Here am I.

And he said to him, Go, I pray thee, see whether it be well with thy brethren, and well with the flocks; and bring me word again. So he sent him out of the vale of Hebron, and he came to Shechem.

And a certain man found him, and, behold, he was wandering in the field: and the man asked him, saying, What seekest thou?

And he said, I seek my brethren: tell me, I pray thee, where they feed their flocks.

And the man said, They are departed hence: for I heard them say, Let us go to Dothan. And Joseph went after his brethren, and found them in Dothan. And when they saw him afar off, even before he came near unto them, they conspired against him to slay him.

And they said one to another, Behold, this dreamer cometh. Come now therefore, and let us slay him, and cast him into some pit; and we will say, Some evil beast hath devoured him: and we shall see what will become of his dreams.

And Reuben heard it, and he delivered him out of their hands; and said, Let us not kill him. Shed no blood, but cast him into this pit that is in the wilderness, and lay no hand upon him; that he might rid him out of their hands, to deliver him to his father again.

And it came to pass, when Joseph was come unto his brethren, that they stript Joseph out of his coat, his coat of many colours that was on him. And they took him, and cast him into a pit: and the pit was empty, there was no water in it. And they sat down to eat bread: and they lifted up their eyes and looked, and, behold, a company of Ishmaelites came from Gilead, with their camels bearing spicery, and balm, and myrrh, going to carry it down to Egypt.

And Judah said unto his brethren, What profit is it if we slay our brother, and conceal his blood? Come, and let us sell him to the Ishmaelites, and let not our hand be upon him; for he is our brother, and our flesh: and his brethren were content.

Then there passed by Midianites, merchant-men; and they drew and lifted up Joseph out of the pit, and sold Joseph to the Ishmaelites for twenty pieces of silver: and they brought Joseph into Egypt.

And Reuben returned unto the pit; and, behold, Joseph was not in the pit; and he rent his clothes. And he returned unto his brethren, and said, The child is not: and I, whither shall I go?

And they took Joseph's coat, and killed a kid of the goats, and dipped the coat in the blood: and they sent the coat of many colours, and they brought it to their father; and said, This have we found: know now whether it be thy son's coat or no.

And he knew it, and said, It is my son's coat; an evil beast hath devoured him: Joseph is without doubt rent in pieces.

And Jacob rent his clothes, and put sackcloth upon his loins, and mourned for his son many days. And all his sons and all his daughters rose up to comfort him; but he refused to be comforted; and he said, For I will go down into the grave unto my son mourning. Thus his father wept for him.

And the Midianites sold him into Egypt unto Potiphar, an officer of Pharaoh's, and captain of the guard.

Joseph and Potiphar's Wife

And Joseph was brought down to Egypt: and Potiphar, an officer of Pharaoh, captain of the guard, an Egyptian, bought him of the hands of the Ishmaelites, which had brought him down thither.

And Joseph found grace in his sight, and he served him: and he made him overseer over his house, and all that he had he put into his hand. And it came to pass from the time that he had made him overseer in his house, and over all that he had, that the Lord blessed the Egyptian's house for Joseph's sake; and the blessing of the Lord was upon all that he had in the house, and in the field. And he left all that he had in Joseph's hand; and he knew not aught he had, save the bread which he did eat. And Joseph was a goodly person, and well-favoured.

And it came to pass after these things, that his master's wife cast her eyes upon Joseph: and she said, Lie with me.

But he refused, and said unto his master's wife, Behold, my master wotteth not what is with me in the house, and he hath committed all that he hath to my hand; there is none greater in this house than I; neither hath he kept back any thing from me, but thee, because thou art his wife: how then can I do this great wickedness, and sin against God?

And it came to pass, as she spake to Joseph day by day, that he hearkened not unto her, to lie by her, or to be with her.

And it came to pass about this time, that Joseph went into the house to do his business; and there was none of the men of the house there within. And she caught him by his garment, saying, Lie with me: and he left his garment in her hand, and fled, and got him out.

And she laid up his garment by her, until his lord came home. And she spake unto him according to these words, saying, The Hebrew servant, which thou hast brought unto us, came in unto me to mock me: and as I lifted up my voice and cried, he left his garment with me, and fled out.

And it came to pass, when his master heard the words of his wife, which she spake unto him, saying, After this manner did thy servant to me; that his wrath was kindled. And Joseph's master took him, and put him into the prison, a place where the king's prisoners were bound: and he was there in the prison.

But the Lord was with Joseph, and shewed him mercy, and gave him favour in the sight of the keeper of the prison. And the keeper of the prison committed to Joseph's hand all the prisoners that were in the prison; and whatsoever they did there, he was the doer of it.

The keeper of the prison looked not to any thing that was under his hand; because the Lord was with him: and that which he did, the Lord made it to prosper.

The Dreams of the Butler and the Baker

And it came to pass after these things, that the butler of the king of Egypt and his baker had offended their lord the king of Egypt. And Pharaoh was wroth against two of his officers, against the chief of the butlers, and against the chief of the bakers. And he put them in ward in the house of the captain of the guard, into the prison, the place where Joseph was bound. And the captain of the guard charged Joseph with them, and he served them; and they continued a season in ward.

And they dreamed a dream both of them, each man his dream in one night, each man according to the interpretation of his dream; the butler and the baker of the king of Egypt, which were bound in the prison.

And Joseph came in unto them in the morning, and looked upon them, and, behold, they were sad. And he asked Pharaoh's officers that were with him in the ward of his lord's house, saying, Wherefore look ye so sadly to-day? And they said unto him, We have dreamed a dream, and there is no interpreter of it. And Joseph said unto them, Do not interpretations belong to God? tell me them, I pray you.

And the chief butler told his dream to Joseph, and said to him, In my dream, behold, a vine was before me; and in the vine were three branches: and it was as though it budded, and her blossoms shot forth; and the clusters thereof brought forth ripe grapes: and Pharaoh's cup was in my hand: and I took the grapes, and pressed them into Pharaoh's cup, and I gave the cup into Pharaoh's hand.

And Joseph said unto him, This is the interpretation of it: the three branches are three days: yet within three days shall Pharaoh lift up thy head, and restore thee unto thy place: and thou shalt deliver Pharaoh's cup into his hand, after the former manner when thou wast his butler.

But think on me when it shall be well with thee, and shew kindness, I pray thee, unto me, and make mention of me unto Pharaoh, and bring me out of this house: for indeed I was stolen away out of the land of the Hebrews: and here also have I done nothing that they should put me into the dungeon.

When the chief baker saw that the interpretation was good, he said unto Joseph, I also was in my dream, and, behold, I had three white baskets on my head: and in the uppermost basket there was of all manner of bake-meats for Pharaoh: and the birds did eat them out of the basket upon my head.

And Joseph answered, and said, This is the interpretation thereof: the three baskets are three days: yet within three days shall Pharaoh lift up thy head from off thee, and shall hang thee on a tree; and the birds shall eat thy flesh from off thee.

And it came to pass the third day, which was Pharaoh's birth-day, that he made a feast unto all his servants: and he lifted up the head of the chief butler and of the chief baker among his servants. And he restored the chief butler unto his butlership again; and he gave the cup into

Pharaoh's hand: but he hanged the chief baker: as Joseph had interpreted to them.

Yet did not the chief butler remember Joseph, but forgat him.

The Dream of Pharaoh

And it came to pass, at the end of two full years, that Pharaoh
dreamed. And he slept and dreamed the second time. And it came to pass
in the morning, that his spirit was troubled; and he sent and called for
all the magicians of Egypt, and all the wise men thereof: and Pharaoh
told them his dream; but there was none that could interpret them unto
Pharaoh.

Then spake the chief butler unto Pharaoh, saying, I do remember my
faults this day: Pharaoh was wroth with his servants, and put me in ward
in the captain of the guard's house, both me and the chief baker: and we
dreamed a dream in one night, I and he: we dreamed each man according
to the interpretation of his dream. And there was there with us a young
man, an Hebrew, servant to the captain of the guard; and we told him,
and he interpreted to us our dreams; to each man according to his dream
he did interpret. And it came to pass, as he interpreted to us, so it was:
me he restored unto mine office, and him he hanged.

Then Pharaoh sent and called Joseph, and they brought him hastily
out of the dungeon: and he shaved himself, and changed his raiment,
and came in unto Pharaoh.

And Pharaoh said unto Joseph, I have dreamed a dream, and there is
none that can interpret it: and I have heard say of thee, that thou canst
understand a dream to interpret it.

And Joseph answered Pharaoh, saying, It is not in me: God shall give
Pharaoh an answer of peace.

And Pharaoh said unto Joseph, In my dream, behold, I stood upon
the bank of the river: and, behold, there came up out of the river seven
kine, fat-fleshed, and well-favoured; and they fed in a meadow: and,
behold, seven other kine came up after them, poor, and very ill-favoured,
and lean-fleshed, such as I never saw in all the land of Egypt for bad-
ness: and the lean and the ill-favoured kine did eat up the first seven fat
kine: and when they had eaten them up, it could not be known that they

had eaten them; but they were still ill-favoured, as at the beginning. So I awoke.

And I saw in my dream, and, behold, seven ears came up in one stalk, full and good: and, behold, seven ears, withered, thin, and blasted with the east wind, spung up after them: and the thin ears devoured the seven good ears: and I told this unto the magicians; but there was none that could declare it to me.

And Joseph said unto Pharaoh, The dream of Pharaoh is one: God hath shewed Pharaoh what he is about to do. The seven good kine are seven years; and the seven good ears are seven years: the dream is one. And the seven thin and ill-favoured kine that came up after them are seven years; and the seven empty ears blasted with the east wind shall be seven years of famine.

This is the thing which I have spoken unto Pharaoh: what God is about to do he sheweth unto Pharaoh. Behold, there come seven years of great plenty thoughout all the land of Egypt: and there shall arise after them seven years of famine; and all the plenty shall be forgotten in the land of Egypt; and the famine shall consume the land; and the plenty shall not be known in the land by reason of that famine following: for it shall be very grievous. And for that the dream was doubled unto Pharaoh twice; it is because the thing is established by God, and God will shortly bring it to pass. Now therefore let Pharaoh look out a man discreet and wise, and set him over the land of Egypt. Let Pharaoh do this, and let him appoint officers over the land, and take up the fifth part of the land of Egypt in the seven plenteous years. And let them gather all the food of those good years that come, and lay up corn under the hand of Pharaoh, and let them keep food in the cities. And that food shall be for store to the land against the seven years of famine, which shall be in the land of Egypt; that the land perish not through the famine.

And Pharaoh said unto Joseph, Forasmuch as God hath shewed thee all this, there is none so discreet and wise as thou art: thou shalt be over my house, and according unto thy word shall all my people be ruled: only in the throne will I be greater than thou. See, I have set thee over all the land of Egypt.

And Pharaoh took off his ring from his hand, and put it upon Joseph's hand, and arrayed him in vestures of fine linen, and put a gold chain about his neck; and he made him to ride in the second chariot which he had: and they cried before him, Bow the knee: and he made him ruler over all the land of Egypt.

And Pharaoh said unto Joseph, I am Pharaoh, and without thee shall no man lift up his hand or foot in all the land of Egypt. And Pharaoh called Joseph's name Zaphnath-paaneah; and he gave him to wife Asenath the daughter of Poti-pherah priest of On. And Joseph went out over all the land of Egypt.

And Joseph was thirty years old when he stood before Pharaoh king of Egypt. And Joseph went out from the presence of Pharaoh, and went throughout all the land of Egypt.

And in the seven plenteous years the earth brought forth by handfuls. And he gathered up all the food of the seven years, which were in the land of Egypt, and laid up the food in the cities: the food of the field, which was round about every city, laid he up in the same.

And the seven years of plenteousness, that was in the land of Egypt, were ended. And the seven years of dearth began to come, according as Joseph had said: and the dearth was in all lands; but in all the land of Egypt there was bread. And all countries came into Egypt to Joseph for to buy corn; because that the famine was so sore in all lands.

Joseph's Brothers Go into Egypt

Now when Jacob saw that there was corn in Egypt, Jacob said unto his sons, Why do ye look one upon another? Behold, I have heard that there is corn in Egypt: get you down thither, and buy for us from thence; that we may live, and not die.

And Joseph's ten brethren went down to buy corn in Egypt. But Benjamin, Joseph's brother, Jacob sent not with his brethren: for he said, Lest peradventure mischief befall him.

And Joseph saw his brethren, and he knew them, but made himself strange unto them, and spake roughly unto them; and he said unto them, Whence come ye? And they said, From the land of Canaan to buy food.

And Joseph knew his brethren, but they knew not him.

And Joseph remembered the dreams which he dreamed of them, and said unto them, Ye are spies; to see the nakedness of the land ye are come.

And they said unto him, Nay, my lord, but to buy food are thy servants come. We are all one man's sons; we are true men; thy servants are no spies.

And he said unto them, Nay, but to see the nakedness of the land ye are come.

And they said, Thy servants are twelve brethren, the sons of one man in the land of Canaan: and behold, the younger is this day with our father, and one is not.

And Joseph said unto them, That is it that I spake unto you, saying, Ye are spies: hereby ye shall be proved: by the life of Pharaoh ye shall not go forth hence, except your youngest brother come hither. Send one of you, and let him fetch your brother, and ye shall be kept in prison, that your words may be proved, whether there be any truth in you: or else, by the life of Pharaoh, surely ye are spies.

And he put them all together into ward three days, and said unto them the third day, This do, and live; for I fear God: if ye be true men, let one of your brethren be bound in the house of your prison: go ye, carry corn for the famine of your houses: but bring your youngest brother unto me; so shall your words be verified, and ye shall not die. And they did so.

And they said one to another, We are verily guilty concerning our brother, in that we saw the anguish of his soul, when he besought us, and we would not hear; therefore is this distress come upon us.

And Reuben answered them, saying, Spake I not unto you, saying, Do not sin against the child; and ye would not hear? therefore, behold, also his blood is required.

And they knew not that Joseph understood them; for he spake unto them by an interpreter. And he turned himself about from them, and wept; and returned to them again, and communed with them, and took from them Simeon, and bound him before their eyes.

Then Joseph commanded to fill their sacks with corn, and to restore every man's money into his sack, and to give them provision for the way: and thus did he unto them. And they laded their asses with the corn, and departed thence. And as one of them opened his sack to give his ass provender in the inn, he espied his money: for, behold, it was in his sack's mouth.

And he said unto his brethren, My money is restored; and, lo, it is even in my sack: and their heart failed them, and they were afraid, saying one to another, What is this that God hath done unto us?

And they came unto Jacob their father unto the land of Canaan, and told him all that befell unto them.

They Return to Egypt

And the famine was sore in the land. And it came to pass, when they had eaten up the corn which they had brought out of Egypt, their father said unto them, Go again, buy us a little food.

And Judah spake unto him, saying, The man did solemnly protest unto us, saying, Ye shall not see my face, except your brother be with you. If thou wilt send our brother with us, we will go down and buy thee food: but if thou wilt not send him, we will not go down: for the man said unto us, Ye shall not see my face, except your brother be with you.

And Israel said, Wherefore dealt ye so ill with me, as to tell the man whether ye had yet a brother?

And they said, The man asked us straitly of our state, and of our kindred, saying, Is your father yet alive? have ye another brother? and we told him according to the tenor of these words: could we certainly know that he would say, Bring your brother down?

And Judah said unto Israel his father, Send the lad with me, and we will arise and go; that we may live, and not die, both we, and thou, and also our little ones. I will be surety for him; of my hand shalt thou require him: if I bring him not unto thee, and set him before thee, then let me bear the blame for ever: for except we had lingered, surely now we had returned this second time.

And their father Israel said unto them, If it must be so now, do this; take of the best fruits in the land in your vessels, and carry down the man a present, a little balm, and a little honey, spices, and myrrh, nuts, and almonds: and take double money in your hand; and the money that was brought again in the mouth of your sacks, carry it again in your hand; peradventure it was an oversight: take also your brother, and arise, go again unto the man: and God Almighty give you mercy before the man, that he may send away your other brother, and Benjamin. If I be bereaved of my children, I am bereaved.

And the men took that present, and they took double money in their hand, and Benjamin; and rose up, and went down to Egypt, and stood before Joseph. And when Joseph saw Benjamin with them, he said to the ruler of his house, Bring these men home, and slay, and make ready; for these men shall dine with me at noon.

And the man did as Joseph bade; and the man brought the men into Joseph's house. And the men were afraid, because they were brought into Joseph's house; and they said, Because of the money that was returned in our sacks at the first time, are we brought in; that he may seek occasion against us, and fall upon us, and take us for bondmen, and our asses.

And they came near to the steward of Joseph's house, and they communed with him at the door of the house, and said, O sir, we came indeed down at the first time to buy food: and it came to pass, when we came to the inn, that we opened our sacks, and behold, every man's money was in the mouth of his sack, our money in full weight: and we have brought it again in our hand. And other money have we brought down in our hands to buy food: we cannot tell who put our money in our sacks.

And he said, Peace be to you, fear not: your God, and the God of your father, hath given you treasure in your sacks: I had your money. And he brought Simeon out unto them.

And the man brought the men into Joseph's house, and gave them water, and they washed their feet; and he gave their asses provender. And they made ready the present against Joseph came at noon: for they heard that they should eat bread there.

And when Joseph came home, they brought him the present which was in their hand into the house, and bowed themselves to him to the earth.

And he asked them of their welfare, and said, Is your father well, the old man of whom ye spake? Is he yet alive?

And they answered, Thy servant our father is in good health, he is yet alive. And they bowed down their heads, and made obeisance.

And he lifted up his eyes, and saw his brother Benjamin, his mother's son, and said, Is this your younger brother, of whom ye spake unto me? And he said, God be gracious unto thee, my son.

And Joseph made haste; for his bowels did yearn upon his brother: and he sought where to weep; and he entered into his chamber, and wept there. And he washed his face, and went out, and refrained himself, and said, Set on bread.

And they set on for him by himself, and for them by themselves, and for the Egyptians, which did eat with him, by themselves: because the Egyptians might not eat bread with the Hebrews; for that is an abomination unto the Egyptians. And they sat before him, the first-born according to his birth-right, and the youngest according to his youth: and the men marvelled one at another. And he took and sent messes unto them from before him: but Benjamin's mess was five times so much as any of theirs. And they drank, and were merry with him.

Joseph and His Brothers Are Reconciled

And he commanded the steward of his house, saying, Fill the men's sacks with food, as much as they can carry, and put every man's money in his sack's mouth. And put my cup, the silver cup, in the sack's mouth of the youngest, and his corn-money. And he did according to the word that Joseph had spoken.

As soon as the morning was light, the men were sent away, they, and their asses. And when they were gone out of the city, and not yet far off, Joseph said unto his steward, Up, follow after the men; and when thou dost overtake them, say unto them, Wherefore have ye rewarded evil for good? Is not this it in which my lord drinketh, and whereby indeed he divineth? ye have done evil in so doing.

And he overtook them, and he spake unto them these same words. And they said unto him, Wherefore saith my lord these words? God forbid that thy servants should do according to this thing: behold, the money which we found in our sacks' mouths, we brought again unto thee out of the land of Canaan: how then should we steal out of thy lord's house silver or gold? With whomsoever of thy servants it be found, both let him die, and we also will be my lord's bond-men.

And he said, Now also let it be according unto your words: he with whom it is found shall be my servant; and ye shall be blameless.

Then they speedily took down every man his sack to the ground, and opened every man his sack. And he searched, and began at the eldest, and left at the youngest: and the cup was found in Benjamin's sack. Then they rent their clothes, and laded every man his ass, and returned to the city.

And Judah and his brethren came to Joseph's house; for he was yet there: and they fell before him on the ground.

And Joseph said unto them, What deed is this that ye have done? wot ye not that such a man as I can certainly divine?

And Judah said, What shall we say unto my lord? what shall we speak? or how shall we clear ourselves? God hath found out the iniquity of thy servants: behold we are my lord's servants, both we, and he also with whom the cup is found.

And he said, God forbid that I should do so: but the man in whose hand the cup is found, he shall be my servant; and as for you, get you up in peace unto your father.

Then Judah came near unto him, and said, O my lord, let thy servant, I pray thee, speak a word in my lord's ears, and let not thine anger burn against thy servant: for thou art even as Pharaoh. My lord asked his servants, saying, Have ye a father, or a brother? And we said unto my lord, We have a father, an old man, and a child of his old age, a little one: and his brother is dead, and he alone is left of his mother, and his father loveth him. And thou saidst unto thy servants, Bring him down unto me, that I may set mine eyes upon him. And we said unto my lord, The lad cannot leave his father: for if he should leave his father, his father would die. And thou saidst unto thy servants, Except your youngest brother come down with you, ye shall see my face no more. And it came to pass, when we came up unto thy servant my father, we told him the words of my lord. And our father said, Go again, and buy us a little food. And we said, We cannot go down: if our youngest brother be with us, then will we go down; for we may not see the man's face, except our youngest brother be with us. And thy servant my father said unto us, Ye know that my wife bare me two sons: and the one went out from me, and I said, Surely he is torn in pieces; and I saw him not since: and if ye take this also from me, and mischief befall him, ye shall bring down my grey hairs with sorrow to the grave. Now therefore when I come to thy servant my father, and the lad be not with us; (seeing that his life is bound up in the lad's life;) he will die: and thy servants shall bring down the grey hairs of thy servant our father with sorrow to the grave. For thy servant became surety for the lad unto my father, saying, If I bring him not unto thee, then I shall bear the blame to my father for ever. Now therefore, I pray thee, let thy servant abide instead of the lad a bondman to my lord; and let the lad go up with his brethren. For how shall I go up to my father, and the lad be not with me? lest peradventure I see the evil that shall come on my father.

Then Joseph could not refrain himself before all them that stood by him; and he cried, Cause every man to go out from me: and there stood no man with him, while Joseph made himself known unto his brethren. And he wept aloud; and the Egyptians and the house of Pharaoh heard.

And Joseph said unto his brethren, I am Joseph; doth my father yet live? And his brethren could not answer him; for they were troubled at his presence.

And Joseph said unto his brethren, Come near to me, I pray you: and they came near: and he said, I am Joseph your brother, whom ye sold into Egypt. Now therefore be not grieved, nor angry with yourselves, that ye sold me hither: for God did send me before you to preserve life. For these two years hath the famine been in the land: and yet there are five years, in the which there shall neither be earing nor harvest. And God sent me before you, to preserve you a posterity in the earth, and to save your lives by a great deliverance. So now it was not you that sent me hither, but God: and he hath made me a father to Pharaoh, and lord of all his house, and a ruler throughout all the land of Egypt. Haste ye, and go up to my father, and say unto him, Thus saith thy son Joseph, God hath made me lord of all Egypt; come down unto me, tarry not: and thou shalt dwell in the land of Goshen, and thou shalt be near unto me, thou, and thy children, and thy children's children, and thy flocks, and thy herds, and all that thou hast: and there will I nourish thee, (for yet there are five years of famine;) lest thou, and thy household, and all that thou hast, come to poverty. And, behold, your eyes see, and the eyes of my brother Benjamin, that it is my mouth that speaketh unto you. And ye shall tell my father of all my glory in Egypt, and of all that ye have seen: and ye shall haste, and bring down my father hither.

And he fell upon his brother Benjamin's neck, and wept; and Benjamin wept upon his neck. Moreover, he kissed all his brethren, and wept upon them: and after that his brethren talked with him.

And the fame thereof was heard in Pharaoh's house, saying, Joseph's brethren are come: and it pleased Pharaoh well, and his servants. And Pharaoh said unto Joseph, Say unto thy brethren, This do ye; lade your beasts, and go, get you unto the land of Canaan; and take your father, and your households, and come unto me: and I will give you the good of the land of Egypt, and ye shall eat the fat of the land. Now thou art commanded, this do ye; take you wagons out of the land of Egypt for your little ones, and for your wives, and bring your father, and come.

Also regard not your stuff: for the good of all the land of Egypt is yours.

And the children of Israel did so: and Joseph gave them wagons, according to the commandment of Pharaoh, and gave them provision for the way. To all of them he gave each man changes of raiment: but to Benjamin he gave three hundred pieces of silver, and five changes of raiment. And to his father he sent after this manner; ten asses laden with the good things of Egypt, and ten she asses laden with corn and bread and meat for his father by the way. So he sent his brethren away, and they departed: and he said unto them, See that ye fall not out by the way.

And they went up out of Egypt, and came into the land of Canaan unto Jacob their father, and told him, saying, Joseph is yet alive, and he is governor over all the land of Egypt. And Jacob's heart fainted, for he believed them not.

And they told him all the words of Joseph, which he had said unto them: and when he saw the wagons which Joseph had sent to carry him, the spirit of Jacob their father revived: and Israel said, It is enough; Joseph my son is yet alive: I will go and see him before I die.

The Tribe of Jacob Goes to Egypt

And they took their cattle, and their goods, which they had gotten in the land of Canaan, and came into Egypt, Jacob, and all his seed with him; his sons, and his sons' sons with him, his daughters, and his son's daughters, and all his seed brought he with him into Egypt.

And he sent Judah before him unto Joseph, to direct his face unto Goshen; and they came into the land of Goshen.

And Joseph made ready his chariot, and went up to meet Israel his father, to Goshen; and presented himself unto him: and he fell on his neck, and wept on his neck a good while.

And Israel said unto Joseph, Now let me die, since I have seen thy face, because thou art yet alive.

Then Joseph came and told Pharaoh, and said, My father and my brethren, and their flocks, and their herds, and all that they have, are come out of the land of Canaan; and, behold, they are in the land of Goshen. And he took some of his brethren, even five men, and presented them unto Pharaoh.

And Pharaoh said unto his brethren, What is your occupation? And they said unto Pharaoh, Thy servants are shepherds, both we, and also our fathers. For to sojourn in the land are we come: for thy servants have no pasture for their flocks, for the famine is sore in the land of Canaan: now therefore, we pray thee, let thy servants dwell in the land of Goshen.

And Pharaoh spake unto Joseph, saying, Thy father and thy brethren are come unto thee: the land of Egypt is before thee; in the best of the land make thy father and brethren to dwell; in the land of Goshen let them dwell: and if thou knowest any men of activity among them, then make them rulers over my cattle.

And Joseph placed his father and his brethren, and gave them a possession in the land of Egypt, in the best of the land, in the land of Rameses, as Pharaoh had commanded.

The Death of Jacob

And Israel said unto Joseph, Behold, I die; but God shall be with you, and bring you again unto the land of your fathers.

And Jacob called unto his sons, and said, Gather yourselves together, that I may tell you that which shall befall you in the last days. Gather yourselves together, and hear, ye sons of Jacob; and hearken unto Israel your father.

Reuben, thou art my first-born, my might, and the beginning of my strength, the excellency of dignity, and the excellency of power: unstable as water, thou shalt not excel; because thou wentest up to thy father's bed; then defilest thou it: he went up to my couch.

Simeon and Levi are brethren; instruments of cruelty are in their habitations. O my soul, come not thou into their secret; unto their assembly, mine honour, be not thou united! for in their anger they slew a man, and in their self-will they digged down a wall. Cursed be their anger, for it was fierce: and their wrath, for it was cruel: I will divide them in Jacob, and scatter them in Israel.

Judah, thou art he whom thy brethren shall praise; thy hand shall be in the neck of thine enemies; thy father's children shall bow down before thee. Judah is a lion's whelp; from the prey, my son, thou art gone up: he stooped down, he couched as a lion, and as an old lion: who shall rouse him up? The sceptre shall not depart from Judah, nor a lawgiver from between his feet, until Shiloh come: and unto him shall the gathering of the people be. Binding his foal unto the vine, and his ass's colt unto the choice vine; he washed his garments in wine, and his clothes in the blood of grapes: his eyes shall be red with wine, and his teeth white with milk.

Zebulun shall dwell at the haven of the sea; and he shall be for an haven of ships; and his border shall be unto Zidon.

Issachar is a strong ass, couching down between two burdens: and he saw that rest was good, and the land that it was pleasant; and bowed his shoulder to bear, and became a servant unto tribute.

Dan shall judge his people, as one of the tribes of Israel. Dan shall be a serpent by the way, an adder in the path, that biteth the horse-heels, so that his rider shall fall backward. I have waited for thy salvation, O Lord!

Gad, a troop shall overcome him: but he shall overcome at the last.

Out of Asher his bread shall be fat, and he shall yield royal dainties.

Naphtali is a hind let loose: he giveth goodly words.

Joseph is a fruitful bough, even a fruitful bough by a well, whose branches run over the wall: the archers have sorely grieved him, and shot at him, and hated him: but his bow abode in strength, and the arms of his hands were made strong by the hands of the mighty God of Jacob: (from thence is the shepherd, the stone of Israel:) even by the God of thy father, who shall help thee, and by the Almighty, who shall bless thee with blessings of heaven above, blessings of the deep that lieth under, blessings of the breasts and of the womb: the blessings of thy father have prevailed above the blessings of my progenitors, unto the utmost bound of the everlasting hills; they shall be on the head of Joseph, and on the crown of the head of him that was separate from his brethren.

Benjamin shall raven as a wolf; in the morning he shall devour the prey, and at night he shall divide the spoil.

All these are the twelve tribes of Israel: and this is it that their father spake unto them, and blessed them: every one according to his blessing he blessed them. And he charged them, and said unto them, I am to be gathered unto my people: bury me with my fathers in the cave that is in the field of Ephron the Hittite, in the cave that is in the field of Machpelah which is before Mamre, in the land of Canaan, which Abraham bought with the field of Ephron the Hittite, for a possession of a burying-place. (There they buried Abraham and Sarah his wife; there they buried Isaac and Rebekah his wife; and there I buried Leah.) The purchase of the field and of the cave that is therein, was from the children of Heth.

And when Jacob had made an end of commanding his sons, he gathered up his feet into the bed, and yielded up the ghost, and was gathered unto his people.

The Death of Joseph

And Joseph dwelt in Egypt, he, and his father's house: and Joseph lived an hundred and ten years. And Joseph saw Ephraim's children of the third generation: the children also of Machir, the son of Manasseh, were brought up upon Joseph's knees.

And Joseph said unto his brethren, I die; and God will surely visit you, and bring you out of this land, unto the land which he sware to Abraham, to Isaac, and to Jacob. And Joseph took an oath of the children of Israel, saying, God will surely visit you, and ye shall carry up my bones from hence.

So Joseph died, being an hundred and ten years old: and they embalmed him, and he was put in a coffin in Egypt.

The Second Book of Moses, Called
EXODUS

The Beginning of Persecution

And the children of Israel were fruitful, and increased abundantly, and multiplied, and waxed exceeding mighty; and the land was filled with them.

Now there arose up a new king over Egypt, which knew not Joseph.

And he said unto his people, Behold, the people of the children of Israel are more and mightier than we. Come on, let us deal wisely with them; lest they multiply, and it come to pass, that, when there falleth out any war, they join also unto our enemies, and fight against us, and so get them up out of the land.

Therefore they did set over them task-masters, to afflict them with their burdens. And they built for Pharaoh treasure-cities, Pithom, and Raamses. But the more they afflicted them, the more they multiplied and grew. And they were grieved because of the children of Israel. And they made their lives bitter with hard bondage, in mortar, and in brick, and in all manner of service in the field: all their service wherein they made them serve was with rigour.

And the king of Egypt spake to the Hebrew midwives (of which the name of the one was Shiphrah, and the name of the other Puah;) and he said, When ye do the office of a midwife to the Hebrew women, and see them upon the stools; if it be a son, then ye shall kill him; but if it be a daughter, then she shall live.

But the midwives feared God, and did not as the king of Egypt commanded them, but saved the men-children alive. And the king of Egypt called for the midwives, and said unto them, Why have you done this thing, and have saved the men-children alive?

And the midwives said unto Pharaoh, Because the Hebrew women are not as the Egyptian women; for they are lively, and are delivered ere the midwives come in unto them.

Therefore God dealt well with the midwives: and the people multiplied, and waxed very mighty.

And Pharaoh charged all his people, saying, Every son that is born ye shall cast into the river, and every daughter ye shall save alive.

The Birth of Moses

And there went a man of the house of Levi, and took to wife a daughter of Levi. And the woman conceived and bare a son: and when she saw him that he was a goodly child, she hid him three months. And when she could not longer hide him, she took for him an ark of bul-rushes, and daubed it with slime and with pitch, and put the child therein; and she laid it on the flags by the river's brink. And his sister stood afar off, to wit what would be done to him.

And the daughter of Pharaoh came down to wash herself at the river; and her maidens walked along by the river's side: and when she saw the ark among the flags, she sent her maid to fetch it. And when she had opened it, she saw the child: and, behold, the babe wept. And she had compassion on him, and said, This is one of the Hebrews' children.

Then said his sister to Pharaoh's daughter, Shall I go, and call to thee a nurse of the Hebrew women, that she may nurse the child for thee?

And Pharaoh's daughter said to her, Go. And the maid went and called the child's mother.

And Pharaoh's daughter said unto her, Take this child away and nurse it for me, and I will give thee thy wages. And the woman took the child and nursed it.

And the child grew, and she brought him unto Pharaoh's daughter, and he became her son. And she called his name Moses: and she said, Because I drew him out of the water.

Moses Becomes Champion of the Jews

And it came to pass in those days, when Moses was grown, that he went out unto his brethren, and looked on their burdens: and he spied an Egyptian smiting an Hebrew, one of his brethren. And he looked this way and that way, and when he saw that there was no man, he slew the Egyptian, and hid him in the sand.

And when he went out the second day, behold, two men of the Hebrews strove together: and he said to him that did the wrong, Wherefore smitest thou thy fellow?

And he said, Who made thee a prince and a judge over us? intendest thou to kill me, as thou killest the Egyptian? And Moses feared, and said, Surely this thing is known.

Now when Pharaoh heard this thing, he sought to slay Moses. But Moses fled from the face of Pharaoh, and dwelt in the land of Midian: and he sat down by a well.

Now the priest of Midian had seven daughters: and they came and drew water, and filled the troughs to water their father's flock. And the shepherds came and drove them away: but Moses stood up and helped them, and watered their flock.

And when they came to Reuel their father, he said, How is it that ye are come so soon to-day?

And they said, An Egyptian delivered us out of the hand of the shepherds, and also drew water enough for us, and watered the flock.

And he said unto his daughters, And where is he? why is it that ye have left the man? call him, that he may eat bread. And Moses was content to dwell with the man: and he gave Moses, Zipporah his daughter. And she bare him a son, and he called his name Gershom; for he said, I have been a stranger in a strange land.

The Burning Bush and the Name of God

Now Moses kept the flock of Jethro his father-in-law, the priest of Midian: and he led the flock to the back side of the desert, and came to the mountain of God, even to Horeb.

And the Angel of the Lord appeared unto him in a flame of fire out of the midst of a bush; and he looked, and, behold, the bush burned with fire, and the bush was not consumed. And Moses said, I will now turn aside, and see this great sight, why the bush is not burnt.

And when the Lord saw that he turned aside to see, God called unto him out of the midst of the bush, and said, Moses, Moses! And he said, Here am I.

And he said, Draw not nigh hither: put off thy shoes from off thy feet; for the place whereon thou standest is holy ground. I am the God of thy father, the God of Abraham, the God of Isaac, and the God of Jacob.

And Moses hid his face; for he was afraid to look upon God.

And the Lord said, I have surely seen the affliction of my people which are in Egypt, and have heard their cry by reason of their taskmasters; for I know their sorrows: and I am come down to deliver them out of the hand of the Egyptians, and to bring them up out of that land, unto a good land, and a large, unto a land flowing with milk and honey; unto the place of the Canaanites, and the Hittites, and the Amorites, and the Perizzites, and the Hivites, and the Jebusites. Come now therefore, and I will send thee unto Pharaoh, that thou mayest bring forth my people, the children of Israel, out of Egypt.

And Moses said unto God, Who am I, that I should go unto Pharaoh, and that I should bring forth the children of Israel out of Egypt?

And he said, Certainly I will be with thee; and this shall be a token unto thee, that I have sent thee: When thou hast brought forth the people out of Egypt, ye shall serve God upon this mountain.

And Moses said unto God, Behold, when I come unto the children of Israel, and shall say unto them, The God of your fathers hath sent me unto you; and they shall say to me, What is his name? what shall I say unto them?

And God said unto Moses, I AM THAT I AM: And he said, Thus shalt thou say unto the children of Israel, I AM hath sent me unto you. Thus shalt thou say unto the children of Israel, The Lord God of your fathers, the God of Abraham, the God of Isaac, and the God of Jacob, hath sent me unto you: this is my name for ever, and this is my memorial unto all generations. Go, and gather the elders of Israel together, and say unto them, The Lord God of your fathers, the God of Abraham, of Isaac, and of Jacob, appeared unto me, saying, I have surely visited you, and seen that which is done to you in Egypt.

And I have said, I will bring you up out of the affliction of Egypt, unto the land of the Canaanites, and the Hittites, and the Amorites, and the Perizzites, and the Hivites, and the Jebusites, unto a land flowing with milk and honey. And they shall hearken to thy voice; and thou shalt come, thou and the elders of Israel, unto the king of Egypt, and ye shall say unto him, The Lord God of the Hebrews hath met with us; and now let us go, we beseech thee, three days' journey into the wilderness, that we may sacrifice to the Lord our God.

And I am sure that the king of Egypt will not let you go, no, not by a mighty hand. And I will stretch out my hand, and smite Egypt with all my wonders which I will do in the midst thereof: and after that he will let you go. And I will give this people favour in the sight of the Egyptians: and it shall come to pass, that, when ye go, ye shall not go empty: but every woman shall borrow of her neighbour, and of her that sojourneth in her house, jewels of silver, and jewels of gold, and raiment: and ye shall put them upon your sons, and upon your daughters; and ye shall spoil the Egyptians.

Moses Is Given Three Miracles

And Moses answered and said, But, behold, they will not believe me, nor hearken unto my voice: for they will say, The Lord hath not appeared unto thee.

And the Lord said unto him, What is that in thine hand? And he said, A rod.

And he said, Cast it on the ground. And he cast it on the ground, and it became a serpent: and Moses fled from before it.

And the Lord said unto Moses, Put forth thine hand, and take it by the tail. And he put forth his hand, and caught it, and it became a rod in his hand: that they may believe that the Lord God of their fathers, the God of Abraham, the God of Isaac, and the God of Jacob, hath appeared unto thee.

And the Lord said furthermore unto him, Put now thine hand into thy bosom. And he put his hand into his bosom: and when he took it out, behold, his hand was leprous as snow. And he said, Put thine hand into thy bosom again. And he put his hand into his bosom again, and plucked it out of his bosom, and, behold, it was turned again as his other flesh.

And it shall come to pass, if they will not believe thee, neither hearken to the voice of the first sign, that they will believe the voice of the latter sign. And it shall come to pass, if they will not believe also these two signs, neither hearken unto thy voice, that thou shalt take of the water of the river, and pour it upon the dry land: and the water which thou takest out of the river shall become blood upon the dry land.

And Moses said unto the Lord, O my Lord, I am not eloquent, neither heretofore, nor since thou hast spoken unto thy servant: but I am slow of speech, and of a slow tongue.

And the Lord said unto him, Who hath made man's mouth? or who maketh the dumb, or deaf, or the seeing, or the blind? have not I the Lord? Now therefore go, and I will be with thy mouth, and teach thee what thou shalt say.

And he said, O my Lord, send, I pray thee, by the hand of him whom thou wilt send.

And the anger of the Lord was kindled against Moses, and he said, Is not Aaron the Levite thy brother? I know that he can speak well. And also, behold, he cometh forth to meet thee: and when he seeth thee, he will be glad in his heart. And thou shalt speak unto him, and put words in his mouth: and I will be with thy mouth, and with his mouth, and will teach you what ye shall do. And he shall be thy spokesman unto the people: and he shall be, even he shall be to thee instead of a mouth, and thou shalt be to him instead of God. And thou shalt take this rod in thine hand, wherewith thou shalt do signs.

Pharaoh Increases the Jews' Burden

And afterward Moses and Aaron went in, and told Pharaoh, Thus saith the Lord God of Israel, Let my people go, that they may hold a feast unto me in the wilderness.

And Pharaoh said, Who is the Lord, that I should obey his voice to let Israel go? I know not the Lord, neither will I let Israel go.

And they said, The God of the Hebrews hath met with us: let us go, we pray thee, three days' journey into the desert, and sacrifice unto the Lord our God; lest he fall upon us with pestilence, or with the sword.

And the king of Egypt said unto them, Wherefore do ye, Moses and Aaron, let the people from their works? get you unto your burdens. Behold, the people of the land now are many, and ye make them rest from their burdens.

And Pharaoh commanded the same day the taskmasters of the people, and their officers, saying, Ye shall no more give the people straw to make brick, as heretofore: let them go and gather straw for themselves. And the tale of the bricks which they did make heretofore, ye shall lay upon them; ye shall not diminish aught thereof: for they be idle; therefore they cry, saying, Let us go and sacrifice to our God. Let there more work be laid upon the men, that they may labour therein: and let them not regard vain words.

And the taskmasters of the people went out, and their officers, and they spake to the people, saying, Thus saith Pharaoh, I will not give you straw. Go ye, get you straw where you can find it: yet not aught of your work shall be diminished. So the people were scattered abroad throughout all the land of Egypt, to gather stubble instead of straw.

The Plague of Bloody Water

And Moses and Aaron went in unto Pharaoh, and they did so as the Lord had commanded: and Aaron cast down his rod before Pharaoh, and before his servants, and it became a serpent.

Then Pharaoh also called the wise men, and the sorcerers: now the magicians of Egypt, they also did in like manner with their enchantments. For they cast down every man his rod, and they became serpents: but Aaron's rod swallowed up their rods. And he hardened Pharaoh's heart that he hearkened not unto them; as the Lord had said.

And the Lord said unto Moses, Pharaoh's heart is hardened, he refuseth to let the people go. Get thee unto Pharaoh in the morning; lo, he goeth out unto the water, and thou shalt stand by the river's brink against he come: and the rod which was turned to a serpent shalt thou take in thine hand. And thou shalt say unto him, The Lord God of the Hebrews hath sent me unto thee, saying, Let my people go, that they may serve me in the wilderness: and behold, hitherto thou wouldest not hear. Thus saith the Lord, In this thou shalt know that I am the Lord: behold, I will smite with the rod that is in my hand upon the waters which are in the river, and they shall be turned to blood.

And Moses and Aaron did so, as the Lord commanded; and he lifted up the rod and smote the waters that were in the river, in the sight of Pharaoh, and in the sight of his servants; and all the waters that were in the river were turned into blood. And the fish that was in the river died; and the river stank, and the Egyptians could not drink of the water of the river; and there was blood throughout all the land of Egypt.

And the magicians of Egypt did so with their enchantments: and Pharaoh's heart was hardened, neither did he hearken unto them; as the Lord had said.

And seven days were fulfilled after that the Lord had smitten the river.

The Plague of Frogs

And the Lord spake unto Moses, Go unto Pharaoh, and say unto him, Thus said the Lord, Let my people go that they may serve me. And if thou refuse to let them go, behold, I will smite all thy borders with frogs: and the river shall bring forth frogs abundantly, which shall go up and come into thine house, and into thy bed-chamber, and upon thy bed, and into the house of thy servants, and upon thy people, and into thine ovens, and into thy kneading-troughs; and the frogs shall come up both on thee, and upon thy people, and upon all thy servants.

And the Lord spake unto Moses, Say unto Aaron, Stretch forth thine hand with thy rod over the streams, over the rivers, and over the ponds, and cause frogs to come up upon the land of Egypt. And Aaron stretched out his hand over the waters of Egypt; and the frogs came up, and covered the land of Egypt.

And the magicians did so with their enchantments, and brought up frogs upon the land of Egypt.

Then Pharaoh called for Moses and Aaron, and said, Entreat the Lord that he may take away the frogs from me, and from my people: and I will let the people go, that they may do sacrifice unto the Lord.

And Moses and Aaron went out from Pharaoh: and Moses cried unto the Lord, because of the frogs which he had brought against Pharaoh. And the Lord did according to the word of Moses: and the frogs died out of the houses, out of the villages, and out of the fields. And they gathered them together upon heaps: and the land stank.

But when Pharaoh saw that there was respite, he hardened his heart, and hearkened not unto them; as the Lord had said.

The Plague of Boils

And the Lord said unto Moses and unto Aaron, Take to you handfuls of ashes of the furnace, and let Moses sprinkle it toward the heaven in the sight of Pharaoh. And it shall become small dust in all the land of Egypt, and shall be a boil breaking forth with blains upon man, and upon beast, throughout all the land of Egypt.

And they took ashes of the furnace, and stood before Pharaoh; and Moses sprinkled it up toward heaven: and it became a boil breaking forth with blains upon man, and upon beast. And the magicians could not stand before Moses, because of the boils: for the boil was upon the magicians, and upon all the Egyptians.

And the Lord hardened the heart of Pharaoh, and he hearkened not unto them; as the Lord had spoken unto Moses.

The Plagues of Locusts and Darkness

And the Lord said unto Moses, Go in unto Pharaoh: for I have hardened his heart, and the heart of his servants; that I might shew these my signs before him: and that thou mayest tell in the ears of thy son, and of thy son's son, what things I have wrought in Egypt, and my signs which I have done among them; that ye may know how that I am the Lord.

And Moses and Aaron came in unto Pharaoh, and said unto him, Thus saith the Lord God of the Hebrews, How long wilt thou refuse to humble thyself before me? Let my people go, that they may serve me. Else, if thou refuse to let my people go, behold, to-morrow will I bring the locusts into thy coast: and they shall cover the face of the earth, that one cannot be able to see the earth: and they shall eat the residue of that which is escaped, which remaineth unto you from the hail, and shall eat every tree which groweth for you out of the field: and they shall fill thy houses, and the houses of all thy servants, and the houses of all the Egyptians; which neither thy fathers, nor thy fathers' fathers have seen, since the day that they were upon the earth unto this day. And he turned himself, and went out from Pharaoh.

And the Lord said unto Moses, Stretch out thine hand over the land of Egypt for the locusts, that they may come up upon the land of Egypt, and eat every herb of the land, even all that the hail hath left.

And Moses stretched forth his rod over the land of Egypt, and the Lord brought an east wind upon the land all that day, and all that night: and when it was morning, the east wind brought the locusts. And the locusts went up over all the land of Egypt, and rested in all the coasts of Egypt: very grievous were they; before them there were no such locusts as they, neither after them shall be such. For they covered the face of the whole earth, so that the land was darkened; and they did eat every herb of the land, and all the fruit of the trees which the hail had left: and there remained not any green thing in the trees, or in the herbs of the field, through all the land of Egypt.

Then Pharaoh called for Moses and Aaron in haste; and he said, I have sinned against the Lord your God, and against you. Now therefore forgive, I pray thee, my sin only this once, and entreat the Lord your God that he may take away from me this death only.

And he went out from Pharaoh, and entreated the Lord. And the Lord turned a mighty strong west wind which took away the locusts, and cast them into the Red sea: there remained not one locust in all the coasts of Egypt.

But the Lord hardened Pharaoh's heart, so that he would not let the children of Israel go.

And the Lord said unto Moses, Stretch out thine hand toward heaven, that there may be darkness over the land of Egypt, even darkness which may be felt.

And Moses stretched forth his hand toward heaven: and there was a thick darkness in all the land of Egypt three days: they saw not one another, neither rose any from his place for three days: but all the children of Israel had light in their dwellings.

But the Lord hardened Pharaoh's heart, and he would not let them go.

And Pharaoh said unto him, Get thee from me, take heed to thyself, see my face no more: for in that day thou seest my face, thou shalt die.

And Moses said, Thou hast spoken well, I will see thy face again no more.

The Passover Is Instituted

And the Lord spake unto Moses and Aaron in the land of Egypt, saying, This month shall be unto you the beginning of months: it shall be the first month of the year to you.

Speak ye unto all the congregation of Israel, saying, In the tenth day of this month they shall take to them every man a lamb according to the house of their fathers, a lamb for an house: and if the household be too little for the lamb, let him and his neighbour next unto his house take it according to the number of the souls: every man according to his eating shall make your count for the lamb.

Your lamb shall be without blemish, a male of the first year: ye shall take it out from the sheep or from the goats: and ye shall keep it up until the fourteenth day of the same month: and the whole assembly of the congregation of Israel shall kill it in the evening. And they shall take of the blood, and strike it on the two side-posts, and on the upper door-post of the houses, wherein they shall eat it. And they shall eat the flesh in that night, roast with fire, and unleavened bread; and with bitter herbs they shall eat it.

Eat not of it raw, nor sodden at all with water, but roast with fire; his head with his legs, and with the purtenance thereof. And ye shall let nothing of it remain until the morning: and that which remaineth of it until the morning ye shall burn with fire.

And thus shall ye eat it; with your loins girded, your shoes on your feet, and your staff in your hand: and ye shall eat it in haste; it is the Lord's passover.

For I will pass through the land of Egypt this night, and will smite all the first-born in the land of Egypt, both man and beast: and against all the gods of Egypt I will execute judgment: I am the Lord. And the blood shall be to you for a token upon the houses where ye are: and when I see the blood, I will pass over you, and the plague shall not be upon you to destroy you, when I smite the land of Egypt.

And this day shall be unto you for a memorial; and ye shall keep it a feast to the Lord throughout your generations: ye shall keep it a feast by an ordinance for ever. Seven days shall ye eat unleavened bread; even the first day ye shall put away leaven out of your houses: for whosoever eateth leavened bread, from the first day until the seventh day, that soul shall be cut off from Israel. And in the first day there shall be an holy convocation, and in the seventh day there shall be an holy convocation to you: no manner of work shall be done in them, save that which every man must eat, that only may be done of you.

And ye shall observe the feast of unleavened bread; for in this self-same day have I brought your armies out of the land of Egypt; therefore shall ye observe this day in your generations by an ordinance for ever. In the first month, on the fourteenth day of the month at even, ye shall eat unleavened bread, until the one and twentieth day of the month at even.

Seven days shall there be no leaven found in your houses: for whosoever eateth that which is leavened, even that soul shall be cut off from the congregation of Israel, whether he be a stranger, or born in the land. Ye shall eat nothing leavened: in all your habitations shall ye eat unleavened bread.

And the children of Israel went away, and did as the Lord had commanded Moses and Aaron, so did they.

And it came to pass, that at midnight the Lord smote all the first-born in the land of Egypt, from the first-born of Pharaoh that sat on his throne, unto the first-born of the captive that was in the dungeon; and all the first-born of cattle.

And Pharaoh rose up in the night, he, and all his servants, and all the Egyptians; and there was a great cry in Egypt: for there was not a house where there was not one dead.

And he called for Moses and Aaron by night, and said, Rise up, and get you forth from among my people, both ye and the children of Israel: and go, serve the Lord, as ye have said. Also take your flocks and your herds, as ye have said, and be gone: and bless me also. And the Egyptians were urgent upon the people, that they might send them out of the land in haste; for they said, We be all dead men.

And the people took their dough before it was leavened, their kneading troughs being bound up in their clothes upon their shoulders. And the children of Israel did according to the word of Moses: and they borrowed of the Egyptians jewels of silver, and jewels of gold, and raiment. And the Lord gave the people favour in the sight of the Egyptians, so that they lent unto them such things as they required: and they spoiled the Egyptians.

And the children of Israel journeyed from Rameses to Succoth, about six hundred thousand on foot that were men, beside children. And a mixed multitude went up also with them; and flocks, and herds, even very much cattle. And they baked unleavened cakes of the dough which they brought forth out of Egypt, for it was not leavened: because they were thrust out of Egypt, and could not tarry, neither had they prepared for themselves any victual.

Now the sojourning of the children of Israel who dwelt in Egypt, was four hundred and thirty years.

They Cross the Red Sea

And the Lord spake unto Moses, saying, Sanctify unto me all the first-born, whatsoever openeth the womb among the children of Israel, both of man and of beast: it is mine.

And Moses said unto the people, Remember this day, in which ye came out from Egypt, out of the house of bondage; for by strength of hand the Lord brought you out from this place: there shall no leavened bread be eaten. This day came ye out, in the month Abib. And it shall be when the Lord shall bring thee into the land of the Canaanites, and the Hittites, and the Amorites, and the Hivites, and the Jebusites, which he sware unto thy fathers to give thee, a land flowing with milk and honey; that thou shalt keep this service in this month. Seven days thou shalt eat unleavened bread, and in the seventh day shall be a feast to the Lord.

And it shall be when the Lord shall bring thee into the land of the Canaanites, as he sware unto thee and to thy fathers, and shall give it thee; that thou shalt set apart unto the Lord all that openeth the matrix; and every firstling that cometh of a beast which thou hast, the males shall be the Lord's. And every firstling of an ass thou shalt redeem with a lamb; and if thou wilt not redeem it, then thou shalt break his neck: and all the first-born of man among thy children shalt thou redeem.

And it shall be when thy son asketh thee in time to come, saying, What is this? that thou shalt say unto him, By strength of hand the Lord brought us out from Egypt, from the house of bondage: and it came to pass, when Pharaoh would hardly let us go, that the Lord slew all the first-born in the land of Egypt, both the first-born of man, and the first-born of beast: therefore I sacrifice to the Lord all that openeth the matrix, being males; but all the first-born of my children I redeem.

And it came to pass, when Pharaoh had let the people go, that God led them not through the way of the land of the Philistines, although that was near; for God said, Lest peradventure the people repent when they see war, and they return to Egypt: but God led the people about, through the way of the wilderness of the Red sea: and the children of Israel went up harnessed out of the land of Egypt.

And Moses took the bones of Joseph with him: for he had straitly sworn the children of Israel, saying, God will surely visit you; and ye shall carry up my bones away hence with you.

And the Lord went before them by day in a pillar of a cloud, to lead them the way; and by night in a pillar of fire, to give them light: to go by day and night.

And it was told the king of Egypt that the people fled: and the heart of Pharaoh and of his servants was turned against the people, and they said, Why have we done this, that we have let Israel go from serving us?

And he made ready his chariot, and took his people with him: and he took six hundred chosen chariots, and all the chariots of Egypt, and captains over every one of them, and he pursued after the children of Israel.

And when Pharaoh drew nigh, the children of Israel lifted up their eyes, and behold, the Egyptians marched after them; and they were sore afraid: and the children of Israel cried out unto the Lord.

And they said unto Moses, Because there were no graves in Egypt, hast thou taken us away to die in the wilderness? Wherefore hast thou dealt thus with us, to carry us forth out of Egypt? Is not this the word that we did tell thee in Egypt, saying, Let us alone, that we may serve the Egyptians? For it had been better for us to serve the Egyptians, than that we should die in the wilderness.

And Moses said unto the people, Fear not, stand still, and see the salvation of the Lord, which he will shew to you to-day: for the Egyptians whom ye have seen to-day, ye shall see them again no more for ever. The Lord shall fight for you, and ye shall hold your peace.

And the Lord said unto Moses, Wherefore criest thou unto me? Speak unto the children of Israel, that they go forward: but lift thou up thy rod, and stretch out thine hand over the sea, and divide it: and the children of Israel shall go on dry ground through the midst of the sea.

And the angel of God which went before the camp of Israel, removed, and went behind them; and the pillar of the cloud went from before their face, and stood behind them: and it came between the camp of the Egyptians and the camp of Israel; and it was a cloud and darkness to them, but it gave light by night to these: so that the one came not near the other all the night.

And Moses stretched out his hand over the sea; and the Lord caused the sea to go back by a strong east wind all that night, and made the sea dry land, and the waters were divided. And the children of Israel went into the midst of the sea upon the dry ground: and the waters were a wall unto them on their right hand, and on their left.

And the Egyptians pursued, and went in after them, to the midst of the sea, even all Pharaoh's horses, his chariots, and his horsemen. And it came to pass, that in the morning-watch the Lord looked unto the host of the Egyptians through the pillar of fire and of the cloud, and troubled the host of the Egyptians, and took off their chariot-wheels, that they drave them heavily: so that the Egyptians said, Let us flee from the face of Israel; for the Lord fighteth for them against the Egyptians.

And the Lord said unto Moses, Stretch out thine hand over the sea, that the waters may come again upon the Egyptians, upon their chariots, and upon their horsemen.

And Moses stretched forth his hand over the sea, and the sea returned to his strength when the morning appeared; and the Egyptians fled against it; and the Lord overthrew the Egyptians in the midst of the sea. And the waters returned, and covered the chariots, and the horsemen, and all the host of Pharaoh that came into the sea after them: there remained not so much as one of them.

But the children of Israel walked upon dry land in the midst of the sea; and the waters were a wall unto them on their right hand, and on their left.

Thus the Lord saved Israel that day out of the hand of the Egyptians: and Israel saw the Egyptians dead upon the sea-shore.

Israel's Song of Deliverance

Then sang Moses and the children of Israel this song unto the Lord:

I will sing unto the Lord, for he hath triumphed gloriously;
The horse and his rider hath he thrown into the sea.

The Lord is my strength and song, and he is become my salvation:
He is my God, and I will prepare him an habitation:
My father's God, and I will exalt him.

The Lord is a man of war:
The Lord is his name.

Pharaoh's chariots and his host hath he cast into the sea:
His chosen captains also are drowned in the Red sea.

The depths have covered them:
They sank into the bottom as a stone.

Thy right hand, O Lord, is become glorious in power:
Thy right hand, O Lord, hath dashed in pieces the enemy.

And in the greatness of thine excellency thou hast overthrown them that
    rose up against thee:
Thou sentest forth thy wrath, which consumed them as stubble.

And with the blast of thy nostrils the waters were gathered together,
The floods stood upright as an heap, and the depths were congealed in
        the heart of the sea.

The enemy said, I will pursue, I will overtake, I will divide the spoil:
My lust shall be satisfied upon them;
I will draw my sword, mine hand shall destroy them.

Thou didst blow with thy wind, the sea covered them:
They sank as lead in the mighty waters.

Who is like unto thee, O Lord, among the gods?
Who is like thee, glorious in holiness, fearful in praises, doing wonders?

Thou stretchedst out thy right hand, the earth swallowed them.

Thou in thy mercy hast led forth the people which thou hast redeemed:
Thou hast guided them in thy strength unto thy holy habitation.

The people shall hear, and be afraid:
Sorrow shall take hold on the inhabitants of Palestina.

Then the dukes of Edom shall be amazed;
The mighty men of Moab, trembling shall take hold upon them;
All the inhabitants of Canaan shall melt away.

Fear and dread shall fall upon them;
By the greatness of thine arm they shall be as still as a stone;
Till thy people pass over, O Lord,
Till the people pass over, which thou hast purchased.

Thou shalt bring them in, and plant them in the mountain of thine
        inheritance,
In the place, O Lord, which thou hast made for thee to dwell in;
In the sanctuary, O Lord, which thy hands have established.

The Lord shall reign for ever and ever.

For the horse of Pharaoh went in with his chariots and with his horse-
        men into the sea,
And the Lord brought again the waters of the sea upon them:
But the children of Israel went on dry land in the midst of the sea.

And Miriam the prophetess, the sister of Aaron, took a timbrel in her hand; and all the women went out after her, with timbrels, and with dances. And Miriam answered them:

Sing ye to the Lord, for he hath triumphed gloriously:
The horse and his rider hath he thrown into the sea.

They Gather Manna

Then said the Lord unto Moses, Behold, I will rain bread from heaven for you; and the people shall go out and gather a certain rate every day, that I may prove them, whether they will walk in my law, or no. And it shall come to pass, that on the sixth day they shall prepare that which they bring in; and it shall be twice as much as they gather daily.

And it came to pass, that at even the quails came up, and covered the camp: and in the morning the dew lay round about the host. And when the dew that lay was gone up, behold, upon the face of the wilderness there lay a small round thing, as small as the hoar frost on the ground: and when the children of Israel saw it, they said one to another, It is manna: for they wist not what it was. And Moses said unto them, This is the bread which the Lord hath given you to eat.

This is the thing which the Lord hath commanded, Gather of it every man according to his eating: an omer for every man according to the number of your persons, take ye every man for them which are in his tents.

And the children of Israel did so, and gathered, some more, some less. And when they did mete it with an omer, he that gathered much had nothing over, and he that gathered little had no lack: they gathered every man according to his eating.

And Moses said, Let no man leave of it till the morning. Notwithstanding, they hearkened not unto Moses; but some of them left of it until the morning, and it bred worms, and stank: and Moses was wroth with them.

And they gathered it every morning, every man according to his eating: and when the sun waxed hot it melted.

And it came to pass, that on the sixth day they gathered twice as much bread, two omers for one man: and all the rulers of the congregation came and told Moses.

And he said unto them, This is that which the Lord hath said, To-morrow is the rest of the holy sabbath unto the Lord: bake that which ye will bake to-day, and seethe that ye will seethe; and that which remaineth over, lay up for you to be kept until the morning.

And they laid it up till the morning, as Moses bade: and it did not stink, neither was there any worm therein.

And Moses said, Eat that to-day; for to-day is a sabbath unto the Lord; to-day ye shall not find it in the field. Six days ye shall gather it; but on the seventh day, which is the sabbath, in it there shall be none.

And it came to pass, that there went out some of the people on the seventh day for to gather, and they found none.

And the children of Israel did eat manna forty years, until they came to a land inhabited: they did eat manna, until they came unto the borders of the land of Canaan.

Moses Gets Water from the Rock

And all the congregation of the children of Israel journeyed from the wilderness of Sin, after their journeys, according to the commandment of the Lord, and pitched in Rephidim: and there was no water for the people to drink. Wherefore the people did chide with Moses, and said, Give us water that we may drink. And Moses said unto them, Why chide ye with me? wherefore do ye tempt the Lord?

And Moses cried unto the Lord, saying, What shall I do unto this people? they be almost ready to stone me.

And the Lord said unto Moses, Go on before the people, and take with thee of the elders of Israel: and thy rod, wherewith thou smotest the river, take in thine hand, and go. Behold, I will stand before thee there upon the rock in Horeb; and thou shalt smite the rock, and there shall come water out of it, that the people may drink. And Moses did so in the sight of the elders of Israel.

And he called the name of the place Massah, and Meribah, because of the chiding of the children of Israel, and because they tempted the Lord, saying, Is the Lord among us, or not?

God Gives Israel the Ten Commandments

In the third month, when the children of Israel were gone forth out of the land of Egypt, the same day came they into the wilderness of Sinai, and there Israel camped before the mount.

And Moses went up unto God, and the Lord called unto him out of the mountain, saying, Thus shalt thou say to the house of Jacob, and tell the children of Israel; ye have seen what I did unto the Egyptians, and how I bare you on eagles' wings, and brought you unto myself. Now therefore, if ye will obey my voice indeed, and keep my covenant, then ye shall be a peculiar treasure unto me above all people: for all the earth is mine: and ye shall be unto me a kingdom of priests, and an holy nation. These are the words which thou shalt speak unto the children of Israel.

And the Lord said unto Moses, Go unto the people, and sanctify them to-day and to-morrow, and let them wash their clothes, and be ready against the third day: for the third day the Lord will come down in the sight of all the people upon mount Sinai. And thou shalt set bounds unto the people round about, saying, Take heed to yourselves, that ye go not up into the mount, or touch the border of it: whosoever toucheth the mount shall be surely put to death: when the trumpet soundeth long, they shall come up to the mount.

And it came to pass on the third day in the morning, that there were thunders and lightnings, and a thick cloud upon the mount, and the voice of the trumpet exceeding loud; so that all the people that was in the camp trembled. And Moses brought forth the people out of the camp to meet with God; and they stood at the nether part of the mount. And mount Sinai was altogether on a smoke, because the Lord descended upon it in fire: and the smoke thereof ascended as the smoke of a furnace, and the whole mount quaked greatly.

And when the voice of the trumpet sounded long, and waxed louder and louder, Moses spake, and God answered him by a voice.

And the Lord came down upon mount Sinai, on the top of the mount: and the Lord called Moses up to the top of the mount; and Moses went up. And the Lord said unto Moses, Go down, charge the people, lest they break through unto the Lord to gaze, and many of them perish. And let the priests also, which come near to the Lord, sanctify themselves, lest the Lord break forth upon them.

And Moses said unto the Lord, The people cannot come up to mount Sinai: for thou chargedst us, saying, Set bounds about the mount, and sanctify it.

And the Lord said unto him, Away, get thee down, and thou shalt come up, thou and Aaron with thee: but let not the priests and the people break through, to come up unto the Lord, lest he break forth upon them.

So Moses went down unto the people, and spake unto them.

And God spake all these words, saying,

I am the Lord thy God, which have brought thee out of the land of Egypt, out of the house of bondage.

Thou shalt have no other gods before me.

Thou shalt not make unto thee any graven image, or any likeness of any thing that is in heaven above, or that is in the earth beneath, or that is in the water under the earth: thou shalt not bow down thyself to them, nor serve them: for I the Lord thy God am a jealous God, visiting the iniquity of the fathers upon the children unto the third and fourth generation of them that hate me; and showing mercy unto thousands of them that love me, and keep my commandments.

Thou shalt not take the name of the Lord thy God in vain: for the Lord will not hold him guiltless that taketh his name in vain.

Remember the sabbath-day to keep it holy. Six days shalt thou labour, and do all thy work: but the seventh day is the sabbath of the Lord thy God: in it thou shalt not do any work, thou, nor thy son, nor thy daughter, thy man-servant, nor thy maid-servant, nor thy cattle, nor thy stranger that is within thy gates: for in six days the Lord made heaven and earth, the sea and all that in them is, and rested the seventh day: wherefore the Lord blessed the sabbath-day and hallowed it.

Honour thy father and thy mother; that thy days may be long upon the land which the Lord thy God giveth thee.

Thou shalt not kill.

Thou shalt not commit adultery.

Thou shalt not steal.

Thou shalt not bear false witness against thy neighbour.

Thou shalt not covet thy neighbour's house, .thou shalt not covet thy neighbour's wife, nor his man-servant, nor his maid-servant, nor his ox, nor his ass, nor any thing that is thy neighbour's.

And the people stood afar off, and Moses drew near unto the thick darkness where God was.

And the Lord said unto Moses, Thus thou shalt say unto the children of Israel; An altar of earth thou shalt make unto me, and shalt sacrifice thereon thy burnt offerings, and thy peace offerings, thy sheep, and thine oxen: in all places where I record my name I will come unto thee, and I will bless thee. And if thou wilt make me an altar of stone, thou shalt not build it of hewn stone, for if thou lift up thy tool upon it, thou hast polluted it. Neither shalt thou go up by steps unto mine altar, that thy nakedness be not discovered thereon.

Further Laws

Now these are the judgments which thou shalt set before them.

He that smiteth a man, so that he die, shall be surely put to death. And if a man lie not in wait, but God deliver him into his hand; then I will appoint thee a place whither he shall flee. But if a man come presumptuously upon his neighbour, to slay him with guile; thou shalt take him from mine altar, that he may die. And he that smiteth his father, or his mother, shall be surely put to death.

If men strive, and hurt a woman with child, so that her fruit depart from her, and yet no mischief follow: he shall be surely punished, according as the woman's husband will lay upon him; and he shall pay as the judges determine. And if any mischief follow, then thou shalt give life for life, eye for eye, tooth for tooth, hand for hand, foot for foot, burning for burning, wound for wound, stripe for stripe.

If a thief be found breaking up, and be smitten that he die, there shall no blood be shed for him. If the sun be risen upon him there shall be blood shed for him: for he should make full restitution; if he have nothing, then he shall be sold for his theft. If the theft be certainly found in his hand alive, whether it be ox, or ass, or sheep; he shall restore double.

If a man shall deliver unto his neighbour money or stuff to keep, and it be stolen out of the man's house; if the thief be found, let him pay double. If the thief be not found, then the master of the house shall be brought unto the judges, to see whether he have put his hand unto his neighbour's goods.

And if a man entice a maid that is not betrothed, and lie with her, he shall surely endow her to be his wife. If her father utterly refuse to give her unto him, he shall pay money according to the dowry of virgins.

Thou shalt not suffer a witch to live.

Whosoever lieth with a beast shall surely be put to death.

He that sacrificeth unto any god, save unto the Lord only, he shall be utterly destroyed.

Thou shalt neither vex a stranger, nor oppress him: for ye were strangers in the land of Egypt.

Ye shall not afflict any widow, or fatherless child. If thou afflict them in any wise, and they cry at all unto me, I will surely hear their cry; and my wrath shall wax hot, and I will kill you with the sword; and your wives shall be widows, and your children fatherless.

If thou lend money to any of my people that is poor by thee, thou shalt not be to him as an usurer, neither shalt thou lay upon him usury.

If thou at all take thy neighbour's raiment to pledge, thou shalt deliver it unto him by that the sun goeth down: for that is his covering only, it is his raiment for his skin: wherein shall he sleep? and it shall come to pass, when he crieth unto me, that I will hear; for I am gracious.

Thou shalt not revile the gods, nor curse the ruler of thy people.

Thou shalt not delay to offer the first of thy ripe fruits, and of thy liquors: the first-born of thy sons shalt thou give unto me. Likewise shalt thou do with thine oxen, and with thy sheep: seven days it shall be with his dam; on the eighth day thou shalt give it me.

And six years thou shalt sow thy land, and shalt gather in the fruits thereof: but the seventh year thou shalt let it rest and lie still; that the poor of thy people may eat: and what they leave the beasts of the field shall eat. In like manner thou shalt deal with thy vineyard, and with thy oliveyard.

And in all things that I have said unto you, be circumspect: and make no mention of the name of other gods, neither let it be heard out of thy mouth.

Three times thou shalt keep a feast unto me in the year. Thou shalt keep the feast of unleavened bread: (thou shalt eat unleavened bread seven days, as I commanded thee, in the time appointed of the month Abib; for in it thou camest out from Egypt: and none shall appear

before me empty:) and the feast of harvest, the first-fruits of thy
labours, which thou hast sown in the field: and the feast of ingathering, which is in the end of the year, when thou hast gathered in thy
labours out of the field. Three times in the year all thy males shall
appear before the Lord God.

Thou shalt not offer the blood of my sacrifice with leavened bread:
neither shall the fat of my sacrifice remain until the morning.

The first of the first-fruits of thy land thou shalt bring into the house
of the Lord thy God.

Thou shalt not seethe a kid in his mother's milk.

Moses Is Given the Tablets of Stone

And he said unto Moses, Come up unto the Lord, thou, and Aaron,
Nadab, and Abihu, and seventy of the elders of Israel; and worship ye
afar off. And Moses alone shall come near the Lord: but they shall not
come nigh; neither shall the people go up with him.

And Moses came and told the people all the words of the Lord, and
all the judgments: and all the people answered with one voice, and
said, All the words which the Lord hath said will we do.

And Moses wrote all the words of the Lord, and rose up early in the
morning, and builded an altar under the hill, and twelve pillars according to the twelve tribes of Israel. And he sent young men of the children of Israel, which offered burnt-offerings, and sacrificed peace-
offerings of oxen unto the Lord. And Moses took half of the blood, and
put it in basins; and half of the blood he sprinkled on the altar. And
he took the book of the covenant, and read in the audience of the people:
and they said, All that the Lord hath said will we do, and be obedient.
And Moses took the blood, and sprinkled it on the people, and said,
Behold the blood of the covenant, which the Lord hath made with you
concerning all these words.

Then went up Moses, and Aaron, Nadab, and Abihu, and seventy of
the elders of Israel: and they saw the God of Israel: and there was
under his feet as it were a paved work of a sapphire-stone, and as it
were the body of heaven in his clearness. And upon the nobles of the
children of Israel he laid not his hand: also they saw God, and did
eat and drink.

And the Lord said unto Moses, Come up to me into the mount, and be there: and I will give thee tables of stone, and a law, and commandments which I have written; that thou mayest teach them. And Moses rose up, and his minister Joshua: and Moses went up into the mount of God. And he said unto the elders, Tarry ye here for us, until we come again unto you: and behold, Aaron and Hur are with you: if any man have any matters to do, let him come unto them.

And Moses went up into the mount, and a cloud covered the mount. And the glory of the Lord abode upon mount Sinai, and the cloud covered it six days: and the seventh day he called unto Moses out of the midst of the cloud. And the sight of the glory of the Lord was like devouring fire on the top of the mount in the eyes of the children of Israel.

And Moses went into the midst of the cloud, and gat him up into the mount: and Moses was in the mount forty days and forty nights.

The Golden Calf

And when the people saw that Moses delayed to come down out of the mount, the people gathered themselves together unto Aaron, and said unto him, Up, make us gods which shall go before us: for as for this Moses, the man that brought us up out of the land of Egypt, we wot not what is become of him.

And Aaron said unto them, Break off the golden ear-rings which are in the ears of your wives, of your sons, and of your daughters, and bring them unto me.

And all the people brake off the golden ear-rings which were in their ears, and brought them unto Aaron. And he received them at their hand, and fashioned it with a graving tool, after he had made it a molten calf: and they said, These be thy gods, O Israel, which brought thee up out of the land of Egypt.

And when Aaron saw it, he built an altar before it; and Aaron made proclamation, and said, To-morrow is a feast to the Lord. And they rose up early on the morrow, and offered burnt-offerings, and brought peace-offerings: and the people sat down to eat and to drink, and rose up to play.

And the Lord said unto Moses, Go, get thee down: for thy people,

which thou broughtest out of the land of Egypt, have corrupted themselves: they have turned aside quickly out of the way which I commanded them: they have made them a molten calf, and have worshipped
it, and have sacrificed thereunto, and said, These be thy gods, O Israel,
which have brought thee up out of the land of Egypt.

And the Lord said unto Moses, I have seen this people, and behold,
it is a stiff-necked people: now therefore let me alone, that my wrath
may wax hot against them, and that I may consume them: and I will
make of thee a great nation.

And Moses besought the Lord, his God, and said, Lord, why doth
thy wrath wax hot against thy people, which thou hast brought forth
out of the land of Egypt, with great power, and with a mighty hand?
Wherefore should the Egyptians speak and say, For mischief did he
bring them out, to slay them in the mountains, and to consume them
from the face of the earth? Turn from thy fierce wrath, and repent of
this evil against thy people. Remember Abraham, Isaac, and Israel, thy
servants, to whom thou swarest by thine own self, and saidst unto them,
I will multiply your seed as the stars of heaven, and all this land that I
have spoken of will I give unto your seed, and they shall inherit it
for ever.

And the Lord repented of the evil which he thought to do unto his
people.

And Moses turned, and went down from the mount, and the two
tables of the testimony were in his hand: the tables were written on
both their sides; on the one side and on the other were they written.
And the tables were the work of God, and the writing was the writing
of God, graven upon the tables.

And when Joshua heard the noise of the people as they shouted, he
said unto Moses, There is a noise of war in the camp. And he said, It
is not the voice of them that shout for mastery, neither is it the voice
of them that cry for being overcome: but the noise of them that sing
do I hear.

And it came to pass as soon as he came nigh unto the camp, that
he saw the calf, and the dancing: and Moses' anger waxed hot, and he
cast the tables out of his hands, and brake them beneath the mount.
And he took the calf which they had made, and burnt it in the fire, and
ground it to powder, and strewed it upon the water, and made the
children of Israel drink of it.

And when Moses saw that the people were naked (for Aaron had made them naked unto their shame among their enemies), then Moses stood in the gate of the camp, and said, Who is on the Lord's side? let him come unto me. And all the sons of Levi gathered themselves together unto him.

And he said unto them, Thus saith the Lord God of Israel, Put every man his sword by his side and go in and out from gate to gate throughout the camp, and slay every man his brother, and every man his companion, and every man his neighbour.

And the children of Levi did according to the word of Moses: and there fell of the people that day about three thousand men.

And it came to pass on the morrow, that Moses said unto the people, Ye have sinned a great sin: and now I will go up unto the Lord; peradventure I shall make an atonement for your sin.

And Moses returned unto the Lord, and said, Oh, this people have sinned a great sin, and have made them gods of gold. Yet now, if thou wilt forgive their sin—; and if not, blot me, I pray thee, out of thy book which thou hast written.

And the Lord said unto Moses, Whosoever hath sinned against me, him will I blot out of my book. Therefore now go, lead the people unto the place of which I have spoken unto thee: behold, mine Angel shall go before thee: nevertheless, in the day when I visit, I will visit their sin upon them.

And the Lord plagued the people, because they made the calf which Aaron made.

The Presence of God

And Moses said unto the Lord, See, thou sayest unto me, Bring up this people: and thou hast not let me know whom thou wilt send with me. Yet thou hast said, I know thee by name, and thou hast also found grace in my sight. Now therefore, I pray thee, if I have found grace in thy sight, shew me now thy way, that I may know thee, that I may find grace in thy sight: and consider that this nation is thy people.

And he said, My presence shall go with thee, and I will give thee rest.

And he said unto him, If thy presence go not with me, carry us not up hence. For wherein shall it be known here that I and thy people have found grace in thy sight? Is it not in that thou goest with us? So shall we be separated, I and thy people, from all the people that are upon the face of the earth.

And the Lord said unto Moses, I will do this thing also that thou hast spoken: for thou hast found grace in my sight, and I know thee by name.

And he said, I beseech thee, shew me thy glory.

And he said, I will make all my goodness pass before thee, and I will proclaim the name of the Lord before thee; and will be gracious to whom I will be gracious, and will shew mercy on whom I will shew mercy. And he said, Thou canst not see my face: for there shall no man see me, and live.

And the Lord said, Behold, there is a place by me, and thou shalt stand upon a rock: and it shall come to pass, while my glory passeth by, that I will put thee in a cleft of the rock; and will cover thee with my hand while I pass by: and I will take away mine hand, and thou shalt see my back parts: but my face shall not be seen.

The Law of the Sabbath

And Moses gathered all the congregation of the children of Israel together, and said unto them, These are the words which the Lord hath commanded, that ye should do them. Six days shall work be done, but on the seventh day there shall be to you an holy day, a sabbath of rest to the Lord: whosoever doeth work therein shall be put to death. Ye shall kindle no fire throughout your habitations upon the sabbath-day.

The Third Book of Moses, Called
LEVITICUS

Various Laws

And the Lord spake unto Aaron, saying,

Do not drink wine nor strong drink, thou, nor thy sons with thee, when ye go into the tabernacle of the congregation, lest ye die: it shall be a statute for ever throughout your generations: and that ye may put difference between holy and unholy, and between unclean and clean; and that ye may teach the children of Israel all the statutes which the Lord hath spoken unto them by the hand of Moses.

And the Lord spake unto Moses and to Aaron, saying unto them, Speak unto the children of Israel, saying, These are the beasts which ye shall eat among all the beasts that are on the earth.

Whatsoever parteth the hoof, and is cloven-footed, and cheweth the cud among the beasts, that shall ye eat.

Nevertheless, these shall ye not eat, of them that chew the cud, or of them that divide the hoof: as the camel, because he cheweth the cud, but divideth not the hoof; he is unclean unto you. And the coney, because he cheweth the cud, but divideth not the hoof; he is unclean unto you. And the hare, because he cheweth the cud, but divideth not the hoof; he is unclean unto you. And the swine, though he divide the hoof, and be cloven-footed, yet he cheweth not the cud; he is unclean unto you. Of their flesh shall ye not eat, and their carcass shall ye not touch; they are unclean to you.

These shall ye eat, of all that are in the waters: whatsoever hath fins and scales in the waters, in the seas, and in the rivers, them shall ye eat. And all that have not fins nor scales in the seas, and in the rivers, of all that move in the waters, and of any living thing which is in the waters, they shall be an abomination unto you.

And these are they which ye shall have in abomination among the fowls; they shall not be eaten, they are an abomination: the eagle, and the ossifrage, and the ospray, and the vulture, and the kite after his kind; every raven after his kind; and the owl, and the night-hawk, and the cuckoo, and the hawk after his kind, and the little owl, and the cormorant, and the great owl, and the swan, and the pelican, and the gier-eagle, and the stork, the heron after her kind, and the lapwing, and the bat. All fowls that creep, going upon all four, shall be an abomination unto you.

Yet these may ye eat, of every flying creeping thing that goeth upon all four, which have legs above their feet, to leap withal upon the earth; even these of them ye may eat: the locust after his kind, and the bald locust after his kind, and the beetle after his kind, and the grasshopper after his kind. But all other flying creeping things, which have four feet, shall be an abomination unto you.

And for these ye shall be unclean: whosoever toucheth the carcass of them shall be unclean until the even. And whosoever beareth aught of the carcass of them shall wash his clothes, and be unclean until the even. The carcasses of every beast which divideth the hoof and is not cloven-footed, nor cheweth the cud, are unclean unto you: every one that toucheth them shall be unclean.

And whatsoever goeth upon his paws, among all manner of beasts that go on all four, those are unclean unto you: whoso toucheth their carcass shall be unclean until the even. And he that beareth the carcass of them shall wash his clothes, and be unclean until the even: they are unclean unto you.

These also shall be unclean unto you among the creeping things that creep upon the earth: the weasel, and the mouse, and the tortoise after his kind, and the ferret, and the chameleon, and the lizard, and the snail, and the mole. These are unclean to you among all that creep: whosoever doth touch them, when they be dead, shall be unclean until the even.

And the Lord spake unto Moses, saying, Speak unto the children of Israel, saying, If a woman have conceived seed, and borne a man-child, then she shall be unclean seven days; according to the days of the separation for her infirmity shall she be unclean. And in the eighth day the flesh of his foreskin shall be circumcised. And she shall then continue in the blood of her purifying three and thirty days: she shall touch no hallowed thing, nor come into the sanctuary, until the days of her purifying be fulfilled.

But if she bear a maid-child, then she shall be unclean two weeks, as in her separation: and she shall continue in the blood of her purifying three-score and six days.

And the Lord spake unto Moses and Aaron, saying, When a man shall have in the skin of his flesh a rising, a scab, or bright spot, and it be in the skin of his flesh like the plague of leprosy; then he shall be brought unto Aaron the priest, or unto one of his sons the priests: and the priest shall look on the plague in the skin of the flesh: and when the hair in the plague is turned white, and the plague in sight be deeper than the skin of his flesh, it is a plague of leprosy: and the priest shall look on him, and pronounce him unclean.

If the bright spot be white in the skin of his flesh, and in sight be not deeper than the skin, and the hair thereof be not turned white; then the priest shall shut up him that hath the plague seven days: and the priest shall look on him again the seventh day: and, behold, if the plague be somewhat dark, and the plague spread not in the skin, the priest shall pronounce him clean: it is but a scab: and he shall wash his clothes, and be clean. But if the scab spread much abroad in the skin, after that he hath been seen of the priest for his cleansing, he shall be seen of the priest again: and if the priest see, that, behold, the scab spreadeth in the skin, then the priest shall pronounce him unclean: it is a leprosy.

And the leper in whom the plague is, his clothes shall be rent, and his head bare, and he shall put a covering upon his upper lip, and shall cry, Unclean, unclean. All the days wherein the plague shall be in him he shall be defiled; he is unclean: he shall dwell alone, without the camp shall his habitation be.

The garment also that the plague of leprosy is in, whether it be a woollen garment, or a linen garment; whether it be in the warp, or woof, of linen, or of woollen: whether in a skin, or in any thing made of skin: and if the plague be greenish or reddish in the garment, or in the skin, either in the warp, or in the woof, or in any thing of skin; it is a plague of leprosy, and shall be shewed unto the priest: and the priest shall look upon the plague, and shut up it that hath the plague seven days: and he shall look on the plague on the seventh day: if the plague be spread in the garment, either in the warp, or in the woof, or in a skin, or in any work that is made of skin; the plague is a fretting leprosy; it is unclean.

He shall therefore burn that garment, whether warp or woof, in woollen or in linen, or any thing of skin, wherein the plague is: for it is a fretting leprosy; it shall be burnt in the fire.

And this shall be his uncleanness in his issue: whether his flesh run with his issue, or his flesh be stopped from his issue, it is his uncleanness. Every bed whereon he lieth that hath the issue, is unclean: and every thing whereon he sitteth, shall be unclean.

And whosoever toucheth his bed, shall wash his clothes, and bathe himself in water, and be unclean until the even. And he that sitteth on any thing whereon he sat that hath the issue, shall wash his clothes, and bathe himself in water, and be unclean until the even. And he that toucheth the flesh of him that hath the issue, shall wash his clothes, and bathe himself in water, and be unclean until the even. And if he that hath the issue spit upon him that is clean; then he shall wash his clothes, and bathe himself in water, and be unclean until the even. And what saddle soever he rideth upon that hath the issue, shall be unclean. And whosoever toucheth any thing that was under him, shall be unclean until the even: and he that beareth any of those things, shall wash his clothes, and bathe himself in water, and be unclean until the even.

And whomsoever he toucheth that hath the issue (and hath not rinsed his hands in water) he shall wash his clothes, and bathe himself in water, and be unclean until the even. And the vessel of earth that he toucheth which hath the issue, shall be broken: and every vessel of wood shall be rinsed in water.

And when he that hath an issue is cleansed of his issue; then he shall number to himself seven days for his cleansing, and wash his clothes, and bathe his flesh in running water, and shall be clean.

And if a woman have an issue, and her issue in her flesh be blood, she shall be put apart seven days: and whosoever toucheth her shall be unclean until the even. And every thing that she lieth upon in her separation shall be unclean: every thing also that she sitteth upon shall be unclean.

And whosoever toucheth her bed shall wash his clothes, and bathe himself in water, and be unclean until the even. And if it be on her bed, or on any thing whereon she sitteth, when he toucheth it he shall be unclean until the even.

And if any man lie with her at all, and her flowers be upon him, he shall be unclean seven days: and all the bed whereon he lieth shall be unclean.

And the Lord spake unto Moses, saying,

Speak unto the children of Israel, and say unto them, I am the Lord your God.

None of you shall approach to any that is near of kin to him, to uncover their nakedness: I am the Lord. The nakedness of thy father, or the nakedness of thy mother, shalt thou not uncover: she is thy mother; thou shalt not uncover her nakedness. The nakedness of thy father's wife shalt thou not uncover: it is thy father's nakedness.

The nakedness of thy sister, the daughter of thy father, or daughter of thy mother, whether she be born at home, or born abroad, even their nakedness thou shalt not uncover. The nakedness of thy son's daughter, or of thy daughter's daughter, even their nakedness thou shalt not uncover: for theirs is thine own nakedness.

The nakedness of thy father's wife's daughter, begotten of thy father, (she is thy sister) thou shalt not uncover her nakedness. Thou shalt not uncover the nakedness of thy father's sister: she is thy father's near kinswoman. Thou shalt not uncover the nakedness of thy mother's sister: for she is thy mother's near kinswoman.

Thou shalt not uncover the nakedness of thy father's brother, thou shalt not approach to his wife: she is thine aunt.

Thou shalt not uncover the nakedness of thy daughter-in-law: she is thy son's wife; thou shalt not uncover her nakedness. Thou shalt not uncover the nakedness of thy brother's wife: it is thy brother's nakedness.

Thou shalt not uncover the nakedness of a woman and her daughter, neither shalt thou take her son's daughter, or her daughter's daughter, to uncover her nakedness; for they are her near kinswomen: it is wickedness.

Neither shalt thou take a wife to her sister, to vex her, to uncover her nakedness, beside the other in her life-time.

Also thou shalt not approach unto a woman to uncover her naked-ness, as long as she is put apart for her uncleanness.

Moreover, thou shalt not lie carnally with thy neighbour's wife, to defile thyself with her.

And thou shalt not let any of thy seed pass through the fire to Molech, neither shalt thou profane the name of thy God: I am the Lord.

Thou shalt not lie with mankind, as with womankind: it is abomina-tion. Neither shalt thou lie with any beast to defile thyself therewith: neither shall any woman stand before a beast to lie down thereto: it is confusion.

And when ye reap the harvest of your land, thou shalt not wholly reap the corners of thy field, neither shalt thou gather the gleanings of thy harvest. And thou shalt not glean thy vineyard, neither shalt thou gather every grape of thy vineyard; thou shalt leave them for the poor and stranger: I am the Lord your God.

Thou shalt not curse the deaf, nor put a stumbling-block before the blind, but shalt fear thy God: I am the Lord.

Ye shall do no unrighteousness in judgment; thou shalt not respect the person of the poor, nor honour the person of the mighty: but in righteousness shalt thou judge thy neighbour.

Thou shalt not go up and down as a tale-bearer among thy people; neither shalt thou stand against the blood of thy neighbour; I am the Lord.

Thou shalt not avenge, nor bear any grudge against the children of thy people, but thou shalt love thy neighbour as thyself: I am the Lord.

Thou shalt not let thy cattle gender with a diverse kind: Thou shalt not sow thy field with mingled seed: neither shall a garment mingled of linen and woollen come upon thee.

Ye shall not round the corners of your heads, neither shalt thou mar the corners of thy beard.

Ye shall not make any cuttings in your flesh for the dead, nor print any marks upon you: I am the Lord.

Do not prostitute thy daughter to cause her to be a whore: lest the land fall to whoredom, and the land become full of wickedness.

Regard not them that have familiar spirits, neither seek after wizards, to be defiled by them: I am the Lord your God.

And if a stranger sojourn with thee in your land, ye shall not vex him. But the stranger that dwelleth with you shall be unto you as one born among you, and thou shalt love him as thyself; for ye were strangers in the land of Egypt: I am the Lord your God.

Whosoever he be of the children of Israel, or of the strangers that sojourn in Israel, that giveth any of his seed unto Molech, he shall surely be put to death: the people of the land shall stone him with stones. And I will set my face against that man, and will cut him off from among his people; because he hath given of his seed unto Molech, to defile my sanctuary, and to profane my holy name.

And if the people of the land do any ways hide their eyes from the man, when he giveth of his seed unto Molech, and kill him not; then I will set my face against that man, and against his family, and will cut him off, and all that go a whoring after him, to commit whoredom with Molech, from among their people.

And the man that committeth adultery with another man's wife, even he that committeth adultery with his neighbour's wife, the adulterer and the adulteress shall surely be put to death.

And the man that lieth with his father's wife hath uncovered his father's nakedness: both of them shall surely be put to death: their blood shall be upon them.

And if a man lie with his daughter-in-law, both of them shall surely be put to death: they have wrought confusion; their blood shall be upon them.

If a man also lie with mankind, as he lieth with a woman, both of them have committed an abomination: they shall surely be put to death; their blood shall be upon them.

And if a man take a wife and her mother, it is wickedness: they shall be burnt with fire, both he and they: that there be no wickedness among you.

And if a man lie with a beast, he shall surely be put to death: and ye shall slay the beast.

And if a woman approach unto any beast, and lie down thereto, thou shalt kill the woman and the beast; they shall surely be put to death; their blood shall be upon them.

And if a man shall take his sister, his father's daughter, or his mother's daughter, and see her nakedness, and she see his nakedness: it is a wicked thing; and they shall be cut off in the sight of their people: he hath uncovered his sister's nakedness; he shall bear his iniquity.

And if a man shall lie with a woman having her sickness, and shall uncover her nakedness; he hath discovered her fountain, and she hath uncovered the fountain of her blood: and both of them shall be cut off from among their people.

Ye shall have one manner of law, as well for the stranger, as for one of your own country: for I am the Lord your God.

And if thy brother be waxen poor, and fallen in decay with thee; then thou shalt relieve him: yea, though he be a stranger, or a sojourner; that he may live with thee. Take thou no usury of him, or increase; but fear thy God; that thy brother may live with thee. Thou shalt not give him thy money upon usury, nor lend him thy victuals for increase.

Both thy bond-men, and thy bond-maids, which thou shalt have, shall be of the heathen that are round about you; of them shall ye buy bond-men and bond-maids. Moreover, of the children of the strangers that do sojourn among you, of them shall ye buy, and of their families that are with you, which they begat in your land: and they shall be your possession. And ye shall take them as an inheritance for your children after you, to inherit them for a possession; they shall be your bond-men for ever: but over your brethren the children of Israel, ye shall not rule one over another with rigour.

And if ye will not for all this hearken unto me, but walk contrary unto me, then I will walk contrary unto you also in fury; and I, even I, will chastise you seven times for your sins.

And ye shall eat the flesh of your sons, and the flesh of your daughters shall ye eat. And I will destroy your high places and cut down your images, and cast your carcasses upon the carcasses of your idols, and my soul shall abhor you. And I will make your cities waste, and bring your sanctuaries unto desolation, and I will not smell the savour of your sweet odours.

And I will bring the land into desolation: and your enemies which dwell therein shall be astonished at it. And I will scatter you among the heathen, and will draw out a sword after you: and your land shall be desolate and your cities waste.

Then shall the land enjoy her sabbaths, as long as it lieth desolate, and ye be in your enemies' land; even then shall the land rest, and enjoy her sabbaths. As long as it lieth desolate it shall rest; because it did not rest in your sabbaths, when ye dwelt upon it.

The Fourth Book of Moses, Called
NUMBERS

Moses Numbers the People

And the Lord spake unto Moses in the wilderness of Sinai, in the tabernacle of the congregation, on the first day of the second month, in the second year after they were come out of the land of Egypt, saying, Take ye the sum of all the congregation of the children of Israel, after their families, by the house of their fathers, with the number of their names, every male by their polls: from twenty years old and upward, all that are able to go forth to war in Israel; thou and Aaron shall number them by their armies. And with you there shall be a man of every tribe; every one head of the house of his fathers.

And Moses and Aaron took these men, and they assembled all the congregation together on the first day of the second month, and they declared their pedigrees after their families, by the house of their fathers, according to the number of the names, from twenty years old and upward, by their polls.

So were all those that were numbered of the children of Israel, by the house of their fathers, from twenty years old and upward, all that were able to go forth to war in Israel; even all they that were numbered, were six hundred thousand and three thousand and five hundred and fifty.

But the Levites, after the tribe of their fathers, were not numbered among them. For the Lord had spoken unto Moses, saying, Only thou shalt not number the tribe of Levi, neither take the sum of them among the children of Israel: but thou shalt appoint the Levites over the tabernacle of testimony, and over all the vessels thereof, and over all things that belong to it: they shall bear the tabernacle, and all the vessels thereof, and they shall minister unto it, and shall encamp round about the tabernacle.

And when the tabernacle setteth forward, the Levites shall take it down; and when the tabernacle is to be pitched, the Levites shall set it up: and the stranger that cometh nigh shall be put to death.

And the children of Israel shall pitch their tents, every man by his own camp, and every man by his own standard, throughout their hosts. But the Levites shall pitch round about the tabernacle of testimony; that there be no wrath upon the congregation of the children of Israel: and the Levites shall keep the charge of the tabernacle of testimony.

And the children of Israel did according to all that the Lord commanded Moses, so did they.

The Law of the Nazarite

And the Lord spake unto Moses, saying, Speak unto the children of Israel, and say unto them, When either man or woman shall separate themselves to vow a vow of a Nazarite, to separate themselves unto the Lord: he shall separate himself from wine and strong drink, and shall drink no vinegar of wine, or vinegar of strong drink, neither shall he drink any liquor of grapes, nor eat moist grapes, or dried. All the days of his separation shall he eat nothing that is made of the vine-tree, from the kernels even to the husk.

All the days of the vow of his separation there shall no razor come upon his head: until the days be fulfilled, in the which he separateth himself unto the Lord, he shall be holy, and shall let the locks of the hair of his head grow.

All the days that he separateth himself unto the Lord, he shall come at no dead body. He shall not make himself unclean for his father, or for his mother, for his brother, or for his sister, when they die: because the consecration of his God is upon his head. All the days of his separation he is holy unto the Lord.

And if any man die very suddenly by him, and he hath defiled the head of his consecration; then he shall shave his head in the day of his cleansing, on the seventh day shall he shave it. And on the eighth day he shall bring two turtles, or two young pigeons, to the priest, to the door of the tabernacle of the congregation: and the priest shall offer the one for a sin-offering, and the other for a burnt-offering, and make an atonement for him, for that he sinned by the dead, and shall hallow his head that same day. And he shall consecrate unto the Lord the days of his separation, and shall bring a lamb of the first year for a trespass-offering: but the days that were before shall be lost, because his separation was defiled.

This is the law of the Nazarite who hath vowed, and of his offering unto the Lord for his separation, besides that that his hand shall get: according to the vow which he vowed, so he must do after the law of his separation.

The Lord's Blessing

And the Lord spake unto Moses, saying, Speak unto Aaron and unto his sons, saying, On this wise ye shall bless the children of Israel, saying unto them,
The Lord bless thee, and keep thee:
The Lord make his face shine upon thee, and be gracious unto thee:
The Lord lift up his countenance upon thee, and give thee peace.
And they shall put my name upon the children of Israel, and I will bless them.

The Cloud and Fire Lead

And on the day that the tabernacle was reared up, the cloud covered the tabernacle, namely, the tent of the testimony: and at even there was upon the tabernacle as it were the appearance of fire, until the morning. So it was always: the cloud covered it by day, and the appearance of fire by night.

And when the cloud was taken up from the tabernacle, then after that the children of Israel journeyed: and in the place where the cloud abode, there the children of Israel pitched their tents. At the commandment of the Lord the children of Israel journeyed; and at the commandment of the Lord they pitched: as long as the cloud abode upon the tabernacle they rested in their tents.

And when the cloud tarried long upon the tabernacle many days, then the children of Israel kept the charge of the Lord, and journeyed not.

And so it was, when the cloud was a few days upon the tabernacle; according to the commandment of the Lord they abode in their tents, and according to the commandment of the Lord they journeyed. And so it was, when the cloud abode from even unto the morning, and that the cloud was taken up in the morning, then they journeyed; whether it was by day or by night that the cloud was taken up, they journeyed. Or whether it were two days, or a month, or a year, that the cloud tarried upon the tabernacle, remaining thereon, the children of Israel abode in their tents, and journeyed not: but when it was taken up, they journeyed.

At the commandment of the Lord they rested in their tents, and at the commandment of the Lord they journeyed: they kept the charge of the Lord, at the commandment of the Lord by the hand of Moses.

Spies Are Sent to Canaan

And the Lord spake unto Moses, saying, Send thou men, that they may search the land of Canaan, which I give unto the children of Israel: of every tribe of their fathers shall ye send a man, every one a ruler among them.

And Moses by the commandment of the Lord sent them from the wilderness of Paran: all those men were heads of the children of Israel.

And Moses sent them to spy out the land of Canaan, and said unto them, Get you up this way southward, and go up into the mountain: and see the land, what it is; and the people that dwelleth therein, whether they be strong or weak, few or many; and what the land is that they dwell in, whether it be good or bad; and what cities they be that they dwell in, whether in tents, or in strong holds; and what the land is, whether it be fat or lean, whether there be wood therein, or not. And be ye of good courage, and bring of the fruit of the land.

Now the time was the time of the first ripe grapes.

So they went up, and searched the land from the wilderness of Zin unto Rehob, as men come to Hamath. And they ascended by the south, and came unto Hebron; where Ahiman, Sheshai, and Talmai, the children of Anak, were. (Now Hebron was built seven years before Zoan in Egypt.)

And they came unto the brook of Eshcol, and cut down from thence a branch with one cluster of grapes, and they bare it between two upon a staff; and they brought of the pomegranates, and of the figs.

And they returned from searching of the land after forty days.

And they went and came to Moses, and to Aaron, and to all the congregation of the children of Israel, unto the wilderness of Paran, to Kadesh; and brought back word unto them, and unto all the congregation, and shewed them the fruit of the land.

And they told him, and said, We came unto the land whither thou sentest us, and surely it floweth with milk and honey; and this is the fruit of it. Nevertheless, the people be strong that dwell in the land, and the cities are walled, and very great: and moreover, we saw the children of Anak there. The Amalekites dwell in the land of the south: and the Hittites, and the Jebusites, and the Amorites, dwell in the mountains; and the Canaanites dwell by the sea, and by the coast of Jordan.

And Caleb stilled the people before Moses, and said, Let us go up at once, and possess it; for we are well able to overcome it. But the men that went up with him said, We be not able to go up against the people; for they are stronger than we. And they brought up an evil report of the land which they had searched unto the children of Israel, saying, The land, through which we have gone to search it, is a land that eateth up the inhabitants thereof; and all the people that we saw in it are men of a great stature. And there we saw the giants, the sons of Anak, which come of the giants: and we were in our own sight as grasshoppers, and so we were in their sight.

The Water of Meribah

Then came the children of Israel, even the whole congregation, into the desert of Zin the first month: and the people abode in Kadesh; and Miriam died there, and was buried there.

And there was no water for the congregation: and they gathered themselves together against Moses and against Aaron. And the people chode with Moses, and spake, saying, Would God that we had died when our brethren died before the Lord!

And why have ye brought up the congregation of the Lord into this wilderness, that we and our cattle should die there? And wherefore have ye made us to come up out of Egypt, to bring us unto this evil place? it is no place of seed, or of figs, or of vines, or of pomegranates; neither is there any water to drink.

And Moses and Aaron went from the presence of the assembly unto the door of the tabernacle of the congregation, and they fell upon their faces and the glory of the Lord appeared unto them.

And the Lord spake unto Moses, saying: Take the rod, and gather thou the assembly together, thou and Aaron thy brother, and speak ye unto the rock before their eyes; and it shall give forth his water, and thou shalt bring forth to them water out of the rock: so thou shalt give the congregation and their beasts drink.

And Moses took the rod from before the Lord, as he commanded him. And Moses and Aaron gathered the congregation together before the rock, and he said unto them, Hear now, ye rebels; must we fetch you water out of this rock?

And Moses lifted up his hand, and with his rod he smote the rock twice: and the water came out abundantly, and the congregation drank, and their beasts also.

And the Lord spake unto Moses and Aaron, Because ye believed me not, to sanctify me in the eyes of the children of Israel, therefore ye shall not bring this congregation into the land which I have given them. This is the water of Meribah; because the children of Israel strove with the Lord, and he was sanctified in them.

The Death of Aaron

And the Lord spake unto Moses and Aaron in mount Hor, by the coast of the land of Edom, saying, Aaron shall be gathered unto his people: for he shall not enter into the land which I have given unto the children of Israel, because ye rebelled against my word at the water of Meribah.

Take Aaron and Eleazar his son, and bring them up unto mount Hor: and strip Aaron of his garments, and put them upon Eleazar his son: and Aaron shall be gathered unto his people, and shall die there.

And Moses did as the Lord commanded: and they went up into mount Hor in the sight of all the congregation.

And Moses stripped Aaron of his garments, and put them upon Eleazar his son; and Aaron died there in the top of the mount: and Moses and Eleazar came down from the mount.

And when all the congregation saw that Aaron was dead, they mourned for Aaron thirty days, even all the house of Israel.

The Bronze Serpent

And when king Arad the Canaanite, which dwelt in the south, heard tell that Israel came by the way of the spies; then he fought against Israel, and took some of them prisoners. And Israel vowed a vow unto the Lord, and said, If thou wilt indeed deliver this people into my hand, then I will utterly destroy their cities. And the Lord hearkened to the voice of Israel, and delivered up the Canaanites; and they utterly destroyed them and their cities: and he called the name of the place Hormah.

And they journeyed from mount Hor by the way of the Red sea, to compass the land of Edom: and the soul of the people was much discouraged because of the way. And the people spake against God, and against Moses, Wherefore have ye brought us up out of Egypt to die in the wilderness? for there is no bread, neither is there any water; and our soul loatheth this light bread.

And the Lord sent fiery serpents among the people, and they bit the people; and much people of Israel died.

Therefore the people came to Moses, and said, We have sinned, for we have spoken against the Lord, and against thee; pray unto the Lord, that he take away the serpents from us. And Moses prayed for the people.

And the Lord said unto Moses, Make thee a fiery serpent, and set it upon a pole: and it shall come to pass, that every one that is bitten, when he looketh upon it, shall live. And Moses made a serpent of brass, and put it upon a pole, and it came to pass, that if a serpent had bitten any man, when he beheld the serpent of brass, he lived.

An Angel Meets Balaam

And the children of Israel set forward, and pitched in the plains of Moab on this side Jordan by Jericho. And Moab was sore afraid of the people, because they were many: and Moab was distressed because of the children of Israel.

And Moab said unto the elders of Midian, Now shall this company lick up all that are round about us, as the ox licketh up the grass of the field.

And Balak the son of Zippor was king of the Moabites at that time. He sent messengers therefore unto Balaam the son of Beor to Pethor, which is by the river of the land of the children of his people, to call him, saying, Behold, there is a people come out from Egypt: behold, they cover the face of the earth, and they abide over against me: come now therefore, I pray thee, curse me this people; for they are too mighty for me: peradventure I shall prevail, that we may smite them, and that I may drive them out of the land: for I wot that he whom thou blessest is blessed, and he whom thou cursest is cursed.

And God came unto Balaam, and said, What men are these with thee?

And Balaam said unto God, Balak the son of Zippor, king of Moab, hath sent unto me, saying, Behold, there is a people come out of Egypt, which covereth the face of the earth: come now, curse me them; peradventure I shall be able to overcome them, and drive them out.

And God said unto Balaam, Thou shalt not go with them; thou shalt not curse the people: for they are blessed.

And Balaam rose up in the morning, and said unto the princes of Balak, Get you into your land: for the Lord refuseth to give me leave to go with you. And the princes of Moab rose up, and they went unto Balak, and said, Balaam refuseth to come with us.

And Balak sent yet again princes, more, and more honourable than they. And they came to Balaam, and said to him, Thus saith Balak the son of Zippor, Let nothing, I pray thee, hinder thee from coming unto me: for I will promote thee unto very great honour, and I will do whatsoever thou sayest unto me: come therefore, I pray thee, curse me this people.

And God came unto Balaam at night, and said unto him, If the men come to call thee, rise up, and go with them; but yet the word which I shall say unto thee, that shalt thou do. And Balaam rose up in the morning, and saddled his ass, and went with the princes of Moab.

And God's anger was kindled because he went: and the angel of the Lord stood in the way for an adversary against him. Now he was riding upon his ass, and his two servants were with him. And the ass saw the angel of the Lord standing in the way, and his sword drawn in his hand: and the ass turned aside out of the way, and went into the field: and Balaam smote the ass, to turn her into the way.

But the angel of the Lord stood in a path of the vineyards, a wall being on this side, and a wall on that side. And when the ass saw the angel of the Lord, she thrust herself unto the wall, and crushed Balaam's foot against the wall: and he smote her again.

And the angel of the Lord went further, and stood in a narrow place where was no way to turn either to the right hand or to the left. And when the ass saw the angel of the Lord, she fell down under Balaam: and Balaam's anger was kindled, and he smote the ass with a staff.

And the Lord opened the mouth of the ass, and she said unto Balaam, What have I done unto thee, that thou hast smitten me these three times?

And Balaam said unto the ass, Because thou hast mocked me: I would there were a sword in mine hand, for now would I kill thee.

And the ass said unto Balaam, Am not I thine ass, upon which thou hast ridden ever since I was thine unto this day? was I ever wont to do so unto thee? And he said, Nay.

Then the Lord opened the eyes of Balaam, and he saw the angel of the Lord standing in the way, and his sword drawn in his hand: and he bowed down his head, and fell flat on his face.

And the angel of the Lord said unto him, Wherefore hast thou smitten thine ass these three times? behold, I went out to withstand thee, because thy way is perverse before me: and the ass saw me, and turned from me these three times: unless she had turned from me, surely now also I had slain thee, and saved her alive.

And Balaam said unto the angel of the Lord, I have sinned; for I knew not that thou stoodest in the way against me: now therefore, if it displease thee, I will get me back again.

And the angel of the Lord said unto Balaam, Go with the men: but only the word that I shall speak unto thee, that thou shalt speak: so Balaam went with the princes of Balak.

And when Balak heard that Balaam was come, he went out to meet him unto a city of Moab, which is in the border of Arnon, which is in the utmost coast.

And it came to pass on the morrow, that Balak took Balaam, and brought him up into the high places of Baal, that thence he might see the utmost part of the people.

Balaam Blesses the Israelites

And Balaam said unto Balak, Build me here seven altars, and prepare me here seven oxen and seven rams. And Balak did as Balaam had spoken; and Balak and Balaam offered on every altar a bullock and a ram.

And Balaam said unto Balak, Stand by thy burnt-offering, and I will go; peradventure the Lord will come to meet me: and whatsoever he sheweth me I will tell thee. And he went to an high place.

And God met Balaam: and he said unto him, I have prepared seven altars, and I have offered upon every altar a bullock and a ram.

And the Lord put a word in Balaam's mouth, and said, Return unto Balak, and thus thou shalt speak. And he returned unto him, and lo, he stood by his burnt-sacrifice, he, and all the princes of Moab.

And he took up his parable, and said, Balak the king of Moab hath brought me from Aram, out of the mountains of the east, saying, Come, curse me Jacob, and come, defy Israel.

How shall I curse, whom God hath not cursed? or how shall I defy, whom the Lord hath not defied?

For from the top of the rocks I see him, and from the hills I behold him: lo, the people shall dwell alone, and shall not be reckoned among the nations.

Who can count the dust of Jacob, and the number of the fourth part of Israel? Let me die the death of the righteous, and let my last end be like his!

And Balak said unto Balaam, What hast thou done unto me? I took thee to curse mine enemies, and behold, thou hast blessed them altogether.

And he answered and said, Must I not take heed to speak that which the Lord hath put in my mouth?

The Law of Inheritance

And the Lord spake unto Moses, saying:

And thou shalt speak unto the children of Israel, saying, If a man die, and have no son, then ye shall cause his inheritance to pass unto his daughter.

And if he have no daughter, then ye shall give his inheritance unto his brethren.

And if he have no brethren, then ye shall give his inheritance unto his father's brethren.

And if his father have no brethren, then ye shall give his inheritance unto his kinsman that is next to him of his family, and he shall possess it: and it shall be unto the children of Israel a statute of judgment, as the Lord commanded Moses.

Joshua Appointed to Succeed Moses

And the Lord said unto Moses, Get thee up into this mount Abarim, and see the land which I have given unto the children of Israel. And when thou hast seen it, thou also shalt be gathered unto thy people, as Aaron thy brother was gathered. For ye rebelled against my commandment in the desert of Zin, in the strife of the congregation, to sanctify me at the water before their eyes: that is the water of Meribah in Kadesh in the wilderness of Zin.

And Moses spake unto the Lord, saying, Let the Lord, the God of the spirits of all flesh, set a man over the congregation, which may go out before them, and which may go in before them, and which may lead them out, and which may bring them in; that the congregation of the Lord be not as sheep which have no shepherd.

And the Lord said unto Moses, Take thee Joshua the son of Nun, a man in whom is the spirit, and lay thine hand upon him; and set him before Eleazar the priest, and before all the congregation: and give him a charge in their sight. And thou shalt put some of thine honour upon him, that all the congregation of the children of Israel may be obedient.

And he shall stand before Eleazar the priest, who shall ask counsel for him after the judgment of Urim before the Lord: at his word shall they go out, and at his word they shall come in, both he, and all the children of Israel with him, even all the congregation.

And Moses did as the Lord commanded him: and he took Joshua, and set him before Eleazar the priest, and before all the congregation: and he laid his hands upon him, and gave him a charge as the Lord commanded by the hand of Moses.

Exogamy Is Discouraged

And Moses commanded the children of Israel according to the word of the Lord, saying, The tribe of the sons of Joseph hath said well.

This is the thing which the Lord doth command concerning the daughters of Zelophehad, saying, Let them marry to whom they think best; only to the family of the tribe of their father shall they marry. So shall not the inheritance of the children of Israel remove from tribe to tribe: for every one of the children of Israel shall keep himself to the inheritance of the tribe of his fathers.

And every daughter, that possesseth an inheritance in any tribe of the children of Israel, shall be wife unto one of the family of the tribe of her father, that the children of Israel may enjoy every man the inheritance of his fathers.

Neither shall the inheritance remove from one tribe to another tribe; but every one of the tribes of the children of Israel shall keep himself to his own inheritance.

These are the commandments and the judgments, which the Lord commanded by the hand of Moses unto the children of Israel in the plains of Moab by Jordan near Jericho.

The Fifth Book of Moses, Called
DEUTERONOMY

*These be the words which Moses spake unto all Israel on this side
Jordan in the wilderness, in the plain over against the Red sea, between
Paran, and Tophel, and Laban, and Hazeroth, and Dizahab.*

The Plea of Moses

And I besought the Lord, saying, O Lord God, thou hast begun to
shew thy servant thy greatness, and thy mighty hand: for what God is
there in heaven or in earth, that can do according to thy works, and
according to thy might? I pray thee, let me go over, and see the good
land that is beyond Jordan, that goodly mountain, and Lebanon.

But the Lord was wroth with me for your sakes, and would not hear
me: and the Lord said unto me, Let it suffice thee; speak no more unto
me of this matter. Get thee up into the top of Pisgah, and lift up thine
eyes westward, and northward, and southward, and eastward, and behold it with thine eyes: for thou shalt not go over this Jordan. But
charge Joshua, and encourage him, and strengthen him: for he shall go
over before this people, and he shall cause them to inherit the land
which thou shalt see.

So we abode in the valley over against Beth-peor.

For a Sign upon Thine Hand

Hear, O Israel: The Lord our God is one Lord:

And thou shalt love the Lord thy God with all thine heart, and with all thy soul, and with all thy might.

And these words which I command thee this day, shall be in thine heart: and thou shalt teach them diligently unto thy children, and shalt talk of them when thou sittest in thine house, and when thou walkest by the way, and when thou liest down, and when thou risest up.

And thou shalt bind them for a sign upon thine hand, and they shall be as frontlets between thine eyes. And thou shalt write them upon the posts of thy house, and on thy gates.

And it shall be, when the Lord thy God shall have brought thee into the land which he sware unto thy fathers, to Abraham, to Isaac, and to Jacob, to give thee great and goodly cities, which thou buildest not, and houses full of all good things which thou filledst not, and wells digged, which thou diggedst not, vineyards and olive-trees, which thou plantedst not; when thou shalt have eaten and be full; then beware lest thou forget the Lord, which brought thee forth out of the land of Egypt, from the house of bondage.

Ye shall diligently keep the commandments of the Lord your God, and his testimonies, and his statutes, which he hath commanded thee. And thou shalt do that which is right and good in the sight of the Lord: that it may be well with thee, and that thou mayest go in and possess the good land which the Lord sware unto thy fathers.

A Warning against Self-Righteousness

Hear, O Israel: Thou art to pass over Jordan this day, to go in to possess nations greater and mightier than thyself, cities great and fenced up to heaven, a people great and tall, the children of the Anakims, whom thou knowest, and of whom thou hast heard say, Who can stand before the children of Anak?

Understand therefore this day, that the Lord thy God is he which goeth over before thee: as a consuming fire he shall destroy them, and he shall bring them down before thy face: so shalt thou drive them out, and destroy them quickly, as the Lord hath said unto thee.

Speak not thou in thine heart, after that the Lord thy God hath cast them out from before thee, saying, For my righteousness the Lord hath brought me in to possess the land: but for the wickedness of these nations the Lord doth drive them out from before thee. Not for thy righteousness, or for the uprightness of thine heart dost thou go to possess their land: but for the wickedness of these nations, the Lord thy God doth drive them out from before thee, and that he may perform the word which the Lord sware unto thy fathers, Abraham, Isaac, and Jacob. Understand therefore, that the Lord thy God giveth thee not this good land to possess it for thy righteousness; for thou art a stiff-necked people.

God's Goodness to Israel

At that time the Lord said unto me, Hew thee two tables of stone like unto the first, and come up unto me into the mount, and make thee an ark of wood. And I will write on the tables the words that were in the first tables which thou brakest, and thou shalt put them in the ark.

And I made an ark of shittim-wood, and hewed two tables of stone like unto the first, and went up into the mount, having the two tables in mine hand. And he wrote on the tables, according to the first writing, the ten commandments, which the Lord spake unto you in the mount, out of the midst of the fire, in the day of the assembly: and the Lord gave them unto me. And I turned myself and came down from the mount, and put the tables in the ark which I had made; and there they be, as the Lord commanded me.

And the children of Israel took their journey from Beeroth of the children of Jaakan to Mosera: there Aaron died, and there he was buried; and Eleazar his son ministered in the priest's office in his stead. From thence they journeyed unto Gudgodah; and from Gudgodah to Jotbath, a land of rivers of waters.

At that time the Lord separated the tribe of Levi, to bear the ark of the covenant of the Lord, to stand before the Lord to minister unto him, and to bless in his name, unto this day. Wherefore Levi hath no part nor inheritance with his brethren; the Lord is his inheritance, according as the Lord thy God promised him.

And I stayed in the mount, according to the first time, forty days and forty nights; and the Lord hearkened unto me at that time also, and the Lord would not destroy thee. And the Lord said unto me, Arise, take thy journey before the people, that they may go in and possess the land which I sware unto their fathers to give unto them.

And now, Israel, what doth the Lord thy God require of thee but to fear the Lord thy God, to walk in all his ways, and to love him, and to serve the Lord thy God with all thy heart and with all thy soul, to keep the commandments of the Lord, and his statutes, which I command thee this day for thy good? Behold, the heaven and the heaven of heavens is the Lord's thy God, the earth also, with all that therein is. Only the Lord had a delight in thy fathers to love them, and he chose their seed after them, even you above all people, as it is this day.

Circumcise therefore the foreskin of your heart, and be no more stiff-necked.

For the Lord your God is God of gods, and Lord of lords, a great God, a mighty, and a terrible, which regardeth not persons, nor taketh reward: he doth execute the judgment of the fatherless and widow, and loveth the stranger, in giving him food and raiment. Love ye therefore the stranger: for ye were strangers in the land of Egypt.

Thou shalt fear the Lord thy God; him shalt thou serve, and to him shalt thou cleave, and swear by his name. He is thy praise, and he is thy God, that hath done for thee these great and terrible things which thine eyes have seen. Thy fathers went down into Egypt with three score and ten persons; and now the Lord thy God hath made thee as the stars of heaven for multitude.

The Law of Release

And the end of every seven years thou shalt make a release. And this is the manner of the release: Every creditor that lendeth aught unto his neighbour shall release it; he shall not exact it of his neighbour, or of his brother; because it is called the Lord's release.

Of a foreigner thou mayest exact it again: but that which is thine with thy brother thine hand shall release: save when there shall be no poor among you; for the Lord shall greatly bless thee in the land which the Lord thy God giveth thee for an inheritance to possess it: only if thou carefully hearken unto the voice of the Lord thy God, to observe to do all these commandments which I command thee this day.

For the Lord thy God blesseth thee, as he promised thee: and thou shalt lend unto many nations, but thou shalt not borrow; and thou shalt reign over many nations, but they shall not reign over thee.

If there be among you a poor man of one of thy brethren within any of thy gates in thy land which the Lord thy God giveth thee, thou shalt not harden thy heart, nor shut thine hand from thy poor brother: but thou shalt open thine hand wide unto him, and shalt surely lend him sufficient for his need, in that which he wanteth.

Beware that there be not a thought in thy wicked heart, saying, The seventh year, the year of release, is at hand; and thine eye be evil against thy poor brother, and thou givest him nought; and he cry unto the Lord against thee, nd it be sin unto thee. Thou shalt surely give him, and thine heart shall not be grieved when thou givest unto him: because that for this thing the Lord thy God shall bless thee in all thy works, and in all that thou puttest thine hand unto.

For the poor shall never cease out of the land: therefore I command thee, saying, Thou shalt open thine hand wide unto thy brother, to thy poor, and to thy needy, in thy land.

The Observance of Holy Days

Observe the month of Abib, and keep the passover unto the Lord thy God: for in the month of Abib the Lord thy God brought thee forth out of Egypt by night. Thou shalt therefore sacrifice the passover unto the Lord thy God, of the flock and the herd, in the place which the Lord shall choose to place his name there.

Thou shalt eat no leavened bread with it; seven days shalt thou eat unleavened bread therewith, even the bread of affliction; (for thou camest forth out of the land of Egypt in haste:) that thou mayest remember the day when thou camest forth out of the land of Egypt, all the days of thy life. And there shall be no leavened bread seen with thee in all thy coasts seven days; neither shall there anything of the flesh, which thou sacrificedst the first day at even, remain all night until the morning.

Thou mayest not sacrifice the passover within any of thy gates, which the Lord thy God giveth thee: but at the place which the Lord thy God shall choose to place his name in, there thou shalt sacrifice the passover at even, at the going down of the sun, at the season that thou camest forth out of Egypt. And thou shalt roast and eat it in the place which the Lord thy God shall choose: and thou shalt turn in the morning, and go unto thy tents. Six days thou shalt eat unleavened bread: and on the seventh day shall be a solemn assembly to the Lord thy God: thou shalt do no work therein.

Seven weeks shalt thou number unto thee: begin to number the seven weeks from such time as thou beginnest to put the sickle to the corn. And thou shalt keep the feast of weeks unto the Lord thy God with a tribute of a free-will-offering of thine hand, which thou shalt give unto the Lord thy God, according as the Lord thy God hath blessed thee: and thou shalt rejoice before the Lord thy God, thou, and thy son, and thy daughter, and thy man-servant, and thy maid-servant, and the Levite that is within thy gates, and the stranger, and the fatherless, and the widow, that are among you, in the place which the Lord thy God hath chosen to place his name there.

And thou shalt remember that thou wast a bond-man in Egypt: and thou shalt observe and do these statutes.

Thou shalt observe the feast of tabernacles seven days, after that thou hast gathered in thy corn, and thy wine. And thou shalt rejoice in thy feast, thou, and thy son, and thy daughter, and thy man-servant, and thy maid-servant, and the Levite, the stranger, and the fatherless, and the widow, that are within thy gates: seven days shalt thou keep a solemn feast unto the Lord thy God in the place which the Lord shall choose: because the Lord thy God shall bless thee in all thine increase, and in all the works of thine hands, therefore thou shalt surely rejoice.

Three times in a year shall all thy males appear before the Lord thy God in the place which he shall choose; in the feast of unleavened bread, and in the feast of weeks, and in the feast of tabernacles: and they shall not appear before the Lord empty: every man shall give as he is able, according to the blessing of the Lord thy God which he hath given thee.

Judges and officers shalt thou make thee in all thy gates, which the

Lord thy God giveth thee, throughout thy tribes: and they shall judge the people with just judgment.

Thou shalt not wrest judgment; thou shalt not respect persons, neither take a gift: for a gift doth blind the eyes of the wise, and pervert the words of the righteous. That which is altogether just shalt thou follow, that thou mayest live, and inherit the land which the Lord thy God giveth thee.

Trial and Punishment

If there be found among you, within any of thy gates which the Lord thy God giveth thee, man or woman that hath wrought wickedness in the sight of the Lord thy God, in transgressing his covenant, and hath gone and served other gods, and worshipped them, either the sun, or moon, or any of the host of heaven, which I have not commanded; and it be told thee, and thou hast heard of it, and inquired diligently, and behold, it be true, and the thing certain, that such abomination is wrought in Israel: then shalt thou bring forth that man or that woman, which have committed that wicked thing, unto thy gates, even that man or that woman, and shalt stone them with stones, till they die.

At the mouth of two witnesses, or three witnesses, shall he that is worthy of death be put to death; but at the mouth of one witness he shall not be put to death. The hands of the witnesses shall be first upon him to put him to death, and afterward the hands of all the people. So thou shalt put the evil away from among you.

The Duty of Kings

When thou art come unto the land which the Lord thy God giveth thee, and shalt possess it, and shalt dwell therein, and shalt say, I will set a king over me, like as all the nations that are about me; thou shalt in any wise set him king over thee whom the Lord thy God shall choose: one from among thy brethren shalt thou set king over thee: thou mayest not set a stranger over thee, which is not thy brother.

But he shall not multiply horses to himself, nor cause the people to return to Egypt, to the end that he should multiply horses: forasmuch as the Lord hath said unto you, Ye shall henceforth return no more that way. Neither shall he multiply wives to himself, that his heart turn not away: neither shall he greatly multiply to himself silver and gold.

And it shall be when he sitteth upon the throne of his kingdom, that he shall write him a copy of this law in a book out of that which is before the priests the Levites. And it shall be with him, and he shall read therein all the days of his life: that he may learn to fear the Lord his God, to keep all the words of this law and these statutes, to do them: that his heart be not lifted up above his brethren, and that he turn not aside from the commandment to the right hand, or to the left: to the end that he may prolong his days in his kingdom, he, and his children, in the midst of Israel.

The Inheritance of Priests

The priests the Levites, and all the tribe of Levi, shall have no part nor inheritance with Israel: they shall eat the offerings of the Lord made by fire, and his inheritance. Therefore shall they have no inheritance among their brethren: the Lord is their inheritance, as he hath said unto them.

And this shall be the priest's due from the people, from them that offer a sacrifice, whether it be ox or sheep; and they shall give unto the priest the shoulder, and the two cheeks, and the maw.

The first-fruit also of thy corn, of thy wine, and of thine oil, and the first of the fleece of thy sheep, shalt thou give him.

For the Lord thy God hath chosen him out of all thy tribes, to stand to minister in the name of the Lord, him and his sons for ever.

The Coming of a Prophet Foretold

And the Lord said unto me, They have well spoken that which they have spoken. I will raise them up a Prophet from among their brethren, like unto thee, and will put my words in his mouth; and he shall speak unto them all that I shall command him. And it shall come to pass, that whosoever will not hearken unto my words which he shall speak in my name, I will require it of him.

But the prophet, which shall presume to speak a word in my name, which I have not commanded him to speak, or that shall speak in the name of other gods, even that prophet shall die.

And if thou say in thine heart, How shall we know the word which the Lord hath not spoken? When a prophet speaketh in the name of the Lord, if the thing follow not, nor come to pass, that is the thing which the Lord hath not spoken, but the prophet hath spoken it presumptuously: thou shalt not be afraid of him.

The Law of False Witness

If a false witness rise up against any man to testify against him that which is wrong; then both the men between whom the controversy is shall stand before the Lord, before the priests and the judges, which shall be in those days; and the judges shall make diligent inquisition; and behold, if the witness be a false witness, and hath testified falsely against his brother; then shall ye do unto him, as he had thought to have done unto his brother: so shalt thou put the evil away from among you.

And those which remain shall hear, and fear, and shall henceforth commit no more any such evil among you. And thine eye shall not pity; but life shall go for life, eye for eye, tooth for tooth, hand for hand, foot for foot.

The God of War

When thou goest out to battle against thine enemies, and seest horses, and chariots, and a people more than thou, be not afraid of them: for the Lord thy God is with thee, which brought thee up out of the land of Egypt.

And it shall be when ye are come nigh unto the battle, that the priest shall approach and speak unto the people, and shall say unto them, Hear, O Israel, ye approach this day unto battle against your enemies: let not your hearts faint, fear not, and do not tremble, neither be ye terrified because of them; for the Lord your God is he that goeth with you, to fight for you against your enemies, to save you.

And the officers shall speak unto the people, saying, What man is there that hath built a new house, and hath not dedicated it? let him go and return unto his house, lest he die in the battle, and another man dedicate it. And what man is he that hath planted a vineyard, and hath not yet eaten of it? let him also go and return unto his house, lest he die in the battle, and another man eat of it. And what man is there that hath betrothed a wife, and hath not taken her? let him go and return unto his house, lest he die in the battle, and another man take her.

And the officers shall speak further unto the people, and they shall say, What man is there that is fearful and faint-hearted? let him go and return unto his house, lest his brethren's heart faint as well as his heart.

And it shall be, when the officers have made an end of speaking unto the people, that they shall make captains of the armies to lead the people.

When thou comest nigh unto a city to fight against it, then proclaim peace unto it. And it shall be, if it make the answer of peace, and open unto thee, then it shall be, that all the people that is found therein, shall be tributaries unto thee, and they shall serve thee.

And if it will make no peace with thee, but will make war against thee, then thou shalt besiege it: and when the Lord thy God hath delivered it into thine hands, thou shalt smite every male thereof with the edge of the sword: but the women, and the little ones, and the cattle, and all that is in the city, even all the spoil thereof, shalt thou take unto thyself: and thou shalt eat the spoil of thine enemies, which the Lord thy God hath given thee.

Thus shalt thou do unto all the cities which are very far off from thee, which are not of the cities of these nations.

But of the cities of these people which the Lord thy God doth give thee for an inheritance, thou shalt save alive nothing that breatheth: but thou shalt utterly destroy them, namely, the Hittites, and the Amorites, the Canaanites, and the Perizzites, the Hivites, and the Jebusites, as the Lord thy God hath commanded thee: that they teach you not to do after all their abominations which they have done unto their gods; so should ye sin against the Lord your God.

When thou shalt besiege a city a long time in making war against it to take it, thou shalt not destroy the trees thereof by forcing an axe against them; for thou mayest eat of them: and thou shalt not cut them down (for the tree of the field is man's life) to employ them in the siege: only the trees which thou knowest that they be not trees for meat, thou shalt destroy and cut them down; and thou shalt build bulwarks against the city that maketh war with thee, until it be subdued.

Of Raiment

The woman shall not wear that which pertaineth unto a man, neither shall a man put on a woman's garment: for all that do so are abomination unto the Lord thy God.

Of Those Emasculated and of Bastards

He that is wounded in the stones, or hath his privy member cut off, shall not enter into the congregation of the Lord.

A bastard shall not enter into the congregation of the Lord; even to his tenth generation shall he not enter into the congregation of the Lord.

Of Sanitation

Thou shalt have a place also without the camp, whither thou shalt go forth abroad: and thou shalt have a paddle upon thy weapon: and it shall be when thou wilt ease thyself abroad, thou shalt dig therewith, and shalt turn back, and cover that which cometh from thee.

Of Sanctuary

Thou shalt not deliver unto his master the servant which is escaped from his master unto thee: he shall dwell with thee, even among you in that place which he shall choose in one of thy gates where it liketh him best: thou shalt not oppress him.

The Law of Divorce

When a man hath taken a wife, and married her, and it come to pass that she find no favour in his eyes, because he hath found some uncleanness in her: then let him write her a bill of divorcement, and give it in her hand, and send her out of his house. And when she is departed out of his house, she may go and be another man's wife.

And if the latter husband hate her, and write her a bill of divorcement, and giveth it in her hand, and sendeth her out of his house; or if the latter husband die, which took her to be his wife; her former husband which sent her away, may not take her again to be his wife, after that she is defiled; for that is abomination before the Lord: and thou shalt not cause the land to sin, which the Lord thy God giveth thee for an inheritance.

Of Master and Servant

Thou shalt not oppress an hired servant that is poor and needy, whether he be of thy brethren, or of thy strangers that are in thy land within thy gates: at his day thou shalt give him his hire, neither shall the sun go down upon it, for he is poor, and setteth his heart upon it: lest he cry against thee unto the Lord, and it be sin unto thee.

Of Individual Responsibility

The fathers shall not be put to death for the children, neither shall the children be put to death for the fathers: every man shall be put to death for his own sin.

The Duty of an Husband's Brother

If brethren dwell together, and one of them die and have no child, the wife of the dead shall not marry without unto a stranger: her husband's brother shall go in unto her, and take her to him to wife, and perform the duty of an husband's brother unto her.

And it shall be, that the first-born which she beareth, shall succeed in the name of his brother which is dead, that his name be not put out of Israel.

And if the man like not to take his brother's wife, then let his brother's wife go up to the gate unto the elders, and say, My husband's brother refuseth to raise up unto his brother a name in Israel, he will not perform the duty of my husband's brother.

Then the elders of his city shall call him, and speak unto him: and if he stand to it, and say, I like not to take her, then shall his brother's wife come unto him in the presence of the elders, and loose his shoe from off his foot, and spit in his face, and shall answer and say, So shall it be done unto that man that will not build up his brother's house. And his name shall be called in Israel, The house of him that hath his shoe loosed.

The Cursed of Israel

And the Levites shall speak, and say unto all the men of Israel with a loud voice,

Cursed be the man that maketh any graven or molten image, an abomination unto the Lord, the work of the hands of the craftsman, and putteth it in a secret place: and all the people shall answer and say, Amen.

Cursed be he that setteth light by his father or his mother: and all the people shall say, Amen.

Cursed be he that removeth his neighbour's land-mark: and all the people shall say, Amen.

Cursed be he that maketh the blind to wander out of the way: and all the people shall say, Amen.

Cursed be he that perverteth the judgment of the stranger, fatherless, and widow: and all the people shall say, Amen.

Cursed be he that lieth with his father's wife; because he uncovereth his father's skirt: and all the people shall say, Amen.

Cursed be he that lieth with any manner of beast: and all the people shall say, Amen.

Cursed be he that lieth with his sister, the daughter of his father, or the daughter of his mother: and all the people shall say, Amen.

Cursed be he that lieth with his mother-in-law: and all the people shall say, Amen.

Cursed be he that smiteth his neighbour secretly: and all the people shall say, Amen.

Cursed be he that taketh reward to slay an innocent person: and all the people shall say, Amen.

Cursed be he that confirmeth not all the words of this law to do them: and all the people shall say, Amen.

The Blessed of Israel

And it shall come to pass, if thou shalt hearken diligently unto the voice of the Lord thy God, to observe and to do all his commandments which I command thee this day: that the Lord thy God will set thee on high above all nations of the earth: and all these blessings shall come on thee, and overtake thee, if thou shalt hearken unto the voice of the Lord thy God.

Blessed shalt thou be in the city, and blessed shalt thou be in the field.

Blessed shall be the fruit of thy body, and the fruit of thy ground, and the fruit of thy cattle, the increase of thy kine, and the flocks of thy sheep.

Blessed shall be thy basket and thy store.

Blessed shalt thou be when thou comest in, and blessed shalt thou be when thou goest out.

The Lord shall cause thine enemies that rise up against thee to be smitten before thy face: they shall come out against thee one way, and flee before thee seven ways.

The Lord shall command the blessing upon thee in thy store-houses, and in all that thou settest thine hand unto: and he shall bless thee in the land which the Lord thy God giveth thee.

The Lord shall establish thee an holy people unto himself, as he hath sworn unto thee, if thou shalt keep the commandments of the Lord thy God, and walk in his ways. The Lord shall open unto thee his good treasure, the heaven to give the rain unto thy land in his season, and to bless all the work of thine hand: and thou shalt lend unto many nations, and thou shalt not borrow.

And the Lord shall make thee the head, and not the tail; and thou shalt be above only, and thou shalt not be beneath; if that thou hearken unto the commandments of the Lord thy God, which I command thee this day, to observe and to do them.

If Thou Wilt Not Hearken

But it shall come to pass, if thou wilt not hearken unto the voice of the Lord thy God, to observe to do all his commandments and his statutes which I command thee this day: that all these curses shall come upon thee, and overtake thee:

Cursed shalt thou be in the city, and cursed shalt thou be in the field. Cursed shall be thy basket and thy store. Cursed shall be the fruit of thy body, and the fruit of thy land, the increase of thy kine, and the flocks of thy sheep. Cursed shalt thou be when thou comest in, and cursed shalt thou be when thou goest out.

And thy heaven that is over thy head shall be brass, and the earth that is under thee shall be iron. The Lord shall make the rain of thy land powder and dust: from heaven shall it come down upon thee, until thou be destroyed.

The Lord shall cause thee to be smitten before thine enemies: thou shalt go out one way against them, and flee seven ways before them; and shalt be removed into all the kingdoms of the earth. And thy carcass shall be meat unto all fowls of the air, and unto the beasts of the earth, and no man shall fray them away.

The Lord will smite thee with the botch of Egypt, and with the emerods, and with the scab, and with the itch, whereof thou canst not be healed.

Thou shalt betroth a wife, and another man shall lie with her: thou shalt build an house, and thou shalt not dwell therein: thou shalt plant a vineyard, and shalt not gather the grapes thereof.

And thou shalt become an astonishment, a proverb, and a by-word, among all nations whither the Lord shall lead thee.

And ye shall be left few in number, whereas ye were as the stars of heaven for multitude; because thou wouldest not obey the voice of the Lord thy God.

And the Lord shall scatter thee among all people from the one end of the earth even unto the other; and there thou shalt serve other gods, which neither thou nor thy fathers have known, even wood and stone.

And among these nations shalt thou find no ease, neither shall the sole of thy foot have rest: but the Lord shall give thee there a trembling heart, and failing of eyes, and sorrow of mind. And thy life shall hang in doubt before thee; and thou shalt fear day and night, and shalt have none assurance of thy life.

In the morning thou shalt say, Would God it were even! and at even thou shalt say, Would God it were morning! for the fear of thine heart wherewith thou shalt fear, and for the sight of thine eyes which thou shalt see.

The Song of Moses

And Moses spake in the ears of all the congregation of Israel the words of this song until they were ended:

Give ear, O ye heavens, and I will speak; and hear, O earth, the words of my mouth.

My doctrine shall drop as the rain, my speech shall distil as the dew, as the small rain upon the tender herb, and as the showers upon the grass:

Because I will publish the name of the Lord: ascribe ye greatness unto our God.

He is the Rock, his work is perfect: for all his ways are judgment: a God of truth and without iniquity, just and right is he.

They have corrupted themselves, their spot is not the spot of his children: they are a perverse and crooked generation.

Do ye thus requite the Lord, O foolish people and unwise? is not he thy father that hath bought thee? hath he not made thee, and established thee?

Remember the days of old, consider the years of many generations: ask thy father, and he will shew thee; thy elders, and they will tell thee.

When the Most High divided to the nations their inheritance, when he separated the sons of Adam, he set the bounds of the people according to the number of the children of Israel.

For the Lord's portion is his people; Jacob is the lot of his inheritance.

He found him in a desert land, and in the waste howling wilderness; he led him about, he instructed him, he kept him as the apple of his eye.

As an eagle stirreth up her nest, fluttereth over her young, spreadeth abroad her wings, taketh them, beareth them on her wings;

So the Lord alone did lead him, and there was no strange god with him.

He made him ride on the high places of the earth, that he might eat the increase of the fields; and he made him to suck honey out of the rock, and oil out of the flinty rock;

Butter of kine, and milk of sheep, with fat of lambs, and rams of the breed of Bashan, and goats, with the fat of kidneys of wheat; and thou didst drink the pure blood of the grape.

But Jeshurun waxed fat, and kicked: thou art waxen fat, thou art grown thick, thou art covered with fatness; then he forsook God which made him, and lightly esteemed the Rock of his salvation.

They provoked him to jealousy with strange gods, with abominations provoked they him to anger.

They sacrificed unto devils, not to God; to gods whom they knew not, to new gods that came newly up, whom your fathers feared not.

Of the Rock that begat thee thou art unmindful, and hast forgotten God that formed thee.

And when the Lord saw it, he abhorred them, because of the provoking of his sons, and of his daughters.

And he said, I will hide my face from them, I will see what their end shall be: for they are a very froward generation, children in whom is no faith.

They have moved me to jealousy with that which is not God; they have provoked me to anger with their vanities: and I will move them to jealousy with those which are not a people; I will provoke them to anger with a foolish nation.

For a fire is kindled in mine anger, and shall burn unto the lowest hell, and shall consume the earth with her increase, and set on fire the foundations of the mountains.

I will heap mischiefs upon them; I will spend mine arrows upon them.

They shall be burnt with hunger, and devoured with burning heat, and with bitter destruction: I will also send the teeth of beasts upon them, with the poison of serpents of the dust.

The sword without, and terror within, shall destroy both the young man and the virgin, the suckling also with the man of grey hairs.

I said, I would scatter them into corners, I would make the remembrance of them to cease from among men;

Were it not that I feared the wrath of the enemy, lest their adversaries should behave themselves strangely, and lest they should say, Our hand is high, and the Lord hath not done all this.

For they are a nation void of counsel, neither is there any understanding in them.

O that they were wise, that they understood this, that they would consider their latter end!

How should one chase a thousand, and two put ten thousand to flight, except their Rock had sold them, and the Lord had shut them up?

For their rock is not as our Rock, even our enemies themselves being judges:

For their vine is of the vine of Sodom, and of the fields of Gomorrah: their grapes are grapes of gall, their clusters are bitter:

Their wine is the poison of dragons, and the cruel venom of asps.

Is not this laid up in store with me, and sealed up among my treasures?

To me belongeth vengeance, and recompense; their foot shall slide in due time, for the day of their calamity is at hand, and the things that shall come upon them make haste.

For the Lord shall judge his people, and repent himself for his servants; when he seeth that their power is gone, and there is none shut up, or left.

And he shall say, Where are their gods, their rock in whom they trusted,

Which did eat the fat of their sacrifices, and drank the wine of their drink-offerings? Let them rise up and help you, and be your protection.

See now that I, even I, am he, and there is no god with me: I kill, and I make alive; I wound, and I heal: neither is there any that can deliver out of my hand.

For I lift up my hand to heaven, and say, I live for ever.

If I whet my glittering sword, and mine hand take hold on judgment; I will render vengeance to mine enemies, and will reward them that hate me.

I will make mine arrows drunk with blood, and my sword shall devour flesh; and that with the blood of the slain and of the captives from the beginning of revenges upon the enemy.

Rejoice, O ye nations, with his people; for he will avenge the blood of his servants, and will render vengeance to his adversaries, and will be merciful unto his land, and to his people.

And Moses made an end of speaking all these words to all Israel.

The Death of Moses

And the Lord spake unto Moses that self-same day, saying, Get thee up into this mountain Abarim, unto mount Nebo, which is in the land of Moab, that is over against Jericho; and behold the land of Canaan which I give unto the children of Israel for a possession: and die in the mount whither thou goest up, and be gathered unto thy people; as Aaron thy brother died in mount Hor, and was gathered unto his people: because ye trespassed against me among the children of Israel at the waters of Meribah-Kadesh, in the wilderness of Zin; because ye sanctified me not in the midst of the children of Israel. Yet thou shalt see the land before thee; but thou shalt not go thither unto the land which I give the children of Israel.

And Moses went up from the plains of Moab, unto the mountain of Nebo, to the top of Pisgah, that is over against Jericho: and the Lord shewed him all the land of Gilead, unto Dan, and all Naphtali, and the land of Ephraim, and Manasseh, and all the land of Judah, unto the utmost sea, and the south, and the plain of the valley of Jericho, the city of palm-trees, unto Zoar.

And the Lord said unto him, This is the land which I sware unto Abraham, unto Isaac, and unto Jacob, saying, I will give it unto thy seed: I have caused thee to see it with thine eye, but thou shalt not go over thither.

So Moses the servant of the Lord died there in the land of Moab, according to the word of the Lord. And he buried him in a valley in the land of Moab, over against Beth-peor: but no man knoweth of his sepulchre unto this day.

And Moses was an hundred and twenty years old when he died: his eye was not dim, nor his natural force abated.

And the children of Israel wept for Moses in the plains of Moab thirty days: so the days of weeping and mourning for Moses were ended.

And Joshua the son of Nun was full of the spirit of wisdom; for Moses had laid his hands upon him: and the children of Israel hearkened unto him, and did as the Lord commanded Moses.

And there arose not a prophet since in Israel like unto Moses, whom the Lord knew face to face, in all the signs and the wonders which the Lord sent him to do in the land of Egypt, to Pharaoh, and to all his servants, and to all his land; and in all that mighty hand, and in all the great terror which Moses shewed in the sight of all Israel.

The Book of Joshua

Joshua Takes Command

Now after the death of Moses, the servant of the Lord, it came to pass, that the Lord spake unto Joshua the son of Nun, Moses' minister, saying, Moses my servant is dead; now therefore arise, go over this Jordan, thou and all this people, unto the land which I do give to them, even to the children of Israel.

Every place that the sole of your foot shall tread upon, that have I given unto you, as I said unto Moses. From the wilderness and this Lebanon even unto the great river, the river Euphrates, all the land of the Hittites, and unto the great sea toward the going down of the sun, shall be your coast.

There shall not any man be able to stand before thee all the days of thy life: as I was with Moses, so I will be with thee: I will not fail thee, nor forsake thee. Be strong and of a good courage: for unto this people shalt thou divide for an inheritance the land which I sware unto their fathers to give them.

The People Cross over Jordan

And Joshua rose early in the morning; and they removed from Shittim, and came to Jordan, he and all the children of Israel, and lodged there before they passed over.

And Joshua said unto the children of Israel, Come hither, and hear the words of the Lord your God. Hereby ye shall know that the living God is among you, and that he will without fail drive out from before you the Canaanites, and the Hittites, and the Hivites, and the Perizzites, and the Girgashites, and the Amorites, and the Jebusites. Behold, the ark of the covenant of the Lord of all the earth passeth over before you into Jordan. Now therefore take you twelve men out of the tribes of Israel, out of every tribe a man. And it shall come to pass, as soon as the soles of the feet of the priests that bear the ark of the Lord, the Lord of all the earth, shall rest in the waters of Jordan, that the waters of Jordan shall be cut off from the waters that come down from above; and they shall stand upon an heap.

And it came to pass, when the people removed from their tents to pass over Jordan, and the priests bearing the ark of the covenant before the people; and as they that bare the ark were come unto Jordan, and the feet of the priests that bare the ark were dipped in the brim of the water, (for Jordan overfloweth all his banks all the time of harvest,) that the waters which came down from above stood and rose up upon an heap very far from the city Adam, that is beside Zaretan; and those that came down toward the sea of the plain, even the salt sea, failed, and were cut off: and the people passed over right against Jericho. And the priests that bare the ark of the covenant of the Lord stood firm on dry ground in the midst of Jordan, and all the Israelites passed over on dry ground, until all the people were passed clean over Jordan.

And it came to pass when Joshua was by Jericho, that he lifted up his eyes and looked, and behold, there stood a man over against him with his sword drawn in his hand: and Joshua went unto him, and said unto him, Art thou for us, or for our adversaries?

And he said, Nay; but as captain of the host of the Lord am I now come.

And Joshua fell on his face to the earth, and did worship, and said unto him, What saith my lord unto his servant?

And the captain of the Lord's host said unto Joshua, Loose thy shoe from off thy foot, for the place whereon thou standest is holy: and Joshua did so.

The Fall of Jericho

Now Jericho was straitly shut up, because of the children of Israel: none went out, and none came in.

And the Lord said unto Joshua, See, I have given into thine hand Jericho, and the king thereof, and the mighty men of valour. And ye shall compass the city, all ye men of war, and go round about the city once: thus shalt thou do six days. And seven priests shall bear before the ark seven trumpets of ram's horns: and the seventh day ye shall compass the city seven times, and the priests shall blow with the trumpets. And it shall come to pass, that when they make a long blast with the ram's horn, and when ye hear the sound of the trumpet, all the people shall shout with a great shout: and the wall of the city shall fall down flat, and the people shall ascend up every man straight before him.

And it came to pass, when Joshua had spoken unto the people, that the seven priests bearing the seven trumpets of ram's horns passed on before the Lord, and blew with the trumpets: and the ark of the covenant of the Lord followed them. And the armed men went before the priests that blew with the trumpets, and the rere-ward came after the ark, the priests going on, and blowing with the trumpets. And Joshua had commanded the people, saying, Ye shall not shout, nor make any noise with your voice, neither shall any word proceed out of your mouth, until the day I bid you shout, then shall ye shout. So the ark of the Lord compassed the city, going about it once: and they came into the camp, and lodged in the camp.

And Joshua rose early in the morning, and the priests took up the ark of the Lord. And seven priests bearing seven trumpets of ram's horns before the ark of the Lord went on continually, and blew with the trumpets: and the armed men went before them; but the rere-ward came after the ark of the Lord, the priests going on, and blowing with the trumpets. And the second day they compassed the city once, and returned into the camp. So they did six days.

And it came to pass on the seventh day, that they rose early about the dawning of the day, and compassed the city after the same manner seven times: only on that day they compassed the city seven times.

And it came to pass at the seventh time, when the priests blew with the trumpets, Joshua said unto the people, Shout; for the Lord hath given you the city. And the city shall be accursed, even it, and all that are therein, to the Lord: only Rahab the harlot shall live, she and all that are with her in the house, because she hid the messengers that we sent. And ye, in any wise keep yourselves from the accursed thing, lest ye make yourselves accursed, when ye take of the accursed thing, and make the camp of Israel a curse, and trouble it. But all the silver, and gold, and vessels of brass and iron, are consecrated unto the Lord: they shall come into the treasury of the Lord.

So the people shouted when the priests blew with the trumpets: and it came to pass, when the people heard the sound of the trumpet, and the people shouted with a great shout, that the wall fell down flat, so that the people went up into the city, every man straight before him, and they took the city. And they burnt the city with fire, and all that was therein: only the silver, and the gold, and the vessels of brass and of iron, they put into the treasury of the house of the Lord.

And Joshua saved Rahab the harlot alive, and her father's household and all that she had; and she dwelleth in Israel even unto this day; because she hid the messengers, which Joshua sent to spy out Jericho.

The Sun Stands Still

And the men of Gibeon sent unto Joshua to the camp to Gilgal, saying, Slack not thy hand from thy servants; come up to us quickly, and save us, and help us: for all the kings of the Amorites that dwell in the mountains are gathered together against us. So Joshua ascended from

Gilgal, he, and all the people of war with him, and all the mighty men of valour.

And the Lord said unto Joshua, Fear them not: for I have delivered them into thine hand; there shall not a man of them stand before thee.

Joshua therefore came unto them suddenly, and went up from Gilgal all night. And the Lord discomfited them before Israel, and slew them with a great slaughter at Gibeon, and chased them along the way that goeth up to Beth-horon, and smote them to Azekah, and unto Makkedah. And it came to pass as they fled from before Israel, and were in the going down to Beth-horon, that the Lord cast down great stones from heaven upon them unto Azekah, and they died: they were more which died with hailstones than they whom the children of Israel slew with the sword.

Then spake Joshua to the Lord in the day when the Lord delivered up the Amorites before the children of Israel, and he said in the sight of Israel, Sun, stand thou still upon Gibeon, and thou Moon, in the valley of Ajalon. And the sun stood still, and the moon stayed, until the people had avenged themselves upon their enemies. Is not this written in the book of Jasher? So the sun stood still in the midst of heaven, and hasted not to go down about a whole day. And there was no day like that before it or after it, that the Lord hearkened unto the voice of a man: for the Lord fought for Israel.

Joshua's Conquest Completed

And all the cities of those kings, and all the kings of them, did Joshua take, and smote them with the edge of the sword, and he utterly destroyed them, as Moses the servant of the Lord commanded. But as for the cities that stood still in their strength, Israel burned none of them, save Hazor only; that did Joshua burn. And all the spoil of these cities, and the cattle, the children of Israel took for a prey unto themselves: but every man they smote with the edge of the sword, until they had destroyed them, neither left they any to breathe.

So Joshua took the whole land, according to all that the Lord said unto Moses, and Joshua gave it for an inheritance unto Israel according to their divisions by their tribes. And the land rested from war.

Joshua Instructs His People

And it came to pass, a long time after that the Lord had given rest unto Israel from all their enemies round about, that Joshua waxed old and stricken in age. And Joshua called for all Israel, and for their elders, and for their heads, and for their judges, and for their officers, and said unto them, I am old and stricken in age: and ye have seen all that the Lord your God hath done unto all these nations because of you; for the Lord your God is he that hath fought for you.

Be ye therefore very courageous to keep and to do all that is written in the book of the law of Moses, that ye turn not aside therefrom to the right hand or to the left; that ye come not among these nations, these that remain among you; neither make mention of the name of their gods, nor cause to swear by them, neither serve them, nor bow yourselves unto them: but cleave unto the Lord your God, as ye have done unto this day. For the Lord hath driven out from before you great nations and strong: but as for you, no man hath been able to stand before you unto this day. One man of you shall chase a thousand: for the Lord your God, he it is that fighteth for you, as he hath promised you. Take good heed therefore unto yourselves, that ye love the Lord your God.

And behold, this day I am going the way of all the earth; and ye know in all your hearts and in all your souls, that not one thing hath failed of all the good things which the Lord your God spake concerning you; all are come to pass unto you, and not one thing hath failed thereof.

When ye have transgressed the covenant of the Lord your God, which he commanded you, and have gone and served other gods, and bowed yourselves to them; then shall the anger of the Lord be kindled against you, and ye shall perish quickly from off the good land which he hath given unto you.

The Death of Joshua

And Joshua gathered all the tribes of Israel to Shechem, and called for the elders of Israel, and for their heads, and for their judges, and for their officers; and they presented themselves before God.

And Joshua said unto all the people, Thus saith the Lord God of Israel, Your fathers dwelt on the other side of the flood in old time, even Terah, the father of Abraham, and the father of Nachor: and they served other gods. And I took your father Abraham from the other side of the flood, and led him throughout all the land of Canaan, and multiplied his seed, and gave him Isaac. I sent Moses also and Aaron, and I plagued Egypt, according to that which I did among them: and afterward I brought you out.

And I brought your fathers out of Egypt: and ye came unto the sea; and the Egyptians pursued after your fathers with chariots and horsemen unto the Red sea. And I brought you into the land of the Amorites, which dwelt on the other side of Jordan; and they fought with you: and I gave them into your hand, that ye might possess their land; and I destroyed them from before you. And I have given you a land for which ye did not labour, and cities which ye built not, and ye dwell in them; of the vineyards and olive-yards which ye planted not do ye eat.

Now therefore fear the Lord, and serve him in sincerity and in truth; and put away the gods which your fathers served on the other side of the flood, and in Egypt; and serve ye the Lord. And if it seem evil unto you to serve the Lord, choose you this day whom ye will serve, whether the gods which your fathers served that were on the other side of the flood, or the gods of the Amorites in whose land ye dwell: but as for me and my house, we will serve the Lord.

And the people answered, and said, God forbid that we should forsake the Lord, to serve other gods; for the Lord our God, he it is that brought us up, and our fathers, out of the land of Egypt, from the house of bondage, and which did those great signs in our sight, and preserved us in all the way wherein we went, and among all the people through whom we passed: and the Lord drave out from before us all the people, even the Amorites which dwelt in the land: therefore will we also serve the Lord; for he is our God.

And Joshua said unto the people, Ye are witnesses against yourselves that ye have chosen you the Lord, to serve him. And they said, We are witnesses.

Now therefore put away (said he) the strange gods which are among you, and incline your heart unto the Lord God of Israel.

And the people said unto Joshua, The Lord our God will we serve, and his voice will we obey.

So Joshua made a covenant with the people that day, and set them a statute and an ordinance in Shechem.

And Joshua wrote these words in the book of the law of God, and took a great stone, and set it up there under an oak that was by the sanctuary of the Lord.

And Joshua said unto all the people, Behold, this stone shall be a witness unto us; for it hath heard all the words of the Lord which he spake unto us; it shall be therefore a witness unto you, lest ye deny your God.

So Joshua let the people depart, every man unto his inheritance.

And it came to pass after these things, that Joshua the son of Nun the servant of the Lord died, being an hundred and ten years old.

The Book of Judges

Israel Takes Tribute

And it came to pass when Israel was strong, that they put the Canaanites to tribute, and did not utterly drive them out. Neither did Ephraim drive out the Canaanites that dwelt in Gezer; but the Canaanites dwelt in Gezer among them. Neither did Zebulun drive out the inhabitants of Kitron, nor the inhabitants of Nahalol; but the Canaanites dwelt among them, and became tributaries. Neither did Asher drive out the inhabitants of Accho, nor the inhabitants of Zidon, nor of Ahlab, nor of Achzib, nor of Helbah, nor of Aphik, nor of Rehob: but the Asherites dwelt among the Canaanites, the inhabitants of the land: for they did not drive them out.

Neither did Naphtali drive out the inhabitants of Beth-shemesh, nor the inhabitants of Beth-anath; but he dwelt among the Canaanites, the inhabitants of the land: nevertheless, the inhabitants of Beth-shemesh and of Beth-anath became tributaries unto them.

And the Amorites forced the children of Dan into the mountain: for they would not suffer them to come down to the valley: but the Amorites would dwell in mount Heres in Aijalon, and in Shaalbim: yet the hand of the house of Joseph prevailed, so that they became tributaries.

And the coast of the Amorites was from the going up to Akrabbim, from the rock, and upward.

The Anger of the Lord

Now these are the nations which the Lord left, to prove Israel by them, (even as many of Israel as had not known all the wars of Canaan; only that the generations of the children of Israel might know to teach them war, at the least such as before knew nothing thereof;) namely, five lords of the Philistines, and all the Canaanites, and the Sidonians, and the Hivites that dwelt in mount Lebanon, from mount Baal-hermon unto the entering in of Hamath. And they were to prove Israel by them, to know whether they would hearken unto the commandments of the Lord, which he commanded their fathers by the hand of Moses.

And the children of Israel dwelt among the Canaanites, Hittites, and Amorites, and Perizzites, and Hivites, and Jebusites: and they took their daughters to be their wives, and gave their daughters to their sons, and served their gods. And the children of Israel did evil in the sight of the Lord, and forgat the Lord their God, and served Baalim, and the groves.

Therefore the anger of the Lord was hot against Israel, and he sold them into the hand of Cushan-rishathaim king of Mesopotamia: and the children of Israel served Cushan-rishathaim eight years.

The Death of Sisera

And the children of Israel again did evil in the sight of the Lord when Ehud was dead. And the Lord sold them into the hand of Jabin king of Canaan that reigned in Hazor, the captain of whose host was Sisera, which dwelt in Harosheth of the Gentiles. And the children of Israel cried unto the Lord; for he had nine hundred chariots of iron; and twenty years he mightily oppressed the children of Israel.

And Deborah, a prophetess, the wife of Lapidoth, she judged Israel at that time. And she dwelt under the palm-tree of Deborah, between Ramah and Beth-el in mount Ephraim: and the children of Israel came up to her for judgment.

And she sent and called Barak the son of Abinoam out of Kedesh-naphtali, and said unto him, Hath not the Lord God of Israel commanded, saying, Go, and draw toward mount Tabor, and take with thee ten thousand men of the children of Naphtali, and of the children of Zebulun? And I will draw unto thee, to the river Kishon, Sisera the captain of Jabin's army, with his chariots and his multitude; and I will deliver him into thine hand.

And Barak said unto her, If thou wilt go with me, then I will go: but if thou wilt not go with me, then I will not go.

And she said, I will surely go with thee: notwithstanding the journey that thou takest shall not be for thine honour; for the Lord shall sell Sisera into the hand of a woman. And Deborah arose, and went with Barak to Kedesh.

And Barak called Zebulun and Naphtali to Kedesh; and he went up with ten thousand men at his feet: and Deborah went up with him.

And Sisera gathered together all his chariots, even nine hundred chariots of iron, and all the people that were with him, from Harosheth of the Gentiles unto the river of Kishon.

So Barak went down from mount Tabor, and ten thousand men after him. And the Lord discomfited Sisera, and all his chariots, and all his host, with the edge of the sword before Barak; so that Sisera lighted down off his chariot, and fled away on his feet. But Barak pursued after the chariots, and after the host, unto Harosheth of the Gentiles: and all the host of Sisera fell upon the edge of the sword: and there was not a man left.

Howbeit, Sisera fled away on his feet to the tent of Jael the wife of Heber the Kenite: for there was peace between Jabin the king of Hazor and the house of Heber the Kenite. And Jael went out to meet Sisera, and said unto him, Turn in, my lord, turn in to me: fear not. And when he had turned in unto her into the tent, she covered him with a mantle.

And he said unto her, Give me, I pray thee, a little water to drink; for I am thirsty. And she opened a bottle of milk, and gave him drink, and covered him.

And he said unto her, Stand in the door of the tent, and it shall be, when any man doth come and inquire of thee, and say, Is there any man here? thou shalt say, No.

Then Jael Heber's wife took a nail of the tent, and took an hammer in her hand, and went softly unto him, and smote the nail into his temples, and fastened it into the ground: for he was fast asleep, and weary. So he died.

And behold, as Barak pursued Sisera, Jael came out to meet him, and said unto him, Come, and I will shew thee the man whom thou seekest. And when he came into her tent, behold, Sisera lay dead, and the nail was in his temples.

Deborah's Song

Then sang Deborah and Barak the son of Abinoam on that day, saying,

Praise ye the Lord for the avenging of Israel, when the people willingly
    offered themselves.
Hear, O ye kings; give ear, O ye princes;
I, even I, will sing unto the Lord;
I will sing praise to the Lord God of Israel.

Lord, when thou wentest out of Seir, when thou marchedst out of the
    field of Edom,
The earth trembled, and the heavens dropped, the clouds also dropped
    water.
The mountains melted from before the Lord,
Even that Sinai from before the Lord God of Israel.

In the days of Shamgar the son of Anath, in the days of Jael,
The highways were unoccupied, and the travellers walked through
    by-ways.
The inhabitants of the villages ceased, they ceased in Israel,
Until that I Deborah arose, that I arose a mother in Israel.

They chose new gods; then was war in the gates:
Was there a shield or spear seen among forty thousand in Israel?
My heart is toward the governors of Israel that offered themselves
    willingly among the people:
Bless ye the Lord.

Speak, ye that ride on white asses,
Ye that sit in judgment, and walk by the way.

They that are delivered from the noise of archers in the places of drawing
      water,
There shall they rehearse the righteous acts of the Lord,
Even the righteous acts toward the inhabitants of his villages in Israel:
Then shall the people of the Lord go down to the gates.

Awake, awake, Deborah;
Awake, awake, utter a song:
Arise, Barak, and lead thy captivity captive,
Thou son of Abinoam.

Then he made him that remaineth have dominion over the nobles among
      the people:
The Lord made me have dominion over the mighty.

Out of Ephraim was there a root of them against Amalek;
After thee, Benjamin, among thy people;
Out of Machir came down governors,
And out of Zebulun they that handle the pen of the writer.

And the princes of Issachar were with Deborah;
Even Issachar, and also Barak:
He was sent on foot into the valley.
For the divisions of Reuben there were great thoughts of heart.

Why abodest thou among the sheep-folds, to hear the bleatings of the
      flocks?
For the divisions of Reuben there were great searchings of heart.

Gilead abode beyond Jordan: and why did Dan remain in ships?
Asher continued on the sea-shore, and abode in his breaches.

Zebulun and Naphtali were a people that jeoparded their lives unto the
      death
In the high places of the field.

The kings came and fought, then fought the kings of Canaan in Taanach
      by the waters of Megiddo;
They took no gain of money.

They fought from heaven;
The stars in their courses fought against Sisera.

The river of Kishon swept them away,
That ancient river, the river Kishon.
O my soul, thou hast trodden down strength.

Then were the horse-hoofs broken by the means of the prancings,
The prancings of their mighty ones.

Curse ye Meroz, said the angel of the Lord,
Curse ye bitterly the inhabitants thereof;
Because they came not to the help of the Lord,
To the help of the Lord against the mighty.

Blessed above women shall Jael the wife of Heber the Kenite be,
Blessed shall she be above women in the tent.
He asked water, and she gave him milk;
She brought forth butter in a lordly dish.

She put her hand to the nail, and her right hand to the workmen's
            hammer;
And with the hammer she smote Sisera,
She smote off his head, when she had pierced and stricken through his
            temples.

At her feet he bowed, he fell, he lay down:
At her feet he bowed, he fell:
Where he bowed, there he fell down dead.

The mother of Sisera looked out at a window, and cried through the
            lattice,
Why is his chariot so long in coming?
Why tarry the wheels of his chariots?

Her wise ladies answered her,
Yea, she returned answer to herself,

Have they not sped? Have they not divided the prey;
To every man a damsel or two; to Sisera a prey of divers colours,
A prey of divers colours of needle-work, of divers colours of needle-
            work on both sides,
Meet for the necks of them that take the spoil?

So let all thine enemies perish, O Lord:
But let them that love him be as the sun when he goeth forth in his
    might.

The Birth of Samson

And the children of Israel did evil again in the sight of the Lord; and
the Lord delivered them into the hand of the Philistines forty years.

And there was a certain man of Zorah, of the family of the Danites,
whose name was Manoah; and his wife was barren, and bare not. And
the angel of the Lord appeared unto the woman, and said unto her,
Behold, now, thou art barren, and bearest not: but thou shalt conceive,
and bear a son. Now therefore beware, I pray thee, and drink not wine,
nor strong drink, and eat not any unclean thing: for lo, thou shalt conceive, and bear a son; and no razor shall come on his head: for the child
shall be a Nazarite unto God from the womb: and he shall begin to
deliver Israel out of the hand of the Philistines.

Then the woman came and told her husband, saying, A man of God
came unto me, and his countenance was like the countenance of an
angel of God, very terrible: but I asked him not whence he was, neither
told he me his name: but he said unto me, Behold, thou shalt conceive,
and bear a son; and now drink no wine nor strong drink, neither eat
any unclean thing: for the child shall be a Nazarite to God from the
womb to the day of his death.

Then Manoah entreated the Lord, and said, O my Lord, let the man
of God which thou didst send come again unto us, and teach us what we
shall do unto the child that shall be born.

And God hearkened to the voice of Manoah; and the angel of God
came again unto the woman as she sat in the field: but Manoah her husband was not with her. And the woman made haste, and ran, and
shewed her husband, and said unto him, Behold, the man hath appeared
unto me, that came unto me the other day.

And Manoah arose, and went after his wife, and came to the man,
and said unto him, Art thou the man that spakest unto the woman? And
he said, I am. And Manoah said, Now let thy words come to pass. How
shall we order the child, and how shall we do unto him? And the angel

of the Lord said unto Manoah, Of all that I said unto the woman, let her beware.

And Manoah said unto the angel of the Lord, What is thy name, that when thy sayings come to pass, we may do thee honour? And the angel of the Lord said unto him, Why askest thou thus after my name, seeing it is secret?

So Manoah took a kid, with a meat offering, and offered it upon a rock unto the Lord; and the angel did wondrously, and Manoah and his wife looked on. For it came to pass, when the flame went up toward heaven from off the altar, that the angel of the Lord ascended in the flame of the altar, and Manoah and his wife looked on it, and fell on their faces to the ground. But the angel of the Lord did no more appear to Manoah and to his wife. Then Manoah knew that he was an angel of the Lord.

And Manoah said unto his wife, We shall surely die, because we have seen God. But his wife said unto him, If the Lord were pleased to kill us, he would not have received a burnt-offering and a meat-offering at our hands, neither would he have shewed us all these things, nor would as at this time have told us such things as these.

And the woman bare a son, and called his name Samson. And the child grew, and the Lord blessed him. And the Spirit of the Lord began to move him at times in the camp of Dan, between Zorah and Eshtaol.

Samson and the Philistine Woman

And Samson went down to Timnath, and saw a woman in Timnath of the daughters of the Philistines. And he came up, and told his father and his mother, and said, I have seen a woman in Timnath of the daughters of the Philistines: now therefore get her for me to wife.

Then his father and his mother said unto him, Is there never a woman among the daughters of thy brethren, or among all my people, that thou goest to take a wife of the uncircumcised Philistines? And Samson said unto his father, Get her for me; for she pleaseth me well.

But his father and his mother knew not that it was of the Lord, that he sought an occasion against the Philistines: for at that time the Philistines had dominion over Israel.

Then went Samson down, and his father and his mother, to Timnath, and came to the vineyards of Timnath, and behold, a young lion roared against him. And the Spirit of the Lord came mightily upon him, and he rent him as he would have rent a kid, and he had nothing in his hand: but he told not his father or his mother what he had done.

And he went down, and talked with the woman; and she pleased Samson well.

And after a time he returned to take her, and he turned aside to see the carcass of the lion: and behold, there was a swarm of bees and honey in the carcass of the lion. And he took thereof in his hands, and went on eating, and came to his father and mother, and he gave them, and they did eat: but he told not them that he had taken the honey out of the carcass of the lion.

So his father went down unto the woman: and Samson made there a feast; for so used the young men to do. And it came to pass, when they saw him, that they brought thirty companions to be with him.

And Samson said unto them, I will now put forth a riddle unto you: if ye can certainly declare it me within the seven days of the feast, and find it out, then I will give you thirty sheets and thirty change of garments: but if ye cannot declare it me, then shall ye give me thirty sheets and thirty change of garments. And they said unto him, Put forth thy riddle, that we may hear it.

And he said unto them, Out of the eater came forth meat, and out of the strong came forth sweetness. And they could not in three days expound the riddle. And it came to pass on the seventh day, that they said unto Samson's wife, Entice thy husband, that he may declare unto us the riddle, lest we burn thee and thy fathers' house with fire: have ye called us to take that we have? is it not so?

And Samson's wife wept before him and said, Thou dost but hate me, and lovest me not: thou hast put forth a riddle unto the children of my people, and hast not told it me. And he said unto her, Behold, I have not told it my father nor my mother, and shall I tell it thee? And she wept before him the seven days, while their feast lasted: and it came to pass on the seventh day, that he told her, because she lay sore upon him: and she told the riddle to the children of her people.

And the men of the city said unto him on the seventh day before the sun went down, What is sweeter than honey? and what is stronger than a lion? And he said unto them, If ye had not ploughed with my heifer, ye had not found out my riddle.

And the Spirit of the Lord came upon him, and he went down to Ashkelon, and slew thirty men of them; and took their spoil, and gave change of garments unto them which expounded the riddle. And his anger was kindled, and he went up to his father's house. But Samson's wife was given to his companion, whom he had used as his friend.

Samson Burns the Philistines' Corn

But it came to pass within a while after, in the time of wheat-harvest, that Samson visited his wife with a kid; and he said, I will go in to my wife into the chamber. But her father would not suffer him to go in.

And her father said, I verily thought that thou hadst utterly hated her; therefore I gave her to thy companion: is not her younger sister fairer than she? take her, I pray thee, instead of her.

And Samson said concerning them, Now shall I be more blameless than the Philistines, though I do them a displeasure.

And Samson went and caught three hundred foxes, and took fire-brands, and turned tail to tail, and put a fire-brand in the midst between two tails. And when he had set the brands on fire, he let them go into the standing corn of the Philistines, and burnt up both the shocks, and also the standing corn, with the vineyards and olives.

Then the Philistines said, Who hath done this? And they answered, Samson, the son-in-law of the Timnite, because he had taken his wife, and given her to his companion. And the Philistines came up, and burnt her and her father with fire.

And Samson said unto them, Though ye have done this, yet will I be avenged of you, and after that I will cease. And he smote them hip and thigh with a great slaughter. And he went down and dwelt in the top of the rock Etam.

Then the Philistines went up, and pitched in Judah, and spread themselves in Lehi. And the men of Judah said, Why are ye come up against us? And they answered, To bind Samson are we come up, to do to him as he hath done to us.

Then three thousand men of Judah went to the top of the rock Etam, and said to Samson, Knowest thou not that the Philistines are rulers over us? what is this that thou hast done unto us? And he said unto them, As they did unto me, so have I done unto them.

And they said unto him, We are come down to bind thee, that we may deliver thee into the hand of the Philistines. And Samson said unto them, Swear unto me, that ye will not fall upon me yourselves. And they spake unto him, saying, No; but we will bind thee fast, and deliver thee into their hand: but surely we will not kill thee. And they bound him with two new cords, and brought him up from the rock.

And when he came unto Lehi, the Philistines shouted against him: and the Spirit of the Lord came mightily upon him, and the cords that were upon his arms became as flax that was burnt with fire, and his bands loosed from off his hands. And he found a new jaw-bone of an ass, and put forth his hand, and took it, and slew a thousand men therewith.

And Samson said, With the jaw-bone of an ass, heaps upon heaps, with the jaw of an ass have I slain a thousand men. And it came to pass when he had made an end of speaking, that he cast away the jaw-bone out of his hand, and called that place Ramath-lehi.

Samson and Delilah

Then went Samson to Gaza, and saw there an harlot, and went in unto her. And it was told the Gazites, saying, Samson is come hither. And they compassed him in, and laid wait for him all night in the gate of the city, and were quiet all the night, saying, In the morning when it is day we shall kill him. And Samson lay till midnight, and arose at midnight, and took the doors of the gate of the city, and the two posts, and went away with them, bar and all, and put them upon his shoulders, and carried them up to the top of an hill that is before Hebron.

And it came to pass afterward, that he loved a woman in the valley of Sorek, whose name was Delilah. And the lords of the Philistines came up unto her, and said unto her, Entice him, and see wherein his great strength lieth, and by what means we may prevail against him, that we may bind him to afflict him: and we will give thee every one of us eleven hundred pieces of silver.

And Delilah said to Samson, Tell me, I pray thee, wherein thy great strength lieth, and wherewith thou mightest be bound to afflict thee.

And Samson said unto her, If they bind me with seven green withs, that were never dried, then shall I be weak, and be as another man.

Then the lords of the Philistines brought up to her seven green withs, which had not been dried, and she bound him with them. (Now there were men lying in wait, abiding with her in the chamber.) And she said unto him, The Philistines be upon thee, Samson. And he brake the withs as a thread of tow is broken when it toucheth the fire. So his strength was not known.

And Delilah said unto Samson, Behold, thou hast mocked me, and told me lies: now tell me, I pray thee, wherewith thou mightest be bound.

And he said unto her, If they bind me fast with new ropes that never were occupied, then shall I be weak, and be as another man.

Delilah therefore took new ropes, and bound him therewith, and said unto him, The Philistines be upon thee, Samson. (And there were liers in wait abiding in the chamber.) And he brake them from off his arms like a thread.

And Delilah said unto Samson, Hitherto thou hast mocked me, and told me lies: tell me wherewith thou mightest be bound. And he said unto her, If thou weavest the seven locks of my head with the web.

And she fastened it with the pin, and said unto him, The Philistines be upon thee, Samson. And he awaked out of his sleep, and went away with the pin of the beam, and with the web.

And she said unto him, How canst thou say, I love thee, when thine heart is not with me? Thou hast mocked me these three times, and hast not told me wherein thy great strength lieth.

And it came to pass when she pressed him daily with her words, and urged him, so that his soul was vexed unto death; that he told her all his heart, and said unto her, There hath not come a razor upon mine head; for I have been a Nazarite unto God from my mother's womb: if I be shaven, then my strength will go from me, and I shall become weak, and be like any other man.

And when Delilah saw that he had told her all his heart, she sent and called for the lords of the Philistines, saying, Come up this once, for he hath shewed me all his heart. Then the lords of the Philistines came up unto her, and brought money in their hand. And she made him sleep upon her knees; and she called for a man, and she caused him to shave off the seven locks of his head; and she began to afflict him, and his strength went from him.

And she said, The Philistines be upon thee, Samson. And he awoke out of his sleep, and said, I will go out as at other times before, and shake myself. And he wist not that the Lord was departed from him. But the Philistines took him, and put out his eyes, and brought him down to Gaza, and bound him with fetters of brass; and he did grind in the prison-house.

Howbeit the hair of his head began to grow again after he was shaven.

Then the lords of the Philistines gathered them together, for to offer a great sacrifice unto Dagon their god, and to rejoice: for they said, Our god hath delivered Samson our enemy into our hand.

And it came to pass, when their hearts were merry, that they said, Call for Samson that he may make us sport. And they called for Samson out of the prison-house; and he made them sport: and they set him between the pillars. And Samson said unto the lad that held him by the hand, Suffer me that I may feel the pillars whereupon the house standeth, that I may lean upon them.

Now the house was full of men and women; and all the lords of the Philistines were there: and there were upon the roof about three thousand men and women, that beheld while Samson made sport.

And Samson called unto the Lord, and said O Lord God, remember me, I pray thee, and strengthen me, I pray thee, only this once, O God, that I may be at once avenged of the Philistines for my two eyes.

And Samson took hold of the two middle pillars upon which the house stood, and on which it was borne up, of the one with his right hand, and of the other with his left. And Samson said, Let me die with the Philistines. And he bowed himself with all his might; and the house fell upon the lords, and upon all the people that were therein. So the dead which he slew at his death were more than they which he slew in his life.

Then his brethren and all the house of his father came down, and took him, and brought him up, and buried him between Zorah and Eshtaol in the burying-place of Manoah his father. And he judged Israel twenty years.

In those days there was no king in Israel: every man did that which was right in his own eyes.

The First Book of Samuel

The Birth of Samuel

Now there was a certain man of Ramathaim-zophim, of mount Ephraim, and his name was Elkanah. And he had two wives; the name of the one was Hannah, and the name of the other Peninnah: and Peninnah had children, but Hannah had no children. And this man went up out of his city yearly to worship and to sacrifice unto the Lord of hosts in Shiloh.

So Hannah rose up after they had eaten in Shiloh, and after they had drunk: (now Eli the priest sat upon a seat by a post of the temple of the Lord:) and she was in bitterness of soul, and prayed unto the Lord, and wept sore. And she vowed a vow, and said, O Lord of hosts, if thou wilt indeed look on the affliction of thine handmaid, and remember me, and not forget thine handmaid, but wilt give unto thine handmaid a man-child, then I will give him unto the Lord all the days of his life, and there shall no razor come upon his head.

Then Eli answered and said, Go in peace: and the God of Israel grant thee thy petition that thou hast asked of him.

And they rose up in the morning early, and worshipped before the Lord, and returned, and came to their house to Ramah: and Elkanah knew Hannah his wife; and the Lord remembered her. Wherefore it came to pass, when the time was come about after Hannah had conceived, that she bare a son, and called his name Samuel, saying, Because I have asked him of the Lord.

And when she had weaned him, she took him up with her, with three bullocks, and one ephah of flour, and a bottle of wine, and brought him unto the house of the Lord in Shiloh: and the child was young. And they slew a bullock, and brought the child to Eli. And she said, O my lord, as thy soul liveth, my lord, I am the woman that stood by thee here, praying unto the Lord. For this child I prayed; and the Lord hath given me my petition which I asked of him. Therefore also I have lent him to the Lord; as long as he liveth he shall be lent to the Lord. And he worshipped the Lord there.

The Lord Calls Samuel

And the child Samuel ministered unto the Lord before Eli. And the word of the Lord was precious in those days; there was no open vision. And it came to pass at that time, when Eli was laid down in his place, and his eyes began to wax dim, that he could not see; and ere the lamp of God went out in the temple of the Lord, where the ark of God was, and Samuel was laid down to sleep; that the Lord called Samuel: and he answered, Here am I.

And he ran unto Eli, and said, Here am I; for thou calledst me. And he said, I called not; lie down again. And he went and lay down.

And the Lord called yet again, Samuel. And Samuel arose and went to Eli, and said, Here am I; for thou didst call me. And he answered, I called not, my son; lie down again. Now Samuel did not yet know the Lord, neither was the word of the Lord yet revealed unto him.

And the Lord called Samuel again the third time. And he arose and went to Eli, and said, Here am I; for thou didst call me. And Eli perceived that the Lord had called the child. Therefore Eli said unto Samuel, Go, lie down: and it shall be, if he call thee, that thou shalt say, Speak, Lord; for thy servant heareth. So Samuel went and lay down in his place.

And the Lord came, and stood and called as at other times, Samuel, Samuel. Then Samuel answered, Speak; for thy servant heareth.

And the Lord said to Samuel, Behold, I will do a thing in Israel, at which both the ears of every one that heareth it shall tingle. In that day I will perform against Eli all things which I have spoken concerning his house: when I begin, I will also make an end. For I have told him, that I will judge his house for ever, for the iniquity which he knoweth: because his sons made themselves vile, and he restrained them not. And therefore I have sworn unto the house of Eli, that the iniquity of Eli's house shall not be purged with sacrifice nor offering for ever.

And Samuel lay until the morning, and opened the doors of the house of the Lord: and Samuel feared to shew Eli the vision.

Then Eli called Samuel, and said, Samuel, my son. And he answered, Here am I.

And he said, What is the thing that the LORD hath said unto thee? I pray thee hide it not from me: God do so to thee, and more also, if thou hide any thing from me, of all the things that he said unto thee.

And Samuel told him every whit, and hid nothing from him. And he said, It is the Lord: let him do what seemeth him good.

And Samuel grew, and the Lord was with him, and did let none of his words fall to the ground. And all Israel, from Dan even to Beer-sheba, knew that Samuel was established to be a prophet of the Lord. And the Lord appeared again in Shiloh: for the Lord revealed himself to Samuel in Shiloh by the word of the Lord.

The Ark Is Taken

And the word of Samuel came to all Israel.

Now Israel went out against the Philistines to battle, and pitched beside Eben-ezer: and the Philistines pitched in Aphek. And the Philistines put themselves in array against Israel: and when they joined battle, Israel was smitten before the Philistines: and they slew of the army in the field about four thousand men.

And when the people were come into the camp, the elders of Israel said, Wherefore hath the Lord smitten us to-day before the Philistines? Let us fetch the ark of the covenant of the Lord out of Shiloh unto us, that when it cometh among us, it may save us out of the hand of our enemies.

So the people sent to Shiloh, that they might bring from thence the ark of the covenant of the Lord of hosts, which dwelleth between the cherubims: and the two sons of Eli, Hophni and Phinehas, were there with the ark of the covenant of God. And when the ark of the covenant of the Lord came into the camp, all Israel shouted with a great shout, so that the earth rang again.

And when the Philistines heard the noise of the shout, they said, What meaneth the noise of this great shout in the camp of the Hebrews? And they understood that the ark of the Lord was come into the camp. And the Philistines were afraid, for they said, God is come into the camp.

And they said, Woe unto us! for there hath not been such a thing heretofore. Woe unto us! who shall deliver us out of the hand of these mighty Gods? these are the Gods that smote the Egyptians with all the plagues in the wilderness. Be strong, and quit yourselves like men, O ye Philistines, that ye be not servants unto the Hebrews, as they have been to you: quit yourselves like men, and fight.

And the Philistines fought, and Israel was smitten, and they fled every man into his tent: and there was a very great slaughter, for there fell of Israel thirty thousand footmen. And the ark of God was taken; and the two sons of Eli, Hophni and Phinehas, were slain.

And there ran a man of Benjamin out of the army, and came to Shiloh the same day with his clothes rent, and with earth upon his head.

And when he came, lo, Eli sat upon a seat by the way-side watching: for his heart trembled for the ark of God. And when the man came into the city and told it, all the city cried out.

And when Eli heard the noise of the crying, he said, What meaneth the noise of this tumult? And the man came in hastily, and told Eli. Now Eli was ninety and eight years old; and his eyes were dim, that he could not see. And the man said unto Eli, I am he that came out of the army, and I fled to-day out of the army. And he said, What is there done, my son? And the messenger answered and said, Israel is fled before the Philistines, and there hath been also a great slaughter among the people, and thy two sons also, Hophni and Phinehas, are dead, and the ark of God is taken.

And it came to pass, when he made mention of the ark of God, that he fell from off the seat backward by the side of the gate, and his neck brake, and he died: for he was an old man, and heavy. And he had judged Israel forty years.

And his daughter-in-law, Phinehas' wife, was with child near to be delivered: and when she heard the tidings that the ark of God was taken, and that her father-in-law and her husband were dead, she bowed herself, and travailed; for her pains came upon her. And about the time of her death, the women that stood by her said unto her, Fear not; for thou hast borne a son. But she answered not, neither did she regard it.

And she named the child I-chabod, saying, The glory is departed from Israel: (because the ark of God was taken, and because of her father-in-law and her husband.) And she said, The glory is departed from Israel: for the ark of God is taken.

The People Want a King

And it came to pass, when Samuel was old, that he made his sons judges over Israel. Now the name of his first-born was Joel: and the name of his second, Abiah: they were judges in Beer-sheba. And his sons walked not in his ways, but turned aside after lucre, and took bribes, and perverted judgment.

Then all the elders of Israel gathered themselves together, and came to Samuel unto Ramah, and said unto him, Behold, thou art old, and thy sons walk not in thy ways: now make us a king to judge us like all the nations.

But the thing displeased Samuel, when they said, Give us a king to judge us: and Samuel prayed unto the Lord. And the Lord said unto Samuel, Hearken unto the voice of the people in all that they say unto thee: for they have not rejected thee, but they have rejected me, that I should not reign over them. According to all the works which they have done since the day that I brought them up out of Egypt even unto this day, wherewith they have forsaken me, and served other gods, so do they also unto thee. Now therefore hearken unto their voice: howbeit, yet protest solemnly unto them, and shew them the manner of the king that shall reign over them.

And Samuel told all the words of the Lord unto the people that asked of him a king. And he said, This will be the manner of the king that shall reign over you: He will take your sons, and appoint them for himself, for his chariots, and to be his horsemen; and some shall run before his chariots. And he will appoint him captains over thousands, and captains over fifties; and will set them to ear his ground, and to reap his harvest, and to make his instruments of war, and instruments of his chariots. And he will take your daughters to be confectionaries, and to be cooks, and to be bakers.

And he will take your fields, and your vineyards, and your olive-yards, even the best of them, and give them to his servants. And he will take the tenth of your seed, and of your vineyards, and give to his officers, and to his servants. And he will take your men-servants, and your maid-servants, and your goodliest young men, and your asses, and put them to his work. He will take the tenth of your sheep: and ye shall be his servants.

And ye shall cry out in that day because of your king which ye shall have chosen you; and the Lord will not hear you in that day.

Nevertheless, the people refused to obey the voice of Samuel; and they said, Nay; but we will have a king over us, that we also may be like all the nations; and that our king may judge us, and go out before us, and fight our battles.

And Samuel heard all the words of the people, and he rehearsed them in the ears of the Lord. And the Lord said to Samuel, Hearken unto their voice, and make them a king. And Samuel said unto the men of Israel, Go ye every man unto his city.

Saul Comes to Samuel

Now there was a man of Benjamin whose name was Kish, the son of Abiel, the son of Zeror, the son of Bechorath, the son of Aphiah, a Benjamite, a mighty man of power. And he had a son, whose name was Saul, a choice young man, and a goodly: and there was not among the children of Israel a goodlier person than he: from his shoulders and upward he was higher than any of the people.

And the asses of Kish, Saul's father, were lost. And Kish said to Saul his son, Take now one of the servants with thee, and arise, go seek the asses. And he passed through mount Ephraim, and passed through the land of Shalisha, but they found them not; then they passed through the land of Shalim, and there they were not: and he passed through the land of the Benjamites, but they found them not.

And when they were come to the land of Zuph, Saul said to his servant that was with him, Come, and let us return; lest my father leave caring for the asses, and take thought for us.

And he said unto him, Behold now, there is in this city a man of God, and he is an honourable man; all that he saith cometh surely to pass: now let us go thither; peradventure he can shew us our way that we should go. And they went up into the city: and when they were come into the city, behold, Samuel came out against them, for to go up to the high place.

Now the Lord had told Samuel in his ear a day before Saul came, saying, To-morrow about this time, I will send thee a man out of the land of Benjamin, and thou shalt anoint him to be captain over my people Israel, that he may save my people out of the hand of the Philistines: for I have looked upon my people, because their cry is come unto me.

And when Samuel saw Saul, the Lord said unto him, Behold the man whom I spake to thee of! this same shall reign over my people.

God Save the King!

Then Samuel took a vial of oil, and poured it upon his head, and kissed him, and said, Is it not because the Lord hath anointed thee to be captain over his inheritance? When thou art departed from me to-day, then thou shalt find two men by Rachel's sepulchre in the border of Benjamin at Zelzah; and they will say unto thee, The asses which thou wentest to seek are found: and lo, thy father hath left the care of the asses, and sorroweth for you, saying, What shall I do for my son?

Then shalt thou go on forward from thence, and thou shalt come to the plain of Tabor, and there shall meet thee three men going up to God to Beth-el, one carrying three kids, and another carrying three loaves of bread, and another carrying a bottle of wine: and they will salute thee, and give thee two loaves of bread; which thou shalt receive of their hands. After that thou shalt come to the hill of God, where is the garrison of the Philistines: and it shall come to pass, when thou art come thither to the city, that thou shalt meet a company of prophets coming down from the high place with a psaltery, and a tabret, and a pipe, and a harp before them; and they shall prophesy: and the Spirit of the Lord will come upon thee, and thou shalt prophesy with them, and shalt be turned into another man. And let it be, when these signs are come unto thee, that thou do as occasion serve thee; for God is with thee. And thou shalt go down before me to Gilgal; and behold, I will come down unto thee, to offer burnt-offerings, and to sacrifice sacrifices of peace-offerings: seven days shalt thou tarry, till I come to thee, and shew thee what thou shalt do.

And it was so, that when he had turned his back to go from Samuel, God gave him another heart: and all those signs came to pass that day.

And when they came thither to the hill, behold, a company of prophets met him; and the Spirit of God came upon him, and he prophesied among them.

And Samuel said to all the people, See ye him whom the Lord hath chosen, that there is none like him among all the people? And all the people shouted, and said, God save the king.

The Lord Accuses Saul

Then came the word of the Lord unto Samuel, saying, It repenteth me that I have set up Saul to be king: for he is turned back from following me, and hath not performed my commandments. And it grieved Samuel; and he cried unto the Lord all night.

And Samuel came to Saul: and Saul said unto him, Blessed be thou of the Lord: I have performed the commandment of the Lord.

Then Samuel said unto Saul, Stay, and I will tell thee what the Lord hath said to me this night. And he said unto him, Say on.

And Samuel said, When thou wast little in thine own sight, wast thou not made the head of the tribes of Israel, and the Lord anointed thee king over Israel? And the Lord sent thee on a journey, and said, Go, and utterly destroy the sinners the Amalekites, and fight against them until they be consumed. Wherefore then didst thou not obey the voice of the Lord, but didst fly upon the spoil, and didst evil in the sight of the Lord?

And Saul said unto Samuel, I have sinned: for I have transgressed the commandment of the Lord, and thy words: because I feared the people, and obeyed their voice. Now therefore, I pray thee, pardon my sin, and turn again with me, that I may worship the Lord.

And Samuel said unto Saul, I will not return with thee: for thou hast rejected the word of the Lord, and the Lord hath rejected thee from being king over Israel. And as Samuel turned about to go away, he laid hold upon the skirt of his mantle, and it rent. And Samuel said unto him, The Lord hath rent the kingdom of Israel from thee this day, and hath given it to a neighbour of thine that is better than thou.

And Samuel came no more to see Saul until the day of his death: nevertheless Samuel mourned for Saul: and the Lord repented that he had made Saul king over Israel.

Samuel Anoints David

And the Lord said unto Samuel, How long wilt thou mourn for Saul, seeing I have rejected him from reigning over Israel? Fill thy horn with oil, and go, I will send thee to Jesse the Beth-lehemite: for I have provided me a king among his sons.

And Samuel said, How can I go? if Saul hear it, he will kill me. And the Lord said, Take an heifer with thee, and say, I am come to sacrifice to the Lord. And call Jesse to the sacrifice, and I will shew thee what thou shalt do: and thou shalt anoint unto me him whom I name unto thee.

And Samuel did that which the Lord spake, and came to Beth-lehem. And he sanctified Jesse and his sons, and called them to the sacrifice.

And it came to pass when they were come, that he looked on Eliab, and said, Surely the Lord's anointed is before him.

But the Lord said unto Samuel, Look not on his countenance, or on the height of his stature; because I have refused him: for the LORD seeth not as man seeth; for man looketh on the outward appearance, but the Lord looketh on the heart.

Then Jesse called Abinadab, and made him pass before Samuel. And he said, Neither hath the Lord chosen this. Then Jesse made Shammah to pass by. And he said, Neither hath the Lord chosen this. Again, Jesse made seven of his sons to pass before Samuel: and Samuel said unto Jesse, The Lord hath not chosen these.

And Samuel said unto Jesse, Are here all thy children? And he said, There remaineth yet the youngest, and behold, he keepeth the sheep. And Samuel said unto Jesse, Send and fetch him: for we will not sit down till he come hither. And he sent, and brought him in.

Now he was ruddy, and withal of a beautiful countenance, and goodly to look to. And the Lord said, Arise, anoint him: for this is he. Then Samuel took the horn of oil, and anointed him in the midst of his brethren: and the Spirit of the Lord came upon David from that day forward.

So Samuel rose up, and went to Ramah.

But the Spirit of the Lord departed from Saul, and an evil spirit from the Lord troubled him. And Saul's servants said unto him, Behold now, an evil spirit from God troubleth thee. Let our lord now command thy servants, which are before thee, to seek out a man who is a cunning player on an harp: and it shall come to pass, when the evil spirit from God is upon thee, that he shall play with his hand, and thou shalt be well.

And Saul said unto his servants, Provide me now a man that can play well, and bring him to me.

Then answered one of the servants, and said, Behold, I have seen a son of Jesse the Beth-lehemite, that is cunning in playing, and a mighty valiant man, and a man of war, and prudent in matters, and a comely person, and the Lord is with him.

Wherefore Saul sent messengers unto Jesse, and said, Send me David thy son, which is with the sheep. And Jesse took an ass laden with bread, and a bottle of wine, and a kid, and sent them by David his son unto Saul. And David came to Saul, and stood before him: and he loved him greatly; and he became his armour-bearer. And Saul sent to Jesse, saying, Let David, I pray thee, stand before me; for he hath found favour in my sight.

And it came to pass, when the evil spirit from God was upon Saul, that David took an harp, and played with his hand: so Saul was refreshed, and was well, and the evil spirit departed from him.

David Kills Goliath

Now the Philistines gathered together their armies to battle, and were gathered together at Shochoh, which belongeth to Judah, and pitched between Shochoh and Azekah, in Ephes-dammim. And Saul and the men of Israel were gathered together, and pitched by the valley of Elah, and set the battle in array against the Philistines.

And there went out a champion out of the camp of the Philistines, named Goliath, of Gath, whose height was six cubits and a span. And he stood and cried unto the armies of Israel, and said unto them, I defy the armies of Israel this day; give me a man that we may fight together. When Saul and all Israel heard those words of the Philistine, they were dismayed and greatly afraid. And the Philistine drew near morning and evening, and presented himself forty days.

And Jesse said unto David his son, Take now for thy brethren an ephah of this parched corn, and these ten loaves, and run to the camp to thy brethren: and carry these ten cheeses unto the captain of their thousand, and look how thy brethren fare, and take their pledge.

And David rose up early in the morning, and left the sheep with a keeper, and took, and went, as Jesse had commanded him; and he came to the trench, as the host was going forth to the fight, and shouted for the battle. For Israel and the Philistines had put the battle in array, army against army. And David left his carriage in the hand of the keeper of the carriage, and ran into the army, and came and saluted his brethren.

And as he talked with them, behold, there came up the champion, the Philistine of Gath, Goliath by name, out of the armies of the Philistines, and spake according to the same words: and David heard them. And all the men of Israel, when they saw the man, fled from him, and were sore afraid.

And David said to Saul, Let no man's heart fail because of him; thy servant will go and fight with this Philistine.

And Saul said to David, Thou art not able to go against this Philistine to fight with him: for thou art but a youth, and he a man of war from his youth.

And David said unto Saul, Thy servant kept his father's sheep, and there came a lion, and a bear, and took a lamb out of the flock: and I went out after him and smote him, and delivered it out of his mouth: and when he arose against me, I caught him by his beard, and smote him, and slew him. Thy servant slew both the lion and the bear: and this uncircumcised Philistine shall be as one of them, seeing he hath defied the armies of the living God. The Lord that delivered me out of the paw of the lion, and out of the paw of the bear, he will deliver me out of the hand of this Philistine. And Saul said unto David, Go, and the Lord be with thee.

And Saul armed David with his armour, and he put an helmet of brass upon his head; also he armed him with a coat of mail. And David girded his sword upon his armour, and he assayed to go; for he had not proved it. And David said unto Saul, I cannot go with these, for I have not proved them. And David put them off him. And he took his staff in his hand, and chose him five smooth stones out of the brook and put them in a shepherd's bag which he had, even in a scrip; and his sling was in his hand: and he drew near to the Philistine. And the Philistine came on, and drew near unto David; and the man that bare the shield went before him. And when the Philistine looked about, and saw David, he disdained him: for he was but a youth, and ruddy, and of a fair countenance.

And the Philistine said unto David, Am I a dog, that thou comest to me with staves? and the Philistine cursed David by his gods. And the Philistine said to David, Come to me, and I will give thy flesh unto the fowls of the air, and to the beasts of the field.

Then said David to the Philistine, Thou comest to me with a sword, and with a spear, and with a shield: but I come to thee in the name of the Lord of hosts, the God of the armies of Israel, whom thou hast defied. This day will the Lord deliver thee into mine hand; and I will smite thee, and take thine head from thee; and I will give the carcasses of the host of the Philistines this day unto the fowls of the air, and to the wild beasts of the earth: that all the earth may know that there is a God in Israel. And all this assembly shall know that the Lord saveth not with sword and spear: for the battle is the Lord's, and he will give you into our hands.

And it came to pass, when the Philistine arose, and came and drew nigh to meet David, that David hasted, and ran toward the army to meet the Philistine. And David put his hand in his bag, and took thence a stone, and slang it, and smote the Philistine in his forehead, that the stone sunk into his forehead; and he fell upon his face to the earth.

So David prevailed over the Philistine with a sling and with a stone, and smote the Philistine and slew him; but there was no sword in the hand of David. Therefore David ran and stood upon the Philistine, and took his sword, and drew it out of the sheath thereof, and slew him, and cut off his head therewith. And when the Philistines saw their champion was dead, they fled.

And as David returned from the slaughter of the Philistine, Abner took him, and brought him before Saul with the head of the Philistine in his hand.

And Saul said to him, Whose son art thou, thou young man? And David answered, I am the son of thy servant Jesse the Beth-lehemite.

Jonathan and David

And it came to pass, when he had made an end of speaking unto Saul, that the soul of Jonathan was knit with the soul of David, and Jonathan loved him as his own soul. And Saul took him that day, and would let him go no more home to his father's house. Then Jonathan and David made a covenant, because he loved him as his own soul. And Jonathan stripped himself of the robe that was upon him, and gave it to David, and his garments, even to his sword, and to his bow, and to his girdle.

And David went out whithersoever Saul sent him, and behaved himself wisely: and Saul set him over the men of war, and he was accepted in the sight of all the people, and also in the sight of Saul's servants. And it came to pass as they came, when David was returned from the slaughter of the Philistine, that the women came out of all the cities of Israel, singing and dancing, to meet king Saul, with tabrets, with joy, and with instruments of music.

And the women answered one another as they played, and said, Saul hath slain his thousands, and David his ten thousands. And Saul was very wroth, and the saying displeased him; and he said, They have ascribed unto David ten thousands, and to me they have ascribed but thousands: and what can he have more but the kingdom? And Saul eyed David from that day and forward.

And it came to pass on the morrow, that the evil spirit from God came upon Saul, and he prophesied in the midst of the house: and David played with his hand, as at other times: and there was a javelin in Saul's hand. And Saul cast the javelin; for he said, I will smite David even to the wall with it. And David avoided out of his presence twice.

And Saul was afraid of David, because the Lord was with him, and was departed from Saul. Therefore Saul removed him from him, and made him his captain over a thousand; and he went out and came in before the people. And David behaved himself wisely in all his ways; and the Lord was with him. Wherefore when Saul saw that he behaved himself very wisely, he was afraid of him. But all Israel and Judah loved David, because he went out and came in before them.

Jonathan Intercedes for David

And Saul spake to Jonathan his son, and to all his servants, that they should kill David. But Jonathan, Saul's son, delighted much in David: and Jonathan told David, saying, Saul my father seeketh to kill thee: now therefore, I pray thee, take heed to thyself until the morning, and abide in a secret place, and hide thyself: and I will go out and stand beside my father in the field where thou art, and I will commune with my father of thee; and what I see, that I will tell thee.

And Jonathan spake good of David unto Saul his father, and said unto him, Let not the king sin against his servant, against David; because he hath not sinned against thee, and because his works have been to thee-ward very good.

And Saul hearkened unto the voice of Jonathan: and Saul sware, As the Lord liveth, he shall not be slain. And Jonathan called David, and Jonathan shewed him all those things. And Jonathan brought David to Saul, and he was in his presence, as in times past.

And there was war again: and David went out, and fought with the Philistines, and slew them with a great slaughter; and they fled from him. And the evil spirit from the Lord was upon Saul, as he sat in his house with his javelin in his hand: and David played with his hand. And Saul sought to smite David even to the wall with the javelin; but he slipped away out of Saul's presence, and he smote the javelin into the wall: and David fled, and escaped that night. Saul also sent messengers unto David's house, to watch him, and to slay him in the morning: and Michal, David's wife, told him, saying, If thou save not thy life to-night, to-morrow thou shalt be slain.

So Michal let David down through a window: and he went, and fled, and escaped, and came to Samuel to Ramah, and told him all that Saul had done to him. And he and Samuel went and dwelt in Naioth.

Saul and the Witch of En-dor

Now Samuel was dead, and all Israel had lamented him, and buried him in Ramah, even in his own city. And Saul had put away those that had familiar spirits, and the wizards, out of the land.

And the Philistines gathered themselves together, and came and pitched in Shunem: and Saul gathered all Israel together, and they pitched in Gilboa. And when Saul saw the host of the Philistines, he was afraid, and his heart greatly trembled. And when Saul inquired of the Lord, the Lord answered him not, neither by dreams, nor by Urim, nor by prophets.

Then said Saul unto his servants, Seek me a woman that hath a familiar spirit, that I may go to her, and inquire of her. And his servants said unto him, Behold, there is a woman that hath a familiar spirit at En-dor.

And Saul disguised himself, and put on other raiment, and he went, and two men with him, and they came to the woman by night: and he said, I pray thee, divine unto me by the familiar spirit, and bring me him up, whom I shall name unto thee.

And the woman said unto him, Behold, thou knowest what Saul hath done, how he hath cut off those that have familiar spirits, and the wizards, out of the land; wherefore then layest thou a snare for my life, to cause me to die? And Saul sware to her by the Lord, saying, As the Lord liveth, there shall no punishment happen to thee for this thing.

Then said the woman, Whom shall I bring up unto thee? And he said, Bring me up Samuel.

And when the woman saw Samuel, she cried with a loud voice: and the woman spake to Saul, saying, Why hast thou deceived me? for thou art Saul.

And the king said unto her, Be not afraid: for what sawest thou? And the woman said unto Saul, I saw gods ascending out of the earth.

And he said unto her, What form is he of? and she said, An old man cometh up; and he is covered with a mantle. And Saul perceived that it was Samuel, and he stooped with his face to the ground, and bowed himself.

And Samuel said to Saul, Why hast thou disquieted me, to bring me up?

And Saul answered, I am sore distressed; for the Philistines make war against me, and God is departed from me, and answereth me no more, neither by prophets, nor by dreams: therefore I have called thee, that thou mayest make known unto me what I shall do.

Then said Samuel, Wherefore then dost thou ask of me, seeing the Lord is departed from thee, and is become thine enemy? And the Lord hath done to him, as he spake by me: for the Lord hath rent the kingdom out of thine hand, and given it to thy neighbour, even to David: because thou obeyedst not the voice of the Lord, nor executedst his fierce wrath upon Amalek, therefore hath the Lord done this thing unto thee this day. Moreover, the Lord will also deliver Israel with thee into the hand of the Philistines: and to-morrow shalt thou and thy sons be with me: the Lord also shall deliver the host of Israel into the hand of the Philistines.

Then Saul fell straightway all along on the earth, and was sore afraid, because of the words of Samuel: and there was no strength in him; for he had eaten no bread all the day, nor all the night.

And the woman came unto Saul, and saw that he was sore troubled, and said unto him, Behold, thine handmaid hath obeyed thy voice, and I have put my life in mine hand, and have hearkened unto thy words which thou spakest unto me. Now therefore, I pray thee, hearken thou also unto the voice of thine handmaid, and let me set a morsel of bread before thee; and eat, that thou mayest have strength when thou goest on thy way. But he refused, and said, I will not eat.

But his servants, together with the woman, compelled him; and he hearkened unto their voice. So he arose from the earth, and sat upon the bed. And the woman had a fat calf in the house; and she hasted, and killed it, and took flour, and kneaded it, and did bake unleavened bread thereof: and she brought it before Saul, and before his servants; and they did eat. Then they arose up, and went away that night.

The Death of Saul and Jonathan

Now the Philistines fought against Israel: and the men of Israel fled from before the Philistines, and fell down slain in mount Gilboa. And the Philistines followed hard upon Saul and upon his sons; and the Philistines slew Jonathan, and Abinadab, and Melchishua, Saul's sons. And the battle went sore against Saul, and the archers hit him; and he was sore wounded of the archers.

Then said Saul unto his armour-bearer, Draw thy sword, and thrust me through therewith; lest these uncircumcised come and thrust me through, and abuse me. But his armour-bearer would not: for he was sore afraid. Therefore Saul took a sword, and fell upon it. And when his armour-bearer saw that Saul was dead, he fell likewise upon his sword, and died with him. So Saul died, and his three sons, and his armour-bearer, and all his men, that same day together.

And when the men of Israel that were on the other side of the valley, and they that were on the other side Jordan saw that the men of Israel fled, and that Saul and his sons were dead, they forsook the cities, and fled; and the Philistines came and dwelt in them.

The Second Book of Samuel

David Mourns

Now it came to pass after the death of Saul, when David was returned from the slaughter of the Amalekites, and David had abode two days in Ziklag; it came even to pass on the third day, that behold, a man came out of the camp from Saul with his clothes rent, and earth upon his head: and so it was, when he came to David, that he fell to the earth, and did obeisance.

And David said unto him, From whence comest thou? And he said unto him, Out of the camp of Israel am I escaped.

And David said unto him, How went the matter? I pray thee, tell me. And he answered, That the people are fled from the battle, and many of the people also are fallen and dead; and Saul and Jonathan his son are dead also.

And David said unto the young man that told him, How knowest thou that Saul and Jonathan his son be dead?

And the young man that told him said, As I happened by chance upon mount Gilboa, behold, Saul leaned upon his spear; and lo, the chariots and horsemen followed hard after him. And when he looked behind him, he saw me, and called unto me. And I answered, Here am I. And he said unto me, Who art thou? And I answered him, I am an Amalekite. He said unto me again, Stand, I pray thee, upon me, and slay me: for anguish is come upon me, because my life is yet whole in me. So I stood upon him, and slew him, because I was sure that he could not live after that he was fallen: and I took the crown that was upon his head, and the bracelet that was on his arm, and have brought them hither unto my lord.

Then David took hold on his clothes, and rent them; and likewise all the men that were with him. And they mourned and wept, and fasted until even, for Saul and for Jonathan his son, and for the people of the Lord, and for the house of Israel; because they were fallen by the sword.

And David said unto the young man that told him, Whence art thou? And he answered, I am the son of a stranger, an Amalekite.

And David said unto him, How wast thou not afraid to stretch forth thine hand to destroy the Lord's anointed? And David called one of the young men, and said, Go near, and fall upon him. And he smote him that he died.

And David said unto him, Thy blood be upon thy head; for thy mouth hath testified against thee, saying, I have slain the Lord's anointed.

And David lamented with this lamentation over Saul, and over Jonathan his son:

The beauty of Israel is slain upon thy high places:
How are the mighty fallen!

Tell it not in Gath, publish it not in the streets of Askelon,
Lest the daughters of the Philistines rejoice,
Lest the daughters of the uncircumcised triumph.

Ye mountains of Gilboa, let there be no dew, neither let there be rain
upon you, nor fields of offerings:

For there the shield of the mighty is vilely cast away,
The shield of Saul, as though he had not been anointed with oil.

From the blood of the slain, from the fat of the mighty,
The bow of Jonathan turned not back,
And the sword of Saul returned not empty.

Saul and Jonathan were lovely and pleasant in their lives,
And in their death they were not divided:
They were swifter than eagles,
They were stronger than lions.

Ye daughters of Israel, weep over Saul,
Who clothed you in scarlet, with other delights;
Who put on ornaments of gold upon your apparel.

How are the mighty fallen in the midst of the battle!
O Jonathan, thou wast slain in thine high places.

I am distressed for thee, my brother Jonathan:
Very pleasant hast thou been unto me:
Thy love to me was wonderful, passing the love of women.

How are the mighty fallen,
And the weapons of war perished!

The Death of Uzzah

Again, David gathered together all the chosen men of Israel, thirty thousand. And David arose, and went with all the people that were with him from Baale of Judah, to bring up from thence the ark of God, whose name is called by the name of The Lord of hosts that dwelleth between the cherubims.

And they set the ark of God upon a new cart, and brought it out of the house of Abinadab that was in Gibeah: and Uzzah and Ahio the sons of Abinadab drave the new cart. And they brought it out of the house of Abinadab, which was at Gibeah, accompanying the ark of God: and Ahio went before the ark. And David and all the house of Israel played before the Lord on all manner of instruments made of fir-wood, even on harps, and on psalteries, and on timbrels, and on cornets, and on cymbals.

And when they came to Nachon's threshing-floor, Uzzah put forth his hand to the ark of God, and took hold of it: for the oxen shook it. And the anger of the Lord was kindled against Uzzah, and God smote him there for his error; and there he died by the ark of God.

And David was displeased, because the Lord had made a breach upon Uzzah: and he called the name of the place Perez-uzzah to this day.

David and Bath-sheba

And it came to pass in an evening-tide, that David arose from off his bed, and walked upon the roof of the king's house: and from the roof he saw a woman washing herself; and the woman was very beautiful to look upon. And David sent and inquired after the woman. And one said, Is not this Bath-sheba the daughter of Eliam, the wife of Uriah the Hittite?

And David sent messengers and took her: and she came in unto him, and he lay with her; (for she was purified from her uncleanness:) and she returned unto her house. And the woman conceived, and sent and told David, and said, I am with child.

And it came to pass in the morning, that David wrote a letter to Joab, and sent it by the hand of Uriah. And he wrote in the letter, saying, Set ye Uriah in the forefront of the hottest battle, and retire ye from him, that he may be smitten, and die.

And it came to pass, when Joab observed the city, that he assigned Uriah unto a place where he knew that valiant men were. And the men of the city went out, and fought with Joab: and there fell some of the people of the servants of David; and Uriah the Hittite died also.

And when the wife of Uriah heard that Uriah her husband was dead, she mourned for her husband. And when the mourning was past, David sent and fetched her to his house, and she became his wife, and bare him a son. But the thing that David had done displeased the Lord.

Nathan's Parable

And the Lord sent Nathan unto David. And he came unto him, and said unto him, There were two men in one city; the one rich, and the other poor. The rich man had exceeding many flocks and herds: but the poor man had nothing save one little ewe-lamb, which he had bought and nourished up: and it grew up together with him, and with his children; it did eat of his own meat, and drank of his own cup, and lay in his bosom, and was unto him as a daughter. And there came a traveller unto the rich man, and he spared to take of his own flock and of his own herd, to dress for the way-faring man that was come unto him; but took the poor man's lamb, and dressed it for the man that was come to him.

And David's anger was greatly kindled against the man; and he said to Nathan, As the Lord liveth, the man that hath done this thing shall surely die. And he shall restore the lamb four-fold, because he did this thing, and because he had no pity.

And Nathan said to David, Thou art the man. Thus saith the Lord God of Israel, I anointed thee king over Israel, and I delivered thee out of the hand of Saul; and I gave thee thy master's house, and thy master's wives into thy bosom, and gave thee the house of Israel and of Judah; and if that had been too little, I would moreover have given unto thee such and such things. Wherefore hast thou despised the commandment of the Lord, to do evil in his sight? thou hast killed Uriah the Hittite with the sword, and hast taken his wife to be thy wife, and hast slain him with the sword of the children of Ammon. Now therefore the sword shall never depart from thine house; because thou hast despised me, and hast taken the wife of Uriah the Hittite to be thy wife.

Thus saith the Lord, Behold, I will raise up evil against thee out of thine own house, and I will take thy wives before thine eyes, and give them unto thy neighbour, and he shall lie with thy wives in the sight of this sun. For thou didst it secretly: but I will do this thing before all Israel, and before the sun.

And Nathan departed unto his house. And the Lord struck the child that Uriah's wife bare unto David, and it was very sick. David therefore besought God for the child; and David fasted, and went in, and lay all night upon the earth.

And it came to pass on the seventh day, that the child died. And the servants of David feared to tell him that the child was dead. But when David saw that his servants whispered, David perceived that the child was dead: therefore David said unto his servants, Is the child dead? and they said, He is dead.

Then David arose from the earth, and washed, and anointed himself, and changed his apparel, and came into the house of the Lord, and worshipped: then he came to his own house; and when he required, they set bread before him, and he did eat.

Then said his servants unto him, What thing is this that thou hast done? thou didst fast and weep for the child while it was alive; but when the child was dead, thou didst rise and eat bread.

And he said, While the child was yet alive, I fasted, and wept: for I said, Who can tell whether God will be gracious to me, that the child may live? But now he is dead, wherefore should I fast? can I bring him back again? I shall go to him, but he shall not return to me.

And David comforted Bath-sheba his wife, and went in unto her, and lay with her: and she bare a son, and he called his name Solomon: and the Lord loved him.

The Rape of Tamar

And it came to pass after this, that Absalom the son of David had a fair sister, whose name was Tamar; and Amnon the son of David loved her. And Amnon was so vexed, that he fell sick for his sister Tamar; for she was a virgin; and Amnon thought it hard for him to do anything to her.

But Amnon had a friend, whose name was Jonadab, the son of Shimeah David's brother: and Jonadab was a very subtle man. And he said unto him, Why art thou, being the king's son, lean from day to day? wilt thou not tell me? And Amnon said unto him, I love Tamar, my brother Absalom's sister.

And Jonadab said unto him, Lay thee down on thy bed, and make thyself sick: and when thy father cometh to see thee, say unto him, I pray thee, let my sister Tamar come, and give me meat, and dress the meat in my sight, that I may see it, and eat it at her hand.

So Amnon lay down, and made himself sick: and when the king was come to see him, Amnon said unto the king, I pray thee, let Tamar my sister come, and make me a couple of cakes in my sight, that I may eat at her hand. Then David sent home to Tamar, saying, Go now to thy brother Amnon's house, and dress him meat.

So Tamar went to her brother Amnon's house; and he was laid down. And she took flour, and kneaded it, and made cakes in his sight, and did bake the cakes. And she took a pan, and poured them out before him: but he refused to eat. And Amnon said, Have out all men from me. And they went out every man from him.

And Amnon said unto Tamar, Bring the meat into the chamber, that I may eat of thine hand. And Tamar took the cakes which she had made, and brought them into the chamber to Amnon her brother. And when she had brought them unto him to eat, he took hold of her, and said unto her, Come lie with me, my sister.

And she answered him, Nay, my brother, do not force me; for no such thing ought to be done in Israel: do not thou this folly. And I, whither shall I cause my shame to go? and as for thee, thou shalt be as one of the fools in Israel. Now therefore, I pray thee, speak unto the king; for he will not withhold me from thee.

Howbeit, he would not hearken unto her voice: but being stronger than she, forced her, and lay with her.

Then Amnon hated her exceedingly; so that the hatred wherewith he hated her was greater than the love wherewith he had loved her. And Amnon said unto her, Arise, be gone.

And she said unto him, There is no cause: this evil in sending me away is greater than the other that thou didst unto me. But he would not hearken unto her.

Then he called his servant that ministered unto him, and said, Put now this woman out from me, and bolt the door after her.

And she had a garment of divers colours upon her: for with such robes were the king's daughters that were virgins apparelled. Then his servant brought her out, and bolted the door after her.

And Tamar put ashes on her head, and rent her garment of divers colours that was on her, and laid her hand on her head, and went on crying.

And Absalom her brother said unto her, Hath Amnon thy brother been with thee? but hold now thy peace, my sister: he is thy brother;

regard not this thing. So Tamar remained desolate in her brother Absalom's house.

But when king David heard of all these things, he was very wroth.

And Absalom spake unto his brother Amnon neither good nor bad: for Absalom hated Amnon, because he had forced his sister Tamar.

Absalom Avenges Tamar

And it came to pass after two full years, that Absalom had sheep-shearers in Baal-hazor, which is beside Ephraim: and Absalom invited all the king's sons. And Absalom came to the king, and said, Behold now, thy servant hath sheep-shearers: let the king, I beseech thee, and his servants go with thy servant.

And the king said to Absalom, Nay, my son, let us not all now go, lest we be chargeable unto thee. And he pressed him: howbeit he would not go, but blessed him.

Then said Absalom, If not, I pray thee, let my brother Amnon go with us. And the king said unto him, Why should he go with thee? But Absalom pressed him, that he let Amnon and all the king's sons go with him.

Now Absalom had commanded his servants, saying, Mark ye now when Amnon's heart is merry with wine, and when I say unto you, Smite Amnon; then kill him, fear not; have not I commanded you? be courageous, and be valiant.

And the servants of Absalom did unto Amnon as Absalom had commanded. Then all the king's sons arose, and every man gat him up upon his mule, and fled.

So Absalom fled, and went to Geshur, and was there three years. And the soul of king David longed to go forth unto Absalom: for he was comforted concerning Amnon, seeing he was dead.

The Return of Absalom

And the king said unto Joab, Behold now, I have done this thing: go therefore, bring the young man Absalom again. And Joab fell to the ground on his face, and bowed himself, and thanked the king: and Joab said, To-day thy servant knoweth that I have found grace in thy sight, my lord, O king, in that the king hath fulfilled the request of his servant. So Joab arose and went to Geshur, and brought Absalom to Jerusalem.

And the king said, Let him turn to his own house, and let him not see my face. So Absalom returned to his own house, and saw not the king's face.

But in all Israel there was none to be so much praised as Absalom for his beauty: from the sole of his foot even to the crown of his head there was no blemish in him. And when he polled his head, (for it was at every year's end that he polled it; because the hair was heavy on him, therefore he polled it;) he weighed the hair of his head at two hundred shekels after the king's weight.

And unto Absalom there were born three sons, and one daughter, whose name was Tamar: she was a woman of a fair countenance.

So Absalom dwelt two full years in Jerusalem, and saw not the king's face. Therefore Absalom sent for Joab, to have sent him to the king; but he would not come to him: and when he sent again the second time, he would not come. Therefore he said unto his servants, See, Joab's field is near mine, and he hath barley there; go and set it on fire. And Absalom's servants set the field on fire.

Then Joab arose, and came to Absalom unto his house, and said unto him, Wherefore have thy servants set my field on fire? And Absalom answered Joab, Behold, I sent unto thee, saying, Come hither, that I may send thee to the king, to say, Wherefore am I come from Geshur? it had been good for me to have been there still: now therefore let me see the king's face; and if there be any iniquity in me, let him kill me.

So Joab came to the king, and told him: and when he had called for Absalom, he came to the king, and bowed himself on his face to the ground before the king: and the king kissed Absalom.

The Treachery of Absalom

And it came to pass after this, that Absalom prepared him chariots and horses, and fifty men to run before him. And Absalom rose up early, and stood beside the way of the gate: and it was so, that when any man that had a controversy came to the king for judgment, then Absalom called unto him, and said, Of what city art thou? And he said, Thy servant is of one of the tribes of Israel.

And Absalom said unto him, See, thy matters are good and right; but there is no man deputed of the king to hear thee. Oh that I were made judge in the land, that every man which hath any suit or cause might come unto me, and I would do him justice!

And it was so, that when any man came nigh to him to do him obeisance, he put forth his hand, and took him, and kissed him. And on this manner did Absalom to all Israel that came to the king for judgment: so Absalom stole the hearts of the men of Israel.

And it came to pass after forty years, that Absalom said unto the king, I pray thee, let me go and pay my vow, which I have vowed unto the Lord, in Hebron. For thy servant vowed a vow while I abode in Geshur in Syria, saying, If the Lord shall bring me again indeed to Jerusalem, then I will serve the Lord. And the king said unto him, Go in peace. So he arose, and went to Hebron.

But Absalom sent spies throughout all the tribes of Israel, saying, As soon as ye hear the sound of the trumpet, then ye shall say, Absalom reigneth in Hebron. And with Absalom went two hundred men out of Jerusalem, that were called; and they went in their simplicity, and they knew not anything. And Absalom sent for Ahithophel the Gilonite, David's counsellor, from his city, even from Giloh, while he offered sacrifices. And the conspiracy was strong; for the people increased continually with Absalom.

And there came a messenger to David, saying, The hearts of the men of Israel are after Absalom.

And David said unto all his servants that were with him at Jerusalem, Arise, and let us flee; for we shall not else escape from Absalom: make speed to depart, lest he overtake us suddenly, and bring evil upon us, and smite the city with the edge of the sword.

And all the country wept with a loud voice, and all the people passed over: the king also himself passed over the brook Kidron, and all the people passed over, toward the way of the wilderness.

And David went up by the ascent of mount Olivet, and wept as he went up, and had his head covered, and he went barefoot: and all the people that was with him covered every man his head, and they went up, weeping as they went up. And one told David, saying, Ahithophel is among the conspirators with Absalom. And David said, O Lord, I pray thee, turn the counsel of Ahithophel into foolishness.

And it came to pass, that when David was come to the top of the mount, where he worshipped God, behold, Hushai the Archite came to meet him with his coat rent, and earth upon his head: unto whom David said, If thou passest on with me, then thou shalt be a burden unto me: but if thou return to the city, and say unto Absalom, I will be thy servant, O king; as I have been thy father's servant hitherto, so will I now also be thy servant: then mayest thou for me defeat the counsel of Ahithophel.

So Hushai, David's friend, came into the city, and Absalom came into Jerusalem.

The Death of Absalom

Then David came to Mahanaim. And Absalom passed over Jordan, he and all the men of Israel with him.

And David numbered the people that were with him, and set captains of thousands and captains of hundreds over them. And David sent forth a third part of the people under the hand of Joab, and a third part under the hand of Abishai the son of Zeruiah, Joab's brother, and a third part under the hand of Ittai the Gittite. And the king said unto the people, I will surely go forth with you myself also.

But the people answered, Thou shalt not go forth: for if we flee away, they will not care for us; neither if half of us die, will they care for us: but now thou art worth ten thousand of us: therefore now it is better that thou succour us out of the city.

And the king said unto them, What seemeth you best I will do. And the king stood by the gate side, and all the people came out by hundreds and by thousands.

And the king commanded Joab and Abishai and Ittai, saying, Deal gently for my sake with the young man, even with Absalom. And all the people heard when the king gave all the captains charge concerning Absalom.

So the people went out into the field against Israel; and the battle was in the wood of Ephraim; where the people of Israel were slain before the servants of David, and there was there a great slaughter that day of twenty thousand men.

And Absalom met the servants of David. And Absalom rode upon a mule, and the mule went under the thick boughs of a great oak, and his head caught hold of the oak, and he was taken up between the heaven and the earth; and the mule that was under him went away. And a certain man saw it, and told Joab, and said, Behold, I saw Absalom hanged in an oak.

And Joab said unto the man that told him, And behold, thou sawest him, and why didst thou not smite him there to the ground? and I would have given thee ten shekels of silver, and a girdle.

And the man said unto Joab, Though I should receive a thousand shekels of silver in mine hand, yet would I not put forth mine hand against the king's son: for in our hearing the king charged thee and Abishai and Ittai, saying, Beware that none touch the young man Absalom. Otherwise I should have wrought falsehood against mine own life: for there is no matter hid from the king, and thou thyself wouldest have set thyself against me.

Then said Joab, I may not tarry thus with thee. And he took three darts in his hand, and thrust them through the heart of Absalom, while he was yet alive in the midst of the oak. And ten young men that bare Joab's armour compassed about and smote Absalom, and slew him. And Joab blew the trumpet, and the people returned from pursuing after Israel: for Joab held back the people. And they took Absalom, and cast him into a great pit in the wood, and laid a very great heap of stones upon him: and all Israel fled every one to his tent.

And David sat between the two gates: and the watchman went up to the roof over the gate unto the wall, and lifted up his eyes, and looked, and behold a man running alone. And the watchman cried, and told the king. And the king said, If he be alone there is tidings in his mouth. And he came apace, and drew near. And the watchman saw another man running: and the watchman called unto the porter, and said, Behold, another man running alone. And the king said, He also bringeth tidings.

And the watchman said, Methinketh the running of the foremost is like the running of Ahimaaz the son of Zadok. And the king said, He is a good man, and cometh with good tidings. And Ahimaaz called, and said unto the king, All is well. And he fell down to the earth upon his face before the king, and said, Blessed be the Lord thy God, which hath delivered up the men that lifted up their hand against my lord the king. And the king said, Is the young man Absalom safe? And Ahimaaz answered, when Joab sent the king's servant, and me thy servant, I saw a great tumult, but I knew not what it was. And the king said unto him, Turn aside and stand here. And he turned aside, and stood still.

And behold, Cushi came; and Cushi said, Tidings, my lord the king: for the Lord hath avenged thee this day of all them that rose up against thee.

And the king said unto Cushi, Is the young man Absalom safe? And Cushi answered, The enemies of my lord the king, and all that rise against thee to do thee hurt, be as that young man is.

And the king was much moved, and went up to the chamber over the gate, and wept: and as he went, thus he said, O my son Absalom! my son, my son Absalom! would God I had died for thee, O Absalom, my son, my son!

David Numbers the People

And again the anger of the Lord was kindled against Israel, and he moved David against them to say, Go, number Israel and Judah. For the king said to Joab, the captain of the host, which was with him, Go now through all the tribes of Israel, from Dan even to Beer-sheba, and number ye the people, that I may know the number of the people.

And Joab said unto the king, Now the Lord thy God add unto the people, how many soever they be, an hundred-fold, and that the eyes of my lord the king may see it: but why doth my lord the king delight in this thing?

Notwithstanding the king's word prevailed against Joab, and against the captains of the host. And Joab and the captains of the host went out from the presence of the king, to number the people of Israel.

And they passed over Jordan, and pitched in Aroer, on the right side of the city that lieth in the midst of the river of Gad, and toward Jazer: then they came to Gilead, and to the land of Tahtim-hodshi; and they came to Dan-jaan, and about to Zidon, and came to the stronghold of Tyre, and to all the cities of the Hivites, and of the Canaanites: and they went out to the south of Judah, even to Beer-sheba. So when they had gone through all the land, they came to Jerusalem at the end of nine months and twenty days.

And Joab gave up the sum of the number of the people unto the king: and there were in Israel eight hundred thousand valiant men that drew the sword; and the men of Judah were five hundred thousand men.

And David's heart smote him after that he had numbered the people. And David said unto the Lord, I have sinned greatly in that I have done: and now, I beseech thee, O Lord, take away the iniquity of thy servant; for I have done very foolishly.

The First Book of the Kings

Solomon Becomes King

Now king David was old and stricken in years; and they covered him with clothes, but he gat no heat. Wherefore his servants said unto him, Let there be sought for my lord the king a young virgin: and let her stand before the king, and let her cherish him, and let her lie in thy bosom, that my lord the king may get heat. So they sought for a fair damsel throughout all the coast of Israel, and found Abishag a Shunammite, and brought her to the king. And the damsel was very fair, and cherished the king, and ministered to him: but the king knew her not.

Then Adonijah the son of Haggith exalted himself, saying, I will be king: and he prepared him chariots and horsemen, and fifty men to run before him.

Wherefore Nathan spake unto Bath-sheba the mother of Solomon, saying, Hast thou not heard that Adonijah the son of Haggith doth reign, and David our lord knoweth it not?

And Bath-sheba went in unto the king into the chamber: and the king was very old; and Abishag the Shunammite ministered unto the king. And Bath-sheba bowed, and did obeisance unto the king. And the king said, What wouldest thou? And she said unto him, My lord, thou swarest by the Lord thy God unto thine handmaid, saying, Assuredly Solomon thy son shall reign after me, and he shall sit upon my throne. And now, behold, Adonijah reigneth; and now, my lord the king, thou knowest it not.

And king David said, Call me Zadok the priest, and Nathan the prophet, and Benaiah the son of Jehoiada. And they came before the king. The king said unto them, Take with you the servants of your lord, and cause Solomon my son to ride upon mine own mule, and bring him down to Gihon: and let Zadok the priest and Nathan the prophet anoint him there king over Israel: and blow ye with the trumpet, and say, God save king Solomon. Then ye shall come up after him, that he may come and sit upon my throne; for he shall be king in my stead: and I have appointed him to be ruler over Israel and over Judah.

So Zadok the priest, and Nathan the prophet, and Benaiah the son of Jehoiada, and the Cherethites, and the Pelethites, went down, and caused Solomon to ride upon king David's mule, and brought him to Gihon. And Zadok the priest took an horn of oil out of the tabernacle, and anointed Solomon. And they blew the trumpet; and all the people said, God save king Solomon.

The Death of David

Now the days of David drew nigh that he should die; and he charged Solomon his son, saying, I go the way of all the earth: be thou strong therefore, and shew thyself a man; and keep the charge of the Lord thy God, to walk in his ways, to keep his statutes, and his commandments, and his judgments, and his testimonies, as it is written in the Law of Moses, that thou mayest prosper in all that thou doest, and whithersoever thou turnest thyself. That the Lord may continue his word which he spake concerning me, saying, If thy children take heed to their way, to walk before me in truth, with all their heart, and with all their soul, there shall not fail thee (said he) a man on the throne of Israel.

So David slept with his fathers, and was buried in the city of David.

Solomon Chooses an Understanding Heart

In Gibeon the Lord appeared to Solomon in a dream by night: and God said, Ask what I shall give thee.

And Solomon said, Thou hast shewed unto thy servant David my father great mercy, according as he walked before thee in truth, and in righteousness, and in uprightness of heart with thee; and thou hast kept for him this great kindness, that thou hast given him a son to sit on his throne, as it is this day. And now, O Lord my God, thou hast made thy servant king instead of David my father: and I am but a little child: I know not how to go out or come in. And thy servant is in the midst of thy people which thou hast chosen, a great people, that cannot be numbered nor counted for multitude. Give therefore thy servant an understanding heart to judge thy people, that I may discern between good and bad: for who is able to judge this thy so great a people?

And the speech pleased the Lord, that Solomon had asked this thing. And God said unto him, Because thou hast asked this thing, and hast not asked for thyself long life; neither hast asked riches for thyself, nor hast asked the life of thine enemies: but hast asked for thyself understanding to discern judgment; behold, I have done according to thy word: lo, I have given thee a wise and an understanding heart; so that there was none like thee before thee, neither after thee shall any arise like unto thee. And I have also given thee that which thou hast not asked, both riches, and honour: so that there shall not be any among the kings like unto thee all thy days. And if thou wilt walk in my ways, to keep my statutes and my commandments, as thy father David did walk, then I will lengthen thy days.

And Solomon awoke; and behold, it was a dream. And he came to Jerusalem, and stood before the ark of the covenant of the Lord, and offered up burnt-offerings, and offered peace-offerings, and made a feast to all his servants.

Solomon Passes Judgment

Then came there two women, that were harlots, unto the king, and stood before him. And the one woman said, O my lord, I and this woman dwell in one house; and I was delivered of a child with her in the house. And it came to pass the third day after that I was delivered, that this woman was delivered also: and we were together; there was no stranger with us in the house, save we two in the house. And this woman's child died in the night; because she overlaid it. And she arose at midnight, and took my son from beside me, while thine handmaid slept, and laid it in her bosom, and laid her dead child in my bosom. And when I arose in the morning to give my child suck, behold, it was dead: but when I had considered it in the morning, behold, it was not my son, which I did bear.

And the other woman said, Nay; but the living is my son, and the dead is thy son. And this said, No; but the dead is thy son, and the living is my son. Thus they spake before the king.

Then said the king, The one saith, This is my son that liveth, and thy son is the dead; and the other saith, Nay; but thy son is the dead, and my son is the living. Bring me a sword. And they brought a sword before the king.

And the king said, Divide the living child in two, and give half to the one, and half to the other.

Then spake the woman whose the living child was unto the king, for her bowels yearned upon her son, and she said, O my lord, give her the living child, and in no wise slay it. But the other said, Let it be neither mine nor thine, but divide it.

Then the king answered and said, Give her the living child, and in no wise slay it: she is the mother thereof.

And all Israel heard of the judgment which the king had judged; and they feared the king: for they saw that the wisdom of God was in him, to do judgment.

The Building of the Temple

And it came to pass in the four hundred and eightieth year after the children of Israel were come out of the land of Egypt, in the fourth year of Solomon's reign over Israel, in the month Zif, which is the second month, that he began to build the house of the Lord.

And he built the walls of the house within with boards of cedar, both the floor of the house, and the walls of the ceiling: and he covered them on the inside with wood, and covered the floor of the house with planks of fir. And the house, that is, the temple before it, was forty cubits long. And the cedar of the house within was carved with knops and open flowers: all was cedar; there was no stone seen.

So Solomon overlaid the house within with pure gold: and he made a partition by the chains of gold before the oracle; and he overlaid it with gold. And the whole house he overlaid with gold, until he had finished all the house: also the whole altar that was by the oracle he overlaid with gold.

And within the oracle he made two cherubims of olive-tree, each ten cubits high. And he set the cherubims within the inner house: and they stretched forth the wings of the cherubims, so that the wing of the one touched the one wall, and the wing of the other cherub touched the other wall; and their wings touched one another in the midst of the house. And he overlaid the cherubims with gold. And he carved all the walls of the house round about with carved figures of cherubims, and palm-trees, and open flowers, within and without.

And the floor of the house he overlaid with gold, within and without.

And for the entering of the oracle he made doors of olive-tree: the lintel and side-posts were a fifth part of the wall. The two doors also were of olive-tree; and he carved upon them carvings of cherubims, and palm-trees, and open flowers, and overlaid them with gold, and spread gold upon the cherubims, and upon the palm-trees.

And he built the inner court with three rows of hewed stone, and a row of cedar beams.

In the fourth year was the foundation of the house of the Lord laid, in the month Zif. And in the eleventh year, in the month Bul (which is the eighth month) was the house finished throughout all the parts thereof, and according to all the fashion of it. So was he seven years in building it.

And king Solomon made a navy of ships in Ezion-geber, which is beside Eloth, on the shore of the Red sea, in the land of Edom. And Hiram sent in the navy his servants, shipmen that had knowledge of the sea, with the servants of Solomon. And they came to Ophir, and fetched from thence gold, four hundred and twenty talents, and brought it to king Solomon.

Solomon and the Queen of Sheba

And when the queen of Sheba heard of the fame of Solomon concerning the name of the Lord, she came to prove him with hard questions. And she came to Jerusalem with a very great train, with camels that bare spices, and very much gold, and precious stones: and when she was come to Solomon, she communed with him of all that was in her heart. And Solomon told her all her questions: there was not anything hid from the king, which he told her not.

And when the queen of Sheba had seen all Solomon's wisdom, and the house that he had built, and the meat of his table, and the sitting of his servants, and the attendance of his ministers, and their apparel, and his cup-bearers, and his ascent by which he went up unto the house of the Lord; there was no more spirit in her.

And she said to the king, It was a true report that I heard in mine own land of thy acts and of thy wisdom. Howbeit, I believed not the words, until I came, and mine eyes had seen it: and behold, the half was not told me: thy wisdom and prosperity exceedeth the fame which I heard. Happy are thy men, happy are these thy servants, which stand continually before thee, and that hear thy wisdom. Blessed be the Lord thy God, which delighted in thee, to set thee on the throne of Israel: because the Lord loved Israel for ever, therefore made he thee king, to do judgment and justice.

And she gave the king an hundred and twenty talents of gold, and of spices very great store, and precious stones: there came no more such abundance of spices as these which the queen of Sheba gave to king Solomon. And the navy also of Hiram, that brought gold from Ophir, brought in from Ophir great plenty of almug-trees, and precious stones.

And the king made of the almug-trees pillars for the house of the Lord, and for the king's house, harps also and psalteries for singers: there came no such almug-trees, nor were seen unto this day.

And king Solomon gave unto the queen of Sheba all her desire, whatsoever she asked, besides that which Solomon gave her of his royal bounty. So she turned and went to her own country, she and her servants.

The Weakness of Solomon

But king Solomon loved many strange women, together with the daughter of Pharaoh, women of the Moabites, Ammonites, Edomites, Zidonians, and Hittites; of the nations concerning which the Lord said unto the children of Israel, Ye shall not go in to them, neither shall they come in unto you: for surely they will turn away your heart after their gods: Solomon clave unto these in love. And he had seven hundred wives, princesses, and three hundred concubines: and his wives turned away his heart.

For it came to pass, when Solomon was old, that his wives turned away his heart after other gods: and his heart was not perfect with the Lord his God, as was the heart of David his father. For Solomon went after Ashtoreth the goddess of the Zidonians, and after Milcom the abomination of the Ammonites. And Solomon did evil in the sight of the Lord, and went not fully after the Lord, as did David his father.

Then did Solomon build an high place for Chemosh, the abomination of Moab, in the hill that is before Jerusalem, and for Molech, the abomination of the children of Ammon. And likewise did he for all his strange wives, which burnt incense and sacrificed unto their gods.

And the Lord was angry with Solomon, because his heart was turned from the Lord God of Israel, which had appeared unto him twice, and had commanded him concerning this thing, that he should not go after other gods: but he kept not that which the Lord commanded.

Wherefore the Lord said unto Solomon, Forasmuch as this is done of thee, and thou hast not kept my covenant and my statutes which I have commanded thee, I will surely rend the kingdom from thee, and will give it to thy servant. Notwithstanding, in thy days I will not do it for David thy father's sake: but I will rend it out of the hand of thy son. Howbeit, I will not rend away all the kingdom; but will give one tribe to thy son, for David my servant's sake, and for Jerusalem's sake which I have chosen.

And the rest of the acts of Solomon, and all that he did, and his wisdom, are they not written in the book of the acts of Solomon? And the time that Solomon reigned in Jerusalem over all Israel was forty years.

And Solomon slept with his fathers, and was buried in the city of David his father: and Rehoboam his son reigned in his stead.

The Divided Kingdom

And Rehoboam went to Shechem: for all Israel were come to Shechem to make him king.

And it came to pass, when Jeroboam the son of Nebat, who was yet in Egypt, heard of it, (for he was fled from the presence of king Solomon, and Jeroboam dwelt in Egypt;) that they sent and called him. And Jeroboam and all the congregation of Israel came, and spake unto Rehoboam, saying, Thy father made our yoke grievous: now therefore make thou the grievous service of thy father, and his heavy yoke which he put upon us, lighter, and we will serve thee. And he said unto them, Depart yet for three days, then come again to me. And the people departed.

And king Rehoboam consulted with the old men that stood before Solomon his father while he yet lived, and said, How do ye advise that I may answer this people? And they spake unto him, saying, If thou wilt be a servant unto this people this day, and wilt serve them, and answer them, and speak good words to them, then they will be thy servants for ever.

But he forsook the counsel of the old men, which they had given him, and consulted with the young men that were grown up with him, and which stood before him: and he said unto them, What counsel give ye that we may answer this people, who have spoken to me, saying, Make the yoke which thy father did put upon us lighter?

And the young men that were grown up with him spake unto him, saying, Thus shalt thou speak unto this people that spake unto thee, saying, Thy father made our yoke heavy, but make thou it lighter unto us; thus shalt thou say unto them, My little finger shall be thicker than my father's loins. And now whereas my father did lade you with a heavy yoke, I will add to your yoke: my father hath chastised you with whips, but I will chastise you with scorpions.

So Jeroboam and all the people came to Rehoboam the third day, as the king had appointed, saying, Come to me again the third day.

And the king answered the people roughly, and forsook the old men's counsel that they gave him; and spake to them after the counsel of the young men, saying, My father made your yoke heavy, and I will add to your yoke: my father also chastised you with whips, but I will chastise you with scorpions. Wherefore the king hearkened not unto the people: for the cause was from the Lord, that he might perform his saying, which the Lord spake by Ahijah the Shilonite unto Jeroboam the son of Nebat.

So when all Israel saw that the king hearkened not unto them, the people answered the king, saying, What portion have we in David? neither have we inheritance in the son of Jesse: to your tents, O Israel: now see to thine own house, David. So Israel departed unto their tents.

But as for the children of Israel which dwelt in the cities of Judah, Rehoboam reigned over them.

Then king Rehoboam sent Adoram, who was over the tribute; and all Israel stoned him with stones, that he died. Therefore king Rehoboam made speed to get him up to his chariot, to flee to Jerusalem.

So Israel rebelled against the house of David unto this day.

And it came to pass when all Israel heard that Jeroboam was come again, that they sent and called him unto the congregation, and made him king over all Israel: there was none that followed the house of David, but the tribe of Judah only.

And when Rehoboam was come to Jerusalem, he assembled all the house of Judah, with the tribe of Benjamin, an hundred and four score thousand chosen men, which were warriors, to fight against the house of Israel, to bring the kingdom again to Rehoboam the son of Solomon.

But the word of God came unto Shemaiah the man of God, saying, Speak unto Rehoboam the son of Solomon, king of Judah, and unto all the house of Judah and Benjamin, and to the remnant of the people, saying, Thus saith the Lord, Ye shall not go up, nor fight against your brethren the children of Israel: return every man to his house; for this thing is from me. They hearkened therefore to the word of the Lord, and returned to depart, according to the word of the Lord.

Then Jeroboam built Shechem in mount Ephraim, and dwelt therein; and went out from thence, and built Penuel.

And Jeroboam said in his heart, Now shall the kingdom return to the house of David. If this people go up to do sacrifice in the house of the Lord at Jerusalem, then shall the heart of this people turn again unto their lord, even unto Rehoboam king of Judah, and they shall kill me, and go again to Rehoboam king of Judah.

Whereupon the king took counsel, and made two calves of gold, and said unto them, It is too much for you to go up to Jerusalem: behold thy gods, O Israel, which brought thee up out of the land of Egypt. And he set the one in Beth-el, and the other put he in Dan. And this thing became a sin: for the people went to worship before the one, even unto Dan.

And he made an house of high places, and made priests of the lowest of the people, which were not of the sons of Levi.

And Jeroboam ordained a feast in the eighth month, on the fifteenth day of the month, like unto the feast that is in Judah, and he offered upon the altar. So did he in Beth-el, sacrificing unto the calves that he had made: and he placed in Beth-el the priests of the high places which he had made. So he offered upon the altar which he had made in Beth-el the fifteenth day of the eighth month, even in the month which he had devised of his own heart; and ordained a feast unto the children of Israel: and he offered upon the altar, and burnt incense.

Elijah and the Ravens

And Ahab the son of Omri reigned over Israel in Samaria twenty and two years. And it came to pass, as if it had been a light thing for him to walk in the sins of Jeroboam the son of Nebat, that he took to wife Jezebel the daughter of Ethbaal king of the Zidonians, and went and served Baal, and worshipped him.

And Elijah the Tishbite, who was of the inhabitants of Gilead, said unto Ahab, As the Lord God of Israel liveth, before whom I stand, there shall not be dew nor rain these years, but according to my word.

And the word of the Lord came unto him, saying, Get thee hence, and turn thee eastward, and hide thyself by the brook Cherith, that is before Jordan. And it shall be, that thou shalt drink of the brook; and

I have commanded the ravens to feed thee there. So he went and did according unto the word of the Lord: for he went and dwelt by the brook Cherith, that is before Jordan. And the ravens brought him bread and flesh in the morning, and bread and flesh in the evening; and he drank of the brook. And it came to pass after a while, that the brook dried up, because there had been no rain in the land.

And the word of the Lord came unto him, saying, Arise, get thee to Zarephath, which belongeth to Zidon, and dwell there: behold, I have commanded a widow woman there to sustain thee.

So he arose and went to Zarephath. And when he came to the gate of the city, behold, the widow woman was there gathering of sticks: and he called to her, and said, Fetch me, I pray thee, a little water in a vessel, that I may drink. And as she was going to fetch it, he called to her, and said, Bring me, I pray thee, a morsel of bread in thine hand.

And she said, As the Lord thy God liveth, I have not a cake, but an handful of meal in a barrel, and a little oil in a cruse: and behold, I am gathering two sticks, that I may go in and dress it for me and my son, that we may eat it, and die.

And Elijah said unto her, Fear not; go and do as thou hast said: but make me thereof a little cake first, and bring it unto me, and after make for thee and for thy son. For thus saith the Lord God of Israel, The barrel of meal shall not waste, neither shall the cruse of oil fail, until the day that the Lord sendeth rain upon the earth.

And she went and did according to the saying of Elijah: and she, and he, and her house, did eat many days. And the barrel of meal wasted not, neither did the cruse of oil fail, according to the word of the Lord, which he spake by Elijah.

And it came to pass after these things, that the son of the woman, the mistress of the house, fell sick; and his sickness was so sore, that there was no breath left in him.

And she said unto Elijah, What have I to do with thee, O thou man of God? art thou come unto me to call my sin to remembrance, and to slay my son?

And he said unto her, Give me thy son. And he took him out of her bosom, and carried him up into a loft, where he abode, and laid him upon his own bed.

And he cried unto the Lord, and said, O Lord my God, hast thou also brought evil upon the widow with whom I sojourn, by slaying her son? And he stretched himself upon the child three times, and cried unto the Lord, and said, O Lord my God, I pray thee, let this child's soul come into him again. And the Lord heard the voice of Elijah; and the soul of the child came into him again, and he revived.

And Elijah took the child, and brought him down out of the chamber into the house, and delivered him unto his mother: and Elijah said, See, thy son liveth.

And the woman said to Elijah, Now by this I know that thou art a man of God, and that the word of the Lord in thy mouth is truth.

Elijah Proves God

And it came to pass after many days, that the word of the Lord came to Elijah in the third year, saying, Go, shew thyself unto Ahab; and I will send rain upon the earth. And Elijah went to shew himself unto Ahab. And there was a sore famine in Samaria.

And it came to pass when Ahab saw Elijah, that Ahab said unto him, Art thou he that troubleth Israel? And he answered, I have not troubled Israel; but thou, and thy father's house, in that ye have forsaken the commandments of the Lord, and thou hast followed Baalim. Now therefore send, and gather to me all Israel unto mount Carmel, and the prophets of Baal four hundred and fifty, and the prophets of the groves four hundred, which eat at Jezebel's table.

So Ahab sent unto all the children of Israel, and gathered the prophets together unto mount Carmel.

And Elijah came unto all the people, and said, How long halt ye between two opinions? if the Lord be God, follow him: but if Baal, then follow him. And the people answered him not a word.

Then said Elijah unto the people, I, even I only, remain a prophet of the Lord; but Baal's prophets are four hundred and fifty men. Let them therefore give us two bullocks; and let them choose one bullock for themselves, and cut it in pieces, and lay it on wood, and put no fire under: and I will dress the other bullock, and lay it on wood, and put no fire under. And call ye on the name of your gods, and I will call on the name of the Lord: and the God that answereth by fire, let him be God. And all the people answered and said, It is well spoken.

And Elijah said unto the prophets of Baal, Choose you one bullock for yourselves, and dress it first; for ye are many; and call on the name of your gods, but put no fire under.

And they took the bullock which was given them, and they dressed it, and called on the name of Baal from morning even until noon, saying, O Baal, hear us. But there was no voice, nor any that answered. And they leaped upon the altar which was made.

And it came to pass at noon, that Elijah mocked them, and said, Cry aloud: for he is a god: either he is talking, or he is pursuing, or he is in a journey, or peradventure he sleepeth, and must be awaked.

And they cried aloud, and cut themselves after their manner with knives and lancets, till the blood gushed out upon them. And it came to pass, when mid-day was past, and they prophesied until the time of the offering of the evening sacrifice, that there was neither voice, nor any to answer, nor any that regarded.

And Elijah said unto all the people, Come near unto me. And all the people came near unto him. And he repaired the altar of the Lord that was broken down. And Elijah took twelve stones, according to the number of the tribes of the sons of Jacob, unto whom the word of the Lord came, saying, Israel shall be thy name. And with the stones he built an altar in the name of the Lord: and he made a trench about the altar, as great as would contain two measures of seed. And he put the wood in order, and cut the bullock in pieces, and laid him on the wood, and said, Fill four barrels with water, and pour it on the burnt-sacrifice, and on the wood. And he said, Do it the second time. And they did it the second time. And he said, Do it the third time. And they did it the third time. And the water ran round about the altar; and he filled the trench also with water.

And it came to pass at the time of the offering of the evening sacrifice, that Elijah the prophet came near and said, Lord God of Abraham, Isaac, and of Israel, let it be known this day that thou art God in Israel, and that I am thy servant, and that I have done all these things at thy word. Hear me, O Lord, hear me, that this people may know that thou art the Lord God, and that thou hast turned their heart back again.

Then the fire of the Lord fell, and consumed the burnt-sacrifice, and the wood, and the stones, and the dust, and licked up the water that was in the trench. And when all the people saw it, they fell on their faces: and they said, The Lord, he is the God; the Lord, he is the God.

And Elijah said unto them, Take the prophets of Baal; let not one of them escape. And they took them; and Elijah brought them down to the brook Kishon, and slew them there.

And Elijah said unto Ahab, Get thee up, eat and drink; for there is a sound of abundance of rain.

So Ahab went up to eat and to drink. And Elijah went up to the top of Carmel; and he cast himself down upon the earth, and put his face between his knees, and said to his servant, Go up now, look toward the sea. And he went up, and looked, and said, There is nothing. And he said, Go again seven times. And it came to pass at the seventh time, that he said, Behold, there ariseth a little cloud out of the sea, like a man's hand. And he said, Go up, say unto Ahab, Prepare thy chariot, and get thee down, that the rain stop thee not. And it came to pass in the meanwhile, that the heaven was black with clouds and wind, and there was a great rain. And Ahab rode, and went to Jezreel.

And the hand of the Lord was on Elijah; and he girded up his loins, and ran before Ahab to the entrance of Jezreel.

The Still Small Voice of God

And Ahab told Jezebel all that Elijah had done, and withal how he had slain all the prophets with the sword. Then Jezebel sent a messenger unto Elijah, saying, So let the gods do to me, and more also, if I make not thy life as the life of one of them by to-morrow about this time. And when he saw that, he arose, and went for his life, and came to Beer-sheba, which belongeth to Judah, and left his servant there.

But he himself went a day's journey into the wilderness, and came and sat down under a juniper-tree: and he requested for himself that he might die: and said, It is enough; now, O Lord, take away my life; for I am not better than my fathers. And as he lay and slept under a juniper-tree, behold, then an angel touched him, and said unto him, Arise and eat. And he looked, and behold, there was a cake baken on the coals, and a cruse of water at his head: and he did eat and drink, and laid him down again. And the angel of the Lord came again the second time, and touched him, and said, Arise and eat, because the journey is too great for thee. And he arose, and did eat and drink, and went in the strength of that meat forty days and forty nights unto Horeb the mount of God.

And he came thither unto a cave, and lodged there; and behold, the word of the Lord came to him, and he said unto him, What doest thou here, Elijah?

And he said, I have been very jealous for the Lord God of hosts: for the children of Israel have forsaken thy covenant, thrown down thine altars, and slain thy prophets with the sword; and I, even I only, am left; and they seek my life, to take it away.

And he said, Go forth, and stand upon the mount before the Lord. And behold, the Lord passed by, and a great and strong wind rent the mountains, and brake in pieces the rocks before the Lord; but the Lord was not in the wind: and after the wind an earthquake; but the Lord was not in the earthquake; and after the earthquake a fire; but the Lord was not in the fire: and after the fire a still small voice. And it was so, when Elijah heard it, that he wrapped his face in his mantle, and went out, and stood in the entering in of the cave. And behold, there came a voice unto him, and said, What doest thou here, Elijah?

And he said, I have been very jealous for the Lord God of hosts: because the children of Israel have forsaken thy covenant, thrown down thine altars, and slain thy prophets with the sword; and I, even I only, am left; and they seek my life, to take it away.

And the Lord said unto him, Go, return on thy way to the wilderness of Damascus: and when thou comest, anoint Hazael to be king over Syria; and Jehu the son of Nimshi shalt thou anoint to be king over Israel: and Elisha the son of Shaphat of Abel-meholah shalt thou anoint to be prophet in thy room. And it shall come to pass, that him that escapeth the sword of Hazael shall Jehu slay: and him that escapeth from the sword of Jehu shall Elisha slay. Yet I have left me seven thousand in Israel, all the knees which have not bowed unto Baal, and every mouth which hath not kissed him.

So he departed thence, and found Elisha the son of Shaphat, who was ploughing with twelve yoke of oxen before him, and he with the twelfth: and Elijah passed by him, and cast his mantle upon him. And he left the oxen, and ran after Elijah, and said, Let me, I pray thee, kiss my father and my mother, and then I will follow thee. And he said unto him, Go back again: for what have I done to thee?

And he returned back from him, and took a yoke of oxen, and slew them, and boiled their flesh with the instruments of the oxen, and gave unto the people, and they did eat. Then he arose, and went after Elijah, and ministered unto him.

The Story of Jezebel

And it came to pass after these things, that Naboth the Jezreelite had a vineyard, which was in Jezreel, hard by the palace of Ahab king of Samaria.

And Ahab spake unto Naboth, saying, Give me thy vineyard, that I may have it for a garden of herbs, because it is near unto my house: and I will give thee for it a better vineyard than it; or if it seem good to thee, I will give thee the worth of it in money.

And Naboth said to Ahab, The Lord forbid it me, that I should give the inheritance of my fathers unto thee.

And Ahab came into his house heavy and displeased, because of the word which Naboth the Jezreelite had spoken to him: for he had said, I will not give thee the inheritance of my fathers. And he laid him down upon his bed, and turned away his face, and would eat no bread.

But Jezebel his wife came to him, and said unto him, Why is thy spirit so sad, that thou eatest no bread?

And he said unto her, Because I spake unto Naboth the Jezreelite, and said unto him, Give me thy vineyard for money; or else, if it please thee, I will give thee another vineyard for it: and he answered, I will not give thee my vineyard.

And Jezebel his wife said unto him, Dost thou now govern the kingdom of Israel? arise, and eat bread, and let thine heart be merry: I will give thee the vineyard of Naboth the Jezreelite.

So she wrote letters in Ahab's name, and sealed them with his seal, and sent the letters unto the elders and to the nobles that were in his city, dwelling with Naboth. And she wrote in the letters, saying, Proclaim a fast, and set Naboth on high among the people: and set two men, sons of Belial, before him, to bear witness against him, saying, Thou didst blaspheme God and the king. And then carry him out and stone him, that he may die.

And the men of his city, even the elders and the nobles who were the inhabitants in his city, did as Jezebel had sent unto them, and as it was

written in the letters which she had sent unto them. They proclaimed a
fast, and set Naboth on high among the people. And there came in two
men, children of Belial, and sat before him: and the men of Belial witnessed against him, even against Naboth, in the presence of the people,
saying, Naboth did blaspheme God and the king. Then they carried him
forth out of the city, and stoned him with stones, that he died.

Then they sent to Jezebel, saying, Naboth is stoned, and is dead.

And it came to pass, when Jezebel heard that Naboth was stoned, and
was dead, that Jezebel said to Ahab, Arise, take possession of the vineyard of Naboth the Jezreelite, which he refused to give thee for money:
for Naboth is not alive, but dead.

And it came to pass, when Ahab heard that Naboth was dead, that
Ahab rose up to go down to the vineyard of Naboth the Jezreelite, to
take possession of it.

And the word of the Lord came to Elijah the Tishbite, saying, Arise,
go down to meet Ahab king of Israel, which is in Samaria: behold, he
is in the vineyard of Naboth, whither he is gone down to possess it.
And thou shalt speak unto him, saying, Thus saith the Lord, Hast thou
killed, and also taken possession? And thou shalt speak unto him, saying,
Thus saith the Lord, In the place where dogs licked the blood of Naboth
shall dogs lick thy blood, even thine.

And Ahab said to Elijah, Hast thou found me, O mine enemy?

And he answered, I have found thee: because thou hast sold thyself
to work evil in the sight of the Lord. Behold, I will bring evil upon
thee, and will take away thy posterity, and will cut off from Ahab him
that pisseth against the wall, and him that is shut up and left in Israel,
and will make thine house like the house of Jeroboam the son of Nebat,
and like the house of Baasha the son of Ahijah, for the provocation
wherewith thou hast provoked me to anger, and made Israel to sin.

And of Jezebel also spake the Lord, saying, The dogs shall eat Jezebel
by the wall of Jezreel.

Him that dieth of Ahab in the city the dogs shall eat: and him that
dieth in the field shall the fowls of the air eat. But there was none like
unto Ahab, which did sell himself to work wickedness in the sight of
the Lord, whom Jezebel his wife stirred up. And he did very abominably
in following idols, according to all things as did the Amorites, whom
the Lord cast out before the children of Israel.

And it came to pass, when Ahab heard those words, that he rent his clothes, and put sackcloth upon his flesh, and fasted, and lay in sackcloth, and went softly.

The Second Book of the Kings

Elijah Calls Down Fire from Heaven

Then Moab rebelled against Israel after the death of Ahab.

And Ahaziah fell down through a lattice in his upper chamber that was in Samaria, and was sick: and he sent messengers, and said unto them, Go, inquire of Baal-zebub the god of Ekron, whether I shall recover of this disease.

But the angel of the Lord said to Elijah the Tishbite, Arise, go up to meet the messengers of the king of Samaria, and say unto them, Is it not because there is not a God in Israel, that ye go to inquire of Baal-zebub the god of Ekron? Now therefore thus saith the Lord, Thou shalt not come down from that bed on which thou art gone up, but shalt surely die. And Elijah departed.

And when the messengers turned back unto him, he said unto them, Why are ye now turned back?

And they said unto him, There came a man up to meet us, and said unto us, Go, turn again unto the king that sent you, and say unto him, Thus saith the Lord, Is it not because there is not a God in Israel, that thou sendest to inquire of Baal-zebub the god of Ekron? therefore thou shalt not come down from that bed on which thou art gone up, but shalt surely die.

And he said unto them, What manner of man was he which came up to meet you, and told you these words?

And they answered him, He was an hairy man, and girt with a girdle of leather about his loins.

And he said, It is Elijah the Tishbite.

Then the king sent unto him a captain of fifty with his fifty. And he went up to him: and behold, he sat on the top of an hill. And he spake unto him, Thou man of God, the king hath said, Come down.

And Elijah answered and said to the captain of fifty, If I be a man of God, then let fire come down from heaven, and consume thee and thy fifty. And there came down fire from heaven, and consumed him and his fifty.

Again also he sent unto him another captain of fifty with his fifty. And he answered and said unto him, O man of God, thus hath the king said, Come down quickly.

And Elijah answered and said unto them, If I be a man of God, let fire come down from heaven, and consume thee and thy fifty. And the fire of God came down from heaven, and consumed him and his fifty.

And he sent again a captain of the third fifty with his fifty. And the third captain of fifty went up, and came and fell on his knees before Elijah, and besought him, and said unto him, O man of God, I pray thee, let my life, and the life of these fifty thy servants, be precious in thy sight. Behold, there came fire down from heaven, and burnt up the two captains of the former fifties with their fifties: therefore let my life now be precious in thy sight.

And the angel of the Lord said unto Elijah, Go down with him: be not afraid of him. And he arose, and went down with him unto the king.

And he said unto him, Thus saith the Lord, Forasmuch as thou hast sent messengers to inquire of Baal-zebub the god of Ekron (is it not because there is no God in Israel to inquire of his word?), therefore thou shalt not come down off that bed on which thou art gone up, but shalt surely die.

So he died according to the word of the Lord which Elijah had spoken. And Jehoram reigned in his stead in the second year of Jehoram the son of Jehoshaphat king of Judah; because he had no son.

Now the rest of the acts of Ahaziah which he did, are they not written in the book of the Chronicles of the kings of Israel?

Elijah Ascends to Heaven

And it came to pass, when the Lord would take up Elijah into heaven by a whirlwind, that Elijah went with Elisha from Gilgal. And Elijah said unto Elisha, Tarry here, I pray thee; for the Lord hath sent me to Beth-el. And Elisha said unto him, As the Lord liveth, and as thy soul liveth, I will not leave thee. So they went down to Beth-el.

And the sons of the prophets that were at Beth-el came forth to Elisha, and said unto him, Knowest thou that the Lord will take away thy master from thy head to-day? And he said, Yea, I know it; hold ye your peace. And Elijah said unto him, Elisha, tarry here, I pray thee; for the Lord hath sent me to Jericho. And he said, As the Lord liveth, and as thy soul liveth, I will not leave thee. So they came to Jericho.

And the sons of the prophets that were at Jericho came to Elisha, and said unto him, Knowest thou that the Lord will take away thy master from thy head to-day? And he answered, Yea, I know it; hold ye your peace. And Elijah said unto him, Tarry, I pray thee, here; for the Lord hath sent me to Jordan. And he said, As the Lord liveth, and as thy soul liveth, I will not leave thee. And they two went on.

And fifty men of the sons of the prophets went, and stood to view afar off: and they two stood by Jordan. And Elijah took his mantle, and wrapped it together, and smote the waters, and they were divided hither and thither, so that they two went over on dry ground.

And it came to pass, when they were gone over, that Elijah said unto Elisha, Ask what I shall do for thee, before I be taken away from thee. And Elisha said, I pray thee, let a double portion of thy spirit be upon me.

And he said, Thou hast asked a hard thing: nevertheless, if thou see me when I am taken from thee, it shall be so unto thee; but if not, it shall not be so.

And it came to pass, as they still went on, and talked, that behold, there appeared a chariot of fire, and horses of fire, and parted them both asunder; and Elijah went up by a whirlwind into heaven.

And Elisha saw it, and he cried, My father, my father, the chariot of Israel, and the horsemen thereof! And he saw him no more: and he took hold of his own clothes, and rent them in two pieces. He took up also the mantle of Elijah that fell from him, and went back, and stood by the bank of Jordan; and he took the mantle of Elijah that fell from him, and smote the waters, and said, Where is the Lord God of Elijah? And when he also had smitten the waters, they parted hither and thither: and Elisha went over.

And he went up from thence unto Beth-el: and as he was going up by the way, there came forth little children out of the city, and mocked him, and said unto him, Go up, thou bald-head; go up, thou bald-head. And he turned back, and looked on them, and cursed them in the name of the Lord. And there came forth two she-bears out of the wood, and tare forty and two children of them.

And he went from thence to mount Carmel, and from thence he returned to Samaria.

The Cure of Naaman

Now Naaman, captain of the host of the king of Syria, was a great man with his master, and honourable, because by him the Lord had given deliverance unto Syria: he was also a mighty man in valour, but he was a leper.

And the Syrians had gone out by companies, and had brought away captive out of the land of Israel a little maid; and she waited on Naaman's wife. And she said unto her mistress, Would God my lord were with the prophet that is in Samaria! for he would recover him of his leprosy.

And one went in, and told his lord, saying, Thus and thus said the maid that is of the land of Israel.

And the king of Syria said, Go to, go, and I will send a letter unto the king of Israel. And he departed, and took with him ten talents of silver, and six thousand pieces of gold, and ten changes of raiment. And he brought the letter to the king of Israel, saying, Now when this letter is come unto thee, behold, I have therewith sent Naaman my servant to thee, that thou mayest recover him of his leprosy.

And it came to pass, when the king of Israel had read the letter, that he rent his clothes, and said, Am I God, to kill and to make alive, that this man doth send unto me to recover a man of his leprosy? Wherefore consider, I pray you, and see how he seeketh a quarrel against me.

And it was so, when Elisha the man of God had heard that the king of Israel had rent his clothes, that he sent to the king, saying, Wherefore hast thou rent thy clothes? let him come now to me, and he shall know that there is a prophet in Israel.

So Naaman came with his horses and with his chariot, and stood at the door of the house of Elisha.

And Elisha sent a messenger unto him, saying, Go and wash in Jordan seven times, and thy flesh shall come again to thee, and thou shalt be clean.

But Naaman was wroth, and went away, and said, Behold, I thought, He will surely come out to me, and stand, and call on the name of the Lord his God, and strike his hand over the place, and recover the leper. Are not Abana and Pharpar, rivers of Damascus, better than all the waters of Israel? may I not wash in them, and be clean? So he turned and went away in a rage.

And his servants came near, and spake unto him, and said, My father, if the prophet had bid thee do some great thing, wouldest thou not have done it? how much rather then, when he saith to thee, Wash, and be clean?

Then went he down, and dipped himself seven times in Jordan, according to the saying of the man of God: and his flesh came again like unto the flesh of a little child, and he was clean.

And he returned to the man of God, he and all his company, and came and stood before him: and he said, Behold, now I know that there is no God in all the earth, but in Israel: now therefore, I pray thee, take a blessing of thy servant.

But he said, As the Lord liveth, before whom I stand, I will receive none. And he urged him to take it; but he refused.

Jerusalem Spared

And Hezekiah prayed before the Lord and said, O Lord God of Israel, which dwellest between the cherubims, thou art the God, even thou alone, of all the kingdoms of the earth; thou hast made heaven and earth. Lord, bow down thine ear, and hear: open, Lord, thine eyes, and see: and hear the words of Sennacherib, which hath sent him to reproach the living God.

Of a truth, Lord, the kings of Assyria have destroyed the nations and their lands, and have cast their gods into the fire: for they were no gods, but the work of men's hands, wood and stone: therefore they have destroyed them. Now therefore, O Lord our God, I beseech thee, save thou us out of his hand, that all the kingdoms of the earth may know that thou art the Lord God, even thou only.

Then Isaiah the son of Amoz sent to Hezekiah, saying, Thus saith the Lord God of Israel, That which thou hast prayed to me against Sennacherib king of Assyria I have heard. This is the word that the Lord hath spoken concerning him; The virgin the daughter of Zion hath despised thee, and laughed thee to scorn; the daughter of Jerusalem hath shaken her head at thee.

Whom hast thou reproached and blasphemed? and against whom hast thou exalted thy voice, and lifted up thine eyes on high? even against the Holy One of Israel. By thy messengers thou hast reproached the Lord, and hast said, With the multitude of my chariots I am come up to the height of the mountains, to the sides of Lebanon, and will cut down the tall cedar-trees thereof, and the choice fir-trees thereof: and I will enter into the lodgings of his borders, and into the forest of his Carmel. I have digged and drunk strange waters, and with the sole of my feet have I dried up all the rivers of besieged places.

Hast thou not heard long ago how I have done it, and of ancient times that I have formed it? now have I brought it to pass, that thou shouldest be to lay waste fenced cities into ruinous heaps. Therefore their inhabitants were of small power, they were dismayed and confounded; they were as the grass of the field, and as the green herb, as the grass on the house-tops, and as corn blasted before it be grown up. But I know thy abode, and thy going out, and thy coming in, and thy rage against me.

Because thy rage against me and thy tumult is come up into mine ears, therefore I will put my hook in thy nose, and my bridle in thy lips, and I will turn thee back by the way by which thou camest. And this shall be a sign unto thee, Ye shall eat this year such things as grow of themselves, and in the second year that which springeth of the same; and in the third year sow ye, and reap, and plant vineyards, and eat the fruits thereof.

And the remnant that is escaped of the house of Judah shall yet again take root downward, and bear fruit upward. For out of Jerusalem shall go forth a remnant, and they that escape out of mount Zion: the zeal of the Lord of hosts shall do this.

Therefore thus saith the Lord concerning the king of Assyria, He shall not come into this city, nor shoot an arrow there, nor come before it with shield, nor cast a bank against it. By the way that he came, by the same shall he return, and shall not come into this city, saith the Lord. For I will defend this city, to save it, for mine own sake, and for my servant David's sake.

And it came to pass that night, that the angel of the Lord went out, and smote in the camp of the Assyrians an hundred fourscore and five thousand: and when they arose early in the morning, behold, they were all dead corpses.

So Sennacherib king of Assyria departed, and went and returned, and dwelt at Nineveh.

The Discovery of Deuteronomy

And it came to pass in the eighteenth year of king Josiah, that the king sent Shaphan the son of Azaliah, the son of Meshullam, the scribe, to the house of the Lord, saying, Go up to Hilkiah the high priest, that he may sum the silver which is brought into the house of the Lord, which the keepers of the door have gathered of the people: and let them deliver it into the hand of the doers of the work, that have the oversight of the house of the Lord: and let them give it to the doers of the work, which is in the house of the Lord, to repair the breaches of the house, unto carpenters, and builders, and masons, and to buy timber and hewn stone to repair the house.

Howbeit, there was no reckoning made with them of the money that was delivered into their hand, because they dealt faithfully.

And Hilkiah the high priest said unto Shaphan the scribe, I have found the book of the law in the house of the Lord. And Hilkiah gave the book to Shaphan, and he read it.

And Shaphan the scribe came to the king, and brought the king word again, and said, Thy servants have gathered the money that was found in the house, and have delivered it into the hand of them that do the work, that have the oversight of the house of the Lord. And Shaphan the scribe shewed the king, saying, Hilkiah the priest hath delivered me a book. And Shaphan read it before the king.

And the king sent, and they gathered unto him all the elders of Judah and of Jerusalem.

And the king went up into the house of the Lord, and all the men of Judah and all the inhabitants of Jerusalem with him, and the priests, and the prophets, and all the people, both small and great: and he read in their ears all the words of the book of the covenant which was found in the house of the Lord.

And the king stood by a pillar, and made a covenant before the Lord, to walk after the Lord, and to keep his commandments, and his testimonies, and his statutes, with all their heart, and all their soul, to perform the words of this covenant that were written in this book. And all the people stood to the covenant.

And the king commanded Hilkiah the high priest, and the priests of the second order, and the keepers of the door, to bring forth out of the temple of the Lord all the vessels that were made for Baal, and for the grove, and for all the host of heaven: and he burned them without Jerusalem in the fields of Kidron, and carried the ashes of them unto Beth-el. And he put down the idolatrous priests, whom the kings of Judah had ordained to burn incense in the high places in the cities of Judah, and in the places round about Jerusalem; them also that burned incense unto Baal, to the sun, and to the moon, and to the planets, and to all the host of heaven. And he brought out the grove from the house of the Lord, without Jerusalem, unto the brook Kidron, and burned it at the brook Kidron, and stamped it small to powder, and cast the powder thereof upon the graves of the children of the people.

And he brake down the houses of the sodomites that were by the house of the Lord, where the women wove hangings for the grove.

And he brought all the priests out of the cities of Judah, and defiled the high places where the priests had burnt incense, from Geba to Beersheba, and brake down the high places of the gates that were in the entering in of the gate of Joshua the governor of the city, which were on a man's left hand at the gate of the city.

Ezra and Nehemiah

The Proclamation of Cyrus

Now in the first year of Cyrus king of Persia, that the word of the Lord by the mouth of Jeremiah might be fulfilled, the Lord stirred up the spirit of Cyrus king of Persia, that he made a proclamation throughout all his kingdom, and put it also in writing, saying,

Thus saith Cyrus king of Persia, The Lord God of heaven hath given me all the kingdoms of the earth; and he hath charged me to build him an house at Jerusalem, which is in Judah. Who is there among you of all his people? his God be with him, and let him go up to Jerusalem, which is in Judah, and build the house of the Lord God of Israel, (he is the God,) which is in Jerusalem. And whosoever remaineth in any place where he sojourneth, let the men of his place help him with silver, and with gold, and with goods, and with beasts, besides the free-will-offering for the house of God that is in Jerusalem.

Then rose up the chief of the fathers of Judah and Benjamin, and the priests, and the Levites, with all them whose spirit God had raised, to go up to build the house of the Lord which is in Jerusalem. And all they that were about them strengthened their hands with vessels of silver, with gold, with goods, and with beasts, and with precious things, besides all that was willingly offered.

The Altar Is Set Up

And when the seventh month was come, and the children of Israel were in the cities, the people gathered themselves together as one man to Jerusalem. Then stood up Jeshua the son of Jozadak, and his brethren the priests, and Zerubbabel the son of Shealtiel, and his brethren, and builded the altar of the God of Israel, to offer burnt-offerings thereon, as it is written in the law of Moses the man of God. And they set the altar upon his bases; for fear was upon them because of the people of those countries: and they offered burnt-offerings thereon unto the Lord, even burnt-offerings morning and evening. They kept also the feast of tabernacles, as it is written, and offered the daily burnt-offerings by number, according to the custom, as the duty of every day required; and afterward offered the continual burnt-offering, both of the new-moons, and of all the set feasts of the Lord that were consecrated, and of every one that willingly offered a free-will offering unto the Lord.

From the first day of the seventh month began they to offer burnt-offerings unto the Lord. But the foundation of the temple of the Lord was not yet laid.

Now when the adversaries of Judah and Benjamin heard that the children of the captivity builded the temple unto the Lord God of Israel; then they came to Zerubbabel, and to the chief of the fathers, and said unto them, Let us build with you: for we seek your God, as ye do; and we do sacrifice unto him since the day of Esarhaddon king of Assur, which brought us up hither.

But Zerubbabel, and Jeshua, and the rest of the chief of the fathers of Israel, said unto them, Ye have nothing to do with us to build an house unto our God; but we ourselves together will build unto the Lord God of Israel, as king Cyrus the king of Persia hath commanded us.

Then the people of the land weakened the hands of the people of Judah, and troubled them in building, and hired counsellors against them, to frustrate their purpose, all the days of Cyrus king of Persia, even until the reign of Darius king of Persia.

The Temple Is Finished

And the elders of the Jews builded, and they prospered through the prophesying of Haggai the prophet and Zechariah the son of Iddo. And they builded, and finished it, according to the commandment of the God of Israel, and according to the commandment of Cyrus, and Darius, and Artaxerxes king of Persia. And this house was finished on the third day of the month Adar, which was in the sixth year of the reign of Darius the king.

And the children of Israel, the priests, and the Levites, and the rest of the children of the captivity, kept the dedication of this house of God with joy, and offered at the dedication of this house of God an hundred bullocks, two hundred rams, four hundred lambs; and for a sin-offering for all Israel, twelve he-goats, according to the number of the tribes of Israel.

And they set the priests in their divisions, and the Levites in their courses, for the service of God, which is at Jerusalem; as it is written in the book of Moses.

And the children of the captivity kept the passover upon the fourteenth day of the first month. For the priests and the Levites were purified together, all of them were pure, and killed the passover for all the children of the captivity, and for their brethren the priests, and for themselves.

And the children of Israel, which were come again out of captivity, and all such as had separated themselves unto them from the filthiness of the heathen of the land, to seek the Lord God of Israel, did eat, and kept the feast of unleavened bread seven days with joy: for the Lord had made them joyful, and turned the heart of the king of Assyria unto them, to strengthen their hands in the work of the house of God, the God of Israel.

Artaxerxes' Letter

Now this is the copy of the letter that the king Artaxerxes gave unto Ezra the priest, the scribe, even a scribe of the words of the commandments of the Lord, and of his statutes to Israel.

Artaxerxes, king of kings, Unto Ezra the priest, a scribe of the law of the God of heaven, perfect peace, and at such a time.

Whatsoever is commanded by the God of heaven, let it be diligently done for the house of the God of heaven: for why should there be wrath against the realm of the king and his sons? Also we certify you, that touching any of the priests and Levites, singers, porters, Nethinims, or ministers of this house of God, it shall not be lawful to impose toll, tribute, or custom, upon them.

And thou, Ezra, after the wisdom of thy God, that is in thine hand, set magistrates and judges, which may judge all the people that are beyond the river, all such as know the laws of thy God; and teach ye them that know them not. And whosoever will not do the law of thy God, and the law of the king, let judgment be executed speedily upon him, whether it be unto death, or to banishment, or to confiscation of goods, or to imprisonment.

Ezra's Prayer

Now the princes came to me, saying, The people of Israel, and the priests, and the Levites, have not separated themselves from the people of the lands, doing according to their abominations, even of the Canaanites, the Hittites, the Perizzites, the Jebusites, the Ammonites, the Moabites, the Egyptians, and the Amorites. For they have taken of their daughters for themselves, and for their sons: so that the holy seed have mingled themselves with the people of those lands: yea, the hand of the princes and rulers hath been chief in this trespass.

And when I heard this thing, I rent my garment and my mantle, and plucked off the hair of my head and of my beard, and sat down astonied. Then were assembled unto me every one that trembled at the words of the God of Israel, because of the transgression of those that had been carried away; and I sat astonied until the evening sacrifice.

And at the evening sacrifice I arose up from my heaviness; and having rent my garment and my mantle, I fell upon my knees, and spread out my hands unto the Lord my God, and said, O my God, I am ashamed and blush to lift up my face to thee, my God: for our iniquities are increased over our head, and our trespass is grown up unto the heavens.

Since the days of our fathers have we been in a great trespass unto this day; and for our iniquities have we, our kings, and our priests, been delivered into the hand of the kings of the lands, to the sword, to captivity, and to a spoil, and to confusion of face, as it is this day. And now for a little space grace hath been shewed from the Lord our God, to leave us a remnant to escape, and to give us a nail in his holy place, that our God may lighten our eyes, and give us a little reviving in our bondage.

For we were bond-men; yet our God hath not forsaken us in our bondage, but hath extended mercy unto us in the sight of the kings of Persia, to give us a reviving, to set up the house of our God, and to repair the desolations thereof, and to give us a wall in Judah and in Jerusalem.

And now, O our God, what shall we say after this? for we have forsaken thy commandments, which thou hast commanded by thy servants the prophets, saying, The land unto which ye go to possess it, is an unclean land with the filthiness of the people of the lands, with their abominations, which have filled it from one end to another with their uncleanness. Now therefore give not your daughters unto their sons, neither take their daughters unto your sons, nor seek their peace or their wealth for ever: that ye may be strong, and eat the good of the land, and leave it for an inheritance to your children for ever.

And after all that is come upon us for our evil deeds, and for our great trespass, seeing that thou our God hast punished us less than our iniquities deserve, and hast given us such deliverance as this; should we again break thy commandments, and join in affinity with the people of these abominations? wouldest not thou be angry with us till thou hadst consumed us, so that there should be no remnant nor escaping?

O Lord God of Israel, thou art righteous: for we remain yet escaped, as it is this day: behold, we are before thee in our trespasses; for we cannot stand before thee because of this.

The Strange Wives Put Away

Now when Ezra had prayed, and when he had confessed, weeping and casting himself down before the house of God, there assembled unto him out of Israel a very great congregation of men and women and children: for the people wept very sore.

And Shechaniah the son of Jehiel, one of the sons of Elam, answered and said unto Ezra, We have trespassed against our God, and have taken strange wives of the people of the land: yet now there is hope in Israel concerning this thing. Now therefore let us make a covenant with our God to put away all the wives, and such as are born of them, according to the counsel of my lord, and of those that tremble at the commandment of our God; and let it be done according to the law. Arise; for this matter belongeth unto thee: we also will be with thee: be of good courage, and do it.

Then arose Ezra, and made the chief priests, the Levites, and all Israel, to swear that they should do according to this word. And they sware.

And they made proclamation throughout Judah and Jerusalem unto all the children of the captivity, that they should gather themselves together unto Jerusalem; and that whosoever would not come within three days, according to the counsel of the princes and the elders, all his substance should be forfeited, and himself separated from the congregation of those that had been carried away.

Then all the men of Judah and Benjamin gathered themselves together unto Jerusalem within three days. It was the ninth month, on the twentieth day of the month; and all the people sat in the street of the house of God, trembling because of this matter, and for the great rain. And Ezra the priest stood up, and said unto them, Ye have transgressed, and have taken strange wives to increase the trespass of Israel. Now therefore make confession unto the Lord God of your fathers, and do his pleasure: and separate yourselves from the people of the land, and from the strange wives.

And the children of the captivity did so. And Ezra the priest, with certain chief of the fathers, after the house of their fathers, and all of them by their names, were separated, and sat down in the first day of the tenth month to examine the matter. And they made an end with all the men that had taken strange wives by the first day of the first month.

And among the sons of the priests there were found that had taken strange wives: namely, of the sons of Jeshua the son of Jozadak, and his brethren; Maaseiah, and Eliezer, and Jarib, and Gedaliah. And they gave their hands that they would put away their wives; and being guilty they offered a ram of the flock for their trespass.

The Jews Complain

The words of Nehemiah the son of Hachaliah.

And there was a great cry of the people and of their wives against their brethren the Jews. For there were that said, We, our sons, and our daughters, are many: therefore we take up corn for them, that we may eat, and live. Some also there were that said, We have mortgaged our lands, vineyards, and houses, that we might buy corn, because of the dearth. There were also that said, We have borrowed money for the king's tribute, and that upon our lands and vineyards. Yet now our flesh is as the flesh of our brethren, our children as their children: and lo, we bring into bondage our sons and our daughters to be servants, and some of our daughters are brought into bondage already: neither is it in our power to redeem them; for other men have our lands and vineyards.

And I was very angry when I heard their cry and these words. Then I consulted with myself, and I rebuked the nobles, and the rulers, and said unto them, Ye exact usury, every one of his brother. And I set a great assembly against them. And I said unto them, We, after our ability, have redeemed our brethren the Jews, which were sold unto the heathen; and will ye even sell your brethren? or shall they be sold unto us? Then held they their peace, and found nothing to answer.

Also I said, It is not good that ye do: ought ye not to walk in the fear of our God because of the reproach of the heathen our enemies? I likewise, and my brethren, and my servants, might exact of them money and corn: I pray you, let us leave off this usury. Restore, I pray you, to them, even this day, their lands, their vineyards, their olive-yards, and their houses, also the hundredth part of the money, and of the corn, the wine, and the oil, that ye exact of them.

Then said they, We will restore them, and will require nothing of them; so will we do as thou sayest. Then I called the priests, and took an oath of them, that they should do according to this promise. Also I shook my lap, and said, So God shake out every man from his house, and from his labour, that performeth not this promise, even thus be he shaken out, and emptied. And all the congregation said, Amen, and praised the Lord. And the people did according to this promise.

Moreover, from the time that I was appointed to be their governor in the land of Judah, from the twentieth year even unto the two and thirtieth year of Artaxerxes the king, that is, twelve years, I and my brethren have not eaten the bread of the governor. But the former governors that had been before me were chargeable unto the people, and had taken of them bread and wine, beside forty shekels of silver; yea, even their servants bare rule over the people: but so did not I, because of the fear of God.

Ezra Reads from the Law

And all the people gathered themselves together as one man into the street that was before the water-gate; and they spake unto Ezra the scribe to bring the book of the law of Moses, which the Lord had commanded to Israel. And Ezra the priest brought the law before the congregation both of men and women, and all that could hear with understanding, upon the first day of the seventh month.

And Ezra opened the book in the sight of all the people; (for he was above all the people;) and when he opened it, all the people stood up: and Ezra blessed the Lord, the great God. And all the people answered, Amen, Amen, with lifting up their hands: and they bowed their heads, and worshipped the Lord with their faces to the ground.

Also Jeshua, and Bani, and Sherebiah, Jamin, Akkub, Shabbethai, Hodijah, Maaseiah, Kelita, Azariah, Jozabad, Hanan, Pelaiah, and the Levites, caused the people to understand the law: and the people stood in their place. So they read in the book in the law of God distinctly, and gave the sense, and caused them to understand the reading.

And Nehemiah, which is the Tirshatha, and Ezra the priest the scribe, and the Levites that taught the people, said unto all the people, This day is holy unto the Lord your God; mourn not, nor weep. For all the people wept, when they heard the words of the law.

Then he said unto them, Go your way, eat the fat, and drink the sweet, and send portions unto them for whom nothing is prepared: for this day is holy unto our Lord: neither be ye sorry; for the joy of the Lord is your strength.

So the Levites stilled all the people, saying, Hold your peace, for the day is holy; neither be ye grieved. And all the people went their way to eat, and to drink, and to send portions, and to make great mirth, because they had understood the words that were declared unto them.

And on the second day were gathered together the chief of the fathers of all the people, the priests, and the Levites, unto Ezra the scribe, even to understand the words of the law. And they found written in the law which the Lord had commanded by Moses, that the children of Israel should dwell in booths in the feast of the seventh month; and that they should publish and proclaim in all their cities, and in Jerusalem, saying,

Go forth unto the mount, and fetch olive-branches, and pine-branches, and myrtle-branches, and palm-branches, and branches of thick trees, to make booths, as it is written.

So the people went forth, and brought them, and made themselves booths, every one upon the roof of his house, and in their courts, and in the courts of the house of God, and in the street of the water-gate, and in the street of the gate of Ephraim. And all the congregation of them that were come again out of the captivity made booths, and sat under the booths; for since the days of Jeshua the son of Nun unto that day had not the children of Israel done so. And there was very great gladness.

Also day by day, from the first day unto the last day, he read in the book of the law of God. And they kept the feast seven days; and on the eighth day was a solemn assembly, according unto the manner.

They Repent and Fast

Now in the twenty and fourth day of this month the children of Israel were assembled with fasting, and with sackclothes, and earth upon them. And the seed of Israel separated themselves from all strangers, and stood and confessed their sins, and the iniquities of their fathers.

And they stood up in their place, and read in the book of the law of the Lord their God one fourth part of the day; and another fourth part they confessed, and worshipped the Lord their God.

The Book of Esther

Vashti's Disobedience

Now it came to pass in the days of Ahasuerus, (this is Ahasuerus which reigned from India even unto Ethiopia, over an hundred and seven and twenty provinces:) that in those days, when the king Ahasuerus sat on the throne of his kingdom, which was in Shushan the palace, in the third year of his reign, he made a feast unto all his princes and his servants; the power of Persia and Media, the nobles and princes of the provinces, being before him; when he shewed the riches of his glorious kingdom and the honour of his excellent majesty many days, even an hundred and fourscore days.

And when these days were expired, the king made a feast unto all the people that were present in Shushan the palace, both unto great and small, seven days, in the court of the garden of the king's palace. Also Vashti the queen made a feast for the women in the royal house which belonged to king Ahasuerus.

On the seventh day, when the heart of the king was merry with wine, he commanded Mehuman, Biztha, Harbona, Bigtha, and Abagtha, Zethar, and Carcas, the seven chamberlains that served in the presence of Ahasuerus the king, to bring Vashti the queen before the king with the crown royal, to shew the people and the princes her beauty: for she was fair to look on. But the queen Vashti refused to come at the king's commandment by his chamberlains: therefore was the king very wroth, and his anger burned in him.

Then the king said to the wise men, which knew the times, (for so was the king's manner toward all that knew law and judgment:) What shall we do unto the queen Vashti according to law, because she hath not performed the commandment of the king Ahasuerus by the chamberlains?

And Memucan answered before the king and the princes, Vashti the queen hath not done wrong to the king only, but also to all the princes, and to all the people that are in all the provinces of the king Ahasuerus. For this deed of the queen shall come abroad unto all women, so that they shall despise their husbands in their eyes, when it shall be reported, The king Ahasuerus commanded Vashti the queen to be brought in before him, but she came not. Likewise shall the ladies of Persia and Media say this day unto all the king's princes, which have heard of the deed of the queen. Thus shall there arise too much contempt and wrath. If it please the king, let there go a royal commandment from him, and let it be written among the laws of the Persians and the Medes, that it be not altered, That Vashti come no more before Ahasuerus: and let the king give her royal estate unto another that is better than she. And when the king's decree which he shall make shall be published throughout all

his empire, (for it is great,) all the wives shall give to their
honour, both to great and small.

And the saying pleased the king and the princes; and the k\
according to the word of Memucan: for he sent letters into all the\
provinces, into every province according to the writing thereof, ai
every people after their language, that every man should bear rule in his
own house; and that it should be published according to the language of
every people.

A New Queen Is Found

Then said the king's servants that ministered unto him, Let there be
fair young virgins sought for the king. And let the king appoint officers
in all the provinces of his kingdom, that they may gather together all
the fair young virgins unto Shushan the palace, to the house of the
women, unto the custody of Hege the king's chamberlain, keeper of the
women; and let their things for purification be given them. And let the
maiden which pleaseth the king be queen instead of Vashti.

And the thing pleased the king; and he did so.

Now in Shushan the palace there was a certain Jew, whose name was
Mordecai, the son of Jair, the son of Shimei, the son of Kish, a Benjamite, who had been carried away from Jerusalem with the captivity
which had been carried away with Jeconiah king of Judah, whom
Nebuchadnezzar the king of Babylon had carried away. And he brought
up Hadassah, (that is, Esther,) his uncle's daughter: for she had neither
father nor mother, and the maid was fair and beautiful; whom Mordecai,
when her father and mother were dead, took for his own daughter.

So it came to pass, when the king's commandment and his decree was
heard, and when many maidens were gathered together unto Shushan
the palace, to the custody of Hegai, that Esther was brought also unto the
king's house, to the custody of Hegai, keeper of the women. And the
maiden pleased him, and she obtained kindness of him; and he speedily
gave her her things for purification, with such things as belonged to her,
and seven maidens which were meet to be given her, out of the king's
house: and he preferred her and her maids unto the best place of the
house of the women.

Esther had not shewed her people nor her kindred: for Mordecai had charged her that she should not shew it. And Mordecai walked every day before the court of the women's house, to know how Esther did, and what should become of her.

Now when every maid's turn was come to go in to king Ahasuerus, after that she had been twelve months, according to the manner of the women, (for so were the days of their purifications accomplished, to wit, six months with oil of myrrh, and six months with sweet odours, and with other things for the purifying of the women;) then thus came every maiden unto the king; whatsoever she desired was given her to go with her out of the house of the women unto the king's house. In the evening she went, and on the morrow she returned into the second house of the women, to the custody of Shaashgaz, the king's chamberlain, which kept the concubines: she came in unto the king no more, except the king delighted in her, and that she were called by name.

Now when the turn of Esther, the daughter of Abihail the uncle of Mordecai, who had taken her for his daughter, was come to go in unto the king, she required nothing but what Hegai the king's chamberlain, the keeper of the women, appointed. And Esther obtained favour in the sight of all them that looked upon her,

So Esther was taken unto king Ahasuerus into his house-royal in the tenth month, which is the month Tebeth, in the seventh year of his reign. And the king loved Esther above all the women, and she obtained grace and favour in his sight more than all the virgins; so that he set the royal crown upon her head, and made her queen instead of Vashti.

Then the king made a great feast unto all his princes and his servants, even Esther's feast; and he made a release to the provinces, and gave gifts, according to the state of the king. And when the virgins were gathered together the second time, then Mordecai sat in the king's gate.

Esther had not yet shewed her kindred, nor her people, as Mordecai had charged her: for Esther did the commandment of Mordecai, like as when she was brought up with him.

In those days, while Mordecai sat in the king's gate, two of the king's chamberlains, Bigthan and Teresh, of those which kept the door, were wroth, and sought to lay hand on the king Ahasuerus. And the thing was known to Mordecai, who told it unto Esther the queen; and Esther certified the king thereof in Mordecai's name. And when inquisition was made of the matter, it was found out; therefore they were both hanged to a tree: and it was written in the book of the Chronicles before the king.

Haman Seeks to Slay the Jews

After these things did king Ahasuerus promote Haman the son of Hammedatha the Agagite, and advanced him, and set his seat above all the princes that were with him. And all the king's servants that were in the king's gate, bowed, and reverenced Haman; for the king had so commanded concerning him. But Mordecai bowed not, nor did him reverence. Then the king's servants which were in the king's gate, said unto Mordecai, Why transgressest thou the king's commandment? Now it came to pass, when they spake daily unto him, and he hearkened not unto them, that they told Haman, to see whether Mordecai's matters would stand: for he had told them that he was a Jew.

And when Haman saw that Mordecai bowed not, nor did him reverence, then was Haman full of wrath. And he thought scorn to lay hands on Mordecai alone; for they had shewed him the people of Mordecai: wherefore Haman sought to destroy all the Jews that were throughout the whole kingdom of Ahasuerus, even the people of Mordecai.

And Haman said unto king Ahasuerus, There is a certain people scattered abroad and dispersed among the people in all the provinces of thy kingdom; and their laws are diverse from all people; neither keep they the king's laws: therefore it is not for the king's profit to suffer them. If it please the king, let it be written that they may be destroyed: and I will pay ten thousand talents of silver to the hands of those that have the charge of the business, to bring it into the king's treasuries.

And the king took his ring from his hand, and gave it unto Haman the son of Hammedatha the Agagite, the Jews' enemy.

And the king said unto Haman, The silver is given to thee, the people also, to do with them as it seemeth good to thee.

Then were the king's scribes called on the thirteenth day of the first month, and there was written according to all that Haman had commanded unto the king's lieutenants, and to the governors that were over every province, and to the rulers of every people of every province, according to the writing thereof, and to every people after their language; in the name of king Ahasuerus was it written, and sealed with the king's ring. And the letters were sent by posts into all the king's provinces, to destroy, to kill, and to cause to perish, all Jews, both young and old, little children and women, in one day, even upon the thirteenth day of the twelfth month, which is the month Adar, and to take the spoil of them for a prey.

Mordecai Asks Esther to Help

When Mordecai perceived all that was done, Mordecai rent his clothes, and put on sackcloth with ashes, and went out into the midst of the city, and cried with a loud and a bitter cry; and came even before the king's gate: for none might enter into the king's gate clothed with sackcloth. And in every province whithersoever the king's commandment and his decree came, there was great mourning among the Jews, and fasting, and weeping, and wailing; and many lay in sackcloth and ashes.

So Esther's maids and her chamberlains came and told it her. Then was the queen exceedingly grieved; and she sent raiment to clothe Mordecai, and to take away his sackcloth from him: but he received it not. Then called Esther for Hatach, one of the king's chamberlains, whom he had appointed to attend upon her, and gave him a commandment to Mordecai, to know what it was, and why it was. So Hatach went forth to Mordecai, unto the street of the city, which was before the king's gate. And Mordecai told him of all that had happened unto him, and of the sum of the money that Haman had promised to pay to the king's treasuries for the Jews, to destroy them. Also he gave him the copy of the writing of the decree that was given at Shushan to destroy them, to shew it unto Esther, and to declare it unto her, and to charge her that she should go in unto the king, to make supplication unto him, and to make request before him for her people. And Hatach came and told Esther the words of Mordecai.

Again Esther spake unto Hatach, and gave him commandment unto Mordecai: All the king's servants, and the people of the king's provinces, do know, that whosoever, whether man or woman, shall come unto the king into the inner court, who is not called, there is one law of his to put him to death, except such to whom the king shall hold out the golden sceptre, that he may live: but I have not been called to come in unto the king these thirty days. And they told to Mordecai Esther's words.

Then Mordecai commanded to answer Esther, Think not with thyself that thou shalt escape in the king's house, more than all the Jews. For if

thou altogether holdest thy peace at this time, then shall there enlargement and deliverance arise to the Jews from another place; but thou and
thy father's house shall be destroyed: and who knoweth, whether thou
art come to the kingdom for such a time as this?

Then Esther bade them return Mordecai this answer, Go, gather
together all the Jews that are present in Shushan, and fast ye for me, and
neither eat nor drink three days, night or day: I also and my maidens
will fast likewise: and so will I go in unto the king, which is not according to the law; and if I perish, I perish.

So Mordecai went his way, and did according to all that Esther had
commanded him.

Esther Entertains

Now it came to pass on the third day, that Esther put on her royal
apparel, and stood in the inner court of the king's house, over against
the king's house: and the king sat upon his royal throne in the royal
house, over against the gate of the house. And it was so, when the king
saw Esther the queen standing in the court, that she obtained favour in
his sight: and the king held out to Esther the golden sceptre that was in
his hand. So Esther drew near, and touched the top of the sceptre.

Then said the king unto her, What wilt thou, queen Esther? and what
is thy request? it shall be even given thee to the half of the kingdom.

And Esther answered, If it seem good unto the king, let the king and
Haman come this day unto the banquet that I have prepared for him.

Then the king said, Cause Haman to make haste, that he may do as
Esther hath said. So the king and Haman came to the banquet that
Esther had prepared.

And the king said unto Esther at the banquet of wine, What is thy
petition? and it shall be granted thee: and what is thy request? even to
the half of the kingdom it shall be performed.

Then answered Esther, and said, My petition and my request is: If I
have found favour in the sight of the king, and if it please the king to
grant my petition, and to perform my request, let the king and Haman
come to the banquet that I shall prepare for them, and I will do
to-morrow as the king hath said.

Then went Haman forth that day joyful and with a glad heart: but when Haman saw Mordecai in the king's gate, that he stood not up, nor moved for him, he was full of indignation against Mordecai. Nevertheless, Haman refrained himself: and when he came home, he sent and called for his friends, and Zeresh his wife. And Haman told them of the glory of his riches, and the multitude of his children, and all the things wherein the king had promoted him, and now he had advanced him above the princes and servants of the king. Haman said, moreover, Yea, Esther the queen did let no man come in with the king unto the banquet that she had prepared but myself; and to-morrow am I invited unto her also with the king. Yet all this availeth me nothing, so long as I see Mordecai the Jew sitting at the king's gate.

Then said Zeresh his wife and all his friends unto him, Let a gallows be made of fifty cubits high, and to-morrow speak thou unto the king that Mordecai may be hanged thereon: then go thou in merrily with the king unto the banquet. And the thing pleased Haman; and he caused the gallows to be made.

The Triumph of Mordecai

On that night could not the king sleep, and he commanded to bring the book of records of the chronicles; and they were read before the king. And it was found written, that Mordecai had told of Bigthana and Teresh, two of the king's chamberlains, the keepers of the door, who sought to lay hand on the king Ahasuerus.

And the king said, What honour and dignity hath been done to Mordecai for this? Then said the king's servants that ministered unto him, There is nothing done for him.

And the king said, Who is in the court? (Now Haman was come into the outward court of the king's house, to speak unto the king to hang Mordecai on the gallows that he had prepared for him.)

And the king's servants said unto him, Behold, Haman standeth in the court. And the king said, Let him come in. So Haman came in.

And the king said unto him, What shall be done unto the man whom the king delighteth to honour? (Now Haman thought in his heart, To whom would the king delight to do honour more than to myself?)

And Haman answered the king, For the man whom the king delighteth to honour, let the royal apparel be brought which the king useth to wear, and the horse that the king rideth upon, and the crown royal which is set upon his head. And let this apparel and horse be delivered to the hand of one of the king's most noble princes, that they may array the man withal whom the king delighteth to honour, and bring him on horseback through the street of the city, and proclaim before him, Thus shall it be done to the man whom the king delighteth to honour.

Then the king said to Haman, Make haste, and take the apparel and the horse, as thou hast said, and do even so to Mordecai the Jew, that sitteth at the king's gate: let nothing fail of all that thou hast spoken.

Then took Haman the apparel and the horse, and arrayed Mordecai, and brought him on horseback through the street of the city, and proclaimed before him, thus shall it be done unto the man whom the king delighteth to honour.

And Mordecai came again to the king's gate. But Haman hasted to his house mourning, and having his head covered. And Haman told Zeresh his wife and all his friends every thing that had befallen him. Then said his wise men and Zeresh his wife unto him, If Mordecai be of the seed of the Jews, before whom thou hast begun to fall, thou shalt not prevail against him, but shalt surely fall before him. And while they were yet talking with him, came the king's chamberlains, and hasted to bring Haman unto the banquet that Esther had prepared.

The Usefulness of Haman's Gallows

So the king and Haman came to banquet with Esther the queen.

And the king said again unto Esther on the second day at the banquet of wine, What is thy petition, queen Esther? and it shall be granted thee: and what is thy request? and it shall be performed, even to the half of the kingdom.

Then Esther the queen answered and said, If I have found favour in thy sight, O king, and if it please the king, let my life be given me at my petition, and my people at my request. For we are sold, I and my people, to be destroyed, to be slain, and to perish. But if we had been sold for bond-men and bond-women, I had held my tongue, although the enemy could not countervail the king's damage.

Then the king Ahasuerus answered and said unto Esther the queen, Who is he, and where is he, that durst presume in his heart to do so?

And Esther said, The adversary and enemy is this wicked Haman. Then Haman was afraid before the king and the queen.

And the king arising from the banquet of wine in his wrath went into the palace-garden: and Haman stood up to make request for his life to Esther the queen; for he saw that there was evil determined against him by the king.

Then the king returned out of the palace-garden into the place of the banquet of wine; and Haman was fallen upon the bed whereon Esther was. Then said the king, Will he force the queen also before me in the house? As the word went out of the king's mouth, they covered Haman's face.

And Harbonah, one of the chamberlains, said before the king, Behold also the gallows fifty cubits high, which Haman had made for Mordecai, who had spoken good for the king, standeth in the house of Haman. Then the king said, Hang him thereon.

So they hanged Haman on the gallows that he had prepared for Mordecai. Then was the king's wrath pacified.

The Book of Ruth

Ruth and Naomi

Now it came to pass in the days when the judges ruled, that there was a famine in the land. And a certain man of Beth-lehem-judah went to sojourn in the country of Moab, he, and his wife, and his two sons. And the name of the man was Elimelech, and the name of his wife Naomi, and the name of his two sons Mahlon and Chilion, Ephrathites of Beth-lehem-judah. And they came into the country of Moab, and continued there. And Elimelech Naomi's husband died; and she was left, and her two sons. And they took them wives of the women of Moab; the name of the one was Orpah, and the name of the other Ruth: and they dwelt there about ten years. And Mahlon and Chilion died also both of them; and the woman was left of her two sons and her husband.

Then she arose with her daughters-in-law, that she might return from the country of Moab: for she had heard in the country of Moab how that the Lord had visited his people in giving them bread. Wherefore she went forth out of the place where she was, and her two daughters-in-law with her; and they went on the way to return unto the land of Judah.

And Naomi said unto her two daughters-in-law, Go, return each to her mother's house: the Lord deal kindly with you, as ye have dealt with the dead, and with me. The Lord grant you that ye may find rest, each of you in the house of her husband. Then she kissed them; and they lifted up their voice, and wept.

And they said unto her, Surely we will return with thee unto thy people.

And Naomi said, Turn again, my daughters: why will ye go with me? are there yet any more sons in my womb, that they may be your husbands? Turn again, my daughters, go your way; for I am too old to have an husband. If I should say, I have hope, if I should have an husband also tonight, and should also bear sons; would ye tarry for them till they were grown? would ye stay for them from having husbands? nay, my daughters; for it grieveth me much for your sakes, that the hand of the Lord is gone out against me.

And they lifted up their voice, and wept again. And Orpah kissed her mother-in-law; but Ruth clave unto her.

And she said, Behold, thy sister-in-law is gone back unto her people, and unto her gods: return thou after thy sister-in-law.

And Ruth said, Entreat me not to leave thee, or to return from following after thee: for whither thou goest, I will go; and where thou lodgest, I will lodge; thy people shall be my people, and thy God my God: where thou diest, will I die, and there will I be buried: the Lord do so to me, and more also, if aught but death part thee and me.

When she saw that she was steadfastly minded to go with her, then she left speaking unto her. So they two went until they came to Beth-lehem. And it came to pass, when they were come to Beth-lehem, that all the city was moved about them, and they said, Is this Naomi?

And she said unto them, Call me not Naomi, call me Mara: for the Almighty hath dealt very bitterly with me. I went out full, and the Lord hath brought me home again empty: why then call ye me Naomi, seeing the Lord hath testified against me, and the Almighty hath afflicted me?

So Naomi returned, and Ruth the Moabitess her daughter-in-law with her, which returned out of the country of Moab: and they came to Beth-lehem in the beginning of barley-harvest.

Boaz Reaps and Ruth Gleans

And Naomi had a kinsman of her husband's, a mighty man of wealth, of the family of Elimelech; and his name was Boaz.

And Ruth the Moabitess said unto Naomi, Let me now go to the field, and glean ears of corn after him in whose sight I shall find grace. And she said unto her, Go, my daughter.

And she went, and came, and gleaned in the field after the reapers; and her hap was to light on a part of the field belonging unto Boaz, who was of the kindred of Elimelech.

And behold, Boaz came from Beth-lehem, and said unto the reapers, The Lord be with you: and they answered him, The Lord bless thee. Then said Boaz unto his servant that was set over the reapers, Whose damsel is this? And the servant that was set over the reapers answered and said, It is the Moabitish damsel that came back with Naomi out of the country of Moab: and she said, I pray you, let me glean and gather after the reapers among the sheaves: so she came, and hath continued even from the morning until now, that she tarried a little in the house.

Then said Boaz unto Ruth, Hearest thou not, my daughter? Go not to glean in another field, neither go from hence, but abide here fast by my maidens: let thine eyes be on the field that they do reap, and go thou after them: have I not charged the young men that they shall not touch thee? and when thou art athirst, go unto the vessels, and drink of that which the young men have drawn.

Then she fell on her face, and bowed herself to the ground, and said unto him, Why have I found grace in thine eyes, that thou shouldest take knowledge of me, seeing I am a stranger?

And Boaz answered and said unto her, It hath fully been shewed me, all that thou hast done unto thy mother-in-law since the death of thine husband: and how thou hast left thy father and thy mother, and the land of thy nativity, and art come unto a people which thou knewest not heretofore. The Lord recompense thy work, and a full reward be given thee of the Lord God of Israel, under whose wings thou art come to trust.

Then she said, Let me find favour in thy sight, my lord; for that thou hast comforted me, and for that thou hast spoken friendly unto thine handmaid, though I be not like unto one of thy handmaidens.

And Boaz said unto her, At meal-time come thou hither, and eat of the bread, and dip thy morsel in the vinegar. And she sat beside the reapers: and he reached her parched corn, and she did eat, and was sufficed, and left.

And when she was risen up to glean, Boaz commanded his young men, saying, Let her glean even among the sheaves, and reproach her not: and let fall also some of the handfuls of purpose for her, and leave them, that she may glean them, and rebuke her not.

So she gleaned in the field until even, and beat out that she had gleaned: and it was about an ephah of barley. And she took it up, and went into the city: and her mother-in-law saw what she had gleaned: and she brought forth, and gave to her that she had reserved after she was sufficed.

And her mother-in-law said unto her, Where hast thou gleaned to-day? and where wroughtest thou? blessed be he that did take knowledge of thee. And she shewed her mother-in-law with whom she had wrought, and said, The man's name with whom I wrought to-day is Boaz.

And Naomi said unto her daughter-in-law, Blessed be he of the Lord, who hath not left off his kindness to the living and to the dead. And Naomi said unto her, The man is near of kin unto us, one of our next kinsmen.

And Ruth the Moabitess said, He said unto me also, Thou shalt keep fast by my young men, until they have ended all my harvest.

And Naomi said unto Ruth her daughter-in-law, It is good, my daughter, that thou go out with his maidens, that they meet thee not in any other field.

So she kept fast by the maidens of Boaz to glean unto the end of barley-harvest and of wheat-harvest; and dwelt with her mother-in-law.

Naomi Counsels Ruth

Then Naomi her mother-in-law said unto her, My daughter, shall I not seek rest for thee, that it may be well with thee? And now is not Boaz of our kindred, with whose maidens thou wast? Behold, he winnoweth barley to-night in the threshing floor. Wash thyself therefore, and anoint thee, and put thy raiment upon thee, and get thee down to the floor: but make not thyself known unto the man, until he shall have done eating and drinking. And it shall be when he lieth down, that thou shalt mark the place where he shall lie, and thou shalt go in, and uncover his feet, and lay thee down; and he will tell thee what thou shalt do.

And she said unto her, All that thou sayest unto me I will do.

And she went down unto the floor, and did according to all that her mother-in-law bade her. And when Boaz had eaten and drunk, and his heart was merry, he went to lie down at the end of the heap of corn: and she came softly, and uncovered his feet, and laid her down.

And it came to pass at midnight, that the man was afraid, and turned himself: and behold, a woman lay at his feet.

And he said, Who art thou? And she answered, I am Ruth thine handmaid: spread therefore thy skirt over thine handmaid; for thou art a near kinsman.

And he said, Blessed be thou of the Lord, my daughter: for thou hast shewed more kindness in the latter end than at the beginning, inasmuch as thou followedst not young men, whether poor or rich. And now, my daughter, fear not; I will do to thee all that thou requirest: for all the city of my people doth know that thou art a virtuous woman. And now it is true that I am thy near kinsman: howbeit there is a kinsman nearer than I. Tarry this night, and it shall be in the morning, that if he will perform unto thee the part of a kinsman, well; let him do the kinsman's part: but if he will not do the part of a kinsman to thee, then will I do the part of a kinsman to thee, as the Lord liveth: lie down until the morning.

And she lay at his feet until the morning: and she rose up before one could know another. And he said, Let it not be known that a woman came into the floor. Also he said, Bring the vail that thou hast upon thee, and hold it. And when she held it, he measured six measures of barley, and laid it on her: and she went into the city.

And when she came to her mother-in-law, she said, Who art thou, my daughter? and she told her all that the man had done to her. And she said, These six measures of barley gave he me; for he said to me, Go not empty unto thy mother-in-law.

Then said she, Sit still, my daughter, until thou know how the matter will fall: for the man will not be in rest, until he have finished the thing this day.

So Boaz Took Ruth

Then went Boaz up to the gate, and sat him down there: and behold, the kinsman of whom Boaz spake came by; unto whom he said, Ho, such a one! turn aside, sit down here. And he turned aside, and sat down. And he took ten men of the elders of the city, and said, Sit ye down here. And they sat down.

And he said unto the kinsman, Naomi, that is come again out of the country of Moab, selleth a parcel of land, which was our brother Elimelech's: and I thought to advertise thee, saying, Buy it before the inhabitants, and before the elders of my people. If thou wilt redeem it, redeem it: but if thou wilt not redeem it, then tell me, that I may know: for there is none to redeem it besides thee; and I am after thee. And he said, I will redeem it.

Then said Boaz, What day thou buyest the field of the hand of Naomi, thou must buy it also of Ruth the Moabitess, the wife of the dead, to raise up the name of the dead upon his inheritance.

And the kinsman said, I cannot redeem it for myself, lest I mar mine own inheritance: redeem thou my right to thyself; for I cannot redeem it.

Now this was the manner in former time in Israel concerning redeeming and concerning changing, for to confirm all things; a man plucked off his shoe, and gave it to his neighbour: and this was a testimony in Israel. Therefore the kinsman said unto Boaz, Buy it for thee. So he drew off his shoe.

And Boaz said unto the elders, and unto all the people, Ye are witnesses this day, that I have bought all that was Elimelech's, and all that was Chilion's and Mahlon's, of the hand of Naomi. Moreover, Ruth the Moabitess, the wife of Mahlon, have I purchased to be my wife, to raise up the name of the dead upon his inheritance, that the name of the dead be not cut off from among his brethren, and from the gate of his place: ye are witnesses this day.

And all the people that were in the gate, and the elders, said, We are witnesses. The Lord make the woman that is come into thine house like Rachel and like Leah, which two did build the house of Israel: and do thou worthily in Ephratah and be famous in Beth-lehem: and let thine house be like the house of Pharez, whom Tamar bare unto Judah, of the seed which the Lord shall give thee of this young woman.

So Boaz took Ruth, and she was his wife: and when he went in unto her, the Lord gave her conception, and she bare a son.

And the women said unto Naomi, Blessed be the Lord, which hath not left thee this day without a kinsman, that his name may be famous in Israel. And he shall be unto thee a restorer of thy life, and a nourisher of thine old age: for thy daughter-in-law, which loveth thee, which is better to thee than seven sons, hath borne him.

And Naomi took the child, and laid it in her bosom, and became nurse unto it. And the women her neighbours gave it a name, saying, There is a son born to Naomi; and they called his name Obed: he is the father of Jesse, the father of David.

The Book of Job

The Holiness of Job

There was a man in the land of Uz whose name was Job; and that man was perfect and upright, and one that feared God, and eschewed evil. And there were born unto him seven sons and three daughters. His substance also was seven thousand sheep, and three thousand camels, and five hundred yoke of oxen, and five hundred she-asses, and a very great household; so that this man was the greatest of all the men of the east.

And his sons went and feasted in their houses, every one his day; and sent and called for their three sisters to eat and to drink with them.

And it was so, when the days of their feasting were gone about, that Job sent and sanctified them, and rose up early in the morning, and offered burnt-offerings according to the number of them all: for Job said, It may be that my sons have sinned, and cursed God in their hearts. Thus did Job continually.

Now there was a day when the sons of God came to present themselves before the Lord, and Satan came also among them. And the Lord said unto Satan, Whence comest thou? Then Satan answered the Lord, and said, From going to and fro in the earth, and from walking up and down in it.

And the Lord said unto Satan, Hast thou considered my servant Job, that there is none like him in the earth, a perfect and an upright man, one that feareth God, and escheweth evil?

Then Satan answered the Lord and said, Doth Job fear God for nought? Hast not thou made an hedge about him, and about his house, and about all that he hath on every side? thou hast blessed the work of his hands, and his substance is increased in the land. But put forth thine hand now, and touch all that he hath, and he will curse thee to thy face.

And the Lord said unto Satan, Behold, all that he hath is in thy power; only upon himself put not forth thine hand. So Satan went forth from the presence of the Lord.

And there was a day when his sons and his daughters were eating and drinking wine in their eldest brother's house; and there came a messenger unto Job, and said, The oxen were ploughing, and the asses feeding beside them, and the Sabeans fell upon them, and took them away; yea, they have slain the servants with the edge of the sword; and I only am escaped alone to tell thee.

While he was yet speaking, there came also another, and said, The fire of God is fallen from heaven, and hath burned up the sheep and the servants, and consumed them; and I only am escaped alone to tell thee.

While he was yet speaking, there came also another, and said, The Chaldeans made out three bands, and fell upon the camels, and have carried them away, yea, and slain the servants with the edge of the sword; and I only am escaped alone to tell thee.

While he was yet speaking, there came also another, and said, Thy sons and thy daughters were eating and drinking wine in their eldest brother's house, and behold, there came a great wind from the wilderness, and smote the four corners of the house, and it fell upon the young men, and they are dead; and I only am escaped alone to tell thee.

Then Job arose, and rent his mantle, and shaved his head, and fell down upon the ground, and worshipped, and said, Naked came I out of my mother's womb, and naked shall I return thither: The Lord gave, and the Lord hath taken away; blessed be the name of the Lord.

In all this Job sinned not, nor charged God foolishly.

Job Is Afflicted with Boils

Again there was a day when the sons of God came to present themselves before the Lord, and Satan came also among them to present himself before the Lord.

And the Lord said unto Satan, From whence comest thou? And Satan answered the Lord, and said, From going to and fro in the earth, and from walking up and down in it.

And the Lord said unto Satan, Hast thou considered my servant Job, that there is none like him in the earth, a perfect and an upright man, one that feareth God, and escheweth evil? and still he holdeth fast his integrity, although thou movedst me against him, to destroy him without cause.

And Satan answered the Lord, and said, Skin for skin, yea, all that a man hath will he give for his life. But put forth thine hand now, and touch his bone and his flesh, and he will curse thee to thy face.

And the Lord said unto Satan, Behold, he is in thine hand; but save his life.

So went Satan forth from the presence of the Lord, and smote Job with sore boils from the sole of his foot unto his crown. And he took him a potsherd to scrape himself withal; and he sat down among the ashes.

Then said his wife unto him, Dost thou still retain thine integrity? curse God, and die. But he said unto her, Thou speakest as one of the

foolish women speaketh. What! shall we receive good at the ha[...]
God, and shall we not receive evil? In all this did not Job sin [...]
his lips.

Now when Job's three friends heard of all this evil that was co[...]
upon him, they came every one from his own place; Eliphaz the
Temanite, and Bildad the Shuhite, and Zophar the Naamathite: for
they had made an appointment together to come to mourn with him,
and to comfort him. And when they lifted up their eyes afar off, and
knew him not, they lifted up their voice, and wept; and they rent every
one his mantle, and sprinkled dust upon their heads toward heaven.

So they sat down with him upon the ground seven days and seven
nights, and none spake a word unto him: for they saw that his grief
was very great.

Job Curses His Day

After this opened Job his mouth, and cursed his day. And Job spake,
and said, Let the day perish wherein I was born, and the night in which
it was said, There is a man child conceived. Let that day be darkness;
let not God regard it from above, neither let the light shine upon it.
Let darkness and the shadow of death stain it; let a cloud dwell upon
it; let the blackness of the day terrify it.

As for that night, let darkness seize upon it; let it not be joined unto
the days of the year; let it not come into the number of the months.
Lo, let that night be solitary; let no joyful voice come therein. Let them
curse it that curse the day, who are ready to raise up their mourning.
Let the stars of the twilight thereof be dark; let it look for light, but
have none; neither let it see the dawning of the day. Because it shut not
up the doors of my mother's womb, nor hid sorrow from mine eyes.

Why died I not from the womb? why did I not give up the ghost when
I came out of the belly? Why did the knees prevent me? or why the
breasts that I should suck? For now should I have lain still and been
quiet, I should have slept; then had I been at rest, with kings and
counsellors of the earth, which built desolate places for themselves; or
with princes that had gold, who filled their houses with silver; or as an
hidden untimely birth I had not been; as infants which never saw light.

There the wicked cease from troubling; and there the weary be at rest. There the prisoners rest together; they hear not the voice of the oppressor. The small and great are there; and the servant is free from his master.

Wherefore is light given to him that is in misery, and life unto the bitter in soul, which long for death, but it cometh not; and dig for it more than for hid treasures, which rejoice exceedingly, and are glad, when they can find the grave? Why is light given to a man whose way is hid, and whom God hath hedged in?

For my sighing cometh before I eat, and my roarings are poured out like the waters. For the thing which I greatly feared is come upon me, and that which I was afraid of is come unto me.

I was not in safety, neither had I rest, neither was I quiet; yet trouble came.

Eliphaz Reproves Job

Then Eliphaz the Temanite answered and said, If we assay to commune with thee, wilt thou be grieved? but who can withhold himself from speaking?

Behold, thou hast instructed many, and thou hast strengthened the weak hands. Thy words have upholden him that was falling, and thou hast strengthened the feeble knees. But now it is come upon thee, and thou faintest; it toucheth thee, and thou art troubled.

Is not this thy fear, thy confidence, thy hope, and the uprightness of thy ways?

Remember, I pray thee, who ever perished, being innocent? or where were the righteous cut off? Even as I have seen, they that plough iniquity, and sow wickedness, reap the same. By the blast of God they perish, and by the breath of his nostrils are they consumed.

Now a thing was secretly brought to me, and mine ear received a little thereof. In thoughts from the visions of the night, when deep sleep falleth on men, fear came upon me, and trembling, which made all my bones to shake. Then a spirit passed before my face; the hair of my flesh stood up: it stood still, but I could not discern the form thereof: an image was before mine eyes, there was silence, and I heard a voice, saying, Shall mortal man be more just than God? shall a man be more pure than his maker?

Call now, if there be any that will answer thee; and to which of the saints wilt thou turn? For wrath killeth the foolish man, and envy slayeth the silly one.

I have seen the foolish taking root: but suddenly I cursed his habitation. His children are far from safety, and they are crushed in the gate, neither is there any to deliver them, whose harvest the hungry eateth up, and taketh it even out of the thorns, and the robber swalloweth up their substance.

Although affliction cometh not forth of the dust, neither doth trouble spring out of the ground; yet man is born unto trouble, as the sparks fly upward.

I would seek unto God, and unto God would I commit my cause: which doeth great things and unsearchable; marvellous things without number; who giveth rain upon the earth, and sendeth waters upon the fields; to set up on high those that be low; that those which mourn may be exalted to safety.

He disappointeth the devices of the crafty, so that their hands cannot perform their enterprise. He taketh the wise in their own craftiness: and the counsel of the froward is carried headlong. They meet with darkness in the day-time, and grope in the noon-day as in the night.

But he saveth the poor from the sword, from their mouth, and from the hand of the mighty. So the poor hath hope, and iniquity stoppeth her mouth.

Behold, happy is the man whom God correcteth: therefore despise not thou the chastening of the Almighty: for he maketh sore, and bindeth up: he woundeth, and his hands make whole. He shall deliver thee in six troubles: yea, in seven there shall no evil touch thee. Thou shalt come to thy grave in a full age, like as a shock of corn cometh in in his season.

Lo this, we have searched it, so it is; hear it, and know thou it for thy good.

Job Justifies His Complaint

But Job answered and said, Oh that my grief were thoroughly weighed, and my calamity laid in the balances together! For now it would be heavier than the sand of the sea: therefore my words are swallowed up.

For the arrows of the Almighty are within me, the poison whereof drinketh up my spirit: the terrors of God do set themselves in array against me.

Doth the wild ass bray when he hath grass? or loweth the ox over his fodder? Can that which is unsavoury be eaten without salt? or is there any taste in the white of an egg? The things that my soul refused to touch are as my sorrowful meat.

Oh that I might have my request; and that God would grant me the thing that I long for! Even that it would please God to destroy me; that he would let loose his hand, and cut me off! Then should I yet have comfort; yea, I would harden myself in sorrow: let him not spare; for I have not concealed the words of the Holy One.

Therefore I will not refrain my mouth; I will speak in the anguish of my spirit; I will complain in the bitterness of my soul.

Bildad Reproves Him

Then answered Bildad the Shuhite, and said, How long wilt thou speak these things? and how long shall the words of thy mouth be like a strong wind? Doth God pervert judgment? or doth the Almighty pervert justice?

If thy children have sinned against him, and he have cast them away for their transgression; if thou wouldest seek unto God betimes, and make thy supplication to the Almighty; if thou wert pure and upright, surely now he would awake for thee, and make the habitation of thy righteousness prosperous. Though thy beginning was small, yet thy latter end should greatly increase.

For inquire, I pray thee, of the former age, and prepare thyself to the search of their fathers: (for we are but of yesterday, and know nothing, because our days upon earth are a shadow:) Shall not they teach thee, and tell thee, and utter words out of their heart?

Can the rush grow up without mire? can the flag grow without water? Whilst it is yet in his greenness, and not cut down, it withereth before any other herb.

So are the paths of all that forget God; and the hypocrite's hope shall perish: whose hope shall be cut off, and whose trust shall be a spider's web.

The Strength of God

Then Job answered and said, I know it is so of a truth: but how should man be just with God? If he will contend with him, he cannot answer him one of a thousand.

He is wise in heart, and mighty in strength: who hath hardened himself against him, and hath prospered? which removeth the mountains, and they know not: which overturneth them in his anger; which shaketh the earth out of her place, and the pillars thereof tremble; which commandeth the sun, and it riseth not; and sealeth up the stars; which alone spreadeth out the heavens, and treadeth upon the waves of the sea; which maketh Arcturus, Orion, and Pleiades, and the chambers of the south; which doeth great things past finding out; yea, and wonders without number.

Lo, he goeth by me, and I see him not: he passeth on also, but I perceive him not. Behold, he taketh away, who can hinder him? who will say unto him, What doest thou?

If God will not withdraw his anger, the proud helpers do stoop under him. How much less shall I answer him, and choose out my words to reason with him? whom, though I were righteous, yet would I not answer, but I would make supplication to my judge.

If I had called, and he had answered me; yet would I not believe that he had hearkened unto my voice. For he breaketh me with a tempest, and multiplieth my wounds without cause. He will not suffer me to take my breath, but filleth me with bitterness.

If I speak of strength, lo, he is strong: and if of judgment, who shall set me a time to plead? If I justify myself, mine own mouth shall condemn me: If I say I am perfect, it shall also prove me perverse. Though I were perfect, yet would I not know my soul: I would despise my life.

This is one thing, therefore I said it, He destroyeth the perfect and the wicked.

Zophar Speaks

Then answered Zophar the Naamathite, and said, Should not the multitude of words be answered? and should a man full of talk be justified? Should thy lies make men hold their peace? and when thou mockest, shall no man make thee ashamed?

For thou hast said, My doctrine is pure, and I am clean in thine eyes.

But oh that God would speak, and open his lips against thee; and that he would shew thee the secrets of wisdom, that they are double to that which is! Know therefore that God exacteth of thee less than thine iniquity deserveth.

Canst thou by searching find out God? canst thou find out the Almighty unto perfection? It is as high as heaven; what canst thou do? deeper than hell; what canst thou know? The measure thereof is longer than the earth, and broader than the sea. If he cut off, and shut up, or gather together, then who can hinder him? For he knoweth vain men: he seeth wickedness also; will he not then consider it?

Job Reproves His Friends and Entreats God

And Job answered and said, No doubt but ye are the people, and wisdom shall die with you. But I have understanding as well as you; I am not inferior to you: yea, who knoweth not such things as these?

I am as one mocked of his neighbour, who calleth upon God, and he answereth him: the just upright man is laughed to scorn. He that is ready to slip with his feet is as a lamp despised in the thought of him that is at ease. The tabernacles of robbers prosper, and they that provoke God are secure; into whose hand God bringeth abundantly.

But ask now the beasts, and they shall teach thee; and the fowls of the air, and they shall tell thee; or speak to the earth, and it shall teach thee; and the fishes of the sea shall declare unto thee.

Who knoweth not in all these that the hand of the Lord hath wrought this?

Lo, mine eye hath seen all this, mine ear hath heard and understood it. What ye know, the same do I know also: I am not inferior unto you. Surely I would speak to the Almighty, and I desire to reason with God.

But ye are forgers of lies, ye are all physicians of no value. O that ye would altogether hold your peace; and it should be your wisdom. Hear now my reasoning, and hearken to the pleadings of my lips.

Will ye speak wickedly for God? and talk deceitfully for him? Will ye accept his person? will ye contend for God? Is it good that he should search you out? or as one man mocketh another, do ye so mock him? He will surely reprove you, if ye do secretly accept persons. Shall not his excellency make you afraid? and his dread fall upon you?

Your remembrances are like unto ashes, your bodies to bodies of clay. Hold your peace, let me alone, that I may speak, and let come on me what will.

Wherefore do I take my flesh in my teeth, and put my life in mine hand?

Though he slay me, yet will I trust in him: but I will maintain mine own ways before him. He also shall be my salvation: for an hypocrite shall not come before him.

Hear diligently my speech, and my declaration with your ears. Behold, now, I have ordered my cause; I know that I shall be justified.

Who is he that will plead with me? for now, if I hold my tongue, I shall give up the ghost.

Only do not two things unto me: then will I not hide myself from thee. Withdraw thine hand far from me: and let not thy dread make me afraid.

Man that is born of a woman is of few days, and full of trouble. He cometh forth like a flower, and is cut down: he fleeth also as a shadow, and continueth not.

And dost thou open thine eyes upon such an one, and bringest me into judgment with thee? Who can bring a clean thing out of an unclean? not one.

Seeing his days are determined, the number of his months are with thee, thou hast appointed his bounds that he cannot pass; turn from him, that he may rest, till he shall accomplish, as an hireling, his day. For there is hope of a tree, if it be cut down, that it will sprout again, and that the tender branch thereof will not cease.

Though the root thereof wax old in the earth, and the stock thereof die in the ground; yet through the scent of water it will bud, and bring forth boughs like a plant. But man dieth, and wasteth away: yea, man giveth up the ghost, and where is he?

As the waters fail from the sea, and the flood decayeth and drieth up: so man lieth down, and riseth not: till the heavens be no more, they shall not awake, nor be raised out of their sleep.

Eliphaz Chides Him Again

Then answered Eliphaz the Temanite, and said, Should a wise man utter vain knowledge, and fill his belly with the east wind? Should he reason with unprofitable talk? or with speeches wherewith he can do no good?

Yea, thou castest off fear, and restrainest prayer before God. For thy mouth uttereth thine iniquity, and thou choosest the tongue of the crafty. Thine own mouth condemneth thee, and not I: yea, thine own lips testify against thee.

Art thou the first man that was born? or wast thou made before the hills? Hast thou heard the secret of God? and dost thou restrain wisdom to thyself? What knowest thou that we know not? what understandest thou, which is not in us?

With us are both the grey-headed and very aged men, much elder than thy father. Are the consolations of God small with thee? is there any secret thing with thee?

Why doth thine heart carry thee away? and what do thine eyes wink at, that thou turnest thy spirit against God, and lettest such words go out of thy mouth?

What is man, that he should be clean? and he which is born of a woman, that he should be righteous? Behold, he putteth no trust in his saints; yea, the heavens are not clean in his sight. How much more abominable and filthy is man, which drinketh iniquity like water?

Job Cries for Pity

Then Job answered and said, How long will ye vex my soul, a[n]̲ ̲ ̲ ̲ ̲ ̲ ̲
me in pieces with words? These ten times have ye reproached me: ye are
not ashamed that ye make yourselves strange to me. And be it indeed
that I have erred, mine error remaineth with myself.

If indeed ye will magnify yourselves against me, and plead against
me my reproach: know now that God hath overthrown me, and hath
compassed me with his net. Behold, I cry out of wrong, but I am not
heard: I cry aloud, but there is no judgment.

My kinsfolk have failed, and my familiar friends have forgotten me.
They that dwell in mine house, and my maids, count me for a stranger:
I am an alien in their sight. I called my servant, and he gave me no
answer; I entreated him with my mouth. My breath is strange to my
wife, though I entreated for the children's sake of mine own body. Yea,
young children despised me; I arose, and they spake against me.

Have pity upon me, have pity upon me, O ye my friends; for the
hand of God hath touched me. Why do ye persecute me as God, and
are not satisfied with my flesh?

O that my words were now written! O that they were printed in a
book! that they were graven with an iron pen and lead in the rock
for ever!

For I know that my Redeemer liveth, and that he shall stand at the
latter day upon the earth, and though after my skin worms destroy this
body, yet in my flesh shall I see God.

Hear diligently my speech, and let this be your consolations. Suffer
me that I may speak; and after that I have spoken, mock on. As for me,
is my complaint to man? and if it were so, why should not my spirit be
troubled? Mark me, and be astonished, and lay your hand upon your
mouth.

Even when I remember I am afraid, and trembling taketh hold on
my flesh.

Wherefore do the wicked live, become old, yea, are mighty in power?
Their seed is established in their sight with them, and their offspring
before their eyes. Their houses are safe from fear, neither is the rod of
God upon them. They spend their days in wealth, and in a moment go

down to the grave. Therefore they say unto God, Depart from us; for we desire not the knowledge of thy ways.

What is the Almighty, that we should serve him? and what profit should we have, if we pray unto him?

Lo, their good is not in their hand: the counsel of the wicked is far from me. How oft is the candle of the wicked put out? and how oft cometh their destruction upon them? God distributeth sorrows in his anger.

They are as stubble before the wind, and as chaff that the storm carrieth away.

God layeth up his iniquity for his children: he rewardeth him, and he shall know it. His eyes shall see his destruction, and he shall drink of the wrath of the Almighty. For what pleasure hath he in his house after him, when the number of his months is cut off in the midst?

Shall any teach God knowledge? seeing he judgeth those that are high.

Behold, I know your thoughts, and the devices which ye wrongfully imagine against me. How then comfort ye me in vain, seeing in your answers there remaineth falsehood?

Eliphaz Speaks Again

Then Eliphaz the Temanite answered and said, Can a man be profitable unto God, as he that is wise may be profitable unto himself?

Is it any pleasure to the Almighty, that thou art righteous? or is it gain to him, that thou makest thy ways perfect? Will he reprove thee for fear of thee? will he enter with thee into judgment?

Is not thy wickedness great? and thine iniquities infinite? For thou hast taken a pledge from thy brother for nought, and stripped the naked of their clothing. Thou hast not given water to the weary to drink, and thou hast withholden bread from the hungry.

But as for the mighty man, he had the earth; and the honourable man dwelt in it. Thou hast sent widows away empty, and the arms of the fatherless have been broken. Therefore snares are round about thee, and sudden fear troubleth thee; or darkness, that thou canst not see; and abundance of waters cover thee.

If thou return to the Almighty, thou shalt be built up, thou shalt put away iniquity far from thy tabernacles. Then shalt thou lay up gold as dust, and the gold of Ophir as the stones of the brooks. Yea, the Almighty shall be thy defence, and thou shalt have plenty of silver. For then shalt thou have thy delight in the Almighty, and shalt lift up thy face unto God.

The Invisibility of God

Then Job answered and said, Even to-day is my complaint bitter: my stroke is heavier than my groaning. Oh that I knew where I might find him! that I might come even to his seat! I would order my cause before him, and fill my mouth with arguments. I would know the words which he would answer me, and understand what he would say unto me.

Will he plead against me with his great power? No; but he would put strength in me. There the righteous might dispute with him; so should I be delivered for ever from my judge.

Behold, I go forward, but he is not there; and backward, but I cannot perceive him: on the left hand, where he doth work, but I cannot behold him: he hideth himself on the right hand, that I cannot see him: but he knoweth the way that I take: when he hath tried me, I shall come forth as gold.

My foot hath held his steps, his way have I kept, and not declined. Neither have I gone back from the commandment of his lips; I have esteemed the words of his mouth more than my necessary food.

But he is in one mind, and who can turn him? and what his soul desireth, even that he doeth.

Bildad Questions

Then answered Bildad the Shuhite, and said, Dominion and fear are with him, he maketh peace in his high places.

Is there any number of his armies? and upon whom doth not his light arise? How then can man be justified with God? or how can he be clean that is born of a woman?

Behold even to the moon, and it shineth not; yea, the stars are not pure in his sight. How much less man, that is a worm; and the son of man which is a worm?

Job Reproves Bildad

But Job answered and said, How hast thou helped him that is without power? How savest thou the arm that hath no strength? How hast thou counselled him that hath no wisdom? and how hast thou plentifully declared the thing as it is? To whom hast thou uttered words? and whose spirit came from thee?

As God liveth, who hath taken away my judgment; and the Almighty, who hath vexed my soul; all the while my breath is in me, and the spirit of God is in my nostrils; my lips shall not speak wickedness, nor my tongue utter deceit.

God forbid that I should justify you: till I die I will not remove mine integrity from me. My righteousness I hold fast, and will not let it go: my heart shall not reproach me so long as I live.

Let mine enemy be as the wicked, and he that riseth up against me as the unrighteous. For what is the hope of the hypocrite, though he hath gained, when God taketh away his soul?

Surely there is a vein for the silver, and a place for gold where they fine it. Iron is taken out of the earth, and brass is molten out of the stone.

He setteth an end to darkness, and searcheth out all perfection: the stones of darkness, and the shadow of death. The flood breaketh out from the inhabitant; even the waters forgotten of the foot: they are dried up, they are gone away from men. As for the earth, out of it cometh bread: and under it is turned up as it were fire. The stones of it are the place of sapphires: and it hath dust of gold.

There is a path which no fowl knoweth, and which the vulture's eye hath not seen: the lion's whelps have not trodden it, nor the fierce lion passed by it.

He putteth forth his hand upon the rock; he overturneth the mountains by the roots. He cutteth out rivers among the rocks; and his eye seeth every precious thing. He bindeth the floods from overflowing; and the thing that is hid bringeth he forth to light.

But where shall wisdom be found? and where is the place of under-standing? Man knoweth not the price thereof; neither is it found in the land of the living. The depth saith, It is not in me: and the sea saith, It is not with me. It cannot be gotten for gold, neither shall silver be weighed for the price thereof. It cannot be valued with the gold of Ophir, with the precious onyx, or the sapphire.

Whence then cometh wisdom? and where is the place of understand-ing? seeing it is hid from the eyes of all living, and kept close from the fowls of the air. Destruction and death say, We have heard the fame thereof with our ears.

God understandeth the way thereof, and he knoweth the place thereof. For he looketh to the ends of the earth, and seeth under the whole heaven; to make the weight for the winds; and he weigheth the waters by measure.

When he made a decree for the rain, and a way for the lightning of the thunder; then did he see it, and declare it; he prepared it, yea, and searched it out. And unto man he said, Behold, the fear of the Lord, that is wisdom; and to depart from evil is understanding.

Is not destruction to the wicked? and a strange punishment to the workers of iniquity? Doth not he see my ways, and count all my steps?

If I have walked with vanity, or if my foot hath hasted to deceit; let me be weighed in an even balance, that God may know mine integrity. If my step hath turned out of the way, and mine heart walked after mine eyes, and if any blot hath cleaved to my hands; then let me sow, and let another eat; yea, let mine offspring be rooted out. If mine heart have been deceived by a woman, or if I have laid wait at my neighbour's door; then let my wife grind unto another, and let others bow down upon her.

If I covered my transgressions as Adam, by hiding mine iniquity in my bosom: did I fear a great multitude, or did the contempt of families terrify me, that I kept silence, and went not out of the door?

Oh that one would hear me! behold, my desire is, that the Almighty would answer me, and that mine adversary had written a book. Surely I would take it upon my shoulder, and bind it as a crown to me. I would declare unto him the number of my steps; as a prince would I go near unto him. If my land cry against me, or that the furrows likewise thereof complain: if I have eaten the fruits thereof without money, or have caused the owners thereof to lose their life: let thistles grow instead of wheat, and cockle instead of barley. The words of Job are ended.

God Speaks

Then the Lord answered Job out of the whirlwind, and said, Who is this that darkeneth counsel by words without knowledge?

Gird up now thy loins like a man; for I will demand of thee, and answer thou me.

Where wast thou when I laid the foundations of the earth? declare, if thou hast understanding. Who hath laid the measures thereof, if thou knowest? or who hath stretched the line upon it? Whereupon are the foundations thereof fastened? or who laid the corner-stone thereof: when the morning stars sang together, and all the sons of God shouted for joy?

Or who shut up the sea with doors, when it brake forth, as if it had issued out of the womb? When I made the cloud the garment thereof, and thick darkness a swaddling band for it, and brake up for it my decreed place, and set bars and doors, and said, Hitherto shalt thou come, but no further: and here shall thy proud waves be stayed?

Hast thou commanded the morning since thy days; and caused the day-spring to know his place; that it might take hold of the ends of the earth, that the wicked might be shaken out of it?

It is turned as clay to the seal; and they stand as a garment. And from the wicked their light is withholden, and the high arm shall be broken.

Hast thou entered into the springs of the sea? or hast thou walked in the search of the depth? Have the gates of death been opened unto thee? or hast thou seen the doors of the shadow of death? Hast thou perceived the breadth of the earth? declare if thou knowest it all.

Where is the way where light dwelleth? and as for darkness, where is the place thereof, that thou shouldest take it to the bound thereof, and that thou shouldest know the paths to the house thereof? Knowest thou it, because thou wast then born? or because the number of thy days is great?

Hast thou entered into the treasures of the snow? or hast thou seen the treasures of the hail, which I have reserved against the time of trouble, against the day of battle and war?

By what way is the light parted, which scattereth the east wind upon the earth? Who hath divided a watercourse for the overflowing of waters, or a way for the lightning of thunder; to cause it to rain on the earth, where no man is; on the wilderness, wherein there is no man; to satisfy the desolate and waste ground; and to cause the bud of the tender herb to spring forth?

Hath the rain a father? or who hath begotten the drops of dew? Out of whose womb came the ice? and the hoary frost of heaven, who hath gendered it?

The waters are hid as with a stone, and the face of the deep is frozen.

Canst thou bind the sweet influences of Pleiades, or loose the bands of Orion? Canst thou bring forth Mazzaroth in his season? or canst thou guide Arcturus with his sons? Knowest thou the ordinances of heaven? canst thou set the dominion thereof in the earth? Canst thou lift up thy voice to the clouds, that abundance of waters may cover thee? Canst thou send lightnings, that they may go, and say unto thee, Here we are? Who hath put wisdom in the inward parts? or who hath given understanding to the heart? Who can number the clouds in wisdom? or who can stay the bottles of heaven, when the dust groweth into hardness, and the clods cleave fast together? Wilt thou hunt the prey for the lion? or fill the appetite of the young lions, when they couch in their dens, and abide in the covert to lie in wait? Who provideth for the raven his food? when his young ones cry unto God, they wander for lack of meat.

Knowest thou the time when the wild goats of the rock bring forth? or canst thou mark when the hinds do calve? Canst thou number the months that they fulfil? or knowest thou the time when they bring forth?

They bow themselves, they bring forth their young ones, they cast out their sorrows. Their young ones are in good liking, they grow up with corn; they go forth, and return not unto them.

Who hath sent out the wild ass free? or who hath loosed the bands of the wild ass? whose house I have made the wilderness, and the barren land his dwellings.

He scorneth the multitude of the city, neither regardeth he the crying of the driver. The range of the mountains is his pasture, and he search-eth after every green thing.

Will the unicorn be willing to serve thee, or abide by thy crib? Canst thou bind the unicorn with his band in the furrow? or will he harrow the valleys after thee? Wilt thou trust him, because his strength is great? or wilt thou leave thy labour to him? Wilt thou believe him, that he will bring home thy seed, and gather it into thy barn?

Gavest thou the goodly wings unto the peacocks? or wings and feathers unto the ostrich? which leaveth her eggs in the earth, and warmeth them in the dust, and forgetteth that the foot may crush them, or that the wild beast may break them. She is hardened against her young ones, as though they were not hers: her labour is in vain without fear; because God hath deprived her of wisdom, neither hath he imparted to her understanding. What time she lifteth up herself on high, she scorneth the horse and his rider.

Hast thou given the horse strength? hast thou clothed his neck with thunder? Canst thou make him afraid as a grasshopper? the glory of his nostrils is terrible. He paweth in the valley, and rejoiceth in his strength: he goeth on to meet the armed men.

He mocketh at fear, and is not affrighted; neither turneth he back from the sword. The quiver rattleth against him, the glittering spear and the shield. He swalloweth the ground with fierceness and rage; neither believeth he that it is the sound of the trumpet. He saith among the trumpets, Ha! ha! and he smelleth the battle afar off, the thunder of the captains, and the shouting.

Doth the hawk fly by thy wisdom, and stretch her wings toward the south? Doth the eagle mount up at thy command, and make her nest on high? She dwelleth and abideth on the rock, upon the crag of the rock, and the strong place. From thence she seeketh the prey, and her eyes behold afar off. Her young ones also suck up blood: and where the slain are, there is she.

Shall he that contendeth with the Almighty instruct him? he that reproveth God, let him answer it.

Then Job answered the Lord, and said, Behold, I am vile; what shall I answer thee? I will lay my hand upon my mouth. Once have I spoken; but I will not answer: yea, twice; but I will proceed no further.

Then answered the Lord unto Job out of the whirlwind, and said, Gird up thy loins now like a man: I will demand of thee, and declare thou unto me.

Wilt thou also disannul my judgment? wilt thou condemn me, that thou mayest be righteous? Hast thou an arm like God? or canst thou thunder with a voice like him?

Deck thyself now with majesty and excellency; and array thyself with glory and beauty. Cast abroad the rage of thy wrath: and behold every one that is proud, and abase him. Look on every one that is proud, and bring him low; and tread down the wicked in their place. Hide them in the dust together; and bind their faces in secret. Then will I also confess unto thee that thine own right hand can save thee.

Behold now Behemoth, which I made with thee; he eateth grass as an ox. Lo now, his strength is in his loins, and his force is in the navel of his belly. He moveth his tail like a cedar; the sinews of his stones are wrapped together. His bones are as strong pieces of brass; his bones are like bars of iron. He is the chief of the ways of God: he that made him can make his sword to approach unto him. Surely the mountains bring him forth food, where all the beasts of the field play. He lieth under the shady trees, in the covert of the reed, and fens. The shady trees cover him with their shadow; the willows of the brook compass him about. Behold, he drinketh up a river, and hasteth not: he trusteth that he can draw up Jordan into his mouth. He taketh it with his eyes: his nose pierceth through snares.

Canst thou draw out leviathan with an hook? or his tongue with a cord which thou lettest down? Canst thou put an hook into his nose? or bore his jaw through with a thorn? Will he make many supplications unto thee? will he speak soft words unto thee? Will he make a covenant with thee? wilt thou take him for a servant for ever? Wilt thou play with him as with a bird? or wilt thou bind him for thy maidens? Shall thy companions make a banquet of him? shall they part him among the merchants? Canst thou fill his skin with barbed irons? or his head with fish-spears?

Lay thine hand upon him, remember the battle, do no more. Behold, the hope of him is in vain: shall not one be cast down even at the sight of him? None is so fierce that dare stir him up: who then is able to stand before me?

Who hath prevented me that I should repay him? whatsoever is under the whole heaven is mine. I will not conceal his parts, nor his power, nor his comely proportion.

Who can discover the face of his garment? or who can come to him with his double bridle? who can open the doors of his face? his teeth are terrible round about.

His scales are his pride, shut up together as with a close seal. One is so near to another, that no air can come between them. They are joined one to another, they stick together, that they cannot be sundered. By his neesings a light doth shine, and his eyes are like the eyelids of the morning. Out of his mouth go burning lamps, and sparks of fire leap out. Out of his nostrils goeth smoke, as out of a seething pot or cauldron. His breath kindleth coals, and a flame goeth out of his mouth. In his neck remaineth strength, and sorrow is turned into joy before him. The flakes of his flesh are joined together: they are firm in themselves; they cannot be moved. His heart is as firm as a stone; yea, as hard as a piece of the nether millstone.

When he raiseth up himself, the mighty are afraid: by reason of breakings they purify themselves. The sword of him that layeth at him cannot hold: the spear, the dart, nor the habergeon. He esteemeth iron as straw, and brass as rotten wood. The arrow cannot make him flee: sling-stones are turned with him into stubble. Darts are counted as stubble: he laugheth at the shaking of a spear.

Sharp stones are under him: he spreadeth sharp-pointed things upon the mire.

He maketh the deep to boil like a pot: he maketh the sea like a pot of ointment. He maketh a path to shine after him; one would think the deep to be hoary.

Upon earth there is not his like, who is made without fear.

He beholdeth all high things: he is a king over all the children of pride.

Job Is Restored in God's Favour

Then Job answered the Lord, and said, I know that thou canst do everything, and that no thought can be withholden from thee.

Who is he that hideth counsel without knowledge? therefore have I uttered that I understood not; things too wonderful for me, which I knew not. Hear, I beseech thee, and I will speak: I will demand of thee, and declare thou unto me. I have heard of thee by the hearing of the ear: but now mine eye seeth thee: wherefore I abhor myself, and repent in dust and ashes.

And it was so, that after the Lord had spoken these words unto Job, the Lord said to Eliphaz the Temanite, My wrath is kindled against thee, and against thy two friends: for ye have not spoken of me the thing that is right, as my servant Job hath. Therefore take unto you now seven bullocks and seven rams, and go to my servant Job, and offer up for yourselves a burnt-offering; and my servant Job shall pray for you: for him will I accept: lest I deal with you after your folly, in that ye have not spoken of me the thing which is right, like my servant Job.

So Eliphaz the Temanite and Bildad the Shuhite and Zophar the Naamathite went, and did according as the Lord commanded them: the Lord also accepted Job. And the Lord turned the captivity of Job, when he prayed for his friends: also the Lord gave Job twice as much as he had before.

Then came there unto him all his brethren, and all his sisters, and all they that had been of his acquaintance before, and did eat bread with him in his house: and they bemoaned him, and comforted him over all the evil that the Lord had brought upon him: every man also gave him a piece of money, and every one an ear-ring of gold.

So the Lord blessed the latter end of Job more than his beginning: for he had fourteen thousand sheep, and six thousand camels, and a thousand yoke of oxen, and a thousand she-asses.

He had also seven sons, and three daughters. And he called the name of the first, Jemima; and the name of the second, Kezia; and the name of the third, Keren-happuch. And in all the land were no women found so fair as the daughters of Job: and their father gave them inheritance among their brethren.

After this lived Job an hundred and forty years, and saw his sons, and his sons' sons, even four generations.

So Job died, being old and full of days.

The Book of Psalms

The Godly and the Ungodly

Blessed is the man that walketh not in the counsel of the ungodly, nor standeth in the way of sinners, nor sitteth in the seat of the scornful.

But his delight is in the law of the Lord; and in his law doth he meditate day and night.

And he shall be like a tree planted by the rivers of water, that bringeth forth his fruit in his season; his leaf also shall not wither; and whatsoever he doeth shall prosper.

The ungodly are not so: but are like the chaff which the wind driveth away.

Therefore the ungodly shall not stand in the judgment, nor sinners in the congregation of the righteous.

For the Lord knoweth the way of the righteous: but the way of the ungodly shall perish.

Prophecy of a Son of God

Why do the heathen rage, and the people imagine a vain thing?

The kings of the earth set themselves, and the rulers take counsel together, against the Lord, and against his Anointed, saying,

Let us break their bands asunder, and cast away their cords from us.

He that sitteth in the heavens shall laugh: the Lord shall have them in derision.

Then shall he speak unto them in his wrath, and vex them in his sore displeasure.

Yet have I set my King upon my holy hill of Zion.

I will declare the decree: the Lord hath said unto me, Thou art my Son; this day have I begotten thee.

Ask of me, and I shall give thee the heathen for thine inheritance, and the uttermost parts of the earth for thy possession.

Thou shalt break them with a rod of iron; thou shalt dash them in pieces like a potter's vessel.

Be wise now therefore, O ye kings: be instructed, ye judges of the earth.

Serve the Lord with fear, and rejoice with trembling.

Kiss the Son, lest he be angry, and ye perish from the way, when his wrath is kindled but a little. Blessed are all they that put their trust in him.

When I Consider Thy Heavens

O Lord our Lord, how excellent is thy name in all the earth! who hast set thy glory above the heavens.

Out of the mouth of babes and sucklings hast thou ordained strength because of thine enemies, that thou mightest still the enemy and the avenger.

When I consider thy heavens, the work of thy fingers; the moon and the stars, which thou hast ordained;

What is man, that thou art mindful of him? and the son of man, that thou visitest him?

For thou hast made him a little lower than the angels, and hast crowned him with glory and honour.

Thou madest him to have dominion over the works of thy hands; thou hast put all things under his feet:

All sheep and oxen, yea, and the beasts of the field;

The fowl of the air, and the fish of the sea, and whatsoever passeth through the paths of the seas.

O Lord our Lord, how excellent is thy name in all the earth!

Hymn of Trust

In the Lord put I my trust: how say ye to my soul, Flee as a bird to your mountain?

For lo, the wicked bend their bow, they make ready their arrow upon the string, that they may privily shoot at the upright in heart.

If the foundations be destroyed, what can the righteous do?

The Lord is in his holy temple, the Lord's throne is in heaven: his eyes behold, his eyelids try the children of men.

The Lord trieth the righteous: but the wicked and him that loveth violence his soul hateth.

Upon the wicked he shall rain snares, fire and brimstone, and an horrible tempest: this shall be the portion of their cup.

For the righteous Lord loveth righteousness; his countenance doth behold the upright.

The Way of a Fool

The fool hath said in his heart, There is no God. They are corrupt, they have done abominable works, there is none that doeth good.

The Lord looked down from heaven upon the children of men, to see if there were any that did understand, and seek God.

They are all gone aside, they are all together become filthy; there is none that doeth good, no, not one.

Have all the workers of iniquity no knowledge? who eat up my people as they eat bread, and call not upon the Lord.

There were they in great fear: for God is in the generation of the righteous.

Ye have shamed the counsel of the poor, because the Lord is his refuge.

Oh that the salvation of Israel were come out of Zion! when the Lord bringeth back the captivity of his people, Jacob shall rejoice, and Israel shall be glad.

Who Walks Uprightly

Lord, who shall abide in thy tabernacle? who shall dwell in thy holy hill?

He that walketh uprightly, and worketh righteousness, and speaketh the truth in his heart.

He that backbiteth not with his tongue, nor doeth evil to his neighbour, nor taketh up a reproach against his neighbour.

In whose eyes a vile person is contemned; but he honoureth them that fear the Lord. He that sweareth to his own hurt, and changeth not.

He that putteth not out his money to usury, nor taketh reward against the innocent. He that doeth these things shall never be moved.

A Hymn of Praise

I will love thee, O Lord, my strength.

The Lord is my rock, and my fortress, and my deliverer; my God, my strength, in whom I will trust; my buckler, and the horn of my salvation, and my high tower.

I will call upon the Lord, who is worthy to be praised: so shall I be saved from mine enemies.

The sorrows of death compassed me, and the floods of ungodly men made me afraid.

The sorrows of hell compassed me about: the snares of death prevented me.

In my distress I called upon the Lord, and cried unto my God: he heard my voice out of his temple, and my cry came before him, even into his ears.

Then the earth shook and trembled; the foundations also of the hills moved and were shaken, because he was wroth.

There went up a smoke out of his nostrils, and fire out of his mouth devoured: coals were kindled by it.

He bowed the heavens also, and came down: and darkness was under his feet.

And he rode upon a cherub and did fly; yea, he did fly upon the wings of the wind.

He made darkness his secret place; his pavilion round about him were dark waters and thick clouds of the skies.

At the brightness that was before him his thick clouds passed, hailstones and coals of fire.

The Lord also thundered in the heavens, and the Highest gave his voice; hail-stones and coals of fire.

Yea, he sent out his arrows, and scattered them; and he shot out lightnings and discomfited them.

Then the channels of waters were seen, and the foundations of the world were discovered at thy rebuke, O Lord, at the blast of the breath of thy nostrils.

He sent from above, he took me, he drew me out of many waters.

He delivered me from my strong enemy, and from them which hated me: for they were too strong for me.

They prevented me in the day of my calamity, but the Lord was my stay.

He brought me forth also into a large place: he delivered me, because he delighted in me.

The Lord rewarded me according to my righteousness; according to the cleanness of my hands hath he recompensed me.

For I have kept the ways of the Lord, and have not wickedly departed from my God.

For all his judgments were before me, and I did not put away his statutes from me.

I was also upright before him; and I kept myself from mine iniquity.

Therefore hath the Lord recompensed me according to my righteousness, according to the cleanness of my hands in his eyesight.

With the merciful thou wilt shew thyself merciful; with an upright man thou wilt shew thyself upright;

With the pure thou wilt shew thyself pure; and with the froward thou wilt shew thyself froward.

For thou wilt save the afflicted people; but wilt bring down high looks.

For thou wilt light my candle: the Lord my God will enlighten my darkness.

For by thee I have run through a troop; and by my God have I leaped over a wall.

As for God, his way is perfect: the word of the Lord is tried: he is a buckler to all those that trust in him.

For who is God save the Lord? or who is a rock save our God?

It is God that girdeth me with strength, and maketh my way perfect.

He maketh my feet like hinds' feet, and setteth me upon my high places.

He teacheth my hands to war, so that a bow of steel is broken by mine arms.

Thou hast also given me the shield of thy salvation: and thy right hand hath holden me up, and thy gentleness hath made me great.

Thou hast enlarged my steps under me, that my feet did not slip.

I have pursued mine enemies, and overtaken them: neither did I turn again till they were consumed.

I have wounded them that they were not able to rise: they are fallen under my feet.

For thou hast girded me with strength unto the battle: thou hast subdued under me those that rose up against me.

Thou hast also given me the necks of mine enemies; that I might destroy them that hate me.

They cried, but there was none to save them: even unto the Lord, but he answered them not.

Then did I beat them small as the dust before the wind: I did cast them out as the dirt in the streets.

Thou hast delivered me from the strivings of the people; and thou hast made me the head of the heathen: a people whom I have not known shall serve me.

As soon as they hear of me, they shall obey me; the strangers shall submit themselves unto me.

The strangers shall fade away, and be afraid out of their close places.

The Lord liveth; and blessed be my Rock; and let the God of my salvation be exalted.

It is God that avengeth me, and subdueth the people under me.

He delivereth me from mine enemies: yea, thou liftest me up above those that rise up against me: thou hast delivered me from the violent man.

Therefore will I give thanks unto thee, O Lord, among the heathen, and sing praises unto thy name.

Great deliverance giveth he to his king; and sheweth mercy to his anointed, to David, and to his seed for evermore.

The Glory of God

The heavens declare the glory of God; and the firmament sheweth his handywork.

Day unto day uttereth speech, and night unto night sheweth knowledge.

There is no speech nor language, where their voice is not heard.

Their line is gone out through all the earth, and their words to the end of the world. In them hath he set a tabernacle for the sun,

Which is as a bridegroom coming out of his chamber, and rejoiceth as a strong man to run a race.

His going forth is from the end of the heaven, and his circuit unto the ends of it: and there is nothing hid from the heat thereof.

The law of the Lord is perfect, converting the soul: the testimony of the Lord is sure, making wise the simple.

The statutes of the Lord are right, rejoicing the heart: the commandment of the Lord is pure, enlightening the eyes.

The fear of the Lord is clean, enduring for ever: the judgments of the Lord are true and righteous altogether.

More to be desired are they than gold, yea, than much fine gold: sweeter also than honey and the honey-comb.

Moreover, by them is thy servant warned; and in keeping of them there is great reward.

Who can understand his errors? cleanse thou me from secret faults.

Keep back thy servant also from presumptuous sins; let them not have dominion over me: then shall I be upright, and I shall be innocent from the great transgression.

Let the words of my mouth, and the meditation of my heart, be acceptable in thy sight, O Lord, my strength, and my redeemer.

The Lord Saveth His Anointed

The Lord hear thee in the day of trouble; the name of the God of Jacob defend thee.

Send thee help from the sanctuary, and strengthen thee out of Zion.

Remember all thy offerings, and accept thy burnt-sacrifice.

Grant thee according to thine own heart, and fulfil all thy counsel.

We will rejoice in thy salvation, and in the name of our God we will set up our banners: the Lord fulfil all thy petitions.

Now know I that the Lord saveth his anointed; he will hear him from his holy heaven with the saving strength of his right hand.

Some trust in chariots, and some in horses: but we will remember the name of the Lord our God.

They are brought down and fallen; but we are risen, and stand upright.

Save, Lord: let the king hear us when we call.

A Cry of Despair

My God, my God, why hast thou forsaken me? why art thou so far from helping me, and from the words of my roaring?

O my God, I cry in the day-time, but thou hearest not; and in the night season, and am not silent.

But thou art holy, O thou that inhabitest the praises of Israel.

Our fathers trusted in thee: they trusted, and thou didst deliver them.

They cried unto thee, and were delivered: they trusted in thee, and were not confounded.

But I am a worm, and no man; a reproach of men, and despised of the people.

All they that see me laugh me to scorn: they shoot out the lip, they shake the head, saying,

He trusted on the Lord that he would deliver him: let him deliver him, seeing he delighted in him.

But thou art he that took me out of the womb: thou didst make me hope when I was upon my mother's breasts.

I was cast upon thee from the womb: thou art my God from my mother's belly.

Be not far from me; for trouble is near; for there is none to help.

Many bulls have compassed me: strong bulls of Bashan have beset me round.

They gaped upon me with their mouths, as a ravening and a roaring lion.

I am poured out like water, and all my bones are out of joint; my heart is like wax: it is melted in the midst of my bowels.

My strength is dried up like a potsherd; and my tongue cleaveth to my jaws; and thou hast brought me into the dust of death.

For dogs have compassed me: the assembly of the wicked have inclosed me: they pierced my hands and my feet.

I may tell all my bones: they look and stare upon me.

They part my garments among them and cast lots upon my vesture.

But be not thou far from me, O Lord: O my strength, haste thee to help me.

Deliver my soul from the sword, my darling from the power of the dog.

Save me from the lion's mouth: for thou hast heard me from the horns of the unicorns.

I will declare thy name unto my brethren: in the midst of the congregation will I praise thee.

Ye that fear the Lord, praise him; all ye the seed of Jacob, glorify him; and fear him, all ye the seed of Israel.

For he hath not despised nor abhorred the affliction of the afflicted; neither hath he hid his face from him; but when he cried unto him, he heard.

My praise shall be of thee in the great congregation: I will pay my vows before them that fear him.

The meek shall eat and be satisfied: they shall praise the Lord that seek him: your heart shall live for ever.

All the ends of the world shall remember and turn unto the Lord: and all the kindreds of the nations shall worship before thee.

For the kingdom is the Lord's: and he is the governor among the nations.

All they that be fat upon earth shall eat and worship: all they that go down to the dust shall bow before him: and none can keep alive his own soul.

A seed shall serve him; it shall be accounted to the Lord for a generation.

They shall come, and shall declare his righteousness unto a people that shall be born, that he hath done this.

The Shepherd's Psalm

The Lord is my shepherd; I shall not want.

He maketh me to lie down in green pastures: he leadeth me beside the still waters.

He restoreth my soul: he leadeth me in the paths of righteousness for his name's sake.

Yea, though I walk through the valley of the shadow of death, I will fear no evil: for thou art with me; thy rod and thy staff they comfort me.

Thou preparest a table before me in the presence of mine enemies: thou anointest my head with oil; my cup runneth over.

Surely goodness and mercy shall follow me all the days of my life; and I will dwell in the house of the Lord for ever.

The King of Glory

The earth is the Lord's and the fulness thereof; the world, and they that dwell therein.

For he hath founded it upon the seas, and established it upon the floods.

Who shall ascend into the hill of the Lord? and who shall stand in his holy place?

He that hath clean hands, and a pure heart; who hath not lifted up his soul unto vanity, nor sworn deceitfully.

He shall receive the blessing from the Lord, and righteousness from the God of his salvation.

This is the generation of them that seek him, that seek thy face, O Jacob.

Lift up your heads, O ye gates; and be ye lifted up, ye everlasting doors; and the King of glory shall come in.

Who is this King of glory? the Lord strong and mighty, the Lord mighty in battle.

Lift up your heads, O ye gates; even lift them up, ye everlasting doors; and the King of glory shall come in.

Who is this King of glory? the Lord of hosts, he is the King of glory.

A Prayer for Forgiveness and Help

Unto thee, O Lord, do I lift up my soul.

O my God, I trust in thee: let me not be ashamed, let not mine enemies triumph over me.

Yea, let none that wait on thee be ashamed: let them be ashamed which transgress without cause.

Shew me thy ways, O Lord; teach me thy paths.

Lead me in thy truth, and teach me: for thou art the God of my salvation: on thee do I wait all the day.

Remember, O Lord, thy tender mercies and thy loving-kindnesses; for
they have been ever of old.

Remember not the sins of my youth, nor my transgressions: according
to thy mercy remember thou me for thy goodness' sake, O Lord.

Good and upright is the Lord: therefore will he teach sinners in
the way.

The meek will he guide in judgment: and the meek will he teach
his way.

All the paths of the Lord are mercy and truth unto such as keep his
covenant and his testimonies.

For thy name's sake, O Lord, pardon mine iniquity; for it is great.

What man is he that feareth the Lord? him shall he teach in the way
that he shall choose.

His soul shall dwell at ease; and his seed shall inherit the earth.

The secret of the Lord is with them that fear him; and he will shew
them his covenant.

Mine eyes are ever toward the Lord; for he shall pluck my feet out
of the net.

Turn thee unto me, and have mercy upon me; for I am desolate and
afflicted.

The troubles of my heart are enlarged: O bring thou me out of my
distresses.

Look upon mine affliction and my pain; and forgive all my sins.

Consider mine enemies; for they are many; and they hate me with
cruel hatred.

O keep my soul, and deliver me: let me not be ashamed; for I put my
trust in thee.

Let integrity and uprightness preserve me; for I wait on thee.

Redeem Israel, O God, out of all his troubles.

A Hymn of Faith

The Lord is my light and my salvation; whom shall I fear? the Lord
is the strength of my life; of whom shall I be afraid?

When the wicked, even mine enemies and my foes, came upon me to eat up my flesh, they stumbled and fell.

Though an host should encamp against me, my heart shall not fear: though war should rise against me, in this will I be confident.

One thing have I desired of the Lord, that will I seek after; that I may dwell in the house of the Lord all the days of my life, to behold the beauty of the Lord, and to inquire in his temple.

For in the time of trouble he shall hide me in his pavilion: in the secret of his tabernacle shall he hide me; he shall set me up upon a rock.

And now shall mine head be lifted up above mine enemies round about me: therefore will I offer in his tabernacle sacrifices of joy; I will sing, yea, I will sing praises unto the Lord.

Hear, O Lord, when I cry with my voice: have mercy also upon me, and answer me.

When thou saidst, Seek ye my face; my heart said unto thee, Thy face, Lord, will I seek.

Hide not thy face far from me; put not thy servant away in anger; thou hast been my help; leave me not, neither forsake me, O God of my salvation.

When my father and my mother forsake me, then the Lord will take me up.

Teach me thy way, O Lord, and lead me in a plain path, because of mine enemies.

Deliver me not over unto the will of mine enemies: for false witnesses are risen up against me, and such as breathe out cruelty.

I had fainted, unless I had believed to see the goodness of the Lord in the land of the living.

Wait on the Lord: be of good courage, and he shall strengthen thine heart: wait, I say, on the Lord.

A Call to Worship

Give unto the Lord, O ye mighty, give unto the Lord glory and strength.

Give unto the Lord the glory due unto his name; worship the Lord in the beauty of holiness.

The voice of the Lord is upon the waters: the God of glory thundereth: the Lord is upon many waters.

The voice of the Lord is powerful; the voice of the Lord is full of majesty.

The voice of the Lord breaketh the cedars; yea, the Lord breaketh the cedars of Lebanon.

He maketh them also to skip like a calf; Lebanon and Sirion like a young unicorn.

The voice of the Lord divideth the flames of fire.

The voice of the Lord shaketh the wilderness; the Lord shaketh the wilderness of Kadesh.

The voice of the Lord maketh the hinds to calve, and discovereth the forests: and in his temple doth every one speak of his glory.

The Lord sitteth upon the flood; yea, the Lord sitteth King for ever.

The Lord will give strength unto his people; the Lord will bless his people with peace.

A Hymn of Promise

I will bless the Lord at all times: his praise shall continually be in my mouth.

My soul shall make her boast in the Lord: the humble shall hear thereof, and be glad.

O magnify the Lord with me, and let us exalt his name together.

I sought the Lord, and he heard me, and delivered me from all my fears.

They looked unto him, and were lightened: and their faces were not ashamed.

This poor man cried, and the Lord heard him, and saved him out of all his troubles.

The angel of the Lord encampeth round about them that fear him, and delivereth them.

O taste and see that the Lord is good: blessed is the man that trusteth in him.

O fear the Lord, ye his saints; for there is no want to them that fear him.

The young lions do lack, and suffer hunger: but they that seek the Lord shall not want any good thing.

Come, ye children, hearken unto me: I will teach you the fear of the Lord.

What man is he that desireth life, and loveth many days, that he may see good?

Keep thy tongue from evil, and thy lips from speaking guile.

Depart from evil, and do good; seek peace, and pursue it.

The eyes of the Lord are upon the righteous, and his ears are open unto their cry.

The face of the Lord is against them that do evil, to cut off the remembrance of them from the earth.

The righteous cry, and the Lord heareth, and delivereth them out of all their troubles.

The Lord is nigh unto them that are of a broken heart; and saveth such as be of a contrite spirit.

Many are the afflictions of the righteous: but the Lord delivereth him out of them all.

He keepeth all his bones: not one of them is broken.

Evil shall slay the wicked: and they that hate the righteous shall be desolate.

The Lord redeemeth the soul of his servants: and none of them that trust in him shall be desolate.

The Wicked and the Godly

Fret not thyself because of evil doers, neither be thou envious against the workers of iniquity.

For they shall soon be cut down like the grass, and wither as the green herb.

Trust in the Lord, and do good; so shalt thou dwell in the land, and verily thou shalt be fed.

Delight thyself also in the Lord; and he shall give thee the desires of thine heart.

Commit thy way unto the Lord; trust also in him; and he shall bring it to pass.

And he shall bring forth thy righteousness as the light, and thy judgment as the noon-day.

Rest in the Lord, and wait patiently for him: fret not thyself because of him who prospereth in his way, because of the man who bringeth wicked devices to pass.

Cease from anger, and forsake wrath: fret not thyself in any wise to do evil.

For evil doers shall be cut off: but those that wait upon the Lord, they shall inherit the earth.

For yet a little while, and the wicked shall not be: yea, thou shalt diligently consider his place, and it shall not be.

But the meek shall inherit the earth; and shall delight themselves in the abundance of peace.

The wicked plotteth against the just, and gnasheth upon him with his teeth.

The Lord shall laugh at him: for he seeth that his day is coming.

The wicked have drawn out the sword, and have bent their bow, to cast down the poor and needy, and to slay such as be of upright conversation.

Their sword shall enter into their own heart, and their bows shall be broken.

A little that a righteous man hath is better than the riches of many wicked.

For the arms of the wicked shall be broken: but the Lord upholdeth the righteous.

The Lord knoweth the days of the upright: and their inheritance shall be for ever.

They shall not be ashamed in the evil time: and in the days of famine they shall be satisfied.

But the wicked shall perish, and the enemies of the Lord shall be as the fat of lambs: they shall consume; into smoke shall they consume away.

The wicked borroweth, and payeth not again: but the righteous sheweth mercy, and giveth.

For such as be blessed of him shall inherit the earth; and they that be cursed of him shall be cut off.

The steps of a good man are ordered by the Lord: and he delighteth in his way.

Though he fall, he shall not be utterly cast down: for the Lord upholdeth him with his hand.

I have been young, and now am old; yet have I not seen the righteous forsaken, nor his seed begging bread.

He is ever merciful, and lendeth; and his seed is blessed.

Depart from evil, and do good; and dwell for evermore.

For the Lord loveth judgment, and forsaketh not his saints; they are preserved for ever: but the seed of the wicked shall be cut off.

The righteous shall inherit the land, and dwell therein for ever.

The mouth of the righteous speaketh wisdom, and his tongue talketh of judgment.

The law of his God is in his heart; none of his steps shall slide.

The wicked watcheth the righteous, and seeketh to slay him.

The Lord will not leave him in his hand, nor condemn him when he is judged.

Wait on the Lord, and keep his way, and he shall exalt thee to inherit the land: when the wicked are cut off, thou shalt see it.

I have seen the wicked in great power, and spreading himself like a green bay-tree.

Yet he passed away, and lo, he was not: yea, I sought him, but he could not be found.

Mark the perfect man, and behold the upright: for the end of that man is peace.

But the transgressors shall be destroyed together: the end of the wicked shall be cut off.

But the salvation of the righteous is of the Lord: he is their strength in the time of trouble.

And the Lord shall help them, and deliver them: he shall deliver them from the wicked, and save them, because they trust in him.

A Psalm of Hope

As the hart panteth after the water-brooks, so panteth my soul after thee, O God.

My soul thirsteth for God, for the living God: when shall I come and appear before God?

My tears have been my meat day and night, while they continually say unto me, Where is thy God?

When I remember these things, I pour out my soul in me: for I had gone with the multitude, I went with them to the house of God, with the voice of joy and praise, with a multitude that kept holy-day.

Why art thou cast down, O my soul? and why art thou disquieted in me? hope thou in God: for I shall yet praise him for the help of his countenance.

O my God, my soul is cast down within me: therefore will I remember thee from the land of Jordan, and of the Hermonites, from the hill Mizar.

Deep calleth unto deep at the noise of thy water-spouts: all thy waves and thy billows are gone over me.

Yet the Lord will command his loving-kindness in the day-time, and in the night his song shall be with me, and my prayer unto the God of my life.

I will say unto God my rock, Why hast thou forgotten me? why go I mourning because of the oppression of the enemy?

As with a sword in my bones, mine enemies reproach me; while they say daily unto me, Where is thy God?

Why art thou cast down, O my soul? and why art thou disquieted within me? hope thou in God: for I shall yet praise him, who is the health of my countenance, and my God.

The Strength of God

God is our refuge and strength, a very present help in trouble.

Therefore will not we fear, though the earth be removed, and though the mountains be carried into the midst of the sea;

Though the waters thereof roar and be troubled, though the mountains shake with the swelling thereof.

There is a river, the streams whereof shall make glad the city of God, the holy place of the tabernacles of the Most High.

God is in the midst of her; she shall not be moved: God shall help her, and that right early.

The heathen raged, the kingdoms were moved: he uttered his voice, the earth melted.

The Lord of hosts is with us; the God of Jacob is our refuge.

Come, behold the works of the Lord, what desolations he hath made in the earth.

He maketh wars to cease unto the end of the earth; he breaketh the bow, and cutteth the spear in sunder; he burneth the chariot in the fire.

Be still, and know that I am God: I will be exalted among the heathen, I will be exalted in the earth.

The Lord of hosts is with us; the God of Jacob is our refuge.

A Hymn of Joy

O clap your hands, all ye people, shout unto God with the voice of triumph.

For the Lord Most High is terrible; he is a great King over all the earth.

He shall subdue the people under us, and the nations under our feet.

He shall choose our inheritance for us, the excellency of Jacob whom he loved.

God is gone up with a shout, the Lord with the sound of a trumpet.

Sing praises to God, sing praises; sing praises unto our King, sing praises.

For God is the King of all the earth: sing ye praises with understanding.

God reigneth over the heathen: God sitteth upon the throne of his holiness.

The princes of the people are gathered together, even the people of the God of Abraham: for the shields of the earth belong unto God: he is greatly exalted.

Have Mercy upon Me!

Have mercy upon me, O God, according to thy loving-kindness: according unto the multitude of thy tender mercies blot out my transgressions.

Wash me thoroughly from mine iniquity, and cleanse me from my sin.

For I acknowledge my transgressions: and my sin is ever before me.

Against thee, thee only, have I sinned, and done this evil in thy sight:

that thou mightest be justified when thou speakest, and be clear when thou judgest.

Behold, I was shapen in iniquity; and in sin did my mother conceive me.

Behold, thou desirest truth in the inward parts: and in the hidden part thou shalt make me to know wisdom.

Purge me with hyssop, and I shall be clean: wash me, and I shall be whiter than snow.

Make me to hear joy and gladness; that the bones which thou hast broken may rejoice.

Hide thy face from my sins, and blot out all mine iniquities.

Create in me a clean heart, O God; and renew a right spirit within me.

Cast me not away from thy presence; and take not thy Holy Spirit from me.

Restore unto me the joy of thy salvation; and uphold me with thy free Spirit.

Then will I teach transgressors thy ways; and sinners shall be converted unto thee.

Deliver me from blood-guiltiness, O God, thou God of my salvation: and my tongue shall sing aloud of thy righteousness.

O Lord, open thou my lips, and my mouth shall shew forth thy praise.

For thou desirest not sacrifice; else would I give it: thou delightest not in burnt-offering.

The sacrifices of God are a broken spirit: a broken and a contrite heart, O God, thou wilt not despise.

Do good in thy good pleasure unto Zion: build thou the walls of Jerusalem.

Then shalt thou be pleased with the sacrifices of righteousness, with burnt-offering and whole burnt-offering: then shall they offer bullocks upon thine altar.

Like Rain upon the Mown Grass

Give the king thy judgments, O God, and thy righteousness unto the king's son.

He shall judge thy people with righteousness, and thy poor with judgment.

The mountains shall bring peace to the people, and the little hills, by righteousness.

He shall judge the poor of the people, he shall save the children of the needy, and shall break in pieces the oppressor.

They shall fear thee as long as the sun and moon endure, throughout all generations.

He shall come down like rain upon the mown grass: as showers that water the earth.

In his days shall the righteous flourish: and abundance of peace so long as the moon endureth.

He shall have dominion also from sea to sea, and from the river unto the ends of the earth.

They that dwell in the wilderness shall bow before him; and his enemies shall lick the dust.

The kings of Tarshish and of the isles shall bring presents: the kings of Sheba and Seba shall offer gifts.

Yea, all kings shall fall down before him: all nations shall serve him.

For he shall deliver the needy when he crieth; the poor also, and him that hath no helper.

He shall spare the poor and needy, and shall save the souls of the needy.

He shall redeem their soul from deceit and violence: and precious shall their blood be in his sight.

And he shall live, and to him shall be given of the gold of Sheba: prayer also shall be made for him continually; and daily shall he be praised.

There shall be an handful of corn in the earth upon the top of the mountains; the fruit thereof shall shake like Lebanon: and they of the city shall flourish like grass of the earth.

His name shall endure for ever: his name shall be continued as long as the sun: and men shall be blessed in him: all nations shall call him blessed.

Blessed be the Lord God, the God of Israel, who only doeth wondrous things.

And blessed be his glorious name for ever: and let the whole earth be filled with his glory; Amen, and Amen.

The prayers of David the son of Jesse are ended.

The House of God

How amiable are thy tabernacles, O Lord of hosts!

My soul longeth, yea, even fainteth for the courts of the Lord: my heart and my flesh crieth out for the living God.

Yea, the sparrow hath found an house, and the swallow a nest for herself, where she may lay her young, even thine altars, O Lord of hosts, my King, and my God.

Blessed are they that dwell in thy house: they will be still praising thee.

Blessed is the man whose strength is in thee; in whose heart are the ways of them,

Who passing through the valley of Baca make it a well; the rain also filleth the pools.

They go from strength to strength, every one of them in Zion appeareth before God.

O Lord God of hosts, hear my prayer: give ear, O God of Jacob.

Behold, O God our shield, and look upon the face of thine anointed.

For a day in thy courts is better than a thousand. I had rather be a doorkeeper in the house of my God, than to dwell in the tents of wickedness.

For the Lord God is a sun and shield: the Lord will give grace and glory; no good thing will he withhold from them that walk uprightly.

O Lord of hosts, blessed is the man that trusteth in thee.

A Prayer of Moses

Lord, thou hast been our dwelling-place in all generations.

Before the mountains were brought forth, or ever thou hadst formed the earth and the world, even from everlasting to everlasting, thou art God.

Thou turnest man to destruction; and sayest, Return, ye children of men.

For a thousand years in thy sight are but as yesterday when it is past, and as a watch in the night.

Thou carriest them away as with a flood; they are as a sleep; in the morning they are like grass which groweth up.

In the morning it flourisheth, and groweth up; in the evening it is cut down, and withereth.

For we are consumed by thine anger, and by thy wrath are we troubled.

Thou hast set our iniquities before thee, our secret sins in the light of thy countenance.

For all our days are passed away in thy wrath: we spend our years, as a tale that is told.

The days of our years are threescore years and ten; and if by reason of strength they be fourscore years, yet is their strength labour and sorrow; for it is soon cut off, and we fly away.

Who knoweth the power of thine anger? even according to thy fear so is thy wrath.

So teach us to number our days, that we may apply our hearts unto wisdom.

Return, O Lord, how long? and let it repent thee concerning thy servants.

O satisfy us early with thy mercy; that we may rejoice and be glad all our days.

Make us glad according to the days wherein thou hast afflicted us, and the years wherein we have seen evil.

Let thy work appear unto thy servants, and thy glory unto their children.

And let the beauty of the Lord our God be upon us: and establish thou the work of our hands upon us; yea, the work of our hands establish thou it.

The Refuge of the Righteous

He that dwelleth in the secret place of the Most High shall abide under the shadow of the Almighty.

I will say of the Lord, He is my refuge and my fortress: my God; in him will I trust.

Surely he shall deliver thee from the snare of the fowler, and from the noisome pestilence.

He shall cover thee with his feathers, and under his wings shalt thou trust: his truth shall be thy shield and buckler.

Thou shalt not be afraid for the terror by night; nor for the arrow that flieth by day;

Nor for the pestilence that walketh in darkness; nor for the destruction that wasteth at noon-day.

A thousand shall fall at thy side, and ten thousand at thy right hand; but it shall not come nigh thee.

Only with thine eyes shalt thou behold and see the reward of the wicked.

Because thou hast made the Lord which is my refuge, even the Most High, thy habitation;

There shall no evil befall thee, neither shall any plague come nigh thy dwelling.

For he shall give his angels charge over thee, to keep thee in all thy ways.

They shall bear thee up in their hands, lest thou dash thy foot against a stone.

Thou shalt tread upon the lion and adder: the young lion and the dragon shalt thou trample under feet.

Because he hath set his love upon me, therefore will I deliver him: I will set him on high, because he hath known my name.

He shall call upon me, and I will answer him: I will be with him in trouble; I will deliver him, and honour him.

With long life will I satisfy him, and shew him my salvation.

Of the Goodness of Praise

It is a good thing to give thanks unto the Lord, and to sing praises unto thy name, O Most High.

To shew forth thy loving-kindness in the morning, and thy faithfulness every night.

Upon an instrument of ten strings, and upon the psaltery; upon the harp with a solemn sound.

For thou, Lord, hast made me glad through thy work: I will triumph in the works of thy hands.

O Lord, how great are thy works! and thy thoughts are very deep.

A brutish man knoweth not; neither doth a fool understand this.

When the wicked spring as the grass, and when all the workers of iniquity do flourish; it is that they shall be destroyed for ever:

But thou, Lord, art most high for evermore.

For lo, thine enemies, O Lord, for lo, thine enemies shall perish; all the workers of iniquity shall be scattered.

But my horn shall thou exalt like the horn of an unicorn: I shall be anointed with fresh oil.

Mine eye also shall see my desire on mine enemies, and mine ears shall hear my desire of the wicked that rise up against me.

The righteous shall flourish like the palm-tree: he shall grow like a cedar in Lebanon.

Those that be planted in the house of the Lord shall flourish in the courts of our God.

They shall still bring forth fruit in old age: they shall be fat and flourishing;

To shew that the Lord is upright: he is my rock, and there is no unrighteousness in him.

The Might of the Lord

The Lord reigneth, he is clothed with majesty; the Lord is clothed with strength, wherewith he hath girded himself: the world also is established, that it cannot be moved.

Thy throne is established of old: thou art from everlasting.

The floods have lifted up, O Lord, the floods have lifted up their voice; the floods lift up their waves.

The Lord on high is mightier than the noise of many waters, yea, than the mighty waves of the sea.

Thy testimonies are very sure: holiness becometh thine house, O Lord, for ever.

A Call to Worship

O come, let us sing unto the Lord: let us make a joyful noise to the rock of our salvation.

Let us come before his presence with thanksgiving, and make a joyful noise unto him with psalms.

For the Lord is a great God, and a great King above all gods.

In his hand are the deep places of the earth: the strength of the hills is his also.

The sea is his, and he made it: and his hands formed the dry land.

O come, let us worship and bow down: let us kneel before the Lord our maker.

For he is our God; and we are the people of his pasture, and the sheep of his hand. To-day if ye will hear his voice,

Harden not your heart, as in the provocation, and as in the day of temptation in the wilderness:

When your fathers tempted me, proved me, and saw my work.

Forty years long was I grieved with this generation, and said, It is a people that do err in their heart, and they have not known my ways:

Unto whom I sware in my wrath, that they should not enter into my rest.

The Majesty of God

O sing unto the Lord a new song: sing unto the Lord, all the earth.

Sing unto the Lord, bless his name; shew forth his salvation from day to day.

Declare his glory among the heathen, his wonders among all people.

For the Lord is great, and greatly to be praised: he is to be feared above all gods.

For all the gods of the nations are idols: but the Lord made the heavens.

Honour and majesty are before him; strength and beauty are in his sanctuary.

Give unto the Lord, O ye kindreds of the people, give unto the Lord glory and strength.

Give unto the Lord the glory due unto his name: bring an offering, and come into his courts.

O worship the Lord in the beauty of holiness: fear before him, all the earth.

Say among the heathen that the Lord reigneth: the world also shall be

established that it shall not be moved: he shall judge the people righteously.

Let the heavens rejoice, and let the earth be glad; let the sea roar, and
the fullness thereof.

Let the field be joyful, and all that is therein: then shall all the trees
of the wood rejoice

Before the Lord; for he cometh, for he cometh to judge the earth: he
shall judge the world with righteousness, and the people with his truth.

Praise the Lord

Make a joyful noise unto the Lord, all ye lands.

Serve the Lord with gladness: come before his presence with singing.

Know ye that the Lord he is God: it is he that hath made us, and not
we ourselves; we are his people, and the sheep of his pasture.

Enter into his gates with thanksgiving, and into his courts with praise;
be thankful unto him, and bless his name.

For the Lord is good; his mercy is everlasting; and his truth endureth
to all generations.

A Vow to the Lord

I will sing of mercy and judgment: unto thee, O Lord, will I sing.

I will behave myself wisely in a perfect way. O when wilt thou come
unto me? I will walk within my house with a perfect heart.

I will set no wicked thing before mine eyes: I hate the work of them
that turn aside; it shall not cleave to me.

A froward heart shall depart from me: I will not know a wicked
person.

Whoso privily slandereth his neighbour, him will I cut off: him that
hath an high look and a proud heart will not I suffer.

Mine eyes shall be upon the faithful of the land, that they may dwell
with me: he that walketh in a perfect way, he shall serve me.

He that worketh deceit shall not dwell within my house: he that
telleth lies shall not tarry in my sight.

I will early destroy all the wicked of the land; that I may cut off all wicked doers from the city of the Lord.

The Gentleness of God

Bless the Lord, O my soul: and all that is within me, bless his holy name.

Bless the Lord, O my soul, and forget not all his benefits:

Who forgiveth all thine iniquities; who healeth all thy diseases;

Who redeemeth thy life from destruction; who crowneth thee with loving-kindness and tender mercies;

Who satisfieth thy mouth with good things; so that thy youth is renewed like the eagle's.

The Lord executeth righteousness and judgment for all that are oppressed.

He made known his ways unto Moses, his acts unto the children of Israel.

The Lord is merciful and gracious, slow to anger, and plenteous in mercy.

He will not always chide; neither will he keep his anger for ever.

He hath not dealt with us after our sins; nor rewarded us according to our iniquities.

For as the heaven is high above the earth, so great is his mercy toward them that fear him.

As far as the east is from the west, so far hath he removed our transgressions from us.

Like as a father pitieth his children, so the Lord pitieth them that fear him.

For he knoweth our frame; he remembereth that we are dust.

As for man, his days are as grass: as a flower of the field, so he flourisheth.

For the wind passeth over it, and it is gone; and the place thereof shall know it no more.

But the mercy of the Lord is from everlasting to everlasting upon them that fear him, and his righteousness unto children's children;

To such as keep his covenant, and to those that remember his commandments to do them.

The Lord hath prepared his throne in the heavens; and his kingdom ruleth over all.

Bless the Lord, ye his angels, that excel in strength, that do his commandments, hearkening unto the voice of his word.

Bless ye the Lord, all ye his hosts; ye ministers of his, that do his pleasure.

Bless the Lord, all his works in all places of his dominion: bless the Lord, O my soul.

The Bounty of God

Bless the Lord, O my soul. O Lord my God, thou art very great; thou art clothed with honour and majesty:

Who coverest thyself with light as with a garment: who stretchest out the heavens like a curtain:

Who layeth the beams of his chambers in the waters: who maketh the clouds his chariot: who walketh upon the wings of the wind:

Who maketh his angels spirits; his ministers a flaming fire:

Who laid the foundations of the earth, that it should not be removed for ever.

Thou coveredst it with the deep as with a garment: the waters stood above the mountains.

At thy rebuke they fled; at the voice of thy thunder they hasted away.

They go up by the mountains; they go down by the valleys unto the place which thou hast founded for them.

Thou hast set a bound that they may not pass over; that they turn not again to cover the earth.

He sendeth the springs into the valleys, which run among the hills.

They give drink to every beast of the field: the wild asses quench their thirst.

By them shall the fowls of the heaven have their habitation, which sing among the branches.

He watereth the hills from his chambers: the earth is satisfied with the fruit of thy works.

He causeth the grass to grow for the cattle, and herb for the service of man: that he may bring forth food out of the earth:

And wine that maketh glad the heart of man, and oil to make his face to shine, and bread which strengtheneth man's heart.

The trees of the Lord are full of sap; the cedars of Lebanon, which he hath planted;

Where the birds make their nests: as for the stork, the fir-trees are her house.

The high hills are a refuge for the wild goats; and the rocks for the conies.

He appointed the moon for seasons: the sun knoweth his going down.

Thou makest darkness, and it is night: wherein all the beasts of the forest do creep forth.

The young lions roar after their prey, and seek their meat from God.

The sun ariseth, they gather themselves together, and lay them down in their dens.

Man goeth forth unto his work and to his labour until the evening.

O Lord, how manifold are thy works! in wisdom hast thou made them all: the earth is full of thy riches.

So is this great and wide sea, wherein are things creeping innumerable, both small and great beasts.

There go the ships: there is that leviathan, whom thou hast made to play therein.

These wait all upon thee; that thou mayest give them their meat in due season.

That thou givest them, they gather: thou openest thine hand, they are filled with good.

Thou hidest thy face, they are troubled: thou takest away their breath, they die, and return to their dust.

Thou sendest forth thy spirit, they are created: and thou renewest the face of the earth.

The glory of the Lord shall endure for ever: the Lord shall rejoice in his works.

He looketh on the earth, and it trembleth: he toucheth the hills, and they smoke.

I will sing unto the Lord as long as I live: I will sing praise to my God while I have my being.

My meditation of him shall be sweet: I will be glad in the Lord.

Let the sinners be consumed out of the earth, and let the wicked be no more. Bless thou the Lord, O my soul. Praise ye the Lord.

A Hymn of Love

I love the Lord, because he hath heard my voice and my supplications.

Because he hath inclined his ear unto me, therefore will I call upon him as long as I live.

The sorrows of death compassed me, and the pains of hell gat hold upon me: I found trouble and sorrow.

Then called I upon the name of the Lord; O Lord, I beseech thee, deliver my soul.

Gracious is the Lord, and righteous; yea, our God is merciful.

The Lord preserveth the simple: I was brought low, and he helped me.

Return unto thy rest, O my soul; for the Lord hath dealt bountifully with thee.

For thou hast delivered my soul from death, mine eyes from tears, and my feet from falling.

I will walk before the Lord in the land of the living.

I believed, therefore have I spoken: I was greatly afflicted:

I said in my haste, All men are liars.

What shall I render unto the Lord for all his benefits toward me?

I will take the cup of salvation, and call upon the name of the Lord.

I will pay my vows unto the Lord now in the presence of all his people.

Precious in the sight of the Lord is the death of his saints.

O Lord, truly I am thy servant; I am thy servant, and the son of thy handmaid: thou hast loosed my bonds.

I will offer to thee the sacrifice of thanksgiving, and will call upon the name of the Lord.

I will pay my vows unto the Lord now in the presence of all his people.

In the courts of the Lord's house, in the midst of thee, O Jerusalem. Praise ye the Lord.

The Endurance of Truth

O praise the Lord, all ye nations; praise him, all ye people.

For his merciful kindness is great toward us: and the truth of the Lord endureth for ever. Praise ye the Lord.

A Prayer for Peace

In my distress I cried unto the Lord, and he heard me.

Deliver my soul, O Lord, from lying lips, and from a deceitful tongue.

What shall be given unto thee? or what shall be done unto thee, thou false tongue?

Sharp arrows of the mighty, with coals of juniper.

Woe is me, that I sojourn in Mesech, that I dwell in the tents of Kedar!

My soul hath long dwelt with him that hateth peace.

I am for peace: but when I speak, they are for war.

Whence Help Cometh

I will lift up mine eyes unto the hills, from whence cometh my help.

My help cometh from the Lord, which made heaven and earth.

He will not suffer thy foot to be moved: he that keepeth thee will not slumber.

Behold, he that keepeth Israel shall neither slumber nor sleep.

The Lord is thy keeper: the Lord is thy shade upon thy right hand.

The sun shall not smite thee by day, nor the moon by night.

The Lord shall preserve thee from all evil: he shall preserve thy soul.

The Lord shall preserve thy going out and thy coming in from this time forth, and even for evermore.

Peace Be within Thee

I was glad when they said unto me, Let us go into the house of the Lord.

Our feet shall stand within thy gates, O Jerusalem.

Jerusalem is builded as a city that is compact together:

Whither the tribes go up, the tribes of the Lord unto the testimony of Israel, to give thanks unto the name of the Lord.

For there are set thrones of judgment, the thrones of the house of David.

Pray for the peace of Jerusalem: they shall prosper that love thee.

Peace be within thy walls, and prosperity within thy palaces.

For my brethren and companions' sakes, I will now say, Peace be within thee.

Because of the house of the Lord our God I will seek thy good.

Adoration of God

Unto thee lift I up mine eyes, O thou that dwellest in the heavens.

Behold, as the eyes of servants look unto the hand of their masters, and as the eyes of a maiden unto the hand of her mistress; so our eyes wait upon the Lord our God, until that he have mercy upon us.

Have mercy upon us, O Lord, have mercy upon us: for we are exceedingly filled with contempt.

Our soul is exceedingly filled with the scorning of those that are at ease, and with the contempt of the proud.

He Giveth His Beloved Sleep

Except the Lord build the house, they labour in vain that build it: except the Lord keep the city, the watchman waketh but in vain.

It is vain for you to rise up early, to sit up late, to eat the bread of sorrows: for so he giveth his beloved sleep.

Lo, children are an heritage of the Lord: and the fruit of the womb is his reward.

As arrows are in the hand of a mighty man; so are children of the youth.

Happy is the man that hath his quiver full of them: they shall not be ashamed, but they shall speak with the enemies in the gate.

He That Fears the Lord

Blessed is every one that feareth the Lord; that walketh in his ways.

For thou shalt eat the labour of thine hands: happy shalt thou be, and it shall be well with thee.

Thy wife shall be as a fruitful vine by the sides of thine house: thy children like olive-plants round about thy table.

Behold, that thus shall the man be blessed that feareth the Lord.

The Lord shall bless thee out of Zion: and thou shalt see the good of Jerusalem all the days of thy life.

Yea, thou shalt see thy children's children, and peace upon Israel.

The Mercy of God

Out of the depths have I cried unto thee, O Lord.

Lord, hear my voice: let thine ears be attentive to the voice of my supplications.

If thou, Lord, shouldest mark iniquities, O Lord, who shall stand?

But there is forgiveness with thee, that thou mayest be feared.

I wait for the Lord, my soul doth wait, and in his word do I hope.

My soul waiteth for the Lord more than they that watch for the morning: I say, more than they that watch for the morning.

Let Israel hope in the Lord: for with the Lord there is mercy, and with him is plenteous redemption.

And he shall redeem Israel from all his iniquities.

The Goodness of Unity

Behold, how good and how pleasant it is for brethren to dwell together in unity!

It is like the precious ointment upon the head, that ran down upon the beard, even Aaron's beard: that went down to the skirts of his garments;

As the dew of Hermon, and as the dew that descended upon the mountains of Zion: for there the Lord commanded the blessing, even life for evermore.

A Hymn of Thanksgiving

O give thanks unto the Lord; for he is good: for his mercy endureth for ever.

O give thanks to the God of gods: for his mercy endureth for ever.

O give thanks to the Lord of lords: for his mercy endureth for ever.

To him who alone doeth great wonders: for his mercy endureth for ever.

To him that by wisdom made the heavens: for his mercy endureth for ever.

To him that stretched out the earth above the waters: for his mercy endureth for ever.

To him that made great lights: for his mercy endureth for ever:

The sun to rule by day: for his mercy endureth for ever:

The moon and stars to rule by night: for his mercy endureth for ever.

To him that smote Egypt in their first-born: for his mercy endureth for ever:

And brought out Israel from among them: for his mercy endureth for ever:

With a strong hand, and with a stretched-out arm: for his mercy endureth for ever.

To him which divided the Red sea into parts: for his mercy endureth for ever:

And made Israel to pass through the midst of it: for his mercy endureth for ever:

But overthrew Pharaoh and his host in the Red sea: for his mercy endureth for ever:

To him which led his people through the wilderness: for his mercy endureth for ever.

To him which smote great kings: for his mercy endureth for ever:

And slew famous kings: for his mercy endureth for ever:

Sihon king of the Amorites: for his mercy endureth for ever:

And Og the king of Bashan: for his mercy endureth for ever:

And gave their land for an heritage: for his mercy endureth for ever:

Even an heritage unto Israel his servant: for his mercy endureth for ever.

Who remembered us in our low estate: for his mercy endureth for ever.

And hath redeemed us from our enemies: for his mercy endureth for ever.

Who giveth food to all flesh: for his mercy endureth for ever.

O give thanks unto the God of heaven: for his mercy endureth for ever.

By the Rivers of Babylon

By the rivers of Babylon, there we sat down, yea, we wept, when we remembered Zion.

We hanged our harps upon the willows in the midst thereof.

For there they that carried us away captive required of us a song; and they that wasted us required of us mirth, saying, Sing us one of the songs of Zion.

How shall we sing the Lord's song in a strange land?

If I forget thee, O Jerusalem, let my right hand forget her cunning.

If I do not remember thee, let my tongue cleave to the roof of my mouth; if I pefer not Jerusalem above my chief joy.

Remember, O Lord, the children of Edom in the day of Jerusalem; who said, Rase it, rase it, even to the foundation thereof.

O daughter of Babylon, who art to be destroyed; happy shall he be, that rewardeth thee as thou hast served us.

Happy shall he be that taketh and dasheth thy little ones against the stones.

The Truth of His Word

I will praise thee with my whole heart: before the gods will I sing praise unto thee.

I will worship toward thy holy temple, and praise thy name for thy loving-kindness and for thy truth; for thou hast magnified thy word above all thy name.

In the day when I cried thou answeredst me, and strengthenedst me with strength in my soul.

All the kings of the earth shall praise thee, O Lord, when they hear the words of thy mouth.

Yea, they shall sing in the ways of the Lord: for great is the glory of the Lord.

Though the Lord be high, yet hath he respect unto the lowly: but the proud he knoweth afar off.

Though I walk in the midst of trouble, thou wilt revive me: thou shalt stretch forth thine hand against the wrath of mine enemies, and thy right hand shall save me.

The Lord will perfect that which concerneth me: thy mercy, O Lord, endureth for ever; forsake not the works of thine own hands.

The Omnipresence of God

O Lord, thou hast searched me, and known me.

Thou knowest my down-sitting and mine up-rising, thou understandest my thought afar off.

Thou compassest my path and my lying down, and art acquainted with all my ways.

For there is not a word in my tongue, but lo, O Lord, thou knowest it altogether.

Thou hast beset me behind and before, and laid thine hand upon me.

Such knowledge is too wonderful for me; it is high, I cannot attain unto it.

Whither shall I go from thy Spirit? or whither shall I flee from thy presence?

If I ascend up into heaven, thou art there: if I made my bed in hell, behold thou art there.

If I take the wings of the morning, and dwell in the uttermost parts of the sea;

Even there shall thy hand lead me, and thy right hand shall hold me.

If I say, Surely the darkness shall cover me; even the night shall be light about me.

Yea, the darkness hideth not from thee; but the night shineth as the day: the darkness and the light are both alike to thee.

For thou hast possessed my reins: thou hast covered me in my mother's womb.

I will praise thee; for I am fearfully and wonderfully made: marvellous are thy works; and that my soul knoweth right well.

My substance was not hid from thee, when I was made in secret, and curiously wrought in the lowest parts of the earth.

Thine eyes did see my substance, yet being unperfect; and in thy book all my members were written, which in continuance were fashioned, when as yet there was none of them.

How precious also are thy thoughts unto me, O God! how great is the sum of them!

If I should count them, they are more in number than the sand: when I awake, I am still with thee.

Surely thou wilt slay the wicked, O God: depart from me therefore, ye bloody men.

For they speak against thee wickedly, and thine enemies take thy name in vain.

Do not I hate them, O Lord, that hate thee? and am not I grieved with those that rise up against thee?

I hate them with perfect hatred: I count them mine enemies.

Search me, O God, and know my heart: try me, and know my thoughts:

And see if there be any wicked way in me, and lead me in the way everlasting.

Praise Ye the Lord

Praise ye the Lord. Praise ye the Lord from the heavens: praise him in the heights.

Praise ye him, all his angels: praise ye him, all his hosts.

Praise ye him, sun and moon: praise him, all ye stars of light.

Praise him, ye heavens of heavens, and ye waters that be above the heavens.

Let them praise the name of the Lord: for he commanded, and they were created.

He hath also established them for ever and ever: he hath made a decree which shall not pass.

Praise the Lord from the earth, ye dragons and all deeps:

Fire, and hail; snow, and vapour: stormy wind fulfilling his word:

Mountains, and all hills; fruitful trees, and all cedars:

Beasts, and all cattle; creeping things, and flying fowl:

Kings of the earth, and all people; princes, and all judges of the earth:

Both young men, and maidens; old men, and children:

Let them praise the name of the Lord: for his name alone is excellent; his glory is above the earth and heaven.

He also exalteth the horn of his people, the praise of all his saints; even of the children of Israel, a people near unto him. Praise ye the Lord.

Praise God in His Sanctuary

Praise ye the Lord. Praise God in his sanctuary: praise him in the firmament of his power.

Praise him for his mighty acts: praise him according to his excellent greatness.

Praise him with the sound of the trumpet: praise him with the psaltery and harp.

Praise him with the timbrel and dance; praise him with stringed instruments and organs.

Praise him upon the loud cymbals: praise him upon the high-sounding cymbals.

Let every thing that hath breath praise the Lord. Praise ye the Lord.

The Proverbs

The proverbs of Solomon the son of David, king of Israel:

The fear of the Lord is the beginning of knowledge: but fools despise wisdom and instruction.

Wisdom crieth without; she uttereth her voice in the streets; she crieth in the chief places of concourse, in the openings of the gates: in the city she uttereth her words, saying, How long, ye simple ones, will ye love simplicity? and the scorners delight in their scorning, and fools hate knowledge? Turn you at my reproof: behold, I will pour out my spirit unto you, I will make known my words unto you.

When wisdom entereth into thine heart, and knowledge is pleasant unto thy soul; discretion shall preserve thee, understanding shall keep thee: to deliver thee from the way of the evil man, from the man that speaketh froward things; who leave the paths of uprightness, to walk in the ways of darkness; who rejoice to do evil, and delight in the frowardness of the wicked; whose ways are crooked, and they froward in their paths: to deliver thee from the strange woman, even from the stranger which flattereth with her words, which forsaketh the guide of her youth, and forgetteth the covenant of her God. For her house inclineth unto death, and her paths unto the dead. None that go unto her return again, neither take they hold of the paths of life.

Let not mercy and truth forsake thee: bind them about thy neck; write them upon the table of thine heart.

My son, despise not the chastening of the Lord; neither be weary of his correction, for whom the Lord loveth he correcteth; even as a father the son in whom he delighteth.

Happy is the man that findeth wisdom, and the man that getteth understanding. For the merchandise of it is better than the merchandise of silver, and the gain thereof than fine gold. She is more precious than rubies: and all the things thou canst desire are not to be compared unto her. Length of days is in her right hand; and in her left hand riches and honour. Her ways are ways of pleasantness, and all her paths are peace. She is a tree of life to them that lay hold upon her: and happy is every one that retaineth her.

The Lord by wisdom hath founded the earth; by understanding hath he established the heavens. By his knowledge the depths are broken up, and the clouds drop down the dew.

Be not afraid of sudden fear, neither of the desolation of the wicked, when it cometh.

Wisdom is the principal thing; therefore get wisdom: and with all thy getting get understanding. Exalt her, and she shall promote thee: she shall bring thee to honour, when thou dost embrace her. She shall give to thine head an ornament of grace: a crown of glory shall she deliver to thee.

My son, attend unto my wisdom, and bow thine ear to my understanding: that thou mayest regard discretion, and that thy lips may keep knowledge.

For the lips of a strange woman drop as an honey-comb, and her mouth is smoother than oil: but her end is bitter as wormwood, sharp as a two-edged sword. Her feet go down to death; her steps take hold on hell. Lest thou shouldest ponder the path of life, her ways are moveable, that thou canst not know them.

Drink waters out of thine own cistern, and running waters out of thine own well. Let thy fountains be dispersed abroad, and rivers of waters in the streets. Let them be only thine own, and not strangers' with thee. Let thy fountain be blessed: and rejoice with the wife of thy youth.

Let her be as the loving hind and pleasant roe; let her breasts satisfy thee at all times; and be thou ravished always with her love.

Go to the ant, thou sluggard; consider her ways, and be wise; which having no guide, overseer, or ruler, provideth her meat in the summer, and gathereth her food in the harvest. How long wilt thou sleep, O sluggard? when wilt thou arise out of thy sleep?

Yet a little sleep, a little slumber, a little folding of the hands to sleep: so shall thy poverty come as one that travelleth, and thy want as an armed man.

These six things doth the Lord hate; yea, seven are an abomination unto him: a proud look, a lying tongue, and hands that shed innocent blood, an heart that deviseth wicked imaginations, feet that be swift in running to mischief, a false witness that speaketh lies, and he that soweth discord among brethren.

Can a man take fire in his bosom, and his clothes not be burned? Can one go upon hot coals, and his feet not be burned? So he that goeth in to his neighbour's wife; whosoever toucheth her shall not be innocent.

Men do not despise a thief, if he steal to satisfy his soul when he is hungry; but if he be found, he shall restore seven-fold; he shall give all the substance of his house. But whoso committeth adultery with a woman, lacketh understanding: he that doeth it, destroyeth his own soul. For jealousy is the rage of a man: therefore he will not spare in the day of vengeance. He will not regard any ransom; neither will he rest content, though thou givest many gifts.

I Wisdom dwell with prudence, and find out knowledge of witty inventions. By me kings reign, and princes decree justice. By me princes rule, and nobles, even all the judges of the earth. I love them that love me: and those that seek me early shall find me. I lead in the way of righteousness, in the midst of the paths of judgment.

The Lord possessed me in the beginning of his way, before his works of old. I was set up from everlasting, from the beginning, or ever the earth was. When there were no depths, I was brought forth; when there were no fountains abounding with water. Before the mountains were settled, before the hills was I brought forth: while as yet he had not made the earth, nor the fields, nor the highest part of the dust of the world. When he prepared the heavens, I was there: when he set a compass upon the face of the depth: when he established the clouds above: when he strengthened the fountains of the deep: when he gave to the sea his decree, that the waters should not pass his commandment; when he appointed the foundations of the earth: then I was by him, as one brought up with him: and I was daily his delight, rejoicing always before him.

Hatred stirreth up strifes: but love covereth all sins.

Where no counsel is, the people fall: but in the multitude of counsellors there is safety.

As a jewel of gold in a swine's snout, so is a fair woman which is without discretion.

He that tilleth his land shall be satisfied with bread: but he that followeth vain persons is void of understanding.

He that spareth his rod hateth his son: but he that loveth him chasteneth him betimes.

The heart knoweth his own bitterness: and a stranger doth not intermeddle with his joy.

Even in laughter the heart is sorrowful; and the end of that mirth is heaviness.

A soft answer turneth away wrath: but grievous words stir up anger.

Better is little with the fear of the Lord, than great treasure and trouble therewith.

Better is a dinner of herbs where love is, than a stalled ox and hatred therewith.

Pride goeth before destruction, and an haughty spirit before a fall.

The hoary head is a crown of glory, if it be found in the way of righteousness.

Better is a dry morsel, and quietness therewith, than an house full of sacrifices with strife.

Whoso mocketh the poor reproacheth his Maker: and he that is glad at calamities shall not be unpunished.

A reproof entereth more into a wise man than an hundred stripes into a fool.

A merry heart doeth good like a medicine: but a broken spirit drieth the bones.

Even a fool, when he holdeth his peace, is counted wise: and he that shutteth his lips is esteemed a man of understanding.

He that answereth a matter before he heareth it, it is folly and shame unto him.

A man that hath friends must shew himself friendly: and there is a friend that sticketh closer than a brother.

Wine is a mocker, strong drink is raging: and whosoever is deceived thereby is not wise.

The glory of young men is their strength: and the beauty of old men is the grey head.

It is better to dwell in a corner of the housetop, than with a brawling woman in a wide house.

Whoso keepeth his mouth and his tongue, keepeth his soul from troubles.

A good name is rather to be chosen than great riches, and loving favour rather than silver and gold.

Train up a child in the way he should go: and when he is old, he will not depart from it.

The slothful man saith, There is a lion without, I shall be slain in the streets.

Make no friendship with an angry man; and with a furious man thou shalt not go: lest thou learn his ways, and get a snare to thy soul.

Seest thou a man diligent in his business? he shall stand before kings; he shall not stand before mean men.

Withhold not correction from the child: for if thou beatest him with a rod, he shall not die. Thou shalt beat him with the rod, and shalt deliver his soul from hell.

Who hath woe? who hath sorrow? who hath contentions? who hath babbling? who hath wounds without cause? who hath redness of eyes? They that tarry long at the wine; they that go to seek mixed wine.

Look not thou upon the wine when it is red, when it giveth his colour in the cup, when it moveth itself aright. At the last it biteth like a serpent, and stingeth like an adder. Thine eyes shall behold strange women, and thine heart shall utter perverse things. Yea, thou shalt be as he that lieth down in the midst of the sea, or as he that lieth upon the top of a mast. They have stricken me, shalt thou say, and I was not sick; they have beaten me, and I felt it not: when shall I awake? I will seek it yet again.

Rejoice not when thine enemy falleth, and let not thine heart be glad when he stumbleth: lest the Lord see it, and it displease him, and he turn away his wrath from him.

It is not good to have respect of persons in judgment.

The heaven for height, and the earth for depth, and the heart of kings is unsearchable.

If thine enemy be hungry, give him bread to eat; and if he be thirsty, give him water to drink: for thou shalt heap coals of fire upon his head, and the Lord shall reward thee.

He that hath no rule over his own spirit is like a city that is broken down, and without walls.

A whip for the horse, a bridle for the ass, and a rod for the fool's back.

As a dog returneth to his vomit, so a fool returneth to his folly.

He that passeth by, and meddleth with strife belonging not to him, is like one that taketh a dog by the ears.

Where no wood is, there the fire goeth out: so where there is no tale-bearer, the strife ceaseth.

Whoso diggeth a pit shall fall therein: and he that rolleth a stone, it will return upon him.

Let another man praise thee, and not thine own mouth; a stranger, and not thine own lips.

A continual dropping in a very rainy day and a contentious woman are alike.

Whoso keepeth the fig-tree shall eat the fruit thereof: so he that waiteth on his master shall be honoured.

Where there is no vision, the people perish: but he that keepeth the law, happy is he.

Seest thou a man that is hasty in his words? there is more hope of a fool than of him.

The words of Agur the son of Jakeh, even the prophecy: the man spake unto Ithiel, even unto Ithiel and Ucal:

Who hath ascended up into heaven, or descended? who hath gathered the wind in his fists? who hath bound the waters in a garment? who hath established all the ends of the earth? what is his name, and what is his son's name, if thou canst tell?

Every word of God is pure: he is a shield unto them that put their trust in him. Add thou not unto his words, lest he reprove thee, and thou be found a liar.

Two things have I required of thee; deny me them not before I die: remove far from me vanity and lies; give me neither poverty nor riches; feed me with food convenient for me, lest I be full, and deny thee, and say, Who is the Lord? or lest I be poor, and steal, and take the name of my God in vain.

There are three things that are never satisfied, yea, four things say not, It is enough: the grave; and the barren womb; the earth that is not filled with water; and the fire that saith not, It is enough.

There be three things which are too wonderful for me, yea, four which I know not: the way of an eagle in the air; the way of a serpent upon a rock; the way of a ship in the midst of the sea; and the way of a man with a maid.

For three things the earth is disquieted, and for four which it cannot bear: for a servant when he reigneth; and a fool when he is filled with meat; for an odious woman when she is married; and an handmaid that is heir to her mistress.

There be four things which are little upon the earth, but they are exceeding wise: the ants are a people not strong, yet they prepare their meat in the summer; the conies are but a feeble folk, yet make they their houses in the rocks; the locusts have no king, yet go they forth all of them by bands; the spider taketh hold with her hands, and is in kings' palaces.

There be three things which go well, yea, four are comely in going: a lion, which is strongest among beasts, and turneth not away for any; a greyhound; an he-goat also; and a king, against whom there is no rising up.

If thou hast done foolishly in lifting up thyself, or if thou hast thought evil, lay thine hand upon thy mouth.

Surely the churning of milk bringeth forth butter, and the wringing of the nose bringeth forth blood: so the forcing of wrath bringeth forth strife.

The words of king Lemuel, the prophecy that his mother taught him. What, my son? and what, the son of my womb? and what, the son of my vows?

Give not thy strength unto women, nor thy ways to that which destroyeth kings.

It is not for kings, O Lemuel, it is not for kings to drink wine; nor for princes strong drink: lest they drink, and forget the law, and pervert the judgment of any of the afflicted.

Give strong drink unto him that is ready to perish, and wine unto those that be of heavy hearts. Let him drink, and forget his poverty, and remember his misery no more.

Open thy mouth for the dumb in the cause of all such as are appointed to destruction. Open thy mouth, judge righteously, and plead the cause of the poor and needy.

Who can find a virtuous woman? for her price is far above rubies. The heart of her husband doth safely trust in her, so that he shall have no need of spoil. She will do him good and not evil all the days of her life. She seeketh wool, and flax, and worketh willingly with her hands. She is like the merchants' ships; she bringeth her food from afar.

She riseth also while it is yet night, and giveth meat to her household, and a portion to her maidens. She considereth a field, and buyeth it; with the fruit of her hands she planteth a vineyard. She girdeth her loins with strength, and strengtheneth her arms. She perceiveth that her merchandise is good: her candle goeth not out by night. She layeth her hands to the spindle, and her hands hold the distaff.

She stretcheth out her hand to the poor: yea, she reacheth forth her hands to the needy. She is not afraid of the snow for her household: for all her household are clothed with scarlet. She maketh herself coverings of tapestry; her clothing is silk and purple.

Her husband is known in the gates, when he sitteth among the elders of the land.

She maketh fine linen, and selleth it; and delivereth girdles unto the merchant.

Strength and honour are her clothing; and she shall rejoice in time to come.

She openeth her mouth with wisdom; and in her tongue is the law of kindness. She looketh well to the ways of her household, and eateth not the bread of idleness.

Her children arise up, and call her blessed; her husband also, and he praiseth her. Many daughters have done virtuously, but thou excellest them all.

Favour is deceitful, and beauty is vain: but a woman that feareth the Lord, she shall be praised. Give her of the fruit of her hands; and let her own works praise her in the gates.

Ecclesiastes

I

The words of the Preacher, the son of David, king in Jerusalem.

Vanity of vanities, saith the Preacher, vanity of vanities; all is vanity.

What profit hath a man of all his labour which he taketh under the sun?

One generation passeth away, and another generation cometh: but the earth abideth for ever.

The sun also ariseth, and the sun goeth down, and hasteth to his place where he arose. The wind goeth toward the south, and turneth about unto the north; it whirleth about continually, and the wind returneth again according to his circuits. All the rivers run into the sea; yet the sea is not full: unto the place from whence the rivers come, thither they return again.

All things are full of labour; man cannot utter it: the eye is not satisfied with seeing, nor the ear filled with hearing.

The thing that hath been, it is that which shall be; and that which is done is that which shall be done: and there is no new thing under the sun. Is there anything whereof it may be said, See, this is new? it hath been already of old time, which was before us. There is no remembrance of former things; neither shall there be any remembrance of things that are to come with those that shall come after.

I have seen all the works that are done under the sun; and behold, all is vanity and vexation of spirit.

II

I said in mine heart, Go to now, I will prove thee with mirth; therefore enjoy pleasure: and behold, this also is vanity. I said of laughter, It is mad: and of mirth, What doeth it?

I sought in mine heart to give myself unto wine, yet acquainting mine heart with wisdom; and to lay hold on folly, till I might see what was that good for the sons of men, which they should do under the heaven all the days of their life.

I made me great works; I builded me houses; I planted me vineyards; I made me gardens and orchards, and I planted trees in them of all kind of fruits; I made me pools of water, to water therewith the wood that bringeth forth trees; I got me servants and maidens, and had servants born in my house; also I had great possessions of great and small cattle above all that were in Jerusalem before me; I gathered me also silver and gold, and the peculiar treasure of kings, and of the povinces; I gat me men-singers and women-singers, and the delights of the sons of men, as musical instruments, and that of all sorts.

So I was great, and increased more than all that were before me in Jerusalem: also my wisdom remained with me. And whatsoever mine eyes desired I kept not from them, I withheld not my heart from any joy; for my heart rejoiceth in all my labour: and this was my portion of all my labour.

Then I looked on all the works that my hands had wrought, and on the labour that I had laboured to do: and behold, all was vanity and vexation of spirit, and there was no profit under the sun.

And I turned myself to behold wisdom, and madness, and folly: for what can the man do that cometh after the king? even that which hath been already done. Then I saw that wisdom excelleth folly, as far as light excelleth darkness. The wise man's eyes are in his head; but the fool walketh in darkness: and I myself perceived also that one event happeneth to them all.

Then said I in my heart, As it happeneth to the fool, so it happeneth even to me; and why was I then more wise? Then I said in my heart, that this also is vanity.

For there is no remembrance of the wise more than of the fool for ever; seeing that which now is in the days to come shall all be forgotten. And how dieth the wise man? as the fool. Therefore I hated life; because the work that is wrought under the sun is grievous unto me: for all is vanity, and vexation of spirit.

Yea, I hated all my labour which I had taken under the sun: because

I should leave it unto the man that shall be after me. And who knoweth whether he shall be a wise man or a fool? yet shall he have rule over all my labour wherein I have laboured, and wherein I have shewed myself wise under the sun. This is also vanity. Therefore I went about to cause my heart to despair of all the labour which I took under the sun.

For there is a man whose labour is in wisdom, and in knowledge, and in equity; yet to a man that hath not laboured therein shall he leave it for his portion. This also is vanity and a great evil.

For what hath man of all his labour, and of the vexation of his heart, wherein he hath laboured under the sun? For all his days are sorrows, and his travail grief; yea, his heart taketh not rest in the night. This is also vanity.

There is nothing better for a man than that he should eat and drink, and that he should make his soul enjoy good in his labour. This also I saw, that it was from the hand of God. For who can eat, or who else can hasten hereunto more than I?

For God giveth to a man that is good in his sight, wisdom, and knowledge, and joy: but to the sinner he giveth travail, to gather and to heap up, that he may give to him that is good before God. This also is vanity and vexation of spirit.

III

To every thing there is a season, and a time to every purpose under the heaven: a time to be born, and a time to die; a time to plant, and a time to pluck up that which is planted; a time to kill, and a time to heal; a time to break down, and a time to build up; a time to weep, and a time to laugh; a time to mourn, and a time to dance; a time to cast away stones, and a time to gather stones together; a time to embrace, and a time to refrain from embracing; a time to get, and a time to lose; a time to keep, and a time to cast away; a time to rend, and a time to sew; a time to keep silence, and a time to speak; a time to love, and a time to hate; a time of war, and a time of peace.

IV

So I returned, and considered all the oppressions that are done under the sun: and behold the tears of such were oppressed, and they had no comforter; and on the side of their oppressors there was power; but they had no comforter.

Wherefore I praised the dead which are already dead more than the living which are yet alive. Yea, better is he than both they, which hath not yet been, who hath not seen the evil work that is done under the sun.

Two are better than one; because they have a good reward for their labour. For if they fall, the one will lift up his fellow: but woe to him that is alone when he falleth; for he hath not another to help him up. Again, if two lie together, then they have heat: but how can one be warm alone? And if one prevail against him, two shall withstand him; and a threefold cord is not quickly broken.

V

He that loveth silver shall not be satisfied with silver; nor he that loveth abundance with increase: this is also vanity. When goods increase they are increased that eat them: and what good is there to the owners thereof, saving the beholding of them with their eyes?

The sleep of a labouring man is sweet, whether he eat little or much: but the abundance of the rich will not suffer him to sleep.

There is a sore evil which I have seen under the sun, namely, riches kept for the owners thereof to their hurt. But those riches perish by evil travail: and he begetteth a son, and there is nothing in his hand. As he came forth of his mother's womb, naked shall he return to go as he came, and shall take nothing of his labour, which he may carry away in his hand.

And this also is a sore evil, that in all points as he came, so shall he go: and what profit hath he that hath laboured for the wind? All his days also he eateth in darkness, and he hath much sorrow and wrath with his sickness.

Behold that which I have seen: it is good and comely for one to eat and to drink, and to enjoy the good of all his labour that he taketh under the sun all the days of his life.

VI

There is an evil which I have seen under the sun, and it is common among men: a man to whom God hath given riches, wealth, and honour, so that he wanteth nothing for his soul of all that he desireth, yet God giveth him not power to eat thereof, but a stranger eateth it: this is vanity, and it is an evil disease.

If a man beget an hundred children, and live many years, so that the days of his years be many, and his soul be not filled with good, and also that he have no burial; I say, that an untimely birth is better than he. For he cometh in with vanity, and departeth in darkness, and his name shall be covered with darkness. Moreover he hath not seen the sun, nor known any thing: this hath more rest than the other.

VII

A good name is better than precious ointment; and the day of death than the day of one's birth. It is better to go to the house of mourning, than to go to the house of feasting: for that is the end of all men; and the living will lay it to his heart. Sorrow is better than laughter: for by the sadness of the countenance the heart is made better.

All things have I seen in the days of my vanity: there is a just man that perisheth in his righteousness, and there is a wicked man that prolongeth his life in his wickedness.

Be not righteous over much; neither make thyself over wise: why shouldest thou destroy thyself? Be not over much wicked, neither be thou foolish: why shouldest thou die before thy time?

I applied mine heart to know, and to search, and to seek out wisdom, and the reason of things, and to know the wickedness of folly, even of foolishness and madness. And I find more bitter than death the woman whose heart is snares and nets, and her hands as bands.

Behold, this have I found, saith the Peacher, counting one by one, to find out the account; which yet my soul seeketh, but I find not: one man among a thousand have I found; but a woman among all those have I not found.

VIII

There is no man that hath power over the spirit to retain the spirit: neither hath he power in the day of death: and there is no discharge in that war; neither shall wickedness deliver those that are given to it.

All this have I seen, and applied my heart unto every work that is done under the sun: there is a time wherein one man ruleth over another to his own hurt.

And so I saw the wicked buried, who had come and gone from the place of the holy, and they were forgotten in the city where they had so done: this is also vanity.

Then I commended mirth, because a man hath no better thing under the sun, than to eat, and to drink, and to be merry.

IX

There is one event to the righteous and to the wicked; to the good, and to the clean, and to the unclean; to him that sacrificeth, and to him that sacrificeth not: as is the good, so is the sinner; and he that sweareth, as he that feareth an oath.

Go thy way, eat thy bread with joy, and drink thy wine with a merry heart. Live joyfully with the wife whom thou lovest all the days of the life of thy vanity, which He hath given thee under the sun, all the days of thy vanity: for that is thy portion in this life, and in thy labour which thou takest under the sun. Whatsoever thy hand findeth to do, do it with thy might; for there is no work, nor device, nor knowledge, nor wisdom, in the grave, whither thou goest.

I returned, and saw under the sun, that the race is not to the swift, nor the battle to the strong, neither yet bread to the wise, nor yet riches to men of understanding, nor yet favour to men of skill; but time and chance happeneth to them all. For man also knoweth not his time: as the fishes that are taken in an evil net, and as the birds that are caught in the snare; so are the sons of men snared in an evil time, when it falleth suddenly upon them.

There was a little city, and few men within it; and there came a great king against it, and besieged it, and built great bulwarks against it. Now there was found in it a poor wise man, and he by his wisdom delivered the city; yet no man remembered that same poor man.

X

He that diggeth a pit shall fall into it; and whoso breaketh an hedge, a serpent shall bite him. Whoso removeth stones shall be hurt therewith; and he that cleaveth wood shall be endangered thereby.

If the iron be blunt, and he do not whet the edge, then must he put to more strength: but wisdom is profitable to direct.

XI

Cast thy bread upon the waters: for thou shalt find it after many days. Give a portion to seven, and also to eight; for thou knowest not what evil shall be upon the earth.

If the clouds be full of rain, they empty themselves upon the earth: and if the tree fall toward the south, or toward the north, in the place where the tree falleth, there it shall be.

He that observeth the wind shall not sow; and he that regardeth the clouds shall not reap.

Thou knowest not what is the way of the spirit, nor how the bones do grow in the womb of her that is with child.

In the morning sow thy seed, and in the evening withhold not thine hand: for thou knowest not whether shall prosper, either this or that, or whether they both shall be alike good.

Truly the light is sweet, and a pleasant thing it is for the eyes to behold the sun:

Rejoice, O young man, in thy youth; and let thy heart cheer thee in the days of thy youth, and walk in the ways of thine heart, and in the sight of thine eyes. Therefore remove sorrow from thy heart, and put away evil from thy flesh: for childhood and youth are vanity.

XII

Remember now thy Creator in the days of thy youth, while the evil days come not, nor the years draw nigh, when thou shalt say, I have no pleasure in them; while the sun, or the light, or the moon, or the stars, be not darkened, nor the clouds return after the rain: in the day when the keepers of the house shall tremble, and the strong men shall bow themselves, and the grinders cease because they are few, and those that look out of the windows be darkened, and the doors shall be shut in the streets, when the sound of the grinding is low, and he shall rise up at the voice of the bird, and all the daughters of music shall be brought low. Also when they shall be afraid of that which is high, and fears shall be in the way, and the almond-tree shall flourish, and the grasshopper shall be a burden, and desire shall fail: because man goeth to his long home, and the mourners go about the streets: or ever the silver cord be loosed, or the golden bowl be broken, or the pitcher be broken at the fountain, or the wheel broken at the cistern. Then shall the dust return to the earth as it was: and the spirit shall return unto God who gave it.

Vanity of vanities, saith the Preacher; all is vanity.

And further, by these, my son, be admonished: of making many books there is no end; and much study is a weariness of the flesh.

Let us hear the conclusion of the whole matter: Fear God, and keep his commandments: for this is the whole duty of man. For God shall bring every work into judgment, with every secret thing, whether it be good, or whether it be evil.

The Song of Solomon

I

The Song of songs, which is Solomon's.

Let him kiss me with the kisses of his mouth: for thy love is better than wine.

Because of the savour of thy good ointments thy name is as ointment poured forth, therefore do the virgins love thee.

Draw me, we will run after thee: the King hath brought me into his chambers: we will be glad and rejoice in thee, we will remember thy love more than wine: the upright love thee.

I am black, but comely, O ye daughters of Jerusalem, as the tents of Kedar, as the curtains of Solomon. Look not upon me, because I am black, because the sun hath looked upon me: my mother's children were angry with me; they made me the keeper of the vineyards; but mine own vineyard have I not kept.

Tell me, O thou whom my soul loveth, where thou feedest, where thou makest thy flock to rest at noon: for why should I be as one that turneth aside by the flocks of thy companions?

If thou know not, O thou fairest among women, go thy way forth by the footsteps of the flock, and feed thy kids beside the shepherds' tents.

I have compared thee, O my love, to a company of horses in Pharaoh's chariots.

Thy cheeks are comely with rows of jewels, thy neck with chains of gold.

We will make thee borders of gold with studs of silver.

While the King sitteth at his table, my spikenard sendeth forth the smell thereof.

A bundle of myrrh is my well-beloved unto me; he shall lie all night betwixt my breasts. My beloved is unto me as a cluster of camphire in the vineyards of En-gedi.

Behold, thou art fair, my love; behold, thou art fair; thou hast doves' eyes. Behold, thou art fair, my beloved, yea, pleasant: also our bed is green.

The beams of our house are cedar, and our rafters of fir.

II

I am the rose of Sharon, and the lily of the valleys.

As the lily among thorns, so is my love among the daughters. As the apple-tree among the trees of the wood, so is my beloved among the sons.

I sat down under his shadow with great delight, and his fruit was sweet to my taste. He brought me to the banqueting house, and his banner over me was love.

Stay me with flagons, comfort me with apples: for I am sick of love.

His left hand is under my head, and his right hand doth embrace me.

I charge you, O ye daughters of Jerusalem, by the roes, and by the hinds of the field, that ye stir not up, nor awake my love, till he please.

The voice of my beloved! behold, he cometh leaping upon the mountains, skipping upon the hills.

My beloved is like a roe, or a young hart: behold, he standeth behind our wall, he looketh forth at the windows, shewing himself through the lattice.

My beloved spake, and said unto me, Rise up, my love, my fair one, and come away. For lo, the winter is past, the rain is over and gone; the flowers appear on the earth; the time of the singing of birds is come, and the voice of the turtle is heard in our land; the fig-tree putteth forth her green figs, and the vines with the tender grape give a good smell. Arise, my love, my fair one, and come away.

O my dove, that art in the clefts of the rock, in the secret places of the stairs, let me see thy countenance, let me hear thy voice; for sweet is thy voice, and thy countenance is comely.

Take us the foxes, the little foxes, that spoil the vines: for our vines have tender grapes.

My beloved is mine, and I am his: he feedeth among the lilies.

Until the day break, and the shadows flee away, turn, my beloved, and be thou like a roe or a young hart upon the mountains of Bether.

III

By night on my bed I sought him whom my soul loveth: I sought him, but I found him not. I will rise now, and go about the city in the streets, and in the broad ways I will seek him whom my soul loveth: I sought him, but I found him not.

The watchmen that go about the city found me: to whom I said, Saw ye him whom my soul loveth?

It was but a little that I passed from them, but I found him whom my soul loveth: I held him, and would not let him go, until I had brought him into my mother's house, and into the chamber of her that conceived me.

I charge you, O ye daughters of Jerusalem, by the roes, and by the hinds of the field, that ye stir not up, nor awake my love, till he please.

Who is this that cometh out of the wilderness like pillars of smoke, perfumed with myrrh and frankincense, with all powders of the merchant?

Behold his bed, which is Solomon's: threescore valiant men are about it, of the valiant of Israel. They all hold swords, being expert in war: every man hath his sword upon his thigh because of fear in the night.

King Solomon made himself a chariot of the wood of Lebanon. He made the pillars thereof of silver, the bottom thereof of gold, the covering of it of purple, the midst thereof being paved with love, for the daughters of Jerusalem.

Go forth, O ye daughters of Zion, and behold king Solomon with the crown wherewith his mother crowned him in the day of his espousals, and in the day of the gladness of his heart.

IV

Behold, thou art fair, my love; behold, thou art fair; thou hast doves' eyes within thy locks: thy hair is as a flock of goats, that appear from mount Gilead. Thy teeth are like a flock of sheep that are even shorn, which came up from the washing; whereof every one bear twins, and none is barren among them. Thy lips are like a thread of scarlet, and thy speech is comely: thy temples are like a piece of a pomegranate within thy locks. Thy neck is like the tower of David builded for an armoury, whereon there hang a thousand bucklers, all shields of mighty men. Thy two breasts are like two young roes that are twins, which feed among the lilies.

Until the day break, and the shadows flee away, I will get me to the mountain of myrrh, and to the hill of frankincense. Thou art all fair, my love; there is no spot in thee.

Come with me from Lebanon, my spouse, with me from Lebanon: look from the top of Amana, from the top of Shenir and Hermon, from the lions' dens, from the mountains of the leopards.

Thou hast ravished my heart, my sister, my spouse; thou hast ravished my heart with one of thine eyes, with one chain of thy neck.

How fair is thy love, my sister, my spouse! how much better is thy love than wine! and the smell of thine ointments than all spices!

Thy lips, O my spouse, drop as the honey-comb: honey and milk are under thy tongue; and the smell of thy garments is like the smell of Lebanon. A garden enclosed is my sister, my spouse; a spring shut up, a fountain sealed. Thy plants are an orchard of pomegranates, with pleasant fruits; camphire, with spikenard, spikenard and saffron; calamus and cinnamon, with all trees of frankincense; myrrh and aloes, with all the chief spices: a fountain of gardens, a well of living waters, and streams from Lebanon.

Awake, O north wind; and come, thou south; blow upon my garden, that the spices thereof may flow out. Let my beloved come into his garden, and eat his pleasant fruits.

V

I am come into my garden, my sister, my spouse: I have gathered my myrrh with my spice; I have eaten my honey-comb with my honey; I have drunk my wine with my milk: eat, O friends; drink, yea, drink abundantly, O beloved.

I sleep, but my heart waketh: it is the voice of my beloved that knocketh, saying, Open to me, my sister, my love, my dove, my undefiled: for my head is filled with dew, and my locks with the drops of the night.

I have put off my coat; how shall I put it on? I have washed my feet; how shall I defile them?

My beloved put in his hand by the hole of the door, and my bowels were moved for him. I rose up to open to my beloved; and my hands dropped with myrrh, and my fingers with sweet-smelling myrrh, upon the handles of the lock. I opened to my beloved; but my beloved had withdrawn himself, and was gone: my soul failed when he spake: I sought him, but I could not find him; I called him, but he gave me no answer.

The watchmen that went about the city found me, they smote me, they wounded me: the keepers of the walls took away my veil from me.

I charge you, O daughters of Jerusalem, if ye find my beloved, that ye tell him, that I am sick of love.

What is thy beloved more than another beloved, O thou fairest among women? what is thy beloved more than another beloved, that thou dost so charge us?

My beloved is white and ruddy, the chiefest among ten thousand. His head is as the most fine gold, his locks are bushy, and black as a raven. His eyes are as the eyes of doves by the rivers of waters, washed with milk, and fitly set. His cheeks are as a bed of spices, as sweet flowers: his lips like lilies, dropping sweet-smelling myrrh. His hands are as gold rings set with the beryl: his belly is as bright ivory overlaid with sapphires. His legs are as pillars of marble, set upon sockets of fine gold: his countenance is as Lebanon, excellent as the cedars. His mouth is most sweet: yea, he is altogether lovely.

This is my beloved, and this is my friend, O daughters of Jerusalem.

VI

Whither is thy beloved gone, O thou fairest among women? whither is thy beloved turned aside? that we may seek him with thee.

My beloved is gone down into his garden, to the beds of spices, to feed in the gardens, and to gather lilies.

I am my beloved's and my beloved is mine: he feedeth among the lilies.

Thou art beautiful, O my love, as Tirzah, comely as Jerusalem, terrible as an army with banners. Turn away thine eyes from me, for they have overcome me: thy hair is as a flock of goats that appear from Gilead. Thy teeth are as a flock of sheep which go up from the washing, whereof every one beareth twins, and there is not one barren among them. As a piece of a pomegranate are thy temples within thy locks.

There are threescore queens, and fourscore concubines, and virgins without number. My dove, my undefiled is but one; she is the only one of her mother, she is the choice one of her that bare her. The daughters saw her, and blessed her; yea, the queens and the concubines, and they praised her.

Who is she that looketh forth as the morning, fair as the moon, clear as the sun, and terrible as an army with banners?

I went down into the garden of nuts to see the fruits of the valley, and to see whether the vine flourished, and the pomegranates budded.

Or ever I was aware, my soul made me like the chariots of Amminadib.

Return, return, O Shulamite; return, return, that we may look upon thee. What will ye see in the Shulamite? As it were the company of two armies.

VII

How beautiful are thy feet with shoes, O prince's daughter! the joints of thy thighs are like jewels, the work of the hands of a cunning workman. Thy navel is like a round goblet, which wanteth not liquor; thy belly is like an heap of wheat set about with lilies. Thy two breasts are like two young roes that are twins. Thy neck is as a tower of ivory; thine eyes like the fish-pools in Heshbon, by the gate of Bathrabbim:

thy nose is as the tower of Lebanon which looketh toward Damascus. Thine head upon thee is like Carmel, and the hair of thine head like purple; the King is held in the galleries.

How fair and how pleasant art thou, O love, for delights! This thy stature is like to a palm-tree, and thy breasts to clusters of grapes.

I said, I will go up to the palm-tree, I will take hold of the boughs thereof: now also thy breasts shall be as clusters of the vine, and the smell of thy nose like apples; and the roof of thy mouth like the best wine for my beloved, that goeth down sweetly, causing the lips of those that are asleep to speak.

I am my beloved's, and his desire is toward me.

Come, my beloved, let us go forth into the field; let us lodge in the villages. Let us get up early to the vineyards; let us see if the vine flourish, whether the tender grape appear, and the pomegranates bud forth: there will I give thee my loves.

The mandrakes give a smell, and at our gates are all manner of pleasant fruits, new and old, which I have laid up for thee, O my beloved.

VIII

O that thou wert as my brother, that sucked the breasts of my mother! when I should find thee without, I would kiss thee; yea, I should not be despised. I would lead thee, and bring thee into my mother's house, who would instruct me: I would cause thee to drink of spiced wine of the juice of my pomegranate.

His left hand should be under my head, and his right hand should embrace me.

I charge you, O daughters of Jerusalem, that ye stir not up, nor awake my love, until he please.

Who is this that cometh up from the wilderness, leaning upon her beloved? I raised thee up under the apple-tree: there thy mother brought thee forth: there she brought thee forth that bare thee.

Set me as a seal upon thine heart, as a seal upon thine arm: for love is strong as death; jealousy is cruel as the grave: the coals thereof are coals of fire, which hath a most vehement flame. Many waters cannot quench love, neither can the floods drown it: if a man would give all the substance of his house for love, it would utterly be contemned.

We have a little sister, and she hath no breasts: what shall we do for our sister in the day when she shall be spoken for?

If she be a wall, we will build upon her a palace of silver: and if she be a door, we will enclose her with boards of cedar.

I am a wall, and my breasts like towers: then was I in his eyes as one that found favour.

Solomon had a vineyard at Baal-hamon; he let out the vineyard unto keepers; every one for the fruit thereof was to bring a thousand pieces of silver.

My vineyard which is mine, is before me: thou, O Solomon, must have a thousand, and those that keep the fruit thereof two hundred.

Thou that dwellest in the gardens, the companions hearken to thy voice: cause me to hear it.

Make haste, my beloved, and be thou like to a roe or to a young hart upon the mountains of spices.

Amos

God's Judgments of Syria

The words of Amos, who was among the herdsmen of Tekoa, which he saw concerning Israel in the days of Uzziah king of Judah, and in the days of Jeroboam the son of Joash king of Israel, two years before the earthquake. And he said, The Lord will roar from Zion, and utter his voice from Jerusalem; and the habitations of the shepherds shall mourn, and the top of Carmel shall wither.

Thus saith the Lord; For three transgressions of Damascus, and for four, I will not turn away the punishment thereof; because they have threshed Gilead with threshing instruments of iron; but I will send a fire into the house of Hazael, which shall devour the palaces of Ben-hadad. I will break also the bar of Damascus, and cut off the inhabitant from the plain of Aven, and him that holdeth the sceptre from the house of Eden: and the people of Syria shall go into captivity unto Kir, saith the Lord.

Thus saith the Lord; For three transgressions of Gaza, and for four, I will not turn away the punishment thereof: because they carried away captive the whole captivity, to deliver them up to Edom: but I will send a fire on the wall of Gaza, which shall devour the palaces thereof: and I will cut off the inhabitant from Ashdod, and him that holdeth the sceptre from Ashkelon, and I will turn mine hand against Ekron: and the remnant of the Philistines shall perish, saith the Lord God.

Thus saith the Lord; For three transgressions of Tyrus, and for four, I will not turn away the punishment thereof: because they delivered up the whole captivity to Edom, and remembered not the brotherly covenant; but I will send a fire on the wall of Tyrus, which shall devour the palaces thereof.

Thus saith the Lord; For three transgressions of Edom, and for four, I will not turn away the punishment thereof: because he did pursue his brother with the sword, and did cast off all pity, and his anger did tear perpetually, and he kept his wrath for ever; but I will send a fire upon Teman, which shall devour the palaces of Bozrah.

Thus saith the Lord; For three transgressions of the children of Ammon, and for four, I will not turn away the punishment thereof: because they have ripped up the women with child, of Gilead, that they might enlarge their border; but I will kindle a fire in the wall of Rabbah, and it shall devour the palaces thereof, with shouting in the day of battle, with a tempest in the day of the whirlwind; and their king shall go into captivity, he and his princes together, saith the Lord.

The Reasons for God's Punishments

Hear this word that the Lord hath spoken against you, O children of Israel, against the whole family which I brought up from the land of Egypt, saying, You only have I known of all the families of the earth: therefore I will punish you for all your iniquities.

Can two walk together, except they be agreed? Will a lion roar in the forest, when he hath no prey? will a young lion cry out of his den, if he have taken nothing? Can a bird fall in a snare upon the earth, where no gin is for him? shall one take up a snare from the earth, and have taken nothing at all? shall a trumpet be blown in the city, and the people not be afraid? shall there be evil in a city, and the Lord hath not done it?

Surely the Lord God will do nothing, but he revealeth his secret unto his servants the prophets. The lion hath roared, who will not fear? the Lord God hath spoken, who can but prophesy?

Publish in the palaces at Ashdod, and in the palaces in the land of Egypt, and say, Assemble yourselves upon the mountains of Samaria, and behold the great tumults in the midst thereof, and the oppressed in the midst thereof. For they know not to do right, saith the Lord, who store up violence and robbery in their palaces.

Therefore thus saith the Lord God; An adversary there shall be even round about the land; and he shall bring down thy strength from thee, and thy palaces shall be spoiled. Thus saith the Lord: As the shepherd taketh out of the mouth of the lion two legs, or a piece of an ear: so shall the children of Israel be taken out that dwell in Samaria in the corner of a bed, and in Damascus in a couch.

Hear ye, and testify in the house of Jacob, saith the Lord God, the God of hosts, that, in the day that I shall visit the transgressions of Israel upon him, I will also visit the altars of Beth-el: and the horns of the altar shall be cut off, and fall to the ground. And I will smite the winter-house with the summer-house; and the houses of ivory shall perish, and the great houses shall have an end, saith the Lord.

A Lament for Israel

Hear ye this word which I take up against you, even a lamentation, O house of Israel. The virgin of Israel is fallen; she shall no more rise: she is forsaken upon her land: there is none to raise her up. For thus saith the Lord God; The city that went out by a thousand shall leave an hundred, and that which went forth by an hundred shall leave ten, to the house of Israel.

For thus saith the Lord unto the house of Israel, Seek ye me, and ye shall live. But seek not Beth-el, nor enter into Gilgal, and pass not to Beer-sheba: for Gilgal shall surely go into captivity, and Beth-el shall come to nought.

Seek the Lord, and ye shall live; lest he break out like fire in the house of Joseph, and devour it, and there be none to quench it in Beth-el. Ye who turn judgment to wormwood, and leave off righteousness in the earth, seek him that maketh the seven stars and Orion, and turneth the shadow of death into the morning, and maketh the day dark with night: that calleth for the waters of the sea, and poureth them out upon the face of the earth: The Lord is his name; that strengtheneth the **spoiled** against the strong, so that the spoiled shall come against the fortress.

They hate him that rebuketh in the gate, and they abhor him that speaketh uprightly.

Forasmuch, therefore, as your treading is upon the poor, and ye take from him burdens of wheat: ye have built houses of hewn stone, but ye shall not dwell in them; ye have planted pleasant vineyards, but ye shall not drink wine of them.

For I know your manifold transgressions and your mighty sins: they afflict the just, they take a bribe, and they turn aside the poor in the gate from their right. Therefore, the prudent shall keep silence in that time; for it is an evil time.

Seek good, and not evil, that ye may live: and so the Lord, the God of hosts, shall be with you, as ye have spoken. Hate the evil, and love the good, and establish judgment in the gate: it may be that the Lord God of hosts will be gracious unto the remnant of Joseph.

Therefore, the Lord, the God of hosts, the Lord, saith thus; Wailing shall be in all streets; and they shall say in all the highways, Alas! alas! and they shall call the husbandmen to mourning, and such as are skilful of lamentation to wailing. And in all vineyards shall be wailing: for I will pass through thee, saith the Lord.

Woe unto you that desire the day of the Lord! to what end is it for you? the day of the Lord is darkness, and not light. As if a man did flee from a lion, and a bear met him; or went into the house, and leaned his hand on the wall, and a serpent bit him. Shall not the day of the Lord be darkness, and not light? even very dark, and no brightness in it?

I hate, I despise your feast days, and I will not smell in your solemn assemblies. Though ye offer me burnt-offerings and your meat-offerings, I will not accept them; neither will I regard the peace-offerings of your fat beasts. Take thou away from me the noise of thy songs; for I will not hear the melody of thy viols. But let judgment run down as waters, and righteousness as a mighty stream.

Have ye offered unto me sacrifices and offerings in the wilderness forty years, O house of Israel? But ye have borne the tabernacle of your Moloch and Chiun your images, the star of your god, which ye made to yourselves. Therefore, will I cause you to go into captivity beyond Damascus, saith the Lord, whose name is The God of hosts.

The Vengeance of the Lord

I saw the Lord standing upon the altar: and he said, Smite the lintel of the door, that the posts may shake: and cut them in the head all of them; and I will slay the last of them with the sword: he that fleeth of them shall not flee away, and he that escapeth of them shall not be delivered. Though they dig into hell, thence shall mine hand take them; though they climb up to heaven, thence will I bring them down. And though they hide themselves in the top of Carmel, I will search and take them out thence; and though they be hid from my sight in the bottom of the sea, thence will I command the serpent, and he shall bite them. And though they go into captivity before their enemies, thence will I command the sword, and it shall slay them: and I will set mine eyes upon them for evil, and not for good.

And the Lord God of hosts is he that toucheth the land, and it shall melt, and all that dwell therein shall mourn: and it shall rise up wholly like a flood; and shall be drowned, as by the flood of Egypt. It is he that buildeth his stories in the heaven, and hath founded his troop in the earth; he that calleth for the waters of the sea, and poureth them out upon the face of the earth: The Lord is his name.

Are ye not as the children of the Ethiopians unto me, O children of Israel? saith the Lord. Have not I brought up Israel out of the land of Egypt? and the Philistines from Caphtor, and the Syrians from Kir?

Behold, the eyes of the Lord God are upon the sinful kingdom, and I will destroy it from off the face of the earth; saving that I will not utterly destroy the house of Jacob, saith the Lord. For lo, I will command, and I will sift the house of Israel among all nations, like as corn is sifted in a sieve, yet shall not the least grain fall upon the earth. All the sinners of my people shall die by the sword, which say, The evil shall not overtake nor prevent us.

In that day will I raise up the tabernacle of David that is fallen, and close up the breaches thereof; and I will raise up his ruins, and I will build it as in the days of old; that they may possess the remnant of Edom, and of all the heathen which are called by my name, saith the Lord that doeth this.

Behold, the days come, saith the Lord, that the ploughman shall overtake the reaper, and the treader of grapes him that soweth seed; and the mountains shall drop sweet wine, and all the hills shall melt. And I will bring again the captivity of my people of Israel, and they shall build the waste cities, and inhabit them; and they shall plant vineyards, and drink the wine thereof; they shall also make gardens, and eat the fruit of them. And I will plant them upon their land, and they shall no more be pulled up out of their land which I have given them, saith the Lord thy God.

Hosea

I

The word of the Lord that came unto Hosea, the son of Beeri, in the days of Uzziah, Jotham, Ahaz, and Hezekiah, kings of Judah, and in the days of Jeroboam the son of Joash king of Israel.

The beginning of the word of the Lord by Hosea. And the Lord said to Hosea, Go, take unto thee a wife of whoredoms and children of whoredoms; for the land hath committed great whoredom, departing from the Lord.

So he went and took Gomer the daughter of Diblaim; which conceived, and bare him a son.

And the Lord said unto him, Call his name Jezreel; for yet a little while, and I will avenge the blood of Jezreel upon the house of Jehu, and will cause to cease the kingdom of the house of Israel. And it shall come to pass at that day, that I will break the bow of Israel in the valley of Jezreel.

And she conceived again, and bare a daughter. And God said unto him, Call her name Lo-ruhamah: for I will no more have mercy upon the house of Israel; but I will utterly take them away. But I will have mercy upon the house of Judah, and will save them by the Lord their God, and will not save them by bow, nor by sword, nor by battle, by horses, nor by horsemen.

Now when she had weaned Lo-ruhamah, she conceived, and bare a son. Then said God, Call his name Lo-ammi; for ye are not my people, and I will not be your God. Yet the number of the children of Israel shall be as the sand of the sea, which cannot be measured nor numbered; and it shall come to pass, that in the place where it was said unto them, Ye are not my people, there it shall be said unto them, Ye are the sons of the living God. Then shall the children of Judah and the children of Israel be gathered together, and appoint themselves one head, and they shall come up out of the land: for great shall be the day of Jezreel.

II

Say ye unto your brethren, Ammi; and to your sisters, Ruhamah. Plead with your mother, plead; for she is not my wife, neither am I her husband: let her therefore put away her whoredoms out of her sight, and her adulteries from between her breasts; lest I strip her naked, and set her as in the day that she was born, and make her as a wilderness, and set her like a dry land, and slay her with thirst. And I will not have mercy upon her children; for they be the children of whoredoms.

For their mother hath played the harlot: she that conceived them hath done shamefully: for she said, I will go after my lovers, that give me my bread and my water, my wool and my flax, mine oil and my drink.

Therefore, behold, I will hedge up thy way with thorns, and make a wall, that she shall not find her paths. And she shall follow after her lovers, but she shall not overtake them; and she shall seek them, but shall not find them: then shall she say, I will go and return to my first husband; for then was it better with me than now. For she did not know that I gave her corn, and wine, and oil, and multiplied her silver and gold, which they prepared for Baal.

Therefore, will I return, and take away my corn in the time thereof, and my wine in the season thereof, and will recover my wool and my flax given to cover her nakedness.

And now will I discover her lewdness in the sight of her lovers, and none shall deliver her out of mine hand. I will also cause all her mirth to cease, her feast days, her new-moons, and her sabbaths, and all her solemn feasts. And I will destroy her vines and her fig-trees, whereof she hath said, These are my rewards that my lovers have given me: and I will make them a forest, and the beasts of the field shall eat them.

And I will visit upon her the days of Baalim, wherein she burned incense to them, and she decked herself with her ear-rings and her jewels, and she went after her lovers, and forgat me, saith the Lord. Therefore, behold, I will allure her, and bring her into the wilderness, and speak comfortably unto her. And I will give her her vineyards from thence, and the valley of Achor for a door of hope: and she shall sing there, as in the days of her youth, and as in the day when she came up out of the land of Egypt. And it shall be at that day, saith the Lord, that thou shalt call me Ishi; and shalt call me no more Baali. For I will take away the names of Baalim out of her mouth, and they shall no more be remembered by their name.

And in that day will I make a covenant for them with the beasts of the field, and with the fowls of heaven, and with the creeping things of the ground; and I will break the bow and the sword and the battle out of the earth, and will make them to lie down safely. And I will betroth thee unto me for ever; yea, I will betroth thee unto me in righteousness, and in judgment, and in loving-kindness, and in mercies. I will even betroth thee unto me in faithfulness: and thou shalt know the Lord.

And it shall come to pass in that day, I will hear, saith the Lord, I will hear the heavens, and they shall hear the earth; and the earth shall hear the corn, and the wine, and the oil; and they shall hear Jezreel. And I will sow her unto me in the earth; and I will have mercy upon her that had not obtained mercy; and I will say to them which were not my people, Thou art my people; and they shall say, Thou art my God.

III

Then said the Lord unto me, Go yet, love a woman beloved of her friend, yet an adulteress, according to the love of the Lord toward the children of Israel, who look to other gods, and love flagons of wine.

So I bought her to me for fifteen pieces of silver, and for an homer of barley, and an half homer of barley: and I said unto her, Thou shalt abide for me many days; thou shalt not play the harlot, and thou shalt not be for another man: so will I also be for thee.

For the children of Israel shall abide many days without a king, and without a prince, and without a sacrifice, and without an image, and without an ephod, and without teraphim: afterwards shall the children of Israel return, and seek the Lord their God, and David their king; and shall fear the Lord and his goodness in the latter days.

IV

Hear the word of the Lord, ye children of Israel: for the Lord hath a controversy with the inhabitants of the land, because there is no truth, nor mercy, nor knowledge of God in the land.

By swearing, and lying, and killing, and stealing, and committing adultery, they break out, and blood toucheth blood. Therefore, shall the land mourn, and every one that dwelleth therein shall languish, with the beasts of the field, and with the fowls of heaven; yea, the fishes of the sea also shall be taken away. Yet let no man strive, nor reprove another; for thy people are as they that strive with the priest. Therefore, shalt thou fall in the day, and the prophet also shall fall with thee in the night, and I will destroy thy mother.

My people are destroyed for lack of knowledge: because thou hast rejected knowledge, I will also reject thee, that thou shalt be no priest to me: seeing thou hast forgotten the law of thy God, I will also forget thy children. As they were increased, so they sinned against me: therefore will I change their glory into shame. They eat up the sin of my people, and they set their heart on their iniquity.

And there shall be, like people, like priest: and I will punish them for their ways, and reward them their doings. For they shall eat, and not have enough: they shall commit whoredom, and shall not increase: because they have left off to take heed to the Lord.

I will not punish your daughters when they commit whoredom, nor your spouses when they commit adultery: for themselves are separated with whores, and they sacrifice with harlots: therefore the people that doth not understand shall fall.

Though thou, Israel, play the harlot, yet let not Judah offend; and come not ye unto Gilgal, neither go ye up to Beth-aven, nor swear, The Lord liveth. For Israel slideth back as a backsliding heifer: now the Lord will feed them as a lamb in a large place.

Ephraim is joined to idols: let him alone.

Their drink is sour: they have committed whoredom continually: her rulers with shame do love, Give ye.

The wind hath bound her up in her wings, and they shall be ashamed because of their sacrifices.

V

Come, and let us return unto the Lord: for he hath torn, and he will heal us; he hath smitten, and he will bind us up. After two days will he revive us: in the third day he will raise us up, and we shall live in his sight. Then shall we know, if we follow on to know the Lord: his going forth is prepared as the morning; and he shall come unto us as the rain, as the latter and former rain unto the earth.

O Ephraim, what shall I do unto thee? O Judah, what shall I do unto thee? for your goodness is as a morning cloud, and as the early dew it goeth away. Therefore have I hewed them by the prophets; I have slain them by the words of my mouth; and thy judgments are as the light that goeth forth. For I desired mercy, and not sacrifice; and the knowledge of God more than burnt-offerings. But they like men have transgressed the covenant; there have they dealt treacherously against me.

Gilead is a city of them that work iniquity, and is polluted with blood. And as troops of robbers wait for a man, so the company of priests murder in the way by consent: for they commit lewdness.

I have seen an horrible thing in the house of Israel: there is the whoredom of Ephraim, Israel is defiled. Also, O Judah, he hath set an harvest for thee, when I returned the captivity of my people.

VI

When Israel was a child, then I loved him, and called my son out of Egypt.

As they called them, so they went from them: they sacrificed unto Baalim, and burned incense to graven images.

I taught Ephraim also to go, taking them by their arms; but they knew not that I healed them.

I drew them with cords of a man, with bands of love: and I was to them as they that take off the yoke on their jaws, and I laid meat unto them.

He shall not return into the land of Egypt, but the Assyrian shall be his king, because they refused to return. And the sword shall abide on his cities, and shall consume his branches, and devour them, because of their own counsels.

And my people are bent to backsliding from me: though they called them to the Most High, none at all would exalt him.

How shall I give thee up, Ephraim? how shall I deliver thee, Israel? how shall I make thee as Admah? how shall I set thee as Zeboim? mine heart is turned within me, my repentings are kindled together. I will not execute the fierceness of mine anger, I will not return to destroy Ephraim: for I am God, and not man; the Holy One in the midst of thee: and I will not enter into the city.

They shall walk after the Lord: he shall roar like a lion; when he shall roar, then the children shall tremble from the west. They shall tremble as a bird out of Egypt, and as a dove out of the land of Assyria: and I will place them in their houses, saith the Lord.

Ephraim compasseth me about with lies, and the house of Israel with deceit: but Judah yet ruleth with God, and is faithful with the saints.

VII

O Israel, return unto the Lord thy God; for thou hast fallen by thine iniquity. Take with you words, and turn to the Lord: say unto him, Take away all iniquity, and receive us graciously: so will we render the calves of our lips.

Asshur shall not save us; we will not ride upon horses: neither will we say any more to the work of our hands, Ye are our gods: for in thee the fatherless findeth mercy.

I will heal their backsliding, I will love them freely: for mine anger is turned away from him. I will be as the dew unto Israel: he shall grow as the lily, and cast forth his roots as Lebanon. His branches shall spread, and his beauty shall be as the olive-tree, and his smell as Lebanon. They that dwell under his shadow shall return; they shall revive as the corn, and grow as the vine: the scent thereof shall be as the wine of Lebanon.

Ephraim shall say, What have I to do any more with idols? I have heard him, and observed him: I am like a green fir-tree. From me is thy fruit found.

Who is wise, and he shall understand these things? prudent, and he shall know them? for the ways of the Lord are right, and the just shall walk in them: but the transgressors shall fall therein.

Micah

Accusation of the Princes

And I said, Hear, I pray you, O heads of Jacob, and ye princes of the house of Israel: Is it not for you to know judgment? Who hate the good, and love the evil; who pluck off their skin from off them, and their flesh from off their bones; who also eat the flesh of my people, and flay their skin from off them; and they break their bones, and chop them in pieces, as for the pot, and as flesh within the cauldron. Then shall they cry unto the Lord, but he will not hear them: he will even hide his face from them at that time, as they have behaved themselves ill in their doings.

Thus saith the Lord concerning the prophets that make my people err, that bite with their teeth, and cry, Peace; and he that putteth not into their mouths, they even prepare war against him. Therefore, night shall be unto you, that ye shall not have a vision; and it shall be dark unto you, that ye shall not divine; and the sun shall go down over the prophets, and the day shall be dark over them. Then shall the seers be ashamed, and the diviners confounded; yea, they shall all cover their lips; for there is no answer of God.

But truly I am full of power by the Spirit of the Lord, and of judgment, and of might, to declare unto Jacob his transgression, and to Israel his sin.

Hear this, I pray you, ye heads of the house of Jacob, and princes of the house of Israel, that abhor judgment, and pervert all equity. They build up Zion with blood, and Jerusalem with iniquity. The heads thereof judge for reward, and the priests thereof teach for hire, and the prophets thereof divine for money: yet will they lean upon the Lord, and say, Is not the Lord among us? none evil can come upon us. Therefore, shall Zion for your sake be ploughed as a field, and Jerusalem shall become heaps, and the mountain of the house as the high places of the forest.

The Establishment of the Kingdom of God

But in the last days it shall come to pass, that the mountain of the house of the Lord shall be established in the top of the mountains, and it shall be exalted above the hills; and people shall flow unto it. And many nations shall come, and say, Come, and let us go up to the mountain of the Lord, and to the house of the God of Jacob; and he will teach us of his ways, and we will walk in his paths: for the law shall go forth of Zion, and the word of the Lord from Jerusalem.

And he shall judge among many people, and rebuke strong nations afar off; and they shall beat their swords into plough-shares, and their spears into pruning-hooks: nation shall not lift up a sword against nation, neither shall they learn war any more. But they shall sit every man under his vine and under his fig-tree; and none shall make them afraid: for the mouth of the Lord of hosts hath spoken it. For all people will walk every one in the name of his god, and we will walk in the name of the Lord our God for ever and ever.

In that day, saith the Lord, will I assemble her that halteth, and I will gather her that is driven out, and her that I have afflicted; and I will make her that halted a remnant, and her that was cast far off a strong nation: and the Lord shall reign over them in mount Zion from henceforth, even for ever.

And thou, O tower of the flock, the strong hold of the daughter of Zion, unto thee shall it come, even the first dominion; the kingdom shall come to the daughter of Jerusalem.

Now why dost thou cry out aloud? is there no king in thee? is thy counsellor perished? for pangs have taken thee as a woman in travail. Be in pain, and labour to bring forth, O daughter of Zion, like a woman in travail: for now shalt thou go forth out of the city, and thou shalt dwell in the field, and thou shalt go even to Babylon; there shalt thou be delivered; there the Lord shall redeem thee from the hand of thine enemies.

Now also many nations are gathered against thee, that say, Let her be defiled, and let our eye look upon Zion. But they know not the thoughts of the Lord: neither understand they his counsel: for he shall gather them as the sheaves into the floor.

Arise and thresh, O daughter of Zion: for I will make thy horn iron, and I will make thy hoofs brass: and thou shalt beat in pieces many people: and I will consecrate their gain unto the Lord, and their substance unto the Lord of the whole earth.

Promise of a Leader

Now gather thyself in troops, O daughter of troops: he hath laid siege against us: they shall smite the judge of Israel with a rod upon the cheek. But thou, Beth-lehem Ephratah, though thou be little among the thousands of Judah, yet out of thee shall he come forth unto me that is to be Ruler in Israel; whose goings forth have been from of old, from everlasting. Therefore will he give them up until the time that she which travaileth hath brought forth: then the remnant of his brethren shall return unto the children of Israel.

And he shall stand and feed in the strength of the Lord, in the majesty of the name of the Lord his God; and they shall abide: for now shall he be great unto the ends of the earth. And this man shall be the peace, when the Assyrian shall come into our land: and when he shall tread in our palaces, then shall we raise against him seven shepherds, and eight principal men.

And they shall waste the land of Assyria with the sword, and the land of Nimrod in the entrances thereof: thus shall he deliver us from the Assyrian, when he cometh into our land, and when he treadeth within our borders. And the remnant of Jacob shall be in the midst of many people as a dew from the Lord, as the showers upon the grass, that tarrieth not for man, nor waiteth for the sons of men.

What the Lord Requires of Thee

Hear ye now what the Lord saith; Arise, contend thou before the mountains, and let the hills hear thy voice. Hear ye, O mountains, the Lord's controversy, and ye strong foundations of the earth: for the Lord hath a controversy with his people, and he will plead with Israel.

O my people, what have I done unto thee? and wherein have I wearied thee? testify against me. For I brought thee up out of the land of Egypt, and redeemed thee out of the house of servants; and I sent before thee Moses, Aaron, and Miriam. O my people, remember now what Balak king of Moab consulted, and what Balaam the son of Beor answered him from Shittim unto Gilgal; that ye may know the righteousness of the Lord.

Wherewith shall I come before the Lord, and bow myself before the high God? shall I come before him with burnt-offerings, with calves of a year old? Will the Lord be pleased with thousands of rams, or with ten thousands of rivers of oil? shall I give my first-born for my transgression, the fruit of my body for the sin of my soul?

He hath shewed thee, O man, what is good; and what doth the Lord require of thee, but to do justly, and to love mercy, and to walk humbly with thy God? The Lord's voice crieth unto the city, and the man of wisdom shall see thy name: hear ye the rod, and who hath appointed it.

Are there yet the treasures of wickedness in the house of the wicked, and the scant measure that is abominable? Shall I count them pure with the wicked balances, and with the bag of deceitful weights?

For the rich men thereof are full of violence, and the inhabitants thereof have spoken lies, and their tongue is deceitful in their mouth. Therefore, also will I make thee sick in smiting thee, in making thee desolate because of thy sins. Thou shalt eat, but not be satisfied; and thy casting down shall be in the midst of thee; and thou shalt take hold, but shalt not deliver; and that which thou deliverest will I give up to the sword. Thou shalt sow, but thou shalt not reap; thou shalt tread the olives, but thou shalt not anoint thee with oil; and sweet wine, but shalt not drink wine.

For the statutes of Omri are kept, and all the works of the house of Ahab, and ye walk in their counsels; that I should make thee a desolation, and the inhabitants thereof an hissing: therefore ye shall bear the reproach of my people.

The Book of the First Isaiah

Isaiah Warns Israel

The vision of Isaiah the son of Amoz, which he saw concerning Judah and Jerusalem in the days of Uzziah, Jotham, Ahaz, and Hezekiah, kings of Judah.

Hear, O heavens, and give ear, O earth: for the Lord hath spoken, I have nourished and brought up children, and they have rebelled against me. The ox knoweth his owner, and the ass his master's crib: but Israel doth not know, my people doth not consider. Ah sinful nation, a people laden with iniquity, a seed of evil-doers, children that are corrupters! they have forsaken the Lord, they have provoked the Holy One of Israel unto anger, they are gone away backward.

Why should ye be stricken any more? ye will revolt more and more: the whole head is sick, and the whole heart faint. From the sole of the foot even unto the head there is no soundness in it; but wounds, and bruises, and putrifying sores: they have not been closed, neither bound up, neither mollified with ointment. Your country is desolate, your cities are burned with fire: your land, strangers devour it in your presence, and it is desolate, as overthrown by strangers. And the daughter of Zion is left as a cottage in a vineyard, as a lodge in a garden of cucumbers, as a besieged city. Except the Lord of hosts had left unto us a very small remnant, we should have been as Sodom, and we should have been like unto Gomorrah.

Hear the word of the Lord, ye rulers of Sodom: give ear unto the law of our God, ye people of Gomorrah.

To what purpose is the multitude of your sacrifices unto me? saith the Lord: I am full of the burnt-offerings of rams, and the fat of fed beasts; and I delight not in the blood of bullocks, or of lambs, or of he-goats. When ye come to appear before me, who hath required this at your hand, to tread my courts? Bring no more vain oblations: incense is an abomination unto me; the new-moons and sabbaths, the calling of assemblies, I cannot away with; it is iniquity, even the solemn meeting. Your new-moons and your appointed feasts my soul hateth: they are a trouble unto me; I am weary to bear them. And when ye spread forth your hands, I will hide mine eyes from you; yea, when ye make many prayers, I will not hear: your hands are full of blood.

Wash you, make you clean: put away the evil of your doings from before mine eyes; cease to do evil; learn to do well; seek judgment, relieve the oppressed, judge the fatherless, plead for the widow.

Come now, and let us reason together, saith the Lord: though your sins be as scarlet, they shall be as white as snow; though they be red like crimson, they shall be as wool.

If ye be willing and obedient, ye shall eat the good of the land: but if ye refuse and rebel, ye shall be devoured with the sword: for the mouth of the Lord hath spoken it.

And it shall come to pass in the last days, that the mountain of the Lord's house shall be established in the top of the mountains, and shall be exalted above the hills; and all nations shall flow unto it.

And many people shall go and say, Come ye, and let us go up to the mountain of the Lord, to the house of the God of Jacob; and he will teach us of his ways, and we will walk in his paths: for out of Zion shall go forth the law, and the word of the Lord from Jerusalem. And he shall judge among the nations, and shall rebuke many people: and they shall beat their swords into plough-shares, and their spears into pruning-hooks: nation shall not lift up sword against nation, neither shall they learn war any more.

O house of Jacob, come ye, and let us walk in the light of the Lord.

Enter into the rock, and hide thee in the dust, for fear of the Lord, and for the glory of his majesty.

The lofty looks of man shall be humbled, and the haughtiness of men shall be bowed down, and the Lord alone shall be exalted in that day.

Vision of the Six-Winged Seraphims

In the year that king Uzziah died I saw also the Lord sitting upon a throne, high and lifted up, and his train filled the temple. Above it stood the seraphims: each one had six wings; with twain he covered his face, and with twain he covered his feet, and with twain he did fly. And one cried unto another, and said, Holy, holy, holy, is the Lord of hosts: the whole earth is full of his glory. And the posts of the door moved at the voice of him that cried, and the house was filled with smoke.

Then said I, Woe is me! for I am undone; because I am a man of unclean lips, and I dwell in the midst of a people of unclean lips: for mine eyes have seen the King, the Lord of hosts.

Then flew one of the seraphims unto me, having a live coal in his hand, which he had taken with the tongs from off the altar. And he laid it upon my mouth, and said, Lo, this hath touched thy lips; and thine iniquity is taken away, and thy sin purged.

Also I heard the voice of the Lord, saying, Whom shall I send, and who will go for us? Then said I, Here am I; send me.

And he said, Go, and tell this people, Hear ye indeed, but understand not; and see ye indeed, but perceive not. Make the heart of this people fat, and make their ears heavy, and shut their eyes; lest they see with their eyes, and hear with their ears, and understand with their heart, and convert, and be healed.

Then said I, Lord, how long? And he answered, Until the cities be wasted without inhabitant, and the houses without man, and the land be utterly desolate, and the Lord have removed men far away, and there be a great forsaking in the midst of the land.

But yet in it shall be a tenth, and it shall return, and shall be eaten: as a teil-tree, and as an oak, whose substance is in them, when they cast their leaves: so the holy seed shall be the substance thereof.

Prophecy of Immanuel

And it came to pass in the days of Ahaz the son of Jotham, the son of Uzziah, king of Judah, that Rezin the king of Syria, and Pekah the son of Remaliah, king of Israel, went up toward Jerusalem to war against it, but could not prevail against it. And it was told the house of David, saying, Syria is confederate with Ephraim. And his heart was moved, and the heart of his people, as the trees of the wood are moved with the wind.

Then said the Lord unto Isaiah, Go forth now to meet Ahaz, thou, and Shearjashub thy son, at the end of the conduit of the upper pool in the highway of the fuller's field. And say unto him, Take heed, and be quiet; fear not, neither be faint-hearted for the two tails of these smoking fire-brands, for the fierce anger of Rezin with Syria, and of the son of Remaliah. Because Syria, Ephraim, and the son of Remaliah, have taken evil counsel against thee, saying, Let us go up against Judah, and vex it, and let us make a breach therein for us, and set a king in the midst of it, even the son of Tabeal.

Thus saith the Lord God, It shall not stand, neither shall it come to pass. For the head of Syria is Damascus, and the head of Damascus is Rezin; and within threescore and five years shall Ephraim be broken, that it be not a people. And the head of Ephraim is Samaria, and the head of Samaria is Remaliah's son. If ye will not believe, surely ye shall not be established.

Moreover, the Lord spake again unto Ahaz, saying, Ask thee a sign of the Lord thy God; ask it either in the depth, or in the height above.

But Ahaz said, I will not ask, neither will I tempt the Lord.

And he said, Hear ye now, O house of David; Is it a small thing for you to weary men, but will ye weary my God also? Therefore the Lord himself shall give you a sign; Behold, a virgin shall conceive, and bear a son, and shall call his name Immanuel. Butter and honey shall he eat, that he may know to refuse the evil, and choose the good. For before the child shall know to refuse the evil, and choose the good, the land that thou abhorrest shall be forsaken of both her kings.

Moreover, the Lord said unto me, Take thee a great roll, and write in it with a man's pen concerning Maher-shalal-hash-baz. And I took unto me faithful witnesses to record, Uriah the priest, and Zechariah the son of Jeberechiah.

And I went unto the prophetess; and she conceived, and bare a son. Then said the Lord to me, Call his name Maher-shalal-hash-baz. For before the child shall have knowledge to cry, My father, and my mother, the riches of Damascus and the spoil of Samaria shall be taken away before the king of Assyria.

The Lord spake also unto me again, saying,

The people that walked in darkness have seen a great light: they that dwell in the land of the shadow of death, upon them hath the light shined. Thou hast multiplied the nation, and not increased the joy: they joy before thee according to the joy in harvest, and as men rejoice when they divide the spoil. For thou hast broken the yoke of his burden, and the staff of his shoulder, the rod of his oppressor, as in the day of Midian. For every battle of the warrior is with confused noise, and garments rolled in blood; but this shall be with burning and fuel of fire.

For unto us a child is born, unto us a son is given: and the government shall be upon his shoulder: and his name shall be called Wonderful, Counsellor, The Mighty God, The Everlasting Father, The Prince of Peace. Of the increase of his government and peace there shall be no end, upon the throne of David, and upon his kingdom, to order it, and to establish it with judgment and with justice from henceforth even for ever. The zeal of the Lord of hosts will perform this.

And there shall come forth a rod out of the stem of Jesse, and a Branch shall grow out of his roots. And the Spirit of the Lord shall rest upon him, the spirit of wisdom and understanding, the spirit of counsel and might, the spirit of knowledge and of the fear of the Lord, and shall make him of quick understanding in the fear of the Lord: and he shall not judge after the sight of his eyes, neither reprove after the hearing of his ears, but with righteousness shall he judge the poor, and reprove with equity for the meek of the earth: and he shall smite the earth with the rod of his mouth, and with the breath of his lips shall he slay the wicked. And righteousness shall be the girdle of his loins, and faithfulness the girdle of his reins.

The wolf also shall dwell with the lamb, and the leopard shall lie down with the kid; and the calf and the young lion and the fatling together; and a little child shall lead them. And the cow and the bear shall feed; their young ones shall lie down together: and the lion shall eat straw like the ox. And the suckling child shall play on the hole of the asp, and the weaned child shall put his hand on the cockatrice's den. They shall not hurt nor destroy in all my holy mountain: for the earth shall be full of the knowledge of the Lord, as the waters cover the sea.

And in that day there shall be a root of Jesse, which shall stand for an ensign of the people; to it shall the Gentiles seek: and his rest shall be glorious.

And in that day thou shalt say, O Lord, I will praise thee: though thou wast angry with me, thine anger is turned away, and thou comfortedst me.

Behold, God is my salvation; I will trust, and not be afraid: for the Lord JEHOVAH is my strength and my song; he also is become my salvation. Therefore with joy shall ye draw water out of the wells of salvation.

And in that day shall ye say, Praise the Lord, call upon his name, declare his doings among the people, make mention that his name is exalted. Sing unto the Lord; for he hath done excellent things: this is known in all the earth. Cry out and shout, thou inhabitant of Zion; for great is the Holy One of Israel in the midst of thee.

The Destinies of the Evil and the Righteous

Come near, ye nations, to hear; and hearken, ye people: let the earth hear, and all that is therein; the world, and all things that come forth of it. For the indignation of the Lord is upon all nations, and his fury upon all their armies; he hath utterly destroyed them, he hath delivered them to the slaughter. Their slain also shall be cast out, and their stink shall come up out of their carcasses, and the mountains shall be melted with their blood.

And all the host of heaven shall be dissolved, and the heavens shall be rolled together as a scroll: and all their hosts shall fall down, as the leaf falleth off from the vine, and as a falling fig from the fig-tree.

For my sword shall be bathed in heaven: behold, it shall come down upon Idumea, and upon the people of my curse, to judgment. The sword of the Lord is filled with blood, it is made fat with fatness, and with the blood of lambs and goats, with the fat of the kidneys of rams: for the Lord hath a sacrifice in Bozrah, and a great slaughter in the land of Idumea.

And the unicorns shall come down with them, and the bullocks with the bulls; and their land shall be soaked with blood. and their dust made fat with fatness. For it is the day of the Lord's vengeance, and the year of recompenses for the controversy of Zion.

And the streams thereof shall be turned into pitch, and the dust thereof into brimstone, and the land thereof shall become burning pitch. It shall not be quenched night nor day; the smoke thereof shall go up for ever: from generation to generation it shall lie waste; none shall pass through it for ever and ever.

But the cormorant and the bittern shall possess it; the owl also and the raven shall dwell in it: and he shall stretch out upon it the line of confusion, and the stones of emptiness. They shall call the nobles thereof to the kingdom, but none shall be there, and all her princes shall be nothing. And thorns shall come up in her palaces, nettles and brambles in the fortresses thereof: and it shall be an habitation of dragons, and a court for owls. The wild beasts of the desert shall also meet with the wild beasts of the island, and the satyr shall cry to his fellow; the screech-owl also shall rest there, and find for herself a place of rest. There shall the great owl make her nest, and lay, and hatch, and gather under her shadow: there shall the vultures also be gathered, every one with her mate.

Seek ye out of the book of the Lord, and read: no one of these shall fail, none shall want her mate: for my mouth, it hath commanded, and his spirit, it hath gathered them.

And he hath cast the lot for them, and his hand hath divided it unto them by line: they shall possess it for ever, from generation to generation shall they dwell therein.

The wilderness and the solitary place shall be glad for them; and the desert shall rejoice, and blossom as the rose. It shall blossom abundantly, and rejoice, even with joy and singing: the glory of Lebanon shall be given unto it, the excellency of Carmel and Sharon, they shall see the glory of the Lord, and the excellency of our God.

Strengthen ye the weak hands and confirm the feeble knees. Say to them that are of a fearful heart, Be strong, fear not; behold, your God will come with vengeance, even God, with a recompense; he will come and save you.

Then the eyes of the blind shall be opened, and the ears of the deaf shall be unstopped. Then shall the lame man leap as an hart, and the tongue of the dumb sing: for in the wilderness shall waters break out, and streams in the desert. And the parched ground shall become a pool, and the thirsty land springs of water: in the habitation of dragons, where each lay, shall be grass with reeds and rushes. And an highway shall be there, and a way, and it shall be called, The way of holiness; the unclean shall not pass over it; but it shall be for those: the way-faring men, though fools, shall not err therein. No lion shall be there, nor any ravenous beast shall go up thereon, it shall not be found there; but the redeemed shall walk there.

And the ransomed of the Lord shall return, and come to Zion with songs and everlasting joy upon their heads: they shall obtain joy and gladness, and sorrow and sighing shall flee away.

Three Prophecies of Destruction

Zephaniah

The word of the Lord which came unto Zephaniah, the son of Cushi, the son of Gedaliah, the son of Amariah, the son of Hizkiah, in the days of Josiah the son of Amon, king of Judah.

I will utterly consume all things from off the land, saith the Lord. I will consume man and beast; I will consume the fowls of the heaven, and the fishes of the sea, and the stumbling-blocks with the wicked; and I will cut off man from off the land, saith the Lord.

The great day of the Lord is near, it is near, and hasteth greatly, even the voice of the day of the Lord: the mighty man shall cry there bitterly. That day is a day of wrath, a day of trouble and distress, a day of waste-ness and desolation, a day of darkness and gloominess, a day of clouds and thick darkness, a day of the trumpet and alarm against the fenced cities, and against the high towers.

And I will bring distress upon men, that they shall walk like blind men, because they have sinned against the Lord: and their blood shall be poured out as dust, and their flesh as the dung. Neither their silver nor their gold shall be able to deliver them in the day of the Lord's wrath; but the whole land shall be devoured by the fire of his jealousy: for he shall make even a speedy riddance of all them that dwell in the land.

Gather yourselves together, yea, gather together, O nation not desired; before the decree bring forth, before the day pass as the chaff, before the fierce anger of the Lord come upon you, before the day of the Lord's anger come upon you.

Seek ye the Lord, all ye meek of the earth, which have wrought his judgment; seek righteousness, seek meekness: it may be ye shall be hid in the day of the Lord's anger.

Nahum

The burden of Nineveh. The book of the vision of Nahum the Elkoshite.

God is jealous, and the Lord revengeth; the Lord revengeth, and is furious; the Lord will take vengeance on his adversaries, and he reserveth wrath for his enemies. The Lord is slow to anger, and great in power, and will not at all acquit the wicked: the Lord hath his way in the whirlwind and in the storm, and the clouds are the dust of his feet. He rebuketh the sea, and maketh it dry, and drieth up all the rivers: Bashan languisheth, and Carmel, and the flower of Lebanon languisheth. The mountains quake at him, and the hills melt, and the earth is burned at his presence, yea, the world, and all that dwell therein.

Who can stand before his indignation? and who can abide in the fierceness of his anger? his fury is poured out like fire, and the rocks are thrown down by him.

The Lord is good, a strong hold in the day of trouble; and he knoweth them that trust in him. But, with an overrunning flood he will make an utter end of the place thereof, and darkness shall pursue his enemies.

What do ye imagine against the Lord? he will make an utter end: affliction shall not rise up the second time. For while they be folden together as thorns, and while they are drunken as drunkards, they shall be devoured as stubble fully dry.

There is one come out of thee, that imagineth evil against the Lord, a wicked counsellor.

Thus saith the Lord: Though they be quiet, and likewise many, yet thus shall they be cut down, when he shall pass through. Though I have afflicted thee, I will afflict thee no more. For now will I break his yoke from off thee, and will burst thy bonds in sunder. And the Lord hath given a commandment concerning thee, that no more of thy name be sown: out of the house of thy gods will I cut off the graven image and the molten image: I will make thy grave; for thou art vile.

Behold upon the mountains the feet of him that bringeth good tidings, that publisheth peace! O Judah, keep thy solemn feasts, perform thy vows: for the wicked shall no more pass through thee: he is utterly cut off.

Habakkuk

The burden which Habakkuk the prophet did see.

O Lord, how long shall I cry, and thou wilt not hear! even cry out unto thee of violence, and thou wilt not save! Why dost thou shew me iniquity, and cause me to behold grievance? for spoiling and violence are before me: and there are that raise up strife and contention. Therefore, the law is slacked, and judgment doth never go forth: for the wicked doth compass about the righteous; therefore wrong judgment proceedeth.

I will stand upon my watch, and set me upon the tower, and will watch to see what he will say unto me, and what I shall answer when I am reproved.

And the Lord answered me, and said, Write the vision, and make it plain upon tables, that he may run that readeth it. For the vision is yet for an appointed time, but at the end it shall speak, and not lie: though it tarry, wait for it; because it will surely come, it will not tarry. Behold, his soul which is lifted up, is not upright in him: but the just shall live by his faith.

Yea, also, because he transgresseth by wine, he is a proud man, neither keepeth at home, who enlargeth his desire as hell, and is as death, and cannot be satisfied, but gathereth unto him all nations, and heapeth unto him all people. Shall not all these take up a parable against him, and a taunting proverb against him, and say, Woe to him that increaseth that which is not his! how long? and to him that ladeth himself with thick clay! Shall they not rise up suddenly that shall bite thee, and awake that shall vex thee, and thou shalt be for booties unto them?

Because thou hast spoiled many nations, all the remnant of the people shall spoil thee; because of men's blood, and for the violence of the land, of the city, and of all that dwell therein.

Woe to him that coveteth an evil covetousness to his house, that he may set his nest on high, that he may be delivered from the power of evil!

Thou hast consulted shame to thy house by cutting off many people, and hast sinned against thy soul. For the stone shall cry out of the wall, and the beam out of the timber shall answer it.

Woe to him that buildeth a town with blood, and establisheth a city by iniquity!

Behold, is it not of the Lord of hosts that the people shall labour in the very fire, and the people shall weary themselves for very vanity? For the earth shall be filled with the knowledge of the glory of the Lord, as the waters cover the sea.

The Book of the Prophet Jeremiah

Jeremiah Chosen as Prophet

The words of Jeremiah the son of Hilkiah, of the priests that were in Anathoth in the land of Benjamin, to whom the word of the Lord came in the days of Josiah the son of Amon king of Judah, in the thirteenth year of his reign. It came also in the days of Jehoiakim the son of Josiah king of Judah, unto the end of the eleventh year of Zedekiah the son of Josiah king of Judah, unto the carrying away of Jerusalem captive in the fifth month.

Then the word of the Lord came unto me, saying: Before I formed thee in the belly, I knew thee; and before thou camest forth out of the womb I sanctified thee, and I ordained thee a prophet unto the nations.

Then said I, Ah, Lord God! behold, I cannot speak: for I am a child.

But the Lord said unto me, Say not, I am a child: for thou shalt go to all that I shall send thee, and whatsoever I command thee thou shalt speak. Be not afraid of their faces: for I am with thee to deliver thee, saith the Lord.

Then the Lord put forth his hand, and touched my mouth. And the Lord said unto me, Behold, I have put my words in thy mouth. See, I have this day set thee over the nations and over the kingdoms, to root out, and to pull down, and to destroy, and to throw down, to build, and to plant.

Moreover the word of the Lord came unto me, saying, Jeremiah, what seest thou? And I said, I see a rod of an almond-tree.

Then said the Lord unto me, Thou hast well seen: for I will hasten my word to perform it.

Then the Lord said unto me, Out of the north an evil shall break forth upon all the inhabitants of the land. For lo, I will call all the families of the kingdoms of the north, saith the Lord; and they shall come, and they shall set every one his throne at the entering of the gates of Jerusalem, and against all the walls thereof round about, and against all the cities of Judah. And I will utter my judgments against them touching all their wickedness, who have forsaken me, and have burned incense unto other gods, and worshipped the works of their own hands.

Thou therefore gird up thy loins, and arise, and speak unto them all that I command thee: be not dismayed at their faces, lest I confound thee before them. For behold, I have made thee this day a defenced city, and an iron pillar, and brazen walls against the whole land, against the kings of Judah, against the princes thereof, against the priests thereof, and against the people of the land. And they shall fight against thee; but they shall not prevail against thee; for I am with thee, saith the Lord, to deliver thee.

A Call for Repentance

The word that came to Jeremiah from the Lord, saying, Stand in the
gate of the Lord's house, and proclaim there this word, and say, Hear
the word of the Lord, all ye of Judah, that enter in at these gates to
worship the Lord. Thus saith the Lord of hosts, the God of Israel,
Amend your ways and your doings, and I will cause you to dwell in
this place.

Trust ye not in lying words, saying, The temple of the Lord, the
temple of the Lord, the temple of the Lord, are these. For if ye thoroughly amend your ways and your doings; if ye thoroughly execute
judgment between a man and his neighbour; if ye oppress not the
stranger, the fatherless, and the widow, and shed not innocent blood in
this place, neither walk after other gods to your hurt; then will I cause
you to dwell in this place, in the land that I gave to your fathers, for
ever and ever.

Behold, ye trust in lying words, that cannot profit. Will ye steal,
murder, and commit adultery, and swear falsely, and burn incense unto
Baal, and walk after other gods whom ye know not?

Seest thou not what they do in the cities of Judah and in the streets of
Jerusalem? The children gather wood, and the fathers kindle the fire,
and the women knead their dough, to make cakes to the queen of heaven,
and to pour out drink-offerings unto other gods, that they may provoke
me to anger. Do they provoke me to anger? saith the Lord: do they not
provoke themselves to the confusion of their own faces?

Therefore thus saith the Lord God; Behold, mine anger and my fury
shall be poured out upon this place, upon man, and upon beast, and
upon the trees of the field, and upon the fruit of the ground; and it
shall burn, and shall not be quenched.

Peace! Peace! and There Is No Peace

At that time, saith the Lord, they shall bring out the bones of the
kings of Judah, and the bones of his princes, and the bones of the priests,

and the bones of the prophets, and the bones of the inhabitants of Jerusalem, out of their graves. And they shall spread them before the sun, and the moon, and all the host of heaven, whom they have loved, and whom they have served, and after whom they have walked, and whom they have sought, and whom they have worshipped: they shall not be gathered, nor be buried; they shall be for dung upon the face of the earth. And death shall be chosen rather than life by all the residue of them that remain of this evil family, which remain in all the places whither I have driven them, saith the Lord of hosts.

Yea, the stork in the heaven knoweth her appointed times; and the turtle, and the crane, and the swallow, observe the time of their coming; but my people know not the judgment of the Lord. For they have healed the hurt of the daughter of my people slightly, saying, Peace, peace; when there is no peace.

Were they ashamed when they had committed abomination? nay, they were not at all ashamed, neither could they blush: therefore shall they fall among them that fall: in the time of their visitation they shall be cast down, saith the Lord.

We looked for peace, but no good came; and for a time of health, and behold, trouble!

The harvest is past, the summer is ended, and we are not saved. For the hurt of the daughter of my people am I hurt; I am black; astonishment hath taken hold on me. Is there no balm in Gilead; is there no physician there? why then is not the health of the daughter of my people recovered?

The Clay and the Potter

The word which came to Jeremiah from the Lord, saying, Arise and go down to the potter's house, and there I will cause thee to hear my words.

Then I went down to the potter's house, and behold, he wrought a work on the wheels. And the vessel that he made of clay was marred in the hand of the potter: so he made it again another vessel, as seemed good to the potter to make it.

Then the word of the Lord came to me, saying, O house of Israel, cannot I do with you as this potter? saith the Lord. Behold, as the clay is in the potter's hand, so are ye in mine hand, O house of Israel. At what instant I shall speak concerning a nation, and concerning a kingdom, to pluck up, and to pull down, and to destroy it, if that nation against whom I have pronounced, turn from their evil, I will repent of the evil that I thought to do unto them.

And at what instant I shall speak concerning a nation, and concerning a kingdom, to build and to plant it, if it do evil in my sight, that it obey not my voice, then I will repent of the good, wherewith I said I would benefit them.

Now therefore go to, speak to the men of Judah, and to the inhabitants of Jerusalem, saying, Thus saith the Lord; Behold, I frame evil against you, and devise a device against you; return ye now every one from his evil way, and make your ways and your doings good.

Pashur Persecutes Jeremiah

Now Pashur the son of Immer the priest, who was also chief governor in the house of the Lord, heard that Jeremiah prophesied these things. Then Pashur smote Jeremiah the prophet, and put him in the stocks that were in the high gate of Benjamin, which was by the house of the Lord.

And it came to pass on the morrow, that Pashur brought forth Jeremiah out of the stocks. Then said Jeremiah unto him, The Lord hath not called thy name Pashur, but Magor-missabib. For thus saith the Lord, Behold, I will make thee a terror to thyself, and to all thy friends: and they shall fall by the sword of their enemies, and thine eyes shall behold it: and I will give all Judah into the hand of the king of Babylon, and he shall carry them captive into Babylon, and shall slay them with the sword.

Moreover I will deliver all the strength of this city, and all the labours thereof, and all the precious things thereof, and all the treasures of the kings of Judah will I give into the hand of their enemies, which shall spoil them, and take them, and carry them to Babylon. And thou, Pashur, and all that dwell in thine house shall go into captivity: and thou shalt come to Babylon, and there thou shalt die, and shalt be buried there, thou, and all thy friends, to whom thou hast prophesied lies.

O Lord, thou hast deceived me, and I was deceived: thou art stronger than I, and hast prevailed: I am in derision daily, every one mocketh me. For since I spake, I cried out, I cried violence and spoil; because the word of the Lord was made a reproach unto me, and a derision, daily. Then I said, I will not make mention of him, nor speak any more in his name. But his word was in my heart as a burning fire shut up in my bones, and I was weary with forbearing, and I could not stay.

Cursed be the day wherein I was born: let not the day wherein my mother bare me be blessed. Cursed be the man who brought tidings to my father, saying, A man-child is born unto thee; making him very glad. And let that man be as the cities which the Lord overthrew, and repented not: and let him hear the cry in the morning, and the shouting at noon-tide, because he slew me not from the womb; or that my mother might have been my grave, and her womb to be always great with me. Wherefore came I forth out of the womb to see labour and sorrow, that my days should be consumed with shame?

Zedekiah Asks for Advice

The word which came unto Jeremiah from the Lord, when king Zedekiah sent unto him Pashur the son of Melchiah, and Zephaniah the son of Maaseiah the priest, saying, Inquire, I pray thee, of the Lord for us; for Nebuchadrezzar king of Babylon maketh war against us; if so be that the Lord will deal with us according to all his wondrous works, that he may go up from us.

Then said Jeremiah unto them, Thus shall ye say to Zedekiah: Thus saith the Lord God of Israel: Behold, I will turn back the weapons of war that are in your hands, wherewith ye fight against the king of Babylon, and against the Chaldeans, which besiege you without the walls, and I will assemble them into the midst of this city. And I myself will fight against you with an out-stretched hand and with a strong arm, even in anger, and in fury, and in great wrath. And I will smite the inhabitants of this city, both man and beast: they shall die of a great pestilence.

And afterward, saith the Lord, I will deliver Zedekiah king of Judah, and his servants, and the people, and such as are left in this city from the pestilence, from the sword, and from the famine, into the hand of Nebuchadrezzar king of Babylon, and into the hand of their enemies, and into the hand of those that seek their life: and he shall smite them with the edge of the sword; he shall not spare them, neither have pity, nor have mercy.

Denunciation of False Pastors

Woe be unto the pastors that destroy and scatter the sheep of my pasture! saith the Lord. Ye have scattered my flock, and driven them away, and have not visited them: behold, I will visit upon you the evil of your doings, saith the Lord.

And I will gather the remnant of my flock out of all countries whither I have driven them, and will bring them again to their folds; and they shall be fruitful and increase. And I will set up shepherds over them, which shall feed them: and they shall fear no more, nor be dismayed, neither shall they be lacking, saith the Lord.

Behold, I am against the prophets, saith the Lord, that use their tongues, and say, He saith. Behold, I am against them that prophesy false dreams, saith the Lord, and do tell them, and cause my people to err by their lies, and by their lightness; yet I sent them not, nor commanded them; therefore they shall not profit this people at all, saith the Lord.

Therefore behold, I, even I, will utterly forget you, and I will forsake you, and the city that I gave you and your fathers, and cast you out of my presence: and I will bring an everlasting reproach upon you, and a perpetual shame, which shall not be forgotten.

Jeremiah Is Taken

In the beginning of the reign of Jehoiakim the son of Josiah, king of Judah, came this word from the Lord, saying: Thus saith the Lord; Stand in the court of the Lord's house, and speak unto all the cities of Judah, which come to worship in the Lord's house, all the words that I command thee to speak unto them; diminish not a word: if so be they will hearken, and turn every man from his evil way, that I may repent me of the evil, which I purpose to do unto them because of the evil of their doings.

So the priests and the prophets and all the people heard Jeremiah speaking these words in the house of the Lord.

Now it came to pass, when Jeremiah had made an end of speaking all that the Lord had commanded him to speak unto all the people, that the priests and the prophets and all the people took him, saying, Thou shalt surely die. Why hast thou prophesied in the name of the Lord, saying, This house shall be like Shiloh, and this city shall be desolate without an inhabitant? And all the people were gathered against Jeremiah in the house of the Lord.

When the princes of Judah heard these things, then they came up from the king's house unto the house of the Lord, and sat down in the entry of the new gate of the Lord's house.

Then spake the priests and the prophets unto the princes and to all the people, saying, This man is worthy to die; for he hath prophesied against this city, as ye have heard with your ears.

Then spake Jeremiah unto all the princes, and to all the people, saying, The Lord sent me to prophesy against this house and against this city all the words that ye have heard. Therefore now amend your ways and your doings, and obey the voice of the Lord your God; and the Lord will repent him of the evil that he hath pronounced against you. As for me, behold, I am in your hand: do with me as seemeth good and meet unto you. But know ye for certain, that if ye put me to death, ye shall surely bring innocent blood upon yourselves, and upon this city, and upon the inhabitants thereof: for of a truth the Lord hath sent me unto you to speak all these words in your ears.

Nevertheless, the hand of Ahikam the son of Shaphan was with Jeremiah, that they should not give him into the hand of the people to put him to death.

The Kings Made Subject to Nebuchadnezzar

In the beginning of the reign of Jehoiakim the son of Josiah king of Judah came this word unto Jeremiah from the Lord, saying, Thus saith the Lord to me: Make thee bonds and yokes, and put them upon thy neck, and send them to the king of Edom, and to the king of Moab, and to the king of the Ammonites, and to the king of Tyrus, and to the king of Zidon, by the hand of the messengers which come to Jerusalem unto Zedekiah king of Judah. And command them to say unto their masters, Thus saith the Lord of hosts, the God of Israel: Thus shall ye say unto your masters: I have made the earth, the man and the beast that are upon the ground, by my great power and by my out-stretched arm, and have given it unto whom it seemed meet unto me. And now have I given all these lands into the hand of Nebuchadnezzar the king of Babylon, my servant; and the beasts of the field have I given him also to serve him. And all nations shall serve him, and his son, and his son's son, until the very time of his land come: and then many nations and great kings shall serve themselves of him.

And it shall come to pass, that the nation and kingdom which will not serve the same Nebuchadnezzar the king of Babylon, and that will not put their neck under the yoke of the king of Babylon, that nation will I punish, saith the Lord, with the sword, and with the famine, and with the pestilence, until I have consumed them by his hand.

Therefore hearken not ye to your prophets, nor to your diviners, nor to your dreamers, nor to your enchanters, nor to your sorcerers, which speak unto you, saying, Ye shall not serve the king of Babylon. For they prophesy a lie unto you, to remove you far from your land; and that I should drive you out, and ye should perish.

But the nations that bring their neck under the yoke of the king of Babylon, and serve him, those will I let remain still in their own land, saith the Lord; and they shall till it, and dwell therein.

I spake also to Zedekiah king of Judah according to all these words, saying, Bring your necks under the yoke of the king of Babylon, and serve him and his people, and live.

Also I spake to the priests and to all this people, saying, Thus saith the Lord; Hearken not to the words of your prophets that prophesy unto you, saying, Behold, the vessels of the Lord's house shall now shortly be brought again from Babylon: for they prophesy a lie unto you. Hearken not unto them; serve the king of Babylon, and live: wherefore should this city be laid waste? But if they be prophets, and if the word of the Lord be with them, let them now make intercession to the Lord of hosts, that the vessels which are left in the house of the Lord, and in the house of the king of Judah, and at Jerusalem, go not to Babylon.

For thus saith the Lord of hosts concerning the pillars, and concerning the sea, and concerning the bases, and concerning the residue of the vessels that remain in this city, which Nebuchadnezzar king of Babylon took not, when he carried away captive Jeconiah the son of Jehoiakim king of Judah from Jerusalem to Babylon, and all the nobles of Judah and Jerusalem: They shall be carried to Babylon, and there shall they be until the day that I visit them, saith the Lord; then will I bring them up, and restore them to this place.

Zedekiah Imprisons Jeremiah

The word that came to Jeremiah from the Lord in the tenth year of Zedekiah king of Judah, which was the eighteenth year of Nebuchadrezzar. For then the king of Babylon's army besieged Jerusalem: and Jeremiah the prophet was shut up in the court of the prison, which was in the king of Judah's house. For Zedekiah king of Judah had shut him up, saying, Wherefore dost thou prophesy, and say, Thus saith the Lord, Behold, I will give this city into the hand of the king of Babylon, and he shall take it?

Then came the word of the Lord unto Jeremiah, saying, Behold, I am the Lord, the God of all flesh: is there any thing too hard for me? Behold, I will give this city into the hand of the Chaldeans, and into the hand of Nebuchadrezzar king of Babylon, and he shall take it. And the Chaldeans, that fight against this city, shall come and set fire on this city, and burn it with the houses, upon whose roofs they have offered incense unto Baal, and poured out drink-offerings unto other gods, to provoke me to anger. For the children of Israel and the children of Judah have only done evil before me from their youth: for the children of Israel have only provoked me to anger with the work of their hands, saith the Lord.

This is the word that came unto Jeremiah from the Lord, after that the king Zedekiah had made a covenant with all the people which were at Jerusalem, to proclaim liberty unto them; that every man should let his man-servant, and every man his maid-servant, being an Hebrew or an Hebrewess, go free; that none should serve himself of them, to wit, of a Jew his brother.

Now when all the princes, and all the people which had entered into the covenant, heard that every one should let his man-servant, and every one his maid-servant, go free, that none should serve themselves of them any more, then they obeyed, and let them go. But afterwards they turned, and caused the servants and the handmaids, whom they had let go free, to return, and brought them into subjection for servants and for hand-maids.

Therefore the word of the Lord came to Jeremiah, from the Lord, saying, I made a covenant with your fathers in the day that I brought them forth out of the land of Egypt, out of the house of bond-men, say-ing, At the end of seven years, let ye go every man his brother an Hebrew, which hath been sold unto thee; and when he hath served thee six years, thou shalt let him go free from thee; but your fathers hearkened not unto me, neither inclined their ear. And ye were now turned, and had done right in my sight, in proclaiming liberty every man to his neighbour; and ye had made a covenant before me in the house which is called by my name. But ye turned and polluted my name, and caused every man his servant, and every man his handmaid, whom he had set at liberty at their pleasure, to return, and brought them into subjection, to be unto you for servants and for handmaids.

Therefore thus saith the Lord: Ye have not hearkened unto me, in proclaiming liberty, every one to his brother, and every man to his neighbour: behold, I proclaim a liberty for you, saith the Lord, to the sword, to the pestilence, and to the famine; and I will make you to be removed into all the kingdoms of the earth.

Baruch Writes Jeremiah's Words

And it came to pass in the fourth year of Jehoiakim the son of Josiah king of Judah, that this word came unto Jeremiah from the Lord, saying, Take thee a roll of a book, and write therein all the words that I have spoken unto thee against Israel, and against Judah, and against all the nations, from the day I spake unto thee, from the days of Josiah, even unto this day. It may be that the house of Judah will hear all the evil which I purpose to do unto them; that they may return every man from his evil way; that I may forgive their iniquity and their sin.

Then Jeremiah called Baruch the son of Neriah: and Baruch wrote from the mouth of Jeremiah all the words of the Lord, which he had spoken unto him, upon a roll of a book.

And Jeremiah commanded Baruch, saying, I am shut up, I cannot go into the house of the Lord. Therefore go thou and read in the roll, which thou hast written from my mouth, the words of the Lord in the ears of the people in the Lord's house upon the fasting day: and also thou shalt read them in the ears of all Judah that come out of their cities. It may be they will present their supplication before the Lord, and will return every one from his evil way: for great is the anger and the fury that the Lord hath pronounced against this people.

And Baruch the son of Neriah did according to all that Jeremiah the prophet commanded him, reading in the book the words of the Lord in the Lord's house.

When Michaiah the son of Gemariah, the son of Shaphan, had heard out of the book all the words of the Lord, then he went down into the king's house, into the scribe's chamber: and lo, all the princes sat there, even Elishama the scribe, and Delaiah the son of Shemaiah, and Elnathan the son of Achbor, and Gemariah the son of Shaphan, and Zedekiah the son of Hananiah, and all the princes. Then Michaiah declared unto them all the words that he had heard, when Baruch read the book in the ears of the people.

Therefore all the princes sent Jehudi the son of Nethaniah, the son of Shelemiah, the son of Cushi, unto Baruch, saying, Take in thine hand the roll wherein thou hast read in the ears of the people, and come. So Baruch the son of Neriah took the roll in his hand, and came unto them.

And they said unto him, Sit down now, and read it in our ears. So Baruch read it in their ears.

Now it came to pass, when they had heard all the words, they were afraid both one and other, and said unto Baruch, We will surely tell the king of all these words.

And they asked Baruch, saying, Tell us now, How didst thou write all these words at his mouth?

Then Baruch answered them, He pronounced all these words unto me with his mouth, and I wrote them with ink in the book.

Then said the princes unto Baruch, Go, hide thee, thou and Jeremiah; and let no man know where ye be.

And they went in to the king into the court, but they laid up the roll in the chamber of Elishama the scribe, and told all the words in the ears of the king. So the king sent Jehudi to fetch the roll: and he took it out of Elishama the scribe's chamber. And Jehudi read it in the ears of the king, and in the ears of all the princes which stood beside the king.

Now the king sat in the winter-house in the ninth month: and there was a fire on the hearth burning before him. And it came to pass, that when Jehudi had read three or four leaves, he cut it with the penknife, and cast it into the fire that was on the hearth, until all the roll was consumed in the fire that was on the hearth.

Yet they were not afraid, nor rent their garments, neither the king, nor any of his servants that heard all these words.

Nevertheless Elnathan and Eliaiah and Gemariah had made intercession to the king that he would not burn the roll: but he would not hear them.

But the king commanded Jerahmeel the son of Hammelech, and Seraiah the son of Azriel, and Shelemiah the son of Abdeel, to take Baruch the scribe and Jeremiah the prophet: but the Lord hid them.

Then the word of the Lord came to Jeremiah, after that the king had burned the roll, and the words which Baruch wrote at the mouth of Jeremiah, saying, Take thee again another roll, and write in it all the former words that were in the first roll, which Jehoiakim the king of Judah hath burned. And thou shalt say to Jehoiakim king of Judah, Thus saith the Lord; Thou hast burned this roll, saying, Why hast thou written therein, saying, The king of Babylon shall certainly come and destroy this land, and shall cause to cease from thence man and beast?

Then took Jeremiah another roll, and gave it to Baruch the scribe, the son of Neriah; who wrote therein from the mouth of Jeremiah all the words of the book which Jehoiakim king of Judah had burned in the fire: and there were added besides unto them many like words.

Jeremiah Is Taken Again

And king Zedekiah the son of Josiah reigned instead of Coniah the son of Jehoiakim, whom Nebuchadrezzar king of Babylon made king in the land of Judah. But neither he, nor his servants, nor the people of the land, did hearken unto the words of the Lord, which he spake by the prophet Jeremiah.

And Zedekiah the king sent Jehucal the son of Shelemiah, and Zephaniah the son of Maaseiah the priest to the prophet Jeremiah, saying, Pray now unto the Lord our God for us. Now Jeremiah came in and went out among the people: for they had not put him into prison.

Then Pharaoh's army was come forth out of Egypt: and when the

Chaldeans that besieged Jerusalem heard tidings of them, they departed from Jerusalem.

Then came the word of the Lord unto the prophet Jeremiah, saying, Thus saith the Lord, the God of Israel; Thus shall ye say to the king of Judah, that sent you unto me to inquire of me; Behold, Pharaoh's army, which is come forth to help you, shall return to Egypt into their own land. And the Chaldeans shall come again, and fight against this city, and take it, and burn it with fire. Thus saith the Lord; Deceive not yourselves, saying, The Chaldeans shall surely depart from us: for they shall not depart. For though ye had smitten the whole army of the Chaldeans that fight against you, and there remained but wounded men among them, yet should they rise up every man in his tent, and burn this city with fire.

And it came to pass, that when the army of the Chaldeans was broken up from Jerusalem for fear of Pharaoh's army, then Jeremiah went forth out of Jerusalem to go into the land of Benjamin, to separate himself thence in the midst of the people. And when he was in the gate of Benjamin, a captain of the ward was there, whose name was Irijah, the son of Shelemiah, the son of Hananiah; and he took Jeremiah the prophet, saying, Thou fallest away to the Chaldeans. Then said Jeremiah, It is false; I fall not away to the Chaldeans. But he hearkened not to him: so Irijah took Jeremiah, and brought him to the princes.

Wherefore the princes were wroth with Jeremiah, and smote him, and put him in prison in the house of Jonathan the scribe: for they had made that the prison.

When Jeremiah was entered into the dungeon, and into the cabins, and Jeremiah had remained there many days, then Zedekiah the king sent, and took him out: and the king asked him secretly in his house, and said, Is there any word from the Lord? And Jeremiah said, There is: for, said he, thou shalt be delivered into the hand of the king of Babylon.

Moreover, Jeremiah said unto king Zedekiah, What have I offended against thee, or against thy servants, or against this people, that ye have put me in prison? Where are now your prophets which prophesied unto you, saying, The king of Babylon shall not come against you, nor against this land? Therefore hear now, I pray thee, O my lord the king: let my supplication, I pray thee, be accepted before thee; that thou cause me not to return to the house of Jonathan the scribe, lest I die there.

Then Zedekiah the king commanded that they should commit Jeremiah into the court of the prison, and that they should give him daily a piece of bread out of the bakers' street, until all the bread in the city were spent. Thus Jeremiah remained in the court of the prison.

Then Shephatiah the son of Mattan, and Gedaliah the son of Pashur the son of Malchiah, heard the words that Jeremiah had spoken unto all the people, saying, Thus saith the Lord, He that remaineth in this city shall die by the sword, by the famine, and by the pestilence: but he that goeth forth to the Chaldeans shall live; for he shall have his life for a prey, and shall live. Thus saith the Lord, This city shall surely be given into the hand of the king of Babylon's army, which shall take it.

Therefore the princes said unto the king, We beseech thee, let this man be put to death; for thus he weakeneth the hands of the men of war that remain in this city, and the hands of all the people, in speaking such words unto them: for this man seeketh not the welfare of this people, but the hurt.

Then Zedekiah the king said, Behold, he is in your hand: for the king is not he that can do any thing against you.

Then took they Jeremiah, and cast him into the dungeon of Malchiah the son of Hammelech, that was in the court of the prison: and they let down Jeremiah with cords. And in the dungeon there was no water, but mire: so Jeremiah sunk in the mire.

Now when Ebed-melech the Ethiopian, one of the eunuchs which was in the king's house, heard that they had put Jeremiah in the dungeon; the king then sitting in the gate of Benjamin, Ebed-melech went forth out of the king's house, and spake to the king, saying, My lord the king, these men have done evil in all that they have done to Jeremiah the prophet, whom they have cast into the dungeon; and he is like to die for hunger in the place where he is: for there is no more bread in the city.

Then the king commanded Ebed-melech the Ethiopian, saying, Take from hence thirty men with thee, and take up Jeremiah the prophet out of the dungeon, before he die.

So Ebed-melech took the men with him, and went into the house of the king under the treasury, and took thence old cast clouts and old rotten rags, and let them down by cords into the dungeon to Jeremiah. And Ebed-melech the Ethiopian said unto Jeremiah, Put now these old cast clouts and rotten rags under thine arm-holes under the cords. And Jeremiah did so.

So they drew up Jeremiah with cords, and took him up out of the dungeon: and Jeremiah remained in the court of the prison.

Then Zedekiah the king sent, and took Jeremiah the prophet unto him into the third entry that is in the house of the Lord: and the king said unto Jeremiah, I will ask thee a thing; hide nothing from me.

Then Jeremiah said unto Zedekiah, If I declare it unto thee, wilt thou not surely put me to death? and if I give thee counsel, wilt thou not hearken unto me?

So Zedekiah the king sware secretly unto Jeremiah, saying, As the Lord liveth, that made us this soul, I will not put thee to death, neither will I give thee into the hand of these men that seek thy life.

Then said Jeremiah unto Zedekiah, Thus saith the Lord, the God of hosts, the God of Israel; If thou wilt assuredly go forth unto the king of Babylon's princes, then thy soul shall live, and this city shall not be burnt with fire; and thou shalt live, and thine house; but if thou wilt not go forth to the king of Babylon's princes, then shall this city be given into the hand of the Chaldeans, and they shall burn it with fire, and thou shalt not escape out of their hand.

And Zedekiah the king said unto Jeremiah, I am afraid of the Jews that are fallen to the Chaldeans, lest they deliver me into their hand, and they mock me.

But Jeremiah said, They shall not deliver thee. Obey, I beseech thee, the voice of the Lord, which I speak unto thee: so it shall be well unto thee, and thy soul shall live. But if thou refuse to go forth, this is the word that the Lord hath shewed me: and behold, all the women that are left in the king of Judah's house shall be brought forth to the king of Babylon's princes, and those women shall say, Thy friends have set thee on, and have prevailed against thee: thy feet are sunk in the mire, and they are turned away back. So they shall bring out all thy wives and thy children to the Chaldeans: and thou shalt not escape out of their hand, but shalt be taken by the hand of the king of Babylon: and thou shalt cause this city to be burned with fire.

Then said Zedekiah unto Jeremiah, Let no man know of these words, and thou shalt not die. But if the princes hear that I have talked with thee, and they come unto thee, and say unto thee, Declare unto us now what thou hast said unto the king, hide it not from us, and we will not put thee to death; also what the king said unto thee: then thou shalt say unto them, I presented my supplication before the king, that he would not cause me to return to Jonathan's house to die there.

Then came all the princes unto Jeremiah, and asked him: and he told them according to all these words that the king had commanded. So they left off speaking with him; for the matter was not perceived.

So Jeremiah abode in the court of the prison until the day that Jerusalem was taken: and he was there when Jerusalem was taken.

The Fall of Jerusalem

In the ninth year of Zedekiah king of Judah, in the tenth month, came Nebuchadrezzar king of Babylon and all his army against Jerusalem, and they besieged it. And in the eleventh year of Zedekiah, in the fourth month, the ninth day of the month, the city was broken up. And all the princes of the king of Babylon came in, and sat in the middle gate, even Nergal-sharezer, Samgar-nebo, Sarse-chim, Rab-saris, Nergal-sharezer, Rab-mag, with all the residue of the princes of the king of Babylon.

And it came to pass, that when Zedekiah the king of Judah saw them, and all the men of war, then they fled, and went forth out of the city by night, by the way of the king's garden, by the gate betwixt the two walls: and he went out the way of the plain. But the Chaldeans' army pursued after them, and overtook Zedekiah in the plains of Jericho: and when they had taken him, they brought him up to Nebuchadnezzar king of Babylon to Riblah in the land of Hamath, where he gave judgment upon him. Then the king of Babylon slew the sons of Zedekiah in Riblah before his eyes: also the king of Babylon slew all the nobles of Judah. Moreover he put out Zedekiah's eyes, and bound him with chains, to carry him to Babylon.

And the Chaldeans burned the king's house, and the houses of the people, with fire, and brake down the walls of Jerusalem. Then Nebuzar-adan the captain of the guard carried away captive into Babylon the remnant of the people that remained in the city, and those that fell away, that fell to him, with the rest of the people that remained. But Nebuzar-adan the captain of the guard left of the poor of the people, which had nothing, in the land of Judah, and gave them vineyards and fields at the same time.

Now Nebuchadrezzar king of Babylon gave charge concerning Jere‑ miah to Nebuzar-adan the captain of the guard, saying, Take him, and look well to him, and do him no harm; but do unto him even as he shall say unto thee.

So Nebuzar-adan the captain of the guard sent, and Nebushasban, Rab-saris, and Nergal-sharezer, Rab-mag, and all the king of Babylon's princes, even they sent, and took Jeremiah out of the court of the prison, and committed him unto Gedaliah the son of Ahikam the son of Shaphan, that he should carry him home: so he dwelt among the people.

The Book of the Prophet Ezekiel

Ezekiel's Vision

Now it came to pass in the thirtieth year, in the fourth month, in the fifth day of the month, as I was among the captives by the river of Chebar, that the heavens were opened, and I saw visions of God. The word of the Lord came expressly unto Ezekiel the priest, the son of Buzi, in the land of the Chaldeans by the river Chebar; and the hand of the Lord was there upon him.

And I looked, and behold, a whirlwind came out of the north, a great cloud, and a fire infolding itself, and a brightness was about it, and out of the midst thereof as the colour of amber, out of the midst of the fire. Also out of the midst thereof came the likeness of four living creatures.

And this was their appearance; they had the likeness of a man. And every one had four faces, and every one had four wings. And their feet were straight feet; and the sole of their feet was like the sole of a calf's foot; and they sparkled like the colour of burnished brass. And they had the hands of a man under their wings on their four sides; and they four had their faces and their wings. Their wings were joined one to another; they turned not when they went; they went every one straight forward.

As for the likeness of their faces, they four had the face of a man and the face of a lion, on the right side: and they four had the face of an ox on the left side; they four also had the face of an eagle. Thus were their faces: and their wings were stretched upward; two wings of every one were joined one to another, and two covered their bodies. And they went every one straight forward; whither the spirit was to go, they went; and they turned not when they went.

As for the likeness of the living creatures, their appearance was like burning coals of fire, and like the appearance of lamps: it went up and down among the living creatures; and the fire was bright, and out of the fire went forth lightning. And the living creatures ran and returned as the appearance of a flash of lightning.

Now as I beheld the living creatures, behold one wheel upon the earth by the living creatures, with his four faces. The appearance of the wheels and their work was like unto the colour of a beryl: and they four had one likeness: and their appearance and their work was as it were a wheel in the middle of a wheel. When they went, they went upon their four sides: and they turned not when they went. As for their rings, they were so high that they were dreadful; and their rings were full of eyes round about them four.

And when the living creatures went, the wheel went by them: and when the living creatures were lifted up from the earth, the wheels were lifted up. Whithersoever the spirit was to go, they went, thither was their spirit to go; and the wheels were lifted up over against them: for the spirit of the living creature was in the wheels. When those went, these went; and when those stood, these stood; and when those were lifted up from the earth, the wheels were lifted up over against them: for the spirit of the living creature was in the wheels.

And the likeness of the firmament upon the heads of the living creature was as the colour of the terrible crystal, stretched forth over their heads above. And under the firmament were their wings straight, the one toward the other: every one had two, which covered on this side, and every one had two, which covered on that side, their bodies.

And when they went, I heard the noise of their wings, like the noise of great waters, as the voice of the Almighty, the voice of speech, as the noise of an host: when they stood, they let down their wings. And there was a voice from the firmament that was over their heads, when they stood, and had let down their wings.

And above the firmament that was over their heads was the likeness of a throne, as the appearance of a sapphire stone: and upon the likeness of the throne was the likeness as the appearance of a man above upon it. And I saw as the colour of amber, as the appearance of fire round about within it, from the appearance of his loins even upward, and from the appearance of his loins even downward, I saw as it were the appearance of fire, and it had brightness round about.

As the appearance of the bow that is in the cloud in the day of rain, so was the appearance of the brightness round about. This was the appearance of the likeness of the glory of the Lord. And when I saw it, I fell upon my face, and I heard a voice of one that spake.

And he said unto me, Son of man, stand upon thy feet, and I will speak unto thee. And the spirit entered into me when he spake unto me, and set me upon my feet, that I heard him that spake unto me.

And he said unto me, Son of man, I send thee to the children of Israel, to a rebellious nation that hath rebelled against me: they and their fathers have transgressed against me, even unto this very day. For they are impudent children and stiff-hearted. I do send thee unto them; and thou shalt say unto them, Thus saith the Lord God.

And when I looked, behold, an hand was sent unto me; and lo, a roll of a book was therein; and he spread it before me: and it was written within and without: and there was written therein lamentations, and mourning, and woe.

Moreover he said unto me, Son of man, eat that thou findest; eat this roll, and go speak unto the house of Israel. So I opened my mouth, and he caused me to eat that roll. And it was in my mouth as honey for sweetness.

Then the spirit took me up, and I heard behind me a voice of a great rushing, saying, Blessed be the glory of the Lord from his place. I heard also the noise of the wings of the living creatures that touched one another, and the noise of the wheels over against them, and a noise of a great rushing. So the spirit lifted me up, and took me away, and I went in bitterness, in the heat of my spirit; but the hand of the Lord was strong upon me.

Exhortation to the Faithful

And the word of the Lord came unto me, saying, Son of man, set thy face toward the mountains of Israel, and prophesy against them, and say, Ye mountains of Israel, hear the word of the Lord God: Thus saith the Lord God to the mountains, and to the hills, to the rivers, and to the valleys; Behold, I, even I, will bring a sword upon you, and I will destroy your high places. And your altars shall be desolate, and your images shall be broken: and I will cast down your slain men before your idols. And I will lay the dead carcasses of the children of Israel before their idols; and I will scatter your bones round about your altars.

Yet will I leave a remnant, that ye may have some that shall escape the sword among the nations, when ye shall be scattered through the countries. And they that escape of you shall remember me among the nations whither they shall be carried captives, because I am broken with their whorish heart, which hath departed from me, and with their eyes which go a-whoring after their idols: and they shall loathe themselves for the evils which they have committed in all their abominations. And they shall know that I am the Lord, and that I have not said in vain that I would do this evil unto them.

Warning to the Sun-Worshippers

And it came to pass in the sixth year, in the sixth month, in the fifth day of the month, as I sat in mine house, and the elders of Judah sat before me, that the hand of the Lord God fell there upon me. Then I beheld, and lo a likeness as the appearance of fire: from the appearance of his loins even downward, fire; and from his loins even upward, as the appearance of brightness, as the colour of amber. And he put forth the form of an hand, and took me by a lock of mine head; and the spirit lifted me up between the earth and the heaven, and brought me in the visions of God to Jerusalem, to the door of the inner gate that looketh toward the north; where was the seat of the image of jealousy, which provoketh to jealousy. And, behold, the glory of the God of Israel was there, according to the vision that I saw in the plain.

And he brought me into the inner court of the Lord's house, and behold, at the door of the temple of the Lord, between the porch and the altar, were about five and twenty men, with their backs toward the temple of the Lord, and their faces toward the east; and they worshipped the sun toward the east.

Then he said unto me, Hast thou seen this, O son of man? Is it a light thing to the house of Judah that they commit the abominations which they commit here? for they have filled the land with violence, and have returned to provoke me to anger: and lo, they put the branch to their nose. Therefore will I also deal in fury: mine eye shall not spare, neither will I have pity: and though they cry in mine ears with a loud voice, yet will I not hear them.

God's Way toward the Penitent

Again the word of the Lord came unto me, saying, Son of man, speak to the children of thy people, and say unto them, When I bring the sword upon a land, if the people of the land take a man of their coasts, and set him for their watchman: if when he seeth the sword come upon the land, he blow the trumpet, and warn the people, then whosoever heareth the sound of the trumpet, and taketh not warning, if the sword come and take him away, his blood shall be upon his own head. He heard the sound of the trumpet, and took not warning; his blood shall be upon him.

But he that taketh warning shall deliver his soul.

But if the watchman see the sword come, and blow not the trumpet, and the people be not warned; if the sword come, and take any person from among them, he is taken away in his iniquity; but his blood will I require at the watchman's hand.

So thou, O son of man, I have set thee a watchman unto the house of Israel; therefore thou shalt hear the word at my mouth, and warn them from me.

Therefore, O thou son of man, speak unto the house of Israel; thus ye speak, saying, If our transgressions and our sins be upon us, and we pine away in them, how should we then live?

Say unto them, As I live, saith the Lord God, I have no pleasure in the death of the wicked; but that the wicked turn from his way and live:

turn ye, turn ye from your evil ways; for why will ye die, O house of Israel?

Therefore, thou son of man, say unto the children of thy people, The righteousness of the righteous shall not deliver him in the day of his transgression: as for the wickedness of the wicked, he shall not fall thereby in the day that he turneth from his wickedness: neither shall the righteous be able to live for his righteousness in the day that he sinneth.

When I shall say to the righteous, that he shall surely live; if he trust to his own righteousness, and commit iniquity, all his righteousness shall not be remembered; but for his iniquity that he hath committed, he shall die for it. Again, when I say unto the wicked, Thou shalt surely die; if he turn from his sin, and do that which is lawful and right; if the wicked restore the pledge, give again that he had robbed, walk in the statutes of life, without committing iniquity; he shall surely live, he shall not die. None of his sins that he hath committed shall be mentioned unto him: he hath done that which is lawful and right; he shall surely live.

Yet the children of thy people say, The way of the Lord is not equal: but as for them, their way is not equal.

When the righteous turneth from his righteousness, and committeth iniquity, he shall even die thereby. But if the wicked turn from his wickedness, and do that which is lawful and right, he shall live thereby.

Yet ye say, The way of the Lord is not equal. O ye house of Israel, I will judge you every one after his ways.

God's Promise

And the word of the Lord came unto me, saying, Son of man, prophesy against the shepherds of Israel, prophesy, and say unto them, Thus saith the Lord God unto the shepherds; Woe be to the shepherds of Israel that do feed themselves! should not the shepherds feed the flocks? Ye eat the fat, and ye clothe you with the wool, ye kill them that are fed: but ye feed not the flock.

The diseased have ye not strengthened, neither have ye healed that which was sick, neither have ye bound up that which was broken, neither have ye brought again that which was driven away, neither have ye sought that which was lost; but with force and with cruelty have ye ruled them. And they were scattered, because there is no shepherd: and they became meat to all the beasts of the field, when they were scattered.

My sheep wandered through all the mountains, and upon every high hill: yea, my flock was scattered upon all the face of the earth, and none did search or seek after them.

Therefore, ye shepherds, hear the word of the Lord; As I live, saith the Lord God, surely because my flock became a prey, and my flock became meat to every beast of the field, because there was no shepherd, neither did my shepherds search for my flock, but the shepherds fed themselves, and fed not my flock; therefore, O ye shepherds, hear the word of the Lord: Behold, I am against the shepherds; and I will require my flock at their hand, and cause them to cease from feeding the flock; neither shall the shepherds feed themselves any more; for I will deliver my flock from their mouth, that they may not be meat for them.

For thus saith the Lord God; Behold, I, even I, will both search my sheep, and seek them out. As a shepherd seeketh out his flock in the day that he is among his sheep that are scattered; so will I seek out my sheep, and will deliver them out of all places where they have been scattered in the cloudy and dark day.

And I will bring them out from the people, and gather them from the countries, and will bring them to their own land, and feed them upon the mountains of Israel by the rivers, and in all the inhabited places of the country. I will feed them in a good pasture, and upon the high mountains of Israel shall their fold be: there shall they lie in a good fold, and in a fat pasture shall they feed upon the mountains of Israel. I will feed my flock, and I will cause them to lie down, saith the Lord God.

I will seek that which was lost, and bring again that which was driven away, and will bind up that which was broken, and will strengthen that which was sick: but I will destroy the fat and the strong; I will feed them with judgment.

And I will set up one Shepherd over them, and he shall feed them, even my servant David; he shall feed them, and he shall be their shepherd. And I the Lord will be their God, and my servant David a prince among them; I the Lord have spoken it.

And I will make with them a covenant of peace, and will cause the evil beasts to cease out of the land: and they shall dwell safely in the wilderness, and sleep in the woods. And I will make them and the places round about my hill a blessing; and I will cause the shower to come down in his season; there shall be showers of blessing. And the tree of the field shall yield her fruit, and the earth shall yield her increase, and they shall be safe in their land, and shall know that I am the Lord, when I have broken the bands of their yoke, and delivered them out of the hand of those that served themselves of them. And they shall no more be a prey to the heathen, neither shall the beasts of the land devour them; but they shall dwell safely, and none shall make them afraid.

The Valley of Dry Bones

The hand of the Lord was upon me, and carried me out in the Spirit of the Lord, and set me down in the midst of the valley which was full of bones, and caused me to pass by them round about: and behold, there were very many in the open valley; and lo, they were very dry.

And he said unto me, Son of man, can these bones live? and I answered, O Lord God, thou knowest.

Again he said unto me, Prophesy upon these bones, and say unto them, O ye dry bones, hear the word of the Lord. Thus saith the Lord God unto these bones; Behold, I will cause breath to enter into you, and ye shall live: and I will lay sinews upon you, and will bring up flesh upon you, and cover you with skin, and put breath in you, and ye shall live; and ye shall know that I am the Lord.

So I prophesied as I was commanded: and as I prophesied, there was a noise, and behold a shaking, and the bones came together, bone to his bone. And when I beheld, lo, the sinews and the flesh came up upon them, and the skin covered them above: but there was no breath in them.

Then said he unto me, Prophesy unto the wind, prophesy, son of man, and say to the wind, Thus saith the Lord God: Come from the four winds, O breath, and breathe upon these slain, that they may live.

So I prophesied as he commanded me, and the breath came into them, and they lived, and stood up upon their feet, an exceeding great army.

Then he said unto me, Son of man, these bones are the whole house of Israel: behold, they say, Our bones are dried, and our hope is lost; we are cut off for our parts. Therefore prophesy and say unto them, Thus saith the Lord God: Behold, O my people, I will open your graves, and cause you to come up out of your graves, and bring you into the land of

Israel. And ye shall know that I am the Lord, when I have opened your graves, O my people, and brought you up out of your graves, and shall put my Spirit in you, and ye shall live, and I shall place you in your own land: then shall ye know that I the Lord have spoken it, and performed it, saith the Lord.

The word of the Lord came again unto me, saying, Moreover, thou son of man, take thee one stick, and write upon it, For Judah and for the children of Israel his companions: then take another stick, and write upon it, For Joseph, the stick of Ephraim, and for all the house of Israel his companions: and join them one to another into one stick; and they shall become one in thine hand.

And when the children of thy people shall speak unto thee, saying, Wilt thou not shew us what thou meanest by these? say unto them, Thus saith the Lord God; Behold, I will take the stick of Joseph, which is in the hand of Ephraim, and the tribes of Israel his fellows, and will put them with him, even with the stick of Judah, and make them one stick, and they shall be one in mine hand. And the sticks whereon thou writest shall be in thine hand before their eyes.

And say unto them, Thus saith the Lord God; Behold, I will take the children of Israel from among the heathen, whither they be gone, and will gather them on every side, and bring them into their own land: and I will make them one nation in the land upon the mountains of Israel; and one king shall be king to them all: and they shall be no more two nations, neither shall they be divided into two kingdoms any more at all: neither shall they defile themselves any more with their idols, nor with their detestable things, nor with any of their transgressions: but I will save them out of all their dwelling-places, wherein they have sinned, and will cleanse them: so shall they be my people, and I will be their God.

And David my servant shall be king over them; and they all shall have one shepherd: they shall also walk in my judgments, and observe my statutes, and do them. And they shall dwell in the land that I have given unto Jacob my servant, wherein your fathers have dwelt, and they shall dwell therein, even they, and their children, and their children's children for ever: and my servant David shall be their prince for ever.

Moreover I will make a covenant of peace with them; it shall be an everlasting covenant with them: and I will place them, and multiply them, and will set my sanctuary in the midst of them for evermore. My tabernacle also shall be with them: yea, I will be their God, and they shall be my people.

And the heathen shall know that I the Lord do sanctify Israel, when my sanctuary shall be in the midst of them for evermore.

The Book of the Second Isaiah

A Voice in the Wilderness

Comfort ye, comfort ye my people, saith your God. Speak ye comfortably to Jerusalem, and cry unto her, that her warfare is accomplished, that her iniquity is pardoned: for she hath received of the Lord's hand double for all her sins.

The voice of him that crieth in the wilderness, Prepare ye the way of the Lord, make straight in the desert a highway for our God. Every valley shall be exalted, and every mountain and hill shall be made low: and the crooked shall be made straight, and the rough places plain. And the glory of the Lord shall be revealed, and all flesh shall see it together: for the mouth of the Lord hath spoken it.

The voice said, Cry.

And he said, What shall I cry? All flesh is grass, and all the goodliness thereof is as the flower of the field. The grass withereth, the flower fadeth: because the spirit of the Lord bloweth upon it: surely the people is grass. The grass withereth, the flower fadeth: but the word of our God shall stand for ever.

O Zion, that bringest good tidings, get thee up into the high mountain. O Jerusalem, that bringest good tidings, lift up thy voice with strength; lift it up, be not afraid; say unto the cities of Judah, Behold your God! Behold the Lord God will come with strong hand, and his arm shall rule for him: behold, his reward is with him, and his work before him. He shall feed his flock like a shepherd: he shall gather the lambs with his arm, and carry them in his bosom, and shall gently lead those that are with young.

Who hath measured the waters in the hollow of his hand, and meted out heaven with the span, and comprehended the dust of the earth in a measure, and weighed the mountains in scales, and the hills in a balance? Who hath directed the Spirit of the Lord, or being his counsellor hath taught him? With whom took he counsel, and who instructed him, and taught him in the path of judgment, and taught him knowledge, and shewed to him the way of understanding?

Behold, the nations are as a drop of a bucket, and are counted as the small dust of the balance: behold, he taketh up the isles as a very little thing. And Lebanon is not sufficient to burn, nor the beasts thereof sufficient for a burnt-offering. All nations before him are as nothing; and they are counted to him less than nothing, and vanity.

To whom then will ye liken God? or what likeness will ye compare unto him?

The workman melteth a graven image, and the goldsmith spreadeth it over with gold, and casteth silver chains. He that is so impoverished that he hath no oblation chooseth a tree that will not rot; he seeketh unto him a cunning workman to prepare a graven image that shall not be moved.

Have ye not known? have ye not heard? hath it not been told you from the beginning? have ye not understood from the foundations of the earth?

It is he that sitteth upon the circle of the earth, and the inhabitants thereof are as grasshoppers; that stretcheth out the heavens as a curtain, and spreadeth them out as a tent to dwell in; that bringeth the princes to nothing; he maketh the judges of the earth as vanity.

Yea, they shall not be planted: yea, they shall not be sown: yea, their stock shall not take root in the earth: and he shall also blow upon them, and they shall wither, and the whirlwind shall take them away as stubble.

To whom then will ye liken me, or shall I be equal? saith the Holy One.

Lift up your eyes on high, and behold who hath created these things, that bringeth out their host by number: he calleth them all by names, by the greatness of his might, for that he is strong in power; not one faileth.

Why sayest thou, O Jacob, and speakest, O Israel, My way is hid from the Lord, and my judgment is passed over from my God?

Hast thou not known, hast thou not heard, that the everlasting God, the Lord, the Creator of the ends of the earth, fainteth not, neither is weary? there is no searching of his understanding. He giveth power to the faint; and to them that have no might he increaseth strength. Even the youths shall faint and be weary, and the young men shall utterly fall. But they that wait upon the Lord shall renew their strength; they shall mount up with wings as eagles; they shall run, and not be weary; and they shall walk, and not faint.

Keep silence before me, O islands; and let the people renew their strength: let them come near; then let them speak: let us come near together to judgment.

Who raised up the righteous man from the east, called him to his foot, gave the nations before him, and made him rule over kings? he gave them as the dust to his sword, and as driven stubble to his bow. He pursued them, and passed safely; even by the way that he had not gone with his feet.

Who hath wrought and done it, calling the generations from the beginning? I the Lord, the first, and with the last; I am he.

The isles saw it, and feared; the ends of the earth were afraid, drew near, and came. They helped every one his neighbour; and every one said to his brother, Be of good courage. So the carpenter encouraged the goldsmith, and he that smootheth with the hammer him that smote the anvil, saying, It is ready for the sodering; and he fastened it with nails, that it should not be moved.

But thou, Israel, art my servant, Jacob whom I have chosen, the seed of Abraham my friend. Thou whom I have taken from the ends of the earth, and called thee from the chief men thereof, and said unto thee, Thou art my servant; I have chosen thee, and not cast thee away.

Fear thou not; for I am with thee: be not dismayed; for I am thy God: I will strengthen thee; yea, I will help thee; yea, I will uphold thee with the right hand of my righteousness.

The Omnipotence of God

Thus saith the Lord to his anointed, to Cyrus, whose right hand I have holden, to subdue nations before him; and I will loose the loins of kings, to open before him the two-leaved gates, and the gates shall not be shut. I will go before thee, and make the crooked places straight: I will break in pieces the gates of brass, and cut in sunder the bars of iron. And I will give thee the treasures of darkness, and hidden riches of secret places, that thou mayest know that I, the Lord, which call thee by thy name, am the God of Israel. For Jacob my servant's sake, and Israel mine elect, I have even called thee by thy name: I have surnamed thee, though thou hast not known me.

I am the Lord, and there is none else, there is no God besides me: I girded thee, though hast not known me, that they may know from the rising of the sun, and from the west, that there is none besides me. I am the Lord, and there is none else. I form the light, and create darkness; I make peace, and create evil; I the Lord do all these things. Drop down, ye heavens, from above, and let the skies pour down righteousness: let the earth open, and let them bring forth salvation, and let righteousness spring up together; I the Lord have created it.

Woe unto him that striveth with his Maker! Let the potsherd strive with the potsherds of the earth. Shall the clay say to him that fashioneth it, What makest thou? or thy work, He hath no hands?

Woe unto him that saith unto his father, What begettest thou? or to the woman, What hast thou brought forth?

Thus saith the Lord, the Holy One of Israel, and his Maker, Ask me of things to come concerning my sons, and concerning the work of my hands command ye me. I have made the earth, and created man upon it: I, even my hands, have stretched out the heavens, and all their host have I commanded. I have raised him up in righteousness, and I will direct all his ways: he shall build my city, and he shall let go my captives, not for price nor reward, saith the Lord of hosts.

Awake, O Zion!

Awake, awake, put on thy strength, O Zion; put on thy beautiful garments, O Jerusalem, the holy city: for henceforth there shall no more come into thee the uncircumcised and the unclean. Shake thyself from the dust; arise, and sit down, O Jerusalem: loose thyself from the bands of thy neck, O captive daughter of Zion.

How beautiful upon the mountains are the feet of him that bringeth good tidings, that publisheth peace; that bringeth good tidings of good, that publisheth salvation; that saith unto Zion, Thy God reigneth! Thy watchmen shall lift up the voice; with the voice together shall they sing: for they shall see eye to eye, when the Lord shall bring again Zion.

Break forth into joy, sing together, ye waste places of Jerusalem: for the Lord hath comforted his people, he hath redeemed Jerusalem. The Lord hath made bare his holy arm in the eyes of all the nations: and all the ends of the earth shall see the salvation of our God.

Depart ye, depart ye, go ye out from thence, touch no unclean thing; go ye out of the midst of her; be ye clean, that bear the vessels of the Lord. For ye shall not go out with haste, nor go by flight: for the Lord will go before you; and the God of Israel will be your rere-ward.

A Promise of Joy and Peace

Ho, every one that thirsteth, come ye to the waters, and he that hath no money; come ye, buy, and eat; yea, come, buy wine and milk without money and without price.

Wherefore do ye spend money for that which is not bread? and your labour for that which satisfieth not? hearken diligently unto me, and eat ye that which is good, and let your soul delight itself in fatness.

Incline your ear, and come unto me; hear, and your soul shall live; and I will make an everlasting covenant with you, even the sure mercies of David. Behold, I have given him for a witness to the people, a leader and commander to the people. Behold, thou shalt call a nation that thou knowest not, and nations that knew not thee shall run unto thee, because of the Lord thy God, and for the Holy One of Israel; for he hath glorified thee.

Seek ye the Lord while he may be found, call ye upon him while he is near. Let the wicked forsake his way, and the unrighteous man his thoughts: and let him return unto the Lord, and he will have mercy upon him; and to our God, for he will abundantly pardon.

For my thoughts are not your thoughts, neither are your ways my ways, saith the Lord. For as the heavens are higher than the earth, so are my ways higher than your ways, and my thoughts than your thoughts.

For as the rain cometh down, and the snow from heaven, and returneth not thither, but watereth the earth, and maketh it bring forth and bud, that it may give seed to the sower, and bread to the eater, so shall my word be that goeth forth out of my mouth: it shall not return unto me void, but it shall accomplish that which I please, and it shall prosper in the thing whereto I sent it.

For ye shall go out with joy, and be led forth with peace: the mountains and the hills shall break forth before you into singing, and all the trees of the field shall clap their hands. Instead of the thorn shall come up the fir-tree, and instead of the brier shall come up the myrtle-tree: and it shall be to the Lord for a name, for an everlasting sign that shall not be cut off.

Arise, shine; for thy light is come, and the glory of the Lord is risen upon thee. For behold, the darkness shall cover the earth, and gross darkness the people: but the Lord shall arise upon thee, and his glory shall be seen upon thee. And the Gentiles shall come to thy light, and kings to the brightness of thy rising.

Lift up thine eyes round about, and see: all they gather themselves together, they come to thee: thy sons shall come from far, and thy daughters shall be nursed at thy side. Then thou shalt see, and flow together, and thine heart shall fear, and be enlarged, because the abundance of the sea shall be converted unto thee, the forces of the Gentiles shall come unto thee.

The multitude of camels shall cover thee, the dromedaries of Midian and Ephah; all they from Sheba shall come: they shall bring gold and incense; and they shall shew forth the praises of the Lord. All the flocks of Kedar shall be gathered together unto thee, the rams of Nebaioth shall minister unto thee: they shall come up with acceptance on mine altar, and I will glorify the house of my glory.

Who are these that fly as a cloud, and as the doves to their windows? Surely the isles shall wait for me, and the ships of Tarshish first, to bring thy sons from far, their silver and their gold with them, unto the name of the Lord thy God, and to the Holy One of Israel, because he hath glorified thee.

And the sons of strangers shall build up thy walls, and their kings shall minister unto thee: for in my wrath I smote thee, but in my favour have I had mercy on thee. Therefore thy gates shall be open continually; they shall not be shut day nor night; that men may bring unto thee the forces of the Gentiles, and that their kings may be brought.

For the nation and kingdom that will not serve thee shall perish; yea, those nations shall be utterly wasted.

The glory of Lebanon shall come unto thee, the fir-tree, the pine-tree, and the box together, to beautify the place of my sanctuary; and I will make the place of my feet glorious. The sons also of them that afflicted thee shall come bending unto thee; and all they that despised thee shall bow themselves down at the soles of thy feet; and they shall call thee, The city of the Lord, The Zion of the Holy One of Israel.

Whereas thou hast been forsaken and hated, so that no man went through thee, I will make thee an eternal excellency, a joy of many generations. Thou shalt also suck the milk of the Gentiles, and shalt suck the breast of kings: and thou shalt know that I the Lord am thy Saviour and thy Redeemer, the mighty One of Jacob.

For brass I will bring gold, and for iron I will bring silver, and for wood brass, and for stones iron: I will also make thy officers peace, and thine exactors righteousness. Violence shall no more be heard in thy land, wasting nor destruction within thy borders; but thou shalt call thy walls Salvation, and thy gates Praise.

The sun shall be no more thy light by day: neither for brightness shall the moon give light unto thee: but the Lord shall be unto thee an ever-lasting light, and thy God thy glory. Thy sun shall no more go down; neither shall thy moon withdraw itself; for the Lord shall be thine everlasting light, and the days of thy mourning shall be ended.

Thy people also shall be all righteous: they shall inherit the land for ever, the branch of my planting, the work of my hands, that I may be glorified. A little one shall become a thousand, and a small one a strong nation: I the Lord will hasten it in his time.

Three Prophecies of Restoration

Haggai

In the seventh month, in the one and twentieth day of the month, came the word of the Lord by the prophet Haggai, saying, Speak now to Zerubbabel the son of Shealtiel, governor of Judah, and to Joshua the son of Josedech the high priest, and to the residue of the people, saying, Who is left among you that saw this house in her first glory? and how do ye see it now? is it not in your eyes in comparison of it as nothing? Yet now be strong, O Zerubbabel, saith the Lord; and be strong, O Joshua, son of Josedech the high priest; and be strong, all ye people of the land, saith the Lord, and work: for I am with you, saith the Lord of hosts: according to the word that I covenanted with you when ye came out of Egypt, so my Spirit remaineth among you; fear ye not.

For thus saith the Lord of hosts; Yet once, it is a little while, and I will shake the heavens, and the earth, and the sea, and the dry land; and I will shake all nations, and the Desire of all nations shall come: and I will fill this house with glory, saith the Lord of hosts. The silver is mine, and the gold is mine, saith the Lord of hosts. The glory of this latter house shall be greater than of the former, saith the Lord of hosts: and in this place will I give peace, saith the Lord of hosts.

Zechariah

Upon the four and twentieth day of the eleventh month, which is the month Sebat, in the second year of Darius, came the word of the Lord unto Zechariah, the son of Barachiah, the son of Iddo the prophet, saying, I saw by night, and behold a man riding upon a red horse, and he stood among the myrtle-trees that were in the bottom; and behind him were there red horses, speckled, and white.

Then said I, O my lord, what are these? And the angel that talked with me said unto me, I will shew thee what these be. And the man that stood among the myrtle-trees answered and said, These are they whom the Lord hath sent to walk to and fro through the earth.

And they answered the angel of the Lord that stood among the myrtle-trees, and said, We have walked to and fro through the earth, and behold, all the earth sitteth still, and is at rest.

Then the angel of the Lord answered and said, O Lord of hosts, how long wilt thou not have mercy on Jerusalem and on the cities of Judah, against which thou hast had indignation these threescore and ten years?

And the Lord answered the angel that talked with me with good words and comfortable words.

So the angel that communed with me said unto me, Cry thou, saying, Thus saith the Lord of hosts; I am jealous for Jerusalem and for Zion with a great jealousy. And I am very sore displeased with the heathen that are at ease: for I was but a little displeased, and they helped forward the affliction. Therefore thus saith the Lord; I am returned to Jerusalem with mercies: mine house shall be built in it, saith the Lord of hosts, and a line shall be stretched forth upon Jerusalem. Cry yet, saying, Thus saith the Lord of hosts; My cities through prosperity shall yet be spread abroad; and the Lord shall yet comfort Zion, and shall yet choose Jerusalem.

Then lifted I up mine eyes, and saw, and behold four horns. And I said unto the angel that talked with me, What be these? And he answered me, These are the horns which have scattered Judah, Israel, and Jerusalem.

And the Lord shewed me four carpenters. Then said I, What come these to do? And he spake, saying, These are the horns which have scattered Judah, so that no man did lift up his head: but these are come to fray them, to cast out the horns of the Gentiles, which lifted up their horn over the land of Judah to scatter it.

I lifted up mine eyes again, and looked, and behold a man with a measuring line in his hand. Then said I, Whither goest thou? And he said unto me, To measure Jerusalem, to see what is the breadth thereof, and what is the length thereof.

And behold, the angel that talked with me went forth, and another angel went out to meet him, and said unto him, Run, speak to this young man, saying, Jerusalem shall be inhabited as towns without walls for the multitude of men and cattle therein. For I, saith the Lord, will be unto her a wall of fire round about, and will be the glory in the midst of her.

Ho, ho, come forth, and flee from the land of the north, saith the Lord: for I have spread you abroad as the four winds of the heaven, saith the Lord. Deliver thyself, O Zion, that dwellest with the daughter of Babylon.

For thus saith the Lord of hosts: After the glory hath he sent me unto the nations which spoiled you: for he that toucheth you, toucheth the apple of his eye. For behold, I will shake my hand upon them, and they shall be a spoil to their servants: and ye shall know that the Lord of hosts hath sent me.

Sing and rejoice, O daughter of Zion; for lo, I come, and I will dwell in the midst of thee, saith the Lord. And many nations shall be joined to the Lord in that day, and shall be my people: and I will dwell in the midst of thee, and thou shalt know that the Lord of hosts hath sent me unto thee. And the Lord shall inherit Judah his portion in the holy land, and shall choose Jerusalem again. Be silent, O all flesh, before the Lord: for he is raised up out of his holy habitation.

And the angel that talked with me came again, and waked me, as a man that is wakened out of his sleep. And said unto me, What seest thou? And I said, I have looked, and behold a candlestick, all of gold, with a bowl upon the top of it, and his seven lamps thereon, and seven pipes to the seven lamps, which are upon the top thereof, and two olive-trees by it, one upon the right side of the bowl, and the other upon the left side thereof.

So I answered and spake to the angel that talked with me, saying, What are these, my lord? Then the angel that talked with me answered and said unto me, Knowest thou not what these be? And I said, No, my lord.

Then he answered and spake unto me, saying, This is the word of the Lord unto Zerubbabel, saying, Not by might, nor by power, but by my Spirit, saith the Lord of hosts. Who art thou, O great mountain? before Zerubbabel thou shalt become a plain: and he shall bring forth the headstone thereof with shoutings, crying, Grace, grace, unto it.

Moreover the word of the Lord came unto me, saying, The hands of

Zerubbabel have laid the foundation of this house; his hands shall also finish it; and thou shalt know that the Lord of hosts hath sent me unto you. For who hath despised the day of small things? for they shall rejoice, and shall see the plummet in the hand of Zerubbabel with those seven; they are the eyes of the Lord, which run to and fro through the whole earth.

Then answered I, and said unto him, What are these two olive-trees upon the right side of the candlestick and upon the left side thereof? And I answered again, and said unto him, What be these two olive branches which through the two golden pipes empty the golden oil out of themselves?

And he answered me and said, Knowest thou not what these be? And I said, No, my lord. Then said he, These are the two anointed ones, that stand by the Lord of the whole earth.

Then I turned, and lifted up mine eyes, and looked, and behold a flying roll. And he said unto me, What seest thou? And I answered, I see a flying roll; the length thereof is twenty cubits, and the breadth thereof ten cubits. Then said he unto me, This is the curse that goeth forth over the face of the whole earth; for every one that stealeth shall be cut off as on this side, according to it; and every one that sweareth shall be cut off as on that side, according to it. I will bring it forth, saith the Lord of hosts, and it shall enter into the house of the thief, and into the house of him that sweareth falsely by my name: and it shall remain in the midst of his house, and shall consume it with the timber thereof and the stones thereof.

And I turned, and lifted up mine eyes, and looked, and behold, there came four chariots out from between two mountains; and the mountains were mountains of brass. In the first chariot were red horses; and in the second chariot black horses; and in the third chariot white horses; and in the fourth chariot grizzled and bay horses.

Then I answered and said unto the angel that talked with me, What are these, my lord?

And the angel answered and said unto me, These are the four spirits of the heavens, which go forth from standing before the Lord of all the earth. The black horses which are therein go forth into the north country; and the white go forth after them; and the grizzled go forth toward the south country.

And the bay went forth, and sought to go that they might walk to and fro through the earth: and he said, Get ye hence, walk to and fro through the earth. So they walked to and fro through the earth.

Then cried he upon me, and spake unto me, saying, Behold, these that go toward the north country have quieted my spirit in the north country.

Again the word of the Lord of hosts came to me, saying, Thus saith the Lord of hosts; I was jealous for Zion with great jealousy, and I was jealous for her with great fury. I am returned unto Zion, and will dwell in the midst of Jerusalem: and Jerusalem shall be called, A city of truth; and the mountain of the Lord of hosts, the holy mountain. There shall yet old men and old women dwell in the streets of Jerusalem, and every man with his staff in his hand for very age. And the streets of the city shall be full of boys and girls playing in the streets thereof.

Thus saith the Lord of hosts; If it be marvellous in the eyes of the remnant of this people in these days, should it also be marvellous in mine eyes? Behold, I will save my people from the east country, and from the west country; and I will bring them, and they shall dwell in the midst of Jerusalem: and they shall be my people, and I will be their God, in truth and in righteousness.

Thus saith the Lord of hosts; Let your hands be strong, ye that hear in these days these words by the mouth of the prophets, which were in the day that the foundation of the house of the Lord of hosts was laid, that the temple might be built. For before these days there was no hire for man, nor any hire for beast; neither was there any peace to him that went out or came in because of the affliction: for I set all men every one against his neighbour. But now I will not be unto the residue of this people as in the former days, for the seed shall be prosperous; the vine shall give her fruit, and the ground shall give her increase, and the heavens shall give their dew; and I will cause the remnant of this people to possess all these things. And it shall come to pass, that as ye were a curse among the heathen, O house of Judah, and house of Israel; so will I save you, and ye shall be a blessing: fear not, but let your hands be strong.

For thus saith the Lord of hosts; As I thought to punish you, when your fathers provoked me to wrath, and I repented not: so again have I thought in these days to do well unto Jerusalem and to the house of Judah: fear ye not.

These are the things that ye shall do; Speak ye every man the truth to his neighbour; execute the judgment of truth and peace in your gates. And let none of you imagine evil in your hearts against his neighbour; and love no false oath; for all these are things that I hate, saith the Lord.

Rejoice greatly, O daughter of Zion; shout, O daughter of Jerusalem: behold, thy King cometh unto thee: he is just, and having salvation; lowly, and riding upon an ass, and upon a colt the foal of an ass. And I will cut off the chariot from Ephraim, and the horse from Jerusalem, and the battle-bow shall be cut off: and he shall speak peace unto the heathen: and his dominion shall be from sea even to sea, and from the river even to the ends of the earth.

Malachi

The burden of the word of the Lord to Israel by Malachi.

From the rising of the sun even unto the going down of the same, my name shall be great among the Gentiles; and in every place incense shall be offered unto my name, and a pure offering: for my name shall be great among the heathen, saith the Lord of hosts.

And now, O ye priests, this commandment is for you. If ye will not hear, and if ye will not lay it to heart, to give glory unto my name, saith the Lord of hosts, I will even send a curse upon you, and will curse your blessings; yea, I have cursed them already, because ye do not lay it to heart. Behold I will corrupt your seed, and spread dung upon your faces, even the dung of your solemn feasts; and one shall take you away with it. And ye shall know that I have sent this commandment unto you, that my covenant might be with Levi, saith the Lord of hosts.

Behold, I will send my messenger, and he shall prepare the way before me: and the Lord, whom ye seek, shall suddenly come to his temple, even the messenger of the covenant, whom ye delight in: behold, he shall come, saith the Lord of hosts.

But who may abide the day of his coming? and who shall stand when he appeareth? for he is like a refiner's fire, and like fullers' soap. And he shall sit as a refiner and purifier of silver: and he shall purify the sons of Levi, and purge them as gold and silver, that they may offer unto the Lord an offering in righteousness. Then shall the offering of Judah and

Jerusalem be pleasant unto the Lord, as in the days of old, and as in former years.

For behold, the day cometh, that shall burn as an oven; and all the proud, yea, and all that do wickedly, shall be stubble: and the day that cometh shall burn them up, saith the Lord of hosts, that it shall leave them neither root nor branch.

But unto you that fear my name, shall the Sun of righteousness arise with healing in his wings; and ye shall go forth, and grow up as calves of the stall. And ye shall tread down the wicked; for they shall be ashes under the soles of your feet in the day that I shall do this, saith the Lord of hosts.

Remember ye the law of Moses my servant, which I commanded unto him in Horeb for all Israel, with the statutes and judgments.

Behold, I will send you Elijah the prophet before the coming of the great and dreadful day of the Lord. And he shall turn the heart of the fathers to the children, and the heart of the children to their fathers, lest I come and smite the earth with a curse.

Joel

The word of the Lord that came to Joel the son of Pethuel. Hear this, ye old men, and give ear, all ye inhabitants of the land. Hath this been in your days, or even in the days of your fathers? Tell ye your children of it, and let your children tell their children, and their children another generation.

That which the palmer-worm hath left hath the locust eaten; and that which the locust hath left hath the canker-worm eaten; and that which the canker-worm hath left hath the caterpillar eaten.

Awake, ye drunkards, and weep; and howl, all ye drinkers of wine, because of the new wine; for it is cut off from your mouth. For a nation is come up upon my land, strong, and without number, whose teeth are the teeth of a lion, and he hath the cheek teeth of a great lion. He hath laid my vine waste, and barked my fig-tree: he hath made it clean bare, and cast it away: the branches thereof are made white.

Blow the trumpet in Zion, sanctify a fast, call a solemn assembly. Gather the people, sanctify the congregation, assemble the elders, gather the children, and those that suck the breasts: let the bridegroom go forth of his chamber, and the bride out of her closet. Let the priests, the ministers of the Lord, weep between the porch and the altar, and let them say, Spare thy people, O Lord, and give not thine heritage to reproach, that the heathen should rule over them: wherefore should they say among the people, Where is their God?

Then will the Lord be jealous for his land, and pity his people. Yea, the Lord will answer and say unto his people, Behold, I will send you corn, and wine, and oil, and ye shall be satisfied therewith: and I will no more make you a reproach among the heathen. But I will remove far off from you the northern army, and will drive him into a land barren and desolate, with his face toward the east sea, and his hinder part toward the utmost sea; and his stink shall come up, and his ill savour shall come up, because he hath done great things.

Fear not, O land; be glad and rejoice: for the Lord will do great things. Be not afraid, ye beasts of the field: for the pastures of the wilderness do spring, for the tree beareth her fruit, the fig-tree and the vine do yield their strength. Be glad then, ye children of Zion, and rejoice in the Lord your God: for he hath given you the former rain moderately, and he will cause to come down for you the rain, the former rain, and the latter rain in the first month.

And the floors shall be full of wheat, and the fats shall overflow with wine and oil. And I will restore to you the years that the locust hath eaten, the canker-worm, and the caterpillar, and the palmer-worm, my great army which I sent among you. And ye shall eat in plenty, and be satisfied, and praise the name of the Lord your God, that hath dealt wondrously with you: and my people shall never be ashamed. And ye shall know that I am in the midst of Israel, and that I am the Lord your God, and none else: and my people shall never be ashamed.

And it shall come to pass afterward, that I will pour out my Spirit upon all flesh; and your sons and your daughters shall prophesy, your old men shall dream dreams, your young men shall see visions. And also upon the servants and upon the handmaids in those days will I pour out my Spirit.

And I will shew wonders in the heavens and in the earth, blood, and fire, and pillars of smoke. The sun shall be turned into darkness, and the moon into blood, before the great and the terrible day of the Lord come. And it shall come to pass, that whosoever shall call on the name of the Lord shall be delivered: for in Mount Zion and in Jerusalem shall be deliverance, as the Lord hath said, and in the remnant whom the Lord shall call.

Jonah

Jonah Is Cast into the Sea

Now the word of the Lord came unto Jonah the son of Amittai, saying, Arise, go to Nineveh, that great city, and cry against it; for their wickedness is come up before me. But Jonah rose up to flee unto Tarshish from the presence of the Lord, and went down to Joppa: and he found a ship going to Tarshish: so he paid the fare thereof, and went down into it, to go with them unto Tarshish from the presence of the Lord.

But the Lord sent out a great wind into the sea, and there was a mighty tempest in the sea, so that the ship was like to be broken. Then the mariners were afraid, and cried every man unto his god, and cast forth the wares that were in the ship into the sea, to lighten it of them. But Jonah was gone down into the sides of the ship: and he lay, and was fast asleep.

So the ship-master came to him, and said unto him, What meanest thou, O sleeper? arise, call upon thy God, if so be that God will think upon us, that we perish not. And they said every one to his fellow, Come, and let us cast lots, that we may know for whose cause this evil is upon us. So they cast lots, and the lot fell upon Jonah.

Then said they unto him, Tell us, we pray thee, for whose cause this evil is upon us; what is thine occupation? and whence comest thou? what is thy country? and of what people art thou? And he said unto them, I am an Hebrew; and I fear the Lord, the God of heaven, which hath made the sea and the dry land. Then were the men exceedingly afraid, and said unto him, Why hast thou done this? For the men knew that he fled from the presence of the Lord, because he had told them.

Then said they unto him, What shall we do unto thee, that the sea may be calm unto us? for the sea wrought and was tempestuous.

And he said unto them, Take me up, and cast me forth into the sea; so shall the sea be calm unto you: for I know that for my sake this great tempest is upon you.

Nevertheless the men rowed hard to bring it to the land; but they could not: for the sea wrought, and was tempestuous against them. Wherefore they cried unto the Lord, and said, We beseech thee, O Lord, we beseech thee, let us not perish for this man's life, and lay not upon us innocent blood: for thou, O Lord, hast done as it pleased thee.

So they took up Jonah, and cast him forth into the sea: and the sea ceased from her raging. Then the men feared the Lord exceedingly, and offered a sacrifice unto the Lord, and made vows.

Now the Lord had prepared a great fish to swallow up Jonah. And Jonah was in the belly of the fish three days and three nights.

Jonah's Prayer

Then Jonah prayed unto the Lord his God out of the fish's belly, and said, I cried by reason of mine affliction unto the Lord, and he heard me; out of the belly of hell cried I, and thou heardest my voice. For thou hadst cast me into the deep, in the midst of the seas; and the floods compassed me about: all thy billows and thy waves passed over me.

Then I said, I am cast out of thy sight; yet I will look again toward thy holy temple.

The waters compassed me about, even to the soul: the depths closed me round about, the weeds were wrapped about my head. I went down to the bottoms of the mountains; the earth with her bars was about me for ever: yet hast thou brought up my life from corruption, O Lord my God.

When my soul fainted within me I remembered the Lord: and my prayer came in unto thee, into thine holy temple.

They that observe lying vanities forsake their own mercy. But I will sacrifice unto thee with the voice of thanksgiving; I will pay that that I have vowed. Salvation is of the Lord.

And the Lord spake unto the fish, and it vomited out Jonah upon the dry land.

Jonah Goes to Nineveh

And the word of the Lord came unto Jonah the second time, saying, Arise, go unto Nineveh, that great city, and preach unto it the preaching that I bid thee.

So Jonah arose, and went unto Nineveh, according to the word of the Lord. Now Nineveh was an exceeding great city of three days' journey. And Jonah began to enter into the city a day's journey, and he cried, and said, Yet forty days, and Nineveh shall be overthrown.

So the people of Nineveh believed God, and proclaimed a fast, and put on sackcloth, from the greatest of them even to the least of them. For word came unto the king of Nineveh, and he arose from his throne, and he laid his robe from him, and covered him with sackcloth, and sat in ashes. And he caused it to be proclaimed and published through Nineveh by decree of the king and his nobles, saying, Let neither man nor beast, herd nor flock, taste anything: let them not feed, nor drink water: but let man and beast be covered with sackcloth, and cry mightily unto God: yea, let them turn every one from his evil way, and from the violence that is in their hands. Who can tell if God will turn and repent, and turn away from his fierce anger, that we perish not?

And God saw their works, that they turned from their evil way; and God repented of the evil that he had said that he would do unto them; and he did it not.

The Lord Reproves Jonah

But it displeased Jonah exceedingly, and he was very angry. And he prayed unto the Lord, and said, I pray thee, O Lord, was not this my saying, when I was yet in my country? Therefore I fled before unto Tarshish: for I knew that thou art a gracious God, and merciful, slow to anger, and of great kindness, and repentest thee of the evil. Therefore now, O Lord, take, I beseech thee, my life from me; for it is better for me to die than to live.

Then said the Lord, Doest thou well to be angry?

So Jonah went out of the city, and sat on the east side of the city, and there made him a booth, and sat under it in the shadow, till he might see what would become of the city. And the Lord God prepared a gourd, and made it to come up over Jonah, that it might be a shadow over his head, to deliver him from his grief. So Jonah was exceeding glad of the gourd. But God prepared a worm when the morning rose the next day, and it smote the gourd that it withered. And it came to pass, when the sun did arise, that God prepared a vehement east wind; and the sun beat upon the head of Jonah, that he fainted, and wished in himself to die, and said, It is better for me to die than to live.

And God said to Jonah, Doest thou well to be angry for the gourd? And he said, I do well to be angry, even unto death.

Then said the Lord, Thou hast had pity on the gourd, for the which thou hast not laboured, neither madest it grow; which came up in a night, and perished in a night. And should not I spare Nineveh, that great city, wherein are more than sixscore thousand persons that cannot discern between their right hand and their left hand, and also much cattle?

The Book of Daniel

Daniel's Loyalty to the Faith of Israel

In the third year of the reign of Jehoiakim king of Judah came Nebuchadnezzar king of Babylon unto Jerusalem, and besieged it. And the Lord gave Jehoiakim king of Judah into his hand, with part of the vessels of the house of God: which he carried into the land of Shinar to the house of his god; and he brought the vessels into the treasure-house of his god.

And the king spake unto Ashpenaz the master of his eunuchs, that he should bring certain of the children of Israel, and of the king's seed, and of the princes, children in whom was no blemish, but well favoured, and skilful in all wisdom, and cunning in knowledge, and understanding science, and such as had ability in them to stand in the king's palace, and whom they might teach the learning and the tongue of the Chaldeans. And the king appointed them a daily provision of the king's meat, and of the wine which he drank: so nourishing them three years, that at the end thereof they might stand before the king.

Now, among these were of the children of Judah, Daniel, Hananiah, Mishael, and Azariah, unto whom the prince of the eunuchs gave names: for he gave unto Daniel the name of Belteshazzar; and to Hananiah, of Shadrach; and to Mishael, of Meshach; and to Azariah, of Abed-nego.

But Daniel purposed in his heart that he would not defile himself with the portion of the king's meat, nor with the wine which he drank: therefore, he requested of the prince of the eunuchs that he might not defile himself.

And the prince of the eunuchs said unto Daniel, I fear my lord the king, who hath appointed your meat and your drink: for why should he see your faces worse liking than the children which are of your sort? then shall ye make me endanger my head to the king.

Then said Daniel to Melzar, whom the prince of the eunuchs had set over Daniel, Hananiah, Mishael, and Azariah, Prove thy servants, I beseech thee, ten days; and let them give us pulse to eat, and water to drink. Then let our countenances be looked upon before thee, and the countenance of the children that eat of the portion of the king's meat: and as thou seest, deal with thy servants.

So he consented to them in this matter and proved them ten days. And at the end of ten days their countenances appeared fairer and fatter in flesh than all the children which did eat the portion of the king's meat.

As for these four children, God gave them knowledge and skill in all learning and wisdom: and Daniel had understanding in all visions and dreams.

The King's Dream

And in the second year of the reign of Nebuchadnezzar, Nebuchadnezzar dreamed dreams, wherewith his spirit was troubled, and his sleep brake from him. Then the king commanded to call the magicians, and the astrologers, and the sorcerers, and the Chaldeans, for to shew the king his dreams. So they came and stood before the king. And the king said unto them, I have dreamed a dream, and my spirit was troubled to know the dream.

Then spake the Chaldeans to the king in Syriac, O king live for ever: tell thy servants the dream, and we will shew the interpretation.

The king answered and said to the Chaldeans, The thing is gone from me: if ye will not make known unto me the dream, with the interpretation thereof, ye shall be cut in pieces, and your houses shall be made a dunghill. But if ye shew the dream, and the interpretation thereof, ye shall receive of me gifts, and rewards and great honour: therefore, shew me the dream, and the interpretation thereof.

The Chaldeans answered before the king, and said, There is not a man upon the earth that can shew the king's matter: therefore there is no king, lord, nor ruler, that asked such things at any magician, or astrologer, or Chaldean.

For this cause the king was angry and very furious, and commanded to destroy all the wise men of Babylon. And the decree went forth that the wise men should be slain; and they sought Daniel and his fellows to be slain.

Then Daniel answered and said to Arioch the king's captain, Why is the decree so hasty from the king? Then Arioch made the thing known to Daniel. Then Daniel went in, and desired of the king that he would give him time, and that he would shew the king the interpretation. Then Daniel went to his house and made the thing known to Hananiah, Mishael, and Azariah, his companions, that they would desire mercies of the God of heaven concerning this secret; that Daniel and his fellows should not perish with the rest of the wise men of Babylon.

Then was the secret revealed unto Daniel in a night vision. Then Daniel blessed the God of heaven.

Therefore, Daniel went in unto Arioch, whom the king had ordained to destroy the wise men of Babylon: he went and said thus unto him; Destroy not the wise men of Babylon: bring me in before the king, and I will shew unto the king the interpretation.

Then Arioch brought in Daniel before the king in haste, and said thus unto him, I have found a man of the captives of Judah, that will make known unto the king the interpretation.

The king answered and said to Daniel, whose name was Belteshazzar, Art thou able to make known unto me the dream which I have seen, and the interpretation thereof?

Daniel answered in the presence of the king, and said, The secret which the king hath demanded cannot the wise men, the astrologers, the magicians, the soothsayers, shew unto the king, but there is a God in heaven that revealeth secrets, and maketh known to the king Nebuchadnezzar what shall be in the latter days. Thy dream, and the visions of thy head upon thy bed, are these:

Thou, O king, sawest, and behold a great image. This great image, whose brightness was excellent, stood before thee; and the form thereof was terrible. This image's head was of fine gold, his breast and his arms of silver, his belly and his thighs of brass, his legs of iron, his feet part of iron and part of clay. Thou sawest till that a stone was cut out without hands, which smote the image upon his feet that were of iron and clay, and brake them to pieces. Then was the iron, the clay, the brass, the silver, and the gold, broken to pieces together, and became like the chaff of the summer threshing-floors; and the wind carried them away, that no place was found for them: and the stone that smote the image became a great mountain, and filled the whole earth.

This is the dream; and we will tell the interpretation thereof before the king. Thou, O king, art a king of kings: for the God of heaven hath given thee a kingdom, power, and strength, and glory. And wheresoever the children of men dwell, the beasts of the field and the fowls of the heaven hath he given into thine hand, and hath made thee ruler over them all. Thou art this head of gold.

And after thee shall arise another kingdom inferior to thee, and another third kingdom of brass, which shall bear rule over all the earth. And the fourth kingdom shall be strong as iron: forasmuch as iron breaketh in pieces and subdueth all things: and as iron that breaketh all these, shall it break in pieces and bruise.

And whereas thou sawest the feet and toes, part of potters' clay, and part of iron, the kingdom shall be divided; but there shall be in it of the strength of the iron, forasmuch as thou sawest the iron mixed with miry clay. And as the toes of the feet were part of iron, and part of clay, so the kingdom shall be partly strong, and partly broken. And whereas thou sawest iron mixed with miry clay, they shall mingle themselves with the seed of men: but they shall not cleave one to another, even as iron is not mixed with clay.

And in the days of these kings shall the God of heaven set up a kingdom, which shall never be destroyed: and the kingdom shall not be left to other people, but it shall break in pieces and consume all these kingdoms, and it shall stand for ever.

Forasmuch as thou sawest that the stone was cut out of the mountain without hands, and that it brake in pieces the iron, the brass, the clay, the silver, and the gold; the great God hath made known to the king what shall come to pass hereafter: and the dream is certain, and the interpretation thereof sure.

Then the king Nebuchadnezzar fell upon his face, and worshipped Daniel, and commanded that they should offer an oblation and sweet odours unto him. The king answered unto Daniel, and said, Of a truth, it is, that your God is a God of gods, and a Lord of kings, and a revealer of secrets, seeing thou couldst reveal this secret.

Then the king made Daniel a great man, and gave him many great gifts, and made him ruler over the whole province of Babylon, and chief of the governors over all the wise men of Babylon.

Then Daniel requested of the king, and he set Shadrach, Meshach, and Abed-nego, over the affairs of the province of Babylon: but Daniel sat in the gate of the king.

Shadrach, Meshach, and Abed-nego

Nebuchadnezzar the king made an image of gold, whose height was threescore cubits, and the breadth thereof six cubits: he set it up in the plain of Dura, in the province of Babylon. Then the princes, the governors, and captains, the judges, the treasurers, the counsellors, the sheriffs, and all the rulers of the provinces, were gathered together unto the dedication of the image that Nebuchadnezzar the king had set up; and they stood before the image that Nebuchadnezzar had set up.

Then an herald cried aloud, To you it is commanded, O people, nations, and languages, that at what time ye hear the sound of the cornet, flute, harp, sackbut, psaltery, dulcimer, and all kinds of music, ye fall down and worship the golden image that Nebuchadnezzar the king hath set up. And whoso falleth not down and worshippeth shall the same hour be cast into the midst of a burning fiery furnace.

Wherefore at that time certain Chaldeans came near, and accused the Jews. They spake and said: There are certain Jews whom thou hast set over the affairs of the province of Babylon, Shadrach, Meshach, and Abed-nego; these men, O king, have not regarded thee: they serve not thy gods, nor worship the golden image which thou hast set up.

Then Nebuchadnezzar in his rage and fury commanded to bring Shadrach, Meshach, and Abed-nego. Then they brought these men before the king.

Then Nebuchadnezzar spake and said unto them, Is it true, O Shadrach, Meshach, and Abed-nego, do not ye serve my gods, nor worship the golden image which I have set up? Now if ye be ready that at what time ye hear the sound of the cornet, flute, harp, sackbut, psaltery, and dulcimer, and all kinds of music, ye fall down and worship the image which I have made; well: but if ye worship not, ye shall be cast the same hour into the midst of a burning fiery furnace; and who is that God that shall deliver you out of my hands?

Shadrach, Meshach, and Abed-nego answered and said to the king, O Nebuchadnezzar, we are not careful to answer thee in this matter. If it be so, our God whom we serve is able to deliver us from the burning fiery furnace, and he will deliver us out of thine hand, O king. But if not, be it known unto thee, O king, that we will not serve thy gods, nor worship the golden image which thou hast set up.

Then was Nebuchadnezzar full of fury, and the form of his visage was changed against Shadrach, Meshach, and Abed-nego: therefore he spake, and commanded that they should heat the furnace one seven times more than it was wont to be heated. And he commanded the most mighty men that were in his army to bind Shadrach, Meshach, and Abed-nego, and to cast them into the burning fiery furnace.

Then these men were bound in their coats, their hosen, and their hats, and their other garments, and were cast into the midst of the burning fiery furnace. Therefore because the king's commandment was urgent, and the furnace exceeding hot, the flame of the fire slew those men that took up Shadrach, Meshach, and Abed-nego. And these three men, Shadrach, Meshach, and Abed-nego, fell down bound into the midst of the burning fiery furnace.

Then Nebuchadnezzar the king was astonied, and rose up in haste, and spake, and said unto his counsellors, Did not we cast three men bound into the midst of the fire? They answered and said unto the king, True, O king.

He answered and said, Lo, I see four men loose, walking in the midst of the fire, and they have no hurt: and the form of the fourth is like the Son of God.

Then Nebuchadnezzar came near to the mouth of the burning fiery furnace, and spake, and said, Shadrach, Meshach, and Abed-nego, ye servants of the most high God, come forth, and come hither. Then Shadrach, Meshach, and Abed-nego, came forth of the midst of the fire.

And the princes, governors, and captains, and the king's counsellors, being gathered together, saw these men, upon whose bodies the fire had no power, nor was an hair of their head singed, neither were their coats changed, nor the smell of fire had passed on them.

Then Nebuchadnezzar spake, and said, Blessed be the God of Shadrach, Meshach, and Abed-nego, who hath sent his angel, and delivered his servants that trusted in him, and have changed the king's word, and yielded their bodies, that they might not serve nor worship any god, except their own God. Therefore, I make a decree, that every people, nation, and language, which speak any thing amiss against the God of

Shadrach, Meshach, and Abed-nego, shall be cut in pieces, and their houses shall be made a dunghill: because there is no other god that can deliver after this sort.

Then the king promoted Shadrach, Meshach, and Abed-nego, in the province of Babylon.

One of Nebuchadnezzar's Dreams Comes True

Nebuchadnezzar the king, unto all people, nations, and languages, that dwell in all the earth; Peace be multiplied unto you. I Nebuchadnezzar was at rest in mine house, and flourishing in my palace. I saw a dream which made me afraid, and the thoughts upon my bed and the visions of my head troubled me.

Daniel came in before me, whose name was Belteshazzar, according to the name of my god, and in whom is the spirit of the holy gods: and before him I told the dream, saying, O Belteshazzar, master of the magicians, thus were the visions of mine head in my bed; I saw, and behold a tree in the midst of the earth, and the height thereof was great. The tree grew, and was strong, and the height thereof reached unto heaven, and the sight thereof to the end of all the earth. The leaves thereof were fair, and the fruit thereof much, and in it was meat for all: the beasts of the field had shadow under it, and the fowls of the heaven dwelt in the boughs thereof, and all flesh was fed of it.

I saw in the visions of my head upon my bed, and behold, a watcher and an holy one came down from heaven. He cried aloud, and said thus, Hew down the tree, and cut off his branches, shake off his leaves, and scatter his fruit: let the beasts get away from under it, and the fowls from his branches. Nevertheless, leave the stump of his roots in the earth, even with a band of iron and brass, in the tender grass of the field; and let it be wet with the dew of heaven, and let his portion be with the beasts in the grass of the earth. Let his heart be changed from man's, and let a beast's heart be given unto him; and let seven times pass over him.

Then Daniel, whose name was Belteshazzar, answered, and said, My lord, the dream be to them that hate thee, and the interpretation thereof to thine enemies.

This is the interpretation, O king, and this is the decree of the Most High, which is come upon my lord the king: that they shall drive thee from men, and thy dwelling shall be with the beasts of the field, and they shall make thee to eat grass as oxen, and they shall wet thee with the dew of heaven, and seven times shall pass over thee, till thou know that the Most High ruleth in the kingdom of men, and giveth it to whomsoever he will. And whereas they commanded to leave the stump of the tree roots; thy kingdom shall be sure unto thee, after that thou shalt have known that the heavens do rule. Wherefore, O king, let my counsel be acceptable unto thee, and break off thy sins by righteousness, and thine iniquities by shewing mercy to the poor; if it may be a lengthening of thy tranquillity.

All this came upon the king Nebuchadnezzar. At the end of twelve months he walked in the palace of the kingdom of Babylon. The king spake, and said, Is not this great Babylon, that I have built for the house of the kingdom by the might of my power, and for the honour of my majesty?

While the word was in the king's mouth, there fell a voice from heaven, saying, O king Nebuchadnezzar, to thee it is spoken; The kingdom is departed from thee. And they shall drive thee from men, and thy dwelling shall be with the beasts of the field: they shall make thee to eat grass as oxen, and seven times shall pass over thee, until thou know that the Most High ruleth in the kingdom of men, and giveth it to whomsoever he will.

The same hour was the thing fulfilled upon Nebuchadnezzar: and he was driven from men, and did eat grass as oxen, and his body was wet with the dew of heaven, till his hairs were grown like eagles' feathers, and his nails like birds' claws.

And at the end of the days I Nebuchadnezzar lifted up mine eyes unto heaven, and mine understanding returned unto me, and I blessed the Most High, and I praised and honoured him that liveth for ever, whose dominion is an everlasting dominion, and his kingdom is from generation to generation.

And all the inhabitants of the earth are reputed as nothing: and he doeth according to his will in the army of heaven, and among the inhabitants of the earth: and none can stay his hand, or say unto him, What doest thou?

At the same time my reason returned unto me; and for the glory of my kingdom, mine honour and brightness returned unto me; and my counsellors and my lords sought unto me; and I was established in my king-dcm, and excellent majesty was added unto me. Now I Nebuchadnezzar praise and extol and honour the King of heaven, all whose works are truth, and his ways judgment: and those that walk in pride he is able to abase.

The Handwriting on the Wall

Belshazzar the king made a great feast to a thousand of his lords, and drank wine before the thousand. Belshazzar, while he tasted the wine, commanded to bring the golden and silver vessels which his father Nebuchadnezzar had taken out of the temple which was in Jerusalem; that the king, and his princes, his wives, and his concubines, might drink therein. Then they brought the golden vessels that were taken out of the temple of the house of God which was at Jerusalem; and the king, and his princes, his wives, and his concubines, drank in them. They drank wine, and praised the gods of gold, and of silver, of brass, of iron, of wood, and of stone.

In the same hour came forth fingers of a man's hand, and wrote over against the candlestick upon the plaster of the wall of the king's palace: and the king saw the part of the hand that wrote. Then the king's countenance was changed, and his thoughts troubled him, so that the joints of his loins were loosed, and his knees smote one against another.

The king cried aloud to bring in the astrologers, the Chaldeans, and the soothsayers. And the king spake and said to the wise men of Babylon, Whosoever shall read this writing, and shew me the interpretation thereof, shall be clothed with scarlet, and have a chain of gold about his neck, and shall be the third ruler in the kingdom.

Then came in all the king's wise men: but they could not read the writing, nor make known to the king the interpretation thereof. Then was king Belshazzar greatly troubled, and his countenance was changed in him, and his lords were astonied.

Now, the queen by reason of the words of the king and his lords came into the banquet-house: and the queen spake and said, O king, live for ever: let not thy thoughts trouble thee, nor let thy countenance be changed. There is a man in thy kingdom, in whom is the spirit of the holy gods; and in the days of thy father light and understanding and wisdom, like the wisdom of the gods, was found in him; now let Daniel be called, and he will shew the interpretation.

Then was Daniel brought in before the king. And the king spake and said unto Daniel, Art thou that Daniel, which art of the children of the captivity of Judah, whom the king my father brought out of Jewry? I have heard of thee, that thou canst make interpretations, and dissolve doubts: now if thou canst read the writing, and make known to me the interpretation thereof, thou shalt be clothed with scarlet, and have a chain of gold about thy neck, and shalt be the third ruler in the kingdom.

Then Daniel answered and said before the king, Let thy gifts be to thyself, and give thy rewards to another; yet I will read the writing unto the king, and make known to him the interpretation.

O thou king, the most high God gave Nebuchadnezzar thy father a kingdom, and majesty, and glory, and honour. And thou his son, O Belshazzar, hast not humbled thine heart, though thou knewest all this, but hast lifted up thyself against the Lord of heaven; and they have brought the vessels of his house before thee, and thou, and thy lords, thy wives and thy concubines, have drunk wine in them; and thou hast praised the gods of silver, and gold, of brass, iron, wood, and stone, which see not, nor hear, nor know: and the God in whose hand thy breath is, and whose are all thy ways, hast thou not glorified. Then was the part of the hand sent from him; and this writing was written.

And this is the writing that was written, MENE, MENE, TEKEL, UPHARSIN.

This is the interpretation of the thing: MENE; God hath numbered thy kingdom, and finished it. TEKEL; Thou art weighed in the balances, and art found wanting. PERES; Thy kingdom is divided and given to the Medes and Persians.

Then commanded Belshazzar, and they clothed Daniel with scarlet, and put a chain of gold about his neck, and made a proclamation concerning him, that he should be the third ruler in the kingdom.

In that night was Belshazzar the king of the Chaldeans slain. And Darius the Median took the kingdom, being about threescore and two years old.

Daniel in the Lions' Den

It pleased Darius to set over the kingdom an hundred and twenty princes, which should be over the whole kingdom, and over these three presidents; of whom Daniel was first: that the princes might give accounts unto them, and the king should have no damage. Then this Daniel was preferred above the presidents and princes, because an excellent spirit was in him; and the king thought to set him over the whole realm.

Then the presidents and princes sought to find occasion against Daniel concerning the kingdom; but they could find none occasion nor fault; forasmuch as he was faithful, neither was there any error or fault found in him. Then said these men, We shall not find any occasion against this Daniel, except we find it against him concerning the law of his God.

Then these presidents and princes assembled together to the king, and said thus unto him, King Darius, live for ever. All the presidents of the kingdom, the governors, and the princes, the counsellors, and the captains, have consulted together to establish a royal statute, and to make a firm decree, that whosoever shall ask a petition of any god or man for thirty days, save of thee, O king, he shall be cast into the den of lions. Now, O king, establish the decree, and sign the writing, that it be not changed, according to the law of the Medes and Persians, which altereth not. Wherefore king Darius signed the writing and the decree.

Now when Daniel knew that the writing was signed, he went into his house; and his windows being open in his chamber toward Jerusalem, he kneeled upon his knees three times a day, and prayed, and gave thanks before his God, as he did aforetime. Then these men assembled, and found Daniel praying and making supplication before his God.

Then they came near, and spake before the king concerning the king's decree; Hast thou not signed a decree, that every man that shall ask a petition of any god or man within thirty days, save of thee, O king, shall be cast into the den of lions? The king answered and said, The thing is true, according to the law of the Medes and Persians, which altereth not.

Then answered they and said before the king, That Daniel, which is of the children of the captivity of Judah, regardeth not thee, O king, nor the decree that thou hast signed, but maketh his petition three times a day.

Then the king, when he heard these words, was sore displeased with himself, and he set his heart on Daniel to deliver him: and he laboured till the going down of the sun to deliver him.

Then these men assembled unto the king, and said unto the king, Know, O king, that the law of the Medes and Persians is, That no decree nor statute which the king establisheth may be changed.

Then the king commanded, and they brought Daniel, and cast him into the den of lions. Now the king spake and said unto Daniel, Thy God whom thou servest continually, he will deliver thee.

And a stone was brought, and laid upon the mouth of the den; and the king sealed it with his own signet, and with the signet of his lords; that the purpose might not be changed concerning Daniel.

Then the king went to his palace, and passed the night fasting: neither were instruments of music brought before him: and his sleep went from him. Then the king arose very early in the morning, and went in haste unto the den of lions. And when he came to the den, he cried with a lamentable voice unto Daniel: and the king spake and said unto Daniel, O Daniel, servant of the living God, is thy God, whom thou servest continually, able to deliver thee from the lions?

Then said Daniel unto the king, O king, live for ever. My God hath sent his angel, and hath shut the lions' mouths, that they have not hurt me: forasmuch as before him innocency was found in me; and also before thee, O king, have I done no hurt.

Then was the king exceeding glad for him, and commanded that they should take Daniel up out of the den. So Daniel was taken up out of the den, and no manner of hurt was found upon him, because he believed in his God.

And the king commanded, and they brought those men which had accused Daniel, and they cast them into the den of lions, them, their children, and their wives; and the lions had the mastery of them, and brake all their bones in pieces or ever they came at the bottom of the den.

Then king Darius wrote unto all people, nations, and languages, that dwell in all the earth; Peace be multiplied unto you. I make a decree, That in every dominion of my kingdom men tremble and fear before the God of Daniel: for he is the living God, and steadfast for ever, and his kingdom that which shall not be destroyed, and his dominion shall be even unto the end. He delivereth and rescueth, and he worketh signs and wonders in heaven and in earth, who hath delivered Daniel from the power of the lions.

So this Daniel prospered in the reign of Darius, and in the reign of Cyrus the Persian.

Daniel's Two Visions

In the first year of Belshazzar king of Babylon, Daniel had a dream and visions of his head, upon his bed: then he wrote the dream, and told the sum of the matters.

Daniel spake and said, I saw in my vision by night, and behold, the four winds of the heaven strove upon the great sea. And four great beasts came up from the sea, diverse one from another.

The first was like a lion, and had eagle's wings; I beheld till the wings thereof were plucked, and it was lifted up from the earth, and made stand upon the feet as a man, and a man's heart was given to it.

And behold another beast, a second, like to a bear, and it raised up itself on one side, and it had three ribs in the mouth of it between the teeth of it; and they said thus unto it, Arise, devour much flesh.

After this, I beheld, and lo, another, like a leopard, which had upon the back of it four wings of a fowl: the beast had also four heads; and dominion was given to it.

After this I saw in the night visions, and behold a fourth beast, dreadful and terrible, and strong exceedingly; and it had great iron teeth: it devoured and brake in pieces, and stamped the residue with the feet of it: and it was diverse from all the beasts that were before it; and it had ten horns. I considered the horns, and behold there came up among them another little horn, before whom there were three of the first horns plucked up by the roots: and behold, in this horn were eyes like the eyes of man, and a mouth speaking great things.

I beheld till the thrones were cast down, and the Ancient of days did sit, whose garment was white as snow, and the hair of his head like the pure wool: his throne was like the fiery flame, and his wheels as burning fire. A fiery stream issued and came forth from before him: thousand thousands ministered unto him, and ten thousand times ten thousand stood before him: the judgment was set, and the books were opened.

I beheld then because of the voice of the great words which the horn spake: I beheld even till the beast was slain, and his body destroyed, and given to the burning flame. As concerning the rest of the beasts, they had their dominion taken away: yet their lives were prolonged for a season and time.

I saw in the night visions, and behold, one like the Son of man came with the clouds of heaven, and came to the Ancient of days, and they brought him near before him. And there was given him dominion, and glory, and a kingdom, that all people, nations, and languages, should serve him: his dominion is an everlasting dominion, which shall not pass away, and his kingdom, that which shall not be destroyed.

I Daniel was grieved in my spirit in the midst of my body, and the visions of my head troubled me. I came near unto one of them that stood by, and asked him the truth of all this. So he told me, and made me know the interpretation of the things.

These great beasts, which are four, are four kings, which shall arise out of the earth. But the saints of the Most High shall take the kingdom, and possess the kingdom for ever, even for ever and ever.

Then I would know the truth of the fourth beast, which was diverse from all the others, exceeding dreadful, whose teeth were of iron, and his nails of brass; which devoured, brake in pieces, and stamped the residue with his feet; and of the ten horns that were in his head, and of the other which came up, and before whom three fell; even of that horn that had eyes, and a mouth that spake very great things, whose look was more stout than his fellows.

I beheld, and the same horn made war with the saints, and prevailed against them; until the Ancient of days came, and judgment was given to the saints of the Most High; and the time came that the saints possessed the kingdom.

Thus he said, The fourth beast shall be the fourth kingdom upon earth, which shall be diverse from all kingdoms, and shall devour the whole earth, and shall tread it down, and break it in pieces. And the ten horns out of this kingdom are ten kings, that shall arise: and another shall rise after them; and he shall be diverse from the first, and he shall subdue three kings. And he shall speak great words against the Most High, and shall wear out the saints of the Most High, and think to change times and laws: and they shall be given into his hand until a time and times and the dividing of time.

But the judgment shall sit, and they shall take away his dominion to consume and to destroy it unto the end. And the kingdom and dominion, and the greatness of the kingdom under the whole heaven, shall be given to the people of the saints of the Most High, whose kingdom is an everlasting kingdom, and all dominions shall serve and obey him.

Hitherto is the end of the matter. As for me Daniel, my cogitations much troubled me, and my countenance changed in me: but I kept the matter in my heart.

In the third year of the reign of king Belshazzar a vision appeared unto me, even unto me Daniel, after that which appeared unto me at the first.

And I saw in a vision; and it came to pass, when I saw, that I was at Shushan in the palace, which is in the province of Elam; and I saw in a vision, and I was by the river of Ulai.

Then I lifted up mine eyes, and saw, and behold, there stood before the river a ram which had two horns: and the two horns were high; but one was higher than the other, and the higher came up last. I saw the ram pushing westward, and northward, and southward; so that no beasts might stand before him, neither was there any that could deliver out of his hand; but he did according to his will, and became great.

And as I was considering, behold, an he-goat came from the west on the face of the whole earth, and touched not the ground: and the goat had a notable horn between his eyes. And he came to the ram that had two horns, which I had seen standing before the river, and ran unto him in the fury of his power. And I saw him come close unto the ram, and he was moved with choler against him, and smote the ram, and brake his two horns: and there was no power in the ram to stand before him, but he cast him down to the ground, and stamped upon him: and there was none that could deliver the ram out of his hand.

Therefore, the he-goat waxed very great: and when he was strong, the great horn was broken; and for it, came up four notable ones toward the four winds of heaven.

And out of one of them came forth a little horn, which waxed exceeding great, toward the south, and toward the east, and toward the pleasant land. And it waxed great, even to the host of heaven; and it cast down some of the host and of the stars to the ground, and stamped upon them.

Yea, he magnified himself even to the prince of the host, and by him the daily sacrifice was taken away, and the place of his sanctuary was cast down. And an host was given him against the daily sacrifice by reason of transgression, and it cast down the truth to the ground; and it practised, and prospered.

Then I heard one saint speaking, and another saint said unto that certain saint which spake, How long shall be the vision concerning the daily sacrifice, and the transgression of desolation, to give both the sanctuary and the host to be trodden under foot?

And he said unto me, Unto two thousand and three hundred days: then shall the sanctuary be cleansed.

And it came to pass, when I, even I Daniel, had seen the vision, and sought for the meaning, then behold, there stood before me as the appearance of a man. And I heard a man's voice between the banks of Ulai, which called, and said, Gabriel, make this man to understand the vision.

So he came near where I stood: and when he came, I was afraid, and fell upon my face: but he said unto me, Understand, O son of man: for at the time of the end shall be the vision.

Now as he was speaking with me, I was in a deep sleep on my face toward the ground: but he touched me, and set me upright.

And he said, Behold, I will make thee know what shall be in the last end of the indignation: for at the time appointed the end shall be. The ram which thou sawest having two horns are the kings of Media and Persia. And the rough goat is the king of Grecia: and the great horn that is between his eyes is the first king.

Now that being broken, whereas four stood up for it, four kingdoms shall stand up out of the nation, but not in his power.

And in the latter time of their kingdom, when the transgressors are come to the full, a king of fierce countenance, and understanding dark sentences, shall stand up. And his power shall be mighty, but not by his own power: and he shall destroy wonderfully, and shall prosper, and practise, and shall destroy the mighty and the holy people. And through his policy also he shall cause craft to prosper in his hand; and he shall magnify himself in his heart, and by peace shall destroy many: he shall also stand up against the Prince of princes; but he shall be broken without hand.

And the vision of the evening and the morning which was told is true: wherefore shut thou up the vision; for it shall be for many days.

And I Daniel fainted, and was sick certain days; afterward I rose up, and did the king's business; and I was astonished at the vision, but none understood it.

Epilogue

And many of them that sleep in the dust of the earth shall awake, some to everlasting life, and some to shame and everlasting contempt. And they that be wise shall shine as the brightness of the firmament; and they that turn many to righteousness, as the stars for ever and ever.

But thou, O Daniel, shut up the words, and seal the book, even to the time of the end. Many shall run to and fro, and knowledge shall be increased.

Then I Daniel looked, and behold, there stood other two, the one on this side of the bank of the river, and the other on that side of the bank of the river. And one said to the man clothed in linen, which was upon the waters of the river, How long shall it be to the end of these wonders?

And I heard the man clothed in linen, which was upon the waters of the river, when he held up his right hand and his left hand unto heaven, and sware by him that liveth for ever, that it shall be for a time, times, and an half; and when he shall have accomplished to scatter the power of the holy people, all these things shall be finished. And I heard, but I understood not.

Then said I, O my Lord, what shall be the end of these things?

And he said, Go thy way, Daniel: for the words are closed up and sealed till the time of the end. Many shall be purified and made white, and tried; but the wicked shall do wickedly: and none of the wicked shall understand; but the wise shall understand.

THE APOCRYPHAL
OLD TESTAMENT

Tobit

The book of the words of Tobit, son of Tobiel, the son of Ananiel, the son of Aduel, the son of Gabael, of the seed of Asael, of the tribe of Nephthali; who in the time of Enemessar king of the Assyrians was led captive out of Thisbe, which is at the right hand of that city, which is called properly Nephthaliin Galilee above Aser.

I Tobit have walked all the days of my life in the way of truth and justice, and I did many alms-deeds to my brethren, and my nation, who came with me to Nineve, into the land of the Assyrians.

And when I was in mine own country, in the land of Israel, being but young, all the tribe of Nephthali my father fell from the house of Jerusalem, which was chosen out of all the tribes of Israel, that all the tribes should sacrifice there, where the temple of the habitation of the Most High was consecrated and built for all ages. Now all the tribes which together revolted, and the house of my father Nephthali, sacrificed unto the heifer Baal. But I alone went often to Jerusalem at the feasts, as it was ordained unto all the people of Israel by an everlasting decree, having the first-fruits and tenths of increase, with that which was first shorn; and them gave I at the altar to the priests the children of Aaron.

The first tenth part of all increase I gave to the sons of Aaron, who ministered at Jerusalem: another tenth part I sold away, and went, and spent it every year at Jerusalem: and the third I gave unto them to whom it was meet, as Debora my father's mother had commanded me, because I was left an orphan by my father.

Furthermore, when I was come to the age of a man, I married Anna of mine own kindred, and of her I begat Tobias.

And when we were carried away captives to Nineve, all my brethren and those that were of my kindred did eat of the bread of the Gentiles. But I kept myself from eating; because I remembered God with all my heart. And the Most High gave me grace and favour before Enemessar, so that I was his purveyor.

Now when Enemessar was dead Sennacherib his son reigned in his stead.

And in the time of Enemessar I gave many alms to my brethren, and gave my bread to the hungry, and my clothes to the naked: and if I saw any of my nation dead, or cast about the walls of Nineve, I buried him. And if the king Sennacherib had slain any, when he was come, and fled from Judea, I buried them privily; for in his wrath he killed many; but the bodies were not found, when they were sought for of the king.

And when one of the Ninevites went and complained of me to the king, that I buried them, and hid myself; understanding that I was sought for to be put to death, I withdrew myself for fear. Then all my goods were forcibly taken away, neither was there anything left me, besides my wife Anna and my son Tobias.

And there passed not five and fifty days before two of his sons killed him, and they fled into the mountains of Ararath; and Sarchedonus his son reigned in his stead; who appointed over his father's accounts, and over all his affairs, Achiacharus my brother Anael's son. And Achiacharus entreating for me, I returned to Nineve. Now Achiacharus was cup-bearer, and keeper of the signet, and steward and overseer of the accounts: and Sarchedonus appointed him next unto him: and he was my brother's son.

Now when I was come home again, and my wife Anna was restored unto me, with my son Tobias, in the feast of Pentecost, which is the holy feast of the seven weeks, there was a good dinner prepared me, in the which I sat down to eat. And when I saw abundance of meat, I said to my son, Go and bring what poor man soever thou shalt find out of our brethren, who is mindful of the Lord; and lo, I tarry for thee.

But he came again, and said, Father, one of our nation is strangled, and is cast out in the market-place. Then before I had tasted of any meat, I started up, and took him up into a room until the going down of the sun. Then I returned, and washed myself, and ate my meat in heaviness, remembering that prophecy of Amos, as he said, Your feasts shall be turned into mourning, and all your mirth into lamentation. Therefore I wept: and after the going down of the sun I went and made a grave, and buried him.

But my neighbours mocked me, and said, This man is not yet afraid to be put to death for this matter: who fled away; and yet lo, he burieth the dead again.

The same night also I returned from the burial, and slept by the wall of my court-yard, being polluted, and my face was uncovered: and I knew not that there were sparrows in the wall, and mine eyes being open, the sparrows muted warm dung into mine eyes, and a whiteness came in mine eyes; and I went to the physicians, but they helped me not: moreover, Achiacharus did nourish me, until I went into Elymais.

And my wife Anna did take women's works to do. And when she had sent them home to the owners, they paid her wages, and gave her also beside a kid. And when it was in my house, and began to cry, I said unto her, From whence is this kid? is it not stolen? render it to the owners; for it is not lawful to eat any thing that is stolen. But she replied upon me, It was given for a gift more than the wages. Howbeit I did not believe her, but bade her render it to the owners: and I was abashed at her. But she replied upon me, Where are thine alms and thy righteous deeds? behold, thou and all thy works are known.

Then I being grieved did weep, and in my sorrow prayed, saying, O Lord, thou art just, and all thy works and all thy ways are mercy and truth, and thou judgest truly and justly for ever. Remember me, and look on me, punish me not for my sins and ignorances, and the sins of my fathers, who have sinned before thee: for they obeyed not thy commandments: wherefore thou hast delivered us for a spoil, and unto captivity, and unto death, and for a proverb of reproach to all the nations among whom we are dispersed. And now thy judgments are many and true: deal with me according to my sins and my fathers': because we have not kept thy commandments, neither have walked in truth before thee. Now therefore deal with me as seemeth best unto thee, and command my spirit to be taken from me, that I may be dissolved, and become earth: for it is profitable for me to die rather than to live, because I have heard false reproaches, and have much sorrow: command therefore that I may now be delivered out of this distress, and go into the everlasting place: turn not thy face away from me.

It came to pass the same day, that in Ecbatane a city of Media, Sara the daughter of Raguel was also reproached by her father's maids; because that she had been married to seven husbands, whom Asmodeus the evil spirit had killed before they had lain with her. Dost thou not know, said they, that thou hast strangled thy husbands? thou hast had already seven husbands, neither wast thou named after any of them. Wherefore dost thou beat us for them? if they be dead, go thy ways after them, let us never see of thee either son or daughter.

When she heard these things, she was very sorrowful, so that she thought to have strangled herself; and she said, I am the only daughter of my father, and if I do this, it shall be a reproach unto him, and I shall bring his old age with sorrow unto the grave.

Then she prayed towards the window, and said, Blessed art thou, O Lord my God, and thy holy and glorious name is blessed and honourable for ever: let all thy works praise thee for ever. And now, O Lord, I set mine eyes and my face towards thee, and say, Take me out of the earth, that I may hear no more the reproach. Thou knowest, Lord, that I am pure from all sin with man, and that I never polluted my name, nor the name of my father, in the land of my captivity; I am the only daughter of my father, neither hath he any child to be his heir, neither any near kinsman, nor any son of his alive to whom I may keep myself for a wife: my seven husbands are already dead; and why should I live? but if it please not thee that I should die, command some regard to be had of me, and pity taken of me, that I hear no more reproach.

So the prayers of them both were heard before the majesty of the great God. And Raphael was sent to heal them both, that is, to scale away the whiteness of Tobit's eyes, and to give Sara the daughter of Raguel for a wife to Tobias the son of Tobit; and to bind Asmodeus the evil spirit; because she belonged to Tobias by right of inheritance. The self-same time came Tobit home, and entered into his house, and Sara the daughter of Raguel came down from her upper chamber.

And when Tobit had called Tobias, he said, My son, when I am dead, bury me; and despise not thy mother, but honour her all the days of thy life, and do that which shall please her, and grieve her not. Remember, my son, that she saw many dangers for thee, when thou wast in her womb; and when she is dead, bury her by me in one grave.

My son, be mindful of the Lord our God all thy days, and let not thy will be set to sin, or to transgress his commandments: do uprightly all thy life long, and follow not the ways of unrighteousness. For if thou deal truly, thy doings shall prosperously succeed to thee, and to all them that live justly. Give alms of thy substance; and when thou givest alms, let not thine eye be envious, neither turn thy face from any poor, and the face of God shall not be turned away from thee. If thou hast abundance, give alms accordingly: if thou have but a little, be not afraid to give according to that little: for thou layest up a good treasure for thyself against the day of necessity. Because that alms do deliver from death, and suffereth not to come into darkness. For alms is a good gift unto all that give it in the sight of the Most High.

Beware of all whoredom, my son, and chiefly take a wife of the seed of thy fathers, and take not a strange woman to wife, which is not of thy father's tribe: for we are the children of the prophets, Noe, Abraham, Isaac, and Jacob: remember, my son, that our fathers from the beginning, even that they all married wives of their own kindred, and were blessed in their children, and their seed shall inherit the land. Now therefore, my son, love thy brethren, and despise not in thy heart thy brethren, the sons and daughters of thy people, in not taking a wife of them: for in pride is destruction and much trouble, and in lewdness is decay and great want: for lewdness is the mother of famine.

Let not the wages of any man, which hath wrought for thee, tarry with thee, but give him it out of hand: for if thou serve God, he will also repay thee: be circumspect, my son, in all things thou doest, and be wise in all thy conversation. Do that to no man which thou hatest: drink not wine to make thee drunken: neither let drunkenness go with thee in thy journey. Give of thy bread to the hungry, and of thy garments to them that are naked; and according to thine abundance give alms; and let not thine eye be envious, when thou givest alms. Pour out thy bread on the burial of the just, but give nothing to the wicked. Ask counsel of all that are wise, and despise not any counsel that is profitable.

Bless the Lord thy God always, and desire of him that thy ways may be directed, and that all thy paths and counsels may prosper: for every nation hath not counsel; but the Lord himself giveth all good things,

and he humbleth whom he will, as he will; now therefore, my son, remember my commandments, neither let them be put out of thy mind.

And fear not, my son, that we are made poor: for thou hast much
wealth, if thou fear God, and depart from all sin, and do that which is
pleasing in his sight.

Judith

And in the eighteenth year, the two and twentieth day of the first
month, there was talk in the house of Nabuchodonosor king of the
Assyrians, that he should, as he said, avenge himself on all the earth.
So he called unto him all his officers, and all his nobles, and communicated with them his secret counsel, and concluded the afflicting of the
whole earth out of his own mouth. Then they decreed to destroy all flesh
that did not obey the commandment of his mouth.

And when he had ended his counsel, Nabuchodonosor king of the
Assyrians called Holofernes the chief captain of his army, which was
next unto him, and said unto him, Thus saith the great king, the lord of
the whole earth, Behold, thou shalt go forth from my presence, and take
with thee men that trust in their own strength, of footmen a hundred
and twenty thousand; and the number of horses with their riders twelve
thousand. And thou shalt go against all the west country, because they
disobeyed my commandment. And thou shalt declare unto them, that
they prepare for me earth and water: for I will go forth in my wrath
against them, and will cover the whole face of the earth with the feet of
mine army, and I will give them for a spoil unto them: so that their slain
shall fill their valleys and brooks, and the river shall be filled with their
dead, till it overflow: and I will lead them captives to the utmost parts
of all the earth. Thou therefore shalt go forth, and take beforehand for
me all their coasts: and if they will yield themselves unto thee, thou shalt

reserve them for me till the day of their punishment. But concerning them that rebel, let not thine eye spare them; but put them to the slaughter, and spoil them wheresoever thou goest. For as I live, and by the power of my kingdom, whatsoever I have spoken, that will I do by my hand. And take thou heed that thou transgress none of the commandments of thy lord, but accomplish them fully, as I have commanded thee, and defer not to do them.

Then Holofernes went forth from the presence of his Lord, and called all the governors and captains, and the officers of the army of Assur; and he mustered the chosen men for the battle, as his lord had commanded him, unto a hundred and twenty thousand, and twelve thousand archers on horseback; and he ranged them, as a great army is ordered for the war.

Then came he down toward the sea-coast, both he and his army, and set garrisons in the high cities, and took out of them chosen men for aid. So they and all the country round about received them with garlands, with dances, and with timbrels. Yet he did cast down their frontiers, and cut down their groves: for he had decreed to destroy all the gods of the land, that all nations should worship Nabuchodonosor only, and that all tongues and tribes should call upon him as god.

Then Holofernes commanded all his army, and all his people which were come to take his part, that they should remove their camp against Bethulia, to take aforehand the ascents of the hill-country, and to make war against the children of Israel. Then their strong men removed their camps in that day, and the army of the men of war was a hundred and seventy thousand footmen, and twelve thousand horsemen, besides the baggage, and other men that were afoot among them, a very great multitude. And they camped in the valley near unto Bethulia, by the fountain, and they spread themselves in breadth over Dothaim.

Now the children of Israel, when they saw the multitude of them, were greatly troubled, and said every one to his neighbour, Now will these men lick up the face of the earth; for neither the high mountains, nor the valleys, nor the hills, are able to bear their weight. Then every man took up his weapons of war, and when they had kindled fires upon their towers, they remained and watched all that night.

But in the second day Holofernes brought forth all his horsemen in the sight of the children of Israel which were in Bethulia; and viewed the passages up to the city, and came to the fountains of their waters, and took them, and set garrisons of men of war over them, and he himself removed toward his people.

Then came unto him all the chief of the children of Esau, and all the governors of the people of Moab, and the captains of the sea-coast, and said, Let our lord now hear a word, that there be not an overthrow in thine army. For this people of the children of Israel do not trust in their spears, but in the height of the mountains wherein they dwell, because it is not easy to come up to the tops of their mountains. Now therefore, my lord, fight not against them in battle-array, and there shall not so much as one man of thy people perish. Remain in thy camp, and keep all the men of thine army, and let thy servants get into their hands the fountain of water, which issueth forth of the foot of the mountain: for all the inhabitants of Bethulia have their water thence: so shall thirst kill them, and they shall give up their city; and we and our people shall go up to the tops of the mountains that are near, and will camp upon them, to watch that none go out of the city.

And these words pleased Holofernes and all his servants, and he appointed to do as they had spoken. So the camp of the children of Ammon departed, and with them five thousand of the Assyrians, and they pitched in the valley, and took the waters, and the fountains of the waters of the children of Israel. Then the children of Esau went up with the children of Ammon, and camped in the hill-country over against Dothaim: and they sent some of them toward the south, and toward the east, over against Ekrebel, which is near unto Chusi, that is upon the brook Mochmur; and the rest of the army of the Assyrians camped in the plain, and covered the face of the whole land; and their tents and carriages were pitched to a very great multitude.

Then the children of Israel cried unto the Lord their God, because their heart failed, for all their enemies had compassed them round about, and there was no way to escape out from among them.

Thus all the company of Assur remained about them, both their footmen, chariots, and horsemen, four and thirty days, so that all their vessels of water failed all the inhabitants of Bethulia. And the cisterns were emptied, and they had not water to drink their fill for one day; for they gave them drink by measure. Therefore their young children were out of heart, and their women and young men fainted for thirst, and fell down in the streets of the city, and by the passages of the gates, and there was no longer any strength in them.

Then all the people assembled to Ozias, and to the chief of the city, both young men, and women, and children, and cried with a loud voice, and said before all the elders, God be judge between us and you: for ye have done us great injury, in that ye have not required peace of the children of Assur. For now we have no helper; but God hath sold us into their hands, that we should be thrown down before them with thirst and great destruction. Now therefore call them unto you, and deliver the whole city for a spoil to the people of Holofernes, and to all his army. For it is better for us to be made a spoil unto them, than to die for thirst: for we will be his servants, that our souls may live, and not see the death of our infants before our eyes, nor our wives nor our children to die. We take to witness against you the heaven and the earth, and our God and Lord of our fathers, which punisheth us according to our sins and the sins of our fathers, that he do not according as we have said this day.

Then there was great weeping with one consent in the midst of the assembly; and they cried unto the Lord God with a loud voice.

Then said Ozias to them, Brethren, be of good courage, let us yet endure five days, in the which space the Lord our God may turn his mercy toward us; for he will not forsake us utterly. And if these days pass, and there come no help unto us, I will do according to your word.

And he dispersed the people, every one to their own charge; and they went unto the walls and towers of their city, and sent the women and children into their houses: and they were very low brought in the city.

Now at that time Judith heard thereof, which was the daughter of Merari, the son of Ox, the son of Joseph, the son of Oziel, the son of Elcia, the son of Ananias, the son of Gideon, the son of Raphaim, the son of Acitho, the son of Eliu, the son of Eliab, the son of Nathanael, the son of Samael, the son of Salasadai, the son of Israel.

And Manasses was her husband, of her tribe and kindred, who died in the barley-harvest. For as he stood overseeing them that bound sheaves in the field, the heat came upon his head, and he fell on his bed, and died in the city of Bethulia; and they buried him with his fathers in the field between Dothaim and Balamo. So Judith was a widow in her house three years and four months.

And she made her a tent upon the top of her house, and put on sack-cloth upon her loins, and ware her widow's apparel. And she fasted all the days of her widowhood, save the eves of the sabbaths, and the sabbaths, and the eves of the new moons, and the new moons, and the feasts and solemn days of the house of Israel.

She was also of a goodly countenance, and very beautiful to behold: and her husband Manasses had left her gold, and silver, and men-servants, and maid-servants, and cattle, and lands; and she remained upon them. And there was none that gave her an ill word; for she feared God greatly.

Now when she heard the evil words of the people against the governor, that they fainted for lack of water; for Judith had heard all the words that Ozias had spoken unto them, and that he had sworn to deliver the city unto the Assyrians after five days; then she sent her waiting-woman, that had the government of all things that she had, to call Ozias and Chabris and Charmis, the ancients of the city.

And they came unto her, and she said unto them, Hear me now, O ye governors of the inhabitants of Bethulia: for your words that ye have spoken before the people this day are not right, touching this oath which ye made and pronounced between God and you, and have promised to deliver the city to our enemies, unless within these days the Lord turn to help you. And now who are ye that have tempted God this day, and stand instead of God among the children of men?

And now try the Lord Almighty, but ye shall never know any thing. For ye cannot find the depth of the heart of man, neither can ye perceive the things that he thinketh: then how can ye search out God, that hath made all these things, and know his mind, or comprehend his purpose? Nay, my brethren, provoke not the Lord our God to anger. For if he will not help us within these five days, he hath power to defend us when he will, even every day, or to destroy us before our enemies.

Then said Ozias to her, All that thou hast spoken, hast thou spoken with a good heart, and there is none that may gainsay thy words. For this is not the first day wherein thy wisdom is manifested; but from the beginning of thy days all the people have known thy understanding, because the disposition of thy heart is good. But the people were very thirsty, and compelled us to do unto them as we have spoken, and to bring an oath upon ourselves, which we will not break. Therefore now pray thou for us, because thou art a godly woman, and the Lord will send us rain to fill our cisterns, and we shall faint no more.

Then said Judith unto them, Hear me, and I will do a thing which shall go throughout all generations to the children of our nation. Ye shall stand this night in the gate, and I will go forth with my waiting-woman: and within the days that ye have promised to deliver the city to our enemies, the Lord will visit Israel by my hand. But inquire not ye of mine act: for I will not declare it unto you, till the things be finished that I do.

Then said Ozias and the princes unto her, Go in peace, and the Lord God be before thee, to take vengeance on our enemies.

So they returned from the tent, and went to their wards.

Then Judith fell upon her face, and put ashes upon her head, and uncovered the sackcloth wherewith she was clothed; and about the time that the incense of that evening was offered in Jerusalem, in the house of the Lord, Judith cried with a loud voice, and said, O Lord God of my father Simeon, to whom thou gavest a sword to take vengeance of the strangers, who loosened the girdle of a maid to defile her, and discovered the thigh to her shame, and polluted her virginity to her reproach: O God, O my God, hear me also a widow.

For, behold, the Assyrians are multiplied in their power; they are exalted with horse and man; they glory in the strength of their footmen; they trust in shield and spear, and bow and sling; and know not that thou art the Lord that breakest the battles: the Lord is thy name. Throw down their strength in thy power, and bring down their force in thy wrath: for they have purposed to defile thy sanctuary, and to pollute the tabernacle where thy glorious name resteth, and to cast down with the sword the horn of thine altar.

Behold their pride, and send thy wrath upon their heads: give into my hand, which am a widow, the power that I have conceived. Smite by the deceit of my lips the servant with the prince, and the prince with the servant: break down their stateliness by the hand of a woman. For thy power standeth not in multitude, nor thy might in strong men: for thou art a God of the afflicted, a helper of the oppressed, an upholder of the weak, a protector of the forlorn, a saviour of them that are without hope. I pray thee, I pray thee, O God of my father, and God of the inheritance of Israel, Lord of the heavens and earth, Creator of the waters, King of every creature, hear thou my prayer: and make my speech and deceit to be their wound and stripe, who have purposed cruel things against thy covenant, and thy hallowed house, and against the top of Sion, and against the house of the possession of thy children. And make every nation and tribe to acknowledge that thou art the God of all power and might, and that there is none other that protecteth the people of Israel but thou.

Now after that she had ceased to cry unto the God of Israel, and had made an end of all these words, she rose where she had fallen down, and called her maid, and went down into the house, in the which she abode in the sabbath-days, and in her feast-days, and pulled off the sackcloth which she had on, and put off the garments of her widowhood, and washed her body all over with water, and anointed herself with precious ointment, and braided the hair of her head, and put on a tire upon it, and put on her garments of gladness, wherewith she was clad during the life of Manasses her husband. And she took sandals upon her feet, and put about her her bracelets, and her chains, and her rings, and her ear-rings, and all her ornaments, and decked herself bravely, to allure the eyes of all men that should see her. Then she gave her maid a bottle of wine, and a cruse of oil, and filled a bag with parched corn, and lumps of figs, and with fine bread; so she folded all these things together, and laid them upon her.

Thus they went straight forth in the valley: and the first watch of the Assyrians met her, and took her, and asked her, Of what people art thou? and whence comest thou? and whither goest thou? And she said, I am a woman of the Hebrews, and am fled from them: for they shall be given you to be consumed: and I am coming before Holofernes the chief captain of your army, to declare words of truth; and I will shew him a way whereby he shall go, and win all the hill-country, without losing the body or life of any one of his men.

Then they chose out of them a hundred men to accompany her and her maid; and they brought her to the tent of Holofernes.

And they that lay near Holofernes went out, and all his servants, and they brought her into the tent. Now Holofernes rested upon his bed under a canopy, which was woven with purple, and gold, and emeralds, and precious stones. So they shewed him of her; and he came out before his tent with silver lamps going before him. And when Judith was come before him and his servants, they all marvelled at the beauty of her countenance; and she fell down upon her face, and did reverence unto him: and his servants took her up.

Then said Holofernes unto her, Woman, be of good comfort, fear not in thy heart: for I never hurt any that was willing to serve Nabuchodono-sor, the king of all the earth. Now therefore, if thy people that dwelleth in the mountains had not set light by me, I would not have lifted up my spear against them: but they have done these things to themselves. But now tell me wherefore art thou fled from them, and art come unto us: for thou art come for safeguard; be of good comfort, thou shalt live this night, and hereafter: for none shall hurt thee, but entreat thee well, as they do the servants of king Nabuchodonosor my lord.

Then Judith said unto him, Receive the words of thy servant, and suffer thy handmaid to speak in thy presence, and I will declare no lie to my lord this night. And if thou wilt follow the words of thy handmaid, God will bring the thing perfectly to pass by thee; and my lord shall not fail of his purposes. As Nabuchodonosor king of all the earth liveth, and as his power liveth, who hath sent thee for the upholding of every living thing: for not only men shall serve him by thee, but also the beasts of the field, and the cattle, and the fowls of the air, shall live by thy power under Nabuchodonosor and all his house. For we have heard of thy wisdom and thy policies, and it is reported in all the earth, that thou only art excellent in all the kingdom, and mighty in knowledge, and wonderful in feats of war.

Now as concerning the matter, which Achior did speak in thy council, we have heard his words; for the men of Bethulia saved him, and he declared unto them all that he had spoken unto thee. Therefore, O lord and governor, reject not his word; but lay it up in thy heart, for it is true; for our nation shall not be punished, neither can the sword prevail against them, except they sin against their God.

And now, that my lord be not defeated and frustrate of his purpose, even death is now fallen upon them, and their sin hath overtaken them, wherewith they will provoke their God to anger, whensoever they shall do that which is not fit to be done: for their victuals fail them, and all their water is scant, and they have determined to lay hands upon their cattle, and purposed to consume all those things, that God hath for-bidden them to eat by his laws: and are resolved to spend the first-fruits of the corn, and the tenths of wine and oil, which they had sanctified, and reserved for the priests that serve in Jerusalem before the face of our God; the which things it is not lawful for any of the people so much as to touch with their hands. For they have sent some to Jerusalem, because they also that dwell there have done the like, to bring them a license from the senate. Now when they shall bring them word, they will forthwith do it, and they shall be given thee to be destroyed the same day.

Wherefore I thy handmaid, knowing all this, am fled from their presence; and God hath sent me to work things with thee, whereat all the earth shall be astonished, and whosoever shall hear it. For thy servant is religious, and serveth the God of heaven day and night: now therefore, my lord, I will remain with thee, and thy servant will go out by night into the valley, and I will pray unto God, and he will tell me when they have committed their sins: and I will come and shew it unto thee: then thou shalt go forth with all thine army, and there shall be none of them that shall resist thee. And I will lead thee through the midst of Judea, until thou come before Jerusalem; and I will set thy throne in the midst thereof; and thou shalt drive them as sheep that have no shepherd, and a dog shall not so much as open his mouth at thee: for these things were told me according to my foreknowledge, and they were declared unto me, and I am sent to tell thee.

Then her words pleased Holofernes and all his servants; and they marvelled at her wisdom, and said, There is not such a woman from one end of the earth to the other, both for beauty of face, and wisdom of words.

Likewise Holofernes said unto her, God hath done well to send thee before the people, that strength might be in our hands, and destruction upon them that lightly regard my lord. And now thou art both beautiful in thy countenance, and witty in thy words: surely if thou do as thou hast spoken, thy God shall be my God, and thou shalt dwell in the house of king Nabuchodonosor, and shalt be renowned through the whole earth.

Then the servants of Holofernes brought her into the tent, and she slept till midnight, and she arose when it was toward the morning watch, and sent to Holofernes, saying, Let my lord now command that thy handmaid may go forth unto prayer. Then Holofernes commanded his guard that they should not stay her.

Thus she abode in the camp three days, and went out in the night into the valley of Bethulia, and washed herself in a fountain of water by the camp. And when she came out, she besought the Lord God of Israel to direct her way to the raising up of the children of her people. So she came in clean, and remained in the tent, until she did eat her meat at evening.

And in the fourth day Holofernes made a feast to his own servants only, and called none of the officers to the banquet. Then said he to Bagoas the eunuch, who had charge over all that he had, Go now, and persuade this Hebrew woman which is with thee, that she come unto us, and eat and drink with us. For lo, it will be a shame for our person, if we shall let such a woman go, not having had her company; for if we draw her not unto us, she will laugh us to scorn.

Then went Bagoas from the presence of Holofernes, and came to her, and he said, Let not this fair damsel fear to come to my lord, and to be honoured in his presence, and drink wine, and be merry with us, and be made this day as one of the daughters of the Assyrians, which serve in the house of Nabuchodonosor.

Then said Judith unto him, Who am I now, that I should gainsay my lord? surely whatsoever pleaseth him I will do speedily, and it shall be my joy unto the day of my death. So she arose, and decked herself with her apparel, and all her woman's attire, and her maid went and laid soft skins on the ground for her over against Holofernes, which she had received of Bagoas for her daily use, that she might sit and eat upon them.

Now when Judith came in and sat down, Holofernes' heart was ravished with her, and his mind was moved, and he desired greatly her company; for he waited a time to deceive her, from the day that he had seen her. Then said Holofernes unto her, Drink now, and be merry with us. So Judith said, I will drink now, my lord, because my life is magnified in me this day more than all the days since I was born. Then she took and ate and drank before him what her maid had prepared.

And Holofernes took great delight in her, and drank much more wine than he had drunk at any time in one day since he was born.

Now when the evening was come, his servants made haste to depart, and Bagoas shut his tent without, and dismissed the waiters from the presence of his lord; and they went to their beds: for they were all weary, because the feast had been long. And Judith was left alone in the tent, and Holofernes lying along upon his bed: for he was filled with wine.

Then Judith, standing by his bed, said in her heart, O Lord God of all power, look at this present upon the works of my hands for the exaltation of Jerusalem. For now is the time to help thine inheritance, and to execute mine enterprises to the destruction of the enemies which are risen against us.

Then she came to the pillar of the bed which was at Holofernes' head, and took down his falchion from thence, and approached to his bed, and took hold of the hair of his head, and said, Strengthen me, O Lord God of Israel, this day. And she smote twice upon his neck with all her might, and she took away his head from him, and tumbled his body down from the bed, and pulled down the canopy from the pillars, and anon after she went forth, and gave Holofernes' head to her maid; and she put it in her bag of meat: so they twain went together according to their custom unto prayer: and when they passed the camp, they compassed the valley, and went up the mountain of Bethulia, and came to the gates thereof.

Then said Judith afar off to the watchmen at the gate, Open, open now the gate: God, even our God, is with us, to shew his power yet in Jerusalem, and his forces against the enemy, as he hath even done this day.

Now when the men of her city heard her voice, they made haste to go down to the gate of their city, and they called the elders of the city. And then they ran all together, both small and great, for it was strange unto them that she was come: so they opened the gate, and received them, and made a fire for a light, and stood round about them.

Then she said to them with a loud voice, Praise, praise God, praise God, I say, for he hath not taken away his mercy from the house of Israel, but hath destroyed our enemies by my hands this night. So she took the head out of the bag, and shewed it, and said unto them, Behold the head of Holofernes, the chief captain of the army of Assur, and behold the canopy, wherein he did lie in his drunkenness; and the lord hath smitten him by the hand of a woman. As the Lord liveth, who hath kept me in my way that I went, my countenance hath deceived him to his destruction, and yet hath he not committed sin with me, to defile and shame me.

Then said Judith unto them, Hear me now, my brethren, and take this head, and hang it upon the highest place of your walls. And so soon as the morning shall appear, and the sun shall come forth upon the earth, take ye every one his weapons, and go forth every valiant man out of the city, and set ye a captain over them, as though ye would go down into the field toward the watch of the Assyrians; but go not down. Then they shall take their armour, and shall go into their camp, and raise up the captains of the army of Assur, and they shall run to the tent of

Holofernes, but shall not find him: then fear shall fall upon them, and they shall flee before your face. So ye, and all that inhabit the coast of Israel, shall pursue them, and overthrow them as they go.

And as soon as the morning arose, they hanged the head of Holofernes upon the wall, and every man took his weapons, and they went forth by bands unto the straits of the mountain. But when the Assyrians saw them, they sent to their leaders, which came to their captains and tribunes, and to every one of their rulers. So they came to Holofernes' tent, and said to him that had the charge of all his things, Waken now our lord: for the slaves have been bold to come down against us to battle, that they may be utterly destroyed.

Then went in Bagoas, and knocked at the door of the tent; for he thought that he had slept with Judith. But because none answered, he opened it, and went into the bed-chamber, and found him cast upon the floor dead, and his head was taken from him. Therefore he cried with a loud voice, with weeping, and sighing, and a mighty cry, and rent his garments. After, he went into the tent where Judith lodged: and when he found her not, he leaped out to the people, and cried, These slaves have dealt treacherously; one woman of the Hebrews hath brought shame upon the house of king Nabuchodonosor: for behold, Holofernes lieth upon the ground without a head.

When the captains of the Assyrians' army heard these words, they rent their coats, and their minds were wonderfully troubled, and there was a cry and a very great noise throughout the camp.

And when they that were in the tents heard, they were astonished at the thing that was done. And fear and trembling fell upon them, so that there was no man that durst abide in the sight of his neighbour, but rushing out all together, they fled into every way of the plain, and of the hill-country. They also that had camped in the mountains round about Bethulia fled away. Then the children of Israel, every one that was a warrior among them, rushed out upon them. Then sent Ozias to Betomasthem, and to Bebai, and Chobai, and Cola, and to all the coasts of Israel, such as should tell the things that were done, and that all should rush forth upon their enemies to destroy them.

Now when the children of Israel heard it, they all fell upon them with one consent, and slew them unto Chobai: likewise also they that came from Jerusalem, and from all the hill-country, (for men had told them what things were done in the camp of their enemies,) and they that were in Galaad, and in Galilee, chased them with a great slaughter, until they were passed Damascus and the borders thereof.

Then Judith began to sing this thanksgiving in all Israel, and all the people sang after her this song of praise. And Judith said,

Begin unto my God with timbrels,
Sing unto my Lord with cymbals: tune unto him a new psalm:
Exalt him, and call upon his name.
For God breaketh the battles:
For among the camps in the midst of the people
He hath delivered me out of the hands of them that persecuted me.

Assur came out of the mountains from the north,
He came with ten thousands of his army,
The multitude whereof stopped the torrents,
And their horsemen have covered the hills.
He bragged that he would burn up my borders,
And kill my young men with the sword,
And dash the sucking children against the ground,
And make mine infants as a prey, and my virgins as a spoil.

But the Almighty Lord hath disappointed them by the hand of a woman.
For the mighty one did not fall by the young men,
Neither did the sons of the Titans smite him,
Nor high giants set upon him:
But Judith, the daughter of Merari, weakened him with the beauty of
      her countenance.

For she put off the garment of her widowhood
For the exaltation of those that were oppressed in Israel,
And anointed her face with ointment,
And bound her hair in a tire,
And took a linen garment to deceive him.
Her sandals ravished his eyes,
Her beauty took his mind prisoner,
And the falchion passed through his neck.
The Persians quaked at her boldness,
And the Medes were daunted at her hardiness.

Then my afflicted shouted for joy, and my weak ones cried aloud;
But they were astonished:

These lifted up their voices, but they were overthrown.
The sons of the damsels have pierced them through, and wounded them
      as fugitives' children:
They perished by the battle of the Lord.

I will sing unto the Lord a new song;
O Lord, thou art great and glorious,
Wonderful in strength, and invincible.
Let all creatures serve thee;
For thou spakest, and they were made,
Thou didst send forth thy spirit, and it created them,
And there is none that can resist thy voice.

For the mountains shall be moved from their foundations with the
      waters,
The rocks shall melt as wax at thy presence:
Yet thou art merciful to them that fear thee.
For all sacrifice is too little for a sweet savour unto thee,
And all the fat is not sufficient for thy burnt-offering:
But he that feareth the Lord is great at all times.

Woe to the nations that rise up against my kindred!
The Lord Almighty will take vengeance of them in the day of judgment,
In putting fire and worms in their flesh;
And they shall feel them, and weep for ever.

Now as soon as they entered into Jerusalem, they worshipped the
Lord; and as soon as the people were purified, they offered their burnt-
offerings, and their free-offerings, and their gifts. Judith also dedicated
all the stuff of Holofernes, which the people had given her, and gave the
canopy, which she had taken out of his bed-chamber, for a gift unto the
Lord. So the people continued feasting in Jerusalem before the sanctuary for the space of three months, and Judith remained with them.

After this time every one returned to his own inheritance, and Judith
went to Bethulia, and remained in her own possession, and was in her
time honourable in all the country.

And many desired her, but none knew her all the days of her life,
after that Manasses her husband was dead, and was gathered to his
people. But she increased more and more in honour, and waxed old in
her husband's house, being a hundred and five years old, and made her

maid free; so she died in Bethulia: and they buried her in the cave of her husband Manasses.

The History of Susanna

There dwelt a man in Babylon, called Joacim: and he took a wife, whose name was Susanna, the daughter of Chelcias, a very fair woman, and one that feared the Lord. Her parents also were righteous, and taught their daughter according to the law of Moses.

Now Joacim was a great rich man, and had a fair garden joining unto his house: and to him resorted the Jews; because he was more honourable than all others.

The same year were appointed two of the ancients of the people to be judges, such as the Lord spake of, that wickedness came from Babylon from ancient judges, who seemed to govern the people. These kept much at Joacim's house: and all that had any suits in law came unto them.

Now when the people departed away at noon, Susanna went into her husband's garden to walk.

And the two elders saw her going in every day, and walking; so that their lust was inflamed toward her. And they perverted their own mind, and turned away their eyes, that they might not look unto heaven, nor remember just judgments. And albeit they both were wounded with her love, yet durst not one shew another his grief. For they were ashamed to declare their lust, that they desired to have to do with her. Yet they watched diligently from day to day to see her.

And the one said to the other, Let us now go home: for it is dinnertime. So when they were gone out, they parted the one from the other, and turning back again they came to the same place; and after they had asked one another the cause, they acknowledged their lust: then appointed they a time both together, when they might find her alone.

And it fell out, as they watched a fit time, she went in as before with two maids only, and she was desirous to wash herself in the garden: for it was hot. And there was nobody there save the two elders, that had hid themselves, and watched her. Then she said to her maids, Bring me oil and washing-balls, and shut the garden-doors, that I may wash me. And they did as she bade them, and shut the garden-doors, and went out themselves at privy doors to fetch the things that she had commanded them: but they saw not the elders, because they were hid.

Now when the maids were gone forth, the two elders rose up, and ran unto her, saying, Behold, the garden-doors are shut, that no man can see us, and we are in love with thee; therefore consent unto us, and lie with us. If thou wilt not, we will bear witness against thee, that a young man was with thee: and therefore thou didst send away thy maids from thee.

Then Susanna sighed, and said, I am straitened on every side: for if I do this thing, it is death unto me: and if I do it not, I cannot escape your hands. It is better for me to fall into your hands, and not to do it, than to sin in the sight of the Lord. With that Susanna cried with a loud voice: and the two elders cried out against her. Then ran the one, and opened the garden-door.

So when the servants of the house heard the cry in the garden, they rushed in at a privy door, to see what was done unto her. But when the elders had declared their matter, the servants were greatly ashamed: for there never was such a report made of Susanna.

And it came to pass the next day, when the people were assembled to her husband Joacim, the two elders came also full of mischievous imagination against Susanna to put her to death; and said before the people, Send for Susanna, the daughter of Chelcias, Joacim's wife. And so they sent. So she came with her father and mother, her children, and all her kindred.

Now Susanna was a very delicate woman, and beauteous to behold. And these wicked men commanded to uncover her face, (for she was covered) that they might be filled with her beauty. Therefore her friends and all that saw her wept.

Then the two elders stood up in the midst of the people, and laid their hands upon her head, and she weeping looked up toward heaven: for her heart trusted in the Lord.

And the elders said, As we walked in the garden alone, this woman came in with two maids, and shut the garden-doors, and sent the maids away. Then a young man, who there was hid, came unto her, and lay with her. Then we that stood in a corner of the garden, seeing this wickedness, ran unto them. And when we saw them together, the man we could not hold: for he was stronger than we, and opened the door, and leaped out. But having taken this woman, we asked who the young man was, but she would not tell us: these things do we testify.

Then the assembly believed them, as those that were the elders and judges of the people: so they condemned her to death.

Then Susanna cried out with a loud voice, and said, O everlasting God, that knowest the secrets, and knowest all things before they be: thou knowest that they have borne false witness against me; and behold, I must die; whereas I never did such things as these men have maliciously invented against me.

And the Lord heard her voice.

Therefore when she was led to be put to death, the Lord raised up the holy spirit of a young youth, whose name was Daniel: who cried with a loud voice, I am clear from the blood of this woman.

Then all the people turned them toward him, and said, What mean these words that thou hast spoken?

So he standing in the midst of them said, Are ye such fools, ye sons of Israel, that without examination or knowledge of the truth, ye have condemned a daughter of Israel? Return again to the place of judgment: for they have borne false witness against her.

Wherefore all the people turned again in haste, and the elders said unto him, Come, sit down among us, and shew it us, seeing God hath given thee the honour of an elder.

Then said Daniel unto them, Put these two aside one far from another, and I will examine them.

So when they were put asunder one from another, he called one of them, and said unto him, O thou that art waxen old in wickedness, now thy sins which thou hast committed aforetime are come to light. For thou hast pronounced false judgment, and hast condemned the innocent, and hast let the guilty go free; albeit the Lord saith, The innocent and righteous shalt thou not slay. Now then, if thou hast seen her, tell me, Under what tree sawest thou them companying together? Who answered, Under a mastick-tree. And Daniel said, Very well; thou hast lied against thine own head; for even now the angel of God hath received the sentence of God to cut thee in two.

So he put him aside, and commanded to bring the other, and said unto

him, O thou seed of Chanaan, and not of Juda, beauty hath deceived
thee, and lust hath perverted thy heart. Thus have ye dealt with the
daughters of Israel, and they for fear companied with you: but the
daughter of Juda would not abide your wickedness. Now therefore tell
me, Under what tree didst thou take them companying together? Who
answered, Under a holm-tree. Then said Daniel unto him, Well; thou
hast also lied against thine own head: for the angel of God waiteth with
the sword to cut thee in two, that he may destroy you.

With that all the assembly cried out with a loud voice, and praised
God, who saveth them that trust in him. And they arose against the two
elders, for Daniel had convicted them of false witness by their own
mouth: and according to the law of Moses they did unto them in such
sort as they maliciously intended to do to their neighbour: and they put
them to death. Thus the innocent blood was saved the same day.

Therefore Chelcias and his wife praised God for their daughter
Susanna, with Joacim her husband, and all the kindred, because there
was no dishonesty found in her.

From that day forth was Daniel had in great reputation in the sight of
the people.

THE NEW TESTAMENT

The Life and Acts of Jesus

(COMPILED FROM THE FOUR GOSPELS)

The Miraculous Conceptions of John the Baptist and of Jesus

(*According to Luke*)

There was in the days of Herod, the king of Judea, a certain priest named Zacharias, of the course of Abia: and his wife was of the daughters of Aaron, and her name was Elisabeth. And they were both righteous before God, walking in all the commandments and ordinances of the Lord blameless. And they had no child, because that Elisabeth was barren; and they both were now well stricken in years.

And it came to pass, that, while he executed the priest's office before God in the order of his course, according to the custom of the priest's office, his lot was to burn incense when he went into the temple of the Lord. And the whole multitude of the people were praying without at the time of incense.

And there appeared unto him an angel of the Lord standing on the right side of the altar of incense. And when Zacharias saw him, he was troubled, and fear fell upon him.

But the angel said unto him, Fear not, Zacharias: for thy prayer is heard; and thy wife Elisabeth shall bear thee a son, and thou shalt call his name John. And thou shalt have joy and gladness; and many shall rejoice at his birth. For he shall be great in the sight of the Lord, and shall drink neither wine nor strong drink; and he shall be filled with the Holy Ghost, even from his mother's womb. And many of the children of Israel shall he turn to the Lord their God. And he shall go before him in the spirit and power of Elias, to turn the hearts of the fathers to the children, and the disobedient to the wisdom of the just; to make ready a people prepared for the Lord.

And Zacharias said unto the angel, Whereby shall I know this? for I am an old man, and my wife well stricken in years.

And the angel answering said unto him, I am Gabriel, that stand in the presence of God; and am sent to speak unto thee, and to show thee these glad tidings. And, behold, thou shalt be dumb, and not able to speak, until the day that these things shall be performed, because thou believest not my words, which shall be fulfilled in their season.

And the people waited for Zacharias, and marvelled that he tarried so long in the temple. And when he came out, he could not speak unto them: and they perceived that he had seen a vision in the temple; for he beckoned unto them, and remained speechless.

And it came to pass, that, as soon as the days of his ministration were accomplished, he departed to his own house.

And after those days his wife Elisabeth conceived, and hid herself five months, saying, Thus hath the Lord dealt with me in the days wherein he looked on me, to take away my reproach among men.

And in the sixth month the angel Gabriel was sent from God unto a city of Galilee, named Nazareth, to a virgin espoused to a man whose name was Joseph, of the house of David; and the virgin's name was Mary.

And the angel came in unto her, and said, Hail, thou that art highly favoured, the Lord is with thee: blessed art thou among women.

And when she saw him, she was troubled at his saying, and cast in her mind what manner of salutation this should be.

And the angel said unto her, Fear not, Mary: for thou hast found favour with God. And, behold, thou shalt conceive in thy womb, and bring forth a son, and shalt call his name JESUS. He shall be great, and shall be called the Son of the Highest; and the Lord God shall give unto him the throne of his father David: and he shall reign over the house of Jacob for ever; and of his kingdom there shall be no end.

Then said Mary unto the angel, How shall this be, seeing I know not a man?

And the angel answered and said unto her, The Holy Ghost shall come upon thee, and the power of the Highest shall overshadow thee: therefore also that holy thing which shall be born of thee shall be called the Son of God. And, behold, thy cousin Elisabeth, she hath also conceived a son in her old age; and this is the sixth month with her, who was called barren. For with God nothing shall be impossible.

And Mary said, Behold the handmaid of the Lord; be it unto me according to thy word. And the angel departed from her.

And Mary arose in those days, and went into the hill country with haste, into a city of Juda; and entered into the house of Zacharias, and saluted Elisabeth.

And it came to pass, that, when Elisabeth heard the salutation of Mary, the babe leaped in her womb; and Elisabeth was filled with the Holy Ghost: and she spake out with a loud voice, and said, Blessed art thou among women, and blessed is the fruit of thy womb. And whence is this to me, that the mother of my Lord should come to me? For, lo, as soon as the voice of thy salutation sounded in mine ears, the babe leaped in my womb for joy. And blessed is she that believed: for there shall be a performance of those things which were told her from the Lord.

And Mary said, My soul doth magnify the Lord, and my spirit hath rejoiced in God my Saviour. For he hath regarded the low estate of his handmaiden: for, behold, from henceforth all generations shall call me blessed. For he that is mighty hath done to me great things; and holy is his name. And his mercy is on them that fear him from generation to generation. He hath showed strength with his arm; he hath scattered the proud in the imagination of their hearts. He hath put down the mighty from their seats, and exalted them of low degree. He hath filled the hungry with good things; and the rich he hath sent empty away. He hath holpen his servant Israel, in remembrance of his mercy; as he spake to our fathers, to Abraham, and to his seed for ever.

And Mary abode with her about three months, and returned to her own house.

Now Elisabeth's full time came that she should be delivered; and she brought forth a son. And her neighbours and her cousins heard how the Lord had showed great mercy upon her; and they rejoiced with her.

And it came to pass, that on the eighth day they came to circumcise the child; and they called him Zacharias, after the name of his father. And his mother answered and said, Not so; but he shall be called John. And they said unto her, There is none of thy kindred that is called by this name.

And they made signs to his father, how he would have him called. And he asked for a writing table, and wrote, saying, His name is John. And they marvelled all.

And his mouth was opened immediately, and his tongue loosed, and he spake, and praised God.

And the child grew, and waxed strong in spirit, and was in the deserts till the day of his showing unto Israel.

The Birth of Jesus

(*According to Luke*)

And it came to pass in those days, that there went out a decree from Caesar Augustus, that all the world should be taxed. (And this taxing was first made when Cyrenius was governor of Syria.) And all went to be taxed, every one into his own city.

And Joseph also went up from Galilee, out of the city of Nazareth, into Judea, unto the city of David, which is called Bethlehem, (because he was of the house and lineage of David,) to be taxed with Mary his espoused wife, being great with child.

And so it was, that, while they were there, the days were accomplished that she should be delivered. And she brought forth her firstborn son, and wrapped him in swaddling clothes, and laid him in a manger; because there was no room for them in the inn.

And there were in the same country shepherds abiding in the field, keeping watch over their flock by night. And, lo, the angel of the Lord came upon them, and the glory of the Lord shone round about them; and they were sore afraid.

And the angel said unto them, Fear not: for, behold, I bring you good tidings of great joy, which shall be to all people. For unto you is born this day in the city of David a Saviour, which is Christ the Lord. And this shall be a sign unto you; Ye shall find the babe wrapped in swaddling clothes, lying in a manger.

And suddenly there was with the angel a multitude of the heavenly host praising God, and saying, Glory to God in the highest, and on earth peace, good will toward men.

And it came to pass, as the angels were gone away from them into heaven, the shepherds said one to another, Let us now go even unto Bethlehem, and see this thing which is come to pass, which the Lord hath made known unto us.

And they came with haste, and found Mary and Joseph, and the babe lying in a manger.

And when they had seen it, they made known abroad the saying which was told them concerning this child. And all they that heard it wondered at those things which were told them by the shepherds.

But Mary kept all these things, and pondered them in her heart.

And the shepherds returned, glorifying and praising God for all the things that they had heard and seen, as it was told unto them.

And when eight days were accomplished for the circumcising of the child, his name was called JESUS, which was so named of the angel before he was conceived in the womb.

The Genealogy of Jesus

(*According to Matthew*)

The book of the generation of Jesus Christ, the son of David, the son of Abraham.

Abraham begat Isaac; and Isaac begat Jacob; and Jacob begat Judas and his brethren; and Judas begat Phares and Zara of Thamar; and Phares begat Esrom; and Esrom begat Aram; and Aram begat Aminadab; and Aminadab begat Naasson; and Naasson begat Salmon; and Salmon begat Booz of Rachab; and Booz begat Obed of Ruth; and Obed begat Jesse; and Jesse begat David the king.

And David the king begat Solomon of her that had been the wife of Urias; and Solomon begat Roboam; and Roboam begat Abia; and Abia begat Asa; and Asa begat Josaphat; and Josaphat begat Joram; and Joram begat Ozias; and Ozias begat Joatham; and Joatham begat Achaz; and Achaz begat Ezekias; and Ezekias begat Manasses; and Manasses begat Amon; and Amon begat Josias; and Josias begat Jechonias and his brethren, about the time they were carried away to Babylon.

And after they were brought to Babylon, Jechonias begat Salathiel; and Salathiel begat Zorobabel; and Zorobabel begat Abiud; and Abiud begat Eliakim; and Eliakim begat Azor; and Azor begat Sadoc; and Sadoc begat Achim; and Achim begat Eliud; and Eliud begat Eleazar; and Eleazar begat Matthan; and Matthan begat Jacob; and Jacob begat Joseph the husband of Mary, of whom was born Jesus, who is called Christ.

So all the generations from Abraham to David are fourteen generations; and from David until the carrying away into Babylon are fourteen generations; and from the carrying away into Babylon unto Christ are fourteen generations.

The Flight into Egypt

(*According to Matthew*)

Now when Jesus was born in Bethlehem of Judea in the days of Herod the king, behold, there came wise men from the east to Jerusalem, saying, Where is he that is born King of the Jews? for we have seen his star in the east, and are come to worship him.

When Herod the king had heard these things, he was troubled, and all Jerusalem with him.

And when he had gathered all the chief priests and scribes of the people together, he demanded of them where Christ should be born.

And they said unto him, In Bethlehem of Judea: for thus it is written by the prophet, And thou Bethlehem, in the land of Juda, art not the least among the princes of Juda: for out of thee shall come a Governor, that shall rule my people Israel.

Then Herod, when he had privily called the wise men, inquired of them diligently what time the star appeared. And he sent them to Bethlehem, and said, Go and search diligently for the young child; and when

ye have found him, bring me word again, that I may come and worship
him also.

When they had heard the king, they departed; and, lo, the star, which
they saw in the east, went before them, till it came and stood over where
the young child was. When they saw the star, they rejoiced with exceeding great joy.

And when they were come into the house, they saw the young child
with Mary his mother, and fell down, and worshipped him: and when
they had opened their treasures, they presented unto him gifts; gold, and
frankincense, and myrrh. And being warned of God in a dream that they
should not return to Herod, they departed into their own country another
way.

And when they were departed, behold, the angel of the Lord appeareth to Joseph in a dream, saying, Arise, and take the young child and his
mother, and flee into Egypt, and be thou there until I bring thee word:
for Herod will seek the young child to destroy him.

When he arose, he took the young child and his mother by night, and
departed into Egypt, and was there until the death of Herod: that it
might be fulfilled which was spoken of the Lord by the prophet, saying,
Out of Egypt have I called my son.

Then Herod, when he saw that he was mocked of the wise men, was
exceeding wroth, and sent forth, and slew all the children that were in
Bethlehem, and in all the coasts thereof, from two years old and under,
according to the time which he had diligently inquired of the wise men.
Then was fulfilled that which was spoken by Jeremy the prophet, saying, In Rama was there a voice heard, lamentation, and weeping, and
great mourning, Rachel weeping for her children, and would not be
comforted, because they are not.

But when Herod was dead, behold, an angel of the Lord appeareth in
a dream to Joseph in Egypt, saying, Arise, and take the young child and
his mother, and go into the land of Israel: for they are dead which
sought the young child's life. And he arose, and took the young child
and his mother, and came into the land of Israel.

But when he heard that Archelaus did reign in Judea in the room of
his father Herod, he was afraid to go thither: notwithstanding, being
warned of God in a dream, he turned aside into the parts of Galilee.
And he came and dwelt in a city called Nazareth: that it might be fulfilled which was spoken by the prophets, He shall be called a Nazarene.

The Childhood of Jesus

(*According to Luke*)

And when the days of her (Mary's) purification according to the law of Moses were accomplished, they brought him to Jerusalem, to present him to the Lord, (as it is written in the law of the Lord, Every male that openeth the womb shall be called holy to the Lord;) and to offer a sacrifice according to that which is said in the law of the Lord, A pair of turtledoves, or two young pigeons.

And, behold, there was a man in Jerusalem, whose name was Simeon; and the same man was just and devout, waiting for the consolation of Israel: and the Holy Ghost was upon him. And it was revealed unto him by the Holy Ghost, that he should not see death, before he had seen the Lord's Christ. And he came by the Spirit into the temple.

And when the parents brought in the child Jesus, to do for him after the custom of the law, then took he him up in his arms, and blessed God, and said, Lord, now lettest thou thy servant depart in peace, according to thy word, for mine eyes have seen thy salvation, which thou hast prepared before the face of all people, a light to lighten the Gentiles, and the glory of thy people Israel.

And Joseph and his mother marvelled at those things which were spoken of him. And Simeon blessed them, and said unto Mary his mother, Behold, this child is set for the fall and rising again of many in Israel; and for a sign which shall be spoken against; (yea, a sword shall pierce through thy own soul also;) that the thoughts of many hearts may be revealed.

And there was one Anna, a prophetess, the daughter of Phanuel, of the tribe of Aser: she was of a great age, and had lived with a husband seven years from her virginity, and she was a widow of about fourscore and four years, which departed not from the temple, but served God with fastings and prayers night and day. And she coming in that instant gave thanks likewise unto the Lord, and spake of him to all them that looked for redemption in Jerusalem.

And when they had performed all things according to the law of the Lord, they returned into Galilee, to their own city of Nazareth. And the child grew, and waxed strong in spirit, filled with wisdom; and the grace of God was upon him.

The Instruction of Jesus

(*According to Luke*)

Now his parents went to Jerusalem every year at the feast of the passover. And when he was twelve years old, they went up to Jerusalem after the custom of the feast.

And when they had fulfilled the days, as they returned, the child Jesus tarried behind in Jerusalem; and Joseph and his mother knew not of it. But they, supposing him to have been in the company, went a day's journey; and they sought him among their kinsfolk and acquaintance. And when they found him not, they turned back again to Jerusalem, seeking him.

And it came to pass, that after three days they found him in the temple, sitting in the midst of the doctors, both hearing them, and asking them questions. And all that heard him were astonished at his understanding and answers.

And when they saw him, they were amazed: and his mother said unto him, Son, why hast thou thus dealt with us? behold, thy father and I have sought thee sorrowing.

And he said unto them, How is it that ye sought me? wist ye not that I must be about my Father's business?

And they understood not the saying which he spake unto them.

And he went down with them, and came to Nazareth, and was subject unto them: but his mother kept all these sayings in her heart. And Jesus increased in wisdom and stature, and in favour with God and man.

The Baptism of Jesus

(*According to Matthew*)

In those days came John the Baptist, preaching in the wilderness of Judea, and saying, Repent ye: for the kingdom of heaven is at hand. For this is he that was spoken of by the prophet Esaias, saying, The voice of one crying in the wilderness, Prepare ye the way of the Lord, make his paths straight.

And the same John had his raiment of camel's hair, and a leathern girdle about his loins; and his meat was locust and wild honey.

Then went out to him Jerusalem, and all Judea, and all the region round about Jordan, and were baptized of him in Jordan, confessing their sins.

But when he saw many of the Pharisees and Sadducees come to his baptism, he said unto them, O generation of vipers, who hath warned you to flee from the wrath to come? Bring forth therefore fruits meet for repentance. And think not to say within yourselves, We have Abraham to our father: for I say unto you, that God is able of these stones to raise up children unto Abraham.

And now also the axe is laid unto the root of the trees: therefore every tree which bringeth not forth good fruit is hewn down, and cast into the fire.

I indeed baptize you with water unto repentance: but he that cometh after me is mightier than I, whose shoes I am not worthy to bear: he shall baptize you with the Holy Ghost, and with fire, whose fan is in his hand, and he will thoroughly purge his floor, and gather his wheat into the garner; but he will burn up the chaff with unquenchable fire.

Then cometh Jesus from Galilee to Jordan unto John, to be baptized of him. But John forbade him, saying, I have need to be baptized of thee, and comest thou to me?

And Jesus answering said unto him, Suffer it to be so now: for thus it becometh us to fulfil all righteousness. Then he suffered him.

And Jesus, when he was baptized, went up straightway out of the water: and, lo, the heavens were opened unto him, and he saw the Spirit of God descending like a dove, and lighting upon him. And lo a voice from heaven, saying, This is my beloved Son, in whom I am well pleased.

The Baptism of Jesus

(*According to John*)

In the beginning was the Word, and the Word was with God, and the Word was God. The same was in the beginning with God. All things were made by him; and without him was not anything made that was made. In him was life; and the life was the light of men. And the light shineth in darkness; and the darkness comprehended it not.

There was a man sent from God, whose name was John. The same came for a witness, to bear witness of the Light, that all men through him might believe. He was not that Light, but was sent to bear witness of that Light.

That was the true Light, which lighteth every man that cometh into the world. He was in the world, and the world was made by him, and the world knew him not. He came unto his own, and his own received him not. But as many as received him, to them gave he power to become the sons of God, even to them that believe on his name, which were born, not of blood, nor of the will of the flesh, nor of the will of man, but of God.

And the Word was made flesh, and dwelt among us, (and we beheld his glory, the glory as of the only begotten of the Father,) full of grace and truth.

John bare witness of him, and cried, saying, This was he of whom I spake, He that cometh after me is preferred before me; for he was before me. And of his fulness have all we received, and grace for grace. For the law was given by Moses, but grace and truth came by Jesus Christ.

No man hath seen God at any time; the only begotten Son, which is in the bosom of the Father, he hath declared him.

And this is the record of John, when the Jews sent priests and Levites from Jerusalem to ask him, Who art thou?

And he confessed, and denied not; but confessed, I am not the Christ.

And they asked him, What then? Art thou Elias? And he saith, I am not. Art thou that Prophet? And he answered, No.

Then said they unto him, Who art thou? that we may give an answer to them that sent us. What sayest thou of thyself?

He said, I am the voice of one crying in the wilderness, Make straight the way of the Lord, as said the prophet Esaias.

And they which were sent were of the Pharisees.

And they asked him, and said unto him, Why baptizest thou then, if thou be not that Christ, nor Elias, neither that Prophet?

John answered them, saying, I baptize with water: but there standeth one among you, whom ye know not. He it is, who coming after me is preferred before me, whose shoe-latchet I am not worthy to unloose.

These things were done in Bethabara beyond Jordan, where John was baptizing.

The next day John seeth Jesus coming unto him, and saith, Behold the Lamb of God, which taketh away the sin of the world! This is he of whom I said, After me cometh a man which is preferred before me; for he was before me. And I knew him not: but that he should be made manifest to Israel, therefore am I come baptizing with water.

And John bare record, saying, I saw the Spirit descending from heaven like a dove, and it abode upon him. And I knew him not: but he that sent me to baptize with water, the same said unto me, Upon whom thou shalt see the Spirit descending, and remaining on him, the same is he which baptizeth with the Holy Ghost. And I saw, and bare record that this is the Son of God.

Jesus Is Tempted by the Devil

(*According to Luke*)

And Jesus being full of the Holy Ghost returned from Jordan, and was led by the Spirit into the wilderness, being forty days tempted of the devil. And in those days he did eat nothing: and when they were ended, he afterward hungered.

And the devil said unto him, If thou be the Son of God, command this stone that it be made bread.

And Jesus answered him, saying, It is written, That man shall not live by bread alone, but by every word of God.

And the devil, taking him up into a high mountain, showed unto him all the kingdoms of the world in a moment of time. And the devil said unto him, All this power will I give thee, and the glory of them: for that

is delivered unto me; and to whomsoever I will, I give it. If thou therefore wilt worship me, all shall be thine.

And Jesus answered and said unto him, Get thee behind me, Satan:
for it is written, Thou shalt worship the Lord thy God, and him only
shalt thou serve.

And he brought him to Jerusalem, and set him on a pinnacle of the
temple, and said unto him, If thou be the Son of God, cast thyself down
from hence, for it is written, He shall give his angels charge over thee,
to keep thee, and in their hands they shall bear thee up, lest at any time
thou dash thy foot against a stone.

And Jesus answering said unto him, It is said, Thou shalt not tempt
the Lord thy God.

And when the devil had ended all the temptation, he departed from
him for a season.

Acknowledgment of Divinity

(*According to Luke*)

And Jesus returned in the power of the Spirit into Galilee: and there
went out a fame of him through all the region round about. And he
taught in their synagogues, being glorified of all.

And he came to Nazareth, where he had been brought up: and, as his
custom was, he went into the synagogue on the sabbath day, and stood
up for to read. And there was delivered unto him the book of the
prophet Esaias. And when he had opened the book, he found the place
where it was written, The Spirit of the Lord is upon me, because he hath
anointed me to preach the gospel to the poor; he hath sent me to heal the
broken-hearted, to preach deliverance to the captives, and recovering of
sight to the blind, to set at liberty them that are bruised, to preach the
acceptable year of the Lord.

And he closed the book, and he gave it again to the minister, and sat
down. And the eyes of all them that were in the synagogue were fastened
on him. And he began to say unto them, This day is this Scripture fulfilled in your ears.

And all bare him witness, and wondered at the gracious words which
proceeded out of his mouth. And they said, Is not this Joseph's son?

And he said unto them, Ye will surely say unto me this proverb, Physician, heal thyself: whatsoever we have heard done in Capernaum, do also here in thy country. And he said, Verily I say unto you, No prophet is accepted in his own country. But I tell you of a truth, many widows were in Israel in the days of Elias, when the heaven was shut up three years and six months, when great famine was throughout all the land, but unto none of them was Elias sent, save unto Sarepta, a city of Sidon, unto a woman that was a widow. And many lepers were in Israel in the time of Eliseus the prophet; and none of them was cleansed, saving Naaman the Syrian.

And all they in the synagogue, when they heard these things, were filled with wrath, and rose up, and thrust him out of the city, and led him unto the brow of the hill whereon their city was built, that they might cast him down headlong. But he, passing through the midst of them, went his way.

The Spirit of the Lord Is Manifest

(*According to John*)

And the third day there was a marriage in Cana of Galilee; and the mother of Jesus was there. And both Jesus was called, and his disciples, to the marriage.

And when they wanted wine, the mother of Jesus saith unto him, They have no wine.

Jesus saith unto her, Woman, what have I to do with thee? mine hour is not yet come.

His mother saith unto the servants, Whatsoever he saith unto you, do it.

And there were set there six waterpots of stone, after the manner of the purifying of the Jews, containing two or three firkins apiece.

Jesus saith unto them, Fill the waterpots with water. And they filled them up to the brim.

And he saith unto them, Draw out now, and bear unto the governor of the feast. And they bare it.

When the ruler of the feast had tasted the water that was made wine, and knew not whence it was, (but the servants which drew the water

knew,) the governor of the feast called the bridegroom, and saith unto
him, Every man at the beginning doth set forth good wine; and when
men have well drunk, then that which is worse: but thou hast kept the
good wine until now.

This beginning of miracles did Jesus in Cana of Galilee, and manifested forth his glory; and his disciples believed on him.

After this he went down to Capernaum, he, and his mother, and his
brethren and his disciples; and they continued there not many days.

And the Jews' passover was at hand, and Jesus went up to Jerusalem,
and found in the temple those that sold oxen and sheep and doves, and
the changers of money sitting, and when he had made a scourge of small
cords, he drove them all out of the temple, and the sheep, and the oxen;
and poured out the changers' money, and overthrew the tables, and said
unto them that sold doves, Take these things hence; make not my
Father's house a house of merchandise.

Then answered the Jews and said unto him, What sign showest thou
unto us, seeing that thou doest these things?

Jesus answered and said unto them, Destroy this temple, and in three
days I will raise it up.

Then said the Jews, Forty and six years was this temple in building,
and wilt thou rear it up in three days?

But he spake of the temple of his body.

When therefore he was risen from the dead, his disciples remembered
that he had said this unto them; and they believed the Scripture, and the
word which Jesus had said.

The Healer

(*According to Luke*)

And (he) came down to Capernaum, a city of Galilee, and taught
them on the sabbath days, and they were astonished at his doctrine: for
his word was with power.

And in the synagogue there was a man, which had a spirit of an
unclean devil, and cried out with a loud voice, saying, Let us alone; what
have we to do with thee, thou Jesus of Nazareth? art thou come to
destroy us? I know thee who thou art; the Holy One of God.

And Jesus rebuked him, saying, Hold thy peace, and come out of him. And when the devil had thrown him in the midst, he came out of him, and hurt him not.

And they were all amazed, and spake among themselves, saying, What a word is this! for with authority and power he commandeth the unclean spirits, and they come out.

And the fame of him went out into every place of the country round about.

And he arose out of the synagogue, and entered into Simon's house. And Simon's wife's mother was taken with a great fever; and they besought him for her. And he stood over her, and rebuked the fever; and it left her: and immediately she arose and ministered unto them.

Now when the sun was setting, all they that had any sick with divers diseases brought them unto him; and he laid his hands on every one of them, and healed them. And devils also came out of many, crying out, and saying, Thou art Christ the Son of God. And he rebuking them suffered them not to speak: for they knew that he was Christ.

And when it was day, he departed and went into a desert place: and the people sought him, and came unto him, and stayed him, that he should not depart from them. And he said unto them, I must preach the kingdom of God to other cities also: for therefore am I sent.

And he preached in the synagogues of Galilee.

The First Disciples

(*According to Luke*)

And it came to pass, that, as the people pressed upon him to hear the word of God, he stood by the lake of Gennesaret, and saw two ships standing by the lake: but the fishermen were gone out of them, and were washing their nets. And he entered into one of the ships, which was Simon's, and prayed him that he would thrust out a little from the land. And he sat down, and taught the people out of the ship.

Now when he had left speaking, he said unto Simon, Launch out into the deep, and let down your nets for a draught.

And Simon answering said unto him, Master, we have toiled all the night, and have taken nothing: nevertheless at thy word I will let down the net.

And when they had this done, they enclosed a great multitude of f.shes: and their net brake. And they beckoned unto their partners, which were in the other ship, that they should come and help them. And they came, and filled both the ships, so that they began to sink.

When Simon Peter saw it, he fell down at Jesus' knees, saying, Depart from me; for I am a sinful man, O Lord. For he was astonished, and all that were with him, at the draught of the fishes which they had taken. And so was also James, and John, the sons of Zebedee, which were partners with Simon.

And Jesus said unto Simon, Fear not; from henceforth thou shalt catch men.

And when they had brought their ships to land, they forsook all, and followed him.

And it came to pass, when he was in a certain city, behold a man full of leprosy; who seeing Jesus fell on his face, and besought him, saying, Lord, if thou wilt, thou canst make me clean. And he put forth his hand, and touched him, saying, I will: be thou clean. And immediately the leprosy departed from him. And he charged him to tell no man: but go, and show thyself to the priest, and offer for thy cleansing, according as Moses commanded, for a testimony unto them.

But so much the more went there a fame abroad of him: and great multitudes came together to hear, and to be healed by him of their infirmities.

And he withdrew himself into the wilderness, and prayed.

The First Disciples

(*According to Matthew*)

Now when Jesus had heard that John was cast into prison, he departed into Galilee; and leaving Nazareth, he came and dwelt in Capernaum, which is upon the seacoast, in the borders of Zabulon and Nephthalim, that it might be fulfilled which was spoken by Esaias the prophet, saying, The land of Zabulon, and the land of Nephthalim, by the way of the sea, beyond Jordan, Galilee of the Gentiles; the people which sat in darkness saw great light; and to them which sat in the region and shadow of death light is sprung up.

From that time Jesus began to preach, and to say, Repent: for the kingdom of heaven is at hand.

And Jesus, walking by the sea of Galilee, saw two brethren, Simon called Peter, and Andrew his brother, casting a net into the sea: for they were fishers. And he saith unto them, Follow me, and I will make you fishers of men. And they straightway left their nets, and followed him.

And going on from thence, he saw other two brethren, James the son of Zebedee, and John his brother, in a ship with Zebedee their father, mending their nets; and he called them. And they immediately left the ship and their father, and followed him.

The First Disciples

(*According to Mark*)

Now as he walked by the sea of Galilee, he saw Simon and Andrew his brother casting a net into the sea: for they were fishers. And Jesus said unto them, Come ye after me, and I will make you to become fishers of men. And straightway they forsook their nets, and followed him.

And when he had gone a little further thence, he saw James the son of Zebedee, and John his brother, who also were in the ship mending their nets. And straightway he called them: and they left their father Zebedee in the ship with the hired servants, and went after him.

The First Disciples

(*According to John*)

Again the next day (after John's baptism of Jesus) after, John stood, and two of his disciples; and looking upon Jesus as he walked, he saith, Behold the Lamb of God! And the two disciples heard him speak, and they followed Jesus.

Then Jesus turned, and saw them following, and saith unto them,

`What seek ye? They said unto him, Rabbi, (which is to say, being interpreted, Master,) where dwellest thou?

He saith unto them, Come and see. They came and saw where he dwelt, and abode with him that day: for it was about the tenth hour.

One of the two which heard John speak, and followed him, was Andrew, Simon Peter's brother. He first findeth his own brother Simon, and saith unto him, We have found the Messias, which is, being interpreted, the Christ. And he brought him to Jesus. And when Jesus beheld him, he said, Thou art Simon the son of Jona: thou shalt be called Cephas, which is by interpretation, a stone.

The day following Jesus would go forth into Galilee, and findeth Philip, and saith unto him, Follow me. Now Philip was of Bethsaida, the city of Andrew and Peter.

Philip findeth Nathanael, and saith unto him, We have found him, of whom Moses in the law, and the prophets, did write, Jesus of Nazareth, the son of Joseph. And Nathanael said unto him, Can there any good thing come out of Nazareth? Philip saith unto him, Come and see.

A Crippled Man Is Healed

(*According to Luke*)

And it came to pass on a certain day, as he was teaching, that there were Pharisees and doctors of the law sitting by, which were come out of every town of Galilee, and Judea, and Jerusalem: and the power of the Lord was present to heal them.

And, behold, men brought in a bed a man which was taken with a palsy: and they sought means to bring him in, and to lay him before him. And when they could not find by what way they might bring him in because of the multitude, they went upon the housetop, and let him down through the tiling with his couch into the midst before Jesus.

And when he saw their faith, he said unto him, Man, thy sins are forgiven thee.

And the scribes and the Pharisees began to reason, saying, Who is this which speaketh blasphemies? Who can forgive sins, but God alone?

But when Jesus perceived their thoughts, he answering said unto them, What reason ye in your hearts? Whether is easier, to say, Thy sins be forgiven thee; or to say, Rise up and walk? But that ye may know that the Son of man hath power upon earth to forgive sins, (he said unto the sick of the palsy,) I say unto thee, Arise, and take up thy couch, and go into thine house.

And immediately he rose up before them, and took up that whereon he lay, and departed to his own house, glorifying God.

And they were all amazed, and they glorified God, and were filled with fear, saying, We have seen strange things to-day.

And after these things he went forth, and saw a publican, named Levi, sitting at the receipt of custom: and he said unto him, Follow me. And he left all, rose up, and followed him.[1]

And Levi made him a great feast in his own house: and there was a great company of publicans and of others that sat down with them. But their scribes and Pharisees murmured against his disciples, saying, Why do ye eat and drink with publicans and sinners?

And Jesus answering said unto them, They that are whole need not a physician; but they that are sick. I came not to call the righteous, but sinners to repentance.

A Crippled Man Is Healed

(*According to John*)

After this there was a feast of the Jews; and Jesus went up to Jerusalem.

Now there is at Jerusalem by the sheep market a pool, which is called in the Hebrew tongue Bethesda, having five porches. In these lay a great multitude of impotent folk, of blind, halt, withered, waiting for the moving of the water. For an angel went down at a certain season into the pool, and troubled the water: whosoever then first after the troubling of the water stepped in was made whole of whatsoever disease he had.

And a certain man was there, which had an infirmity thirty and eight years. When Jesus saw him lie, and knew that he had been now a long time in that case, he saith unto him, Wilt thou be made whole? The impotent man answered him, Sir, I have no man, when the water is

---

[1] "And as Jesus passed forth from thence, he saw a man, named Matthew, sitting at the receipt of custom: and he saith unto him, Follow me. And he arose, and followed him."—Matthew IX.

troubled, to put me into the pool: but while I am coming, another step-peth down before me. Jesus saith unto him, Rise, take up thy bed, and walk. And immediately the man was made whole, and took up his bed, and walked: and on the same day was the sabbath.

The Jews therefore said unto him that was cured, It is the sabbath day: it is not lawful for thee to carry thy bed. He answered them, He that made me whole, the same said unto me, Take up thy bed, and walk.

Then asked they him, What man is that which said unto thee, Take up thy bed, and walk? And he that was healed wist not who it was: for Jesus had conveyed himself away, a multitude being in that place.

Afterward Jesus findeth him in the temple, and said unto him, Behold, thou art made whole: sin no more, lest a worse thing come unto thee.

The man departed, and told the Jews that it was Jesus, which had made him whole. And therefore did the Jews persecute Jesus, and sought to slay him, because he had done these things on the sabbath day.

The Two Blind Men and the Dumb Man

(*According to Matthew*)

And when Jesus departed thence, two blind men followed him, cry-ing, and saying, Thou Son of David, have mercy on us.

And when he was come into the house, the blind men came to him: and Jesus saith unto them, Believe ye that I am able to do this? They said unto him, Yea, Lord. Then touched he their eyes, saying, According to your faith be it unto you. And their eyes were opened; and Jesus straitly charged them, saying, See that no man know it.

But they, when they were departed, spread abroad his fame in all that country.

As they went out, behold, they brought to him a dumb man possessed with a devil. And when the devil was cast out, the dumb spake: and the multitudes marvelled, saying, It was never so seen in Israel.

But the Pharisees said, He casteth out devils through the prince of the devils.

And Jesus went about all the cities and villages, teaching in their synagogues, and preaching the gospel of the kingdom, and healing every sickness and every disease among the people.

The Woman of Samaria

(*According to John*)

When therefore the Lord knew how the Pharisees had heard that Jesus made and baptized more disciples than John, (though Jesus himself baptized not, but his disciples,) he left Judea, and departed again into Galilee. And he must needs go through Samaria.

Then cometh he to a city of Samaria, which is called Sychar, near to the parcel of ground that Jacob gave to his son Joseph.

Now Jacob's well was there. Jesus therefore, being wearied with his journey, sat thus on the well: and it was about the sixth hour.

There cometh a woman of Samaria to draw water: Jesus saith unto her, Give me to drink. (For his disciples were gone away unto the city to buy meat.)

Then saith the woman of Samaria unto him, How is it that thou, being a Jew, askest drink of me, which am a woman of Samaria? for the Jews have no dealings with the Samaritans.

Jesus answered and said unto her, If thou knewest the gift of God, and who it is that saith to thee, Give me to drink; thou wouldest have asked of him, and he would have given thee living water.

The woman saith unto him, Sir, thou hast nothing to draw with, and the well is deep: from whence then hast thou that living water? Art thou greater than our father Jacob, which gave us the well, and drank thereof himself, and his children, and his cattle?

Jesus answered and said unto her, Whosoever drinketh of this water shall thirst again, but whosoever drinketh of the water that I shall give him shall never thirst; but the water that I shall give him shall be in him a well of water springing up into everlasting life.

The woman saith unto him, Sir, give me this water, that I thirst not, neither come hither to draw.

Jesus saith unto her, Go, call thy husband, and come hither.

The woman answered and said, I have no husband.

Jesus said unto her, Thou hast well said, I have no husband; for thou hast had five husbands; and he whom thou now hast is not thy husband: in that saidst thou truly.

The woman saith unto him, Sir, I perceive that thou art a prophet. Our fathers worshipped in this mountain; and ye say, that in Jerusalem is the place where men ought to worship.

Jesus saith unto her, Woman, believe me, the hour cometh, when ye shall neither in this mountain, nor yet at Jerusalem, worship the Father. Ye worship ye know not what: we know what we worship; for salvation is of the Jews. But the hour cometh, and now is, when the true worshippers shall worship the Father in spirit and in truth: for the Father seeketh such to worship him. God is a Spirit: and they that worship him must worship him in spirit and in truth.

The woman saith unto him, I know that Messias cometh, which is called Christ: when he is come, he will tell us all things.

Jesus saith unto her, I that speak unto thee am he.

And upon this came his disciples, and marvelled that he talked with the woman: yet no man said, What seekest thou? or, Why talkest thou with her?

The woman then left her waterpot, and went her way into the city, and saith to the men, Come, see a man, which told me all things that ever I did: is not this the Christ?

Then they went out of the city, and came unto him.

To Keep Holy the Sabbath

(*According to Luke*)

I

And it came to pass on the second sabbath after the first, that he went through the corn fields; and his disciples plucked the ears of corn, and did eat, rubbing them in their hands. And certain of the Pharisees said unto them, Why do ye that which is not lawful to do on the sabbath days?

And Jesus answering them said, Have ye not read so much as this, what David did, when himself was ahungered, and they which were with him, how he went into the house of God, and did take and eat the showbread, and gave also to them that were with him; which it is not lawful to eat but for the priests alone? And he said unto them, That the Son of man is Lord also of the sabbath.

And it came to pass also on another sabbath, that he entered into the synagogue and taught: and there was a man whose right hand was withered. And the scribes and Pharisees watched him, whether he would heal on the sabbath day; that they might find an accusation against him. But he knew their thoughts, and said to the man which had the withered hand, Rise up, and stand forth in the midst. And he arose and stood forth.

Then said Jesus unto them, I will ask you one thing; Is it lawful on the sabbath days to do good, or to do evil? to save life, or to destroy it?

And looking round about upon them all, he said unto the man, Stretch forth thy hand. And he did so: and his hand was restored whole as the other.

And they were filled with madness; and communed one with another what they might do to Jesus.

And it came to pass in those days, that he went out into a mountain to pray, and continued all night in prayer to God.

And when it was day, he called unto him his disciples: and of them he chose twelve, whom also he named apostles; Simon, (whom he also named Peter,) and Andrew his brother, James and John, Philip and Bartholomew, Matthew and Thomas, James the son of Alpheus, and Simon called Zelotes, and Judas the brother of James, and Judas Iscariot, which also was the traitor.

And he came down with them, and stood in the plain, and the company of his disciples, and a great multitude of people out of all Judea and Jerusalem, and from the seacoast of Tyre and Sidon, which came to hear him, and to be healed of their diseases, and they that were vexed with unclean spirits: and they were healed.

And the whole multitude sought to touch him: for there went virtue out of him, and healed them all.

II

And, behold, there was a woman which had a spirit of infirmity eighteen years, and was bowed together, and could in no wise lift up herself. And when Jesus saw her, he called her to him, and said unto her,

Woman, thou art loosed from thine infirmity. And he laid his hands on her: and immediately she was made straight, and glorified God.

And the ruler of the synagogue answered with indignation, because that Jesus had healed on the sabbath day, and said unto the people, There are six days in which men ought to work: in them therefore come and be healed, and not on the sabbath day.

The Lord then answered him, and said, Thou hypocrite, doth not each one of you on the sabbath loose his ox or his ass from the stall, and lead him away to watering? And ought not this woman, being a daughter of Abraham, whom Satan hath bound, lo, these eighteen years, be loosed from this bond on the sabbath day?

And when he had said these things, all his adversaries were ashamed: and all the people rejoiced for all the glorious things that were done by him.

III

And it came to pass, as he went into the house of one of the chief Pharisees to eat bread on the sabbath day, that they watched him. And, behold, there was a certain man before him which had the dropsy.

And Jesus answering spake unto the lawyers and Pharisees, saying, Is it lawful to heal on the sabbath day?

And they held their peace. And he took him, and healed him, and let him go, and answered them, saying, Which of you shall have an ass or an ox fallen into a pit, and will not straightway pull him out on the sabbath day?

And they could not answer him again to these things.

Who Is This That Forgiveth Sins?

(According to Luke)

Now when he had ended all his sayings in the audience of the people, he entered into Capernaum. And a certain centurion's servant, who was dear unto him, was sick, and ready to die. And when he heard of Jesus, he sent unto him the elders of the Jews, beseeching him that he would come and heal his servant.

And when they came to Jesus, they besought him instantly, saying, That he was worthy for whom he should do this, for he loveth our nation, and he hath built us a synagogue.

Then Jesus went with them. And when he was now not far from the house, the centurion sent friends to him, saying unto him, Lord, trouble not thyself; for I am not worthy that thou shouldest enter under my roof; wherefore neither thought I myself worthy to come unto thee: but say in a word, and my servant shall be healed. For I also am a man set under authority, having under me soldiers, and I say unto one, Go, and he goeth; and to another, Come, and he cometh; and to my servant, Do this, and he doeth it.

When Jesus heard these things, he marvelled at him, and turned him about, and said unto the people that followed him, I say unto you, I have not found so great faith, no, not in Israel.

And they that were sent, returning to the house, found the servant whole that had been sick.

And it came to pass the day after, that he went into a city called Nain; and many of his disciples went with him, and much people.

Now when he came nigh to the gate of the city, behold, there was a dead man carried out, the only son of his mother, and she was a widow: and much people of the city was with her.

And when the Lord saw her, he had compassion on her, and said unto her, Weep not. And he came and touched the bier: and they that bare him stood still. And he said, Young man, I say unto thee, Arise.

And he that was dead sat up, and began to speak. And he delivered him to his mother.

And there came a fear on all: and they glorified God, saying, That a great prophet is risen up among us; and, That God hath visited his people. And this rumour of him went forth throughout all Judea, and throughout all the region round about. And the disciples of John showed him of all these things.

And John calling unto him two of his disciples sent them to Jesus, saying, Art thou he that should come? or look we for another?

And in that same hour he cured many of their infirmities and plagues, and of evil spirits; and unto many that were blind he gave sight.

Then Jesus answering said unto them, Go your way, and tell John what things ye have seen and heard; how that the blind see, the lame walk, the lepers are cleansed, the deaf hear, the dead are raised, to the poor the gospel is preached. And blessed is he, whosoever shall not be offended in me.

And when the messengers of John were departed, he began to speak unto the people concerning John, What went ye out into the wilderness for to see? A reed shaken with the wind?

But what went ye out for to see? A man clothed in soft raiment? Behold, they which are gorgeously apparelled, and live delicately, are in kings' courts.

But what went ye out for to see? A prophet? Yea, I say unto you, and much more than a prophet. This is he, of whom it is written, Behold, I send my messenger before thy face, which shall prepare thy way before thee. For I say unto you, Among those that are born of women there is not a greater prophet than John the Baptist: but he that is least in the kingdom of God is greater than he.

And all the people that heard him, and the publicans, justified God, being baptized with the baptism of John. But the Pharisees and lawyers rejected the counsel of God against themselves, being not baptized of him.

And the Lord said, Whereunto then shall I liken the men of this generation? and to what are they like? They are like unto children sitting in the market place, and calling one to another, and saying, We have piped unto you, and ye have not danced; we have mourned to you, and ye have not wept.

For John the Baptist came neither eating bread nor drinking wine; and ye say, He hath a devil. The Son of man is come eating and drinking; and ye say, Behold a gluttonous man, and a winebibber, a friend of publicans and sinners! But wisdom is justified of all her children.

And one of the Pharisees desired him that he would eat with him. And he went into the Pharisee's house, and sat down to meat. And, behold, a woman in the city, which was a sinner, when she knew that Jesus sat at meat in the Pharisee's house, brought an alabaster box of ointment, and stood at his feet behind him weeping, and began to wash his feet with tears, and did wipe them with the hairs of her head, and kissed his feet, and anointed them with the ointment.

Now when the Pharisee which had bidden him saw it, he spake within himself, saying, This man, if he were a prophet, would have known who and what manner of woman this is that toucheth him; for she is a sinner.

And Jesus answering said unto him, Simon, I have somewhat to say unto thee. And he saith, Master, say on.

There was a certain creditor which had two debtors: the one owed five hundred pence, and the other fifty. And when they had nothing to pay, he frankly forgave them both. Tell me therefore, which of them will love him most?

Simon answered and said, I suppose that he, to whom he forgave most. And he said unto him, Thou hast rightly judged.

And he turned to the woman, and said unto Simon, Seest thou this woman? I entered into thine house, thou gavest me no water for my feet: but she hath washed my feet with tears, and wiped them with the hairs of her head. Thou gavest me no kiss: but this woman, since the time I came in, hath not ceased to kiss my feet. My head with oil thou didst not anoint: but this woman hath anointed my feet with ointment. Wherefore I say unto thee, Her sins, which are many, are forgiven; for she loved much: but to whom little is forgiven, the same loveth little.

And he said unto her, Thy sins are forgiven.

And they that sat at meat with him began to say within themselves, Who is this that forgiveth sins also?

And he said to the woman, Thy faith hath saved thee; go in peace.

Mary and Martha

(*According to Luke*)

Now it came to pass, as they went, that he entered into a certain village: and a certain woman named Martha received him into her house. And she had a sister called Mary, which also sat at Jesus' feet, and heard his word.

But Martha was cumbered about much serving, and came to him, and said, Lord, dost thou not care that my sister hath left me to serve alone? bid her therefore that she help me.

And Jesus answered and said unto her, Martha, Martha, thou art careful and troubled about many things; but one thing is needful; and Mary hath chosen that good part, which shall not be taken away from her.

Jesus, Thou Son of God!

(*According to Luke*)

And it came to pass afterward, that he went throughout every city and village, preaching and showing the glad tidings of the kingdom of God.

And the twelve were with him, and certain women, which had been healed of evil spirits and infirmities, Mary called Magdalene, out of whom went seven devils, and Joanna the wife of Chuza Herod's steward, and Susanna, and many others, which ministered unto him of their substance.

Then came to him his mother and his brethren, and could not come at him for the press. And it was told him by certain which said, Thy mother and thy brethren stand without, desiring to see thee. And he answered and said unto them, My mother and my brethren are these which hear the word of God, and do it.

Now it came to pass on a certain day, that he went into a ship with his disciples: and he said unto them, Let us go over unto the other side of the lake. And they launched forth.

But as they sailed, he fell asleep: and there came down a storm of wind on the lake; and they were filled with water, and were in jeopardy. And they came to him, and awoke him, saying, Master, Master, we perish. Then he arose, and rebuked the wind and the raging of the water: and they ceased, and there was a calm.

And he said unto them, Where is your faith? And they being afraid wondered, saying one to another, What manner of man is this! for he commandeth even the winds and water, and they obey him.

And they arrived at the country of the Gadarenes, which is over against Galilee. And when he went forth to land, there met him out of the city a certain man, which had devils long time, and ware no clothes, neither abode in any house, but in the tombs. When he saw Jesus, he cried out, and fell down before him, and with a loud voice said, What have I to do with thee, Jesus, thou Son of God most high? I beseech thee, torment me not. (For he had commanded the unclean spirit to come out of the man. For oftentimes it had caught him: and he was kept bound with chains and in fetters; and he brake the bands, and was driven of the devil into the wilderness.)

And Jesus asked him, saying, What is thy name? And he said, Legion: because many devils were entered into him. And they besought him that he would not command them to go out into the deep.

And there was there a herd of many swine feeding on the mountain: and they besought him that he would suffer them to enter into them. And he suffered them.

Then went the devils out of the man, and entered into the swine: and the herd ran violently down a steep place into the lake, and were choked.

When they that fed them saw what was done, they fled, and went and told it in the city and in the country. Then they went out to see what was done; and came to Jesus, and found the man, out of whom the devils were departed, sitting at the feet of Jesus, clothed, and in his right mind: and they were afraid. They also which saw it told them by what means he that was possessed of the devils was healed.

Then the whole multitude of the country of the Gadarenes round about besought him to depart from them; for they were taken with great fear: and he went up into the ship, and returned back again.

Now the man, out of whom the devils were departed, besought him that he might be with him: but Jesus sent him away, saying, Return to thine own house, and show how great things God hath done unto thee. And he went his way, and published throughout the whole city how great things Jesus had done unto him. And it came to pass, that, when Jesus was returned, the people gladly received him, for they were all waiting for him.

And, behold, there came a man named Jairus, and he was a ruler of the synagogue; and he fell down at Jesus' feet, and besought him that he would come into his house, for he had one only daughter, about twelve years of age, and she lay a dying. But as he went the people thronged him.

And a woman having an issue of blood twelve years, which had spent all her living upon physicians, neither could be healed of any, came behind him, and touched the border of his garment: and immediately her issue of blood stanched.

And Jesus said, Who touched me? When all denied, Peter and they that were with him said, Master, the multitude throng thee and press thee. and sayest thou, Who touched me?

And Jesus said, Somebody hath touched me: for I perceive that virtue is gone out of me.

And when the woman saw that she was not hid, she came trembling, and falling down before him, she declared unto him before all the people for what cause she had touched him, and how she was healed immediately.

And he said unto her, Daughter, be of good comfort: thy faith hath made thee whole; go in peace.

While he yet spake, there cometh one from the ruler of the synagogue's house, saying to him, Thy daughter is dead; trouble not the Master.

But when Jesus heard it, he answered him, saying, Fear not: believe only, and she shall be made whole.

And when he came into the house, he suffered no man to go in, save Peter, and James, and John, and the father and the mother of the maiden. And all wept, and bewailed her: but he said, Weep not; she is not dead, but sleepeth.

And they laughed him to scorn, knowing that she was dead.

And he put them all out, and took her by the hand, and called, saying, Maid, arise.

And her spirit came again, and she arose straightway: and he commanded to give her meat. And her parents were astonished: but he charged them that they should tell no man what was done.

The Twelve Apostles Named

(*According to Matthew*)

And when he had called unto him his twelve disciples, he gave them power against unclean spirits, to cast them out, and to heal all manner of sickness and all manner of disease.

Now the names of the twelve apostles are these; The first, Simon, who is called Peter, and Andrew his brother; James the son of Zebedee, and John his brother; Philip, and Bartholomew; Thomas, and Matthew the publican; James the son of Alpheus, and Lebbeus, whose surname was Thaddeus; Simon the Canaanite, and Judas Iscariot, who also betrayed him.

He Instructs His Disciples

(*According to Luke*)

I

The Twelve

Then he called his twelve disciples together, and gave them power and authority over all devils, and to cure diseases. And he sent them to preach the kingdom of God, and to heal the sick. And he said unto them, Take nothing for your journey, neither staves, nor scrip, neither bread, neither money; neither have two coats apiece. And whatsoever house ye enter into, there abide, and thence depart. And whosoever will not receive you, when ye go out of that city, shake off the very dust from your feet for a testimony against them.

And they departed, and went through the towns, preaching the gospel, and healing everywhere.

II

The Seventy

After these things the Lord appointed other seventy also, and sent them two and two before his face into every city and place, whither he himself would come. Therefore said he unto them, The harvest truly is great, but the labourers are few: pray ye therefore the Lord of the harvest, that he would send forth labourers into his harvest. Go your ways: behold, I send you forth as lambs among wolves. Carry neither purse, nor scrip, nor shoes: and salute no man by the way. And into whatsoever house ye enter, first say, Peace be to this house. And if the son of peace be there, your peace shall rest upon it: if not, it shall turn to you again.

And in the same house remain, eating and drinking such things as they give: for the labourer is worthy of his hire. Go not from house to house.

And into whatsoever city ye enter, and they receive you, eat such things as are set before you, and heal the sick that are therein, and say unto them, The kingdom of God is come nigh unto you.

But into whatsoever city ye enter, and they receive you not, go your ways out into the streets of the same, and say, Even the very dust of your city, which cleaveth on us, we do wipe off against you: notwithstanding, be ye sure of this, that the kingdom of God is come nigh unto you. But I say unto you, that it shall be more tolerable in that day for Sodom, than for that city.

Woe unto thee, Chorazin! woe unto thee, Bethsaida! for if the mighty works had been done in Tyre and Sidon, which have been done in you, they had a great while ago repented, sitting in sackcloth and ashes. But it shall be more tolerable for Tyre and Sidon at the judgment, than for you. And thou, Capernaum, which art exalted to heaven, shalt be thrust down to hell.

He that heareth you heareth me; and he that despiseth you despiseth me; and he that despiseth me despiseth him that sent me.

And the seventy returned again with joy, saying, Lord, even the devils are subject unto us through thy name.

And he said unto them, I beheld Satan as lightning fall from heaven. Behold, I give unto you power to tread on serpents and scorpions, and over all the power of the enemy; and nothing shall by any means hurt you. Notwithstanding, in this rejoice not, that the spirits are subject unto you; but rather rejoice, because your names are written in heaven.

In that hour Jesus rejoiced in spirit, and said, I thank thee, O Father, Lord of heaven and earth, that thou hast hid these things from the wise and prudent, and hast revealed them unto babes: even so, Father; for so it seemed good in thy sight.

All things are delivered to me of my Father: and no man knoweth who the Son is, but the Father; and who the Father is, but the Son, and he to whom the Son will reveal him.

The Rock of the Christian Church

(*According to Matthew*)

When Jesus came into the coasts of Caesarea Philippi, he asked his disciples, saying, Whom do men say that I, the Son of man, am?

And they said, Some say that thou art John the Baptist; some, Elias; and others, Jeremias, or one of the prophets.

He saith unto them, But whom say ye that I am?

And Simon Peter answered and said, Thou art the Christ, the Son of the living God.

And Jesus answered and said unto him, Blessed art thou, Simon Barjona: for flesh and blood hath not revealed it unto thee, but my Father which is in heaven. And I say also unto thee, That thou art Peter, and upon this rock I will build my church; and the gates of hell shall not prevail against it. And I will give unto thee the keys of the kingdom of heaven: and whatsoever thou shalt bind on earth shall be bound in heaven; and whatsoever thou shalt loose on earth shall be loosed in heaven.

Then charged he his disciples that they should tell no man that he was Jesus the Christ.

From that time forth began Jesus to show unto his disciples, how that he must go unto Jerusalem, and suffer many things of the elders and chief priests and scribes, and be killed, and be raised again the third day.

Then Peter took him, and began to rebuke him, saying, Be it far from thee, Lord: this shall not be unto thee.

But he turned, and said unto Peter, Get thee behind me, Satan: thou art an offence unto me: for thou savourest not the things that be of God, but those that be of men.

The Death of John the Baptist

(*According to Matthew*)

At that time Herod the tetrarch heard of the fame of Jesus, and said unto his servants, This is John the Baptist; he is risen from the dead; and therefore mighty works do show forth themselves in him.

For Herod had laid hold on John, and bound him, and put him in prison for Herodias' sake, his brother Philip's wife. For John said unto him, It is not lawful for thee to have her.

And when he would have put him to death, he feared the multitude, because they counted him as a prophet.

But when Herod's birthday was kept, the daughter of Herodias danced before them, and pleased Herod. Whereupon he promised with an oath to give her whatsoever she would ask. And she, being before instructed of her mother, said, Give me here John Baptist's head in a charger.

And the king was sorry: nevertheless for the oath's sake, and them which sat with him at meat, he commanded it to be given her. And he sent, and beheaded John in the prison. And his head was brought in a charger, and given to the damsel: and she brought it to her mother.

And his disciples came, and took up the body, and buried it, and went and told Jesus.

The Loaves and Fishes

(*According to Mark*)

And the apostles gathered themselves together unto Jesus, and told him all things, both what they had done, and what they had taught. And he said unto them, Come ye yourselves apart into a desert place, and rest a while: for there were many coming and going, and they had no leisure so much as to eat. And they departed into a desert place by ship privately.

And the people saw them departing, and many knew him, and ran afoot thither out of all cities, and outwent them, and came together unto him. And Jesus, when he came out, saw much people, and was moved with compassion toward them, because they were as sheep not having a shepherd: and he began to teach them many things.

And when the day was now far spent, his disciples came unto him, and said, This is a desert place, and now the time is far passed. Send them away, that they may go into the country round about, and into the villages, and buy themselves bread: for they have nothing to eat.

He answered and said unto them, Give ye them to eat.

And they say unto him, Shall we go and buy two hundred pennyworth of bread, and give them to eat?

He saith unto them, How many loaves have ye? go and see.

And when they knew, they say, Five, and two fishes.

And he commanded them to make all sit down by companies upon the green grass. And they sat down in ranks, by hundreds, and by fifties. And when he had taken the five loaves and the two fishes, he looked up to heaven, and blessed, and brake the loaves, and gave them to his disciples to set before them; and the two fishes divided he among them all. And they did all eat, and were filled. And they took up twelve baskets full of the fragments, and of the fishes. And they that did eat of the loaves were about five thousand men.

Jesus Walks on the Water

(*According to Matthew*)

And straightway Jesus constrained his disciples to get into a ship, and to go before him unto the other side, while he sent the multitudes away. And when he had sent the multitudes away, he went up into a mountain apart to pray: and when the evening was come, he was there alone. But the ship was now in the midst of the sea, tossed with waves: for the wind was contrary.

And in the fourth watch of the night Jesus went unto them, walking on the sea. And when the disciples saw him walking on the sea, they were troubled, saying, It is a spirit; and they cried out for fear.

But straightway Jesus spake unto them, saying, Be of good cheer; it is I; be not afraid.

And Peter answered him and said, Lord, if it be thou, bid me come unto thee on the water.

And he said, Come.

And when Peter was come down out of the ship, he walked on the water, to go to Jesus. But when he saw the wind boisterous, he was afraid; and beginning to sink, he cried, saying, Lord, save me.

And immediately Jesus stretched forth his hand, and caught him, and said unto him, O thou of little faith, wherefore didst thou doubt?

And when they were come into the ship, the wind ceased. Then they that were in the ship came and worshipped him, saying, Of a truth thou art the Son of God.

The Transfiguration

(*According to Luke*)

And he took Peter and John and James, and went up into a mountain to pray. And as he prayed, the fashion of his countenance was altered, and his raiment was white and glistening. And, behold, there talked with him two men, which were Moses and Elias, who appeared in glory, and spake of his decease which he should accomplish at Jerusalem.

But Peter and they that were with him were heavy with sleep: and when they were awake, they saw his glory, and the two men that stood with him.

And it came to pass, as they departed from him, Peter said unto Jesus, Master, it is good for us to be here: and let us make three tabernacles; one for thee, and one for Moses, and one for Elias: not knowing what he said.

While he thus spake, there came a cloud, and overshadowed them: and they feared as they entered into the cloud. And there came a voice out of the cloud, saying, This is my beloved Son: hear him.

And when the voice was past, Jesus was found alone. And they kept it close, and told no man in those days any of those things which they had seen.

Let the Children First Be Filled

(*According to Mark*)

And . . . he . . . went into the borders of Tyre and Sidon, and entered into a house, and would have no man know it: but he could not be hid.

For a certain woman, whose young daughter had an unclean spirit, heard of him, and came and fell at his feet: the woman was a Greek, a Syrophenician by nation; and she besought him that he would cast forth the devil out of her daughter.

But Jesus said unto her, Let the children first be filled: for it is not meet to take the children's bread, and to cast it unto the dogs.

And she answered and said unto him, Yes, Lord: yet the dogs under the table eat of the children's crumbs.

And he said unto her, For this saying go thy way; the devil is gone out of thy daughter.

And when she was come to her house, she found the devil gone out, and her daughter laid upon the bed.

And again, departing from the coasts of Tyre and Sidon, he came unto the sea of Galilee, through the midst of the coasts of Decapolis.

And they bring unto him one that was deaf, and had an impediment in his speech; and they beseech him to put his hand upon him. And he took him aside from the multitude, and put his fingers into his ears, and he spit, and touched his tongue; and looking up to heaven, he sighed, and saith unto him, Ephphatha, that is, Be opened. And straightway his ears were opened, and the string of his tongue was loosed, and he spake plain.

And he charged them that they should tell no man: but the more he charged them, so much the more a great deal they published it; and were beyond measure astonished, saying, He hath done all things well: he maketh both the deaf to hear, and the dumb to speak.

The Lunatic Son

(*According to Matthew*)

And when they were come to the multitude, there came to him a certain man, kneeling down to him, and saying, Lord, have mercy on my son; for he is lunatic, and sore vexed: for ofttimes he falleth into the fire, and oft into the water. And I brought him to thy disciples, and they could not cure him.

Then Jesus answered and said, O faithless and perverse generation, how long shall I be with you? how long shall I suffer you? bring him hither to me.

And Jesus rebuked the devil; and he departed out of him: and the child was cured from that very hour.

Then came the disciples to Jesus apart, and said, Why could not we cast him out?

And Jesus said unto them, Because of your unbelief: for verily I say unto you, If ye have faith as a grain of mustard seed, ye shall say unto this mountain, Remove hence to yonder place; and it shall remove: and nothing shall be impossible unto you. Howbeit this kind goeth not out but by prayer and fasting.

The Tribute Money

(*According to Matthew*)

And while they abode in Galilee, Jesus said unto them, The Son of man shall be betrayed into the hands of men: and they shall kill him, and the third day he shall be raised again. And they were exceeding sorry.

And when they were come to Capernaum, they that received tribute money came to Peter, and said, Doth not your master pay tribute?

He saith, Yes.

And when he was come into the house, Jesus prevented him, saying, What thinkest thou, Simon? of whom do the kings of the earth take custom or tribute? of their own children, or of strangers?

Peter saith unto him, Of strangers.

Jesus saith unto him, Then are the children free. Notwithstanding, lest we should offend them, go thou to the sea, and cast a hook, and take up the fish that first cometh up; and when thou hast opened his mouth, thou shalt find a piece of money: that take, and give unto them for me and thee.

The Son of Man Hath No Place

(*According to Luke*)

Then there arose a reasoning among them, which of them should be greatest. And Jesus, perceiving the thought of their heart, took a child, and set him by him, and said unto them, Whosoever shall receive this child in my name receiveth me; and whosoever shall receive me, receiveth him that sent me: for he that is least among you all, the same shall be great.

And John answered and said, Master, we saw one casting out devils in thy name; and we forbade him, because he followeth not with us.

And Jesus said unto him, Forbid him not: for he that is not against us is for us.

And it came to pass, when the time was come that he should be received up, he steadfastly set his face to go to Jerusalem, and sent messengers before his face: and they went, and entered into a village of the Samaritans, to make ready for him. And they did not receive him, because his face was as though he would go to Jerusalem.

And when his disciples James and John saw this, they said, Lord, wilt thou that we command fire to come down from heaven, and consume them, even as Elias did?

But he turned, and rebuked them, and said, Ye know not what manner of spirit ye are of. For the Son of man is not come to destroy men's lives, but to save them.

And they went to another village.

And it came to pass, that, as they went in the way, a certain man said unto him, Lord, I will follow thee whithersoever thou goest.

And Jesus said unto him, Foxes have holes, and birds of the air have nests; but the Son of man hath not where to lay his head.

And he said unto another, Follow me. But he said, Lord, suffer me first to go and bury my father.

Jesus said unto him, Let the dead bury their dead: but go thou and preach the kingdom of God.

And another also said, Lord, I will follow thee; but let me first go bid them farewell, which are at home at my house.

And Jesus said unto him, No man, having put his hand to the plough, and looking back, is fit for the kingdom of God.

The Sons of Zebedee

(According to Matthew)

Then came to him the mother of Zebedee's children with her sons, worshipping him, and desiring a certain thing of him.

And he said unto her, What wilt thou? She saith unto him, Grant that these my two sons may sit, the one on thy right hand, and the other on the left, in thy kingdom.

But Jesus answered and said, Ye know not what ye ask. Are ye able to drink of the cup that I shall drink of, and to be baptized with the baptism that I am baptized with?

They say unto him, We are able.

And he saith unto them, Ye shall drink indeed of my cup, and be baptized with the baptism that I am baptized with: but to sit on my right hand, and on my left, is not mine to give, but it shall be given to them for whom it is prepared of my Father.

And when the ten heard it, they were moved with indignation against the two brethren.

But Jesus called them unto him, and said, Ye know that the princes of the Gentiles exercise dominion over them, and they that are great exercise authority upon them. But it shall not be so among you: but whosoever will be great among you, let him be your minister; and whosoever will be chief among you, let him be your servant: even as the Son of man came not to be ministered unto, but to minister, and to give his life a ransom for many.

Suffer the Little Children

(According to Mark)

And they brought young children to him, that he should touch them; and his disciples rebuked those that brought them.

But when Jesus saw it, he was much displeased, and said unto them, Suffer the little children to come unto me, and forbid them not; for of such is the kingdom of God. Verily I say unto you, Whosoever shall not receive the kingdom of God as a little child, he shall not enter therein.

And he took them up in his arms, put his hands upon them, and blessed them.

A Face toward Jerusalem

(According to Luke)

I

And it came to pass, as he went to Jerusalem, that he passed through the midst of Samaria and Galilee. And as he entered into a certain village, there met him ten men that were lepers, which stood afar off. And they lifted up their voices, and said, Jesus, Master, have mercy on us.

And when he saw them, he said unto them, Go show yourselves unto the priests.

And it came to pass, that, as they went, they were cleansed. And one of them, when he saw that he was healed, turned back, and with a loud voice glorified God, and fell down on his face at his feet, giving him thanks: and he was a Samaritan.

And Jesus answering said, Were there not ten cleansed? but where are the nine? There are not found that returned to give glory to God, save this stranger. And he said unto him, Arise, go thy way: thy faith hath made thee whole.

II

Then he took unto him the twelve, and said unto them, Behold, we go up to Jerusalem, and all things that are written by the prophets concerning the Son of man shall be accomplished. For he shall be delivered unto the Gentiles, and shall be mocked, and spitefully entreated, and spitted on. And they shall scourge him, and put him to death; and the third day he shall rise again.

And they understood none of these things: and this saying was hid from them, neither knew they the things which were spoken.

III

And Jesus entered and passed through Jericho. And, behold, there was a man named Zaccheus, which was the chief among the publicans, and he was rich. And he sought to see Jesus who he was; and could not for the press, because he was little of stature. And he ran before, and climbed up into a sycamore tree to see him; for he was to pass that way.

And when Jesus came to the place, he looked up, and saw him, and said unto him, Zaccheus, make haste, and come down; for to-day I must abide at thy house.

And he made haste, and came down, and received him joyfully. And when they saw it, they all murmured, saying, That he was gone to be guest with a man that is a sinner.

And Zaccheus stood, and said unto the Lord; Behold, Lord, the half of my goods I give to the poor; and if I have taken any thing from any man by false accusation, I restore him fourfold.

And Jesus said unto him, This day is salvation come to this house, forasmuch as he also is a son of Abraham. For the Son of man is come to seek and to save that which was lost.

The Woman Taken in Adultery

(*According to John*)

Jesus went unto the mount of Olives.

And early in the morning he came again into the temple, and all the people came unto him; and he sat down, and taught them.

And the scribes and Pharisees brought unto him a woman taken in adultery; and when they had set her in the midst, they say unto him, Master, this woman was taken in adultery, in the very act. Now Moses in the law commanded us, that such should be stoned: but what sayest thou? This they said, tempting him, that they might have to accuse him.

But Jesus stooped down, and with his finger wrote on the ground, as though he heard them not. So when they continued asking him, he lifted up himself, and said unto them, He that is without sin among you, let him first cast a stone at her. And again he stooped down, and wrote on the ground.

And they which heard it, being convicted by their own conscience, went out one by one, beginning at the eldest, even unto the last: and Jesus was left alone, and the woman standing in the midst.

When Jesus had lifted up himself, and saw none but the woman, he said unto her, Woman, where are those thine accusers? hath no man condemned thee? She said, No man, Lord. And Jesus said unto her, Neither do I condemn thee: go, and sin no more.

The Blind Man Stood on the Road and Cried

(*According to John*)

And as Jesus passed by, he saw a man which was blind from his birth. And his disciples asked him, saying, Master, who did sin, this man, or his parents, that he was born blind?

Jesus answered, Neither hath this man sinned, nor his parents: but that the works of God should be made manifest in him. I must work the works of him that sent me, while it is day: the night cometh, when no man can work. As long as I am in the world, I am the light of the world.

When he had thus spoken, he spat on the ground, and made clay of the spittle, and he anointed the eyes of the blind man with the clay, and said unto him, Go, wash in the pool of Siloam, (which is by interpretation, Sent.) He went his way therefore, and washed, and came seeing.

The neighbours therefore, and they which before had seen him that he was blind, said, Is not this he that sat and begged? Some said, This is he: others said, He is like him: but he said, I am he. Therefore said they unto him, How were thine eyes opened?

He answered and said, A man that is called Jesus made clay, and anointed mine eyes, and said unto me, Go to the pool of Siloam, and wash: and I went and washed, and I received sight.

Then said they unto him, Where is he? He said, I know not.

They brought to the Pharisees him that aforetime was blind. And it was the sabbath day when Jesus made the clay, and opened his eyes.

Then again the Pharisees also asked him how he had received his sight. He said unto them, He put clay upon mine eyes, and I washed, and do see.

Therefore said some of the Pharisees, This man is not of God, because he keepeth not the sabbath day. Others said, How can a man that is a sinner do such miracles? And there was a division among them.

They say unto the blind man again, What sayest thou of him, that he hath opened thine eyes? He said, He is a prophet.

But the Jews did not believe concerning him, that he had been blind, and received his sight, until they called the parents of him that had received his sight. And they asked them, saying, Is this your son, who ye say was born blind? how then doth he now see?

His parents answered them and said, We know that this is our son, and that he was born blind, but by what means he now seeth, we know not; or who hath opened his eyes, we know not. He is of age; ask him: he shall speak for himself. These words spake his parents, because they feared the Jews: for the Jews had agreed already, that if any man did confess that he was Christ, he should be put out of the synagogue. Therefore said his parents, He is of age; ask him.

Then again called they the man that was blind, and said unto him, Give God the praise: we know that this man is a sinner.

He answered and said, Whether he be a sinner or no, I know not: one thing I know, that, whereas I was blind, now I see.

Then said they to him again, What did he to thee? how opened he thine eyes?

He answered them, I have told you already, and ye did not hear: wherefore would ye hear it again? will ye also be his disciples?

Then they reviled him, and said, Thou art his disciple; but we are Moses' disciples. We know that God spake unto Moses: as for this fellow, we know not from whence he is.

The man answered and said unto them, Why herein is a marvellous thing, that ye know not from whence he is, and yet he hath opened mine eyes. Now we know that God heareth not sinners: but if any man be a worshipper of God, and doeth his will, him he heareth. Since the world began was it not heard that any man opened the eyes of one that was born blind. If this man were not of God, he could do nothing.

They answered and said unto him, Thou wast altogether born in sins, and dost thou teach us? And they cast him out.

Jesus heard that they had cast him out; and when he had found him, he said unto him, Dost thou believe on the Son of God?

He answered and said, Who is he, Lord, that I might believe on him?

And Jesus said unto him, Thou hast both seen him, and it is he that talketh with thee.

And he said, Lord, I believe. And he worshipped him.

And Jesus said, For judgment I am come into this world, that they which see not might see; and that they which see might be made blind.

And some of the Pharisees which were with him heard these words, and said unto him, Are we blind also?

Jesus said unto them, If ye were blind, ye should have no sin: but now ye say, We see; therefore your sin remaineth.

Lazarus Arises from Death

(*According to John*)

Now a certain man was sick, named Lazarus, of Bethany, the town of Mary and her sister Martha. (It was that Mary which anointed the Lord with ointment, and wiped his feet with her hair, whose brother Lazarus was sick.) Therefore his sisters sent unto him, saying, Lord, behold, he whom thou lovest is sick.

When Jesus heard that, he said, This sickness is not unto death, but for the glory of God, that the Son of God might be glorified thereby.

Now Jesus loved Martha, and her sister, and Lazarus. When he had heard therefore that he was sick, he abode two days still in the same place where he was. Then after that saith he to his disciples, Let us go into Judea again.

His disciples say unto him, Master, the Jews of late sought to stone thee; and goest thou thither again?

Jesus answered, Are there not twelve hours in the day? If any man walk in the day, he stumbleth not, because he seeth the light of this world. But if a man walk in the night, he stumbleth, because there is no light in him. These things said he: and after that he saith unto them, Our friend Lazarus sleepeth; but I go, that I may awake him out of sleep.

Then said his disciples, Lord, if he sleep, he shall do well. Howbeit Jesus spake of his death: but they thought that he had spoken of taking of rest in sleep.

Then said Jesus unto them plainly, Lazarus is dead. And I am glad for your sakes that I was not there, to the intent ye may believe; nevertheless let us go unto him.

Then said Thomas, which is called Didymus, unto his fellow disciples, Let us also go, that we may die with him.

Then when Jesus came, he found that he had lain in the grave four days already.

Now Bethany was nigh unto Jerusalem, about fifteen furlongs off. And many of the Jews came to Martha and Mary, to comfort them concerning their brother. Then Martha, as soon as she heard that Jesus was coming, went and met him: but Mary sat still in the house.

Then said Martha unto Jesus, Lord, if thou hadst been here, my brother had not died. But I know, that even now, whatsoever thou wilt ask of God, God will give it thee.

Jesus saith unto her, Thy brother shall rise again.

Martha saith unto him, I know that he shall rise again in the resurrection at the last day.

Jesus said unto her, I am the resurrection, and the life: he that believeth in me, though he were dead, yet shall he live. And whosoever liveth and believeth in me shall never die. Believest thou this?

She saith unto him, Yea, Lord: I believe that thou art the Christ, the Son of God, which should come into the world.

And when she had so said, she went her way, and called Mary her sister secretly, saying, The Master is come, and calleth for thee.

As soon as she heard that, she arose quickly, and came unto him. Now Jesus was not yet come into the town, but was in that place where Martha met him.

The Jews then which were with her in the house, and comforted her, when they saw Mary, that she rose up hastily and went out, followed her, saying, She goeth unto the grave to weep there.

Then when Mary was come where Jesus was, and saw him, she fell down at his feet, saying unto him, Lord, if thou hadst been here, my brother had not died.

When Jesus therefore saw her weeping, and the Jews also weeping which came with her, he groaned in the spirit, and was troubled, and said, Where have ye laid him? They say unto him, Lord, come and see.

Jesus wept.

Then said the Jews, Behold how he loved him! And some of them said, Could not this man, which opened the eyes of the blind, have caused that even this man should not have died?

Jesus therefore again groaning in himself cometh to the grave. It was a cave, and a stone lay upon it. Jesus said, Take ye away the stone. Martha, the sister of him that was dead, saith unto him, Lord, by this time he stinketh: for he hath been dead four days.

Jesus saith unto her, Said I not unto thee, that, if thou wouldest believe, thou shouldest see the glory of God?

Then they took away the stone from the place where the dead was laid. And Jesus lifted up his eyes, and said, Father, I thank thee that thou hast heard me. And I knew that thou hearest me always, but because of the people which stand by I said it, that they may believe that thou hast sent me. And when he thus had spoken, he cried with a loud voice, Lazarus, come forth.

And he that was dead came forth, bound hand and foot with graveclothes; and his face was bound about with a napkin. Jesus saith unto them, Loose him, and let him go.

Then many of the Jews which came to Mary, and had seen the things which Jesus did, believed on him. But some of them went their ways to the Pharisees, and told them what things Jesus had done.

Then gathered the chief priests and the Pharisees a council, and said, What do we? for this man doeth many miracles. If we let him thus alone, all men will believe on him; and the Romans shall come and take away both our place and nation.

And one of them, named Caiaphas, being the high priest that same year, said unto them, Ye know nothing at all, nor consider that it is expedient for us, that one man should die for the people, and that the whole nation perish not.

And this spake he not of himself: but being high priest that year, he prophesied that Jesus should die for that nation, and not for that nation only, but that also he should gather together in one the children of God that were scattered abroad.

Then from that day forth they took counsel together for to put him to death.

Jesus therefore walked no more openly among the Jews, but went thence unto a country near to the wilderness, into a city called Ephraim, and there continued with his disciples.

And the Jews' passover was nigh at hand: and many went out of the country up to Jerusalem before the passover, to purify themselves. Then sought they for Jesus, and spake among themselves, as they stood in the temple, What think ye, that he will not come to the feast?

Now both the chief priests and the Pharisees had given a commandment, that, if any man knew where he were, he should show it, that they might take him.

The Poor Ye Have Always

(*According to John*)

Then Jesus six days before the passover came to Bethany, where Lazarus was which had been dead, whom he raised from the dead. There they made him a supper; and Martha served: but Lazarus was one of them that sat at the table with him.

Then took Mary a pound of ointment of spikenard, very costly, and anointed the feet of Jesus, and wiped his feet with her hair: and the house was filled with the odour of the ointment.

Then saith one of his disciples, Judas Iscariot, Simon's son, which should betray him, Why was not this ointment sold for three hundred pence, and given to the poor? This he said, not that he cared for the poor; but because he was a thief, and had the bag, and bare what was put therein.

Then said Jesus, Let her alone: against the day of my burying hath she kept this. For the poor always ye have with you; but me ye have not always.

Much people of the Jews therefore knew that he was there: and they came not for Jesus' sake only, but that they might see Lazarus also, whom he had raised from the dead.

But the chief priests consulted that they might put Lazarus also to death, because that by reason of him many of the Jews went away, and believed on Jesus.

Entry into Jerusalem

(*According to Luke*)

And when he had thus spoken, he went before, ascending up to Jerusalem. And it came to pass, when he was come nigh to Bethphage and Bethany, at the mount called the mount of Olives, he sent two of his disciples, saying, Go ye into the village over against you; in the which at your entering ye shall find a colt tied, whereon yet never man sat: loose him, and bring him hither. And if any man ask you, Why do ye loose him? thus shall ye say unto him, Because the Lord hath need of him.

And they that were sent went their way, and found even as he had said unto them. And as they were loosing the colt, the owners thereof said unto them, Why loose ye the colt? And they said, The Lord hath need of him.

And they brought him to Jesus: and they cast their garments upon the colt, and they set Jesus thereon.

And as he went, they spread their clothes in the way. And when he was come nigh, even now at the descent of the mount of Olives, the whole multitude of the disciples began to rejoice and praise God with a loud voice for all the mighty works that they had seen, saying, Blessed be the King that cometh in the name of the Lord: peace in heaven, and glory in the highest.[1]

· And some of the Pharisees from among the multitude said unto him, Master, rebuke thy disciples.

---

[1] "And when they drew nigh unto Jerusalem, and were come to Bethphage, unto the mount of Olives, then sent Jesus two disciples, saying unto them, Go into the village over against you, and straightway ye shall find an ass tied, and a colt with her: loose them, and bring them unto me. And if any man say aught unto you, ye shall say, The Lord hath need of them; and straightway he will send them.

All this was done, that it might be fulfilled which was spoken by the prophet, saying, Tell ye the daughter of Sion, Behold, thy King cometh unto thee, meek, and sitting upon an ass, and a colt the foal of an ass.

And the disciples went, and did as Jesus commanded them, and brought the ass, and the colt, and put on them their clothes, and they set him thereon.

And a very great multitude spread their garments in the way; others cut down branches from the trees, and strewed them in the way. And the multitudes that went before, and that followed, cried, saying, Hosanna to the Son of David: Blessed is he that cometh in the name of the Lord; Hosanna in the highest."—Matt. 21:1-9.

And he answered and said unto them, I tell you that, if these should hold their peace, the stones would immediately cry out.

And when he was come near, he beheld the city, and wept over it, saying, If thou hadst known, even thou, at least in this thy day, the things which belong unto thy peace! but now they are hid from thine eyes. For the days shall come upon thee, that thine enemies shall cast a trench about thee, and compass thee round, and keep thee in on every side, and shall lay thee even with the ground, and thy children within thee; and they shall not leave in thee one stone upon another; because thou knewest not the time of thy visitation.

And he went into the temple, and began to cast out them that sold therein, and them that bought, saying unto them, It is written, My house is the house of prayer; but ye have made it a den of thieves.

And he taught daily in the temple. But the chief priests and the scribes and the chief of the people sought to destroy him, and could not find what they might do: for all the people were very attentive to hear him.

The Fig Tree Cursed

(*According to Matthew*)

Now in the morning, as he returned into the city, he hungered. And when he saw a fig tree in the way, he came to it, and found nothing thereon, but leaves only, and said unto it, Let no fruit grow on thee henceforward for ever. And presently the fig tree withered away. And when the disciples saw it, they marvelled, saying, How soon is the fig tree withered away!

Jesus answered and said unto them, Verily I say unto you, If ye have faith, and doubt not, ye shall not only do this which is done to the fig tree, but also if ye shall say unto this mountain, Be thou removed, and be thou cast into the sea; it shall be done. And all things, whatsoever ye shall ask in prayer, believing, ye shall receive.

And when he was come into the temple, the chief priests and the elders of the people came unto him as he was teaching, and said, By what authority doest thou these things? and who gave thee this authority?

And Jesus answered and said unto them, I also will ask you one thing, which if ye tell me, I in like wise will tell you by what authority I do these things. The baptism of John, whence was it? from heaven, or of men?

And they reasoned with themselves, saying, If we shall say, From heaven; he will say unto us, Why did ye not then believe him? But if we shall say, Of men; we fear the people; for all hold John as a prophet.

And they answered Jesus, and said, We cannot tell.

And he said unto them, Neither tell I you by what authority I do these things.

The Widow's Mites

(*According to Luke*)

And he looked up, and saw the rich men casting their gifts into the treasury. And he saw also a certain poor widow casting in thither two mites.

And he said, Of a truth I say unto you, that this poor widow hath cast in more than they all; for all these have of their abundance cast in unto the offerings of God: but she of her penury hath cast in all the living that she had.

The Things That Are Caesar's

(*According to Matthew*)

Then went the Pharisees, and took counsel how they might entangle him in his talk. And they sent out unto him their disciples with the Herodians, saying, Master, we know that thou art true, and teachest the way of God in truth, neither carest thou for any man: for thou regardest not the person of men. Tell us therefore, What thinkest thou? Is it lawful to give tribute unto Caesar, or not?

But Jesus perceived their wickedness, and said, Why tempt ye me, ye hypocrites? Show me the tribute money.

And they brought unto him a penny.

And he saith unto them, Whose is this image and superscription? They say unto him, Caesar's.

Then saith he unto them, Render therefore unto Caesar the things which are Caesar's; and unto God the things that are God's.

When they had heard these words, they marvelled, and left him, and went their way.

The Price of a Saviour

I

(*According to Luke*)

Now the feast of unleavened bread drew nigh, which is called the passover. And the chief priests and scribes sought how they might kill him; for they feared the people.

Then entered Satan into Judas surnamed Iscariot, being of the number of the twelve. And he went his way, and communed with the chief priests and captains, how he might betray him unto them. And they were glad, and covenanted to give him money. And he promised, and sought opportunity to betray him unto them in the absence of the multitude.

Then came the day of unleavened bread, when the passover must be killed. And he sent Peter and John, saying, Go and prepare us the passover, that we may eat.

And they said unto him, Where wilt thou that we prepare? And he said unto them, Behold, when ye are entered into the city, there shall a man meet you, bearing a pitcher of water; follow him into the house where he entereth in. And ye shall say unto the goodman of the house, The Master saith unto thee, Where is the guest chamber, where I shall eat the passover with my disciples? And he shall show you a large upper room furnished: there make ready.

And they went, and found as he had said unto them: and they made ready the passover.

II

(*According to Matthew*)

Then one of the twelve, called Judas Iscariot, went unto the chief priests, and said unto them, What will ye give me, and I will deliver him unto you? And they covenanted with him for thirty pieces of silver. And from that time he sought opportunity to betray him.

The Last Supper

I

(*According to Luke*)

And when the hour was come, he sat down, and the twelve apostles with him. And he said unto them, With desire I have desired to eat this passover with you before I suffer: for I say unto you, I will not any more eat thereof, until it be fulfilled in the kingdom of God.

And he took the cup, and gave thanks, and said, Take this, and divide it among yourselves: for I say unto you, I will not drink of the fruit of the vine, until the kingdom of God shall come.

And he took bread, and gave thanks, and brake it, and gave unto them, saying, This is my body which is given for you: this do in remembrance of me.

Likewise also the cup after supper, saying, This cup is the new testament in my blood, which is shed for you.

But, behold, the hand of him that betrayeth me is with me on the table. And truly the Son of man goeth, as it was determined: but woe unto that man by whom he is betrayed! And they began to inquire among themselves, which of them it was that should do this thing.

II

(*According to John*)

And supper being ended, the devil having now put into the heart of Judas Iscariot, Simon's son, to betray him; Jesus knowing that the Father had given all things into his hands, and that he was come from God, and went to God; he riseth from supper, and laid aside his garments; and took a towel, and girded himself.

After that he poureth water into a basin, and began to wash the disciples' feet, and to wipe them with the towel wherewith he was girded.

Then cometh he to Simon Peter: and Peter saith unto him, Lord, dost thou wash my feet? Jesus answered and said unto him, What I do thou knowest not now; but thou shalt know hereafter.

Peter saith unto him, Thou shalt never wash my feet. Jesus answered him, If I wash thee not, thou hast no part with me. Simon Peter saith unto him, Lord, not my feet only, but also my hands and my head.

Jesus saith to him, He that is washed needeth not save to wash his feet, but is clean every whit: and ye are clean, but not all. For he knew who should betray him; therefore said he, Ye are not all clean.

So after he had washed their feet, and had taken his garments, and was set down again, he said unto them, Know ye what I have done to you? Ye call me Master and Lord: and ye say well; for so I am. If I then, your Lord and Master, have washed your feet; ye also ought to wash one another's feet. For I have given you an example, that ye should do as I have done to you. Verily, verily, I say unto you, The servant is not greater than his lord; neither he that is sent greater than he that sent him. If ye know these things, happy are ye if ye do them.

I speak not of you all: I know whom I have chosen: but that the Scripture may be fulfilled, He that eateth bread with me hath lifted up his heel against me.

Now I tell you before it come, that, when it is come to pass, ye may believe that I am he. Verily, verily, I say unto you, He that receiveth whomsoever I send receiveth me; and he that receiveth me receiveth him that sent me.

When Jesus had thus said, he was troubled in spirit, and testified, and said, Verily, verily, I say unto you, that one of you shall betray me.

Then the disciples looked one on another, doubting of whom he spake.

Now there was leaning on Jesus' bosom one of his disciples, whom Jesus loved. Simon Peter therefore beckoned to him, that he should ask who it should be of whom he spake.

He then lying on Jesus' breast saith unto him, Lord, who is it? Jesus answered, He it is, to whom I shall give a sop, when I have dipped it. And when he had dipped the sop, he gave it to Judas Iscariot, the son of Simon.

And after the sop Satan entered into him. Then said Jesus unto him, That thou doest, do quickly. Now no man at the table knew for what intent he spake this unto him. For some of them thought, because Judas had the bag, that Jesus had said unto him, Buy those things that we have need of against the feast; or, that he should give something to the poor. He then, having received the sop, went immediately out; and it was night.

Therefore, when he was gone out, Jesus said, Now is the Son of man glorified, and God is glorified in him. If God be glorified in him, God shall also glorify him in himself, and shall straightway glorify him.

Little children, yet a little while I am with you. Ye shall seek me; and as I said unto the Jews, Whither I go, ye cannot come; so now I say to you. A new commandment I give unto you, That ye love one another; as I have loved you, that ye also love one another. By this shall all men know that ye are my disciples, if ye have love one to another.

Simon Peter said unto him, Lord, whither goest thou? Jesus answered him, Whither I go, thou canst not follow me now; but thou shalt follow me afterward. Peter said unto him, Lord, why cannot I follow thee now? I will lay down my life for thy sake. Jesus answered him, Wilt thou lay down thy life for my sake? Verily, verily, I say unto thee, The cock shall not crow, till thou hast denied me thrice.

Gethsemane

(*According to Luke*)

And he came out, and went, as he was wont, to the mount of Olives; and his disciples also followed him. And when he was at the place, he said unto them, Pray that ye enter not into temptation.

And he was withdrawn from them about a stone's cast, and kneeled down, and prayed, saying, Father, if thou be willing, remove this cup from me: nevertheless, not my will, but thine, be done.

And there appeared an angel unto him from heaven, strengthening him.

And being in an agony he prayed more earnestly: and his sweat was as it were great drops of blood falling down to the ground.

And when he rose up from prayer, and was come to his disciples, he found them sleeping for sorrow, and said unto them, Why sleep ye? rise and pray, lest ye enter into temptation.[1]

And while he yet spake, behold a multitude, and he that was called Judas, one of the twelve, went before them, and drew near unto Jesus to kiss him. But Jesus said unto him, Judas, betrayest thou the Son of man with a kiss?

When they which were about him saw what would follow, they said unto him, Lord shall we smite with the sword? And one of them smote the servant of the high priest, and cut off his right ear.[2] And Jesus answered and said, Suffer ye thus far. And he touched his ear, and healed him.

Then Jesus said unto the chief priests, and captains of the temple, and the elders, which were come to him, Be ye come out, as against a thief, with swords and staves? When I was daily with you in the temple, ye stretched forth no hands against me: but this is your hour, and the power of darkness.

Then took they him, and led him, and brought him into the high priest's house. And Peter followed afar off.[3]

And when they had kindled a fire in the midst of the hall, and were set down together, Peter sat down among them. But a certain maid beheld him as he sat by the fire, and earnestly looked upon him, and said,

---

[1] "Then cometh Jesus with them unto a place called Gethsemane, and saith unto the disciples, Sit ye here, while I go and pray yonder. And he took with him Peter and the two sons of Zebedee, and began to be sorrowful and very heavy. Then saith he unto them, My soul is exceeding sorrowful, even unto death: tarry ye here, and watch with me. And he went a little further, and fell on his face, and prayed, saying, O my Father, if it be possible, let this cup pass from me: nevertheless, not as I will, but as thou wilt. And he cometh unto the disciples, and findeth them asleep, and saith unto Peter, What, could ye not watch with me one hour?"—Matthew XXVI.

[2] "Then Simon Peter having a sword drew it, and smote the high priest's servant, and cut off his right ear. The servant's name was Malchus. Then said Jesus unto Peter, Put up thy sword into the sheath: the cup which my Father hath given me, shall I not drink it?"—John XVIII.

[3] "Then the band and the captain and officers of the Jews took Jesus, and bound him, and led him away to Annas first; for he was father-in-law to Caiaphas, which was the high priest that same year. Now Caiaphas was he, which gave counsel to the Jews, that it was expedient that one man should die for the people."—John XVIII.

This man was also with him. And he denied him, saying, Woman, I know him not.

And after a little while another saw him, and said, Thou art also of them. And Peter said, Man, I am not.

And about the space of one hour after another confidently affirmed, saying, Of a truth this fellow also was with him; for he is a Galilean. And Peter said, Man, I know not what thou sayest. And immediately, while he yet spake, the cock crew.

And the Lord turned, and looked upon Peter. And Peter remembered the word of the Lord, how he had said unto him, Before the cock crow, thou shalt deny me thrice. And Peter went out and wept bitterly.[1]

And the men that held Jesus mocked him, and smote him. And when they had blind-folded him, they struck him on the face, and asked him, saying, Prophesy, who is it that smote thee? And many other things blasphemously spake they against him.[2]

And as soon as it was day, the elders of the people and the chief priests and the scribes came together, and led him into their council, saying, Art thou the Christ? tell us. And he said unto them, If I tell you, ye will not believe: and if I also ask you, ye will not answer me, nor let me go. Hereafter shall the Son of man sit on the right hand of the power of God.

Then said they all, Art thou then the Son of God? And he said unto them, Ye say that I am. And they said, What need we any further witness? for we ourselves have heard of his own mouth.[3]

---

[1] "Now Peter sat without in the palace: and a damsel came unto him, saying, Thou also wast with Jesus of Galilee. But he denied before them all, saying, I know not what thou sayest. And when he was gone out into the porch, another maid saw him, and said unto them that were there, This fellow was also with Jesus of Nazareth. And again he denied with an oath, I do not know the man. And after a while came unto him they that stood by, and said to Peter, Surely thou also art one of them; for thy speech betrayeth thee. Then began he to curse and to swear, saying, I know not the man. And immediately the cock crew. And Peter remembered the word of Jesus, which said unto him, Before the cock crow, thou shalt deny me thrice. And he went out, and wept bitterly."— Matthew XXVI.

[2] "The high priest then asked Jesus of his disciples, and of his doctrine. Jesus answered him, I spake openly to the world; I ever taught in the synagogue, and in the temple, whither the Jews always resort; and in secret have I said nothing. Why askest thou me? ask them which heard me, what I have said unto them: behold, they know what I said. And when he had thus spoken, one of the officers which stood by struck Jesus with the palm of his hand, saying, Answerest thou the high priest so? Jesus answered him, If I have spoken evil, bear witness of the evil: but if well, why smitest thou me?"—John XVIII.

[3] "Now the chief priests, and elders, and all the council, sought false witness against Jesus, to put him to death; but found none: yea, though many false witnesses came, yet found they none. At the last came two false witnesses, and said, This fellow said, I am able to destroy the temple of God, and to build it in three days.

The Trial of Jesus

(*According to John*)

Pilate then went out unto them, and said, What accusation bring ye against this man?

They answered and said unto him, If he were not a malefactor, we would not have delivered him up unto thee.

Then said Pilate unto **them,** Take ye him, and judge him according to your law.

The Jews therefore said unto him, It is not lawful for us to put any man to death; that the saying of Jesus might be fulfilled, which he spake, signifying what death he should die.

Then Pilate entered into the judgment hall again, and called Jesus, and said unto him, Art thou the King of the Jews?

Jesus answered him, Sayest thou this thing of thyself, or did others tell it thee of me?

Pilate answered, Am I a Jew? Thine own nation and the chief priests have delivered thee unto me: what hast thou done?

Jesus answered, My kingdom is not of this world; if my kingdom were of this world, then would my servants fight, that I should not be delivered to the Jews: but now is my kingdom not from hence.

Pilate therefore said unto him, Art thou a king then?

Jesus answered, Thou sayest that I am a king. To this end was I born, and for this cause came I into the world, that I should bear witness unto the truth. Every one that is of the truth heareth my voice.

Pilate saith unto him, What is truth? And when he had said this, he went out again unto the Jews, and saith unto them, I find in him no

---

"And the high priest arose, and said unto him, Answerest thou nothing? what is it which these witness against thee? But Jesus held his peace. And the high priest answered and said unto him, I adjure thee by the living God, that thou tell us whether thou be the Christ, the Son of God. Jesus saith unto him, Thou hast said: nevertheless I say unto you, Hereafter shall ye see the Son of man sitting on the right hand of power, and coming in the clouds of heaven.

"Then the high priest rent his clothes, saying, He hath spoken blasphemy; what further need have we of witnesses? behold, now ye have heard his blasphemy. What think ye? They answered and said, He is guilty of death."—Matthew XXVI.

fault at all.[1] But ye have a custom, that I should release unto you one at the passover: will ye therefore that I release unto you the King of the Jews?

Then cried they all again, saying, Not this man, but Barabbas. Now Barabbas was a robber.[2]

Condemnation

(*According to John*)

Then Pilate therefore took Jesus, and scourged him. And the soldiers platted a crown of thorns, and put it on his head, and they put on him a purple robe, and said, Hail, King of the Jews! and they smote him with their hands.

Pilate therefore went forth again, and saith unto them, Behold, I bring him forth to you, that ye may know that I find no fault in him.

Then came Jesus forth, wearing the crown of thorns, and the purple robe. And Pilate saith unto them, Behold the man!

When the chief priests therefore and officers saw him, they cried out, saying, Crucify him, crucify him. Pilate saith unto them, Take ye him, and crucify him: for I find no fault in him. The Jews answered him, We have a law, and by our law he ought to die, because he made himself the Son of God.

---

[1] "Then said Pilate to the chief priests and to the people, I find no fault in this man.

"And they were the more fierce, saying, He stirreth up the people, teaching throughout all Jewry, beginning from Galilee to this place.

"When Pilate heard of Galilee, he asked whether the man were a Galilean. And as soon as he knew that he belonged unto Herod's jurisdiction, he sent him to Herod, who himself also was at Jerusalem at that time.

"And when Herod saw Jesus, he was exceeding glad: for he was desirous to see him of a long season, because he had heard many things of him; and he hoped to have seen some miracle done by him. Then he questioned with him in many words; but he answered him nothing. And the chief priests and scribes stood and vehemently accused him. And Herod with his men of war set him at nought, and mocked him, and arrayed him in a gorgeous robe, and sent him again to Pilate.

"And the same day Pilate and Herod were made friends together; for before they were at enmity between themselves."—Luke XXIII.

[2] "And they cried out all at once, saying, Away with this man, and release unto us Barabbas: (who for a certain sedition made in the city, and for murder, was cast into prison.)

"Pilate therefore, willing to release Jesus, spake again to them. But they cried, saying, Crucify him, crucify him.

"And he said unto them the third time, Why, what evil hath he done? I have found no cause of death in him: I will therefore chastise him, and let him go.

"And they were instant with loud voices, requiring that he might be crucified: and the voices of them and of the chief priests prevailed."—Luke XXIII.

When Pilate therefore heard that saying, he was the more afraid; and went again into the judgment hall, and saith unto Jesus, Whence art thou? But Jesus gave him no answer. Then saith Pilate unto him, Speakest thou not unto me? Knowest thou not that I have power to crucify thee, and have power to release thee? Jesus answered, Thou couldest have no power at all against me, except it were given thee from above: therefore he that delivered me unto thee hath the greater sin. And from thenceforth Pilate sought to release him: but the Jews cried out, saying, If thou let this man go, thou art not Caesar's friend: whosoever maketh himself a king speaketh against Caesar.

When Pilate therefore heard that saying, he brought Jesus forth, and sat down in the judgment seat in a place that is called the Pavement, but in the Hebrew, Gabba-tha. And it was the preparation of the passover, and about the sixth hour: and he saith unto the Jews, Behold your King!

But they cried out, Away with him, away with him, crucify him. Pilate saith unto them, Shall I crucify your King? The chief priests answered, We have no king but Caesar.

Then delivered he him therefore unto them to be crucified. And they took Jesus, and led him away.

The Way to Calvary

(*According to Luke*)

And there followed him a great company of people, and of women, which also bewailed and lamented him.

But Jesus turning unto them said, Daughters of Jerusalem, weep not for me, but weep for yourselves, and for your children. For, behold, the days are coming, in the which they shall say, Blessed are the barren, and the wombs that never bare, and the paps which never gave suck. Then shall they begin to say to the mountains, Fall on us; and to the hills, Cover us. For if they do these things in a green tree, what shall be done in the dry?

And there were also two others, malefactors, led with him to be put to death.

The Crucifixion

I

(*According to John*)

And he bearing his cross[1] went forth into a place called the place of a skull, which is called in the Hebrew Golgotha: where they crucified him, and two others with him, on either side one, and Jesus in the midst.

And Pilate wrote a title, and put it on the cross. And the writing was, JESUS OF NAZARETH THE KING OF THE JEWS. This title then read many of the Jews; for the place where Jesus was crucified was nigh to the city: and it was written in Hebrew, and Greek, and Latin. Then said the chief priests of the Jews to Pilate, Write not, The King of the Jews; but that he said, I am King of the Jews. Pilate answered, What I have written I have written.

II

(*According to Luke*)

And when they were come to the place, which is called Calvary, there they crucified him, and the malefactors, one on the right hand, and the other on the left.

Then said Jesus, Father, forgive them; for they know not what they do.

And they parted his raiment, and cast lots. And the people stood beholding. And the rulers also with them derided him, saying, He saved others; let him save himself, if he be Christ, the chosen of God. And the soldiers also mocked him, coming to him, and offering him vinegar, and saying, If thou be the King of the Jews, save thyself.

And one of the malefactors which were hanged railed on him, saying, If thou be Christ, save thyself and us.

But the other answering rebuked him, saying, Dost not thou fear God, seeing thou art in the same condemnation? And we indeed justly; for we receive the due reward of our deeds: but this man hath done

---

[1] "And as they led him away, they laid hold upon one Simon, a Cyrenian, coming out of the country, and on him they laid the cross, that he might bear it after Jesus."—Luke XXIII. (Matthew and Mark agree with Luke in this.)

nothing amiss. And he said unto Jesus, Lord, remember me when thou comest into thy kingdom.

And Jesus said unto him, Verily I say unto thee, To-day shalt thou be with me in paradise.

"Woman, Behold Thy Son!"

(*According to John*)

Then the soldiers, when they had crucified Jesus, took his garments, and made four parts, to every soldier a part; and also his coat: now the coat was without seam, woven from the top throughout. They said therefore among themselves, Let us not rend it, but cast lots for it, whose it shall be: that the Scripture might be fulfilled, which saith, They parted my raiment among them, and for my vesture they did cast lots. These things therefore the soldiers did.

Now there stood by the cross of Jesus his mother, and his mother's sister, Mary the wife of Cleophas, and Mary Magdalene. When Jesus therefore saw his mother, and the disciple standing by, whom he loved, he saith unto his mother, Woman, behold thy son! Then saith he to the disciple, Behold thy mother! And from that hour that disciple took her unto his own home.

Death on the Cross

(*According to Matthew*)

Now from the sixth hour there was darkness over all the land unto the ninth hour. And about the ninth hour Jesus cried with a loud voice, saying, Eli, Eli, lama sabachtha-ni? that is to say, My God, my God, why hast thou forsaken me?

Some of them that stood there, when they heard that, said, This man calleth for Elias. And straightway one of them ran, and took a sponge, and filled it with vinegar, and put it on a reed, and gave him to drink. The rest said, Let be, let us see whether Elias will come to save him.

Jesus, when he had cried again with a loud voice, yielded up the ghost.

And, behold, the veil of the temple was rent in twain from the top to the bottom; and the earth did quake, and the rocks rent; and the graves were opened; and many bodies of the saints which slept arose, and came out of the graves after his resurrection, and went into the holy city, and appeared unto many.

Now when the centurion, and they that were with him, watching Jesus, saw the earthquake, and those things that were done, they feared greatly, saying, Truly this was the Son of God.

And many women were there beholding afar off, which followed Jesus from Galilee, ministering unto him: among which was Mary Magdalene, and Mary the mother of James and Joses, and the mother of Zebedee's children.

Burial

(*According to John*)

The Jews therefore, because it was the preparation, that the bodies should not remain upon the cross on the sabbath day, (for that sabbath day was a high day,) besought Pilate that their legs might be broken, and that they might be taken away. Then came the soldiers, and brake the legs of the first, and of the other which was crucified with him.

But when they came to Jesus, and saw that he was dead already, they brake not his legs: but one of the soldiers with a spear pierced his side, and forthwith came there out blood and water. And he that saw it bare record, and his record is true; and he knoweth that he saith true, that ye might believe. For these things were done, that the Scripture should be fulfilled, A bone of him shall not be broken. And again another Scripture saith, They shall look on him whom they pierced.

And after this Joseph of Arimathea, being a disciple of Jesus, but secretly for fear of the Jews, besought Pilate that he might take away the body of Jesus: and Pilate gave him leave. He came therefore, and took the body of Jesus.[1]

---

[1] "Joseph of Arimathea, an honourable counsellor, which also waited for the kingdom of God, came, and went in boldly unto Pilate, and craved the body of Jesus. And Pilate marvelled if he were already dead: and calling unto him the centurion, he asked him whether he had been any while dead. And when he knew it of the centurion, he gave the body to Joseph."—Mark XV.

And there came also Nicodemus, which at the first came to Jesus by night, and brought a mixture of myrrh and aloes, about a hundred pound weight.

Then took they the body of Jesus, and wound it in linen clothes with the spices, as the manner of the Jews is to bury. Now in the place where he was crucified there was a garden; and in the garden a new sepulchre, wherein was never man yet laid. There laid they Jesus therefore because of the Jews' preparation day; for the sepulchre was nigh at hand.[1]

The Tomb Is Sealed

(*According to Matthew*)

Now the next day, that followed the day of the preparation, the chief priests and Pharisees came together unto Pilate, saying, Sir, we remember that that deceiver said, while he was yet alive, After three days I will rise again. Command therefore that the sepulchre be made sure until the third day, lest his disciples come by night, and steal him away, and say unto the people, He is risen from the dead: so the last error shall be worse than the first.

Pilate said unto them, Ye have a watch: go your way, make it as sure as ye can.

So they went, and made the sepulchre sure, sealing the stone, and setting a watch.

The Resurrection

I

(*According to Matthew*)

In the end of the sabbath, as it began to dawn toward the first day of the week, came Mary Magdalene and the other Mary to see the sepulchre. And, behold, there was a great earthquake: for the angel of the Lord

---

[1] "And the women also, which came with him from Galilee, followed after, and beheld the sepulchre, and how his body was laid. And they returned, and prepared spices and ointments; and rested the sabbath day according to the commandment."—Luke XXIII.

descended from heaven, and came and rolled back the stone from the door, and sat upon it. His countenance was like lightning, and his raiment white as snow: and for fear of him the keepers did shake, and became as dead men.

And the angel answered and said unto the women, Fear not ye: for I know that ye seek Jesus, which was crucified. He is not here: for he is risen, as he said. Come, see the place where the Lord lay. And go quickly, and tell his disciples that he is risen from the dead; and, behold, he goeth before you into Galilee; there shall ye see him: lo, I have told you.

And they departed quickly from the sepulchre with fear and great joy; and did run to bring his disciples word.

And as they went to tell his disciples, behold, Jesus met them, saying, All hail. And they came and held him by the feet, and worshipped him. Then said Jesus unto them, Be not afraid: go tell my brethren that they go into Galilee, and there shall they see me.

Now when they were going, behold, some of the watch came into the city, and showed unto the chief priests all the things that were done. And when they were assembled with the elders, and had taken counsel, they gave large money unto the soldiers, saying, Say ye, His disciples came by night, and stole him away while we slept. And if this come to the governor's ears, we will persuade him, and secure you.

So they took the money, and did as they were taught: and this saying is commonly reported among the Jews until this day.

II

(*According to John*)

The first day of the week cometh Mary Magdalene early, when it was yet dark, unto the sepulchre, and seeth the stone taken away from the sepulchre. Then she runneth, and cometh to Simon Peter, and to the other disciple, whom Jesus loved, and saith unto them, They have taken away the Lord out of the sepulchre, and we know not where they have laid him.

Peter therefore went forth, and that other disciple, and came to the sepulchre. So they ran both together: and the other disciple did outrun

Peter, and came first to the sepulchre. And he stooping down, and looking in, saw the linen clothes lying; yet went he not in.

Then cometh Simon Peter following him, and went into the sepulchre, and seeth the linen clothes lie, and the napkin, that was about his head, not lying with the linen clothes, but wrapped together in a place by itself. Then went in also that other disciple, which came first to the sepulchre, and he saw, and believed. For as yet they knew not the Scripture, that he must rise again from the dead.

Then the disciples went away again unto their own home.

But Mary stood without at the sepulchre weeping: and as she wept, she stooped down, and looked into the sepulchre, and seeth two angels in white sitting, the one at the head, and the other at the feet, where the body of Jesus had lain.

And they say unto her, Woman, why weepest thou? She saith unto them, Because they have taken away my Lord, and I know not where they have laid him. And when she had thus said, she turned herself back, and saw Jesus standing, and knew not that it was Jesus.

Jesus saith unto her, Woman, why weepest thou? whom seekest thou? She, supposing him to be the gardener, saith unto him, Sir, if thou have borne him hence, tell me where thou hast laid him, and I will take him away. Jesus saith unto her, Mary. She turned herself, and saith unto him, Rabboni; which is to say, Master.

Jesus saith unto her, Touch me not; for I am not yet ascended to my Father: but go to my brethren, and say unto them, I ascend unto my Father, and your Father; and to my God, and your God.

Mary Magdalene came and told the disciples that she had seen the Lord, and that he had spoken these things unto her.

The Risen Christ

I

(*According to Matthew*)

Then the eleven disciples went away into Galilee, into a mountain where Jesus had appointed them. And when they saw him, they worshipped him: but some doubted.

And Jesus came and spake unto them, saying, All power is given unto me in heaven and in earth. Go ye therefore, and teach all nations, baptizing them in the name of the Father, and of the Son, and of the Holy Ghost: teaching them to observe all things whatsoever I have commanded you: and, lo, I am with you alway, even unto the end of the world. Amen.

II

(*According to Mark*)

Now when Jesus was risen early the first day of the week, he appeared first to Mary Magdalene, out of whom he had cast seven devils. And she went and told them that had been with him, as they mourned and wept. And they, when they had heard that he was alive, and had been seen of her, believed not.

After that he appeared in another form unto two of them, as they walked, and went into the country. And they went and told it unto the residue: neither believed they them.

Afterward he appeared unto the eleven as they sat at meat, and upbraided them with their unbelief and hardness of heart, because they believed not them which had seen him after he was risen. And he said unto them, Go ye into all the world, and preach the gospel to every creature. He that believeth and is baptized shall be saved; but he that believeth not shall be damned.

And these signs shall follow them that believe; In my name shall they cast out devils; they shall speak with new tongues; they shall take up serpents; and if they drink any deadly thing, it shall not hurt them; they shall lay hands on the sick, and they shall recover.

So then, after the Lord had spoken unto them, he was received up into heaven, and sat on the right hand of God. And they went forth, and preached everywhere, the Lord working with them, and confirming the word with signs following. Amen.

III

(*According to Luke*)

And, behold, two of them went that same day to a village called Emmaus, which was from Jerusalem about threescore furlongs. And they talked together of all these things which had happened. And it came to pass, that, while they communed together and reasoned, Jesus himself drew near, and went with them. But their eyes were holden that they should not know him.

And he said unto them, What manner of communications are these that ye have one to another, as ye walk, and are sad? And the one of them, whose name was Cleopas, answering said unto him, Art thou only a stranger in Jerusalem, and hast not known the things which are come to pass there in these days? And he said unto them, What things?

And they said unto him, Concerning Jesus of Nazareth, which was a prophet mighty in deed and word before God and all the people: and how the chief priests and our rulers delivered him to be condemned to death, and have crucified him. But we trusted that it had been he which should have redeemed Israel: and beside all this, to-day is the third day since these things were done. Yea, and certain women also of our company made us astonished, which were early at the sepulchre; and when they found not his body, they came, saying, that they had also seen a vision of angels, which said that he was alive. And certain of them which were with us went to the sepulchre, and found it even so as the women had said: but him they saw not.

Then he said unto them, O fools, and slow of heart to believe all that the prophets have spoken: ought not Christ to have suffered these things, and to enter into his glory? And beginning at Moses and all the prophets, he expounded unto them in all the Scriptures the things concerning himself.

And they drew nigh unto the village, whither they went: and he made as though he would have gone further. But they constrained him, saying, Abide with us; for it is toward evening, and the day is far spent. And he went in to tarry with them.

And it came to pass, as he sat at meat with them, he took bread, and blessed it, and brake, and gave to them. And their eyes were opened, and they knew him; and he vanished out of their sight.

And they said one to another, Did not our heart burn within us, while he talked with us by the way, and while he opened to us the Scriptures?

And they rose up the same hour, and returned to Jerusalem, and found the eleven gathered together, and them that were with them, saying, The Lord is risen indeed, and hath appeared to Simon. And they told what things were done in the way, and how he was known of them in breaking of bread.

And as they thus spake, Jesus himself stood in the midst of them, and saith unto them, Peace be unto you. But they were terrified and affrighted, and supposed that they had seen a spirit. And he said unto them, Why are ye troubled? and why do thoughts arise in your hearts? Behold my hands and my feet, that it is I myself: handle me, and see; for a spirit hath not flesh and bones, as ye see me have. And when he had thus spoken, he showed them his hands and his feet.

And while they yet believed not for joy, and wondered, he said unto them, Have ye here any meat? And they gave him a piece of a broiled fish, and of a honeycomb. And he took it, and did eat before them.

And he said unto them, These are the words which I spake unto you, while I was yet with you, that all things must be fulfilled, which were written in the law of Moses, and in the prophets, and in the psalms, concerning me.

Then opened he their understanding, that they might understand the Scriptures, and said unto them, Thus it is written, and thus it behooved Christ to suffer, and to rise from the dead the third day: and that repentance and remission of sins should be preached in his name among all nations, beginning at Jerusalem. And ye are witnesses of these things.

And, behold, I send the promise of my Father upon you: but tarry ye in the city of Jerusalem, until ye be endued with power from on high.

And he led them out as far as to Bethany, and he lifted up his hands, and blessed them. And it came to pass, while he blessed them, he was parted from them, and carried up into heaven.

And they worshipped him, and returned to Jerusalem with great joy: and were continually in the temple, praising and blessing God. Amen.

IV

(*According to John*)

Then the same day at evening, being the first day of the week, when the doors were shut where the disciples were assembled for fear of the Jews, came Jesus and stood in the midst, and saith unto them, Peace be unto you. And when he had so said, he showed unto them his hands and his side. Then were the disciples glad, when they saw the Lord.

Then said Jesus to them again, Peace be unto you: as my Father hath sent me, even so send I you.

And when he had said this, he breathed on them, and saith unto them, Receive ye the Holy Ghost: whosoever sins ye remit, they are remitted unto them; and whosoever sins ye retain, they are retained.

But Thomas, one of the twelve, called Didymus, was not with them when Jesus came. The other disciples therefore said unto him, We have seen the Lord. But he said unto them, Except I shall see in his hands the print of the nails, and put my finger into the print of the nails, and thrust my hand into his side, I will not believe.

And after eight days again his disciples were within, and Thomas with them: then came Jesus, the doors being shut, and stood in the midst, and said, Peace be unto you.

Then saith he to Thomas, Reach hither thy finger, and behold my hands; and reach hither thy hand, and thrust it into my side; and be not faithless, but believing. And Thomas answered and said unto him, My Lord and my God. Jesus saith unto him, Thomas, because thou hast seen me, thou hast believed: blessed are they that have not seen, and yet have believed.

And many other signs truly did Jesus in the presence of his disciples, which are not written in this book: but these are written, that ye might believe that Jesus is the Christ, the Son of God; and that believing ye might have life through his name.

After these things Jesus showed himself again to the disciples at the sea of Tiberias; and on this wise showed he himself.

There were together Simon Peter, and Thomas called Didymus, and Nathanael of Cana in Galilee, and the sons of Zebedee, and two other of his disciples. Simon Peter saith unto them, I go a fishing. They say unto him, We also go with thee. They went forth, and entered into a ship immediately; and that night they caught nothing.

But when the morning was now come, Jesus stood on the shore; but the disciples knew not that it was Jesus. Then Jesus saith unto them, Children, have ye any meat? They answered him, No. And he said unto them, Cast the net on the right side of the ship, and ye shall find. They cast therefore, and now they were not able to draw it for the multitude of fishes.

Therefore that disciple whom Jesus loved saith unto Peter, It is the Lord. Now when Simon Peter heard that it was the Lord, he girt his fisher's coat unto him, (for he was naked,) and did cast himself into the sea.

And the other disciples came in a little ship, (for they were not far from land, but as it were two hundred cubits,) dragging the net with fishes. As soon then as they were come to land, they saw a fire of coals there, and fish laid thereon, and bread. Jesus saith unto them, Bring of the fish which ye have now caught. Simon Peter went up, and drew the net to land full of great fishes, a hundred and fifty and three: and for all there were so many, yet was not the net broken. Jesus saith unto them, Come and dine. And none of the disciples durst ask him, Who art thou? knowing that it was the Lord. Jesus then cometh, and taketh bread, and giveth them, and fish likewise.

This is now the third time that Jesus showed himself to his disciples, after that he was risen from the dead.

So when they had dined, Jesus saith to Simon Peter, Simon, son of Jonas, lovest thou me more than these? He saith unto him, Yea, Lord; thou knowest that I love thee. He saith unto him, Feed my lambs. He saith to him again the second time, Simon, son of Jonas, lovest thou me? He saith unto him, Yea, Lord; thou knowest that I love thee. He saith unto him, Feed my sheep. He saith unto him the third time, Simon, son of Jonas, lovest thou me? Peter was grieved because he said unto him the third time, Lovest thou me? And he said unto him, Lord, thou knowest all things; thou knowest that I love thee. Jesus saith unto him, Feed my sheep. Verily, verily, I say unto thee, When thou wast young, thou girdedst thyself, and walkedst whither thou wouldest: but when thou shalt be old, thou shalt stretch forth thy hands, and another shall gird thee, and carry thee whither thou wouldest not. This spake he, signifying by what death he should glorify God. And when he had spoken this, he saith unto him, Follow me.

Then Peter, turning about, seeth the disciple whom Jesus loved following; which also leaned on his breast at supper, and said, Lord, which is he that betrayeth thee? Peter seeing him saith to Jesus, Lord, and what shall this man do? Jesus saith unto him, If I will that he tarry till I come, what is that to thee? follow thou me.

Then went this saying abroad among the brethren, that that disciple should not die: yet Jesus said not unto him, He shall not die; but, If I will that he tarry till I come, what is that to thee?

This is the disciple which testifieth of these things, and wrote these things: and we know that his testimony is true.

And there are also many other things which Jesus did, the which, if they should be written every one, I suppose that even the world itself could not contain the books that should be written. Amen.

The Sermons and Sayings of Jesus

(COMPILED FROM THE FOUR GOSPELS)

The Sermon on the Mount

(According to Matthew)

And seeing the multitudes, he went up into a mountain: and when he was set, his disciples came unto him: and he opened his mouth, and taught them, saying:

Blessed are the poor in spirit: for theirs is the kingdom of heaven. Blessed are they that mourn: for they shall be comforted. Blessed are the meek: for they shall inherit the earth. Blessed are they which do hunger and thirst after righteousness: for they shall be filled. Blessed are the merciful: for they shall obtain mercy. Blessed are the pure in heart: for they shall see God. Blessed are the peacemakers: for they shall be called the children of God. Blessed are they which are persecuted for righteousness' sake: for theirs is the kingdom of heaven. Blessed are ye, when men shall revile you, and persecute you, and shall say all manner of evil against you falsely, for my sake. Rejoice, and be exceeding glad: for great is your reward in heaven: for so persecuted they the prophets which were before you.

Ye are the salt of the earth: but if the salt have lost his savour, wherewith shall it be salted? it is thenceforth good for nothing, but to be cast out, and to be trodden under foot of men.

Ye are the light of the world. A city that is set on a hill cannot be hid. Neither do men light a candle, and put it under a bushel, but on a candlestick; and it giveth light unto all that are in the house. Let your light so shine before men, that they may see your good works, and glorify your Father which is in heaven.

Think not that I am come to destroy the law, or the prophets: I am not come to destroy, but to fulfil. For verily I say unto you, Till heaven and earth pass, one jot or one tittle shall in no wise pass from the law, till all be fulfilled. Whosoever therefore shall break one of these least commandments, and shall teach men so, he shall be called the least in the kingdom of heaven: but whosoever shall do and teach them, the same shall be called great in the kingdom of heaven. For I say unto you, That except your righteousness shall exceed the righteousness of the scribes and Pharisees, ye shall in no case enter into the kingdom of heaven.

Ye have heard that it was said by them of old time, Thou shalt not kill; and whosoever shall kill shall be in danger of the judgment. But I say unto you, That whosoever is angry with his brother without a cause shall be in danger of the judgment: and whosoever shall say to his brother, Raca, shall be in danger of the council: but whosoever shall say, Thou fool, shall be in danger of hell fire. Therefore if thou bring thy gift to the altar, and there rememberest that thy brother hath aught against thee, leave there thy gift before the altar, and go thy way; first be reconciled to thy brother, and then come and offer thy gift.

Agree with thine adversary quickly, while thou art in the way with him; lest at any time the adversary deliver thee to the judge, and the judge deliver thee to the officer, and thou be cast into prison. Verily I say unto thee, Thou shalt by no means come out thence, till thou hast paid the uttermost farthing.

Ye have heard that it was said by them of old time, Thou shalt not commit adultery. But I say unto you, That whosoever looketh on a woman to lust after her hath committed adultery with her already in his heart.

And if thy right eye offend thee, pluck it out, and cast it from thee: for it is profitable for thee that one of thy members should perish, and not that thy whole body should be cast into hell. And if thy right hand offend thee, cut it off, and cast it from thee: for it is profitable for thee that one of thy members should perish, and not that thy whole body should be cast into hell.

It hath been said, Whosoever shall put away his wife, let him give her a writing of divorcement. But I say unto you, That whosoever shall put away his wife, saving for the cause of fornication, causeth her to commit adultery: and whosoever shall marry her that is divorced committeth adultery.

Again, ye have heard that it hath been said by them of old time, Thou shalt not forswear thyself, but shalt perform unto the Lord thine oaths. But I say unto you, Swear not at all; neither by heaven; for it is God's throne; nor by the earth; for it is his footstool; neither by Jerusalem; for it is the city of the great King. Neither shalt thou swear by thy head, because thou canst not make one hair white or black. But let your communication be, Yea, yea; Nay, nay: for whatsoever is more than these cometh of evil.

Ye have heard that it hath been said, An eye for an eye, and a tooth for a tooth. But I say unto you, That ye resist not evil: but whosoever shall smite thee on thy right cheek, turn to him the other also. And if any man will sue thee at the law, and take away thy coat, let him have thy cloak also. And whosoever shall compel thee to go a mile, go with him twain. Give to him that asketh thee, and from him that would borrow of thee turn not thou away.

Ye have heard that it hath been said, Thou shalt love thy neighbour, and hate thine enemy. But I say unto you, Love your enemies, bless them that curse you, do good to them that hate you, and pray for them which despitefully use you, and persecute you, that ye may be the children of your Father which is in heaven: for he maketh his sun to rise on the evil and on the good, and sendeth rain on the just and on the unjust.

For if ye love them which love you, what reward have ye? do not even the publicans the same? And if ye salute your brethren only, what do ye more than others? do not even the publicans so?

Be ye therefore perfect, even as your Father which is in heaven is perfect.

Take heed that ye do not your alms before men, to be seen of them: otherwise ye have no reward of your Father which is in heaven. Therefore when thou doest thine alms, do not sound a trumpet before thee, as the hypocrites do in the synagogues and in the streets, that they may have glory of men. Verily I say unto you, They have their reward. But when thou doest alms, let not thy left hand know what thy right hand doeth, that thine alms may be in secret: and thy Father which seeth in secret himself shall reward thee openly.

And when thou prayest, thou shalt not be as the hypocrites are: for they love to pray standing in the synagogues and in the corners of the streets, that they may be seen of men. Verily I say unto you, They have their reward. But thou, when thou prayest, enter into thy closet, and when thou hast shut thy door, pray to thy Father which is in secret; and thy Father which seeth in secret shall reward thee openly. But when ye pray, use not vain repetitions, as the heathen do: for they think that they shall be heard for their much speaking. Be not ye therefore like unto them, for your Father knoweth what things ye have need of, before ye ask him.

After this manner therefore pray ye:

Our Father which art in heaven, Hallowed be thy name. Thy kingdom come. Thy will be done in earth, as it is in heaven. Give us this day our daily bread. And forgive us our debts, as we forgive our debtors. And lead us not into temptation, but deliver us from evil: For thine is the kingdom, and the power, and the glory, for ever. Amen.[1]

For if ye forgive men their trespasses, your heavenly Father will also forgive you. But if ye forgive not men their trespasses, neither will your Father forgive your trespasses.

Moreover when ye fast, be not, as the hypocrites, of a sad countenance: for they disfigure their faces, that they may appear unto men to fast. Verily I say unto you, They have their reward. But thou, when thou fastest, anoint thine head, and wash thy face, that thou appear not unto men to fast, but unto thy Father which is in secret: and thy Father which seeth in secret shall reward thee openly.

Lay not up for yourselves treasures upon earth, where moth and rust doth corrupt, and where thieves break through and steal. But lay up for yourselves treasures in heaven, where neither moth nor rust doth

---

[1] "And he said unto them, When ye pray, say, Our Father which art in heaven, Hallowed be thy name. Thy kingdom come. Thy will be done, as in heaven, so in earth. Give us day by day our daily bread. And forgive us our sins; for we also forgive every one that is indebted to us. And lead us not into temptation; but deliver us from evil."— Luke XI.

corrupt, and where thieves do not break through nor steal; for where your treasure is, there will your heart be also.

The light of the body is the eye: if therefore thine eye be single, thy whole body shall be full of light. But if thine eye be evil, thy whole body shall be full of darkness. If therefore the light that is in thee be darkness, how great is that darkness!

No man can serve two masters: for either he will hate the one, and love the other; or else he will hold to the one, and despise the other. Ye cannot serve God and mammon.

Therefore I say unto you, Take no thought for your life, what ye shall eat, or what ye shall drink; nor yet for your body, what ye shall put on. Is not the life more than meat, and the body than raiment? Behold the fowls of the air: for they sow not, neither do they reap, nor gather into barns; yet your heavenly Father feedeth them. Are ye not much better than they? Which of you by taking thought can add one cubit unto his stature? And why take ye thought for raiment? Consider the lilies of the field, how they grow; they toil not, neither do they spin, and yet I say unto you, That even Solomon in all his glory was not arrayed like one of these. Wherefore, if God so clothe the grass of the field, which to-day is, and to-morrow is cast into the oven, shall he not much more clothe you, O ye of little faith?

Therefore take no thought, saying, What shall we eat? or, What shall we drink? or, Wherewithal shall we be clothed? (For after all these things do the Gentiles seek:) for your heavenly Father knoweth that ye have need of all these things. But seek ye first the kingdom of God, and his righteousness; and all these things shall be added unto you. Take therefore no thought for the morrow: for the morrow shall take thought for the things of itself. Sufficient unto the day is the evil thereof.

Judge not, that ye be not judged. For with what judgment ye judge, ye shall be judged: and with what measure ye mete, it shall be measured to you again. And why beholdest thou the mote that is in thy brother's eye, but considerest not the beam that is in thine own eye? Or how wilt thou say to thy brother, Let me pull out the mote out of thine eye; and, behold, a beam is in thine own eye? Thou hypocrite, first cast out the beam out of thine own eye; and then shalt thou see clearly to cast out the mote out of thy brother's eye.

Give not that which is holy unto the dogs, neither cast ye your pearls before swine, lest they trample them under their feet, and turn again and rend you.

Ask, and it shall be given you; seek, and ye shall find; knock, and it shall be opened unto you. For every one that asketh receiveth; and he that seeketh findeth; and to him that knocketh it shall be opened. Or what man is there of you, whom if his son ask bread, will he give him a stone? Or if he ask a fish, will he give him a serpent? If ye then, being evil, know how to give good gifts unto your children, how much more shall your Father which is in heaven give good things to them that ask him?

Therefore all things whatsoever ye would that men should do to you, do ye even so to them: for this is the law and the prophets.

Enter ye in at the strait gate: for wide is the gate, and broad is the way, that leadeth to destruction, and many there be which go in thereat, because strait is the gate, and narrow is the way, which leadeth unto life, and few there be that find it.

Beware of false prophets, which come to you in sheep's clothing, but inwardly they are ravening wolves. Ye shall know them by their fruits. Do men gather grapes of thorns, or figs of thistles? Even so every good tree bringeth forth good fruit; but a corrupt tree bringeth forth evil fruit. A good tree cannot bring forth evil fruit, neither can a corrupt tree bring forth good fruit. Every tree that bringeth not forth good fruit is hewn down, and cast into the fire. Wherefore by their fruits ye shall know them.

Not every one that saith unto me, Lord, Lord, shall enter into the kingdom of heaven; but he that doeth the will of my Father which is in heaven. Many will say to me in that day, Lord, Lord, have we not prophesied in thy name? and in thy name have cast out devils? and in thy name done many wonderful works? And then will I profess unto them, I never knew you: depart from me, ye that work iniquity.

Therefore whosoever heareth these sayings of mine, and doeth them, I will liken him unto a wise man, which built his house upon a rock; and the rain descended, and the floods came, and the winds blew, and beat upon that house; and it fell not: for it was founded upon a rock.

And every one that heareth these sayings of mine, and doeth them not, shall be likened unto a foolish man, which built his house upon the sand;

and the rain descended, and the floods came, and the winds blew, and beat upon that house; and it fell: and great was the fall of it.

And it came to pass, when Jesus had ended these sayings, the people were astonished at his doctrine, for he taught them as one having authority, and not as the scribes.

To the Disciples of Christ

(*According to Matthew*)

Behold, I send you forth as sheep in the midst of wolves: be ye therefore wise as serpents, and harmless as doves. But beware of men: for they will deliver you up to the councils, and they will scourge you in their synagogues, and ye shall be brought before governors and kings for my sake, for a testimony against them and the Gentiles.

But when they deliver you up, take no thought how or what ye shall speak: for it shall be given you in that same hour what ye shall speak. For it is not ye that speak, but the Spirit of your Father which speaketh in you.

And the brother shall deliver up the brother to death, and the father the child: and the children shall rise up against their parents, and cause them to be put to death. And ye shall be hated of all men for my name's sake: but he that endureth to the end shall be saved.

But when they persecute you in this city, flee ye into another: for verily I say unto you, Ye shall not have gone over the cities of Israel, till the Son of man be come.

The disciple is not above his master, nor the servant above his lord. It is enough for the disciple that he be as his master, and the servant as his lord. If they have called the master of the house Beelzebub, how much more shall they call them of his household?

Fear them not therefore: for there is nothing covered, that shall not be revealed; and hid, that shall not be known. What I tell you in darkness, that speak ye in light: and what ye hear in the ear, that preach ye upon the housetops.

And fear not them which kill the body, but are not able to kill the soul: but rather fear him which is able to destroy both soul and body in hell. Are not two sparrows sold for a farthing? and one of them shall not fall on the ground without your Father. But the very hairs of your head are all numbered. Fear ye not therefore, ye are of more value than many sparrows.

Whosoever therefore shall confess me before men, him will I confess also before my Father which is in heaven. But whosoever shall deny me before men, him will I also deny before my Father which is in heaven.

Think not that I am come to send peace on earth: I came not to send peace, but a sword. For I am come to set a man at variance against his father, and the daughter against her mother, and the daughter-in-law against her mother-in-law. And a man's foes shall be they of his own household. He that loveth father or mother more than me is not worthy of me; and he that loveth son or daughter more than me is not worthy of me.

And he that taketh not his cross, and followeth after me, is not worthy of me. He that findeth his life shall lose it: and he that loseth his life for my sake shall find it.

He that receiveth you receiveth me; and he that receiveth me receiveth him that sent me. He that receiveth a prophet in the name of a prophet shall receive a prophet's reward; and he that receiveth a righteous man in the name of a righteous man shall receive a righteous man's reward. And whosoever shall give to drink unto one of these little ones a cup of cold water only in the name of a disciple, verily I say unto you, he shall in no wise lose his reward.

Invitation to Christ

(*According to Matthew*)

I thank thee, O Father, Lord of heaven and earth, because thou hast hid these things from the wise and prudent, and hast revealed them unto babes. Even so, Father; for so it seemed good in thy sight.

All things are delivered unto me of my Father: and no man knoweth the Son, but the Father; neither knoweth any man the Father, save the Son, and he to whomsoever the Son will reveal him.

Come unto me, all ye that labour and are heavy laden, and I will give you rest. Take my yoke upon you, and learn of me; for I am meek and lowly in heart: and ye shall find rest unto your souls. For my yoke is easy, and my burden is light.

A Rebuke to Doubters

(*According to Matthew*)

Every kingdom divided against itself is brought to desolation; and every city or house divided against itself shall not stand. And if Satan cast out Satan, he is divided against himself; how shall then his kingdom stand? And if I by Beelzebub cast out devils, by whom do your children cast them out? therefore they shall be your judges. But if I cast out devils by the Spirit of God, then the kingdom of God is come unto you.

Or else, how can one enter into a strong man's house, and spoil his goods, except he first bind the strong man? and then he will spoil his house.

He that is not with me is against me; and he that gathereth not with me scattereth abroad.

Wherefore I say unto you, All manner of sin and blasphemy shall be forgiven unto men: but the blasphemy against the Holy Ghost shall not be forgiven unto men. And whosoever speaketh a word against the Son of man, it shall be forgiven him: but whosoever speaketh against the Holy Ghost, it shall not be forgiven him, neither in this world, neither in the world to come.

Either make the tree good, and his fruit good; or else make the tree corrupt, and his fruit corrupt: for the tree is known by his fruit.

O generation of vipers, how can ye, being evil, speak good things? for out of the abundance of the heart the mouth speaketh. A good man out of the good treasure of the heart bringeth forth good things: and an evil man out of the evil treasure bringeth forth evil things. But I say unto you, That every idle word that men shall speak, they shall give account thereof in the day of judgment. For by thy words thou shalt be justified, and by thy words thou shalt be condemned.

Then certain of the scribes and of the Pharisees answered, saying, Master, we would see a sign from thee.

But he answered and said unto them,

An evil and adulterous generation seeketh after a sign; and there shall no sign be given to it, but the sign of the prophet Jonas; for as Jonas was three days and three nights in the whale's belly; so shall the Son of man be three days and three nights in the heart of the earth. The men of Nineveh shall rise in judgment with this generation, and shall condemn it: because they repented at the preaching of Jonas; and, behold, a greater than Jonas is here.

The queen of the south shall rise up in the judgment with this generation, and shall condemn it, for she came from the uttermost parts of the earth to hear the wisdom of Solomon; and, behold, a greater than Solomon is here.

When the unclean spirit is gone out of a man, he walketh through dry places, seeking rest, and findeth none. Then he saith, I will return into my house from whence I came out; and when he is come, he findeth it empty, swept, and garnished. Then goeth he, and taketh with himself seven other spirits more wicked than himself, and they enter in and dwell there: and the last state of that man is worse than the first. Even so shall it be also unto this wicked generation.

Of Forms and Meanings

(*According to Matthew*)

Then came to Jesus scribes and Pharisees, which were of Jerusalem, saying, Why do thy disciples transgress the tradition of the elders? for they wash not their hands when they eat bread.

But he answered and said unto them,

Why do ye also transgress the commandment of God by your tradition? For God commanded, saying, Honour thy father and mother: and, He that curseth father or mother, let him die the death. But ye say, Whosoever shall say to his father or his mother, It is a gift, by whatsoever thou mightest be profited by me, and honour not his father or his mother, he shall be free. Thus have ye made the commandment of God of none effect by your tradition.

Ye hypocrites, well did Esaias prophesy of you, saying, This people draweth nigh unto me with their mouth, and honoureth me with their lips; but their heart is far from me. But in vain they do worship me, teaching for doctrines the commandments of men.

And he called the multitude, and said unto them,

Hear, and understand: not that which goeth into the mouth defileth a man; but that which cometh out of the mouth, this defileth a man.

Then came his disciples, and said unto him, Knowest thou that the Pharisees were offended, after they heard this saying?

But he answered and said,

Every plant, which my heavenly Father hath not planted, shall be rooted up. Let them alone; they be blind leaders of the blind. And if the blind lead the blind, both shall fall into the ditch.

Then answered Peter and said unto him, Declare unto us this parable. And Jesus said,

Are ye also yet without understanding? Do not ye yet understand, that whatsoever entereth in at the mouth goeth into the belly, and is cast out into the draught? But those things which proceed out of the mouth come forth from the heart; and they defile the man. For out of the heart proceed evil thoughts, murders, adulteries, fornications, thefts, false witness, blasphemies. These are the things which defile a man: but to eat with unwashen hands defileth not a man.

The Price of Salvation

(*According to Matthew*)

Then said Jesus unto his disciples,

If any man will come after me, let him deny himself, and take up his cross, and follow me. For whosoever will save his life shall lose it: and whosoever will lose his life for my sake shall find it.

For what is a man profited, if he shall gain the whole world, and lose his own soul? or what shall a man give in exchange for his soul?

For the Son of man shall come in the glory of his Father with his angels; and then he shall reward every man according to his works.

Verily I say unto you, There be some standing here, which shall not taste of death, till they see the Son of man coming in his kingdom.

Whatsoever Ye Bind on Earth

(*According to Matthew*)

Moreover if thy brother shall trespass against thee, go and tell him his fault between thee and him alone: if he shall hear thee, thou hast gained thy brother. But if he will not hear thee, then take with thee one or two more, that in the mouth of two or three witnesses every word may be established. And if he shall neglect to hear them, tell it unto the church: but if he neglect to hear the church, let him be unto thee as a heathen man and a publican.

Verily I say unto you, Whatsoever ye shall bind on earth shall be bound in heaven; and whatsoever ye shall loose on earth shall be loosed in heaven.

Again I say unto you, That if two of you shall agree on earth as touching any thing that they shall ask, it shall be done for them of my Father which is in heaven. For where two or three are gathered together in my name, there am I in the midst of them.

Then came Peter to him, and said, Lord, how oft shall my brother sin against me, and I forgive him? till seven times?

Jesus saith unto him,

I say not unto thee, Until seven times, but, Until seventy times seven.

Therefore is the kingdom of heaven likened unto a certain king, which would take account of his servants. And when he had begun to reckon, one was brought unto him, which owed him ten thousand talents. But forasmuch as he had not to pay, his lord commanded him to be sold, and his wife, and children, and all that he had, and payment to be made. The servant therefore fell down, and worshipped him, saying, Lord, have patience with me, and I will pay thee all. Then the lord of that servant was moved with compassion, and loosed him, and forgave him the debt.

But the same servant went out, and found one of his fellow servants, which owed him a hundred pence: and he laid hands on him, and took him by the throat, saying, Pay me that thou owest. And his fellow servant fell down at his feet, and besought him, saying, Have patience with me, and I will pay thee all. And he would not: but went and cast him into prison, till he should pay the debt.

So when his fellow servants saw what was done, they were very sorry, and came and told unto their lord all that was done. Then his lord, after that he had called him, said unto him, O thou wicked servant, I forgave thee all that debt, because thou desiredst me. Shouldest not thou also have had compassion on thy fellow servant, even as I had pity on thee? And his lord was wroth, and delivered him to the tormentors, till he should pay all that was due unto him.

So likewise shall my heavenly Father do also unto you, if ye from your hearts forgive not every one his brother their trespasses.

Of Marriage

(*According to Matthew*)

I

The Pharisees also came unto him, tempting him, and saying unto him, Is it lawful for a man to put away his wife for every cause?
And he answered and said unto them,

Have ye not read, that he which made them at the beginning made them male and female, and said, For this cause shall a man leave father and mother, and shall cleave to his wife: and they twain shall be one flesh? Wherefore they are no more twain, but one flesh. What therefore God hath joined together, let not man put asunder.

They say unto him, Why did Moses then command to give a writing of divorcement, and to put her away?
He saith unto them,

Moses because of the hardness of your hearts suffered you to put away your wives: but from the beginning it was not so. And I say unto you, Whosoever shall put away his wife, except it be for fornication, and shall marry another, committeth adultery: and whoso marrieth her which is put away doth commit adultery.

His disciples say unto him, If the case of the man be so with his wife, it is not good to marry.
But he said unto them,

All men cannot receive this saying, save they to whom it is given. For there are some eunuchs, which were so born from their mother's womb: and there are some eunuchs, which were made eunuchs of men: and there be eunuchs, which have made themselves eunuchs for the kingdom of heaven's sake. He that is able to receive it, let him receive it.

II

The same day came to him the Sadducees, which say that there is no resurrection, and asked him, saying, Master, Moses said, If a man die, having no children, his brother shall marry his wife, and raise up seed unto his brother. Now there were with us seven brethren: and the first, when he had married a wife, deceased, and, having no issue, left his wife unto his brother. Likewise the second also, and the third, unto the seventh. And last of all the woman died also. Therefore in the resurrection, whose wife shall she be of the seven? for they all had her.

Jesus answered and said unto them,

Ye do err, not knowing the Scriptures, nor the power of God. For in the resurrection they neither marry, nor are given in marriage, but are as the angels of God in heaven.

Of Riches

(*According to Matthew*)

And, behold, one came and said unto him, Good Master, what good thing shall I do, that I may have eternal life?

And he said unto him,

Why callest thou me good? there is none good but one, that is, God: but if thou wilt enter into life, keep the commandments.

He saith unto him, Which? Jesus said,

Thou shalt do no murder, Thou shalt not commit adultery, Thou shalt not steal, Thou shalt not bear false witness, Honour thy father and thy mother: and, Thou shalt love thy neighbour as thyself.

The young man saith unto him, All these things have I kept from my youth up: what lack I yet? Jesus said unto him,

If thou wilt be perfect, go and sell that thou hast, and give to the poor, and thou shalt have treasure in heaven: and come and follow me.

But when the young man heard that saying, he went away sorrowful: for he had great possessions.

Then said Jesus unto his disciples,

Verily I say unto you, That a rich man shall hardly enter into the kingdom of heaven. And again I say unto you, It is easier for a camel to go through the eye of a needle, than for a rich man to enter into the kingdom of God.

When his disciples heard it, they were exceedingly amazed, saying, Who then can be saved? But Jesus beheld them, and said unto them,

With men this is impossible; but with God all things are possible.

The Reward of Salvation

(*According to Matthew*)

Then answered Peter and said unto him, Behold, we have forsaken all, and followed thee; what shall we have therefore? And Jesus said unto them,

Verily I say unto you, That ye which have followed me, in the regeneration when the Son of man shall sit in the throne of his glory, ye also shall sit upon twelve thrones, judging the twelve tribes of Israel. And every one that hath forsaken houses, or brethren, or sisters, or father, or mother, or wife, or children, or lands, for my name's sake, shall receive a hundredfold, and shall inherit everlasting life. But many that are first shall be last; and the last shall be first.

Of Resurrection

(*According to Matthew*)

But as touching the resurrection of the dead, have ye not read that which was spoken unto you by God, saying, I am the God of Abraham, and the God of Isaac, and the God of Jacob? God is not the God of the dead, but of the living.

The Great Commandments

(*According to Mark*)

And one of the scribes came, and having heard them reasoning together, and perceiving that he had answered them well, asked him, Which is the first commandment of all? And Jesus answered him,

The first of all the commandments is, Hear, O Israel; The Lord our God is one Lord: and thou shalt love the Lord thy God with all thy heart, and with all thy soul, and with all thy mind, and with all thy strength: this is the first commandment. And the second is like, namely this, Thou shalt love thy neighbour as thyself. There is none other commandment greater than these.

And the scribe said unto him, Well, Master, thou hast said the truth: for there is one God; and there is none other but he: and to love him with all the heart, and with all the understanding, and with all the soul, and with all the strength, and to love his neighbour as himself, is more than all whole burnt offerings and sacrifices.

And when Jesus saw that he answered discreetly, he said unto him,

Thou art not far from the kingdom of God.

And no man after that durst ask him any question.

Of His Identity

(*According to Matthew*)

While the Pharisees were gathered together, Jesus asked them, saying,

What think ye of Christ? whose son is he?

They say unto him, The son of David. He saith unto them,

How then doth David in spirit call him Lord, saying, The Lord said unto my Lord, Sit thou on my right hand, till I make thine enemies thy footstool? If David then call him Lord, how is he his son?

And no man was able to answer him a word, neither durst any man from that day forth ask him any more questions.

He Rebukes the Scribes and Pharisees

(According to Matthew)

Then spake Jesus to the multitude, and to his disciples, saying,

The scribes and the Pharisees sit in Moses' seat. All therefore whatsoever they bid you observe, that observe and do; but do not ye after their works, for they say, and do not. For they bind heavy burdens and grievous to be borne, and lay them on men's shoulders; but they themselves will not move them with one of their fingers. But all their works they do for to be seen of men; they make broad their phylacteries, and enlarge the borders of their garments, and love the uppermost rooms at feasts, and the chief seats in the synagogues, and greetings in the markets, and to be called of men, Rabbi, Rabbi.

But be not ye called Rabbi: for one is your Master, even Christ; and all ye are brethren. And call no man your father upon the earth: for one is your Father, which is in heaven. Neither be ye called masters, for one is your Master, even Christ. But he that is greatest among you shall be your servant. And whosoever shall exalt himself shall be abased; and he that shall humble himself shall be exalted.

But woe unto you, scribes and Pharisees, hypocrites! for ye shut up the kingdom of heaven against men, for ye neither go in yourselves, neither suffer ye them that are entering to go in. Woe unto you, scribes and Pharisees, hypocrites! for ye devour widows' houses, and for a pretense make long prayer: therefore ye shall receive the greater damnation. Woe unto you, scribes and Pharisees, hypocrites! for ye compass sea and land to make one proselyte, and when he is made, ye make him twofold more the child of hell than yourselves.

Woe unto you, ye blind guides, which say, Whosoever shall swear by the temple, it is nothing; but whosoever shall swear by the gold of the temple, he is a debtor! Ye fools and blind: for whether is greater, the gold, or the temple that sanctifieth the gold? And, Whosoever shall swear by the altar, it is nothing; but whosoever sweareth by the gift that is upon it, he is guilty. Ye fools and blind: for whether is greater, the gift, or the altar that sanctifieth the gift? Whoso therefore shall swear by the altar, sweareth by it, and by all things thereon. And whoso shall swear by the temple, sweareth by it, and by him that dwelleth therein. And he that shall swear by heaven, sweareth by the throne of God, and by him that sitteth thereon.

Woe unto you, scribes and Pharisees, hypocrites! for ye pay tithe of mint and anise and cummin, and have omitted the weightier matters of the law, judgment, mercy, and faith: these ought ye to have done, and not to leave the other undone. Ye blind guides, which strain at a gnat, and swallow a camel.

Woe unto you, scribes and Pharisees, hypocrites! for ye make clean the outside of the cup and of the platter, but within they are full of extortion and excess. Thou blind Pharisee, cleanse first that which is within the cup and platter, that the outside of them may be clean also.

Woe unto you, scribes and Pharisees, hypocrites! for ye are like unto whited sepulchres, which indeed appear beautiful outward, but are within full of dead men's bones, and of all uncleanness. Even so ye also outwardly appear righteous unto men, but within ye are full of hypocrisy and iniquity.

Woe unto you, scribes and Pharisees, hypocrites! because ye build the tombs of the prophets, and garnish the sepulchres of the righteous, and say, If we had been in the days of our fathers, we would not have been partakers with them in the blood of the prophets. Wherefore ye be witnesses unto yourselves, that ye are the children of them which killed the prophets. Fill ye up then the measure of your fathers. Ye serpents, ye generation of vipers, how can ye escape the damnation of hell?

Wherefore, behold, I send unto you prophets, and wise men, and scribes: and some of them ye shall kill and crucify; and some of them shall ye scourge in your synagogues, and persecute them from city to city, that upon you may come all the righteous blood shed upon the earth, from the blood of righteous Abel unto the blood of Zacharias son of Barachias, whom ye slew between the temple and the altar. Verily I say unto you, All these things shall come upon this generation.

O Jerusalem, Jerusalem, thou that killest the prophets, and stonest them which are sent unto thee, how often would I have gathered thy children together, even as a hen gathereth her chickens under her wings, and ye would not! Behold, your house is left unto you desolate. For I say unto you, Ye shall not see me henceforth, till ye shall say, Blessed is he that cometh in the name of the Lord.

Second Coming

(*According to Matthew*)

I

*And Jesus went out, and departed from the temple: and his disciples
came to him for to show him the buildings of the temple. And Jesus said
unto them,*

See ye not all these things? verily I say unto you, There shall not be
left here one stone upon another, that shall not be thrown down.

*And as he sat upon the mount of Olives, the disciples came unto him
privately, saying, Tell us, when shall these things be? and what shall be
the sign of thy coming, and of the end of the world? And Jesus answered
and said unto them,*

Take heed that no man deceive you. For many shall come in my name,
saying, I am Christ; and shall deceive many. And ye shall hear of wars
and rumours of wars: see that ye be not troubled: for all these things
must come to pass, but the end is not yet. For nation shall rise against
nation, and kingdom against kingdom: and there shall be famines, and
pestilences, and earthquakes, in divers places. All these are the beginning of sorrows.

Then shall they deliver you up to be afflicted, and shall kill you, and
ye shall be hated of all nations for my name's sake. And then shall many
be offended, and shall betray one another, and shall hate one another.
And many false prophets shall rise, and shall deceive many. And because iniquity shall abound, the love of many shall wax cold. But he that
shall endure unto the end, the same shall be saved.

And this gospel of the kingdom shall be preached in all the world for
a witness unto all nations; and then shall the end come.

When ye therefore shall see the abomination of desolation, spoken of
by Daniel the prophet, stand in the holy place, (whoso readeth, let him
understand,) then let them which be in Judea flee into the mountains.
Let him which is on the housetop not come down to take any thing out
of his house. Neither let him which is in the field return back to take his

clothes. And woe unto them that are with child, and to them that give suck in those days!

But pray ye that your flight be not in the winter, neither on the sabbath day. For then shall be great tribulation, such as was not since the beginning of the world to this time, no, nor ever shall be. And except those days should be shortened, there should no flesh be saved: but for the elect's sake those days shall be shortened.

Then if any man shall say unto you, Lo, here is Christ, or there; believe it not. For there shall arise false Christs, and false prophets, and shall show great signs and wonders; insomuch that, if it were possible, they shall deceive the very elect. Behold, I have told you before. Wherefore if they shall say unto you, Behold, he is in the desert; go not forth: behold, he is in the secret chambers; believe it not. For as the lightning cometh out of the east, and shineth even unto the west; so shall also the coming of the Son of man be. For wheresoever the carcass is, there will the eagles be gathered together.

Immediately after the tribulation of those days shall the sun be darkened, and the moon shall not give her light, and the stars shall fall from heaven, and the powers of the heavens shall be shaken. And then shall appear the sign of the Son of man in heaven: and then shall all the tribes of the earth mourn, and they shall see the Son of man coming in the clouds of heaven with power and great glory. And he shall send his angels with a great sound of a trumpet, and they shall gather together his elect from the four winds, from one end of heaven to the other.

Now learn a parable of the fig tree; When his branch is yet tender, and putteth forth leaves, ye know that summer is nigh. So likewise ye, when ye shall see all these things, know that it is near, even at the doors.

Verily I say unto you, This generation shall not pass, till all these things be fulfilled.

Heaven and earth shall pass away, but my words shall not pass away.

But of that day and hour knoweth no man, no, not the angels of heaven, but my Father only. But as the days of Noe were, so shall also the coming of the Son of man be. For as in the days that were before the flood they were eating and drinking, marrying and giving in marriage, until the day that Noe entered into the ark, and knew not until the flood came, and took them all away; so shall also the coming of the Son of man be.

Then shall two be in the field; the one shall be taken, and the other left. Two women shall be grinding at the mill; the one shall be taken, and the other left.

Watch therefore; for ye know not what hour your Lord doth come. But know this, that if the goodman of the house had known in what watch the thief would come, he would have watched, and would not have suffered his house to be broken up. Therefore be ye also ready, for in such an hour as ye think not the Son of man cometh.

Who then is a faithful and wise servant, whom his lord hath made ruler over his household, to give them meat in due season? Blessed is that servant, whom his lord when he cometh shall find so doing. Verily I say unto you, That he shall make him ruler over all his goods.

But and if that evil servant shall say in his heart, My lord delayeth his coming, and shall begin to smite his fellow servants, and to eat and drink with the drunken, the lord of that servant shall come in a day when he looketh not for him, and in an hour that he is not aware of, and shall cut him asunder, and appoint him his portion with the hypocrites: there shall be weeping and gnashing of teeth.

II

When the Son of man shall come in his glory, and all the holy angels with him, then shall he sit upon the throne of his glory. And before him shall be gathered all nations: and he shall separate them one from another, as a shepherd divideth his sheep from the goats. And he shall set the sheep on his right hand, but the goats on the left.

Then shall the King say unto them on his right hand, Come, ye blessed of my Father, inherit the kingdom prepared for you from the foundation of the world. For I was ahungered, and ye gave me meat; I was thirsty, and ye gave me drink; I was a stranger, and ye took me in; naked, and ye clothed me; I was sick, and ye visited me; I was in prison, and ye came unto me.

Then shall the righteous answer him, saying, Lord, when saw we thee ahungered, and fed thee? or thirsty, and gave thee drink? When saw we thee a stranger, and took thee in? or naked, and clothed thee? Or when saw we thee sick, or in prison, and came unto thee?

And the King shall answer and say unto them, Verily I say unto you,

Inasmuch as ye have done it unto one of the least of these my brethren, ye have done it unto me.

Then shall he say also unto them on the left hand, Depart from me, ye cursed, into everlasting fire, prepared for the devil and his angels. For I was ahungered, and ye gave me no meat; I was thirsty, and ye gave me no drink; I was a stranger, and ye took me not in; naked, and ye clothed me not; sick, and in prison, and ye visited me not.

Then shall they also answer him, saying, Lord, when saw we thee ahungered, or athirst, or a stranger, or naked, or sick, or in prison, and did not minister unto thee?

Then shall he answer them, saying, Verily I say unto you, Inasmuch as ye did it not to one of the least of these, ye did it not to me.

And these shall go away into everlasting punishment: but the righteous into life eternal.

Humble Thyself

(*According to Luke*)

And he put forth a parable to those which were bidden, when he marked how they chose out the chief rooms; saying unto them,

When thou art bidden of any man to a wedding, sit not down in the highest room; lest a more honourable man than thou be bidden of him; and he that bade thee and him come and say to thee, Give this man place; and thou begin with shame to take the lowest room. But when thou art bidden, go and sit down in the lowest room; that when he that bade thee cometh, he may say unto thee, Friend, go up higher: then shalt thou have worship in the presence of them that sit at meat with thee. For whosoever exalteth himself shall be abased; and he that humbleth himself shall be exalted.

Then said he also to him that bade him,

When thou makest a dinner or a supper, call not thy friends, nor thy brethren, neither thy kinsmen, nor thy rich neighbours; lest they also bid thee again, and a recompense be made thee. But when thou makest a feast, call the poor, the maimed, the lame, the blind; and thou shalt be blessed; for they cannot recompense thee; for thou shalt be recompensed at the resurrection of the just.

Of the Requirements for Discipleship

(*According to Luke*)

I

If any man come to me, and hate not his father, and mother, and wife, and children, and brethren, and sisters, yea, and his own life also, he cannot be my disciple. And whosoever doth not bear his cross, and come after me, cannot be my disciple.

For which of you, intending to build a tower, sitteth not down first, and counteth the cost, whether he have sufficient to finish it? Lest haply, after he hath laid the foundation, and is not able to finish it, all that behold it begin to mock him, saying, This man began to build, and was not able to finish.

Or what king, going to make war against another king, sitteth not down first, and consulteth whether he be able with ten thousand to meet him that cometh against him with twenty thousand? Or else, while the other is yet a great way off, he sendeth an ambassage, and desireth conditions of peace.

So likewise, whosoever he be of you that forsaketh not all that he hath, he cannot be my disciple.

II

It is impossible but that offences will come: but woe unto him, through whom they come! It were better for him that a millstone were hanged about his neck, and he cast into the sea, than that he should offend one of these little ones.

Take heed to yourselves: If thy brother trespass against thee, rebuke him; and if he repent, forgive him. And if he trespass against thee seven times in a day, and seven times in a day turn again to thee, saying, I repent; thou shalt forgive him.

And the apostles said unto the Lord, Increase our faith. And the Lord said,

If ye had faith as a grain of mustard seed, ye might say unto this sycamine tree, Be thou plucked up by the root, and be thou planted in the sea; and it should obey you.

But which of you, having a servant ploughing or feeding cattle, will say unto him by and by, when he is come from the field, Go and sit down to meat? And will not rather say unto him, Make ready wherewith I may sup, and gird thyself, and serve me, till I have eaten and drunken; and afterward thou shalt eat and drink? Doth he thank that servant because he did the things that were commanded him? I trow not.

So likewise ye, when ye shall have done all those things which are commanded you, say, We are unprofitable servants: we have done that which was our duty to do.

Of the Rich Man and Lazarus

(*According to Luke*)

There was a certain rich man, which was clothed in purple and fine linen, and fared sumptuously every day. And there was a certain beggar named Lazarus, which was laid at his gate, full of sores, and desiring to be fed with the crumbs which fell from the rich man's table; moreover the dogs came and licked his sores.

And it came to pass, that the beggar died, and was carried by the angels into Abraham's bosom: the rich man also died, and was buried; and in hell he lifted up his eyes, being in torments, and seeth Abraham afar off, and Lazarus in his bosom. And he cried and said, Father Abraham, have mercy on me, and send Lazarus, that he may dip the tip of his finger in water, and cool my tongue; for I am tormented in this flame.

But Abraham said, Son, remember that thou in thy lifetime receivedst thy good things, and likewise Lazarus evil things: but now he is comforted, and thou art tormented. And beside all this, between us and you there is a great gulf fixed, so that they which would pass from hence to you cannot; neither can they pass to us, that would come from thence.

Then he said, I pray thee therefore, father, that thou wouldest send him to my father's house, for I have five brethren, that he may testify unto them, lest they also come into this place of torment.

Abraham saith unto him, They have Moses and the prophets; let them hear them.

And he said, Nay, father Abraham; but if one went unto them from the dead, they will repent.

And he said unto him, If they hear not Moses and the prophets, neither will they be persuaded, though one rose from the dead.

The Birth of the Spirit

(*According to John*)

There was a man of the Pharisees, named Nicodemus, a ruler of the Jews. The same came to Jesus by night, and said unto him, Rabbi, we know that thou art a teacher come from God: for no man can do these miracles that thou doest, except God be with him. Jesus answered and said unto him,

Verily, verily, I say unto thee, Except a man be born again, he cannot see the kingdom of God.

Nicodemus saith unto him, How can a man be born when he is old? can he enter the second time into his mother's womb, and be born? Jesus answered,

Verily, verily, I say unto thee, Except a man be born of water and of the Spirit, he cannot enter into the kingdom of God. That which is born of the flesh is flesh; and that which is born of the Spirit is spirit. Marvel not that I said unto thee, Ye must be born again.

The wind bloweth where it listeth, and thou hearest the sound thereof, but canst not tell whence it cometh, and whither it goeth: so is every one that is born of the Spirit.

Nicodemus answered and said unto him, How can these things be? Jesus answered and said unto him,

Art thou a master of Israel, and knowest not these things? Verily, verily, I say unto thee, We speak that we do know, and testify that we have seen; and ye receive not our witness. If I have told you earthly things, and ye believe not, how shall ye believe, if I tell you of heavenly things? And no man hath ascended up to heaven, but he that came down from heaven, even the Son of man which is in heaven.

And as Moses lifted up the serpent in the wilderness, even so must the Son of man be lifted up, that whosoever believeth in him should not perish, but have eternal life.

For God so loved the world, that he gave his only begotten Son, that whosoever believeth in him should not perish, but have everlasting life. For God sent not his Son into the world to condemn the world; but that the world through him might be saved.

He that believeth on him is not condemned: but he that believeth not is condemned already, because he hath not believed in the name of the only begotten Son of God. And this is the condemnation, that light is come into the world, and men loved darkness rather than light, because their deeds were evil. For every one that doeth evil hateth the light, neither cometh to the light, lest his deeds should be reproved. But he that doeth truth cometh to the light, that his deeds may be made manifest, that they are wrought in God.

Of the Power of Jesus

(*According to John*)

But Jesus answered them,
My Father worketh hitherto, and I work.
Therefore the Jews sought the more to kill him, because he not only had broken the sabbath, but said also that God was his Father, making himself equal with God. Then answered Jesus and said unto them,
Verily, verily, I say unto you, The Son can do nothing of himself, but what he seeth the Father do: for what things soever he doeth, these also doeth the Son likewise. For the Father loveth the Son, and showeth him all things that himself doeth, and he will show him greater works than these, that ye may marvel. For as the Father raiseth up the dead, and quickeneth them; even so the Son quickeneth whom he will.

For the Father judgeth no man, but hath committed all judgment unto the Son, that all men should honour the Son, even as they honour the Father. He that honoureth not the Son honoureth not the Father which hath sent him.

Verily, verily, I say unto you, He that heareth my word, and believeth on him that sent me, hath everlasting life, and shall not come into condemnation; but is passed from death unto life.

Verily, verily, I say unto you, The hour is coming, and now is, when the dead shall hear the voice of the Son of God: and they that hear shall live. For as the Father hath life in himself; so hath he given to the Son to have life in himself, and hath given him authority to execute judgment also, because he is the Son of man.

Marvel not at this, for the hour is coming, in the which all that are in the graves shall hear his voice, and shall come forth; they that have done good, unto the resurrection of life; and they that have done evil, unto the resurrection of damnation.

I can of mine own self do nothing: as I hear, I judge: and my judgment is just; because I seek not mine own will, but the will of the Father which hath sent me. If I bear witness of myself, my witness is not true.

There is another that beareth witness of me; and I know that the witness which he witnesseth of me is true. Ye sent unto John, and he bare witness unto the truth. But I receive not testimony from man: but these things I say, that ye might be saved. He was a burning and a shining light: and ye were willing for a season to rejoice in his light.

But I have greater witness than that of John: for the works which the Father hath given me to finish, the same works that I do, bear witness of me, that the Father hath sent me. And the Father himself, which hath sent me, hath borne witness of me. Ye have neither heard his voice at any time, nor seen his shape. And ye have not his word abiding in you: for whom he hath sent, him ye believe not.

Search the Scriptures; for in them ye think ye have eternal life: and they are they which testify of me. And ye will not come to me, that ye might have life. I receive not honour from men. But I know you, that ye have not the love of God in you. I am come in my Father's name, and ye receive me not: if another shall come in his own name, him ye will receive. How can ye believe, which receive honour one of another, and seek not the honour that cometh from God only?

Do not think that I will accuse you to the Father: there is one that accuseth you, even Moses, in whom ye trust. For had ye believed Moses, ye would have believed me, for he wrote of me. But if ye believe not his writings, how shall ye believe my words?

The Bread of Life

(*According to John*)

Labour not for the meat which perisheth, but for that meat which endureth unto everlasting life, which the Son of man shall give unto you: for him hath God the Father sealed.

Then said they unto him, What shall we do, that we might work the works of God? Jesus answered and said unto them,

This is the work of God, that ye believe on him whom he hath sent.

They said therefore unto him, What sign showest thou then, that we may see, and believe thee? what dost thou work? Our fathers did eat manna in the desert; as it is written, He gave them bread from heaven to eat. Then Jesus said unto them,

Verily, verily, I say unto you, Moses gave you not that bread from heaven; but my Father giveth you the true bread from heaven. For the bread of God is he which cometh down from heaven, and giveth life unto the world.

Then said they unto him, Lord, evermore give us this bread. And Jesus said unto them,

I am the bread of life: he that cometh to me shall never hunger; and he that believeth on me shall never thirst.

But I said unto you, That ye also have seen me, and believe not. All that the Father giveth me shall come to me; and him that cometh to me I will in no wise cast out. For I came down from heaven, not to do mine own will, but the will of him that sent me. And this is the Father's will which hath sent me, that of all which he hath given me I should lose nothing, but should raise it up again at the last day. And this is the will of him that sent me, that every one which seeth the Son, and believeth on him, may have everlasting life: and I will raise him up at the last day.

The Jews then murmured at him, because he said, I am the bread which came down from heaven. And they said, Is not this Jesus, the son of Joseph, whose father and mother we know? how is it then that he saith, I came down from heaven? Jesus therefore answered and said unto them,

Murmur not among yourselves. No man can come to me, except the

Father which hath sent me draw him: and I will raise him up at the last day. It is written in the prophets, And they shall be all taught of God. Every man therefore that hath heard, and hath learned of the Father, cometh unto me. Not that any man hath seen the Father, save he which is of God, he hath seen the Father.

Verily, verily, I say unto you, He that believeth on me hath everlasting life.

I am that bread of life. Your fathers did eat manna in the wilderness, and are dead. This is the bread which cometh down from heaven, that a man may eat thereof, and not die. I am the living bread which came down from heaven. If any man eat of this bread, he shall live for ever: and the bread that I will give is my flesh, which I will give for the life of the world.

The Jews therefore strove among themselves, saying, How can this man give us his flesh to eat? Then Jesus said unto them,

Verily, verily, I say unto you, Except ye eat the flesh of the Son of man, and drink his blood, ye have no life in you. Whoso eateth my flesh, and drinketh my blood, hath eternal life; and I will raise him up at the last day. For my flesh is meat indeed, and my blood is drink indeed. He that eateth my flesh, and drinketh my blood, dwelleth in me, and I in him. As the living Father hath sent me, and I live by the Father; so he that eateth me, even he shall live by me. This is that bread which came down from heaven: not as your fathers did eat manna, and are dead: he that eateth of this bread shall live for ever.

The Light of the World

(*According to John*)

Then spake Jesus again unto them, saying,

I am the light of the world: he that followeth me shall not walk in darkness, but shall have the light of life.

The Pharisees therefore said unto him, Thou bearest record of thyself; thy record is not true. Jesus answered and said unto them,

Though I bear record of myself, yet my record is true: for I know whence I came, and whither I go; but ye cannot tell whence I come, and whither I go.

Ye judge after the flesh; I judge no man. And yet if I judge, my judgment is true: for I am not alone, but I and the Father that sent me. It is also written in your law, that the testimony of two men is true. I am one that bear witness of myself, and the Father that sent me beareth witness of me.

Then said they unto him, Where is thy Father? Jesus answered,

Ye neither know me, nor my Father: if ye had known me, ye should have known my Father also.

These words spake Jesus in the treasury, as he taught in the temple: and no man laid hands on him; for his hour was not yet come. Then said Jesus again unto them,

I go my way, and ye shall seek me, and shall die in your sins: whither I go, ye cannot come.

Then said the Jews, Will he kill himself? because he saith, Whither I go, ye cannot come. And he said unto them,

Ye are from beneath; I am from above: ye are of this world; I am not of this world. I said therefore unto you, that ye shall die in your sins: for if ye believe not that I am he, ye shall die in your sins.

Then said they unto him, Who art thou? And Jesus saith unto them,

Even the same that I said unto you from the beginning. I have many things to say and to judge of you: but he that sent me is true; and I speak to the world those things which I have heard of him.

They understood not that he spake to them of the Father. Then said Jesus unto them,

When ye have lifted up the Son of man, then shall ye know that I am he, and that I do nothing of myself; but as my Father hath taught me, I speak these things. And he that sent me is with me: the Father hath not left me alone; for I do always those things that please him.

As he spake these words, many believed on him. Then said Jesus to those Jews which believed on him,

If ye continue in my word, then are ye my disciples indeed, and ye shall know the truth, and the truth shall make you free.

The Good Shepherd

(*According to John*)

Verily, verily, I say unto you, He that entereth not by the door into the sheepfold, but climbeth up some other way, the same is a thief and a robber. But he that entereth in by the door is the shepherd of the sheep. To him the porter openeth; and the sheep hear his voice: and he calleth his own sheep by name, and leadeth them out. And when he putteth forth his own sheep, he goeth before them, and the sheep follow him: for they know his voice. And a stranger will they not follow, but will flee from him; for they know not the voice of strangers.

This parable spake Jesus unto them; but they understood not what things they were which he spake unto them. Then said Jesus unto them again,

Verily, verily, I say unto you, I am the door of the sheep. All that ever came before me are thieves and robbers: but the sheep did not hear them. I am the door. By me if any man enter in, he shall be saved, and shall go in and out, and find pasture.

The thief cometh not, but for to steal, and to kill, and to destroy: I am come that they might have life, and that they might have it more abundantly. I am the good shepherd; the good shepherd giveth his life for the sheep. But he that is a hireling, and not the shepherd, whose own the sheep are not, seeth the wolf coming, and leaveth the sheep, and fleeth; and the wolf catcheth them, and scattereth the sheep. The hireling fleeth, because he is a hireling, and careth not for the sheep.

I am the good shepherd, and I know my sheep, and am known of mine. As the Father knoweth me, even so know I the Father, and I lay down my life for the sheep. And other sheep I have, which are not of this fold: them also I must bring, and they shall hear my voice; and there shall be one fold, and one shepherd.

Therefore doth my Father love me, because I lay down my life, that I might take it again. No man taketh it from me, but I lay it down of myself. I have power to lay it down, and I have power to take it again. This commandment have I received of my Father.

There was a division therefore again among the Jews for these sayings,

and many of them said, He hath a devil, and is mad; why hear ye him?
Others said, These are not the words of him that hath a devil. Can a devil
open the eyes of the blind?

And it was at Jerusalem the feast of the dedication, and it was winter.
And Jesus walked in the temple in Solomon's porch. Then came the Jews
round about him, and said unto him, How long dost thou make us to
doubt? If thou be the Christ, tell us plainly. Jesus answered them,

I told you, and ye believed not: the works that I do in my Father's
name, they bear witness of me. But ye believe not, because ye are not of
my sheep, as I said unto you. My sheep hear my voice, and I know them,
and they follow me, and I give unto them eternal life; and they shall
never perish, neither shall any man pluck them out of my hand.

My Father, which gave them me, is greater than all; and no man is
able to pluck them out of my Father's hand. I and my Father are one.

That You Walk in the Light

(*According to John*)

Verily, verily, I say unto you, Except a corn of wheat fall into the
ground and die, it abideth alone: but if it die, it bringeth forth much
fruit. He that loveth his life shall lose it; and he that hateth his life in
this world shall keep it unto life eternal. If any man serve me, let him
follow me; and where I am, there shall also my servant be: if any man
serve me, him will my Father honour.

Now is my soul troubled; and what shall I say? Father, save me from
this hour: but for this cause came I unto this hour. Father, glorify thy
name.

Then came there a voice from heaven, saying, I have both glorified it,
and will glorify it again. The people therefore that stood by, and heard
it, said that it thundered: others said, An angel spake to him. Jesus
answered and said,

This voice came not because of me, but for your sakes. Now is the
judgment of this world; now shall the prince of this world be cast out.
And I, if I be lifted up from the earth, will draw all men unto me.

This he said, signifying what death he should die. The people an-

*swered him, We have heard out of the law that Christ abideth for ever:
and how sayest thou, The Son of man must be lifted up? who is this Son
of man? Then Jesus said unto them,*

Yet a little while is the light with you. Walk while ye have the light,
lest darkness come upon you: for he that walketh in darkness knoweth
not whither he goeth. While ye have light, believe in the light, that ye
may be the children of light.

*These things spake Jesus, and departed, and did hide himself from
them.*

To Save the World

(*According to John*)

He that believeth on me, believeth not on me, but on him that sent
me. And he that seeth me seeth him that sent me.

I am come a light into the world, that whosoever believeth on me
should not abide in darkness.

And if any man hear my words, and believe not, I judge him not: for
I came not to judge the world, but to save the world. He that rejecteth
me, and receiveth not my words, hath one that judgeth him: the word
that I have spoken, the same shall judge him in the last day.

For I have not spoken of myself; but the Father which sent me, he
gave me a commandment, what I should say, and what I should speak.
And I know that his commandment is life everlasting: whatsoever I
speak therefore, even as the Father said unto me, so I speak.

Let Not Your Heart Be Troubled

(*According to John*)

Let not your heart be troubled: ye believe in God, believe also in me.
In my Father's house are many mansions: if it were not so, I would have
told you. I go to prepare a place for you. And if I go and prepare a place
for you, I will come again, and receive you unto myself; that where I

am, there ye may be also. And whither I go ye know, and the way ye know.

Thomas saith unto him, Lord, we know not whither thou goest; and how can we know the way? Jesus saith unto him,

I am the way, the truth, and the life: no man cometh unto the Father, but by me. If ye had known me, ye should have known my Father also: and from henceforth ye know him, and have seen him.

Philip saith unto him, Lord, show us the Father, and it sufficeth us. Jesus saith unto him,

Have I been so long time with you, and yet hast thou not known me, Philip? he that hath seen me hath seen the Father; and how sayest thou then, Show us the Father? Believest thou not that I am in the Father, and the Father in me? the words that I speak unto you I speak not of myself: but the Father that dwelleth in me, he doeth the works. Believe me that I am in the Father, and the Father in me: or else believe me for the very works' sake.

Verily, verily, I say unto you, He that believeth on me, the works that I do shall he do also; and greater works than these shall he do; because I go unto my Father.

And whatsoever ye shall ask in my name, that will I do, that the Father may be glorified in the Son. If ye shall ask any thing in my name, I will do it.

If ye love me, keep my commandments. And I will pray the Father, and he shall give you another Comforter, that he may abide with you for ever, even the Spirit of truth; whom the world cannot receive, because it seeth him not, neither knoweth him: but ye know him; for he dwelleth with you, and shall be in you.

I will not leave you comfortless: I will come to you. Yet a little while, and the world seeth me no more; but ye see me: because I live, ye shall live also. At that day ye shall know that I am in my Father, and ye in me, and I in you.

He that hath my commandments, and keepeth them, he it is that loveth me; and he that loveth me shall be loved of my Father, and I will love him, and will manifest myself to him.

Judas saith unto him, not Iscariot, Lord, how is it that thou wilt manifest thyself unto us, and not unto the world? Jesus answered and said unto him,

If a man love me, he will keep my words: and my Father will love him, and we will come unto him, and make our abode with him. He that loveth me not keepeth not my sayings: and the word which ye hear is not mine, but the Father's which sent me.

These things have I spoken unto you, being yet present with you. But the Comforter, which is the Holy Ghost, whom the Father will send in my name, he shall teach you all things, and bring all things to your remembrance, whatsoever I have said unto you.

Peace I leave with you, my peace I give unto you: not as the world giveth, give I unto you. Let not your heart be troubled, neither let it be afraid. Ye have heard how I said unto you, I go away, and come again unto you. If ye loved me, ye would rejoice, because I said, I go unto the Father: for my Father is greater than I.

And now I have told you before it come to pass, that, when it is come to pass, ye might believe. Hereafter I will not talk much with you: for the prince of this world cometh, and hath nothing in me. But that the world may know that I love the Father; and as the Father gave me commandment, even so I do. Arise, let us go hence.

The True Vine

(*According to John*)

I am the true vine, and my Father is the husbandman. Every branch in me that beareth not fruit he taketh away: and every branch that beareth fruit, he purgeth it, that it may bring forth more fruit.

Now ye are clean through the word which I have spoken unto you.

Abide in me, and I in you. As the branch cannot bear fruit of itself, except it abide in the vine; no more can ye, except ye abide in me. I am the vine, ye are the branches. He that abideth in me, and I in him, the same bringeth forth much fruit; for without me ye can do nothing. If a man abide not in me, he is cast forth as a branch, and is withered; and men gather them, and cast them into the fire, and they are burned. If ye abide in me, and my words abide in you, ye shall ask what ye will, and it shall be done unto you.

Herein is my Father glorified, that ye bear much fruit; so shall ye be my disciples. As the Father hath loved me, so have I loved you: continue ye in my love. If ye keep my commandments, ye shall abide in my love; even as I have kept my Father's commandments, and abide in his love. These things have I spoken unto you, that my joy might remain in you, and that your joy might be full.

This is my commandment, That ye love one another, as I have loved you. Greater love hath no man than this, that a man lay down his life for his friends.

Ye are my friends, if ye do whatsoever I command you. Henceforth I call you not servants; for the servant knoweth not what his lord doeth: but I have called you friends; for all things that I have heard of my Father I have made known unto you. Ye have not chosen me, but I have chosen you, and ordained you, that ye should go and bring forth fruit, and that your fruit should remain; that whatsoever ye shall ask of the Father in my name, he may give it you.

These things I command you, that ye love one another.

If the world hate you, ye know that it hated me before it hated you. If ye were of the world, the world would love his own; but because ye are not of the world, but I have chosen you out of the world, therefore the world hateth you.

Remember the word that I said unto you, The servant is not greater than his lord. If they have persecuted me, they will also persecute you; if they have kept my saying, they will keep yours also. But all these things will they do unto you for my name's sake, because they know not him that sent me.

If I had not come and spoken unto them, they had not had sin; but now they have no cloak for their sin.

He that hateth me hateth my Father also.

If I had not done among them the works which none other man did, they had not had sin: but now have they both seen and hated both me and my Father. But this cometh to pass, that the word might be fulfilled that is written in their law, They hated me without a cause.

But when the Comforter is come, whom I will send unto you from the Father, even the Spirit of truth, which proceedeth from the Father, he shall testify of me. And ye also shall bear witness, because ye have been with me from the beginning.

Be of Good Cheer

(*According to John*)

These things have I spoken unto you, that ye should not be offended.

They shall put you out of the synagogues: yea, the time cometh, that whosoever killeth you will think that he doeth God service. And these things will they do unto you, because they have not known the Father, nor me.

But these things have I told you, that when the time shall come, ye may remember that I told you of them. And these things I said not unto you at the beginning, because I was with you. But now I go my way to him that sent me; and none of you asketh me, Whither goest thou? But because I have said these things unto you, sorrow hath filled your heart.

Nevertheless I tell you the truth; It is expedient for you that I go away, for if I go not away, the Comforter will not come unto you; but if I depart, I will send him unto you. And when he is come, he will reprove the world of sin, and of righteousness, and of judgment; of sin, because they believe not on me; of righteousness, because I go to my Father, and ye see me no more; of judgment, because the prince of this world is judged.

I have yet many things to say unto you, but ye cannot bear them now. Howbeit when he, the Spirit of truth, is come, he will guide you into all truth: for he shall not speak of himself; but whatsoever he shall hear, that shall he speak, and he will show you things to come. He shall glorify me, for he shall receive of mine, and shall show it unto you.

All things that the Father hath are mine: therefore said I, that he shall take of mine, and shall show it unto you.

A little while, and ye shall not see me: and again, a little while, and ye shall see me, because I go to the Father.

Then said some of his disciples among themselves, What is this that he saith unto us, A little while, and ye shall not see me: and again, a little while, and ye shall see me: and, Because I go to the Father? They said therefore, What is this that he saith, A little while? we cannot tell what he saith. Now Jesus knew that they were desirous to ask him, and said unto them,

Do ye inquire among yourselves of that I said, A little while, and ye shall not see me: and again, a little while, and ye shall see me? Verily, verily, I say unto you, That ye shall weep and lament, but the world shall rejoice; and ye shall be sorrowful, but your sorrow shall be turned into joy.

A woman when she is in travail hath sorrow, because her hour is come; but as soon as she is delivered of the child, she remembereth no more the anguish, for joy that a man is born into the world. And ye now therefore have sorrow, but I will see you again, and your heart shall rejoice, and your joy no man taketh from you.

And in that day ye shall ask me nothing. Verily, verily, I say unto you, Whatsoever ye shall ask the Father in my name, he will give it you. Hitherto have ye asked nothing in my name: ask, and ye shall receive, that your joy may be full.

These things have I spoken unto you in proverbs: but the time cometh, when I shall no more speak unto you in proverbs, but I shall show you plainly of the Father. At that day ye shall ask in my name: and I say not unto you, that I will pray the Father for you, for the Father himself loveth you, because ye have loved me, and have believed that I came out from God.

I came forth from the Father, and am come into the world: again, I leave the world, and go to the Father.

His disciples said unto him, Lo, now speakest thou plainly, and speakest no proverb. Now are we sure that thou knowest all things, and needest not that any man should ask thee: by this we believe that thou camest forth from God. Jesus answered them,

Do ye now believe? Behold, the hour cometh, yea, is now come, that ye shall be scattered, every man to his own, and shall leave me alone: and yet I am not alone, because the Father is with me.

These things I have spoken unto you, that in me ye might have peace. In the world ye shall have tribulation: but be of good cheer; I have overcome the world.

The Glory Thou Gavest Me

(*According to John*)

These words spake Jesus, and lifted up his eyes to heaven, and said,
Father, the hour is come; glorify thy Son, that thy Son also may
glorify thee, as thou hast given him power over all flesh, that he should
give eternal life to as many as thou hast given him. And this is life
eternal, that they might know thee the only true God, and Jesus Christ,
whom thou hast sent.

I have glorified thee on the earth: I have finished the work which
thou gavest me to do. And now, O Father, glorify thou me with thine
own self with the glory which I had with thee before the world was.

I have manifested thy name unto the men which thou gavest me out
of the world: thine they were, and thou gavest them me; and they
have kept thy word. Now they have known that all things whatsoever
thou hast given me are of thee. For I have given unto them the words
which thou gavest me; and they have received them, and have known
surely that I came out from thee, and they have believed that thou
didst send me.

I pray for them; I pray not for the world, but for them which thou
hast given me; for they are thine. And all mine are thine, and thine are
mine; and I am glorified in them.

And now I am no more in the world, but these are in the world, and
I come to thee. Holy Father, keep through thine own name those whom
thou hast given me, that they may be one, as we are. While I was with
them in the world, I kept them in thy name: those that thou gavest me
I have kept, and none of them is lost, but the son of perdition; that the
Scripture might be fulfilled. And now come I to thee; and these things
I speak in the world, that they might have my joy fulfilled in them-
selves.

I have given them thy word; and the world hath hated them, because
they are not of the world, even as I am not of the world. I pray not that
thou shouldest take them out of the world, but that thou shouldest keep
them from the evil. They are not of the world, even as I am not of the
world. Sanctify them through thy truth; thy word is truth.

As thou hast sent me into the world, even so have I also sent them into the world. And for their sakes I sanctify myself, that they also might be sanctified through the truth.

Neither pray I for these alone, but for them also which shall believe on me through their word, that they all may be one; as thou, Father, art in me, and I in thee, that they also may be one in us: that the world may believe that thou hast sent me.

And the glory which thou gavest me I have given them; that they may be one, even as we are one; I in them, and thou in me, that they may be made perfect in one; and that the world may know that thou hast sent me, and hast loved them, as thou hast loved me.

Father, I will that they also, whom thou hast given me, be with me where I am; that they may behold my glory, which thou hast given me: for thou lovedst me before the foundation of the world. O righteous Father, the world hath not known thee; but I have known thee, and these have known that thou hast sent me. And I have declared unto them thy name, and will declare it; that the love wherewith thou hast loved me may be in them, and I in them.

Parables

Of the Cloth and Wine

(*According to Matthew*)

Then came to him the disciples of John, saying, Why do we and the Pharisees fast oft, but thy disciples fast not? And Jesus said unto them,

Can the children of the bride-chamber mourn, as long as the bridegroom is with them? but the days will come, when the bridegroom shall be taken from them, and then shall they fast.

No man putteth a piece of new cloth unto an old garment; for that which is put in to fill it up taketh from the garment, and the rent is made worse. Neither do men put new wine into old bottles; else the bottles break, and the wine runneth out, and the bottles perish: but they put new wine into new bottles, and both are preserved.

Of the Sower, the Tares, the Mustard Seed, and the Leaven

(According to Matthew)

And he spake many things unto them in parables, saying,

Behold, a sower went forth to sow; and when he sowed, some seeds fell by the wayside, and the fowls came and devoured them up: some fell upon stony places, where they had not much earth: and forthwith they sprung up, because they had no deepness of earth, and when the sun was up, they were scorched; and because they had no root, they withered away. And some fell among thorns; and the thorns sprung up, and choked them; but other fell into good ground, and brought forth fruit, some a hundredfold, some sixtyfold, some thirtyfold.

Who hath ears to hear, let him hear.

And the disciples came, and said unto him, Why speakest thou unto them in parables? He answered and said unto them,

Because it is given unto you to know the mysteries of the kingdom of heaven, but to them it is not given. For whosoever hath, to him shall be given, and he shall have more abundance: but whosoever hath not, from him shall be taken away even that he hath. Therefore speak I to them in parables: because they seeing see not; and hearing they hear not, neither do they understand.

And in them is fulfilled the prophecy of Esaias, which saith, By hearing ye shall hear, and shall not understand; and seeing ye shall see, and shall not perceive. For this people's heart is waxed gross, and their ears are dull of hearing, and their eyes they have closed; lest at any time they should see with their eyes, and hear with their ears, and should understand with their heart, and should be converted, and I should heal them.

But blessed are your eyes, for they see: and your ears, for they hear. For verily I say unto you, That many prophets and righteous men have desired to see those things which ye see, and have not seen them; and to hear those things which ye hear, and have not heard them.

Hear ye therefore the parable of the sower. When any one heareth the word of the kingdom, and understandeth it not, then cometh the wicked one, and catcheth away that which was sown in his heart. This is he which received seed by the wayside. But he that received the seed into stony places, the same is he that heareth the word, and anon with joy receiveth it; yet hath he not root in himself, but dureth for a while; for when tribulation or persecution ariseth because of the word, by and by he is offended. He also that received seed among the thorns is he that heareth the word; and the care of this world, and the deceitfulness of riches, choke the word, and he becometh unfruitful. But he that received seed into the good ground is he that heareth the word, and understandeth it; which also beareth fruit, and bringeth forth, some a hundredfold, some sixty, some thirty.

Another parable put he forth unto them, saying,

The kingdom of heaven is likened unto a man which sowed good seed in his field. But while men slept, his enemy came and sowed tares among the wheat, and went his way. But when the blade was sprung up, and brought forth fruit, then appeared the tares also.

So the servants of the householder came and said unto him, Sir, didst not thou sow good seed in thy field? from whence then hath it tares?

He said unto them, An enemy hath done this.

The servants said unto him, Wilt thou then that we go and gather them up?

But he said, Nay; lest while ye gather up the tares, ye root up also the wheat with them. Let both grow together until the harvest, and in the time of harvest I will say to the reapers, Gather ye together first the tares, and bind them in bundles to burn them: but gather the wheat into my barn.

Another parable put he forth unto them, saying,

The kingdom of heaven is like to a grain of mustard seed, which a man took, and sowed in his field, which indeed is the least of all seeds, but when it is grown, it is the greatest among herbs, and becometh a tree, so that the birds of the air come and lodge in the branches thereof.

Another parable spake he unto them:

The kingdom of heaven is like unto leaven, which a woman took, and hid in three measures of meal, till the whole was leavened.

All these things spake Jesus unto the multitude in parables; and without a parable spake he not unto them, that it might be fulfilled which was spoken by the prophet, saying, I will open my mouth in parables; I will utter things which have been kept secret from the foundation of the world.

Then Jesus sent the multitude away, and went into the house: and his disciples came unto him, saying, Declare unto us the parable of the tares of the field. He answered and said unto them,

He that soweth the good seed is the Son of man; the field is the world; the good seed are the children of the kingdom; but the tares are the children of the wicked one; the enemy that sowed them is the devil; the harvest is the end of the world; and the reapers are the angels. As therefore the tares are gathered and burned in the fire; so shall it be in the end of this world. The Son of man shall send forth his angels, and they shall gather out of his kingdom all things that offend, and them which do iniquity; and shall cast them into a furnace of fire: there shall be wailing and gnashing of teeth. Then shall the righteous shine forth as the sun in the kingdom of their Father. Who hath ears to hear, let him hear.

Again, the kingdom of heaven is like unto treasure hid in a field; the which when a man hath found, he hideth, and for joy thereof goeth and selleth all that he hath, and buyeth that field.

Again, the kingdom of heaven is like unto a merchantman, seeking goodly pearls, who, when he had found one pearl of great price, went and sold all that he had, and bought it.

Again, the kingdom of heaven is like unto a net, that was cast into the sea, and gathered of every kind, which, when it was full, they drew to shore, and sat down, and gathered the good into vessels, but cast the bad away.

So shall it be at the end of the world: the angels shall come forth, and sever the wicked from among the just, and shall cast them into the furnace of fire: there shall be wailing and gnashing of teeth.

Jesus saith unto them,

Have ye understood all these things?

They say unto him, Yea, Lord. Then said he unto them,

Therefore every scribe which is instructed unto the kingdom of heaven, is like unto a man that is a householder, which bringeth forth out of his treasure things new and old.

The Last Shall Be First

(*According to Matthew*)

For the kingdom of heaven is like unto a man that is a householder, which went out early in the morning to hire labourers into his vineyard. And when he had agreed with the labourers for a penny a day, he sent them into his vineyard. And he went out about the third hour, and saw others standing idle in the market place, and said unto them: Go ye also into the vineyard, and whatsoever is right I will give you. And they went their way. Again he went out about the sixth and ninth hour, and did likewise.

And about the eleventh hour he went out, and found others standing idle, and saith unto them, Why stand ye here all the day idle?

They say unto him, Because no man hath hired us.

He saith unto them, Go ye also into the vineyard; and whatsoever is right, that shall ye receive.

So when even was come, the lord of the vineyard saith unto his steward, Call the labourers, and give them their hire, beginning from the last unto the first.

And when they came that were hired about the eleventh hour, they received every man a penny. But when the first came, they supposed that they should have received more; and they likewise received every man a penny. And when they had received it, they murmured against the goodman of the house, saying, These last have wrought but one hour, and thou hast made them equal unto us, which have borne the burden and heat of the day.

But he answered one of them, and said, Friend, I do thee no wrong: didst not thou agree with me for a penny? Take that thine is, and go thy way: I will give unto this last, even as unto thee. Is it not lawful for me to do what I will with mine own? Is thine eye evil, because I am good?

So the last shall be first, and the first last: for many be called, but few chosen.

Of the Two Sons

(*According to Matthew*)

But what think ye? A certain man had two sons; and he came to the first, and said, Son, go work to-day in my vineyard.

He answered and said, I will not; but afterward he repented, and went.

And he came to the second, and said likewise. And he answered and said, I go, sir; and went not.

Whether of them twain did the will of his father?

They say unto him, The first. Jesus saith unto them,

Verily I say unto you, That the publicans and the harlots go into the kingdom of God before you. For John came unto you in the way of righteousness, and ye believed him not; but the publicans and the harlots believed him: and ye, when ye had seen it, repented not afterward, that ye might believe him.

Of the Bad Husbandmen

(*According to Matthew*)

Hear another parable: There was a certain householder, which planted a vineyard, and hedged it round about, and digged a winepress in it, and built a tower, and let it out to husbandmen, and went into a far country.

And when the time of the fruit drew near, he sent his servants to the husbandmen, that they might receive the fruits of it. And the husbandmen took his servants, and beat one, and killed another, and stoned another.

Again, he sent other servants more than the first: and they did unto them likewise.

But last of all he sent unto them his son, saying, They will reverence my son. But when the husbandmen saw the son, they said among themselves, This is the heir; come, let us kill him, and let us seize on his inheritance. And they caught him, and cast him out of the vineyard, and slew him.

When the lord therefore of the vineyard cometh, what will he do unto those husbandmen?

They say unto him, He will miserably destroy those wicked men, and will let out his vineyard unto other husbandmen, which shall render him the fruits in their seasons. Jesus saith unto them,

Did ye never read in the Scriptures, The stone which the builders rejected, the same is become the head of the corner: this is the Lord's doing, and it is marvellous in our eyes?

Therefore say I unto you, The kingdom of God shall be taken from you, and given to a nation bringing forth the fruits thereof. And whosoever shall fall on this stone shall be broken: but on whomsoever it shall fall, it will grind him to powder.

Of the Prince's Wedding

(According to Matthew)

The kingdom of heaven is like unto a certain king, which made a marriage for his son, and sent forth his servants to call them that were bidden to the wedding: and they would not come.

Again, he sent forth other servants, saying, Tell them which are bidden, Behold, I have prepared my dinner; my oxen and my fatlings are killed, and all things are ready: come unto the marriage. But they made light of it, and went their ways, one to his farm, another to his merchandise. And the remnant took his servants, and entreated them spitefully, and slew them.

But when the king heard thereof, he was wroth: and he sent forth his armies, and destroyed those murderers, and burned up their city.

Then saith he to his servants, The wedding is ready, but they which were bidden were not worthy. Go ye therefore into the highways, and as many as ye shall find, bid to the marriage.

So those servants went out into the highways, and gathered together all as many as they found, both bad and good: and the wedding was furnished with guests.

And when the king came in to see the guests, he saw there a man which had not on a wedding garment, and he saith unto him, Friend, how camest thou in hither not having a wedding garment? And he was speechless.

Then said the king to the servants, Bind him hand and foot, and take him away, and cast him into outer darkness; there shall be weeping and gnashing of teeth. For many are called, but few are chosen.

Of the Wise and Foolish Virgins

(According to Matthew)

Then shall the kingdom of heaven be likened unto ten virgins, which took their lamps, and went forth to meet the bridegroom. And five of them were wise, and five were foolish. They that were foolish took their lamps, and took no oil with them. But the wise took oil in their vessels with their lamps.

While the bridegroom tarried, they all slumbered and slept. And at midnight there was a cry made, Behold, the bridegroom cometh; go ye out to meet him.

Then all those virgins arose, and trimmed their lamps. And the foolish said unto the wise, Give us of your oil; for our lamps are gone out. But the wise answered, saying, Not so; lest there be not enough for us and you: but go ye rather to them that sell, and buy for yourselves.

And while they went to buy, the bridegroom came; and they that were ready went in with him to the marriage, and the door was shut.

Afterward came also the other virgins, saying, Lord, Lord, open to us. But he answered and said, Verily I say unto you, I know you not.

Watch therefore; for ye know neither the day nor the hour wherein the Son of man cometh.

The Good and Faithful Servant

(According to Matthew)

For the kingdom of heaven is as a man travelling into a far country, who called his own servants, and delivered unto them his goods. And unto one he gave five talents, to another two, and to another one; to every man according to his several ability; and straightway took his journey.

Then he that had received the five talents went and traded with the same, and made them other five talents. And likewise he that had received two, he also gained other two. But he that had received one went and digged in the earth, and hid his lord's money.

After a long time the lord of those servants cometh, and reckoneth with them.

And so he that had received five talents came and brought other five talents, saying, Lord, thou deliveredst unto me five talents; behold, I have gained beside them five talents more.

His lord said unto him, Well done, thou good and faithful servant: thou hast been faithful over a few things, I will make thee ruler over many things: enter thou into the joy of thy lord.

He also that had received two talents came and said, Lord, thou deliveredst unto me two talents: behold, I have gained two other talents beside them.

His lord said unto him, Well done, good and faithful servant; thou hast been faithful over a few things, I will make thee ruler over many things: enter thou into the joy of thy lord.

Then he which had received the one talent came and said, Lord, I knew thee that thou art a hard man, reaping where thou hast not sown, and gathering where thou hast not strewed, and I was afraid, and went and hid thy talent in the earth: lo, there thou hast that is thine.

His lord answered and said unto him, Thou wicked and slothful servant, thou knewest that I reap where I sowed not, and gather where I have not strewed. Thou oughtest therefore to have put my money to the exchangers, and then at my coming I should have received mine own with usury. Take therefore the talent from him, and give it unto him which hath ten talents. For unto every one that hath shall be given, and he shall have abundance: but from him that hath not shall be taken away even that which he hath. And cast ye the unprofitable servant into outer darkness: there shall be weeping and gnashing of teeth.

Of the Good Samaritan

(According to Luke)

And, behold, a certain lawyer stood up, and tempted him, saying, Master, what shall I do to inherit eternal life? He said unto him,

What is written in the law? how readest thou?

And he answering said, Thou shalt love the Lord thy God with all thy heart, and with all thy soul, and with all thy strength, and with all thy mind; and thy neighbour as thyself. And he said unto him,

Thou hast answered right: this do, and thou shalt live.

But he, willing to justify himself, said unto Jesus, And who is my neighbour? And Jesus answering said,

A certain man went down from Jerusalem to Jericho, and fell among thieves, which stripped him of his raiment, and wounded him, and departed, leaving him half dead. And by chance there came down a certain priest that way; and when he saw him, he passed by on the other side. And likewise a Levite, when he was at the place, came and looked on him, and passed by on the other side. But a certain Samaritan, as he journeyed, came where he was; and when he saw him, he had compassion on him, and went to him, and bound up his wounds, pouring in oil and wine, and set him on his own beast, and brought him to an inn, and took care of him. And on the morrow when he departed, he took out two pence, and gave them to the host, and said unto him, Take care of him: and whatsoever thou spendest more, when I come again, I will repay thee.

Which now of these three, thinkest thou, was neighbour unto him that fell among the thieves?

And he said, He that showed mercy on him. Then said Jesus unto him,

Go, and do thou likewise.

Of One That Layeth Up Treasure

(*According to Luke*)

And he spake a parable unto them, saying,

The ground of a certain rich man brought forth plentifully. And he thought within himself, saying, What shall I do, because I have no room where to bestow my fruits? And he said, This will I do: I will pull down my barns, and build greater; and there will I bestow all my fruits and my goods. And I will say to my soul, Soul, thou hast much goods laid up for many years; take thine ease, eat, drink, and be merry.

But God said unto him, Thou fool, this night thy soul shall be required of thee: then whose shall those things be, which thou hast provided?

So is he that layeth up treasure for himself, and is not rich toward God.

Fear not, little flock; for it is your Father's good pleasure to give you the kingdom. Sell that ye have, and give alms; provide yourselves bags which wax not old, a treasure in the heavens that faileth not, where no thief approacheth, neither moth corrupteth. For where your treasure is, there will your heart be also.

Of the Fig Tree

(*According to Luke*)

A certain man had a fig tree planted in his vineyard; and he came and sought fruit thereon, and found none. Then said he unto the dresser of his vineyard, Behold, these three years I come seeking fruit on this fig tree, and find none: cut it down; why cumbereth it the ground?

And he answering said unto him, Lord, let it alone this year also, till I shall dig about it, and dung it: and if it bear fruit, well: and if not, then after that thou shalt cut it down.

Of the Ninety and Nine

(According to Luke)

What man of you, having a hundred sheep, if he lose one of them, doth not leave the ninety and nine in the wilderness, and go after that which is lost, until he find it? And when he hath found it, he layeth it on his shoulders, rejoicing. And when he cometh home, he calleth together his friends and neighbours, saying unto them, Rejoice with me; for I have found my sheep which was lost.

I say unto you, that likewise joy shall be in heaven over one sinner that repenteth, more than over ninety and nine just persons, which need no repentance.

Of the Ten Pieces of Silver

(According to Luke)

Either what woman having ten pieces of silver, if she lose one piece, doth not light a candle, and sweep the house, and seek diligently till she find it? And when she hath found it, she calleth her friends and her neighbours together, saying, Rejoice with me; for I have found the piece which I had lost.

Likewise, I say unto you, there is joy in the presence of the angels of God over one sinner that repenteth.

Of the Prodigal Son

(According to Luke)

And he said:

A certain man had two sons. And the younger of them said to his father, Father, give me the portion of goods that falleth to me. And he divided unto them his living. And not many days after the younger son gathered all together, and took his journey into a far country, and there wasted his substance with riotous living.

And when he had spent all, there arose a mighty famine in that land; and he began to be in want. And he went and joined himself to a citizen of that country; and he sent him into his fields to feed swine. And he would fain have filled his belly with the husks that the swine did eat: and no man gave unto him.

And when he came to himself, he said, How many hired servants of my father's have bread enough and to spare, and I perish with hunger! I will arise and go to my father, and will say unto him, Father, I have sinned against heaven, and before thee, and am no more worthy to be called thy son: make me as one of thy hired servants.

And he arose, and came to his father. But when he was yet a great way off, his father saw him, and had compassion, and ran, and fell on his neck, and kissed him.

And the son said unto him, Father, I have sinned against heaven, and in thy sight, and am no more worthy to be called thy son.

But the father said to his servants, Bring forth the best robe, and put it on him; and put a ring on his hand, and shoes on his feet, and bring hither the fatted calf, and kill it; and let us eat, and be merry. For this my son was dead, and is alive again; he was lost, and is found. And they began to be merry.

Now his elder son was in the field: and as he came and drew nigh to the house, he heard music and dancing. And he called one of the servants, and asked what these things meant.

And he said unto him, Thy brother is come; and thy father hath killed the fatted calf, because he hath received him safe and sound.

And he was angry, and would not go in; therefore came his father out, and entreated him.

And he answering said to his father, Lo, these many years do I serve thee, neither transgressed I at any time thy commandment; and yet thou never gavest me a kid, that I might make merry with my friends. But as soon as this thy son was come, which hath devoured thy living with harlots, thou hast killed for him the fatted calf.

And he said unto him, Son, thou art ever with me, and all that I have is thine. It was meet that we should make merry, and be glad: for this thy brother was dead, and is alive again; and was lost, and is found.

Of the Widow and the Judge

(According to Luke)

And he spake a parable unto them to this end, that men ought always to pray, and not to faint, saying,

There was in a city a judge, which feared not God, neither regarded man. And there was a widow in that city; and she came unto him, saying, Avenge me of mine adversary.

And he would not for a while: but afterward he said within himself, Though I fear not God, nor regard man, yet because this widow troubleth me, I will avenge her, lest by her continual coming she weary me.

And the Lord said,

Hear what the unjust judge saith. And shall not God avenge his own elect, which cry day and night unto him, though he bear long with them? I tell you that he will avenge them speedily. Nevertheless, when the Son of man cometh, shall he find faith on the earth?

Of the Two Men Who Prayed

(According to Luke)

And he spake this parable unto certain which trusted in themselves that they were righteous, and despised others:

Two men went up into the temple to pray; the one a Pharisee, and the other a publican.

The Pharisee stood and prayed thus with himself, God, I thank thee, that I am not as other men are, extortioners, unjust, adulterers, or even as this publican. I fast twice in the week, I give tithes of all that I possess.

And the publican, standing afar off, would not lift up so much as his eyes unto heaven, but smote upon his breast, saying, God be merciful to me a sinner.

I tell you, this man went down to his house justified rather than the other: for every one that exalteth himself shall be abased; and he that humbleth himself shall be exalted.

The Acts

The Acts of the Apostles

The Apostles' Ministry Begins

The former treatise have I made, O Theophilus, of all that Jesus began both to do and teach, until the day in which he was taken up, after that he through the Holy Ghost had given commandments unto the apostles whom he had chosen; to whom also he shewed himself alive after his passion, by many infallible proofs, being seen of them forty days, and speaking of the things pertaining to the kingdom of God.

And when he had spoken these things, while they beheld, he was taken up; and a cloud received him out of their sight.

Then returned they unto Jerusalem, from the mount called Olivet, which is from Jerusalem a sabbath day's journey. And when they were come in, they went up into an upper room, where abode both Peter and James, and John, and Andrew, Philip, and Thomas, Bartholomew, and Matthew, James the son of Alpheus, and Simon Zelotes, and Judas the brother of James. These all continued with one accord in prayer and supplication, with the women, and Mary the mother of Jesus, and with his brethren.

And in those days Peter stood up in the midst of the disciples, and said, (the number of the names together were about an hundred and twenty,) Men and brethren, this scripture must needs have been fulfilled, which the Holy Ghost by the mouth of David spake before concerning Judas, which was guide to them that took Jesus. For he was numbered with us, and had obtained part of this ministry. Now this man purchased a field with the reward of iniquity; and falling headlong, he burst asunder in the midst, and all his bowels gushed out. And it was known unto all the dwellers at Jerusalem; insomuch as that field is called in their proper tongue, Aceldama, that is to say, The field of blood. For it is written in the book of Psalms, Let his habitation be desolate, and let no man dwell therein: and, His bishoprick let another take.

Wherefore of these men which have companied with us, all the time that the Lord Jesus went in and out among us, beginning from the baptism of John, unto that same day that he was taken up from us, must one be ordained to be a witness with us of his resurrection.

And they appointed two, Joseph called Barsabas, who was surnamed Justus, and Matthias. And they prayed, and said, Thou, Lord, which knowest the hearts of all men, shew whether of these two thou hast chosen, that he may take part of this ministry and apostleship, from which Judas by transgression fell, that he might go to his own place. And they gave forth their lots; and the lot fell upon Matthias; and he was numbered with the eleven apostles.

And when the day of Pentecost was fully come, they were all with one accord in one place. And suddenly there came a sound from heaven, as of a rushing mighty wind, and it filled all the house where they were sitting. And there appeared unto them cloven tongues like as of fire, and it sat upon each of them. And they were all filled with the Holy Ghost, and began to speak with other tongues, as the Spirit gave them utterance.

And there were dwelling at Jerusalem Jews, devout men, out of every nation under heaven. And they were all amazed, and marvelled, saying one to another, Behold, are not all these which speak, Galileans? And how hear we every man in our own tongue, wherein we were born? Parthians, and Medes, and Elamites, and the dwellers in Mesopotamia, and in Judea, and Cappadocia, in Pontus, and Asia, Phrygia, and Pamphylia, in Egypt, and in the parts of Libya about Cyrene, and strangers of Rome, Jews and proselytes, Cretes and Arabians, we do hear them speak in our tongues the wonderful works of God. Others mocking, said, These men are full of new wine.

But Peter, standing up with the eleven, lifted up his voice, and said unto them, Ye men of Judea, and all ye that dwell at Jerusalem, be this known unto you, and hearken to my words: for these are not drunken, as ye suppose, seeing it is but the third hour of the day. But this is that which was spoken by the prophet Joel, And it shall come to pass in the last days, saith God, I will pour out of my Spirit upon all flesh: and your sons and your daughters shall prophesy, and your young men shall see visions, and your old men shall dream dreams. And on my servants and on my handmaidens, I will pour out in those days of my Spirit; and they shall prophesy.

And I will shew wonders in heaven above, and signs in the earth beneath; blood, and fire, and vapour of smoke. The sun shall be turned into darkness, and the moon into blood, before that great and notable day of the Lord come. And it shall come to pass, that whosoever shall call on the name of the Lord, shall be saved.

Ye men of Israel, hear these words; Jesus of Nazareth, a man approved of God among you by miracles, and wonders, and signs, which God did by him in the midst of you, as ye yourselves also know, Him, being delivered by the determinate counsel and foreknowledge of God, ye have taken, and by wicked hands have crucified and slain.

Now when they heard this, they were pricked in their heart, and said unto Peter and to the rest of the apostles, Men and brethren, what shall we do?

Then Peter said unto them, Repent, and be baptized every one of you in the name of Jesus Christ, for the remission of sins, and ye shall receive the gift of the Holy Ghost. And with many other words did he testify and exhort, saying, Save yourselves from this untoward generation.

Then they that gladly received his word, were baptized: and the same day there were added unto them about three thousand souls. And they, continuing daily with one accord in the temple, and breaking bread from house to house, did eat their meat with gladness and singleness of heart, praising God, and having favour with all the people. And the Lord added to the church daily such as should be saved.

Peter's Miracle

Now Peter and John went up together into the temple, at the hour of prayer, being the ninth hour. And a certain man lame from his mother's womb was carried, whom they laid daily at the gate of the temple which is called Beautiful, to ask alms of them that entered into the temple, who, seeing Peter and John about to go into the temple, asked an alms.

And Peter fastening his eyes upon him with John, said, Look on us. And he gave heed unto them, expecting to receive something of them.

Then Peter said, Silver and gold have I none; but such as I have give I thee: In the name of Jesus Christ of Nazareth, rise up and walk.

And he took him by the right hand, and lifted him up: and immediately his feet and ankle-bones received strength. And he, leaping up, stood, and walked, and entered with them into the temple, walking, and leaping, and praising God. And all the people saw him walking and praising God. And they knew that it was he which sat for alms at the Beautiful gate of the temple: and they were filled with wonder and amazement at that which had happened unto him. And as the lame man which was healed held Peter and John, all the people ran together unto them in the porch that is called Solomon's, greatly wondering.

And when Peter saw it, he answered unto the people, Ye men of Israel, why marvel ye at this? or why look ye so earnestly on us, as though by our own power or holiness we had made this man to walk? The God of Abraham, and of Isaac, and of Jacob, the God of our fathers hath glorified his Son Jesus; whom ye delivered up, and denied him in the presence of Pilate, when he was determined to let him go.

Repent ye therefore, and be converted, that your sins may be blotted out, when the times of refreshing shall come from the presence of the Lord. And he shall send Jesus Christ, which before was preached unto you, whom the heaven must receive, until the times of restitution of all things, which God hath spoken by the mouth of all his holy prophets, since the world began.

Peter and John Imprisoned

And as they spake unto the people, the priests, and the captain of the temple, and the Sadducees came upon them, being grieved that they taught the people, and preached through Jesus the resurrection from the dead. And they laid hands on them, and put them in hold unto the next day: for it was now even-tide.

Howbeit, many of them which heard the word, believed; and the number of the men was about five thousand.

And it came to pass on the morrow, that their rulers, and elders, and scribes, called them, and commanded them not to speak at all, nor teach in the name of Jesus. But Peter and John answered and said unto them, Whether it be right in the sight of God to hearken unto you more than unto God, judge ye. For we cannot but speak the things which we have seen and heard.

So, when they had further threatened them, they let them go, finding nothing how they might punish them, because of the people: for all men glorified God for that which was done.

And being let go, they went to their own company, and reported all that the chief priests and elders had said unto them.

And when they had prayed, the place was shaken where they were assembled together; and they were all filled with the Holy Ghost, and they spake the word of God with boldness.

And the multitude of them that believed were of one heart, and of one soul: neither said any of them that aught of the things which he possessed was his own; but they had all things common. Neither was there any among them that lacked: for as many as were possessors of lands or houses sold them, and brought the prices of the things that were sold, and laid them down at the apostles' feet: and distribution was made unto every man according as he had need.

The Lie of Ananias

But a certain man named Ananias, with Sapphira his wife, sold a possession, and kept back part of the price, (his wife also being privy to it,) and brought a certain part, and laid it at the apostles' feet. But Peter said, Ananias, Why hath Satan filled thine heart to lie to the Holy Ghost, and to keep back part of the price of the land?

And Ananias hearing these words, fell down, and gave up the ghost. And great fear came on all them that heard these things. And the young men arose, wound him up, and carried him out, and buried him.

And it was about the space of three hours after, when his wife, not knowing what was done, came in. And Peter answered unto her, Tell me whether ye sold the land for so much? And she said, Yea, for so much.

Then Peter said unto her, How is it that ye have agreed together to tempt the Spirit of the Lord? behold the feet of them which have buried thy husband are at the door, and shall carry thee out. Then fell she down straightway at his feet, and yielded up the ghost. And the young men came in, and found her dead, and carrying her forth, buried her by her husband. And great fear came upon all the church, and upon as many as heard these things.

And by the hands of the apostles were many signs and wonders wrought among the people; (and they were all of one accord in Solomon's porch).

Then the high priest rose up, and all they that were with him, (which is the sect of the Sadducees,) and were filled with indignation, and laid their hands on the apostles, and put them in the common prison. But the angel of the Lord by night opened the prison-doors, and brought them forth, and said, Go, stand and speak in the temple to the people all the words of this life.

And when they heard that, they entered into the temple early in the morning, and taught. Then went the captain with the officers, and brought them without violence: for they feared the people, lest they should have been stoned.

And when they had brought them, they set them before the council: and the high priest asked them, saying, Did not we straitly command you, that ye should not teach in this name? and behold, ye have filled Jerusalem with your doctrine, and intend to bring this man's blood upon us.

Then Peter and the other apostles answered and said, We ought to obey God rather than men.

Then stood there up one in the council, a Pharisee, named Gamaliel, a doctor of the law, had in reputation among all the people, and commanded to put the apostles forth a little space, and said unto them, Ye men of Israel, take heed to yourselves what ye intend to do as touching these men. Refrain from these men, and let them alone: for if this counsel or this work be of men, it will come to nought. But if it be of God, ye cannot overthrow it; lest haply ye be found even to fight against God.

And to him they agreed: and when they had called the apostles, and beaten them, they commanded that they should not speak in the name of Jesus, and let them go.

And they departed from the presence of the council, rejoicing that they were counted worthy to suffer shame for his name. And daily in the temple, and in every house, they ceased not to teach and preach Jesus Christ.

The Death of Stephen

And Stephen, full of faith and power, did great wonders and miracles among the people.

Then there arose certain of the synagogue, which is called the synagogue of the Libertines, and Cyrenians, and Alexandrians, and of them of Cilicia, and of Asia, disputing with Stephen. And they were not able to resist the wisdom and the spirit by which he spake.

Then they suborned men, which said, We have heard him speak blasphemous words against Moses, and against God. And they stirred up the people, and the elders, and the scribes, and came upon him, and caught him, and brought him to the council, and set up false witnesses, which said, This man ceaseth not to speak blasphemous words against this holy place, and the law; for we have heard him say, that this Jesus of Nazareth shall destroy this place, and shall change the customs which Moses delivered us. And all that sat in the council, looking steadfastly on him, saw his face as it had been the face of an angel.

Then said the high priest, Are these things so?

And he said, Ye stiff-necked, and uncircumcised in heart and ears, ye do always resist the Holy Ghost: as your fathers did, so do ye. Which of the prophets have not your fathers persecuted? and they have slain them which shewed before of the coming of the Just One; of whom ye have been now the betrayers and murderers; who have received the law by the disposition of angels, and have not kept it.

When they heard these things, they were cut to the heart, and they gnashed on him with their teeth. But he, being full of the Holy Ghost, looked up steadfastly into heaven, and saw the glory of God, and Jesus standing on the right hand of God, and said, Behold, I see the heavens opened, and the Son of man standing on the right hand of God.

Then they cried out with a loud voice, and stopped their ears, and ran upon him with one accord, and cast him out of the city, and stoned him: and the witnesses laid down their clothes at a young man's feet, whose name was Saul. And they stoned Stephen, calling upon God, and saying, Lord Jesus, receive my spirit. And he kneeled down and cried with a loud voice, Lord, lay not this sin to their charge. And when he had said this, he fell asleep.

And Saul was consenting unto his death. And at that time there was a great persecution against the church which was at Jerusalem; and they were all scattered abroad throughout the regions of Judea and Samaria, except the apostles.

And devout men carried Stephen to his burial, and made great lamentation over him.

As for Saul, he made havoc of the church, entering into every house, and haling men and women, committed them to prison.

Therefore they that were scattered abroad went every where preaching the word.

Saul's Conversion

And Saul, yet breathing out threatenings and slaughter against the disciples of the Lord, went unto the high priest, and desired of him letters to Damascus to the synagogues, that if he found any of this way, whether they were men or women, he might bring them bound unto Jerusalem.

And as he journeyed, he came near Damascus: and suddenly there shined round about him a light from heaven. And he fell to the earth, and heard a voice saying unto him, Saul, Saul, why persecutest thou me?

And he said, Who art thou, Lord? And the Lord said, I am Jesus whom thou persecutest. It is hard for thee to kick against the pricks.

And he trembling, and astonished, said, Lord, what wilt thou have me to do? And the Lord said unto him, Arise, and go into the city, and it shall be told thee what thou must do.

And the men which journeyed with him stood speechless, hearing a voice, but seeing no man.

And Saul arose from the earth; and when his eyes were opened, he saw no man: but they led him by the hand, and brought him into Damascus. And he was three days without sight, and neither did eat nor drink.

And there was a certain disciple at Damascus, named Ananias; and to him said the Lord in a vision, Ananias. And he said, Behold, I am here, Lord.

And the Lord said unto him, Arise, and go into the street which is called Straight, and inquire in the house of Judas for one called Saul of Tarsus: for behold, he prayeth, and hath seen in a vision a man named Ananias, coming in, and putting his hand on him, that he might receive his sight.

And Ananias went his way, and entered into the house: and putting his hands on him, said, Brother Saul, the Lord (even Jesus that appeared unto thee in the way as thou camest) hath sent me, that thou mightest receive thy sight, and be filled with the Holy Ghost.

And immediately there fell from his eyes as it had been scales: and he received sight forthwith, and arose, and was baptized. And when he had received meat, he was strengthened. Then was Saul certain days with the disciples which were at Damascus. And straightway he preached Christ in the synagogues, that he is the Son of God.

Peter's Vision of the Gentiles

As they went on their journey, and drew nigh unto the city, Peter went up upon the house-top to pray, about the sixth hour. And he became very hungry, and would have eaten: but while they made ready, he fell into a trance, and saw heaven opened, and a certain vessel descending unto him, as it had been a great sheet knit at the four corners, and let down to the earth, wherein were all manner of four-footed beasts of the earth, and wild beasts, and creeping things, and fowls of the air.

And there came a voice to him, Rise, Peter; kill, and eat.

But Peter said, Not so, Lord; for I have never eaten anything that is common or unclean.

And the voice spake unto him again the second time, What God hath cleansed, that call not thou common.

This was done thrice: and the vessel was received up again into heaven.

Then Peter opened his mouth, and said, Of a truth I perceive that God is no respecter of persons, but in every nation, he that feareth him and worketh righteousness, is accepted with him. Can any man forbid water, that these should not be baptized, which have received the Holy Ghost as well as we?

And the apostles and brethren that were in Judea, heard that the Gentiles had also received the word of God.

And when Peter was come up to Jerusalem, they that were of the circumcision contended with him, saying, Thou wentest in to men uncircumcised, and didst eat with them.

But Peter rehearsed the matter from the beginning, and expounded it by order unto them.

When they heard these things, they held their peace, and glorified God, saying, Then hath God also to the Gentiles granted repentance unto life.

Now they which were scattered abroad upon the persecution that arose about Stephen, travelled as far as Phenice, and Cyprus, and Antioch, preaching the word to none but unto the Jews only. And some of them were men of Cyprus and Cyrene, which when they were come to Antioch, spake unto the Grecians, preaching the Lord Jesus.

And the hand of the Lord was with them: and a great number believed, and turned unto the Lord.

Then tidings of these things came unto the ears of the church which was in Jerusalem: and they sent forth Barnabas, that he should go as far as Antioch.

Then departed Barnabas to Tarsus, for to seek Saul. And when he had found him, he brought him unto Antioch. And it came to pass, that a whole year they assembled themselves with the church, and taught much people. And the disciples were called Christians first in Antioch.

And in these days came prophets from Jerusalem unto Antioch.

Paul and Barnabas Turn to the Gentiles

And the next sabbath-day came almost the whole city together to hear the word of God. But when the Jews saw the multitudes, they were filled with envy, and spake against those things which were spoken by Paul, contradicting and blaspheming.

Then Paul and Barnabas waxed bold, and said, It was necessary that the word of God should first have been spoken to you: but seeing you put it from you, and judge yourselves unworthy of everlasting life, lo, we turn to the Gentiles. For so hath the Lord commanded us, saying,

I have set thee to be a light of the Gentiles, that thou shouldest be for salvation unto the ends of the earth.

And when the Gentiles heard this, they were glad, and glorified the word of the Lord: and as many as were ordained to eternal life, believed.

And there sat a certain man at Lystra, impotent in his feet, being a cripple from his mother's womb, who never had walked.

The same heard Paul speak: who steadfastly beholding him, and perceiving that he had faith to be healed, said with a loud voice, Stand upright on thy feet. And he leaped and walked.

And when the people saw what Paul had done, they lifted up their voices, saying in the speech of Lycaonia, The gods are come down to us in the likeness of men. And they called Barnabas, Jupiter; and Paul, Mercurius, because he was the chief speaker. Then the priest of Jupiter, which was before their city, brought oxen and garlands unto the gates, and would have done sacrifice with the people.

Which when the apostles, Barnabas and Paul, heard of, they rent their clothes, and ran in among the people, crying out, and saying, Sirs, why do ye these things? We also are men of like passions with you, and preach unto you, that ye should turn from these vanities unto the living God, which made heaven, and earth, and the sea, and all things that are therein: who in times past suffered all nations to walk in their own ways. Nevertheless he left not himself without witness, in that he did good, and gave us rain from heaven, and fruitful seasons, filling our hearts with good and gladness.

And certain men which came down from Judea, taught the brethren, and said, Except ye be circumcised after the manner of Moses, ye cannot be saved.

When therefore Paul and Barnabas had no small dissension and disputation with them, they determined that Paul and Barnabas, and certain other of them, should go up to Jerusalem unto the apostles and elders about this question.

And when they were come to Jerusalem, they were received of the church, and of the apostles and elders, and they declared all things that God had done with them.

And when there had been much disputing, Peter rose up and said unto them, Men and brethren, ye know how that a good while ago, God made choice among us, that the Gentiles, by my mouth, should hear the word of the gospel, and believe. And God, which knoweth the hearts, bare them witness, giving them the Holy Ghost, even as he did unto us, and put no difference between us and them, purifying their hearts by faith. Now therefore why tempt ye God, to put a yoke upon the neck of the disciples, which neither our fathers nor we were able to bear? But we believe, that through the grace of the Lord Jesus Christ, we shall be saved, even as they.

Then all the multitude kept silence, and gave audience to Barnabas and Paul, declaring what miracles and wonders God had wrought among the Gentiles by them.

And after they had held their peace, James answered, saying, Men and brethren, hearken unto me. Simeon hath declared how God at the first did visit the Gentiles, to take out of them a people for his name. And to this agree the words of the prophets; as it is written, After this I will return, and will build again the tabernacle of David which is fallen down; and I will build again the ruins thereof, and I will set it up: that the residue of men might seek after the Lord, and all the Gentiles, upon whom my name is called, saith the Lord, who doeth all these things.

Known unto God are all his works from the beginning of the world. Wherefore my sentence is, that we trouble not them, which from among the Gentiles are turned to God: but that we write unto them that they abstain from pollutions of idols, and from fornication, and from things strangled, and from blood. For Moses of old time hath in every city them that preach him, being read in the synagogues every sabbath-day.

Then pleased it the apostles and elders, with the whole church, to send chosen men of their own company to Antioch, with Paul and Barnabas; namely, Judas surnamed Barsabas, and Silas, chief men among the brethren.

And they wrote letters by them after this manner; The apostles, and elders, and brethren, send greeting unto the brethren which are of the Gentiles in Antioch, and Syria, and Cilicia. Forasmuch as we have heard, that certain which went out from us, have troubled you with words, subverting your souls, saying, Ye must be circumcised, and keep the law; to whom we gave no such commandment: it seemed good unto us, being assembled with one accord, to send chosen men unto you, with our beloved Barnabas and Paul: men that have hazarded their lives for the name of our Lord Jesus Christ. We have sent therefore Judas and Silas, who shall also tell you the same things by mouth. For it seemed good to the Holy Ghost, and to us, to lay upon you no greater burden than these necessary things; that ye abstain from meats offered to idols, and from blood, and from things strangled, and from fornication: from which if ye keep yourselves, ye shall do well. Fare ye well.

Paul Reproves the Athenians

Now while Paul waited for them at Athens, his spirit was stirred in him, when he saw the city wholly given to idolatry. Therefore disputed he in the synagogue with the Jews, and with the devout persons, and in the market daily with them that met with him.

Then certain philosophers of the Epicureans, and of the Stoics, encountered him. And some said, What will this babbler say? other some, He seemeth to be a setter forth of strange gods: because he preached unto them Jesus, and the resurrection.

And they took him, and brought him unto Areopagus, saying, May we know what this new doctrine, whereof thou speakest, is? For thou bringest certain strange things to our ears; we would know therefore what these things mean. (For all the Athenians and strangers which were there, spent their time in nothing else, but either to tell, or to hear some new thing.)

Then Paul stood in the midst of Mars-hill, and said, Ye men of Athens, I perceive that in all things ye are too superstitious. For as I passed by, and beheld your devotions, I found an altar with this inscription, TO THE UNKNOWN GOD. Whom therefore ye ignorantly worship, him declare I unto you.

God that made the world, and all things therein, seeing that he is Lord of heaven and earth, dwelleth not in temples made with hands; neither is worshipped with men's hands, as though he needed any thing, seeing he giveth to all life, and breath, and all things; and hath made of one blood all nations of men for to dwell on all the face of the earth, and hath determined the times before appointed, and the bounds of their habitation; that they should seek the Lord, if haply they might feel after him, and find him, though he be not far from every one of us:

for in him we live, and move, and have our being; as certain also of your own poets have said, For we are also his offspring.

Forasmuch then as we are the offspring of God, we ought not to think that the Godhead is like unto gold, or silver, or stone, graven by art and man's device.

And the times of this ignorance God winked at; but now commandeth all men everywhere to repent: because he hath appointed a day, in the which he will judge the world in righteousness, by that man whom he hath ordained: whereof he hath given assurance unto all men, in that he hath raised him from the dead.

And when they heard of the resurrection of the dead, some mocked; and others said, We will hear thee again of this matter.

So Paul departed from among them.

The Epistles

The Epistle of Paul, the Apostle, to the Romans

Paul, a servant of Jesus Christ, called to be an apostle, separated unto the gospel of God, to all that be in Rome, beloved of God, called to be saints: Grace to you, and peace from God our Father, and the Lord Jesus Christ.

I am debtor both to the Greeks, and to the Barbarians; both to the wise, and to the unwise. So, as much as in me is, I am ready to preach the gospel to you that are at Rome also.

For therein is the righteousness of God revealed from faith to faith: as it is written, The just shall live by faith. For the wrath of God is revealed from heaven against all ungodliness, and unrighteousness of men, who hold the truth in unrighteousness.

Tribulation and anguish, upon every soul of man that doeth evil; of the Jew first, and also of the Gentile; but glory, honour, and peace, to every man that worketh good; to the Jew first, and also to the Gentile. For there is no respect of persons with God.

For as many as have sinned without law, shall also perish without law: and as many as have sinned in the law, shall be judged by the law.

For he is not a Jew, which is one outwardly; neither is that circumcision, which is outward in the flesh. But he is a Jew which is one inwardly; and circumcision is that of the heart, in the spirit, and not in the letter; whose praise is not of men, but of God.

What advantage then hath the Jew? or what profit is there of circumcision? Much every way: chiefly, because that unto them were committed the oracles of God.

But now the righteousness of God without the law is manifested, being witnessed by the law and the prophets; even the righteousness of God, which is by faith of Jesus Christ unto all, and upon all them that believe; for there is no difference: for all have sinned, and come short of the glory of God; being justified freely by his grace, through the redemption that is in Christ Jesus: whom God hath set forth to be a propitiation, through faith in his blood, to declare his righteousness for the remission of sins that are past, through the forbearance of God; to declare, I say, at this time his righteousness: that he might be just, and the justifier of him which believeth in Jesus.

Where is boasting then? It is excluded. By what law? of works? Nay; but by the law of faith. Therefore we conclude, that a man is justified by faith without the deeds of the law.

Is he the God of the Jews only? is he not also of the Gentiles? Yes, of the Gentiles also: seeing it is one God which shall justify the circumcision by faith, and uncircumcision through faith.

Do we then make void the law through faith? God forbid: yea, we establish the law.

Therefore being justified by faith, we have peace with God, through our Lord Jesus Christ, by whom also we have access by faith into this grace wherein we stand, and rejoice in hope of the glory of God. And not only so, but we glory in tribulations also; knowing that tribulation worketh patience; and patience, experience; and experience, hope; and hope maketh not ashamed: because the love of God is shed abroad in our hearts by the Holy Ghost which is given unto us.

For when we were yet without strength, in due time Christ died for the ungodly. For scarcely for a righteous man will one die: yet per-adventure for a good man some would even dare to die. But God commendeth his love towards us, in that while we were yet sinners, Christ died for us.

Much more then, being now justified by his blood, we shall be saved from wrath through him. For if when we were enemies, we were reconciled to God by the death of his Son; much more, being reconciled, we shall be saved by his life. And not only so, but we also joy in God, through our Lord Jesus Christ, by whom we have now received the atonement.

Wherefore as by one man sin entered into the world, and death by sin: and so death passed upon all men, for that all have sinned: there-fore, as by the offence of one, judgment came upon all men to con-demnation; even so by the righteousness of one, the free gift came upon all men unto justification of life. For as by one man's disobedience many were made sinners, so by the obedience of one shall many be made righteous.

Moreover the law entered, that the offence might abound. But where sin abounded, grace did much more abound: that as sin hath reigned unto death, even so might grace reign through righteousness unto eternal life, by Jesus Christ our Lord.

What shall we say then? Shall we continue in sin, that grace may abound? God forbid: how shall we, that are dead to sin, live any longer therein? Know ye not that so many of us as were baptized into Jesus Christ, were baptized into his death? Therefore we are buried with him by baptism into death: that like as Christ was raised up from the dead by the glory of the Father, even so we also should walk in newness of life. For if we have been planted together in the likeness of his death, we shall be also in the likeness of his resurrection.

Wherefore, my brethren, ye also are become dead to the law by the body of Christ; that ye should be married to another, even to him who is raised from the dead, that we should bring forth fruit unto God. For when we were in the flesh, the motions of sins, which were by the law, did work in our members, to bring forth fruit unto death: but now we are delivered from the law, that being dead wherein we were held; that we should serve in newness of spirit, and not in the oldness of the letter. What shall we say then? Is the law sin? God forbid. Nay, I had not known sin, but by the law; for I had not known lust, except the law had said, Thou shalt not covet. But sin, taking occasion by the commandment, wrought in me all manner of concupiscence. For without the law sin was dead.

Was then that which is good made death unto me? God forbid. But sin, that it might appear sin, working death in me by that which is good; that sin by the commandment might become exceeding sinful.

For we know that the law is spiritual: but I am carnal, sold under sin. For that which I do, I allow not: for what I would, that do I not; but what I hate, that do I. If then I do that which I would not, I consent unto the law that it is good.

Now then it is no more I that do it, but sin that dwelleth in me. For I know that in me (that is, in my flesh,) dwelleth no good thing: for to will is present with me; but how to perform that which is good, I find not. For the good that I would, I do not; but the evil which I would not, that I do. Now if I do that I would not, it is no more I that do it, but sin that dwelleth in me.

I find then a law, that when I would do good, evil is present with me. For I delight in the law of God, after the inward man: but I see another law in my members warring against the law of my mind, and bringing me into captivity to the law of sin which is in my members.

O wretched man that I am! who shall deliver me from the body of this death? I thank God, through Jesus Christ our Lord; so then, with the mind I myself serve the law of God; but with the flesh the law of sin.

For to be carnally minded is death; but to be spiritually minded is life and peace: because the carnal mind is enmity against God: for it is not subject to the law of God, neither indeed can be. So then they that are in the flesh cannot please God.

But ye are not in the flesh, but in the Spirit, if so be that the Spirit of God dwell in you. Now, if any man have not the Spirit of Christ, he is none of his. And if Christ be in you, the body is dead because of sin; but the Spirit is life because of righteousness. But if the Spirit of him that raised up Jesus from the dead dwell in you, he that raised up Christ from the dead shall also quicken your mortal bodies by his Spirit that dwelleth in you.

Therefore, brethren, we are debtors not to the flesh, to live after the flesh. For if ye live after the flesh, ye shall die: but if ye through the Spirit do mortify the deeds of the body, ye shall live. For as many as are led by the Spirit of God, they are the sons of God. For ye have not received the spirit of bondage again to fear; but ye have received the Spirit of adoption, whereby we cry, Abba, Father.

The Spirit itself beareth witness with our spirit, that we are the children of God: and if children, then heirs: heirs of God, and joint-heirs with Christ; if so be that we suffer with him, that we may be also glorified together.

For I reckon, that the sufferings of this present time are not worthy to be compared with the glory which shall be revealed in us. For the earnest expectation of the creature waiteth for the manifestation of the sons of God. For the creature was made subject to vanity, not willingly, but by reason of him who hath subjected the same in hope; because the creature itself also shall be delivered from the bondage of corruption, into the glorious liberty of the children of God.

For we know that the whole creation groaneth, and travaileth in pain together until now: and not only they, but ourselves also, which have the first-fruits of the Spirit, even we ourselves groan within ourselves, waiting for the adoption, to wit, the redemption of our body.

For we are saved by hope. But hope that is seen, is not hope: for what a man seeth, why doth he yet hope for? But if we hope for that we see not, then do we with patience wait for it.

Likewise the Spirit also helpeth our infirmities: for we know not what we should pray for as we ought: but the Spirit itself maketh intercession for us with groanings which cannot be uttered.

And he that searcheth the hearts knoweth what is the mind of the Spirit, because he maketh intercession for the saints, according to the will of God. And we know that all things work together for good, to them that love God, to them who are the called according to his purpose.

For whom he did foreknow, he also did predestinate to be conformed to the image of his Son, that he might be the first-born among many brethren. Moreover, whom he did predestinate, them he also called: and whom he called, them he also justified: and whom he justified, them he also glorified.

What shall we then say to these things? If God be for us, who can be against us? He that spared not his own Son, but delivered him up for us all, how shall he not with him also freely give us all things?

Who shall lay any thing to the charge of God's elect? It is God that justifieth: who is he that condemneth? It is Christ that died, yea rather, that is risen again, who is even at the right hand of God, who also maketh intercession for us. Who shall separate us from the love of Christ? shall tribulation, or distress, or persecution, or famine, or nakedness, or peril, or sword? As it is written, For thy sake we are killed all the day long; we are accounted as sheep for the slaughter. Nay, in all these things we are more than conquerors, through him that loved us.

For I am persuaded, that neither death, nor life, nor angels, nor principalities, nor powers, nor things present, nor things to come, nor height, nor depth, nor any other creature, shall be able to separate us from the love of God which is in Christ Jesus our Lord.

I beseech you therefore, brethren, by the mercies of God, that ye present your bodies a living sacrifice, holy, acceptable unto God, which is your reasonable service. And be not conformed to this world: but be ye transformed by the renewing of your mind, that ye may prove what is that good, and acceptable, and perfect will of God. For I say, through the grace given unto me, to every man that is among you, not to think of himself more highly than he ought to think; but to think soberly, according as God hath dealt to every man the measure of faith.

For as we have many members in one body, and all members have not the same office, so we, being many, are one body in Christ, and every one members one of another. Having then gifts, differing according to the grace that is given to us, whether prophecy, let us prophesy according to the proportion of faith, or ministry, let us wait on our ministering: or he that teacheth, on teaching, or he that exhorteth, on exhortation: he that giveth, let him do it with simplicity: he that ruleth, with diligence; he that sheweth mercy, with cheerfulness.

Let love be without dissimulation. Abhor that which is evil; cleave to that which is good. Be kindly affectioned one to another with brotherly love; in honour preferring one another; not slothful in business; fervent in spirit; serving the Lord; rejoicing in hope; patient in tribulation; continuing instant in prayer; distributing to the necessity of saints; given to hospitality.

Bless them which persecute you; bless, and curse not. Rejoice with them that do rejoice, and weep with them that weep.

Be of the same mind one toward another. Mind not high things, but condescend to men of low estate. Be not wise in your own conceits.

Recompense to no man evil for evil. Provide things honest in the sight of all men.

If it be possible, as much as lieth in you, live peaceably with all men.

Dearly beloved, avenge not yourselves, but rather give place unto wrath: for it is written, Vengeance is mine; I will repay, saith the Lord. Therefore, if thine enemy hunger, feed him; if he thirst, give him drink; for in so doing thou shalt heap coals of fire on his head.

Be not overcome of evil, but overcome evil with good.

Let every soul be subject unto the higher powers. For there is no power but of God: the powers that be, are ordained of God. Whosoever therefore resisteth the power, resisteth the ordinance of God: and they that resist shall receive to themselves damnation.

For rulers are not a terror to good works, but to the evil. Wilt thou then not be afraid of the power? do that which is good, and thou shalt have praise of the same: for he is the minister of God to thee for good. But if thou do that which is evil, be afraid; for he beareth not the sword in vain: for he is the minister of God, a revenger to execute wrath upon him that doeth evil.

Wherefore ye must needs be subject, not only for wrath, but also for conscience' sake. For, for this cause pay ye tribute also: for they are God's ministers, attending continually upon this very thing.

Render therefore to all their dues: tribute to whom tribute is due; custom to whom custom; fear to whom fear; honour to whom honour. Owe no man anything, but to love one another; for he that loveth another hath fulfilled the law.

For this, Thou shalt not commit adultery, Thou shalt not kill, Thou shall not steal, Thou shalt not bear false witness, Thou shalt not covet; and if there be any other commandment, it is briefly comprehended in this saying, namely, Thou shalt love thy neighbour as thyself.

The night is far spent, the day is at hand: let us therefore cast off the works of darkness, and let us put on the armour of light. Let us walk honestly, as in the day: not in rioting and drunkenness, not in chambering and wantonness, not in strife and envying.

But put ye on the Lord Jesus Christ, and make not provision for the flesh, to fulfil the lusts thereof.

Who art thou that judgest another man's servant? to his own master he standeth or falleth; yea, he shall be holden up: for God is able to make him stand. Let us not therefore judge one another any more: but judge this rather, that no man put a stumbling-block, or an occasion to fall in his brother's way.

I know, and am persuaded by the Lord Jesus, that there is nothing unclean of itself: but to him that esteemeth any thing to be unclean, to him it is unclean.

But if thy brother be grieved with thy meat, now walkest thou not charitably. Destroy not him with thy meat, for whom Christ died. For the kingdom of God is not meat and drink, but righteousness, and peace, and joy in the Holy Ghost.

Let us therefore follow after the things which make for peace, and things wherewith one may edify another.

The First Epistle of Paul, the Apostle, to the Corinthians

Grace be unto you, and peace from God our Father, and from the Lord Jesus Christ.

God is faithful, by whom ye were called unto the fellowship of his Son Jesus Christ our Lord.

Now I beseech you, brethren, by the name of our Lord Jesus Christ, that ye all speak the same thing, and that there be no divisions among you; but that ye be perfectly joined together in the same mind, and in the same judgment. For it hath been declared unto me of you, my brethren, by them which are of the house of Chloe, that there are contentions among you.

Now this I say, that every one of you saith, I am of Paul; and I of Apollos; and I of Cephas; and I of Christ. Is Christ divided? was Paul crucified for you? or were ye baptized in the name of Paul?

I thank God that I baptized none of you, but Crispus and Gaius; lest any should say that I had baptized in mine own name. And I baptized also the household of Stephanas; besides, I know not whether I baptized any other. For Christ sent me not to baptize, but to preach the gospel: not with wisdom of words, lest the cross of Christ should be made of none effect.

For the preaching of the cross is to them that perish, foolishness; but unto us which are saved, it is the power of God. For it is written, I will destroy the wisdom of the wise, and will bring to nothing the understanding of the prudent.

Where is the wise? where is the scribe? where is the disputer of this world? hath not God made foolish the wisdom of this world? For after that in the wisdom of God the world by wisdom knew not God, it pleased God by the foolishness of preaching to save them that believe.

For the Jews require a sign, and the Greeks seek after wisdom: but we preach Christ crucified, unto the Jews a stumbling-block, and unto the Greeks foolishness; but unto them which are called, both Jews and Greeks, Christ the power of God, and the wisdom of God. Because the foolishness of God is wiser than men; and the weakness of God is stronger than men.

But God hath chosen the foolish things of the world to confound the wise; and God hath chosen the weak things of the world to confound the things which are mighty; and base things of the world, and things which are despised, hath God chosen, yea, and things which are not, to bring to nought things that are.

And I, brethren, could not speak unto you as unto spiritual, but as unto carnal, even as unto babes in Christ. I have fed you with milk, and not with meat: for hitherto ye were not able to bear it, neither yet now are ye able. For ye are yet carnal: for whereas there is among you envying, and strife, and divisions, are ye not carnal, and walk as men?

Know ye not that ye are the temple of God, and that the Spirit of God dwelleth in you? If any man defile the temple of God, him shall God destroy: for the temple of God is holy, which temple ye are.

Now concerning the things whereof ye wrote unto me: It is good for a man not to touch a woman. Nevertheless, to avoid fornication, let every man have his own wife, and let every woman have her own husband. Let the husband render unto the wife due benevolence: and likewise also the wife unto the husband. The wife hath not power of her own body, but the husband: and likewise also the husband hath not power of his own body, but the wife.

Defraud ye not one the other, except it be with consent for a time, that ye may give yourselves to fasting and prayer: and come together again, that Satan tempt ye not for your incontinency. But I speak this by permission, and not of commandment.

For I would that all men were even as I myself. But every man hath his proper gift of God, one after this manner, and another after that. I say therefore to the unmarried and widows, It is good for them if they abide even as I. But if they cannot contain, let them marry: for it is better to marry than to burn.

And unto the married I command, yet not I, but the Lord, Let not the wife depart from her husband. But and if she depart, let her remain unmarried, or be reconciled to her husband: and let not the husband put away his wife.

But to the rest speak I, not the Lord, If any brother hath a wife that believeth not, and she be pleased to dwell with him, let him not put her away. And the woman which hath an husband that believeth not, and if he be pleased to dwell with her, let her not leave him. For the unbelieving husband is sanctified by the wife, and the unbelieving wife is sanctified by the husband: else were your children unclean; but now are they holy.

But as God hath distributed to every man, as the Lord hath called every one, so let him walk. And so ordain I in all churches.

Art thou bound unto a wife? seek not to be loosed. Art thou loosed from a wife? seek not a wife. But and if thou marry, thou hast not sinned: and if a virgin marry, she hath not sinned. Nevertheless, such shall have trouble in the flesh; but I spare you.

But this I say, brethren, The time is short. It remaineth, that both they that have wives, be as though they had none; and they that weep, as though they wept not; and they that rejoice, as though they rejoiced not; and they that buy, as though they possessed not; and they that use this world, as not abusing it. For the fashion of this world passeth away.

As concerning the eating of those things that are offered in sacrifice unto idols, we know that an idol is nothing in the world, and that there is none other God but one. Howbeit, there is not in every man that knowledge: for some with conscience of the idol unto this hour eat it as a thing offered unto an idol: and their conscience, being weak, is defiled.

And through thy knowledge shall the weak brother perish, for whom Christ died? But when ye sin so against the brethren, and wound their weak conscience, ye sin against Christ.

Wherefore, if meat make my brother to offend, I will eat no flesh while the world standeth, lest I make my brother to offend.

But I would have you know, that the head of every man is Christ; and the head of the woman is the man; and the head of Christ is God. Every man praying or prophesying, having his head covered, dishonoureth his head. But every woman that prayeth or prophesieth with her head uncovered, dishonoureth her head: for that is even all one as if she were shaven.

For a man indeed ought not to cover his head, forasmuch as he is the image and glory of God: but the woman is the glory of the man. For the man is not of the woman, but the woman of the man. Neither was the man created for the woman, but the woman for the man.

Let your women keep silence in the churches; for it is not permitted unto them to speak: but they are commanded to be under obedience, as also saith the law. And if they will learn anything, let them ask their husbands at home; for it is a shame for women to speak in the church.

Now in this that I declare unto you, I praise you not, that ye come together not for the better, but for the worse. For first of all, when ye come together in the church, I hear that there be divisions among you; and I partly believe it. For there must be also heresies among you, that they which are approved may be made manifest among you.

When ye come together therefore into one place, this is not to eat the Lord's supper. For in eating every one taketh before other his own supper: and one is hungry, and another is drunken. What! have ye not houses to eat and to drink in? or despise ye the church of God, and shame them that have not? What shall I say to you? shall I praise you in this? I praise you not.

For I have received of the Lord, that which also I delivered unto you, That the Lord Jesus, the same night in which he was betrayed, took bread: and when he had given thanks, he brake it, and said, Take, eat: this is my body, which is broken for you: this do in remembrance of me.

After the same manner also he took the cup, when he had supped, saying, This cup is the new testament in my blood: this do ye, as oft as ye drink it, in remembrance of me. For as often as ye eat this bread, and drink this cup, ye do shew the Lord's death till he come.

Wherefore, whosoever shall eat this bread, and drink this cup of the Lord, unworthily, shall be guilty of the body and blood of the Lord. But let a man examine himself, and so let him eat of that bread, and drink of that cup. For he that eateth and drinketh unworthily, eateth and drinketh damnation to himself, not discerning the Lord's body.

For this cause many are weak and sickly among you, and many sleep. For if we would judge ourselves, we should not be judged. But when we are judged, we are chastened of the Lord, that we should not be condemned with the world.

Wherefore, my brethren, when ye come together to eat, tarry one for another. And if any man hunger, let him eat at home: that ye come not together unto condemnation. And the rest will I set in order when I come.

Now concerning spiritual gifts, brethren, I would not have you ignorant. Ye know that ye were Gentiles, carried away unto these dumb idols, even as ye were led. Wherefore I give you to understand, that no man speaking by the Spirit of God, calleth Jesus accursed: and that no man can say that Jesus is the Lord, but by the Holy Ghost.

Now there are diversities of gifts, but the same Spirit. And there are differences of administrations, but the same Lord. And there are diversities of operations, but it is the same God which worketh all in all. But the manifestation of the Spirit is given to every man to profit withal.

For to one is given by the Spirit the word of wisdom; to another, the word of knowledge by the same Spirit; to another, faith by the same Spirit; to another, the gifts of healing by the same Spirit; to another, the working of miracles; to another, prophecy; to another, discerning of spirits; to another, divers kinds of tongues; to another, the interpretation of tongues: but all these worketh that one and the self-same Spirit, dividing to every man severally as he will.

For as the body is one, and hath many members, and all the members of that one body, being many, are one body: so also is Christ. For by one Spirit are we all baptized into one body, whether we be Jews or Gentiles, whether we be bond or free; and have been all made to drink into one Spirit.

For the body is not one member, but many. If the foot shall say, Because I am not the hand, I am not of the body; is it therefore not of the body? And if the ear shall say, Because I am not the eye, I am not of the body; is it therefore not of the body? If the whole body were an eye, where were the hearing? If the whole were hearing, where were the smelling? But now hath God set the members every one of them in the body, as it hath pleased him.

And if they were all one member, where were the body? But now are they many members, yet but one body. And the eye cannot say unto the hand, I have no need of thee: nor again the head to the feet, I have no need of you.

Nay, much more those members of the body, which seem to be more feeble, are necessary: and those members of the body, which we think to be less honourable, upon these we bestow more abundant honour; and our uncomely parts have more abundant comeliness. For our comely parts have no need: but God hath tempered the body together, having given more abundant honour to that part which lacked: that there should be no schism in the body; but that the members should have the same care one for another. And whether one member suffer, all the members suffer with it; or one member be honoured, all the members rejoice with it.

Now ye are the body of Christ, and members in particular. And God hath set some in the church, first apostles, secondarily prophets, thirdly teachers, after that miracles, then gifts of healings, helps, governments, diversities of tongues.

Are all apostles? are all prophets? are all teachers? are all workers of miracles? have all the gifts of healing? do all speak with tongues? do all interpret?

But covet earnestly the best gifts. And yet shew I unto you a more excellent way.

Though I speak with the tongues of men and of angels, and have not charity, I am become as sounding brass, or a tinkling cymbal. And though I have the gift of prophecy, and understand all mysteries, and all knowledge; and though I have all faith, so that I could remove mountains, and have not charity, I am nothing. And though I bestow all my goods to feed the poor, and though I give my body to be burned, and have not charity, it profiteth me nothing.

Charity suffereth long, and is kind; charity envieth not; charity vaunteth not itself, is not puffed up, doth not behave itself unseemly, seeketh not her own, is not easily provoked, thinketh no evil, rejoiceth not in iniquity, but rejoiceth in the truth; beareth all things, believeth all things, hopeth all things, endureth all things.

Charity never faileth: but whether there be prophecies, they shall fail; whether there be tongues, they shall cease; whether there be knowledge, it shall vanish away.

For we know in part, and we prophesy in part. But when that which is perfect is come, then that which is in part shall be done away.

When I was a child, I spake as a child, I understood as a child, I thought as a child: but when I became a man, I put away childish things. For now we see through a glass, darkly; but then face to face: now I know in part; but then shall I know even as also I am known.

And now abideth faith, hope, charity, these three; but the greatest of these is charity.

Moreover, brethren, I declare unto you the gospel which I preached unto you, which also ye have received, and wherein ye stand; by which also ye are saved, if ye keep in memory what I preached unto you, unless ye have believed in vain.

For I delivered unto you first of all, that which I also received, how that Christ died for our sins according to the scriptures; and that he was buried, and that he rose again the third day according to the scriptures: and that he was seen of Cephas, then of the twelve: after that, he was seen of above five hundred brethren at once; of whom the greater part remain unto this present, but some are fallen asleep. After that, he was seen of James; then of all the apostles. And last of all he was seen of me also, as of one born out of due time.

For I am the least of the apostles, that am not meet to be called an apostle, because I persecuted the church of God. But by the grace of God I am what I am: and his grace which was bestowed upon me, was not in vain; but I laboured more abundantly than they all: yet not I, but the grace of God which was with me.

Therefore whether it were I or they, so we preach, and so ye believed.

Now if Christ be preached that he rose from the dead, how say some among you that there is no resurrection of the dead? But if there be no resurrection of the dead, then is Christ not risen: and if Christ be not risen, then is our preaching vain, and your faith is also vain. Yea, and we are found false witnesses of God; because we have testified of God that he raised up Christ: whom he raised not up, if so be that the dead rise not.

For if the dead rise not, then is not Christ raised: and if Christ be not raised, your faith is vain; ye are yet in your sins. Then they also which are fallen asleep in Christ are perished. If in this life only, we have hope in Christ, we are of all men most miserable.

But now is Christ risen from the dead, and become the first-fruits of them that slept. For since by man came death, by man came also the resurrection of the dead. For as in Adam all die, even so in Christ shall all be made alive.

If after the manner of men I have fought with beasts at Ephesus, what advantageth it me, if the dead rise not? Let us eat and drink; for to-morrow we die.

Be not deceived: evil communications corrupt good manners. Awake to righteousness, and sin not; for some have not the knowledge of God. I speak this to your shame.

But some man will say, How are the dead raised up? and with what body do they come?

Thou fool, that which thou sowest is not quickened except it die. And that which thou sowest, thou sowest not that body that shall be, but bare grain; it may chance of wheat, or of some other grain. But God giveth it a body as it hath pleased him, and to every seed his own body. All flesh is not the same flesh; but there is one kind of flesh of men, another flesh of beasts, another of fishes, and another of birds.

There are also celestial bodies, and bodies terrestrial: but the glory of the celestial is one, and the glory of the terrestrial is another. There is one glory of the sun, and another glory of the moon, and another glory of the stars; for one star differeth from another star in glory.

So also is the resurrection of the dead. It is sown in corruption, it is raised in incorruption: it is sown in dishonour, it is raised in glory; it is sown in weakness, it is raised in power. It is sown a natural body, it is raised a spiritual body. There is a natural body, and there is a spiritual body.

And so it is written, The first man Adam was made a living soul, the last Adam was made a quickening spirit. Howbeit, that was not first which is spiritual, but that which is natural; and afterward that which is spiritual. The first man is of the earth, earthy: the second man is the Lord from heaven. As is the earthy, such are they also that are earthy: and as is the heavenly, such are they also that are heavenly. And as we have borne the image of the earthy, we shall also bear the image of the heavenly.

Now this I say, brethren, that flesh and blood cannot inherit the kingdom of God; neither doth corruption inherit incorruption. Behold, I shew you a mystery; we shall not all sleep, but we shall all be changed, in a moment, in the twinkling of an eye, at the last trump. For the trumpet shall sound, and the dead shall be raised incorruptible, and we shall be changed. For this corruptible must put on incorruption, and this mortal must put on immortality. So when this corruptible shall have put on incorruption, and this mortal shall have put on immortality, then shall be brought to pass the saying that is written, Death is swallowed up in victory.

O death, where is thy sting? O grave, where is thy victory? The sting of death is sin; and the strength of sin is the law. But thanks be to God, which giveth us the victory, through our Lord Jesus Christ.

Therefore, my beloved brethren, be ye steadfast, unmoveable, always abounding in the work of the Lord, forasmuch as ye know that your labour is not in vain in the Lord.

The Second Epistle of Paul, the Apostle, to the Corinthians

Paul, an apostle of Jesus Christ by the will of God, and Timothy our brother, unto the church of God which is at Corinth, with all the saints which are in all Achaia: Grace be to you and peace from God our Father, and from the Lord Jesus Christ. Blessed be God, even the Father of our Lord Jesus Christ, the Father of mercies, and the God of all comfort; who comforteth us in all our tribulation, that we may be able to comfort them which are in any trouble by the comfort wherewith we ourselves are comforted of God. For as the sufferings of Christ abound in us, so our consolation also aboundeth by Christ.

For we preach not ourselves, but Christ Jesus the Lord; and ourselves your servants for Jesus' sake. For God, who commanded the light to shine out of darkness, hath shined in our hearts, to give the light of the knowledge of the glory of God in the face of Jesus Christ. But we have this treasure in earthen vessels, that the excellency of the power may be of God, and not of us.

We are troubled on every side, yet not distressed; we are perplexed, but not in despair; persecuted, but not forsaken; cast down, but not destroyed; always bearing about in the body the dying of the Lord Jesus, that the life also of Jesus might be made manifest in our body.

As the truth of Christ is in me, no man shall stop me of this boasting in the regions of Achaia. Wherefore? because I love you not? God knoweth.

I say again, Let no man think me a fool; if otherwise, yet as a fool receive me, that I may boast myself a little. That which I speak, I speak it not after the Lord, but as it were foolishly, in this confidence of boasting. Seeing that many glory after the flesh, I will glory also. For ye suffer fools gladly, seeing ye yourselves are wise.

For ye suffer, if a man bring you into bondage, if a man devour you, if a man take of you, if a man exalt himself, if a man smite you on the face.

I speak as concerning reproach, as though we had been weak. Howbeit, whereinsoever any is bold (I speak foolishly), I am bold also. Are they Hebrews? so am I. Are they Israelites? so am I. Are they the seed of Abraham? so am I. Are they ministers of Christ? (I speak as a fool) I am more; in labours more abundant, in stripes above measure, in prisons more frequent, in deaths oft.

Of the Jews five times received I forty stripes save one. Thrice was I beaten with rods, once was I stoned, thrice I suffered shipwreck, a night and a day I have been in the deep; in journeyings often, in perils of waters, in perils of robbers, in perils by mine own countrymen, in perils by the heathen, in perils in the city, in perils in the wilderness, in perils in the sea, in perils among false brethren; in weariness and painfulness, in watchings often, in hunger and thirst, in fastings often, in cold and nakedness.

It is not expedient for me doubtless to glory. I will come to visions and revelations of the Lord. I knew a man in Christ above fourteen years ago, (whether in the body, I cannot tell; or whether out of the body, I cannot tell: God knoweth;) such an one caught up to the third heaven. And I knew such a man, (whether in the body, or out of the body, I cannot tell: God knoweth;) how that he was caught up into paradise, and heard unspeakable words, which it is not lawful for a man to utter. Of such an one will I glory: yet of myself I will not glory, but in my infirmities.

For though I would desire to glory, I shall not be a fool; for I will say the truth; but now I forbear, lest any man should think of me above that which he seeth me to be, or that he heareth of me.

And lest I should be exalted above measure through the abundance of the revelations, there was given to me a thorn in the flesh, the messenger of Satan to buffet me, lest I should be exalted above measure. For this thing I besought the Lord thrice, that it might depart from me. And he said unto me, My grace is sufficient for thee: for my strength is made perfect in weakness. Most gladly therefore will I rather glory in my infirmities, that the power of Christ may rest upon me.

Therefore I take pleasure in infirmities, in reproaches, in necessities, in persecutions, in distresses for Christ's sake: for when I am weak, then am I strong.

I am become a fool in glorying; ye have compelled me: for I ought to have been commended of you: for in nothing am I behind the very chiefest apostles, though I be nothing.

The Epistle of Paul,
the Apostle, to the Galatians

Paul, an apostle, (not of men, neither by man, but by Jesus Christ, and God the Father, who raised him from the dead;) and all the brethren which are with me, unto the churches of Galatia: grace be to you, and peace from God the Father, and from our Lord Jesus Christ.

As we said before, so say I now again, If any man preach any other gospel unto you than that ye have received, let him be accursed. For do I now persuade men, or God? or do I seek to please men? for if I yet pleased men, I should not be the servant of Christ. But I certify you, brethren, that the gospel which was preached of me is not after man: for I neither received it of man, neither was I taught it, but by the revelation of Jesus Christ.

For ye have heard of my conversation in time past in the Jews' religion, how that beyond measure I persecuted the church of God, and wasted it; and profited in the Jews' religion above many my equals in mine own nation, being more exceedingly zealous of the traditions of my fathers.

But when it pleased God, who separated me from my mother's womb, and called me by his grace, to reveal his Son in me, that I might preach him among the heathen; immediately I conferred not with flesh and blood: neither went I up to Jerusalem to them which were apostles before me: but I went to Arabia, and returned again unto Damascus.

Then after three years, I went up to Jerusalem to see Peter, and abode with him fifteen days. But other of the apostles saw I none, save James the Lord's brother.

Now the things which I write unto you, behold, before God, I lie not.

Then fourteen years after I went up again to Jerusalem with Barnabas, and took Titus with me also. And I went up by revelation, and communicated unto them that gospel which I preach among the Gentiles, but privately to them which were of reputation, lest by any means I should run, or had run, in vain.

But neither Titus, who was with me, being a Greek, was compelled to be circumcised: and that because of false brethren unawares brought in, who came in privily to spy out our liberty which we have in Christ Jesus, that they might bring us into bondage: to whom we gave place by subjection, no, not for an hour; that the truth of the gospel might continue with you.

And when James, Cephas, and John, who seemed to be pillars, perceived the grace that was given unto me, they gave to me and Barnabas the right hands of fellowship; that we should go unto the heathen, and they unto the circumcision. Only they would that we should remember the poor; the same which I also was forward to do.

But when Peter was come to Antioch, I withstood him to the face, because he was to be blamed. For, before that certain came from James, he did eat with the Gentiles: but when they were come, he withdrew, and separated himself, fearing them which were of the circumcision. And the other Jews dissembled likewise with him; insomuch that Barnabas also was carried away with their dissimulation. But when I saw that they walked not uprightly according to the truth of the gospel, i said unto Peter before them all, If thou, being a Jew, livest after the manner of Gentiles, and not as do the Jews, why compellest thou the Gentiles to live as do the Jews?

For ye are all the children of God by faith in Christ Jesus. For as many of you as have been baptized into Christ, have put on Christ. There is neither Jew nor Greek, there is neither bond nor free, there is neither male nor female: for ye are all one in Christ Jesus.

This I say then, Walk in the Spirit, and ye shall not fulfil the lust of the flesh. For the flesh lusteth against the Spirit, and the Spirit against the flesh: and these are contrary the one to the other: so that ye cannot do the things that ye would. But if ye be led by the Spirit, ye are not under the law.

Now the works of the flesh are manifest, which are these, adultery, fornication, uncleanness, lasciviousness, idolatry, witchcraft, hatred, variance, emulations, wrath, strife, seditions, heresies, envyings, murders, drunkenness, revellings, and such like: of the which I tell you before, as I have also told you in time past, that they which do such things shall not inherit the kingdom of God.

But the fruit of the Spirit is love, joy, peace, long-suffering, gentleness, goodness, faith, meekness, temperance: against such there is no law. And they that are Christ's have crucified the flesh, with the affections and lusts.

If we live in the Spirit, let us also walk in the Spirit. Let us not be desirous of vain glory, provoking one another, envying one another.

Brethren, if a man be overtaken in a fault, ye which are spiritual, restore such an one in the spirit of meekness; considering thyself, lest thou also be tempted. Bear ye one another's burdens, and so fulfil the law of Christ.

For if a man think himself to be something, when he is nothing, he deceiveth himself. But let every man prove his own work, and then shall he have rejoicing in himself alone, and not in another. For every man shall bear his own burden.

Let him that is taught in the word, communicate unto him that teacheth in all good things.

Be not deceived; God is not mocked: for whatsoever a man soweth, that shall he also reap. For he that soweth to his flesh, shall of the flesh reap corruption: but he that soweth to the Spirit, shall of the Spirit reap life everlasting. And let us not be weary in well-doing: for in due season we shall reap if we faint not.

As we have therefore opportunity, let us do good unto all men, especially unto them who are of the household of faith.

Brethren, the grace of our Lord Jesus Christ be with your spirit. Amen.

The Epistle of Paul, the Apostle, to the Ephesians

Paul, an apostle of Jesus Christ by the will of God, to the saints which are at Ephesus, and to the faithful in Christ Jesus: Grace be to you, and peace, from God our Father, and from the Lord Jesus Christ, in whom also we have obtained an inheritance, being predestinated according to the purpose of him who worketh all things after the counsel of his own will, that we should be to the praise of his glory, who first trusted in Christ.

I therefore, the prisoner of the Lord, beseech you that ye walk worthy of the vocation wherewith ye are called, with all lowliness and meekness, with long-suffering, forbearing one another in love, endeavouring to keep the unity of the Spirit in the bond of peace.

There is one body, and one Spirit, even as ye are called in one hope of your calling; one Lord, one faith, one baptism, one God and Father of all, who is above all, and through all, and in you all. But unto every one of us is given grace according to the measure of the gift of Christ.

This I say therefore, and testify in the Lord, that ye henceforth walk not as other Gentiles walk, in the vanity of their mind, having the understanding darkened, being alienated from the life of God through the ignorance that is in them, because of the blindness of their heart, who, being past feeling, have given themselves over unto lasciviousness, to work all uncleanness with greediness.

But ye have not so learned Christ; if so be that ye have heard him, and have been taught by him, as the truth is in Jesus: that ye put off concerning the former conversation the old man, which is corrupt according to the deceitful lusts, and be renewed in the spirit of your mind, and that ye put on the new man, which after God is created in righteousness and true holiness.

Wherefore putting away lying, speak every man truth with his neighbour: for we are members one of another. Be ye angry, and sin not. Let not the sun go down upon your wrath. Neither give place to the devil. Let him that stole, steal no more: but rather let him labour, working with his hands the thing which is good, that he may have to give to him that needeth.

Let all bitterness, and wrath, and anger, and clamour, and evil-speaking, be put away from you, with all malice. And be ye kind one to another, tender-hearted, forgiving one another, even as God for Christ's sake hath forgiven you.

Be ye therefore followers of God as dear children, and walk in love, as Christ also hath loved us, and hath given himself for us an offering and a sacrifice to God for a sweet-smelling savour. But fornication, and all uncleanness, or covetousness, let it not be once named among you, as becometh saints; neither filthiness, nor foolish talking, nor jesting, which are not convenient; but rather giving of thanks.

So ought men to love their wives, as their own bodies. He that loveth his wife loveth himself. For no man ever yet hated his own flesh; but nourisheth and cherisheth it, even as the Lord the church. For we are members of his body, of his flesh, and of his bones. For this cause shall a man leave his father and mother, and shall be joined unto his wife, and they two shall be one flesh.

This is a great mystery. But I speak concerning Christ and the church.

Nevertheless, let every one of you in particular so love his wife even as himself: and the wife see that she reverence her husband.

Children, obey your parents in the Lord: for this is right. Honour thy father and mother (which is the first commandment with promise), that it may be well with thee, and thou mayest live long on the earth. And, ye fathers, provoke not your children to wrath: but bring them up in the nurture and admonition of the Lord.

Servants, be obedient to them that are your masters according to the flesh, with fear and trembling, in singleness of your heart, as unto Christ, not with eye-service, as men-pleasers; but as the servants of Christ, doing the will of God from the heart, with good will doing service, as to the Lord, and not to men, knowing that whatsoever good thing any man doeth, the same shall he receive of the Lord, whether he be bond or free

And, ye masters, do the same things unto them, forbearing threatening: knowing that your Master also is in heaven; neither is there respect of persons with him.

Finally, my brethren, be strong in the Lord, and in the power of his might.

The Epistle of Paul,
the Apostle, to the Philippians

Paul and Timotheus, the servants of Jesus Christ, to all the saints in Christ Jesus which are at Philippi, with the bishops and deacons: Grace be unto you, and peace, from God our Father, and from the Lord Jesus Christ.

Some indeed preach Christ even of envy and strife: and some also of good will. The one preach Christ of contention, not sincerely, supposing to add affliction to my bonds: but the other of love, knowing that I am set for the defence of the gospel. What then? notwithstanding, every way, whether in pretence or in truth, Christ is preached; and I therein do rejoice, yea, and will rejoice.

For I know that this shall turn to my salvation through your prayer, and the supply of the Spirit of Jesus Christ, according to my earnest expectation, and my hope, that in nothing I shall be ashamed, but that with all boldness, as always, so now also, Christ shall be magnified in my body, whether it be by life, or by death.

For to me to live is Christ, and to die is gain.

But if I live in the flesh, this is the fruit of my labour: yet what I shall choose I wot not. For I am in a strait betwixt two, having a desire to depart, and to be with Christ; which is far better: nevertheless, to abide in the flesh is more needful for you.

Do all things without murmurings and disputings, that ye may be blameless and harmless, the sons of God, without rebuke, in the midst of a crooked and perverse nation, among whom ye shine as lights in the world, holding forth the word of life; that I may rejoice in the day of Christ, that I have not run in vain, neither laboured in vain.

Beware of dogs, beware of evil-workers, beware of the concision. For we are the circumcision, which worship God in the Spirit, and rejoice in Christ Jesus, and have no confidence in the flesh.

Though I might also have confidence in the flesh. If any other man thinketh that he hath whereof he might trust in the flesh, I more: circumcised the eighth day, of the stock of Israel, of the tribe of Benjamin, an Hebrew of the Hebrews; as touching the law, a Pharisee; concerning zeal, persecuting the church; touching the righteousness which is in the law, blameless. But what things were gain to me, those I counted loss for Christ.

Yea, doubtless, and I count all things but loss for the excellency of the knowledge of Christ Jesus my Lord: for whom I have suffered the loss of all things, and do count them but dung, that I may win Christ, and be found in him, not having mine own righteousness, which is of the law, but that which is through the faith of Christ, the righteousness which is of God by faith: that I may know him, and the power of his resurrection, and the fellowship of his sufferings, being made conformable unto his death; if by any means I might attain unto the resurrection of the dead.

Not as though I had already attained, either were already perfect: but I follow after, if that I may apprehend that for which also I am apprehended of Christ Jesus.

Brethren, I count not myself to have apprehended; but this one thing I do, forgetting those things which are behind, and reaching forth unto those things which are before, I press toward the mark for the prize of the high calling of God in Christ Jesus.

Therefore, my brethren dearly beloved and longed for, my joy and crown, so stand fast in the Lord, my dearly beloved.

Rejoice in the Lord always: and again I say, Rejoice.

Let your moderation be known unto all men. The Lord is at hand.

Be careful for nothing; but in every thing by prayer and supplication with thanksgiving let your requests be made known unto God. And the peace of God, which passeth all understanding, shall keep your hearts and minds through Christ Jesus.

Finally, brethren, whatsoever things are true, whatsoever things are honest, whatsoever things are just, whatsoever things are pure, whatsoever things are lovely, whatsoever things are of good report; if there be any virtue, and if there be any praise, think on these things.

Those things which ye have both learned, and received, and heard, and seen in me, do: and the God of peace shall be with you.

But I rejoiced in the Lord greatly, that now at the last your care of me hath flourished again; wherein ye were also careful, but ye lacked opportunity. Not that I speak in respect of want: for I have learned, in whatsoever state I am, therewith to be content. I know both how to be abased, and I know how to abound: every where and in all things I am instructed both to be full and to be hungry, both to abound and to suffer need. I can do all things through Christ, which strengtheneth me.

Now unto God and our Father be glory for ever and ever. Amen.

The First Epistle of Paul, the Apostle, to the Thessalonians

Paul, and Silvanus, and Timotheus, unto the church of the Thessalonians which is in God the Father, and in the Lord Jesus Christ: Grace be unto you, and peace, from God our Father and the Lord Jesus Christ.

We give thanks to God always for you all, making mention of you in our prayers, remembering without ceasing your work of faith, and labour of love, and patience of hope in our Lord Jesus Christ, in the sight of God and our Father, knowing, brethren beloved, your election of God.

Ye are witnesses, and God also, how holily, and justly, and unblameably we behaved ourselves among you that believe: as ye know how we exhorted, and comforted, and charged every one of you, as a father doth his children, that ye would walk worthy of God, who hath called you unto his kingdom and glory.

For this cause also thank we God without ceasing, because, when ye received the word of God which ye heard of us, ye received it not as the word of men, but (as it is in truth) the word of God, which effectually worketh also in you that believe. For ye, brethren, became followers of the churches of God which in Judea are in Christ Jesus: for ye also have suffered like things of your own countrymen, even as they have of the Jews: who both killed the Lord Jesus, and their own prophets, and have persecuted us; and they please not God, and are contrary to all men: forbidding us to speak to the Gentiles that they might be saved, to fill up their sins always: for the wrath is come upon them to the uttermost.

Furthermore then we beseech you, brethren, and exhort you by the Lord Jesus, that as ye have received of us how ye ought to walk and to please God, so ye would abound more and more.

But as touching brotherly love ye need not that I write unto you: for ye yourselves are taught of God to love one another. And indeed ye do it toward all the brethren which are in all Macedonia: but we beseech you, brethren, that ye increase more and more; and that ye study to be quiet, and to do your own business, and to work with your own hands, as we commanded you; that ye may walk honestly toward them that are without, and that ye may have lack of nothing.

But I would not have you to be ignorant, brethren, concerning them which are asleep, that ye sorrow not, even as others which have no hope. For if we believe that Jesus died and rose again, even so them also which sleep in Jesus will God bring with him. For this we say unto you by the word of the Lord, that we which are alive and remain unto the coming of the Lord shall not prevent them which are asleep.

For the Lord himself shall descend from heaven with a shout, with the voice of the archangel, and with the trump of God: and the dead in Christ shall rise first: then we which are alive and remain shall be caught up together with them in the clouds, to meet the Lord in the air: and so shall we ever be with the Lord.

Wherefore, comfort one another with these words.

But of the times and the seasons, brethren, ye have no need that I write unto you. For yourselves know perfectly, that the day of the Lord so cometh as a thief in the night.

For when they shall say, Peace and safety; then sudden destruction cometh upon them, as travail upon a woman with child; and they shall not escape.

But ye, brethren, are not in darkness, that that day should overtake you as a thief. Ye are all the children of light, and the children of the day: we are not of the night, nor of darkness. Therefore let us not sleep, as do others; but let us watch and be sober. For they that sleep, sleep in the night; and they that be drunken, are drunken in the night. But let us, who are of the day, be sober, putting on the breast-plate of faith and love; and for an helmet, the hope of salvation.

For God hath not appointed us to wrath, but to obtain salvation by our Lord Jesus Christ, who died for us, that, whether we wake or sleep, we should live together with him. Wherefore comfort yourselves together, and edify one another, even as also ye do.

And we beseech you, brethren, to know them which labour among you, and are over you in the Lord, and admonish you, and to esteem them very highly in love for their work's sake. And be at peace among yourselves.

Now we exhort you, brethren, warn them that are unruly, comfort the feeble-minded, support the weak, be patient toward all men. See that none render evil for evil unto any man; but ever follow that which is good, both among yourselves, and to all men.

Rejoice evermore. Pray without ceasing. In every thing give thanks: for this is the will of God in Christ Jesus concerning you. Quench not the Spirit. Despise not prophesyings. Prove all things; hold fast that which is good. Abstain from all appearance of evil.

And the very God of peace sanctify you wholly; and I pray God your whole spirit, and soul, and body, be preserved blameless unto the coming of our Lord Jesus Christ.

The grace of our Lord Jesus Christ be with you. Amen.

The Second Epistle of Paul,
the Apostle, to the Thessalonians

Paul, and Silvanus, and Timotheus, unto the church of the Thessalonians in God our Father and the Lord Jesus Christ: Grace unto you, and peace, from God our Father and the Lord Jesus Christ.

And to you, who are troubled, rest with us, when the Lord Jesus shall be revealed from heaven with his mighty angels, in flaming fire taking vengeance on them that know not God, and that obey not the gospel of our Lord Jesus Christ: who shall be punished with everlasting destruction from the presence of the Lord, and from the glory of his power; when he shall come to be glorified in his saints, and to be admired in all them that believe (because our testimony among you was believed) in that day.

Now we beseech you, brethren, by the coming of our Lord Jesus Christ, and by our gathering together unto him, that ye be not soon shaken in mind, or be troubled, neither by spirit, nor by word, nor by letter as from us, as that the day of Christ is at hand.

Let no man deceive you by any means: for that day shall not come, except there come a falling away first, and that man of sin be revealed, the son of perdition; who opposeth and exalteth himself above all that is called God, or that is worshipped; so that he, as God, sitteth in the temple of God, shewing himself that he is God. Remember ye not, that when I was yet with you, I told you these things?

And now ye know what withholdeth that he might be revealed in his time. For the mystery of iniquity doth already work: only he who now letteth will let, until he be taken out of the way.

And then shall that Wicked be revealed, whom the Lord shall consume with the spirit of his mouth, and shall destroy with the brightness of his coming: even him, whose coming is after the working of Satan, with all power, and signs, and lying wonders, and with all deceivableness of unrighteousness in them that perish; because they received not the love of the truth, that they might be saved.

And for this cause God shall send them strong delusion, that they should believe a lie: that they all might be damned who believed not the truth, but had pleasure in unrighteousness.

But we are bound to give thanks always to God for you, brethren beloved of the Lord, because God hath from the beginning chosen you to salvation, through sanctification of the Spirit, and belief of the truth: whereunto he called you by our gospel, to the obtaining of the glory of our Lord Jesus Christ.

The salutation of Paul with mine own hand, which is the token in every epistle: so I write. The grace of our Lord Jesus Christ be with you all. Amen.

The First and Second Epistles of Paul, the Apostle, to Timothy

Paul, an apostle of Jesus Christ by the commandment of God our Saviour, and Lord Jesus Christ, which is our hope; unto Timothy, my own son in the faith; Grace, mercy, and peace, from God our Father and Jesus Christ our Lord.

As I besought thee to abide still at Ephesus, when I went into Macedonia, that thou mightest charge some that they teach no other doctrine, neither give heed to fables and endless genealogies, which minister questions, rather than godly edifying which is in faith; so do.

Let no man despise thy youth; but be thou an example of the believers, in word, in conversation, in charity, in spirit, in faith, in purity. Till I come, give attendance to reading, to exhortation, to doctrine. Neglect not the gift that is in thee, which was given thee by prophecy, with the laying on of the hands of the presbytery.

Let as many servants as are under the yoke count their own masters worthy of all honour, that the name of God and his doctrine be not blasphemed. And they that have believing masters, let them not despise them, because they are brethren; but rather do them service, because they are faithful and beloved, partakers of the benefit. These things teach and exhort.

If any man teach otherwise, and consent not to wholesome words, even the words of our Lord Jesus Christ, and to the doctrine which is according to godliness, he is proud, knowing nothing, but doting about questions and strifes of words, whereof cometh envy, strife, railings, evil surmisings, perverse disputings of men of corrupt minds, and destitute of the truth, supposing that gain is godliness: from such withdraw thyself.

But godliness with contentment is great gain.

For we brought nothing into this world, and it is certain we can carry nothing out. And having food and raiment, let us be therewith content.

But they that will be rich, fall into temptation, and a snare, and into many foolish and hurtful lusts, which drown men in destruction and perdition. For the love of money is the root of all evil: which while some coveted after, they have erred from the faith, and pierced themselves through with many sorrows.

But thou, O man of God, flee these things; and follow after righteousness, godliness, faith, love, patience, meekness. Fight the good fight of faith, lay hold on eternal life, whereunto thou art also called, and hast professed a good profession before many witnesses.

Thou therefore, my son, be strong in the grace that is in Christ Jesus. And the things that thou hast heard of me among many witnesses, the same commit thou to faithful men, who shall be able to teach others also.

Thou therefore endure hardness, as a good soldier of Jesus Christ. No man that warreth entangleth himself with the affairs of this life; that he may please him who hath chosen him to be a soldier.

And if a man also strive for masteries, yet is he not crowned, except he strive lawfully. The husbandman that laboureth must be first partaker of the fruits. Consider what I say; and the Lord give thee understanding in all things.

Study to shew thyself approved unto God, a workman that needeth not to be ashamed, rightly dividing the word of truth. But shun profane and vain babblings: for they will increase unto more ungodliness.

I charge thee therefore before God, and the Lord Jesus Christ, who shall judge the quick and the dead at his appearing and his kingdom; preach the word; be instant in season, out of season; reprove, rebuke, exhort with all long-suffering and doctrine. For the time will come, when they will not endure sound doctrine; but after their own lusts shall they heap to themselves teachers, having itching ears; and they shall turn away their ears from the truth, and shall be turned unto fables.

But watch thou in all things, endure afflictions, do the work of an evangelist, make full proof of thy ministry.

For I am now ready to be offered, and the time of my departure is at hand. I have fought a good fight, I have finished my course, I have kept the faith; henceforth there is laid up for me a crown of righteousness, which the Lord, the righteous Judge, shall give me at that day: and not to me only, but unto all them also that love his appearing.

The Lord Jesus Christ be with thy spirit. Grace be with you. Amen.

The Epistle to the Hebrews

God, who at sundry times and in divers manners spake in time past unto the fathers by the prophets, hath in these last days spoken unto us by his Son, whom he hath appointed heir of all things, by whom also he made the worlds; who being the brightness of his glory, and the express image of his person, and upholding all things by the word of his power, when he had by himself purged our sins, sat down on the right hand of the Majesty on high; being made so much better than the angels, as he hath by inheritance obtained a more excellent name than they. For unto which of the angels said he at any time, Thou art my Son, this day have I begotten thee? And again, I will be to him a Father, and he shall be to me a Son?

But one in a certain place testified, saying, What is man, that thou art mindful of him? or the son of man, that thou visitest him? Thou madest him a little lower than the angels; thou crownedst him with glory and honour, and didst set him over the works of thy hands: thou hast put all things in subjection under his feet. For in that he put all in subjection under him, he left nothing that is not put under him. But now we see not yet all things put under him: but we see Jesus, who was made a little lower than the angels for the suffering of death, crowned with glory and honour; that he by the grace of God should taste death for every man.

For verily he took not on him the nature of angels; but he took on him the seed of Abraham. Wherefore in all things it behooved him to be made like unto his brethren; that he might be a merciful and faithful High Priest in things pertaining to God, to make reconciliation for the sins of the people.

Now the just shall live by faith: but if any man draw back, my soul shall have no pleasure in him. But we are not of them who draw back unto perdition; but of them that believe to the saving of the soul.

Now faith is the substance of things hoped for, the evidence of things not seen: for by it the elders obtained a good report.

Through faith we understand that the worlds were framed by the word of God, so that things which are seen were not made of things which do appear.

By faith Abel offered unto God a more excellent sacrifice than Cain, by which he obtained witness that he was righteous, God testifying of his gifts: and by it he being dead yet speaketh.

By faith Enoch was translated, that he should not see death; and was not found, because God had translated him: for before his translation he had this testimony, that he pleased God. But without faith it is impossible to please him: for he that cometh to God must believe that he is, and that he is a rewarder of them that diligently seek him.

By faith Noah, being warned of God of things not seen as yet, moved with fear, prepared an ark to the saving of his house; by the which he condemned the world, and became heir of the righteousness which is by faith.

By faith Abraham, when he was called to go out into a place which he should after receive for an inheritance, obeyed; and he went out, not knowing whither he went. By faith he sojourned in the land of promise, as in a strange country, dwelling in tabernacles with Isaac and Jacob, the heirs with him of the same promise: for he looked for a city which hath foundations, whose builder and maker is God.

Through faith also Sara herself received strength to conceive seed, and was delivered of a child when she was past age, because she judged him faithful who had promised. Therefore sprang there even of one, and him as good as dead, so many as the stars of the sky in multitude, and as the sand which is by the seashore innumerable.

These all died in faith, not having received the promises, but having seen them afar off, and were persuaded of them, and embraced them, and confessed that they were strangers and pilgrims on the earth. For they that say such things declare plainly that they seek a country. And truly, if they had been mindful of that country from whence they came out, they might have had opportunity to have returned. But now they desire a better country, that is, an heavenly: wherefore God is not ashamed to be called their God: for he hath prepared for them a city.

By faith Abraham, when he was tried, offered up Isaac: and he that had received the promises offered up his only-begotten son, of whom it was said, That in Isaac shall thy seed be called: accounting that God was able to raise him up, even from the dead; from whence also he received him in a figure.

By faith Isaac blessed Jacob and Esau concerning things to come.

By faith Jacob, when he was a dying, blessed both the sons of Joseph; and worshipped, leaning upon the top of his staff.

By faith Joseph, when he died, made mention of the departing of the children of Israel; and gave commandment concerning his bones.

By faith Moses, when he was born, was hid three months of his parents, because they saw he was a proper child; and they were not afraid of the king's commandment. By faith Moses, when he was come to years, refused to be called the son of Pharaoh's daughter, choosing rather to suffer affliction with the people of God, than to enjoy the pleasures of sin for a season; esteeming the reproach of Christ greater riches than the treasures in Egypt: for he had respect unto the recompense of the reward.

By faith he forsook Egypt, not fearing the wrath of the king: for he endured, as seeing him who is invisible. Through faith he kept the passover, and the sprinkling of blood, lest he that destroyed the first-born should touch them. By faith they passed through the Red sea as by dry land: which the Egyptians assaying to do were drowned.

By faith the walls of Jericho fell down, after they were compassed about seven days.

By faith the harlot Rahab perished not with them that believed not, when she had received the spies with peace.

And what shall I more say? for the time would fail me to tell of Gedeon, and of Barak, and of Samson, and of Jephthae, of David also, and Samuel, and of the prophets: who through faith subdued kingdoms, wrought righteousness, obtained promises, stopped the mouths of lions, quenched the violence of fire, escaped the edge of the sword, out of weakness were made strong, waxed valiant in fight, turned to flight the armies of the aliens. Women received their dead raised to life again: and others were tortured, not accepting deliverance; that they might obtain a better resurrection: and others had trial of cruel mockings and scourgings, yea, moreover of bonds and imprisonment: they were stoned, they were sawn asunder, were tempted, were slain with the sword: they wandered about in sheep-skins and goat-skins; being destitute, afflicted, tormented (of whom the world was not worthy): they wandered in deserts, and in mountains, and in dens and caves of the earth.

And these all, having obtained a good report through faith, received not the promise: God having provided some better thing for us, that they without us should not be made perfect.

Wherefore, seeing we also are compassed about with so great a cloud of witnesses, let us lay aside every weight, and the sin which doth so easily beset us, and let us run with patience the race that is set before us, looking unto Jesus the author and finisher of our faith; who, for the joy that was set before him, endured the cross, despising the shame, and is set down at the right hand of the throne of God.

For consider him that endured such contradiction of sinners against himself, lest ye be wearied and faint in your minds. Ye have not yet resisted unto blood, striving against sin.

And ye have forgotten the exhortation which speaketh unto you as unto children, My son, despise not thou the chastening of the Lord, nor faint when thou art rebuked of him: for whom the Lord loveth he chasteneth, and scourgeth every son whom he receiveth. If ye endure chastening, God dealeth with you as with sons: for what son is he whom the father chasteneth not? But if ye be without chastisement, whereof all are partakers, then are ye bastards, and not sons.

Wherefore lift up the hands which hang down, and the feeble knees; and make straight paths for your feet, lest that which is lame be turned out of the way; but let it rather be healed. Follow peace with all men, and holiness, without which no man shall see the Lord: looking diligently, lest any man fail of the grace of God; lest any root of bitterness springing up, trouble you, and thereby many be defiled.

Let brotherly love continue. Be not forgetful to entertain strangers: for thereby some have entertained angels unawares. Remember them that are in bonds, as bound with them; and them which suffer adversity, as being yourselves also in the body.

Marriage is honourable in all, and the bed undefiled: but whoremongers and adulterers God will judge.

Let your conversation be without covetousness; and be content with such things as ye have: for he hath said, I will never leave thee, nor forsake thee. So that we may boldly say, The Lord is my helper, and I will not fear what man shall do unto me.

Remember them which have the rule over you, who have spoken unto you the word of God: whose faith follow, considering the end of their conversation: Jesus Christ the same yesterday, and to-day, and for ever.

Be not carried about with divers and strange doctrines: for it is a good thing that the heart be established with grace; not with meats, which have not profited them that have been occupied therein.

Now the God of peace, that brought again from the dead our Lord Jesus, that great Shepherd of the sheep, through the blood of the everlasting covenant, make you perfect in every good work, to do his will, working in you that which is well-pleasing in his sight, through Jesus Christ; to whom be glory for ever and ever. Amen.

The General Epistle of James

James, a servant of God and of the Lord Jesus Christ, to the twelve tribes which are scattered abroad, greeting.

My brethren, count it all joy when ye fall into divers temptations; knowing this, that the trying of your faith worketh patience. But let patience have her perfect work, that ye may be perfect and entire, wanting nothing.

If any of you lack wisdom, let him ask of God, that giveth to all men liberally, and upbraideth not; and it shall be given him. But let him ask in faith, nothing wavering. For he that wavereth is like a wave of the sea driven with the wind and tossed. For let not that man think that he shall receive anything of the Lord. A double-minded man is unstable in all his ways.

Let the brother of low degree rejoice in that he is exalted: but the rich, in that he is made low: because as the flower of the grass he shall pass away. For the sun is no sooner risen with a burning heat, but it withereth the grass, and the flower thereof falleth, and the grace of the fashion of it perisheth: so also shall the rich man fade away in his ways.

Every good gift and every perfect gift is from above, and cometh down from the Father of lights, with whom is no variableness, neither shadow of turning.

Of his own will begat he us with the word of truth, that we should be a kind of first fruits of his creatures. Wherefore, my beloved brethren, let every man be swift to hear, slow to speak, slow to wrath: for the wrath of man worketh not the righteousness of God.

Wherefore lay apart all filthiness, and superfluity of naughtiness, and receive with meekness the ingrafted word, which is able to save your souls.

But be ye doers of the word, and not hearers only, deceiving your own selves. For if any be a hearer of the word, and not a doer, he is like unto a man beholding his natural face in a glass: for he beholdeth himself, and goeth his way, and straightway forgetteth what manner of man he was.

But whoso looketh into the perfect law of liberty, and continueth therein, he being not a forgetful hearer, but a doer of the work, this man shall be blessed in his deed.

If any man among you seem to be religious, and bridleth not his tongue, but deceiveth his own heart, this man's religion is vain.

Pure religion and undefiled before God and the Father is this, To visit the fatherless and widows in their affliction, and to keep himself unspotted from the world.

My brethren, have not the faith of our Lord Jesus Christ, the Lord of glory, with respect of persons. For if there come unto your assembly, a man with a gold ring, in goodly apparel, and there come in also a poor man in vile raiment; and ye have respect to him that weareth the gay clothing, and say unto him, Sit thou here in a good place; and say to the poor, Stand thou there, or sit here under my footstool: are ye not then partial in yourselves, and are become judges of evil thoughts?

Hearken, my beloved brethren, Hath not God chosen the poor of this world rich in faith, and heirs of the kingdom which he hath promised to them that love him? But ye have despised the poor. Do not rich men oppress you, and draw you before the judgment-seats? Do not they blaspheme that worthy name by the which ye are called? If ye fulfil the royal law according to the scripture, Thou shalt love thy neighbour as thyself, ye do well: but if ye have respect to persons, ye commit sin, and are convinced of the law as transgressors. For whosoever shall keep the whole law, and yet offend in one point, he is guilty of all.

What doth it profit, my brethren, though a man say he hath faith, and have not works? can faith save him? If a brother or sister be naked, and destitute of daily food, and one of you say unto them, Depart in peace, be ye warmed and filled; notwithstanding ye give them not those things which are needful to the body; what doth it profit? Even so faith, if it hath not works, is dead, being alone.

Yea, a man may say, Thou hast faith, and I have works: shew me thy faith without thy works, and I will shew thee my faith by my works. Thou believest that there is one God; thou doest well: the devils also believe, and tremble. But wilt thou know, O vain man, that faith without works is dead?

My brethren, be not many masters, knowing that we shall receive the greater condemnation. For in many things we offend all.

If any man offend not in word, the same is a perfect man, and able also to bridle the whole body. Behold, we put bits in the horses' mouths, that they may obey us; and we turn about their whole body. Behold also the ships, which, though they be so great, and are driven of fierce winds, yet are they turned about with a very small helm, whithersoever the governor listeth. Even so the tongue is a little member, and boasteth great things. Behold, how great a matter a little fire kindleth!

And the tongue is a fire, a world of iniquity: so is the tongue among our members, that it defileth the whole body, and setteth on fire the course of nature; and it is set on fire of hell. For every kind of beasts, and of birds, and of serpents, and of things in the sea, is tamed, and hath been tamed, of mankind: but the tongue can no man tame; it is an unruly evil, full of deadly poison.

Therewith bless we God, even the Father; and therewith curse we men, which are made after the similitude of God. Out of the same mouth proceedeth blessing and cursing. My brethren, these things ought not so to be. Doth a fountain send forth at the same place sweet water and bitter? Can the fig-tree, my brethren, bear olive-berries? either a vine, figs? so can no fountain both yield salt water and fresh.

Who is a wise man and endued with knowledge among you? let him shew out of a good conversation his works with meekness of wisdom.

But if ye have bitter envying and strife in your hearts, glory not, and lie not against the truth. This wisdom descendeth not from above, but is earthly, sensual, devilish. For where envying and strife is, there is confusion and every evil work.

But the wisdom that is from above is first pure, then peaceable, gentle, and easy to be entreated, full of mercy and good fruits, without partiality, and without hypocrisy. And the fruit of righteousness is sown in peace of them that make peace.

From whence come wars and fightings among you? come they not hence, even of your lusts that war in your members? Ye lust and have not: ye kill, and desire to have, and cannot obtain: ye fight and war, yet ye have not, because ye ask not. Ye ask, and receive not, because ye ask amiss, that ye may consume it upon your lusts.

Ye adulterers and adulteresses, know ye not that the friendship of the world is enmity with God? whosoever therefore will be a friend of the world is the enemy of God. Do ye think that the scripture saith in vain, The spirit that dwelleth in us lusteth to envy? But he giveth more grace. Wherefore he saith, God resisteth the proud, but giveth grace unto the humble.

Submit yourselves therefore to God. Resist the devil, and he will flee from you. Draw nigh to God, and he will draw nigh to you. Cleanse your hands, ye sinners, and purify your hearts, ye double-minded.

Be afflicted, and mourn, and weep: let your laughter be turned to mourning, and your joy to heaviness. Humble yourselves in the sight of the Lord, and he shall lift you up.

Speak not evil one of another, brethren. He that speaketh evil of his brother, and judgeth his brother, speaketh evil of the law, and judgeth the law: but if thou judge the law, thou art not a doer of the law, but a judge. There is one lawgiver, who is able to save, and to destroy: who art thou that judgest another?

Go to now, ye that say, To-day or to-morrow we will go into such a city, and continue there a year, and buy, and sell, and get gain: whereas ye know not what shall be on the morrow. For what is your life? It is even a vapour, that appeareth for a little time, and then vanisheth away. For that ye ought to say, If the Lord will, we shall live, and do this, or that. But now ye rejoice in your boastings: all such rejoicing is evil.

Therefore to him that knoweth to do good, and doeth it not, to him it is sin.

Go to now, ye rich men, weep and howl for your miseries that shall come upon you. Your riches are corrupted, and your garments are moth-eaten. Your gold and silver is cankered; and the rust of them shall be a witness against you, and shall eat your flesh as it were fire. Ye have heaped treasure together for the last days.

Behold, the hire of the labourers who have reaped down your fields, which is of you kept back by fraud, crieth; and the cries of them which have reaped are entered into the ears of the Lord of sabaoth. Ye have lived in pleasure on the earth, and been wanton; ye have nourished your hearts, as in a day of slaughter. Ye have condemned and killed the just; and he doth not resist you.

Is any among you afflicted? let him pray. Is any merry? let him sing psalms. Is any sick among you? let him call for the elders of the church;

and let them pray over him, anointing him with oil in the name of the Lord: and the prayer of faith shall save the sick, and the Lord shall raise him up; and if he have committed sins, they shall be forgiven him.

Confess your faults one to another, and pray one for another, that ye may be healed. The effectual fervent prayer of a righteous man availeth much.

The First Epistle General of John

That which was from the beginning, which we have heard, which we have seen with our eyes, which we have looked upon, and our hands have handled, of the Word of life; (for the life was manifested, and we have seen it, and bear witness, and shew unto you that eternal life which was with the Father, and was manifested unto us;) that which we have seen and heard declare we unto you, that ye also may have fellowship with us: and truly our fellowship is with the Father, and with his son Jesus Christ. And these things write we unto you, that your joy may be full.

This then is the message which we have heard of him, and declare unto you, that God is light, and in him is no darkness at all. If we say that we have fellowship with him, and walk in darkness, we lie, and do not the truth: but if we walk in the light, as he is in the light, we have fellowship one with another, and the blood of Jesus Christ his Son cleanseth us from all sin.

If we say that we have no sin, we deceive ourselves, and the truth is not in us. If we confess our sins, he is faithful and just to forgive us our sins, and to cleanse us from all unrighteousness. If we say that we have not sinned, we make him a liar, and his word is not in us.

My little children, these things write I unto you, that ye sin not. And if any man sin we have an advocate with the Father, Jesus Christ the righteous: and he is the propitiation for our sins: and not for ours only, but also for the sins of the whole world.

And hereby we do know that we know him, if we keep his commandments. He that saith, I know him, and keepeth not his commandments, is a liar, and the truth is not in him. But whoso keepeth his word, in him verily is the love of God perfected: hereby know we that we are in him. He that saith he abideth in him, ought himself also so to walk, even as he walked.

Brethren, I write no new commandment unto you, but an old commandment which ye had from the beginning: the old commandment is the word which ye have heard from the beginning.

Again, a new commandment I write unto you, which thing is true in him and in you: because the darkness is past, and the true light now shineth. He that saith he is in the light, and hateth his brother, is in darkness even until now. He that loveth his brother abideth in the light, and there is none occasion of stumbling in him. But he that hateth his brother is in darkness, and walketh in darkness, and knoweth not whither he goeth, because that darkness hath blinded his eyes.

I write unto you, little children, because your sins are forgiven you for his name's sake. I write unto you, fathers, because ye have known him that is from the beginning. I write unto you, young men, because ye have overcome the wicked one. I write unto you, little children, because ye have known the Father. I have written unto you, fathers, because ye have known him that is from the beginning. I have written unto you, young men, because ye are strong, and the word of God abideth in you, and ye have overcome the wicked one.

Love not the world, neither the things that are in the world. If any man love the world, the love of the Father is not in him. For all that is in the world, the lust of the flesh, and the lust of the eyes, and the pride of life, is not of the Father, but is of the world. And the world passeth away, and the lust thereof: but he that doeth the will of God abideth for ever.

Behold what manner of love the Father hath bestowed upon us, that we should be called the sons of God! therefore the world knoweth us not, because it knew him not. Beloved, now are we the sons of God, and it doth not yet appear what we shall be: but we know that, when he shall appear, we shall be like him; for we shall see him as he is. And every man that hath this hope in him purifieth himself, even as he is pure.

For this is the message that ye heard from the beginning, that we should love one another. Not as Cain, who was of that wicked one, and slew his brother. And wherefore slew he him? Because his own works were evil, and his brother's righteous.

Marvel not, my brethren, if the world hate you.

We know that we have passed from death unto life, because we love the brethren. He that loveth not his brother, abideth in death. Whosoever hateth his brother, is a murderer: and ye know that no murderer hath eternal life abiding in him. Hereby perceive we the love of God, because he laid down his life for us: and we ought to lay down our lives for the brethren.

But whoso hath this world's good, and seeth his brother have need, and shutteth up his bowels of compassion from him, how dwelleth the love of God in him? My little children, let us not love in word neither in tongue, but in deed and in truth.

Beloved, believe not every spirit, but try the spirits whether they are of God; because many false prophets are gone out into the world. Hereby know ye the Spirit of God: every spirit that confesseth that Jesus Christ is come in the flesh, is of God: and every spirit that confesseth not that Jesus Christ is come in the flesh, is not of God. And this is that spirit of antichrist, whereof ye have heard that it should come; and even now already is it in the world.

Ye are of God, little children, and have overcome them: because greater is he that is in you, than he that is in the world. They are of the world: therefore speak they of the world, and the world heareth them. We are of God. He that knoweth God, heareth us; he that is not of God, heareth not us. Hereby know we the spirit of truth, and the spirit of error.

Beloved, let us love one another: for love is of God; and every one that loveth is born of God, and knoweth God. He that loveth not, knoweth not God; for God is love. In this was manifested the love of God towards us, because that God sent his only begotten Son into the world, that we might live through him. Herein is love, not that we loved God, but that he loved us, and sent his Son to be the propitiation for our sins. Beloved, if God so loved us, we ought also to love one another. No man hath seen God at any time. If we love one another, God dwelleth in us, and his love is perfected in us.

Hereby know we that we dwell in him, and he in us, because he hath given us of his Spirit. And we have seen and do testify, that the Father sent the Son to be the Saviour of the world. Whosoever shall confess that Jesus is the Son of God, God dwelleth in him, and he in God.

And we have known and believed the love that God hath to us. God is love: and he that dwelleth in love, dwelleth in God, and God in him. Herein is our love made perfect, that we may have boldness in the day of judgment: because as he is, so are we in this world. There is no fear in love; but perfect love casteth out fear: because fear hath torment. He that feareth, is not made perfect in love. We love him, because he first loved us.

If a man say, I love God, and hateth his brother, he is a liar. For he that loveth not his brother whom he hath seen, how can he love God, whom he hath not seen? And this commandment have we from him, That he who loveth God, love his brother also.

These things have I written unto you that believe on the name of the Son of God; that ye may know that ye have eternal life, and that ye may believe on the name of the Son of God.

And this is the confidence that we have in him, that if we ask anything according to his will, he heareth us: and if we know that he hear us, whatsoever we ask, we know that we have the petitions that we desired of him.

If any man see his brother sin a sin which is not unto death, he shall ask, and he shall give him life for them that sin not unto death. There is a sin unto death: I do not say that he shall pray for it. All unrighteousness is sin: and there is a sin not unto death.

We know that whosoever is born of God, sinneth not; but he that is begotten of God, keepeth himself, and that wicked one toucheth him not. And we know that we are of God, and the whole world lieth in wickedness.

And we know that the Son of God is come, and hath given us an understanding, that we may know him that is true; and we are in him that is true, even in his Son Jesus Christ. This is the true God, and eternal life.

Little children, keep yourselves from idols. Amen.

The Apocalypse

The Revelation of St. John the Divine

I

I John, who also am your brother, and companion in tribulation, and in the kingdom and patience of Jesus Christ, was in the isle that is called Patmos, for the word of God, and for the testimony of Jesus Christ. I was in the Spirit on the Lord's day, and heard behind me a great voice, as of a trumpet, say, I am Alpha and Omega, the first and the last: and, What thou seest write in a book, and send it unto the seven churches which are in Asia; unto Ephesus, and unto Smyrna, and unto Pergamos, and unto Thyatira, and unto Sardis, and unto Philadelphia, and unto Laodicea.

And I turned to see the voice that spake with me. And being turned, I saw seven golden candlesticks; and in the midst of the seven candlesticks one like unto the Son of man, clothed with a garment down to the foot, and girt about the paps with a golden girdle. His head and his hairs were white like wool, as white as snow; and his eyes were as a flame of fire; and his feet like unto fine brass, as if they burned in a furnace; and his voice as the sound of many waters. And he had in his right hand seven stars: and out of his mouth went a sharp two-edged sword: and his countenance was as the sun shineth in his strength.

And when I saw him, I fell at his feet as dead. And he laid his right hand upon me, saying unto me, Fear not; I am the first and the last: I am he that liveth, and was dead; and behold, I am alive for evermore, Amen; and have the keys of hell and of death. Write the things which thou hast seen, and the things which are, and the things which shall be hereafter; the mystery of the seven stars which thou sawest in my right hand, and the seven golden candlesticks. The seven stars are the angels of the seven churches: and the seven candlesticks which thou sawest are the seven churches.

II

After this I looked, and behold, a door was opened in heaven: and the first voice which I heard, was as it were of a trumpet talking with me; which said, Come up hither, and I will shew thee things which must be hereafter.

And immediately I was in the Spirit: and behold, a throne was set in heaven, and one sat on the throne. And he that sat was to look upon like a jasper and a sardine stone: and there was a rainbow round about the throne in sight like unto an emerald.

And round about the throne were four and twenty seats; and upon the seats I saw four and twenty elders sitting, clothed in white raiment; and they had on their heads crowns of gold. And out of the throne proceeded lightnings, and thunderings, and voices. And there were seven lamps of fire burning before the throne, which are the seven Spirits of God. And before the throne there was a sea of glass like unto crystal: and in the midst of the throne, and round about the throne, were four beasts full of eyes before and behind.

And the first beast was like a lion, and the second beast like a calf, and the third beast had a face as a man, and the fourth beast was like a flying eagle. And the four beasts had each of them six wings about him; and they were full of eyes within: and they rest not day and night, saying, Holy, holy, holy, Lord God Almighty, which was, and is, and is to come.

And when those beasts give glory, and honour, and thanks to him that sat on the throne, who liveth for ever and ever, the four and twenty elders fall down before him that sat on the throne, and worship him that liveth for ever and ever, and cast their crowns before the throne, saying, Thou art worthy, O Lord, to receive glory, and honour, and power: for thou hast created all things, and for thy pleasure they are and were created.

III

And I saw in the right hand of him that sat on the throne a book written within and on the backside, sealed with seven seals. And I saw a strong angel proclaiming with a loud voice, Who is worthy to open the book, and to loose the seals thereof? And no man in heaven, nor in earth, neither under the earth, was able to open the book, neither to look thereon. And I wept much, because no man was found worthy to open, and to read the book, neither to look thereon.

And one of the elders saith unto me, Weep not: behold, the Lion of the tribe of Juda, the Root of David, hath prevailed to open the book, and to loose the seven seals thereof. And I beheld, and lo, in the midst of the throne, and of the four beasts, and in the midst of the elders, stood a Lamb as it had been slain, having seven horns, and seven eyes, which are the seven Spirits of God sent forth into all the earth. And he came and took the book out of the right hand of him that sat upon the throne.

And when he had taken the book, the four beasts, and four and twenty elders fell down before the Lamb, having every one of them harps, and golden vials full of odours, which are the prayers of saints. And they sung a new song, saying, Thou art worthy to take the book, and to open the seals thereof; for thou wast slain, and hast redeemed us to God by thy blood out of every kindred, and tongue, and people, and nation; and hast made us unto our God kings and priests: and we shall reign on the earth.

And I beheld, and I heard the voice of many angels round about the throne, and the beasts, and the elders: and the number of them was ten thousand times ten thousand, and thousands of thousands; saying with a loud voice, Worthy is the Lamb that was slain to receive power, and riches, and wisdom, and strength, and honour, and glory, and blessing.

And every creature which is in heaven, and on the earth, and under the earth, and such as are in the sea, and all that are in them, heard I saying, Blessing, and honour, and glory, and power, be unto him that sitteth upon the throne, and unto the Lamb, for ever and ever.

And the four beasts said, Amen. And the four and twenty elders fell down and worshipped him that liveth for ever and ever.

IV

And I saw when the Lamb opened one of the seals, and I heard, as it were the noise of thunder, one of the four beasts, saying, Come and see. And I saw, and behold, a white horse: and he that sat on him had a bow; and a crown was given unto him: and he went forth conquering, and to conquer.

And when he had opened the second seal, I heard the second beast say, Come and see. And there went out another horse that was red: and power was given to him that sat thereon to take peace from the earth, and that they should kill one another: and there was given unto him a great sword.

And when he had opened the third seal, I heard the third beast say, Come and see. And I beheld, and lo, a black horse; and he that sat on him had a pair of balances in his hand. And I heard a voice in the midst of the four beasts say, A measure of wheat for a penny, and three measures of barley for a penny; and see thou hurt not the oil and the wine.

And when he had opened the fourth seal, I heard the voice of the fourth beast say, Come and see. And I looked, and behold, a pale horse: and his name that sat on him was Death, and hell followed with him. And power was given unto them over the fourth part of the earth, to kill with sword, and with hunger, and with death, and with the beasts of the earth.

And when he had opened the fifth seal, I saw under the altar the souls of them that were slain for the word of God, and for the testimony which they held: and they cried with a loud voice, saying, How long, O Lord, holy and true, dost thou not judge and avenge our blood on them that dwell on the earth? And white robes were given unto every one of them; and it was said unto them, that they should rest yet for a little season, until their fellow-servants also and their brethren, that should be killed as they were, should be fulfilled.

And I beheld when he had opened the sixth seal, and lo, there was a great earthquake; and the sun became black as sackcloth of hair, and the moon became as blood: and the stars of heaven fell unto the earth, even as a fig-tree casteth her untimely figs, when she is shaken of a mighty wind. And the heaven departed as a scroll when it is rolled together; and every mountain and island were moved out of their places. And the kings of the earth, and the great men, and the rich men, and the chief captains, and the mighty men, and every bond-man, and every free-man, hid themselves in the dens and in the rocks of the mountains; and said to the mountains and rocks, Fall on us, and hide us from the face of him that sitteth on the throne, and from the wrath of the Lamb: for the great day of his wrath is come; and who shall be able to stand?

V

And when he had opened the seventh seal, there was silence in heaven about the space of half an hour.

And I saw the seven angels which stood before God; and to them were given seven trumpets. And another angel came and stood at the altar, having a golden censer; and there was given unto him much incense, that he should offer it with the prayers of all saints upon the golden altar which was before the throne. And the smoke of the incense, which came with the prayers of the saints, ascended up before God out of the angel's hand. And the angel took the censer, and filled it with fire of the altar, and cast it into the earth: and there were voices, and thunderings, and lightnings, and an earthquake. And the seven angels which had the seven trumpets prepared themselves to sound.

The first angel sounded and there followed hail and fire mingled with blood, and they were cast upon the earth: and the third part of trees was burnt up, and all green grass was burnt up.

And the second angel sounded, and as it were a great mountain burning with fire was cast into the sea: and the third part of the sea became blood; and the third part of the creatures which were in the sea, and had life, died; and the third part of the ships were destroyed.

And the third angel sounded, and there fell a great star from heaven, burning as it were a lamp, and it fell upon the third part of the rivers, and upon the fountains of waters; and the name of the star is called Wormwood: and the third part of the waters became wormwood; and many men died of the waters, because they were made bitter.

And the fourth angel sounded, and the third part of the sun was smitten, and the third part of the moon, and the third part of the stars; so as the third part of them was darkened, and the day shone not for a third part of it, and the night likewise. And I beheld, and heard an angel flying through the midst of heaven, saying with a loud voice, Woe, woe, woe, to the inhabiters of the earth, by reason of the other voices of the trumpet of the three angels, which are yet to sound!

And the fifth angel sounded, and I saw a star fall from heaven unto the earth: and to him was given the key of the bottomless pit.

And he opened the bottomless pit; and there arose a smoke out of the pit, as the smoke of a great furnace; and the sun and the air were darkened by reason of the smoke of the pit. And there came out of the smoke locusts upon the earth: and unto them was given power, as the scorpions of the earth have power.

And it was commanded them that they should not hurt the grass of the earth, neither any green thing, neither any tree; but only those men which have not the seal of God in their foreheads. And to them it was given that they should not kill them, but that they should be tormented five months: and their torment was as the torment of a scorpion, when he striketh a man. And in those days shall men seek death, and shall not find it; and shall desire to die, and death shall flee from them.

And the shapes of the locusts were like unto horses prepared unto battle; and on their heads were as it were crowns like gold, and their faces were as the faces of men. And they had hair as the hair of women, and their teeth were as the teeth of lions. And they had breast-plates, as it were breast-plates of iron; and the sound of their wings was as the sound of chariots of many horses running to battle. And they had tails like unto scorpions, and there were stings in their tails: and their power was to hurt men five months.

And they had a king over them, which is the angel of the bottomless pit, whose name in the Hebrew tongue is Abaddon, but in the Greek tongue hath his name Apollyon.

And the sixth angel sounded, and I heard a voice from the four horns of the golden altar which is before God, saying to the sixth angel which had the trumpet, Loose the four angels which are bound in the great river Euphrates. And the four angels were loosed, which were prepared for an hour, and a day, and a month, and a year, for to slay the third part of men.

And the number of the army of the horsemen were two hundred

thousand thousand: and I heard the number of them. And thus I saw the horses in the vision, and them that sat on them, having breast-plates of fire, and of jacinth, and brimstone: and the heads of the horses were as the heads of lions; and out of their mouths issued fire, and smoke, and brimstone.

By these three was the third part of men killed, by the fire, and by the smoke, and by the brimstone, which issued out of their mouths. For their power is in their mouth, and in their tails: for their tails were like unto serpents, and had heads, and with them they do hurt.

And I saw another mighty angel come down from heaven, clothed with a cloud: and a rainbow was upon his head, and his face was as it were the sun, and his feet as pillars of fire: and he had in his hand a little book open: and he set his right foot upon the sea, and his left foot on the earth, and cried with a loud voice, as when a lion roareth: and when he had cried, seven thunders uttered their voices.

And when the seven thunders had uttered their voices, I was about to write: and I heard a voice from heaven saying unto me, Seal up those things which the seven thunders uttered, and write them not.

And the angel which I saw stand upon the sea and upon the earth, lifted up his hand to heaven, and sware by him that liveth for ever and ever, who created heaven, and the things that therein are, and the earth, and the things that therein are, and the sea, and the things which are therein, that there should be time no longer: but in the days of the voice of the seventh angel, when he shall begin to sound, the mystery of God should be finished, as he hath declared to his servants the prophets.

And the voice which I heard from heaven spake unto me again, and said, Go, and take the little book which is open in the hand of the angel which standeth upon the sea and upon the earth. And I went unto the angel, and said unto him, Give me the little book. And he said unto me, Take it, and eat it up; and it shall make thy belly bitter, but it shall be in thy mouth sweet as honey. And I took the little book out of the angel's hand, and ate it up; and it was in my mouth sweet as honey: and as soon as I had eaten it my belly was bitter. And he said unto me, Thou must prophesy again before many peoples, and nations, and tongues, and kings.

And the seventh angel sounded; and there were great voices in heaven, saying, The kingdoms of this world are become the kingdoms of our Lord, and of his Christ; and he shall reign for ever and ever.

VI

And I looked, and lo, a Lamb stood on the mount Sion, and with him an hundred forty and four thousand, having his Father's name written in their foreheads. And I heard a voice from heaven, as the voice of many waters, and as the voice of a great thunder: and I heard the voice of harpers harping with their harps: and they sung as it were a new song before the throne, and before the four beasts, and the elders: and no man could learn that song but the hundred and forty and four thousand, which were redeemed from the earth.

And I saw another angel fly in the midst of heaven, having the everlasting gospel to preach unto them that dwell on the earth, and to every nation, and kindred, and tongue, and people, saying with a loud voice, Fear God, and give glory to him; for the hour of his judgment is come: and worship him that made heaven, and earth, and the sea, and the fountains of waters.

And there followed another angel, saying, Babylon is fallen, is fallen, that great city, because she made all nations drink of the wine of the wrath of her fornication.

And the third angel followed them, saying with a loud voice, If any man worship the beast and his image, and receive his mark in his forehead, or in his hand, the same shall drink of the wine of the wrath of God, which is poured out without mixture into the cup of his indignation; and he shall be tormented with fire and brimstone in the presence of the holy angels, and in the presence of the Lamb: and the smoke of their torment ascendeth up for ever and ever: and they have no rest day nor night, who worship the beast and his image, and whosoever receiveth the mark of his name.

Here is the patience of the saints: here are they that keep the commandments of God, and the faith of Jesus.

And I heard a voice from heaven, saying unto me, Write, Blessed are the dead which die in the Lord from henceforth: Yea, saith the Spirit, that they may rest from their labours; and their works do follow them. And I looked, and behold, a white cloud, and upon the cloud one sat like unto the Son of man, having on his head a golden crown, and in his hand a sharp sickle.

And another angel came out of the temple, crying with a loud voice to him that sat on the cloud, Thrust in thy sickle, and reap: for the time is come for thee to reap; for the harvest of the earth is ripe.

And he that sat on the cloud thrust in his sickle on the earth; and the earth was reaped.

And another angel came out of the temple which is in heaven, he also having a sharp sickle.

And another angel came out from the altar, which had power over fire; and cried with a loud cry to him that had the sharp sickle, saying, Thrust in thy sharp sickle, and gather the clusters of the vine of the earth; for her grapes are fully ripe. And the angel thrust in his sickle into the earth, and gathered the vine of the earth, and cast it into the great wine-press of the wrath of God.

And the wine-press was trodden without the city, and blood came out of the wine-press, even unto the horse-bridles, by the space of a thousand and six hundred furlongs.

VII

And I heard as it were the voice of a great multitude, and as the voice of many waters, and as the voice of mighty thunderings, saying, Alleluia: for the Lord God omnipotent reigneth. Let us be glad and rejoice, and given honour to him: for the marriage of the Lamb is come, and his wife hath made herself ready. And to her was granted that she should be arrayed in fine linen, clean and white: for the fine linen is the righteousness of saints.

And he saith unto me, Write, Blessed are they which are called unto the marriage-supper of the Lamb. And he saith unto me, These are the true sayings of God. And I fell at his feet to worship him. And he said unto me, See thou do it not: I am thy fellow-servant, and of thy brethren that have the testimony of Jesus: worship God: for the testimony of Jesus is the spirit of prophecy.

And I saw heaven opened, and behold, a white horse; and he that sat upon him was called Faithful and True, and in righteousness he doth judge and make war. His eyes were as a flame of fire, and on his head were many crowns; and he had a name written, that no man knew, but he himself. And he was clothed with a vesture dipped in blood: and his name is called The Word of God. And the armies which were in heaven followed him upon white horses, clothed in fine linen, white and clean.

And out of his mouth goeth a sharp sword, that with it he should smite the nations: and he shall rule them with a rod of iron: and he treadeth the wine-press of the fierceness and wrath of Almighty God. And he hath on his vesture and on his thigh a name written, KING OF KINGS, AND LORD OF LORDS.

And I saw an angel standing in the sun; and he cried with a loud voice, saying to all the fowls that fly in the midst of heaven, Come, and gather yourselves together unto the supper of the great God; that ye may eat the flesh of kings, and the flesh of captains, and the flesh of mighty men, and the flesh of horses, and of them that sit on them, and the flesh of all men, both free and bond, both small and great.

And I saw the beast, and the kings of the earth, and their armies, gathered together to make war against him that sat on the horse, and against his army.

And the beast was taken, and with him the false prophet that wrought miracles before him, with which he deceived them that had received the mark of the beast, and them that worshipped his image. These both were cast alive into a lake of fire burning with brimstone. And the remnant were slain with the sword of him that sat upon the horse, which sword proceeded out of his mouth: and all the fowls were filled with their flesh.

VIII

And I saw an angel come down from heaven, having the key of the bottomless pit and a great chain in his hand. And he laid hold on the dragon, that old serpent, which is the Devil, and Satan, and bound him a thousand years, and cast him into the bottomless pit, and shut him up, and set a seal upon him, that he should deceive the nations no more, till the thousand years should be fulfilled; and after that he must be loosed a little season.

And I saw thrones, and they sat upon them, and judgment was given unto them: and I saw the souls of them that were beheaded for the witness of Jesus, and for the word of God, and which had not worshipped the beast, neither his image, neither had received his mark upon their foreheads, or in their hands; and they lived and reigned with Christ a thousand years. But the rest of the dead lived not again until the thousand years were finished.

This is the first resurrection. Blessed and holy is he that hath part in the first resurrection: on such the second death hath no power, but they shall be priests of God and of Christ, and shall reign with him a thousand years.

And when the thousand years are expired, Satan shall be loosed out of his prison, and shall go out to deceive the nations which are in the four quarters of the earth, Gog and Magog, to gather them together to battle: the number of whom is as the sand of the sea.

And they went up on the breadth of the earth, and compassed the camp of the saints about, and the beloved city: and fire came down from God out of heaven, and devoured them. And the devil that deceived them was cast into the lake of fire and brimstone, where the beast and the false prophet are, and shall be tormented day and night for ever and ever.

And I saw a great white throne, and him that sat on it, from whose face the earth and the heaven fled away; and there was found no place for them.

And I saw the dead, small and great, stand before God; and the books were opened, which is the book of life: and the dead were judged out of those things which were written in the books, according to their works.

And the sea gave up the dead which were in it; and death and hell delivered up the dead which were in them: and they were judged every man according to their works. And death and hell were cast into the lake of fire. This is the second death.

And whosoever was not found written in the book of life was cast into the lake of fire.

IX

And I saw a new heaven and a new earth: for the first heaven and the first earth were passed away; and there was no more sea.

And I John saw the holy city, new Jerusalem, coming down from God out of heaven, prepared as a bride adorned for her husband. And I heard a great voice out of heaven, saying, Behold, the tabernacle of God is with men, and he will dwell with them, and they shall be his people, and God himself shall be with them, and be their God. And God shall wipe away all tears from their eyes; and there shall be no more death, neither sorrow, nor crying, neither shall there be any more pain: for the former things are passed away.

And he that sat upon the throne said, Behold, I make all things new. And he said unto me, Write: for these words are true and faithful. And he said unto me, It is done. I am Alpha and Omega, the beginning and the end. I will give unto him that is athirst of the fountain of the water of life freely. He that overcometh shall inherit all things; and I will be his God, and he shall be my son.

But the fearful, and unbelieving, and the abominable, and murderers, and whoremongers, and sorcerers, and idolaters, and all liars, shall have their part in the lake which burneth with fire and brimstone: which is the second death.

And there came unto me one of the seven angels, which had the seven vials full of the seven last plagues, and talked with me, saying, Come hither, I will shew thee the bride, the Lamb's wife. And he carried me away in the spirit to a great and high mountain, and shewed me that great city, the holy Jerusalem, descending out of heaven from God, having the glory of God: and her light was like unto a stone most precious, even like a jasper stone, clear as crystal; and had a wall great and high, and had twelve gates, and at the gates twelve angels, and names written thereon, which are the names of the twelve tribes of the children of Israel. On the east, three gates; on the north, three gates; on the south, three gates; and on the west, three gates. And the wall of the city had twelve foundations, and in them the names of the twelve apostles of the Lamb.

And he that talked with me, had a golden reed to measure the city, and the gates thereof, and the wall thereof. And the city lieth foursquare, and the length is as large as the breadth: and he measured the city with the reed, twelve thousand furlongs. The length, and the breadth, and the height of it are equal. And he measured the wall thereof, an hundred and forty and four cubits according to the measure of a man, that is, of the angel.

And the building of the wall of it was of jasper: and the city was pure gold, like unto clear glass. And the foundations of the wall of the city were garnished with all manner of precious stones. The first foundation was jasper; the second, sapphire; the third, a chalcedony; the fourth, an emerald; the fifth, sardonyx; the sixth, sardius; the seventh, chrysolite; the eighth, beryl; the ninth, a topaz; the tenth, a chrysoprasus; the eleventh, a jacinth; the twelfth, an amethyst. And the twelve gates were twelve pearls, every several gate was of one pearl; and the street of the city was pure gold, as it were transparent glass.

And I saw no temple therein: for the Lord God Almighty and the Lamb are the temple of it. And the city had no need of the sun, neither of the moon, to shine in it: for the glory of God did lighten it, and the Lamb is the light thereof.

And the nations of them which are saved shall walk in the light of it: and the kings of the earth do bring their glory and honour into it. And the gates of it shall not be shut at all by day: for there shall be no night there. And they shall bring the glory and honour of the nations into it. And there shall in no wise enter into it any thing that defileth, neither whatsoever worketh abomination, or maketh a lie; but they which are written in the Lamb's book of life.

And he shewed me a pure river of water of life, clear as crystal, proceeding out of the throne of God and of the Lamb. In the midst of the street of it, and on either side of the river, was there the tree of life, which bare twelve manner of fruits, and yielded her fruit every month: and the leaves of the tree were for the healing of the nations.

And there shall be no more curse: but the throne of God and of the Lamb shall be in it; and his servants shall serve him: and they shall see his face; and his name shall be in their foreheads. And there shall be no night there; and they need no candle, neither light of the sun; for the Lord God giveth them light: and they shall reign for ever and ever.

And he said unto me, These sayings are faithful and true. And the Lord God of the holy prophets sent his angel to shew unto his servants the things which must shortly be done. Behold, I come quickly: blessed is he that keepeth the sayings of the prophecy of this book.

And I John saw these things, and heard them. And when I had heard and seen, I fell down to worship before the feet of the angel which shewed me these things. Then saith he unto me, See thou do it not: for I am thy fellow-servant, and of thy brethren the prophets, and of them which keep the sayings of this book: worship God.

And he saith unto me, Seal not the sayings of the prophecy of this book: for the time is at hand. He that is unjust, let him be unjust still: and he which is filthy, let him be filthy still: and he that is righteous, let him be righteous still: and he that is holy, let him be holy still. And behold, I come quickly; and my reward is with me, to give every man according as his work shall be. I am Alpha and Omega, the beginning and the end, the first and the last. Blessed are they that do his commandments, that they may have right to the tree of life, and may enter in through the gates into the city. For without are dogs, and sorcerers, and whoremongers, and murderers, and idolaters, and whosoever loveth and maketh a lie.

I Jesus have sent mine angel to testify unto you these things in the churches. I am the root and the offspring of David, and the bright and morning-star.

And the Spirit and the bride say, Come. And let him that heareth say, Come. And let him that is athirst come. And whosoever will, let him take the water of life freely.

For I testify unto every man that heareth the words of the prophecy of this book, If any man shall add unto these things, God shall add unto him the plagues that are written in this book: and if any man shall take away from the words of the book of this prophecy, God shall take away his part out of the book of life, and out of the holy city, and from the things which are written in this book.

He which testifieth these things saith, Surely I come quickly: Amen. Even so, come, Lord Jesus.

The grace of our Lord Jesus Christ be with you all. Amen.

THE APOCRYPHAL
NEW TESTAMENT

The Birth of Mary

In the histories of the twelve tribes of Israel it is written that there was one Ioacim, exceeding rich: and he offered his gifts twofold, saying: That which is of my superfluity shall be for the whole people, and that which is for my forgiveness shall be for the Lord, for a propitiation unto me.

Now the great day of the Lord drew nigh and the children of Israel offered their gifts. And Reuben stood over against him saying: It is not lawful for thee to offer thy gifts first, forasmuch as thou hast gotten no seed in Israel. And Ioacim was sore grieved, and went unto the record of the twelve tribes of the people, saying: I will look upon the record of the twelve tribes of Israel, whether I only have not gotten seed in Israel. And he searched, and found concerning all the righteous that they had raised up seed in Israel. And he remembered the patriarch Abraham, how in the last days God gave him a son, even Isaac. And Ioacim was sore grieved, and showed not himself to his wife, but betook himself into the wilderness, and pitched his tent there, and fasted forty days and forty nights, saying within himself: I will not go down either for meat or for drink until the Lord my God visit me, and my prayer shall be unto me meat and drink.

And his wife Anna was sore grieved and mourned with a great mourning because she was reproached by all the tribes of Israel. And coming to herself she said: What shall I do? I will pray with weeping unto the Lord my God that he visit me. And she put off her mourning garments and cleansed and adorned her head and put on her bridal garments: and about the ninth hour she went down into the garden to walk there. And she saw a laurel-tree and sat down underneath it and besought the Lord saying: O God of our fathers, bless me, and hearken unto my prayer, as thou didst bless the womb of Sarah, and gavest her a son, even Isaac.

And looking up to the heaven she espied a nest of sparrows in the laurel-tree, and made a lamentation within herself, saying: Woe unto me, who begat me? And what womb brought me forth, for I am become a curse before the children of Israel, and I am reproached, and they have mocked me forth out of the temple of the Lord? Woe unto me, unto what am I likened? I am not likened unto the fowls of the heaven, for even the fowls of the heaven are fruitful before thee, O Lord. Woe unto me; unto what am I likened? I am not likened unto the beasts of the earth, for even the beasts of the earth are fruitful before thee, O Lord. Woe unto me, unto what am I likened? I am not likened unto these waters, for even these waters are fruitful before thee, O Lord. Woe unto me, unto what am I likened? I am not likened unto this earth, for even this earth bringeth forth her fruits in due season and blesseth thee, O Lord.

And behold an angel of the Lord appeared, saying unto her: Anna, Anna, the Lord hath hearkened unto thy prayer, and thou shalt conceive and bear, and thy seed shall be spoken of in the whole world. And Anna said: As the Lord my God liveth, if I bring forth either male or female, I will bring it for a gift unto the Lord my God, and it shall be ministering unto him all the days of its life.

And behold there came two messengers saying unto her: Behold Ioacim thy husband cometh with his flocks: for an angel of the Lord came down unto him saying: Ioacim, Ioacim, the Lord God hath hearkened unto thy prayer. Get thee down hence, for behold thy wife Anna shall conceive.

And behold Ioacim came with his flocks, and Anna stood at the gate and saw Ioacim coming, and ran and hung upon his neck, saying: Now know I that the Lord God hath greatly blessed me: for behold the widow is no more a widow, and she that was childless shall conceive. And Ioacim rested the first day in his house.

And her months were fulfilled, and in the ninth month Anna brought forth. And she said unto the midwife: What have I brought forth? And she said: A female. And Anna said: My soul is magnified this day; and she laid herself down. And when the days were fulfilled, Anna purified herself and gave suck to the child and called her name Mary.

The Childhood of Mary

And day by day the child waxed strong, and when she was six months old her mother stood her upon the ground to try if she would stand; and she walked seven steps and returned unto her bosom. And she caught her up, saying: As the Lord my God liveth, thou shalt walk no more upon this ground, until I bring thee into the temple of the Lord. And she made a sanctuary in her bedchamber and suffered nothing common or unclean to pass through it. And she called for the daughters of the Hebrews that were undefiled, and they carried her hither and thither.

And the first year of the child was fulfilled, and Ioacim made a great feast and bade the priests and the scribes and the assembly of the elders and the whole people of Israel. And Ioacim brought the child to the priests, and they blessed her, saying: O God of our fathers, bless this child and give her a name renowned for ever among all generations. And all the people said: So be it, so be it. Amen. And he brought her to the high priests, and they blessed her, saying: O God of the high places, look upon this child, and bless her with the last blessing which hath no successor.

And unto the child her months were added: and the child became two years old. And Ioacim said: Let us bring her up to the temple of the Lord that we may pay the promise which we promised; lest the Lord require it of us and our gift become unacceptable. And Anna said: Let us wait until the third year, that the child may not long after her father or mother. And Ioacim said: Let us wait.

And the child became three years old, and Ioacim said: Call for the daughters of the Hebrews that are undefiled, and let them take every one a lamp, and let them be burning, that the child turn not backward and her heart be taken captive away from the temple of the Lord. And they did so until they were gone up into the temple of the Lord.

And her parents gat them down marvelling, and praising the Lord God because the child was not turned away backward.

And Mary was in the temple of the Lord as a dove that is nurtured: and she received food from the hand of an angel.

And when she was twelve years old, there was a council of the priests, saying: Behold Mary is become twelve years old in the temple of the

Lord. What then shall we do with her? lest she pollute the sanctuary of the Lord. And they said unto the high priest: Thou standest over the altar of the Lord. Enter in and pray concerning her: and whatsoever the Lord shall reveal to thee, that let us do.

And the high priest took the vestment with the twelve bells and went in unto the Holy of Holies and prayed concerning her. And lo, an angel of the Lord appeared saying unto him: Zacharias, Zacharias, go forth and assemble them that are widowers of the people, and let them bring every man a rod, and to whomsoever the Lord shall show a sign, his wife shall she be. And the heralds went forth over all the country round about Judaea, and the trumpet of the Lord sounded, and all men ran thereto.

And Joseph cast down his adze and ran to meet them, and when they were gathered together they went to the high priest and took their rods with them. And he took the rods of them all and went into the temple and prayed. And when he had finished the prayer he took the rods and went forth and gave them back to them: and there was no sign upon them. But Joseph received the last rod: and lo, a dove came forth of the rod and flew upon the head of Joseph. And the priest said unto Joseph: Unto thee hath it fallen to take the virgin of the Lord and keep her for thyself. And Joseph refused, saying: I have sons, and I am an old man, she is but a girl: lest I become a laughing-stock to the children of Israel. And the priest said unto Joseph: Fear the Lord thy God, and remember what things God did unto Dathan and Abiram and Korah, how the earth clave and they were swallowed up because of their gainsaying. And now fear thou, Joseph, lest it be so in thine house. And Joseph was afraid, and took her to keep her for himself. And Joseph said unto Mary: Lo, I have received thee out of the temple of the Lord: and now do I leave thee in my house, and I go away to build my buildings and I will come again unto thee. The Lord shall watch over thee.

Now there was a council of the priests, and they said: Let us make a veil for the temple of the Lord. And the priest said: Call unto me pure virgins of the tribe of David. And the officers departed and sought and found seven virgins. And the priests called to mind the child Mary, that she was of the tribe of David and was undefiled before God: and the officers went and fetched her. And they brought them into the temple of the Lord, and the priest said: Cast me lots, which of you shall weave the gold and the undefiled white and the fine linen and the silk and the hyacinthine, and the scarlet and the true purple. And the lot of the true purple and the scarlet fell unto Mary, and she took them and went unto her house.

And at that season Zacharias became dumb, and Samuel was in his stead until the time when Zacharias spake again.

But Mary took the scarlet and began to spin it.

The Conception of Jesus

And she took the pitcher and went forth to fill it with water: and lo a voice saying: Hail, thou that art highly favoured; the Lord is with thee: blessed art thou among women.

And she looked about her upon the right hand and upon the left, to see whence this voice should be: and being filled with trembling she went to her house and set down the pitcher, and took the purple and sat down upon her seat and drew out the thread.

And behold an angel of the Lord stood before her saying: Fear not, Mary, for thou hast found grace before the Lord of all things, and thou shalt conceive of his word. And she, when she heard it, questioned in herself, saying: Shall I verily conceive of the living God, and bring forth after the manner of all women? And the angel of the Lord said: Not so, Mary, for a power of the Lord shall overshadow thee: wherefore also that holy thing which shall be born of thee shall be called the Son of the Highest. And thou shalt call his name Jesus: for he shall save his people from their sins. And Mary said: Behold the handmaid of the Lord is before him: be it unto me according to thy word.

And she made the purple and the scarlet and brought them unto the priest. And the priest blessed her and said: Mary, the Lord God hath magnified thy name, and thou shalt be blessed among all generations of the earth. And Mary rejoiced and went away unto Elizabeth her kins-woman: and she knocked at the door. And Elizabeth when she heard it cast down the scarlet and ran to the door and opened it, and when she saw Mary she blessed her and said: Whence is this to me that the mother of my Lord should come unto me? for behold that which is in me leaped and blessed thee. And Mary forgat the mysteries which Gabriel the archangel had told her, and she looked up unto the heaven and said: Who am I, Lord, that all the generations of the earth do bless me? And she abode three months with Elizabeth, and day by day her womb grew: and Mary was afraid and departed unto her house and hid herself from the children of Israel. Now she was sixteen years old when these mysteries came to pass.

Now it was the sixth month with her, and behold Joseph came from his building, and he entered into his house and found her great with child. And he smote his face, and cast himself down upon the ground on sackcloth and wept bitterly, saying: With what countenance shall I look unto the Lord my God? and what prayer shall I make concerning this maiden? for I received her out of the temple of the Lord my God a virgin, and have not kept her safe. Who is he that hath ensnared me? Who hath done this evil in mine house and hath defiled the virgin? Is not the story of Adam repeated in me? for as at the hour of his giving thanks the serpent came and found Eve alone and deceived her, so hath it befallen me also. And Joseph arose from off the sackcloth and called Mary and said unto her, O thou that wast cared for by God, why hast thou done this? thou hast forgotten the Lord thy God. Why hast thou humbled thy soul, thou that wast nourished up in the Holy of Holies and didst receive food at the hand of an angel? But she wept bitterly, saying: I am pure and I know not a man. And Joseph said unto her: Whence then is that which is in thy womb? and she said: As the Lord my God liveth, I know not whence it is come unto me.

And Joseph was sore afraid and ceased from speaking unto her, and pondered what he should do with her. And Joseph said: If I hide her sin, I shall be found fighting against the law of the Lord: and if I manifest her unto the children of Israel, I fear lest that which is in her be the seed of an angel, and I shall be found delivering up innocent blood to the judgment of death. What then shall I do? I will let her go from me privily. And the night came upon him. And behold an angel of the Lord appeared unto him in a dream, saying: Fear not this child, for that which is in her is of the Holy Ghost, and she shall bear a son and thou shalt call his name Jesus, for he shall save his people from their sins. And Joseph arose from sleep and glorified the God of Israel which had shown this favour unto her: and he watched over her.

Now Annas the scribe came unto him and said to him: Wherefore didst thou not appear in our assembly? and Joseph said unto him: I was weary with the journey, and I rested the first day. And Annas turned him about and saw Mary great with child. And he went hastily to the priest and said unto him: Joseph, of whom thou bearest witness that he is righteous, hath sinned grievously. And the priest said: Wherein? And he said: The virgin whom he received out of the temple of the Lord, he hath defiled her, and married her by stealth, and hath not declared it to the children of Israel. And the priest answered and said: Hath Joseph done this? And Annas the scribe said: Send officers, and thou shalt find the virgin great with child. And the officers went and found as he had said, and they brought her together with Joseph unto the place of judgment. And the priest said: Mary, wherefore hast thou done this, and wherefore hast thou humbled thy soul and forgotten the Lord thy God, thou that wast nurtured in the Holy of Holies and didst receive food at the hand of an angel and didst hear the hymns and didst dance before the Lord, wherefore hast thou done this?

But she wept bitterly, saying: As the Lord my God liveth I am pure before him and I know not a man. And the priest said unto Joseph: Wherefore hast thou done this? and Joseph said: As the Lord my God liveth I am pure as concerning her. And the priest said: Bear no false witness but speak the truth: thou hast married her by stealth and hast not declared it unto the children of Israel, and hast not bowed thine head under the mighty hand, that thy seed should be blessed. And Joseph held his peace.

And the priest said: Restore the virgin whom thou didst receive out of the temple of the Lord. And Joseph was full of weeping. And the priest said: I will give you to drink of the water of the conviction of the Lord, and it will make manifest your sins before your eyes. And the priest took thereof and made Joseph drink and sent him into the hill-country. And he returned whole. He made Mary also drink and sent her into the hill-country. And she returned whole. And all the people marvelled, because sin appeared not in them. And the priest said: If the Lord God hath not made your sin manifest, neither do I condemn you. And he let them go. And Joseph took Mary and departed unto his house rejoicing, and glorifying the God of Israel.

The Birth of Jesus

Now there went out a decree from Augustus the king that all that were in Bethlehem of Judaea should be recorded. And Joseph said: I will record my sons: but this child, what shall I do with her? how shall I record her? as my wife? nay, I am ashamed. Or as my daughter? but all the children of Israel know that she is not my daughter. This day of the Lord shall do as the Lord willeth. And he saddled the she-ass, and set her upon it, and his son led it, and Joseph followed after. And they drew near unto Bethlehem within three miles: and Joseph turned himself about and saw her of a sad countenance and said within himself: Peradventure that which is within her paineth her. And again Joseph turned himself about and saw her laughing, and said unto her: Mary, what aileth thee that I see thy face at one time laughing and at another time sad? And Mary said unto Joseph: It is because I behold two peoples with mine eyes, the one weeping and lamenting and the other rejoicing and exulting.

And they came to the midst of the way, and Mary said unto him: Take me down from the ass, for that which is within me presseth me, to come forth. And he took her down from the ass and said unto her: Whither shall I take thee to hide thy shame? for the place is desert.

And he found a cave there and brought her into it, and set his sons by her: and he went forth and sought for a midwife of the Hebrews in the country of Bethlehem.

And they stood in the place of the cave: and behold a bright cloud overshadowing the cave. And the midwife said: My soul is magnified this day, because mine eyes have seen marvellous things: for salvation is born unto Israel. And immediately the cloud withdrew itself out of the cave, and a great light appeared in the cave so that their eyes could not endure it. And by little and little that light withdrew itself until the young child appeared: and it went and took the breast of its mother Mary.

And the midwife cried aloud and said: Great unto me to-day is this day, in that I have seen this new sight. And the midwife went forth of the cave and Salome met her. And she said to her: Salome, Salome, a new sight have I to tell thee. A virgin hath brought forth, which her nature alloweth not. And Salome said: As the Lord my God liveth, if I make not trial and prove her nature I will not believe that a virgin hath brought forth.

And the midwife went in and said unto Mary: Order thyself, for there is no small contention arisen concerning thee. And Salome made trial and cried out and said: Woe unto mine iniquity and mine unbelief, because I have tempted the living God, and lo, my hand falleth away from me in fire. And she bowed her knees unto the Lord, saying: O God of my fathers, remember that I am the seed of Abraham and Isaac and Jacob: make me not a public example unto the children of Israel, but restore me unto the poor, for thou knowest, Lord, that in thy name did I perform my cures, and did receive my hire of thee. And lo, an angel of the Lord appeared, saying unto her: Salome, Salome, the Lord hath hearkened to thee: bring thine hand near unto the young child and take him up, and there shall be unto thee salvation and joy. And Salome came near and took him up, saying: I will do him worship, for a great king is born unto Israel. And behold immediately Salome was healed: and she went forth of the cave justified. And lo, a voice saying: Salome, Salome, tell none of the marvels which thou hast seen, until the child enter into Jerusalem.

And behold, Joseph made him ready to go forth into Judaea. And there came a great tumult in Bethlehem of Judaea; for there came wise men, saying: Where is he that is born king of the Jews? for we have seen his star in the east and are come to worship him. And when Herod heard it he was troubled and sent officers unto the wise men. And he sent for the high priests and examined them, saying: How is it written concerning the Christ, where he is born? They say unto him: In Bethlehem of Judaea: for so it is written. And he let them go. And he examined the wise men, saying unto them: What sign saw ye concerning the king that is born? And the wise men said: We saw a very great star shining among those stars and dimming them so that the stars appeared not: and thereby knew we that a king was born unto Israel, and we came to worship him. And Herod said: Go and seek for him, and if ye find him, tell me, that I also may come and worship him. And the wise men went forth. And lo, the star which they saw in the east went before them until they entered into the cave: and it stood over the head of the cave. And the wise men saw the young child with Mary his mother: and they brought out of their scrip gifts, gold and frankincense and myrrh. And being warned by the angel that they should not enter into Judaea, they went into their own country by another way.

But when Herod perceived that he was mocked by the wise men, he was wroth, and sent murderers, saying unto them: Slay the children from two years old and under. And when Mary heard that the children were being slain, she was afraid, and took the young child and wrapped him in swaddling clothes and laid him in an ox-manger.

Miracles of the Child Jesus

I, Thomas the Israelite, have thought it needful to make known unto all the brethren that are of the Gentiles the mighty works of childhood which our Lord Jesus Christ wrought when he was conversant in the body, and came unto the city of Nazareth in the fifth year of his age.

On a certain day when there had fallen a shower of rain he went forth of the house where his mother was and played upon the ground where the waters were running: and he made pools, and the waters flowed down, and the pools were filled with water. Then saith he: I will that ye become clean and wholesome waters. And straightway they did so. But a certain son of Annas the scribe passed by bearing a branch of willow, and he overthrew the pools with the branch, and the waters were poured out. And Jesus turned about and said unto him: O ungodly and disobedient one, what hurt have the pools done thee that thou hast emptied them? Thou shalt not finish thy course, and thou shalt be withered up even as the branch which thou hast in hand. And he went on, and after a little he fell and gave up the ghost. And when the young children that played with him saw it, they marvelled and departed and told the father of him that was dead. And he ran and found the child dead, and went and accused Joseph.

Now Jesus made of that clay twelve sparrows: and it was the sabbath day. And a child ran and told Joseph, saying: Behold, thy child playeth about the brook, and hath made sparrows of the clay, which is not lawful. And he when he heard it went and said to the child; Wherefore doest thou so and profaneth the sabbath? But Jesus answered him not, but looked upon the sparrows and said: Go ye, take your flight, and remember me in your life. And at the word they took flight and went up into the air. And when Joseph saw it he was astonished.

And after these things one day Jesus was playing with other boys upon the top of an house of two stories. And one child was pushed down by another and thrown down to the ground and died. And the boys which were playing with him, when they saw it, fled, and Jesus was left alone standing upon the roof whence the boy was thrown down. And when the parents of the boy that was dead heard of it they ran weeping, and when they found the boy lying dead upon the earth and Jesus standing alone, they supposed that the boy had been thrown down by him, and they looked upon him and reviled him. But Jesus, seeing that, leaped down straightway from the upper story and stood at the head of him that was dead and saith to him: Zeno, did I cast thee down? Arise and tell. For so the boy was called. And with the word the boy rose up and worshipped Jesus and said: Lord, thou didst not cast me down, but when I was dead thou didst make me alive.

And when he came to the eighth year of his age Joseph was required by a certain rich man to build him a bed, for he was a carpenter. And he went forth into the field to gather wood, and Jesus also went with him. And he cut two beams of wood and wrought them with the axe, and set one beside the other and measured and found it too short; and when he saw that he was vexed and sought to find another. But Jesus seeing it saith unto him: set these two together so that the ends of both be even. And Joseph, though he was perplexed concerning this, what the child should mean, did that which was commanded. And he saith again unto him: Take firm hold of the short beam. And Joseph took hold on it, marvelling. Then Jesus also took hold of the other end and pulled the other end thereof and made it also equal to the other beam, and saith unto Joseph: Be no more vexed, but do thy work without hindrance. And he when he saw it was exceedingly amazed, and said within himself: Blessed am I for that God hath given me such a son. And when they departed into the city Joseph told it to Mary, and she when she heard and saw the wonderful mighty works of her son rejoiced, glorifying him.

Worship of the Animals

They came to a cave and wished to rest there. Mary dismounted and sat with Jesus in her lap. There were three boys with Joseph and a girl with Mary. Suddenly a number of dragons came out of the cave, and all cried out in fear. Jesus got down from his mother's lap and stood before the dragons, which worshipped him. Thus was fulfilled the word, Praise the Lord out of the earth, ye dragons and all deeps. Jesus walked before them and bade them hurt no one. Mary was alarmed for him, but he said, Fear not, neither conceive that I am a child, for I always was and am a perfect man, and it is necessary that all the beasts of the forest should grow tame before me.

In like manner lions and leopards adored him and accompanied them, showed them the way, and bowed their heads to Jesus. At first Mary was afraid, but Jesus smiled on her and reassured her. The lions never injured their oxen and asses or the sheep they had brought from Judaea. Wolves, too, came and were harmless. Thus was fulfilled the word, The wolves shall feed with the lambs, the lion and ox shall eat straw together. They had with them two oxen and a cart to carry their necessaries.

There is a road from Jericho to Jordan, at the place where Israel crossed and the ark rested. Jesus, eight years old, went from Jericho to Jordan. On the way there was a vault where was a lioness with whelps. He went in and sat there, and the whelps played about him: the older lions stood at a distance and adored him, wagging their tails. The people who saw it said that he or his parents must have sinned or he would not have delivered himself to the lions. Then he came forth and the lions went before him, and the whelps played before his feet. His parents and the people looked on. Jesus said: How much better than you are the beasts which know me and are tame, while men know me not.

The Miracle of the Palm Tree

On the third day Mary saw a palm and wished to rest under it. When she was seated there she saw fruit on it, and said to Joseph that she should like to have some. Joseph said he was surprised she should say that because the tree was so high: he himself was thinking more about water, of which they had very little left. Jesus sitting in Mary's lap with a joyful countenance bade the palm give his mother of its fruit. The tree bent as low as her feet and she gathered what she would. He bade it rise again, and give them of the water concealed below its roots. A spring came forth and all rejoiced and drank of it.

The Trial of Jesus

In the fifteenth year of the governance of Tiberius Caesar, emperor of the Romans, and of Herod, king of Galilee, in the nineteenth year of his rule, on the eighth of the Kalends of April, which is the 25th of March, in the consulate of Rufus and Rubellio, in the fourth year of the two hundred and second Olympiad, Joseph who is Caiaphas being high priest of the Jews: these be the things which, after the cross and passion of the Lord, Nicodemus recorded and delivered unto the high priest and the rest of the Jews: and the same Nicodemus set them forth in Hebrew.

For the chief priests and scribes assembled in council, even Annas and Caiaphas and Somne and Dothaim and Gamaliel, Judas, Levi and Nepthalim, Alexander and Jairus and the rest of the Jews, and came unto Pilate accusing Jesus for many deeds, saying: We know this man, that he is the son of Joseph the carpenter, begotten of Mary, and he saith that he is the Son of God and a king; moreover he doth pollute the sabbaths and he would destroy the law of our fathers.

Pilate saith: And what things are they that he doeth, and would destroy the law?

The Jews say: We have a law that we should not heal any man on the sabbath: but this man of his evil deeds hath healed the lame and the bent, the withered and the blind and the paralytic, the dumb and them that were possessed, on the sabbath day!

Pilate saith unto them: By what evil deeds?

They say unto him: He is a sorcerer, and by Beelzebub the prince of the devils he casteth out devils, and they are all subject unto him.

Pilate saith unto them: This is not to cast out devils by an unclean spirit, but by the god Asclepius.

The Jews say unto Pilate: We beseech thy majesty that he appear before thy judgment-seat and be heard. And Pilate called them unto him and said: Tell me, how can I that am a governor examine a king? They say unto him: We say not that he is a king, but he saith it of himself.

And Pilate called the messenger and said unto him: Let Jesus be brought hither, but with gentleness. And the messenger went forth, and when he perceived Jesus he worshipped him and took the kerchief that was on his hand and spread it upon the earth and saith unto him: Lord, walk hereon and enter in, for the governor calleth thee. And when the Jews saw what the messenger had done, they cried out against Pilate saying: Wherefore didst thou not summon him by an herald to enter in, but by a messenger? for the messenger when he saw him worshipped him and spread out his kerchief upon the ground and hath made him walk upon it like a king!

Then Pilate called for the messenger and said unto him: Wherefore hast thou done this, and hast spread thy kerchief upon the ground and made Jesus to walk upon it? The messenger saith unto him: Lord, governor, when thou sentest me to Jerusalem unto Alexander, I saw Jesus sitting upon an ass, and the children of the Hebrews held branches in their hands and cried out, and others spread their garments beneath him, saying: Save now, thou that art in the highest: blessed is he that cometh in the name of the Lord.

The governor saith unto the messenger: Go forth and bring him in after what manner thou wilt. And the messenger went forth and did after the former manner and said unto Jesus: Lord, enter in: the governor calleth thee.

Now when Jesus entered in, and the ensigns were holding the standards, the images of the standards bowed and did reverence to Jesus. And when the Jews saw the carriage of the standards, how they bowed themselves and did reverence unto Jesus, they cried out above measure against the ensigns. But Pilate said unto the Jews: Marvel ye not that the images bowed themselves and did reverence unto Jesus? The Jews say unto Pilate: We saw how the ensigns made them to bow and did reverence to him. And the governor called for the ensigns and saith unto them: Wherefore did ye so? They say unto Pilate: We are Greeks and servers of temples, and how could we do him reverence? for indeed, whilst we held the images they bowed of themselves and did reverence unto him.

Now when Pilate saw it he was afraid, and sought to rise up from the judgment-seat. And while he yet thought to rise up, his wife sent unto him, saying: Have thou nothing to do with this just man, for I have suffered many things because of him by night. And Pilate called unto him all the Jews, and said unto them: Ye know that my wife feareth God and favoureth rather the customs of the Jews, with you? They say unto him: Yea, we know it. Pilate saith unto them: Lo, my wife hath sent unto me, saying: Have thou nothing to do with this just man: for I have suffered many things because of him by night. But the Jews answered and said unto Pilate: Said we not unto thee that he is a sorcerer? Behold, he hath sent a vision of a dream unto thy wife.

And Pilate called Jesus unto him and said to him: What is it that these witness against thee? speakest thou nothing? But Jesus said: If they had not had power they would have spoken nothing; for every man hath power over his own mouth, to speak good or evil: they shall see to it.

The elders of the Jews answered and said unto Jesus: What shall we see? Firstly, that thou wast born of fornication; secondly, that thy birth in Bethlehem was the cause of the slaying of children; thirdly, that thy father Joseph and thy mother Mary fled into Egypt because they had no confidence before the people.

Then said certain of them that stood by, devout men of the Jews: We say not that he came of fornication; but we know that Joseph was betrothed unto Mary, and he was not born of fornication.

And Pilate commanded the whole multitude to go out, saving the twelve men which said that he was not born of fornication, and he commanded Jesus to be set apart: and Pilate saith unto them: For what cause do they desire to put him to death? They say unto Pilate: They have jealousy, because he healeth on the sabbath day. Pilate saith: For a good work do they desire to put him to death? They say unto him: Yea.

And Pilate was filled with indignation and went forth without the judgment hall and saith unto them: I call the Sun to witness that I find no fault in this man. The Jews answered and said to the governor: If this man were not a malefactor we would not have delivered him unto thee. And Pilate said: Take ye him and judge him according to your law. The Jews said unto Pilate: It is not lawful for us to put any man to death. Pilate said: Hath God forbidden you to slay, and allowed me?

And Pilate went in again into the judgment hall and called Jesus apart and said unto him: Art thou the King of the Jews? Jesus answered and said to Pilate: Sayest thou this thing of thyself, or did others tell it thee of me? Pilate answered Jesus: Am I also a Jew? thine own nation and the chief priests have delivered thee unto me: what hast thou done? Jesus answered: My kingdom is not of this world; for if my kingdom were of this world, my servants would have striven that I should not be delivered to the Jews: but now is my kingdom not from hence. Pilate said unto him: Art thou a king, then? Jesus answered him: Thou sayest that I am a king; for this cause was I born and am come, that every one that is of the truth should hear my voice. Pilate saith unto him: What is truth? Jesus saith unto him: Truth is of heaven. Pilate saith: Is there not truth upon earth? Jesus saith unto Pilate: Thou seest how that they which speak the truth are judged of them that have authority upon earth.

And Pilate left Jesus in the judgment hall and went forth to the Jews and said unto them: I find no fault in him. The Jews say unto him: This man said: I am able to destroy this temple and in three days to build it up. Pilate saith: What temple? The Jews say: That which Solomon built in forty and six years, but which this man saith he will destroy and build it in three days. Pilate saith unto them: I am guiltless of the blood of this just man: see ye to it. The Jews say: His blood be upon us and on our children.

And Pilate called the elders and the priests and Levites unto him and said to them secretly: Do not so: for there is nothing worthy of death whereof ye have accused him, for your accusation is concerning healing and profaning of the sabbath. The elders and the priests and Levites say: If a man blaspheme against Caesar, is he worthy of death or no? Pilate saith: He is worthy of death. The Jews say unto Pilate: If a man be worthy of death if he blaspheme against Caesar, this man hath blasphemed against God.

Then the governor commanded all the Jews to go out from the judgment hall, and he called Jesus to him and saith unto him: What shall I do with thee? Jesus saith unto Pilate: Do as it hath been given thee. Pilate saith: How hath it been given? Jesus saith: Moses and the prophets did foretell concerning my death and rising again. Now the Jews inquired by stealth and heard, and they say unto Pilate: What needest thou to hear further of this blasphemy? Pilate saith unto the Jews: If this word be of blasphemy, take ye him for his blasphemy, and bring him into your synagogue and judge him according to your law. The Jews say unto Pilate: It is contained in our law, that if a man sin against a man, he is worthy to receive forty stripes save one: but he that blasphemeth against God, that he should be stoned with stoning.

Pilate saith unto them: Take ye him and avenge yourselves of him in what manner ye will. The Jews say unto Pilate: We will that he be crucified. Pilate saith: He deserveth not to be crucified.

Now as the governor looked round about upon the multitude of the Jews which stood by, he beheld many of the Jews weeping, and said: Not all the multitude desire that he should be put to death. The elder of the Jews said: To this end have the whole multitude of us come hither, that he should be put to death. Pilate saith to the Jews: Wherefore should he die? The Jews said: Because he called himself the Son of God, and a king.

But a certain man, Nicodemus, a Jew, came and stood before the governor and said: I beseech thee, good lord, bid me speak a few words.

Pilate saith: Say on. Nicodemus saith: I said unto the elders and the priests and Levites and unto all the multitude of the Jews in the synagogue: Wherefore contend ye with this man? This man doeth many and wonderful signs, which no man hath done, neither will do: let him alone and contrive not any evil against him: if the signs which he doeth are of God, they will stand, but if they be of men, they will come to nought. For verily Moses, when he was sent of God into Egypt did many signs, which God commanded him to do before Pharaoh, king of Egypt; and there were there certain men, servants of Pharaoh, Jannes and Jambres, and they also did signs not a few, of them which Moses did, and the Egyptians held them as gods, even Jannes and Jambres: and whereas the signs which they did were not of God, they perished and those also that believed on them. And now let this man go, for he is not worthy of death.

The Jews say unto Nicodemus: Thou didst become his disciple and thou speakest on his behalf. Nicodemus saith unto them: Is the governor also become his disciple, that he speaketh on his behalf? did not Caesar appoint him unto this dignity? And the Jews were raging and gnashing their teeth against Nicodemus. Pilate saith unto them: Wherefore gnash ye your teeth against him, whereas ye have heard the truth? The Jews say unto Nicodemus: Mayest thou receive his truth and his portion. Nicodemus saith: Amen, Amen: may I receive it as ye have said.

Now one of the Jews came forward and besought the governor that he might speak a word. The governor saith: If thou wilt say aught, speak on. And the Jew said: Thirty and eight years lay I on a bed in suffering of pains, and at the coming of Jesus many that were possessed and laid with divers diseases were healed by him, and certain faithful young men took pity on me and carried me with my bed and brought me unto him; and when Jesus saw me he had compassion, and spake a word unto me: Take up thy bed and walk. And I took up my bed and walked. The Jews say unto Pilate: Ask of him what day it was whereon he was healed? He that was healed saith: On the sabbath. The Jews say: Did we not inform thee so, that upon the sabbath he healeth and casteth out devils?

And another Jew came forward and said: I was born blind: I heard words but I saw no man's face: and as Jesus passed by I cried with a loud voice: Have mercy on me, O son of David. And he took pity on me and put his hands upon mine eyes and I received sight immediately.

And another Jew came forward and said: I was bowed and he made me straight with a word. And another said: I was a leper, and he healed me with a word.

And a certain woman named Bernice crying out from afar off said: I had an issue of blood and I touched the hem of his garment, and the flowing of my blood was stayed which I had twelve years. The Jews say: We have a law that a woman shall not come to give testimony.

And certain others, even a multitude both of men and women, cried out, saying: This man is a prophet and the devils are subject unto him. Pilate saith to them which said: The devils are subject unto him: Wherefore were not your teachers also subject unto him? They say unto Pilate: We know not. Others also said: He raised up Lazarus which was dead out of his tomb after four days. And the governor was afraid and said unto all the multitude of the Jews: Wherefore will ye shed innocent blood?

And he called unto him Nicodemus and those twelve men which said that he was not born of fornication, and said unto them: What shall I do, for there riseth sedition among the people? They say unto him: We know not: let them see to it. Again Pilate called for all the multitude of the Jews and saith: Ye know that ye have a custom that at the feast of unleavened bread I should release unto you a prisoner. Now I have a prisoner under condemnation in the prison, a murderer, Barabbas by name, and this Jesus also which standeth before you, in whom I find no fault: whom will ye that I release unto you? But they cried out: Barabbas. Pilate saith: What shall I do then with Jesus who is called Christ? The Jews say: Let him be crucified. But certain of the Jews answered: Thou art not a friend of Caesar's if thou let this man go; for he called himself the Son of God and a king: thou wilt therefore have him for king and not Caesar.

And Pilate was wroth and said unto the Jews: Your nation is alway seditious and ye rebel against your benefactors. The Jews say: Against what benefactors? Pilate saith: According as I have heard, your God brought you out of Egypt out of hard bondage, and led you safe through the sea as by dry land, and in the wilderness he nourished you with manna and gave you quails, and gave you water to drink out of a rock, and gave unto you a law. And in all these things ye provoked your God to anger, and sought out a molten calf, and angered your God and he sought to slay you: and Moses made supplication for you and ye were not put to death. And now ye do accuse me that I hate the king. And he rose up from the judgment-seat and sought to go forth. And the Jews cried out, saying: We know our king, even Caesar and not Jesus. For indeed the wise men brought gifts from the east unto him as unto a king, and when Herod heard from the wise men that a king was born, he sought to slay him; and when his father Joseph knew that, he took him and his mother and they fled into Egypt. And when Herod heard it he destroyed the children of the Hebrews that were born in Bethlehem.

And when Pilate heard these words he was afraid. And Pilate silenced the multitude, because they cried still, and said unto them: So, then, this is he whom Herod sought? The Jews say: Yea, this is he. And Pilate took water and washed his hands before the sun, saying: I am innocent of the blood of this just man: see ye to it. Again the Jews cried out: His blood be upon us and upon our children.

Then Pilate commanded the veil to be drawn before the judgment-seat whereon he sat, and saith unto Jesus: Thy nation hath convicted thee as being a king: therefore have I decreed that thou shouldest first be scourged according to the law of the pious emperors, and thereafter hanged upon the cross in the garden wherein thou wast taken: and let Dysmas and Gestas the two malefactors be crucified with thee.

The Regret of Pilate

After these things Pilate entered into the temple of the Jews and gathered together all the chief of the priests, and the teachers and scribes and doctors of the law, and went in with them into the holy place of the temple and commanded all the doors to be shut, and said unto them: We have heard that ye have in this temple a certain great Bible; wherefore I ask you that it be presented before us. And when that great Bible adorned with gold and precious jewels was brought by four ministers, Pilate said to them all: I adjure you by the God of your fathers which commanded you to build this temple in the place of his sanctuary, that ye hide not the truth from me. Ye know all the things that are written in this Bible; but tell me now if ye have found in the scriptures that this Jesus whom ye have crucified is the Son of God which should come for the salvation of mankind, and in what year of the times he must come. Declare unto me whether ye crucified him in ignorance or knowingly.

And Annas and Caiaphas when they were thus adjured commanded all the rest that were with them to go out of the temple; and they themselves shut all the doors of the temple and of the sanctuary, and said unto Pilate: Thou hast adjured us, O excellent judge, by the building of this temple to make manifest unto thee the truth and reason. After that we had crucified Jesus, knowing not that he was the Son of God, but supposing that by some chance he did his wondrous works, we made a great assembly in this temple; and as we conferred one with another concerning the signs of the mighty works which Jesus had done, we found many witnesses of our own nation who said that they had seen Jesus alive after his passion, and that he was passed into the height of the heaven. Moreover, we saw two witnesses whom Jesus raised from the dead, who declared unto us many marvellous things which Jesus did among the dead, which things we have in writing in our hands. Now our custom is that every year before our assembly we open this holy Bible and inquire the testimony of God. And we have found in the first book of the seventy how that Michael the angel spake unto the third son of Adam the first man concerning the five thousand and five hundred years, wherein should come the most beloved Son of God, even Christ: and furthermore we have thought that peradventure this same was the God of Israel which said unto Moses: Make thee an ark of the covenant in length two cubits and a half, and in breadth one cubit and a half, and in height one cubit and a half. For by those five cubits and a half we have understood and known the fashion of the ark of the old covenant, for that in five thousand and a half thousand years Jesus Christ should come in the ark of his body: and we have found that he is the God of Israel, even the Son of God. For after his passion, we the chief of the priests, because we marvelled at the signs which came to pass on his account, did open the Bible, and searched out all the generations unto the generation of Joseph, and Mary the mother of Christ, taking her to be the seed of David: and we found that from the day when God made the heaven and the earth and the first man, from that time unto the flood are 2,212 years: and from the flood unto the building of the tower 531 years: and from the building of the tower unto Abraham 606 years: and from Abraham unto the coming of the children of Israel out of Egypt 470 years: and from the going of the children of Israel out of Egypt unto the building of the temple 511 years: and from the building of the temple unto the destruction of the same temple 464 years: so far found we in the Bible of Esdras: and inquiring from the burning of the temple unto the coming of Christ and his birth we found it to be 636 years, which together were five thousand and five hundred years, like as we found it written in the Bible that Michael the archangel declared before unto Seth the third son of Adam, that after five thousand and a half thousand years Christ the Son of God should come. Hitherto we have told no man, lest there should be a schism in our synagogues; and now, O excellent judge, thou hast adjured us by this holy Bible of the testimonies of God, and we do declare it unto thee: and we also have adjured thee by thy life and health that thou declare not these words unto any man in Jerusalem.

And Pilate, when he heard these words of Annas and Caiaphas, laid them all up amongst the acts of the Lord and Saviour in the public books of his judgment hall, and wrote a letter unto Claudius the king of the city of Rome, saying:

Pontius Pilate unto Claudius, greeting.

There befell of late a matter which I myself brought to light: for the Jews through envy have punished themselves and their posterity with fearful judgments of their own fault; for whereas their fathers had promises that their God would send them out of heaven his holy one who should of right be called their king, and did promise that he would send him upon earth by a virgin; he, then, came when I was governor of Judaea, and they beheld him enlightening the blind, cleansing lepers, healing the palsied, driving devils out of men, raising the dead, rebuking the winds, walking upon the waves of the sea dry-shod, and doing many other wonders, and all the people of the Jews calling him the Son of God: the chief priests therefore, moved with envy against him, took him and delivered him unto me and brought against him one false accusation after another, saying that he was a sorcerer and did things contrary to their law.

But I, believing that these things were so, having scourged him, delivered him unto their will: and they crucified him, and when he was buried they set guards upon him. But while my soldiers watched him he rose again on the third day: yet so much was the malice of the Jews kindled that they gave money to the soldiers, saying: Say ye that his disciples stole away his body. But they, though they took the money, were not able to keep silence concerning that which had come to pass, for they also have testified that they saw him arisen and that they received money from the Jews. And these things have I reported unto thy mightiness for this cause, lest some other should lie unto thee and thou shouldest deem right to believe the false tales of the Jews.

The Descent into Hell

After the resurrection from the dead of our Lord Jesus Christ, Bartholomew came unto the Lord and questioned him, saying: Lord, reveal unto me the mysteries of the heavens.

Jesus answered and said unto him: If I put not off the body of the flesh, I shall not be able to teil them unto thee.

Bartholomew therefore drew near unto the Lord and said: I have a word to speak unto thee, Lord.

And Jesus said to him: I know what thou art about to say; say then what thou wilt, and I will answer thee.

And Bartholomew said: Lord, when thou wentest to be hanged upon the cross, I followed thee afar off and saw thee hung upon the cross, and the angels coming down from heaven and worshipping thee. And when there came darkness, I beheld, and I saw thee that thou wast vanished away from the cross, and I heard only a voice in the parts under the earth, and great wailing and gnashing of teeth on a sudden. Tell me, Lord, whither wentest thou from the cross?

And Jesus answered and said: Blessed art thou, Bartholomew, my beloved, because thou sawest this mystery; and now will I tell thee all things whatsoever thou askest me. For when I vanished away from the cross, then went I down into Hades that I might bring up Adam and all them that were with him, according to the supplication of Michael the archangel.

Then said Bartholomew: Lord, what was the voice which was heard?

Jesus saith unto him: Hades said unto Beliar: As I perceive, a God cometh hither.

And the angels cried unto the powers, saying: Remove your gates, ye princes, remove the everlasting doors, for behold the King of Glory cometh down. Hades said: Who is the King of Glory, that cometh down from heaven unto us?

And when I had descended five hundred steps, Hades was troubled, saying: I hear the breathing of the Most High, and I cannot endure it. But the devil answered and said: Submit not thyself, O Hades, but be strong: for God himself hath not descended upon the earth. But when I had descended yet five hundred steps, the angels and the powers cried out: Take hold, remove the doors, for behold the King of Glory cometh down. And Hades said: O, woe unto me, for I hear the breath of God.

And Beliar said unto Hades: Look carefully who it is that cometh, for it is Elias, or Enoch, or one of the prophets that this man seemeth to me to be. But Hades answered Death and said: Not yet are six thousand years accomplished. And whence are these, O Beliar; for the sum of the number is in mine hands.

And Beliar said unto Hades: Be not troubled, make safe thy gates and strengthen thy bars: consider, God cometh not down upon the earth.

Hades saith unto him: These be no good words that I hear from thee: my belly is rent, and mine inward parts are pained: it cannot be but that God cometh hither. Alas, whither shall I flee before the face of the power of the great King? Suffer me to enter into myself: for before thee was I formed.

Then did I enter in and scourged him and bound him with chains that cannot be loosed, and brought forth thence all the patriarchs and came again unto the cross.

Bartholomew saith unto him: Tell me, Lord, who was he whom the angels bare up in their hands, even that man that was very great of stature?

Jesus answered and said unto him: It was Adam the first-formed, for whose sake I came down from heaven upon earth. And I said unto him: I was hung upon the cross for thee and for thy children's sake. And he, when he heard it, groaned and said: So was thy good pleasure, O Lord.

Again Bartholomew said: Lord, I saw the angels ascending before Adam and singing praises. But one of the angels which was very great, above the rest, would not ascend up with them: and there was in his hand a sword of fire, and he was looking steadfastly upon thee only. And all the angels besought him that he would go up with them, but he would not. But when thou didst command him to go up, I beheld a flame of fire issuing out of his hands and going even unto the city of Jerusalem.

And Jesus said unto him: Blessed art thou, Bartholomew my beloved, because thou sawest these mysteries. This was one of the angels of vengeance which stand before my Father's throne: and this angel sent he unto me. And for this cause he would not ascend up, because he desired to destroy all the powers of the world. But when I commanded him to ascend up, there went a flame out of his hand and rent asunder the veil of the temple, and parted it in two pieces for a witness unto the children of Israel for my passion because they crucified me.

And when he had thus spoken, he said unto the apostles: Tarry for me in this place, for to-day a sacrifice is offered in paradise. And Bartholomew answered and said unto Jesus: Lord, what is the sacrifice which is offered in paradise? And Jesus said: There be souls of the righteous which to-day have departed out of the body and go unto paradise, and unless I be present they cannot enter into paradise.

And Bartholomew said: Lord, how many souls depart out of the world daily? Jesus said unto him: Thirty thousand.

Bartholomew saith unto him: Lord, when thou wast with us teaching the word, didst thou receive the sacrifices in paradise? Jesus answered and said unto him: Verily I say unto thee, my beloved, that I both taught the word with you and continually sat with my Father, and received the sacrifices in paradise every day. Bartholomew answered and said unto him: Lord, if thirty thousand souls depart out of the world every day, how many souls out of them are found righteous? Jesus saith unto him: Hardly fifty my beloved. Again Bartholomew saith: And how do three only enter into paradise? Jesus saith unto him: The three enter into paradise or are laid up in Abraham's bosom: but the others go into the place of the resurrection, for the three are not like unto the fifty.

Bartholomew saith unto him: Lord, how many souls above the number are born into the world daily? Jesus saith unto him: One soul only is born above the number of them that depart.

And when he had said this he gave them the peace, and vanished away from them.

Examination of Satan

When Jesus appeared again, Bartholomew saith unto him: Lord, show us the adversary of men that we may behold him, of what fashion he is, and what is his work, and whence he cometh forth, and what power he hath that he spared not even thee, but caused thee to be hanged upon the tree. But Jesus looked upon him and said: Thou bold heart! thou askest for that which thou art not able to look upon. But Bartholomew was troubled and fell at Jesus' feet and began to speak thus: O lamp that cannot be quenched, Lord Jesu Christ, maker of the eternal light, that hast given unto them that love thee the grace that beautifieth all, and hast given us the eternal light by thy coming into the world, that hast . . . the heavenly essence by a word . . . hast accomplished the work of the Father, hast turned the shame-facedness of Adam into mirth, hast done away the sorrow of Eve with a cheerful countenance by thy birth from a virgin: remember not evil against me but grant me the word of mine asking.

And as he thus spake, Jesus raised him up and said unto him: Bartholomew, wilt thou see the adversary of men? I tell thee that when thou beholdest him, not thou only but the rest of the apostles and Mary will fall on your faces and become as dead corpses.

But they all said unto him: Lord, let us behold him.

And he led them down from the Mount of Olives and looked wrathfully upon the angels that keep hell, and beckoned unto Michael to sound the trumpet in the height of the heavens. And Michael sounded, and the earth shook, and Beliar came up, being held by 660 angels and bound with fiery chains. And the length of him was 1,600 cubits and his breadth 40 cubits, and his face was like a lightning of fire and his eyes full of darkness. And out of his nostrils came a stinking smoke; and his mouth was as the gulf of a precipice, and the one of his wings was four-score cubits. And straightway when the apostles saw him, they fell to the earth on their faces and became as dead. But Jesus came near and raised the apostles and gave them a spirit of power, and he saith unto Bartholomew: Come near, Bartholomew, and trample with thy feet on his neck, and he will tell thee his work, what it is, and how he deceiveth men. And Jesus stood afar off with the rest of the apostles. And Bartholomew feared, and raised his voice and said: Blessed be the name of thine immortal kingdom from henceforth even for ever. And when he had spoken, Jesus permitted him, saying: Go and tread upon the neck of Beliar: and Bartholomew ran quickly upon him and trode upon his neck: and Beliar trembled.

And Bartholomew was afraid, and fled, and said unto Jesus: Lord, give me an hem of thy garments that I may have courage to draw near unto him. But Jesus said unto him: Thou canst not take an hem of my garments, for these are not my garments which I wore before I was crucified. And Bartholomew said: Lord, I fear lest, like as he spared not thine angels, he swallow me up also. Jesus saith unto him: Were not all things made by my word, and by the will of my Father the spirits were made subject unto Solomon? thou, therefore, being commanded by my word, go in my name and ask him what thou wilt. And Bartholomew made the sign of the cross and prayed unto Jesus and went behind him. And Jesus said to him: Draw near. And as Bartholomew drew near, fire was kindled on every side, so that his garments appeared fiery. Jesus saith to Bartholomew: As I said unto thee, tread upon his neck and ask him what is his power.

And Bartholomew went and trode upon his neck, and pressed down his face into the earth as far as his ears. And Bartholomew saith unto him: Tell me who thou art and what is thy name. And he said to him: Lighten me a little, and I will tell thee who I am and how I came hither, and what my work is and what my power is. And he lightened him and saith to him: Say all that thou hast done and all that thou doest.

And Beliar answered and said: If thou wilt know my name, at the first I was called Satanael, which is interpreted a messenger of God, but when I rejected the image of God my name was called Satanas, that is, an angel that keepeth hell. And again Bartholomew saith unto him: Reveal unto me all things and hide nothing from me. And he said unto him: I swear unto thee by the power of the glory of God that even if I would hide aught I cannot, for he is near that would convict me. For if I were able I would have destroyed you like one of them that were before you. For, indeed, I was formed the first angel: for when God made the heavens, he took a handful of fire and formed me first, Michael second, Gabriel third, Uriel fourth, Raphael fifth, Nathanael sixth, and other angels of whom I cannot tell the names. For they are the rod-bearers of God, and they smite me with their rods and pursue me seven times in the night and seven times in the day, and leave me not at all and break in pieces all my power.

Suffer me, and I will tell thee how I was cast down into this place and how the Lord did make man. I was going to and fro in the world, and God said unto Michael: Bring me a clod from the four corners of the earth, and water out of the four rivers of paradise. And when Michael brought them God formed Adam in the regions of the east, and shaped the clod which was shapeless, and stretched sinews and veins upon it and established it with joints; and he worshipped him, himself for his own sake first, because he was the image of God, therefore he worshipped him. And when I came from the ends of the earth Michael said: Worship thou the image of God, which he hath made according to his likeness. But I said: I am fire of fire, I was the first angel formed, and shall I worship clay and matter? And Michael saith to me: Worship, lest God be wroth with thee. But I said to him: God will not be wroth with me; but I will set my throne over against his throne, and I will be as he is. Then was God wroth with me and cast me down, having commanded the windows of heaven to be opened. And when I was cast down, he asked also the six hundred that were under me, if they would worship: but they said: Like as we have seen the first angel do, neither will we worship him that is less than ourselves. Then were the six hundred also cast down by him with me.

And when we were cast down upon the earth we were senseless for forty years; and when the sun shone forth seven times brighter than fire, suddenly I awaked; and I looked about and saw the six hundred that were under me senseless. And I awaked my son Salpsan and took him to counsel how I might deceive the man on whose account I was cast out of the heavens. And thus did I contrive it. I took a vial in mine hand and scraped the sweat from off my breast and the hair of mine armpits, and washed myself in the springs of the waters whence the four rivers flow out, and Eve drank of it and desire came upon her: for if she had not drunk of that water I should not have been able to deceive her.

Then Bartholomew commanded him to go into hell.

How Long Shall Death Prevail?

After the Word had told about the end, Salome saith: Until when shall men continue to die? Now the scripture speaks of man in two senses, the one that is seen, and the soul: and again, of him that is in a state of salvation, and him that is not: and sin is called the death of the soul; and it is advisedly that the Lord makes answer: So long as women bear children.

And why do not they who walk by anything rather than the true rule of the Gospel go on to quote the rest of that which was said to Salome: for when she had said, I have done well, then, in not bearing children? (as if childbearing were not the right thing to accept) the Lord answers and says: Every plant eat thou, but that which hath bitterness eat not.

When Salome inquired when the things concerning which she asked should be known, the Lord said: When ye have trampled on the garment of shame, and when the two become one and the male with the female is neither male nor female. In the first place, then, we have not this saying in the four Gospels that have been delivered to us, but in that according to the Egyptians.

The Lord said to Salome when she inquired: How long shall death prevail? As long as ye women bear children; not because life is an ill, and the creation evil: but as showing the sequence of nature: for in all cases birth is followed by decay.

And when the Saviour says to Salome that there shall be death as long as women bear children, he did not say it as abusing birth, for that is necessary for the salvation of believers.

But those who set themselves against God's creation because of continence, which has a fair-sounding name, quote also those words which were spoken to Salome, of which I made mention before. They are contained, I think, in the Gospel according to the Egyptians. For they say that the Saviour himself said: I came to destroy the works of the female.

Satan Creates the World

I, John, your brother and partaker in tribulation, and that shall be also a partaker in the kingdom of heaven, when I lay upon the breast of our Lord Jesus Christ and said unto him: Lord, who is he that shall betray thee? he answered and said: He that dippeth his hand with me in the dish: then Satan entered unto him and he sought how he might betray him.

And I asked of the Lord: When Satan fell, in what place dwelt he? And he answered me: My Father changed his appearance because of his pride, and the light was taken from him, and his face became like unto heated iron, and his face became wholly like that of a man: and he drew with his tail the third part of the angels of God, and was cast out from the seat of God and from the stewardship of the heavens. And Satan came down into this firmament, and he could find no rest for himself nor for them that were with him. And he asked the Father, saying: Have patience with me and I will pay thee all. And the Father had mercy on him and gave him rest and them that were with him, as much as they would even unto seven days.

And so sat he in the firmament and commanded the angel that was over the air and him that was over the waters, and they raised the earth up and it appeared dry: and he took the crown of the angel that was over the waters, and of the half thereof he made the light of the moon and of the half the light of the stars: and of the precious stones he made all the hosts of the stars.

And thereafter he made the angels his ministers according to the order of the form of the Most High, and by the commandment of the invisible Father he made thunder, rain, hail, and snow.

And he sent forth angels to be ministers over them. And he commanded the earth to bring forth every beast for food, and every creeping thing, and trees and herbs: and he commanded the sea to bring forth fishes, and the fowls of the heaven.

And he devised furthermore and made man in his likeness, and commanded the angel of the third heaven to enter into the body of clay. And he took thereof and made another body in the form of a woman, and commanded the angel of the second heaven to enter into the body of the woman. But the angels lamented when they beheld a mortal shape upon them and that they were unlike in shape. And he commanded them to do the deed of the flesh in the bodies of clay, and they knew not how to commit sin.

Then did the contriver of evil devise in his mind to make paradise, and he brought the man and woman into it. And he commanded to bring a reed, and the devil planted it in the midst of paradise, and so did the wicked devil hide his device that they knew not his deceit. And he came in and spake unto them, saying: Of every fruit which is in paradise eat ye, but of the fruit of the knowledge of good and evil eat not. Notwithstanding, the devil entered into a wicked serpent and seduced the angel that was in the form of the woman, and he wrought his lust with Eve in the song of the serpent. And therefore are they called sons of the devil and sons of the serpent that do the lust of the devil their father, even unto the end of this world. And again the devil poured out upon the angel that was in Adam the poison of his lust, and it begetteth the sons of the serpent and the sons of the devil even unto the end of this world.

And after that I, John, asked of the Lord, saying: How say men that

Adam and Eve were created by God and set in paradise to keep the commandments of the Father, and were delivered unto death? And the Lord said to me: Hearken, John, beloved of my Father; foolish men say thus in their deceitfulness that my Father made bodies of clay: but by the Holy Ghost made he all the powers of the heavens, and holy ones were found having bodies of clay because of their transgression, and therefore were delivered unto death.

And again I, John, asked the Lord: How beginneth a man to be in the spirit in a body of flesh? And the Lord said unto me: Certain of the angels which fell do enter unto the bodies of women, and receive flesh from the lust of the flesh, and so is a spirit born of spirit, and flesh of flesh, and so is the kingdom of Satan accomplished in this world and among all nations.

The Appearances of Jesus

When he had chosen Peter and Andrew, which were brethren, he cometh unto me and James my brother, saying: I have need of you, come unto me. And my brother hearing that, said: John, what would this child have that is upon the seashore and called us? And I said: What child? And he said to me again: That which beckoneth to us. And I answered: Because of our long watch we have kept at sea, thou seest not aright, my brother James; but seest thou not the man that standeth there, comely and fair and of a cheerful countenance? But he said to me: Him I see not, brother; but let us go forth and we shall see what he would have.

And so when we had brought the ship to land, we saw him also helping along with us to settle the ship: and when we departed from that place, being minded to follow him, again he was seen of me as having a head rather bald, but the beard thick and flowing, but of James as a youth whose beard was newly come. We were therefore perplexed, both of us, as to what that which we had seen should mean. And after that, as we followed him, both of us were by little and little, yet more, perplexed as we considered the matter.

Yet unto me there then appeared this yet more wonderful thing: for I would try to see him privily, and I never at any time saw his eyes blinking, but only open. And oft-times he would appear to me as a

small man and uncomely, and then again as one reaching unto heaven.
Also there was in him another marvel: when I sat at meat he would take
me upon his own breast; and sometimes his breast was felt of me to be
smooth and tender, and sometimes hard like unto stones, so that I was
perplexed in myself and said: Wherefore is this so unto me?

And at another time he taketh with him me and James and Peter
unto the mountain where he was wont to pray, and we saw in him a
light such as it is not possible for a man that useth mortal speech to
describe what it was like.

Again in like manner he bringeth us three up into the mountain,
saying: Come ye with me. And we went again: and we saw him at a
distance praying. I, therefore, because he loved me, drew nigh unto him
softly, as though he could not see me, and stood looking upon his
hinder parts: and I saw that he was not in any wise clad with garments,
but was seen of us naked, and not in any wise as a man, and that his
feet were whiter than any snow, so that the earth there was lighted up
by his feet, and that his head touched the heaven: so that I was afraid
and cried out, and he, turning about, appeared as a man of small
stature, and caught hold on my beard and pulled it and said to me: John,
be not faithless but believing, and not curious. And I said unto him:
But what have I done, Lord? And I say unto you, brethren, I suffered
so great pain in that place where he took hold on my beard for thirty
days, that I said to him: Lord, if thy twitch when thou wast in sport
hath given me so great pain, what were it if thou hadst given me a
buffet? And he said unto me: Let it be thine henceforth not to tempt
him that cannot be tempted.

But Peter and James were wroth because I spake with the Lord, and
beckoned unto me that I should come unto them and leave the Lord
alone. And I went, and they both said unto me: He, the old man, that
was speaking with the Lord upon the top of the mount, who was he?
for we heard both of them speaking. And I, having in mind his great
grace, and his unity which hath many faces, and his wisdom which
without ceasing looketh upon us, said: That shall ye learn if ye inquire
of him.

Again, once when all we his disciples were at Gennesaret sleeping in
one house, I alone having wrapped myself in my mantle, watched what
he should do: and first I heard him say: John, go thou to sleep. And I
thereon feigning to sleep saw another like unto him, whom also I heard

say unto my Lord: Jesus, they whom thou hast chosen believe not yet on thee. And my Lord said unto him: Thou sayest well: for they are men.

Another glory also will I tell you, brethren: oftentimes when I walked with him, I desired to see the print of his foot, whether it appeared on the earth; for I saw him as it were lifting himself up from the earth: and I never saw it.

The Dance of Praise

Now before he was taken by the lawless Jews, who also had their law from the lawless serpent, he gathered all of us together and said: Before I am delivered up unto them let us sing an hymn to the Father, and so go forth to that which lieth before us. He bade us therefore make as it were a ring, holding one another's hands, and himself standing in the midst he said: Answer Amen unto me. He began, then, to sing an hymn and to say:

Glory be to thee, Father.
And we, going about in a ring, answered him: Amen.
Glory be to thee, Word: Glory be to thee, Grace. Amen.
Glory be to thee, Spirit: Glory be to thee, Holy One:
Glory be to thy glory. Amen.
We praise thee, O Father; we give thanks to thee, O Light, wherein
    darkness dwelleth not. Amen.
Now whereas we give thanks, I say:
I would be saved, and I would save. Amen.
I would be loosed, and I would loose. Amen.
I would be wounded, and I would wound. Amen.
I would be born, and I would bear. Amen.
I would eat, and I would be eaten. Amen.
I would hear, and I would be heard. Amen.
I would be thought, being wholly thought. Amen.
I would be washed, and I would wash. Amen.
Grace danceth. I would pipe; dance ye all. Amen.
I would mourn: lament ye all. Amen.
The number Eight singeth praise with us. Amen.
The number Twelve danceth on high. Amen.

The Whole on high hath part in our dancing. Amen.
Whoso danceth not, knoweth not what cometh to pass. Amen.
I would flee, and I would stay. Amen.
I would adorn and I would be adorned. Amen.
I would be united, and I would unite. Amen.
A house I have not, and I have houses. Amen.
A place I have not, and I have places. Amen.
A temple I have not, and I have temples. Amen.
A lamp am I to thee that beholdest me. Amen.
A mirror am I to thee that perceivest me. Amen.
A door am I to thee that knockest at me. Amen.
A way am I to thee a wayfarer. Amen.

Now answer thou unto my dancing. Behold thyself in me who speak, and seeing what I do, keep silence about my mysteries.

Thou that dancest, perceive what I do, for thine is this passion of the manhood, which I am about to suffer. For thou couldest not at all have understood what thou sufferest if I had not been sent unto thee, as the word of the Father. Thou that sawest what I suffer sawest me as suffering, and seeing it thou didst not abide but wert wholly moved, moved to make wise. Thou hast me as a bed, rest upon me. Who I am, thou shalt know when I depart. What now I am seen to be, that I am not. Thou shalt see when thou comest. If thou hadst known how to suffer, thou wouldest have been able not to suffer. Learn thou to suffer, and thou shalt be able not to suffer. What thou knowest not, I myself will teach thee. Thy God am I, not the God of the traitor. I would keep tune with holy souls. In me know thou the word of wisdom. Again with me say thou: Glory be to thee, Father; glory to thee, Word; glory to thee, Holy Ghost. And if thou wouldst know concerning me, what I was, know that with a word did I deceive all things and I was no whit deceived. I have leaped: but do thou understand the whole, and having understood it, say: Glory be to thee, Father. Amen.

Thus, my beloved, having danced with us the Lord went forth. And we as men gone astray or dazed with sleep fled this way and that.

Correspondence of Abgarus and Jesus

A copy of a letter written by Abgarus the toparch to Jesus, and sent to him by means of Ananias the runner, to Jerusalem:

Abgarus Uchama the toparch to Jesus the good Saviour that hath appeared in the parts of Jerusalem, greeting. I have heard concerning thee and thy cures, that they are done of thee without drugs or herbs: for, as the report goes, thou makest blind men to see again, lame to walk, and cleansest lepers, and castest out unclean spirits and devils, and those that are afflicted with long sickness thou healest, and raisest the dead. And having heard all this of thee, I had determined one of two things, either that thou art God come down from heaven, and so doest these things, or art a Son of God that doest these things. Therefore now have I written and entreated thee to trouble thyself to come to me and heal the affliction which I have. For indeed I have heard that the Jews even murmur against thee and wish to do thee hurt. And I have a very little city but comely, which is sufficient for us both.

The answer, written by Jesus, sent by Ananias the runner to Abgarus the toparch:

Blessed art thou that hast believed in me, not having seen me. For it is written concerning me that they that have seen me shall not believe in me, and that they that have not seen me shall believe and live. But concerning that which thou hast written to me, to come unto thee; it must needs be that I fulfil all things for the which I was sent here, and after fulfilling them should then be taken up unto him that sent me. And when I am taken up, I will send thee one of my disciples, to heal thine affliction and give life to thee and them that are with thee.

A Description of Jesus

(*From a Letter of Lentulus*)

There hath appeared in these times, and still is, a man of great power named Jesus Christ, who is called by the Gentiles the prophet of truth, whom his disciples call the Son of God: raising the dead and healing diseases, a man in stature middling tall, and comely, having a reverend countenance, which they that look upon may love and fear; having hair of the hue of an unripe hazel-nut and smooth almost down to his ears, but from the ears in curling locks somewhat darker and more shining, waving over his shoulders; having a parting at the middle of the head according to the fashion of the Nazareans; a brow smooth and very calm, with a face without wrinkle or any blemish, which a moderate colour makes beautiful; with the nose and mouth no fault at all can be found; having a full beard of the colour of his hair, not long, but a little forked at the chin; having an expression simple and mature, the eyes grey, glancing, and clear; in rebuke terrible, in admonition kind and lovable, cheerful yet keeping gravity; sometimes he hath wept, but never laughed; in stature of body tall and straight, with hands and arms fair to look upon; in talk grave, reserved and modest, so that he was rightly called by the prophet fairer than the children of men.

The Hymn of the Soul

When I was a little child,
And dwelling in my kingdom in my Father's house,
And in the wealth and the glories
Of my nurturers had my pleasure,
From the East, our home,
My parents, having equipped me, sent me forth.
And of the wealth of our treasury
They had already tied up for me a load,
Large it was, yet light,
So that I might bear it unaided—
Gold and silver of Gazzak the great,
And rubies of India,
And agates from the land of Kushan,
And they girded me with adamant
Which can crush iron.
And they took off from me the bright robe,
Which in their love they had wrought for me,
And my purple toga,
Which was measured and woven to my stature.

And they made a compact with me,
And wrote it in my heart that it should not be forgotten:
"If thou goest down into Egypt,
And bringest the one pearl,
Which is in the midst of the sea
Hard by the loud-breathing serpent,
Then shalt thou put on thy bright robe
And thy toga, which is laid over it,
And with thy brother, our next in rank,
Thou shalt be heir in our kingdom."

I quitted the East and went down,
There being with me two messengers,
For the way was dangerous and difficult,
And I was very young to tread it.
I passed the borders of Maishan,
The meeting-place of the merchants of the East,
And I reached the land of Babel.
I went down into Egypt,
And my companions parted from me.
I betook me straight to the serpent,
Hard by his dwelling I abode,
Waiting till he should slumber and sleep,
And I could take my pearl from him.
And when I was single and alone,
A stranger to those with whom I dwelt,
One of my race, a free-born man,
From among the Easterns, I beheld there—
A youth fair and well favoured.

And he came and attached himself to me.
And I made him my intimate,
A comrade with whom I shared my merchandise.
I warned him against the Egyptians
And against consorting with the unclean;
And I put on a garb like theirs,
Lest they should insult me because I had come from afar,
To take away the pearl,

And lest they should arouse the serpent against me.
But in some way or other
They perceived that I was not their countryman;
So they dealt with me treacherously,
Moreover they gave me their food to eat.
I forgot that I was a son of kings,
And I served their king;
And I forgot the pearl,
For which my parents had sent me,
And by reason of the burden
I lay in a deep sleep.

But all these things that befell me
My parents perceived and were grieved for me;
And a proclamation was made in our kingdom,
That all should speed to our gate,
Kings and princes of Parthia
And all the nobles of the East.
So they wove a plan on my behalf,
That I might not be left in Egypt,
And they wrote to me a letter,
And every noble signed his name thereto:
"From thy Father, the King of kings,
And thy Mother, the mistress of the East,
And from thy brother, our next in rank,
To thee our son, who art in Egypt, greeting!
Up and arise from thy sleep,
And listen to the words of our letter!
Call to mind that thou art a son of kings!
See the slavery—whom thou servest!
Remember the pearl
For which thou didst speed to Egypt!
Think of thy bright robe,
And remember thy glorious toga,
Which thou shalt put on as thine adornment,
When thy name hath been read out in the list of the valiant,
And with thy brother,
Thou shalt be in our kingdom."

And my letter was a letter
Which the King sealed with his right hand,
To keep it from the wicked ones, the children of Babel,
And from the savage demons.
It flew in the likeness of an eagle,
The king of all birds;
It flew and alighted beside me,
And became all speech.
At its voice and the sound of its rustling,
I started and arose from my sleep.
I took it up and kissed it,
And loosed its seal, and read;
And according to what was traced on my heart
Were the words of my letter written.
I remembered that I was a son of kings,
And my free soul longed for its natural state.
I remembered the pearl,
For which I had been sent to Egypt,
And I began to charm him,
The terrible loud-breathing serpent.
I hushed him to sleep and lulled him into slumber,
For my Father's name I named over him,
And the name of our next in rank,
And of my Mother, the queen of the East;
And I snatched away the pearl,
And turned to go back to my Father's house.
And their filthy and unclean garb
I stripped off, and left it in their country,
And I took my way straight to come
To the light of our home, the East.
And my letter, my awakener,
I found before me on the road,
And as with its voice it had awakened me,
So too with its light it was leading me,
Shone before me with its form,
And with its voice and its guidance
It also encouraged me to speed,
And with his love was drawing me on.

I went forth,
I left Babel on my left hand,
And reached Maishan the great,
The haven of the merchants,
That sitteth on the shore of the sea.

And my bright robe, which I had stripped off,
And the toga wherein it was wrapped,
From the heights of Hyrcania
My parents sent thither,
By the hand of their treasurers,
Who in their faithfulness could be trusted therewith.
And because I remembered not its fashion—
For in my childhood I had left it in my Father's house—
On a sudden, as I faced it,
The garment seemed to me like a mirror of myself.
I saw it all in my whole self,
Moreover I faced my whole self in facing it,
For we were two in distinction
And yet again one in one likeness.
And the treasurers also,
Who brought it to me, I saw in like manner,
That they were twain yet one likeness,
For one kingly sign was graven on them,
Of his hands that restored to me
My treasure and my wealth by means of them,
My bright embroidered robe,
With glorious colours;
With gold and with beryls,
And rubies and agates
And sardonyxes varied in colour,
It also was made ready in its home on high.
And with stones of adamant
All its seams were fastened;
And the image of the King of kings
Was depicted in full all over it,
And like the sapphire-stone also
Were its manifold hues.

Again I saw that all over it
The motions of knowledge were stirring,
And as if to speak
I saw it also making itself ready.
I heard the sound of its tones,
Which it uttered to those who brought it down,
And in its kingly motions
It was spreading itself out towards me,
And in the hands of its givers
It hastened that I might take it.
And me too my love urged on
That I should run to meet it and receive it,
And I stretched forth and received it,
With the beauty of its colours I adorned myself.
And my toga of brilliant colours
I cast around me, in its whole breadth.
I clothed myself therewith, and ascended
To the gate of salutation and homage;
I bowed my head, and did homage
To the Majesty of my Father who had sent it to me,
For I had done his commandments,
And he too had done what he promised,
And at the gate of his princes
I mingled with his nobles;
For he rejoiced in me and received me,
And I was with him in his kingdom.
All his servants glorify him.
And he promised that also to the gate
Of the King of kings I should speed with him,
And bringing my gift and my pearl
I should appear with him before our King.

MOHAMMEDAN
Scriptures

MOHAMMEDAN SCRIPTURES

The Koran

In the Name of God, the Compassionate, the Merciful[1]

Early Meccan Period

Clots of Blood

Read! in the name of thy Lord who created;—
Created man from CLOTS OF BLOOD:—
Read! For thy Lord is the most beneficent,
Who hath taught the use of the pen;—
Hath taught man that which he knew not.

Nay, verily, man is most extravagant in wickedness
Because he seeth himself possessed of wealth.
Verily unto the Lord is the return of all.
What thinkest thou of him who forbiddeth
A servant of God when he prayeth?
What thinkest thou? that he hath followed the true guidance or enjoined
	piety?
What thinkest thou, if he hath treated the truth as a lie and turned his
	back?
Doth he not know that God seeth?

---

[1] In THE KORAN this formula is prefixed to each "Sura," or Revelation.

Nay, verily, if he desist not, we will assuredly seize him by the forelock,
The lying sinful forelock!
Then let him summon his associates;
We too will summon the guards of hell:
Nay! obey him not; but adore, and draw nigh to God.

The Enwrapped

O thou ENWRAPPED in thy mantle!
Arise and warn!
And thy Lord—magnify him!
And thy raiment—purify it!
And the abomination—flee it!
And bestow not favours that thou mayest receive again with increase;
And for thy Lord wait thou patiently.
For when there shall be a trump on the trumpet,
That then shall be a distressful day,
A day, to the unbelievers, devoid of ease.

Nay, by the moon!
And by the night when it retreateth!
And by the morn when it brighteneth!
Verily, hell is one of the most grievous woes,
Fraught with warning to man,
To him among you who desireth to press forward, or to remain behind.
For its own works lieth every soul in pledge. But they of God's right
        hand
In their gardens make inquiry of the wicked;—
"What hath cast you into hell-fire?"
They will say, "We were not of those who prayed,
And we were not of those who fed the poor,
And we plunged into vain disputes with vain disputers,
And we rejected as a lie the day of reckoning,
Till the certainty came upon us"—
Therefore intercession of interceders shall not avail them.

What then hath come to them that they turn aside from the warning
As if they were affrighted asses fleeing from a lion?
But every one of them would fain have open pages given to him out of
      heaven!
Nay, but they fear not the life to come.
Nay, verily this Koran is a warning, and whoso will, beareth it in mind;
But not unless God please, will they bear it in mind. Meet is he to be
      feared, and meet is forgiveness in him.

The Night

By the NIGHT when she spreadeth her veil;
By the day when it appeareth in glory;
By Him who made male and female;
Verily your aims are indeed different!
As then for him who giveth alms and feareth God,
And yieldeth assent to the good;
To him will we therefore make easy the path to happiness.
But as to him who is covetous and bent on riches,
And calleth the good a lie,
To him will we make easy the path to distress;
And what shall his wealth avail him when he goeth down headlong?
Truly man's guidance is with us,
And ours, the next life and this life present.
I warn you therefore of the flaming fire;
None shall be burned at it but the most wretched,—
Who hath called the truth a lie and turned his back.
But the greatly God-fearing shall escape it,—
Who giveth away his substance that he may become pure;
And who offereth not favours to any one for the sake of recompense,
But only as seeking the face of his Lord the most high.
And assuredly in the end he shall be well content.

The Night-Comer

By the heaven, and by the NIGHT-COMER!
But what shall teach thee what the night-comer is?
'Tis the star of piercing radiance.
Verily every soul has of a surety a guardian over it.
Let man then reflect out of what he was created.
He was created of the poured-forth germs,
Which issue from between the loins and breastbones:
Well able truly is God to restore him to life,—
On the day when all secrets shall be searched out,
And he shall have no other might or helper.

I swear by the heaven which accomplisheth its revolution,
And by the earth which openeth her bosom,
That this Koran is indeed a discriminating discourse,
And that it is not frivolous.
They verily plot a plot against thee,
And I will plot a plot against them.
Deal gently therefore with the infidels; grant them a gentle respite.

He Frowned

HE FROWNED, and he turned his back,
Because the blind man came to him!
But what made thee know whether he would not aim at holiness,
Or be warned, and the warning profit him?
As to him who has become wealthy—
Him therefore thou didst receive with honour:
Yet is it not thy concern that he endeavours not to be pure;
But as to him who cometh to thee in earnest,
And full of fears—
Him dost thou neglect.
Do not so. Verily it (the Koran) is a warning;
(And whoso is willing beareth it in mind)

Written on honoured pages,
Exalted, purified,
By the hands of scribes, honoured, righteous.

Cursed be man! What hath made him unbelieving?
Of what thing did God create him?
Out of moist germs.
He created him and fashioned him,
Then made him an easy passage from the womb,
Then causeth him to die and burieth him;
Then, when he pleaseth, will raise him again to life.
Nay! but man hath not yet fulfilled the bidding of his Lord.
Let man then look at his food:
It was we who rained down the copious rains,
Then cleft the earth with clefts;
So caused we the upgrowth of the grain,
And grapes and healing herbs,
And the olive and the palm,
And enclosed gardens thick with trees,
And fruits and herbage,
Provision for yourselves and for your cattle.

But when the stunning trumpet-blast shall arrive,
On that day shall a man fly from his brother,
And his mother and his father,
And his wife and his children;
For every man of them on that day his own concern shall be enough.
There shall be faces on that day radiant,
Laughing and joyous:
And faces on that day with dust upon them:
Blackness shall cover them!
These are the unbelievers, the impure.

The Most High

Praise the name of thy Lord THE MOST HIGH,
Who hath created and balanced all things,
And who hath fixed their destinies and guided them;

Who bringeth forth the pastures,
Then reduceth them to dusky stubble.
We will teach thee to recite the Koran, nor aught shalt thou forget,
Save what God pleaseth; he verily knoweth alike the manifest and what
      is hidden;
And we will make easy for thee the easiest way.

Warn therefore; verily the warning is profitable:
He that feareth God will receive the warning,—
And the greatest wretch only will turn aside from it,
Who shall be burned at the terrible fire;
Then shall he not die therein, and shall not live.
Happy he who is purified by Islam,
And remembereth the name of his Lord and prayeth.
But ye prefer this present life,
Though the life to come is better and more enduring.
This truly is in the books of old,
The books of Abraham and Moses.

The Folded Up

When the sun shall be FOLDED UP,
And when the stars shall shoot downwards,
And when the mountains shall be set in motion,
And when the camels ten months gone with foal shall be abandoned,
And when the wild beasts shall be gathered together,
And when the seas shall be swollen,
And when souls shall be paired with their bodies,
And when the damsel that had been buried alive shall be asked
For what crime she was put to death,
And when the leaves of the Book shall be unrolled,
And when the heaven shall be stripped away,
And when hell shall be made to blaze,
And when paradise shall be brought near,
Every soul shall know what it hath produced.

And I swear by the stars of retrograde motion,
Which move swiftly and hide themselves away,

And by the night when it cometh darkening on,
And by the dawn when it clears away the darkness by its breath,
That verily this is the word of an illustrious messenger,
Powerful with the Lord of the throne, of established rank,
Obeyed by angels, faithful also to his trust,
And your compatriot is not one possessed by djinn;
For he saw him in the clear horizon:
Nor doth he keep back heaven's secrets,
Nor doth he teach the doctrine of a cursed Satan.
Whither then are ye going?
Verily this Koran is no other than a warning to all creatures;
To him among you who willeth to walk in a straight path:
But will it ye shall not, unless as God willeth it, Lord of the worlds.

The Brightness

By the noon-day BRIGHTNESS,
And by the night when it darkeneth!
Thy Lord hath not forsaken thee, neither hath he hated thee,
And surely the future shall be better for thee than the present,
And thy Lord shall assuredly be bounteous to thee and thou be satisfied.
Did he not find thee an orphan and provide thee a home?
And he found thee erring and guided thee,
And found thee needy and enriched thee.
As to the orphan therefore wrong him not;
And as to him that asketh of thee, chide him not away;
And as for the favours of thy Lord, tell them then abroad.

The Opening

Have we not OPENED thy breast for thee?
And taken off from thee thy burden,
Which galled thy back?
And have we not upraised thy name for thee?
Then verily along with the difficulty cometh ease.
Verily along with the difficulty cometh ease.

But when thou art set at liberty, be instant (in prayer),
And seek thy Lord with fervour.

Those Who Stint

Woe to those who STINT the measure:
Who when they take by measure from others, exact the full;
But when they mete to them or weigh to them, minish—
Have they no thought that they shall be raised again
For a great day,
A day when mankind shall stand before the Lord of the worlds?

Nay, verily, the register of the wicked is in Sidjin;
And what shall make thee understand what Sidjin is?
It is a book distinctly written.
Woe, on that day, to those who treated our signs as lies,
Who treated the day of judgment as a lie!
But none treat it as a lie, save the transgressor, the criminal,
Who, when our signs are rehearsed to him, saith, "Tales of the ancients!"
Nay, but their own works have got the mastery over their hearts:
Yes; they shall surely be shut out as by a veil from their Lord on that day;
Then shall they be surely burned in hell-fire:
Then shall it be said to them, "This is what ye deemed a lie."

Nay, verily the register of the righteous is in Illiyoun;
And what shall make thee understand what Illiyoun is?
A book distinctly written;
The angels who draw nigh unto God attest it.
Surely among delights shall the righteous dwell!
Seated on bridal couches they will gaze around;
Thou shalt mark in their faces the brightness of delight;
Choice sealed wine shall be given them to quaff,—
The seal of musk.—For this let those pant who pant for bliss—
Mingled therewith shall be the waters of Tasnim—
Fount whereof they who draw nigh to God shall drink.
The sinners indeed laugh the faithful to scorn:
And when they pass by them they wink at one another,—
And when they return to their own people, they return jesting,

And when they see them they say, "Verily these are the erring ones."
And yet they have no mission to be their guardians.
Therefore, on that day the faithful shall laugh the infidels to scorn,
As reclining on bridal couches they behold them.
Is there a repayment to the unbelievers in accordance with their deeds?

The Mountain

By the MOUNTAIN,
And by the Book written
On an outspread scroll,
And by the frequented fane,
And by heaven's lofty roof,
And by the swollen sea,
Verily, a chastisement from thy Lord is most imminent,
And none shall put it back.
With reeling on that day the heaven shall reel,
And with moving shall the mountains move,
And woe, on that day, to those who called the apostles liars,
Who plunged for pastime into vain disputes—
On that day shall they be thrust with thrusting to the fire of hell:—
"This is the fire which ye treated as a lie!
Is it magic, then? or, do ye not see it?
Burn ye therein: and bear it patiently or impatiently it will be the same
        to you: ye only receive the reward of your doings."

But 'mid gardens and delights shall they dwell who have feared God,
Rejoicing in what their Lord hath given them; and that from the pain
        of hell-fire hath their Lord preserved them.
"Eat and drink with healthy enjoyment, in recompense for your deeds."
On couches ranged in rows shall they recline; and to the damsels with
        large dark eyes will we wed them.
And to those who have believed, whose offspring have followed them
        in the faith, will we again unite their offspring; nor of the meed
        of their works will we in the least defraud them. Pledged to
        God is every man for his actions.
And fruits in abundance will we bestow on them, and such flesh as they
        shall desire;

Therein shall they present to one another the cup which shall engender
    no light discourse, no motive to sin:
And youths shall go round unto them beautiful as imbedded pearls:
And they shall accost one another and ask mutual questions.
"A time indeed there was," will they say, "when we were full of care
    as to the future lot of our families;
But kind hath God been to us, and from the pestilential torment of the
    scorching wind hath he preserved us;
Verily, heretofore we called upon him—and he of a truth, he is the
    Beneficent, the Merciful."
Warn thou, then. For thou by the favour of thy Lord art neither sooth-
    sayer nor possessed.

Or will they say, "A poet! let us await some adverse turn of his fortune"?
Say, wait ye, and in sooth I too will wait with you.
Or is it their dreams which inspire them with this? or is it that they are
    a perverse people?
Or say they, "He hath forged it (the Koran) himself"? Nay rather, they
    will not believe.
Let them then produce a discourse like it, if they speak the truth.
Or were they created of nothing? or were they the creators of them-
    selves?
Or created they the heavens and earth? Nay rather, they have no faith.
Or hold they thy Lord's treasures? or bear they the rule supreme?
Or have they a ladder for hearing the angels? Then let any one who
    hath heard them bring a clear proof of it.
Or hath God the daughters, and ye the sons?
Or askest thou pay of them? But they are themselves weighed down
    with debts.
Or have they a knowledge of the secret things? Then let them write
    them down.
Or desire they to lay snares for thee? But the snared ones are they who
    do not believe.
Or have they any god beside God? Glory be to God above what they
    join with him.
And should they see a fragment of the heaven falling down, they would
    say, "It is only a dense cloud."

Leave them then until they come face to face with their day wherein
   they shall swoon away;
A day in which their snares shall not at all avail them, neither shall they
   be helped.
And verily, beside this is there a punishment for the evil-doers: but
   most of them know it not.
But wait thou patiently the judgment of thy Lord, for verily thou art in
   our eye; and celebrate the praise of thy Lord when thou risest up,
And in the night-season: and praise him at the waning of the stars.

The Merciful

The God of MERCY hath taught the Koran,
Hath created man,
Hath taught him articulate speech.
The sun and the moon have each their times,
And the plants and the trees bend in adoration.
And the heaven, he hath reared it on high; and he hath appointed the
   balance,
That in the balance ye should not transgress;
Weigh therefore with fairness, and scant not the balance.
And the earth, he hath prepared it for the living tribes:
Therein are fruits, and the palms with sheathed clusters,
And the grain with its husk, and the supports of life.
Which then of the bounties of your Lord will ye twain deny?
He created man of clay like an earthen vessel,
And he created the djinn of pure fire:
Which then of the bounties of your Lord will ye twain deny?
He is Lord of the East,
And He is Lord of the West:
Which then of the bounties of your Lord will ye twain deny?
He hath let loose the two seas which meet each other:
Yet between them is a barrier which they overpass not:
Which then of the bounties of your Lord will ye twain deny?
From each he bringeth up the pearls both great and small:
Which then of the bounties of your Lord will ye twain deny?

And his are the ships towering up at sea like the tall mountains:
Which then of the bounties of your Lord will ye twain deny?
All on the earth passeth away,
But the face of thy Lord abideth in its majesty and glory:
Which then of the bounties of your Lord will ye twain deny?
To him maketh suit all that is in the heaven and the earth; every day
    doth he work:
Which then of the bounties of your Lord will ye twain deny?
We will settle accounts with you, O ye men and djinn:
Which then of the bounties of your Lord will ye twain deny?

Middle Meccan Period

The Poets

Ta. Sin. Mim. These are the signs of the lucid Book.
Haply thou wearest thyself away with grief because they believe not.
Were it our will, we could send down to them a sign from the heaven,
    before which they would ever humbly bow.
But from each fresh warning that cometh to them from the God of
    Mercy they have only turned aside,
And treated it as a lie: But tidings shall reach them which they shall
    not laugh to scorn.
Have they not beheld the earth—how we have caused to spring up
    therein of every noble sort?
Verily, in this is a sign: but most of them believe not.
And truly, thy Lord!—He assuredly is the Mighty, the Merciful.

Verily from the Lord of the worlds hath this Book come down;
The faithful spirit hath come down with it
Upon thy heart, that thou mightest become a warner—
In the clear Arabic tongue:
And truly it is foretold in the scriptures of them of yore.

Shall it not be a sign to them that the learned among the children of
      Israel recognized it?
If we had sent it down unto any foreigner,
And he had recited it to them, they had not believed.
In such sort have we influenced the heart of the wicked ones,
That they will not believe it till they see the grievous chastisement.
And it shall come upon them on a sudden when they look not for it:
And they will say, "Can we be respited?"
Will they then seek to hasten on our chastisement?
How thinkest thou? If after we have given them their fill for years,
That with which they are menaced come upon them at last,
Of what avail will their enjoyments be to them?
We have destroyed no city which had not first its warners
With admonition; nor did we deal unjustly.
The satans were not sent down with this Koran:
It beseemed them not, and they had not the power,
For they are far removed from hearing the discourse of angels.

Call not thou then on any other god with God, lest thou be of those
      consigned to torment:
But warn thy relatives of nearer kin,
And kindly lower thy wing over the faithful who follow thee,
And if they disobey thee, then say: "I verily am clear of your doings";—
And put thy trust in the Mighty, the Merciful,
Who seeth thee when thou standest in prayer,
And thy demeanour among those who worship;
Verily he is the hearer, the knower.

Shall I tell you on whom the satans descend?
They descend on every lying, wicked person:
They impart what they have heard; but most of them are liars.

It is the POETS whom the erring follow:
Seest thou not how they rove distraught in every valley?
And that they say that which they do not?
Save those who believe and do good works, and oft remember God;
And who defend themselves when unjustly treated. But they who treat
      them unjustly shall find out what a lot awaiteth them hereafter.

The Ant

Ta. Sad. These are the signs (verses) of the Koran and of the lucid
    Book;
Guidance and glad tidings to the believers who observe prayer and pay
    the stated alms, and believe firmly—do they—in the life to come.
Verily, as to those who believe not in the life to come, we have made
    their own doings fair-seeming to them, and they are bewildered
    therein.
These are they whom the woe of chastisement awaiteth; and in the next
    life they shall suffer—yes shall they—greatest loss;
But of a truth thou hast certainly received the Koran from a wise, a
    knowing God.

And of old we gave knowledge to David and Solomon: and they said,
    "Praise be to God, who hath made us to excel many of his
    believing servants!"
And in knowledge Solomon was David's heir. And he said, "O men, we
    have been taught the speech of birds, and are endued with every-
    thing. Lo! this is indeed a clear boon from God."

And to Solomon were gathered his hosts of djinn and of men and of
    birds, and they were marched on in order,
Until when they reach the Valley of Ants, saith AN ANT, "O ye ants,
    enter your dwellings, lest Solomon and his army crush you and
    know it not."
Then smiled Solomon, laughing at her words, and he said, "Stir me up,
    O Lord, to be thankful for thy favour which thou hast showed
    upon me and upon my parents, and to do righteousness that shall
    be well pleasing to thee, and bring me in, by thy mercy, among
    thy servants the righteous."

The Queen of Saba

And he reviewed the birds, and said, "How is it that I see not the
    hoopoe? Is it one of the absent?

Surely with a severe chastisement will I chastise it, or I will certainly
   slaughter it, or it shall surely bring me a clear excuse."

Nor tarried it long ere it came and said, "I know what thou knowest not,
   and with sure tidings have I come to thee from Saba:

Lo, I found a woman reigning over them, gifted with everything, and
   she hath a splendid throne;

And I found her and her people worshipping the sun instead of God;
   and Satan hath made their works fair-seeming to them, and
   turned them from the Way; wherefore they are not guided

To the worship of God, who bringeth to light the secret things of heaven
   and earth, and knoweth what men conceal and what they manifest:

God! there is no god but he! Lord of the glorious throne!"

He said, "We shall see whether thou hast spoken truth, or whether thou
   art of them that lie.

Go with this my letter and throw it down to them: then turn away from
   them and await their answer."

She said, "O my nobles! verily an honourable letter hath been thrown
   down to me:

Of a truth it is from Solomon; and lo! it is 'In the name of God, the
   Compassionate, the Merciful!

Set not up yourselves against me, but come to me submitting (Muslims).'"

She said, "O ye nobles, advise me in mine affair: I decide not an affair
   without your concurrence."

They said, "We are endued with strength and are endued with mighty
   valour.—But to command is thine: See therefore what thou wilt
   command us."

She said, "Verily kings, when they enter a city, spoil it, and abase the
   mightiest of its people: and in like manner will these also do.

But I will send to them a gift, and await what the envoys bring back."

And when the messenger came to Solomon, he said, "Would ye increase
   my riches? But what God hath given to me is better than what he
   hath given you: yet ye glory in these your gifts:

Return to them: for we will surely come to them with forces which they
   cannot withstand, and we will assuredly drive them from their
   land humbled; and they shall become contemptible."

Said he, "O nobles, which of you will bring me her throne before they come to me, submitting? (Muslims)."

An Efreet of the djinn said, "I will bring it thee ere thou risest from thy place: for verily I have power for this, and am trusty."

And one who had the knowledge of scripture said, "I will bring it to thee in the twinkling of an eye." And when he saw it set down before him, he said, "This is of the favour of my Lord, to try me whether I will be thankful or unthankful. And he who is thankful is only thankful to his own behoof; and as for him who is unthankful—truly then my Lord is self-sufficient, bounteous!"

Said he, "Make her throne so that she know it not: we shall see whether she hath or hath not Guidance."

And when she came, it was asked, "Is thy throne like this?" She said, "As though it were the same." "And we," said he, "have had knowledge given us before her, and have become Muslims;

But the gods she has worshipped instead of God have led her astray: verily she is of a people who believe not."

It was said to her, "Enter the palace": and when she saw it, she thought it a lake of water, and bared her legs. He said, "Lo! it is a palace smoothly paved with glass."

She said, "O my Lord! verily I have acted wickedly (by worshipping idols), and I resign myself, with Solomon, to God, Lord of the worlds."

Say: Praise be to God, and peace be on his servants whom he hath chosen! Is God the more worthy, or the gods they join with him?

Who hath made the heavens and the earth, and sendeth down the rain to you from heaven, by which we cause luxuriant groves to spring up? Not in your power is it to cause its trees to spring up! What! A god with God? Yet they are a people who find equals for him!

Who hath made the earth firm, and made rivers in its midst, and placed mountains upon it, and put a barrier between the two seas? A god with God? Yet the greater part of them have no knowledge!

Who answereth the oppressed when they cry to him, and taketh off their ills, and hath made you to succeed your sires on the earth? A god with God? How few bear these things in mind!

Who guideth you in the darkness of the land and of the sea? and who

sendeth forth the winds as the forerunners of his mercy? A god
    with God? High be God exalted above what ye join with him!
Who createth a being, then reneweth it? and who supplieth you out of
    the heaven and the earth? A god with God? Say: Bring forth
    your proofs if you speak the truth.

Verily, by his wisdom will thy Lord decide between them: for he is the
    Mighty, the Knowing.
Put thou then thy trust in God: for thou hast clear truth on thy side.
Verily thou shalt not make the dead to hear; neither shalt thou make the
    deaf to hear the call, when they turn their backs upon thee;
Neither art thou the guide of the blind out of their errors: none shalt
    thou make to hear but those who believe our signs: and they are
    Muslims.

The Last Day

And when the doom shall light upon them, we will cause a monster to
    come forth to them out of the earth, and cry to them, that "man-
    kind have not firmly believed our signs" (revelations).
And on that day will we gather out of every nation a company of those
    who have gainsaid our signs, and they shall be kept marching in
    ranks
Till they come before God, who will say, "Treated ye my signs as impos-
    tures, although ye embraced them not in your knowledge? What
    is it that ye have done?"
And doom shall light upon them for their evil deeds, and nought shall
    they have to plead.
See they not that we have ordained the night that they may rest in it, and
    the day with its gift of light? Of a truth herein are signs to people
    who believe.
On that day there shall be a blast on the trumpet, and all that are in the
    heavens, and all that are on the earth, shall be terror-stricken,
    save him whom God pleaseth to deliver; and all shall come to
    him in humble guise.
And thou shalt see the mountains, which thou thinkest so firmly fixed,
    pass away with the passing of a cloud! 'Tis the work of God, who
    ordereth all things! Lo! He is well aware of your actions.

He who shall present himself with good works, shall reap the benefit
    therefrom, and they shall be secure from terror on that day;

And they who shall present themselves with evil shall therefore be flung
    face downwards into the fire. Shall ye be recompensed but as ye
    have wrought?

Say: Specially am I commanded to worship the Lord of this land, which
    he hath sanctified. And all things are his: and I am commanded
    to be one of those who surrender themselves to God (a Muslim),

And to recite the Koran: and whoever is rightly guided, will be rightly
    guided only to his own behoof; and as to him who erreth, then
    say, I truly am a warner only.

And say, Praise be to God! He will show you his signs, and ye shall
    acknowledge them: and of what ye do, thy Lord is not regardless.

The Cave

(*The Story of the Seven Sleepers*)

Praise be to God, who hath sent down the Book to his servant, and hath
    not made it tortuous

But direct; that it may warn of a grievous woe from him, and announce
    to the faithful who do the things that are right, that a goodly
    reward wherein they shall abide for ever, awaiteth them;

And that it may warn those who say, "God hath begotten a son."

No knowledge of this have either they or their fathers! A grievous say-
    ing to come out of their mouths! Verily they speak no other than
    a lie!

Haply, then, if they believe not in this new revelation, thou wilt fret
    thyself to death on their very footsteps, out of vexation.

Verily, we have made all that is on earth as its adornment, that we might
    make trial who among mankind would excel in works:

But verily we are about to reduce all that is thereon to dust bare of
    herbage!

Hast thou reflected that the inmates of THE CAVE and Er-Rakeem were
    one of our wondrous signs?

When the youths betook them to the cave, they said, "O our Lord! grant
us mercy from before thee, and order for us our affair aright."
Then struck we upon their ears with deafness in the cave for many a year:
Then we awaked them that we might know which of the two parties
could best reckon the space of their abiding.

We will relate to thee their tale with truth. Verily they were youths who
believed in their Lord, and in guidance had we increased them;
And we made them stout of heart when they stood up and said, "Our
Lord is Lord of the heavens and of the earth; by no means will
we call on any other god than him; for then we had said a thing
outrageous.
These our people have taken other gods beside him, though they bring
no clear authority for them; but, who more iniquitous than he
who deviseth a lie concerning God?
So when ye have separated yourselves from them and from that which
they worship beside God, then betake you to the cave: Your
Lord will unfold his mercy to you, and will order your affair for
you for the best."

And thou mightest have seen the sun when it arose, pass on the right of
their cave, and when it set, leave them on the left, while they
were in its spacious chamber. This is one of the signs of God.
Guided indeed is he whom God guideth, but for him whom He
misleadeth, thou shalt by no means find a patron, a guide.
And thou wouldst have deemed them awake, though they were sleeping:
and we turned them to the right and to the left. And at the
threshold lay their dog with paws outstretched. Hadst thou come
suddenly upon them, thou wouldst surely have turned thy back
on them in flight, and have been filled with fear at them.

So we awaked them that they might question one another. Said a speaker
among them, "How long have ye tarried here?" They said, "We
have tarried a day or part of a day." They said, "Your Lord
knoweth best how long ye have tarried: send now one of you
with this your coin into the city, and let him mark who therein
hath purest food, and from him let him bring you a supply; and
let him be courteous, and not discover you to any one:
Of a truth they, if they find you out, will stone you or turn you back to
their faith, and in that case it will fare ill with you for ever."

And thus made we their adventure known to their fellow citizens, that
they might learn that the promise of God is true, and that as to
"the Hour" there is no doubt of its coming. When they disputed
among themselves concerning what had befallen them, some
said, "Build a building over them; their Lord knoweth best about
them." Those who prevailed in their matter said, "A place of
worship will we surely raise over them."

They will say, "They were three; their dog the fourth:" and they will
say, "Five; their dog the sixth," doubtfully guessing at the secret:
and they will say, "Seven; and their dog the eighth." Say: My
Lord best knoweth the number: none, save a few, shall know
them.

Therefore be clear in thy discussions about them, and ask not any one
concerning them.

And say not thou of a thing, "I will surely do this to-morrow"; without,
"If God will." And when thou hast forgotten, call thy Lord to
mind; and say, "Haply my Lord will guide me, that I may come
near to the truth of this story with correctness."

And they tarried in their cave 300 years, and they underwent an increase
of nine.

Say: God best knoweth how long they tarried: With him are the secrets
of the heavens and of the earth: Look thou and hearken unto
him alone. Man hath no guardian but him, and none may bear
part in his judgments:—

And publish what hath been revealed to thee of the Book of thy Lord—
none may change his words,—and thou shalt by no means find a
place of refuge other than him:

And be thou patient with those who call upon their Lord at morn and
even, seeking his face: and let not thine eyes be turned away
from them in quest of the pomp of this life; neither obey him
whose heart we have made careless of the remembrance of us,
and who followeth his own lusts, and whose ways are unbridled.

And say: The truth is from your Lord: let him then who will, believe;
and let him who will, be an unbeliever. Verily for these offenders
we have got ready the fire whose smoke shall enwrap them: and
if they implore help, helped shall they be with water like molten

brass which will scald their faces! Wretched the drink! and evil
the couch!

As to those who have believed and done the things that are right,—
Verily we will not suffer the reward of him whose works were
good, to perish!

For them, the gardens of Eden: at their feet shall rivers flow: decked
shall they be therein with bracelets of gold, and green robes of
silk and rich brocade shall they wear, reclining therein on
thrones. Blissful the reward! and a pleasant couch!

Late Meccan Period

God Has No Son

The Book sent down from God, the Mighty, the Wise!

Verily we have sent down the Book to thee with the truth: serve thou
God then, showing forth to him a pure religion—

Is not a pure worship due to God?

But they who have taken others beside him as lords, saying, "We serve
them only that they may bring us near unto God,"—of a truth,
God will judge between them and the faithful, concerning that
wherein they have differed.

Verily God guideth not him who is a liar, an unbeliever.

Had God desired to have had a son, He had surely chosen what he
pleased out of his own creation. But praise be to him! He is God,
the One, the Almighty.

The Spider

Yes, and God is well acquainted with those who have believed, and he is
well acquainted with the hypocrites.

Also the unbelievers say to the faithful, "Follow ye our way, and we will surely bear your sins." But not aught of their sins will they bear— verily they are indeed liars!

But their own burdens, and burdens together with their own burdens shall they surely bear: and inquisition shall surely be made of them on the day of resurrection as to their false devices.

The likeness for those who take to themselves guardians beside God is the likeness of the SPIDER who buildeth her a house: but verily, frailest of all houses surely is the house of the spider. Did they but know this!

God truly hath knowledge of all that they call on beside him; and he is the Mighty, the Wise:

These similitudes have we set forth to men: but none will understand them except the endued with knowledge.

God hath created the heavens and the earth for a serious end. Verily in this is a sign to those who believe.

Recite the portions of the Book which have been revealed to thee and discharge the duty of prayer: verily prayer restraineth from the filthy and the blame-worthy. And assuredly the gravest duty is the remembrance of God; and God knoweth what ye do.

Dispute ye not, unless in kindliest sort, with the people of the Book; save with such of them as have dealt wrongfully with you: and say ye, "We believe in what hath been sent down to us and hath been sent down to you. Our God and your God is one, and to him are we self-surrendered" (Muslims).

And thus have we sent down the Book of the Koran to thee: and they to whom we have given the Book of the law believe in it: and of these Arabians there are those who believe in it: and none, save the infidels, reject our signs.

And thou didst not recite any book (of revelation) before it: with that right hand of thine thou didst not transcribe one: else might they who treat it as a vain thing have justly doubted:

But it is a clear sign in the hearts of those whom "the knowledge" hath reached; and none except the wicked reject our signs.

They say also, "Unless a sign be sent down to him from his Lord. . . ." Say: Signs are in the power of God alone, and I am only an open warner.

Is it not enough for them that we have sent down to thee the Book to be
recited to them? In this verily is a mercy and a warning to those
who believe.

Say: God is a sufficient witness between me and you:
He knoweth all that is in the heavens and the earth, and they who believe
in vain things and disbelieve in God—these shall suffer loss.

And they challenge thee to hasten the punishment: but had there not
been a season fixed for it, that punishment had already come
upon them—but it shall surely overtake them suddenly when
they look not for it—
They challenge thee to hasten the punishment: but verily hell shall be
round about the infidels:
On a certain day the punishment shall come upon them from above them
and from beneath their feet; and God will say, "Taste ye your
own doings."

O my servants who have believed! Vast truly is my earth: me, therefore!
yea worship me.
Every soul shall taste of death: afterwards to us shall ye return.
But those who have believed and wrought righteousness will we assuredly lodge in gardens with lofty apartments, beneath which the
rivers flow, to abide therein for ever. Goodly the reward of those
who labour,
Who patiently endure, and put their trust in their Lord!

And this present life is no other than a pastime and a disport: but truly
the future mansion is life indeed! Would that they knew this!
Then when they embark on shipboard, they call upon God, professing to
him the purity of their faith; but when he bringeth them safe to
land, behold they join partners with him;
Believing not in our revelation, and yet take their fill of good things: but
in the end they shall know their folly.
Do they not see that we have established a safe precinct while all around
them men despoil? Will they then believe in vain idols, and not
own the goodness of God?
But who acteth more wrongly than he who deviseth a lie against God, or

calleth the truth, when it hath come to him, a lie? Is there not an abode for the infidels in hell?

And those who have made efforts for us, in our paths will we surely guide: for verily God is with those who do righteous deeds.

Medinan Period

Relation to Jews and Christians

The unbelievers among the people of the Book, and among the idolaters, do not wish that any good should be sent down to you from your Lord: but God will show his special mercy to whom he will, for God is of great bounty.

Whatever verse we cancel, or cause thee to forget, we bring a better or its like. Knowest thou not that God hath power over all things?

Knowest thou not that the dominion of the heavens and of the earth is God's? and that ye have neither patron nor helper, save God?

Would ye ask of your apostle as of old it was asked of Moses? But he who hath exchanged faith for unbelief, hath already erred from the even way.

Many of those who have scripture would like to bring you back to unbelief after ye have believed, out of selfish envy, even after the truth hath been clearly shown to them. Forgive them then, and shun them till God shall come with his decree. Truly God hath power over all things.

And observe prayer and pay the legal impost: and whatever good thing ye have sent on before for your soul's sake, ye shall find it with God. Verily God seeth what ye do.

And they say, "By no means shall any but Jews or Christians enter paradise:" This is their belief. Say: Give your proofs if ye speak the truth—

But, they who set their face with resignation Godward, and do what is

right,—their reward is therefore with their Lord, and no fear
shall come on them, neither shall they be grieved.

Moreover, the Jews say, "The Christians lean on nought:" "On nought
lean the Jews," say the Christians: Yet both are readers of the
Book. So with like words say they who have no knowledge. But
on the resurrection day, God shall judge between them as to that
in which they have differed.

And who committeth a greater wrong than he who hindereth the temples
of God from having his name mentioned in them, and who
hasteth to ruin them? Such men cannot enter them but with fear.
There is shame for them in this world, and a severe torment in
the next.

The East and the West is God's: therefore, whichever way ye turn, there
is the face of God: Truly God is immense, knowing (omnipresent, omniscient).

And they say, "God hath begotten a son." Glory be to him! Nay rather—
his, whatever is in the heavens and the earth! All obeyeth him,—

Sole maker of the heavens and of the earth! And when he decreeth a
thing, he only saith to it, "Be," and it is.

And they who have no knowledge say, "Why doth not God speak to us,
or thou come to us with a sign?" So spake those who were before
them the like of their words: their hearts are alike: Clear now
have we made the signs (verses) for those who have firm faith:

Verily, with the truth have we sent thee, a bearer of good tidings and a
warner: and concerning the inmates of hell thou shalt not be
questioned.

But until thou follow their religion, neither the Jews nor the Christians
will ever be satisfied with thee. Say: Verily, guidance of God,—
that is the guidance! And if after "the Knowledge" which hath
reached thee, thou follow their desires, thou shalt find from God
neither helper nor protector.

They to whom we have given the Book, and who read it as it ought to
be read,—these believe therein: but whoso believeth not therein,
these are they who shall be the losers.

O children of Israel! remember my favour wherewith I have favoured
you, and that above all creatures have I been bounteous to you:

And dread the day when not in aught shall soul satisfy for soul, nor shall any ransom be taken from it, nor shall any intercession avail, and they shall not be helped.

When his Lord made trial of Abraham by commands which he fulfilled, he said, "I am about to make thee an Imam to mankind:" he said, "Of my offspring also:" "My covenant," said God, "embraceth not the evil-doers."

And remember when we appointed the holy house as man's resort and safe retreat, and said, "Take ye the station of Abraham for a place of prayer." And we commanded Abraham and Ismael, "Purify my house for those who shall go in procession round it, and those who shall abide there for devotion, and those who shall bow down and prostrate themselves."

And when Abraham said, "Lord! make this land secure, and supply its people with fruits, such of them as believe in God and in the last day:" he said, "And whoso believeth not, little therefore will I bestow on him; then will I drive him to the torment of the fire! and ill the passage!"

And when Abraham, with Ismael, raised the foundations of the house, they said, "O our Lord! accept it from us; thou of a truth art the hearer, the knower.

O our Lord! and make us thy Muslims (resigned to thee), and our posterity a Muslim people; and teach us our holy rites, and be turned towards us: verily thou art He who turneth, the Merciful.

O our Lord! and raise up among them an apostle from themselves who may rehearse thy signs unto them, and teach them 'the Book,' and wisdom, and purify them: of a truth thou art the Mighty, the Wise."

And who but he that hath debased his soul to folly will mislike the faith of Abraham, when we have chosen him in this world, and truly in the world to come he shall be assuredly of the just?

When his Lord said to him, "Resign thyself to me" (become a Muslim), he said, "I resign myself to the Lord of the worlds."

And this to his children did Abraham enjoin, and Jacob also, saying, "O my children! truly God hath chosen a religion for you; so die not without having become Muslims."

Were ye present when Jacob was at the point of death? when he said to his sons, "Whom will ye worship when I am gone?" They said, "We will worship thy God and the God of thy fathers Abraham and Ismael and Isaac, one God, and to him are we surrendered (Muslims)."

That people have now passed away; to them the meed of their deeds, and to you the meed of your deeds: but of their doings ye shall not be questioned.

They say, moreover, "Become Jews or Christians, that ye may have the true guidance." Say: Nay! the religion of Abraham, the sound in faith, and not one of those who join gods with God is our religion!

Say ye: "We believe in God, and that which hath been sent down to us, and that which hath been sent down to Abraham and Ismael and Isaac and Jacob and the tribes; and that which hath been given to Moses and to Jesus, and that which was given to the prophets from their Lord. No difference do we make between any of them: and to God are we resigned (Muslims)."

If therefore they believe the like of what ye believe, then have they true guidance; but if they turn back, then verily they are in a state of separation from you; and God will suffice to protect thee against them: and he is the hearer, the knower.

Moral and Ritual Prescriptions

There is no piety in turning your faces toward the east or the west, but he is pious who believeth in God and the last day and the angels and the scriptures and the prophets; who for the love of God disburseth his wealth to his kindred, and to the orphans, and the needy, and the wayfarer, and those who ask, and for ransoming; who observeth prayer, and payeth the legal alms, and who is one of those who are faithful to their engagements when they have engaged in them, and patient under ills and hardships and in time of trouble: these are they who are just, and these are they who fear God.

O believers! retaliation for bloodshedding is prescribed to you: the free man for the free, and the slave for the slave, and the woman for the woman: but he to whom his brother shall make any remission is to be dealt with equitably; and a payment should be made to him with liberality.

This is a relaxation from your Lord and a mercy. For him therefore who after this shall transgress, a sore punishment!

But in this law of retaliation is your security for life, O men of understanding! Haply ye will fear God.

It is prescribed to you when any one of you is at the point of death, that if he leave goods, he bequeath equitably to his parents and kindred; this is binding on those who fear God:—

Whoso then after he hath heard what a bequest is shall change it, the guilt of this shall be on those only who alter it; verily, God heareth, knoweth:

But he who feareth from the testator any mistake or wrong, and shall make a settlement between the parties—that then shall be no guilt in him; verily, God is forgiving, merciful.

O believers! a fast is prescribed to you, as it was prescribed to those before you, that ye may fear God,

For certain days. But he among you who shall be sick, or on a journey, shall fast that same number of other days: and for those who are able to keep it and yet break it, there shall be as an expiation the maintenance of a poor man. And he who of his own accord performeth a good work, shall derive good from it: and that ye fast is good for you—if ye but knew it.

As to the month Ramadhan in which the Koran was sent down to be man's guidance, and an explanation of that guidance, and an illumination, as soon as any one of you observeth the moon, let him set about the fast; but he who is sick, or upon a journey, shall fast a like number of other days. God wisheth you ease and wisheth not your discomfort, and that you fulfil the number of days, and that you glorify God for his guidance: and haply you will be thankful.

And when my servants ask thee concerning me, then verily will I be nigh unto them—will answer the cry of him that crieth, when he crieth unto me: but let them hearken unto me, and believe in me. Haply they will proceed aright.

You are allowed on the night of the fast to approach your wives: they
are your garment and ye are their garment. God knoweth that ye
have mutually defrauded yourselves therein; so he turneth unto
you and remitteth unto you. Now, therefore, go in unto them
with full desire for that which God hath ordained for you; and
eat and drink until ye can discern a white thread from a black
thread by the daybreak: afterwards fast strictly till night, and go
not in unto them, but pass the time in the Mosques. These are
the bounds set up by God: therefore come not near to transgress
them. Thus God maketh his signs clear to men: haply they will
fear him.

Consume not your wealth among yourselves in vain things; nor offer it to
judges as a bribe that ye may consume a part of men's wealth
unjustly, while ye know the sin which ye commit.

They will ask thee of the new moons. Say: They are periods fixed for
man's service and for the pilgrimage. But there is no piety in
entering your houses at the back, but piety consists in the fear of
God. Enter your houses then by their doors; and fear God: haply
ye shall be prosperous.

The Holy War

And fight for the cause of God against those who fight against you: but
commit not the injustice of attacking them first: verily God
loveth not the unjust:

And kill them wherever ye shall find them, and eject them from whatever place they have ejected you; for seduction from the truth is
worse than slaughter: yet attack them not at the sacred Mosque,
until they attack you therein; but if they attack you, then slay
them— Such the recompense of the infidels!—

But if they desist, then verily God is gracious, merciful—

And do battle against them until there be no more seduction from the
truth and the only worship be that of God: but if they desist,
then let there be no hostility, save against wrong-doers.

War is prescribed to you; but to this ye have a repugnance:

Yet haply ye are averse from a thing, though it be good for you, and
haply ye love a thing though it be bad for you: And God knoweth; but ye, ye know not.

They will ask thee concerning war in the sacred month. Say: The act of
fighting therein is a grave crime: but the act of turning others
aside from the path of God, and unbelief in him, and to prevent
access to the sacred Mosque, and to drive out his people, is worse
in the sight of God; and civil strife is worse than bloodshed. But
they will not cease to war against you until they turn you from
your religion, if they be able; but whoever of you shall turn from
his religion and die an infidel, their works shall be fruitless in
this world and in the next: and they shall be consigned to the
fire; therein to abide for aye.

But they who believe, and who fly their country, and fight in the cause
of God, may hope for God's mercy: and God is gracious,
merciful.

Wives

And marry not idolatresses until they believe; for assuredly a slave who
believeth is better than an idolatress, though she please you more.
And wed not your daughters to idolaters until they believe; for a
slave who is a believer is better than an idolater, even though he
please you.

They invite to the fire; but God inviteth to paradise, and to pardon, if he
so will, and maketh clear his signs to men: perchance they will
be monished.

They will also question thee as to the courses of women. Say: They are a
pollution. Separate yourselves therefore from women and approach them not, until they be cleansed. But when they are
cleansed, go in unto them as God hath ordained for you. Verily
God loveth those who turn in penitence to him, and loveth those
who purify themselves.

Your wives are your field: go in therefore to your field in what way so
ever ye will; but do first some act for your souls' good: and fear
ye God, and know that ye must meet him; and bear these tidings
to the faithful.

For those who intend to separate from their wives shall be a period of waiting for four months; but if they go back from their purpose, then verily God is gracious, merciful:

And if they resolve on a divorce, then verily God is he who heareth, knoweth:

And the divorced shall await the result by themselves until they have had their courses thrice, nor is it allowable for them to conceal what God hath created in their wombs, if they believe in God and the last day; and it will be more just in their husbands to bring them back when in this state, if they desire a reconciliation. And it is for the women to act as they (the husbands) act towards them with all fairness; yet are the men a step above them; and God is mighty, wise.

Ye may divorce your wives twice: but after that, ye must either retain them with kindness or put them away with benefits. But it is not allowed you to appropriate to yourselves aught of what ye have given to them, unless both fear that they cannot keep within the bounds set up of God. And if ye fear that they cannot observe the ordinances of God, then no blame shall attach to either of you for what the wife shall herself give for her redemption. These are the bounds of God: therefore overstep them not; for whoever oversteppeth the bounds of God are evil-doers.

Then if the husband divorce her a third time, it is not lawful for him to take her again, until she shall have married another husband; and if he also divorce her, then shall no blame attach to them if they return to each other, thinking that they can keep within the bounds fixed of God. And these are the bounds fixed of God; he maketh them clear to those who have knowledge.

And when ye divorce women, and they have reached the prescribed time, either retain them with generosity, or put them away with generosity: but retain them not by constraint so as to be unjust towards them. He who doth so, doth in fact injure himself. And make not the signs of God a jest; but remember God's favour toward you, and the Book and the wisdom which he hath sent down to you for your warning, and fear God, and know that God hath knowledge of everything.

And when ye divorce your wives, and they have reached the prescribed time, hinder them not from marrying their husbands when they have agreed among themselves in an honourable way. This warning is for him among you who believeth in God and in the last day. This is most pure for you, and most decent. And God hath knowledge, but ye know not.

Other Prophets

Some of the apostles we have endowed more highly than others: to some God hath spoken, and he hath raised others of them to the loftiest grade; and to Jesus the son of Mary we gave manifest proofs of his mission, and we strengthened him with the Holy Spirit. And if God had pleased, they who came after them would not have wrangled, after the clear proofs had reached them. But into disputes they fell: some of them believed, and some were unbelievers; yet if God had pleased, they would not have thus wrangled: but God doth what he will.

Praise of God

God! There is no god but he; the Living, the Self-subsisting; neither slumber seizeth him, nor sleep; his, whatsoever is in the heavens and whatsoever is in the earth! Who is he that can intercede with him but by his own permission? He knoweth what is present with his creatures, and what is yet to befall them; yet nought of his knowledge do they comprehend, save what he willeth. His throne reacheth over the heavens and the earth, and the upholding of both burdeneth him not; and he is the High, the Great!

Let there be no compulsion in religion. Now is the right way made distinct from error; whoever therefore denieth Taghoot and believeth in God hath taken hold on a strong handle that hath no flaw therein: and God is he who heareth, knoweth.

God is the patron of believers: he bringeth them out of darkness into light:

As to those who believe not, their patrons are Taghoot: they bring them out of light into darkness: they shall be inmates of hell-fire: they shall abide therein for ever.

War Captives

O prophet! stir up the faithful to the fight. Twenty of you who stand
firm shall vanquish two hundred: and if there be a hundred of
you, they shall vanquish a thousand of the infidels, for they are a
people devoid of understanding.

Now hath God made your work easy, for he knoweth that there is weakness among you. If therefore there be a hundred of you who
endure resolutely, they shall vanquish two hundred; and if there
be a thousand of you, they shall vanquish two thousand by God's
permission; for God is with those who are resolute to endure.

No prophet hath been enabled to take captives until he hath made great
slaughter in the earth. Ye desire the passing fruitions of this
world, but God desireth the next life for you. And God is
mighty, wise.

Had there not been a previous ordinance from God, a severe chastisement had certainly befallen you, on account of the ransom which
ye took.

Eat therefore of the spoils ye have taken that which is lawful and good;
and fear God: verily God is gracious, merciful.

O prophet! say to the captives who are in your hands, "If God shall know
good to be in your hearts, he will give you good beyond all that
hath been taken from you, and will forgive you: for God is forgiving, merciful."

But if they seek to deal treacherously with thee—they have already dealt
treacherously with God before! Therefore hath he given you
power over them. And God is knowing, wise.

Refugees

Verily, they who believe and have fled their homes and spent their substance and themselves for the cause of God, and they who have
taken in the prophet and been helpful to him, shall be near of
kin the one to the other. And they who have believed, but have
not fled their homes, shall have no rights of kindred with you at

all, until they too fly their country. Yet if they seek aid from you on account of the faith, your part it is to give them aid, except against a people between whom and yourselves there may be a treaty. And God beholdeth your actions.

And the infidels have the like relationships one with another. Unless ye do the same, there will be discord in the land and great corruption.

But as for those who have believed and fled their country, and fought in the cause of God, and provided the prophet an asylum and been helpful to him, these are the faithful; mercy is their due and a noble provision.

And they who have believed and have since fled their country, and fought at your side, these also are of you. Those who are united by ties of blood are the nearest of kin to each other. This is in the Book of God. Verily, God knoweth all things.

The Table

(*Concerning Infidels*)

O believers! take not the Jews or Christians as friends. They are but friends to one another; and if any one of you taketh them for his friends, then surely he is one of them! Verily God will not guide the evil-doers.

So shalt thou see the diseased at heart speed away to them, and say, "We fear lest a change of fortune befall us." But haply God will of himself bring about some victory or event of his own ordering; then soon will they become repentant for their secret imaginings:

And the faithful will say, "Are these they who swore by God their most solemn oath, that they were surely on your side?" Vain their works; and they themselves shall come to ruin.

O ye who believe! should any of you desert his religion, God will then raise up a people whom he loveth, and who love him, lowly towards the faithful, haughty towards the unbelievers. For the cause of God will they contend, and not fear the blame of the blamer. This is the grace of God! On whom he will he bestoweth it! And God is all-embracing, omniscient!

Verily, your protector is God and his apostle, and those who believe, who observe prayer, and pay the alms of obligation, and who bow in worship.

And whoso take God and his apostle and those who believe for friends, they truly are the people of God! they shall have the upper hand.

O ye who believe! take not such of those who have received the scriptures before you, as scoff and jest at your religion, or the infidels, for your friends; but fear God if ye are believers:

Nor those who when ye call to prayer, make it an object of raillery and derision. This they do because they are a people who have no understanding.

Say: O people of the Book! do ye not disavow us only because we believe in God, and in what he hath sent down to us, and in what he hath sent down aforetime, and because most of you are doers of ill?

Say: Can I announce to you any retribution worse than that which awaiteth them with God? They whom God hath cursed and with whom he hath been angry—and some of whom he hath changed into apes and swine,—and the worshippers of Taghoot, are in evil plight, and have gone farthest astray from the right path!

When they presented themselves to you they said, "We believe"; but infidels they came in unto you, and infidels they went forth! God well knew what they concealed.

Many of them shalt thou see hasten together to wickedness and malice, and to eat unlawful things. Bad indeed is what they do!

Had not their doctors and teachers forbidden their uttering wickedness, and their eating unlawful food, bad indeed would have been their doings!

"Moreover, the hand of God," say the Jews, "is tied up." Their own hands shall be tied up—and for that which they have said shall they be cursed. Nay! outstretched are both his hands! At his own pleasure doth he bestow gifts, and that which hath been sent down to thee from thy Lord will surely increase the rebellion and unbelief of many of them; and we have put enmity and hatred between them that shall last till the day of the resurrection. Oft as they kindle a beacon fire for war shall God quench it! and they strive after violence on the earth: but God loveth not the abettors of violence.

But if the people of the Book believe and have the fear of God, we will surely put away their sins from them and bring them into gardens of delight: and if they observe the law and the evangel, and what hath been sent down to them from their Lord, they shall surely have their fill of good things from above them and from beneath their feet. Some there are among them who keep the right path; but many of them—evil are their doings!

O apostle! proclaim all that hath been sent down to thee from thy Lord: for if thou do it not, thou hast not proclaimed his message at all. And God will protect thee from evil men: verily, God guideth not the unbelievers.

Say: O people of the Book! ye have no ground to stand on, until ye observe the law and the evangel, and that which hath been sent down to you from your Lord. That which hath been sent down to thee from thy Lord will certainly increase the rebellion and unbelief of many of them; but, be not thou troubled for the unbelievers.

Verily, they who believe, and the Jews, and the Sabeites, and the Christians—whoever of them believeth in God and in the last day, and doth what is right, on them shall come no fear, neither shall they be put to grief.

Of old we accepted the covenant of the children of Israel, and sent apostles to them. Oft as an apostle came to them with that for which they had no desire, some they treated as liars, and some they slew;

And they reckoned that no harm would come of it:—so they became blind and deaf! Then was God turned unto them: then many of them again became blind and deaf! but God beheld what they did.

Surely now are they infidels who say, "God is the Messiah son of Mary"; for the Messiah said, "O children of Israel! worship God, my Lord and your Lord." Verily, those who join other gods with God, God doth exclude from paradise, and their abode the fire; and for the wicked no helpers!

They surely are infidels who say, "God is a third of three": for there is no god but one God: and if they refrain not from what they say, a grievous chastisement shall assuredly befall such of them as believe not.

Will they not, therefore, turn unto God, and ask pardon of him? since God is forgiving, merciful!

The Messiah, son of Mary, is but an apostle; other apostles have flourished before him; and his mother was a just person: they both ate food. Behold! how we make clear to them the signs! then behold how they turn aside!

Say: Will ye worship, beside God, that which can neither hurt you nor help you? But God! He only heareth, knoweth.

Say: O people of the Book! outstep not bounds of truth in your religion; neither follow the desires of those who have already gone astray, and caused many to go astray, and themselves gone astray from the evenness of the way.

The Masnavi

A Certain Person in the Time of 'Umar—May God Be Pleased with Him!—Imagines He Sees the New Moon

In the time of 'Umar the month of fast came round, and a number of men ran to the top of a hill with him to take an omen from the new moon of the month of fast. Said one of them: "There, 'Umar, is the new moon."

When 'Umar could not see the moon in the sky, he said: "This moon has arisen out of your imagination; for in the celestial spheres I am keener-sighted than you. Why then do I not see the pure crescent?" He continued: "Moisten your hand, and rub your eyebrows, and then look up towards the crescent."

When he had moistened his eyebrows, he could not see the moon. He said: "O King, it is not the moon; it has disappeared."

He answered: "Yea, the hair of your eyebrows had become as a bow, which shot an arrow of surmise at you."

A single hair deflected from his eyebrow led him into error, so that he boastingly claimed to have seen the moon. Since a deflected hair may veil the sky from you, how will it be when all your members have become deflected?

O you who would walk straight, make straight your members by means of the straight; turn not your face from the threshold of the righteous. The balance may make the balance true; the balance too may make the balance false.

Whoever adjusts his weights to those of the untrue, falls into deficiency and falseness, and his intellect becomes confused.

A Companion of Jesus—on Him Be Peace!—Begs Him to Restore Some Bones to Life

A certain fool was accompanying Jesus; he saw some bones in a deep hollow. He said, "O my companion, teach me that exalted name by which you make the dead alive. Teach it to me, in order that I may do a kindness:—that by it I may give life to these bones."

He answered, "Be silent; that business is beyond you: it is incongruous with your breathings and speech. For that business demands a breath more pure than rain; and more subtle in its action than are the angels. Lifetimes are required before the breath is purified, and one becomes thus a custodian of the treasury of the heavens. Supposing you indeed take this rod firmly in your hand, whence would your hand gain the cunning of Moses?"

He rejoined, "If I be not one who should give utterance to such mysteries, then do you utter the name over the bones."

Jesus said, "O Lord, what mystery is this? What means the tendency of this fool towards such contention? Why is not this sick man solicitous about himself? Why has this lifeless carrion no care for life in himself? He leaves his own dead personality, and seeks to restore an alien corpse."

God said, "He who is an alien to grace seeks and finds naught but disgrace and adversity: if thorny brambles grow, it is the requital of his sowing. He who sows the seeds of thorny brambles in the world,—see

you seek him not in a rose-garden. If he take a rose in his hand, it becomes a thorn; if he go towards a friend, that friend becomes a serpent.
That miserable wretch is the alchemy of snake-poison, in contrariety to
the alchemy of the pious man."

God Takes Counsel with the Angels as to the Creation of Man

Counsel was being taken as to the creation of man, when the souls
were still immersed up to the neck in the sea of God's potency. When
the angels objected to that proposal, the Pirs secretly whistled in derision
at them.

They, the Pirs, were acquainted with the picture of everything which
has become existent, even before the Universal Soul became fettered.
Before the skies existed they saw Saturn; before the existence of grains
they saw bread. Without brain and heart, they were full of thought;
without army and war, they were associated with victory.

That actual vision of theirs is, as regards them, thought; though,
indeed, as regards these people of the world, it is intuition. Thought is
in connection with the past and the future; when it is freed from these
two, the difficult is solved.

They saw every conditioned thing as a thing unconditioned; they saw
the pure metal and the impure before the mine existed.

In the heart of the grape they saw the wine; in absolute non-existence
they saw objects. Before the creation of grapes they drank wines, and
shewed the excitement of intoxication.

In hot July they see December; in the rays of the sun they see the
shade. This firmament drinks draughts as they, the Pirs, circulate the
cup; the sun through their generosity puts on gold brocade.

When of these Pirs you see two friends together,—they are even as
one, and also as six hundred thousand. Their numbers are after the
manner of those of the waves: it is the wind which has produced their
multiplicity.

The sun of spirits has become diffused through the windows, the
bodies. When you look at the sun's disk it is indeed one; but he whose
mental vision is veiled by bodies is in doubt.

The diffusion is entailed by the animal spirit; the human spirit is one essence.

Since God sprinkled his light upon them—his light will never become scattered.

A Governor Orders a Man to Dig Up from the Road a Bramble-Bush Which He Has Planted

A certain unfeeling person of pleasant speech planted a bramble-bush in the middle of the road. The passers-by reproached him, and repeatedly told him to dig it up; but he did not do so.

And every moment that bramble-bush was getting larger, and the feet of the people were covered with blood from the wounds it inflicted. The clothes of the people were torn by its thorns; and the feet of the poor were miserably wounded.

When the governor enjoined him seriously to dig it up, he answered, "Yes, I will dig it up some day."

For a good time he promised to do it to-morrow and to-morrow; and in the meantime his bramble-bush grew firm and robust.

The governor said to him one day, "O promise-breaker, come forward in my business; do not creep back." He rejoined, "O uncle, the days are between us." The governor said, "Hasten; defer not the payment of my debt.

"You who say, 'To-morrow,' learn you this, that in every day which time brings, that evil tree grows younger, and this digger of it up gets more old and helpless. The bramble-bush is gaining strength and on the rise; whilst the proposed digger of it up is getting old and on the decline. The bramble-bush every day and every moment more green and fresh; the digger of it up every day more emaciated and withered. It is becoming younger, and you are becoming older; be quick therefore, and do not waste your time."

Consider the bramble-bush as any bad habit of yours; its thorns at last will often wound your feet. You have often been wounded by your evil nature;—you have no sense; you are utterly devoid of sense.

If you are heedless of others' being wounded, which wounding happens through your evil nature,—if you are heedless of that, I say, you are at least not heedless of your own wounds: you are the torment of yourself and of every stranger.

Either take an axe and strike like a man: like 'Ali cut away this gate of Khaibar; or else graft a rose-bush upon this bramble-bush; graft the light of a friend upon this fire; in order that his light may quench your fire; and the grafting of that rose-bush may make your bramble-bush a bed of roses.

The Being of Man Is like a Forest

The being of man is like a forest;—be full of caution of this being if you are of that breath. In our being there are thousands of wolves and hogs. In our being there is the righteous, the unrighteous; the fair and the foul.

That trait which is predominant decides the temperament: when gold exceeds copper in quantity, the substance is gold. The quality which is predominant in your being,—you will have to rise in the very form of that same quality.

At one moment wolfishness comes into man; at another moment, the moon-like beauty of the face of Joseph. Feelings of peace and of enmity go by a hidden road from bosom to bosom.

Nay, indeed, wisdom, knowledge, and skill pass from man even into the ox and the ass. The untrained horse, rough and unformed, becomes of good easy paces and docile; the bear dances, and the goat also salutes. From men the desire of doing something enters into the dog: he becomes a shepherd, or a hunter, or a guard. From those Sleepers a moral nature passed to the dog of the companions of the Cave, so that he became a seeker of God.

Every moment a new species appears in the bosom; sometimes a demon, sometimes an angel, and sometimes wild beasts.

From that wonderful forest with which every lion is acquainted there is a hidden road to that snare, the bosoms of men.

Steal the pearl of the soul from hearts, O you who are less than a dog!—from the hearts, I would say, of the Sufi saints. Since you steal, steal at least that exquisite pearl; since you bear burdens, bear at least a noble one.

The Wisdom of Luqman

A friend is like gold, and trials are like fire: the pure gold is well and happy in the heart of the fire.

Was it not so with Luqman, who was a devoted slave; who day and night was active in service? His master held him as the first and best in service: he considered him as better than his own sons, because Luqman, though the son of a slave, was a master of himself and one free from desire.

Whatever food they brought the master,—he used to send someone to Luqman upon its being brought, in order that Luqman should partake of it,—the master's design being to eat that which he left.

He used to eat his leavings, and go into raptures; whatever food Luqman did not partake of, he, the master, would throw away. And even if he eat of it, it was without heart and appetite:—this is the mark of an infinite union.

They had brought him once a water-melon as a present; he said, "Go, and call my son, Luqman."

When he had cut it and given him a slice, he ate it like sugar and honey. From the pleasure with which he ate it, he gave him a second, and so on till the seventeenth slice was reached. One slice remained, and he said, "I will eat this myself, so that I may see how sweet a melon this is. He eats it with such pleasure that from his enjoyment one's heart is filled with desire and longs for the morsel."

When he had eaten it, fire flamed in him from its bitterness: it both blistered his tongue, and burnt his throat. From its bitterness he became for a while stupefied; afterwards he said to him, "O soul of the world, how have you made all this poison a sweet antidote? How have you thought this harshness kindness? What patience is this? wherefore is this endurance? Or is it perchance that this life of yours is in your opinion a foe? Why did you not plead a reason for abstaining and say, 'I have an excuse to offer; desist a while.' "

He answered, "I have eaten so much from your bountiful hand that I am bent double with shame. When suddenly I received one bitter thing from your hand, I was ashamed to make you acquainted with it. Since all the parts of my body have grown through your bounties, and are deep in your grain and snare,—if I cry out and complain on account of one thing which is bitter, may the dust of a hundred roads be on all parts of my body! It has received the sweetness of your sugar-giving hand; how could that sweetness allow any bitterness in the melon?"

Bitter things become sweet through love; copper things become golden through love. Dregs become clear and bright through love; pains become salutary through love. Through love a dead person is made living; through love a king is made a slave.

The Two Masters

A king said to a Shaikh in conversation: "Ask me for something in the way of a gift."

The Shaikh said, "Are you not ashamed to speak so to me? Be above this. I have two slaves, and despicable they are; but those two are rulers and lords over you."

The king said, "What are those two? This is an error."

He replied, "The one is 'anger' and the other 'sensuality.' "

"Paradise Is Surrounded by Things Unpleasant to Us; the Fires Are Surrounded by Our Carnal Desires"

Green branches are the source of the food of the fire which shall burn you; but he who is burnt by the fire shall be in proximity to Kausar.

Whoever is suffering an affliction in prison,—that is the requital of a morsel or a carnal desire. Whoever has a share of felicity in a palace,—that is the reward of some combat and affliction. Whomsoever you see unequalled in the possession of gold and silver,—know that he has been patient in earning.

He sees without causes when his eyes have become penetrating;—you, who are bound by sense, pay you attention to causes. He whose soul is beyond natural qualities is in the position of breaking through causes.

The spiritual eye sees the spring of the miracles of the prophets as without cause, and not from water and moisture. Cause is like the physician and the patient; cause is like the lamp and the wick. Twist a new wick for your night-lamp. Know that the Lamp, the sun, is devoid of these things. Go, make plaster for the roof of your house. Know that the roof of the sky is devoid of plaster.

Alas! when our Beloved was the dispeller of our care, the privacy of night passed away, and it became day. Except at night the moon has no effulgence. Seek not the heart's desire except through heart's pain.

You have abandoned Jesus and cherished the ass; hence you are necessarily, as an ass, outside of the curtain. The fortune of Jesus is knowledge and deep spiritual knowledge; these are not the fortune of the ass, O asinine one.

You hear the cry of the ass, and you have compassion; then you know not that the ass is enjoining upon you the properties of the ass. Have compassion upon Jesus, and not upon the ass: do not make the carnal soul lord over your intellect.

If you have become sick in heart through Jesus, still health too comes from him; leave him not.

O sweet-breathed Messiah, how are you as to affliction? for there has never been in the world a treasure without a serpent. How are you, Jesus, at the sight of the Jews? How are you, Joseph, at the hands of the crafty and envious? For this raw people, night and day, you are a furtherer of life even as the night and day.

A Mouse Draws the Leading Rein of a Camel, and Gets Conceited

A little mouse seized in its claws the leading rein of a camel and in its conceit moved on with it. From the readiness with which the camel set off with it, the mouse was deluded into thinking itself a mighty creature.

The mouse's thought was reflected upon the camel; it said to itself, "I will show you something soon; good luck to you!" And so till the mouse came to the bank of a big river, at which the mighty elephant would have felt powerless.

The mouse stopped there and remained helpless. The camel said, "O my companion of the hills and plains, what is this stopping? Why this perturbation? Step on valiantly and enter the water. You are my road-guide and leader; do not stop midway and remain motionless."

The mouse replied, "This is a great and deep river; I am afraid, O companion, of being drowned."

The camel said, "Let me see the extent of the water." Then he speedily put his feet into it. He said, "The water is only up to the knees, stupid mouse; why did you become perturbed, and lose your reason?"

The mouse replied, "It is an ant to you, but a dragon to me, for there are differences in the heights of knees. If, O accomplished being, it is only up to your knees, it is a hundred ells above the crown of my head."

The camel said, "Do not another time be so bold, so that your body and soul may not be burnt by these sparks. Vie you with mice like yourself; there can be no business between a mouse and a camel."

The mouse said, "I repent. For the sake of God help me over this perilous water."

The camel felt compassion and said, "Come; jump up, and sit upon my saddle. This passing over has been granted to me; I could help over hundreds of thousands like you."

Since you are not a prophet, follow the road after him who is one, in order that some day you may get from the pit of your carnal nature to the high place of the Shaikh. Be you a subject since you are not a Sultan; do not try to navigate since you are not a captain. When you are not a perfect master do not take a shop by yourself alone. Submit to be kneaded, in order that you may become paste.

Hear the command, "Listen in silence," and be silent: since you have not become the tongue of God, be ears. But if you speak, speak in the form of interrogation: speak with kings of kings as a humble suppliant.

John the Baptist—on Him Be Peace!—in His Mother's Womb Inclines in Worship before Jesus—on Him Be Peace!

The mother of John before giving birth to him said in private to Mary, "I have found for certain that you will give birth to a King, who will be a Lord of constancy, a wise Apostle. When I have happened to be opposite to you, my unborn child at once has inclined in worship. This embryo inclined in worship before that embryo, so that pain affected my body through its inclination."

Mary said, "I also have perceived within myself an inclination on the part of the infant in my womb."

Fools say, "Cancel this story, because it is an untruth and an error; since Mary at the time of her delivery was far both from strangers and from relatives;—until that woman of persuasive eloquence was delivered without the town, she really did not enter it. When she had given birth to him she then took him up in her arms and carried him to her kindred. Where did the mother of John see her to speak these words to her as to the supposed occurrence?"

Let the caviller know this, that to the man of mind that which is absent as to space is present. The mother of John when far from the eyes of Mary might be present to her spiritual vision. With closed eyes she might see a friend when she has made a lattice of the body.

And if she saw her neither without nor in her own mind, pay attention, simpleton, to the spirit of the story.

O my brother, the story is like a measure; the spirit in it is like the grain. The man of intellect takes the grain, the spirit; he does not pay attention to the measure though it be taken away.

The Contention as to Grapes of Four Persons, Each of Whom Knows Grapes by a Different Name

A man gave a diram to four persons. One of them, a Persian, said, "I will spend this on 'angur.' "

Another of them was an Arab; he said, "No, you rogue; I want 'inab,' not 'angur.' "

A third was a Turk; he said, "I do not want 'inab,' dear friend, I want 'uzum.' "

The fourth was a Greek; he said, "Stop this altercation; I wish for 'istafil.' "

Those persons began to fight against one another, because they were ignorant of the secret of the names. Through sheer ignorance they struck one another with their fists; they were full of ignorance and devoid of knowledge.

If one who knew the inner truth, an estimable man versed in many tongues, had been there, he would have reconciled them. He would have said, "With this one diram I will gratify the desire of all of you. If in all sincerity you entrust your hearts to me, this diram of yours will do so much for you. Your one diram will become as four, which is what is wanted; four enemies will become as one by concord. The words of each of you lead you to contention and disagreement; my words bring you agreement. Therefore be you silent, keep silence, in order that I may be your tongue in speech."

Although your words appear uniform and in harmony, they are the source in their effect of contention and anger.

The Forty-Two Traditions of An-Nawawi

1. Actions are to be judged only in accordance with intentions; and every one gets only what he intended; hence he whose emigration is for the sake of Allah and his apostle, his emigration is for the sake of Allah and his apostle; and he who emigrates for a worldly thing, to get it; or for a wife, to marry her; so his emigration is for that for which he emigrated.

2. It was one day when we were sitting with the apostle of Allah, that a man came towards us with very white clothes and very black hair. The traces of travel were not seen on him, and not one of us recognized him. He sat down by the prophet and propped his knees up against his knees, and placed the palms of his hands on his thighs, and said, "O Mohammed, tell me about Islam." And the apostle of Allah said to him, "Islam is that you should give witness that there is no deity except Allah, and that Mohammed is the apostle of Allah; and you should perform the prayer ceremony, and give alms, and fast in Ramadhan; and pilgrimage to the house, if you can manage it." He said, "You are right." We were surprised at his asking, and saying he was right. He said, "Tell me about faith." He said, "You should believe in Allah and his angels and his books and his apostles and in the last day and in predestination (both good and evil)." He said, "You are right; tell me about *ihsan*." He

said, "You should worship Allah, as if you saw him; for although you do not see him, he sees you." He said, "Tell me about the hour." He said, "The one who is questioned does not know more about it than the questioner." He said, "Tell me about its indications." He said, "It is that a female slave will give birth to her master, or mistress; and that thou wilt see the barefoot and the naked and the destitute and the shepherds going so far as to build." Then off he went and I waited a long time. Then he said, "Do you know, 'Umar, who the questioner was?" I said, "Allah and his apostle know better." He said, "It was Gabriel. He came to teach you your religion."

3. Islam is built on five points:—the witness of there being no deity except Allah, and of Mohammed being the apostle of Allah; the performing of prayer; the giving of alms; the pilgrimage to the house; and the fast of Ramadhan.

4. The creation of any one of you is when he is compressed in his mother's womb for forty days as a speck; then he becomes a clot in the same way; then he becomes a coagulation in the same way; then the angel is sent to him, so he breathes the spirit into him: and the angel is bidden to write up his sustenance, the allotted span of his life, his works, and whether he will be wretched or happy after death; and by Allah (than whom there is no deity) indeed any one of you will work the work of the people of paradise, so that there is only a yard between him and it, and then that which is written overtakes him, and he works the work of the people of the fire and enters it; and indeed any one of you works the work of the people of the fire, so that there is but a yard between him and it, and then that which is written overtakes him, and he works the work of the people of paradise and enters it.

5. The one who introduces (as from himself) into our affair that which has nothing to do with it is a reprobate.

6. What is lawful is obvious, and what is unlawful is obvious; and between them are matters which are ambiguous and of which many people are ignorant. Hence, he who is careful in regard to the ambiguous has justified himself in regard to his religion and his honour; but he who stumbles in the ambiguous has stumbled in the forbidden, as the shepherd pasturing around the forbidden land is on the verge of pasturing in it: is it not that every king of the Arabs has protected land, and is not the protected land of Allah that which he has forbidden? Is it not the fact that there is in the body a clot of blood; if it is in good

condition, the whole body is too; and if it is in rotten condition, so too is the whole body; is not this the heart?

7. Religion is good advice. We said, "Whose?" He, the prophet, said, "Allah's and His Book's and His apostle's, and the Imams of the Muslims, and the generality of them."

8. I have been commanded to wage war upon people until they witness that there is no deity except Allah, and that Mohammed is the apostle of Allah; and that they perform the prayer and give alms. Then if they do that, so far as I am concerned, their lives and property will be protected, unless in conflict with the rights of Islam; and their account is with Allah Ta'ala.

9. What I have forbidden you, avoid; and what I have ordered you, comply with to the utmost of your ability; for what destroyed those who were before you was only the quantity of their questions, and their differences over the matter of their prophets.

10. Allah Ta'ala is good; he accepteth only what is good; and Allah gave to the believers the same command that he gave to those whom he sent. For the Almighty said, "O apostles, eat of the good things and do that which is good." And the Almighty said, "O ye who believe, eat of the good things that we have granted to you." Then he remembered the man on the long journey, dusty and with dishevelled hair, stretching out his hands to heaven and saying, O Lord, O Lord; while his food was forbidden and his drink was forbidden and his raiment was forbidden; and he was fed on that which was forbidden—then how should answer be afforded him?

11. Let go the things in which you are in doubt for the things in which there is no doubt.

12. Leaving alone things which do not concern him is one of the good things in a man's Islam.

13. No one of you is a believer until he loves for his brother what he loves for himself.

14. The blood of a Muslim man is not lawful but for one of three reasons:—an adulterous married person; an avenger of blood; and the one who leaves his religion, that is, splits the community.

15. He that believes in Allah and the last day, let him speak good or hold his peace; and he who believes in Allah and the last day, let him honour his neighbour; and he who believes in Allah and the last day, let him honour his guest.

16. A man said to the prophet, "Give me a command." He said, "Do not get angry." The man repeated the question several times, and he said, "Do not get angry."

17. Allah has prescribed *Ihsan* for everything; hence, if you kill, do it well; and if you slaughter, do it well; and let each one of you sharpen his knife and let his victim die at once.

18. Fear Allah, wherever thou art; and follow up bad actions with good, so as to wipe them out; and behave in a decent way to people.

19. I was behind the prophet one day, and he said, "Young man, I will teach you a lesson; keep hold on Allah and he will keep hold on you; keep hold on Allah, and you will find him in front of you; if you ask anything, ask it from Allah; if ye seek help, seek it from Allah. And know that the nation, if it has agreed in benefiting you in anything, will not benefit you in anything, save in what Allah has written for you; and if it has agreed on harming you in anything, will not harm you in anything, save in a thing Allah has written against you;—the pens are discarded and the pages are dry."

20. Among the things which people comprehended from the material of the first prophecy was, If you are not ashamed, then do whatever you wish.

21. I said, "O apostle of Allah, tell me something about Islam, which I could not ask of any one except you." He said, "Say, I believe in Allah; and then go straight."

22. A man asked the apostle of Allah and said, "Is it your opinion, that, if I pray the prescribed prayers; and fast in Ramadhan; and believe firmly in what is allowable; and shun what is forbidden, and do not do anything more than that, I shall enter the garden?" He said, "Yes."

23. Purification is part of religion; and "Praise be to Allah" fills the scales; and "Allah be exalted" and "Praise be to Allah" fill what is between heaven and earth; and prayer is light; and almsgiving is a proof; and patience is brightness; and the Koran is an argument in your favour or against you; and every one goes about his business at the beginning of the day and sells his soul: he either frees it or causes it to perish.

24. It was when he was relating things about his Lord, that he said: "O my servants, I have forbidden myself wickedness, and have made it a forbidden thing in the midst of you, so do not do injustice to one another.

"O my servants, every one of you is in error, except the one I have guided, so ask guidance from me and I will guide you.

"O my servants, every one of you is hungry, except him whom I have fed; so ask food of me and I will feed you.

"O my servants, every one of you is naked except him whom I have clothed; so ask clothing of me and I will clothe you.

"O my servants, you sin day and night; and I pardon your sins; so ask pardon of me and I will pardon you.

"O my servants, you will never reach harming me, so as to harm me; and you will never reach benefiting me, so as to benefit me.

"O my servants, were the first of you and last of you, both of men and *djinn*—were they in accord once with the most godly heart of a single man amongst you—that would not add aught to my kingdom.

"O my servants, were the first of you and the last of you, both of men and *djinn*—were they according to the dissipated heart of any single man amongst you—that would not diminish aught from my kingdom.

"O my servants, were the first of you and the last of you, both of men and *djinn*—were they to rise up in a single spot on the surface of the earth and to ask me something and I gave to each one what he asked, that would not diminish aught from me, except as the needle does not diminish anything from the sea, when it is thrown in.

"O my servants, it is only your works that I take account of for you; then I recompense you for them; and he who finds good, let him praise Allah; and he who finds otherwise, let him blame himself alone."

25. Some of the companions of the prophet said to him: "The people of wealth brought rewards, praying as we pray and fasting as we fast, and giving alms from the superabundance of their properties." He said: "Has not Allah appointed for you of what you should give alms? Surely in every act of adoration there is almsgiving; and in every *takbir* there is almsgiving; and in every *al hamdu lillah,* there is almsgiving; and in every *Hallelujah* there is almsgiving; and in every bidding to do what is right there is almsgiving; and in every prohibition of what is forbidden there is almsgiving; and in the marriage of any one of you there is alms-giving." They said, "O apostle of Allah, will any one of us reach his desire, and there be in it a reward for him?" He said, "Do you think that, were he to put it among the forbidden things, it would be a sin for him; and likewise if he put it among the allowable things, there would be a reward?"

26. Almsgiving is incumbent upon every "bone" of people each day that the sun rises; it is almsgiving if you make adjustment between a couple; and if you help a man in the matter of his riding-animal and mount him upon her or lift his baggage for him upon her. A good word is almsgiving; and in every step you walk towards prayer there is an act of almsgiving; and it is almsgiving when you ward danger off the road.

27. Righteousness is goodness of character; and sinfulness is what is woven in the soul, and you hate that people should ascertain the matter.

I went to the apostle of Allah, and he said: "You have come to ask about righteousness." I said, "Yes." He said, "Ask your heart to decide; righteousness is what the soul and the heart feel tranquil about; and sinfulness is what is fixed in the soul, and roams about in the breast, even if people give their decision in your favour over and over again."

28. The apostle of Allah exhorted us with an exhortation, by which our hearts were distressed and our eyes flowed down with tears; and we said, "O apostle of Allah, it is as if it were a farewell exhortation; give us a 'last will and testament.' " He said, "My behest is your being piously disposed towards Allah (may he be praised and exalted), listening and obeying, even if a 'slave' is invested with authority over you. Indeed the one who lives from you will notice a big 'discord'; and it is for you to keep my *sunna* and the *sunna* of the rightly-guided Khalifas; cling to them as with your molar teeth; and beware of novel affairs, for surely all innovation is error."

29. I, Mu'adh, said, "O apostle of Allah, inform me of a work which will bring me into the garden and keep me far from the fire." He said, "You have indeed made inquiry about something great; but indeed it is easy for one for whom Allah facilitates things; you should worship Allah without joining aught with him; you should perform prayer, give alms, and fast in Ramadhan; and make pilgrimage to the house." Then he said, "Shall I not indicate to you the doors to good. Fasting is a protection, and almsgiving quenches sin as water quenches fire, and the prayer of a man at the dead of night."

Then he said, "Shall I not tell you about the 'pith' of the matter, and its base and the apex of its prominence?" I said, "Of course, O apostle of Allah." He said, "The 'pith' is Islam; and its base is prayer, and apex of its prominence is holy war." Then he said, "Shall I tell you how to get all this?" I said, "Of course, O apostle of Allah." So he took hold of his tongue, and said, "Control this." I said, "O prophet of Allah, we are indeed to blame for what we speak with it." So he said, "Your mother is bereft of you; will people be toppled into the fire on their faces except for the harvest of their tongues?"

30. Allah Ta'ala has enjoined ordinances, and you must not neglect them; and has laid down limits, and you must not transgress them; and has forbidden certain things which you must not violate; and has been silent over certain things as an act of mercy towards you, not out of forgetfulness, so do not investigate these.

31. A man came to the apostle of Allah and said, "O apostle of Allah, indicate me a work, which, were I to do it, Allah would love me for it, and people would love me too." And he said, "Be abstemious in the world, and Allah will love you; and be abstemious in what belongs to people, and people will love you."

32. Let there be no injury in the world and no requital.

33. If people were granted their claims, then men might claim the possessions and blood of any group of people, but the burden of proof is on the one who stakes the claim; and the oath on the one who denies.

34. Whoever of you sees something of which Allah disapproves, then let him change it with his hand; and if that is impossible, then with his tongue; and if that is impossible, then with his heart; and that is faith of the weakest kind.

35. Do not be envious of each other; and do not outbid each other; and do not hate each other; do not oppose each other; and do not undersell each other; and be, O slaves of Allah, as brothers. A Muslim is a brother to a Muslim, not oppressing him and not forsaking him; not lying to him and not despising him. Here is true piety (and he, Mohammed, would point to his breast three times)—it's quite bad enough for a man to despise his brother Muslim. A Muslim's life, property and honour are inviolate to a Muslim.

36. He who dispels from a believer one of the griefs of the world, Allah will dispel for him a grief on the day of resurrection; he who cheers up a person in difficulties, Allah will cheer him in this world and the next; he who shields a Muslim, Allah will shield him in this world and the next. Allah is there to help his slave, so long as he is out to help his brother, and he who walks a path seeking therein knowledge, Allah will make easy for him a path to paradise through it. And when a company meets together in one of the houses of Allah to pore over the book of Allah and to study it together amongst themselves, the

Shechinah comes down to them and mercy overshadows them; and the angels surround them; and Allah remembers them among them that are his; and the one whose work makes him procrastinate will not be hastened along by the nobility of his ancestry.

37. Surely Allah has written down good deeds and evil ones; then he made that clear, so that he who is concerned about a good deed, but does not perform it, Allah has written it down with himself as a perfect good deed; and if he is concerned about it and fulfils it, then Allah has written it down with himself for ten good deeds up to seven hundred-fold—exceeding manifold; and if he is concerned about a bad deed and does not fulfil it, then Allah has written it down with himself as one good, perfect deed; and if he is concerned about it and fulfilled it, then Allah has written it down as a single bad deed.

38. Allah Ta'ala said: Whoever is hostile to a supporter of mine, on him will I declare war; and my slave will not approach me with anything dearer than that which I put on him as an obligation; and he continues presenting me with matters of supererogation, that I may love him. And when I love him, I am his hearing by which he hears; and his sight by which he sees; and his hand by which he strikes for me; and his foot by which he walks. And if he asks me for anything, I will certainly give it to him; and if he takes refuge in me, I will certainly give him refuge.

39. Surely Allah for my sake has overlooked the error of my nation and its forgetfulness, and its being forced to do a thing it does not like.

40. Be in the world as if you were a stranger or a traveller: when evening time comes, expect not the morning; and when morning time comes expect not the evening; and prepare as long as you are in good health for sickness, and so long as you are alive for death.

41. Not one of you is a believer until his passion becomes in line with that which I have brought.

42. Allah Ta'ala said: So long as you call upon me and hope in me, I forgive you all that originates from you; and I will not heed, O son of man, should your sins reach the horizon of the heavens, and then you asked my pardon and I would pardon you. O son of man, were you to come to me with almost an earth-ful of sins, and then you met me without joining anything with me in the godhead, then would I come to you with an earth-ful of forgiveness.

NOTES

HINDU SCRIPTURES

BUDDHIST SCRIPTURES

CONFUCIANIST SCRIPTURES

TAOIST SCRIPTURES

ZOROASTRIAN SCRIPTURES

JUDEO-CHRISTIAN SCRIPTURES

MOHAMMEDAN SCRIPTURES

CONDENSED BIBLIOGRAPHY

BOOKS QUOTED

BOOKS NOT QUOTED

GLOSSARY

INDEX

Notes

In the following notes are (1) a short characterization and history of the scriptures included in the seven basic divisions of THE BIBLE OF THE WORLD, (2) detailed identification of the source from which each text is taken, and (3) some statements of parallels and contrasts between legends and conceptions of the various religions. Such statements are by no means intended to include all the parallels which may be drawn or the comparisons which may be made, but rather to serve as a stimulant for the serious reader to find his own parallels in other parts of the texts, and to suggest a method of reading whereby one subject may be followed consistently through the world's sacred books.

HINDU SCRIPTURES

"Hinduism" is the general name given to the religious creeds and practices of a number of Hindus estimated (by L. D. Barnett, in his monograph *Hinduism*) at 207,000,000. Hume, in *The World's Living Religions*, quotes the 1931 census of India, which gives the number as 239,195,140. It is the oldest living organized religion in the world, and embraces within its many sects a variety of detailed beliefs and a most universal tolerance of all religious belief. Basically its worship is addressed to an Impersonal, all-pervading, never-to-be-completely-comprehended creative and ruling eternal force, which existed before the universe, before there were gods or men, which is in all animate and inanimate objects. Of this force the various gods (Vishnu, Indra, Rudra, etc.) were born, each a symbol of some aspect or power of the all-pervading, unified impersonal force or, as we would like to say, from the point of view of Western theology, each a symbol of the various aspects of the one God.

The age of the Hindu religion is unknown. Certainly its earliest scriptures, the Vedas, preserved and passed on orally for generations before ever they were written down, had accumulated as early as 1000 B.C.—many scholars believe earlier than that.

Next in antiquity are the Brahmana-scriptures, which were compiled probably about 800 B.C., tremendous works recounting the Vedic legends and recording the liturgies and rituals of the four Vedic schools of thought. Some of the speculations of the Vedas were carried further, and modified somewhat.

Out of these speculations grew the Upanishads (eighth or seventh century B.C.) in which religious questioning was carried further and a new importance given to the attainment of knowledge as the way to spiritual freedom. This period was one of the richest of all in the history of Hinduism, both in religious thought and in the production of creative religious literature. In the older Upanishads the conception of the one absolute supreme being, the basic conception of monotheism, was given an emphasis which no religion has ever surpassed.

The next great addition to the sacred books of the Hindus was the gigantic epic poem, the Mahabharata, which was begun about 500 B.C. and into which was inserted—perhaps as late as the second or third century A.D.—the Bhagavad-Gita (or, the Lord's Song), its best known and, from the religious point of view, its most important, part. In the Gita the importance of activity and devotion are stressed.

The Puranas (of which we have included representative parts from the Vishnu, the Garuda, and the Markandeya) are later, most of them having been composed during the first ten centuries A.D. In their original form they are poems of great length, and in simple popular style recount myths of cosmology and a vast miscellany of social and religious instruction.

Sri Ramakrishna, who lived and wrote in the nineteenth century, is an example of recent Hindu thought which has been somewhat modified by Western theology. Here, as in the non-dogmatic, non-sectarian utterances of those whom May Lamberton Becket has called "the unchurched spiritual" of the modern Western world, we find strong evidence of the gradual amalgamation of all deep religious thought throughout the world, which may eventually do away with religious sectarianism.

Page 3. *The Rig-Veda.* "Veda, meaning knowledge, is the name given to certain ancient Sanskrit works which express the early religious beliefs of the Hindus. These are the Rig-Veda, the Sama-Veda, the Yajur-Veda, and the Atharva-Veda. Of these, the Rig-Veda—so called because its Sanhita or collection of Mantras or hymns consists of Richas or verses intended for loud recitation—is the oldest, the most important, and the most generally interesting, some of its hymns being rather Indo-European than Hindu, and representing the condition of the Aryans before their final settlement in India. These four Vedas are considered to be of divine origin and to have existed from all eternity, the Rishis or sacred poets to whom the hymns are ascribed being merely inspired seers who saw or received them by sight directly from the supreme Creator. In accordance with this belief these sacred books have been orally preserved and handed down with the most reverential care from generation to generation.
Of these hymns there are more than a thousand, arranged in ten mandalas, circles, or books, each of which is ascribed to one poet or seer, or to one family."
    —From the preface to *Hymns of the Rig-Veda,* by Ralph T. H. Griffith.
    The Hymns of the Rig-Veda are reprinted from *The Hymns of the Rig-Veda,* 2 volumes, translated by Ralph T. H. Griffith. Benares, E. J. Lazarus and Company, 1896.
    Page 3. *Creation.* Rig-Veda X, 129.
    Page 3. *"That One Thing."* "Tatekam." Tat = neuter personal pronoun. Nameless power beyond and between all things. The essence and substance as well as the source of life. The only true reality behind the supposed reality of our error-bound experiences. Ekam = the One, as it is understood in all mysticism, Unity. "That One Thing" and "that unit" are attempts in translation to indicate the meaning of the Sanskrit which speaks of the single primordial substance out of which the universe has developed. It is that which, in all Indian religious literature, is above men and gods alike, centre and motivator of the universe and all its details.
    Page 4. *To Dawn.* Rig-Veda I, 113.
    Page 4. *Savitar.* Stimulator, vivifier; the god who personifies generative power. Here, the sun. "Her white offspring" are the clouds which attend her. "Both the heavens" are day and night.
    Page 5. *To Indra.* Rig-Veda I, 32.
    Page 5. *Tvashtar* in ordinary diction means carpenter. In the Vedas it is the appellation of a god, the divine artificer.
    Page 7. *To Varuna.* Rig-Veda II, 28.
    Page 7. *Aditya* is the sun, child of infinity, that is, of *Aditi* of verse 3 of this hymn.
    Page 8. *To Varuna.* Rig-Veda V, 85.
    Page 9. *"If we have sinned,"* etc. Cf. "Forgive us our trespasses," in the Lord's Prayer, p. 1126.
    Page 10. *To Agni.* Rig-Veda X, 88.
    Page 10. *"Agni was born,"* etc. Agni here personifies the sun.
    Page 12. *To Agni, in Praise of Night and Day.* Rig-Veda VI, 9.
    Page 13. *"All gods of one accord,"* etc. Here is another statement of the monistic note of Hinduism. See selection from the Brihadaranyaka Upanishad, "How Many Gods?" p. 54.
    Page 13. *To the Waters.* Rig-Veda VII, 49.
    Page 13. *To Varuna.* Rig-Veda VII, 86.
    Page 14. *"Free us from sins,"* etc. Here is the doctrine of hereditary sin contained in the Old Testament conception, "Visiting the iniquity of the fathers upon the children unto the third and fourth generation."
    Page 15. *To Frogs.* Rig-Veda VII, 103. Professor F. Max Müller wrote of this hymn: "The hymn, which is called a panegyric of the frogs, is clearly a satire on the priests. It is curious to observe that the same animals should have been chosen by the Vedic satirist which were selected by the earliest satirist of Greece, i.e., Aristophanes, as the representatives of the Homeric heroes."
    Page 16. *To Indra.* Rig-Veda VIII, 6. (Somewhat cut.)
    Page 17. *Dialogue between Yama and Yami.* Rig-Veda X, 10. "Yama and Yami" = forming a pair. Twin son and daughter of Vivasvat, the "shining forth" god of the

NOTES   1347

morning sun. "They are," says von Roth, "twin brother and sister, and are the first human pair, originators of the race. As the Hebrew conception [Genesis. See p. 644] closely connects the parents of mankind by making the woman formed from a portion of the body of the man, so, by Indian tradition, they are placed in the relation of twins." Professor F. Max Müller, on the other hand, considers this an unsound speculation and interprets them as representing Day and Night. The Atharva-Veda, however, speaks of Yama as "the first man that died, and the first that departed to the celestial world." Because of this he was early regarded as the god who rules over the departed fathers in heaven. Later he is regarded as the god of death, presiding in the lower region (see Katha Upanishad, "The House of Death," p. 43). His name is thought to mean "subduer" or "punisher." He is the regent of the South, and younger brother of Manu, reputed author of hymns and the books of laws, The Ordinances of Manu. Compare the name "Yama" with "Yima," the good shepherd and earliest man of Zoroastrianism (p. 581). It is also of interest that Yama and Yami, Adam and Eve of the Jewish Old Testament, Mashyoi and Mashya of Zoroastrianism (pp. 625, 635) are, in each case, of one flesh. It is interesting also to find in all these stories and also in the Buddhist story of mankind's assumption of physical form (p. 264) that each records the first manifestation of sexual attraction in the human race, and each records shame in connexion with it, as does also the story of the conception of Zarathushtra (p. 609). See also Upanishad story, p. 38, and note referring to this page.

Page 18. *Funeral Hymn.* Rig-Veda X, 154.
Page 19. *Prayer of a Gambler.* Rig-Veda X, 34. The dice used at this time were made from nuts "sprung from tall trees, whose single point is final." The singer apparently had an unlucky habit of throwing two aces, commonly called in modern crap-shooters' language, "snake-eyes."
Page 20. *To Purusha.* Rig-Veda X, 90. "Purusha," meaning literally "person," "man," here means soul, the universal soul, highest personal principle, supreme spirit, "All that yet hath been," etc.—one of the many attempts in the Vedas and Upanishads to express the Indian conception of the final universal divine principle behind the gods, men, and the universe.
Page 21. *To Liberality.* Rig-Veda X, 117.
Page 22. *To Night.* Rig-Veda X, 127.
Page 23. *To Aranyani, the Woods Goddess.* Rig-Veda X, 46.
Page 23. *The Atharva-Veda.* The Atharva-Veda hymns, pp. 23 ff., are taken from *The Hymns of the Atharva-Veda,* translated by Ralph T. H. Griffith (2 volumes). Benares, E. J. Lazarus and Company, 1895.
Page 23. *Blessing for a Child.* Atharva-Veda II, 28.
Page 24. *A Love Charm.* Atharva-Veda III, 22.
Page 25. *To a Magical Plant, That It Heal a Broken Bone.* Atharva-Veda IV, 12.
Page 25. *A Charm to Destroy Hostile Priests.* Atharva-Veda V, 7.
Page 26. *To Heaven and Earth.* Atharva-Veda V, 7.
Page 26. *A Charm against Witchcraft.* Atharva-Veda V, 14. "A wild boar dug thee." Obviously this charm was used in connexion with a plant supposed to possess magical powers, or the root of such a plant.
Page 27. *A Charm to Grow Hair.* Atharva-Veda VI, 22.
Page 27. *To Bless a Child's First Teeth.* Atharva-Veda VI, 140.
Page 28. *A Water Charm.* Atharva-Veda II, 3.
Page 28. *A Charm against Fear.* Atharva-Veda II, 15.
Page 28. *A Charm against Sterility.* Atharva-Veda III, 22.
Page 29. *A Blessing on Barley.* Atharva-Veda VI, 142.
Page 29. *One Common Spirit.* Atharva-Veda VII, 19.
Page 30. *To Time.* Atharva-Veda XIX, 53.
Page 31. *The Satapatha-Brahmana.* Selections from the Satapatha-Brahmana are from the translation by Julius Eggeling according to the text of the Madhandina School. From *The Sacred Books of the East,* edited by F. Max Müller. Reprinted here by permission of the publishers, the Clarendon Press, Oxford.
Page 31. *The Creation of Prajapati and the Gods.* Satapatha-Brahmana, Kanda XI, Adhyaya I, Brahmana VI.
Page 32. *Manu's Escape from the Flood.* Satapatha-Brahmana, Kanda I, Adhyaya VIII, Brahmana I. This is the Hindu legend of the deluge, of folk-tradition throughout the world—a legend the basic fact of which geologic research is just now beginning to

authenticate. For versions in other scriptures, see the Old Testament story of Judeo-Christianity, p. 648; the two Zoroastrian accounts, pp. 583 and 628; and the mention in the Chinese classics on pp. 384 and 445. Also of interest is the extract from the Babylonian Epic of Gilgamesh in the note to p. 648. The Egyptian account declares that Tem, or Atem, the sun god, let loose a flood of waters to destroy mankind, and only those who were with the god in his boat escaped. In the account of the Arawak Indians of northern Brazil the flood was loosed when a monkey removed a basket placed by the god Sigu over the hollow stump of a tree filled with water. Sigu led the animals to a mountain top and kept them while a terrible storm ensued. One human being survived the flood and re-peopled the earth by changing stones into human beings. The Athapascan Indians of North America tell how Yetl, the raven who created the world and man, saved the first men from the flood. A legend of the Caribs of the Antilles tells how mankind was saved from the flood by an ibis.

Page 34. *The Fire-Altar, the Universe.* Satapatha-Brahmana, Kanda X, Adhyaya V, Brahmana IV.

Page 37. *The Sacrificial Horse, the Universe.* Satapatha-Brahmana, Kanda X, Adhyaya VI, Brahmana IV.

Page 38. *The Upanishads.* Save where otherwise noted, selections from the Upanishads are taken from the translation by F. Max Müller in *The Sacred Books of the East,* and are here reprinted by permission of the publishers, the Clarendon Press, Oxford. These selections are also available in *Hindu Scriptures,* edited by Dr. Nicol Macnicol, Everyman's Library 944; London, Dent; New York, Dutton.

Page 38. *The Universal Self.* Brihadaranyaka Upanishad. Adhyaya I, Brahmana IV; Adhyaya II, Brahmana IV.

Page 38. *"He then made this his Self to fall in two,"* etc. In this story of the creation of woman there is a close analogy to the Adam and Eve story of Genesis, and the Zoroastrian propagation legend, for here woman and man are made by a division of one person (as Eve is made from Adam's rib). In this Hindu legend there is a closer identification of man with creation, since the first man is "Self alone," that is, "Atman," the creative universal essence which, in Hindu religious philosophy, is the core of our being. Here the Atman, in the shape of the first man, creates woman, and then, through various changes and further divisions, other animals.

It is interesting to note, however, that here, as in the myths of the beginning of human propagation in the other religions, as well as in the Yama and Yami legend of the Rig-Veda, the consciousness of sexual attraction is immediately followed by a sense of shame. See note referring to p. 17.

Page 41. *"He who knows this, obtains all this."* Note the emphasis on knowing here and elsewhere. Indians divide their history into three periods, (1) Karmamarga, or activity path, (2) Jnanamarga, or knowledge path, (3) Bhaktimarga, or devotion path. The Vedas represent the first, the Upanishads the second, and the Bhagavad-Gita and modern philosophies the third.

Page 43. *"There is no more knowledge."* Other translations read: "After death there is no consciousness."

Page 43. *The House of Death.* Katha Upanishad, complete. Slightly rearranged and edited to preserve its natural dramatic form. Note that here Yama appears, not as the first man (see p. 17 and note referring to that page) but in his later form as Death and ruler of the nether regions.

Page 48. *"This one does not kill,"* etc. Further explained by Krishna in the Bhagavad-Gita. See pp. 87, 88.

Page 49. *"The sharp edge of a razor is difficult to pass over."* Cf. Zoroastrian account of the Chinvad Bridge, p. 621.

Page 52. *"The sun does not shine there."* Cf. Revelations: "And the city had no need of the sun, neither of the moon, to shine in it; for the glory of God did lighten it" (p. 1245).

Page 53. *"He is."* Cf. Old Testament name of Jehovah, "I am that I am," p. 698. Both of these passages conform to the tendency in all religions to derive the name of God from the verb "to be."

Page 54. *How Many Gods?* Brihadaranyaka Upanishad, Adhyaya III, Brahmana IX. This is one of the most forceful expressions of the basic monotheism of the Hindu religion.

Page 54. *The Light of Man.* Brihadaranyaka Upanishad, Adhyaya IV, Brahmana IV.

Page 59. *"No, no!"* The Sanskrit is "Neti, neti" = "Not this, not that," that is, not anything to which a precise name or description may be applied. Cf. first line of the Tao-Te-King, p. 471.

Page 59. *My Self within the Heart.* Chhandogya Upanishad, Prapathaka III, Khanda XIV.

Page 60. *When the Sun Rises.* Chhandogya Upanishad, Prapathaka IV, Khanda XIX.

Page 61. *Quarrel of the Senses.* Chhandogya Upanishad, Prapathaka V, Khanda I.

Page 62. *The Education of Svetaketu.* Chhandogya Upanishad, Prapathaka VI, complete.

Page 64. *"No one can henceforth mention"* etc. Cf. Ecclesiastes, "There is no new thing under the sun," p. 926.

Page 68. *The Power of God.* From the Svetasvatara Upanishad.

Page 70. "The sun does not shine there," etc. See note referring to page 52.

Page 71. *Father and Son.* I—From Kaushitaki Upanishad, reprinted here, by permission of the publishers, from *The Thirteen Principal Upanishads,* translated from the Sanskrit by Robert Ernest Hume. London, Humphrey Milford, 1934.

Page 72. *II*—from same source as *I.*

Page 73. *III*—Brihadaranyaka Upanishad, Adhyaya I, Brahmana V.

Page 74. *The Blessed Triad.* Brihadaranyaka Upanishad, Adhyaya V, Brahmana II.

Page 74. *The Way of Truth.* From Mundaka Upanishad, as translated by Robert Ernest Hume in *The Thirteen Principal Upanishads,* listed in note to page 71.

Page 75. *The Glory of God.* Isa Upanishad, complete. Reprinted by permission of the publishers, from *Himalayas of the Soul,* translated by J. Mascaro. New York, E. P. Dutton and Company, 1938.

Page 77. *The Ordinances of Manu.* Selections reprinted from *The Ordinances of Manu,* translated from the Sanskrit by Arthur Coke Burnell. London, Kegan Paul, Trench, Trubner and Company, 1891.

Page 77. *Creation.* From the Ordinances of Manu, Lecture I.

Page 79. *Laws I.* From the Ordinances of Manu, Lecture IV.

Page 79. *"A twice-born man"* is one who has been "born again" through the enlightenment he has received from his guru, or spiritual leader; therefore, general appellation for a man of the Brahmana-caste. The conception is not dissimilar to Christ's "Except a man be born again." See p. 1147.

Page 80. *II.* From the Ordinances of Manu, Lecture V.

Page 81. *"No act is to be done,"* etc. Cf. St. Paul's attitude toward women in the Epistles of the New Testament.

Page 82. *III.* From the Ordinances of Manu, Lecture VIII.

Page 84. *IV.* From the Ordinances of Manu, Lecture IX.

Page 85. *The Bhagavad-Gita, or, The Lord's Song.* The Bhagavad-Gita selections reprinted by permission of the publishers, from *The Bhagavad-Gita, or, The Lord's Song,* translated by Annie Besant. Wheaton, Illinois, the Theosophical Press, 1929; London, the Theosophical Publishing House.

Page 85. *Revolt against War.* From the Bhagavad-Gita, first and second discourses.

Page 88. *The Rule of Action.* From the Bhagavad-Gita, third discourse.

Page 91. *The Rule of Wisdom.* From the Bhagavad-Gita, fourth discourse.

Page 92. *The Nature of God.* From the Bhagavad-Gita, seventh discourse.

Page 93. *The Imperishable.* From the Bhagavad-Gita, eighth discourse.

Page 95. *The Lord of All.* From the Bhagavad-Gita, ninth discourse.

Page 96. *The Form of God.* From the Bhagavad-Gita, eleventh discourse.

Page 97. *The Rule of Devotion.* From the Bhagavad-Gita, twelfth discourse.

Page 99. *The Good Man and the Evil.* From the Bhagavad-Gita, sixteenth discourse.

Page 100. *The Way of Deliverance.* From the Bhagavad-Gita, eighteenth discourse.

Page 102. *The Vishnu Purana.* Selections from the Vishnu Purana reprinted from *The Vishnupuranam,* edited by Manmatha Nath Dutt from translation by H. H. Wilson. Calcutta, H. C. Dass, 1894.

Page 102. *The Sacred Ganges.* From Vishnu Purana, Section VIII, Part II.

Page 102. *The General Duties of Man.* From Vishnu Purana.

Page 104. *The Duties of Householders.* From Vishnu Purana, Section X, Part III.

Page 109. *The Burden of Life.* From Vishnu Purana, Section V, Part VI.

Page 112. *Benediction.* From Vishnu Purana, Section VIII, Part VI.

Page 113. *The Garuda Purana.* Selections from the Garuda Purana are taken from

The Garuda Puranam, edited and published by Manmatha Nath Dutt. Calcutta, Society for the Resuscitation of Indian Literature, 1908.

Page 113. *The Duties of the Four Castes.* From Garuda Purana, Chapter XLIX.

Page 114. *The Worship of Ancestors.* From Garuda Purana, Chapters LXXXIII, LXXXIV, LXXXV.

Page 119. *Of Associates.* From Garuda Purana, Chapters CXII, CXIII, CXIV.

Page 121. *"Crooked trees," etc.* Cf. stories of the crooked trees in the works of Chuang Tze, pp. 513, 514.

Page 121. *Karma.* From Garuda Purana, Chapters CXIII, CXV.

Page 124. *A Duty to Children.* From Garuda Purana, Chapter CXV.

Page 124. *The Markandeya Purana.* Selections are taken from *The Markandeya Puranam,* edited by Manmatha Nath Dutt. Calcutta, H. C. Dass, 1896.

Page 124. *Sumati Instructs His Father.* Markandeya Purana, Chapters 10, 11, 12, 13, 14, 15, 16.

Page 132. *"It so happened," etc.* Note the striking similarity between this scene and the corresponding one in Dante's *Inferno.* It is highly doubtful that Dante had access to this story. It is probably rather an important example of the psychological phenomenon by which the same conceptions arise in different minds at different times and places.

Page 136. *The Development of Creatures.* Markandeya Purana, Chapter XLIX.

Page 139. *Brahma's Petition to the Sun.* Markandeya Purana, Chapter CIII.

Page 141. *Sankaracharya's Atma Bodha.* Reprinted from *Sankaracharya; His Life and Teachings,* a translation of Atma Bodha by Sitha Nath Dutta. Calcutta, H. C. Dass, Elysium Press, for the Society for the Resuscitation of Indian Literature, 1899. Atma Bodha, or, Knowledge of Spirit, is one of the best-known and most reverenced of the many works of Sankaracharya (more commonly known as Sankara), a Hindu philosopher and religious organizer of the ninth century A.D. He was essentially a reformer, working against those Hindu sects who neglected, or dissented from, the conception of the divine origin of the Vedas. His greatest opponents were the Buddhists, and he contributed largely to the decline of Buddhism in India. Atma Bodha is especially interesting in the light of the contemporary doctrine of Christian Science.

Page 142. *The Hathayoga Pradipika.* Selections are taken from *The Hatha-Yoga Pradipika of Swatmaram Swami,* translated by Shrinivas Iyangar. Bombay, the Bombay Theosophical Publication Fund, 1893.

Page 146. *The Yoga Sutras of Patanjali.* Reprinted, with the permission of the publishers, from *The Light of the Soul, Its Science and Effect,* a paraphrase of the Yoga Sutras of Patanjali, with commentary, by Alice A. Bailey. New York, Lucis Publishing Company, 1927. The Yoga Sutras comprise the basic teaching of the school of Raja-Yoga—a development of Yoga for which the Hatha-Yoga practices (a few of which are outlined in selections from the Hathayoga Pradipika given immediately before the Yoga Sutras) are a preparation. The age of these practices is unknown. Even the date of the birth of Patanjali is uncertain. Most occidental authorities suggest a date between 820 B.C. and 300 B.C., though some believe he was born after the time of Christ.

Page 151. *The Sarva-Darsana-Samgraha.* Selections are taken from *The Sarva-Darsana-Samgraha,* or *Review of the Different Systems of Hindu Philosophy,* by Madhava Acharya, translated by E. B. Cowell, M.A., and A. E. Gough, M.A. London, Kegan Paul, Trench, Trubner and Company, 1894.

Page 155. *The Hitopadesa.* Selections are taken from *The Hitopadesa,* translated from the Sanskrit by Francis Johnson. London, Chapman and Hall, 1928.

Page 161. *The Works of Sri Ramakrishna.* Selections are reprinted, with permission of the publishers, from *The Sayings of Sri Ramakrishna,* compiled by Swami Abhedananda. New York, the Vedanta Society, 1903.

BUDDHIST SCRIPTURES

The early sacred books of the Buddhists are contained in the Tripitaka or Three Baskets, the Vinaya Pitaka (Discipline Basket), the Sutta Pitaka (Instruction Basket), and Abhidhamma Pitaka (Metaphysical Basket). These are in Pali, a composite language related to that spoken by the common people of North-Central India, the homeland of Gotama, the Buddha. In addition to these Pali books there are many later scriptures in the Sanskrit language.

Original Buddhism was founded in the teachings of Gotama (Gautama in Sanskrit), born 560 B.C., a prince of the Sakya clan who, at the age of twenty-nine, leaving his wife, child, and prospects of future status as a ruler (see p. 192 for legendary account), retired to the forest. There, after seven years' meditation, seated under a tree (see pp. 204 ff.) he came to those conclusions which, as founder and leader of an order of followers called bhikkhus, he expounded to them and to the world. It is because of this that he received the title Buddha, which is not a name but an appellation meaning "the Enlightened" or "the Knowing" One (bodhi = knowledge). There is a parallel for this in the appellation "Christ," the Messiah, as applied to Jesus of Nazareth.

Gotama's doctrine is a composite of ethical rules and philosophical approach to the riddle of human existence and the problem of human misery. It does not recognize the Hindu caste system, denies, or evades, the conclusions of Hinduism concerning an intangible supreme being with its coterie of personified powers in the form of gods, and exalts renunciation of all desires as the way to achieve cessation of misery through Nirvana (a state variously explained by interpretative scholars as "passionless peace," "extinction of individual consciousness through merging with the infinite," "complete extinction," etc.). It places the blame for an undesired continuation of existence through rebirth not upon fate, God, the devil, or heredity, but on the individual through the operation of the law of Karma (the continuing effect of one's deeds). The world about us, according to much Buddhist doctrine, is delusion, the ego is not genuine, not a true reality, but only a degrading composite of temporary, obstructive delusions.

Yet with all of the socially negative emphasis upon renunciation of the world, withdrawal from society, celibacy, and a materially non-productive life, there is in the Buddha's teaching perhaps a higher degree of human compassion than exists in any other religion save that of Christ. (See "The Story of Kisagotami," as an example, p. 306). Indeed, more parallels have been drawn between the teachings of Christ and of Buddha than between those of any other two religious leaders.

After the death of the Buddha, the Buddhist order in India eventually degenerated and was subsequently almost completely driven out by the onward sweep of Islam. To-day there is only a small group of Buddhists (2000 according to Robert Ernest Hume in *The World's Living Religions*, Scribner's, 1938) left in the homeland of the Buddha. However, the religion had meanwhile spread to Ceylon and to the north and east into Tibet, China, Japan, and south-eastern Asia, where it has flourished continuously since. Its followers are variously estimated. Robert Ernest Hume (*op. cit.*) says the "nearest estimate is 137,000,000." But he also quotes T. W. Rhys Davids's figure of 500,000,000. Much depends upon the mode of reckoning.

Page 181. *The Conception and Birth of the Buddha.* From the Introduction to the Jataka. Reprinted, by permission of the publishers, from *Buddhism in Translations*, by Henry Clarke Warren. Cambridge, Harvard University Press, 1915. For other accounts of immaculate or otherwise miraculous conceptions, see pp. 383, 609, 1051, 1247 ff.

Page 183. *"The four guardian angels," etc.* Cf. the visitation of the angel of the Lord to the Virgin Mary, p. 1052, to Anna, p. 1248, to Zacharias, p. 1052, to the infant Zarathushtra, p. 611 and to Joseph, p. 1252. Throughout the history of religion there is a tendency to associate heavenly visitations and miraculous ethereal and terrestrial phenomena with the births and deaths of its most sacred figures. This story of the miraculous conception of the Buddha has another significant parallel with the story of the conception of Jesus. Buddha, in the form of a white elephant, seems, in the Buddhist story, to have conceived himself; "by striking her on the right side, he seemed to enter her womb." If the Christian trinity of Father, Son, and Holy Ghost as one, is taken into consideration, something of the implication of self-fatherhood is contained in the story of Christ's conception by the Holy Ghost (p. 1051). See also pp. 605 ff. for elements of divinity and the miraculous in the birth of Zarathushtra, and p. 383, for instance, in the Chinese classics.

Page 184. *"Be not anxious, great king!"* Cf. the words of the angel to Zacharias, p. 1052, and to Joseph, p. 1252.

Page 185. *"Womb . . . can never be occupied again."* In the early days of Christianity a significant controversy was waged over the question of whether Jesus had brothers or sisters, those on the negative side holding, as do the Buddhists, that the body of the Saviour's Mother was sacred to the holy birth alone. This formed a part of the increasing "Mary worship" of the fourth century A.D., and is a part of the foundation of the position of the Virgin Mary in contemporary Catholic theology. On the other side were those who minimized the value of sexual abstinence and held that other children were born to Mary. See St. Paul's mention of "the Lord's brother" (p. 1207) and "Mary, the mother of Jesus, with his brethren" (p. 1176).

Page 185. *"He sent her away,"* etc. It is interesting to note that Jesus was also born, not at Mary's home, but while she was on a journey. See the Gospel account, p. 1054, and the Apocryphal story, p. 1253.

Page 186. *"Two streams of water from the sky."* An example of celestial phenomena connected with the birth of a sacred or divine being; cf. the star of Bethlehem (p. 1056), and "the glory of the Lord" and "the heavenly hosts" (pp. 1054–1055). See also p. 611 for the visitation of archangels to the infant Zarathushtra, and p. 183 and note referring to that page.

Page 186. *"The chief am I,"* etc. Buddha shouts "the shout of victory" upon being born. Zarathushtra laughs out loud. (See p. 611.)

Page 187. *The Holy Child.* From the Introduction to the Jataka. Reprinted (as above) from Warren's *Buddhism in Translations.*

Page 187. "Entered the dwelling of the king." Cf. visit of the Magi (who Robert Ernest Hume, in *The World's Living Religions,* says "may be identified with Zoroastrian priests") to the new-born Jesus (p. 1056).

Page 188. *He Sees the Four Signs.* From the Introduction to the Jataka. Reprinted (as above) from Warren's *Buddhism in Translations.*

Page 190. *The World about Him.* From *The Buddha-Charita,* Books III and IV. Reprinted here, with the permission of the publishers, from *Buddhist Mahayana Texts, Part I. The Buddha-Karita of Asvaghosha,* translated from the Sanskrit by E. B. Cowell. Being Vol. XLIV of *The Sacred Books of the East,* edited by F. Max Müller. Oxford, Clarendon Press, 1894.

Page 192. *The Great Retirement.* From the Introduction to the Jataka, reprinted (as above) from Warren's *Buddhism in Translations.*

Page 196. *"At that moment came Mara,"* etc. This is the first of several attempts which Mara, the evil one, makes to turn Buddha back from his mission. (See p. 205.) Cf. attempts by the personified forces of evil to destroy Zarathushtra, pp. 586, 606, 611, 615, et al., and Christ's temptation by Satan, p. 1062.

Page 197. *Buddha Is Instructed and Instructs.* From *The Buddha-Charita,* Book VI. Reprinted (as above) from *The Sacred Books of the East.*

Page 198. "Uttered his inward thought," etc. Cf. Christ teaching the elders in the temple.

Page 199. *Sad Homecoming.* From *The Buddha-Charita,* Book VIII. Reprinted (as above) from *The Sacred Books of the East.*

Page 200. *Gautami's Lament.* From *The Buddha-Charita,* Book VIII. Reprinted (as above) from *The Sacred Books of the East.*

Page 201. *The Plaint of Yasodhara.* From *The Buddha-Charita,* Book VIII. Reprinted (as above) from *The Sacred Books of the East.*

Page 203. *The Firm Resolve.* From *The Buddha-Charita,* Book XII. Reprinted (as above) from *The Sacred Books of the East.*

Page 205. *Assault by Mara.* From *The Buddha-Charita,* Book XIII. Reprinted (as above) from *The Sacred Books of the East.* See p. 196 and note referring to that page.

Page 206. *"Suryaka, the enemy of the fish,"* because he dried up the world ocean. So is Buddha drying up the ocean of passions by stopping the flow of the waters of desire.

Page 208. *Attainment of Knowledge.* From *The Buddha-Charita,* Book XIV. Reprinted (as above) from *The Sacred Books of the East.*

Page 209. *The Aliment of Joy.* From *The Buddha-Charita,* Book XV. Reprinted (as above) from *The Sacred Books of the East.*

Page 210. *The Great Ministry Begins.* From *The Buddha-Charita,* Book XV. Reprinted (as above) from *The Sacred Books of the East.*

Page 212. *The Foundation of the Kingdom of Righteousness.* From *The Mahavagga of the Vinaya Texts.* Reprinted, by permission of the publishers, from *The Life of Gotama the Buddha* (compiled exclusively from the Pali Canon), by E. H. Brewster, introductory note by C. A. F. Rhys Davids. London, Kegan Paul, Trench, Trubner and Co., Ltd.; New York, E. P. Dutton and Co., 1926.

Page 214. *Return.* From *The Buddha-Charita,* Book XVII. Reprinted (as above) from *The Sacred Books of the East.*

Page 215. *The Buddha's Daily Habits.* From *The Sumagala-Vilasini,* Buddhaghosha's commentary on *The Digha-Nikaya.* Reprinted (as above) from Warren's *Buddhism in Translations.*

Page 218. *The Gift of Ambapali.* From *The Maha Parinibbana Suttanta.* Reprinted with the permission of the publishers from *Dialogues of the Buddha, Part II,* translated from the Pali of the *Digha-Nikaya* by T. W. and C. A. F. Rhys Davids. Being Volume III of *Sacred Books of the Buddhists,* translated by various oriental scholars and edited by T. W. Rhys Davids. London, Henry Frowde, Oxford University Press, 1938.

Page 219. *Hold Fast to the Truth.* From *The Maha Parinibbana Suttanta.* Reprinted (as above) from *Dialogues of the Buddha, Part II.*

Page 221. *Announcement of Death.* From *The Maha Parinibbana Suttanta.* Reprinted (as above) from *Dialogues of the Buddha, Part II.*

Page 223. *"A mighty earthquake."* Cf. account of earthquake at the time of Jesus's crucifixion (p. 1114).

Page 225. *"The passing away of the Tathagata,"* etc. Cf. Christ's announcement of his coming death, p. 1092.

Page 226. *"They are these,"* etc. T. W. and C. A. F. Rhys Davids, the translators of the text from which this selection is taken, add this valuable footnote: It is of great interest to notice what are the points upon which Gotama, in this last address to his disciples, and at the solemn time, when death was so near at hand, is reported to have laid such emphatic stress. Unfortunately we have only a fragment of the address, and, as it would seem from its commencement, only the closing fragment. This, however, is in the form of a summary, consisting of an enumeration of certain aggregates, the details of which must have been as familiar to the early Buddhists as the details of similar numerical terms—such as the ten commandments, the twelve tribes, the seven deadly sins, the four gospels, and so on—afterwards were to the Christians. This summary of the Buddha's last address may fairly be taken as a summary of Buddhism, which thus appears to be simply a system of earnest self-culture and self-control.

The following are the details of the aggregate technical terms used in the above summary, but it will be understood that the English equivalents used give rather a general than an exact representation of the ideas expressed by the Pali ones. To attempt more would demand a treatise rather than a note.

The four Earnest Meditations are:
1. Meditation on the body.
2. Meditation on the sensations.
3. Meditation on the ideas.
4. Meditation on reason and character.

The fourfold Great Struggle against evil is divided into:
1. The struggle to prevent evil arising.
2. The struggle to put away evil states which have arisen.
3. The struggle to produce goodness not previously existing.
4. The struggle to increase goodness when it does exist.

The four Roads to Saintship are four means by which Iddhi is to be acquired. They are:
1. The will to acquire it united to earnest meditation and the struggle against evil.
2. The necessary exertion united to earnest meditation and the struggle against evil.
3. The necessary preparation of the heart united to earnest meditation and the struggle against evil.
4. Investigation united to earnest meditation and the struggle against evil.

The five moral powers (balani) are said to be the same as the next class, called organs (indriyani). The details of both classes are:
1. Faith. 2. Energy. 3. Thought. 4. Contemplation. 5. Wisdom.

The seven kinds of Wisdom are:
1. Energy. 2. Thought. 3. Contemplation. 4. Investigation (of Scripture). 5. Joy. 6. Repose. 7. Serenity.

The Aryan Eightfold Path consists of:
1. Right views. 2. High aims. 3. Right speech. 4. Upright conduct. 5. A harmless livelihood. 6. Perseverance in well-doing. 7. Intellectual activity. 8. Right rapture.

Page 226. *The Food of Chunda the Smith.* From *The Maha Parinibbana Suttanta.* Reprinted (as above) from *Dialogues of the Buddha, Part II.*

Page 228. *Preparation for Death.* From *The Maha Parinibbana Suttanta.* Reprinted (as above) from *Dialogues of the Buddha, Part II.*

Page 229. *"It is he who rightly honours,"* etc. Cf. the words of Christ: "Not every one that saith unto me Lord, Lord," etc. (p. 1128), and "For I was an hungered," etc. (p. 1143).

Page 230. *The Establishment of Pilgrimage Places.* From *The Maha Parinibbana Suttanta.* Reprinted (as above) from *Dialogues of the Buddha, Part II.*

Page 231. *"Hinder not yourselves,"* etc. Cf. Mat. 8:22: "Let the dead bury their dead."

Page 232. *Ananda Weeps.* From *The Maha Parinibbana Suttanta.* Reprinted (as above) from *Dialogues of the Buddha, Part II.*

Page 233. *Admission of Women.* From *The Chullavagga, Tenth Khandhaka, Vinaya Texts.* Reprinted (as above) from *The Life of Gotama the Buddha.*

Page 237. *The Last Conversion.* From *The Maha Parinibbana Suttanta.* Reprinted (as above) from *Dialogues of the Buddha, Part II.*

Page 238. *Arahants.* T. W. and C. A. F. Rhys Davids supply the following footnote: Arahants are those who have reached Nirvana, the "supreme goal, the highest fruit," of the Aryan Eightfold Path. To live "the Life that's Right" (samma) is to live in the Noble Path, each of the eight divisions of which is to be samma, round, right and perfect, normal and complete. To live right (samma) is therefore to have: (1) right views, free from superstition; (2) right aims, high and worthy of the intelligent and earnest man; (3) right speech, kindly, open, truthful; (4) right conduct, in all concerns of life; (5) right livelihood, bringing hurt or danger to no living thing; (6) right perseverance, in all the other seven; (7) right mindfulness, the watchful, active mind; (8) right contemplation, earnest thought on the deep mysteries of life. In each of these the word right is samma, and the whole paragraph being on the Aryan Path, the allusion is certainly to this central doctrine of the Buddhist Dhamma.

Page 239. *Death of the Buddha.* From *The Maha Parinibbana Suttanta.* Reprinted (as above) from *Dialogues of the Buddha, Part II.*

Page 241. *"Passing out of the state,"* etc. For the meaning of these four stages see discussion of the four Jhanas, p. 250.

Page 242. *The Thirty-Two Marks.* From *The Lakkhana Suttanta.* Reprinted by permission of the publishers from *Dialogues of the Buddha, Part III,* translated from the Pali of the *Digha-Nikaya* by T. W. and C. A. F. Rhys Davids, being Vol. IV of *The Sacred Books of the Buddhists,* edited by T. W. Rhys Davids. London, Humphrey Milford, Oxford University Press, 1921. Corrections in the text have been made by Mrs. Rhys Davids for THE BIBLE OF THE WORLD, to make the translation conform to that of the revised edition which will soon be published by the Oxford University Press.

Page 244. *The Nine Incapabilities.* From *The Pasadika Suttanta.* Reprinted (as above) from *Dialogues of the Buddha, Part III.*

Page 244. *Setting-Up of Mindfulness.* From *The Maha Satipatthana Suttanta.* Reprinted (as above) from *Dialogues of the Buddha, Part II.*

Page 251. *The Perfect Net.* From *The Brahma-Gala Sutta.* Reprinted here by permission of the publishers from *Dialogues of the Buddha,* translated from the Pali by T. W. Rhys Davids, being Vol. II of *The Sacred Books of the Buddhists,* translated by various oriental scholars and edited by F. Max Müller. London, Henry Frowde, Oxford University Press, 1899.

Page 256. *Questions Which Tend Not to Edification.* From *The Majjhima-Nikaya, Sutta 63.* Reprinted (as above) from Warren's *Buddhism in Translations.*

Page 259. *Discussion of Dependent Origination.* From *The Maha-Nidana-Sutta of the Digha-Nikaya.* Reprinted (as above) from Warren's *Buddhism in Translations.*

NOTES 1355

Page 261. *On Theology.* From *The Tevigga Sutta.* Reprinted (as above) from *Dialogues of the Buddha.*

Page 263. *The Passing Away and Becoming of the World.* From *The Aggana Suttanta.* Reprinted (as above) from *Dialogues of the Buddha, Part III.*

Page 266. *"And beings seeing them so doing,"* etc. Here is an ancient explanation of the still extant custom of throwing rice, confetti, and old shoes at a bride and groom. Also see note referring to p. 17.

Page 269. *The Fall and Rise of Social Behaviour.* From *The Chakkavatti Sihanada Suttanta.* Reprinted (as above) from *Dialogues of the Buddha, Part III.*

Page 273. *"Let us now abstain,"* etc. Compare with the ten commandments of Judeo-Christianity, p. 714.

Page 274. *The Buddha and the Elephant.* From the *Udana,* Sec. V, Chap. IV. Reprinted with permission of the publishers from *Minor Anthologies of the Pali Canon, Part II,* translated by F. L. Woodward, M.A. London, Humphrey Milford, Oxford University Press, 1935.

Page 275. *The Mighty Ocean of Dhamma.* From the *Udana,* Sec. V, Chap. V. Reprinted (as above) from *Minor Anthologies of the Pali Canon, Part II.*

Page 277. *The Elephant and the Blind Men.* From the *Udana,* Sec. IV, Chap. VI. Reprinted (as above) from *Minor Anthologies of the Pali Canon, Part II.*

Page 279. *Death of the Insects.* From the *Udana,* Sec. IX, Chap. VI. Reprinted (as above) from *Minor Anthologies of the Pali Canon, Part II.*

Page 280. *The Sorrow of Visakha.* From the *Udana,* Sec. VIII, Chap. VIII. Reprinted (as above) from *Minor Anthologies of the Pali Canon, Part II.*

Page 281. *A Sermon to the Monks.* From the *Itivuttaka.* Reprinted (as above) from *Minor Anthologies of the Pali Canon, Part II.*

Page 286. *"I am a Brahmana,"* etc. This is not literally true if Brahmana is understood as the Hindu caste designation. Gotama was born a Kshatriya. But he refused to acknowledge the Hindu caste system. For explanation of the Buddhist use of the term, see the Dhammapada, p. 303.

Page 287. *Rebirth and Karma.* From *Payasi Suttanta.* Reprinted (as above) from *Dialogues of the Buddha, Part II.*

Page 295. *The Dhammapada.* All selections from the Dhammapada are reprinted from *Lectures on the Science of Religion, with a Paper on Buddhist Nihilism and a Translation of the Dhammapada or Path of Virtue,* by Max Müller, M.A. New York, Charles Scribner and Company, 1872.

Page 296. *"Hatred ceases by love."* Cf. Christ's words: "Love your enemies," etc. (p. 1125). Cf. also pp. 475, 500, 504, 558, in Taoism, and pp. 920 *et al.* in the Old Testament and 1138 *et al.* in the New Testament.

Page 298. *"One is the road that leads to wealth,"* etc. Cf. Christ's words: "It is easier for a camel to go through the eye of a needle than for a rich man to enter into the kingdom of God" (p. 1137).

Page 299. *"Do not speak harshly,"* etc. Cf. "A soft answer turneth away wrath," etc. (p. 921).

Page 300. *"This tabernacle."* Here, as in Christ's figure of speech (p. 1065 and elsewhere), the tabernacle or temple is the body.

Page 300. *"Overcome anger by love,"* etc. See note to p. 296.

Page 301. *"What ought to be done is neglected,"* etc. Cf. the general confession in the Book of Common Prayer of the Protestant Episcopal Church in the United States of America: "We have left undone those things which we ought to have done; and we have done those things which we ought not to have done; and there is no health in us."

Page 304. *Buddhaghosha's Parables.* All selections from Buddhaghosha's Parables reprinted by permission of the publishers from *Buddhaghosha's Parables,* translated by Captain T. Rogers, R.E. London, Trubner and Co., 1870.

Page 304. *Gotama.* Captain Rogers in his translation from the Burmese uses here and elsewhere the phrase "Para Taken," which is Burmese for the "Lord" or "Master." We have changed it throughout in this text to "Gotama," to keep the identity of the Buddha clear.

Page 305. *"Had the boy carried into one of the outer rooms of the house."* Funeral ceremonies in Burma begin with a gathering very like an Irish wake, with hired music and the wailing of paid professional mourners. The father in this story was afraid that if his son died in one of the principal rooms his mourning guests would see his plate and jewels.

Page 305. *"Tavatinsa Nat country."* Dwelling place of the "Nats," a class of beings between men and gods.

Page 310. *The Path of Purity (Buddhaghosha's Visuddhimagga)*. All selections are taken from *The Path of Purity, Part I,* being a translation of Buddhaghosha's Visuddhimagga by Pe Maung Tin. London (for the Pali Text Society), Oxford University Press, 1922.

Page 313. *Shrichakrasambhara Tantra.* The selections under this head are from the *Shrichakrasambhara Tantra,* edited by Kazi Dawa-Samdup, being Vol. VII of *Tantrik Texts,* under the general editorship of Arthur Avalon. London, Luzac and Company, 1919.

Page 316. *The Lotus of the True Law.* Selections under this head, with the exception of "Of the Regarder-of-the-Cries-of-the-World," p. 330, reprinted here with permission of the publishers from *The Saddharma-Pundarika* or *Lotus of the True Law,* translated by H. Kern, being Vol. XXI of *The Sacred Books of the East,* edited by F. Max Müller. Oxford, the Clarendon Press, 1884.

Page 322. *"Hear the dire results,"* etc. Cf. Christ's warning to those who scorn his teachings or mistreat his disciples (p. 1083).

Page 322. *"Thou shalt not expound a sutra like this to foolish people."* A reflection of the Hindu rule against imparting the scriptures to any not fit to understand them. See also Christ's words: "All men cannot receive this saying" (p. 1136).

Page 323. *"A certain man went away from his father,"* etc. Cf. the story of the prodigal son (p. 1173).

Page 327. *"A great cloud big with rain."* Cf. the 72nd Psalm, p. 898, "Like Rain upon the Mown Grass."

Page 328. *"I shall refresh,"* etc. Cf. the words of Christ: "Come unto me all ye who labour and are heavy laden, and I will give you rest" (p. 1130).

Page 330. *Of the Regarder-of-the-Cries-of-the-World.* This selection on Kuan Yin reprinted from *The Lotus of the Wonderful Law,* or *The Lotus Gospel; Saddharma Pundarika Sutra; Miao-fa Lien Hua Ching,* by W. E. Soothill. Oxford, Clarendon Press, 1930.

Page 331. *The Diamond Sutra.* Condensation reprinted from *The Diamond Sutra (Chin-Kang-Ching)* or *Prajna-Paramita,* translated from the Chinese by William Gemmell. London, Kegan Paul, Trench, Trubner and Company, 1912.

Page 336. *Asvaghosha's Discourse on the Awakening of Faith.* Selections reprinted from *Acvaghosha's Discourse on the Awakening of Faith in the Mahayana,* translated from Chinese by Teitaro Suzuki. Chicago, Open Court Publishing Company, 1900.

Page 341. *The Tibetan Doctrine.* The first ten stanzas here given are selected from stanzas 20–228 of a re-rendering in English by W. Y. Evans-Wentz of Alexander Csoma de Koros's (Hungarian) translation of the Subhashita Ratna Nidhi, attributed to the Grand Lama of Saskya, otherwise known as the Saskya Pandita, recognized as the head of the Lamaist Church in A.D. 1270 by the Chinese emperor, Kublai (Khubilai) Khan. The next seven verses are from a similar collection entitled *The Staff of Wisdom* (Tib.: *Sheo-rab-Sdou-bu;* Skt.: *Prajna-Danda*) attributed to Nagarjuna, the learned expounder of the Mahayana, and translated by the late Lama Kazi Dawa-Samdup. The next fifteen are from the Lama Kazi Dawa-Samdup's translation of *The Ocean of Delight for the Wise* (Tib.: *Lodan-Gawai-Roltso*). The last group of short proverbs is from *The Voice of the Silence.* All are reprinted, by permission of the publishers, from *Tibetan Yoga and Secret Doctrines, or Seven Books of Wisdom of the Great Path,* according to the Late Lama Kazi Dawa-Samdup's English rendering, arranged and edited with introductions and annotations to serve as a commentary, by W. Y. Evans-Wentz, with foreword by Dr. R. R. Marett. London, Oxford University Press, Humphrey Milford, 1935.

Page 345. *Jaina Sutras.* A word of explanation for the inclusion of a part of the scriptures of Jainism within the Buddhist scriptures. Jainism, one of the lesser known of the Eastern religions, is associated with Buddhism in that, like the latter, it arose in India as a reform movement growing out of dissatisfaction with the social and philosophical implications of Hinduism. Its rise was practically contemporary with that of Buddhism, and many of its teachings are similar. Its founder, Mahavira, began his ministry about thirty years before that of Buddha. He was also virtually a contemporary of the founders of three other great living religions, Confucius and Lao Tze in China, and Zarathushtra (Zoroaster) in Persia. It was during this period also that the great Jewish prophets Jeremiah, Ezekiel, and Isaiah of the Exile made such a deep impress on the Jewish religion, which, in its turn, so profoundly conditioned the religion of Christ.

The editors of THE BIBLE OF THE WORLD, desiring to represent the scriptures of Jainism, yet, because of pressure of space, not wanting to add another section to the work, have included these selections from the Akaranga Sutra within the Buddhist scriptures.

Page 345. *Who Knows One Thing.* From Akaranga Sutra, Book I, Lecture I, Lesson 4. Reprinted, by permission of the publishers, from *Gaina Sutras,* translated from Prakit by Hermann Jacobi. *Part I: The Akaranga Sutra, The Kalpa Sutra,* being Vol. XXII of *The Sacred Books of the East,* edited by F. Max Müller. Oxford, the Clarendon Press, 1884.

Page 346. *The Way of a Jaina Monk.* From Akaranga Sutra (as above), Book I, Lecture VII, Lesson 8.

Page 347. *The Five Vows.* From Akaranga Sutra (as above), Book II, Lecture XV.

Page 351. *A Manual of Zen Buddhism.* Zen Buddhism is perhaps as much an outgrowth of Taoism as of Buddhism. For better understanding of this section, the Taoist scriptures should be read before the Zen material. All selections in this section reprinted from *A Manual of Zen Buddhism,* by Daisetz Teitaro Suzuki. Kyoto, the Eastern Buddhist Society, 1935.

Page 351. *The Lankavatara Sutra.* From Sections XVIII, XIX, XXIV, and XXV of *The Lankavatara Sutra.*

Page 354. *On Believing in Mind.* From *Shinjin-no-mei* by Seng-t'san (Sosan in Japanese), who died 606 C.E. Mind = *hsin.* Hsin is one of those Chinese words which defy translation. When the Indian scholars were trying to translate the Buddhist Sanskrit works into Chinese, they discovered that there were five classes of Sanskrit terms which could not be satisfactorily rendered into Chinese. We thus find in the Chinese Tripitaka such words as *prajna, bodhi, buddha, nirvana, dhyana, bodhisattva,* etc., almost always untranslated; and they now appear in their original Sanskrit form among the technical Buddhist terminology. If we could leave *hsin* with all its nuances of meaning in this translation, it would save us from the many difficulties that face us in its English rendering. For *hsin* means "mind," "heart," "soul," "spirit"—each singly as well as all inclusively. In the present composition by the third patriarch of Zen, it has sometimes an intellectual connotation but at other times it can properly be translated by "heart."

Page 358. *On the Absolute.* From *Hui-Neng's Tan-Ching.*

Page 367. *The Ten Ox-Herding Pictures.* In various forms, current in the scriptures of Zen Buddhism since the fifteenth century. The ox is symbolic of the self or soul being subjected to Zen discipline. The gradual whitening process which goes on in the ox, and his final disappearance from the consciousness of the man, represent the gradual advance of purification. The artist who drew the sixteenth-century pictures here reproduced is unknown.

CONFUCIANIST SCRIPTURES

Confucius, sage of the principal religion of modern China, was born in 551 B.C. in the province of Shantung, China, married at nineteen, and devoted his life to teaching and government. He sought to preserve and improve the Chinese traditions of conduct according to those humanitarian and ethical principles which are embodied in his words in the Confucianist scriptures. He and his disciples edited and made available to the world in their present form the Chinese classics: the *Shu King,* or *Book of History;* the *Shih King,* or *Book of Poetry;* the *I King,* or *Book of Changes;* the *Li Ki,* or *Book of Ceremonial Rites;* the *Hsiao King,* or *Book of Filial Piety;* and wrote the *Chun Chiu* or *Spring and Autumn Annals.*

The group of Confucianist scriptures with which the Western world is more familiar consists of four books written about Confucius or his doctrines, by his followers. They are the *Lun Yu* or *Analects of Confucius,* the *Chung Yung* or *Doctrine of the Steadfast Mean,* the *Ta Hsio* or *Great Learning,* and *Meng-tze* or *The Works of Mencius.*

Perhaps it may be said that the basic teachings of Confucius centre in what has often been called the Chinese golden rule of reciprocity, "What you do not want done to yourself, do not do to others" (see p. 413), and in Confucius's interpretations of the importance of propriety, ceremonial ritual, and filial piety.

Although it has often been denied by Western critics that Confucianism is a religion at all, because of its emphasis upon sheer ethical conduct and Confucius's own reticence upon subjects connected with deity, prayer, and immortality, there is a strong religious content in his conception of the divine source of the goodness inherent in human nature, and in the very insistence upon religious ceremonial which is strongly marked throughout Confucian writings.

Hume (*op. cit.*) places the number of modern Confucianists at 250,000,000.

Page 379. *The Li Ki.* Selections from the Li Ki reprinted, by permission of the publishers, from *Sacred Books of China, Texts of Confucianism,* Parts III and IV, translated by James Legge, being Vols. XXVII and XXVIII of *The Sacred Books of the East.* Oxford, the Clarendon Press, 1885.

Page 383. *The Shih King.* Selections from the Shih King reprinted, by permission of the publishers, from *Sacred Books of China, Texts of Confucianism,* Part I, translated by James Legge, being Vol. III of *Sacred Books of the East,* Oxford, the Clarendon Press, 1879; and from *The Chinese Classics,* translated by James Legge, Vol. IV, *The Shih King,* Parts I and II, London, Trubner and Company, 1871.

Page 383. *The Song of How-tsieh.* Reprinted (as above) from *The Chinese Classics,* Vol. IV, Part II.

Page 383. "*Trod on a toe-print made by God,*" etc. Apparently a miraculous conception, common in the stories of divine or greatly revered beings. Cf. Jesus, Zarathushtra, Gotama Buddha, *et al.* See notes referring to pp. 181, 183.

Page 384. *The Wisdom of Yu.* Reprinted (as above) from *Sacred Books of China, Texts of Confucianism,* Part I.

Page 384. "*The deluge.*" See p. 445 and note referring to p. 32.

Page 385. *Spring Song.* Page 385 *Plea to an Ancestor.* Page 386. *Lamentation.* Page 386. *Heavenly Disaster.* Page 387. *Accusation of Heaven.* Page 388. *Warning to Governors.* Page 390. *How Vast Is God!* Page 390. *Drought.* Page 391. *Widow's Plaint.* Reprinted (as above) from *Sacred Books of China, Texts of Confucianism,* Part I.

Page 392. *Brothers Are Best.* Reprinted (as above) from *The Chinese Classics,* Vol. IV, Part II.

Page 393. *Blessing.* Reprinted (as above) from *The Chinese Classics,* Vol. IV, Part II.

Page 394. *In Praise of Ancestors.* Reprinted (as above) from *The Chinese Classics,* Vol. IV, Part II.

Page 394. *On Letting Alone.* Reprinted (as above) from *The Chinese Classics,* Vol. IV, Part II. This short poem, and "Admonition" on p. 396, show that the basic philosophy of Taoism has sound roots in the Chinese classics.

Page 394. *The Nature of People and Things.* Reprinted (as above) from *The Chinese Classics,* Vol. IV, Part II.

Page 395. *The Necessity of Propriety.* Reprinted (as above) from *The Chinese Classics,* Vol. IV, Part I.

Page 396. *Sorrow.* Reprinted (as above) from *The Chinese Classics,* Vol. IV, Part I.

Page 396. *Admonition.* Reprinted (as above) from *The Chinese Classics,* Vol. IV, Part I. See note referring to p. 394.

Page 396. *Beauty.* Reprinted (as above) from *The Chinese Classics,* Vol. IV, Part I.

Page 397. *The King's Affairs.* Reprinted (as above) from *The Chinese Classics,* Vol. IV, Part I.

Page 398. *Pattern.* Reprinted (as above) from *The Chinese Classics,* Vol. IV, Part I.

Page 398. *The Analects of Confucius.* Selections from *The Analects of Confucius, The Great Learning, The Doctrine of the Mean,* and *The Works of Mencius,* are from a translation by Charles A. Wong published in China without the imprint of a publisher or date.

Page 413. *"What you do not want done to yourself,"* etc. This is, of course, almost an exact parallel to the golden rule of Judeo-Christianity. There is, however, this significant difference, that here it is expressed in negative terms, which is much more in accordance with the oriental doctrine of *wu wei,* that is, refraining from inappropriate action (even though the action may be intended to do good) ; whereas the Judeo-Christian religion, which places much emphasis on the active doing of good, states the rule positively.

Page 415. *"Have you learned the Odes?"* See pp. 383 ff. for examples of the odes. *"Have you learned the rules of propriety?"* See pp. 379 ff. for examples from the book of proprieties.

Page 445. *"Of the great inundation."* See p. 384, and note referring to p. 32.

Page 451. *"Man's Nature Is Good."* An important doctrine of Confucianism, and the direct antithesis of the Judeo-Christian doctrine of original sin.

Page 463. *The Book of Filial Piety.* Selections from the *Hsiao King* are reprinted, by permission of the publishers, from *The Book of Filial Duty,* translated from the Chinese by Ivan Chen, London, John Murray; New York, E. P. Dutton, 1920.

TAOIST SCRIPTURES

Taoism, the religion of the *Tao,* or way, is closely associated with the name of Lao Tze, who is traditionally called its founder, and who was the reputed author of the Tao-Te-King, its oldest basic sacred book. Little is known of Lao Tze. Indeed the story of his life partakes of the vagueness of legend. According to one story, Lao Tze was born in 604 B.C. in humble circumstances in the province of Honan, Central China, and died about 517 B.C.—no one knows where. For in his old age, according to this account, when he foresaw the coming decay of his state, he left it. When he reached the frontier the customs-house officer asked him not to depart from the country without leaving his wisdom behind. Thereupon Lao Tze wrote quickly the Tao-Te-King. After this he left and was never heard of again. Some scholars doubt, however, that he is the author of this puzzling, profound, and beautiful book.

The central concept of Taoism is *Tao,* meaning "the way," "the path." It is also interpreted as "the word" as used in the Gospel of John, corresponding somewhat to the Greek "Logos." Indeed the translation into Chinese of the Gospel according to John begins: "In the beginning was the Tao, and the Tao was with God, and the Tao was God." (Robert Ernest Hume, *The World's Living Religions.*)

This is the central belief of Taoism: that the universe is ruled by a supreme intangible force within and about and beyond every detail. In the words of the Tao-Te-King itself (see p. 481):

> "There is a thing inherent and natural,
> Which existed before heaven and earth.
> Motionless and fathomless,
> It stands alone and never changes;
> It pervades everywhere and never becomes exhausted.
> It may be regarded as the Mother of the Universe.
> I do not know its name.
> If I am forced to give it a name,
> I call it Tao, and I name it as supreme."

The Taoist conception of man's relation to God and to his fellow-men is contained largely in the precept "to let alone." According to this doctrine, man's nature is essentially good, and Tao, if not interfered with by human thought and action, will work through human nature to its proper end. Yet for all its emphasis on "letting alone," Taoism teaches recompensing evil with good in much the same way as Christianity does, save that good effort is not, as in Christ's teachings, connected with the idea of a compassionate, personal Father-God.

Taoism has degenerated greatly since the days in which Lao Tze and Chuang Tze lived. Its present adherents, according to Robert Ernest Hume (*The World's Living Religions*), constitute 43,000,000 people, most of whom are Chinese.

An interesting development of the Taoist philosophy, however, flourishes in Japan under the name of Zen Buddhism, which owes as much to the doctrines of Lao Tze and Chuang Tze as to those of the Buddha. Because of its classification as Zen Buddhism, examples of its writings are included in the Buddhist section of *The Bible of the World* (p. 351). For better understanding of this section, the Taoist section should be read first.

Page 471. *The Tao-Te-King.* The complete Tao-Te-King here reprinted, by the permission of the publishers, from *Tao Te Ching,* a new translation by Ch'u Ta-Kao. London, the Buddhist Lodge, 1937.

The Tao Te Ching or Tao-Te-King was probably written at about the time of Confucius, by Lao Tze. It has greatly influenced the life and thought of the Chinese people, but because of its disagreement with Confucian principles, it was for a long time denied a place among the classics by most Confucian scholars, and failed to receive the careful preservation and dissemination which were accorded Confucian scriptures.

Ch'u Ta-Kao, whose translation of the Tao-Te-King we have used, calls attention to the many difficulties facing a translator of this ancient work. Among them is the fact that, before paper was invented in China, books were usually written on bamboo-tablets and fastened with strings or strips of leather. While being handed down from generation to generation the tablets were sometimes displaced, and the disarrangement caused distortions in the text. Ch'u Ta-Kao has therefore in several cases transferred the passages of one chapter to another in such a way as to make the sense more coherent, on the ground that they may very likely have been misread or become disarranged in their frequent handling. For example, he has omitted the last three lines from Chapter II and added them to Chapter LI; and the last two lines of Chapter XVII have been transferred to the end of Chapter XXXVII. Throughout he has compared all the available translations, and many such changes are in accord with the work of earlier translators. The cumulative work of Ch'en Chu, a contemporary Tao-Te-King scholar, has been this translator's principal source.

In his introduction to the translation, Dr. Lionel Giles writes: "The wording of the original is extraordinarily vigorous and terse; never, surely, has so much thought been compressed into so small a space. Throughout the universe there are scattered a certain number of stars belonging to a class known as 'white dwarfs.' They are usually very small, yet the atoms of which they consist are crushed together so closely that their weight is enormous in relation to their size, and this entails the radiation of so much energy that the surface is kept at a temperature vastly hotter than that of the sun. The Tao-Te-King may fitly be called a 'white dwarf' of philosophical literature, so weighty is it, so compact, and so suggestive of a mind radiating thought at a white heat."

Page 471. *"Non-existence is called,"* etc. Reminiscent of the Hinduist controversy as to whether existence or non-existence preceded the creation. See the Vedic conception that at first there was neither (p. 3).

Page 472. *"Tao . . . seems to be the origin of all things."* Considering "Tao" as "the Word" in the sense of the Gospel of John, we have here the parallel to the beginning of the Gospel: "In the beginning was the Word," etc. See note at the beginning of this section of the Notes.

Page 474. *"Handling and sharpening a blade."* See "Prince Hui's Excellent Cook," p. 513.

Page 475. *"He who loves the world,"* etc. Cf. Christ's commandment: "Love thy neighbour as thyself," pp. 1136, 1138.

Page 479. *"Be humble, and you will remain entire,"* etc., throughout verse. See the words of Christ: "Blessed are the meek," etc., p. 1123.

Page 491. *"When going to a battle,"* etc. It is said that the Chinese who fought in the Boxer uprising were Taoists and went into battle sure that they could not be hurt by the bullets of their enemies because of this statement in the Tao-Te-King.

Page 493. *"What is embraced,"* etc. Cf. Psalm 127: "Except the Lord build the house," p. 911.

Page 500. *"For he who fights with love,"* etc. Cf. St. Paul's definition of love (charity), p. 1201.

Page 501. *"My words are . . . easy to practise."* Cf. words of Christ: "My yoke is easy," etc., p. 1131.

Page 503. "The yielding can overcome the hard," etc. Cf. words of Christ: "Blessed are the meek," p. 1123.

Page 504. "Return love for great hatred," cf. words of Christ: "Love your enemies," etc., p. 1125. Also the same thought in the Dhammapada, p. 296.

Page 505. *The Works of Chuang Tze.* Selections from the works of Chuang Tze reprinted by permission of the publishers from *Chuang Tzu, Mystic, Moralist, and Social Reformer,* translated from the Chinese by Herbert A. Giles. London, Bernard Quaritch, 1889.

Chuang Tze belongs to the third and fourth centuries B.C. Influenced by the mysticism and idealism of the Tao-Te-King, he inveighed against the factualism and worldliness of Confucius. Chuang Tze is of the greatest importance to Taoists, upon whose religion he has had as impressive an influence as had St. Paul on Christianity.

Page 513. *The Worthless Tree.* See also pp. 514 and 121.

Page 524. "At the beginning of the beginning," etc. Cf. first lines of Vedic creation hymn, p. 3.

Page 555. *"If you could be as a child,"* etc. Cf. words of Christ: "Whosoever shall not receive the kingdom of God as a little child," p. 1092.

Page 557. "At the beginning there was nothing." Cf. opening of Genesis, p. 641, and Vedic creation hymn, p. 3.

ZOROASTRIAN SCRIPTURES

Of all the Eastern religions, that most closely associated with Judeo-Christianity is Zoroastrianism, founded by Zoroaster (Zarathushtra), who was born in Persia at an unknown date. "There has been uncertainty and variety of opinion concerning the actuality and date of his existence, whether 6000 B.C., or 1400 B.C., or 1000 B.C.," writes Robert Ernest Hume, in *The World's Living Religions;* but he quotes Professor A. V. Williams Jackson as saying that "the latest possible and most probable" dates of Zoroaster are 660–583 B.C. This, the more generally accepted time of his ministry, makes him an approximate contemporary of Gotama Buddha, Confucius, Lao Tze, Mahavira, and Jeremiah, Ezekiel, and the Isaiah of the Israelite Exile.

Zoroastrianism is not specifically mentioned in the Judeo-Christian scriptures, but there are many evidences of its influence upon Judaism and through that upon Christianity. In Isaiah, the Lord addresses the Zoroastrian King Cyrus of Persia as his "Messiah" and his "Shepherd." The wise men from the East, the Magi who came to the manger in which the infant Jesus lay, are, according to Hume, generally believed to have been Zoroastrian priests. The sun worshippers described in Ezekiel (p. 985) were probably carrying out Zoroastrian rites.

The idea of an evil antagonist to the omniscient, omnipotent God, which becomes more prominent in the later Old Testament, is probably influenced by Zoroastrian teachings. And the idea of a life after death, as found in the later Old Testament scriptures, is undoubtedly traceable to Zoroastrian influence. These are among the most forceful contributions of the Parsi religion to the world's religious thought.

But more peculiar to the Avesta and Pahlavi Texts which make up these sacred books of Persia are a robust adoration of Earth and its fruits, a reverence for work, and a humanity toward man and beast which give them a timeless value for all peoples.

Just as remnants of Zoroastrianism are found in Judaism, so are remains of the early Vedic religion of India found in Zoroastrianism, survivals of those days when the Hindus and the Persians were one people. The *Devas* of Hinduism are the *Daevas* of Zoroastrianism (see *Daevas* in Glossary), the *Soma* of the Vedas is the *Haoma* of the Avesta, etc.

About six centuries after the birth of Christ, the religion of Zarathushtra was supplanted in Persia by Mohammedanism and is now completely non-existent in the country of its birth. As a living organized religion Zoroastrianism is represented by a mere 100,000, most of whom are in India.

Page 561. *The Hymns of Zoroaster.* Selections from the Gathas reprinted by permission of the translator from *The Hymns of Zoroaster,* translated by Kenneth Sylvan Guthrie. London, George Bell; Brooklyn, Comparative Literature Press, 1914. The

Gathas consist of those yasnas, or hymns, which are thought to have been written by Zoroaster himself.

Page 561. *Exhortation to the Faithful.* Yasna 45.

Page 563. *A Prayer for Guidance.* Yasna 44.

Page 565. *The Choice between Right and Wrong.* Yasna 30.

Page 567. *A Prayer for Enlightenment.* Yasna 31.

Page 571. *The Zendavesta.* All selections from the Zendavesta (except for "The Earth," p. 574, and "Funerals and Purification," p. 577) reprinted by permission of the publishers, from the following books: *The Zendavesta, Part I, The Vendidad;* translated by James Darmsteter, being Vol. IV of *The Sacred Books of the East,* edited by F. Max Müller. Oxford, the Clarendon Press, 1895. *The Zendavesta, Part II. The Sirozahs, Yasts, and Nyayis;* translated by James Darmsteter, being Vol. XXIII of *The Sacred Books of the East,* 1883. *The Zendavesta, Part III, The Yasna, Visparad, Afrinagan, Gahs, and Miscellaneous Fragments;* translated by L. H. Mills, being Vol. XXXI of *The Sacred Books of the East,* 1887.

Page 571. *The Fatherhood of God.* Yasna XLV.

Page 572. *The Mazdayasnian Confession.* Yasna XII.

Page 574. *The Earth.* From the *Vendidad,* Fargard III (I, II, and III). Reprinted from *Sacred Books of the East,* a volume of *The World's Great Classics* (Zendavesta selections translated by James Darmsteter). Colonial Press, New York and London, 1900.

Page 577. *Funerals and Purification.* From the *Vendidad,* Fargard VIII (I and II). Reprinted from *Sacred Books of the East,* as listed in preceding reference.

Page 578. *The Sixteen Perfect Lands.* From Chap. I, the *Vendidad.*

Page 580. *The First Man.* From Chap. II, the *Vendidad.* See note referring to p. 17.

Page 583. *The Evil Winters.* From Chap. II, the *Vendidad.* This is obviously one version of the Zoroastrian flood story—the flood resulting from the melting snow. Note in the instructions to take into the Vara two seeds of every kind of plant as well as of men and animals a reflection of the importance the Zoroastrian religion places on cultivation of trees and plants. The most significant difference between this and the Judaistic legend is that in Genesis God sends the flood as a punishment for wickedness, while in the Zoroastrian *Vendidad* the hosts of darkness send it in an attempt to overcome the power of Ahura Mazda. For the other Zoroastrian flood story, see p. 628. See also p. 32 and note referring to that page.

Page 586. *Assault on Zarathushtra.* From Chap. XXX, the *Vendidad.* It is interesting to compare the Buddhist and Christian conceptions of attempts made by the forces of evil to turn Gotama and Jesus aside from their missions. See pp. 196, 205, and 1062. For other Zoroastrian accounts, see pp. 606, 611, 612, and 615.

Page 589. *The One of Whom Questions Are Asked.* From the *Ormazd Yast.*

Page 590. *The Best Healing.* From the *Ormazd Yast.*

Page 591. *Hymn to the Sun.* From the *Khorshed Yast.*

Page 592. *The Glory of God.* From the *Zamyad Yast.*

Page 593. *The Praise of Holiness.* From *Yast Fragment XXI.*

Page 594. *The Fravashis of the Faithful.* From the *Farvardin Yast* I, XIV, XV, XVI, XXII, XXX. *The Fravashi* is the inner power in every being that maintains it and makes it grow and subsist. Originally the Fravashis were the same as the Pitris of the Hindus or the Manes of the Latins, that is to say, the everlasting and deified souls of the dead; but in course of time they gained a wider domain, and not only men, but gods and even physical objects, such as the sky and the earth, had each a Fravashi.

Page 598. *The Abodes of the Soul.* From *Yast XXII.*

Page 601. *Of the Dog.* From Chaps. XIII and XV, the *Vendidad.*

Page 605. *The Pahlavi Texts.* All selections from Pahlavi Texts reprinted with the permission of the publishers from the following books: *Pahlavi Texts, Part I, The Bundahis, Bahman Yast, and Shayast La-Shayast;* translated by E. W. West, being Vol. V of *The Sacred Books of the East,* edited by F. Max Müller. Oxford, the Clarendon Press, 1880. *Pahlavi Texts, Part II, The Dadistan-i-Dinik and the Epistles of Manuskihar;* translated by E. W. West, being Vol. XVIII of *The Sacred Books of the East,* 1882. *Pahlavi Texts, Part V, Marvels of Zoroastrianism;* translated by E. W. West, being Vol. XLVII of *The Sacred Books of the East,* 1897.

Page 605. *The Conception and Birth of Zarathushtra.* From the *Dinkard,* Book VII, Chaps. I, II, III. See notes referring to pp. 17 and 181.

Page 609. *"Two of those cows,"* etc. A strange attenuation of the idea that a holy being must be as far removed from natural sexual processes as possible, strongly exemplified in the immaculate conception of Jesus. Here one of the elements influential in the forming of Zarathushtra is milk miraculously produced by virgin cows. See note referring to pp. 181, 183, 185.

Page 609. *"Keshmak . . . growled."* Here, as in other episodes in the life of Zarathushtra (see pp. 586, 611, 612, 615), as in the temptation of Jesus by Satan (p. 1062), and as in Mara's attempts to overthrow Gotama Buddha (pp. 192, 205), is a typical example of the personified forces of evil in contest with the personified forces of righteousness.

Page 610. *"People who are ashamed."* See note referring to p. 17.

Page 611. *"He laughed."* Gotama Buddha "shouted the shout of victory." See p. 186.

Page 611. *Hazards of the Infant Zarathushtra.* From the *Zad-Sparam,* Chap. XVI.

Page 611. *"The Karap,"* etc. See note referring to Keshmak, p. 609.

Page 612. *The Vision of the Child.* From the *Zad-Sparam.* Chap. XVIII.

Page 612. *"Looked a long while."* Gotama, too, at birth, looked in all directions. See p. 186.

Page 613. *Announcement of Purpose.* From the *Dinkard,* Chaps. III and IV, and the *Zad-Sparam,* Chap. XXI.

Page 615. *Temptation by a Demon.* From the *Dinkard,* Chap. IV. See note referring to Keshmak, p. 609.

Page 616. *The Joyousness of Religion.* From the *Dinkard,* Chap. V.

Page 616. *The Death of Zarathushtra.* From the *Zad-Sparam,* Chap. XXIII.

Page 616. *The Apostasy of the Iron Age.* From the *Dinkard,* Chap. VII.

Page 617. *The Essence of Zarathushtra's Religion.* From the *Zad-Sparam,* Chap. XXIV.

Page 619. *The Function of the Righteous.* From the *Dadistan-i-Dinik,* III.

Page 620. *Evil to the Good.* From the *Dadistan-i-Dinik,* VI.

Page 621. *The Chinvad Bridge.* From the *Dadistan-i-Dinik,* XXI.

Page 622. *The Nature of Heaven.* From the *Dadistan-i-Dinik,* XXI.

Page 623. *The Nature of Hell.* From the *Dadistan-i-Dinik,* XXVII.

Page 624. *Reception in Heaven.* From the *Dadistan-i-Dinik,* XXXI.

Page 625. *The Sin of Profiteering.* From the *Dadistan-i-Dinik,* XLIX.

Page 625. *The First Man.* From the *Dadistan-i-Dinik,* LXII.

Page 626. *"Connected together."* Eve was made of Adam's rib (p. 644); Mashya and Mashyoi were likewise of one flesh (p. 635). Also see note referring to p. 17.

Page 626. *The Propagation of Man.* From the *Dadistan-i-Dinik,* LXV.

Page 627. *The Rainbow.* From the *Dadistan-i-Dinik.* See Jehovah's covenant with Noah: "I do set my bow in the sky," etc., p. 651.

Page 627. *The Two Regions.* From the *Zad-Sparam,* Chap. I: "Light above and darkness below," the heaven and hell of Judeo-Christianity.

Page 627. *The Order of Creation.* From the *Bundahis,* Chaps. I and II. Cf. the very similar order (with man created sixth, as here) in the Genesis story, p. 641.

Page 628. *The Flood.* From the *Bundahis,* Chaps. VI and VII. See also "The Evil Winters," p. 583; the Hindu story of the flood, p. 32; the Genesis story, p. 648; and the mention of it in the Chinese classics, pp. 384 and 445. Also see the notes referring to these pages.

Page 630. *The Resurrection.* From the *Bundahis,* Chap. XXX.

Page 634. *The Reproduction of Species.* From the *Bundahis,* Chap. XVI. See note referring to p. 17.

Page 635. *The Ancestry of the World.* From the *Bundahis,* Chap. XV. See note referring to p. 17.

Page 637. *"When I see thy shame."* See note referring to p. 610, and note referring to p. 17.

Page 637. *The Independence of the Dog.* From the *Bundahis,* Chap. XIV.

JUDEO-CHRISTIAN SCRIPTURES

The convenient but somewhat inaccurate phrase, Judeo-Christian scriptures, is used in *The Bible of the World* to designate the four groups of books known to us as the Old Testament, the Old Testament Apocrypha, the New Testament, and the New Testament Apocrypha. All these scriptures owe their beings, either directly or indirectly, to Hebrew origins, though only one of them, the Old Testament, contains scriptures of orthodox Judaism. Among them the New Testament is the only one which is both an exclusive contribution of Christianity and now recognized as canonical scripture by the entire Christian Church. To it has been added in the Christian Church canon the books of the Old Testament, taken over from Judaism. The Greek and Latin Christian Churches also consider the Old Testament Apocrypha (discarded by most Protestant sects) as canonical.

The New Testament Apocrypha is not now a part of the canon of any organized church, but contains rejected books which tell stories of the life, words, and acts of Jesus and his disciples, some of which conflict with accounts in the canonical New Testament. Although these books have been eliminated from the Christian canon, several of the stories contained in them (such as the birth of Anna, mother of the Virgin Mary, Christ's descent into hell, etc.) are imperishable parts of Christian tradition.

Some of these *New Testament Apocryphal* books comprise a part of the scriptures of Manichæism, the religion of Mani, a Persian of the third century A.D., who taught a dualism combining the concept of opposed light and darkness of Zoroastrianism and his own interpretation of the meaning of Christ. In his doctrine, man's body was considered the product of darkness (evil) but his soul the offspring of light (good). The later Manichæans distinguished the historical Christ from the spiritual Christ, maintaining that the former was a physical incarnation of the forces of darkness, but the latter was a divine deliverer.

The sacred books of Judaism consist of twenty-four documents divided into three groups called the Law, the Prophets, and the Writings. Of these, the Law or the Torah, consisting of the first five books, Genesis, Exodus, Leviticus, Numbers, and Deuteronomy, is considered especially sacred by orthodox Jews.

The religion of Judaism may be said to have been founded by Moses before or about 1200 B.C. under circumstances of which there is no better account than that given in Exodus (see pp. 694 ff.). Roots of the religion he taught were planted in the primitive religious beliefs of the Semites, nomadic ancestors of the modern Bedouins. Theirs was largely a tribal and local worship. Moses brought the Israelites to belief in Jehovah alone, as the nation's God, while still recognizing the respect due to the gods of other peoples. (See "Thou shalt not revile the gods," etc., p. 716.) Thus, original Judaism was not strictly monotheism, but rather, henotheism.

Year by year and century by century the conception of Jehovah changed until, from being the most powerful of gods and the only God worship of whom had the sanction of the dominant Mosaic tradition, he became the one and only existing God of universal power. With this development came a gradual change in the conception of his personality. Instead of the vengeful, humanly fallible, sometimes weak, sometimes even petulant, God of early legends, he became the all-pervading, merciful God of the second Isaiah and Daniel, who logically developed into the loving Father-God of Rabbinic Judaism and the New Testament.

The congregation of Judaism is now scattered over the face of the earth. Hume estimates their number as 11,000,000, and adds that more than half of this scattered remnant is in Russia.

It is a mistake to think of Christianity as a religion separate from Judaism in its concepts. It is true that orthodox Jews have never accepted Jesus as the long-prophesied Messiah of the Old Testament, that, as an organized body, they denied and persecuted him during his lifetime and (if we may accept the evidence of the Gospels) were responsible for his crucifixion. But Jesus himself, born a Jew, was first and foremost a protestant of the basic religion of Judaism. A purist in religion, as in all things, his mission was to reform, not to overthrow, the organized religion of Judaism, and to bring mankind into closer harmony with his interpretation of the Father-God Jehovah, that the Kingdom of Heaven might reign on earth.

There is little in Christ's teachings which does not have its roots in the Old Testament. Thus, the Christian Church could not have considered its scriptures complete without the inclusion of the older basic canon of Judaism and the fundamental religious concepts of the religion of the Jews.

Such scriptural record of Jesus's life and teachings as we have is contained in *The Bible of the World*. The two sections headed "The Life and Acts of Jesus" (p. 1051) and "The Sermons and Sayings of Jesus" (p. 1123) are compiled from the four Gospels, Matthew, Mark, Luke, and John, in an attempt to eliminate repetitions and point out the differences which exist in the four canonical accounts. Written between A.D. 65 and 150 (Robert Ernest Hume, *The World's Living Religions*), they were preceded by the Pauline writings, the Epistles, which were written between A.D. 50 and 65 (Hume), the earliest Christian writings.

Christianity has, according to Hume, 557,000,000 adherents, located in all the countries of the world, but principally in Europe and the Americas.

All selections from the canonical Old Testament and New Testament are reprinted from the authorized version of the King James translation of the Holy Bible. For explanation of the arrangement of the books of the Old Testament and the Gospel material in *The Bible of the World*, see the Introduction.

Page 641. *The Creation.* From Genesis I. Compare the very similar order of creation in the Zoroastrian legend, pp. 627, 628. Cf. also the Babylonian creation story, a part of which follows:

> "When in the height heaven was not named
> And the earth beneath did not yet bear a name,
> And the primeval Apsu, who begat them,
> And Chaos, Tiamat, the Mother of them both,—
> Their waters were mingled together,
> And no field was formed, no marsh was to be seen;
> When of the gods none had been called into being,
> And none bore a name, and no destinies were ordained;
> Then were created the gods in the midst of heaven . . ."
>   *(From the first tablet)*

> "And the Lord (Marduk) stood upon Tiamat's hinder parts.
> And with his merciless club he smashed her skull.

.   .   .   .

> Then the Lord rested, gazing upon her dead body,
> While he divided the flesh . . . and devised a cunning plan.
> He split her up like a flat fish into two halves;
> One half of her he stablished as a covering for heaven.
> He fixed a bolt, he stationed a watchman,
> And bade them not to let her waters come forth."
>   *(From the fourth tablet)*

> "He (Marduk) made the stations for the great gods;
> The stars, their images, as the stars of the Zodiac he fixed.
> He ordained the year and into sections he divided it;
> For the twelve months he fixed three stars.

.   .   .   .

> The moon-god he caused to shine forth, the night he entrusted to him."
>   *(From the fifth tablet)*

> "When Marduk heard the words of the gods,

.   .   .   .

> He opened his mouth and unto Ea he spake,

.   .   .   .

'My blood will I take and bone will I fashion,

.   .   .   .

I will create man who shall inhabit the earth.' "

(From the sixth tablet)

—From "The Seven Tablets of The History of Creation."
(The Seven Tablets of Creation, or The Babylonian
and Assyrian Legends concerning the Creation of the
World and of Mankind, edited by L. W. King. London,
Luzac and Company, 1902.)

Page 643. *The Garden of Eden.* From Genesis II.
Page 644. *"Took one of his ribs."* See note referring to Yama and Yami, p. 17.
Page 644. *The Fall of Man.* From Genesis III. See note on Yama and Yami, p. 17.
Page 646. *The Murder of Abel.* From Genesis IV.
Page 647. *The Making of the Ark.* From Genesis VI.
Page 648. *The Flood.* From Genesis VII and VIII. See version of this story in the Hindu scriptures, p. 32, and note referring to that page for other references. The account in Genesis obviously owes a great deal to the account in the older Babylonian *Epic of Gilgamesh,* a part of which follows:

"On the fifth day I drew its design,
In its plan 120 cubits high on each of its sides.
By 120 cubits it corresponded on each edge of its roof.
I laid down its form, I enclosed it,
I constructed it in six stories,
Dividing it into seven parts.
Its interior I divided into nine parts,
Water plugs I fastened within it.
I prepared a rudder, and supplied what was necessary.
Three sars of bitumen I poured over the outside,
Three sars of bitumen I poured over the inside,

.   .   .   .

I put on board my family and relatives,
The cattle of the field, the beasts of the field,
. . . I put on board.

.   .   .   .

The appointed time arrived,
The ruler of darkness at eventide sent a heavy rain.

.   .   .   .

I entered the ship and shut my door.

.   .   .   .

Like an onslaught in battle it rushed in on the people.
No man beheld his fellow,
No longer could men know each other. In heaven
The gods were dismayed at the flood.

.   .   .   .

For six days and nights
The wind blew, the flood, the tempest overwhelmed the land.
When the seventh day drew near, the tempest, the flood,
Ceased from the battle in which it had fought like a host.
Then the sea rested and was still, and the wind storm and the flood ceased.
I opened the window and daylight fell upon my face,
I bowed myself down and sat a-weeping.

.   .   .   .

After twelve days an island arose.
To the land of Nisir the ship took its course,

The mountain of the land of Nisir held fast the ship and suffered it not to stir.

. . .

When the seventh day drew nigh
I sent forth a dove and let her go,
The dove went to and fro,
But there was no resting place, and she returned.
Then I sent forth a swallow and let her go,
The swallow went to and fro,
But there was no resting place, and she returned.
Then I sent forth a raven and let her go,
The raven flew away, she beheld the abatement of the waters,
And she came near, wading and croaking, but did not return.
Then I sent everything forth to the four quarters of heaven, I offered sacrifice,
I made a libation on the peak of the mountain.

. . .

The gods smelt the sweet savour,
The gods gathered like flies about him that offered up the sacrifice."
                    —From *The Epic of Gilgamesh*, Canto XI.
                    Babylonian Flood Stories, Percy Handcock, M.A.
                    London, Society for Promoting Christian Knowledge,
                    1921.

Page 650. *God's Covenant with Noah*. From Genesis IX.
Page 651. *"I do set my bow in the cloud."* See Zoroastrian explanation of the rainbow, p. 627.
Page 651. *The Tower of Babel*. From Genesis XI.
Page 652. *God's Promise to Abraham*. From Genesis XII.
Page 653. *Sarai and Hagar*. From Genesis XVI.
Page 654. *The Law of Circumcision*. From Genesis XVII.
Page 655. *Abraham Entertains the Lord*. From Genesis XVIII.
Page 656. *Abraham Intercedes for Sodom*. From Genesis XVIII.
Page 657. *The Destruction of Sodom and Gomorrah*. From Genesis XIX.
Page 659. *The Birth of Isaac*. From Genesis XX and XXI.
Page 660. *Abraham Offers Isaac*. From Genesis XXII.
Page 661. *Rebekah at the Well*. From Genesis XXIV.
Page 664. *Esau Sells His Birthright*. From Genesis XXV.
Page 665. *Isaac Blesses Jacob*. From Genesis XXVII.
Page 668. *The Vision of Jacob's Ladder*. From Genesis XXVIII.
Page 669. *Jacob Earns Two Wives*. From Genesis XXIX.
Page 671. *The Birth of Joseph*. From Genesis XXX.
Page 673. *Jacob and Laban Are Estranged*. From Genesis XXXI.
Page 674. *Jacob and Esau Make Peace*. From Genesis XXXI, XXXII, XXXIII.
Page 676. *The Family of Jacob*. From Genesis XXV.
Page 677. *Joseph Is Sold by His Brothers*. From Genesis XXXVII.
Page 679. *Joseph and Potiphar's Wife*. From Genesis XXXIX.
Page 680. *The Dreams of the Butler and the Baker*. From Genesis XL.
Page 682. *The Dream of Pharaoh*. From Genesis XLI.
Page 684. *Joseph's Brothers Go into Egypt*. From Genesis XLII.
Page 686. *They Return to Egypt*. From Genesis XLIII.
Page 688. *Joseph and His Brothers Are Reconciled*. From Genesis XLIV and XLV.
Page 691. *The Tribe of Jacob Goes to Egypt*. From Genesis XLV and XLVII.
Page 692. *The Death of Jacob*. From Genesis XLVIII and XLIX.
Page 694. *The Death of Joseph*. From Genesis L.
Page 694. *The Beginning of Persecution*. From Exodus I.
Page 695. *The Birth of Moses*. From Exodus II.
Page 696. *Moses Becomes Champion of the Jews*. From Exodus II.
Page 697. *The Burning Bush and the Name of God*. From Exodus III.
Page 698. *"I AM THAT I AM."* See, in Hindu scriptures, the appellation of God, "He is," p. 53.

George A. Barton (in *The Religions of the World*, University of Chicago Press, 1920)
says that these grew out of an early code of "Ten Commands" of nomadic days, which
"appear to have been as follows":
1. Thou shalt worship no other god.
2. Thou shalt make thee no molten gods.
3. The feast of the Passover thou shalt keep.
4. The firstling of an ass thou shalt redeem with a lamb; all the first born of thy sons
   thou shalt redeem.
5. None shall appear before me empty.
6. Six days thou shalt work, but on the seventh thou shalt rest.
7. Thou shalt observe the feast of ingathering (of dates).
8. Thou shalt not offer the blood of my sacrifice with leavened bread, neither shall
   the sacrifice of the Passover remain until the morning.
9. The firstlings of the flocks thou shalt bring unto Jahweh, thy God.
10. Thou shalt not seethe a kid in its mother's milk.

The tenth law is obviously the source of the prohibition against eating butter or milk
with meat in orthodox Jewish dietary laws. Ten was a convenient number of rules,
because they could be designated on the ten fingers and thus easily remembered. "There
is much reason to believe that these commands were not written down, but were committed to tradition," Barton writes. "This fact made it easier for later prophets to reinter-
pret the covenant and to make its basis ethical."

Page 716. *"Thou shalt not revile the gods,"* etc. This is one of the most outspoken evidences of henotheism (that is, worshipping only one God while recognizing conceptions
of other gods) in the Old Testament.

Page 743. *A Warning against Self-Righteousness.* From Deuteronomy IX.

Page 744. *God's Goodness to Israel.* From Deuteronomy X.

Page 745. *"Forty days and forty nights."* Note that Jesus also stayed in the wilderness forty days and forty nights. See p. 1062.

Page 745. *The Law of Release.* From Deuteronomy XV.

Page 746. *The Observance of Holy Days.* From Deuteronomy XVI.

Page 748. *Trial and Punishment.* From Deuteronomy XVII.

Page 748. *The Duty of Kings.* From Deuteronomy XVII.

Page 749. *The Inheritance of Priests.* From Deuteronomy XVIII.

Page 749. *The Coming of a Prophet Foretold.* From Deuteronomy XVIII.

Page 750. *The Law of False Witness.* From Deuteronomy XIX.

Page 750. *"Eye for eye,"* etc. One of many residues in the Old Testament of the ancient Code of Hammurabi (probably the Amraphel of Genesis XIV, 1), sixth king of the First Dynasty of Babylon, who reigned about 2250 B.C. Robert Francis Harper (in *The Code of Hammurabi, King of Babylon,* University of Chicago Press, 1904) translates paragraphs 196 and 200 as follows: "If a man destroy the eye of another man, they shall destroy his eye. If a man knock out the tooth of a man of his own rank, they shall knock out his tooth."

Page 750. *The God of War.* From Deuteronomy XX.

Page 752. *Of Raiment.* From Deuteronomy XXII.

Page 752. *Of Those Emasculated and of Bastards.* From Deuteronomy XXIII. "Bastard" here means one born of a forbidden marriage or of incest, not one merely born out of wedlock.

Page 752. *Of Sanitation.* From Deuteronomy XXIII.

Page 752. *Of Sanctuary.* From Deuteronomy XXIII.

Page 753. *The Law of Divorce.* From Deuteronomy XXIV.

Page 753. *Of Master and Servant.* From Deuteronomy XXIV.

Page 753. *Of Individual Responsibility.* From Deuteronomy XXIV.

Page 753. *The Duty of an Husband's Brother.* From Deuteronomy XXV.

Page 754. *The Cursed of Israel.* From Deuteronomy XXVII.

Page 755. *The Blessed of Israel.* From Deuteronomy XXVII.

Page 756. *If Thou Wilt Not Hearken.* From Deuteronomy XXVIII.

Page 757. *"The Lord shall scatter,"* etc. A woefully accurate prophecy of the position of the Jew to-day and in previous centuries.

Page 757. *The Song of Moses.* From Deuteronomy XXXI and XXXII.

Page 760. *The Death of Moses.* From Deuteronomy XXXII and XXXIV.

Page 761. *Joshua Takes Command.* From Joshua I.

Page 762. *The People Cross over Jordan.* From Joshua III and V.

Page 763. *The Fall of Jericho.* From Joshua VI.

Page 764. *The Sun Stands Still.* From Joshua X.

Page 765. *Joshua's Conquest Completed.* From Joshua XI.

Page 766. *Joshua Instructs His People.* From Joshua XXIII.

Page 766. *The Death of Joshua.* From Joshua XXIV.

Page 768. *Israel Takes Tribute.* From Judges I.

Page 769. *The Anger of the Lord.* From Judges III.

Page 769. *The Death of Sisera.* From Judges IV.

Page 771. *Deborah's Song.* Judges V.

Page 774. *The Birth of Samson.* Judges XIII.

Page 775. *Samson and the Philistine Woman.* From Judges XIV.

Page 777. *Samson Burns the Philistines' Corn.* From Judges XV.

Page 778. *Samson and Delilah.* From Judges XVI and XXI.

Page 781. *The Birth of Samuel.* From I Samuel I.

Page 782. *The Lord Calls Samuel.* From I Samuel III.

Page 783. *The Ark Is Taken.* I Samuel IV.

Page 785. *The People Want a King.* I Samuel VIII.

Page 786. *Saul Comes to Samuel.* From I Samuel IX.

Page 787. *God Save the King!* From I Samuel X.

Page 788. *The Lord Accuses Saul.* From I Samuel XV.

Page 789. *Samuel Anoints David.* From I Samuel XVI.

Page 917. *Praise God in His Sanctuary*. Psalm CL.

Page 918. *Proverbs*. From various chapters of the Book of Proverbs.

Page 920. *"Love covereth all sins."* See Dhammapada, p. 296; also Tao-Te-King, pp. 475, 500, 504, 558; also words of Jesus, p. 1125.

Page 921. "A soft answer turneth away wrath." See Dhammapada, "Do not speak harshly," etc., p. 299.

Page 926. *Ecclesiastes*. Selections are from the chapters corresponding to the numbers used for the different sections.

Page 933. *The Song of Solomon*. The Song of Songs is reprinted without cutting. For centuries the Christian Church taught that this was an expression of the love of Christ for the Church, in spite of the fact that it was written some four centuries before the birth of Jesus. These songs were probably originally composed to be sung at marriage ceremonies, according to Raymond C. Knox, in *Knowing the Bible* (New York, the Macmillan Company, 1927).

Page 940. *God's Judgments of Syria*. From Amos I.

Page 941. *The Reasons for God's Punishments*. From Amos III.

Page 942. *A Lament for Israel*. From Amos V.

Page 944. *The Vengeance of the Lord*. From Amos IX.

Page 945. *Hosea I*. From Hosea I.

Page 946. *II*. From Hosea II.

Page 947. *III*. From Hosea III.

Page 948. *IV*. From Hosea IV.

Page 949. *V*. From Hosea VI.

Page 949. *VI*. From Hosea XI.

Page 950. *VII*. From Hosea XIV.

Page 951. *Accusation of the Princes*. From Micah III.

Page 952. *The Establishment of the Kingdom of God*. From Micah IV.

Page 953. *Promise of a Leader*. From Micah V. "But thou, Bethlehem," etc. This is one of the many passages in the Old Testament quoted by Christians as prophesying the coming of Jesus. The Jews, however, do not so regard it.

Page 954. *What the Lord Requires of Thee*. From Micah VI.

Page 955. *The Book of the First Isaiah*. The book of Isaiah, as it occurs in the King James Bible, is now thought to consist principally of two books written by two men separated in time by nearly two centuries and by the Exile. The first part (represented here) was probably written between 800 and 700 B.C., and consists of chapters I–XXXIX, inclusive. The second part, consisting of the rest, probably written between 600 and 500 B.C., is represented by the text which begins on p. 991.

Page 955. *Isaiah Warns Israel*. From Isaiah I and II.

Page 957. *Vision of the Six-Winged Seraphims*. From Isaiah V.

Page 957. *Prophecy of Immanuel*. From Isaiah VII, VIII, IX, XI, XII.

Page 959. *"A rod out of the stem of Jesse,"* etc. This is one of the many passages in the Old Testament quoted by Christians in evidence of their belief that Jesus was the oft-prophesied Messiah.

Page 960. *The Destinies of the Evil and the Righteous*. From Isaiah XXXIV.

Page 962. *Zephaniah*. From Zephaniah I and II.

Page 963. *Nahum*. From Nahum I.

Page 964. *Habakkuk*. From Habakkuk I and II.

Page 965. *Jeremiah Chosen as Prophet*. From Jeremiah I.

Page 967. *A Call for Repentance*. From Jeremiah VII.

Page 967. *Peace! Peace! and There Is No Peace*. From Jeremiah VIII.

Page 968. *The Clay and the Potter*. From Jeremiah XVIII.

Page 969. *Pashur Persecutes Jeremiah*. From Jeremiah XX.

Page 970. *Zedekiah Asks for Advice*. From Jeremiah XXI and XXII.

Page 971. *Denunciation of False Pastors*. From Jeremiah XXIII.

Page 971. *Jeremiah Is Taken*. From Jeremiah XXVI.

Page 972. *The Kings Made Subject to Nebuchadnezzar*. From Jeremiah XXVII.

Page 974. *Zedekiah Imprisons Jeremiah*. Jeremiah XXXII, XXXIV.

Page 975. *Baruch Writes Jeremiah's Words*. From Jeremiah XXXVI.

Page 977. *Jeremiah Is Taken Again*. From Jeremiah XXXVII, XXXVIII.

Page 981. *The Fall of Jerusalem*. From Jeremiah XXXIX.

Page 982. *Ezekiel's Vision.* From Ezekiel I, II, III.

Page 985. *Exhortation to the Faithful.* From Ezekiel VI.

Page 985. *Warning to the Sun-Worshippers.* From Ezekiel VIII. "Sun-worshippers" probably Zoroastrians.

Page 986. *God's Way toward the Penitent.* From Ezekiel XXXIII.

Page 987. *God's Promise.* From Ezekiel XXXIII.

Page 989. *The Valley of Dry Bones.* From Ezekiel XXXVII.

Page 991. *The Book of the Second Isaiah.* See note referring to p. 955, *The Book of the First Isaiah.*

Page 991. *A Voice in the Wilderness.* From Isaiah XL, XLI.

Page 993. *The Omnipotence of God.* From Isaiah XLV.

Page 994. *Awake, O Zion!* From Isaiah LII.

Page 995. *A Promise of Joy and Peace.* From Isaiah LV.

Page 998. *Haggai.* From Haggai II.

Page 998. *Zechariah.* From Zechariah I, II, IV, V, VI, VIII.

Page 1003. *Malachi.* From Malachi I, III, IV.

Page 1004. *Joel.* From Chaps. I and II of *Joel.*

Page 1006. *Jonah Is Cast into the Sea.* From Jonah I.

Page 1007. *Jonah's Prayer.* Jonah II.

Page 1008. *Jonah Goes to Nineveh.* Jonah III.

Page 1009. *The Lord Reproves Jonah.* Jonah IV.

Page 1010. *Daniel's Loyalty to the Faith of Israel.* Daniel I.

Page 1011. *The King's Dream.* Daniel II.

Page 1014. *Shadrach, Meshach, and Abed-nego.* Daniel III.

Page 1016. *One of Nebuchadnezzar's Dreams Comes True.* Daniel IV.

Page 1018. *The Handwriting on the Wall.* Daniel V.

Page 1020. *Daniel in the Lions' Den.* Daniel VI.

Page 1022. *Daniel's Two Visions.* Daniel VII, VIII.

Page 1026. *Epilogue.* Daniel XII.

Page 1027. *The Apocryphal Old Testament.* Selections from the Apocryphal Old Testament are reprinted from *The Holy Bible, containing the Old and New Testaments, together with the Apocrypha,* translated out of the original tongues, and with the former translations diligently compared and revised, with Canne's marginal notes and references. Concord, New Hampshire, published by Luther Roby, 1843.

The first separation of the books represented here as Apocryphal, from the other books of the Old Testament, occurred when Martin Luther printed his Bible in 1534, including after the other books of the Old Testament those books not found in the Hebrew, under the title "Apocrypha, that is, books which are not held equal to the sacred scriptures, and nevertheless are useful and good to read." Thus they were printed for decades between the books of the *Old Testament* and those of the New. The Church of England recognized them in 1571 as books "to read for example of life and instruction of manners." In 1615 action was taken by the Church of England prohibiting the omission of the Apocryphal books from any edition of the Bible. But their inclusion was opposed by the Puritans and Presbyterianism, and in 1648 the Westminster Confession was adopted, which declared that the books of the Apocrypha, "not being of divine inspiration, are no part of the Canon of the Scripture; and therefore are of no authority in the Church of God, nor to be in any otherwise approved, or made use of, than other human writings." In 1827 the British and Foreign Bible Society decided to exclude the Apocrypha from all its printed Bibles. These books are, however, still retained in the Vulgate Bible used by the Roman Catholic Church.

Page 1048. *"I am clear from the blood of this woman,"* etc. This explains the line, "A Daniel come to judgment," in Shakespeare's *The Merchant of Venice.*

Page 1051. For explanation of the handling of Gospel Material in THE BIBLE OF THE WORLD see Introduction.

Page 1051. *The Miraculous Conceptions of John the Baptist and of Jesus.* From Luke I. Cf. stories of the conception and birth of Gotama Buddha, pp. 181 ff., and of Zarathushtra, pp. 605 ff., 611. See notes referring to pp. 181, 183, 185.

Page 1052. *"A virgin espoused to a man,"* etc. For the story of Mary's birth and her relationship to Joseph, see the Apocryphal story, pp. 1247 ff.

Page 1054. *The Birth of Jesus.* From Luke II.

Page 1054. "In a manger." According to the Apocryphal story, Jesus was born in a cave near Bethlehem and hidden in a manger later in order to escape Herod. See pp. 1253 ff.

Page 1055. "Heavenly host." See p. 186 and notes referring to that page and to pp. 181, 183, 185.

Page 1055. The Genealogy of Jesus. Matthew I. "Jesse begat David." See "Out of the stem of Jesse," p. 959. This is a part of the documentation for the Christian belief that Jesus was the Messiah whose coming was prophesied in the Old Testament.

Page 1056. The Flight into Egypt. Matthew II. "Wise men": probably, according to Hume, Zoroastrian priests.

Page 1058. The Childhood of Jesus. Luke II.

Page 1058. "Took him up in his arms and blessed God." Cf. similar recognition by a sage of the divinity of the infant Gotama, p. 187.

Page 1059. The Instruction of Jesus. Luke II.

Page 1059. "Both hearing them and asking them questions." Cf. similar evidences of wisdom in the young Gotama and Zoroaster, pp. 188 ff. and 612.

Page 1059. The Baptism of Jesus. Matthew III.

Page 1061. The Baptism of Jesus. John I.

Page 1061. "In the beginning was the Word." Herein lies a theology new to the Gospels of Christianity and partaking of the influence of Greek philosophy and Eastern mysticism. "Word" is here used in much the same sense as "Tao" of Taoism. Indeed the translation of John into Chinese begins (according to Robert Ernest Hume, in The World's Living Religions): "In the beginning was the Tao, and the Tao was with God, and the Tao was God." See verse XXV, the Tao-Te-King, p. 481.

Page 1062. Jesus Is Tempted by the Devil. Luke IV. See similar attempts by the personified forces of evil to turn aside the personified forces of good in stories of the lives of Gotama Buddha (p. 196) and Zarathushtra (pp. 586, 606, 611, 615).

Page 1063. Acknowledgment of Divinity. Luke IV. Cf. Buddha's and Zarathushtra's announcements of purpose, pp. 192 ff. and 613 ff.

Page 1064. The Spirit of the Lord Is Manifest. John II.

Page 1065. "This temple." Cf. "this tabernacle," p. 300.

Page 1065. The Healer. Luke IV.

Page 1066. The First Disciples. Luke V.

Page 1067. The First Disciples. Matthew IV.

Page 1068. The First Disciples. Mark I.

Page 1068. The First Disciples. John I.

Page 1069. A Crippled Man Is Healed. Luke V.

Page 1070. A Crippled Man Is Healed. John V.

Page 1071. The Two Blind Men and the Dumb Man. Matthew IX.

Page 1072. The Woman of Samaria. John IV.

Page 1072. "How is it that thou," etc. There is a story of Ananda, disciple of Gotama Buddha, who asked a woman for a drink of water. She protested that she was of low caste. He said: "I asked thee not for thy caste, but for a drink of water."

Page 1073. "Salvation is of the Jews." See note referring to p. 1088.

Page 1073. To Keep Holy the Sabbath. I. Luke VI.

Page 1074. II. Luke XIII.

Page 1075. III. Luke XIV.

Page 1075. Who Is This That Forgiveth Sins? Luke VII.

Page 1076. "A dead man," etc. In similar circumstances Gotama Buddha did not try to restore life to the dead, but by a wise and effective lesson taught the bereaved mother to accept the universality of death. See the story of Kisagotami, p. 306.

Page 1078. Mary and Martha. Luke X.

Page 1079. Jesus, Thou Son of God! Luke VIII.

Page 1079. "Thy mother and thy brethren." This is significant to the controversy in the early Christian Church as to whether or not Jesus had brothers and sisters. See note referring to p. 185. See also St. Paul's reference to "James, the Lord's brother," p. 1207.

Page 1081. The Twelve Apostles Named. Matthew X.

Page 1082. He Instructs His Disciples. I. Luke IX.

Page 1082. II. Luke X.

Page 1083. *The Rock of the Christian Church.* Matthew XVI.
Page 1084. *"Thou art Peter . . . this rock."* In the Greek this constitutes a play on words, since *Petros* means both "Peter" and "rock."
Page 1084. *The Death of John the Baptist.* Matthew XIV.
Page 1085. *The Loaves and Fishes.* Mark VI.
Page 1086. *Jesus Walks on the Water.* Matthew XIV.
Page 1087. *The Transfiguration.* Luke IX.
Page 1087. *Let the Children First Be Filled.* Mark VII.
Page 1088. *"Let the children first be filled."* This is one of the faint scraps of evidence that Jesus considered himself a Messiah to the Jews, but not to the Gentiles. See also reference to Gentiles, p. 1127. See also "Salvation is of the Jews," p. 1073.
Page 1088. *The Lunatic Son.* Matthew XVII.
Page 1089. *The Tribute Money.* Matthew XVII.
Page 1089. *The Son of Man Hath No Place.* Luke IX.
Page 1091. *The Sons of Zebedee.* Matthew XX.
Page 1091. *Suffer the Little Children.* Mark X.
Page 1092. *"As a little child."* Cf. Chuang Tze: "If you could be as a child," etc. p. 555.
Page 1092. *A Face toward Jerusalem. I.* Luke XVII.
Page 1092. *II.* Luke XVII.
Page 1092. *"Put . . . to death."* Cf. Buddha's announcement of his death, p. 225.
Page 1093. *III.* Luke XIX.
Page 1093. *The Woman Taken in Adultery.* John VIII.
Page 1094. *The Blind Man Stood on the Road and Cried.* John IX.
Page 1096. *Lazarus Arises from Death.* John XI.
Page 1099. *The Poor Ye Have Always.* John XII.
Page 1100. *Entry into Jerusalem.* Luke XIX.
Page 1101. *The Fig Tree Cursed.* Matthew XXI.
Page 1102. *The Widow's Mites.* Luke XXI.
Page 1102. *The Things That Are Caesar's.* Matthew XXII.
Page 1103. *The Price of a Saviour. I.* Luke XXII.
Page 1103. *II.* Matthew XXVI.
Page 1104. *The Last Supper. I.* Luke XXII.
Page 1104. *II.* John XIII.
Page 1106. *Gethsemane.* Luke XXII.
Page 1109. *The Trial of Jesus.* John XVIII. See also the more detailed Apocryphal account, pp. 1258 ff.
Page 1110. *Condemnation.* John XIX.
Page 1111. *The Way to Calvary.* Luke XXIII.
Page 1112. *The Crucifixion. I.* John XIX.
Page 1112. *II.* Luke XXIII.
Page 1113. *"Woman, Behold Thy Son!"* John XIX.
Page 1113. *Death on the Cross.* Matthew XXVII.
Page 1114. *"The earth did quake,"* etc. Cf. earthquake which accompanied Gotama's announcement of his coming death, p. 223.
Page 1114. *Burial.* John XIX.
Page 1115. *The Tomb Is Sealed.* Matthew XXVII.
Page 1115. *The Resurrection. I.* Matthew XXVIII.
Page 1116. *II.* John XX.
Page 1117. *The Risen Christ. I.* Matthew XXVIII.
Page 1118. *II.* Mark XVI.
Page 1118. *III.* Luke XXIV.
Page 1120. *IV.* John XX, XXI.
Page 1123. *The Sermon on the Mount.* Matthew V, VI, VII.
Page 1123. *"Blessed are the meek."* See Tao-Te-King, verse XXII, p. 479; also p. 503.
Page 1125. *"Love your enemies."* Cf. Dhammapada, p. 296; also Old Testament, "love covereth all sins," p. 920; also Tao-Te-King, "return love for great hatred," p. 504, and pp. 475, 500, 558, and 920.
Page 1127. *"For after all these things do the Gentiles seek."* See note referring to p. 1088.

Page 1128. *"Not everyone,"* etc. Cf. similar conditions of true discipleship imposed by the Buddha, p. 229.

Page 1129. *To the Disciples of Christ.* Matthew X. This is a part of Matthew's version of Christ's instructions to his disciples. Luke's much shorter version (given in the section headed "The Life and Acts of Jesus") seems more especially directed to his living followers. This fuller and more general utterance seems intended for followers of the Christian religion everywhere.

Page 1130. *Invitation to Christ.* Matthew XI.

Page 1131. *"For my yoke is easy."* Cf. Buddha, "My words are easy," p. 501.

Page 1131. *A Rebuke to Doubters.* Matthew XII.

Page 1132. *Of Forms and Meanings.* Matthew XV.

Page 1133. *The Price of Salvation.* Matthew XVI.

Page 1134. *Whatsoever Ye Bind on Earth.* Matthew XVIII.

Page 1135. *Of Marriage. I.* Matthew XIX.

Page 1136. *II.* Matthew XXII.

Page 1136. *Of Riches.* Matthew XIX.

Page 1136. *"Thou shalt love thy neighbour,"* etc. Cf. "he who loves the world," p. 475. Also pp. 296, 500, 504, 558, 920, 1125, *et al.*

Page 1137. *"A rich man,"* etc. Cf. Dhammapada, p. 298.

Page 1137. *The Reward of Salvation.* Matthew XIX.

Page 1137. *Of Resurrection.* Matthew XXII.

Page 1138. *The Great Commandments.* Mark XII. "Thou shalt love thy neighbour," etc. Cf. Tao-Te-King, p. 475. "Thou shalt love the Lord thy God," cf. p. 743. Also see pp. 296, 500, 504, 558, 920, 1125.

Page 1138. *Of His Identity.* Matthew XXII.

Page 1139. *He Rebukes the Scribes and Pharisees.* Matthew XXIII.

Page 1141. *Second Coming. I.* Matthew XXIV.

Page 1142. *"Shall the sun be darkened,"* etc. Cf. the "Buddha Uproar," p. 181.

Page 1143. *II.* Matthew XXV.

Page 1144. *Humble Thyself.* Luke XIV.

Page 1145. *Of the Requirements for Discipleship. I.* Luke XIV.

Page 1145. *II.* Luke XVII.

Page 1146. *Of the Rich Man and Lazarus.* Luke XVI.

Page 1147. *The Birth of the Spirit.* John III.

Page 1147. *"Born again."* Cf. "twice born man" of the Hindu scriptures. See p. 79 and note referring to that page.

Page 1148. *Of the Power of Jesus.* John V.

Page 1150. *The Bread of Life.* John VI.

Page 1151. *The Light of the World.* John VIII.

Page 1153. *The Good Shepherd.* John X.

Page 1154. *That You Walk in the Light.* John XII.

Page 1155. *To Save the World.* John XII.

Page 1155. *Let Not Your Heart Be Troubled.* John XIV.

Page 1157. *The True Vine.* John XV.

Page 1159. *Be of Good Cheer.* John XVI.

Page 1161. *The Glory Thou Gavest Me.* John XVII.

Page 1162. *Of the Cloth and Wine.* Matthew IX.

Page 1163. *Of the Sower, the Tares, the Mustard Seed, and the Leaven.* Matthew XIII.

Page 1166. *The Last Shall Be First.* Matthew XX.

Page 1167. *Of the Two Sons.* Matthew XXI.

Page 1167. *Of the Bad Husbandmen.* Matthew XXI.

Page 1168. *Of the Prince's Wedding.* Matthew XXII.

Page 1169. *Of the Wise and Foolish Virgins.* Matthew XXV.

Page 1169. *The Good and Faithful Servant.* Matthew XXV.

Page 1171. *Of the Good Samaritan.* Luke X.

Page 1172. *Of One That Layeth Up Treasure.* Luke XII.

Page 1172. *Of the Fig Tree.* Luke XIII.

Page 1173. *Of the Ninety and Nine.* Luke XV.

Page 1173. *Of the Ten Pieces of Silver.* Luke XV.

Page 1173. *Of the Prodigal Son.* Luke XV. Cf. similar parable in Buddhism, p. 323.

Page 1175. *Of the Widow and the Judge.* Luke XVIII.
Page 1175. *Of the Two Men Who Prayed.* Luke XVIII.
Page 1176. *The Apostles' Ministry Begins.* Acts I, II.
Page 1176. *"Purchased a field."* According to Matthew XXVII, 1–6, Judas attempted to return the money to the chief priests and elders, before Jesus was crucified, saying that he had betrayed an innocent man; and when the priests refused to accept it, he threw the silver down, went out of the temple, and hanged himself.
Page 1178. *Peter's Miracle.* Acts III.
Page 1179. *Peter and John Imprisoned.* Acts IV.
Page 1180. *The Lie of Ananias.* Acts V.
Page 1182. *The Death of Stephen.* Acts VI, VII, VIII.
Page 1183. *Saul's Conversion.* Acts IX.
Page 1184. *Peter's Vision of the Gentiles.* Acts X, XI.
Page 1185. *Paul and Barnabas Turn to the Gentiles.* Acts XIII, XIV, XV.
Page 1188. *Paul Reproves the Athenians.* Acts XVII.
Page 1189. *The Epistle of Paul to the Romans.* Selections from all the Epistles are made from the various chapters of each, respectively.
Page 1201. *"Have not charity."* Cf. Tao-Te-King LXVII, pp. 499, 500.
Page 1233. *The Revelation of St. John the Divine. I.* From Revelation I.
Page 1234. *II.* From Revelation IV.
Page 1235. *III.* From Revelation V.
Page 1236. *IV.* From Revelation VI.
Page 1237. *V.* From Revelation VIII, IX, X.
Page 1240. *VI.* From Revelation XIV.
Page 1241. *VII.* From Revelation XIX.
Page 1242. *VIII.* From Revelation XX.
Page 1243. *IX.* From Revelation XXI, XXII.
Page 1245. *"The city had no need of the sun."* See p. 52 for parallel in Hindu scriptures.
Page 1247. *The Apocryphal New Testament.* Selections from the Apocryphal New Testament, with the exception of "The Song of the Soul," are reprinted, with the permission of the publishers, from *The Apocryphal New Testament,* translated by Montague Rhodes James. Oxford, the Clarendon Press, 1926.
Page 1247. *The Birth of Mary.* From *The Book of James,* or *Protevangelium,* which has been found in an original Greek and several oriental versions, the oldest of which is Syriac. It was probably written during the second century A.D. The author is unknown.
Page 1249. *The Childhood of Mary.* From the Book of James.
Page 1251. *The Conception of Jesus.* From the Book of James.
Page 1253. *The Birth of Jesus.* From the Book of James.
Page 1256. *Miracles of the Child Jesus.* From the Gospel of Thomas, mentioned as early as A.D. 348 by Cyril of Jerusalem (according to Montague Rhodes James), who warns against reading it, saying: "It is not by one of the twelve apostles but by one of the three wicked disciples of Manes." James, however, says: "Very likely the Manichæans used it, but it was older than their sect."
Page 1257. *Worship of the Animals.* This and "The Miracle of the Palm Tree" which follows are from *The Gospel of Pseudo-Matthew,* a Latin compilation probably of the eighth or ninth century A.D. Its unknown compiler issued it as a secret work of Matthew, who, it was said, was unwilling to have its contents known during his lifetime. The same compiler charged the Manichæans with having issued a false copy of it. It is, however, generally considered spurious, according to Montague James.
Page 1258. *The Miracle of the Palm Tree.* From *The Gospel of Pseudo-Matthew.* This legend appears in several forms. In an old Kentucky mountain song, probably of old English origin, it is a cherry tree under which Mary rests, and it is before Jesus is born. Joseph flatly refuses to pick the cherries for her, whereupon the unborn Jesus commands the cherry tree to bend down, and it does so. See also the account of the sal tree which bent down for the mother of Gotama Buddha (pp. 185, 186).
Page 1258. *The Trial of Jesus.* This and "The Regret of Pilate" which follows it are from *The Gospel of Nicodemus,* or *Acts of Pilate,* which has been found in early Greek, Latin, Coptic, Syriac, and Armenian. It is perhaps not earlier than the fourth century A.D., but many of its conceptions are undoubtedly earlier.

Page 1268. *The Descent into Hell.* This and "Examination of Satan" which follows it are taken from *The Gospel of Bartholomew,* found in Greek, Latin, and Slavonic. Jerome mentions it in his commentary on Matthew. Montague Rhodes James thinks the Greek version not older than the fifth century A.D. The story of the descent into hell is apparently the source of the statement, "He descended into hell," in some versions of "The Apostles' Creed."

Page 1273. *How Long Shall Death Prevail?* From a letter by Clement of Alexandria discussing the lost *Gospel according to the Egyptians.*

Page 1274. *Satan Creates the World.* From the Book of John the Evangelist, of unknown origin, but probably, according to Montague James, of the sixth or seventh century A.D.

Page 1276. *The Appearances of Jesus.* From the Acts of John.

Page 1278. *The Dance of Praise.* From the Acts of John.

Page 1280. *Correspondence of Abgarus and Jesus.* From Eusebius's *Ecclesiastical History.*

Page 1280. *A Description of Jesus.* A fragment which Montague James believes to be an invention contained in a letter, probably of the thirteenth century, supposed to have been written by "a certain Lentulus" to the Roman Senate. "This follows," James writes, "the traditional portraits closely, and no doubt was written in the presence of one."

Page 1281. *The Hymn of the Soul.* Reprinted from *The Hymn of the Soul,* edited by J. Armitage Robinson. Cambridge, the University Press, 1897. This is also included in the Apocryphal New Testament within the Acts of Thomas, but is considered much older than this book, into which it was inserted. Indeed, in the Acts of Thomas it is introduced by "and he [Thomas] began to utter a psalm in this wise," intimating that it was then in existence, and that Thomas was quoting from memory. The hymn is originally Syriac, according to Montague James, who mentions also a Greek manuscript containing it.

MOHAMMEDAN SCRIPTURES

The last to come into being of the living religions represented in *The Bible of the World* is Mohammedanism, founded by Mohammed. The prophet of Islam was born in Mecca, in A.D. 570, son of a member of the Arabian Koreish tribe of shepherds and traders. During his youth, trading expeditions took him to Syria and Palestine, where he came into frequent contact with Jews and Christians.

It was not until he was in middle age (thirty-five to forty, according to Hume, in *The World's Living Religions*) that he entered upon his religious mission. From the Jews and Christians he had gained a conception of monotheism, which he later carried further, denouncing the idea of the Christian *trinity* as polytheistic, and teaching his followers to abhor "those who join gods with God." He did, however, always accept Jesus as one of the prophets of God. At forty, during a period of deep mental depression, he became convinced that he was appointed by God to be a great religious leader. But his preachings met with scant success and even persecution, from which he fled to Medinah in 622, when he was fifty-two years of age. There his early failure was followed by success, not only as the promulgator of a new religion, but as a warring leader who assured his followers that Allah would protect the faithful who fought in holy war. Formerly he had been friendly towards the Jews. Now he began to persecute and to kill them. For a number of years he held political sway over the whole of Arabia.

Mohammed died without leaving a successor. Four comrades of the prophet, among whom was his son-in-law Ali, kept the followers intact until the assassination of Ali, twenty-eight years after Mohammed's death. Thereupon the religion became split into warring sects.

The main scripture of Mohammedanism is the Koran, written by Mohammed himself, as a transcription of the revelations conveyed to him by the Angel Gabriel. It is arranged in 114 chapters or Suras which, *in toto,* are about one-fourth the length of the Old Testament. The influences of Judaism, Christianity, and, in a lesser degree, Zoroastrianism, are apparent throughout the book.

According to Hume, there are approximately 230,000,000 Mohammedans in the world to-day, among whom the largest single group consists of approximately 68,000,000 in

India—the land of the Vedas and Gotama Buddha. The rest are in Arabia, Persia, other Asiatic countries, and Africa.

Page 1289. *The Koran.* All selections from the Koran are reprinted, by permission of the publisher, from *El Kor'an,* or, *The Koran,* translated from the Arabic by J. M. Rodwell. London, Bernard Quaritch, 1876.
Page 1289. *Clot. of Blood.* Sura 96.
Page 1290. *The Enwrapped.* Sura 74.
Page 1291. *The Night.* Sura 92.
Page 1292. *The Night-Comer.* Sura 86.
Page 1292. *He Frowned.* Sura 80.
Page 1293. *The Most High.* Sura 87.
Page 1294. *The Folded Up.* Sura 81.
Page 1295. *The Brightness.* Sura 93.
Page 1295. *The Opening.* Sura 94.
Page 1296. *Those Who Stint.* Sura 83.
Page 1297. *The Mountain.* Sura 52.
Page 1299. *The Merciful.* Sura 55.
Page 1300. *The Poets.* Sura 26.
Page 1302. *The Ant.* Sura 27.
Page 1302. *The Queen of Saba.* Sura 27.
Page 1305. *The Last Day.* Sura 27.
Page 1306. *The Cave.* Sura 18.
Page 1309. *God Has No Son.* Sura 39.
Page 1309. *The Spider.* Sura 29.
Page 1312. *Relation to Jews and Christians.* Sura 2.
Page 1315. *Moral and Ritual Prescriptions.* Sura 2.
Page 1317. *The Holy War.* Sura 2.
Page 1318. *Wives.* Sura 2.
Page 1320. *Other prophets.* Sura 2.
Page 1320. *Praise of God.* Sura 2.
Page 1321. *War Captives.* Sura 8.
Page 1321. *Refugees.* Sura 8.
Page 1322. *The Table.* Sura 5.
Page 1325. *The Masnavi,* from the second book of which selections have been taken, is the work of Jalalu 'D-Din Rumi, the most famous of the Sufi poets, who was born at Balkh in A.D. 1207, and died in A.D. 1273. He was the founder of the Order of Maulavi Darvishes. The selections here given are from the first English translation of the work, made in 1910 by C. E. Wilson, Professor of Persian, University College, London. Reprinted here by permission of the publishers, Probsthain and Company, London.
Page 1335. *The Forty-Two Traditions of An-Nawawi.* Reprinted, by permission of the translator and the editor, from *The Forty-Two Traditions of An-Nawawi,* translated by Eric F. F. Bishop. *The Moslem World,* April 1939. Published by the Hartford Seminary Foundation, Hartford, Connecticut.

Condensed Bibliography

BOOKS QUOTED

Abhedananda, Swami (compiler). *The Sayings of Sri Ramakrishna.* New York, Vedanta Society, 1903.

Bailey, Alice A. *The Light of the Soul. A Paraphrase of the Yoga Sutras of Patanjali, with Commentary.* New York, Lucis Publishing Company, 1927.

Barnett, L. D. *Hinduism.* London, Constable and Company, 1913.

Barton, George A. *The Religions of the World.* Chicago, University of Chicago Press, 1920.

Besant, Annie (translator). *The Bhagavad-Gita, or The Lord's Song.* Wheaton, Illinois, Theosophical Press, 1929.

Bishop, Eric F. F. (translator). *The Forty-Two Traditions of An-Nawawi.* Hartford, Connecticut, Hartford Seminary Foundation, *The Moslem World* for April 1939.

Brewster, E. H. (compiler). *The Life of Gotama, the Buddha.* London, Kegan Paul, Trench, Trubner and Company; New York, E. P. Dutton and Company, 1926.

Burnell, Arthur Coke (translator). *The Ordinances of Manu.* London, Kegan Paul, Trench, Trubner and Company, 1891.

Ch'u Ta-Kao (translator). *Tao Te Ching.* London, Buddhist Lodge, 1937.

Cowell, E. B. (translator). *Buddhist Mahayana Texts, Part I, The Buddha Karita of Asvaghosha. Being Vol. XLIX of Sacred Books of the East,* edited by F. Max Müller. Oxford, Clarendon Press, 1894.

Cowell, E. B., and Gough, A. E. (translators). *The Sarva-Darsana-Samgraha, by Madhava Acharya.* London, Kegan Paul, Trench, Trubner and Company, 1894.

Daisetz Teitaro Suzuki. *A Manual of Zen Buddhism.* Kyoto, Eastern Buddhist Society, 1935.

Darmsteter, James (translator). *The Zend-Avesta, Part I, The Vendidad. Being Vol. IV of Sacred Books of the East,* edited by F. Max Müller, Oxford, Clarendon Press, 1895.

Darmsteter, James (translator). *The Zend-Avesta, Part II, The Sirozahs, Yasts, and Nyayis. Being Vol. XXIII of Sacred Books of the East,* edited by F. Max Müller. Oxford, Clarendon Press, 1883.

Dutt, Manmatha Nath (editor). *The Garuda Puranam.* Calcutta, Society for the Resuscitation of Indian Literature, 1908.

Dutt, Manmatha Nath (editor). *The Markandeya Puranam.* Calcutta, H. C. Dass, 1896.

Dutt, Manmatha Nath (editor). *The Vishnu Puranam,* from translation by H. H. Wilson. Calcutta, H. C. Dass, 1894.

Dutta, Sita Nath. *Sankaracharya, His Life and Teachings. A Translation of Atma-Bodha.* Calcutta, for the Society for the Resuscitation of Indian Literature, H. C. Press, 1899.

Eggeling, Julius (translator). *The Satapatha Brahmana, Part I, Books I and II. Being Vol. XII of Sacred Books of the East,* edited by F. Max Müller. Oxford, Clarendon Press, 1882.

Eggeling, Julius (translator). *The Satapatha Brahmana, Part IV, Books VIII, IX, and X. Being Vol. XLIII of Sacred Books of the East,* edited by F. Max Müller. Oxford, Clarendon Press, 1897.

Eggeling, Julius (translator). *The Satapatha Brahmana, Part V, Books XI, XII, XIII, and XIV. Being Vol. XLIV of Sacred Books of the East,* edited by F. Max Müller. Oxford, Clarendon Press, 1900.

Evans-Wentz, W. Y. (editor). *Tibetan Yoga and Secret Doctrines, or Seven Books of Wisdom of the Great Path, according to the late Lama Kazi-Dawa-Samdup's English rendering,* with foreword by Dr. R. R. Marett. London, Humphrey Milford, Oxford University Press, 1935.

Gemmell, William (translator). *The Diamond Sutra, or Prajna-Paramita.* London, Kegan Paul, Trench, Trubner and Company, 1912.

Giles, Herbert A. (translator). *Chuang Tzu, Mystic, Moralist, and Social Reformer.* London, Bernard Quaritch, 1889.

Griffith, Ralph T. H. (translator). *The Hymns of the Atharva-Veda.* 2 Vols., Benares, E. J. Lazarus and Company, 1895.

Griffith, Ralph T. H. (translator). *The Hymns of the Rig-Veda.* 2 Vols., Benares, E. J. Lazarus and Company, 1896–97.

Guthrie, Kenneth Sylvan (translator). *The Hymns of Zoroaster.* Brooklyn, Comparative Literature Press; London, George Bell, 1914.

Handcock, Percy. *Early Babylonian Flood Stories.* London, Society for Promoting Christian Knowledge, 1921.

Harper, Robert Francis (translator). *The Code of Hammurabi.* Chicago, University of Chicago Press, 1904.

Hume, Robert Ernest (translator). *The Thirteen Principal Upanishads.* London, Humphrey Milford, 1934.

Hume, Robert Ernest. *The World's Living Religions.* New York, Charles Scribner's Sons, 1938.

Ivan Chen (translator). *The Book of Filial Duty (Hsiao Ching).* London, John Murray; New York, E. P. Dutton and Company, 1920.

Iyangar, Shrinivas (translator). *The Hatha-Yoga Pradipika of Swatmaram Swami.* Bombay, Bombay Theosophical Publication Fund, 1893.

Jacobi, Herman (translator). *Gaina Sutras, Part I, The Akaranga Sutra, The Kalpa Sutra. Being Vol. XXII of Sacred Books of the East,* edited by F. Max Müller. Oxford, Clarendon Press, 1884.

James, Montague Rhodes (translator). *The Apocryphal New Testament.* Oxford, Clarendon Press, 1924.

Johnson, Francis (translator). *The Hitopadesa.* London, Chapman and Hall, 1928.

Kazi Dawa-Samdup (editor). *Shrichakrasambhara Tantra. Being Vol. VII of Tantrik Texts,* edited by Arthur Avalon. London, Luzac and Company, 1919.

Kern, H. (translator). *The Saddharma-Pundarika, or The Lotus of the True Law. Being Vol. XXI of Sacred Books of the East,* edited by F. Max Müller. Oxford, Clarendon Press, 1884.

King James Translation of the Bible. Authorized Version.

Legge, James (translator). *The Chinese Classics.* 7 Vols., London, Trubner and Company, 1871.

Legge, James (translator). *Sacred Books of China, Part I, The Shih King. Being Vol. III of Sacred Books of the East,* edited by F. Max Müller. Oxford, Clarendon Press, 1879.

Legge, James (translator). *Sacred Books of China, Part III, The Li Ki. Being Vol. XXVII of Sacred Books of the East,* edited by F. Max Müller. Oxford, Clarendon Press, 1885.

Legge, James (translator). *Sacred Books of China. Part IV, The Li Ki. Being Vol. XXVIII of Sacred Books of the East,* edited by F. Max Müller. Oxford, Clarendon Press, 1885.

Macnicol, Nicol (editor). *Hindu Scriptures.* Everyman's Library, No. 944. New York, E. P. Dutton and Company, 1938.

Mascaro, J. (translator). *Himalayas of the Soul.* New York, E. P. Dutton and Company, 1938. London, John Murray.

Mills, L. H. (translator). *The Zend-Avesta, Part III, The Yasna, Visparad, Afrinagan, Gako, and Miscellaneous Fragments. Being Vol. XXXI of Sacred Books of the East,* edited by F. Max Müller. Oxford, Clarendon Press, 1887.

Müller, F. Max. *Lectures on the Science of Religion, with a Paper on Buddhist Nihilism and a Translation of the Dhammapada.* New York, Charles Scribner and Company, 1872.

Müller, F. Max (translator). *The Upanishads, Part I. Being Vol. I of Sacred Books of the East,* edited by F. Max Müller. Oxford, Clarendon Press, 1879.

Müller, F. Max (translator). *The Upanishads, Part II. Being Vol. XV of Sacred Books of the East,* edited by F. Max Müller. Oxford, Clarendon Press, 1884.

Pe Maung Tin (translator). *The Path of Purity. Buddhaghosha's Visuddimagga. Part I.* London (for the Pali Text Society), Oxford University Press, 1922.

Robinson, J. Armitage (editor). *The Hymn of the Soul.* Cambridge, University Press, 1897.

Rodwell, J. M. (translator). *El Kor'an, or The Koran.* London, Bernard Quaritch, 1876.

Rogers, Capt. T. (translator). *Buddhaghosha's Parables*. London, Trubner and Company, 1870.
Rhys Davids, T. W. (translator). *Dialogues of the Buddha. Being Vol. II of the Sacred Books of the Buddhists*, edited by F. Max Müller. London, Henry Frowde, Oxford University Warehouse, 1899.
Rhys Davids, T. W. and C. A. F. (translators). *Dialogues of the Buddha, Part II. Being Vol. III of Sacred Books of the Buddhists*, edited by T. W. Rhys Davids. London, Henry Frowde, Oxford University Press, 1938.
Rhys Davids, T. W. and C. A. F. (translators). *Dialogues of the Buddha, Part III. Being Vol. IV of Sacred Books of the Buddhists*, edited by T. W. Rhys Davids. London, Humphrey Milford, Oxford University Press, 1921.
Soothill, W. E. *The Lotus of the Wonderful Law*. Oxford, Clarendon Press, 1930.
Teitaro Suzuki (translator). *Acvaghosha's Discourse on the Awakening of Faith in the Mahayana*. Chicago, Open Court Publishing Company, 1900.
Warren, Henry Clarke (translator). *Buddhism in Translations*. Cambridge, Harvard University Press, 1915.
West, E. W. (translator). *Pahlavi Texts, Part I, the Bundahis, Bahman Yast, and Shayast La-Shayast. Being Vol. V. of Sacred Books of the East*, edited by F. Max Müller. Oxford, Clarendon Press, 1880.
West, E. W. (translator). *Pahlavi Texts, Part II. The Dadistan-i-Dinik and the Epistles of Manuskihar. Being Vol. XVIII of Sacred Books of the East*, edited by F. Max Müller. Oxford, Clarendon Press, 1882.
West, E. W. (translator). *Pahlavi Texts, Part V. Marvels of Zoroastrianism. Being Vol. XLVII of Sacred Books of the East*, edited by F. Max Müller. Oxford, Clarendon Press, 1897.
Wilson, C. E. (translator). *The Masnavi, Book II*. By Jalalu 'D-Din Rumi. London, Probsthain and Company, 1910.
Wilson, Epiphanius (editor). *Sacred Books of the East. Being a volume of The World's Great Classics*, edited by Julian Hawthorne and Clarence Cook. New York and London, Colonial Press, 1900.
Wong, Charles A. (translator). *Confucian Analects; The Great Learning; The Doctrine of the Mean; The Works of Mencius*. No publisher. No date.
Woodward, F. L. (translator). *The Minor Anthologies of the Pali Canon. Part II*. London, Humphrey Milford, Oxford University Press, 1935.

BOOKS NOT QUOTED
(Suggested for further reading)

Anwyl, Edward. *Celtic Religion in Pre-Christian Times*. London, Archibald Constable and Company, 1906.
Bell, Richard (translator). *The Qur'an*. Edinburgh, T. and T. Clark, 1937.
Besant, Annie. *The Wisdom of the Upanishats*. Benares and London, Theosophical Publishing Society, 1907.
Box, G. H. *Early Christianity and Its Rivals*. New York, Jonathan Cape and Harrison Smith, 1929.
Brief Glossary of Buddhist Terms. London, Buddhist Lodge, 1937.
Brown, Brian. *The Story of Buddha and Buddhism*. Philadelphia, David McKay, 1927.
Brown, Brian. *The Story of Confucius*. Philadelphia, David McKay, 1927.
Browne, Lewis. *This Believing World*. New York, Macmillan Company, 1926.
Burkitt, F. Crawford. *Early Eastern Christianity*. London, John Murray, 1904.
Case, Shirley Jackson. *The Evolution of Early Christianity*. Chicago, University of Chicago Press, 1917.
Cheira, Edward. *They Wrote on Clay*. Chicago, University of Chicago Press, 1938.
Coomaraswamy, Ananda K. *A New Approach to the Vedas*. London, Luzac and Company, 1933.
Dadachanyi, Faredun K. *Light of the Avesta and the Gathas*. Bombay, Faredun K. Dadachanyi, 1913.
Dowson, John. *A Classical Dictionary of Hindu Literature*. London, Kegan Paul, Trench, Trubner and Company, 1928.

Edmunds, Albert J. *Buddhist and Christian Gospels, now first compared from the originals.* 2 Vols., Philadelphia, Innes and Sons, 1909.
Edwardes, Marian, and Spence, Lewis. *A Dictionary of Non-Classical Mythology.* London and Toronto, J. M. Dent and Sons, Ltd., New York, E. P. Dutton and Company, Everyman's Library.
Farquhar, J. N. *A Primer of Hinduism.* London, Henry Frowde, Oxford University Press, 1912.
Field, Dorothy. *The Religion of the Sikhs.* New York, E. P. Dutton and Company, 1928.
Finney, Ross L. (editor). *Huck's Synopsis of the First Three Gospels.* Cincinnati, Jennings and Graham; New York, Eaton and Mains, 1907.
Francis, H. T., and Thomas, E. J. (editors). *Jataka Tales.* Cambridge, University Press, 1916.
Goddard, Dwight (editor). *A Buddhist Bible.* Thetford, Vermont, Goddard, 1938.
Guignebert, Charles. *Christianity, Past and Present.* New York, Macmillan Company, 1927.
Holy Scriptures (The) According to the Masoretic Text, a New Translation. Philadelphia, Jewish Publication Society, 1937.
Horner, George (translator). *Pistis Sophia.* London, Society for Promoting Christian Knowledge; New York and Toronto. Macmillan Company, 1924.
Hume, Robert Ernest (compiler and editor). *Treasure House of the Living Religions. Selections from their sacred scriptures.* New York, Charles Scribner's Sons, 1933.
Lani, D. J. *The Divine Songs of Zarathushtra.* With an Introduction by Rabindranath Tagore, London, George Allen and Unwin, Ltd.; New York, Macmillan Company, 1924.
Jennings, Wm. (translator). *The Confucian Analects.* London, George Routledge and Sons.
King, L. W. (editor). *The Seven Tablets of Creation.* London, Luzac and Company, 1902.
Knox, Raymond C. *Knowing the Bible.* New York, Macmillan Company, 1927.
Langdon, S. *Babylonian Penitential Psalms.* Paris, Librairie Orientaliste Paul Geuthner, 1927.
Leonard, William Ellery (translator). *Gilgamesh. Epic of Old Babylonia.* New York, Viking Press, 1934.
Leuba, James H. *The Psychological Origin and the Nature of Religion.* London, Constable and Company, 1915.
Lewis, Frank Grant. *How the Bible Grew.* Chicago, University of Chicago Press, 1936.
Lin Yutang (editor). *The Wisdom of Confucius.* New York, Modern Library, 1938.
Martin, Alfred W. *Great Religious Teachers of the East.* New York, Macmillan Company, 1911.
Mead, G. R. S. *Fragments of a Faith Forgotten.* London, John M. Watkins, 1931.
Nyogen Senzaki, and Saladin Reps (translators). *The Gateless Gate.* London, John Murray, 1934.
Phythian-Adams, W. J. *Mithraism.* Chicago, Open Court Publishing Co.
Redfield, Bessie G. *Gods; a Dictionary of the Deities of All Lands.* New York, London, G. P. Putnam's Sons, 1931.
Rice, Stanley. *Ancient Indian Fables and Stories from the Panchatantra.* New York, E. P. Dutton and Company, 1924.
Ross, Peter V. *A Digest of the Bible.* New York, Prentice Hall and Company, 1938.
Ryder, Arthur W. (translator). *The Bhagavad-Gita.* Chicago, University of Chicago Press, 1929.
Ryder, Arthur W. (translator). *The Panchatantra.* Chicago, University of Chicago Press, 1925.
Sale, George (translator). *The Koran.* New York, American Book Exchange, 1880.
Saunders, Kenneth. *Buddhism.* New York, Jonathan Cape and Harrison Smith, 1930.
Smith, J. M. Powis (editor and translator, with others). *The Old Testament; an American Translation.* Chicago, University of Chicago Press, 1927.
Smith, Margaret. *The Persian Mystics.* London, John Murray, 1932.
Shree Purohit Swami, and Yeats, W. B. *The Ten Principal Upanishads.* London, Faber and Faber, 1937.
Smith, Sidney. *The Babylonian Legends of the Creation and the Fight between Bel and the Dragon.* London, British Museum, 1931.

Starr, Frederick. *Confucianism*. New York, Covici Friede, 1930.

Sung, Z. D. (translator). *The Text of the Yi King and Its Appendices*. Shanghai, China Modern Education Company, 1935.

Teitaro Suzuki, and Carus, Dr. Paul (translators). *Tai-Shang Kan-Ying P'ien. Treatise of the Exalted One on Response and Retribution*. Chicago, Open Court Publishing Company, 1906.

Thomas, E. J. (translator). *Buddhist Scriptures*. London, John Murray, 1913.

Thompson, R. Campbell (translator). *The Epic of Gilgamesh*. London, Luzac and Company, 1928.

Wagiswara, W. D. C., and Saunders, K. J. (translators). *The Buddha's Way of Virtue. A Translation of the Dhammapada*. London, John Murray, 1912.

Wilson, Epiphanius (editor). *Babylonian and Assyrian Literature*. New York, Colonial Press, 1901.

Wilson, Epiphanius (editor). *Chinese Literature*. New York, Colonial Press, 1900.

Wilson, Epiphanius (editor). *Egyptian Literature*. New York, Colonial Press, 1901.

GLOSSARY

(Key to abbreviations used: H = Hindu Scriptures; B = Buddhist Scriptures; J = Jainist Scriptures; C = Confucianist Scriptures; T = Taoist Scriptures; Z = Zoroastrian Scriptures; M = Mohammedan Scriptures. One of these symbols is used with each reference to designate only in what scripture the word occurs in *The Bible of the World*, not to intimate that it is exclusive to the language of this scripture. In general, definitions are confined to the meanings of the word as used in this book.)

Acarya. (B) A spiritual teacher or guide.

Achyuta. (H) "Unfallen." A characterization of Vishnu or Krishna.

Adhvaryu. (H) A priest who recites the prayers of the Yajur-Veda.

Aditi. (H) "Free, unbounded." Infinity. The boundless heaven. Deva-Matri, Mother of the gods.

Aditya. (H) A group of gods, sons of Aditi, of whom Varuna was chief; therefore he was *the* Aditya. Sustainers of the light of sun, moon, stars, dawn, etc.

Advaita-Vadins. (H) "Workers against twoness." Followers of the doctrine of universal unity.

Aesha. (Z) The power of wishing personified.

Aeshm, Aeshma. (Z) Rage. Also the demon of rage. Asmodeus of the Book of Tobit.

Agamas. (H) Not contradicting the sense of scripture; orthodox, canonical; a group of Hindu religious treatises.

Agni. (B) (H) (nom. Agnis = Ignis) Fire. One of the three great Vedic deities, Agni, Vayu (or Indra), and Surya, ruling earth, air, and sky.

Agnihotra. (H) A priest of Agni, or Agni as priest.

Ahamkara. (H) Self-consciousness. The function in the soul which produces falsely the conception of an ego.

Ahriman. (Z) See Angra Mainyu.

Ahuna-Vairya. (Z) Personification of prayer.

Ahura Mazda. (Z) The supreme principle; the single, omnipotent, omniscient God of Zoroastrianism. For origin of name, see Asura.

Airyana. (Z) Same as Sanskrit *Aryan*, the basic race which was divided into Indian and Persian.

Alaka. (B) Capital of Kuvera and home of Gandharvas (which see) on Mount Meru (which see).

Alakananda. (H) One of the four branches of the sacred river Ganges, or Ganga.

'Ali. (M) Mohammed's son-in-law, one of the successors of the prophet in leading the community. After 'Ali's assassination, Islam became permanently divided into sects.

Allah. (M) Proper name of the one all-knowing and all-powerful God, whom Mohammed exalted in contradistinction to the many nature-spirits worshipped before his time by the Arabs.

Amerodad. (Z) Immortality. Proper name of one of the Amesha Spentas, which see.

Amesha-Spentas. (Z) Saints, or seven superior genii which may be compared to the Indian Adityas (which see) and to the archangels of the Hebrew Old Testament.

Ananda. (H) "Joy, Happiness." An appellation of Siva in Hinduism and a suffix to many Hindu teachers' names. (B) Name of Buddha's personal attendant and beloved disciple.

Anathapindika. (B) "Nourisher of the unprotected." Given name of Sudatta, who was the main lay-follower of the Buddha, giver of the Jetavana monastery-park.

Angirasa. (H) (B) Member of a class of Pitris, that is, sacred ancestors, Patres, the Manes.

Angra Mainyu. (Z) The embodiment of evil in Zoroastrian belief. King of all evil and unclean spirits. Counterpart of Satan. Later called Ahriman.

Antariksha. (H) The atmosphere between heaven and earth, realm of the Gandharvas, Apsarases, and Yakshas, which see.

Anuttarasamyaksambodhicitta. (B) Most-perfect-knowledge-mind.

Apagadha. (Z) A serious illness.

Apaosh. (Z) The evil spirit of drought.

Apsaras. (H) "Moving in the water." A nymph of Indra's heaven. Plural: —es,

1385

—as. Wives or mistresses of the Gandharvas, and leading a love life with them.

Arahant. (B) One who has followed the
eightfold path to enlightenment.

Arahat. (B) See Arahant.

Aranyani. (H) Vedic goddess of the forest.

Arbudasikhara. (H) Serpent Mountain.

Arhat. (B) Pali equivalent of Sanskrit Arahant, which see. (H) A deserving, worthy
person. See Arahant.

Arjuna. (H) "White." Name of the third
Pandu prince, son of Indra. The episode in
the Bhagavad-Gita is but one of many in
his long career as a brave warrior.

Arundhati. (H) The morning star, espoused
to the Rishi Vasishtha, and a paragon of
wifely virtues.

Aryans. (B) Originally, "faithfully devoted"
comrades; later, self-nomination of the in-
vaders into India in contradistinction to the
aboriginals. In Buddhism, spiritualized, or
noble, well formed.

Asana. (H) The third stage of Yoga practice, including physical postures as a background for meditation.

Asavas. (B) Mental intoxication; defilement.

Asha. (Z) Pure. The cosmic righteous order
pervading all things pure. Piety. Purity.
Also the god of purity.

Ashaist. (Z) One who follows the order of
Asha and worships the spirit of Asha,
which see.

Ashavahist. (Z) Ashavan. Provided with
order. Belonging to the holy order. See
Asha.

Ashavahisto. (Z) See Vahista.

Ashem vohu. (Z) The first words of the second holiest prayer. Translated: "Purity is
the best treasure."

Ashemaogha. (Z) Interfering with purity.
Force working against goodness.

Ashramas, Asramas. (H) Stages in the life
of a Brahmana.

Ashvins. (H) See Asvins.

Asperena. (Z) A measure of weight used on
a scale.

Asto-vidhotu. (Z) The genius of death. Ver-
bally, to separate.

Asu. (H) Breath, life, vitality, spirit world.

Asura. (H) "Spiritual, Divine." In the earliest portion of the Rig-Veda the name denotes the supreme spirit and is equivalent
to Ahura in Zoroastrianism. It was then
applied to Indra, Agni, Varuna, and other
important deities. Later it acquired an opposite meaning and signified a demon, or
enemy of the gods.

Asvaghosha. (B) One of the most celebrated
of Buddhist philosophers, who lived about
six hundred years after the death of Gotama
Buddha.

Asvins. (H) "Horsemen." Two Vedic deities,
twin sons of the sun or the sky. The car-
riers of light to the morning sky.

Atar. (Z) A chief of the Yazatas. The genius
of fire. The ninth month and the ninth day
of the month were named after him in
Persia.

Atharva, Atharvan. (H) The fourth Veda.

In early times somehow considered as un-
canonical because mostly containing magic
spells. But these popular practices were
later taken over by the priests (atharvans)
and they, claiming the only right to handle
them, called the fourth Veda specially
Atharva-Veda, i.e., the Veda belonging to
the Atharvans.

Atharvan. (H) Name of a priest in the Rig-
Veda, the oldest son of Brahma. Inspired
author of the Atharva-Veda. Also general
name for priests in Vedic times.

Atharvangirases. (H) Descendants of Atharvan and Angiras, or the Angirasas alone,
who are associated with the Atharva-
Veda; hence the hymns of that Veda.

Athravan. (Z) Same as Sanskrit Atharvan.
Priest, fire priest.

Atman. (H) The universal soul. The divine
principle, especially as manifested within
the human self. Often inadequately translated as "the self." The Higher Self, the
real Self, the divine spark in man; the
Reality of the Ego, which stands in the
background as the essence of this only supposed reality. See footnote on page 38.

Atta. (B) Pali equivalent of Sanskrit Atman
(which see). In Buddhist literature, however, used more in the secular meaning of
personality, and denied in many of the
Scriptures.

Aum, Om. (H) Symbol of the Lord of created beings. The mystic word which precedes all prayers. Compounded of the letters A U M, symbolic of the three major
Vedas. In later times a monosyllabic representation of union of Vishnu, Siva, and
Brahma. The word is declared to exert
mystic power when meditated upon.

Avaoirista. (Z) The sin of inflicting pain on
another through uncontrolled rage.

Avatara. (B) (H) "A descent." Incarnation
of a deity, especially of Vishnu. In Buddhism, used for the coming to birth in the
world of a Bodhisattva.

Avesta. (Z) The Zendavesta. The original
scriptures of the Zoroastrians.

Avidya. (H) "Not knowing." The active
principle of ignorance within us which must
be overcome by religious practices directed
toward enlightenment.

Ayatanas. (B) "Dwelling place." In philosophical doctrines, the six sense-organs and
their objective stimulators.

Az. (Z) To lead. To walk.

Azi Dahaka, Az-i Dahak. (Z) Name of a
tyrant who, descended from Ahriman on
his mother's side, troubled the earth for a
thousand years.

Bakhdhi. (Z) Lot. Fate.

Baresma. (Z) Name of a group of branches
which the priest held during ritual observances.

Bauddha. (H) Buddhists.

Bhadra. (H) Wife of Utathya, a Brahmana
of the race of Angiras. Bhadra was stolen
by Varuna because of her great beauty.
Utathya, by drinking up all the water of

the sea and making the rivers dry up, forced Varuna to return her.

Bhaga. (H) A Vedic deity of wealth and marriage. Classed with the Adityas and Visvadevas.

Bhagavat. (H) "Possessing a happy lot." The Venerable, the Adorable, the Lord.

Bhakta. (H) A devoted worshipper.

Bharadvaga. (B) (H) A Rishi to whom many Vedic hymns are attributed.

Bharata. (H) A king from whom descended the warriors called Bharatas.

Bhikkhu. (B) Pali equivalent of Sanskrit Bhikshu. Originally a beggar; later, general appellation for the followers of the Buddha who had left worldly life. The usual translation as "monk" does not quite cover the meaning of bhikkhu, because "monk" is too much coloured by Christian traditions.

Bhikshu. (H) A mendicant. A Brahmana in the fourth and highest stage of his religious life.

Bhishma. (H) "The terrible." Son of King Santanu by the River Goddess Ganga. His son also was named Bhishma or Santanava.

Bhrigu. (H) A Vedic sage. A great Rishi. Founder of the race of Bhrigus or Bhargavas.

Bhuh, Bhumi. (H) "The underlying." The earth. See Prithivi.

Bhur. (H) See Vyahritis.

Bhuvah. (H) See Vyahritis.

Bimbisara. (B) King of Magadha at the time of Gotama Buddha. Built city of Rajagaha. Convert to Buddhism. Presented Veluvana (the Bamboo Grove) to Gotama for use of the Order.

Bodhi. (B) Enlightenment.

Bodhi tree, or Bo-tree. (B) The tree under which Gotama attained enlightenment at Buddha Gaya. A kind of fig tree, popularly called pipal tree.

Bodhisatta. (B) Pali equivalent of Sanskrit Bodhisattva, which see.

Bodhisattva. (B) One whose being or essence is bodhi, that is, wisdom arising from direct perception of truth. A being which through its incarnations in many forms and in many realms of existence prepares itself to become a Buddha, a teacher of the enlightening doctrine on earth. In Hinayana Buddhism, an aspirant for Buddhahood, one who is to be a Buddha. In Mahayana Buddhism, one who, having attained enlightenment, nevertheless renounces Nirvana in order to help humanity.

Bo-tree. (B) See Bodhi tree.

Brahma. (H) (masculine) A personification of the essential principle Brahman (which see) as the creator god, the Prajapati, or lord and father of all creatures. In later times, one of the trinity Brahma, Vishnu, and Siva. Brahma is usually shown in sculpture with four heads looking in the four directions.

Brahmacharins. (H) Brahmana students.

Brahma-mimansa. (H) A philosophical system which teaches the art of reasoning, with the express purpose of aiding in the interpretation of the Vedas.

Brahman. (H) (neuter) The supreme essence, the central principle or soul of the universe, the all-pervading force, incorporeal, immaterial, invisible, uncreated, unborn, with neither beginning nor end, and infinite in its manifestations, in all existing creatures and things. To achieve knowledge of and identification with it is the highest goal of Hindu religious meditation and other practices.

Brahmana. (H) 1. Member of the Brahmana class, the first of the four castes, the sacerdotal class, whose members may or may not act as priests. His person is inviolate and he is held to be entitled to greater honour than royalty. 2. "Belonging to the Brahmanas." Works composed by and for the Brahmanas.

Brahmanaspati, Brihaspati. (H) Name of a deity who intercedes with the gods for the welfare of mankind.

Brahma-yoni. (H) Yoni = the female organ. Hence, Brahma-yoni = the holy, or the worshipful female organ of Brahma which, alone or in combination with the linga or male organ (phallus), is an object of worship by the Saktis. A sacred mountain cleft through which pilgrims pass to gain religious merit.

Brihaspati. (H) See Brahmanaspati.

Buddha. (B) A title derived from the root budh, "to know." The enlightened one. The title given to Gotama, founder of the Buddhist order and religion, and to others. (H) The Buddha is sometimes considered as being Vishnu's ninth incarnation.

Buddha Vajra-Sattva. (H) Vajra = thunderbolt, also male organ. Sattva = the essence of being. Therefore, the Buddha with the virility of the male organ and the pushing power of the thunderbolt, as the driving force in his being.

Buddhaghosha. (B) "Voice of Buddha." Name of several Buddhist writers. The most noted, author of the Visuddhimagga and other works, and Chief Hinayana commentator was born in north India early in the fifth century A.D.

Buddhi. (B) (H) The vehicle of enlightenment, bodhi, the faculty of supreme understanding.

Buiti. (Z) Proper name of one of the Daevas (which see).

Chakshu. (H) Eye or sight. Chakshusha = the sixth Manu.

Champa. (B) (H) Name of a city in India, the capital of Anga.

Chandala. (H) Name of a woman. "The shining one."

Charvaka. (H) 1. Name of a materialistic philosopher. 2. Name of the philosophical system professed by his followers.

Ch'i. (T) The great breath, the life, the soul, the spirit of the living universe.

Chinvad Bridge. (Z) Chinvad = "to be desirous." The bridge between heaven and earth.

Chitta. (B) (H) The inner world of man. The focus of his emotions and intellect. Also understood in Yoga as "mind stuff," that is, the substance in which thoughts take form.

Chou (Chow) dynasty. (C) A celebrated dynasty which lasted from 1122 B.C. to 255 B.C. The *chow le*, or chow ritual, is assigned to this period.

Chuang Tze. (T) A Chinese sage who lived about 400 B.C. His works, together with the Tao-Te-King, constitute the basic scriptures of philosophical Taoism. See Tao.

Chung Yung. (C) The doctrine of the middle course which varies neither to one side nor the other.

Citta. See Chitta.

Confucius. (C) Latinized form of Confutzee, i.e., Kung the Master, or Master Kung. The great ethical teacher who lived 551–479 B.C. and who founded Confucianism.

Daevaists. (Z) Followers of the Daevas (which see).

Daevas. (Z) Malevolent spirits. Demons of darkness. Originally the same as "devas" in Hinduism (Veda). But, as often in the history of religions, the gods of one tribe, because of mutually hostile attitudes, became the demons of the other tribe.

Dahak. (Z) See Azi Dahaka.

Daiti. (Z) Preparation.

Daitya. (Z) 1. Right, justice. 2. Name of the river which flows under the Chinvad Bridge.

Daityas. (H) Titans who warred against the gods along with the Danavas, with whom they are closely associated. See Danu.

Dakhmas. (Z) A container for bones. The name of the "towers of silence" where the bodies of the dead are left to be devoured by birds.

Dakshina. (H) A gift made to Brahmanas in recognition of their services at a sacrifice. Personified as a goddess.

Danu. (H) Mother of the danavas, giants who warred against the gods. Also a danava.

Darsana. (H) "Demonstration," or school of philosophy.

Dasaratha. (B) (H) Name of a prince of the Solar race, son of Aja, and king of Ayodhya.

Dasas. (H) "Slaves." Indian tribes who opposed the intrusive Aryans.

Deva, Devata. (H) (nom. Devas = Deus, from the root *div*, to shine) A divine being or god.

Devas. (B) "Shining ones," celestial beings, with good, bad, and indifferent characteristics; in Buddhism, however, considered to be mortal and subject to reincarnation, in need of the releasing doctrine of the Buddha.

Dhamma. (B) Pali equivalent of Dharma. In Buddhism the word may mean, according to its context, any of the following: system, doctrine, religion, virtue, moral quality, righteousness, justice, duty, law, standard, norm, ideal, truth, form, condition, cause, phenomenon, thing, cosmic order.

Dhammapada. (B) Verses on Dhamma. See Dhamma.

Dhananjaya. (H) "Conqueror of riches." Used as a title for Arjuna and others.

Dharana. (H) A stage of Yoga practice in which the mind is fixed on one single object of meditation. "To hold fast."

Dharma. (H) (Pali equivalent, Dhamma) 1. Justice. 2. A name of Yama as the judge of the dead. 3. Moral or religious duty. See Yama.

Dharmakaya. (B) The embodied law. The Buddha as personification of truth.

Dharmaraja. (B) "Justice ruler." Therefore, (1) Yama (which see), (2) Yudhishthira, mythical son of Yama.

Dharmaranya. (H) A sacred grove.

Dharma-Yupa. (H) Yupa = beam or stake. Therefore, the stake of Dharma, which see.

Dhrita-rashtra. (H) First son of Vichitra-virya. Born blind, he renounced a throne and precipitated a war among his hundred sons.

Dhruva. (H) The pole star.

Dhyana. (B) (H) Mystic states of serene contemplation attained by meditation. Translated in Chinese as Ch'an, in Japanese, Zen, but this gives a wrong conception of Zen, which see.

Digha Nikaya. (B) "Collection of long discourses." The first section of the Sutta Pitaka.

Djinn. (M) Same as jinn, which see.

Draupadeyas. (H) Sons or followers of Draupadi.

Druj. (Z) From the verb meaning "to lie" or "to betray." The name of a group of female demons.

Drujust. (Z) A follower of the Druj (which see).

Drupada. (H) King of Panchala. Father-in-law of Arjuna.

Duryodhana. (H) "Hard to conquer." Eldest son of King Dhrita-rashtra.

Duskara. (H) "Hard to achieve."

Duzak. (Z) Hell.

Dyaus. (H) The sky, heaven. A masculine Vedic deity. Etymologically related to Greek Zeus; and to Latin Deus, Jovis.

Eightfold Path. (B) The Buddhist formula of moral and intellectual development leading to enlightenment.

Frashaostra. (Z) Proper name. Brother of Yamaspa.

Fravashis. (Z) Spirits of the departed. Some correspondence to the Manes, but of greater spiritual elevation apparently. One legend tells that they took mortal shape to further Ahura Mazda's cause on earth.

Gadha. (Z) 1, a cudgel for slaying; 2, a murderer; 3, illness.

Gandhara. (H) A city and country famous for its horses, situated on the Indus. Its

people are referred to as Gandarii by He-
rodotus. Today famous through recent discoveries of hellenistic art influence on Indian, and especially Buddhist, art.

Gandharvas. (B) (H) Vedic deities of the atmosphere, one of whose duties was to prepare the soma juice for the gods.

Ganga. (B) (H) The sacred river Ganges.

Ganges. (B) (H) The sacred river, sometimes
called Ganga.

Garuda. (B) (H) A mythical half-bird, half-
man, on which Vishnu rides. The king of
birds.

Gatha. (B) (H) (Z) A song or one verse
of a song. Same as Sanskrit Gita. In Zoroastrian scriptures there are five Avestan
songs called Gathas. These are the oldest
in this religion, and are believed to have
been composed by Zarathushtra himself.

Gautama. (B) Sanskrit equivalent of Pali
Gotama, the clan name of the Buddha. (H)
1. A common proper name. 2. Name of the
husband of Ahalya, who was seduced by
Indra. 3. Author of a Dharma-sastra.

Gaya. (B) Buddha Gaya. Situated about six
miles from the town of Gaya. The place
where Gotama attained enlightenment under
the Bodhi tree. Site now of the Maha-
Bodhi Temple. (H) One of seven sacred
cities. Situated in Bihar and still an objective for pilgrimages.

Gayatri. (H) 1. An especially sacred verse
of the Rig-Veda in worship of the sun,
which it is the duty of every Brahmana
to repeat silently every morning and evening. 2. A name of Sata-rupa, Brahma's
female half, daughter, and consort. 3. Siva's
consort in the Hari-vansa.

Gayomard. (Z) The first created man, according to Zoroastrian mythology.

Ghee. (H) Sacred melted butter used in sacrificial rites.

Gita. (H) Song.

Gita-govinda. (H) A lyrical poem by Jaya-
deva on the early life of Krishna as Govinda the cowherd.

Gotama. (B) Pali equivalent of Sanskrit
Gautama, which see.

Govinda. (H) "Cow-keeper." One of the
names of Krishna.

Gudakesha. (H) "Whose hair is in tufts."
An appellation of Arjuna.

Guna. (H) Name of each one of the three
constituents of matter, sattva (good qualities), rajas (rage), and tamas (dullness).
Sattva is depicted in symbolic art as yellow, rajas as red, and tamas as black.

Gupta. (H) One of a dynasty of kings who
reigned in Magadha.

Guru. (H) A spiritual leader or tutor, whose
complete spiritual authority a student must
accept.

Hadha-naepata. (Z) Proper name of a plant
of pleasant odour with the branches of
which the Haoma juice (which see) was
extracted by pounding.

Haetumant. (Z) Proper name. A country.
Modern Hindmand.

Haoma. (Z) The personified sacred plant of
Persian mythology, from which juice was
extracted for sacred rites. Its worship is
believed to have been common to Indians
and Iranians before the two races separated.
See Soma.

Haptok-ring. (Z) Name of constellation of
the Great Bear. Considered the leader of
the Northern Star Regiment, and especially
the adversary of the planet Mars. Surrounds the portal of Hell.

Harahvaiti. (Z) The name of a mountain.
Perhaps Armenian Mount Ararat. Perhaps
meaning mountain of the Aryans.

Hari. (B) (H) A name usually used to designate Vishnu, but sometimes other gods.

Hatha-Yoga. (H) A system of Yoga (which
see) by which physical practices are empha-
sized as prerequisite to meditation. A system preparatory to Raja-Yoga (which see).

Hemachandra. (H) Name of the author of
a Sanskrit vocabulary.

Heruka. (H) A name of Garuda (which see).

Himavat. (B) (H) Personification of the
Himalaya Mountains.

Hiranyagarbha. (H) The golden egg from
which the universe was created.

Hom. (Z) Same as Haoma (which see).

Horvadad. (Z) "Plenty." "Wholeness."
Proper name of a feminine Amesha-Spenta
(which see) who protects the waters and
gives wealth.

Hotar. (H) Priest.

Hrishikesha. (H) "With erect hair." A name
of Krishna or Vishnu.

Hsiao King. (C) "The Book of Filial Piety."
A collection of moral tales extolling the
virtues of devotion to one's parents.

Ida. (B) (H) Food, refreshment, or a libation of milk; hence a stream of praise,
personified as the goddess of speech.

Indra. (B) (H) The god of the firmament.
In early Vedic times a god of the first
rank, later chief of all the gods not of the
triad.

Indriya. (B) Originally, belonging to Indra.
Faculty, sense-power.

Iran. (Z) Persia.

Isana, Ishana. (H) A name of Siva or Rudra.

Islam. (M) Name of Mohammed's religious
system, meaning "Submission to Allah."

Isvara. (H) "Lord." A title of Siva.

Itihasa. (H) A legendary poem or heroic history. Especially applied to the Maha-
bharata.

Jaina. (H) A school of Hindu philosophy
characterized by its followers' refusal to
kill anything, even vermin.

Jalalu 'D-Din Rumi. (M) Persian mystic, the
most famous Sufi (which see). A.D. 1207–
1273.

Janaloka. (H) That division of the universe
in which Brahma's sons, Sanaka, Sananda,
and Sanat-Kumara, live.

Janardana. (H) "The adored of mankind." A
name of Krishna.

Jataka. (B) A birth story. A book purporting to be accounts of former lives of the Buddha.

Jatavedas. (H) A Vedic epithet for fire.

Jhana. (B) Pali equivalent for Sanskrit Dhyana (which see).

Jinn. (M) A group of spirits between men and angels. They are both good and evil. One of the jinn is Satan.

Jiva. (H) Life. The principle of life within us. "The spark of life."

Jivita. (H) A living being. See Jiva.

Jnana. (H) Superior knowledge or wisdom.

Jnana Sannyasin. (H) See Jnana. See Sannyasin. A recluse following the path of knowledge and wisdom.

Jnanendriyas. (H) Organ of perception or sense.

Ka-'ba. (M) The main worship and pilgrimage spot of Islam at Mecca. The temple there contains a black cubic tent, the Kaaba, in which is a black meteorite, a stone which is left in Islam of the ancient Arab stone-worship.

Kahapana. (B) Small coin.

Kala. (H) "Time," addressed in the Atharva as the source of all. Also a name of Yama. Also a form of Vishnu.

Kaleshvara. (H) A title of time personified as a god.

Kalinga. (B) (H) The country along the Coromandel coast north of Madras.

Kali-Yuga. (H) The fourth and present age of the world which began in 3102 B.C. to endure 432,000 years. In Hindu prophecy marked by violence, bloodshed, and wars.

Kalpa. (B) (H) A day and night of Brahma —4,320,000,000 years.

Kama. (B) (H) The god of love. Eros. Cupid.

Kamadeva. (B) (H) Kama.

Kammatthana. (B) Spot of activity, object of spiritual exercise, of meditation.

Kanva. (H) Name of a Rishi.

Kapila. (B) (H) A famous sage, founder of Sankhya philosophy.

Kapila. (B) (H) Kapila-Vastu, a town on the river Rohini, home of Suddhodana, father of Gotama Buddha.

Karap. (Z) One who is deaf to the doctrine.

Karma. (B) (H) (Pali equivalent, Kamma) Action and the inevitable result of action. The law of cause and effect. The doctrine of rebirth according to deeds is a corollary to that of Karma.

Karma Sannyasin. (H) Sannyasin = a recluse. Therefore, a recluse following the way of Karma (which see).

Karshvares. (Z) Name of the seven parts of the world.

Kasi. (B) (H) Benares.

Kasyapa. (H) "Tortoise." A Vedic sage to whom some hymns are attributed. One of the seven great Rishis.

Kaustubha-Jewel. (H) A celebrated jewel produced by churning the ocean, and worn on the breast of Krishna or Vishnu.

Keresaspa. (Z) Proper name. One of the clan

of Cama. He killed a dragon and followed a sinful love.

Kesava. (H) "Having much or fine hair." A name of Vishnu or Krishna.

Khattiya. (B) Same as Sanskrit Kshatriya (which see).

Khnenta. (Z) Name of a river which flows into the Caspian Sea.

Khrafstras. (Z) Bad. Poor. Objectionable creeping animals, lice; destructive worms.

Khshathra. (Z) A Regiment, Government, King. Proper name of one of the Amesha-Spentas (which see) who is guardian of metals. Same as Sanskrit Kshatra (which see).

Khshathra Vairya. (Z) The power of wishing.

Kinnaras. (B) (H) "What men?" Mythical beings with human bodies and horses' heads. Sprung from the toe of Brahma, they are musicians to the gods.

Kosala. (B) (H) 1. A country on the Sarayu River. Also applied to other Indian countries. 2. The ruling clan in the Kingdom of Kosala (corresponding to modern Nepal) at the time of Gotama Buddha.

Krishna. (H) "Black." The eighth incarnation of Vishnu.

Kshatra. (H) Power, might, military power.

Kshatriya. (B) (H) The second or regal and warrior class.

Kuan Chung. (T) The Chinese god of war.

Kuan Yin. (T) The Chinese goddess of mercy, capable of assuming all forms. In Chinese Buddhism a form of the Bodhisattva Avalokitesvara. In Buddhist times sometimes considered a form of the Buddha.

Kunti. (H) 1. Daughter of the Yadava Prince Sura, wife of Pandu, and mother of Arjuna. 2. Name of a country and a people of upper India.

Kuru Panchalas. (H) A tribe of the Panchala country.

Kurus. (B) (H) Princes of the Lunar race. Also a people of India dwelling about Kuru-Kshetra, and associated with Prince Kuru.

Kusavati. (B) (H) Capital of southern Kosala.

Kuvera. (B) (H) In the Vedas, a chief of evil spirits. Vaisravana. Hindu god of wealth.

Li. (C) (T) 1. A measurement of distance equal to about a third of an English mile. 2. Absolute right. 3. Etiquette. Propriety.

Lakshmana. (H) Son of King Dasa-ratha, twin brother of Satru-ghna and half-brother of Rama-chandra. He was thought to partake of some of Vishnu's divinity.

Lankavatara Sutra. (B) One of the most important of the texts of Mahayana Buddhism. An exposition of the basic principles to which Zen Buddhism refers.

Lao Tze. (C) (T) A Chinese philosopher who, according to tradition, lived about 600 B.C., and to whom is doubtfully ascribed the writing of the Tao-Te-King and the founding of Taoism. See Tao.

Lokya. (H) Bestowing worlds or freedom.

Lumbini Grove. (B) The grove in Lumbini Park near Kapilavatthu. It was in this grove that Gotama Buddha was born.

Madhava. (H) Name of a celebrated fourteenth-century religious teacher of Tuluva.

Madhusudana. (H) "Slayer of Madhu." A name of Krishna, who killed the demon Madhu.

Madyamika. (B) The middle doctrine. Between two extremes.

Magadha. (B) (H) The country of south Bihar where the Pali language, or rather, a dialect closely related to Pali—the Magadhi—was spoken.

Maghavan. (H) A name of Indra.

Maha-bharata. (H) The great epic poem of the Hindus, probably the longest ever written, describing the great war of the Bharatas.

Mahakalpa. (H) A measurement of time. A cosmic era.

Mahamaya. (B) The name of Gotama Buddha's mother. (H) A name of the sacred city Gaya.

Mahamoha. (H) The great Moha (which see).

Mahat. (H) The great intellect produced at the creation.

Mahayana. (B) The Buddhist school of "the great vehicle" of salvation, as opposed to the Hinayana school of "the little vehicle." Also (incorrectly) called the "northern school." Geographically it includes Tibet, Mongolia, China, Japan, Korea, and Hawaii. The Mahayana glorifies the Bodhisattva's ideal of the renunciation of Nirvana in order to help humanity.

Maitreya, Metteya. (B) The compassionate Buddha who is to come in the distant future. Foretold by Gotama, as Christ foretold his second coming. (H) Name of a Rishi, son of Kusarava and disciple of Parasara.

Manas. (B) (H) Sanskrit equivalent of Pali *mano*. Mind, in the widest sense, as the seat of intellectual operations and emotions.

Manasa. (H) "The Intellectual." Name of a primeval god.

Mandala. (B) "Circle." 1. A division of a literary work. 2. A geometrical design into which representations of deities are worked. Through meditation on the Mandala, first as a map of the world, second as one's own self, the worshipper seeks identification of himself with the cosmos, thus achieving samadhi (which see).

Mandara. (H) The great mountain used by the gods for churning the ocean.

Mantra. (H) The part of the Veda made up of hymns. A formula which, by the power of its sound, creates certain conditions in the world of one's soul.

Manu. (H) The name given to each of fourteen progenitors of the human race. To the first is attributed the Ordinances of Manu. The seventh is he who is mentioned in the story of the flood.

Mara. (B) The killer, murderer, death, personification of death-power and of evil principle, the tempter. Note etymological relation to Latin "mors" and English "night-mare."

Maruts. (H) The storm gods, allies of Indra. They wield the lightning and thunder, ride the chariot of the wind, and direct the course of the storm.

Mathra. (Z) The holy word. A spot in the holy scriptures. The same as Sanskrit Mantra (which see).

Maya. (H) 1. A Daitya who was architect and carpenter for the gods. 2. "Illusion, Deception, the Demoniac Power." Personified as a female of celestial birth whose purpose is to delude humanity. 3. Also a name of Gaya, a sacred city.

Mazda. (Z) The great wisdom; wisdom and plenty. The name of the one god of Zoroastrianism, Ahura Mazda. Related to Sanskrit Maha = great.

Mazdayasnian. (B) A worshipper of Ahura Mazda.

Mecca. (M) The birthplace of Mohammed, where his family were in charge of the Ka-'ba (which see). When he preached worship of Allah he was persecuted and fled to Medina.

Mencius. (C) The philosopher Meng, often spoken of by Confucianists as the second sage, Confucius being the first. Lived 372–289 B.C. His works form one of the classics of Confucianism.

Meru. (B) A mountain.

Mithra. (Z) The Persian sun-god.

Mitra. (H) A son of Aditi. A manifestation of the sun. Probably connected with Persian Mithra. He rules the day, Varuna the night.

Moha. (H) Bewilderment, making men believe falsely in the reality of the world.

Mouru. (Z) Name of an ancient city on the edge of the desert.

Mow, or Mou. (C) Chinese measurement of land. About one-sixth of an acre.

Mrityu. (H) "Death." A name of Yama.

Muni. (H) A holy sage. A pious and learned man. A title applied to the Rishis.

Muslim. (M) Derived from the same Arabic root as Islam (which see). Is used for designation of the followers of Islam, meaning "those who submit."

Naga. (B) (H) A snake, especially the cobra de capello. A legendary semi-divine being with human face and the tail of a serpent. A race of people said to have been descended from these beings. Snake worship was widespread among the pre-Aryan aboriginal tribes of India, as archæological discoveries prove.

Nagarjuna. (B) Buddhist philosopher and saint. Probably of the beginning of the second century A.D. Some considered him a reincarnation of Ananda.

Nakshatras. (H) Lunar feminine deities, twenty-eight in number, daughters of the moon by Daksha.

Namuki. (B) (H) A demon slain by Indra, who smothered him with foam after having promised not to kill him "by wet or dry."

Nana-dassana. (B) Vision of recognition.

Nandana. (B) (H) The grove of Indra, lying north of Meru.

Nara. (H) "Man." The original eternal man.

Narada. (H) One of the seven great Rishis. Some hymns of the Rig-Veda are ascribed to him.

Narayana. (H) 1. Son of Nara, the original Man. 2. Brahma, the Creator. 3. Vishnu.

Nasu. (Z) Corpse.

Nats. (H) (B) Celestial spirits of a higher rank than human beings, but lower than gods.

Nemovanta. (Z) Woven rushes.

Nibbana. (B) Pali equivalent of Sanskrit Nirvana (which see).

Nirvana. (B) The supreme goal of the Buddhist. Release from the limitations of existence. Release from the necessity to be born again. That state in which all attributes relating to phenomenal existence cease.

Nivid. (H) Formula.

Niyama. (H) The second stage of Yoga practice.

Nyaya. (H) A philosophical school marked by its insistence on logic.

Om. (H) See Aum.

Padma. (H) A name of Lakshmi, the goddess of beauty.

Pairikas. (Z) Name of a class of evil female beings who mislead men, seducing them with their great beauty. In later Persian mythology they become beautiful fairies.

Pali. (B) The language in which the Buddhist Pitakas were first written.

Pandavas. (H) Descendants of Pandu.

Pandu. (H) "The pale." Brother of Dhritarashtra, King of Hastina-pura.

Parameshthika. (H) The highest wish. "Heart's desire," or the most ardent wisher.

Parameshthin. (H) "Stander in the highest place." A title of gods and great mortals. In the Vedas a son or creation of Prajapati.

Paramita. (B) Perfection. There are six (or ten) paramitas or stages of spiritual perfection through which the Bodhisattva must progress in his rise to Buddhahood.

Parasara. (H) A Rishi thought to have written some of the Vedic hymns.

Parinirvana. (B) The complete Nirvana (which see), as sealed by bodily death.

Parjanya. (H) 1. The rain god of the Vedas. 2. One of the Adityas.

Partha. (H) Son of Pritha or Kunti. An appellation of Arjuna.

Pasupata. (H) "Lord of creatures." An appellation of Rudra.

Patimokkha. (B) The 227 rules followed by the Buddhist Bhikkhu.

Peshotanu. (Z) A sinful person. A body afflicted with sin.

Picacas, Pisaca. (H) A demon, who moves rapidly and emanates light. A will-o'-the-wisp.

Pisachas. Same as Picacas.

Pitakas. (B) (Pitaka = basket) "The three baskets" divisions of the Buddhist Pali scriptures.

Pradhana. (H) Primary matter as opposed to spirit.

Pradipika. (H) "Lamp." An enlightening commentary.

Prajapati. (H) "Lord of Creatures," applied to several creative gods.

Prajna. (B) Sanskrit equivalent of Pali "panna." Transcendental wisdom, divine intuition. One of the six paramitas (which see). (H) Intelligence, knowledge.

Prana. (H) Breath or life.

Pranayama. (H) The fourth stage of Yoga practice. The Yoga breathing exercises.

Prathama. (H) Foremost chief.

Pratyahara. (H) The fifth stage of Yoga practice. The process of freeing the senses from all objectivity.

Pratyekabuddha. (B) A Buddha who works out his individual salvation (Nirvana) only, without teaching his doctrine and without dedicating all his efforts to the delivery of all other beings, as the Sammasambuddha does.

Pravritti. (H) Activity. Function.

Prayaga. (H) Where the rivers Ganges, Jumna, and the legendary subterranean Saraswati unite. A famous pilgrimage place. The modern Allahabad.

Pretashila. (H) A stone of the dead, where funeral cakes are offered.

Prithivi, Prithi, Prithu. (H) "The wide." The earth. Personified as the mother of all beings. See bhuh, bhumi.

Purana. (H) "Old." Hence an ancient legend or story.

Purusha. (H) "Person." The original eternal man. The supreme being. Soul of the universe. A name of Brahma.

Purushottamas. (B) (H) "Best of men." In its mystic sense, the soul of the universe, the supreme god. A title of Vishnu.

Pushan. (H) A Vedic deity. Keeper of flocks and herds and bringer of prosperity. He surveys all things and acts as a conductor on journeys and on all paths.

Putra. (H) Son.

Qibla. (M) The "facing" in prayer; formerly towards Jerusalem; changed by Mohammed towards Mecca.

Qur'an. (M) The Koran.

Raga. (B) Passion. Uncontrolled lust of every kind. One of the three cardinal blemishes of character. (H) A musical mode or melody personified. The Ragas have consorts names Reginis.

Ragha. (Z) Name of a town near Teheran,

whose ruins are still extant. According to some traditions Zarathushtra was born there.

Rahula. (B) "Impediment." The name of Gotama Buddha's son.

Raja (B) (H) Ruler. King. Also a republican chieftain of the Sakyan clan. Gotama Buddha's father was such a chieftain, according to tradition. (H) General name for a king.

Rajagriha. (H) Name of the capital of Magadha.

Rajanya. (H) A Vedic designation of the Kshatriya class.

Rajas. (H) One of the gunas, which see.

Rajasuya. (H) A royal sacrifice performed at the installation of a king.

Raja-Yoga. (H) An advanced system of Yoga (which see) which, through higher meditation, stimulates consciousness of the difference between the true inner self and that which the person believes to be himself through the evidence of sensory perception.

Rakshasa. (H) A goblin or evil spirit.

Rama. (H) Rama-chandra, seventh incarnation of Vishnu.

Ramadan, Ramadhan. (M) The holy month of Islam, wherein all Muslims have to fast and in which the pilgrimages to Mecca are carried out. The order is abstinence from eating, drinking, smoking, and cohabitation from sunrise until sunset, but not during the night.

Ramayana. (H) "The Adventures of Rama." Oldest of the Sanskrit epic poems, partly composed about 500 B.C.

Rangha. (Z) Name of a river (the Araxes of the Greeks), the outside limit of the then known country.

Rashnu. (Z) Proper name of one of the Yazatas (which see) who is the spirit of lawfulness and is the judge of the dead with Mithra and Craosha. The dead are put on a scale, where the soul is weighed.

Rata. (Z) Gift. Name of a genius.

Rati. (B) (H) "Love, Desire." The Venus of Hindus. The goddess of sexual pleasures, wife of Kama, god of love. Daughter of Daksha, (which see). In Buddhism, the daughter of Mara.

Ratu. (Z) The fixed time. The rule. May be Lord and Master. The priest who attends the sacrifice.

Ravana. (H) A demon king of Lanka or Ceylon, expelled by his half-brother Kuvera.

Ric. (H) The Rig-Veda. The first and most important of the four Vedas, earliest verse-collections of the Aryans, probably in part older than even their immigration into India, which goes back to the third millennium B.C.

Rishi. (B) (H) An inspired poet or sage. Seven are deified and represented in the sky by the seven stars of the Great Bear.

Rudra. (B) (H) "Howler." The god of storms. Father of the Rudras and Maruts. Sometimes identified with the god of fire.

Etymologically, "the red one," because of the colour of desert dust-storms.

Sad-Guru. (H) A good teacher.

Sadhu. (H) "Leading to the goal." The honourable one. The venerable one. Saint.

Sakalya. (H) Name of an early Hindu grammarian and expositor of the Vedas.

Sakya. (B) The clan to which Gotama Buddha belonged. It was told later that they were not ruled by kings but were republicans led by chieftains called rajas, of whom Gotama's father was one. They are said to have made their own laws, meeting in a common hall for this purpose, to have been monogamous, and not to have recognized the Hindu caste rules.

Sakyamuni. (B) "Sage of the Sakyas." A title often applied to Gotama Buddha by those outside the clan.

Sama. (H) "The chanted." The Sama-Veda.

Samadhi. (B) Contemplation of reality; the state of spiritual ecstasy achieved through the complete elimination of all sense of separateness, and continued meditation of reality. (H) The highest stage of meditation in Yoga practice.

Samana. (B) Pali equivalent for Sanskrit "Sramana" (ascetic), one who makes an effort to gain salvation.

Sama-Veda. (H) The third Veda, composed of 1549 metrical verses.

Samma. (B) Supreme, the highest point or summit. Relatively it is used to describe each step of the noble eightfold path.

Samvatsara. (H) "Year." The era of Vikramaditya, dating from 57 B.C.

Sandhya. (H) "Dusk." Personified as the daughter of Brahma.

Sandilya. (H) A descendant of Sandila, a sage connected with the Chhandogya Upanishad.

Sankaracharya (Sankara-acharya). (H) Name of a great religious teacher of the eighth or ninth century A.D.

Sankhyas. (H) Followers of the Sankhya school of Hindu philosophy, which has deeply influenced Buddhist philosophy and its psychological vocabulary.

Sannyasin. (H) A Brahmana who has reached the highest stage of his religious life.

Saoshyant. (Z) Same as Soshyans (which see).

Sariputra. (B) Sanskrit equivalent of Pali Sariputta. Also called Upatissa. One of the two chief disciples of Gotama Buddha.

Sariputta. (B) See Sariputra.

Sarva. (H) "The destroyer." A deity of the Vedas. Later a name of Siva and of one of the Rudras.

Sarvajna Vishnu. (H) "All-knowing Vishnu."

Sarvatsara. (H) Name of one of the Upanishads.

Sastra. (B) (H) A rule book or treatise. Any book of divine authority, but especially a law book.

Sat-chit-ananda. (H) He who is blessed by a personal inner world of the highest qualities.

Savitar. (H) "Generator. Stimulator." 1. A Vedic appellation for the sun. 2. An Aditya.

Sayana. (H) A famous commentator on the Rig-Veda, usually called Sayanacharya.

Shrichakrasambhara Tantra. (B) The scripture which explains the holy Mandala (which see) as depicted in many temples.

Shun. See Yao and Shun.

Siddha. (H) Supernatural power, or one who has achieved it. One of 88,000 semi-divine beings of great holiness who dwell between the earth and the sun.

Siddhattha. (B) First name of the Buddha, meaning: having attained one's object, the efficient one.

Sindhu. (H) The Indus River and the country which borders it. Also the people living near it. Also a river in Malwa.

Sita. (H) "A furrow." Worshipped as the personification of husbandry. Wife of Rama.

Siva. (H) The third deity of the Hindu triad. A development of the Vedic Rudra. The name means "gracious," and is given to him because one tries by addressing him thus to prevent the outbreak of his destructive qualities. Siva represents the divine reality in its negative aspect as destroying the mere secular and harmonious vision of the world.

Slokas. (H) The most commonly used metre in Sanskrit verse.

˘ — ˘ — ˘ — ˘ — | ˘ — ˘ — ˘ — ˘ —
˘ — ˘ — ˘ — ˘ — | ˘ — ˘ — ˘ — ˘ —

Soma. (H) The intoxicating milk-like juice of a sacred plant used in sacrificial rites. Personified, the god who animated the soma juice. Also see the Zoroastrian Haoma.

Soshyans. (Z) To be useful. The future Saviour, The Messiah.

Sotapan, Sotapatti. (B) Pali equivalent for Sanskrit Srotapatti, (which see.)

Spendarmad. (Z) See Spenta Armaiti.

Spenta. (Z) A name of the increasers of Ahura Mazda's powers.

Spenta Armaiti. (Z) One of the Amesha-Spentas (which see) who is in conflict with Angra Mainyu, increasing the power of Ahura Mazda.

Spenta-Mainyu. (Z) Name of the Gathas which begin with these words.

Spitama. (Z) The name of Zarathushtra's clan.

Sraddha. (H) 1. Faith, personified in the Vedas. 2. Name of a daughter of the sage Daksha, wife of the god Dharma, and mother of Kamadeva, god of love.

Sramana. (H) Mendicant.

Sraosha. (Z) Obedience. Proper name of one of the Yazatas who first taught the law. As a heavenly guard of the world he wakes at the third hour of night. He wakes the cock who drives away the demon of sleep from mankind.

Sraosho-karana. (Z) Sraosh = obedience. Sraosho-karana = a spur for horses. The instrument for stimulating obedience. A whip.

Srotapatti. (B) "Entering the stream," which at the very end is bound to carry into the ocean of salvation, into Nirvana.

Sruti. (H) That which has been heard in oral tradition. The revealed message. The most sacred of the scriptures.

Stupa. (B) A mound of earth or brick in which the ashes or bodies of important persons were deposited.

Sudras. (B) (H) The fourth caste, that is, the servant class.

Sufi. (M) A sect of Moslems who are named for their original clothing of *suf* or coarse wool. They developed the idea of God's incarnation in men, who in turn may become almost divine through asceticism and mysticism. The Sufis lived mostly in Persia and India.

Sukha. (B) Smooth, agreeable, sweet. The word and its contrary, "dukkha" (pain), go back to nomadic times, when the carriage and its quality meant everything; original meanings of the words: having a good, and a bad, hub ("kha") of the wheel, respectively.

Sumeru. (B) (H) The World Mountain. Early Indian geographical conception of the earth was that it was a mountain standing in the midst of the World-Ocean.

Sunna. (M) Originally, way. Name of the main part of Islam, after its dissolution into sects. The followers of the Sunna claim that their doctrine comes down continuously from the founder. The Turkish Moslems are mostly Sunna Moslems.

Sura. (M) Name of the single chapters or revelations of the Koran. There are 114.

Surya. (H) The Sun, the Sun-god.

Sushupti. (H) Deep sleep.

Sutra. (B) (H) Sanskrit equivalent of Pali "Sutta." A thread or string on which jewels are strung. A verse, as something worked together as on a thread. In Buddhism, applied to that part of the Pali Canon containing narratives about dialogues of the Buddha.

Sutratman. (H) "Thread soul." Intellect conditioned by the aggregate and therefore passing through all things like a thread.

Sutta. (B) See Sutra.

Svar. (H) See Vyahritis.

Svastika. (H) A mystic symbol in the form of a Greek cross with the end of each member bent at a right angle.

Svayam. (H) Self-existent. (Used with Manu, "Manu Svayam.")

Svetasvatara. (H) Name of a Upanishad attached to the Yajur-Veda.

Swar. (H) See Vyahritis.

Tamas. (H) The "black" guna, which see.

Tantra. (H) "Rule, Ritual." Any one of a large class of religious and magical treatises. Mostly applied to a group of later Hindu texts, compiled about A.D. 1300.

Tao. (B) (C) (T) Originally meant "highway." Later used by Taoists and Buddhists somewhat as the "Logos" of Greek philosophy. May be understood as "the way" or "the law" of life.

Taoism. (T) The religious doctrine of Tao (which see). Its two chief early exponents were Lao Tze and Chuang Tze.

Tao-Te-King. (T) The basic scripture of Taoism, supposedly composed by Lao Tze, but now assigned by some to the fourth, or third century B.C. The legend tells that in old age he left western China to go into India. At the frontier he was stopped and not permitted to leave the country until he had written down all his wisdom. This he did in a few days in the Tao-Te-King.

Tapasa. (H) One who has produced tapas, an inner heat kindled by meditation.

Tathagata. (B) A title of Gotama Buddha used by his followers and also by himself of himself. Its derivation is doubtful, but it is variously interpreted as "thus come," "thus gone," that is, following the path of former Buddhas, and "neither comes from anywhere nor goes to anywhere."

Tirtham. (H) A stone marking a spot dedicated to the worship of a particular deity, spirit, or hero.

Treta-Yuga. (H) A period of 1,296,000 years representing the second age of the world.

Tukhara. (B) Member of a northern tribe called Tukharas or Tusharas.

Tvashtar. (H) A Vedic deity. The ideal artist and artisan.

Upanishads. (H) "Esoteric doctrine." A group of ancient Hindu scriptures.

Usanas. (H) 1. The planet Venus. 2. Name of the author of a law-book.

Vadhaghna. (Z) Name of an evil ruler, the power of whom Angra Mainyu promised to give Zarathushtra on condition that he would curse Ahura Mazda.

Vahista. (Z) The best. Asha Vahista = the superlative asha (which see).

Vaiseshika. (H) The atomic school of philosophy.

Vaisvanara. (H) A name of Agni.

Vaisyas, Vaishyas. (B) (H) The third caste, consisting of tradesmen and farmers.

Vaitarini, Vaitaraini. (H) "To be crossed." The river which must be crossed in order to reach the infernal regions. It is filled with blood, ordure, and other filth, and runs swiftly. (Cf. the Styx, and the River Jordan in Christian symbolism.) Also a river in the country of the Kalingas.

Vaivasvata. (H) A name of the seventh Manu. An appellation of Yama.

Vamadeva. (H) A Rishi to whom are attributed several Vedic hymns.

Vara. (Z) A garden.

Varshneya. (H) A name of Krishna.

Varuna. (H) One of the oldest of the Vedic gods. "The universal encompasser. The all-embracer." Bearer of the moral order, attributed to the night and to the waters, and to the symbolically corresponding subconscious regions of the soul, which con-

tain the creative power for everything which later becomes visible.

Vasishta. (H) "Wealthiest." Name of a sage to whom many Vedic hymns are attributed.

Vasu. (H) One of a class of deities who attend upon Indra. In Vedic times there were eight, each of whom personified a natural phenomenon, fire, water, pole-star, etc.

Vata. (H) The wind, Vayu.

Vayu. (H) See Vata.

Vayu. (Z) Air as a genius. The same as Sanskrit Vayu (which see).

Veda. (H) "Knowledge." The holy books regarded as the primal revelation of the Hindu religion. See Appendix note.

Vedanta. (H) "The end of the Veda." An orthodox school of philosophy, teaching the doctrine of Advaita, which see.

Videha. (B) (H) An ancient country and clan of which the capital was Mithilia. It corresponds with modern Tirhut, or North Bihar.

Vidya. (H) Knowledge. The opposite of Avidya, which see.

Vihara. (B) A dwelling place, also a state of life or condition of heart. The houses presented to the Buddha for the use of the Sangha, or Order, were called Viharas, and the name is now generally used for a Buddhist retreat or monastery.

Vijnana. (B) Conscious recognition.

Vindhya. (B) (H) The mountains which stretch across India dividing Hindustan from the Dakhin. Also the forest which covers those mountains.

Vinnana. (B) Pali equivalent of Sanskrit Vijnana. The normal consciousness. The empirical mind, by which one recognizes the phenomenal world and gains the experience of life.

Viraj. (H) The male half of Brahma, typifying all male creatures.

Visankhara. (B) Dissolution, destruction.

Vishnu. (H) From vish, "to pervade." Second god of the Hindu triad. Later supposed to reveal himself through various incarnations called avataras (which see).

Visuddhimagga. (B) "The Path of Purity." A famous Buddhist work by Buddhaghosha.

Visva Devas. (H) Deities of inferior rank.

Vizaresha. (Z) Proper name of a Daeva who drags souls into hell.

Vohu-gaona. (Z) Beautifully coloured. A fragrant wood used for incense.

Vohu-mano. (Z) The spirit of goodness. One of the Amesha-Spentas, which see.

Vouru-kasha. (Z) Name of the Caspian Sea.

Vritra. (H) The Vedic demon of drought, clogging up the flux of the waters, and hence symbolic of ascetic, restricting practices. Was slain by Indra.

Vrittis. (H) "The turning of a wheel." Turbulences in the Chitta (which see) which produce false impressions of reality.

Vyahritis. (H) The three mystical words said by Manu to have been "milked" by Prajapati from the Vedas: bhur, which became the earth, *bhuvah*, which became "this firmament," and *swar*, which became "that sky."

Yajnavalkya. (H) The Lord of Sacrifice. A famous sage to whom is ascribed authorship of several of the Hindu scriptures, including the Satapatha-Brahmana.

Yajur Veda, or Yajush. (H) The second Veda.

Yakshas. (B) (H) A class of supernatural beings attendant upon Kuvera, the god of wealth. Vegetation deities.

Yama. (H) Twin brother of Yami, and with her progenitor of the race. The first human being to die; therefore ruler of death and the land of death. Death personified.

Yami. (H) See Yama.

Yamuna. (B) The river Jumna personified in Hinduism as the daughter of the Sun. The sister of Yama.

Yang. (C) (T) See Yin and Yang.

Yao. (C) A monarch of antiquity held up by the Chinese as a model of piety and virtue. He ruled, according to tradition, from 2356 until 2280 B.C., when he abdicated in favour of Shun on account of Shun's reputation for filial piety and brotherly affection.

Yatha ahu vairyo. (Z) The beginning of one of the holiest prayers of Zoroastrianism.

Yazatas. (Z) Venerable. Given name of various higher beings. There are heavenly, invisible Yazatas, of whom the head is Ahura Mazda, and earthly ones, of whom the head is Zarathushtra. To them belong the Amesha-Spentas. There are exactly 100,000 of them.

Yellow Emperor (C) (T) Hwang-Ti, a legendary ruler who is said to have lived nearly 3000 years before Christ and to have been the pioneer of the early civilization of mankind by the invention of wheeled carriages, a medium of exchange, music, astronomical instruments, etc.

Yin. (C) (T) The shade, as opposed to light.

Yin and Yang. (C) (T) North and south banks of a river, light and shade, male and female, the primeval forces from the interaction of which all things have been evolved.

Yoga. (B) (H) "Yoke"—that which unites. A school of philosophy especially marked by regulated physical postures in connexion with meditation. There are two great Yoga systems, Hatha-Yoga, psycho-physiological training along ascetic lines, and Raja-Yoga, the development of inner powers by meditation, etc.

Yogi, Yogin. (B) (H) One who practises Yoga, which see.

Yoyana (Yojana). (H) Nine English miles.

Yu. (C) A semi-mythological emperor and hero who ruled 2300 B.C. and drained the empire after a great flood, which has been identified by some as the world-wide deluge of Genesis and other scriptures.

Yugandhara rocks. (B) Rocks near or in Yugandhara, a city in the Punjab.

Zen. (B) A Chinese and Japanese school of Buddhism, perhaps more closely related to Taoism than to Indian Buddhism. It urges dependence upon (without seeking or avoiding) one's inner nature. It places no importance on doctrine or the written word, for these are mere ideas of truth rather than truth itself. Zen is the philosophy of discovery by being simply what one is.

INDEX

Abbreviations are used throughout the index to indicate the source of the material referred to. Symbols in parentheses, as (H), indicate the main scriptural divisions. Those following the parentheses, such as Rv., indicate the single works within these scriptures. Abbreviations are listed below as nearly as possible in the order in which the texts occur in *The Bible of the World*. Entries in italics indicate titles of scriptures, books, or selections.

SS   = Song of Solomon
Am.   = Amos
Ho.   = Hosea
Mi.   = Micah
I.I   = Book of the First Isaiah
Ze.   = Zephaniah
Na.   = Nahum
Ha.   = Habakkuk
Je.   = Jeremiah
El.   = Ezekiel
I.II = Book of the Second Isaiah
Ha.   = Haggai
Zc.   = Zechariah
Ma.   = Malachi
Jl.   = Joel
Jh.   = Jonah
Da.   = Daniel
OA   = Apocryphal Old Testament
Mat. = Gospel of Matthew
Lu.   = Gospel of Luke
Mar. = Gospel of Mark
Jhn. = Gospel of John
AA   = Acts of the Apostles
PR   = Epistle of Paul to the
         Romans
PC.I = First Epistle of Paul to the
         Corinthians

PC.II = Second Epistle of Paul to the
         Corinthians
PG   = Epistle of Paul to the
         Galatians
PE   = Epistle of Paul to the
         Ephesians
PP   = Epistle of Paul to the Philip-
         pians
PT.I = First Epistle of Paul to the
         Thessalonians
PT.II = Second Epistle of Paul to
         the Thessalonians
Ti.   = Paul's First and Second
         Epistles to Timothy
H   = Epistle to the Hebrews
Ja.   = General Epistle of James
I.J. = First Epistle General of John
Re.   = Revelation of St. John the
         Divine

NA   = New Testament Apocrypha

(M)   = Mohammedan Scriptures
K   = Koran
MA   = Masnavi
An.   = Forty-Two Traditions of An-
         Nawawi

Aaron, the death of (JC), N 735
Abed-nego, Shadrach, and Meshach (JC),
 Da. 1014
Abel and Cain, their birth (JC), Ge. 646
Abel, his murder (JC), Ge. 646
Abgarus, his correspondence with Jesus (JC),
 NA 1280
Abib, the month of (JC), D 746
Abodes of the Soul, The (Z), Z 598
Abraham Entertains the Lord (JC), Ge.
 655
Abraham: God's promise to him (JC), Ge.
 652; death of (JC), Ge. 664; mention of
 (M), K 1314
Abraham Intercedes for Sodom (JC), Ge.
 656
Abraham Offers Isaac (JC), Ge. 660
Absalom: (JC), his men kill Amnon, S.II
 804; he flees to Geshur, S.II 804; he re-
 turns from Geshur, S.II 804; his treach-
 ery, S.II 805; his death, S.II 807
Absalom Avenges Tamar (JC), S.II 804
Accusation of Heaven (C), SK 387
Accusation of the Princes (C), Mi. 951
Acknowledgment of Divinity (JC), Lu. 1063
Action: relation to inaction, as explained by
 Krishna (H), Bg. 91; Yoga by, as ex-
 plained by Krishna (H), Bg. 89
Acts of the Apostles, The (JC), AA 1176
Adam and Eve are clothed (JC), Ge. 645
Adam, creation of (JC), Ge. 642, 643
Admission of Women (B), Ch. 233
Admonition (C), SK 396
Adoration of God (JC), Ps. 911
Adultery: law of (H), OM 83; law of
 (JC), L 728; the woman taken in adul-
 tery (JC), Jhn. 1093
Agni: (H), Rv. 10, 12; creation of (H),
 SB 32; in the fire-altar (H), SB 34
Agriculture, of co-operation in (C), WM
 441

Agur, son of Jakeh, his prophecy (JC), Pr.
 923
Ahuna-Vairya (Z), Z 586
Air, creation of (H), Rv. 21
Akaranga Sutra (B), (J) Ak. 345
Aliment of Joy, The (B), BC 209
All Things after Their Kind (T), CT 547
All Things Are Complete in Us (C), WM
 459
Altar Is Set Up, The (JC), Ez. 835
Ambapali, the gift of (B), MS 218
Amnon: rapes Tamar (JC), S.II 803; is
 killed by Absalom's men (JC), S.II 804
Amos (JC), Am. 940
Analects of Confucius, The (C), AC 398
Ananda Weeps (B), MS 232
Ananias, the lie of (JC), AA 1180
Ancestors: in praise of (C), SK 394; wor-
 ship of (H), GP 114
Ancestry of the World, The (Z), P 635
Andrew, Simon, James, and John become
 disciples of Jesus (JC), Mat. 1067
Angel: appears to Joshua (JC), J 762; ap-
 pears to shepherds (JC), Lu. 1054; ap-
 pears to Mary (JC), Lu. 1052; to Zac-
 harias (JC), Lu. 1052; at the birth of
 Buddha (B), IJ 183, 184; to the infant
 Zarathushtra (Z), P 611; to Joseph (JC),
 AN 1252
Angel Meets Balaam, An (JC), N 737
Anger (B), Dh. 300
Anger of the Lord, The (JC), Ju. 769
Angra Mainyu: his evil creations (Z), Z
 578; his assault on Zarathushtra (Z), Z
 586
Animals, creation of: (H), Rv. 20, U 39;
 (JC), Ge. 642
Anna, mother of the Virgin Mary (JC), NA
 1247
Anna recognizes Jesus as Saviour (JC), Lu.
 1058